Lifespan Developmental Psychology

Lifespan Developmental Psychology

Donald B. Irwin
Des Moines Area Community College

Janet A. Simons
The University of Iowa

 Brown &
Benchmark
PUBLISHERS

Madison, Wisconsin · Dubuque, Iowa

Book Team

Executive Editor *Michael Lange*
Developmental Editor *Sheralee Connors*
Production Editor *Marlys Nekola*
Designer *Eric Engelby*
Art Editor/Processor *Joseph P. O'Connell*
Photo Editor *Robin Storm*
Permissions Coordinator *LouAnn K. Wilson*
Visuals/Design Developmental Consultant *Marilyn A. Phelps*
Visuals/Design Freelance Specialist *Mary L. Christianson*
Marketing Manager *Steven Yetter*
Advertising Manager *Susie Butler*

 Brown &
Benchmark

A Division of Wm. C. Brown Communications, Inc.

Executive Vice President/General Manager *Thomas E. Doran*
Vice President/Editor in Chief *Edgar J. Laube*
Vice President/Sales and Marketing *Eric Ziegler*
Director of Production *Vickie Putman Caughron*
Director of Custom and Electronic Publishing *Chris Rogers*

Wm. C. Brown Communications, Inc.

President and Chief Executive Officer *G. Franklin Lewis*
Corporate Senior Vice President and Chief Financial Officer *Robert Chesterman*
Corporate Senior Vice President and President of Manufacturing *Roger Meyer*

The credits section for this book begins on page 561 and is considered an extension of the copyright page.

Interior design by Mark Christianson

Cover image © Camile Przewodek. Represented by Gerald and Cullen Rapp, Inc.

Copyedited by Mary Monner

A Times Mirror Company

Library of Congress Catalog Card Number: 93–70480

ISBN 0–697–06430–1

Printed in the United States of America by Wm. C. Brown Communications, Inc., 2460 Kerper Boulevard, Dubuque, IA 52001

10 9 8 7 6 5 4 3 2 1

Brief Contents

Contents

Preface

Welcome to our lifespan developmental psychology textbook. The preface is a good place to begin your exploration of a book because it points out the main features and topics of the book, and helps you to browse through the book in a more informed manner. We encourage students and faculty to scan the various chapters of the book before settling down to learn the material in more depth. Look for the following features as you explore the chapters.

The study guide is incorporated in the textbook. Students who actively read textbooks—quizzing themselves along the way, doing periodical mini-reviews, and using mnemonics to remember material learn more than students who just read the chapter from start to finish. For many textbooks, students can buy study guides that help in learning and reviewing material, but buying both a book and a study guide is fairly expensive. This textbook includes guided reviews, practice multiple choice items, and study suggestions for each chapter without adding to the cost of the textbook. In addition to twenty review multiple choice questions at the end of the chapters, you will find several suggestions for activities and discussion in the *Exploring Human Development* and *Discussing Human Development* sections. Using these suggestions will make the material more engaging and meaningful for you.

The book features multicultural information. Each chapter includes a boxed feature on a cultural aspect of developmental psychology. Some of the boxes feature ethnic diversity in the United States while others feature a global approach to cultural diversity. More importantly, multicultural information is included throughout each chapter rather than limited to just the boxed feature. Some of the multicultural information is theoretical in nature, such as coverage of racial identity theory, while other information features a specific research study, such as the extensive long-term nutritional research being conducted in China. The authors have selected a variety of cultural topics and important research studies.

The book also looks at gender and age effects in development. In every chapter, important aspects of gender effects are covered, while also emphasizing that men and women are more similar than different. Biological, psychological, and socialized gender effects are discussed.

Every lifespan developmental book explores issues of age, but sometimes the effects of aging and age stereotypes are glossed over. This textbook devotes greater than average space to development during adulthood and looks at both the positive and negative aspects of being various ages. Infancy, childhood, and adulthood are explored in terms of physical development, cognitive development, and psychosocial development. The authors also look at the effects of gender and ethnicity on persons of various ages.

The book carefully balances research findings and practical information. It is important to cover well-known and informative research findings as well as to describe some of these studies in depth so that students get a sense of how psychology is "done." It is also important that students understand how psychological findings can be usefully applied. Therefore, we have chosen several topics and research studies that many students will find relevant to their own lives. Each chapter, for example, has a boxed feature on some aspect of parent-child interaction. These boxed features cover a wide variety of topics, ranging from the effects of parent-child bonding to caring for aging parents. Family issues, such as parenting newborns and stepfamily adjustments, are covered throughout the chapters. Moreover, we have included information on a variety of problems that many individuals face during their lifetime, such as eating disorders, domestic violence, substance abuse, mourning, divorce, and religious issues.

Supplementary Materials

We have worked with our publisher to produce an outstanding, integrated teaching package to accompany our text. We know how important these materials can be in teaching effectively, so we wrote the major ancillaries ourselves. We have already mentioned the many features of the built-in study guide feature of the textbook.

Another key element of the teaching package is the *Instructor's Course Planner*. This flexible planner provides a variety of useful tools to enhance teaching efforts, reduce workload, and increase enjoyment. For each chapter of the text, the *Planner* provides a summary outline, learning objectives, key terms, research projects, classroom activities, discussion topics, minilecture topics, essay questions, and a transparency guide. The *Planner* also contains a section on "Ethical Practices in Research with Human Subjects" and a chapter-by-chapter videotape list. The *Instructor's Course Planner* is conveniently housed within an attractive 11″ × 13″ × 9″ carrying case. This case is designed to accommodate the complete ancillary package by containing each chapter's material within a separate hanging file. This allows instructors to keep all of their class materials organized at their fingertips.

Because we are committed to all aspects of this text project, we also wrote all the questions for the printed *Test Item File*. This comprehensive test bank includes over 1,800 multiple-choice test questions that are keyed to the text and learning objectives. Each item is also designated as factual, conceptual, or applied, based upon the first three levels of Benjamin Bloom's *Taxonomy of Educational Objectives*.

The *Brown and Benchmark Developmental Psychology Transparency/Slide Set* consists of 100 newly developed acetate transparencies or slides. These full-color illustrations include graphics from various outside sources. Created by Lynne Blesz-Vestal, these transparencies were expressly designed to provide comprehensive coverage of all major topic areas generally covered in developmental psychology. A comprehensive annotated guide provides a brief description of each transparency and helpful suggestions for classroom use.

The *Brown and Benchmark Customized Reader* allows instructors to select up to 100 journal or magazine articles from a menu provided by Brown and Benchmark sales representatives. The selected readings are then custom printed for students and bound into an attractive 8 1/4″ × 11″ book, giving instructors the opportunity to create their own student reader.

TestPak 3.0 is an integrated computer program designed to print test masters; to permit on-line computerized testing; to help students review text material through an interactive self-testing, self-scoring quiz program; and to provide instructors with a gradebook program for classroom management. Test questions can be found in the *Test Item File,* or instructors may create their own. Professors may choose to use Testbank A for exam questions and Testbank B in conjunction with the quiz program. Printing the exam requires access to a personal computer—an IBM that uses 5.25- or 3.5-inch diskettes, an Apple IIe or IIc, or a Macintosh. TestPak requires two disk drives and will work with any printer. Diskettes are available through a local Brown and Benchmark sales representative or by phoning Educational Services at 1–800–338–5371. The package contains complete instructions for making up an exam.

A large selection of videotapes is also available to adopters, based on the number of textbooks ordered directly from Brown and Benchmark Publishers.

Acknowledgments

The authors acknowledge a wonderful team at Brown and Benchmark, a division of Wm. C. Brown Communications, Inc. We felt informed and nurtured every step of the way during the considerable and arduous task of developing a textbook. Special thanks goes to our editor Michael Lange and to our developmental editor Sheralee Connors. We are grateful, also, to our bookteam: Marlys Nekola, production editor, Eric Engelby, designer, Joe O'Connell, art editor/processor, Robin Storm, photo editor, and LouAnn Wilson, permissions editor.

We are also sincerely thankful to the following academic reviewers, who read various drafts of the book and provided helpful suggestions, constructive criticisms, new references, and endless encouragement:

- Wade Bedwell, Harding University
- Peggy De Cooke, Northern Illinois University
- James R. Council, North Dakota State University
- David F. Filak, El Paso Community College
- Regina Mace, El Paso Community College
- Betty Millin, Middlesex Community College
- Sandy Osborne, Montana State University
- Suzanne Pasch, University of Wisconsin–Milwaukee
- Sharon Paulsen, Ball State University
- Kathryn Quina, University of Rhode Island
- Robert R. Rainey, Florida Community College
- Donald M. Stanley, North Harris County College
- Roxanne Sullivan, Bellevue College
- Marc Wayner, Hocking Technical College
- Patrick S. Williams, University of Houston–Downtown

We dedicate this book to:

My wife Marilyn, and son, Ben,
who add each day to my
understanding of human development.
Donald B. Irwin

My family, my teachers,
my colleagues, and my students.
Janet A. Simons

Lifespan
Developmental
Psychology

chapter 1

The Study of Human Development

Key Terms

Lifespan developmental psychology
Nurture
Nature
Biological perspective
Behavioral-learning perspective
Cognitive perspective
Psychodynamic perspective
Humanistic-existential perspective
Organismic model
Mechanistic model
Contextual model
Zeitgeist
Ortgeist
Cross-sectional studies
Longitudinal studies
Sequential designs
Cephalocaudal principle
Proximodistal principle
Maturation
Critical periods

Learning Objectives

1. Discuss the philosophical roots and the scientific beginnings of the study of human development.
2. Describe beliefs about historical views of children.
3. Describe the characteristics of each of the five psychological perspectives, and list the advantages and disadvantages of each approach.
4. Compare and contrast the five psychological perspectives in terms of their overemphasized and de-emphasized factors.
5. Define the organismic, mechanical, and contextual models, and explain which perspectives emphasize these different developmental models.
6. Describe each of the major research methods, and list their advantages and disadvantages.
7. Explain the basic features of the experimental method.
8. Describe the basic features of cross-sectional, longitudinal, and sequential studies, and explain how each of these studies is useful in developmental research.
9. List and explain the general features of ethical research.
10. Discuss how and why experimenters control problems associated with vague terminology, experimenter bias, and subject bias.
11. Compare and contrast the various sources for psychological information.
12. Debate the role of nature and of nurture in human development.
13. List and describe general principles of physical development.
14. Compare and contrast qualitative and quantitative development.
15. Describe how the Ortgeist and Zeitgeist influence development.

> One cannot step in the same river twice. (*Heraclitus*)
> You can't go home again. (*Wolfe*)
> The only constant is change. (*Swift*)

As philosophers, scientists, and writers, both ancient and modern, have recognized, everything is constantly changing—nothing remains the same. **Lifespan developmental psychology** is the study of changes in peoples' lives from conception to death. You were conceived, nurtured in a womb, born, and cared for in infancy. You grew through childhood, experienced adolescence, and are now somewhere in your adult years. Thus far, your development has involved a mind-boggling number of changes, and many changes are yet to come. Developmental psychologists try to unravel the complex interaction of factors that constitutes development across the lifespan.

Exploring Your Own Development

In this chapter, you will learn about different perspectives on lifespan development, but no perspective is more important than your personal perspective. The information and ideas presented throughout this text will only become meaningful as you relate them to the events of your life. One way to do this is by personalizing the developmental timelines presented in Figure 1.1. The divisions on each timeline represent a typical course of events across the lifespan for that dimension. Space has been left between each line for you to write in significant events in your life.

Begin with the chronological age line. Above the zero at the left, write your birthdate; then, above each decade marker, write the year you were that age. Place a marker at the appropriate spot to mark today's date, and write today's date above it (e.g., if you are now 25, the mark would go halfway between the markers for 20 and 30). For each decade, write in any significant political/economic/cultural events that occurred during that time period. For example, if you were born in 1965, a major event of the next 10 years was the Vietnam War.

Above and below the occupational timeline, write information and dates for your school attendance, graduations, first job, part-time jobs, career decisions, college or vocational training, career achievements (promotions, pay raises, etc.), and job and career changes. Repeat the process with information and dates for the family cycle timeline. Finally, on the economic cycle timeline, write dates for when you achieved partial or complete financial independence. Also include dates for any major purchases, such as a car, boat, stereo, or home.

For fun, on the unused portions of your developmental timelines, write other significant life events that you anticipate. Some markers, such as graduating from college by a certain date, may become personal goals, while others may represent anticipated outcomes, such as retirement at a particular age or the arrival of your first grandchild.

Compare your markers with the "typical" ones presented in Figure 1.1. These markers represent society's norms for when these events and changes occur (Atchley, 1975). Although your markers may differ significantly from the typical ones presented, your own sense of being "on time" or "out of sync" is influenced by your perceptions of the appropriateness of the timing of your life events. Your perceptions of this may be different from someone else's perceptions. The difference is analogous to the difference in perspectives between a biography and an autobiography (Olney, 1980). Only you have the inner awareness of what living your particular life is like.

This exercise of defining the contexts of your development can become even more meaningful if you compare your markers with those of your classmates. If your class is typical of many today, you may be comparing information with a 39-year-old grandmother, a 39-year-old father of a toddler, and a 19-year-old with 39-year-old parents. By comparing your markers with those of others, you may begin to sense that development is less a regular, inevitable sequence of changes and more a multifaceted series of complex decisions and circumstances. Developmental psychologists use many types of research methods to understand the factors that influence change across the lifespan. In this book, you will learn about developmental psychology across the lifespan, but more importantly, you may gain a better understanding of your own development.

The Study of Human Development Through the Ages

From the earliest times, philosophers have speculated about the nature of human existence and the factors that affect human lives. Over the centuries, three models emerged to describe the course of human development (Pongratz, 1967). The circular model, prominent in the classical period of ancient Greece, held that humans were static and embodied the idea that "nothing was ever new under the sun" (see Figure 1.2). The semicircular model, found in various historical periods, depicted development as birth, growth, decline, and death. The spiral model, appearing first in the 18th century, viewed development as cyclical but progressive. Thus, today when you say, "Like father, like son," or "People are no different now than they were then," you are expressing ideas that fit with the circular model. When someone mentions that "Forgetfulness is a sign of aging," the person is evoking the semicircular model. Finally, when you hear, "Kids are sure a lot smarter today," the speaker is stating a view consistent with the spiral model.

The emergence of the spiral model, with its optimistic outlook that development showed progressive improvement from generation to generation, followed the period of Enlightenment, during which there were major advances in the natural sciences. Increasingly, the scientists of the time sought to classify and develop relationships between all living and nonliving things (Butterfield, 1957). As they linked ideas together, the concept of evolution or

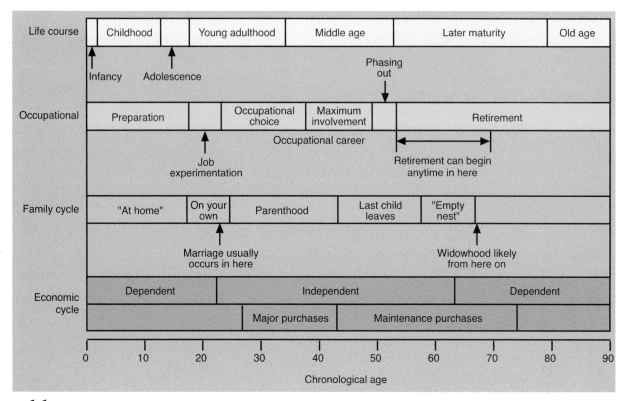

Figure 1.1

Developmental timelines. The divisions on each timeline represent a typical course of events across the lifespan for that dimension. Of course, each of us writes our own "script" for life that is influenced by many other factors and circumstances.

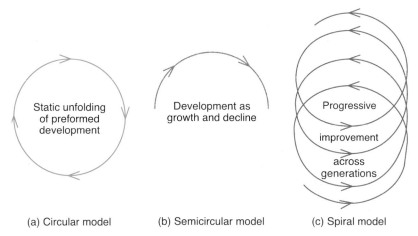

Figure 1.2

Three historical models of development.

development across time began to take shape. Progressive change began to replace the idea of static unfolding.

Philosophical Roots

Two scholars from the Enlightenment period—John Locke (1632–1704) and Jean-Jacques Rousseau (1712–1778)—were most influential in establishing the spiral model in the thinking of the time. Interestingly, while both Locke and Rousseau shared a belief in progressive developmental change, they held differing views about the nature of children. Locke proposed that children's early experiences shaped their later lives. He believed that, at birth, children

were a blank slate (a *tabula rasa*) and that experiences after birth filled in the blank slate and determined the course of later development. Locke acknowledged that individual differences were present at birth in intellect and temperament but argued that children were rational beings and highly receptive to the teachings of their parents. He emphasized that **nurture** (the effects of environmental experience and learning) was far more important than **nature** (innate hereditary factors) in determining a child's abilities and character. According to Locke, by careful instruction, parents could write upon a child's blank slate any characteristics they desired for the child. Thus, Locke viewed the child as the passive recipient of the teachings of parents or experiences. He believed that nurture was at the core of the child's development.

Unlike Locke, Rousseau proposed that children were active, self-willed determiners of their own development. Rousseau countered Locke's emphasis on nurture with a focus on the child's internal nature. He maintained that children were not vases waiting to be filled from their parents' nurturing. Instead, he believed that children's internal natures should be allowed to grow unconstrained by their parents and that, in due time, children would develop into logical beings.

Rousseau's view of children as internally driven and innately good differed from Locke's idea that children's internal nature was neither good nor bad but merely a blank slate. Together, Locke and Rousseau built the foundation for the modern era of the study of human development. At the same time, they provided the philosophical bases for two modern developmental perspectives: the biological and behavioral-learning perspectives discussed later in this chapter.

successful study tip

Linking Together Ideas and Images

One way to successfully learn and remember important points is to link the ideas or concepts with visual images. For example, Locke's idea of the *tabula rasa* provides an easy visualization of a blank slate. You can add to the content of your image by visualizing parents writing the word *nurture* on the child's blank slate. In a similar way, you can visualize Rousseau's ideas in the form of a spring-driven toy car, one that is driven by its own internal nature. You can further add to the information in your image by visualizing the car's vanity license plate to read *nature*. Successful study tips like this one are interspersed throughout each chapter to help you more easily learn important concepts.

Historical Views of Children

Before we discuss historical antecedents to the modern era of developmental psychology, consider what life was like for children of earlier periods of history—for example, children in ancient Sparta or in medieval Europe. Social historians have tried to reconstruct the lifestyles of children and the child-rearing practices of earlier times but are not unanimous in their conclusions.

After examining medieval paintings from the 16th and 17th centuries and other historical documents, Philippe Aries (1962) concluded that a separate concept of childhood did not exist until the 1600s. Aries maintained that, before 1600, early childhood was a characteristically pleasant time, with few constraints on a child's behavior. He further concluded that, with the evolution of childhood as a separate concept from adulthood, children experienced increasingly less freedom and increasingly severe punishments. Much of Aries's argument is based

Infancy and early childhood years have always been viewed as a special period of growth, exploration, and play.

on his speculations about the lives of medieval children. The actual data are very fragmentary.

In contrast to Aries's position, Lloyd deMause (1974) maintained that "(t)he history of childhood is a nightmare from which we have only recently begun to awaken. The further back in history one goes, the lower the level of child care, and the more likely children are to be killed, abandoned, beaten, terrorized, and sexually abused" (p. 1). DeMause emphasized the prevalence of child neglect and abandonment, abuse (both physical and sexual), infanticide, and exploitation. While he examined a much wider range of historical documents than did Aries, historical records of childhood and child-rearing practices from before the 18th century are sparse and generally inspire much speculation on the part of social historians.

Even though the historical record is slim, parents of earlier centuries were not all ignorant of their children's needs, mean-spirited, lacking in compassion, and continually abusive to their children (Borstelmann, 1983). Indeed, some historical documents record the kindness and affection of parents of earlier eras toward their children (Pollock, 1983). The obvious fact is that, even though infant mortality rates were high until recent times, over the centuries, the world's population increased as more and more children survived to adulthood. Social historians may not be able to agree on the conditions of these children's lives, but clearly, progressive improvement in child-rearing practices supported the population increase.

While the progressive improvement in child-rearing practices suggests that society's concept of childhood has changed over the centuries, some commonalities across the generations suggest that the first 5 to 7 years of childhood always have been given special status (Elkind, 1987a). The children of ancient Babylon began their schooling at age 6. In Sparta of ancient Greece, males did not enter the military barracks for training and education until age 7. During the Middle Ages in Europe, children did not begin to wear adult-styled clothing, discarding their gowns of earlier childhood, until about the age of 6. Also, European boys (girls stayed at home to learn to be homemakers) did not become apprentices to learn a trade until the age of 6 or 7.

The dawning of the Industrial Age of the late 18th and early 19th centuries, even with its abuses of child labor, did not result in children younger than 5 to working in the factories, mills, and mines. Today, parents still send their children to school at about age 6.

The common thread among these observations is that the first few years of life always have been viewed as different from the years that follow. Thus, children younger than 5 years of age have been treated differently from older children and adults. They have been viewed as immature and as dependent on the care of others. This recognition of the first years of childhood as different from the ensuing years provided the foundation for consideration of other special periods during the lifespan, with their own special needs and characteristics. For example, by the early 1800s, the idea of an awkward period between childhood and adulthood was well accepted, although the actual concept of adolescence was not considered by some to have achieved its special status until the period from 1870 to 1900 (Gillis, 1974).

With the recognition of early childhood as distinct from the rest of the lifespan came the awareness of the unique features of each age of life. The 18th and 19th centuries were a particularly fertile time for scientific discoveries in general, but especially for the scientific study of lifespan development.

The Scientific Beginnings of Lifespan Development

The cornerstone of science is careful observation. The budding scientists of the 18th and 19th centuries became careful observers of nature and, eventually, of human nature. The philosophical foundation built by Locke and Rousseau regarding the study of human development was strengthened by two other German philosophers—Johann Nicolaus Tetens (1736–1807) and Friedrich August Carus (1770–1808). In their writings, Tetens and Carus examined ideas about human development that covered the entire lifespan. They now are recognized as the first major theoretical and methodological advocates of the study of lifespan development (Baltes, 1983).

The Early Child Study Movement

The study of children and human development in general was given a major boost in 1859 when Charles Darwin (1809–1882) published his treatise *The Origin of Species.* Darwin's theory of evolution radically changed the way scientists viewed the development of species. The ideas of ontogeny (the development of individuals within a generation) and phylogeny (the evolution of species across generations—a major example of the spiral model of development) were linked together in the memorable phrase, "Ontogeny recapitulates phylogeny." In the mistaken belief that, within the development of an individual of a species, you can see repeated the evolution of that species, scientists, academicians, and laypersons began searching for examples of the principle. The early development of humans

was closely scrutinized because, in the sequence of beginning in a watery existence in the womb through crawling, creeping, and eventually walking, the Darwinians believed that the phylogeny of humans was being repeated in their ontogeny. The Darwinians were wrong in their beliefs about developmental recapitulation, but their efforts established the scientific value of studying children (Charlesworth, 1986).

Scientific child study was well established in Europe by the late 1800s. The tradition of scientists studying their own children also continued. Over the years, many psychology notables have made their children the focus of their scientific investigations. Wilhelm Wundt, the acknowledged founder of experimental psychology, kept a diary of his observations of his two oldest children during the late 1870s. Armande Binet, whose father (Alfred Binet) founded the intelligence testing movement; Polly Watson, daughter of behaviorist John Watson; Jacqueline Piaget, daughter of renowned Swiss cognitive-developmental psychologist Jean Piaget; and Denise Skinner, daughter of radical behaviorist B.F. Skinner, were all subjects of their scientist/fathers' investigations.

Developmental Psychology in the United States

Two factors were instrumental in bringing the child study movement to the United States: (1) interest in Darwin's ideas of evolution and (2) growth in public education for the masses. One person, G. Stanley Hall (1844–1924), combined these factors while enthusiastically advancing the fledgling science of developmental psychology. Hall chose children to illustrate the central ideas of evolutionary theory: that change across time (development) occurs throughout nature; that continuity between dissimilar species exists; and that individual differences are important because, through them, differences in adaptation and survival occur. Scientific child study became the method for discovering the basic ways in which all children change, the continuity between childhood and adulthood, and the individual differences in children.

At the same time, this data base of information was used to improve teaching and to meet the needs of children in school. For example, intrigued by similar research in Germany, Hall began in 1882 to study what 5- and 6-year-olds knew when they entered school (Hall, 1883). The title of Hall's work was "The Contents of Children's Minds." Hall developed the questionnaire method, which could be administered to hundreds of children at a time. He discovered that kindergartners knew less than many teachers expected and that what they knew contained much misinformation (e.g., that butter came from buttercups!). John Hancock, a colleague of Hall's at Clark University, investigated children's motor abilities. He discovered that kindergartners were not capable of the fine motor movements often expected of them in school (Hancock, 1894). He advocated that children be given tasks and games that involved large muscle movement.

Exploring Cultural Diversity: What Shall We Call Ourselves?

As the history of developmental psychology shows, modern developmentalists draw upon a rich background of diverse information sources to explain human development. Today, developmentalists are very aware of the need to explain developmental change in different cultural settings. From the beginning, the United States has encompassed people from many other countries of origin, as well as many nations of native Americans. These diverse origins have created a multicultural kaleidoscope that is beautiful to behold but difficult with which to work.

The difficulties arise at many different levels. Do the results of a study of preschoolers at a day-care center in suburban Houston apply equally well to preschoolers living in a Polish neighborhood of Chicago, in Chinatown in San Francisco, and in rural Montana? When they read about studies comparing Japanese and American teens, do Canadian teenagers think that their experiences are being considered? To whom does the term *Latino* refer to? To what extent do cultural differences result in developmental differences? Putting aside Americans' multicultural heritage, how successfully can studies in one country explain developmental change in citizens of countries elsewhere on the planet?

A basic difficulty we face, as the authors of this textbook, is how to address cultural diversity accurately and appropriately. We strongly believe in the need for a cross-cultural perspective for the global society in which all of us live. We also strongly believe that a multicultural perspective is needed to explain adequately the development of all of us living in the United States. But, what labels should be used to refer to the many cultural/ethnic groups here and worldwide?

In this text, we have consciously sought to limit the use of terms referring to skin color. We recognize that American society is a rainbow of skin colors but that color is often the least effective way to identify group membership. There is significant cultural diversity among "Blacks" as well as among "Whites."

We have chosen to use specific references, such as Mexican Americans or Swedish Americans, whenever possible. We refer to Hispanic Americans, African Americans, and Asian-Pacific-Islander Americans only when more specific designations are not possible. We have attempted to be sensitive to the preferences of different groups but recognize that we may not always have been successful in our efforts.

What shall we, as Americans, call ourselves? In terms of our cultural diversity, we think WONDERFUL is a great label!

Hall and his colleagues conducted hundreds of questionnaire studies with thousands of children. By present standards, Hall's methods left much to be desired. Little attempt was made to assure reliable sampling techniques; therefore, accurate interpretations of the data were difficult. Nonetheless, Hall popularized child study in the United States. His enthusiasm for his work (despite its lack of rigor) established developmental psychology as a scientific discipline with practical benefits for society.

The developmental ideas of James Mark Baldwin (1861–1934), another American psychologist, have not received the recognition they deserve (Broughton & Freeman-Moir, 1982; White, 1983). Unlike Hall, who investigated many widely varying subjects, Baldwin was a grand theorist. Baldwin proposed a stage theory of cognitive development and a comprehensive stage theory of development (Baldwin, 1895; 1906–1915). He applied Darwin's principles of biological organization and adaptation to the human mind and viewed thinking as the result of evolutionary processes. While now recognized as an important developmentalist, Baldwin was undoubtedly overshadowed in his day by his friend William James and his contemporary G. Stanley Hall. His lack of recognition also is likely due in part to his forced resignation from Johns Hopkins University after being discovered in a Baltimore brothel in 1909 (Dewsbury, 1984).

guided review

1. In the 17th century, John Locke proposed that an infant's mind was a *tabula rasa* and that a child's development was largely influenced by _____, while Rousseau later viewed infants as primarily influenced by their own active _____.
2. From studying paintings, Aries concluded that the concept of _____ began during the 1600s; from studying more general information, deMause concluded that early parenting was quite _____.
3. The early child study movement in the United States was most influenced by ideas of _____ and the growth in _____ for the masses.

answers (LO=learning objective):

1. experience (or: nurture, learning); nature (or: biology) [LO-1].
2. childhood; poor (or: abusive, neglectful) [LO-2].
3. evolution (or: Darwin); public education [LO-1].

Theoretical Perspectives of Human Development

Developmental psychologists share with all psychologists the goals of description, explanation, prediction, control, and application. To aid them in reaching these goals, developmental psychologists have adopted various theoretical perspectives on behavior and development. Theoretical perspectives provide frameworks within which data (sources of descriptive information about development) can be organized. These frameworks not only serve to organize information from scientific studies and specific theories but also are the basis for generating new, testable hypotheses, predictions about possible explanations for development. Thus, the frameworks provide systematic ways to test ideas about development and to apply the information gained to better understand development. Ultimately, the goal is that individuals will be better able to control their own development.

Major Psychological Perspectives

Five major perspectives have emerged from the scientific study of human behavior. A useful way to think about these frameworks is to consider the different views you have when you sit in different sections of a football stadium (Simons, Irwin, & Drinnin, 1987). Fans who sit on the 50–yd line see the game differently from those who sit near the goal lines. Although each group of fans can better describe certain aspects of the game, both can give accurate descriptions of the entire game. However, your understanding of the game would be more complete if you listened to information from both groups.

Likewise, the different psychological perspectives focus on different aspects of development. The observations and conclusions that developmental psychologists reach are influenced by their views of the playing field (i.e., by the particular perspectives they adopt). Knowledge of each perspective will help you to achieve a more complete understanding of lifespan development.

The sections that follow highlight major developmental perspectives. A summary of the lives and ideas of important researchers and theorists from each of the perspectives is included in Appendix A. Because this guide provides easy access to concise information about many theories, the specific theories found within each psychological perspective are not discussed in detail at this time.

The Biological Perspective

The **biological perspective** emphasizes the relationships of biological systems to behavior and mental processes. Within developmental psychology, this perspective began with Darwin's influence in the mid-1800s. Darwin's theory of evolution stressed the role of biogenetic factors in determining the development of individuals and, consequently, the evolution of species. Darwin's ideas about the causal influences of hereditary factors had an enormous impact on later developmentalists. The idea of heredity as the inborn determiner of development meshed well with the earlier philosophical ideas of Rousseau about the importance of innate factors in human nature.

In the United States, Darwin's ideas were supported by G. Stanley Hall and one of Hall's students at Clark University, Arnold Gesell (1880–1961). Gesell believed that development was the result of inherited factors that directed the development of the individual's anatomy and physiology. Maturation—the unfolding of the individual's genetic characteristics—was thought to occur with little influence from the environment.

By the 1950s, another theoretical approach within the biological perspective was developing. Ethology, the comparative study across species of the biological bases of behavior, began with the studies of European zoologists Niko Tinbergen and Konrad Lorenz (Lorenz, 1957; Tinbergen, 1951). Tinbergen and Lorenz were less interested in physical maturation and more interested in the biological causes of behavior. They studied animals in their natural environments, comparing their results to human behavior.

Another theoretical approach within the biological perspective has recently emerged. Advocates of sociobiology maintain that social behaviors represent inherited genetic patterns of behavior that enhance the survival of the organism's genes (Kitchener, 1985; Wilson, 1975). According to this theory, altruistic social behaviors have evolved and occur whenever self-sacrificing will enhance the survival of the gene pool (e.g., parents sacrificing to protect their children helps to assure that their genes will survive through their children).

A common thread among the various approaches within the biological perspective is that development is a function of biological factors determined by one's genetic inheritance. The biological perspective emphasizes understanding human biogenetics in order to understand human development.

The Behavioral-Learning Perspective

The **behavioral-learning perspective** emphasizes environmental factors in explaining development. While this position acknowledges the presence of hereditary factors, it views development as largely determined by one's environment. Hereditary factors are believed to provide a blueprint for development, with the environment providing the actual materials. Developmental psychologists adopting this perspective focus on the role of learning and experience in shaping development.

The first proponent of the behavioral-learning perspective was John B. Watson (1878–1958). In 1913, he focused the attention of psychologists on the importance of studying observable, overt behavior, the process of learning, and the influences of the environment on an individual's behavior. Like Locke, Watson believed that infants were born with a blank slate that was waiting to be filled with associations between environmental stimuli and behavioral responses. Development, for Watson, was the continuous amassing of new behaviors as the result of learning.

Watson studied the effects of classical conditioning, a basic form of learning originally studied by Ivan Pavlov, on the acquisition of emotions in young children. Another behaviorist, B. F. Skinner (1904–1990), studied operant conditioning. Classical conditioning involves learning to respond to cues, or signals, in the environment, while in operant conditioning, the environmental consequences received for certain behaviors are believed to be instrumental in shaping development. Skinner believed that the consequences available in an individual's environment determine that person's behavior (Skinner, 1953).

In addition to classical and operant conditioning, a third way in which learning can occur is through observation: Learners can observe the behavior of models and, later, imitate that behavior. Albert Bandura (1977), a leading advocate of observational learning, based his social learning theory on the concepts of modeling and imitation. Bandura's theory represented a departure from the strict environmental determinism of Watson and Skinner. Bandura included internal thought processes, such as mental representations and decision making, as important determiners of what behaviors a person chooses to imitate and when the individual chooses to imitate them.

Another important idea in social learning theory is that of the reciprocal interaction between the individual and his or her environment. The developing person is believed to be actively involved in determining the environment that ultimately shapes the person's behavior. Bandura's ideas represent a bridge between behaviorism and other perspectives, especially the cognitive perspective.

The Cognitive Perspective

Unlike the behavioral-learning perspective, which in its extreme form sees humans as passive responders to their environment, the **cognitive perspective** emphasizes the individual's active role in influencing his or her development. Generally, this perspective focuses on the development of thinking and related intellectual abilities. Cognitive development occurs as you attempt to make sense of your world. From the cognitive viewpoint, humans actively select and process information about the world and construct a meaningful internal representation of their knowledge.

A leading theorist in this area was Jean Piaget (1896–1980), who proposed a cognitive developmental theory (Piaget, 1952b). Piaget maintained that, from birth onward, mental development was the result of an active construction process by the individual. He proposed that cognitive development proceeds through an invariant series of stages in which a person constructs increasingly more complex and realistic internal representations of the world. Piaget made major contributions to the study of cognitive development. His theory is covered in greater detail in later chapters.

Another important influence on the cognitive perspective has been information-processing theory. Information-processing theorists believe that the individual elements of cognition (attending, perceiving, learning, and remembering) are organized into a series of sequential mental transformations that result in internal mental representations (Dodd & White, 1980). Many of the ideas in information-processing theory have been derived from applying concepts gained through computer technology and programming.

The Psychodynamic Perspective

The **psychodynamic perspective** stresses that development is the result of dynamic inner forces of which you are normally unaware. Developmental psychologists adopting this point of view maintain that humans are born with an innate

The founder of psychoanalytic theory, Sigmund Freud, is seen here with his daughter Anna, who was also a well-known psychoanalyst.

set of forces that shape and determine later development. This framework generally focuses on personality development, with Freud's psychoanalytic theory as the historical basis for many of the perspective's key ideas. Freud's stages of psychosexual development represent one of the first modern formal theories of development.

Freud's ideas were revised and extended by a number of his students, including his daughter Anna. Many of these neo-Freudians moved away from Freud's strongly held innate, biological views in favor of a greater role for social influences on personality development. Erik Erikson's ideas are notable in this regard because his stages of personality development include the entire lifespan (Erikson, 1963). In both Freud's and Erikson's views, each succeeding stage is fundamentally different from the previous one. A common idea among all psychodynamic views is that you are always in a state of conflict between your internal urges and society's constraints on your behavior.

The Humanistic-Existential Perspective

The **humanistic-existential perspective** emphasizes individuals' active roles in their ongoing development. Social and personality development are of primary interest from this perspective. An underlying belief is that you make conscious choices that directly affect how you develop. Development results from striving to fulfill your potential for growth. This position is influenced by the earlier philosophical movements of existentialism (the analysis of the meaning of existence) and phenomenology (the analysis of experience).

Abraham Maslow (1908–1970) and Carl Rogers (1902–1987), two of the founders of humanistic psychology, proposed separate theories that, while not directly developmental in nature, did incorporate ideas of progressive, developmental change. Maslow's metamotivational theory of personality underscored the universal tendency for growth (Maslow, 1968). The tendency to grow is illustrated in people's creativity and inventiveness, as well as in the way children naturally enjoy learning new skills and abilities. Carl Rogers, in his self theory, assumed that all people possess a tendency to grow in positive ways, once circumstances are supportive (Rogers, 1951). Rogers emphasized that people are the best judges of what they should do with their lives and that all have the capacity for self-improvement.

Rogers was not the first to suggest the idea of self-fulfillment in personality development. In 1929, Charlotte Buhler (1893–1974) proposed five stages in the attainment of self-fulfillment and positive development. Her stages went from childhood to old age and defined self-fulfillment in terms of identifying and attaining personal goals (Buhler, 1968). The ideas of Maslow, Rogers, and Buhler share the humanistic-existential perspective belief that each of us has the capacity to make our own choices and to change if we so choose.

successful study tip

Key Words for Remembering the Perspectives

When you need to remember several terms, cue yourself with a nonsense sentence in which the key words begin with the initial letters of the terms you need to remember. To remember the five psychological perspectives presented in this chapter, use the following sentence:

The B.B.C. produced Heidi.

The first *B* stand for biological, the second *B* for behavioral-learning, the *C* for cognitive, the *P* in *produced* for psychodynamic, and the *H* in *Heidi* for humanistic-existential. Don't laugh at this technique until you've tried it; it works!

Comparing the Perspectives

Each of the five psychological perspectives has its own set of assumptions, basic concepts, major theorists, and favorite methods for studying human behavior. The theories within each perspective represent sets of coordinated statements about how best to organize information about behavior. (Concise summaries of these and other theories are presented in Appendix A.) Each perspective provides important insights about developmental changes in behavior. However, the beneficial contributions come with the risk of overemphasizing some factors in developmental change, while de-emphasizing or ignoring other relevant factors present in other perspectives. None of these viewpoints is mutually exclusive. Common elements can be found among all of them.

In focusing on biogenetic factors, the biological perspective has contributed to understanding the physical and evolutionary bases of all development. But, in stressing hereditary factors and physical maturation, developmentalists who use this perspective risk not seeing how the environment influences behavior development. In reverse, the

same remarks can be made about the behavioral-learning perspective. In emphasizing the environment's active role in developmental change, behavioral-learning theorists have organized voluminous data about how people acquire new behaviors, but they often overlook the interaction of biogenetic factors.

The cognitive developmentalists have placed active mental processes at the core of developmental change. Interestingly, this perspective combines elements of both the biological and behavioral-learning approaches and makes its important contribution by stressing the interaction of the two. Cognitive development is seen as an active construction process through the interaction of innate mental processes and the environment.

Similarly, the psychodynamic perspective also stresses interaction—the interaction of innate psychic forces and social constraints. Freud contributed the focus on biological factors and childhood, while Erikson stressed social influences and developmental change across the lifespan. The idea of the ability to change at any age is also found in the humanistic-existential perspective, as is the concept that each individual is unique and possesses an inner striving for self-fulfillment.

While each of these perspectives provides a definite view of the developmental landscape, none—nor all of them collectively—offers a complete picture of human development. Where the perspectives overlap, the view is sometimes clearer and sometimes more cloudy about the nature of human development. For these reasons, grouping the perspectives under major models of development is useful.

Major Developmental Models

Because none of the psychological perspectives provides an exclusive, or conclusive, way to understand human development, elements of each of the perspectives can be found in three fundamental models of development (see Table 1.1). The underlying themes of the **organismic model** are biological structure and the self-directed activity of living systems (Fischer & Silvern, 1985). In contrast, the **mechanistic model** considers living systems to be reactive to their environments, more like machines whose actions can be comprehended by an analysis of their functional parts and the environmental factors that influence them. Fundamental to the **contextual model** are the ideas that living systems act upon their environments and are reactive to them and that each individual develops in a unique set of bio-socio-historical circumstances, the context of development (Lerner, 1985).

A theory that proposes innate, inherited factors as important contributors to human development is using the organismic model. Thus, the theories found within the biological perspective are in the mainstream of the organismic model; but elements of the cognitive, psychodynamic, and humanistic-existential perspectives also fall within this model. For example, Piaget's idea of innate mental operations, Freud's concept of dynamic inner forces, and Rogers's notion of an inner drive toward self-fulfillment all stem from the structural aspects of the organismic model.

Table 1.1
Summary Chart for Three Developmental Models

Model	Perspectives	Themes
Organismic model	Biological Cognitive Psychodynamic Humanistic- existential	Biological structure Self-directed activity Inherited factors Innate behaviors
Mechanistic model	Behavioral-learning	Effects of the environment on behavior Reactive behaviors Operant and respondent conditioning
Contextual model	All perspectives	Development within a bio-socio- historical context Individuals acting upon and reacting to their environments Synthesis of organismic and mechanistic models

In addition, the influence of the organismic model is seen in the active, self-directed roles given to people in the cognitive and humanistic-existential perspectives.

The basic connection between the mechanistic model and the behavioral-learning perspective should be obvious. Behaviorists have steadfastly maintained that people are fundamentally reactive to their environments. Behaviorists' analysis of learning into its basic elements of environmental stimuli and the effects of these stimuli on behavioral responses is the second major link to the mechanistic model. While neither the psychodynamic nor humanistic-existential perspectives view individuals in the reactive mode of the mechanistic model, elements of the model are present in their theories. The mechanistic influences of the environment are seen in Erikson's ideas about the effects of social constraints on behavior and in the humanists' views on environmental factors in the choices for growth or safety.

The contextual model has its basis in the dialectical philosophies of Hegel and Marx, the ideas that society is in a continual state of imbalance and that individuals reflect this state of flux in their actions and reactions (Riegel, 1976). In arguing for the contextual model, Soviet psychologist Lev Vygotsky rejected the idea that neither internal factors nor external factors were more important and favored the suggestion that both proceed in continual interaction. In the United States, Klaus Riegel and Urie Bronfenbrenner contributed to the model by emphasizing the broader contexts in which development occurs (Bronfenbrenner, 1979; Riegel, 1979). Both have maintained that development does not take place in a vacuum.

They believe that development can best be understood when the biological, social, cultural, and historical contexts in which the individual exists are considered.

In some ways, the contextual model represents a synthesis of the best features of the organismic and mechanistic models. The synthesis is achieved by stressing interactionism, the continuing cycle of action and reaction between the individual and his or her environment within a specific bio-socio-historical context. Elements of the contextual model are found in the biological, behavioral-learning, cognitive, psychodynamic, and humanistic-existential perspectives.

While each of the three developmental models brings the various psychological perspectives together in different ways, the contextual model has been particularly useful in helping to define a lifespan developmental perspective.

A Lifespan Developmental Perspective

As you have already learned in this chapter, lifespan developmental ideas have been proposed by persons both ancient and modern. The ideas of Tetens and Carus from the 18th and 19th centuries were historically important, as were those of some early 20th-century writers. In the mid-20th century, the Committee on Human Development at the University of Chicago was instrumental in advancing the lifespan developmental perspective (Havighurst, 1948, 1956; Neugarten, 1964, 1969). During the 1970s, this position was clarified as a result of several factors.

Interest in adult development and aging caused researchers to look for models to explain developmental changes during the adult years (Lerner, 1983). The biological perspective of growth and maturation worked well through adolescence but was not sufficient to explain adult development (Baltes, Reese, & Lipsitt, 1980; Baltes & Schaie, 1973). Studies of adult cognitive development highlighted increasing individual differences in intellectual change as people aged (Baltes, 1979a; Baltes & Schaie, 1974; Schaie, Labouvie, & Buech, 1973). The observed changes in adult development appeared to be more the result of the context in which the development was occurring than the result of simply being a certain age (Baltes et al., 1980). These factors were important in defining a perspective that could organize information about these non-age-related influences.

According to one of the leading proponents of this position, the lifespan developmental perspective incorporates the following major ideas:

> The potential for developmental change is seen to be present across all of life; the human life course is held to be potentially multidirectional and necessarily multidimensional (Baltes, 1979b; Baltes et al., 1980). In addition, the sources of the potentially continual changes across life are seen to involve both the inner-biological and outer-ecological levels of the context within which the organism is embedded. Indeed, although an orientation *to* the study of development and not a specific theory *of*

Each generation is unique. The hippies of the 1960s experienced different significant events than did the yuppies of the 1980s.

development (Baltes, 1979b), it is clear that lifespan developmentalists are disposed to a reciprocal model of organism-context relations. (Lerner, 1983, p. 13)

Lerner, Baltes, and others proposed that the organismic and mechanistic models were inadequate to account for developmental changes across the entire lifespan. Therefore, developmental psychologists looked to other models, especially the contextual model, for more adequate explanations. The result was a perspective that views human development as reciprocally linked to historically changing contexts across one's lifetime. A prominent feature of this approach is the attempt to understand the effect of the timing of life events on development.

The Zeitgeist: The Spirit of the Times

Before the current interest in lifespan development, when children were the primary focus, developmentalists typically investigated age-related factors, such as the motor development of 2-year-olds and children's cognitive development. These normative age-graded factors were held to be generally true for most individuals of certain age (Baltes et al., 1980; Baltes & Reese, 1984). For example, the norms for onset of puberty acknowledged some individual and cultural differences in timing but generally assumed that the onset corresponded to one's chronological age or time since birth and that the experience was essentially the same for everyone. However, the contextual model suggests that the experience is different, depending on the timing of the event (Neugarten, 1980b). Nonnormative life events, such as beginning puberty much earlier or later than the norm, produce differential effects.

In addition, normative history-graded factors—events commonly experienced by the majority of a culture—also produce different effects in people in different age groups, or cohorts. The impact of the Vietnam War on your development depends on how old you were at the time. Each era of history is marked by major events that serve to define the period. The German word for these markers is the **Zeitgeist,** the spirit of the age or the sign of the times. You probably recall some earlier Zeitgeists, such as the Dark Ages and the Elizabethan period. The Zeitgeist is another example of the importance of context in human development.

The Ortgeist: The Spirit of the Place

Another German word—the **Ortgeist,** the spirit of the place—describes another significant aspect of context in the lifespan developmental perspective. People not only experience life events at different chronological ages and at different historical times, but also at different geographical locations. Imagine what your life would have been like if you had been a 24-year-old male in 1944. Around the world, many men of that age were soldiers at that time. How would your experiences have been different if you were living in Germany, England, Russia, Argentina, Rhodesia, India, or Japan at the time? The effect of the Ortgeist is not always so global. Developmental differences in the onset of puberty in females have been noted between rural and urban settings (Zacharias & Wurtman, 1969). You may have noticed that people who live as little as 250 mi away from you speak a somewhat different dialect from your own. Like the Zeitgeist, the Ortgeist points out the great importance of contexts on development.

> ## successful study tip
>
> ### *Remembering the Zeitgeist and Ortgeist*
>
> Try visual imagery to help you remember these two foreign terms. One translation of "geist" is ghost. Picture in your mind a fantastic haunted house with old father time with his hourglass at the door. Father time is the Zeitgeist—the spirit of the age—and the haunted house is the Ortgeist—the spirit of the place.

Complexity of Human Development

As you have read this chapter, you may have recognized occasional examples of the circular, semicircular, and spiral models of development. For instance, Gesell's ideas about maturation coincide with the circular model. However, after considering the contextual nature of the lifespan developmental perspective, you may have concluded that even the elegant spiral model cannot adequately describe the complexities of lifespan development. If you have, you have reached the same conclusion as lifespan developmentalists.

Developmental psychologists who study the lifespan have rejected as too simplistic one-factor perspectives, such as the biological perspective, and one-dimensional models, such as the semicircular model of growth and decline. To more accurately describe the complexities of normative age-graded factors, normative history-graded factors, nonnormative life events, and the place and timing of significant life events, developmental psychologists created multidimensional (contexts), multidirectional (interactions), multigenerational (Zeitgeists), and multicultural (Ortgeists) concepts.

You were introduced to these complex factors at the beginning of the chapter, when you personalized the timelines in Figure 1.1. While complexity of this degree may seem mind-boggling, the end result is a perspective on development that does a better job of describing, predicting, explaining, and applying information about development to individuals' lives. In the sections that follow, we discuss the methods scientists use to understand these complex factors.

guided review

4. The _____ perspective includes such areas as maturation, ethology, sociobiology, and biogenetics.
5. The behavioral-learning perspective emphasizes that behavior is largely determined by the _____, while the cognitive perspective focuses on the development of _____.
6. The cognitive and _____ perspectives both propose active interaction of innate mental processes and the environment.
7. The _____ model combines features of both the organismic and mechanistic models.

answers (LO = learning objective):

4. biological [LO-3]. 5. environment; thinking [LO-3].
6. psychodynamic [LO-4]. 7. contextual [LO-5].

Research Methodologies

In the next few pages, you will learn about the basic research designs and methodologies of the developmental psychologies. These designs are summarized in Table 1.2. By learning how psychologists conduct their research, you become aware of both the difficulties of designing good studies and the limitations of all research. The information in this book and your developmental psychology course are based on thousands of research studies.

Naturalistic Observation and Case Studies

Naturalistic Observation

Naturalistic observation is a descriptive technique in which psychologists record the behaviors of persons (or animals) in natural settings. In these studies, a trained observer collects data without manipulating or changing the events that occur during the observation. Objectively and accurately describing behavior is difficult. The observer must disregard personal biases and opinions that could influence observations, refrain from interpretations and note only actual observed behaviors, and be accurate in observing all relevant behaviors. Naturalistic observation is often the beginning point of other research. Although naturalistic observations cannot be used to make scientific predictions or to determine cause-effect relationships, the information can be helpful in deciding which possibilities seem most likely and in developing testable hypotheses (tentative explanations about relationships among variables).

Sometimes, naturalistic observation is the preferred method for studying behavior. For example, some cross-cultural studies can utilize *only* naturalistic observation techniques; other methods would interfere with the existing culture. Margaret Mead (1935) used naturalistic observa-

tion to study gender roles in nonwestern cultures of New Guinea. She described alternative gender-role patterns than those generally found in the United States at the time (e.g., the Arapesh culture had very aggressive males and females; the women of the Tchambuli culture were more aggressive than the men).

Another naturalistic observation study that provided informative data unavailable with other methods was conducted by Anna Freud and Sophie Dann (1951) on the development of six German-Jewish 3-year-olds, who were orphaned when their parents were executed in Hitler's gas chambers. From early infancy until they were liberated from the Tereszin concentration camp, these youngsters had minimal contact with adults. When the six youngsters were placed together for a year in an English home, the children were restless, uncontrollable, noisy, and destructive toward toys and furniture. However, they also exhibited strong bonds with each other. The six children did not want to be separated, shared possessions, and protected each other. Despite their initial exclusive attention to each other, over time, they responded to adults and formed modest attachments with them. Freud and Dann concluded that the children were remarkably psychologically intact. As adults, all six led effective lives (Hartup, 1983). The naturalistic observation study of unconventional early childhood of these six youngsters revealed information about the resilience of human nature, the ability of peer relationships to help in socialization, and the adaptability of individuals to radical environmental changes.

Case Studies

An intensive study of one person is called a case study or the clinical method. Case studies are especially useful in studying therapy effects, behavioral changes after an event or disease, and personalities of atypical individuals.

The chief advantages of case studies are that psychologists can investigate unusual problems or unique events and can gather intensive, in-depth information about individuals. The main disadvantages of case studies are that objectivity is difficult and that case studies may not be representative of a group.

Surveys and Interviews

Surveys and interviews are research methods for measuring many people on several variables. Using either written questionnaires or personal interviews, researchers ask about people's attitudes, beliefs, and behaviors.

A survey of a population involves questioning every person in a group. A population survey is possible with a small group, such as "Mr. Freytag's sixth-grade class" or "Dr. Sutton's general psychology class," but with large populations, a complete survey is impractical. Therefore, most psychology research is done with a representative sample of the population. A representative sample contains the same essential characteristics and proportions as the population. One way to create a representative sample is to do random sampling, in which every individual in the population has an equal chance of being selected for the sample.

Table 1.2
Summary of Research Methods in Developmental Psychology

Method	General Definition	Advantages	Disadvantages
Naturalistic observation	Observed behavior in natural settings without interference by the observer	Provides descriptions of behavior in realistic settings. Good source of hypotheses for generating experimental research. Complexity of actual behavioral settings is captured.	Cause-effect explanations are only speculation. Complexity of setting may result in confusion about what variables are important.
Case study	Careful description of one individual's relevant behaviors	Provides intensive study of the individual. Good source of ideas for theory and research hypotheses. Allows investigation of the unusual.	The individual studied may not be typical. Information may be more anecdotal than representative.
Surveys and interviews	Gathering of systematic descriptions of thoughts, attitudes, and behaviors	Systematic data collection that can help detect differences in variables.	Wording of survey or interview may result in certain answers. Persons may misrepresent themselves on some items.
Correlational	Statistical procedures that can determine relationships among variables	Can help discover relationships among variables.	Cannot determine causality, yet correlations are commonly mistaken as cause-and-effect.
Experiment	Scientific comparison of groups under different conditions either in a laboratory or field setting	Allows direct control over variables, which permits looking at causality.	Sometimes, to gain control over variables, the resulting variables are not the most critical or the most applicable to real life. Cannot distinguish effects of age from cohort.
Cross-Sectional	Comparison of groups of different ages on one or more variables	Data gathering is fairly easy and allows a look at the effect of age on results.	Because different groups of individuals are compared, the age effect is confounded by cohort effects.
Longitudinal	Research in which the same individuals are tested at different times in their lives	The same individuals are followed over time to see how age and experience change results.	Because the same individuals are studied, results may be confused by experiences particular to that generation. May be too expensive to run, and there may be a large subject dropout rate.
Sequential	Combination of longitudinal and cross-sectional approaches	Allows examination of both age and cohort effects. Data are obtained as quickly as a cross-sectional study, with more data over time.	May be impractical and very expensive. Requires extensive planning and a large subject pool.

The population involved influences the interpretation of survey results. Table 1.3 presents results from a *Ms.* magazine survey on money. How might results be influenced by those responding to the questionnaire? For example, only 6 percent of respondents had high school or less education, while 37 percent had graduate degrees. Also, 54 percent of the women who responded had personal incomes exceeding $25,000, compared to the average income at the time for American women of $10,618. Would what was typical for this group be typical for all American women? While some comparisons in general changes in women's attitudes and practices regarding money could be made by comparing percentages in 1977 and 1988, could not many of the changes be due to differences in average age of the respondents? In 1977, the median age of survey respondents was 29; in 1988, the median age was 37. Indeed, survey data interpretation is often difficult.

In addition to securing a representative sample, researchers need to carefully word questions to minimize answer biases. For example, how would you be influenced by

the wording of the following questions: "In what *unacceptable* sexual behaviors have you engaged?" and "Do you believe that *babies* should be *killed* by abortion?" The wording of these two questions might influence the answers people give or provide cues to what answers the researchers want respondents to state. In the questionnaire results of Table 1.3, changing the wording of "When *poverty* comes in at the door, love flies out by the window" to "When total household income is reduced, love also decreases" might radically change the percentage agreeing with the statement.

Many respondents have a courtesy bias—that is, they try to provide responses that are socially acceptable to and/or that they believe the researcher wants. For example, they may give different responses to surveys done by the Democratic and the Republican political parties.

Another problem with some survey topics and questions is that people cannot accurately answer them. Questions about aspects of development that cannot be consciously remembered or that are difficult to calculate accurately often are "guessed at," even when people want

Table 1.3
Results of the 1977 and 1988 *Ms.* Magazine Surveys on Money

I. Which of the following do you have in your name?	1977	1988
1. Checking account	90%	94%
2. Credit card(s)	77	93
3. Savings account(s)	89	84
4. Life insurance	56	70
5. Real estate	28	46
6. A will	25	44
7. Mortgage	24	43
8. Bank loan	34	42
9. Stocks	24	33
10. Certificates of deposit		29
11. Mutual funds		26
12. Annuities		17
13. T-bills, notes, bonds		10

II. Do you agree with the following statements?	1977	1988
1. "Money can't buy happiness."	66%	73%
2. "When poverty comes in at the door, love flies out by the window."	49	32

From: "Smart Money," money survey in *Ms.*, November 1989, pp. 53–57.
Copyright © 1989 Lang Communications, New York, NY.

to answer accurately. For example, how exactly could you answer, "What were your favorite play activities when you were 2 years old?", "How many lies do you tell in a week?", and "How many times a day do you think about sex?"

Despite these flaws, carefully constructed and conducted surveys provide both good description and data that can be used to predict behaviors. However, survey data do not yield explanations of behavior.

The Correlational Method

The correlational method involves statistical procedures that establish relationships between two or more variables, such as traits, behaviors, or events. Correlational studies may be used to investigate such factors as the relationship between television viewing and aggressive behaviors (as more television is watched, children display more aggressive behaviors) and the relationship between weddings and suicides (most weddings and suicides occur in May and June).

In correlational studies, factors are examined for their "co-relations" (correlations), or links. Correlations are calculated from statistical procedures that yield numbers

called correlation coefficients. The correlation coefficients can vary from –1.00 to +1.00 and indicate the degree of association between variables. As a coefficient approaches +1.00, a positive relationship exists, and the two variables "vary" in the same direction. Research has found positive correlations between heights of monozygotic twins, between adult age and reaction time, and between IQ scores of siblings.

As a coefficient approaches –1.00, a negative relationship exists, and the two variables "vary" in opposite directions. Negative correlations have been found between anxiety levels and IQ test scores, between amount of parental criticism and children's positive self-image, and between golf experience and golf scores.

The coefficient indicates the strength of a correlation, with numbers closer to 1 (+1 or –1) indicating stronger relationships. A number close to zero indicates no relationship or a very weak relationship. An example of a nonsignificant correlation is the relationship between foot size and degree of honesty.

Strong correlation coefficients do not prove causation, even though they indicate a relationship. For example, statistician George Snedecor found a correlation coefficient of over +.90 in the United States between the number of divorces per year and the number of bananas imported (Strahan, 1978). If strong correlations proved cause-and-effect, you would have to conclude that eating bananas causes marital problems and divorces; or you might conclude that divorced individuals eat bananas to relieve depression or to bring luck in new relationships. The high correlation between bananas and divorces probably is caused by increasing population size over the years, resulting in both greater numbers of bananas eaten and greater numbers of divorces (Simons et al., 1987).

The Experimental Method: Basic Research Design

The most important methodology in psychology is the experimental method because it can be used to provide explanations of behavior and also information about causation. In experiments, psychologists establish the relationship between manipulated variables (independent variables) and measured variables (dependent variables). Experiments basically answer the question, "Does the independent variable influence the dependent variable?" (e.g., "Does an aggressive cartoon influence the amount of aggression displayed during children's play?"). The independent variable is the possible cause in the experiment. The dependent variable is the measured outcome of the experiment, or the effects of the independent variable.

Experiments involve experimental and control groups. Experimental groups receive specific amounts of the independent variable (e.g., a cartoon with one aggressive act every 30 sec). Control groups provide a baseline against which the behavior of subjects in the experimental groups is compared. Control groups receive no independent variable (e.g., do not see any cartoons) or a typical amount of the independent variable (e.g., see nonaggressive cartoons). Otherwise, control groups and experimental groups are treated alike.

Statistical procedures determine whether the independent variable produces a significant change in the dependent variable. Statistically significant results mean that the differences between experimental and control groups are unlikely to be the result of chance factors.

Experimental Techniques Used with Developmental Research

Cross-Sectional Studies

Developmental researchers want to explore how behaviors change over time. **Cross-sectional studies** allow researchers to look at how people of various ages differ on one or more factors, while providing the convenience of measuring all age groups in one time period (see Figure 1.3). Most developmental studies of children are cross-sectional in design (Clarke-Stewart, 1988). For example, to study how thinking skills change from age 4 to age 10, a researcher could locate comparable 4-, 6-, 8-, and 10-year-olds and measure them. One of the main advantages of cross-sectional studies is the brief amount of time needed for doing the research. However, this design ignores individuals' unique patterns of growth and development.

Longitudinal Studies

Longitudinal studies follow the same subjects over an extended period of time to note developmental changes in variables (see Figure 1.3). To study with a longitudinal design how thinking skills change from age 4 to age 10, a researcher could measure thinking skills in 4-year-olds and then remeasure every 2 years until the children were 10 years old. An advantage of this design is that researchers can assess continuity for individuals. However, time and

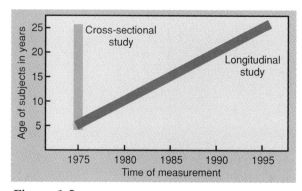

Figure 1.3

Cross-sectional and longitudinal methods. Cross-sectional studies are measurements across ages at one point or slice of time, while longitudinal studies follow the same individuals across time.

money commitments over a long period are required. Additional problems include the loss of subjects over the course of the study (the longer the study, the more likely that subjects will drop out) and the difficulty of generalizing from one cohort group to another.

In one longitudinal study, Donald Zytowski (1976) reassessed 882 adults who had taken the Kuder Occupational Interest Survey (KOIS) in high school. He found that, 12 to 19 years later, just over half of the subjects were employed in an area suggested by the interest inventory. Unlike some preplanned longitudinal studies, this KOIS study was not originally scheduled as a longitudinal study. In this case, the researcher had access to old KOIS surveys and decided to locate subjects, at much effort and expense, more than a decade after they had taken the test. Yet, the effort resulted in unique information about career continuity and satisfaction.

More typically, researchers set out to do longitudinal studies from the start. In medical research, the majority of studies are longitudinal. For example, a longitudinal study on whether the drug tamoxifen can prevent breast cancer will take 10 years and require 10,000 women from age 40 to 70 who are at high risk for breast cancer but who at the beginning of the study are healthy (Shereff, 1989).

Sequential Studies

Sequential designs are combinations of cross-sectional and longitudinal research designs in which individuals of different age groups are observed repeatedly over an extended period of time. A model of a sequential design is shown in Figure 1.4. Sequential studies allow researchers to have all the benefits of both cross-sectional and longitudinal designs and provide data that can be statistically analyzed to avoid the limitations of those designs.

A researcher might use a sequential design to study the thinking skills of 4-year-olds. Two years later, the subjects are remeasured, plus a new group of 4-year-olds are measured. Every 2 years of the study, former subjects are measured again and a new group of 4-year-olds is studied. Thus, each time the longitudinal group is studied, additional cross-sectional data are also collected.

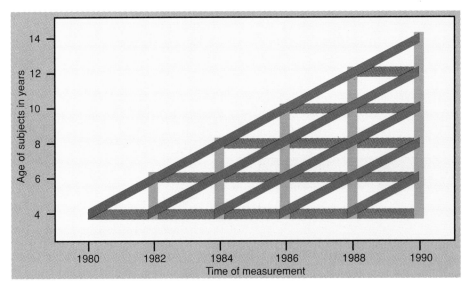

Figure 1.4
In this sequential design, both cross-sectional (vertical) and longitudinal (diagonal) comparisons are possible, as well as comparisons of 4-year-olds, 6-year-olds, and so forth (horizontal).

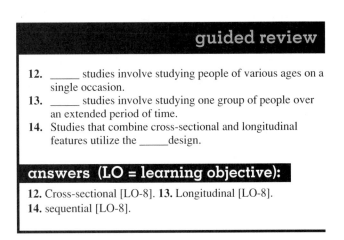

guided review

12. _____ studies involve studying people of various ages on a single occasion.
13. _____ studies involve studying one group of people over an extended period of time.
14. Studies that combine cross-sectional and longitudinal features utilize the _____ design.

answers (LO = learning objective):

12. Cross-sectional [LO-8]. **13.** Longitudinal [LO-8].
14. sequential [LO-8].

Research Limitations

Research Ethics

Psychologists are committed to increasing knowledge about human behavior, but in pursuing this goal, they must respect the dignity and worth of their subjects and avoid inflicting physical or psychological harm. Three important concerns in ethical research are deception, invasion of privacy, and lasting effects.

Deception

Deception in research studies involves misleading subjects about some aspect of the research in which they are participating. Subjects might be directly misled through directions or statements about the purpose of the research. They can also be indirectly misled by the general appearance of the research. For example, subjects might be given a bogus psychological assessment inventory or interact with an experimental confederate, a person employed by the researcher to pretend to be a "real" subject.

Most studies are done without the use of deception, but some studies require it. Conformity studies, for example, often involve the use of confederates who provide an "artificial consensus" for the real subject. However, deception in psychology experiments should be minimized, and as soon as the experiment is over, the subjects should be told about the deception and its possible effects.

Invasion of Privacy

Research should be designed to avoid the invasion of privacy of subjects' lives; the subjects' responses should be confidential, and all research materials (e.g., written materials, audiotapes, videotapes) should be kept in ways that keep identities of subjects private. Respecting subjects' privacy can be especially challenging in naturalistic observation because this design may involve subjects who do not know they have participated in a psychological study.

Lasting Effects

Psychological research should minimize the distress experienced by subjects. Researchers also need to ensure that their subjects do not suffer lasting effects from experiments. Informed consent allows subjects to be told about the study's basic characteristics and possible exposure to unpleasant stimuli before they agree to participate. In addition, subjects should be informed that they may withdraw their consent at any time during the study.

Another process that helps to eliminate lasting effects is debriefing. At the conclusion of participation in the experiment, subjects are reinformed about the study's purpose and told about any of the deceptions that were used. Subjects are often allowed to evaluate their experience, and researchers sometimes offer to inform subjects about study results.

When infants and children are research subjects, their parents must give fully informed consent for them to participate.

Rights of Children as Subjects

All of the ethical guidelines used with adult subjects apply to children, along with some additional concerns (Cryan, 1985). With young children, parental permission is required. With school-age or older children, both parent and child must agree to the research participation. The objection of either parent or child is sufficient to exclude a child from research. In addition, federal law protects high school students from research in the schools on such sensitive topics as sexual behavior and drug use.

The use of deception with children is highly discouraged because children may not have the cognitive capacity to understand the deception, even after debriefing. They may not be able to dismiss the deception, for example, of being told that they scored below average or that they did poorly on a task. Children may interpret lying by adult researchers as a betrayal. Studies that encourage children to behave in socially undesirable manners may have longer lasting effects on participating children than participating adults. Researchers should also avoid using tangible rewards, such as candy bars and small toys, to solicit young subjects.

Rights of Anencephalic Infants

One currently debated area is the use of anencephalic infants in medical research (e.g., Botkin, 1988; Fost, 1988; Landwirth, 1988; Milunsky, 1988; Nolan, 1988; Walters & Ashwal, 1988). Anencephalic infants are born without cerebral hemispheres but with active brain stems. Of the 1,800 American babies born each year with anencephaly, 55 to 75 percent are stillborn. Of the living anencephalic infants, 95 percent die within the first week.

The debate on the rights of anencephalic infants centers on their use as organ donors. Can anencephalic infants be used for donor organs because they are essentially "brain-absent beings"? Or, does the primacy of respect for persons, regardless of cognitive capacity or life expectancy, mean that anencephalic infants' organs cannot be used until there is total brain death?

Currently, 450 children need kidney transplants, 800 need livers, and 600 could benefit from heart transplants. These needy recipients could use the organs of anencephalic infants. Kidneys of anencephalic victims have even been successfully transplanted into a 12-year-old (Holzgreve, Beller, & Buchholz, 1987). What do you think is the proper choice? How would you define "human" and "death"?

An anencephalic newborn could be kept alive with mechanical ventilation until a recipient was found (Landwirth, 1988). This technology suggests further uses of anencephalic infants in research. Suppose anencephalic infants were legally ruled "dead," but basic functions could be maintained by technological means. Under what conditions could anencephalic infants be used for studying drug effects, classical conditioning, and other scientific concerns? What ethical restrictions would you place on such use of anencephalic newborns? Of embryos or fetuses?

Research Problems

Every psychologist must cope with an assortment of research problems. Three research problems are clarity of definitions, experimenter biases, and subject biases.

Operational Definitions

Definitions need to be precise so that psychologists can understand each other's works. For example, as a student, if your classmate says, "I did poorly on the test," what grade do you suppose your classmate received? *Poor* is an ambiguous term. For your classmate, *poor* might mean a B because this person only considers As to be worthwhile grades. On the other hand, the grade might have been a D, and a C would have been considered terrific.

The same is true in psychology. Vague definitions are confusing in communication. Therefore, psychologists use operational definitions, words defined with precise, observable, measurable criteria. For example, an extravert is defined as someone who scores 75 or more on the "Here I Am" Personality Scale; a couch potato is someone who averages more than 21 hr of television a week. You can disagree with operational definitions, but at least you can specifically define how the researcher used the terms.

Experimenter Bias

Experimenter bias occurs when experimenters inadvertently produce biased results. Possible sources of experimenter bias include subtle, nonverbal gestures during an experiment and slight differences in how the experimenter reads directions to subjects. If experimenters communicate their expectations to subjects, many subjects behave according to those expectations (i.e., there is a self-fulfilling prophecy in that the subject behaves in line with the expectation conveyed).

Subject Bias

Subject bias occurs when subjects fail to behave objectively or naturally in an experimental setting. Some subjects try to please the experimenter and provide desired results, rather than behaving as they typically would. Other subjects are more concerned with appearing "normal" to the psychologist than in providing true responses. A small number of subjects deliberately try to provide misleading and unhelpful responses.

Researchers use techniques that help them to minimize experimenter and subject bias. For example, many research studies are double-blind studies, in which neither the experimenter nor the subjects know which is the experimental group and which is the control group.

Research Limitations

Statistical Concerns

In the 1880s and 1890s, Francis Galton took growth measurements on 17,000 individuals. He analyzed his data during the pioneering days of descriptive statistics. Now, more than a century later, psychologists use an array of sophisticated statistical procedures. Yet, today's researcher still has one big problem that Galton also faced: "Statistics can support logical and illogical relations with equal significance and strength; it's up to us to distinguish which is which" (Clarke-Stewart, 1988, p. 71).

The Limits of Knowledge

In addition to improved methods of data analysis, psychologists need better methods of data collection. More efforts need to be made to collect data that are *meaningful*, in addition to being reliable, valid, and collectible (Clarke-Stewart, 1988). In all areas of developmental psychology, the amount of "fairly certain" knowledge is currently quite small. The "Exploring the Parent/Child Relationship" feature provides information about what psychologists currently know about parental effects on infants and preschoolers. Although thousands of studies have been done in this area, future psychologists have much to discover.

Using Research

Research Articles

The material in this book is based on the research findings of hundreds of studies. To learn more about any of the studies cited in the book, you may wish to read the original report. You can get the complete citation in the "References" section at the back of this book, and your college librarian can help you to obtain a copy of the journal article. Use the guidelines in Table 1.4 to help you understand the content of the article.

Psychology and the Mass Media

The results of psychological research are often covered in newspapers, magazines, and television reports. During this course and for the rest of your life, the mass media will partially inform you about psychological ideas. Sometimes, the popular press does an outstanding job of covering psychology. At other times, however, articles and reports are erroneous. The following guidelines can help you to become aware of and to deal with typical reporting errors (Simons, Irwin, & Drinnin, 1987):

1. Sensational studies are reported more than ordinary findings. This tendency can give you a false impression of typical research results. To understand a psychological topic better, you need to read review articles, scientific books, or several studies on the topic.
2. Because of time or space restraints, media reports usually give only partial information about a study. You may not be told essential elements of an experiment, what subjects were involved, and the research method used. Additional information can be located in the original report.
3. Correlational studies may be described erroneously as cause-and-effect relationships. Consider the other factors that may have contributed to a significant correlation.
4. Learn to distinguish among experiments, correlational studies and surveys, case studies, and "armchair" observations. Often, an individual's opinion or a dramatic anecdote is offered as proof for a conclusion. Ask yourself, "How good is the evidence?"

Exploring the Parent/Child Relationship: Current Knowledge About the Effects of Parents on Infants and Preschoolers

One goal of developmental psychology is to understand the parent-child relationship, and much research has been done on how parents affect their children's development. Reviews (e.g., Clarke-Stewart, 1979, 1988) of parent-child research suggest that a little is known, much is guessed, and most remains unknown for future psychologists to explore. The following brief look at the main points known about early parent-child interactions in several areas illustrates the limited but promising state of developmental psychology today. Current psychologists are moving away from overly simple generalizations about parents' effects on children's development, but unfortunately, they are left with new complexities and uncertainties, rather than definitive answers.

Infant Temperament

Researchers are confident that individual differences in activity level, inhibition, cuddliness, and irritability exist and that substantial stability in temperament exists from infancy through childhood. But, do parents influence temperament? Well, infants who become more "easy" in temperament have involved, expressive mothers, and infants who become more "difficult" have more insensitive mothers (Matheny, 1986; Washington, Minde, & Goldberg, 1986).

However, psychologists now believe in a two-way interaction between parent and child on temperament changes. One theory proposes that parents influence infants with moderate temperaments but that infants with extreme temperaments are more likely to influence their parents (Buss & Plomin, 1984). Another theory suggests that "goodness of fit" between parental behavior and expectations and the infant's temperament is important. Therefore, an assertive mother does better with a "difficult" baby than an "easy" baby, while a mother whose self-confidence is low does better with an "easy" than with a "difficult" baby (Lerner, 1984; Thomas & Chess, 1977).

Early Socialization

Much research on early socialization is in the area of parental discipline style. An authoritative parental style of being warm, reasonable, nonpunitive, and firm has traditionally been associated with children who are reasonable and compliant. However, some recent studies suggest that reasonable, compliant children promote authoritative parenting more than authoritative parenting results in reasonable, compliant children. Other research findings suggest that prosocial behaviors appear before parents attempt to teach prosocial behaviors and that children's temperament influences parents' socialization efforts (Clarke-Stewart, 1988).

As with temperament and attachment, early socialization is now viewed as a two-way interaction between parent and child. For example, what is the effect of parental use of aggressive discipline? The answer depends on the child's characteristics. A fairly nonaggressive child becomes less aggressive when punished, but an aggressive child becomes more aggressive when punished (Eron, 1982).

Cognitive Development

Research indicates that parents who instruct their children increase their children's cognitive performance. However, a parental teaching style that is directive, dominating, and cognitively undemanding is less helpful than a parental teaching style that is verbal, explanatory, and cognitively demanding (Clarke-Stewart, 1988).

Language Acquisition

One obvious influence that parents have on their children's language acquisition is the determination of which language their children learn. In addition, parental verbalization (e.g., complexity, variety, responsiveness) and verbal prodding (i.e., accepting children's language and asking children questions) influence children's comprehension and vocabulary. "Baby talk" or "motherese," however, is a response to the infant's talking style, rather than a way in which parents teach language to their offspring (Clarke-Stewart, 1988).

Conclusions

As with earlier research, current research does suggest that parental behaviors influence children's development, but little is known about the kinds of effects various behaviors have. Early research explored differences between lower- and middle-class parents or the effects of simple, brief manipulations in psychology laboratories. These kinds of research do not provide enough information for learning the complexity of parent-child influences. Today's researchers explore the effects of the child on the parent, as well as the effects of the parent on the child. The process of development requires more study, and researchers are relying more on such methodologies as longitudinal and sequential studies. Because subtle parental influences and complex interactions need to be explored, researchers are using more complex analyses, such as multivariate designs and meta-analyses. Demanding issues, such as nature-nurture, require large subject pools and more specific kinds of subjects, such as twins reared apart (Clarke-Stewart, 1988).

Much remains to be known about how parents influence their offspring. As Clarke-Stewart wrote in 1988:

> We have clearly increased our knowledge about parents' effects on children's development over the last decade. But what we have found out, it seems, is that the issue of parents' effects is more complex than we had thought. We have opened up that complexity by demonstrating the contributions of the child and the context to development and by tapping into an apparent myriad of factors in each of the three categories—parent, child, and context. The more we have found out, the more we have discovered there is to learn. Our progress has been expansive and expanding, divergent rather than convergent, question finding rather than question answering. (p. 65)

Table 1.4
How to Read a Research Report

Here are several tips for understanding research reports in professional journals:

1. The title of the study sometimes helps you to identify the independent and dependent variables. Many titles are in this format: "The effects of [independent variable] on the [dependent variable]." The title also identifies the subject matter of the study.

2. The abstract, which briefly summarizes the entire research study, provides a quick way to decide if the article is relevant to what you want to study. The abstract also helps you to organize your reading of the report by summarizing the report's important information.

3. The introduction gives the historical background of the research topic, provides a summary of relevant earlier research findings, offers theoretical explanations, and introduces the hypothesis of the present study.

4. The methods section contains a detailed description of how the study was conducted. The subjects used in the study are described, and the procedures of the study—the apparatus, directions to the subjects, and directions for conducting the experiment—are given. The methods section may mention assessment instruments or measuring devices used by the researchers.

5. The results section gives information about the data collected and the statistical procedures used. This section often includes charts, frequency tables, and bar graphs illustrating the results. Your mathematical and statistical background will determine how comfortable you are with the results section. You might want to pay attention to information about the level of significance as determined by statistical procedures. If the level of significance is given as $p < .05$, the results of the experiment would be found by chance fewer than 5 times in a 100. Similarly, if the level of significance is given as $p < .01$ the experimental results would be due to chance less than 1 time in 100.

6. The discussion section features the researchers' personal assessments of the results. They may interpret their results from a particular theoretical perspective, or they may present alternative explanations for their data. The discussion section often includes comments about the limitations of the present research study and may suggest future research studies.

7. Finally, the references give bibliographic information about research studies reviewed and used by the authors. This section provides good sources of information if you want to learn more about the research topic.

From: J. A. Simons, et al., in *Psychology: The Search for Understanding*, 1987, p. 50. Copyright © 1987 West Publishing, St. Paul, MN.

5. Results are sometimes oversimplified or overgeneralized. Check what is left out or overdone.
6. Reports may fail to distinguish accurately between observations and inferences. Check whether the report's conclusions are logically reached. If you want to be certain of the research findings, locate the original research report.

15. Ethical research minimizes use of _____, the deliberate misleading of subjects, but when it is used, its effects are minimized by _____ immediately following the experiment.
16. Researchers who use school-age children in their studies need the children's permission as well as _____ permission.
17. Precise, measurable definitions are called _____ definitions.
18. Both experimenter and subject biases can be minimized by using a _____ study procedure.
19. The textbook authors got their information from _____.

answers (LO = learning objective):

15. deception; debriefing [LO-9]. 16. parental [LO-9].
17. operational [LO-10]. 18. double-blind [LO-10].
19. psychological journals [LO-11].

General Developmental Issues and Principles

The Nature Versus Nurture Issue

A major developmental issue is the effect of the interaction of heredity (nature) and environment (nurture) on behavior. One popular idea is that psychological development must be preceded by an increment in biological maturation—that is, that genetic influences are first and environmental influences second (Scarr & McCartney, 1983). In fact, one general developmental principle is: "Physiological development precedes behavioral development." As you progress through the chapters in this text, you will encounter this principle in such topics as reading readiness and the effects of early versus late maturation in adolescence.

Some psychologists believe that genetic factors are so important that some genotypes are more likely to receive and to select certain environments and environmental features. For example, if a correlational study suggested that nearsighted people get higher grades and are more likely to go to college, then two conclusions are possible: Myopia may be related to genetic intelligence, or books may be more interesting to nearsighted persons because the books can be held close to the eyes. In another example, babies who inherit an easygoing, sociable temperament are more likely to be cuddled than more difficult babies, thereby increasing their opportunities to become even more sociable (Chess & Thomas, 1987). Clearly, nature and nurture interact with each other, increasing the effects of genetic differences among people.

Research: Twin Studies

How much of intelligence, personality, and mental well-being is genetically determined? Twin studies, which investigate the similarities and differences in identical and fraternal twins (including sets raised together and sets separated at birth and raised apart), provide one way to estimate these effects. Several studies found that monozygotic (i.e., identical) twins are more similar than dizygotic (i.e., fraternal) twins on the major personality dimensions of emotional stability and extraversion (Floderus-Myrhed, Pedersen & Rasmuson, 1980; Loehlin & Nichols, 1976; Martin & Jardine, 1986; Rose, Koskenvuo, Kaprio, Sarna, & Langinvainio, 1988). In addition to their identical genetic backgrounds, it could be argued that monozygotic twins, similar physical appearance and similar treatment from others could cause their similar personalities. However, several studies have found that similar treatment (e.g., dressed alike, in same classes) does not increase similarity in personality of monozygotic twins (Loehlin & Nichols, 1976; Rowe, Clapp, & Wallis, 1987).

The best methodology for studying genetic-environmental influences is to study twins who have been reared apart, since these twins maximize the genetic component and minimize the shared-family-context component. However, even many monozygotic twins have biological differences. These twins are "mirror images" of each other—their fingerprints are reversed, one is left-handed and the other is right-handed, and one has language skills dominated by the left hemisphere of the brain, while the other has the reverse (DeAngelis, 1986). Even height of monozygotic twins is only a ratio of 0.94 (0.90 if reared apart), meaning that about 10 percent of height is environmental, rather than genetic. Psychologist Nancy Segal explains the significance of this ratio:

> We don't say that 90 percent of your height is influenced by genetic factors and the other 10 percent by environmental factors. Rather, that ratio represents the proportion of differences among people that can be explained by genes or by environmental influences.
>
> Just because a characteristic is genetically influenced does not mean it can't be modified. By altering elements of our environment, we can alter genetic expression in any number of ways. (Rosen, 1987, p. 40)

Recent studies have found remarkable similarities in the characteristics, intelligence, temperaments, mannerisms, and preferences of reared-apart twins. Regardless of the personality trait studied, genetic contributions appear to be significant in these twins (Farber, 1981; Goldsmith, 1983; Holden, 1987).

One unique study compared 217 monozygotic and 114 dizygotic twins who were reared apart with 44 monozygotic and 27 dizygotic twins who were reared together on several personality dimensions (Tellegen et al., 1988). The researchers suggested that family-environment factors are much smaller influences than genetic components:

> Consistent with previous reports, but contrary to widely held beliefs, the overall contribution of a common family-environment component was small and negligible for all but 2 of the 14 personality measures. (p. 1031)

Table 1.5
Correlations for Scales of the Multidimensional Personality Questionnaire for Monozygotic Twin Pairs Reared Apart (MZA), Dizygotic Twin Pairs Reared Apart (DZA), Monozygotic Twin Pairs Reared Together (MZT), and Dizygotic Twin Pairs Reared Together (DZT)

Scale	MZA	DZA	MZT	DZT
Primary:				
Well-being	.48	.18	.58	.23
Social potency	.56	.27	.65	.08
Achievement	.36	.07	.51	.13
Social closeness	.29	.30	.57	.24
Stress reaction	.61	.27	.52	.24
Alienation	.48	.18	.55	.38
Aggression	.46	.06	.43	.14
Control	.50	.03	.41	−.06
Harm avoidance	.49	.24	.55	.17
Traditionalism	.53	.39	.50	.47
Absorption	.61	.21	.49	.41
Higher Order:				
Positive emotionality	.34	−.07	.63	.18
Negative emotionality	.61	.29	.54	.41
Constraint	.57	.04	.58	.25

From: A. Tellegen, et al., "Personality Similarity in Twins Reared Apart and Together" in *Journal of Personality and Social Psychology, 54*, Table 3, p. 1035, 1988. Copyright © 1988 American Psychological Association. Reprinted by permission.

As shown in Table 1.5, about 50 percent of measured personality diversity can be attributed to genetic diversity. In this study, the most important shared family-environment effects were positive emotionality and social closeness. However, the environmental influence on these factors was lower than the genetic effects on the genetically influenced traits of aggression, control, social closeness, positive emotionality, and achievement. The characteristics most influenced by genetic factors were constraint, negative emotionality, harm avoidance, social potency, stress reaction, and absorption.

A similar design was used in a study that looked at the neuroticism and extraversion in adult twins reared apart and reared together. Earlier studies had suggested that extraversion was .50 to .74 due to genetic factors and that neuroticism was .41 to .60. However, in this study, the proportion of variance attributable to all genetic sources was .41 for extraversion and .31 for neuroticism. These numbers are significant but much lower than the earlier studies, probably because the average age of the twins in this study was nearly 60. The findings suggest that genetic factors of personality are less important in later life than in early life (Pedersen, Plomin, McClearn, & Friberg, 1988).

Research with twins provides important information about the roles of heredity and environment on development and behavior.

Other Research Methods

In addition to twin studies, other techniques may be used to study the relative effects of heredity and environment. One possibility is children of twins studies (Clarke-Stewart, 1988). This subject pool allows study of the correlations between children and their parents and the aunts or uncles who are their parents' identical twin. Similar correlations between children and parents and between children and aunt/uncle twins demonstrate a strong genetic contribution. In one study of twins' children, the children's correlation with the twin parents and with the twin aunts/uncles on a nonverbal intelligence test was quite similar, suggesting that genetics is a large contributor to nonverbal intelligence (Rose, 1979).

Consanguinity studies (studies of biologically related individuals) examine as many biological relatives as possible to assess the degree to which they share characteristics and how closeness of relationship affects the degree of similarity. Heredity can also be studied by selective breeding in animals or by manipulating environments of either animals or people.

Other Psychobiological Developmental Issues

Outmoded Psychobiological Developmental Principles

A view of development as determined by either heredity or environment is outmoded. You do not need to decide if your personality and intelligence are due to nature *or* nurture—life is an interaction between these two factors. You may wish to think in terms of a gene-behavior pathway in which genetic aspects set limits or constraints on behavioral development and in which some characteristics will develop under certain environmental conditions. For example, PKU, or phenylketonuria, is an inherited condition in which infants lack the genetic material to provide the enzyme system that metabolizes phenylalanine, an amino acid. With a normal diet, severe mental retardation results; however, if foods with phenylalanine are kept from the infants' diet, there is no buildup that interferes with normal growth and function of the brain (Gottlieb, 1983).

Another outmoded conception of development is the biogenetic law, learned by numerous students as "ontogeny recapitulates phylogeny." Proposed by Haeckel in 1891, the biogenetic law implies that evolution occurs by terminal addition—that is, that in prenatal development, humans pass through a series of physical characteristics that reflect stages through which all their evolutionary ancestors passed (e.g., have gills during their "fish" stage and tails during their "animal" stage). However, if biogenetic law was correct, fetuses would develop teeth before tongues, yet these develop in the opposite order prenatally (Gottlieb, 1983).

Although a popular term in the 1920s, *instinct* (a fixed, innate, goal-directed pattern of behavior for a species) is not a useful term today. It is better to think of species-typical actions or species-specific genetic material that increases the likelihood of certain behavioral capabilities. While the term *instinct* implied universal and unlearned behaviors, the term *species-typical actions* acknowledges that few behaviors are fixed across the species and that behaviors are a complex interaction of internal states, environmental conditions, and past experiences (Bindra, 1985).

Current Psychobiological Developmental Principles

The following general principles are currently accepted as characteristics of human development (Baltes, Featherman, & Lerner, 1986; Gottlieb, 1983; Kagan, 1984):

1. Individuals have forward referencing—that is, physical development precedes behavioral development. Individuals have "preadapted" qualities. For example, all the behavioral capacities needed by newborns are developed during the prenatal phase.
2. Development follows the **cephalocaudal principle** of being from head to toe. Development occurs first and strongest in the head region and proceeds down the body trunk. This principle is illustrated by the size of the infant's head at birth in relationship to the rest of its body.
3. Development follows the **proximodistal principle**—that is, development occurs from the center of the body outward. Note, for example, how much more the center of the infant's body at birth is developed compared to its arms and legs.
4. Development involves differentiation. Virtually all behavior becomes more highly differentiated and versatile with development. In infants and children, increases in the perception of fine detail, finer muscular movements, and greater cognitive achievements illustrate this principle.
5. Development involves large and significant individual differences in all quantitative aspects of behavioral development. Quantitative change involves increases or decreases in size and number, such as physical height or the size of one's vocabulary.
6. Qualitative changes involve changes in process or function. Your problem-solving skills and memory

strategies as a college student are different from the ones you used in elementary school. Qualitative change that occurs as the unfolding of one's unique genetic plan is known as **maturation.**

7. Optimal stages exist when there is maximum susceptibility or ease of mastery for various tasks or situations. **Critical periods** refer to the time periods of most sensitivity to environmental influences.

8. The sequence of behavioral stages is remarkably consistent. For example, across such species as chickens, ducks, guinea pigs, sheep, and humans, the order of development of sensory systems is touch, balance, hearing, and then vision. Developmental psychologists vary in their emphasis on stages and qualitative changes in development.

9. Functioning—use, exercise, practice, stimulation, experience—may be necessary to maintain aspects of development. Experience contributes to species-typical development in three ways. Maintenance is the preservation of already-developed achievements. For example, young infants can babble the sounds found in all languages, but with the passage of time, only sounds common to one's native language are maintained. Facilitation accelerates the emergence of achievements that would eventually be reached otherwise. Induction refers to experience that is essential if the species-typical endpoint is to be fully achieved. Facilitative experiences regulate maturation and behavioral development; inductive experiences determine whether a behavioral or physical aspect is ever present.

10. Development involves canalization, or the movement from a wide range of behavior potential (plasticity) to a narrowed channelled behavior potential. As development continues, there are fewer diffuse, random options and more focused and specific development. Initial plasticity allows for recovery from early deprivation and for optimal adaptation to diverse environmental circumstances; yet, even plasticity likely has predetermined paths of development. Psychologists would like to know the degree of modifiability and reversibility in human development.

11. Developmental psychology is interested in the continuity and discontinuity of development. Are there abrupt changes that signal the emergence of reading readiness, or the ability to do algebra? Is there stability between childhood personality and adult personality? This complex discontinuity-continuity issue is being researched and argued. Data from the Berkeley studies beginning in the 1920s can support the concept that individuals have much stability between childhood and adult ratings (Block, 1981), as well as the idea that childhood characteristics are poor predictors of adult characteristics (MacFarlane, 1964). At the very least, factors that influence development express themselves cumulatively. The underlying structure is

there, but the expressive behaviors change with age and roles. An 8-year-old who persists at building Lego structures may persist in studying for final exams in college—the persistence is the underlying variable, but it is expressed differently throughout life.

12. Development is influenced by one's cultural context (the Ortgeist), historical time (the Zeitgeist), and lifetime. Development occurs over one's entire lifespan. Developmental tasks arise from three sources: physical maturation, cultural pressures, and individual aspirations and values.

You will encounter these principles throughout the remainder of this book as you read about development across the lifespan.

guided review

20. Studies of _____, especially ones reared apart, are useful in studies of nature versus nurture.
21. _____ development precedes behavioral development.
22. The sequence of behavioral stages is fairly _____.
23. One's Ortgeist, or _____ context, and one's Zeitgeist, or _____ time period, influence one's development.

answers (LO = learning objective):

20. twins [LO-12]. **21.** Physical [LO-13]. **22.** constant (or: consistent, predictable, regular) [LO-14]. **23.** cultural (or: place); historical (or: generational) [LO-15].

Exploring Human Development

1. Write your developmental autobiography, following the suggestions given in Appendix B. Collect oral biographies from persons of generations different from your own. Compare their experiences and contexts for development with your own. How different are the generational reactions to the same historical events?

2. If you have not already done so, add your personal markers to the developmental timelines in Figure 1.1. Make copies of the timelines, and ask family members and friends of different ages to complete them. Comparing your markers with those of your parents and grandparents can be especially interesting.

3. To better understand the different perspectives presented in this chapter, hold a minidebate with your classmates, presenting the pros and cons of each of the perspectives.

4. Explore the Ortgeist by seeking out students from different countries and with cultural experiences different from your own. Compare the similarities and differences in your experiences at different ages of development and your perceptions of significant life events and the appropriate ages for when they should occur.

5. Make two visits to a public setting (e.g., a city park or zoo, a shopping mall, a college student center). On the first visit, observe the behaviors of others. On the second visit, get ready to do objective observation (e.g., choose a specific

topic to observe, know ahead of time how you will record information accurately and void of personal biases). How did the two observation visits differ?

6. Locate surveys in popular magazines (e.g., *Ms., Ladies Home Journal, Money, Psychology Today*). How well written are the questionnaire items? Do you think the results will contain a representative sample of the general public?

Discussing Human Development

1. In what ways are the ideas of Locke and Rousseau still present in contemporary child-rearing practices? Which of these two philosophical views do you favor? Why?

2. In your opinion, which one of the psychological perspectives has the most positive, optimistic view of human development, and which one has the most negative, pessimistic view? Support your choices with examples.

3. An old conundrum questions whether the people make the times or the times make the people (i.e., is a political leader judged great by virtue of his or her own characteristics or the characteristics of the age in which he or she lived?). Using the Zeitgeist and the Ortgeist, make the case that the times make the people.

4. With regard to discussion topic 3, a key point of the contextual approach is that neither the times nor the people are exclusive causes; instead, the interaction of people and times is emphasized. Discuss examples from history that illustrate this interactive effect.

5. In what kinds of research studies would you refuse to participate? What research guidelines would you establish to ensure ethical conduct in research? What topics do you think are most important for psychologists to study currently? Why?

6. Do psychologists have a responsibility to monitor the applications of psychological theory? Are psychologists obligated to make certain that psychological findings are used in ethical ways?

Reading and Viewing More About Human Development

Baltes, P. B., & Brim, O. G. (Eds.). (1977–1984). *Life-span development and behavior* (Vols. 1–6). New York: Academic.

Kagan, J. (1984). *The nature of the child.* New York: Basic Books.

Kessen, W. (Ed.), & Mussen, P. H. (Series Ed.). (1983). *Handbook of child psychology: Vol. 1. History, theory and methods.* New York: Wiley. (See Chapter 1 by L. J. Borstelmann, "Children before psychology: Ideas about children from antiquity to the late 1800s," and Chapter 2 by R. B. Cairns, "The emergence of developmental psychology.")

Markey, P. (Prod.), and Redford, R. (Dir.). (1992). *A river runs through it.* PG, 123 min.

Pollock, L. (1983). *Forgotten children: Parent-child relations from 1500 to 1900.* Cambridge, England: Cambridge University Press.

Thomas, J. (Prod.), and Bertolucci, B. (Dir.). (1987). *The last emperor.* PG-13, 140 min.

Summary

I. The study of human development through the ages
   A. Before science, philosophers developed views about human nature and people's development.
      1. The circular, semicircular, and spiral models emerged to describe the course of human development.
      2. During the 17th century, Locke proposed that children were passively shaped by environmental experience and learning.
      3. On the other hand, Rousseau emphasized children's active, self-determining inner nature in influencing the course of development.
   B. Scientists are interested in the views of childhood and in the parenting styles of earlier generations.
      1. By studying paintings of children, Aries concluded that the concept of childhood first developed in the 1600s.
      2. DeMause viewed parenting in earlier centuries as involving high levels of neglect, abuse, infanticide, and exploitation.
      3. Evidence indicates that many early cultures saw the first few years of life as a special period, and during the 1800s, adolescence began to receive a separate status.
   C. The scientific beginnings of lifespan development began in the 19th century, as philosophical positions were combined with careful observation of the scientific method.
      1. Evolutionist Charles Darwin's mistaken belief that individual development included a repetition of the species' evolution contributed to the increased interest in researching infants.
      2. Scientific child study was well established by the late 1800s.
   D. The early child study movement in the United States was influenced by ideas of evolution and by public education.
      1. Hall studied children to learn about their development over time and about individual differences in children, and many of his findings were used by educators.
      2. Baldwin proposed an important stage theory of cognitive development.

II. Theoretical perspectives of human development
   A. Five major perspectives have emerged from the scientific study of human behavior, and each has added to the understanding of lifespan development.
      1. Influenced by the early work of Rousseau, Darwin, Gesell, and Hall, the biological perspective emphasizes the relationships of biological systems to behavior and mental processes in such areas as maturation, ethology, sociobiology, and biogenetics.
      2. The behavioral-learning perspective emphasizes that behavior is largely determined by environment and studies learning in terms of classical conditioning, operant conditioning, observational learning, and social learning.
      3. The cognitive perspective focuses on the role of thinking in an individual's active development,

with two influential theories being Piaget's cognitive developmental theory and information-processing theory.

    4. The psychodynamic perspective of Freud and Erikson emphasizes the role of dynamic inner forces of which the individual is normally unaware.

    5. The humanistic-existential perspective, typified by Maslow, Rogers, and Buhler, emphasizes the human potential for directly influencing ongoing development.

B. A comparison of the five perspectives of human development shows that, while each has important contributions, each overemphasizes some factors of development while de-emphasizing others.

    1. The biological perspective emphasizes heredity and maturation but minimizes environmental influences, while the behavioral-learning perspective exhibits the opposite bias.

    2. In many ways, the cognitive perspective combines elements of the biological and behavioral-learning approaches.

    3. Both the cognitive and psychodynamic approaches propose active interaction of innate mental processes and the environment.

    4. The humanistic-existential perspective focuses on ability to change across the lifespan, uniqueness of individuals, and striving for self-fulfillment.

C. Three major developmental models are the organismic, mechanistic, and contextual.

    1. The organismic model features biological structure; therefore, the biological perspective is typical, but elements of the other perspectives are also organismic.

    2. The mechanistic model views living systems as reactive to their environments; the behavioral-learning perspective is most fitting to this model.

    3. The contextual model considers aspects of biology and one's socio-historical circumstances, as emphasized by Vygotsky, Riegel, and Bronfenbrenner.

D. A lifespan developmental perspective considers the potential for developmental change across all of one's life, as well as in several directions and in many dimensions.

    1. The Zeitgeist, the spirit of the times, suggests that one's development is influenced by the beliefs that exist and the events that occur during one's lifetime.

    2. The Ortgeist, the spirit of one's place, suggests that one's culture influences the course of development.

    3. Human development, and the study of this development, involves much complexity.

III. Research methodologies

A. Often a beginning point of other research because it leads to testable hypotheses, naturalistic observation involves careful observation of nonmanipulated events.

B. The intensive study of one person is called a case study or the clinical method, and its primary uses are in studying the unusual situation or learning about an individual in-depth.

C. Using representative or random sampling with the survey method and interviews, psychologists can measure many people on several variables.

D. Correlational methods involve statistical procedures that establish relationships between variables; strong relationships do not prove causation, however.

E. The most important methodology in psychology is the experimental method because it can provide explanations of behavior.

    1. In experiments, psychologists study the effects of the independent variable on the dependent variable.

    2. All experiments involve at least one experimental group and one control group.

IV. Experimental techniques used with developmental research

A. Cross-sectional studies involve studying people of various ages on a single occasion.

B. Longitudinal studies follow the same persons over an extended time period.

C. Sequential designs combine features of cross-sectional and longitudinal research designs and study persons of varying ages over an extended time period.

V. Research limitations

A. Psychologists are committed to increasing knowledge through ethical research.

    1. Deception, or misleading subjects, should be kept to a minimum, and subjects should be told about the deception after the experiment.

    2. Research should be designed to avoid the invasion of privacy of subjects' lives.

    3. Subjects should be told about the basic nature of the study and any possible unpleasant experiences before participation, and debriefing should follow every experiment.

    4. Both parent and child must grant permission before children can be research subjects.

    5. An example of controversial research ethics is doing medical research with anencephalic infants.

B. Researchers must deal with a variety of research problems to conduct high-quality and meaningful research.

    1. Precise operational definitions are necessary for good research measurements and for communications with other psychologists.

    2. Researchers try to minimize experimenter bias that can influence subject performance.

    3. Psychologists want subjects to behave naturally rather than exhibiting such biases as wanting to be normal, helpful, or disruptive.

    4. Double-blind studies help researchers to control for some research problems.

C. Research has its limits, both in terms of how data are collected and in how they are statistically analyzed.

D. In addition to the information presented in your textbook, you can learn about research findings in psychological journals and through newspaper, magazine, and television coverage.

VI. General developmental issues and principles

A. Psychologists often conduct research studies to better understand the interaction between heredity (nature) and environment (nurture).

    1. Twin studies, especially ones comparing twins raised apart with those reared together, provide useful heredity-environment information.

    2. A more complex model involves comparing the offspring of twins with various blood relatives.

3. Consanguinity studies compare many biological relatives on shared characteristics.

B. Psychologists want to develop general developmental principles.

   1. Outmoded principles include the biogenetic law and the concept of instincts.

   2. Physical development precedes behavioral development, with physical development following the cephalocaudal and the proximodistal principles.

   3. The sequence of behavioral stages is remarkably consistent, and optimal time periods exist for some aspects of development.

   4. Developmental psychologists study both qualitative and quantitative changes and continuity and discontinuity aspects of development.

   5. Development is influenced by one's cultural context (the Ortgeist) and historical time (the Zeitgeist), as well as by physical maturation and individual decisions.

Chapter Review Test

1. Which of the following statements is consistent with the circular model of human development?
   - **a.** "Forgetfulness is a sign of aging."
   - **b.** "Kids are sure a lot smarter today."
   - **c.** "People are no different now than ever before."
   - **d.** "Humankind is going to the dogs."

2. Which of the following is *not* associated with the philosophical viewpoint of John Locke?
   - **a.** emphasis on nature
   - **b.** concept of *tabula rasa*
   - **c.** child as a passive recipient
   - **d.** experience and learning as cores of development

3. Which of the following accurately reflects beliefs about historical views of children?
   - **a.** Aries suggested that childhood received more emphasis prior to the 1600s than it currently receives.
   - **b.** deMause believed that parenting in earlier times involved higher rates of neglect, abuse, and exploitation.
   - **c.** Until the 20th century, adults failed to recognize that the first few years of childhood are special.
   - **d.** The concept of adolescence was well accepted by the 18th century.

4. _____ is the comparative study across species of the biological bases of behavior.
   - **a.** Sociobiology
   - **b.** Biogenetics
   - **c.** Maturational theory
   - **d.** Ethology

5. Concepts from computer technology and programming have influenced _____ theory.
   - **a.** metamotivational
   - **b.** information-processing
   - **c.** psychodynamic
   - **d.** cognitive developmental

6. The _____ perspective emphasizes that development results from striving to fulfill one's potential.
   - **a.** humanistic-existential
   - **b.** organismic
   - **c.** psychodynamic
   - **d.** behavioral-learning

7. The cognitive perspective combines elements of both the _____ and _____ perspectives.
   - **a.** biological; behavioral-learning
   - **b.** psychodynamic; biological
   - **c.** humanistic-existential; behavioral-learning
   - **d.** psychodynamic; humanistic-existential

8. The behavioral-learning perspective is most compatible with the _____ model.
   - **a.** contextual
   - **b.** organismic
   - **c.** mechanistic
   - **d.** interaction

9. When Carole is people-watching at the shopping mall, she is engaging in behavior that is most similar to the research methodology of
   - **a.** the survey method.
   - **b.** the case study.
   - **c.** experimentation.
   - **d.** naturalistic observation.

10. Case study is to _____ as survey method is to _____.
   - **a.** several subjects; several variables
   - **b.** one variable; several subjects
   - **c.** one subject; several subjects
   - **d.** several variables; one variable

11. The correlational method
   - **a.** is identical to the experimental method.
   - **b.** can be used to determine causation.
   - **c.** is no longer used in the field of psychology.
   - **d.** shows the degree of relationship between two or more variables.

12. In an experiment in which caffeine consumption is manipulated to learn about caffeine's effects on college students' ability to memorize key terms in developmental psychology, the independent variable is the
   - **a.** number of key terms that are memorized.
   - **b.** amount of caffeine consumed.
   - **c.** number of college students.
   - **d.** field of developmental psychology.

13. Control groups receive
   - **a.** no dependent variable.
   - **b.** the highest level of independent variable.
   - **c.** no independent variable.
   - **d.** the lowest level of dependent variable.

14. Which of the following developmental research experimental techniques can be done in the shortest time period?
    a. cross-sectional studies
    b. longitudinal studies
    c. sequential studies
    d. naturalistic observation studies
15. Effects of deception are minimized by
    a. getting parental permission.
    b. using confederates.
    c. experimenter bias.
    d. debriefing.
16. Which of the following is an example of an operational definition?
    a. A heavy smoker smokes several cigarettes daily.
    b. A good student has a grade point average of at least 2.85.
    c. Anger is an emotional response to thinking that one has been attacked.
    d. Developmental psychology is a useful course for the majority of students.
17. Which of the following is *not* primarily associated with the nature aspect of development?
    a. maturation
    b. heredity
    c. parenting
    d. genotypes
18. In the Tellegen et al. (1988) study of monozygotic and dizygotic twins reared together or apart, one personality trait influenced more by family-environment effects than by genetics was
    a. social closeness.
    b. stress reaction.
    c. aggression.
    d. achievement.

19. Which of the following statements is *not* consistent with general principles of development?
    a. Physical development comes before behavioral development.
    b. Development occurs first and strongest in the lower region of the body and then moves upward.
    c. The sequence of behavioral development is fairly consistent.
    d. Experience and practice aid the emergence, maintenance, and full achievement of developmental aspects.
20. Peter's school-age son Joey is more interested in recycling than is Peter. Joey has learned more about environmental concerns from teachers and television than his father did as a child. The difference in attitudes between Peter and Joey is influenced by their
    a. nature.
    b. Ortgeist.
    c. Gestalt.
    d. Zeitgeist.

Answers

(LO = learning objective)

1. C [LO-1].	8. C [LO-5].	15. D [LO-9].
2. A [LO-1].	9. D [LO-6].	16. B [LO-10].
3. B [LO-2].	10. C [LO-6].	17. C [LO-12].
4. D [LO-3].	11. D [LO-6].	18. A [LO-12].
5. B [LO-3].	12. B [LO-7].	19. B [LO-13, 14].
6. A [LO-3].	13. C [LO-7].	20. D [LO-15].
7. A [LO-4].	14. A [LO-8].	

chapter 2

Prenatal
Development

Key Terms

Fertilization
Ovulation
Ultrasound
Germinal stage
Implantation
Placenta
Amniotic sac
Embryonic stage
Fetal Stage
Reflexes
Quickening
Teratogens
Fetal Alcohol Syndrome (FAS)
Spontaneous abortion
Abortion
Genetics
Heredity
Chromosomes
Genes
DNA
Gametes
Phenotype
Genotype
Dominant inheritance
Recessive inheritance
Sex-linked inheritance
Sex-limited inheritance
Polygenic inheritance
Amniocentesis

Learning Objectives

1. Describe the process of fertilization, and list possible obstacles to the process.
2. Compare androsperm and gynosperm, and relate how their differences play a role in the gender of the developing organism.
3. List the major causes of infertility.
4. Compare and contrast the major kinds of technologies used to overcome fertility problems.
5. List the primary characteristics of the germinal stage.
6. List the primary characteristics of the embryonic stage.
7. List the primary characteristics of the fetal stage.
8. Describe some of the major teratogens and their potential effects on the developing organism.
9. Explain the effects that alcohol, cigarettes, and other drugs can have on the developing organism.
10. Differentiate between the terms *spontaneous abortion* and *voluntary abortion.*
11. Describe typical effects of the pregnancy on the expectant parents.
12. Explain the primary mechanisms of heredity.
13. Compare and contrast dominant inheritance, recessive inheritance, sex-linked inheritance, sex-limited inheritance, and abnormal chromosomes, and provide examples of each form.
14. Define genetic counseling and its uses.

Life has a flow to it. It flows across generations and within your own lifetime. Developmental psychologists recognize that life began flowing a long time ago and that each new life carries on the life flow of its ancestors. In this chapter, as we focus on the beginnings of life in individuals, we also look at how the life flow is carried forward through heredity and how heredity and environmental influences interact to begin the development that flows in each of us.

Exploring Your Own Development

How aware are you of the beginnings of your own development? What were the circumstances at the time you were conceived? Some of you may already know this information, others of you may want to know these things, and still others of you may wish for this information to remain a mystery. Regardless of your situation, you undoubtedly have acquired some knowledge and folklore about conceiving a child.

Every culture develops folklore about behaviors or signs that can influence the characteristics, health, and gender of the developing fetus. Some folklore seems to have persisted for generations and in many cultures. For example, researchers found a persistent, widespread belief that heartburn during pregnancy is associated with having a hairy child. Other folklore is specific to one or a few cultures. Sometimes, two unlikely cultures share an uncommon bit of pregnancy folklore. For example, both European Jews now living in New York and Catholics in Panama believe that putting a red ribbon on a newborn will ward off the evil eye (Goldfarb, 1988).

Researchers who collected 121 examples of pregnancy folklore in contemporary America found that the examples fit into three categories: (1) practices that influence the fetus (e.g., eating fish for an intelligent baby), (2) behaviors that ensure a healthy baby and a safe delivery (e.g., labor will be easy if a knife is kept beside the woman), and (3) practices that determine gender (e.g., eating lots of broccoli is associated with boy babies) (Kruger & Maetzold, 1983).

What pregnancy folklore do you know? Perhaps you have heard that male babies are carried high or to the front, while girl babies are carried low or to the back. At a baby shower, you may have placed a wedding ring on a string and held it over the expectant mother's palm. If the ring moved in a circle, you proclaimed the impending birth of a girl, but if the ring moved back and forth, you predicted a boy (Goldfarb, 1988).

Most pregnancy folklore seems unfounded, trite, but also harmless. However, some cultural beliefs about the pregnancy experience do seem to influence the expectant

Pregnancy folklore, may be exhibited at celebrations of an impending birth. One example says the number of ribbons a woman breaks opening packages indicates the number of children she will eventually have.

woman's actual pregnancy. Margaret Mead (1949), for example, found that cultures with the belief that pregnant women would experience morning sickness had the most expectant mothers experiencing morning sickness. In some other cultures, morning sickness was very rare; it was not an expected component of pregnancy and therefore was not experienced. Mead even found cultures in which morning sickness occurred only in the first pregnancy, as was expected from folklore.

As you continue reading about prenatal development, check your already acquired knowledge with that determined by developmental psychologists in their research.

The Process of Conception

Conception, or **fertilization,** occurs when a sperm penetrates the ovum, or egg. Scientists have known about fertilization since 19th-century zoologist Hermmann Fol saw the fertilization of a starfish egg through a microscope (Wassarman, 1988). Although knowledge about fertilization has grown considerably since Fol, the process of conception still remains one of life's most striking miracles.

Although most people become parents without much difficulty, the growing number of infertile couples suggests that conception cannot be viewed as a simple, matter-of-fact process. In fact, a closer look suggests that fertilization is an amazing process because little in human anatomy seems constructed to encourage its occurrence.

The Female Reproductive System

Each woman is born with approximately 400,000 immature ova (or oocytes) in her two ovaries; by puberty, about 100,000 ooctyes remain (see Figure 2.1a). Each oocyte is in a small, saclike structure called a follicle. A hormone called

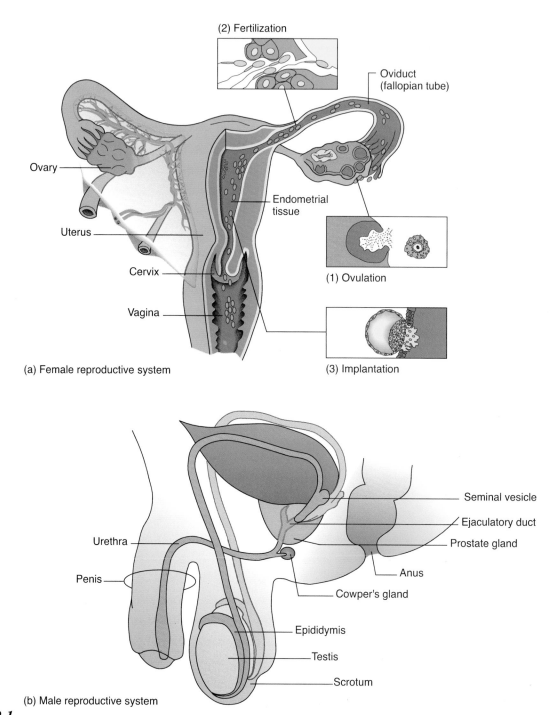

(2) Fertilization

Oviduct
(fallopian tube)

Ovary

Endometrial
tissue

Uterus

(1) Ovulation

Cervix

Vagina

(3) Implantation

(a) Female reproductive system

Seminal vesicle

Ejaculatory duct

Urethra

Prostate gland

Penis

Anus

Cowper's gland

Epididymis

Testis

Scrotum

(b) Male reproductive system

Figure 2.1

(a) Frontal view of female reproductive system, with insets showing the (1) site of ovulation, (2) site of fertilization, and (3) site of implantation. (b) Side view of male reproductive system.

follicle-stimulating hormone (FSH) causes the monthly maturation of an ovum. Another hormone—luteinizing hormone (LH)—triggers **ovulation,** the release of the mature ovum from its follicle. Women usually ovulate about every 28 days, but ovulation can fail to occur, may be ahead of schedule, or can be delayed by a variety of factors, including stress and illness. Although women have thousands of ova, only a few hundred of them become mature and are released over a lifetime. After ovulation, fertilization must occur within 24 hr, or the egg begins to physically deteriorate. Thus, more than 90 percent of the time, conditions are not right for fertilization to occur.

After ovulation, the egg emerges from the follicle through a rupture in the ovarian wall. Despite what might seem a useful, practical way to construct the body, the ovaries are not directly connected to the fallopian tubes, the desired site of fertilization. As shown in Figure 2.1a, the released egg must find its way into one of the fallopian tubes and is then carried through the tube toward the uterus, or womb. The mature egg is about the size of a period in this book, and the opening to the fallopian tubes is about the size of a printed hyphen. The ovum has no self-mobility and so is dependent on currents from the cilia of the fallopian tubes to pull it into this small opening. Once in the fallopian tube, cilia move the ovum toward the uterus. However, the fertilization process can further be impeded or made impossible by fallopian tube constrictions or scar tissue caused by an anatomical defect, infection, or disease.

The Male Reproductive System

Men whose testicles (testes) are healthy and mature usually produce several hundred million sperm (or spermatozoa) each day (see Figure 2.1b for the major components of the male reproductive system). Some men produce fewer sperm, due to physical conditions (e.g., an undescended testicle), illnesses (e.g., mumps during adulthood), or lifestyle practices (e.g., marijuana smoking). Only one sperm needs to fuse with an ovum to cause fertilization.

Fertilization

During intercourse, the sperm are released in semen during ejaculation. Once released in the vagina, the sperm, making whiplike tail movements, must try to swim through the narrow, mucus-filled cervix, through the uterus, and up into a fallopian tube. This journey is quite a task for a sperm, since its entire length is about 1/600th inch. Navigating these few inches to the fallopian tube is difficult, not only because of the length of the journey but also because of the anatomical obstacles along the way. The journey is so difficult that, unless the man releases at least 20 million sperm during ejaculation, fertilization is unlikely.

The general environment of the female's reproductive tract is hostile to sperm. The vagina's acidic pH level protects against bacteria and germs entering the reproductive tract, and this pH level also is not conducive to long life for the sperm. Approximately half of the sperm die shortly after ejaculation. In addition, the opening of the cervix is quite small and is filled with a mucous plug that provides another barrier to disease organisms. Many sperm expend all their energy and die while swimming against the physical barriers of the vagina, the cervix, and the uterus. Although sperm can travel very fast by moving their tail, they are not constructed with steering gear. Any sperm that miss a clear route are destroyed by the female's white blood cells.

Of the remaining sperm, some migrate into each fallopian tube, further reducing the number of sperm available for fertilization (assuming, of course, that ovulation has oc-

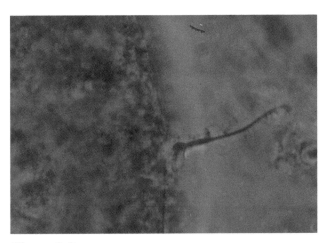

Figure 2.2
One human sperm enters the egg through the zona pellucida, a jelly-like coating around the ovum.

curred and that the ovum has moved into one of the fallopian tubes!). In addition, the sperm must swim upstream (so to speak) against the current since, from the cilia in the fallopian tubes to the mucus in the cervix, movement in the female reproductive system is outward toward the vagina. Sperm that somehow manage to reach the ovum must try to penetrate the zona pellucida, the outer coating of the egg, as shown in Figure 2.2. Only a few hundred sperm may remain to penetrate this coating, and only one sperm is able to fuse its genetic material with that of the egg. This fusion is fertilization, and the newly fertilized egg is called a zygote (Wassarman, 1988).

One reason for the difficulty of the fertilization process is that the female anatomy is better designed to facilitate pregnancy than fertilization. More importantly, fertilization difficulties help to safeguard against high rates of genetic disorders and poor-quality offspring. The least healthy sperm never make it near the egg and therefore cannot influence the next generation.

Despite the seeming obstacles, conception occurs with remarkable ease for many couples. For most couples planning to conceive (and for many who are not!), the timing of intercourse to coincide with ovulation is the major concern. Sperm are likely to be active and plentiful enough to be able to fertilize the egg for about 48 hr, and since the egg remains capable of being fertilized for about 24 hr, fertilization from sexual intercourse is feasible for about 2 days out of each menstrual cycle (usually around the middle of each menstrual cycle).

Timing of Intercourse and Gender

People once thought that chances of producing a boy child could be enhanced by tying a string around the right testicle and eating salt and that chances of producing a girl child could be enhanced by tying a string around the left testicle and eating sweets (Ericsson & Glass, 1982; Fraser, 1986). Scientists now know, however, that timing of intercourse can influence the likelihood of conceiving a male or a female.

Sperm that unite with the egg to produce a female child are called gynosperm (X sperm), while those that lead to the production of a male child are called androsperm (Y sperm). The testes produce about 3 percent more androsperm than gynosperm, which may be one reason why more boys than girls are conceived (Maranto, 1984). Androsperm have longer tails and weigh less than gynosperm. Therefore, a higher proportion of androsperm reach the site of fertilization faster than slower swimming gynosperm (gynosperm have a heavier load to push and a shorter tail with which to push). If ovulation has already occurred at the time of intercourse, more male children are conceived because androsperm are in the majority among the sperm that reach the egg first. However, gynosperm remain active longer than the faster swimming androsperm. If intercourse occurs before ovulation, more female children are conceived because a higher percentage of gynosperm will have survived to penetrate the later-arriving egg. Timing of intercourse does not guarantee the birth of a female or male offspring; it just changes the odds.

The technology of gametrics can be used to improve gender selection odds even further. In gametrics, gynosperm and androsperm are physically separated by putting the semen in different solutions. When sperm are placed in a column of albumin solution, androsperm reach the bottom first. When sperm are placed in a column that has a gelatinous powder on top, the heavier gynosperm fall and reach the bottom ahead of the androsperm (Ericsson & Glass, 1982). Although some worry that this type of technology will increase the birth of male babies over female babies, in the United States, the most common use of gametrics is to choose the gender of a later-born child so that it will be the opposite of the child or children already in the family. In addition, gender selection may be useful in helping families to decrease their chances of passing on sex-linked disorders, such as hemophilia and Duchenne's muscular dystrophy (Schaeffer, 1987).

Fertility and Fertility Problems

Current Fertility Rates

According to the U.S. Bureau of the Census, only 37 percent of American families have children currently living with them, a drop of 8 percent since 1970. Moreover, only 8 percent of these families have three children, and just 4 percent have four or more children. In 1960, 21 percent of families had three or more children. Despite the low percentage of families with children, nearly 90 percent of all American women ages 35 to 44 have given birth to at least one child. African-American women tend to have earlier timing of first births. For example, in 1980, 30 percent of 18- to 19-year-old African-American women had at least one child, while only 12 percent of their European-American counterparts had borne children. By age 25, over half of all African-American women but only a third of European-American women have had at least one child. Overall, the birthrate is quite similar for both groups—about 2.2 for European Americans and 2.5 for

African Americans. For both groups, more than 85 percent of births occur before age 35 (Hogan, 1987).

Involuntary Childlessness

Does your image of the typical American family include Mom, Dad, two kids, and a pet? Although, fewer than 10 percent of families fit this stereotype, considerable pressure exists to include child raising in one's life. Only 15 percent of European-American women and 10 percent of all other American women remain childless (Hogan, 1987). Few couples voluntarily decide to remain childless. Some couples, however, find that one of the partners is infertile, or incapable of biologically conceiving a child. Infertility probably affects 1 in 10 couples (Miall, 1986).

Infertility can be caused by a number of factors, such as aging, infections (e.g., pelvic inflammatory disease, which can be caused by untreated sexually transmitted diseases), anatomical defects (e.g., blocked fallopian tubes), and prior medical treatment. For example, childhood and adolescent cancer treatment may affect survivors' fertility, especially for males. Radiation therapy directed below the diaphragm has been shown to reduce fertility in both sexes by 25 percent, while certain types of chemotherapy affect the fertility of 60 percent of males. The most significant drops in fertility rates have been associated with Hodgkin's disease and male genital cancer (Byrne, Mulvihill, Myers, & Connelly, 1987).

Reproductive Technologies

Since the 1950s, the number of options for overcoming infertility problems has been growing. These options currently include fertility drugs, artificial insemination by husband (AIH) or donor (AID), in vitro fertilization (IVF), embryo transfer, and surrogate pregnancy (Planned Parenthood, 1985; Sher and Marriage, 1988). Each kind of reproductive technology involves moral and legal issues.

Fertility Drugs

Fertility drugs are used to increase ovulation, assist in implantation of the embryo, or lower the risk of miscarriage (spontaneous ending of the pregnancy). Some modern fertility drugs are considered low risk, with one of the more serious side effects being an increased possibility of multiple births. However, some scientists fear that today's fertility drugs and supplemental hormones may lead to serious damage years from now for either the mother or her offspring (Direcks & Holmes, 1986).

Scientists are concerned about delayed side effects primarily because one drug went from being a blessing to being a monster. In 1957, diethylstilbestrol (DES) was advertised as producing "Bigger and stronger babies, too." First synthesized in 1938, DES in the 1950s became the standard treatment for threatened miscarriages. The versatile and supposedly safe DES was also used in high doses as "morning-after" pills to keep a possibly fertilized egg from implanting in the uterus and as a livestock feed supplement, and in low doses as a milk suppressant and as therapy for breast cancer and prostate cancer (Direcks & Holmes, 1986).

DES was used to prevent miscarriages on the basis of one poorly designed research study, and its use in this area continued even after better research showed that it was not effective. Up to 3 million pregnant American women and 380,000 pregnant women in the Netherlands received DES (Direcks & Holmes, 1986). By the late 1960s, researchers were noticing that a rare cancer of the vagina called clear-cell adenocarcinoma was much more common in DES-daughters (daughters of mothers who used DES) than in other females the same age. These women's lives could only be saved by removing their reproductive tracts. Other damage from the DES treatment included the following:

- Between 70 and 90 percent of DES-daughters in their teens have benign adenosis, which is misplaced glandular tissue in the vagina.
- Two-thirds of DES-daughters have structural abnormalities in the upper reproductive tract. These abnormalities include T-shaped uteruses and cervixes that open up under the weight of pregnancy.
- Two of every ten DES-sons either have undescended testes or cysts in the testes.
- DES-sons also have higher rates of hypospadias (a defect where the opening of the penis is not properly positioned), constricted urethra, and microphallus (very small penis).
- Pathological sperm are found in 25 percent of DES-sons.
- DES-mothers have higher breast cancer rates than other women.

Because of delayed side effects such as these, doctors and scientists are very cautious in their recommendations of fertility drugs to couples experiencing infertility. Even so, fertility drugs remain a major form of treatment for infertility and are often part of the treatment involving other reproductive technologies.

Artificial Insemination

Artificial insemination, by which a husband's (AIH) or donor's (AID) sperm are collected and then used to fertilize the woman's egg, was first performed in the United States in 1890 and has since become a common procedure (Andrews, 1984).

Of current techniques, artificial insemination may be one of the easiest medical procedures for overcoming fertility problems, but psychological, moral, and legal issues are numerous. Some men may feel inadequate or may be unable to cope with their feelings about the donor. An Israeli study of 44 infertile couples who chose the AID procedure found that 80 percent of the husbands felt guilty about not "proving manhood" or "being a real father" (Andrews, 1984).

The decision about whether to tell offspring about their AID conception is even more complex. Will telling the child change the relationship with the parenting father? Will not telling the child withhold potentially critical medical information? Will an informed child attempt to develop a relationship with the biological father?

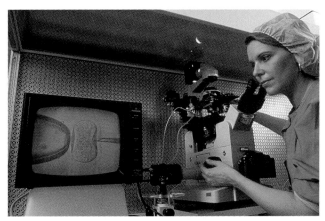

This medical researcher is using a needle to inject sperm cells directly into a human egg (shown on screen). A light microscope allows her to carefully monitor the process.

In Vitro Fertilization

Nearly everyone refers to in vitro fertilization (IVF) as "test tube babies," and this catchy nickname may lead people to believe that IVF is a simple and highly successful procedure. In reality, IVF has a pregnancy rate for a single attempt of just 10 percent and involves complex procedures (Barol, 1987).

Developed in the 1970s with the successful birth of Louise Brown in July 1978, the IVF procedure is stressful, costly, and time consuming (Barol, 1987; Halpern, 1989). The woman is first given up to 12 days of drug injections to stimulate multiple ovulation. Her side effects from these drugs usually include headaches and severe mood swings. During this time, the couple is asked to abstain from sex so that the man's sperm count can build up.

Next, the woman is anesthetized, and the mature eggs are surgically removed from her ovaries with the aid of either a laparoscope or an ultrasound scanner. Commonly, six to eight eggs are retrieved and placed in glass containers along with the man's sperm. The man's sperm are usually obtained fresh by masturbation but must be specially treated to duplicate the conditions found in the woman's reproductive tract.

If cell division occurs, one or more embryos are transferred to the uterus. The woman must lie still for several hours and limit movement for most of the next day. She must also undergo injections of progesterone (a hormone) that help prepare the uterus to receive the fertilized embryo. Procedures such as these may cost as much as $8,000, with a success rate between 10 and 25 percent (Menning, 1988).

Embryo Transfer

During the 1980s, the procedure called embryo transfer (ET) was developed. ET involves the removal of an embryo from a woman's uterus and the insertion of the embryo into the uterus of the woman who will bear the child. The fertilized egg must be removed from the first uterus from 4 to 6 days after fertilization. One variation of this procedure involves frozen embryos (Andrews, 1984; Planned

Reprinted by permission of Doug Marlette and Creators Syndicate.

Parenthood, 1985). Frozen embryo transfers have already resulted in identical twins who are more than a year apart in age and a custody battle over frozen embryos.

Surrogate Parenting

One of the most emotionally charged and controversial reproductive alternatives is surrogate pregnancy. In this procedure, one woman carries a pregnancy for another. Often, the surrogate mother is inseminated with the parenting father's sperm, although donor sperm or an embryo resulting from IVF can be used (Planned Parenthood, 1985). Despite many public discussions about this technique and legal controversies, little research has been conducted on the psychological aspects of surrogate pregnancy. One study of 30 surrogate mothers found that they typically experienced 4 to 6 weeks of grief following the birth (Andrews, 1984).

Ethical and Legal Issues

Each of the foregoing reproductive technologies involves complex ethical and legal issues. While in one study involving 450 couples, only 8 were rejected for artificial insemination (Andrews, 1984), some service providers routinely refuse to artificially inseminate single women. As more single women and men and gay and lesbian couples, as well as infertile couples, choose to have or to adopt children through the use of these technologies, society will need to clarify the rights of donors and surrogates, the rights of individuals to have access to these technologies, and even the legal meaning of such basic terms as *mother, father, son,* and *daughter.*

Future Conception Technology

The current level of conception technology is complex, and the future may hold even more promising, or alarming, possibilities. The following is just a short list of fertilization techniques that many scientists believe will become feasible in the future (Kirby, 1987; Ostling, 1987a). Which techniques do you think should be encouraged, discouraged, or forbidden?

- Cloning (creation of identical individuals from a single cell)
- Artificial wombs
- Parthogenesis (reproduction from unfertilized eggs)
- Gestation of human embryos within animals
- Twin fusion (the surgical splitting of embryos to produce twins)
- Hybrids of humans and animals
- Development of human embryos for medical research purposes
- Ectogenesis (the growth of the fetus outside of the body)

Technologies to Help Ongoing Pregnancies

Reproductive technology is also invaluable in helping to maintain pregnancies to full term. In **ultrasound,** acoustic pulses are sent into the pregnant woman's body from a probe placed on the abdomen, and then a computer analyzes reflected pulses to map the fetus's body structure. Ultrasound techniques are so sophisticated that structures as small as the pupil on the eye of a second-trimester fetus can be examined (Miller, 1985; Rothman, Grant, & Strahorn, 1988). Not only can an ultrasound scanner detect the fetus's location and fetal structural problems, some researchers also believe that it can provide information about normal brain functioning. For example, by 28 weeks, normal fetuses respond to a buzzer by forcefully clenching their eyelids. In a study of 680 fetuses that were at least 28 weeks old, ultrasound showed that 8 fetuses had no buzzer response. Two of these eight fetuses were deaf, four had major structural abnormalities of the nervous system, and two were stillborn (Miller, 1985).

Transtelephonic monitoring, which records and transmits vital information over the telephone to medical personnel, is useful for high-risk mothers. A pregnant mother wears a 3-inch sensor below the navel for a 1-hr recording in the morning and again in the evening. Each hour's worth of information can be transmitted by telephone in only 3 min. These data are analyzed by a computer, and if early labor is detected, prompt use of drugs is often effective in stopping preterm labor.

A second type of transtelephonic monitoring device can transmit fetal heart-rate tracings over the telephone. This device is most useful with pregnant women who have diabetes or hypertension, who are in preterm labor, or who have been pregnant longer than 40 weeks (Garcio-Barrio, 1988).

Treating Fetuses

Medical and surgical treatment of fetuses is new and experimental. An early procedure first used in New Zealand in the early 1960s involved blood transfusions to the fetus. More complex and recent procedures involve surgery in utero. For example, in some cases, a shunt, or catheter, has been successfully added to a hydrocephalic fetus to allow normal head growth (Crooks, 1988).

As in other reproductive technologies, the medical personnel involved need to consider the risk to the mother, the potential benefit to the fetus, and whether preterm labor can be avoided. Important ethical issues are raised by these procedures. For example, under what circumstances should a medical doctor choose a fetus's interests over a mother's decision (Crooks, 1988; Fost, Bartholome, & Bell, 1988)?

Stages of Prenatal Development

Throughout gestation—the time from fertilization to birth—an ever increasingly complex individual develops from the interactions of a genetic plan and the individual's environment. (These interactions are discussed in the sections that follow this one.) During prenatal development, the single-cell zygote undergoes thousands of cell divisions, and it changes and grows as it passes through three prenatal stages: the germinal, embryonic, and fetal stages.

The Germinal Stage

The first 2 weeks of prenatal development are called the **germinal stage.** During these 2 weeks, the fertilized egg goes from the single-celled zygote to a mass of approximately 150 cells.

From Zygote to Blastocyst

In the first 3 or 4 days, the beginning organism moves down the fallopian tube and into the uterus and begins cell division. By this time, it has taken on the form of a blastocyst, a fluid-filled sphere, which helps to protect the developing organism. For the next day or two, the blastocyst floats freely in the uterus.

One side of the blastocyst forms a thickened cluster of cells called the embryonic disk, from which the baby develops. The embryonic disk first divides into two layers, the ectoderm and the endoderm. The ectoderm is the upper layer, and it develops into the skin, nails, teeth, hair, nervous system, and sensory organs. The lower layer, or endoderm, evolves into the major organs—digestive system, respiratory system, liver, pancreas, and salivary glands. Soon, a middle layer called the mesoderm appears and develops into the inner skin, muscles, skeleton, and circulatory system.

successful study tip

Visualizing the Three Layers of the Blastocyst

Take a moment to develop some visual images of the three layers of the blastocyst so that you will remember their layer order and what they develop into. Begin with the ectoderm. Visualize the word *ectoderm* lying on the skin of your arm, then on your hair, and finally on your teeth; this pairing will help you to remember what the ectoderm becomes. Next, see yourself swallowing the word *endoderm* to help you remember that it becomes the digestive system; likewise, you can remember that it forms the respiratory system by visualizing yourself inhaling and exhaling the word *endoderm*. Then, see the word *mesoderm* imprinted on your biceps muscle, because one of the important things the mesoderm forms is your muscular system.

Finally, visualize the three words out in front of you, with *ectoderm* on top and *endoderm* on the bottom. (Remember the order by letting the "end" of *endoderm* remind you of "bottom.") Place *mesoderm* in the middle of *ectoderm* and *endoderm*. (Because *mesoderm* and *middle* both start with *m*, you'll easily remember this.) This visualization helps you to recall the order of the layers of the blastocyst. Be sure to add *mesoderm* last to your visualization, since it is also the last to develop in the germinal stage.

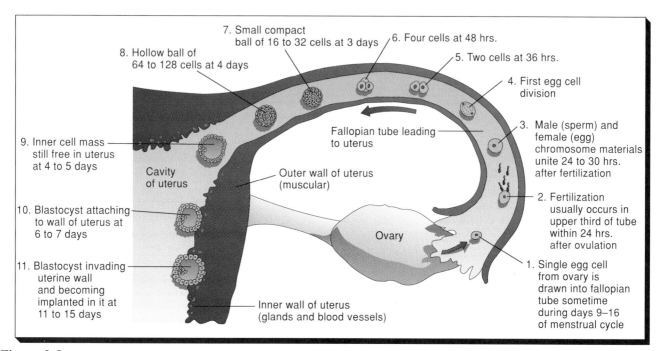

Figure 2.3
Significant developments in the germinal stage.

Development of the Nurturing and Protective Mechanisms

During the second half of the germinal stage, other parts of the blastocyst develop a complex system that nourishes and protects the developing organism. The trophoblast, the outer cell layer of the blastocyst, grows threadlike tendrils that penetrate the lining of the uterine wall by secreting digestive enzymes. This allows the blastocyst to implant in the wall and to begin receiving nourishment from the mother's body. When the process of **implantation** is completed, the developing organism is called an embryo (see Figure 2.3).

As implantation occurs, the **placenta** (the transfer organ between the mother's system and the developing baby), the umbilical cord (which connects the baby to the placenta), and the **amniotic sac** and chorionic sac (membranes that surround and protect the baby) begin to develop and continue developing during the embryonic stage.

The placenta provides for the transfer of oxygen, nourishment, and waste products to and from the maternal system and the baby via the umbilical cord. The placenta also provides protection from infections and foreign substances and forms a barrier against thyroid-stimulating and growth hormones, nucleic acids, neutral fats, bacteria, and viruses (Silver, 1987). A third function of the placenta is producing hormones needed during pregnancy for readying the breasts for lactation and for producing uterine contractions during childbirth (Silver, 1987).

Surrounding the developing organism is the amniotic sac, a membrane filled with amniotic fluid that both protects the baby and produces room for the fetus to float and move. The baby will urinate into the amniotic fluid; from there, the waste substances enter the placenta and are eliminated by the mother. The fetus also exchanges amniotic fluid by swallowing it. The exchange between the baby and the amniotic fluid is slow, but the mother has fairly rapid exchange of amniotic fluid and completely replaces it every 2 or 3 hr (Newton & Modahl, 1978).

The end of the germinal stage coincides with the mother's expected menstrual period. If the expectant parents are not already looking for signs of pregnancy, the absence of menstruation may be the first sign that fertilization has occurred and that a pregnancy has begun. Soon, the woman may notice other indicators of pregnancy (e.g., nausea and vomiting, tingling sensations in the breasts, changes in frequency of urination). A visit to a medical clinic for testing or the use of a pregnancy home test kit can confirm what the woman's body is signaling to her. Whether performed at a clinic or at home, the tests are an accurate way to detect pregnancy (Hale, 1984).

The Embryonic Stage

During the second stage of gestation—the **embryonic stage**—all of the major body systems and individual organs develop. This 6-week period usually ends around the eighth week of gestation, but it may last longer. Because of the tremendous physical changes during the embryonic stage, it is the stage of greatest vulnerability to developmental birth defects.

The First Month

At 1 month, the embryo is from 1/4 to 1/2 inch long. Both the cephalocaudal principle (the head develops faster than the lower parts of the body) and the proximodistal principle (the central area develops faster than the extremities) are evident in the 1-month-old embryo's appearance. The embryo has a head and a trunk and just the beginnings of the arms and legs on the trunk. At this stage, the embryo also has a tail, a feature that soon recedes. A primitive heart is already beating about 65 times a minute, sending blood through tiny arteries and veins. The brain, kidneys, liver, and digestive tract have also begun to develop. Head swellings will develop into eyes, ears, mouth, and nose.

The Second Month

At the end of the embryonic stage, the organism is just under 1 inch long and weighs about 1/13 oz. At this point, the head is about half of the total body length and has recognizable features. The embryo even has a tongue and taste buds. The embryo's brain is sending messages that coordinate the functions of the organ systems—the heartbeat is steady, the stomach can produce digestive juices, the kidneys can filter the blood, and the liver produces blood cells. The limbs have developed significantly. The arms have hands and fingers, and the legs have knees, ankles, and toes. Around the start of the ninth week, bone cells start to form; this is the marker that indicates the start of the third stage of prenatal development.

The Fetal Stage

The third and longest stage, the **fetal stage,** is one of continuing development and growth. Monthly changes in the fetus are summarized in Table 2.1. During the fetal stage, the fetus typically grows to over 19 inches and more than 7 lb. Many behaviors, including all of the **reflexes** (automatic behaviors in response to external stimulation), also appear during the fetal stage.

The developing fetus's internal environment consists of the amniotic fluid and its constituents, the embryonic membranes, and the uterus. The fetus also has a life-support system made up of the umbilical cord, the placenta, the uterus, and the maternal circulatory system (Smotherman & Robinson, 1987). The environment outside the mother influences the fetus via the physical transmission of mechanical stimuli through the mother's abdomen (Smotherman & Robinson, 1987). During the fetal stage, mothers often find that the fetus responds with movement to music and voices. Toward the 29th week of gestation, all healthy fetuses respond to a loud, external noise with blinking, a head turn, waved arms, and leg extension (Birnholz & Benacerraf, 1983; Madison, Madison, & Adubato, 1986). Some researchers even believe that the brain mechanisms responsible for musical ability are activated before birth and might be influenced by the musical sounds that penetrate the uterine wall (Wein, 1988).

The fetus is also affected by the external environment in that chemicals in the mother's diet, medications she may use, and environmental toxins can penetrate the placental barrier and affect the fetus (Smotherman & Robinson, 1987). The next section discusses some of these factors.

Table 2.1
Fetal Development

Time After Conception	Fetal Developments
3 months	At 3 months, the fetus weighs 1 oz and is about 3 inches long. The head is about one third of its total length and features a prominent nose. The fetus has a number of detailed features, including fingernails, toenails, vocal chords, and closed eyelids.
	Male and female fetuses are different in appearance at this time. The internal reproductive organs also contain primitive egg or sperm cells.
	The fetus breathes, swallows amniotic fluid into its lungs, and urinates into the amniotic fluid. The fetus also moves its legs, head, and thumbs.
4 months	Additional growth in the body means that the head is now just one fourth of the total body length, the proportion that will exist at birth. The 4-month-old fetus is between 6 and 10 inches long and weighs about 7 oz.
	The placenta is now fully developed, and the umbilical cord is as long as the fetus itself.
	Reflexes that appeared in the third month are stronger at this point, due to better muscle development. The fetus is much more physically active, and around this time, the mother feels the fetus kicking, an experience called **quickening.**
5 months	A 5-month-old fetus weighs from 12 to 16 oz and is about a foot long. At this time, sweat and sebaceous glands are functioning, hair is growing on the eyebrows and eyelashes, and there is fine hair on the head. The rest of the fetus is covered with a hair called lanugo.
	At this stage, the fetus has developed an individual preference for sleep-wake patterns and a favorite position within the uterus (called its lie), may hiccup and squirm, and is an active kicker and stretcher.
6 months	At 6 months, the fetus weighs about 1 1/4 lb and is about 14 inches long. Fat pads are developing under the skin, and the eyes are completely developed. The most immature system is the respiratory system.
7 months	The 7-month-old fetus weighs from 3 to 5 lb and averages 16 inches in length. All of the reflex behaviors are fully developed. Everyday behaviors include crying and sucking its thumb.
8 months	Movement is curtailed by now because, at 18 to 20 inches long and between 5 and 7 1/2 lb, there is little room for movement. From now until birth, the most important growth is a layer of fat that will help the newborn to survive the varying temperatures outside the uterus.
9 months	About a week before birth, the average baby of 7 1/2 lb and 20 inches in length stops growing. Approximately 266 days after conception, a full-term baby is born.

Source: From N. Newton and C. Modahl, "Pregnancy: The Closest Human Relationship" in *Human Nature,* March, 40–49, 1978.

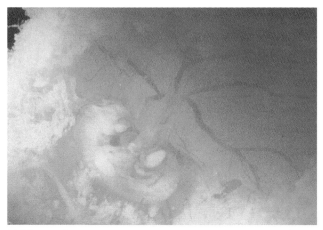

(a) Five weeks

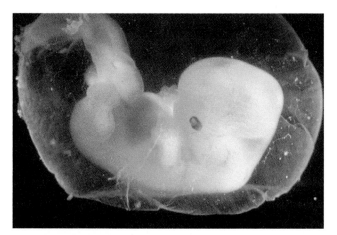

(b) Six weeks

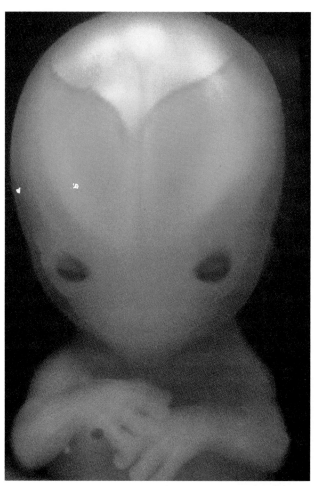

(d) Twelve weeks

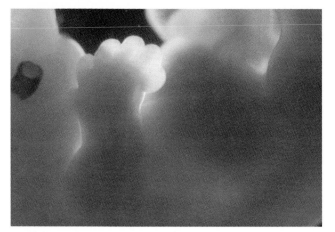

(c) Eight weeks

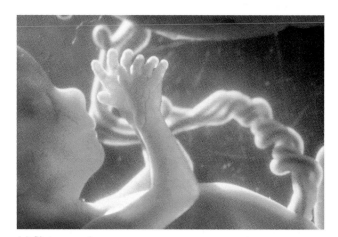

(e) Sixteen weeks

Human development from the 5th to the 16th week. (a) In the 5-week-old embryo, the body is flexed and c-shaped. (b) At the end of 6 weeks, the head becomes disproportionately large. (c) In the 8-week-old embryo, the nose is flat, and the eyes are far apart. (d) At twelve weeks the fetus has more developed fingers. (e) At 16 weeks, the blood vessels are easily visible through the transparent skin, and the eyes are closer together.

Remembering the Three Stages of Prenatal Development

To remember the order of the three stages of prenatal development, simply use the acronym GEF—germinal, embryonic, fetal. Try to use short phrases to help you remember the length of each stage, as in:

Germinal—"2 weeks"
Embryonic—"To 2 months"
Fetal—"To birth"

guided review

6. The time from fertilization to birth is called _____.
7. The single-celled fertilized cell, or _____, of the fluid-filled _____ are the structures of the _____ stage.
8. The _____ is the transfer organ between the mother's system and the developing baby, and the _____ is a fluid-filled membrane around the organism that provides protection.
9. The second stage of prenatal development, the _____ stage, is the time period in which the organs develop; this stage ends when _____ cells start to form.
10. In the longest and final _____ stage, automatic behaviors called _____ develop, and the mother experiences _____ when she feels the fetus moving.

answers

6. gestation (or: pregnancy) [LO-5]. 7. zygote; blastocyst; germinal [LO-5]. 8. placenta; amniotic sac [LO-5]. 9. embryonic; bone [LO-6]. 10. fetal; reflexes; quickening [LO-7].

Environmental Factors and Prenatal Development

Teratogens

Teratogens (from *tera*, the Greek word for "monsters") are any agents that may pass from the mother through the placental barrier and affect the fetus. Teratogens are a major cause of birth defects (Norwood, 1985). Table 2.2 lists many suspected teratogens. Since many common items are on this list and most babies are born without defects, the placenta must be a fairly effective barrier, even when some exposure to substances and viruses occurs.

Teratogens and Organ Vulnerability

The timing of the exposure to a teratogen is critical to the impact the teratogen may have on prenatal development. As shown in Figure 2.4, the vulnerability of different organ

Table 2.2
A Partial List of Probable Teratogens

Diseases

Chlamydia	Pneumonia
Gonorrhea	Rubella (Measles)
Herpes Viruses	Scarlet Fever
Human Immunodeficiency Virus	Syphilis
	Toxoplasmosis
Mumps	Tuberculosis

Drugs

Accutane (Acne Medicine)	Hexachlorophene
Alcohol	Iodides
Amphetamines	Lithium
Antibiotics	LSD
Anticancer Drugs	Opiates (e.g., Heroin)
Anticoagulant Drugs	Poliomyelitis Immunization
Anticonvulsive Drugs	Quinine
Aspirin	Sedatives
Barbiturates	Smallpox Vaccination
Caffeine	Thalidomide
Cigarettes	Tranquilizers
Cocaine	Vitamins A, C, or D in Excess
Diethylstibestrol (DES)	

Environmental Factors

Cadmium	Mercury
Cat Feces	Nickel
Fumes from Paints, Solvents, Glues, Dry-Cleaning Fluids, and So Forth	Pesticides, Herbicides, and Insecticides
	Polychlorinated Biphenyls (PCBs)
Hair Dyes	
Lead	Radiation (X rays, Video Display Terminals)
Manganese	

Noninfectious Maternal Conditions

Alcoholism and Chemical Dependency	Phenylketonuria
	Rh$^+$ Factor
Anemia	Stress
Diabetes Mellitus	

Source: Data from Benson, 1983; Norwood, 1985; Plotkin, et al., 1988; Quilligan & Kretchmer, 1980; Raymond, 1989; Vaughan, McKay, & Behrman, 1984.

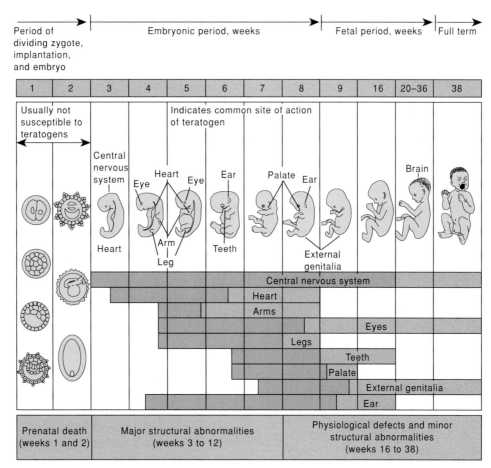

Figure 2.4

The vulnerability of different organ systems to the influence of teratogens during prenatal development (darkest section of bar reflects greatest vulnerability). Organ vulnerability to teratogens varies through the course of pregnancy with cephalocaudal and proximodistal trends—that is, regions closer to the head and in central locations are most vulnerable early in pregnancy.

systems to teratogens changes throughout prenatal development (Moore, 1979). Overall, more damage is likely early in the pregnancy, when organ systems are just developing. Unfortunately, women who are using drugs, taking medicines, or exposing themselves to chemicals and heavy metals may not yet realize that they are pregnant during the time when damage can be greatest. Whenever possible, women should plan for their pregnancy by avoiding suspected teratogens *before* becoming pregnant.

Medical Teratogens

As indicated in Table 2.2, many commonly used medicines can have adverse effects on developing embryos and fetuses. Aspirin, for example, is associated with birth defects and increased miscarriage rates. Although only a couple of dozen drugs have been proven to cause birth defects, only a dozen drugs have been ruled safe for pregnancy. Mostly, the effects are unknown (Dowie, 1985). The best advice during pregnancy is to use medications sparingly, if at all.

In the late 1950s and early 1960s, thalidomide was one of the first medications to be clearly identified as causing serious birth defects. Thalidomide was given to reduce morning sickness and other unpleasant symptoms during pregnancy, but women who took this medication during the critical period for fetal limb development gave birth to babies with seriously deformed arms or legs. While on the market, thalidomide was responsible for at least 8,000 seriously deformed babies.

More recently, accutane, an effective acne medication used since 1982, has been found to cause birth defects and to increase the rate of miscarriages. By 1988, researchers realized that accutane created a one in four chance of babies being born with malformed faces, heart defects, or severe retardation (Raymond, 1989).

Lifestyle Teratogens

Other significant teratogens are associated with individuals' lifestyles. For example, women (and men) may choose to use alcohol or other drugs that may have teratogenic effects prenatally. Even the choice of where to live carries some risk. Birth defects do not occur in equal numbers across all areas of the United States. Several hundred localities, such as the Love Canal area in New York, have been identified as birth defect clusters (Norwood, 1985).

Especially during pregnancy, decisions about the use of alcohol, tobacco, and other chemical substances can affect the potential for prenatal developmental hazards. For example, numerous studies have found significant correlations between a history of heavy alcohol use in pregnancy and physical abnormalities, growth retardation, delayed mental development, and delayed motor development in infants (Barr, Streissguth, Martin, & Herman, 1984; Cooper, 1987; Golden, Sokol, Kuhnert, & Bottoms, 1982; Hanson, Streissguth, & Smith, 1978; Rosett et al., 1983; Streissguth, Barr, & Martin, 1983; Streissguth, Martin, Sandman, Kirchner, & Darby, 1984). As maternal alcohol consumption increases during pregnancy, the risk of significant malformations increases. A pregnant woman who averages 1 to 2 oz of alcohol a day has about a 10 percent risk of having a baby with a significant malformation. A pregnant woman who drinks 2 oz or more of alcohol daily has at least a 20 percent risk (Hanson et al., 1978).

The pattern of problems is so typical in babies whose mothers abuse alcohol that it has been labeled **fetal alcohol syndrome (FAS).** Women who drink heavily during pregnancy have twice as many miscarriages and give birth to babies with average IQs of 68 (average IQs for normal infants are 90 to 110). These babies are also more likely to be hyperactive and distractible, with poorer reaction times and other motor impairments (Cooper, 1987; Streissguth et al., 1983; Streissguth et al., 1984). In addition, alcohol use in early pregnancy is related to smaller infant size at 8 months (Barr et al., 1984).

Smoking during pregnancy also affects fetal development, and fetal tobacco syndrome is associated with congenital malformations, neonatal pneumonia, and higher newborn mortality, partly because smoking constricts uterine blood vessels, thereby reducing nutrients to the fetus (Fried & Oxorn, 1980; Naeye, 1981). Birth weight is affected significantly: Newborns whose mothers smoked weigh about 200 g less than do other babies. The more cigarettes the mother consumed, the lower the birthweight (Naeye, 1981). Smoking by fathers or other family members also has an effect, lowering the weight of newborn infants by two thirds as much as does smoking by mothers ("Fetuses weigh less," 1986).

In addition, pregnant women who smoke tend to gain either less or more than the average nonsmoking woman during the course of pregnancy. Smokers who gain over 35 percent of their weight during pregnancy tend to have much longer and more difficult labors (Shepard, Hellenbrand, & Bracken, 1986).

Illicit drugs, such as heroin, cocaine, and marijuana, also affect fetal development. Not only do these drugs increase the risk of miscarriage and stillbirth, they lead to high incidences of neonatal physical addiction, health problems, and long-term defects. Cocaine, for example, is associated with disordered neurological function, lowered birthweight, smaller head size, shorter birth length, and congenital malformations (Frank, Zuckerman, & Amaro, 1988).

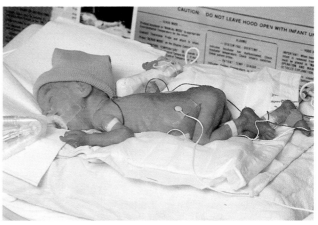

This cocaine baby and others affected by lifestyle teratogens often face a lifetime of medical problems.

Sensitization Factors

An incompatibility between the mother's blood type and the fetal blood type results in a different type of teratogen. For example, if the mother is Rh- and the fetus is Rh+, the fetus's blood contains a protein substance that the mother's blood does not. The mother's body interprets the Rh+ as a foreign substance and builds antibodies to attack it. The first Rh+ fetus is usually not affected, but each succeeding pregnancy in which the fetus's blood is Rh+ has increasing risk of miscarriage, jaundice, heart defects, mental retardation, and death. In earlier years, blood transfusions (either after birth or in utero) were the most effective way to increase the baby's odds of surviving. Now, a vaccine called rhogam can be given within 3 days of the first childbirth or abortion involving an Rh+ fetus. This vaccine prevents Rh- mothers from making antibodies.

Reducing the Risks

Monitoring of newborns since 1970 indicates that serious birth defects are on the rise. A small percentage of the increase is attributable to the medical technology that helps an increasing number of premature babies to survive, but the major reason for the increase in birth defects is teratogens (Norwood, 1985). Part of the long-term solution needs to be a reduction in environmental waste hazards and pollution and the development of safer technologies. However, each pregnant woman can take several steps to lower the risks for her developing fetus. Frank Duffey of the March of Dimes has suggested that "we can cut the birth defect rate in half in this country just by convincing women not to smoke, drink, or take any kind of prescription or nonprescription drug, and to eat a proper diet while they are pregnant" (Dowie, 1985, p. 20).

In addition to avoiding known teratogens, pregnant women should follow good nutrition guidelines and receive adequate prenatal health care because both of these result in healthier babies. For years, folk wisdom held that malnourishment harmed the mother but not the fetus. People believed that the fetus fed from the mother's bodily resources, but by the 1940s, research was suggesting a different picture. We now know that malnourishment has the least effect early in the pregnancy, when the embryo's nutritional needs are quite small. The negative effects of maternal malnourishment increase throughout prenatal development, especially affecting development of the brain (Storfer, 1990).

Good prenatal health care can make women aware of the need to protect their fetuses from potential teratogens and, thus, avert many potential problems. Regular checkups also can detect developing problems with the pregnancy and treat them before they damage the fetus or the mother. Health-care providers can assist the pregnant woman in planning a nutritious diet and can monitor her weight gain. Physicians changed their advice on weight gain during pregnancy after research showed that women who gain too little have more low-birthweight babies and more still-births. Women are now advised to gain at least 24 lb during their pregnancies.

Miscarriages and Abortions

Spontaneous Abortions
Spontaneous abortions, or miscarriages, occur when a pregnancy ends and the fetus is expelled by the 25th week of pregnancy. (After the 25th week, the more appropriate term is *stillborn.*) Three out of four spontaneous abortions occur during the first trimester. Between 10 and 14 percent of U.S. women are estimated to have lost a fetus by miscarriage (Day & Hooks, 1987). Risk factors for spontaneous abortions include a history of previous abortions, smoking, and the age of the mother (being under 20 or older than 29). Research also suggests that women in nursing, food service, and sales may have higher incidences of spontaneous abortions than women in other occupations. The most consistent risk factors at work are heavy lifting, physical effort, noise, and cold (McDonald, Armstrong, & Cherry, 1986).

At least half of all spontaneous abortions involve genetic mix-ups: chromosomal mutations and other abnormal changes in genetic material during cell division. Other causes of miscarriages include poor implantation, abnormal development of the umbilical cord, and maternal physiological problems. Couples whose genetic makeups contain a gene called transferrin C3 are more likely to have spontaneous abortions and babies with neural-tube defects (Weitkamp & Schachter, 1985). The herpes virus can also cause some spontaneous abortions (Goldsmith, 1985). Despite the persistence of some folklore beliefs, noises, jostling, and jolts are not likely causes of miscarriages.

Abortions
Each year in the United States, about 1.6 million women choose voluntarily to end a pregnancy with a surgical procedure that results in the **abortion** of the fetus. These women come from diverse backgrounds and have abortions for a variety of reasons. Adolescents obtain about one fourth of all abortions, while married women account for about one fifth of the total (Kantrowitz, 1987; Sachs, 1988). Some women have abortions because the fetus has been exposed to possible teratogens or might have a genetic defect; others decide that this is the wrong time to begin parenthood or to have an additional child in the family.

Americans hold strong beliefs about women's right to an abortion, as shown by these demonstrators in Washington, D.C.

Most women who have undergone an abortion handle the emotional burden of the decision fairly well. Research suggests that career-oriented women are the least likely to regret their decision to have an abortion, while traditionally feminine women are slightly more likely to regret their decision (Alter, 1984).

The morality and legality of abortions is a highly emotional issue. What are your views and attitudes about abortion? A poll in October 1988 found that 64 percent of American adults want to keep abortions legal (Sachs, 1988); over 80 percent would permit abortions if the fetus had a major defect. The issue is debated worldwide. The "Exploring Cultural Diversity" feature examines the effects of denied abortions in the former Czechoslovakia.

The Expectant Parents

Gender Expectations
As a couple plans for having a baby, they each may have a preference for the gender of the anticipated child. As in many societies, some Americans prefer that their firstborn child be a boy. As shown in Table 2.3, when asked about their gender preferences for their future first two children, nonparent college students exhibited a strong preference for the firstborn to be a boy and for the second child to be a girl (Goldfarb, 1988). Interestingly, parents who are adopting show some preference for getting a baby girl (Pogrebin, 1980).

The societal bias against female babies may be weakening. In one study, 140 women pregnant with their first baby were questioned during the third trimester of their pregnancy. Most of them indicated no gender preference for their baby; the rest split between the preference for a girl or a boy (Steinbacher & Gilroy, 1986).

One recent change in gender expectations is that many parents no longer have to wait until the delivery room to know if "It's a boy!" or "It's a girl!" Medical technology such as ultrasound and amniocentesis can determine the baby's sex during the pregnancy. How does this early knowledge affect expectant parents? Would you want to know prior to birth the gender of your baby? Why?

Do women who are denied abortions go on to love and care for their babies equally as much as women who wanted their babies all along? One unique longitudinal study done on 440 Czechoslovakian children suggests that the effects of unwanted pregnancy influence children into their young adult years (David, Dytryck, Matejcek, & Schuller, 1988).

In the early 1960s, abortions in the former Czechoslovakia were strictly controlled. Women who were denied access to an abortion at the local level could appeal the government decision; 2 percent of those who appealed were turned down a second time. Researchers compared 220 offspring from these twice-denied women with 220 wanted offspring with similar backgrounds. Mothers of UP (unwanted pregnancy) children were more likely than other mothers to rate their children as naughty, stubborn, and bad-tempered during the preschool years. At age 9, UP children had fewer friends and lower language skills than AP (acceptable pregnancy) children. More UP than AP children disliked school. At age 15, more UP children were in counseling, more were hyperactive, and they tended to be less social. UP boys rated themselves as more neglected or rejected by their mothers than by their fathers, which was opposite the pattern of AP boys.

In their early twenties, more UP adults were dissatisfied with their lives than were AP adults. They had less satisfactory love relationships, more marital problems, more psychiatric disorders, and more criminal offenses. Of course, many UP offspring did have satisfactory, productive lives.

How would you apply the results of this study to American society? On the one hand, the findings suggest that women should be allowed to end unwanted pregnancies. However, alternative solutions would be to encourage mothers of unwanted babies in giving up the babies for adoption or to provide family counseling shortly after the birth for mothers who were negative or ambivalent about the pregnancy.

Table 2.3
Gender Preferences of 1,169 College Students (Nonparents) for Firstborn and Second-Born Children (1978–1986)

Gender:	First/Second	College Students	
		Females	**Males**
	Girl/Girl	5.0%	9.2%
	Boy/Boy	21.4	12.7
	Girl/Boy	14.8	29.2
	Boy/Girl	51.7	42.6

Reproduced with permission of author and publisher from: Goldfarb, Connie S. "The folklore of pregnancy." *Psychological Reports, 62,* 891–900. Copyright © Psychological Reports, 1988.

Relationship Changes

Both men and women are emotionally affected by pregnancy and the advent of parenthood. In a study of 227 expectant and recent fathers, researchers found that many of them felt fear and ambivalence about the pregnancy or approaching parenthood, but few of them believed that they could express their concerns. At least 40 percent of the sample felt each of the following concerns: a queasiness or fear of the birth process itself, a feeling of increased responsibility in parenting and in financial concerns, questions about uncertain paternity, a fear of loss of spouse or the child, a fear of being replaced, and more awareness of their human fragility and mortality. For many, becoming a father signaled a move from the younger to older generation (Shapiro, 1987).

Pregnancy has a strong impact on the relationship between the expectant father and expectant mother. In many relationships, new parents become less likely to define themselves as "partners" or "lovers" and focus more on their roles as "parents." In some couples, parenthood ushers in an increased tendency to define household tasks along traditional gender roles (Cowan et al., 1985a).

Several studies found that marital satisfaction often decreases after parenthood (Awalt, Snowden, & Schott, 1987; Belsky, Lang, & Rovine, 1985; Cowan et al., 1985a). Marital dissatisfaction during the time of pregnancy itself especially is associated with continuing marital dissatisfaction and dissatisfaction with the parenting role. A study of 106 married pregnant women associated the following factors with increased marital satisfaction during parenthood: high certainty and intention about the pregnancy, self-confidence, birth of a first child, and strong religious values (Snowden, Schott, Awalt, & Gillis-Knox, 1988).

A couple's sexual relationship also is affected by pregnancy and the initial parenting period. For most couples, sexual interest, sexual activity, and sexual satisfaction declines during the pregnancy, especially during the third trimester (the last 3 months) (Fisher & Gray, 1988). After the birth of the child, many couples resume sexual activity within 6 weeks to 2 months, but some couples report lessened activity and interest for up to 1 year. Interestingly, breast-feeding mothers report the most rapid return of sexual interest and activity.

The Developing Parent-to-Fetus Relationship

Throughout pregnancy, expectant parents build a growing relationship with the developing fetus. Especially after quickening, parents become more attached to and have

Rothman (1987) proposed that modern technology has given rise to the "tentative pregnancy," the time period during which expectant parents wait for news from their physician about the genetic quality of their fetus. Until they know that their fetus is not a Down syndrome baby or afflicted with one of the other serious genetic defects, they do not fully count on becoming parents. According to Rothman:

> The significance of maternity clothing and pregnancy announcement lies in the public announcement of the pregnancy status. Feeling movement, in contrast, marks the private or psychological acknowledgment

not so much of the *pregnancy* as of the *baby*. Before the widespread availability of prenatal diagnosis, there was no distinction to be made between a wanted pregnancy and a wanted fetus. . . .

> The new technology of reproduction puts many women into a difficult social state, the condition I think of as a "tentative pregnancy." A woman's commitment to her pregnancy under the conditions imposed by amniocentesis [a procedure for examining the condition of the fetus] can only be tentative. She cannot ignore it, but neither can she wholeheartedly embrace it. . . . The tentatively pregnant

woman has entered the pregnant status, she is a pregnant woman, but she knows that she may not be carrying a baby but a genetic accident, a mistake. The pregnancy may not be leading to a baby, but to an abortion. The pregnancy is medically acknowledged, made socially real, but the fetus/baby is not. (pp. 100–101)

The tentative pregnancy condition may be relieved as earlier reliable diagnostic techniques are developed or as fetal treatments become more common and effective. Meanwhile, many expectant parents are afraid that their pregnancy will end before a baby is born.

Will this woman's baby show a preference for Beatrix Potter's "A Book About Baby" because mom read it to her when she was a fetus?

dreams and hopes for their soon-to-be offspring. They often talk to the fetus, and the fetus hears them, as indicated by voice recognition studies after birth. Research has shown that newborns even show a preference for stories read to them while they were still in the womb. The babies indicate their preferences by changing their patterns or timing of sucking on pressure-sensitive nipples that, in turn, change what stories the babies hear their mothers reading. In fact, one study showed that 10 of 12 infants chose *The Cat in the Hat* over other Dr. Seuss stories when that book had been read to them while in the womb (Nelson, 1985).

Some parents put their relationship with the developing fetus on hold until modern medical technology informs them that the fetus is without serious defects. Rothman (1987) suggested that the result is a "tentative pregnancy," the topic of the next "Exploring the Parent/Child Relationship" feature.

guided review

11. Any agent that might pass through the placenta and affect the developing organism is called a _____.
12. A pattern of problems associated with alcohol abuse during pregnancy is called _____.
13. _____, or miscarriages, most often occur in the first trimester, and the most common cause is _____.
14. A Czechoslovakian study involving denied _____ found that the adult offspring from _____ pregnancies were more dissatisfied with life.
15. College students' most common gender preferences for future offspring are that the first be a _____ and the second be a _____.
16. The time period between finding out about one's pregnancy and being technologically reassured that the fetus is healthy is called the "_____."

answers

11. teratogen [LO-8]. **12.** fetal alcohol syndrome [LO-9]. **13.** Spontaneous abortions; genetic [LO-10]. **14.** abortions; unwanted [LO-10]. **15.** boy; girl [LO-11]. **16.** tentative pregnancy [LO-11].

Genetic Blueprints for Development

One major topic remains to be discussed in this chapter. In this final section, we examine the genetic background and hereditary factors in prenatal development.

Mechanisms of Heredity

Genes and Chromosomes

Genetics is the study of **heredity,** the inborn influences on development from the genes inherited from parents. Its roots trace back to Mendel, who in the 1860s developed the first modern laws of inheritance. This advancing science is now involved in learning the entire human genetic map, or human genome, through analysis of the structure of all 46 **chromosomes.** The chromosomes are composed of over 150,000 **genes,** the basic building blocks of life. The smallest chromosome consists of over 2,000 genes, made up from 50,000 base pairs of nucleotides (basic proteins), strung together in strands of **DNA** (deoxyribonucleic acid). By 1992, researchers had successfully mapped two chromosomes: the Y or male chromosome and chromosome 21, which houses genes involved in neurological diseases, such as Down syndrome and Alzheimer's (Roberts, 1992).

A genome map—a genetic blueprint—would allow researchers and medical doctors to diagnose, prevent, and treat diseases related to defective genes. Specific genetic blueprints have already been identified for some cases of Alzheimer's disease, biological depression, and cystic fibrosis. Someday, this monumental mapping effort may provide genetic information about causes of schizophrenia, cancer, and heart disease.

Geneticists also know that only some of a person's many genes are working at any one time. Someday, scientists will understand the switching mechanism that activates different genes throughout the lifespan and perhaps will be able to manipulate the switches (Ptashne, 1989). What is currently known about the mechanisms of heredity allows us to marvel at the complex messages that go into making each person.

DNA Duplication

You start as a single-celled fertilized egg and develop into a fully grown human being. In the process, your genome replicates itself about a million billion times. To create a healthy, functioning human being, this duplication of DNA must be very accurate. For example, if DNA duplication involved an error rate of one error per million, each person would have 3,000 genetic mistakes! Instead, DNA duplication is so accurate that the error rate is no higher than 1 in 10 billion (Radman & Wagner, 1988).

Multiple Births

The nucleus of almost every cell in your body has the genetic information provided by 23 pairs of chromosomes. Your **gametes** (either eggs or sperm), however, have only half as much genetic information. When your father's sperm and your mother's egg united at fertilization, the 23 single chromosomes provided by each gamete combined to form the 23 pairs of chromosomes that are uniquely you.

Most people are genetically unique. Sometimes, however, two (or more) babies are born with the identical genetic heritage. Popularly called "identical twins," genetically identical twins are more properly labeled monozygotic twins. Monozygotic twins are produced when the cell division after fertilization begins two individuals instead of one.

Monozygotic twins comprise only one fourth to one third of all twins that are born. Much more common are dizygotic twins. Dizygotic twins are produced when the mother ovulates two eggs in a short time period, and both of the eggs are fertilized. Genetically, dizygotic twins are no more similar than siblings who developed in different pregnancies. As discussed in Chapter 1, researchers like to compare monozygotic and dizygotic twins on personality, intelligence, achievement, and physical characteristics because it helps them to learn about the relative influence of heredity and environment on behavior.

What factors increase the likelihood of multiple births? Ethnic background seems to play a role. Twins occur in 1 in 70 births among African Americans, but account for only 1 in 150 births among the Japanese and 1 in 300 births among the Chinese. Older women, third or later pregnancies, families with a history of twin births, and use of fertility drugs all increase the odds of multiple births (Vaughan, McKay, & Behrman, 1984).

Genetic Gender

Genetically speaking, the difference between a boy and a girl is that a boy's sex chromosomes (1 pair of the 23 pairs of chromosomes) are XY, and a girl's sex chromosomes are XX. The other 22 pairs, called autosomes, do not influence gender. This explanation, however, is not entirely accurate. The sex chromosomes XX and XY do play a role, but rather than the whole chromosome being important, gender is determined by just one gene on the sex chromosomes. This important gene, called TDF, or testes determining factor, is just one fifth of 1 percent of the sex chromosomes. In other words, men and women are 99.8 percent genetically the same. What a difference just 1 of 150,000 genes makes ("Identity crises," 1988)!

Until about the seventh week after conception, all embryos appear the same. Then the TDF gene triggers the additive principle, which results in additional hormones directing some embryos to become males, rather than following the initial course to become females. (Note that prenatal development suggests that "Eve" preceded "Adam"—that is, if TDF is not present, a female continues to develop.) The TDF gene usually is found on the Y of an XY embryo, and XY babies become boys; no TDF gene is found on almost all XX embryos, and these babies become girls. The TDF gene, rather than the presence of a Y chromosome, is the critical component. Men can be XX if a bit of Y chromosome with TDF is attached, and women can be XY if no TDF gene is present. These genetically rare individuals are infertile but otherwise appear normal (Lemonick, 1988).

It's a boy! The testes determining factor gene (TDF) on the Y chromosome is triggered about the third month of prenatal development.

Genetic Similarities

If the genetic similarity between males and females surprises you, this may be even more astonishing—chimpanzees and humans share genetic structures that are more than 98 percent identical. In fact, chimpanzees are more closely related to humans than they are to any other primate. For example, while chimps and humans are 98.4 percent genetically similar, chimps and gorillas are only 97.9 percent similar (Mereson, 1988).

When it comes to genes, small changes can produce rather big and important differences! The high degree of genetic similarity between chimpanzees and humans does not mean that humans are descended from the apes (although some researchers think that a genetic split between ancestral hominids and chimpanzees occurred about 8 million years ago). However, some scientists believe that the entire human race has a common female ancestor who lived about 200,000 years ago (somewhere around our 10,000th great grandmother!). Researchers base their theory on the study of 147 placentas from America, Africa, Europe, the Middle East, and Asia (Kozlov, 1988). Obviously, genetic research is helpful in understanding the past as well as in developing techniques for the future.

Patterns of Genetic Transmission

Mendel's Pioneering Work

While today's genetic researchers have sophisticated knowledge and technology, in the 1860s, Austrian monk Gregor Mendel discovered the fundamental laws of heredity under basic, primitive conditions. He developed his ideas about heredity before terms like *genes* and *chromosomes* existed by observing the results of crossbreeding experiments with peas. By noting the consistent inherited patterns in the offspring of the parent pea plants, Mendel proposed two important laws of heredity: the law of dominant inheritance and the law of independent segregation.

The law of dominant inheritance states that some traits (dominant ones) need only be inherited from one parent to influence outward appearance, or **phenotype.** Other traits (recessive ones) must be inherited from both parents to appear in a phenotype. The law of independent segregation states that each trait is inherited separately. Therefore, even though you exhibit a dominant trait in your phenotype, one of the two genes you carry in your **genotype** (your actual genetic makeup) may be recessive and passed on to your offspring.

Dominant and Recessive Inheritance

Phenotypes are your observable traits, such as brown eyes, curly hair, and freckles. The underlying genetic composition of these expressed traits is your genotype. Different genotypes may produce the same phenotype. For a simple example, you have a pair of alleles, a pair of inherited genes, that affect your eye color. If you have brown eyes, you have inherited a gene for brown eyes (we'll label it B) from either one or both parents. If your inheritance is homozygous for brown eyes, you got a B from each parent, and your genotype for eye coloring is BB. If your inheritance is heterozygous for brown eyes, you got a B from one parent and a less dominant color, such as blue (b), from the other parent. The resulting genotype is Bb. Although the phenotype in both cases is the same, two different genotypes (BB, Bb) produce the same eye color. **Dominant inheritance** occurs when either one or both alleles carries the dominant trait. **Recessive inheritance** occurs only if both alleles carry information for the recessive trait. Recessive inheritance is always homozygous. Figure 2.5 illustrates the patterns of dominant and recessive inheritance for the curious trait of how people roll their tongues.

Dominant genetic characteristics include curly hair, brown eyes, nearsightedness and farsightedness, polydactylism (extra fingers and toes), dark hair, long eyelashes, and broad lips. Recessive genetic characteristics include straight hair, blue or hazel eyes, color blindness, light or red hair, and thin lips. If you have any of the recessive characteristics, you know that you are homozygous in that trait. However, if you possess some of the dominant characteristics, your genotype might be either homozygous or heterozygous. Can you explain now why two blue-eyed parents cannot give birth to a brown-eyed baby, but two brown-eyed parents can give birth to a blue-eyed baby?

Sex-Linked and Sex-Limited Inheritance

In **sex-linked inheritance,** relevant information is carried on the sex chromosomes—usually, the X chromosome. Therefore, recessive sex-linked characteristics are much more likely to show up in males than females. As shown in Figure 2.6, if the mother carries a faulty gene, a male offspring has a 50-50 chance of inheriting the faulty gene and the disorder. A female offspring is protected from the disorder by inheriting a normal X from her father. However, the female has a 50-50 risk of inheriting the faulty gene and

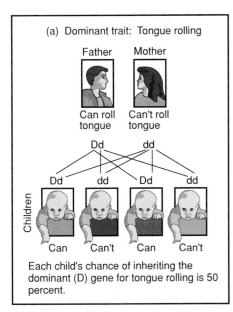

(a) Dominant trait: Tongue rolling

Father — Can roll tongue — Dd
Mother — Can't roll tongue — dd

Children: Dd, dd, Dd, dd
Can, Can't, Can, Can't

Each child's chance of inheriting the dominant (D) gene for tongue rolling is 50 percent.

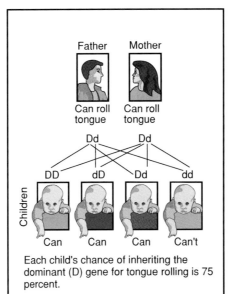

Father — Can roll tongue — Dd
Mother — Can roll tongue — Dd

Children: DD, dD, Dd, dd
Can, Can, Can, Can't

Each child's chance of inheriting the dominant (D) gene for tongue rolling is 75 percent.

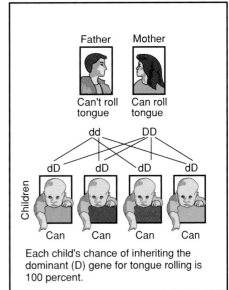

Father — Can't roll tongue — dd
Mother — Can roll tongue — DD

Children: dD, dD, dD, dD
Can, Can, Can, Can

Each child's chance of inheriting the dominant (D) gene for tongue rolling is 100 percent.

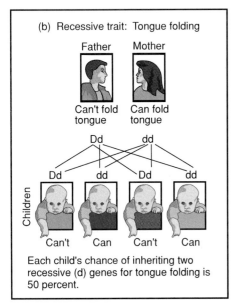

(b) Recessive trait: Tongue folding

Father — Can't fold tongue — Dd
Mother — Can fold tongue — dd

Children: Dd, dd, Dd, dd
Can't, Can, Can't, Can

Each child's chance of inheriting two recessive (d) genes for tongue folding is 50 percent.

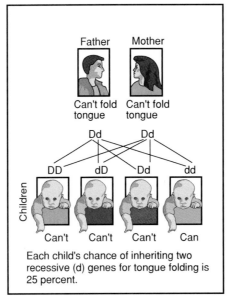

Father — Can't fold tongue — Dd
Mother — Can't fold tongue — Dd

Children: DD, dD, Dd, dd
Can't, Can't, Can't, Can

Each child's chance of inheriting two recessive (d) genes for tongue folding is 25 percent.

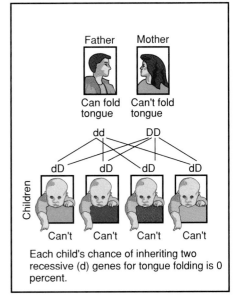

Father — Can fold tongue — dd
Mother — Can't fold tongue — DD

Children: dD, dD, dD, dD
Can't, Can't, Can't, Can't

Each child's chance of inheriting two recessive (d) genes for tongue folding is 0 percent.

Figure 2.5

Patterns of dominant and recessive inheritance. Some individuals can roll up the sides of their tongues to form tubes (tongue rolling); others can fold up the tips of their tongues when they stick out their tongues (tongue folding). (a) Tongue rolling is a dominant trait. Persons with at least one dominant gene can roll their tongue, while those who lack the dominant gene cannot. (b) Tongue folding is a recessive trait. Persons with two recessive genes can fold their tongues, while those who do not have two recessive genes cannot. Some people can both fold and roll their tongues, while others can do neither. Can you figure out how this can be?

being a carrier like her mother. Hemophilia and red-green color blindness are sex-linked characteristics, and these disorders are primarily exhibited in males but carried by females.

Some characteristics are **sex-limited inheritance,** rather than sex-linked. In these cases, both males and females may inherit the characteristic, but usually only one gender displays the trait because it is triggered by specific levels of hormones. Baldness is a good example. The high levels of androgen in males activate the baldness characteristic, while only a few women have high enough levels of androgen to become bald.

Polygenic Inheritance

Actually, only a few traits involve a simple pair of alleles and fit the dominant-recessive trait pattern. Many more traits, such as height and weight, involve **polygenic inheritance,** or multiple alleles. In the near future, polygenic inheritance patterns may be better understood because of the work in mapping the human genome. However, what is currently known about dominant, recessive, and sex-linked inheritance is important in understanding genetic defects.

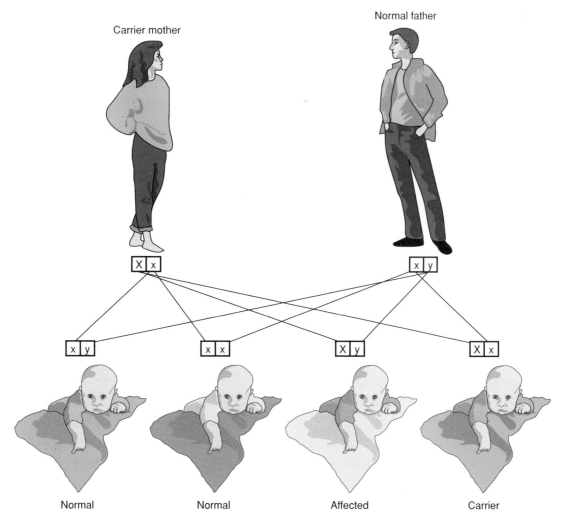

Figure 2.6

Sex-linked inheritance (X = faulty gene; x, y = normal genes). For each male child, the odds are 50-50: (1) 50 percent risk of inheriting the faulty X and the disorder, and (2) 50 percent chance of inheriting the normal x and y chromosomes. For each female child, the odds also are 50-50: (1) 50 percent risk of inheriting one faulty X, to be a carrier like mother; and (2) 50 percent chance of inheriting no faulty gene.

Genetic and Chromosomal Abnormalities

About 1,500 genetic disorders are known, and the average person has four to eight recessive genes that can pass on a genetic disorder. In fact, about 2 percent of all newborns have a genetic disorder, and many genetic disorders result in miscarriage in early pregnancy (Schaeffer, 1987).

One difficulty is that some defects have multiple causes. Cleft lip and palate, for example, is the fourth most common birth defect and affects 1 in 700 babies. Yet, heredity is the cause only one fourth of the time. Another cause is environmental hazards, but for most cases, the specific cause remains unknown. Fortunately for those affected, this disorder can be surgically repaired during infancy (Jimenez, 1988).

Defects Transmitted by Dominant Inheritance

Defects transmitted by dominant inheritance often are either not life threatening or develop late in life because, otherwise, the characteristic would not survive into the next generation. An example of a nonlethal dominant trait defect is achondroplasia, a type of dwarfism.

An example of a fatal dominant trait defect is Huntington's disease, a progressive neural disease affecting 25,000 individuals. Because Huntington's disease does not usually develop until the victim is 35 years of age or older, many people with Huntington's have children, who then have a 50-50 risk for the disease. The early symptoms of the disease are irritability, clumsiness, depression, and forgetfulness. Later, chorea (constant and uncontrollable movement) develops, causing slurred speech, grimaces, flinging arms and legs, clenching and unclenching fists, and falling down. Over time, the individual loses the ability to talk, swallow, and remember recent events. Within 20 years, the person usually dies. An even earlier death is likely if the condition is inherited from one's father rather than from one's mother (Grady, 1987; Schaeffer, 1987).

While 25,000 individuals know that they have Huntington's disease, about 125,000 relatives are at risk for the disorder. Recently, a genetic test was developed that can identify which individuals are destined to get the disease. Few have chosen to take the test. Would you? You run a

50-50 chance of being told that you will get this disease, but you also run a 50-50 chance of being told that you and your offspring are free of this dreaded inheritable curse. Many individuals must now weigh the advantages and disadvantages of being tested.

Defects Transmitted by Recessive Inheritance

Genetic defects transmitted by recessive inheritance include cystic fibrosis, sickle-cell anemia, and Tay-Sachs disease. Sickle-cell anemia affects 1 in 600 African Americans. About 1 in 25 European Americans is a carrier for cystic fibrosis, and these 10 million carriers give birth annually to nearly 2,000 affected babies, who usually survive into early childhood (Rothman, 1987; Schaeffer, 1987). Tay-Sachs disease is a deteriorative disease of the central nervous system that is found principally among Jewish people of Eastern European ancestry (Schaeffer, 1987). Tay-Sachs disease often includes 6 months of "normal" infancy before the dying process begins (Rothman, 1987).

Defects Transmitted by Sex-Linked Inheritance

Other genetic disorders are sex-linked. One such disorder—hemophilia—is a severe bleeding disorder that affects 1 in 5,000 to 10,000 males. Another sex-linked disorder is Duchenne's muscular dystrophy, the most common and severe form of muscular dystrophy (Schaeffer, 1987).

Fragile X syndrome is the second leading cause of retardation. Along with mental retardation, this genetic pattern causes physical abnormalities, such as oversized ears, an elongated forehead, enlarged testes, and double-jointedness. This syndrome is also considered to be the cause of about 10 percent of autism cases. Autism involves an extreme withdrawal from other people and a refusal to communicate. Surprisingly, about 20 percent of males who inherit the fragile X gene are unaffected carriers, and nearly one third of female carriers are affected. These figures do not fit the typical sex-linked disorder (Murphy, 1987).

Defects Transmitted by Abnormal Chromosomes

Some defects are caused by accidental chromosomal abnormalities, such as a missing sex chromosome (e.g., Turner's syndrome) or an extra sex chromosome (e.g., Klinefelter's syndrome). Chromosomal abnormalities involving the sex chromosomes often produce sterility or contradictory secondary sex characteristics.

The most common chromosomal disorder is Down syndrome, which involves an extra chromosome 21. This disorder affects about 1 in 800 babies. Although most Down syndrome people have low intelligence (IQ of 35 to 55), 10 to 15 percent of them can be successful in normal school classes with about a 1-year delay (Miller, 1987; Siwolop & Mohs, 1985).

A number of factors have been linked to the incidence of Down syndrome. As women grow older, they are at increasing risk of conceiving a child with Down syndrome. The incidence of Down syndrome is only 1 in 3,000 births for women under age 30, but the rate rises to 1 in 600 births for women between the ages of 30 and 34, 1 in 80 for

Singer Arlo Guthrie's father Woodie Guthrie died of Huntington disease. Although Arlo could be tested to see if he is a carrier, he has chosen not to find out if he is doomed to this disease.

women ages 40 to 44, and 1 in 40 for women over age 44 (Apgar & Beck, 1974). One explanation for these age-related data is that older women's developing eggs have been exposed to teratogens for longer periods of time, thereby increasing the risk that the 21st pair will not split correctly or that a portion of chromosome 21 will translocate to another chromosome.

However, in as many as one third of the cases of Down syndrome, the man contributes the extra chromosome (Magenis, Overton, Chamberlin, Brady, & Lorrein, 1977). The risk of fathering a child with Down syndrome also increases with age, especially for men over age 50 (Abroms & Bennett, 1981). Recent research has implicated a gene involved in protein synthesis on chromosome 21 in causing the disorder (Allore et al., 1988). In this area, as well as in many others, couples soon may be able to get better information about the likelihood of their transmitting this defect to their offspring.

Genetic Counseling

Genetic counseling provides information about potential genetic problems and offers alternatives based on genetic tests. About 350 tests are available to identify

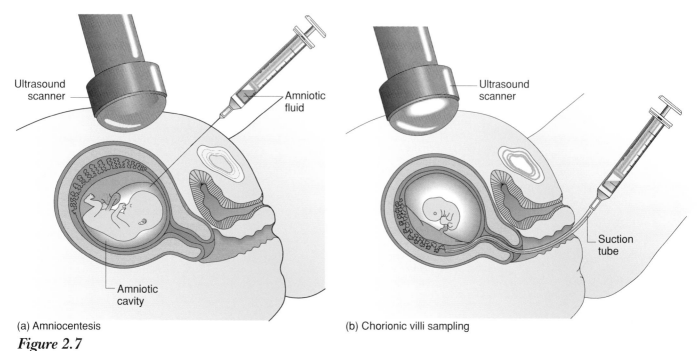

Ultrasound scanner — Amniotic fluid

Amniotic cavity

(a) Amniocentesis

Ultrasound scanner

Suction tube

(b) Chorionic villi sampling

Figure 2.7

(a) Amniocentesis and (b) chorionic villi sampling, along with ultrasound monitoring, are commonly used tests to detect genetic disorders.

approximately 100 genetic defects (Levoy, 1987). Experts debate whether prenatal genetic screening should be routine or done only if a potential problem is likely (Elias & Annas, 1987). When genetic counseling is chosen, it is expensive. The most common genetic tests include amniocentesis, chorionic villus sampling, alpha-fetoprotein screening, and ultrasonography.

Amniocentesis, performed around the 16th week of pregnancy, consists of inserting a large, hollow needle through the mother's abdomen into the amniotic sac and withdrawing a sample of amniotic fluid (see Figure 2.7a). Although ultrasound pictures help to guide the insertion of the needle so that the fetus is not harmed, amniocentesis still carries a small risk of causing a miscarriage. Without amniocentesis, miscarriage occurs in 32 of 1,000 pregnancies after the 16th week of pregnancy; with amniocentesis, the rate of miscarriage rises to 35 in 1,000 pregnancies (Rothman, 1987). For many, the test is worth the small additional risk because it can detect over 80 disorders and check lung development (Schaeffer, 1987).

A newer, but similar test, is chorionic villus sampling, in which a long, thin tube is inserted through the vagina and used to remove some uterine cells for analysis (see Figure 2.7b). The cells are analyzed for the same chromosomal and developmental disorders as those found with amniocentesis. While this technique has about the same risk for miscarriage as amniocentesis, it has the advantage of being able to be done from the 9th to 11th week of pregnancy (Schaeffer, 1987).

Alpha-fetoprotein screening (AFP) is a maternal blood test that allows the detection of defects in the formation of the brain and spinal cord, such as spina bifida. The test assesses the level of AFP in the blood, with high levels associated with nervous system defects. It also can detect about a third of all fetuses with Down syndrome because these fetuses have low levels of alpha-fetoprotein (Elias & Annas, 1987). Because blood samples are routinely taken during pregnancy, many physicians may perform this test without consulting the woman or her partner.

One of the more popular monitoring techniques is ultrasonography, or more commonly, ultrasound. As many as 40 percent of pregnant women may receive ultrasound monitoring. This technique reveals soft tissue, organ development, and the skeleton of the fetus (Rothman, 1987). Ultrasound during the second trimester can fairly accurately detect Down syndrome when examiners observe skin-fold thickness, femur length, and other characteristics of Down syndrome fetuses (Benacerraf, Gelman, & Frigoletto, 1987).

Only the couple involved can decide whether they want genetic counseling and screening. Its value goes up when the couple can identify specific genetic disorders in their family histories, but many factors need to be considered. Can the counselor provide definitive answers to the concerns? Are the techniques relatively safe? Does the couple need the reassurance that most prenatal screenings provide? Does early knowledge of a genetic defect change anything—for example, would the couple have an abortion? Are the available procedures worth the cost, risk, and time involved? No one answer fits everybody (Rothman, 1987).

In the next chapter, you learn about one of life's most important transitions—the transition from the womb to the world. In addition to childbirth, Chapter 3 explores the neonatal period, the first month after birth.

17. _____, the study of _____, which is the inborn influences on development due to genes, is currently an important area of science, as shown by the _____ project that is analyzing all 150,000 genes that make up a human being.
18. Ova and sperm, also called the _____, have half as much genetic information as other chromosomes, called _____.
19. The _____ principle, triggered by the gene called the _____, is the release of extra hormones needed to have embryos develop into males.
20. In _____ inheritance, both genes in your _____ must have this trait for it to influence your outward appearance, called the _____.
21. _____ inheritance involves sex-linked characteristics that are only displayed under specific levels of hormones.
22. Huntington's disease is an example of a _____ trait defect, sickle-cell anemia is due to _____ inheritance, hemophilia and fragile X syndrome are examples of _____ inheritance, and Down syndrome is an example of a defect due to an abnormal _____.
23. With 350 tests to identify about 100 genetic defects, _____ counseling can help potential parents to make decisions about future offspring.
24. _____ examines amniotic fluid and is done around the 16th week of pregnancy, but a newer test, called _____, can be done earlier and involves analyzing uterine cells.
25. A maternal blood test that helps to detect spina bifida and Down syndrome is _____ screening.

answers

17. Genetics; heredity; human genome [LO-12]. 18. gametes (or: sex chromosomes); autosomes [LO-12]. 19. additive; testes determining factor (or: TDF) [LO-12]. 20. recessive; genotype; phenotype [LO-13]. 21. Sex-limited [LO-13].
22. dominant; recessive; sex-linked; chromosome [LO-13].
23. genetic [LO-14]. 24. Amniocentesis; chorionic villus sampling [LO-14]. 25. alpha-fetoprotein [LO-14].

Exploring Human Development

1. Visit a family planning center, such as Planned Parenthood. Find out what kinds of services are offered, who uses these services, and the cost of these services. Review any written materials provided.
2. Visit a library and locate books about pregnancy and the developing baby that are written for siblings and other books that are for expectant parents. Of the books you found, which do you think are best? Why?
3. Conduct a short, confidential survey among several college students on one of the controversial topics in this chapter, such as abortion, fertility clinics, in vitro fertilization, surrogate parenting, or medical treatment of fetuses. Summarize your findings in a written report.

Discussing Human Development

1. What are the advantages and disadvantages of knowing fetal gender before birth?
2. What do you think medical technology will be able to do 20 years from now in the area of fetal development?
3. If the technology for cloning was well developed, would you be tempted to be cloned? What would be the advantages and disadvantages of raising a child genetically identical to yourself?
4. What could be done to reduce the risks of teratogens on an individual basis? What could society do to lower the number of birth defects caused by teratogens?
5. What, if any, criteria should be established for the donor and recipient in (a) artificial insemination by donor and (b) surrogate mothers? Why?
6. How many uses can you think of for information gained from mapping the human genome? Can you think of uses in criminology? mental health? advertising?

Reading More About Human Development

Corea, G. (1985). *The mother machine: Reproductive technologies from artificial insemination to artificial wombs*. New York: Harper & Row.

Eisenberg, A., Murkoff, H.E., & Hathaway, S.E. (1984). *What to expect when you're expecting*. New York: Workman.

Greer, G. (1984). *Sex and destiny: The politics of human fertility*. New York: Harper & Row.

Hartman, B. (1987). *Reproductive rights and wrongs*. New York: Harper & Row.

Summary

I. The process of conception
  A. Conception, or fertilization, occurs when a sperm penetrates the ovum.
    1. In women, follicle-stimulating hormone (FSH) causes the monthly maturation of an ovum, and luteinizing hormone (LH) triggers ovulation.
    2. Fertilization needs to occur within 24 hr of ovulation.
    3. The fallopian tube is the preferred site for fertilization, after which the fertilized egg is moved toward the uterus by cilia.
    4. While women have a lifetime number of approximately 400,000 ova, most men produce several hundred million sperm daily in their testicles.
    5. Once released during ejaculation, sperm make whiplike tail movements to try to swim through the cervix, uterus, and fallopian tube.
    6. Most sperm die before reaching the ova because of the vagina's acidic pH level, the mucous plug of the cervix, choosing the wrong fallopian tube, and sperm defects.
    7. Some obstacles to conception exist because the female anatomy is better designed to facilitate pregnancy than to facilitate conception.

8. The faster, longer androsperm (Y sperm), which produce males, are just slightly more common than the heavier, female-producing gynosperm (X sperm).

9. When ovulation occurs prior to intercourse, a higher proportion of males are conceived; when the order is reversed, more females are conceived.

B. Even though most couples conceive easily, many fertility problems exist.

1. Current American fertility rates are lower than just a couple of decades ago. Statistics show that most births occur before the mother is 35 years old, and few differences exist in European-American and African-American fertility rates.

2. Involuntary childlessness, or infertility, affects about 1 in 10 couples.

3. Causes of infertility include aging, infections, anatomical defects, and prior medical treatment.

C. Several reproductive technologies have been developed to help overcome fertility problems.

1. A variety of fertility drugs, with varying strengths and side effects, are available.

2. Diethylstilbestrol (DES) had serious long-term effects for offspring, including vaginal and testicular cancers.

3. First performed in 1890, artificial insemination has become a common procedure to overcome fertility problems.

4. A complex procedure, in vitro fertilization involves drug injections to stimulate multiple ovulation, surgical removal of mature eggs from the ovaries, fertilization in the laboratory, and implantation of fertilized embryos in the uterus.

5. Less commonly used fertility procedures include embryo transfer and surrogate parenting.

6. Future conception technologies may include cloning, artificial wombs, parthogenesis, twin fusion, and ectogenesis.

7. Just as important as fertility technologies are the technologies that help ongoing pregnancies, such as ultrasound, transtelephonic monitoring, and fetal surgery.

II. Stages of prenatal development

A. The germinal stage is the first two weeks of prenatal development.

1. During this stage, the single-celled zygote travels down the fallopian tube into the uterus, where it develops into a 150-cell blastocyst.

2. One side of the blastocyst becomes the embryonic disk, which divides into the ectoderm, endoderm, and later, the mesoderm layers; the baby develops from the embryonic disk.

3. The blastocyst also develops tendrils that penetrate the uterine wall, resulting in implantation; at this time, the placenta, umbilical cord, and amniotic and chorionic sacs also begin to develop.

B. The embryonic stage is the 6 weeks following the germinal stage.

1. At 1 month, the 1/2-inch-long embryo has a head and trunk but just the start of arms and legs; it also has a temporary tail, a primitive heart, and the beginnings of organs and facial features.

2. At 2 months, the 1-inch-long embryo weighs about 1/13 oz, is half head, coordinates functioning organs, and has more evident limbs.

3. Around the start of the ninth week, the development of bone cells signals the end of the embryonic stage.

C. The fetal stage is the third and longest prenatal stage and is marked by many physical developments, as well as the appearance of reflexes.

1. Early in this period, organ and sense development are prominent.

2. In the last several months, the fetus gains much weight.

3. The fetus is influenced by several levels of prenatal environment—the local environment of amniotic fluid and the uterus; the life-support system of placenta, umbilical cord, uterus, and maternal circulatory system; and the environment outside the mother.

III. Environmental factors and prenatal development

A. Teratogens are any agents that may pass from the mother through the placental barrier and affect the fetus.

1. Teratogens are a major cause of birth defects, with both amount of exposure and the timing of the exposure affecting vulnerability of the various organs.

2. Some medicines, such as thalidomide and accutane, can have adverse effects on developing embryos and fetuses.

3. Lifestyle teratogens involve fetal exposure due to maternal choices, such as drinking alcohol, using drugs, and smoking cigarettes.

4. Pregnant women who drink moderately have a 10 percent risk of having a baby with a significant malformation; with heavy drinking, many risks increase: the risk of miscarriages doubles, and a pattern labeled fetal alcohol syndrome is common.

5. Smoking during pregnancy can result in fetal tobacco syndrome.

6. Illicit drugs increase the risk of miscarriage and stillbirth, neonatal physical addiction, health problems, and long-term defects.

7. A different type of teratogen problem can develop when a mother with Rh- blood has more than one child with Rh+ blood. Fortunately, the use of rhogam can prevent this problem.

8. The number of birth defects is on the rise, indicating a need for reduced environmental hazards, safer lifestyles, better maternal health care/nutrition, and improved technologies.

B. Each year, many pregnancies end in miscarriages and abortions.

1. Spontaneous abortions, or miscarriages, occur during the first 25 weeks of pregnancy; after 25 weeks, the term *stillborn* is used.

2. At least half of spontaneous abortions involve genetic problems, and other causes are physiological problems and lifestyle choices.

3. Each year in the United States, about 1.6 million women have a voluntary abortion.

4. Most women handle the emotional burden of abortion, but a minority regret the decision.

5. A longitudinal Czechoslovakian study on the effects of denied abortions found that, as young adults, children from unwanted pregnancies were more dissatisfied with their lives than were comparable young adults whose parents had been accepting of the pregnancy.

C. Parenting begins before the birth of a child, as expectant parents formulate their preferences and expectations.
   1. Some parents have a gender preference for their future baby.
   2. Pregnancy affects the relationship between the pregnant couple.
   3. Expectant parents build a growing relationship with the developing fetus, especially after quickening.
   4. The period of time between knowing one is pregnant and having medical technology reassurance of the fetus's health is called the "tentative pregnancy."

IV. Genetic blueprints for development
   A. The primary mechanisms of heredity are genes and chromosomes.
      1. Genetics is the study of heredity, to the inborn influences on development from the genes inherited from parents.
      2. A human genetic map, or human genome, will be able to analyze the structure of the over 150,000 genes on the 46 human chromosomes.
      3. The genes that compose the chromosomes are made up of thousands of pairs of nucleotides strung together in strands of DNA (deoxyribonucleic acid).
      4. To become a human being, the genome has to replicate itself a million billion times, and the error rate of this replication is no higher than 1 in 10 billion.
      5. Except for monozygotic twins, each person is genetically unique.
      6. The gametes, or sex chromosomes, determine genetic gender, with the Y chromosome having one gene—the testes determining factor (TDF)—that determines gender.
      7. Human males and females are 99.8 percent genetically the same; chimpanzees and humans are about 98 percent genetically the same.
   B. Patterns of genetic transmission determine which traits people have.
      1. Mendel did pioneering work in the field of genetics and developed the law of dominant inheritance and the law of independent segregation.
      2. Different genotypes may produce the same phenotype.
      3. Dominant inheritance occurs if one of both alleles carries the dominant trait; recessive inheritance occurs only if both alleles carry the recessive trait.
      4. Sex-linked inheritance involves information carried on the sex chromosome, usually the X chromosome; sex-limited inheritance involves an interaction of genetic pattern and hormonal level.
      5. Most traits involve polygenic inheritance, or multiple alleles.

C. Genetic and chromosomal abnormalities are quite common, with about 1,500 genetic disorders known.
   1. Some defects, such as Huntington's disease, are caused by dominant inheritance.
   2. Other genetic defects, such as sickle-cell anemia and Tay-Sachs disease, are transmitted by recessive inheritance.
   3. Genetic defects transmitted by sex-linked inheritance include hemophilia, Duchenne's muscular dystrophy, and fragile X syndrome.
   4. Still other genetic disorders, including Down syndrome, Turner's syndrome, and Klinefelter's syndrome, are transmitted by accidental chromosomal abnormalities.

D. Genetic counseling provides information about potential genetic problems and offers alternatives based on genetic tests.
   1. Currently, approximately 350 tests can be used to identify about 100 genetic disorders.
   2. Commonly used tests include amniocentesis, chorionic villus sampling, and alpha-fetoprotein screening.
   3. Often, medical tests reassure expectant parents that everything is going well, but sometimes, the results require difficult decision making.

Chapter Review Test

1. The hormone that triggers ovulation, the release of a mature ovum from the follicle, is called
   a. follicle-stimulating hormone (FSH).
   b. estrogen.
   c. luteinizing hormone (LH).
   d. oxytocin.

2. Sperm are produced in the
   a. testicles.
   b. penis.
   c. prostate gland.
   d. vas deferens.

3. Which of the following aspects of female anatomy makes it difficult for the sperm to survive and penetrate the ova?
   a. the acidic pH level of the vagina
   b. the mucous plug of the cervix
   c. cilia movement in the fallopian tubes
   d. all of the above

4. The outer coating of the ova is called the
   a. shell.
   b. zona pellucida.
   c. zygote.
   d. albumen.

5. Gynosperm is to _____ as androsperm is to _____.
   a. male; female
   b. faster; slower
   c. lighter; heavier
   d. shorter; longer

6. In the 1950s, a common fertility drug was diethylstilbestrol (DES). Since then, it has been associated with numerous medical problems, the most serious being
   a. respiratory problems.
   b. vaginal cancer.

c. larger than normal penis.

d. digestive tract abnormalities.

7. AIH differs from AID in that, in AIH,

    a. a surrogate mother is utilized during pregnancy.

    b. the gender of the baby is prechosen.

    c. the sperm donor is the husband.

    d. the sperm are frozen for a time period before being used.

8. Which of the following future conception technologies could be used only to produce female babies?

    a. parthogenesis

    b. cloning

    c. twin fusion

    d. ectogenesis

9. Which of the following is *not* an appropriate name for a structure during the germinal stage?

    a. zygote

    b. embryonic disk

    c. blastocyst

    d. embryo

10. Which layer of the blastocyst develops into the major organs, including the digestive and respiratory systems?

    a. ectoderm

    b. endoderm

    c. mesoderm

    d. destoderm

11. Which of the following is a function of the placenta?

    a. transferring oxygen, nourishment, and waste products to and from the maternal system and the fetus

    b. protecting from infections and foreign substances

    c. producing hormones needed during pregnancy

    d. all of the above

12. What signals the end of the embryonic period?

    a. the start of the ninth week after conception, regardless of the embryo's development

    b. formation of the first bone cells

    c. sex differentiation due to the additive principle

    d. quickening, or the experience of the expectant mother noticing fetal movements

13. Teratogens usually do the most damage

    a. during the first 2 weeks of pregnancy.

    b. during the embryonic stage, when organ systems are just developing.

    c. during the fetal stage because this is the period of greatest height and weight change.

    d. throughout the entire gestation.

14. The pattern of fetal alcohol syndrome (FAS) includes all of the following *except*

    a. below average IQ.

    b. poorer reaction time.

    c. hyperactivity and overattending to a stimulus.

    d. lower birthweight.

15. Which of the following is a result of the study in the former Czechoslovakia of offspring from unwanted pregnancies?

    a. Their mothers rated them as naughty, stubborn, and bad-tempered preschoolers.

    b. They tended to excel in the classroom, probably as a way to deal with mixed messages from parents.

    c. They were higher in social and language skills but were also more hyperactive.

    d. Although somewhat less social and more problematic as children, these offspring did not differ from others by age 20.

16. Samantha and Stephano are typical nonparent college students in that they would each like their first two children to reflect which of the following birth orders?

    a. Girl/Girl

    b. Boy/Boy

    c. Boy/Girl

    d. Girl/Boy

17. The additive principle describes the process that determines the _____ of babies.

    a. intelligence

    b. sex

    c. size

    d. sexual orientation

18. Which of the following is the most common form of genetic inheritance?

    a. polygenic

    b. sex-linked

    c. dominant

    d. recessive

19. Sex-limited inheritance indicates that

    a. only females can have this characteristic.

    b. only males can have this characteristic.

    c. the characteristic comes from the Y chromosome rather than the X chromosome.

    d. hormonal level determines if an inherited characteristic is exhibited.

20. Which of the following disorders is paired *incorrectly* with a type of inheritance?

    a. Huntington's disease—sex-linked inheritance

    b. Cystic fibrosis—recessive inheritance

    c. Baldness—sex-limited inheritance

    d. Down syndrome—abnormal chromosome

Answers

1. C [LO-1].	**8.** A [LO-4].	**15.** A [LO-10].
2. A [LO-1].	**9.** D [LO-5].	**16.** C [LO-11].
3. D [LO-1].	**10.** B [LO-5].	**17.** B [LO-12].
4. B [LO-1].	**11.** D [LO-6].	**18.** A [LO-13].
5. D [LO-2].	**12.** B [LO-6,7].	**19.** D [LO-13].
6. B [LO-4].	**13.** B [LO-8].	**20.** A [LO-13].
7. C [LO-4].	**14.** C [LO-9].	

chapter 3

Childbirth and the Neonatal Period

Learning Objectives

1. List the primary characteristics of each of the three stages of birthing.
2. Describe the biological changes that take place during birthing.
3. Summarize the main features of typical medical deliveries.
4. Describe cesarean deliveries and the primary reasons for using this method.
5. Compare and contrast the Lamaze and Leboyer birthing techniques.
6. Discuss the varieties of childbirth procedures, including hospital deliveries, home deliveries, birth centers, midwives, and practices in other cultures.
7. Summarize the major factors associated with low birthweight, and describe typical care for low-birthweight babies.
8. Compare and contrast instruments for medically assessing neonates, especially the Apgar Scale and the Brazelton Neonatal Behavioral Assessment Scale.
9. Describe the general physical appearance of neonates.
10. Discuss the neonate's reflexes and other movements.
11. Summarize the neonate's sense abilities in smell, taste, touch, hearing, and vision.
12. Discuss whether neonates are capable of imitation.
13. Describe how culture influences parenting.
14. Discuss how parents communicate with and comfort their newborns.

An average of 266 days after conception, birth occurs. In this chapter, you will learn about the birth process, techniques and customs of childbirth, characteristics and treatment of low-birthweight babies, and general aspects of the neonatal period of life.

Exploring Your Own Development

One way to make the material in this chapter more meaningful is to explore the circumstances of your own birth. Your biological mother, if available, is the best source of information. Your biological father can also provide some insights, as can grandparents, aunts, uncles, older siblings, and close family friends. You might be able to interview the physician or other persons who attended your birth. Sometimes, a baby book or other family records can provide information about where you were born and the length of the birthing process. As you gather information, note what aspects of your birth were influenced by medical and popular beliefs of the era. Do you know the answers to the following questions?

1. What were the conditions throughout the pregnancy? Were there any medical complications? What were the high points and low points of the pregnancy?
2. What prenatal care was given? How often was the doctor visited? What level of activity did the doctor advise? Were medications or diets prescribed or recommended?
3. Who made the decisions about prenatal care and the method of childbirth—the doctor? the mother? the father? someone else?
4. Where did the birth take place? How was this decision made? When labor began, how did the transport to the hospital (or other setting) take place?
5. Who was present at the birthing? Who decided who would be present? What were the reactions and behaviors of those present?
6. What was the labor and actual birth like? How did it compare to what was expected?
7. What medicines and technology were part of the labor process?
8. Was the birth a fairly normal one? If not, what aspects were atypical?
9. Were any of the following procedures or situations involved in your birth: obstetric medications, forceps, cesarean delivery, home birth, birth centers, episiotomy, birthing chair, midwife, Lamaze techniques, Leboyer techniques, fetal monitor, ultrasound, birthing room, intensive neonatal nursery?
10. What was the reaction to the birth? What emotions were prevalent over the next few weeks (e.g., fatigue, depression)?

Your birth was a remarkable happening. Knowing the answers to the previous questions should not detract from, but instead enhance, your appreciation for just how remarkable birth is.

The Birth Process

Stages of Birthing

Childbirth, or **parturition,** is divided into three basic stages, as depicted in Figure 3.1.

The First Stage

The first stage begins with labor contractions that last between 15 and 25 sec. As the stage progresses, the contractions become more severe and uncomfortable, as the lower part of the uterus is stretched. Early on, the woman's "water breaks" as the amniotic membrane is broken; if the membrane stays intact, medical personnel break it. Two important processes are occurring during this first stage: **effacement** (cervical thinning) and **dilation** (the enlargement of the cervical opening). Dilation continues until the opening is large enough for the baby's head to pass through.

With the first child, the first stage averages between 12 and 24 hr, during which time the expectant parents must deal with a variety of overwhelming physical and emotional sensations:

> When labor begins, even the best prepared parents tend to be taken by surprise. It is not that the beginning of the process is difficult to recognize; it is that even the most careful words cannot describe the overwhelmingly physical nature of the birth process nor prepare you for the extraordinary feeling of having your body taken over by forces which are outside your conscious control. We are brought up to control and manage our bodies' functions, holding back coughs and yawns, fending off sleep in public. . . . But childbirth cannot be controlled in this sense. Once labor begins, your baby is going to get himself born with or without your conscious cooperation. The contractions will go on at their appointed rate and strength until the birth canal is fully open. (Leach, 1982, p. 27)

The Second Stage

The second stage of childbirth begins when the cervix is completely dilated and lasts until the baby is born. This usually takes an average of 50 min with the first baby and less time with later births. During this stage, the mother bears down with abdominal muscles during the contractions to help the baby leave the birth canal. Typically, babies are born headfirst (a cephalic presentation), and the appearance of the baby's head is called the **crowning.** Less often, the baby comes out buttocks first (a breech presentation) or in a crosswise position (a transverse presentation).

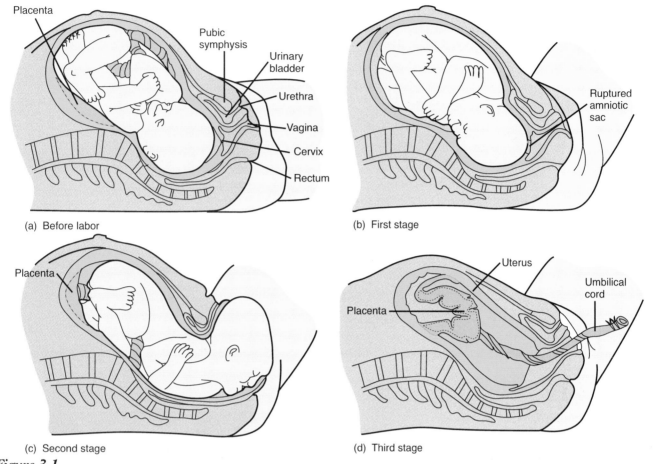

(a) Before labor

Placenta
Pubic symphysis
Urinary bladder
Urethra
Vagina
Cervix
Rectum

(b) First stage

Ruptured amniotic sac

(c) Second stage

Placenta

(d) Third stage

Uterus
Umbilical cord
Placenta

Figure 3.1

Three stages of parturition. (a) Position of fetus just before birth begins. (b) The first stage: Dilation of the cervix. (c) The second stage: Birth of the baby. (d) The third stage: Expulsion.

In a cephalic presentation, the head pushes its way through the birth canal, and bruises and swelling of the head are not unusual. The narrowness and complexity of the pelvic passage also mean that the infant must twist, bend, turn, and extend itself to get through the birth canal.

Many doctors perform an **episiotomy,** a surgical incision designed to enlarge the birth canal and to minimize vaginal tearing, during the second stage of labor. However, episiotomies have become a controversial procedure since some women have experienced difficult and painful healing of the incision. Episiotomies are much more common in the United States than in Europe.

The Third Stage

The third stage of birthing involves the expulsion of the afterbirth, which includes the umbilical cord, placenta, and fetal membranes. This stage lasts an average of only 8 min (Holmes, Reich, Pasternak, 1984). The entire placenta and membranes must be expelled so that the mother can begin the involutional process, the return of the reproductive organs to their original state.

successful study tip

Birth Stages
Try making a mental outline of this information: Stage 1: Labor Effacement Dilation Stage 2: Delivery Stage 3: Afterbirth Delivery of placenta and fetal membranes

Biological Changes During Birthing

Much remains mysterious about the biological changes during both pregnancy and childbirth. Over the next several years, exciting discoveries and connections are likely. For example, recent research suggests that women who experience panic attacks have fewer panic symptoms throughout their pregnancy and that this reduction may be associated with the lessening of adrenaline responses or effects on barbiturate receptors (George, Ladenheim, & Nutt, 1987).

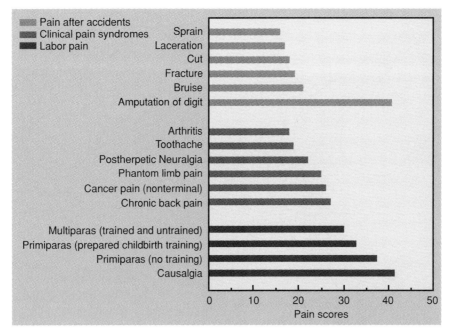

Figure 3.2

Comparison of pain during first childbirth (primaparous) and later childbirth experiences (multiparous) with pain of other conditions, using the McGill Pain Index.

Initiation of Childbirth

Researchers are not sure what initiates uterine contractions during childbirth, but hormones called prostaglandins may be very important. Fetal urine released into the amniotic fluid may trigger these prostaglandins, which then may initiate labor (Strickland, Saeed, Casey, & Mitchell, 1983). Women who have had dysmenorrhea (painful menstrual periods) tend to have more prostaglandins and are at risk for higher than usual labor pain (Melzack, 1984).

Pain of Childbirth

Pain seems to be unavoidable for women in labor. The pelvis of the upright human female makes birthing more complex and more painful than is birthing for four-legged animals. Figure 3.2 shows scores on the McHill Pain Index for a variety of painful conditions. Women in labor experience a wide range of individual pain levels, but average scores for labor pain are exceeded only by causalgia in chronic-pain patients and amputation of digits in acute-pain patients. On the whole, primiparas, or first childbirth, is more painful than later childbirth experiences (multiparas). Prepared childbirth techniques may reduce the pain, but they do not eliminate it (Melzack, 1984).

Release of Stress Hormones in Babies

During the birthing process, babies may spend an hour getting through the birth canal, may experience periods of intermittent oxygen deprivation, and must adapt to the radical environmental changes involved in moving from the womb to the outside world. Babies release high levels of stress hormones (adrenaline and noradrenaline) during birth, but, instead of signaling distress and unfavorable complications, this hormone release seems to help babies to survive the birthing process (Lagercrantz & Slotkin, 1986). For

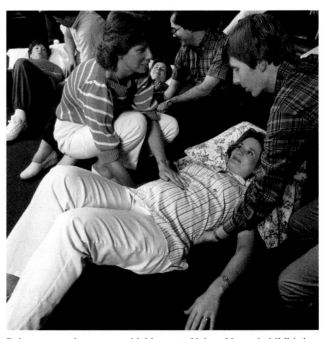

Pain seems to be an unavoidable part of labor. Natural childbirth classes, like this Lamaze training session, help expectant mothers to learn breathing and relaxation techniques that may reduce the pain, but certainly not eliminate it.

example, the release of these hormones helps to clear the lungs of liquid for breathing, increases blood flow to the vital organs, and helps to ready nourishment for the cells. The major adaptational effects are shown in Table 3.1. In general, the hormonal release helps the baby to achieve *homeostasis,* or stable functioning, during the transition to independent functioning (Lagercrantz & Slotkin, 1986).

Table 3.1
Adaptational Effects of the Release of Stress Hormones
During Childbirth

Improves Breathing
Increases lung surfactant (a soaplike substance that helps air sacs in the lungs to stay open)
Increases lung-liquid absorption
Dilates bronchioles

Protects Heart and Brain
Increases blood flow to vital organs

Mobilizes Fuel
Increases metabolism
Breaks down normal fat into fatty acids
Breaks down glycogen (in liver) to glucose
Stimulates new production of glucose by liver

Prepares for Attentiveness/Bonding
Dilates pupils
Appears to increase alertness

Source: Data from Langercrantz and Slotkin, "The Stress of Being Born" in *Scientific American,* 100–107, April 1986.

Abnormal stresses and complications during childbirth may have long-lasting effects on the baby. For example, infants who were high birth risks are at increased risk to commit suicide during adolescence. In one study, about 60 percent of victims of adolescent suicide had one to three major risk factors at birth: respiratory disease, lack of prenatal care, and birth mother with a chronic disease (Greenberg, 1985).

Psychological Effects of Childbirth on the Mother

Most mothers and fathers find childbirth to be a positive experience. Within one day after childbirth, 29 percent of women describe birth as "the best experience of my life," and only 1 percent identify birth as "the worst experience of my life" (Ball, 1987). However, for many women, childbearing is followed by a period of negative emotions.

A significant minority of women experience depression and other psychiatric symptoms following childbirth. Throughout history, these psychiatric disturbances have been called puerperal fever, milk fever, lactation psychosis, and more recently, **postpartum depression.**

Postpartum depression influences mother-infant interactions. At 1 and 3 months after birth, depressed mothers are less likely to talk with their babies and to provide affectionate contact. More depressed mothers bottle-feed their infants by the third month. Fortunately, differences in mother-infant interactions disappear by the 16th month (Fleming et al., 1988).

Categories of Postpartum Depression

The current trend is to distinguish between severe psychotic reactions and milder and more frequent "maternity blues" (Murray & Gallahue, 1987). The most severe category of postpartum depression is called puerperal psychosis, a rare disorder occurring in about 1 of 1,000 deliveries and typically beginning 2 or 3 weeks after childbirth. The symptoms are severe enough to be considered a psychotic reaction associated with childbirth and are similar to those found in mania disorder or major depressive disorder (Murray & Gallahue, 1987).

About 10 to 15 percent of new mothers are affected by mild to moderately severe postpartum depression. This category of postpartum depression begins within a few weeks of childbirth, lasts from a few weeks to over a year, and has symptoms that are similar to other depressive disorders (Murray & Gallahue, 1987).

The third category of postpartum depression is called postnatal maternity blues. More than half of new mothers experience this level of depression. Characteristics include frequent and quick mood swings, intense and prolonged crying, despondency, anxiety, irritability, and feelings of inadequacy. Postnatal maternity blues begin within a few days of childbirth and are usually transient (Murray & Gallahue, 1987).

Causes of Postpartum Depression

Causes of postpartum depression remain unclear. Biological causes are possible, since childbearing involves stress, pain, and hormonal changes, but researchers cannot pinpoint a specific biological cause. A few studies have found that levels of various substances (e.g., progesterone, estradial, estrogen, tryptophan, norepinephrine, serotonin) differ between depressed mothers and nondepressed mothers, but other studies do not find the same differences. In addition, the amount and kind of drugs used to aid delivery do not seem to be related to postpartum depression (Murray & Gallahue, 1987).

Other studies focus on the woman's desire to be a mother, the social support network available to the new mother, the loneliness and inner-directed anger of the mother, the quality of the marital relationship, and stress levels. These studies suggest that such factors play a role in postpartum depression, but no one factor can be used to predict who will become depressed following childbirth (Murray & Gallahue, 1987). Prior experience with children seems to play a role (Fleming, Ruble, Flett, & Shaul, 1988). That is, women who have had prior practical experience with children (younger siblings, baby-sitting, previous births) are less likely to experience postpartum depression. Overall, however, maternal emotional reactions are an interaction of biological, personality, and situational factors (Murray & Gallahue, 1987).

1. The first stage of birth involves several hours of _____ (the thinning of the cervix) and _____ (the enlargement of the cervical opening).
2. The baby is born during the _____ stage of birthing; during this stage, most babies are born headfirst in a _____ presentation, but some are born buttocks first (a _____ presentation) or in a crosswise position (a _____ presentation).
3. Sometimes, to minimize vaginal tearing, doctors make a surgical incision called an _____ to enlarge the birth canal.
4. The third and shortest stage of birthing involves the expulsion of the umbilical cord, fetal membranes, and the _____.
5. Hormones called _____ seem to be very important in initiating uterine contractions.
6. During birthing, babies release high levels of _____ hormones, which aid in achieving _____, or stable functioning.
7. Most women view childbirth as a _____ experience; however, more than half experience depression, with the most common category called _____ and a mild to moderately severe form called _____.

answers

1. effacement; dilation [LO-1]. **2.** second; cephalic; breech; transverse [LO-1]. **3.** episiotomy [LO-1]. **4.** placenta (afterbirth) [LO-1]. **5.** prostaglandins [LO-2]. **6.** stress; homeostasis [LO-2]. **7.** positive; postnatal maternity blues; postpartum depression [LO-2].

Methods of Childbirth

The birthing process itself has changed very little over the centuries, but where childbirth takes place and details of childbearing methods have changed with each generation.

Medicated Deliveries

Approximately 95 percent of current deliveries involve some medications—from general anesthesia to spinal blocks (injections of an anesthetic into the membranes surrounding the spinal cord; these block pain from below the point of injection). Medications first became available in the mid-1880s, when both ether and chloroform were used. At that time, however, the British clergy discouraged the use of painkillers, believing that God wanted women to have labor pain (a biblical interpretation based on Eve's misdeed with the apple, Genesis 3:16). Queen Victoria used chloroform when she gave birth to her eighth child in 1853, though, and the use of anesthetics soon became popular (Melzack, 1984).

Today, many individuals believe that obstetric medication should be avoided whenever possible and that prepared childbirth techniques can make childbirth painless (Lamaze, 1970). However, even women who have learned prepared childbirth techniques may experience high levels of pain. Effective use of obstetric medications often can reduce the pain involved in labor. For example, epidural

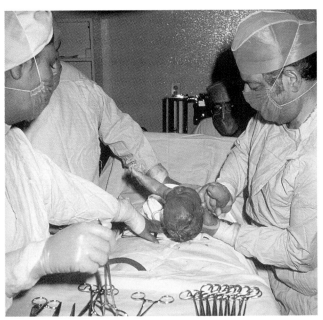

Like a growing number of babies, this infant was delivered by cesarean section.

blocks (a type of spinal block) are able to reduce pain scores an average of 89 percent (Melzack, 1984).

Opponents of obstetric medications argue that medicated newborns are more sluggish and not as alert as nonmedicated infants. They believe that motor development, language and cognitive development, and weight gain are all negatively affected by these medications (Brackbill, 1982). Some professionals state that routine use of medications has contributed to the high infant mortality rate in the United States. Others believe that the effects of obstetric medications are minimal if small doses are used (Stechler & Halton, 1982).

The use of hospitals and medical procedures for birthing is expensive. In 1987, total delivery cost for a 3-day stay with a routine birth averaged about $2,560, and for a cesarean delivery about $5,500 (Roha, 1987).

Cesarean Delivery

A **cesarean section (C-section)** is a surgical procedure to remove the baby from the uterus. It is major abdominal surgery, and mothers have longer hospital stays, longer recovery periods, higher rates of depression, and greater risk of infection after cesarean deliveries (Sachs et al., 1983).

Incidence of Cesarean Deliveries
Recent decades have been marked by a tremendous growth in cesarean deliveries. In 1970, only 1 in 20 babies was born by cesarean delivery; now, 1 in 5 is a common ratio. C-sections are second only to biopsy as the most common surgical procedure in the United States (Entwisle & Alexander, 1988). Why the increase?

Reasons for and Effects of Cesarean Deliveries
One common (over 33 percent) reason for cesarean delivery is that the labor is failing to progress properly. The two other most common reasons are that the mother has had a

previous C-section (although the majority of these women could have a successful vaginal delivery) and that the baby is in the breech or transverse position. Other reasons include doctors' convenience and concerns (because of potential malpractice suits) about being medically conservative. Although C-sections generally provide safe deliveries, many critics now believe that more cesarean deliveries are performed than are needed.

Many doctors use a **fetal monitor,** a sensing device placed around the woman's abdomen, to measure fetal heart rate and contractions. Another type of fetal monitor is attached to the fetus's scalp to measure oxygen in the bloodstream. While this monitoring has been useful in detecting serious birth complications, fetal heart monitoring may also lead to an overestimate of the need for cesarean births. Doctors may interpret the data produced by the stresses of normal birth as birth complications and choose to do C-sections. As a result, babies born by C-section miss out on the normal birthing process surge of stress hormones. As detailed in Table 3.1 earlier, stress hormones help to absorb liquid in the lungs and aid production of surfactant (Lagercrantz & Slotkin, 1986). Without the stress hormones, C-section babies have a higher incidence of breathing problems.

What are the long-term effects of a cesarean birth? An extensive study found no correlation between delivery method and 4-year-old children's Stanford-Binet IQ scores. In addition, most studies of parent-child interactions are positive in outcome. In one study, first-graders showed no differences based on delivery mode for ability in reading and math, but the parents of cesarean-born children, as well as the cesarean-born children themselves, had higher expectations with regard to school grades (Entwisle & Alexander, 1987).

Natural and Prepared Childbirth

Natural or prepared childbirth training (PCT) teaches mothers how to cope with the stress and pain of labor and delivery by using exercises and breathing techniques. PCT also helps fathers to feel more involved because they serve as labor coaches (McNurlen, 1986). Until PCT became popular, most hospitals had banned fathers from delivery rooms since the end of World War I. Today, nearly all hospitals allow fathers into the labor and delivery rooms (Wideman & Singer, 1984).

Lamaze Techniques

PCT was popularized by Fernand Lamaze (1970) in his book *Painless Childbirth: Psychoprophylactic Method.* Lamaze based his psychoprophylactic methods on the 1914 writings of physician Grantly Dick-Read, who proposed a theory of natural childbirth (childbirth without medications and with breathing exercises), and also on his observations of childbirth in the Soviet Union, where women gave birth by Pavlovian classical conditioning techniques (associating aspects of birth with pleasant feelings and positive, calming mental images). Lamaze promoted teaching accurate information about reproduction and childbirth and providing instruction in breathing and relaxation techniques. He also advocated cognitive restructuring strategies, such as visual focusing, sucking on ice, and focusing on foot massages.

The Lamaze method typically is taught in six weekly classes, starting in the woman's 7th month of pregnancy. The husband or another person serves as a coach and monitor for the process. The coach times contractions, helps in regulating breathing and focusing attention, and provides messages. More than 500,000 U.S. couples take Lamaze training each year, and doctors tend to be supportive of this method (Wideman & Singer, 1984).

One problem with the Lamaze strategy is that it seems to promise painless childbirth. In actuality, pain is diminished but still can be severe (see Figure 3.2). An effective instruction in Lamaze techniques may reduce women's labor pain by approximately 30 percent. Many expectant mothers trained in Lamaze techniques, however, do not understand that pain is an unavoidable aspect of labor. Thus, they believe that the pain they experience represents their failure to perform well during labor (Melzack, 1984). Some women may want to consider combining PCT with conservative use of obstetric medicines.

Lamaze training does have several benefits. Although the training does not affect pregnant women's anxiety levels, it does seem to be associated with more positive feelings about pregnancies, fewer negative labor memories, and more positive feelings toward themselves (Tanzer & Block, 1976). In addition, having a supportive partner during childbirth is associated with shorter labors and more interaction with newborns (Sosa, Kennell, Klaus, Robertson, & Urrutia, 1980). One large study comparing 500 Lamaze-trained women with 500 nontrained women found that the Lamaze-trained women had only one third the number of toxemia cases, one half the number of premature births, and one fourth as many cesarean deliveries (Hughey, McElin, & Young, 1978).

Leboyer Techniques

In his book *Birth Without Violence,* Frederick Leboyer (1975) argued the need to minimize the trauma of leaving the womb and entering a noisy, overstimulating world. Therefore, Leboyer advocated giving birth in a darkened and warm room, placing the newborn on the mother's stomach immediately after birth, delaying the cutting of the umbilical cord for awhile, and later, giving the baby a gentle massage and a warm bath. Leboyer's **gentle birth hypothesis** was that such a warm and personal birthing procedure would produce babies born with joy rather than with distress and that this difference would help to develop happier people.

For nearly 10 years, the Leboyer technique was viewed as a superior alternative to the sterile and cold operating room delivery. However, early criticisms of this birthing method focused on problems with details. For example, the low lighting during this delivery could cause doctors to miss vital signs of a medical complication. Also, babies could be exposed to more infections when lying on the mother's abdomen or in the warm bathwater (Cohn, 1975).

More recently, critics have suggested that the Leboyer method has no demonstrable short-term or long-term positive effects. In one study, 56 pregnant women

Bonding, or strong, emotional attachment between parents and newborn in the first minutes of life, was popularized by Klaus and Kennell (1976) in their book *Maternal-Infant Bonding.* The two pediatricians stressed that immediate, prolonged contact between parents and their babies in the period immediately after birth had strong, positive effects on parent-child relationships. They also theorized that parents deprived of early contact were less emotionally attached to their infants, which was believed to have an adverse effect on child development and parent-child relationships.

Klaus and Kennell based their concept of parent-infant bonding on animal studies. Among many mammals other than humans, mothers tend to nurture their own young but ignore or even mistreat the young of other mammals. Maternal hormones released during the birth process, the offspring's smell, and the critical period immediately after birth apparently combine to form a bond between mother and baby. If an animal baby is removed from its mother at birth and returned in a few hours, the mother often rejects it. However, if the baby is removed after mother and offspring have been together for even just a few minutes, the mother will nurture the baby when it is returned in a few hours (Klaus & Kennell, 1976). Klaus and Kennell expanded this animal phenomenon to humans.

Similar hypotheses exist today. For example, oxytocin, a hormone secreted by the brain prior to labor, has been proposed as the biological basis for mothering behaviors. Once again, animal studies are used as support for this idea. When oxytocin is injected into the brain of a rat that has never given birth, the rat builds a nest and cares for the offspring of other rats. If oxytocin is removed from female rats, their maternal behavior ends (Baker, 1987).

But does the concept of bonding pertain to human beings? The research on bonding since Klaus and Kennell published their book suggests that no long-term effects result from the quality of initial bonding. In fact, early contact has no significant impact on parenting (Lamb & Hwang, 1982; Myers, 1984).

The concept of bonding was widely reported in the media during the 1970s, but the research findings that suggest that bonding is not important have received much less media coverage. When asked, many people report that they believe bonding is a very real phenomenon. They may even believe that failure to bond at birth increases the risk for child abuse and neglect.

While research has not supported the bonding concept, its effects on hospital procedures in maternity wards probably will remain. The bonding concept encouraged hospitals to allow parents of newborns to spend more time with the new child.

were randomly assigned to either a Leboyer method delivery or a traditional delivery group. Researchers found no differences in crying among the two groups of newborns. No assessment differences were found at 24 hr, 72 hr, or 8 months (Nelson et al., 1980). The Leboyer technique may even rob newborns of the healthy stresses of the birth process (Lagercrantz & Slotkin, 1986). Over the last few years, the idea of gentle birth has waned in popularity, as has the concept of bonding, the topic of the "Exploring the Parent/Child Relationship" feature.

Childbirth Settings

Hospital Settings

Today, hospitals are seen as providing the safest and most convenient sites for childbirth. This attitude has not always been prevalent. Obstetrics first became a part of a physician's training in the mid-18th century, and only poor and unmarried women were likely to give birth in hospital settings. In those times, many maternity patients died in hospitals—about one in four mothers died of childbed fever until Ignaz Semmelweis discovered that germs caused childbed fever. Until the 1840s, medical students often dissected corpses and then attended women in childbirth without washing their hands in between. Once Semmelweis made hand washing a common practice, childbed fever was reduced (Crano, 1986).

Currently, 98 percent of childbirths occur in a hospital setting, and 95 percent of all births are attended to by physicians (McNurlen, 1986). In recent years, however,

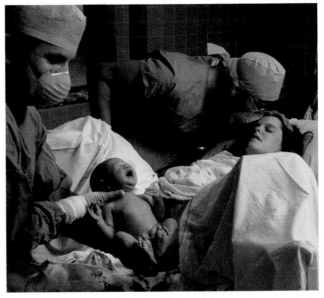

The doctor holds a newborn child in a birthing room at a hospital, while the father congratulates the mother.

more women have insisted on being part of the decision-making process, rather than letting physicians have total control (Savage, 1986). Partly because of this change, some hospitals have been offering more options in procedures and settings, such as having homey, comfortable "birthing rooms" and allowing fathers to stay overnight with the mother and infant.

Throughout history, childbirth procedures have varied. In the 1500s, nearly all births took place at home; now, nearly all births take place in the hospital. Once, midwives assisted in the majority of births; now physicians are the major attendants. In the 19th century, women were discouraged from using medicines to affect their pain levels; now the debate centers around whether too many drugs and medical procedures are used. People once assumed that birthing came naturally; now, the majority of expectant parents participate in training programs. Most 20th-century men were excluded from the birthing process; now, expectant fathers are encouraged to participate. Just as customs have changed over time, different cultures have developed unique birthing practices. The variations include couvades, doulas, and public births.

Couvades

Males in some preindustrial societies manifest many signs of labor and delivery, including pains, groans, moans, "mock delivery," and a lengthy recovery period (longer than the mother's recovery). This practice among expectant fathers is called a couvade. Perhaps, the couvade serves as a way for men to deal with their envy of women's biological creative power (Bettelheim, 1962). Or, the couvade may be a practical way of claiming paternity of the newborn (Paige & Paige, 1973).

Doulas

Guatemalans sometimes have doulas at the birthing process. Doulas are untrained attendants who stay with the mother throughout the labor to provide emotional support. Women who have a doula average 7.7 hr of labor, while unattended women average 15.4 hr of labor (Goodell & Gurin, 1984). Research in the United States also shows that women who have a

supportive labor coach have shorter labors (Sosa et al., 1980).

Public Births

In the United States, birthing is a fairly private affair. Outside of medical personnel, usually only the mother and father are present. Before the 1960s, even fathers were not usually allowed in the delivery room. In some places, however, public births, or well-attended births, are the custom. On Easter Island, villagers gather around a woman in labor. In the Japanese court in previous centuries, births were well-attended so that the audience could frighten away undesirable spirits (Sorel, 1984). Perhaps, the current parallel would be individuals who choose to videotape the birthing process for later viewing with friends or relatives.

An increasing awareness of birthing practices throughout the world may result in even more changes in the common birthing procedures used in the United States.

Floridian midwife, Gladys Miller, is representative of one trend in delivery practices. No longer learned by apprenticeships, midwives are now registered nurses with specialized training.

Home Deliveries

Although almost all childbirths occur in the hospital, some individuals use alternative settings for birthing. One to two percent of babies are born in home deliveries. Most doctors do not recommend home deliveries because about 20 percent of "low-risk" mothers have to be transferred to a hospital during or after delivery. Most insurance policies do not pay the expenses of home deliveries, and most physicians will not attend home deliveries (Goodell & Gurin, 1984; McNurlen, 1986).

Birth Centers

An alternative childbirth setting is the birth center, which provides doctor-assisted childbirth with minimal medicinal intervention. Birth centers are established near hospitals so that unforeseen complications can be dealt with quickly and are feasible for healthy women with low risks of complications. Mother and newborn usually are home within 24 hr of birth. Birthing expenses are typically less at birth centers than at hospitals, but expectant parents need to check whether their insurance covers birth center costs (Goodell & Gurin, 1984; McNurlen, 1986).

Midwives

The use of midwives, trained women who assist births, predates the use of doctors to assist births. Until recently, lay midwives (or "granny midwives") played an important role in assisting poor, rural, and isolated women to have safe childbirths. Until 1950, for example, half of black babies born in southern states were delivered by "granny midwives." "Granny midwives" trained by self-study and apprenticeship, and many in the medical profession believe that they should not practice (Holland, 1987; Holmes, 1987). While lay midwives are a diminishing group, certified nurse-midwives (CNM), who are registered nurses with extra training, are gaining in popularity. Many are employed at birth centers. Currently, these certified nurse-midwives deliver about 3 percent of all U.S. babies (Holmes, 1987). The "Exploring Cultural Diversity" feature provides a cross-cultural look at childbirthing.

Low-Birthweight Babies

Low-birthweight babies are all newborns who weigh less than 5 1/2 lb. These infants make up nearly 7 percent of all babies born in the United States. In 1986, about 245,000 low-birthweight babies were born, and approximately 10,000 of these infants weighed less than 1,000 g (2.3 lb). Surprisingly, at intensive-care nurseries, even babies who weigh less than 750 g have a 24 percent chance of survival.

From 750 to 1,000 g, survival rate improves to 70 percent. Babies who weigh at least 1,000 g have a 98 percent rate of survival with the best medical care (Behrman, 1987; Holmes et al., 1984).

Low-birthweight babies form a high percentage of the medically-at-risk infants. About 10 percent of all babies (or 350,000 infants each year) spend some time in intensive-care nurseries (Holmes et al., 1984). The annual costs for these intensive-care units is about $2 billion (Grady, 1985; Kantrowitz, Wingert, & Hager, 1988).

About 92 percent of low-birthweight babies are **premature** or **preterm**. These babies (also called "preemies") have a short gestation period, generally defined as under 38 weeks. Eight percent of low-birthweight babies are not premature but are **small-for-gestational-age (SGA)** infants. These full-term but SGA babies have more mature central nervous systems (maturity can be assessed by infants' reflexes and by external features, such as skin texture and ear form) than do preterm babies (Holmes et al., 1984). Some babies are both preterm and SGA; some babies are preterm and **AGA (appropriate-for-gestational-age)**.

Although less frequent than low-birthweight babies, some babies are **large-for-gestational-age (LGA)**. LGA babies often have diabetic mothers and are prone to respiratory problems, metabolic imbalances, and birth complications (Holmes et al., 1984).

Factors Affecting Low Birthweight

While several specific factors are associated with low birthweight, at least half of all small or medically-at-risk infants are the result of uncomplicated pregnancies in which contributing factors are hard to distinguish. In another 10 percent of the cases, the primary cause seems to be iatrogenic; that is, the physician is largely responsible. The most common iatrogenic cause is induced labor (Holmes et al., 1984).

Several maternal conditions during pregnancy add to the probability of giving birth prematurely and increasing the risk for low-birthweight babies: hypertension, rubella during the first 16 weeks of pregnancy (although 69 percent of babies are unaffected), urogenital infections, diabetes, more than four previous pregnancies, pregnancy as a teenager or over age 35, being underweight, little weight gain during pregnancy, cigarette or marijuana smoking, having had two or more abortions, maternal malnutrition

Highly trained nurses in well-equipped neonatal intensive care units have improved the survival rate of premature infants.

Caring for Low-Birthweight Babies

Medical Care

In the 1980s, the medical specialty of **neonatology** (the care of newborn babies) made tremendous strides in helping "preemies" survive. For example, more than 9 of 10 infants who weigh only 2 to 3 lb at birth now survive; in 1960, more than half of these infants died.

A typical medical advance can be illustrated by looking at how premature babies are aided in respiratory difficulties. "Preemies" used to be given pure oxygen to breathe; this aided survival, but the pure oxygen resulted in retrolental fibroplasia, which caused blindness. Today, preterm infants breathe by means of a mechanical ventilator. Mechanical ventilators decrease the risk of blindness but sometimes damage fragile lungs. Researchers want to develop a synthetic lubricant that could be directly applied to the lungs (Kantrowitz et al., 1988).

Parental Care

Advanced medical care is not enough. Low-birthweight infants also need much parental care, yet parents of preterm infants interact less with their babies than do parents of full-term infants. They provide less body contact, spend less time smiling at their babies, talk to them less, and hold them for shorter time periods. These differences may be due to parents feeling (1) apprehensive about a baby's fragile appearance and health, (2) intimidated by intensive-care nurseries, (3) a need to distance themselves when the baby's life is endangered, or (4) guilt and incompetence for not carrying the baby full term (Campos, Barrett, Lamb, Goldsmith, & Stenberg, 1983; Goldberg, 1979; Schwartzberg, 1988a).

Medical experience and research studies suggest several activities for parents of low-birthweight babies to help them cope well with their situations:

- Parents have to work harder to get responses from preterm babies. Then, once the "preemies" are responding, the babies have a harder time turning off. Parents aware of this difference can more successfully avoid temperamental displays (Schwartzberg, 1988a).
- Preterm infants need more time to distinguish visually between objects. Therefore, parents should not barrage the infants with novel items. Instead, they should repeat activities several times and play slowly (Schwartzberg, 1988a).
- Preterm babies need extra pacifier-sucking opportunities. This extra sucking helps them to gain weight and to leave the hospital sooner, and may reduce complications up to 2 years later (Anderson, Burroughs, & Measel, 1983).
- Premature infants need extra touch and movement stimulation, and parents can achieve this by stroking and flexing limbs, rocking, and doing gentle massages. These activities seem to reduce babies' stress and to lower levels of cortisol, a stress-related compound (Scafidi et al., 1986).

during the last trimester, anemia, and exposure to teratogens (Behrman, 1987; Grady, 1985; Holmes et al., 1984; Lieberman, Ryan, Monson, & Schoenbaum, 1987; Monmaney, 1988; Pascoe, Chessare, Baugh, Urich, & Ialongo, 1987; Stein, Susser, Saenger, & Marolla, 1975).

Some studies have found that African Americans, Hispanic Americans, and Native Americans have higher percentages of low-birthweight babies than do European Americans (Behrman, 1987; Kleinman & Kessel, 1987). Researchers do not attribute this to biological differences between racial/ethnic groups but to associated social-economic factors, such as less prenatal medical care, younger age of mothers, lower socioeconomic factors, and malnutrition (Lieberman et al., 1987).

One major preventive factor with regard to low-birthweight babies seems to be good prenatal care. If all pregnant women could participate in regular prenatal medical care by the 12th week of pregnancy, the rate of low-birthweight babies would be cut in half. Good prenatal care would also increase the survival rate among the remaining half. Every low birthweight that could be prevented by prenatal care would save from $14,000 to $30,000 (Monmaney, 1988).

Another maternal factor associated with low-birthweight babies is drug consumption. Approximately 95 percent of pregnant women take at least one potentially harmful prescription or over-the-counter medication drug. About 6 percent of pregnant women take at least 10 drugs. Drugs are most damaging when used during the first 45 days after conception (Holmes et al., 1984). In other words, women may harm their fetuses before they even realize they are pregnant.

Finally, low birthweight seems to be associated with family factors, such as how much help the pregnant woman gets in household tasks, amount of family stress, and family dysfunction. Fetuses may serve as "symptom bearers" for dysfunctional family situations (Pascoe et al., 1987; Ramsey, Abell, & Baker, 1986).

- Premature infants sleep better if provided with tape-recorded human heartbeat sounds (Rose, 1983a, 1983b).
- Because preterm babies cannot self-regulate body temperature, parents need to be careful to maintain sufficient warmth (Grady, 1985).
- Parents should imitate expressions, movements, and sounds made by their premature babies (Field, 1981).
- Because of weak lungs, preterm babies need to avoid smoke and dust, including baby powder (Schwartzberg, 1988a).

The Neonatal Period

Even full-term babies have to make major adjustments in the transition from womb to outside world environment. The most striking comparisons between prenatal and postnatal life are summarized in Table 3.2. Because newborns must make such tremendous transitions at a time when their body systems still need some time to stabilize, the first few weeks of life are a special phase of infancy. Infants in this month-long phase are called **neonates** (from "neo-" for *new* and "nate" for *born*).

Medical Assessment

At birth, all neonates should be assessed for any medical conditions that require attention. Assessment tools include the Apgar Scale and the Brazelton Neonatal Behavioral Assessment Scale.

Apgar Scale

One quick assessment tool employed in almost all hospitals is the **Apgar Scale,** developed by Virginia Apgar (1953; Apgar, Holaday, James, Weisbrot, & Berrier, 1958). As shown in Table 3.3, the Apgar Scale measures infant response in five areas: heart rate, respiration, muscle tone, reflex irritability (nervous system functioning), and color. The test is given 1 min after birth and again at 5 min after birth, and infant responses are scored 0, 1, or 2. Ninety percent of all infants receive at least a 7 out of a possible 10 points (Apgar & Beck, 1973).

Table 3.2
A Comparison of Prenatal and Postnatal Life

Characteristic	Prenatal Life	Postnatal Life
Physical environment	Fluid (amniotic fluid)	Gaseous (air)
External temperature	Fairly constant	Fluctuates with atmosphere
Sensory stimulation	Minimal (mostly kinesthetic and vibratory)	Variety of stimuli to all senses
Nutrition	Dependent on nutrients in mother's blood	Dependent on external food and functioning digestive system
Oxygen supply	Passed from maternal bloodstream at the placental surface	Passed from lung surface to pulmonary blood vessels
Metabolic elimination	Passed into maternal bloodstream via placenta	Eliminated by lungs, skin, kidneys, and gastrointestinal tract

Reprinted with the permission of Macmillan Publishing Company, a division of Macmillan, Inc. from *Developmental Physiology and Aging* by Paolas. Timiras. Copyright © 1972 P. S. Timiras.

Table 3.3
The Apgar Scale

Aspect Tested	Score 0	Score 1	Score 2
1. Heart rate	Absent	Slow (<100)	Fast (>100)
2. Respiration	Absent	Slow, irregular	Good, crying
3. Muscle tone	Limp	Weak, inactive	Strong, active
4. Reflex irritability	No response	Grimace	Cough or sneeze
5. Color	Blue or pale	Body pink, limbs blue	Entirely pink

Adapted from V.A. Apgar, "A Proposal for a New Method of Evaluation of a Newborn Infant" in *Anesthesia and Analgesia . . . Current Research, 32,* 260–267. 1953. International Anesthesia Research Society, Cleveland, OH.

The score at 5 min is more useful in indicating neonatal progress and long-term prognosis. Low-birthweight babies often receive low scores because of their physical immaturity, but an improved score from the first to second testing is a good sign for "preemies" (Koops & Battaglia, 1987). Scores can also be temporarily affected by obstetric medications that were given to the mother during labor (Apgar et. al., 1958).

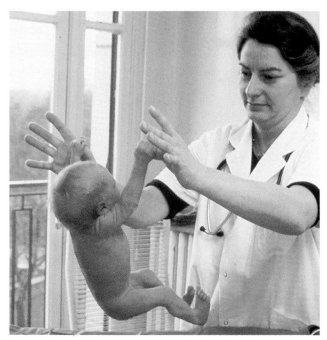

This neonate scores an "A" on its grasping reflex test.

Babies who initially receive a 7 and remain high on the second testing can immediately be given to the mother. Intermediate scores of 4 to 6 may require some respiratory intervention if test scores are not higher at the second testing. Most infants who score low need immediate intervention, such as aid with respiration, cardiac massage, larnynoscope, or umbilical catheterization (Koops & Battaglia, 1987).

The Apgar Scale is widely used because it is easy, fast, and indicates medical conditions requiring immediate action. For example, infants with little reflex irritability may have central nervous system impairment, and individuals who retain some cyanosis, or blue coloring, instead of becoming entirely pink may have respiratory or heart problems. However, the scale is unable to detect long-term developmental concerns (Drotar, 1987; Gorski et al., 1987).

Brazelton Neonatal Behavioral Assessment Scale
Terry Brazelton (1973, 1978) developed the **Brazelton Neonatal Behavioral Assessment Scale (BNAS),** a scale that tests 26 categories in 30 min. The test is administered on the third or fourth day after birth and repeated on the ninth or tenth day. Since the goal is to obtain optimal scores, assessors are encouraged to give the BNAS when infants are alert and active. Items can be repeated to determine the highest performance level (Gorski, Lewkowicz, & Huntington, 1987).

This ambitious scale measures various aspects of physiological, motor, state of consciousness, and social interaction behavior. The 26 categories measure six main areas: (1) habituation (diminishing response to a stimulus presented over time), (2) orientation (ability to attend to and focus on stimuli), (3) motor maturity (coordination and control of muscles), (4) variation (responses to dealing with changes in color, activity, and state), (5) self-quieting (ability to quiet oneself after activity), and (6) cuddliness (measures of social interaction). Compared with the Apgar Scale, the BNAS is a more sensitive index of the central nervous system maturity of neonates, yet it, too, has shortcomings in detecting most developmental outcomes (Gorski et al., 1987).

One study using the BNAS investigated the effects of obstetric medications on newborns (Murray, Dolby, Nation, & Thomas, 1981). The researchers found that the effects of the medications are strongest on the first day, still noticeable on the fifth day, and still affecting mother-infant interaction for the first month.

One of the most important uses of the BNAS has been in pointing out behaviors that may influence parent-infant interaction. For example, the BNAS can show individual differences in infant cuddliness, which can clue parents into the need for compensatory behavior in this area (Als, Tronick, Lester, & Brazelton, 1979). Parents can be taught ways to stimulate and comfort babies in areas in which the infants are fairly unresponsive.

Some parents have been given "Brazelton training": They learn how to administer the BNAS to their babies, and in the process of measuring their newborns' gazing abilities, smiling and cooing responses, and so forth, they learn how to better elicit pleasant interactions with their infants. In addition to the babies learning to be more responsive to their parents, the parents gain in knowledge about infant abilities, feel more competent and confident about their parenting skills, and are more satisfied with their parenting roles (Myers, 1982; Widmayer & Field, 1980; Worobey & Belsky, 1982).

Other Assessments
Barry Lester has suggested that medical cues can be derived from neonates' crying patterns. For example, a pattern called "cri du chat," a steady crying at approximately 800 cycles, is a distinctive cry of brain-damaged infants. This steady cry contrasts with normal infants' crying, which starts at 200 cycles and rises to 600 cycles, holds steady, and then drops off (Angier, 1984; Lester & Boukydis, 1985). Malnourished infants have high-pitched, arhythmatic crying that is low in intensity and high in duration (Angier, 1984). Infants with Down syndrome have pain cries that are lower in pitch than normal infants (Zeskind & Marshall, 1988). Asphyxiated babies have shorter cries, higher fundamental frequencies, and less stable cry signals (Campos et al., 1983).

Researchers believe that higher pitches and frequency variability can be used as assessment tools in detecting subtle differences in neurological functioning. For example, infants with great variability in cry pitch need more visits with health-care personnel during their first month after hospital discharge (Zeskind & Marshall, 1988). Eventually, analysis of crying sounds may become part of standard neonatal exams (Turkington, 1984).

New techniques allow medical personnel to detect neonatal eye and ear impairments. One vision test, called visually evoked potential (or VEP), measures the brain's responses to a checkerboard pattern that reverses colors. By measuring the time between brain-wave peaks and the wave amplitudes, researchers can test neonates' eyes for defects. The VEP can pick up strabismus, or cross-eye, a condition that leads to amblyopia, or "lazy eye" blindness. A related technique, called brain-stem evoked response (BSER), can be used to detect loss of hearing in one ear (Patrusky, 1980).

Neonates are also screened for the enzyme disorder phenylketonuria (PKU), which occurs once in 14,000 births. Babies who inherit this condition become mentally retarded unless they are placed on a special diet during the first month of life. Other medical conditions, such as hypothyroidism, can be detected by medical tests.

Although useful assessment and screening devices have been developed, more sensitive tests that can detect other developmental biological risks, such as sudden infant death syndrome (SIDS) and mental retardation, are needed (Drotar, 1987; Eldredge & Salamy, 1988; Gorski et al., 1987).

General Appearance and Characteristics of Neonates

On television shows and in the movies, newborns are quite attractive creatures, so new parents may be quite surprised by some of their neonate's physical features. Temporarily, their new "bundle of joy" may have a flattened or cone-shaped head, patchy coloring, and squinty eyes that create a look only "its parents could love." Some of the temporary features of newborns are summarized in Table 3.4. In addition, newborns have an oily covering called the vernix caseosa, which serves as a temporary protection against infection.

The general physical appearance of newborns reflects the cephalocaudal principle ("cephalo" means *head;* "caudal" means *tail*), which states that development proceeds from the head to lower body parts. The head is one fourth of newborns' total body length, and the brain is already 25 percent of its adult weight (McAuliffe, 1985).

The average newborn is 20 inches long and weighs over 7 lb. Male babies tend to be longer and heavier, and later borns tend to weigh more than firstborns. Over the first few days, neonates lose an average of 10 percent of their birthweight; about the fifth day, neonates start to gain weight back. By the end of the second week, most neonates are back to their original birthweight (Leach, 1982).

Reflexes and Motor Abilities

Reflexes

Newborns exhibit several **reflexes,** automatic responses to external stimulation. Most of the reflexes disappear during the first year of life, as indicated in Table 3.5, but some, such as blinking, gagging, yawning, and sneezing, are life-long reflexes. One explanation for the number of reflexes in neonates is that newborns are functioning primarily from

---

Table 3.4
Physical Features of Newborns

1. Bluish hands and feet. Color is caused by baby's inefficient circulation. Typically occurs when baby has been asleep for awhile. Pink color returns when the baby is picked up and moved.

2. Blue patches. These are temporary accumulations of pigment under the skin. They are most common in babies that will have fairly dark skin.

3. Cradle cap. Some babies have a thick, cap-shaped layer of skin that peels, and this layer is called a cradle cap. Other babies have more moderate skin peeling on the head and other areas, especially the palms and soles.

4. Body hair. Some babies temporarily have a fuzzy body hair called lanugo, which drops off in a few days. Head hair of the newborn also often falls out and is replaced, sometimes with hair of a different color.

5. Oddly shaped head. Misshapen heads are due to the pressures of pushing through the birth canal. They correct themselves in a few months.

6. Soft spots. Soft areas, or fontanels, in the head are areas where the bones of the skull have not yet fused together. A "sunken" spot means that the baby needs liquids; a bulging fontanel should be checked by a physician.

7. "Tongue tie." More of a newborn's tongue is anchored to the mouth than is true of older individuals. This condition corrects itself since most of the tongue's growth in the first year is in the tip.

8. Sucking blisters and white tongue. Some babies have white tongues due to their milk diet. While they are milk-fed, some babies get temporary "sucking blisters."

9. Swollen breasts. In the first 5 days after birth, some babies have swollen breasts, resulting from maternal hormones preceding birth. Some babies even have some secretion, which in the Middle Ages was referred to as "witch's milk" and thought to have healing powers.

10. Eliminations and secretions. Newborns have a variety of temporary secretions, including meconium, a greenish-black, sticky substance that is eliminated during the first day of life. Vaginal bleeding, which is caused by maternal estrogens just before birth, may occur during the first week. Newborns urinate frequently—30 times a day is normal. Also, newborns cry without tears; the first tears come at around 4 to 6 weeks.

Data from Penelope Leach, *Your Baby & Child: From Birth to Age Five,* 1989. Copyright © 1989 Dorling Kindersley Adult, London, England. Reprinted by permission.

---

the brain stem and subcortex; as the cortex develops, the reflexes disappear, and infants turn toward more voluntary control of their behavior (McAuliffe, 1985).

Newborn Movements

Of course, neonates are not limited to reflexive behaviors. Researchers in a recent study observed the movements of 25 normal newborns between their third and sixth day of life and also captured these movements on film through the use of an automatic movement mattress that triggered a

Table 3.5
Reflexes in the Neonate

Name of Reflex	Triggering Stimulation	Infant's Response	Reflex Ends
Babinski	Stroking of sole of foot	Toes spread out, and foot twists in.	6 to 9 months
Darwinian (grasping)	Stroking of palm of hand	Hand makes a strong fist; if around, a stick can be lifted.	2 months
Moro (startle)	A sudden noise, being dropped, sudden contact	Head drops backward, neck extends, arms and legs extend, and back arches.	3 months
Placing	Drawing of backs of feet against flat surface	Foot is withdrawn.	1 month
Rooting	Stroking of cheek	Head turns, mouth opens, and infant makes sucking movements.	9 months
Swimming	Placing infant in water facedown	Infant makes swimming movements.	6 months
Tonic neck	Laying infant down on back	Head turns to one side, limbs are extended on preferred side, and other limbs are flexed.	2 months
Walking	Holding infant under arm and having infant's bare feet touch a flat surface	Feet make steplike motions.	2 months

camera (Weggemann, Brown, Fulford, & Minns, 1987). The study found about 80 individual movements that were grouped into several movement forms, such as those shown in Figure 3.3.

Usually after feeding, infants have relaxed faces (no smiles or frowns) and exhibit a few slow, progressive movements (alternating movements of flexion and extension of the limbs) and bursts of noninitiative sucking. After falling asleep, frowns and sucking movements are exhibited, along with irregular respiration and REM (rapid eye movement). Athetoid movements (fingers and toes) and movement of a single limb are common. After a half hour, infants are in quiet sleep, which is marked by more regular respiration, no eye movement, and little body movement. When hunger awakens infants, there are isolated progression movements and, later, almost continuous movement. Infants that are supine exhibit more stretch movements and head turns than those in prone positions.

Movements are not affected by infant gender or type of feeding, but they are related to state of arousal, gestational age, positioning, and temperature and light factors. Babies are more active when lying on their back than when lying facedown. Premature babies exhibit more limb movements than full-term babies.

One study electronically recorded the activity of 50 neonates and then used mobile microcomputers to monitor the children when they were between the ages of 4 and 8 (Korner et al., 1985). The most active, vigorous neonates grew into the young children with the highest daytime activity rates. Parents rated these same active neonates as more likely to approach, rather than to retreat from, new experiences as young children.

Sensation and Cognitive Abilities

At birth, all of the sensory systems are working to some degree, with new capabilities developing over the first months of life. Researchers exploring the sensory capacities of neonates have had to be creative because, obviously, they could not rely on their subjects to provide verbal comments about their experiences. From testing neonates during an alert state (when in an upright versus lying-down position) to using brain-wave recordings or sucking responses on a pacifier, neonate researchers have learned much since the 1950s about innate sensory functions.

Smell

Newborns can distinguish between pleasant and unpleasant odors. They exhibit positive expressions for vanilla and fruity smells but negative expressions for rotten egg and fishy smells. Moreover, infants less than one week old will turn away from ammonia odor (Lipsitt, Engen, & Kaye, 1963; Rieser, Yonas, & Wilkner, 1976).

When the same smell is repeatedly presented, neonates show diminished response to the smell (a response pattern called **habituation**); however, if a new smell is presented, neonates intensify their responses. By noting when habituation and renewed interest occurs, researchers have determined that neonates can distinguish among such smells as garlic, vinegar, alcohol, and anise (Lipsitt et al., 1963).

In one of the more intriguing studies, mothers of neonates wore breast pads. Then, neonates had their own mother's breast pad placed to one side of them and a stranger's breast pad placed to the other side. Neonates who were 6 days old typically turned toward their own mother's pad (MacFarlane, 1978). Neonates who were only 2 days

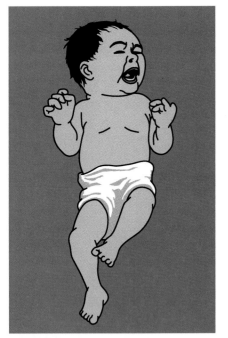

(a) Progressive movements

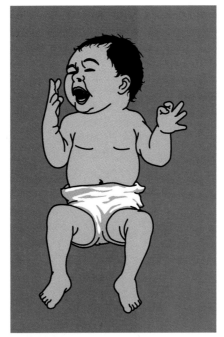

(b) Startle response

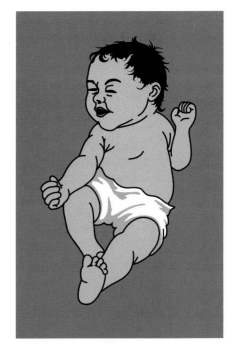

(c) Asymmetrical tonic neck reflex

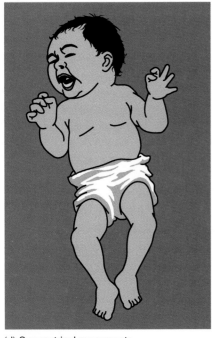

(d) Symmetrical movements

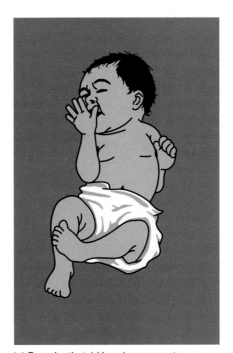

(e) Pseudoathetoid hand movements

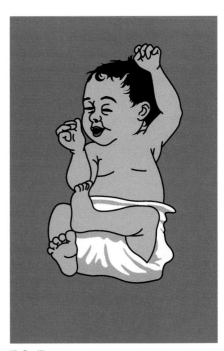

(f) Smiling

Figure 3.3

Typical newborn movements. (a) Progressive movements. (b) Startle response. (c) Asymmetrical tonic neck reflex. (d) Symmetrical movements. (e) Pseudoathetoid hand movements. (f) Smiling.

old did not exhibit this preference. In a study using 2-week-old babies, breast-fed babies were able to recognize their mother's smell on gauze pads worn under the mother's arm. They were unable to recognize the gauze pads worn by their fathers. Non-breast-fed children could not distinguish the gauze pads of either parent (Cernoch & Porter, 1985).

Taste

Like many adults, newborns prefer sweet tastes. They choose a sugar solution over plain water and even show a preference for sucrose over glucose. Neonates also can distinguish sweet substances from sour, bitter, and salty ones. When a sugar solution or water is placed on their tongues, neonates show more tongue movement to the side for sugar

Breastfeeding is a close, shared experience between mother and child.

(Weiffenbach & Thach, 1975). Newborns will suck two different-tasting liquids at varying speeds, even if the liquids have identical smells (Lipsitt, 1977). Babies that are just a few days old display different sucking and swallowing patterns for artificial milk versus breast milk and sterile water versus salty water (Johnson & Salisbury, 1975).

Newborn full-term babies have different facial expressions for various tastes. Very sweet liquids usually elicit smiles and eager sucking. Sour solutions, however, elicit pursed lips, wrinkled noses, and eye blinking. Bitter liquids cause newborns to stick out their tongues and attempt to spit. On the other hand, distilled water (which is tasteless) elicits no expression (Steiner, 1979).

Touch
Touch is probably the first sense to develop in the fetus, with the rooting reflex developed 2 months after conception. All areas of the body are touch-sensitive by 32 weeks of gestation. The area around the mouth is the most sensitive region.

Perhaps the most important area of touch that needs to be understood is the neonate's experience of pain. Until recently, almost all circumcisions (the optional surgical procedure performed on male babies to remove the foreskin of the penis) and other neonate surgical procedures were done without use of anesthetic drugs; sometimes, medications are still not provided, even though narcotic fentanyl and lidocaine are considered safe for newborns (Anand &

Hickey, 1987; Fletcher, 1987). Many doctors and families assumed that neonates perceive minimal or no pain during these procedures. However, this required ignoring some obvious signs of pain in newborns, as stated by one physician:

> It has generally been assumed that the ability of a child to feel pain increases with age and that neonates may not perceive pain or may perceive it only minimally. Assumed by whom? Certainly not by those of us at the bedside of critically ill infants, who see them flinch from procedures, startle in response to loud noises, and turn from bright lights and various other forms of stimulation. Not by those who have heard infants' anguished cries and seen their vigorous withdrawals from painful stimuli. Not by those who have observed their increasing heart and respiratory rates and profuse sweating in response to heel sticks or circumcision. And finally, not by those who have seen babies gasp for every breath as they die from incurable chronic lung disease. (Fletcher, 1987, p. 1347)

Although researchers have difficulty in researching pain in neonates, the following findings suggest that newborns experience pain (Anand & Hickey, 1987):

- Skin pain receptors are as dense in newborns as in adults. These nerve endings start to appear in the 7th week of gestation and are on all skin surfaces by the 20th week of gestation.
- Pain pathways to both the brain stem and thalamus are myelinated by 30 weeks of gestation.
- Substance P, one of several brain neurochemicals associated with experiencing pain, appears by the 16th week of gestation. There are higher densities of substance P in neonates than in adults.
- The endogenous opioid system, which plays a role in the control of pain, releases endorphin substances during the birth process in response to fetal distress. Babies born by the more difficult breech presentation have higher endorphin levels. Functionally mature cells of this system are found in the pituitary gland by the 15th week of gestation.
- Both preterm and full-term neonates undergoing circumcision or heel lancing exhibit marked increases in heart rate and blood pressure unless they are given local anesthesia beforehand.
- Neonates undergoing surgery with minimal or no anesthesia have a suppression of insulin secretion and increased release of a variety of substances, including cortisol, growth hormone, and catecholamines, compared to neonates who receive adequate medication.
- Neonates undergoing unpleasant, painful procedures, including pinpricks, have behavioral responses, including crying; facial expressions associated with sadness, surprise, and pain; diffuse body movement; reflex withdrawal; grimacing; and prolonged wakefulness and irritability.

Of course, researchers cannot tell if the subjective experience of pain in neonates is similar to that experienced by children and adults, but the research findings seem to support medical personnel using medications for surgical and other unpleasant procedures with newborns.

Hearing

The middle and inner ears of neonates are adult-size, and neonates have well-developed auditory ability. However, at birth, the middle-ear passages are filled with amniotic fluid that lessens initial hearing. For the first 6 months, an infant's hearing is not quite as good as an adult's.

Neonates turn or look toward the source of sound, can differentiate loudness of sounds, and prefer high-pitched sounds to lower-pitched sounds (MacFarlane, 1978). Continuous sounds tend to have soothing effects on neonates (Brackbill, 1970). By 1 month, infants can differentiate between sounds, such as *P* and *B* (Eimas, 1975).

Although neonates can locate the direction from which a sound is coming, they are not as accurate in this as are older individuals. Even 30-week-old infants can only discriminate sound displacements of about 19 degrees, whereas adults discriminate differences of only 1 to 2 degrees (Ashmead, Clifton, & Perris, 1987). Neonates are also confused when trying to locate sounds that come from more than one source. When a second sound coming from the opposite direction is added a fraction of a second later than the first sound, neonates fail to locate either sound correctly. Instead of turning toward either the first sound or the second sound, neonates act as if they are hearing a single sound coming directly from ahead. In contrast, adults tend to turn toward the first sound and ignore the second sound; this characteristic response is called the precedence effect (Clifton, Morrongiello, Kulig, & Dowd, 1981).

Neonates prefer human voices to other sounds—for example, neonates prefer female voices to bell sounds (Freedman, 1971). Three-day-old infants can distinguish their own mother's voice from the voice of a stranger. They are willing to suck on a pacifier longer when the behavior triggers a recording of their mother's voice reading a Dr. Seuss story than if it triggers the story being read by a different voice (DeCasper & Fifer, 1980). This recognition was eliminated in a study in which mothers were told to read a passage without intonation. When mothers did this, their babies no longer recognized their voices (Mehler, Bertoncini, Barriere, & Jassik-Gerschenfeld, 1978).

Newborns synchronize their movements to adult speech patterns. Filming infants under 2 weeks old while they were exposed to English or Chinese speech, researchers found that the infants began to synchronize their movements to coincide with the structure of speech (regardless of which language was used). The neonates started and stopped their movements to match the speech, but they did not synchronize their movements when exposed to recordings of either tapping sounds or disconnected vowel sounds. Newborns appear to be prewired biologically to respond to human speech (Condon & Sander, 1974).

Vision

What is the newborn's visual capabilities? **Visual acuity,** or the ability to detect the separate parts of an object, is limited in newborns. Early studies measured visual acuity by involuntary eye movements and estimated that newborn perceptual abilities were 20/400 to 20/800. These findings meant that newborns could see at 20 ft what most people could see from 400 to 800 ft (Kiff & Lepard, 1966). Later, with more accurate technology, the estimate of visual acuity for newborns was changed to 20/150 (Lewis & Maurer, 1977). Over the first 6 to 12 months of life, visual acuity greatly improves (Banks & Salapatek, 1983; Cohen, DeLoache, & Strauss, 1979).

Neonates also have limited **visual accommodation,** the ability to focus. Although newborns can accommodate, they tend to overaccommodate for distant objects and underaccommodate for near objects. Accuracy improves during the neonatal period. Neonates focus best at approximately 7 1/2 inches, which, coincidentally, happens to be the distance from mother's face to baby's face during feeding. Peripheral vision ability also doubles from the 2nd to 10th week of life (Banks & Salapatek, 1983).

Although most studies of depth perception are conducted with babies with locomotion skills, research suggests that neonates can perceive depth and tell when objects are getting closer. At 10 days old, they can react defensively when objects move toward their faces. These young subjects exhibit a stronger response when the objects are heading directly at them than when the objects are off to one side (Bower, Broughten, & Moore, 1970).

Neonates visually scan objects differently than older persons. Shown a figure such as a triangle or star, neonates tend to scan only a small portion of the figure. By 2 months, infants are scanning a larger portion of the figure, and unlike their younger counterparts, they look at the figure's center as well as the edge (Salapatek, 1975). A similar pattern is found when infants are shown a picture of a human face: One-month-olds scan a smaller portion of the face than do 2-month-olds. The older infants explore internal features—the nose, mouth, and especially the eyes—more (Maurer & Salapatek, 1976).

Although newborns have some color preferences, their color vision is still developing in the first few months of life (Banks & Salapatek, 1983). Neonates also prefer curved to straight lines, three-dimensional to two-dimensional objects, novel to familiar objects, and faces to other patterns (Fantz, 1961, 1965). Visual preferences found in one study are shown in Figure 3.4. Scientists debate whether the preference for human faces represents biological prewiring or a preference for complex figures.

Although 1-month-olds can recognize their mother's voice, they are less successful at recognizing their mother's face. One study found that 1-month-olds did not pay more attention to their mother's face than to a stranger's face. In fact, neonates tend to prefer dark-haired faces to the familiar face (Melhuish, 1982).

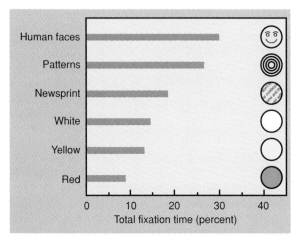

Figure 3.4
Visual preferences of neonates. Neonates from 10 hr to 5 days old look longer at patterns than they do at solid colors. Neonates prefer human faces to other patterns.

Even among newborns, one sense's input can influence another sense's input. Two-day-old infants prefer a light of intermediate intensity. However, if white noise is played simultaneously, neonates prefer low-intensity lighting (Lewkowicz & Turkewitz, 1981). Either neonates have trouble differentiating sound and sight, or they have a preference for a certain level of total stimulation.

Imitation

Imitation (modeling) requires coordinated motor activity and a mental representation of what one wants to imitate. Until recently, imitation was considered a cognitive ability that could not be observed until toward the end of the first year. However, research in the 1970s suggested that 1-week-old infants imitate adults when the adults stick out their tongues or open their mouths wide (Meltzoff & Moore, 1977).

Other research also indicated that neonates could imitate facial expressions. In one study, 2-day-old infants seemed to be able to imitate three emotions: happiness, sadness, and surprise (Field, Woodson, Greenberg, & Cohen, 1982). The emotion of surprise (wide opening of the mouth) was the most imitated expression. Widened lips were most likely to follow the model's expression of happiness, and pouting lips were most likely to follow the model's expression of sadness.

However, not all research findings consistently show that neonates can imitate facial expressions. One recent study found that infants could imitate tongue protrusion (successful imitation occurred in 60 percent of the trials), but not emotional facial expressions of happy, sad, and surprise (Kaitz, Meschulach-Sarfaty, & Auerbach, 1988). The results of this study are shown in Figure 3.5. The authors suggest that neonates stick their tongues out frequently and smile, frown, or appear surprised less spontaneously; thus, they believe that imitation of tongue protrusion is more

likely. Tongue protrusion may represent a built-in response to stick out the tongue to all slender objects—a mother's nipple, a felt-tip pen, or another's tongue (Jacobson & Kagan, 1979). Other critics think that imitation results may look like imitation but may really be the result of an excitement response of the part of the infants (Olson & Sherman, 1983b).

On the other hand, since several studies did report imitation of facial gestures before the age of 2 months, imitation may actually exist. If so, neonatal imitation may play a preparatory role in later cognitive development. Neonatal imitation may aid survival in infancy and then disappear when no longer necessary.

Parenting the Newborn

Cultural Influences

Unfortunately, all babies are not joyously welcomed into the world. Only when people can freely choose when to become parents and have the means (i.e., effective birth control) to act on these choices are most babies viewed as precious, valuable creatures. In earlier times, unwanted babies could put an unbearable strain on limited supplies, and sometimes, families did not let newborns survive. Until the 19th century, **infanticide** (the killing of babies) was common. In the Middle Ages, infanticide was not considered a crime by state or church. Biological birth did not mean the social birth of a *person*—that distinction was marked only by acceptance into the family (Belmont, 1976).

Throughout history, parental priority has changed from child quantity to child quality. This change occurred because of (1) control of fertility through contraceptive technology and (2) industrialization and urbanization, which meant fewer children were needed to help out with family economics (Aries, 1973). The current emphasis on child quality has sparked research into child-care practices.

Reactions to a new family member are influenced by population growth patterns, which vary from one country to another. Currently, 42 percent of Mexico's population is under 15 years of age, while West Germany has a large elderly population and more deaths than births each year (negative population growth). By the 21st century, several countries will have negative population growth, including Austria, Belgium, Britain, Bulgaria, the former Czechoslovakia, Denmark, East Germany, France, Greece, Italy, Luxembourg, the Netherlands, Sweden, and Switzerland. Probably by the year 2035, the United States will change to negative population growth. Countries with negative population growth are more likely to encourage positive attitudes about having additional children. For example, China has a growing population, and China's government policy is to encourage late marriages and one-child families. Meanwhile, France, facing a declining population, has begun offering 10,000 francs to couples who choose to have three or more children (Rossi, 1987).

Availability of prenatal care and child care also influences how couples feel about becoming parents. Even government policies about care for the aged have an impact on

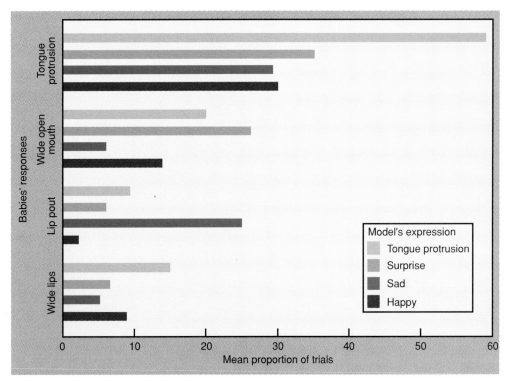

Figure 3.5
Mean proportion of trials during which neonates made mouth movements while each of four facial expressions was modeled.

the number of children families desire. Countries in which adult children care for the elderly are more likely to retain high birth rates (Rossi, 1987).

Impact of Neonates on New Parents
In a 1953 magazine article, Erik and Joan Erikson commented on how becoming a parent is a transition that redefines one's identity, and their comments still appear timely (Schlein, 1987a):

> Babies control and bring up their families as much as they are controlled by them. In fact, we might say that the family brings up a baby by being brought up by him. (p. 569)
>
> This makes of the young mother a most strategic being, and this entirely on her and her baby's terms, for no other woman's charm, vigor, or intelligence can be for her baby what she can be. She is his first day and night, his first sky and earth, his first love—and also his deepest, most desperate anger. (p. 571)
>
> Let us also not forget that every man, quite secretly, is something of a frustrated mother; for every man was once part of a mother and at one time wanted to be like her. Self-assured men . . . can be quite maternal in a firm and cautious way if permitted by changing mores. Chances are that our culture will permit them more and more part in baby care and that men will be better men for it. (p. 572)

Many fathers now meet their children by attending their births. Almost all fathers who are at the birth process and have early and extended contact with their offspring evaluate their experiences as positive. However, no consistent effect of this early interaction can be found for either father or child (Palkovitz, 1985). Still, even if long-term positive consequences cannot be found, the experience seems to be worth it for its immediate effects on fathers.

Others' Questions About the Newborn
What do you think most people ask first about a newborn? In one study, 80 percent of the initial questions were about the baby's gender. More people phrased the question "Is it a boy?" rather than "Is it a girl?", and more asked "Is it a boy or girl?" than asked "Is it a girl or a boy?" The next most common questions involved the health of the mother and baby, followed by questions about the baby's characteristics (Intons-Peterson & Reddel, 1984).

Communicating With Babies
Parents often seem to shift their behavior to match preferences of their new babies. For example, as you read earlier, neonates prefer higher pitches to lower ones, and parents tend to raise the pitch of their voices when they speak to their babies. Infants are more likely to start vocalizing during or after maternal vocalization than in its absence. Mothers tend to vocalize and respond more when girl babies vocalize, and when boy babies move. Girl babies vocalize more than boy babies, especially while their mothers gaze at them, and boy babies move more. Even during the

Right from the start, family members engage the infant in communication.

22. The _____ Scale is administered twice shortly after birth to determine medical concerns; it measures infant responses in _____, _____, muscle tone, color, and _____ irritability.
23. The longer _____ Scale measures six main areas of functioning, including _____ (the diminishing response to a stimulus presented over time), _____ (the ability to attend to and focus on stimuli), and _____ (a measure of social interaction).
24. Barry Lester suggested that medical cues can be derived from _____ patterns, including the distinctive "_____," a steady crying of brain-damaged infants.
25. Screening for _____, an enzyme disorder, allows an infant to be placed on a special diet to avoid mental retardation.
26. Newborns have an oily covering called the _____ that serves as a temporary protection against infection; other physical features can include _____ (a fuzzy body hair) and _____ (soft areas on the head where bones of the skull have not yet fused).
27. Newborns exhibit _____ (automatic responses to external stimulation), including the _____ reflex, when the sole of the foot is stroked, and the _____ reflex, which is a response to a sudden noise.
28. Neonates prefer _____ tastes, are more sensitive to touch in the _____ region, and prefer listening to _____ and looking at _____.
29. Some researchers believe that neonates can imitate _____ protrusions and possibly even _____.
30. A country with a higher death rate than birth rate is experiencing _____ population growth.
31. Parents _____ the pitch of their voices when talking to their babies.

22. Apgar; heart rate; respiration; reflex [LO-8]. 23. Brazelton Neonatal Behavioral Assessment; habituation; orientation; cuddliness [LO-8]. 24. crying; cri du chat [LO-8]. 25. phenylketonuria [LO-8]. 26. vernix caseosa; lanugo; fontanels (or: soft spots) [LO-9]. 27. reflexes; Babinski; Moro [LO-10]. 28. sweet; mouth; human voices (or: a mother's voice, high pitches); human faces [LO-11]. 29. tongue; facial expressions [LO-12]. 30. negative [LO-13]. 31. raise [LO-14].

neonatal period, mother and infant communication patterns involve both synchronization and reciprocity. These behaviors can be interpreted as precursors of later verbal communication (Rosenthal, 1982).

The most frequent maternal behavior during breast-feeding is probably gazing at the infant, which, observers note, occurs an average of 86 percent of the feeding time. Talking to the baby occurs from none of the time to non-stop during the feeding time period (Rosenthal, 1982).

Comforting Babies

Responsive mothers soon learn conditions that prevent crying and that are helpful in terminating crying that does begin. For the most part, parents should attend quickly to their baby's crying. Ignoring babies actually increases the amount of crying in the first year, while quickly responding to cries decreases it (Bell & Ainsworth, 1972). Techniques that comfort and soothe infants include rocking, pacifiers, humming sounds, and warm baths (Byrne & Horowitz, 1981). One of the most comforting techniques is to pick the infant up and place it to the shoulder, supporting its head just above the shoulder. This position provides both personal contact and increased visual alertness (Thoman, Korner, & Beason-Williams, 1977).

Babies fall asleep more quickly when they have additional tryptophan (an amino acid), and tryptophan can be increased by adding sugar to an infant's diet. Nursing mothers who eat candy before the baby's evening feeding have babies who fall asleep faster (Yogman & Zeisel, 1983).

Exploring Human Development

1. Compare the information you found out about the circumstances of your birth with that gathered by other members of the class. Are there trends based on decade of birth?
2. Test the reflexes of a neonate and an older infant. Use Table 3.5 for descriptions of the appropriate reflexes and how to trigger them. What differences do you find between younger and older infants?
3. Find out what birthing options are available in your community. For example, are there birthing centers, certified midwives, and prepared childbirth training courses?
4. Interview women about their childbirth experiences. Write up your observations from these interviews.

Childbirth and the Neonatal Period **79**

5. Read several parenting guides for their advice regarding the transition into parenting and caring for newborns. What advice is typical? Do most of the books present what seems like good advice to you?

Discussing Human Development

1. How should a woman choose her obstetrician and pediatrician? Why?
2. How would you treat a case of "maternity blues?" Why do you think depression is a fairly common response shortly after childbirth?
3. What medical procedures should be used to keep low-birthweight babies and other medically-at-risk infants alive? Are there times when some medical procedures should not be used? Why?
4. Based on what you have read about neonatal perceptual ability, what characteristics would you build into an infant's room? What "play" activities might you develop for infants?
5. What information from this chapter do you think would be most valuable to new parents? Why?

Reading More About Human Development

Ball, J. A. (1987). *Reacting to motherhood.* New York: Cambridge University Press.
Brinkley, G., Goldberg, L., & Kukar, J. (1982). *Your child's first journey.* Wayne, N.J.: Avery Publishing.
Goldberg, S., & Divitto, B. A. (1983). *Born too soon: Preterm birth and early development.* San Francisco: W. H. Freeman.
Sorel, N. (1984) *Ever since Eve: Personal reflections on childbirth.* New York: Oxford University Press.

Summary

I. The birth process
   A. Childbirth, or parturition, is divided into three basic stages.
      1. The first stage is the longest; effacement, dilation, and the breaking of the amniotic membrane occur during this stage.
      2. The second stage begins when the cervix is completely dilated and lasts until the baby is born.
      3. The third stage involves expulsion of the placenta, fetal membranes, and umbilical cord.
   B. Researchers are interested in learning about the biological changes during pregnancy and childbirth.
      1. Prostaglandins seem to initiate the uterine contractions.
      2. The design of the human female pelvis makes birthing complex and painful.
      3. The hour-long journey through the birth canal is accompanied by release of high levels of stress hormones to help babies survive and adapt to the outside environment.
   C. Despite women's common belief that childbirth was the best experience of their life, some women feel depressed after childbirth.
      1. Postnatal maternity blues is common (more than 50 percent), while mild to moderately severe postpartum depression and puerperal psychosis are less common (10 percent and 0.1 percent, respectively).
      2. Causes of postpartum depression are unclear but appear to be an interaction of biological, personality, and situational factors.

II. Methods of childbirth
   A. About 95 percent of current deliveries involve medications.
   B. Cesarean section is a surgical procedure to remove the baby from the uterus.
      1. C-sections are done more frequently now than in the past.
      2. The most common reasons for performing C-sections are: labor is failing to progress properly, the mother has had a previous C-section, and baby is in the breech or transverse position.
      3. Fetal monitors may be used during labor to help detect birth complications.
   C. Natural or prepared childbirth training (PCT) teaches mothers how to cope with the stress and pain of labor and delivery.
      1. One of the most popular training procedures is the Lamaze method, which may reduce labor pain by about 30 percent.
      2. The Leboyer technique, or gentle birth hypothesis, has failed to demonstrate either short-term or long-term benefits, and a criticism is that the procedure may increase errors in noticing medical complications.
      3. Research on bonding concludes that the quality of initial bonding has no long-term effects on either the offspring's characteristics or on parenting.
   D. Although most babies are born in hospitals, others are born at home or in birth centers.
      1. Historically, hospitals were an unsafe setting for birthing because one in four new mothers died of childbed fever.
      2. One to two percent of babies are born at home.
      3. Birth centers allow doctor-assisted childbirth with minimal medical intervention.
      4. Traditionally, lay midwives, or "granny midwives," have assisted in births; now, certified nurse-midwives are gaining in popularity.
      5. Societal childbirth practices vary and include traditions of couvade, doulas, and public births.

III. Low-birthweight babies
   A. Low-birthweight newborns weigh less than 5 1/2 lb and often are at high medical risk.
      1. Most low-birthweight babies are premature.
      2. Some are small-for-gestational-age; these full-term babies have a more mature central nervous system.
      3. Less frequent is the large-for-gestational-age baby, who is prone to respiratory problems and metabolic imbalances.

B. Maternal factors associated with low-birthweight babies include hypertension, rubella in early pregnancy, urogenital infections, diabetes, pregnancy as a teenager or over age 35, being underweight, substance use or abuse, and teratogens.

C. Great advances in the field of neonatology mean that more "preemies" now survive.
1. Medical advances include greater success in dealing with respiratory difficulties.
2. Parents also need prompting to care properly for such fragile-looking infants and can be instructed in activities that help their low-birthweight baby to develop.

IV. The neonatal period
A. The neonatal period is the first month of life and is marked by tremendous transitions.
B. Medical assessment of the newborn allows early detection of medical complications and rapid treatment.
1. The Apgar Scale measures heart rate, respiration, muscle tone, reflex irritability, and color at 1 min and 5 min after birth.
2. The Brazelton Neonatal Behavioral Assessment Scale evaluates newborns in 26 categories that measure various aspects of physiological, motor, state, and social interaction behavior.
3. Other neonatal assessments include analyzing crying patterns and brain-wave patterns.

C. Newborns have many striking physical characteristics, including the vernix caseosa, lanugo, oddly shaped heads, soft spots, and temporary skin colors due to circulation or pigment.
1. The general physical appearance of newborns reflects the cephalocaudal principle.
2. At birth, the average baby is 20 inches long and weighs over 7 lb; initially, some body weight is lost, but the neonate usually is back to its original birthweight by the end of the second week.

D. Reflexes, or automatic responses to external stimulation, are present in newborns, along with some voluntary movements.
E. At birth, all of the sensory systems are working to some degree, with new capabilities developing over the first months of life.
1. Neonates can distinguish between pleasant and unpleasant odors and can also identify their own mothers by smell.
2. Newborns have a preference for sweet tastes; they also show different facial responses to sour and bitter tastes.
3. Touch is the first sense to develop in the fetus, and for neonates, the most sensitive region is the mouth.
4. Neonates experience pain, including the pain of a circumcision done without anesthetic drugs.
5. Neonates can roughly locate the source of sounds, are affected by the loudness of sounds, and have a preference for high pitches.
6. Neonates prefer human voices to other sounds, and their mother's voice to the voices of others.

7. Neonates have limited visual acuity and accommodation; yet, they have an impressive ability to perceive depth and can tell when objects are getting closer.
8. Research results on the ability of neonates to imitate tongue protrusions and facial expressions have been mixed.

F. Parenting a newborn represents a major life transition that redefines one's identity.
1. Parenting has changed throughout history, as noted by the acceptance of infanticide in the Middle Ages and the more recent change in priorities from child quantity to child quality.
2. Reactions to a new family member are influenced by family resources and family size, as well as by whether one's culture is in a negative or positive population growth period.
3. Society now encourages more paternal involvement with infants.
4. Parents change their behaviors to match preferences of their babies; they speak differently to babies and learn what helps to soothe a crying infant.

Chapter Review Test

1. The thinning of the cervix during the first stage of birthing is called
   a. effacement.
   b. dilation.
   c. crowning.
   d. parturition.

2. Typically and preferably, the first part of the baby to be born is the
   a. buttocks.
   b. feet.
   c. head.
   d. arms.

3. The birth of the baby occurs during the _____ stage of birthing.
   a. first
   b. second
   c. third
   d. fourth

4. A controversial surgical incision of the vagina is called
   a. an episiotomy.
   b. a cesarean section.
   c. a V-cut.
   d. an effacement.

5. The involutional process is the
   a. medical term for the birth process.
   b. expulsion of the umbilical cord and placenta in the third stage of childbirth.
   c. uterine contractions during the first two stages of childbirth.
   d. return of the female reproductive organs to their original state following childbirth.

6. The hormones that play an important role in initiating uterine contractions are the
    a. estrogens.
    b. prostaglandins.
    c. luteinizing hormones.
    d. oxytocins.
7. Which of the following provides the greatest reduction in pain during labor and delivery?
    a. Lamaze method
    b. cesarean section
    c. obstetric medications
    d. hypnosis
8. Which of the following is the most common experience of depression following childbirth?
    a. no depression
    b. postnatal maternity blues
    c. puerperal psychosis
    d. postpartum depression
9. Childbed fever in hospital births declined once Semmelweiss made _____ a common practice.
    a. birth control and family planning
    b. prenatal care
    c. cesarean sections
    d. hand washing by hospital staff
10. Which of the following is a reason for the current high rates of cesarean sections being performed?
    a. baby is in a breech or transverse presentation.
    b. the mother had a previous cesarean delivery.
    c. labor is not progressing properly.
    d. all of the above are correct.
11. The Lamaze method is to _____ as the Leboyer method is to _____.
    a. mother; baby
    b. breathing; thinking
    c. mother; father
    d. short-term benefits; long-term benefits
12. Which of the following is not someone who might assist at a birth?
    a. doulas
    b. "granny midwives"
    c. couvades
    d. certified nurse-midwives
13. Low-birthweight neonates are always
    a. preterm babies.
    b. under 5 1/2 lb.
    c. at medical risk.
    d. all of the above

14. Which of the following ethnic groups has the lowest incidence of low-birthweight babies?
    a. African American
    b. Native American
    c. European American
    d. Hispanic American
15. Which of the following is *not* measured by the Apgar Scale?
    a. heart rate
    b. reflex irritability
    c. muscle tone
    d. habituation
16. Which of the following is an *incorrect* pairing of neonatal physical appearance?
    a. blue patches/poor circulation
    b. lanugo/body hair
    c. meconium/body secretion
    d. fontanel/skull
17. An infant exhibits the _____ reflex when its facial cheek is stroked; the reflex consists of the baby turning its head, opening its mouth, and beginning to suck.
    a. rooting
    b. placing
    c. babinski
    d. moro
18. Which of the following could 10-day-old Yvette probably accomplish?
    a. recognize her mother's smell
    b. turn away from an unpleasant smell, such as ammonia
    c. distinguish among garlic, vinegar, alcohol, and anise
    d. all of the above
19. Which of the following is an *incorrect* visual preference of newborns?
    a. three-dimensional objects over two-dimensional objects
    b. straight lines over curved lines
    c. novel objects over familiar objects
    d. faces over checkered patterns
20. Which of the following questions about a newborn are people most likely to ask *first?*
    a. "Is the baby healthy?"
    b. "How long was the labor?"
    c. "Is it a boy or a girl?"
    d. "What name have you decided on?"

Answers

1. A [LO-1].	8. B [LO-2].	15. D [LO-8].
2. C [LO-1].	9. D [LO-3].	16. A [LO-9].
3. B [LO-1].	10. D [LO-4].	17. A [LO-10].
4. A [LO-1].	11. A [LO-5].	18. D [LO-11].
5. D [LO-1].	12. C [LO-6].	19. B [LO-11].
6. B [LO-2].	13. B [LO-7].	20. C [LO-13].
7. C [LO-2,3,4,5].	14. C [LO-7].	

chapter 4

Infancy: Physical and Cognitive Development

Key Terms

Maturation
Brain lateralization
Motor skills
Depth perception
Perceptual constancy
Exploratory systems
Classical conditioning
Operant conditioning
Modeling (imitation)
Adaptation
Schema
Assimilation
Accommodation
Equilibration
Sensorimotor stage
Object permanence
Egocentrism
Enactive mode
Iconic mode
Symbolic mode
Infantile amnesia
Receptive language
Expressive language
Innate theory of language development
Learning theory of language development
Babbling
Baby-talk register

Learning Objectives

1. Describe the general aspects of physical growth in infancy, including the role of maturation.
2. Discuss the cephalocaudal and proximodistal principles of physical growth.
3. Explain how nutritional needs change during infancy and how generational factors have influenced how infants are fed.
4. Describe the typical order and timing of motor development, and compare infants' abilities in gross versus fine motor movements.
5. Summarize gender and ethnic similarities and differences in motor development.
6. Discuss current ideas about toilet training, and be familiar with the procedure developed by Azrin and Foxx.
7. List the main aspects of visual and auditory sensory development during infancy.
8. Define proprioception, and describe its development during infancy.
9. Describe and differentiate the three phases of Gibson's exploratory system.
10. Explain the role of classical conditioning, operant conditioning, and modeling during infancy.
11. Describe infants' main achievements during Piaget's sensorimotor stage, including the changes over the six substages and the development of object permanence.
12. Discuss Bower's explanation of object permanence, and be able to compare self-related code and landmark code.
13. Define each of Jerome Bruner's modes (enactive, iconic, and symbolic), and explain when each mode is important in development.
14. Define infantile amnesia, and provide alternative explanations for its occurrence.
15. Compare and contrast receptive language and expressive language.
16. Distinguish the main features of Chomsky's and Skinner's theories of language development.
17. List the major milestones of language development.
18. Describe baby-talk register.
19. Discuss parental influences on the development of competence.

In Chapter 3, we discussed the beginning of the infancy period—the neonatal period. In this chapter and in Chapter 5, you will learn about the rest of infancy, the first 2 years of life. Infancy can be subdivided into the first year and toddlerhood, the second year.

This chapter focuses on physical development (physical growth and motor, sensory, and exploratory development) and on cognitive development (Piaget's sensorimotor stage, learning, memory and language development). Chapter 5 discusses emotional, personality, and social development during infancy. During these 2 years, infants grow and change tremendously in each of these areas.

Exploring Your Own Development

Although you do not have vivid memories of your personal experience of infancy, you may be able to relate the material in this chapter better to your first 2 years of life by reviewing your baby pictures or by watching any home movies or videos that were taken of you. If you can, ask parents, older siblings or cousins, other relatives, family friends, or neighbors about their memories of your infancy. What stories do family members like to tell about when you were a baby? Use this material to help you learn and understand the concepts in this chapter and Chapter 5. You may also want to use the information you gather about your infancy to begin a psychobiography, as outlined in Appendix B.

Another way to make this material more relevant is to observe current infants more closely. What can a 6-month-old infant do? How does a 1-year-old view the world? How do the cognitive abilities of a 1-year-old differ from those of a 2-year-old? How does the infant learn to understand language and use speech? Watch babies and their parents when you are at the supermarket, at the mall, or at other social activities. Visit a day-care center that serves infants as well as preschoolers. Talk with the staff about their observations of the many changes during the first 2 years of life.

Physical Development

Physical Growth

Maturation

Physical growth includes changes in height, weight, and internal characteristics. Much of physical growth involves **maturation,** or age-related physical changes that involve genetically programmed patterns of physical development. These biological aspects determine the maximal potential of growth, while environmental factors, such as nutrition, may temporarily detour this biological programming. Except under extreme circumstances, when environmental obstacles are removed, growth returns to the programmed maturational path. For example, your physical height today is a function of genetically programmed maturation. However, how quickly you grew and when you grew were not

Exploring family photo albums is an excellent way to learn more about oneself.

just a matter of heredity; what you ate and childhood illnesses (environmental factors) interacted with your genetic program to determine how tall you would actually become.

Body Proportions

Physical growth modifies body proportions. Body proportions strongly reflect the principle of cephalocaudal development (i.e., physical development is from head to toe). Even before birth, the embryo's head develops earlier than the rest of the body, and at 2 months into its prenatal development, an embryo's head is one half its body length. At birth, the neonate's head is about one fourth of entire body length. By the end of infancy, the child's head is only one fifth of entire body length. As the legs become comparatively longer, the proportion of the head to body continues to drop, to one sixth at age 6, one seventh at age 12, and about one eighth or less by young adulthood. Another way to conceptualize this change in body proportion is in terms of one's belly button. At birth, approximately 45 percent of one's body length is below the belly button. By the end of infancy, this percentage is 50, and by adulthood, it is 60.

Similarly, the infant versus adult body proportions reflect the proximodistal principle (i.e., development begins at the center of the body and moves to the extremities). The

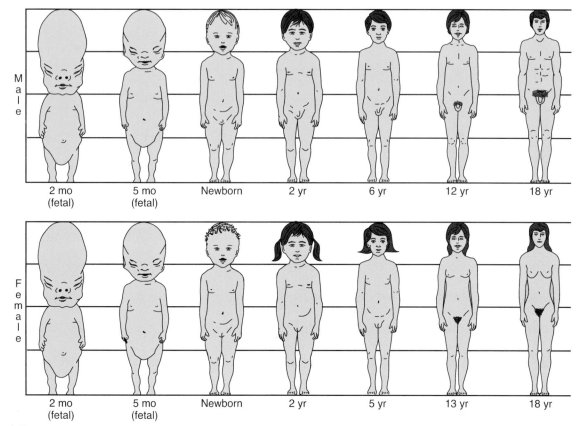

Figure 4.1
Changes in body form during prenatal and postnatal growth reflect cephalocaudal and proximodistal development.

embryo's head and trunk develop before the arms and legs. The arms and legs develop before the hands and feet. A neonate's arms and legs are small in proportion to trunk length, and in comparison to arm length, the baby's hands and fingers are small. A baby's legs are only one fourth of total body length, while an adult's legs are about one half of total body length. Consistent with the cephalocaudal and proximodistal principles, from birth to adulthood, the size of the head only doubles, while the feet grow to about 5 times their initial size (see Figure 4.1).

Compared to adults, infants have a larger surface area per unit weight. As a result, infants have more potential for heat loss and for dehydration than do adults. Babies need more warm clothing and more frequent drinks than adults do. In addition, the larger proportion of surface area means that infants need proportionately more calories to maintain their basal metabolism (Eichorn, 1979).

Other physical differences between babies and adults are the body weight percentages of water, fat, and protein. As shown in Table 4.1, babies have a higher proportion of water than adults. During the first year of life, body water composition drops from 75 to 65 percent (Ashburn, 1986). From infancy to adulthood, females change most dramatically in percentage of body fat, while males change most in percentage of body protein (Eichorn, 1979).

Table 4.1
Make-Up of Body Weight for Infants and Adults

Percentage of Body Weight			
	At Birth	*Adult Female*	*Adult Male*
Water	75%	52%	62%
Fat	11	31	14
Protein	11	16	33

Source: Data from D. H. Eichorn, "Physical Development: Current Foci of Research" in *Handbook of Infant Development,* 1979, edited by J. D. Osofsky. John Wiley & Sons, New York, NY.

Height and Weight

Carrie, an average infant, doubled her birthweight in the first 4 months of her life and tripled her birthweight by her first birthday. During the first 6 months of life, Carrie made almost a 150 percent increment in height (Osofsky, 1987). On her second birthday, she matched the average 2-year-old American's weight of 30 lb and height of 34 1/2 inches. Typically, 2-year-olds are nearly one fifth of their adult weight and about one half of their adult height.

Overall, smaller-than-average babies do a lot of catch-up growth during the first months of life. Despite their proportionately greater weight gain during the first 2 years of life, however, babies with lower birthweights are likely to remain shorter and weigh less than average or above-average birthweight babies.

While lower birthweight babies tend to remain smaller, high birthweight babies have an increased risk of experiencing childhood obesity (Binkin, Yip, Fleshood, & Trowbridge, 1988).

During infancy, babies also experience much growth in height. On average, infants grow more than 5 inches in their first 6 months of life and then add another 3 inches in the next 3 months. During their second year, most infants grow another 4 inches in height. As with weight, smaller-than-average babies do some catch-up in height during the first few months.

Biochemical and Anatomical Differences

In addition to the obvious developmental variations in height and weight among individuals are great internal biochemical and anatomical differences (Williams, 1956). Some of the biochemical differences may contribute to individual differences in mood states and the experience of depression and mental disorders, such as schizophrenia. Charting individual external differences in height and weight is easy, compared to noting individual biochemical and anatomical differences.

Anatomically, there are many possible shapes for organs such as the stomach, and locations of arteries and veins within the body vary from person to person. These internal physical aspects of human beings also grow and change through the years. Researchers have studied both about how these factors vary among individuals and how they change across an individual's lifespan. An area of internal physical development that is of special interest is the brain, where many changes in activity and specialization occur during infancy.

Brain Maturation

At birth, the brain is already 25 percent of its adult weight, and by the end of infancy, that percentage has grown to about 75. By comparison, a 2-year-old's body weight is only 20 percent of normal adulthood weight. Researchers believe that the newborn's brain contains its full number of neurons and that brain growth consists mainly of making more connecting networks among the neurons and of *myelination* of neurons. Myelination occurs when neurons become coated with a fatty insulating substance called myelin. Myelinated neurons can transmit impulses faster than nonmyelinated neurons. Myelination occurs more rapidly for the neurons processing sensory information than for neurons involved with producing body movement. Thus, infants' sensory capabilities are ahead of their abilities to control body movement.

Brain Activity

Researchers have been able to use *PET scans* (*positron emission tomography,* a technologically advanced process for studying the body internally) of infants of various ages,

Bright as this infant appears, she has much lower cerebral cortex activity than adults.

to learn about brain activity. Among 5-day-old neonates, the most active areas of the brain are the primary motor (control of body movement) and sensory areas, the basal ganglia (a center for integrating information from various areas of the brain), the brain stem (control of automatic activities, such as blood circulation and breathing), and the cerebellum (coordination of movement). PET scans reveal little other activity in the cerebral cortex of 5-day-old infants (Chugani & Phelps, 1986).

By 11 weeks, PET scans reveal that activity is spreading into other areas, with additional activity in the primary motor and sensory areas. By 4 months, brain activity in the cerebral cortex is common, allowing infants to develop more voluntary movement. PET scans of 7-month-olds reveal that brain activity is now common in cortical areas that allow infants to coordinate their senses and movements. From this age on, infants have the intellectual capacity to begin to think in terms of purposeful behavior. Less than a month later, the activity in infants' brains appears similar to that in adults' brains (Chugani & Phelps, 1986).

Brain Lateralization

Brain lateralization refers to the separation and integration of functional systems within the cerebral hemispheres of the brain. The left cerebral hemisphere receives sensory information from the right side of the body and also controls voluntary body movements in the right half of the body. Likewise, the right cerebral hemisphere receives sensory information from and controls movement on the left side of the body.

By age 5, children have developed a dominant cerebral hemisphere—usually the left hemisphere—which is specialized for speech and other language functions. For right-handers, the left hemisphere is the dominant speech/language hemisphere 95 percent of the time. This coordination between handedness and language functions in the left hemisphere is not a simple relationship. If it was, you could predict that most left-handed individuals would have speech and language functions localized in the right hemisphere. However, for left-handers, the left hemisphere is the dominant speech/language hemisphere 70 percent of the time. Brain lateralization also occurs in the right hemisphere. For most individuals, emotional information is processed more accurately by the nondominant right hemisphere (Lenneberg, 1967; Saxby & Bryden, 1985).

Sucking is one of the most pleasurable activities of infancy.

---

successful study tip

Remembering the Lateralization of the Left and Right Hemispheres

It's been said that "Left-handed people are the only persons in their right mind!" However, as you have just read, a majority of left-handers also use their left hemispheres to organize speech and other language functions. To remember that "*L*"anguage functions are "*L*"ocalized in the "*L*"eft hemisphere for most people, associate the "*L*" in language with the "*L*" in left. To remember that the processing of emotional information is localized in the right hemisphere for most people, recall this sentence: I just *LOVE* my right hemisphere and would *HATE* to be without it.

Infants' Nutritional Needs

Breast Milk, Formulas, and Solid Food
For the first 6 months, infants' nutritional needs can be met either with breast milk or with formulas based on soy protein with added vitamins, carbohydrates, and vegetable oils. Cow's milk is not an adequate nutritional source for infants (Ashburn, 1986). Both breast milk and formulas have about 20 cal/oz.

Around 6 months of age, babies have additional needs for iron and vitamins A, B, C, and D, and vitamin preparations are often added to the diet. Infants who develop iron-deficiency anemia may experience a variety of problems, including delayed growth, faulty immune systems, and diminished learning capacity (Fomon, Filer, Anderson, & Ziegler, 1979).

In different eras, solid foods have been introduced to babies at varying times of infancy. In the 18th century, even neonates might be fed a mixture of butter, sugar, oil, and spiced bread and a warm drink of gruel and wine, but today, parents wait several months before adding any solid foods to the diet. Although babies a few weeks old can tolerate cereals, the introduction of solid foods should be delayed for three reasons: (1) breast milk or formula is a more efficient food source, (2) babies given solid foods early tend to be overfed, and (3) early introduction increases the risk of food allergies, especially for wheat, citrus juices, and egg whites (Ashburn, 1986).

Feeding Schedules and Amounts of Food
The behaviorists of the 1920s encouraged parents to stick to a strict regime in the care of their infants, establishing firm times for sleeping, holding, and feeding. Today, infants are more likely to be fed on a *flexible, demand-feeding schedule*

rather than a *rigid feeding schedule*. The more flexible eating schedule helps in avoiding both the underfeeding and the overfeeding of infants, and is associated with shorter periods of infant crying (Barr & Elias, 1988). Young infants may "demand" as many as eight feedings a day, but by 4 to 5 months of age, four daily feedings are more typical.

With a flexible schedule, parents should not force additional food on infants who indicate that they are satisfied; young infants show satiation by slowing their sucking activity, turning their heads to the side, letting milk run from the mouth, or falling asleep. Older infants may indicate that they are full by pushing their spoons away or drawing their heads back (Ashburn, 1986).

In the 1970s, many scientists and medical doctors emphasized that overfeeding infants was a primary cause of childhood and adult obesity (Knittle, 1972), but this belief has been questioned by more recent research findings. In a review of several studies, no connection was found between infant obesity and adolescent obesity (Roche, 1981). However, feeding and activity styles developed in toddlerhood and early childhood do influence later weight. Basically, parents increase their children's odds of dealing with obesity if they (1) "push" additional food on their children, (2) overrestrict their children's food so that the children do not learn internal control over intake, (3) allow children to eat and chew too quickly, and (4) permit an inactive lifestyle of television watching (Drabman, Cordus,

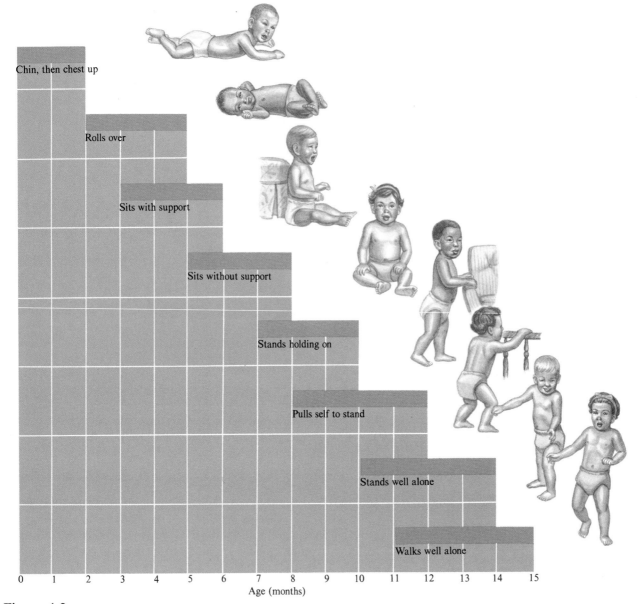

Chin, then chest up

Rolls over

Sits with support

Sits without support

Stands holding on

Pulls self to stand

Stands well alone

Walks well alone

0 1 2 3 4 5 6 7 8 9 10 11 12 13 14 15
Age (months)

Figure 4.2
Sequence of motor development and average age of achievement.

Hammer, Jarvie, & Horton, 1979; Kolata, 1986; Rodin & Hall, 1987). Genetic factors also play a large role in whether individuals become overweight.

Motor Development

During the 2 years of infancy, babies move from reflexes (involuntary reactive movements) to voluntary active behaviors, gradually mastering a wide range of **motor skills** (controlled and coordinated movements of various parts of their bodies).

The General Order of Development

Figure 4.2 illustrates the typical order and average ages at which motor skills develop. As you can see, motor abilities tend to follow both the cephalocaudal and proximodistal developmental principles described earlier. Therefore, an early motor ability of infants is holding their heads erect for

several seconds. A little later, infants gain control over their shoulders and then their arms. When motor development accelerates in the leg region, babies gain better control over their knees before they develop good control over their toes.

Proximodistal motor development is demonstrated in how infants and toddlers develop their skills in playing with balls. Infants who can sit on the floor with their legs apart can be rolled a large ball. If the ball is rolled directly between their legs, the infants learn to push the ball back. However, young infants completely miss balls rolled somewhat off-center. Likewise, toddlers tend to use the center of their bodies more than their arms when they first throw a ball. Rather than moving their arm like a baseball pitcher, they propel the ball by turning their body at the waist and heaving the ball like a shot-putter.

Table 4.2
Motor Development Tasks Accomplished by a 1 1/2-Year-Old

Fills a cup with cubes

Hurls a ball

Sits down in a small chair

Turns pages of a book, two or three pages at a time

Builds a tower of three blocks

Identifies a picture

Pulls a toy on a string

Source: Data from H. Knobloch and B. Pasamanick, *Gesell and Amatruda's Developmental Diagnosis*, 3rd edition, pp. 82–83, 1974.

The physically accelerated growth of the upper part and center of the body influences the order of motor development. Internally, myelination of nerves also follows a cephalocaudal direction—from head, to shoulders, to arms, to upper chest, to abdomen, to legs, to feet. These internal changes also illustrate that biological development precedes behavioral development. Therefore, motor development occurs in an order that reflects physiological development.

Gross and Fine Motor Development

Infants perform *gross* (large body segment) *movements* before they can do *fine motor* actions well. For example, it is easier for young infants to move large toy vehicles along the floor than to pick up small objects. At 6 months, infants can use a whole-hand grasp to voluntarily pick up objects. The skill of voluntarily letting go of objects develops about a month later. At 9 months, infants acquire the *pincer grasp* and are able to use their thumbs in opposition to their fingers, but they still must use their fingers in unison. Nevertheless, the pincer grasp allows infants to pick up Cheerios, pull lint off sweaters, and capture crawling bugs. At 18 months, infants have enough fine motor control that they can turn book pages, but they usually turn them a couple of pages at a time. Table 4.2 provides some examples of the motor abilities of an 18-month-old. As the infant's motor abilities grow, the infant has increased ways to explore the environment.

Infants vary in the rates at which motor skills develop, but the range of normal development is quite small. Infants who reach the milestones of motor development much later than others should be checked for potential physical problems but may only be developing at a much slower than normal rate. The age at which a baby starts to crawl or walk appears to be unrelated to later intelligence.

The order of motor ability development is basically universal. Some babies may pick an unorthodox way of crawling, such as "buttocks walking," for awhile, but nearly all babies crawl before they walk. As long as there is a minimal level of environmental stimulation, the rate and order of motor development cannot be altered much. In exploring your development in infancy, did you discover whether you tried creeping (scooting along on your stomach by moving your arms and legs) before crawling (pushing yourself up on your arms and knees and then moving)?

Exceptions to the standard order of development can sometimes be traced to cultural variations in child-rearing practices, as discussed in the "Exploring Cultural Diversity" feature. Are any of these practices similar to ones found in your own family and cultural background?

Gender Differences in Motor Development

Boy and girl babies are very similar, except for some small differences in physical and motor abilities. Mark each of the following statements for whether you think the statement is more typical of B (boys) or G (girls). Then check whether your impressions match research findings (Feldman, Brody, & Miller, 1980; Kalat, 1981; Korner, 1973; Tanner, 1970).

B G   1. Sits at an earlier age

B G   2. Better large-muscle movements, such as kicking

B G   3. Performs more rhythmic behaviors, such as sucking and smiling

B G   4. Tends to be toilet trained sooner

B G   5. Can lift head higher at birth

B G   6. Walks at an earlier age

B G   7. At birth, is 4 weeks more advanced in skeletal development

B G   8. Talks at an earlier age

B G   9. Weighs more and is taller at birth

Did you think these statements are more typical of boys or of girls? Since many people tend to view boy babies as stronger and bigger than girl babies, you may have marked more *B*s than *G*s, but six of these statements are true of girls. Only 2, 5, and 9 are true of boy babies.

Interestingly, despite the small advantages female babies have in physical development, most parents perceive their infant daughters as weaker than their infant sons. Parents tend to describe baby boys as "sturdy," "alert," and "athletic" and baby girls as "weak" and "delicate" (Rubin, Provenzano, & Luria, 1974). Even when infants are the same physical size, male babies are described in stronger, healthier words. Why do you think these expectations exist?

Although parents treat their male and female infant children fairly similarly, the gender differences that do occur may accentuate gender differences in later motor development. Male toddlers are allowed more assertive behaviors, while female toddlers are more reinforced for verbal behaviors (Fagot, Hagan, Leinbach, & Kronsberg, 1985). Male toddlers receive more rewards for physical play that involves gross motor skills than do female toddlers (Smith & Lloyd, 1978). When you watch infants at play, what would you see differently if you did not know their gender?

Accelerating Walking

Proud parents not only want their children to be normal, they often want their children to excel, to be ahead of normal. Therefore, they may try to accelerate their children's

The nearly universal sequence of motor developments can be explained by the strong influence of genetic programming on maturation. However, the differences that do exist can be traced to the influence of environmental or cultural practices on child-rearing. For example, Margaret Mead found that New Guinea's Arapesh babies often stood before they were able to sit alone. Mead observed that the Arapesh usually held their babies in a standing position instead of sitting them on their laps; therefore, standing was practiced, while sitting was not (Mead, 1935).

Another example of cultural influence on motor development is the finding that Southeast Asian children often score very low on three specific tasks of the Denver Developmental Screening Test, a test designed to identify children not developing normally (Miller, Onotera, & Deinard, 1984). These tasks are performing pat-a-cake, picking up raisins, and dressing oneself. The Southeast Asian children's abnormal performance in these areas is easily understood in terms of their culture. Their performance in pat-a-cake is poor because pat-a-cake is not a game in their Asian culture. The infants avoid picking up raisins because the raisins look similar to a bitter-tasting medicine common to their culture, and the infants are motivated to avoid any similarly looking object. Finally, Asian infants are less likely to be able to dress themselves because their culture does not encourage early self-dressing.

A traditional practice among many Hopi and Navaho Indians is to wrap babies in cloth and strap them to a cradleboard until they are about 6 months old.

Usually, diverse cultural practices have no impact on motor development. For example, a study of Hopi infants compared the development of walking in babies who were swaddled and placed on cradleboards with other babies who were allowed to freely move their arms and legs during their first months of life. In spite of quite differing amounts of physical freedom, the two child-rearing practices did not result in a different timeline for beginning to walk (Dennis & Dennis, 1940).

In addition to differences in cultural practices, the genetically determined rate of motor development may vary with ethnic background. As a group, African-American babies have an earlier rate of development of gross motor skills than do European-American babies, who typically develop gross motor skills before Asian-American babies (Kaplan & Dove, 1987).

One interesting study investigated influences on motor development by comparing Ugandan, European, and Indian infants born in Africa. The Ugandan babies had the best muscle tone and were ahead of the other infants in raising their heads, sitting without support, standing, and walking. By 20 months, however, the other babies caught up to the Ugandan babies (Geber, 1962; Geber & Dean, 1957). How would you explain these results? One explanation is that genetic differences produce these results. A second explanation is that child-rearing practices aid the Ugandan babies in developing their motor abilities. Ugandan parents often use a dashiki, a carrier that holds young infants upright while providing support for their heads. This practice may strengthen muscles and accelerate early motor development.

Even when ethnic-genetic background and culture-specific child-rearing practices result in motor development differences, remember that the similarities in motor development between diverse groups of children are far greater than the differences.

development. Most research in the area of accelerating motor development suggests that parents could better spend their time enriching their children's lives in other ways.

As a case in point, the study comparing swaddled and freely moving Hopi infants (Dennis & Dennis, 1940) suggested that the primary influence on motor development is physical maturation, rather than the amount of practice in moving one's legs. However, daily practice can modify motor development slightly. Researchers compared the rate of motor development for neonates who were given daily practice based on the stepping reflex with other neonates who were given passive exercise and a control group of neonates. As mentioned in Chapter 3, the stepping reflex is the automatic walking motion made by newborns when their feet touch a flat surface.

The researchers found that the strength of the stepping reflex is a function of age and exercise (Zelazo, Zelazo, & Kolb, 1972). In this study, without exercise, the stepping reflex disappeared by 8 weeks, as expected. The passive exer-

cise group, who had their arms and legs pumped 12 min a day, retained a stepping reflex rate of 3 steps per minute. The group of babies who practiced 12 min of stepping exercise daily for 7 weeks, however, exhibited a strong stepping reflex. At 8 weeks, this group averaged 30 steps per minute. The stepping reflex practice group eventually walked a little earlier than the other two groups, but the difference was small and seemingly was not worth the extra effort.

Some parents buy infant walkers for their prewalking infants. Although parents often believe that these walkers will help prepare babies for walking, the walkers do not seem to accelerate the age at which independent walking occurs. In one study in which the subjects were 4-month-old twins, one of each pair of twins was placed in a walker for an hour each day, and the other twin did not receive any walker experience. Despite this daily difference, the twin pairs began to walk at the same age (Ridenour, 1982). In addition to not accelerating walking, infant walkers can

Exploring the Parent/Child Relationship: Toilet Training in One Day

Fifty years ago, many parents tried to toilet train their infants by their first birthday. In contrast, some modern parents wait until their babies are 3 years old (Eden, 1988). What is the best timing? From 12 to 18 months of age, most babies become aware of their bowel movements, yet they are not ready for training procedures. Between 18 and 21 months of age, most infants have regular bowel movements, stay dry for 2 to 3 hr at a time, and understand the meaning of praise. Therefore, parents might want to wait until their infants are at least 20 months old (Azrin & Foxx, 1981; Eden, 1988).

Azrin and Foxx (1981) are the authors of the optimistically titled book *Toilet Training in Less Than a Day,* and although training often runs over the 1-day limit, the book provides the following helpful suggestions for combining physical readiness and behavior modification techniques:

1. Before training, encourage the toddler to try self-dressing and to watch others at the toilet; help them to understand toilet words.
2. Buy training pants, a potty-chair, and a doll that wets.
3. Observe your child for bladder control (stays dry for 3 hr), understanding of directions, and ability to assist in undressing. Also observe "warning signals" that precede bowel movements and urination, such as reddening of face, straining noises, squatting, crossed legs, or a sudden stop in playing.
4. During toilet training, use lots of rewards, including snacks, drinks, praise, hugs, and smiling.
5. Dress your child in training pants, and help your child to learn to put them on and take them off.
6. Put training pants on the doll, and illustrate the doll using the potty-chair correctly. Let your child also teach the doll.
7. Use shaping procedures. For example, have your child tell you when he or she is dry, and provide a reinforcer for reporting this. Let the child try the potty-chair, sitting on it with pants down for several minutes, and reinforce this behavior.
8. Praise the beginning of urination or defecation.
9. Have the child remove his or her own wet pants when "accidents" occur and put them in the laundry hamper. Make certain that disapproval is mild, and rely mostly on reward of desired responses. Most children have many accidents until age 3, and night bladder control comes last.

Parents can be creative in finding ways that children enjoy toilet training and learn procedures quickly. One mother put a small amount of bubble-bath liquid in her son's potty-chair, and he enjoyed making bubbles when he urinated. The only drawback to her technique was when her son walked into the bathroom while she was taking a bubble bath.

Using behavior modification techniques to toilet train toddlers seems preferable to the overly rigid methods used in previous generations or to overpermissive techniques of waiting until the child is 3 years old. If you are faced with the task of toilet training a child, you may wish to ask other parents what worked when their children were learning to control bodily functions and use the toilet.

By waiting until the infant is about two years old, toilet training can be a fairly simple and pleasant learning experience.

cause serious injuries to infants, both due to the walker's design and to unsupervised use in home environments with such hazards as stairs.

Toilet Training

Sometime during infancy or early preschool, parents want to modify aspects of motor ability involving defecation and urination. One important task for toddlers is to learn control over toilet behaviors. Although some parents strive for toilet training when their child is about a year old, most experts believe that toddlers have better physical maturation of the sphincter muscle after 20 months. In fact, early-trained infants may merely indicate that the parents watch for signals of coming bowel movements, such as strained facial expression, a pause in playing, crossed legs, and squatting, and then rush the child to the potty-chair. In other words, the young babies are not toilet-trained—their parents are.

An early study of urinary control training used two twin pairs (McGraw, 1940). One infant from each pair began training at 2 months, while the other waited. The twins who received later training were easier to train and had complete dryness about the same time as the early-trained infants. Early attempts at toilet training seem to be a hassle for parents and beyond the bodily control of infants.

For parents who wait until at least 20 months of age, toilet training can be relatively simple and not involve a lot of time. In fact, the "Exploring the Parent/Child Relationship" feature describes a procedure that promises "toilet training in one day." Actually, 1-day toilet training is feasible—*if* parents choose the right day.

Sensory Development

At the same time that physical and motor changes are occurring in infancy, sensory development is also making major advances. The interaction of developments in these areas is incorporated into and advances cognitive development. The infant uses information gained from each of five major sensory systems, as well as other sense data, to guide its exploration and understanding of the external world. How the infant makes sense of the wealth of sensory information available is not entirely clear.

Perceptual Theories

Two differing positions have been put forth to explain how infants (as well as the rest of us) perceive (i.e., make sense of sensory information) and act on perceptions. The earlier position was developed over 100 years ago in Europe by Helmholtz (1962). Helmholtz's position is labeled unconscious inference theory and is based on the idea that infants first must be able to retain memories of past experiences before they can begin to make sense of present sensory information. Theorists favoring this position maintain that perception is based, in part, on incoming sensory information and, in part, on unconscious inferences about that information from past experience. Previous experience with sensory information is necessary for you to understand what it is that you are experiencing now and to react appropriately to the experience. As you see the printing in this textbook, what you read is a function not only of what is printed on the page but also of inferences you are making about the words and phrases you are seeing, based on your past experiences stored in memory. When you encounter a word you do not know, you use these inferences to help you to perceive the meaning of the word.

J. J. Gibson's (1979) theory of direct perception (*ecological approach*) states that perceptions are formed directly from the information provided by the stimulus. According to this theory, you make sense of sensory information directly from the information you receive from your senses. While inferences from information stored in memory may alter the experience, they are not necessary for making sense of the situation (Aslin & Smith, 1988). Gibson maintained that the environment affords all the information you need through your senses to make sense of the world. When you look up and see an object in the room closer to you than another object, do you "know" that the one object is closer to you because of inferences you have made based on past experience or because there were cues in the information taken in by your eyes that allowed you to "know" that the object is closer?

The implications of these theoretical positions for development in infancy center on how much, if any, experi-

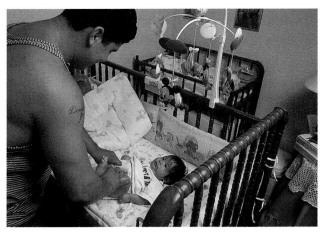

Sensory exploration is an important activity for infants, and colorful mobiles are an attractive nursery feature.

ence is necessary before, as an infant, you could make sense of your world. Commonsense observations tend to support the unconscious inference theory, but research evidence also supports the theory of direct perception. How would you interpret the results of a study in which 5-month-olds were able to make sense of and integrate auditory and visual information? Infants heard either a sound track of a car becoming louder or a car becoming quieter. They were simultaneously shown a film of an approaching car and a film of a car driving away. The infants tended to watch the film that appropriately fit the sounds they heard (Walker-Andrews & Lennon, 1985). Do 5-month-olds have enough visual and auditory experiences stored in memory to unconsciously infer which film went with the sound track? Or, were the infants able to directly make sense of the information from the films and the sound track? The researchers maintain that their findings support the theory of direct perception.

Physical Development of the Eye and Visual Cortex

As an adult, much sensory information comes to you from the visual system; yet, vision is one of the least developed senses at birth. Although the human *retina,* where the sense receptors for vision are located, is more mature at birth than many species, including the cat, rat, and dog, major retinal structures are not anatomically similar to an adult's until the 11th month (Banks & Salapatek, 1983).

Other physical aspects of the eyes also change during the first year. During the first 3 months, the optic nerve becomes fully myelinated; myelination of the brain's visual cortex occurs somewhat later (Banks & Salapatek, 1983). Babies begin to develop binocular vision (coordinated use of both eyes) in the fifth month as cells in the visual cortex mature and further differentiate (Pines, 1982).

Aspects of Visual Development

As physical development of the eye, optic nerve, and visual cortex improves, and as infants have more perceptual experience with the world, infants' visual capabilities expand.

Table 4.3
Chronology of Visual Development

Age	Level of Development
Birth	Awareness of light and dark. Infant closes eyelids in bright light.
Neonatal	Looks at near objects (3 to 30 inches away).
2 weeks	Looks with one eye at farther objects (3 ft away).
4 weeks	Follows large, conspicuously moving objects.
6 weeks	Briefly looks at moving objects with both eyes.
8 weeks	Follows moving objects with jerky eye movements.
12 weeks	Visual following is now a combination of head and eye movements.
	The use of both eyes together (convergence) improves. Enjoys light objects and bright colors.
16 weeks	Inspects own hands.
	Looks immediately at a 1-inch cube brought within 1 to 2 ft of eye.
	Visual acuity (focusing ability) improves from 20/3000 to 20/200.
20 weeks	Coordinates the focusing of both lenses (accommodation) during convergence.
	Visually pursues lost rattle.
	Shows interest in stimuli more than 3 ft away.
24 weeks	Retrieves a dropped 1-inch cube.
	Can maintain looking at a stationary object even in the presence of a competing moving stimulus.
	Hand-eye coordination begins.
26 weeks	Will look at a string.
28 weeks	Coordinated looking with both eyes (binocular fixation) is clearly established.
36 weeks	Depth perception begins.
40 weeks	Displays marked interest in tiny objects.
	Tilts head backward to gaze up.
	Visual acuity is 20/200.
1 year	Discriminates simple geometric forms (squares and circles).
	Visual acuity is 20/180.
1 to 1.5 years	Looks at pictures with interest.
1.5 years	Convergence is well established.
	Localization in distance crude—runs into large objects.
2 years	Accommodation is well developed.
	Visual acuity is 20/40 (reaches 20/20 by 4 years).

Form H. K. Silver, "Growth & Development" in *Current Pediatric Diagnosis & Treatment*, Table 2.8, p. 25, 1987. Edited by C. H. Kempe, et al. Copyright © 1987 Appleton & Lange, Norwalk, CT.

Table 4.3 summarizes the typical chronology of visual development. Note that visual abilities improve both in infancy and the preschool years. Given the information in the table, how might you decorate a nursery to match an infant's visual abilities? At what age might babies exhibit an increased interest in picture books? What kinds of toys and room decorations are unnecessary for infants and seem to be more designed for parents' interest than infant development?

Overall, research indicates that visual perception proceeds from parts to wholes—that is, young infants are especially sensitive to components of their visual field, while older infants are beginning to perceive relationships between parts of their visual field. One of the first areas in which infants begin to pay attention to wholes rather than just to segments is when motion is involved (Aslin & Smith, 1988). For example, 4-month-olds who are shown parts of objects that move together, even if different shapes, tend to treat these parts as a single object (Kellman, Spelke, & Short, 1986). Among older infants, the preference for "parts" switches to a preference for "wholes."

Color Vision and Color Preferences
Color vision develops during the first 3 months (Pines, 1982). Do young infants prefer certain colors? Newborns show little color preference; in fact, newborns look as long at a gray stimulus as they do at any particular color. By 3 months of age, green is of no greater interest than gray, but definite color preferences have appeared. Three-month-olds prefer the long wavelengths of red and yellow to short wavelengths of blue and green (R. J. Adams, 1987).

Interestingly, color preferences among adults tend to be the reverse of young infants. More adults prefer the short-wavelength colors, particularly blue, to the longer wavelengths (R. J. Adams, 1987). Over the years, has your color preference switched from red to blue? Do you think you could replicate the findings of this color preference study among college students?

Depth and Constancy Perception
Some researchers believe that infants younger than 3 months are limited to two-dimensional vision (Aslin & Smith, 1988). Young infants do not alter focus as object distance changes, so perhaps, distances greater than about 30 inches are blurred (Haynes, White, & Held, 1965). How do infants develop **depth perception,** and how can researchers study infants' responses to depth?

The visual cliff apparatus shown in Figure 4.3 has been used in a number of infant depth perception studies (Gibson & Walk, 1960). The visual cliff consists of a thick sheet of glass placed on a table. The "shallow" side of the visual cliff is created by putting a checkerboard pattern directly under the glass top, and a "deep" side is created by placing the checkerboard pattern several feet below the glass. Infants as young as 2 months exhibit a decreased heart rate if placed on the "deep" end but a steady heart rate if placed on the "shallow" end, suggesting some recognition of depth (Campos, Langer, & Krowitz, 1970).

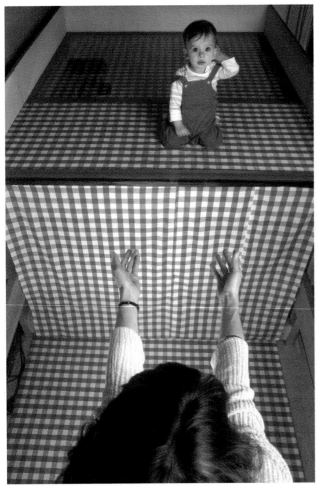

Figure 4.3

The visual cliff. An infant who has reached the crawling stage will crawl from the center of the table across the shallow end, but not across the deep end, to reach his or her mother. This indicates that, by 6 months of age, infants can perceive depth.

Infants also make a visual placing response of extension of arms plus fanning the fingers before making tactual contact with the glass surface when lowered on the "shallow" side but do not make this response when lowered on the "deep" side (Campos et al., 1978). Most crawling babies refuse to move from the "shallow" side to the "deep" side of the visual cliff. Interestingly, the pace of visual development, combined with early motor development, leads to early-crawling babies being more likely to cross to the "deep" side than late crawlers (Richards & Rader, 1981).

One reliable depth cue is created by *retinal disparity,* the fact that the two eyes send slightly different images to the brain. *Stereopsis,* the sense of depth based solely on retinal disparity, does not seem to emerge until the fourth month because maturation in the visual cortex must occur first (Aslin & Smith, 1988; Pines, 1982).

Other depth cues, called *pictorial cues to depth,* can be pointed out in two-dimensional pictures (see Figure 4.4). Young infants use pictorial cues, too. For example, when 4-month-old infants begin to reach for objects, they reliably reach for the nearer of two simultaneously presented objects (Granrud, Yonas, & Pettersen, 1984). From 5 to 7 months, infants can use shading, relative size, familiar size, interposition, and linear perspective cues (Aslin & Smith, 1988).

Perceptual constancy results when infants are able to perceptually adapt to the changing and many times distorted information from their sense receptors by perceiving some aspects of their perceptions as constant or unchanging. Perceptual constancies help in perceiving a stable world. One type of constancy is *size constancy,* the ability to know that an object remains the same size despite changes in the size of the retinal image. Newborns possess only a basic size constancy, which is reorganized in the first 4 months as stereopsis emerges (Aslin & Smith, 1988; Granrud, 1987). Until this more advanced perceptual size constancy is achieved, as a parent moves toward a 2-month-old, the increasing size of the image on the infant's retina may be seen as the parent's head expanding!

Perception of Faces

Babies prefer to view human faces over most other stimuli. For the youngest infants, the outer outline or contour of the facial image is more crucial than the realism of the features. At 1 month, infants tend to inspect one external area, such as the hairline, the chin, or an ear, for the longest time (Haaf, 1974; Maurer & Salapatek, 1976).

At 5 to 7 weeks, infants tend to focus more on the internal features, especially the eyes, than on the external features (Haith, Bergman, & Moore, 1977). Under 3 months, however, babies are as likely to smile at scrambled faces as they are to more realistic faces (Fantz, 1970). However, even 3-month-olds look longer at attractive faces than at unattractive faces, leaving researchers wondering how cultural beauty standard preferences could be known so young (Langlois et al., 1987). Finally, around the sixth or seventh month, infants can recognize individual faces (Caron, Caron, Caldwell, & Weiss, 1973). When babies can reliably differentiate Mom from the babysitter, they may start to fuss when someone other than Mom is their primary caretaker.

Another study examined infants' preferences for inanimate objects with scrambled facial features, store mannequins, and a live 20-year-old female (Langsdorf, Izard, Rayias, & Hembree, 1983). As shown in Figure 4.5, a preference for the real person was found at 2, 4, 6, and 8 months of age.

The preference for a real human being over a store mannequin may not surprise you. This preference may be genetically preprogrammed or learned through the reinforcers of food and touch. However, you may be surprised to learn that 5-month-old infants are most likely to base memory for face photos on age and sex characteristics, rather than on facial features. Until infants are 7 months old, feature differences are not enough to help them recognize a face if the two photos are of the same sex and age (Fagan & Singer, 1979). In fact, babies prefer to look at same-sex babies, and 13-month-olds gaze more at same-sex babies, even if the baby is wearing gender-inappropriate clothing—a task

(a) Linear perspective

(d) Relative size

(b) Interposition

(e) Shading

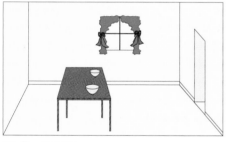

(c) Familiar size

Figure 4.4

Pictorial cues to depth. (a) Linear perspective (railroad tracks). (b) Interposition. (c) Familiar size. (d) Relative size. (e) Shading.

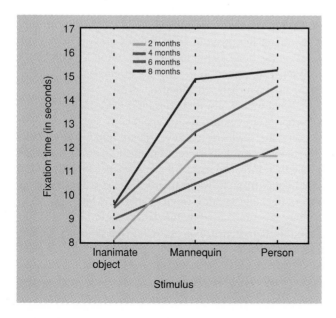

Figure 4.5

Interest by infants in various stimuli.

that adults cannot accomplish (Friedrich, 1983). Researchers have not discovered how infants are able to perceive gender differences.

Visual Problems

About 3 percent of preschoolers suffer from *amblyopia,* which is a functional loss of seeing ability due to disruption of the normal development of the visual pathway. In one type of amblyopia, *strabismic amblyopia,* the visual deficit is caused by the two eyes not being parallel. When this occurs, the child consistently uses one eye for looking, and if early preventive measures are not taken, the nonfixating eye eventually becomes nonfunctional. With early eye screening, doctors can prescribe a program that exercises the weaker eye by patching the "good eye" for several hours a day (Aoki & Siekevitz, 1988; Atkinson & Braddick, 1988).

A refractive screening program in Cambridge, Massachusetts, examined all 6-month-old infants in the community. About 5 percent of the infants exhibited marked farsightedness, about 1.6 percent had marked nearsightedness, and nearly 3 percent had amblyopia. Those with problems had regular checkups into the preschool years (Atkinson & Braddick, 1988). This screening process allowed doctors to follow the course of the visual problems and to treat them. Many of the early nearsighted and farsighted problems disappeared with further developmental changes.

Hearing Abilities

Six-month-old infants have amazing hearing abilities. They can distinguish consonant and vowel sounds, and even sounds that are not part of their native language (Friedrich, 1983; Kuhl & Miller, 1982). They can distinguish among tones of different frequency about as well as adults (Olsho, Schoon, Sakai, Turpin, & Sperduto, 1982). They are also adept at locating the source of auditory and visual information (Morrongiello & Rocca, 1987).

In one study, infants from 6 to 18 months of age were placed in a dark room with 10 loudspeakers arranged in a semicircle. When auditory clicking cues and visual light cues were both given, even the youngest infants were able to turn their heads within a few degrees of the sound source. By 18 months, infants were quite accurate in locating the sound source, even without accompanying visual cues (Morrongiello & Rocca, 1987).

Hearing Problems

Of course, not all children can hear well and accurately. A small percentage of infants have significant hearing loss, and about 1 in 500 children under the age of 16 has some permanent hearing loss. Profound hearing loss is usually detected by age 2, but partial hearing loss in one ear often goes unnoticed until the child is in school. Attentive parents and professionals can use the warning signs in Table 4.4 to help detect hearing problems sooner (Calkins, 1988).

The most striking difference between hearing babies and hearing-impaired babies is the timetable for babbling, one of the beginning stages of speech development. Most babies start to babble around the 6th or 7th month, but severely hearing-impaired babies may not begin until the 11th

Table 4.4 Warning Signs of Hearing Loss	
Age	**Symptoms**
Birth to 3 months	Baby is not startled by hand-clapping within 3 to 6 ft. Is not soothed by mother's voice.
3 to 6 months	Baby does not search for source of sound by turning eyes and head. Does not respond to mother's voice. Does not imitate own noises, such as "ooh," "ba-bas," etc. Does not seem to enjoy sound-making toys.
6 to 10 months	Baby does not respond to own name or to telephone ringing or to someone's voice when not loud. Is unable to understand words, such as "no" and "bye-bye."
10 to 15 months	Baby cannot point to or look at familiar objects or people when asked to do so. Cannot imitate simple words and sounds.
15 to 18 months	Baby is unable to follow simple spoken directions and is not progressing in word comprehension.
Any age	Baby does not awaken or is not disturbed by loud sounds. Does not respond when called. Pays no attention to ordinary crib noises. Uses gestures almost exclusively to establish needs rather than verbalizing, or watches parents' faces intently.

From Diane Calkins, "The Hidden Handicap." Reprinted with permission from *American Baby Magazine,* August 1988 issue. Copyright © 1988 Cahners Publishing USA.

to 25th month. Even then, hearing-impaired babies tend to babble less and use fewer syllables (Calkins, 1988).

Many factors can contribute to early hearing loss. Some families have a hereditary history of childhood deafness. Malformations in the ear, low birthweight, and congenital infections such as rubella and herpes also can cause deafness (Calkins, 1988). As with vision, hearing should be checked by a professional early in life.

Proprioception

Proprioception is the receptor system that provides information about the position of each body part in relation to the rest of the body and in relation to gravity. You probably take your proprioception skills for granted—that is why you are no longer labeled a toddler.

When infants are first learning to stand, they use visual proprioceptive information about body sway more than the nonvisual proprio-receptors in the inner ear to help them maintain stable posture. Manipulation of visual information, therefore, can make infants sway or even fall.

Infants from 13 to 16 months of age were placed in an experimental "moving room"—that is, while they were standing, the room could be moved forward or backward in relation to their stance. For example, when the experimental room was moved forward, the infants felt as if they were swaying backward. Although the infants were actually standing still, when the three walls and ceiling were moved

Infants enjoy exploring their environment, and simple experiences like playing with water provide much pleasure.

forward, the infants compensated by moving their bodies forward. As a result, they swayed forward and often fell. Moving the room backward resulted in the opposite effect. That is, infants thought that they were swaying forward and compensated by leaning backward, again often falling (Lee & Aronson, 1974). Similar swaying was achieved with younger infants who were seated in the experimental moving room (Butterworth & Hicks, 1977).

That infants and small children cannot stand well or walk easily with their eyes shut demonstrates the importance of visual information in proprioception. Remember how hard it used to be to do well at "Pin the Tail on the Donkey"? Although you probably do much better at this game now, even adults have trouble walking a straight line without visual information (E. J. Gibson, 1988).

Exploratory Behavior

Physical, perceptual, and motor development in infants expands their world. As a result of these coordinated and interacting developments, infants become active explorers. Infants are programmed with action systems and sensory systems that allow them to discover what the world is like. Eleanor Gibson (1988) proposed that **exploratory systems** develop in three orderly phases during the first year. In contrast to some psychologists, who believe that neonates are limited to reflexive, compulsory behaviors, Gibson argued that young infants engage in spontaneous and self-directed exploratory behaviors.

Phase 1: Exploring Events
Eleanor Gibson (1988) suggested that, during the first phase, infants explore events. Neonates are preprogrammed to search for and focus attention on events in their immediate visual environment. Stationary, static objects and scenes arouse less interest than visually presented movement. For example, infants pay more attention to a flickering light than to a steady light. Exploratory behaviors are aided by the apparent coordination of looking and listening systems at birth.

Babies also learn about basic properties of objects via the *haptic exploratory system*—by examining them with their tongues, sucking on them, and tasting them. Haptic information allows 1-month-olds to distinguish nipples on the basis of texture and 3-month-olds to distinguish nipples on the basis of shape (Rochat, 1983). Visual-haptic coordination increases the ease with which babies bring objects into their mouths for gathering information about the objects.

Exploratory skills build up rapidly in Phase 1. Fifteen-week-olds are more likely to reach for closer targets than for farther ones, and in a few weeks, they master reaching for stationary objects and even catching slowly moving objects (Field, 1976; von Hofsten & Lindhagen, 1979). Such skills, along with stereopsis development and biological maturation of muscles that allow reaching, grasping, and fingering, provide the setting for moving into Phase 2.

Phase 2: Attention to Affordance and Object Features
Around the fourth or fifth month, infants enter Phase 2 of exploratory behavior development. In this phase, infants engage in more purposeful and self-determined object exploration and pay close attention to objects' distinctive features. They also focus on the *affordances* of the environment. Affordances are what objects offer to an individual. For example, infants learn that a cup is an object from which to drink and that a rug provides a comfortable crawling surface.

A new emphasis in Phase 2 is the exploration of objects to determine their functions. Eventually, this type of exploration leads young children to classify objects, but at first, this exploration of function is accomplished one object at a time (E. J. Gibson, 1988).

Early in Phase 2, infants may learn functions by trial and error. For example, while playing, 6-month-old Bruce may pull a cloth toward himself and accidentally bring a stuffed toy sitting on the cloth within reach. Bruce may learn to use the cloth as a tool to bring other objects within reach. Eight-month-old Barbara, however, has enough previous experience using fabric as a tool that she immediately gives an intentional pull on a cloth to bring a doll laying on the cloth closer (Willats, 1985).

In Phase 1, visual and haptic exploration predominates. In Phase 2, information from these senses is used to facilitate information processing in less developed modes, such as touch (E. J. Gibson, 1988). At 5 months, tactile habituation is almost 3 times longer than visual habituation, illustrating that infants are less skilled and less familiar with tactile information (Steri & Pecheux, 1986).

Phase 3: Ambulatory Exploration
Phase 2 is limited by infants having to depend on others to move them from place to place to explore new areas. By 9 months of age, however, infants can add locomotion to their highly competent explorations. Locomotion allows infants to attend to a larger world (E. J. Gibson, 1988).

In Phase 3, infants begin spontaneous, self-initiated locomotion and can now explore around corners, look behind obstacles, and turn around to see behind them. Eleanor Gibson (1988) stressed that "*steering*" around obstacles has a biological basis, as even young infants exhibit avoidance responses in "looming" experiments in which objects seem to be approaching infants on a collision course (Yonas, 1981).

During Phase 3, infants exhibit a new ability—carrying objects—that, according to Eleanor Gibson (1988), is a built-in response. Toddlers love to carry objects and enjoy giving objects to others and then taking them back. Carrying objects allows more opportunity to explore objects in the environment, to develop new functions for the objects, and to build social relationships.

These exploratory skills provide the basis for successful navigation in the world. They also allow infants to make major advancements in their cognitive abilities and language skills. Although the exploration fundamentals develop during the first year, exploration of the environment is still inefficient and redundant and continues to improve for several years.

Cognitive Development

Parental Beliefs

Although parents have often underestimated infant abilities and overestimated the abilities of preschoolers and school-age children, a recent trend is for parents to expect early infant cognitive development. Western parents, especially highly educated mothers, are being influenced by cultural beliefs and research findings about infant cognitive abilities, and compared to earlier generations, have adopted accelerated timetables of cognitive development (Ninio, 1988). In addition, many modern parents attempt to provide environments that will enhance cognitive development. In its extreme form, this type of influence results in efforts to produce precocious, intellectual superbabies.

Most parents, however, are more interested in providing a home environment and activities that enhance the natural emergence of cognitive skills. Picture books are a common teaching tool in the home, and mothers, rather than babies, control interactions about the pictures in books. Mothers tend to ask questions that they think can be answered, and older infants are asked for more labels and information than younger infants (DeLoache & DeMendoza, 1987). Also, mothers and fathers use picture books to convey cultural information to their children.

Burton White (1986) suggested one reasonable approach to helping infants develop their cognitive abilities. According to White, simple, colorful mobiles and such everyday items as measuring cups, pots, and pans provide the types of stimulation that help babies to explore the world, making enrollment in expensive courses and the purchase of expensive toys unnecessary.

How Infants Learn

During infancy, babies learn in many ways, including through classical and operant conditioning and modeling. As they grow older, infants become more efficient in their learning skills, and the kinds and amounts of learning that occur are truly staggering (Sameroff & Cavanagh, 1979).

Classical Conditioning

Classical conditioning involves learning to respond to signals (stimuli) that have previously been associated with stimuli that produce automatic or involuntary responses. In Pavlov's classic studies of this type of learning, dogs learned to salivate to the sound of a bell because the bell sound was paired with food, which naturally elicited salivation.

Young infants can learn through classical conditioning under some circumstances. In a study by Fitzgerald & Brackbill (1976), newborns were classically conditioned in 177 trials to turn their heads to a signal. Older infants learned more quickly: Three-month-olds were conditioned in 42 trials, and 5-month-olds were conditioned in only 28 trials. Interestingly, all three ages reached *extinction,* the point where the signal no longer elicits a response, in only 25 to 27 trials (Papousek, 1967).

Picture books are a common teaching tool to enhance the natural emergence of cognitive skills in infants.

When this child calls the cat a "doggie," assimilation is occurring. Accommodation will take place when she learns to differentiate between "kitties" and "doggies."

Operant Conditioning

Babies also learn through **operant conditioning**—that is, babies increase responses that are followed by pleasant consequences (*reinforcers*) and decrease responses that are followed by unpleasant consequences (*punishers*). Therefore, a baby who is picked up and cuddled (a reinforcer) after she starts to coo is likely to coo again to receive more cuddling. Likewise, reinforcers can be used to increase specific behaviors, such as smiling, crying, kicking, and sucking (Lancioni, 1980). Any infant behavior can be increased by giving reinforcers immediately following the behavior.

Research studies have shown that 3-month-olds with one end of a ribbon attached to their leg and the other end attached to a crib mobile are capable of learning to kick their leg to move the mobile (Dunst & Lingerfelt, 1985; Rovee-Collier, Sullivan, Enright, Lucas, & Fagen, 1980). The relevant stimuli are the presence of the ribbon and the mobile, and the response is leg kicking. In this example, the reinforcer is the baby's pleasure in producing and perceiving mobile movement. With 3-month-olds, this type of learning is forgotten in 8 days.

Modeling (Imitation)

A third way in which infants learn is by using **modeling** or **imitation** (the copying of another's behavior), a skill infants become capable of near the end of the first year. At first, infants can only imitate another's behavior if they perform the behavior right after seeing it. During the second year, however, they can delay their imitation for a period of time. In one study, 14-month-olds were able to pull apart a small toy 24 hr after observing an adult take the toy apart (Meltzoff, 1985).

Piagetian Theory of Cognitive Development

Jean Piaget (1896-1980) was a Swiss psychologist who became well-known for his ingenious work in the area of cognitive development and for his lifelong interest in studying children's explanations (Evans, 1981). A biographical sketch of Piaget and a summary of the concepts and stages of his theory of cognitive development are found in Appendix A. To learn about children's cognitions, Piaget observed children in natural settings while they performed tasks he presented to them.

According to Piaget, the goal of all organisms is **adaptation,** the process of adjusting to the environment. Piaget focused on the mental operations that process information from the environment and that represent the information in internal schemas. **Schemas** are mental structures that denote what is essential about category membership. Your world makes sense because you use schemas to help you classify novel objects and to determine their functions. For example, regardless of height, width, color, material, or decoration, you have no trouble choosing a glass instead of a bowl from which to drink. Young infants, however, must learn what attributes indicate "a drinking tool" and which do not.

Infants and older individuals form schemas by using the mental processes of assimilation and accommodation. **Assimilation** is the process by which a new experience is incorporated into an already existing schema. The toddler who knows characteristics of his "doggie" Rover may correctly generalize to other dogs in the neighborhood. He learns that collies, poodles, boxers, and schnauzers all can be labeled "doggie."

However, assimilation often leads to overgeneralization, in which cows and cats are also called "doggie." At this point, the process of accommodation enters the picture. **Accommodation** occurs when infants learn to modify a schema to fit a new experience or to create an entirely new schema. In accommodation, the schemas become "doggies," "moo-cows," and "kitties." Piaget believed that assimilation and accommodation occur because people want to make sense of their experiences in light of what they already know. He called the drive to maintain a balance between existing cognitive schemas and current experience **equilibration.** In other words, equilibration is an internal drive that assures, through processes of assimilation and accommodation, that our schemas are sufficient to make sense of our experiences.

Table 4.5
A Brief Description of Piaget's Sensorimotor Stage of Development

Stage	Approximate Age Range	Representative Skills
Sensorimotor	Birth to 24 Months	Coordination of Simple Behaviors and Perceptions
		Simple Means-Ends
		Separation
		Object Permanence

Primary source: Newton, N., & Modahl, C. (1978, March). Pregnancy: The closest human relationship. *Human Nature,* pp. 40-49.

Piaget believed that children of various ages think differently about the world. He grouped these characteristically different ways of thinking into four stages (see Appendix A). The characteristics of the **sensorimotor stage** of cognitive development, which coincides with infancy, are presented in Table 4.5. Piaget's other three stages (preoperational, ages 2 to 7; concrete operational, ages 7 to 12; and formal operational, age 12 on) are discussed in detail in later chapters.

The Sensorimotor Stage
Piaget's sensorimotor stage of cognitive development lasts from birth to approximately 2 years of age and is so named because infants develop their cognitive abilities through their sensory and motor abilities. During these 2 years, infants learn to coordinate simple behaviors, learn how to have purposeful behaviors, and learn that objects in the physical world are permanent. They also acquire a sense of self. The newborn begins life in a state of *adualism,* in which there is no distinction between the self and the outer world (Harris, 1983). By 18 months, however, toddlers express self-recognition and self-awareness when viewing themselves in a mirror.

Piaget divided the sensorimotor stage into six substages. The first substage lasts for about 1 month and centers around *reflex activity.* Piaget regarded reflexes as the building blocks of cognitive growth. With time, these reflexes become more efficient and more voluntary.

The second substage is called *primary circular reactions* because babies from 1 to 4 months old repeatedly (i.e., circularly) do activities with their bodies (i.e., primary). For example, babies repeatedly suck fingers and rattles because sucking is a pleasurable activity.

The third substage lasts from the fourth to eighth month and is called *secondary circular reactions.* The word *secondary* indicates that the focus has shifted from the body to objects. Now, actions are repeated because babies find pleasure in the results of their actions. For example, a rattle is shaken to hear the sound. These young infants pay such good attention during object exploration that, if they play with a toy that makes a sound, they can later look at the correct toy when the sound is reproduced (Lyons-Ruth, 1977).

The fourth substage is called *coordination of secondary schemes* and lasts until 12 months of age. The most significant cognitive development during this stage is the appearance of intentional behavior. An example mentioned earlier in the chapter was a child intentionally pulling a cloth so that the doll resting on it was brought within reach. Such purposeful behavior often occurs during this substage. By now, infants can combine actions, have means-ends behavior (they associate their present activities with reaching the goals they have in mind), and try different actions to reach a goal. They also can coordinate information from different senses well. An example of this higher level of complex organization was seen in 8-month-olds who held but did not see an object that produced a sound and who were later able to visually choose this object over another object (Bryant, Jones, Claxton, & Perkins, 1972).

From ages 12 to 18 months, infants are in Piaget's fifth substage—the *tertiary circular reactions* substage. The word *circular* indicates that infants in this stage still repeat actions, and the word *tertiary* emphasizes that these infants have an expanded world due to locomotion and are busy exploring many novel situations. Piaget viewed the 1-year-old as an active trial-and-error experimenter who learned about the world by trying out "variations on a theme." For example, today's lunchtime theme might be "What happens when I drop food from my high chair?" The variations include dropping *this* food item versus *that* food item, dropping from my hand versus dropping from my spoon, and simply letting go versus flinging an object. Trying different versions of the same basic action helps infants to really understand how the world operates.

The sixth and final substage of the sensorimotor stage is the *beginning of representational thought.* Piaget maintained that, from 18 months on, infants are capable of retaining mental images of objects and events. This ability allows infants to move from trial-and-error strategies to more efficient problem-solving strategies. It also increases infants' abilities to use deferred imitation, symbolic play, and language. The accomplishments of this substage mark, in many ways, the move from infancy to early childhood.

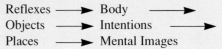
successful study tip

The Six Substages of the Sensorimotor Stage

Students usually find it difficult to remember the six substages of Piaget's sensorimotor stage. You can learn this material more easily if you think about each substage building upon the earlier ones. Regardless of the substage, infants learn by repeatedly practicing their new skills. First, they begin with reflexes, then with other body movements. To this repertoire, infants add learning about objects, intentions, and places. Finally, they develop the ability to form long-lasting mental images about the world.

Reflexes ⟶ Body ⟶
Objects ⟶ Intentions ⟶
Places ⟶ Mental Images

Table 4.6
Descriptions of Object Permanence Conceptualization During the Six Substages of the Sensorimotor Stage

First 4 Months:

Substage 1	Infant has no apparent object permanence. Infant will follow object across the visual field, but the object is ignored when it disappears.
Substage 2	Infant exhibits primitive object permanence. Infant looks briefly at location where the object disappeared (i.e., there is passive expectancy).

4 to 8 Months:

Substage 3	Infant searches for a missing object by sustained visual (and manual) examination of the spot where the object seemed to disappear.

8 to 12 Months:

Substage 4	Infant actively searches for a disappeared object. For example, infant will pull a cover away or crawl around an object to search for the missing item. However, if the object is moved to a new hiding place in full view of the infant, the infant still searches first the location in which the item disappeared.

12 to 18 Months:

Substage 5	Infant can track an object that disappears and reappears in several locations quickly. Now, when an object is visible when being moved to a new location, the infant can find the object in its new hiding place.

18 to 24 Months:

Substage 6	Infants can now search in appropriate places even when object is hidden from view as it is moved. Apparently, the infant can "image" the object and follow this image from one location to another (i.e., the infant is able to consider "invisible movement").

Source: Data from P. L. Harris, "Infant Cognition" in *Handbook of Child Psychology,* 4th edition, 1983, edited by P. H. Mussen. From M. H. Harth and J. J. Campes (Vol. ed.), *Infancy and Developmental Psychobiology,* John Wiley & Sons, NY. From P. L. Harris, "Perseverative Search at a Visibly Empty Place By Young Infants" in *Journal of Experimental Child Psychology,* 18, 535–542, 1974. From G. Gratch, "Responses to Hidden Persons and Things By 5, 9, and 16-Month-Old Infants in a Visual Tracking Situation" in *Developmental Psychology,* 18, 232–237, 1982.

Development of Object Permanence

What must a young infant think when his or her mother disappears from the nursery and then reappears some time later? As an adult, you realize that the appearance, disappearance, and reappearance of a person or object represents changes in the person or object's location but not its existence. For young infants, this type of situation might represent changes in existence (i.e., literally, out of sight, out of mind). When objects are not in the baby's perceptual field, the objects no longer exist. When they come back into view, the objects once again have an existence. Even in the fourth substage, infants may misinterpret events and believe that it is their act of searching for the object that is responsible for bringing the object back into existence (Harris, 1983).

Object permanence is acquired when infants have the capacity to recognize that people and objects continue to exist even when the infants are not in sensory contact with those people and objects. Acquiring complete object

Object permanence is acquired when an infant has the capacity to recognize that people and objects continue to exist even when the infant is not in sensory contact with them. Object permanence plays an important role in this father-son game of hide-and-seek.

permanence is a 2-year task, according to Piaget. Table 4.6 summarizes the development of object permanence through the six substages of the sensorimotor stage.

Although research studies confirm Piaget's developmental sequence of object permanence, other psychologists have suggested alternative explanations. Piaget assumed that infants had to learn that objects "continue to exist" when not being perceived (Harris, 1983). Bower (1982) suggested that the real task involved may be learning "where to search" for objects.

According to Bower, young infants may use a *self-related code* to determine the location of objects. The code of an object's position to the self at a given moment is something like "to my left, within reaching distance," and objects can be found if the relationship to the self remains constant (Butterworth, 1978). Since young infants cannot crawl and therefore alter their position relative to the object, a self-related code is practical and fairly reliable (Bremner, 1980).

After crawling, babies need another way in which to reliably find objects and thus develop a *landmark code (framework code),* such as "It's in this room" or "It's under the table" (Bower, 1982). When first switching to the framework code in substage 4, infants make many errors because the environment is complex and they are not yet able to retain temporal order information (Harris, 1983). Therefore, a common error during substage 4 is to search in the initial, rather than current, location.

Infant Egocentrism

Piaget and other scientists have assumed that toddlers and preschoolers exhibit **egocentrism,** an inability to view or experience the world from another's point of view. Although small infants and children are limited by egocentrism in complex perceptual and social situations, researchers have found surprising understanding of others' perceptions in some simple situations (Flavell, 1985; Flavell, Shipstead, & Croft, 1978). Eighteen-month-old Devan was asked to show her picture to her cousins, and Devan held the picture flat to allow them to see. In response to the same request, 2-year-old April even turned the picture around so that the back faced her and the front was visible to her cousins. Both girls understood that others could not see without their eyes so they pried Billy's hands from his eyes so that he could see their pictures.

The Neo-Piagetians
As you have read in this chapter and will encounter in succeeding chapters, Piaget's ideas have been criticized but not dismissed. They remain the major framework for organizing ideas about cognitive development. New researchers into Piaget's ideas—neo-Piagetians—continue to expand theory into new areas, such as the role of social, affective, and cultural factors on cognitive development (Berthenthal, 1987). Researchers are revising Piaget's original qualitative stage ideas to include quantitative increases in thinking strategies, memory, and automatic processing. They also are attempting to combine Piaget's ideas with ideas from the information-processing approach (Pascual-Leone, 1980).

Information-Processing Approach
The information-processing approach views cognitive development from the perspective that individuals are active manipulators of perceptions and symbols, and research focuses on what is done with information from perceptions. Information-processing theorists build upon and modify the Piaget framework regarding cognitive development.

Bruner's Modes of Cognitive Representation
Jean Piaget's work influenced American psychologist Jerome S. Bruner, who is best known for looking at the modes that children use to represent the world. According to Bruner, during the sensorimotor period, the primary way infants represent the world internally is the **enactive mode.** In this mode, the world is represented in terms of motor acts. Therefore, a rattle is not an object but, rather, an action, a series of movements. Children older than 2 begin to use the **iconic mode** more often. The iconic mode involves representing the world through mental images. By the school years, children prefer to use the **symbolic mode,** especially language (Bruner, Olver, & Greenfield, 1966).

As an adult, you use all three modes well. For example, how would you describe your car to another person? First, you might use the symbolic mode and give a brief description of the car: "Well, it's a 1982 tan Chevy Citation with an Iowa license plate. It's got about 85,000 miles on it." Then, you might pause and form a mental image of the car (the iconic mode) to see what else you could add: "Oh yeah, there's a bumper sticker that says *Another Ho-Hum Day in Paradise* and another that says *If You Can Read This, Thank a Teacher.*" If the other person asks, "Where's the ignition?", you would probably shift into the enactive mode and actively point out its location with gestures.

Early Counting Skills
Another important way you learn to represent the world internally is in terms of quantities. At what age can children count? Even before you could count to 10 or add 2 plus 2, you had some sense of number. It's a rare toddler, for example, who does not know how to choose the bigger of two pieces of cake or choose the larger pile of M&Ms.

A few studies suggest that even neonates have some ability to differentiate number of objects up to three. Neonates were habituated (allowed to be accustomed) to patterns of dots on cards. Some cards had the same number of dots, but the dots were arranged in a different order. Babies who first saw a card with three dots exhibited more interest in a card with two dots than in another card of three dots arranged differently. The opposite was also true. Babies habituated to two dots increased interest when shown a card with three dots. Neonatal ability to differentiate numbers stopped at three (Antell & Keating, 1983). Even at 4 and 7 months, babies could only tell the difference in numbers up through three (Starkey & Cooper, 1980).

Why do you think babies can distinguish among 1, 2, and 3? Some psychologists (e.g., Flavell, 1985) believe that babies have an inborn neurological process that regulates behavioral counting. Others (e.g., Antell & Keating, 1983; Gibson, 1966) suggest that a baby's ability to discriminate among these three numbers is tied into general perceptual abilities to attend to unchanging features in the environment.

Memory Development

Infantile Amnesia
What was your infancy like? What memories do you have of being fed? Did you like to soil your diapers? What feelings did you have about your toilet training? In fact, you have no firsthand memories about your own infancy. **Infantile amnesia** (having little or no memory for one's own life before age 3) is a fairly universal experience for both children and adults (Kail, 1984).

One study that overwhelmingly illustrated infantile amnesia involved asking parents and their older offspring about the birth of a later child. Children were asked such questions as "When your brother/sister was born, did you visit your mother while she was in the hospital?" As expected, when children were less than 3 years older than the sibling, they did not recall the sibling's birth (Sheingold & Tenney, 1982).

Several explanations for infantile amnesia are possible. One explanation is that early coded information is stored in memory in a different, more primitive format than later on. When individuals try to retrieve early material, they cannot because they use an overly sophisticated material search. Bruner's concept that infants use an enactive mode to represent their experiences, while older individuals prefer iconic and symbolic modes may play a role. Another explanation is that the brain maturation during the first years may change physiological structures of the brain and change or delete early memories. Finally, Freud believed that early memories were repressed because the memory of them caused anxiety.

Is anything retained for the long term during the first 2 years of life? Yes, infants build a vocabulary and skill package that continues through the years. But words and skills are frequently practiced, while *episodic memories* of life events may go unpracticed. Events from infancy may be better recalled if young children reexperience similar situations and events to rehearse episodic memories. For

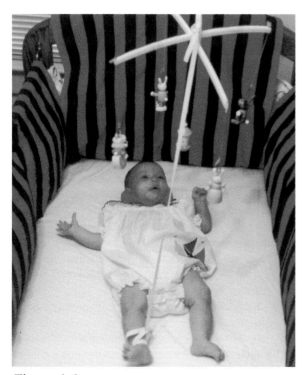

Figure 4.6

Studying infant memory. Shown here is the technique used in Rovee-Collier's investigation of infant memory. The mobile is connected to the infant's ankle by the ribbon and moves in direct proportion to the frequency and vigor of the infant's kicks.

example, children between 2 1/2 and 3 years of age were put into a laboratory they had visited at least 15 times between 6 and 40 weeks of age. Compared to a control group who had never been in the laboratory, measures on these children suggested that they remembered some of their earlier experiences (Myers, Clifton, & Clarkson, 1987). Likewise, your early memories may be influenced by photographs, videotapes, or family stories about your early years. These are the events that you got to rehearse over and over—like returning to the laboratory—and, therefore, are "remembered."

Characteristics of Early Memory

What are the capabilities of infants' memories? Some research findings suggest that infants can retain information for minutes but that they cannot remember as much or as long as older children (Olson & Sherman, 1983a; Werner & Perlmutter, 1979). When parents of infants from 7 to 11 months of age were asked about instances that revealed memory recall in their babies, they related examples in which infants seemed to anticipate where household items were kept, exhibited surprise when items were not in their typical location, correctly remembered game rituals such as peek-a-boo, and seemed to search for people (Ashmead & Perlmutter, 1980).

Carolyn Rovee-Collier and her colleagues hung a mobile over an infant's crib and attached a ribbon to one of the baby's limbs (Borovsky, Hill, & Rovee-Collier, 1987; Rovee-Collier, 1987). Six-week-old infants quickly discovered which arm or leg would move the mobile (see Figure 4.6). Two weeks later, the infants were placed in the same situation. They *remembered* which arm or leg to

move, even though they were not attached to the mobile. These early signs of memory are the basis for the kinds of learning from experience that continues throughout our lifetime. Ongoing investigation of such abilities underscores the surprising competence of young infants (Boller & Rovee-Collier, 1992; Rovee-Collier, 1992).

By the end of infancy, memory skills are much better. As parents are well aware, 2-year-olds remember parents' promises about treats about 80 percent of the time. They also begin to grow rapidly in their abilities to remind parents to do tasks and to remember advertising jingles and nursery rhymes (Somerville, Wellman, & Cultice, 1983).

How important are early memory capabilities? Some memory researchers believe that visual memory and attentiveness in infants correlates with intelligence at school age (Kolata, 1987). Yet, memory can be enhanced by parenting methods. Young children's memories are added if parents ask them lots of questions that encourage generation of stored information. Storytelling also helps to build memory abilities (Price, 1984).

guided review

9. Parents are still likely to _____ the cognitive abilities of infants while _____ those of preschoolers and school-age children.
10. Infants learn in many ways, including through _____ conditioning, _____ conditioning, and _____.
11. According to Jean Piaget's theory of cognitive development, _____ is used to place new experiences into existing schemas, and _____ is the process of modifying schemas to fit a new experience.
12. In the _____ stage of cognitive development, infants learn simple behavior coordination, purposeful behaviors, a rudimentary sense of self, and _____ (knowing that persons and objects still exist even when infants are not in sensory contact with them).
13. In the first substage of the sensorimotor stage, _____ are the building blocks of cognitive growth, and by the sixth substage, infants are able to retain _____, allowing deferred imitation, symbolic play, and language.
14. According to Bower, young infants may use a _____ code to determine the location of objects and, after acquiring locomotion skills, move to a _____ code.
15. According to Bruner, infants largely use the _____ mode, preschoolers move more to an _____ mode, and older children rely primarily on the _____ mode.
16. Young infants may have a built-in mechanism that provides some ability to differentiate number of objects up to _____.
17. _____ is the term used for having little or no memory of one's life before age 3.

answers

9. underestimate; overestimating [LO-10]. 10. classical; operant; modeling [LO-10]. 11. assimilation; accommodation [LO-11]. 12. sensorimotor; object permanence [LO-11]. 13. reflexes; mental images [LO-11]. 14. self-related; landmark (framework) [LO-12]. 15. enactive; iconic, symbolic [LO-13]. 16. three [LO-13]. 17. Infantile amnesia [LO-14].

Language Development

Speech Perception and Infant Vocalization

Language development and speech can be viewed as an "object of perception." Comprehending speech is basically a product of auditory perception, but visual perception is important, too, since listeners can pick up cues to speech sounds by watching the speaker's face and to speech meanings by observing gestures (Kuhl & Meltzoff, 1988).

Comprehension Versus Production

Two major aspects of speech perception develop during infancy. One aspect is learning to comprehend speech, or acquiring **receptive language.** The other aspect is to be able to produce speech, or acquiring **expressive language.** Both processes begin early, but "meaningful" comprehension remains ahead of "meaningful" speech (Crystal, 1986).

By 4 months, infants are able to recognize some differences among basic sounds, such as *a* sounds with open, wide mouths; *i* sounds with mouths with retracted lips; and *u* sounds with mouths whose lips are protruded and pursed. This is an important step in language development because infants must be able to identify sound parts of speech and put these parts together (Kuhl & Meltzoff, 1988).

Speech Perception and Culture

Adults often have difficulty learning to speak foreign languages because they cannot distinguish phonemic sounds (the basic sounds in a language culture) not native to their own language. Many English-speaking people, for example, have trouble understanding and producing the gutteral sounds that are common in the German language, and Japanese-speaking people have trouble distinguishing the *r* and *l* sounds of the English language. Infants, however, begin life able to produce and distinguish a wider range of phonemic sounds than can children and adults (Eimas, 1985; Werker & Tees, 1984). Six-month-old infants in English-speaking homes are able to distinguish Hindi and Salish sounds foreign to English speech. However, they lose this ability over the next 6 months because older infants pay increasing attention to everyday sounds and decreasing attention to sounds without meaning within their language culture (Eimas, 1985; Werker & Tees, 1984).

Theories of Language Development

Noam Chomsky (1972, 1978) and B. F. Skinner (1957) presented two diverse theories of language acquisition. Chomsky, a nativist who believes in an inborn biological capacity underlying the use of language, asserts that, regardless of language, culture, and parenting style, babies everywhere acquire similar language skills at about the same age. According to psycholinguists such as Chomsky, the universal similarity of language development is strong evidence for the **innate theory of language development,** the idea that the development of language is built into every human's system and that the order of language acquisition is at least partly determined by brain maturation. According to Chomsky, biological mechanisms are important in learning the properties of speech because all young infants pay attention to a wide range of speech sounds and patterns, even if these are not part of their everyday environment.

On the other hand, the behaviorist Skinner proposed that language is a product of social interaction in which adults systematically reinforce babies for language acquisition. According to Skinner, at first, adults respond to any vocalization by young infants, and over time, social reinforcers shape vocalizations into meaningful speech. Therefore, Skinner's **learning theory approach to language development** emphasizes the environmental factors that shape the particular language an infant learns.

Although innate factors may play a bigger role than Skinner would support, even nativists would agree that reinforcement plays a major role in language acquisition. Parental pleasure in infant vocalization encourages infants to vocalize more. As parents smile and react more to sounds that come close to "real words," babies learn to discriminate some sounds better than others.

Thus, babies probably are biologically predisposed to vocalize, and parents teach babies that their randomly produced "da-da, da-da" is a special vocalization and babies respond by saying "da-da" more and relating this sound to their father. The best theory of language acquisition will probably combine many features of the innate theory and learning theory approaches (Gelman, 1986).

Stages of Language Development

The First Year

Because all babies develop language in similar ways and about the same time, psychologists talk about milestones of language development (see Table 4.7). During the first year, infants develop the building blocks of language (Crystal, 1986). Babies begin with basic noises, such as crying, fussing, sucking, and coughing, and learn to coo by 6 to 8 weeks. *Cooing* consists of vowel sounds and is a major vocalization from 2 months on. Soon, infants string a series of up to a dozen cooing sounds (Stark, 1986).

At approximately 6 months, babies add consonant sounds to cooing and begin **babbling,** producing consonant/vowel sound combinations. Initially, the most common consonant sounds are *h* and *d*, which is one reason why "da-da" is often a baby's first word. Other commonly used consonants are *b, m, q, w,* and *j*. Do you know what your parents heard as your first words? "Ma-ma," "ba" (i.e., ball), and "wa-wa" (i.e., water) are common first words in addition to "da-da." Interestingly, most babbling consists of consonant-vowel combinations, rather than vowel-consonant—for example, "am-am," "ab," and "aw-aw"—combinations (Crystal, 1986).

Toward the end of the first year, babies rehearse long strings of sounds, developing a rhythmic, songlike tone of voice called the *melodic utterance.* From ages 9 to 18 months, babies commonly entertain themselves while lying in their cribs and singsonging their babbling. These infants time their "chunks" of babble sounds to give the impression of communication. This *"scribble talk"* sounds like normal conversation, except that meaning is mostly absent (Crystal, 1986).

Table 4.7
Sequence of Language Development

Age	Language Development
Early	All babies make the same sounds.
6 months	Adds consonants to cooing, which then becomes *babbling*.
	Begins more frequent practice of phonemes of own language (*phonetic drift*).
12 months	Imitates sounds (*echolalia*).
	Produces first words.
	Understands some words. Over the next year, will understand about 22 new words per month but vocalize only 10 new words a month.
	Uses *holophrasing*, or one-word sentences.
	Exhibits *melodic utterance*, or singsonging words and sounds.
18 months (1.5 years)	Has a vocabulary of 3 to 50 words.
	Uses patterns of sounds and innotations that resemble speech (*"scribble talk"*).
	Makes good advances in understanding words.
24 months (2 years)	Has vocabulary of more than 50 words.
	Most commonly uses two-word phrases.
	No longer engages in babbling.
	Exhibits increased interest in verbal communication.
	Uses *telegraphic speech* (subject-verb-object communiqués).
30 months (2.5 years)	Uses new words almost daily.
	Has vocabulary of over a thousand words.
	Grammar ability is almost equal to colloquial adult usage.
	Exhibits fewer syntactic mistakes.
114 months (9.5 years)	Uses 28,142 words a day—including 3,825 different words.
	Has a speaking vocabulary of 50,000 words.
	Understands about 100,000 words.
	Uses about 1,000 rules of grammar.

Source: Data from D. Crystal, *Listen to Your Child: A Parent's Guide to Children's Language,* 1986, Penguin Press, England. From E. H. Lenneberg, *Biological Functions of Language,* 1967, John Wiley & Sons, NY.

The Second Year

Although in the first year, babies comprehend some language, real spoken language begins at the start of the second year. Children probably understand at least 50 words clearly before they can even produce 10 words. By 18 months, most babies have an expressive vocabulary of about 50 words but can typically comprehend about 250 words.

Parent-Child Talk

Parents simplify their grammar and pronunciation to aid infant comprehension. In addition, when adults speak to babies, they alter tone and inflection in their speech (Grieser

Table 4.8
Characteristics of the Baby-Talk Register

1. Adults speak to babies using a higher than normal pitch.
2. Adults speak to babies using a greater than normal range of pitch.
3. Adults use a rising final intonation on imperatives when they are speaking to infants ("Come here?").
4. Adults occasionally speak to babies in whispered sounds.
5. When adults speak to infants, they use longer than normal duration in speaking separable verbs ("Cooome-here").
6. Adults talking to babies often use two main syllabic stresses on words calling for one ("Co-ome here").

From O. K. Garnica, "Some Prosodic and Paralinguistic Features of Speech to Young Children" in *Talking to Children,* 1977, edited by C. E. Snow and C. A. Ferguson. Copyright © 1977 Cambridge University Press, North American Branch, New York, NY.

& Kuhl, 1988; Phillips, 1973). Basic characteristics of this **baby-talk register** are summarized in Table 4.8.

In infancy and during the rest of childhood, much of what children learn comes from experiences. Children's language learning proceeds from action to concept and then to words. Children's vocabulary builds as situations and objects become meaningful (Genishi, 1988). Therefore, parents who use picture books or who interact with their toddlers during play help their youngsters to build larger, relevant vocabularies (DeLoache & DeMendoza, 1987; O'Brien & Nagle, 1987).

guided review

18. _____ language involves comprehending speech, while ability to produce speech is called _____ language.
19. _____ believes in an inborn biological capacity underlying the use of language, as evidenced by the universal similarities in language acquisition, but _____ believed in a learning theory approach, emphasizing the reinforcement of language in social interactions.
20. At about 2 months of age, infants engage in _____ of vowel sounds; 4 months later, cooing becomes _____, as consonant sounds are added. Soon, _____ is evident as infants begin to more frequently practice the sounds of their own native language.
21. Around one year of age, infants produce their first words; other developments that quickly occur are _____ (use of one-word sentences), singsonging words and sounds called _____, and "_____," which sounds like normal conversation but basically has no meaning.
22. When speaking to infants, adults often use _____, which is characterized by higher pitch, wider range of pitch, and changes in intonation.

answers

18. Receptive; expressive [LO-15]. 19. Chomsky; Skinner [LO-16]. 20. cooing; babbling; phonetic drift [LO-17].
21. holophrasing; melodic utterance, scribble talk [LO-17].
22. baby-talk register [LO-18].

Developing Competence

The physical, motor, perceptual, cognitive, and language development in infancy culminates in advancing levels of competency for the child. The complex interactions of these individual areas yield an emerging preschooler who thinks, remembers, uses language, solves problems, and changes daily. At this point, different contexts affect individual development. Consider how the context of interactions with parents influences development competence.

Some children develop better cognitive skills and persevere longer in problem solving than do other children. What aspects of infancy start to influence these individual differences in competence? Beginning at about 8 months of age, when infants are starting to crawl and to understand language, parenting styles seem to influence babies' competencies. Preschoolers who get along well with children and adults, who take pride in their accomplishments, and who persevere at tasks come from homes with frequent parent-child communication, reasonable limits on child behavior, and interesting environments to explore and experience (White, Kaban, & Attanucci, 1979).

Parents of competent toddlers and preschoolers serve as "consultants" for their children—providing them with a safe home, showing them interesting objects and events, and utilizing common items in creative ways. Parents who foster greater competency in their infants also apply rules consistently, display both love and respect for their children, and are good at creatively distracting children from unwanted situations. These parents seem to enjoy their children and the parenting experience (White, 1985; White et al., 1979).

The best time period for enhancing the development of competence is from 6 months to 2 years, although some modifications also can be made after that age. Suggestions for parents who wish to help their infants and preschoolers become more competent explorers and learners include:

1. Allow infants to have some physical freedom, but establish reasonable, safe limits.
2. Let infants learn how to gain positive attention. Do not hover over them and provide constant attention, or they will not learn attention-seeking skills. When children request attention, try to be prompt in being with them, and provide quality interaction.
3. Interact with infants and talk with young children about their interests, rather than redirecting them to your own interests. Use distraction mainly to get them interested in good activities and away from forbidden tasks.
4. Use personal communication more than television and audiocassettes to teach language. Use picture books and storybooks to build communication skills, knowledge, and social interaction.

Parents of competent toddlers and preschoolers serve as "consultants" for their children, promoting communication, applying consistent rules and limits on behavior, and displaying love and respect.

5. See everyday household items as educational toys. Help infants to learn about the world by exploring readily available items.
6. Allow children to play creatively. Toys can be used in more than one way. It is more important to play freely with colors and shapes than to color within the lines in a coloring book.
7. Enjoy your children's efforts. Appreciate the differences among children. Try to find the enjoyments of parenting rather than the burdens.
8. Find substitute caretakers, whether relatives or babysitters, that have similar attitudes about child-rearing and children.

As you reflect on your past development, a word of caution is in order. If you find aspects of your past development where your parents or other significant caregivers did not necessarily follow the advice given in this and other chapters, try not to be too harsh in your judgment of their child-rearing. Remember that you have made it thus far in your life, an accomplishment that has required a fair degree of competency on your part. Be glad that you have learned some things that will help you to better foster competency in the children in your own family and the families of your friends. The issue of competency continues in Chapter 5, where you will learn about infants' developing personality and social skills.

23. Parenting styles that enhance a sense of competence include frequent parent-child _____, reasonable _____ on child behavior, and interesting environments to explore and experience.
24. Parents can foster competence by serving as their children's "_____," providing a safe home, showing interesting objects and events, and utilizing common objects in creative ways.

answers

23. communication; limits [LO-19]. 24. consultants [LO-19].

Exploring Human Development

1. Look at photographs of yourself during infancy, and examine the characteristics that reflect the cephalocaudal and proximodistal principles of development.
2. Design and conduct a study of object permanence with infants.
3. Design a short survey dealing with adult expectations for infants' perceptual, motor, or cognitive development, and collect data from college students.
4. Make a collection of articles from recent magazines about infants. Indicate which articles seem to be accurate, which seem to overgeneralize, and which contain faulty or out-of-date information. What topics are "hot" topics in the popular press?

Discussing Human Development

1. How would you design a baby's nursery to aid perceptual and cognitive development?
2. Early psychologists did more research on physical and motor development than on perceptual and cognitive development. Today, the opposite is true. Why the change? Do you think it reflects changes in what society values? Do you think it reflects changes in what researchers are able to study?
3. Name five pieces of information presented in this chapter that you think are most important for parents of infants to know. Why did you choose these particular items?
4. What involvement should others have in how parents raise their children? For example, if parents are not doing activities that increase their children's competency, should others in society step in to enhance the opportunities for these children? If your answer is "yes," how should this involvement be accomplished? If your answer is "no," what is the basis for your decision?

Reading More About Human Development

Chess, S., & Thomas, A. (1987). *Know your child.* New York: Basic Books.
Crystal, D. (1986). *Listen to your child: A parent's guide to children's language.* Harmondsworth, England: Penguin.
Evans, R.I. (1981). *Dialogue with Jean Piaget* (Eleanor Dickworth, Trans.). New York: Praeger.
Kagan, J. (1984). *The nature of the child.* New York: Basic Books.
White, B. (1985). *The first three years* (rev. ed.). New York: Prentice-Hall.

Summary

I. Physical development
  A. During infancy, physical growth includes changes in height, weight, and internal characteristics.
    1. Maturation is age-related physical change that is genetically programmed and that represents one's optimal potential for growth.
    2. Body proportions reflect the cephalocaudal and proximodistal principles of development.
    3. Compared to adults, infants have a larger surface area per unit weight, making them more susceptible to heat loss and to dehydration, as well as increasing their caloric need.
    4. Infants have a higher percentage of body water than do older individuals; from infancy to adulthood, females change most dramatically in percentage of body fat, while males change most in percentage of body protein.
    5. By the end of infancy, infants are about one fifth of their adult weight and one half of their adult height.
    6. At birth, the brain is already one fourth of its adult weight, and by the end of infancy, it is three fourths of its final size.
    7. For neonates, brain activity is largely in the motor and sensory areas, the basal ganglia, the brain stem, and the cerebellum; over the next 8 months, activity in the cerebral cortex increases so that it becomes similar to that of an adults' brain.
    8. Brain lateralization refers to the separation and integration of functional systems within the cerebral hemispheres of the brain.
  B. Nutritional needs of infants change, from about 6 months of breast milk or formulas to the gradual addition of other foods to meet additional iron and vitamin needs.
    1. Throughout history, solid foods have been introduced at varying times of infancy, with the current trend being to delay solid foods for several months.
    2. Today, infants are more likely to be fed on a flexible, demand-feeding schedule than on a rigid feeding schedule.
    3. Recent studies suggest no relationship between infant obesity and adolescent obesity; however, genetic factors, along with parents who "push" additional foods on their children, overrestrict their children's foods, allow fast eating, and permit an inactive lifestyle, are associated with later weight problems.
  C. Motor development moves from reflexes and involuntary reactive movements to more voluntary active behaviors.
    1. There is a typical order and timing to motor development that tends to follow the cephalocaudal and proximodistal principles.

2. Internal changes, including myelination of nerves, also follow these developmental principles.

3. Biological development precedes motor and other behavioral development.

4. Gross motor movements are performed before fine motor ones.

5. The sequence of motor development is basically universal, with a few differences due to cultural practices; rate of development is influenced by ethnic background.

6. Female infants have a small advantage in physical development, but parents view baby boys as stronger.

7. Practicing the stepping reflex does not accelerate walking, and swaddling does not hinder the development of walking.

8. Toilet training is often easier if the toddler is at least 20 months old because the sphincter muscle can then be more easily controlled; there are many styles of toilet training, including a behavior modification technique designed by Azrin and Foxx.

D. Sensory development makes major advances during infancy.

1. Two prominent perceptual theories are Helmholtz's unconscious perceptual theory and Gibson's theory of direct perception.

2. At birth, vision is one of the least developed senses, and it takes 11 months for the major retinal structures to become anatomically similar to an adult's; perceptual abilities improve into the preschool years.

3. Overall, visual perception proceeds from parts to wholes.

4. Color preferences are present among 3-month-old infants, who prefer the long wavelengths of red and yellow to short wavelengths of blue and green; the preferences reverse by adulthood.

5. The visual cliff apparatus is used to test depth perception, an aspect that develops over several months and involves both anatomical cues, such as retinal disparity, and pictorial cues, such as shading, interposition, and linear perspective.

6. Perceptual constancies help in perceiving a stable world.

7. Babies prefer to view human faces over most other stimuli.

8. In infancy, amblyopia can be diagnosed and visual deficits minimized.

9. At 6 months, infants can distinguish consonant and vowel sounds, sounds that are not part of their native language, different tones, and the locations of sounds.

10. Profound hearing loss is usually detected by age 2; other losses often go undetected until the school years.

11. The most significant clue to an infant's hearing impairment is a different timetable in babbling.

12. Toddlers learn to use their proprioception system to maintain stable posture.

E. Eleanor Gibson proposed an orderly, self-directed, three-phase exploratory system during the first year of infancy.

1. Phase 1 involves the exploration of events, using a coordinated looking and listening system and the haptic exploratory system.

2. During these first 4 months, infants show more interest in visually presented movement and changing stimuli than in static objects, and they build skills in reaching for stationary objects and may even catch slowly moving objects.

3. In the fourth or fifth month, infants enter Phase 2, in which they focus on affordance and object features. The new emphasis in this phase is on the exploration of objects to determine their functions.

4. Tactile exploration becomes very important in Phase 2.

5. By around 9 months of age, infants have some locomotion, and they enter Phase 3: ambulatory exploration; this phase enlarges the area of possible exploration and includes the skill of carrying objects, which adds to infants' exploration abilities.

II. Cognitive development

A. Parents have often underestimated infant abilities, yet overestimated preschool and school-age abilities; some parents now are aware of early infant cognitive development.

1. Parents may purposely provide an environment designed to enhance cognitive development; in its extreme form, the attempt is to produce a "superbaby."

2. Ideally, the home environment and daily activities allow the natural emergence of cognitive skills; picture books, colorful mobiles, and everyday items such as cups and pans allow this development.

B. Infants learn through classical conditioning, operant conditioning, and modeling.

1. Acquisition of a classically conditioned response of head turning to a signal takes fewer trials as infants get older, but extinction is not age-related.

2. Any infant behavior can be increased by giving reinforcers immediately following the behavior (operant conditioning).

3. Near the end of the first year, infants can imitate another's behavior if they perform it immediately; during the second year, they become capable of delayed imitation.

C. In Jean Piaget's influential theory of cognitive development, infants are in the sensorimotor stage.

1. With the goal of adaptation, infants use the processes of assimilation and accommodation of their schemas to experience equilibration.

2. The most important skills of the sensorimotor stage are the coordination of simple behaviors and perceptions, simple means-ends, separation of self from others, and object permanence.

3. Piaget divided the 2-year sensorimotor stage into six substages: during these substages, infants move from reflex behaviors to other body movements, add learning about objects and then novel situations while gaining in intentional behavior, and finally develop the ability to form long-lasting mental images about the world.
4. Gradually developed during this stage is object permanence, the capacity to recognize that people and objects continue to exist even when the self is not in sensory contact with them.
5. Bower suggested that object permanence involves moving from a self-related code to locate objects to a landmark code (or framework code).
6. In complex perceptual and social situations, small infants and children are limited by egocentrism.
7. Neo-Piagetians continue to expand Piaget's theory into new areas, such as the role of social, affective, and cultural factors on cognitive development.

D. The information-processing approach builds upon Piaget's ideas and views individuals as active manipulators of perceptions and symbols.
1. Bruner suggested that the primary way infants represent the world internally is the enactive mode, or in terms of motor acts.
2. After infancy, children are more likely to use the iconic mode, or representation through mental images; school-age children prefer the symbolic mode, especially language.
3. Studies measuring rates of habituation find that even very young infants seem to sense a difference in number of objects up to three; other early counting skills include toddlers' ability to choose bigger dessert slices or bigger piles of candies.

E. Memory development in infancy is difficult to study, partly because researchers and other adults have no firsthand memories of their own infancy to aid in developing hypotheses.
1. A fairly universal experience is infantile amnesia, having little or no memory for one's own life before 3 years of age.
2. Explanations for infantile amnesia include (1) making a wrong type of memory search (e.g., symbolic or iconic instead of enactive), (2) brain maturation that has changed physiological structures, and (3) lack of practice of episodic memories.
3. Early remembered episodic memories are likely to be those that are repetitive or that are reviewed by "family stories" or media storage.
4. Memory is longer lasting in older infants than in younger infants, and memory abilities are built through activities, such as asking lots of questions and storytelling.

III. Language development
A. Two important aspects of speech perception are speech comprehension (receptive language) and infant vocalization (expressive language).
1. "Meaningful" comprehension remains ahead of "meaningful" speech.
2. By 4 months of age, infants can recognize differences among basic sounds.
3. Infants are able to produce and distinguish a wider range of phonemic sounds than children and adults.

B. Two diverse theories of language development were proposed by Noam Chomsky and B. F. Skinner.
1. Noam Chomsky proposed that the universal similarity of language development means that there are innate biological mechanisms that structure the process.
2. On the other hand, B. F. Skinner concluded that language is a product of social interaction in which adults systematically reinforce babies for language acquisition.

C. Regardless of culture, all babies develop language in similar ways and at about the same time.
1. At about 2 months of age, cooing begins; 4 months later, consonant sounds are added, and infants begin babbling. Babbling is later rehearsed as melodic utterance and as "scribble talk."
2. Although, in the first year, babies comprehend some language, real spoken language begins at the start of the second year.

D. Parents and other adults change their wording, tone, and inflection when speaking to infants.
1. Characteristics of this baby-talk register include higher pitch and many changes in inflection.
2. Children's language learning proceeds from action to concept and then to words; therefore, parents who use picture books or who interact with their toddlers during play help their youngsters to build larger, relevant vocabularies.

IV. Developing competence
A. During infancy, the child gains competency in physical, motor, perceptual, cognitive, and language areas.
B. Frequent parent-child communication, reasonable limits on child behavior, and interesting environments to explore are associated with higher levels of competence.
C. The best time period for enhancing the development of competence is from 6 months to 2 years of age.

Chapter Review Test

1. Maturation refers to
   a. the effects of environmental obstacles on growth.
   b. how development begins at the center of the body and moves to the extremities.
   c. genetically programmed patterns of physical development.
   d. the brain lateralization that begins during infancy.

2. Which of the following is *not* an example of the cephalocaudal principle?
   a. A young infant who can roll a ball back will miss the ball completely if it is rolled somewhat off-center toward the infant.
   b. An infant can hold its head erect and steady before being able to sit with support.
   c. At the end of the embryo stage, the head is half of the total length of the developing organism.
   d. When the infant weighs one fifth of its eventual adult weight, the brain is three fourths of its adult weight.

3. Which of the following is an example of proximodistal motor development?
   a. Infants can sit up before they can stand up.
   b. Infants see with their eyes before they hear with their ears.
   c. Toddlers tend to use the centers of their bodies more than their arms when they first throw a ball.
   d. Infants play with their fingers more than their toes.

4. Which of the following is a result of infants' larger surface area per unit weight than older individuals?
   a. higher caloric intake to maintain basal metabolism
   b. warmer clothing needed due to greater heat loss
   c. more frequent drinks to avoid dehydration
   d. all of the above

5. Which of the following is a correct statement about nutrition during infancy?
   a. Infants use fewer calories than adults to maintain basal metabolism.
   b. Young infants indicate food satiation by slower sucking, by turning the head sideways, or by falling asleep.
   c. A rigid feeding schedule helps in avoiding underfeeding, overfeeding, and long periods of crying.
   d. Research shows a connection between infant and adolescent obesity.

6. As a group, which babies have the earliest rate of development of gross motor skills?
   a. African-American babies
   b. European-American babies
   c. Asian-American babies
   d. There are no ethnic differences in gross motor development.

7. Which perceptual theory suggests that infants must be able to retain memories of past experiences prior to making sense of present sensory information?
   a. J.J. Gibson's theory of direct perception
   b. Chomsky's innate theory
   c. Helmholtz's unconscious inference theory
   d. E. Gibson's three-phase exploratory system

8. Which of the following is a typical color preference of a 3-month-old?
   a. green
   b. yellow
   c. blue
   d. gray

9. The visual cliff apparatus is used to measure
   a. exploratory behavior.
   b. object permanence.
   c. gross motor movements.
   d. depth perception.

10. Which of the following does a several-month-old infant *most prefer* to look at?
    a. a store mannequin
    b. a strange adult
    c. a same-sex baby
    d. a scrambled face

11. The haptic exploratory system involves
    a. using one's tongue and mouth to explore and learn about objects.
    b. paying attention to the functions of particular objects.
    c. being able to explore a larger area due to having locomotor abilities.
    d. using iconic mode, rather than being limited to enactive mode.

12. In a classical conditioning experiment in which infants were conditioned to turn their heads to a signal, older infants
    a. could be conditioned, but younger infants could not.
    b. reached extinction with fewer trials than younger infants.
    c. were faster than younger infants in both acquisition and extinction.
    d. took fewer trials to acquire the conditioning than younger infants, but extinction took about the same number of trials.

13. What did Jean Piaget call the mental structures that denote what is essential about category membership?
    a. affordances
    b. schemas
    c. circular reactions
    d. iconic mode

14. Which of the following behaviors is characteristic of Piaget's tertiary circular reactions substage?
    a. trying different versions of the same basic action
    b. being able to retain mental images of objects and events
    c. initial appearance of intentional behavior
    d. fundamental shift from paying attention to the body to paying attention to objects

15. Which of the following is an example of a self-related code?
    a. "It's in my room."
    b. "It's under the chair."
    c. "I think I can remember where it is."
    d. "It's to my right, within reaching distance."

16. Which mode did Jerome Bruner propose as most typical of infancy?
    a. symbolic
    b. iconic
    c. enactive
    d. none of the above

17. Which of the following is proposed as an explanation for infantile amnesia?
    a. Brain maturation changes the physiological structures of the brain, deleting early memories.
    b. Early memories are repressed due to anxiety.
    c. Memories are stored in a simple enactive mode, and symbolic mode is used to try to retrieve the memories.
    d. All of the above are correct.
18. Which of the following occurs at the youngest age?
    a. holophrasing
    b. melodic utterance
    c. babbling
    d. "scribble talk"
19. Which of the following is typical of a 2-year-old?
    a. has a vocabulary of more than 50 words
    b. commonly uses two-word phrases
    c. no longer engages in babbling
    d. all of the above
20. The 2-year-old's sense of competence is
    a. apparently unrelated to parenting style.
    b. aided by frequent parent-child communication.
    c. associated with infants being in environments without limitations.
    d. almost entirely determined by maturation.

Answers

1. C [LO-1,2].
2. A [LO-2].
3. C [LO-2].
4. D [LO-1].
5. B [LO-3].
6. A [LO-5].
7. C [LO-7].
8. B [LO-7].
9. D [LO-7].
10. C [LO-7].
11. A [LO-9].
12. D [LO-10].
13. B [LO-11].
14. A [LO-11].
15. D [LO-12].
16. C [LO-13].
17. D [LO-14].
18. C [LO-17].
19. D [LO-17].
20. B [LO-19].

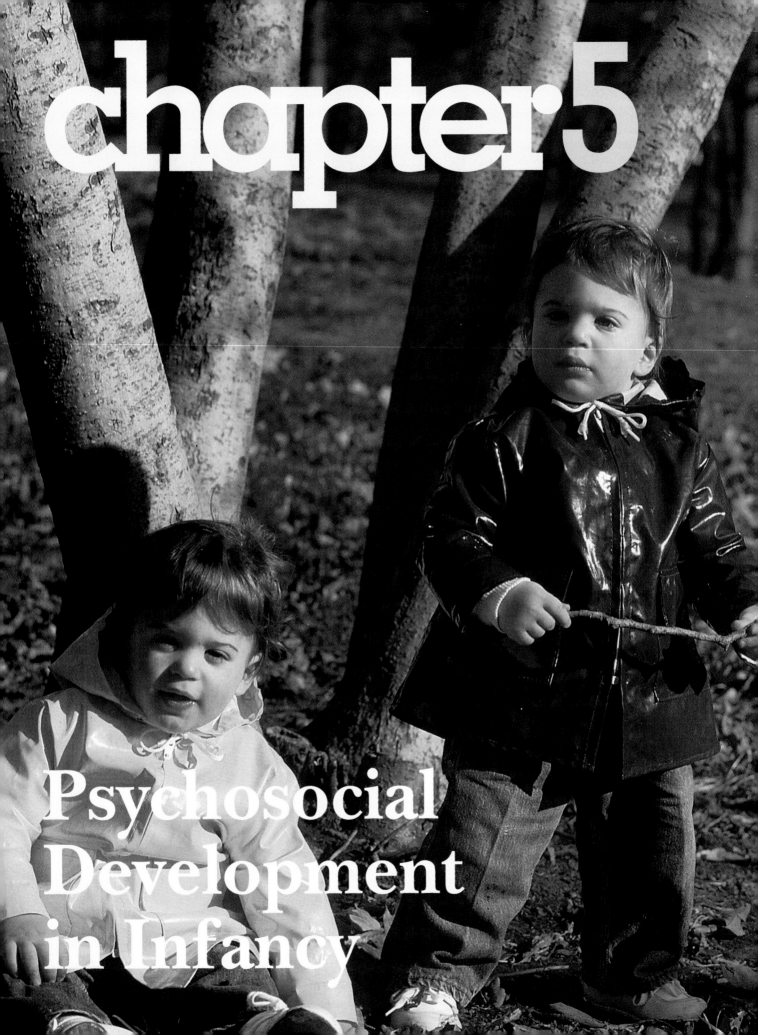

chapter 5

Psychosocial Development in Infancy

Learning Objectives

1. Describe the basic normal and abnormal cries and their role in infancy.
2. Explain the role of social smiles in infant development.
3. List the main aspects of emotional expression development during infancy, and discuss cultural and familial influences.
4. Compare and contrast the theories of emotional development proposed by Sroufe and Izard.
5. Discuss the general pattern of fear development and the role of culture and ethnic background in fear experiences.
6. Describe the major aspects of temperament, and compare "easy," "slow-to-warm," and "difficult" babies on parent-infant interactions and personality characteristics.
7. Explain Freud's ideas about the oral and anal stages of personality development, and give examples of possible adult personality traits due to fixations.
8. Compare and contrast the basic features of Freud's psychoanalytic theory and Erikson's psychosocial theory.
9. Describe the basic features of Erikson's first two psychosocial stages.
10. Compare and contrast the ideas of Mahler and Stern on how infants develop a sense of self.
11. Discuss the role of racial identity in individual development.
12. Define attachment, and compare and contrast the attachment theories of Bowlby, Schaffer and Emerson, and Mahler.
13. Describe the research conducted by Ainsworth, and differentiate between the three patterns of attachment that she found.
14. Explain how attachment influences parental relationships, peer relationships, and personality characteristics.
15. Discuss the difficulties involved in the transition to parenthood.
16. Compare and contrast maternal and paternal communication and interaction with infants.
17. Describe the general features of appropriate toys, art experiences, and books for infants.
18. Characterize the first peer relationships.

Chapter 4 described physical and cognitive development during the first 2 years of life. As you will discover in this chapter, however, infancy also involves tremendous changes in emotions, personality, and social interaction.

Exploring Your Own Development

When did you last cry? Did your favorite comic bring a smile to your face today? Emotional responses are part of our daily lives, but from where do they come, and what role do they play in our lives? Your first emotional reactions may be recorded in a baby book but not in your own memory. Asking your parents or others who knew you as a baby about your early emotional behavior can be insightful. Do these same people see parallels between your temperament as a baby and your characteristic emotional responses as an adult? This anecdotal information about yourself can help you to relate to the information presented in this chapter.

Emotional Development

Crying and Smiling

The Language of Cries

Cries are both an emotional expression and a primitive way to communicate. Therefore, babies use different crying styles to communicate different messages. The three basic cries—the *hunger cry,* the *pain cry,* and the *anger cry*—are described in Table 5.1 (Wolf, 1969). In addition, babies in extreme distress, such as babies suffering from malnutrition, exhibit distinctive cries related to their distress.

Caretaker Responses to Crying

Parents learn to respond differently to infants' various cries. For example, mothers of 4- to 6-month-olds who listened to taped cries of 12 unrelated infants made different assumptions based on the type of crying sounds. The tapes of the most irritating cries—those with longer pauses within and between cry sounds—were judged to be cries of difficult or spoiled babies (Lounsbury & Bales, 1982).

Parents are especially interested in dealing with nighttime crying. Among 9-month-olds, only 16 percent tend to sleep through the night; some of the remaining infants wake up but do not cry to wake up their parents (Anders, 1982). Many infants over a year old still exhibit frequent nocturnal spontaneous awakenings.

One study of 33 older babies who had about 14 spontaneous awakenings per week explored strategies for reducing nighttime crying. Both scheduled awakenings and systematic ignoring produced more immediate and long-term reduction in nighttime crying than parents keeping their regular routine. Scheduled awakenings involved having parents wake their infants to feed and console them at least 15 min before their typical spontaneous awakening times. Systematic ignoring involved parents allowing infants to "cry it out" without parental attention except to ensure the infants' physical well-being. Although systematic ignoring was the faster strategy, both it and scheduled

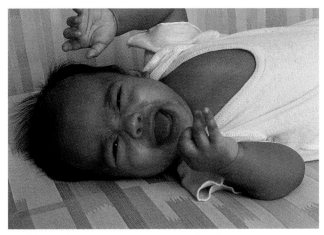

Parents, and most adults, are able to distinguish among hunger, anger, and pain cries.

Table 5.1
Types of Infant Cries

Three Basic Infant Cries

1. Anger cry: Loud and prolonged vocalization
2. Hunger cry (basic cry): Rhythmic and repetitive vocalization
3. Pain cry: Sudden onset, initial long cry, extended breath holding

Two Abnormal Infant Cries

1. Malnourished cry: Varies more in the basic pitches produced and is more distorted
2. Asphyxiated cry: Shorter cries, higher basic pitches, less stable cries

Source: Data from P. H. Wolf, "The Natural History of Crying and Other Vocalizations in Early Infancy" in *Determinants of Infant Behavior,* Vol. 4, 1969, edited by B. Fuss, Wiley and Sons, NY.

awakenings significantly reduced both awakenings and crying during the 8-week treatment period and at 3-week and 6-week follow-ups (Rickert & Johnson, 1988). Which strategy would you rather employ to deal with a nighttime crier?

Results of another study suggested that shifting infants' daily schedules can influence nighttime crying (Weissbluth, 1985). During the first 4 to 6 months, parents should probably respond quickly to nighttime crying. However, an older infant who displays "trained night crying" between midnight and 5 A.M. usually reduces his or her crying time if parents (1) wake the baby early, (2) do not allow naps after 11 A.M., (3) set bedtime at 9 P.M., (4) keep the baby's bedroom dark and quiet at night, and (5) do not attend to nighttime crying. Of course, if the baby shows difficulty in breathing, a pediatrician should be consulted.

For daytime crying, one parenting strategy that results in less crying is increasing the amount of time the baby is carried (Hunziker & Barr, 1986). When 6-week-olds were carried an additional 2 hr daily, their crying and fussing was reduced by 43 percent. Being carried in the arms or in a "baby backpack" seems to soothe infants.

Infants also learn to have some self-control over their own crying and negative emotions. Infant coping behaviors or **self-directed regulatory behaviors** when upset or unhappy include: looking away, self-comforting, and self-stimulation. Thumb sucking is an example of an effective coping strategy for infants (Tronick, 1989). What adult versions of these infant self-directed regulatory behaviors do you exhibit when upset?

Smiles

Although parents may perceive smiles in their newborn babies, neonatal smiles are largely reflexive, rather than an intentional response to parental attention. Vocalization is the first regular stimulus to produce genuine smiling; a little later, faces stimulate smiles in infants (Wolff, 1963).

Social smiles make their appearance between the fourth and sixth weeks (Trotter, 1983). One explanation for why they emerge around this time is that social smiles are largely a prewired biological development. Other psychologists focus on perceptual influences on the development of social smiles. Early on, primitive circle faces stimulate infant smiles; with age and experience, the human face becomes the most important discriminating stimulus for a smile response.

From a behavioristic perspective, social smiles may be the result of classical conditioning. That is, smiles become associated with pleasant experiences, such as feeding and cuddling. Or, in combination of operant conditioning and cognitive development, infants learn that their smiles influence the responses they get from adults and children.

Infants' ability to influence parents through smiling and other emotions seems to be important in the development of good parent-child relationships. Failure in this regard is associated with long-term negative emotions (e.g., depression) for infants (Tronick, 1989).

Facial Expressions

Biological Basis of Emotions

Some theorists believe that facial patterns evolved from biologically adaptive behaviors connected with basic activities, such as fighting, grooming, respiration, and vision (Campos et al., 1983). Charles Darwin (1872), for example, proposed that the look for disgust is universal among humans because it is rooted in the muscular configuration that people have when they are about to vomit. Darwin and others believed that the basic emotions were biologically determined but that cultural variables resulted in modifications of universal expression patterns (Adelmann & Zajonc, 1989; Campos, Barrett, Lamb, Goldsmith, & Stenberg, 1983).

Support for a biological basis for emotions comes from (1) research that has found that the basic emotions are recognizable across cultures, (2) the predictability of the emergence of specific emotions at various ages during infancy, (3) young infants' capability to use the same muscle movements as adults to express emotions, and (4) emotions becoming more complex and diverse with age as socialization influences subtle differences in emotions. Indeed, compared to older children and adults, infants are less likely to display complex combinations of emotional expressions and are unlikely to hide their emotions. The deliberate disguise of emotions likely does not develop until the second year, when infants are also capable of deferred imitation (Campos et al., 1983; Ekman & Oster, 1979; Tronick, 1989).

Emergence of Emotional Expressions

Although psychologists are not in full agreement about the timing of the emergence of various emotions, Table 5.2 provides some good estimates. Modern disagreements are usually over subtle differences in definitions, but early researchers differed especially about how many emotions were present at birth. Watson (1919) argued that there were three basic emotions: love, rage, and fear. Bridges (1932), however, proposed one initial emotion, called undifferentiated excitement or distress. Although current researchers do not believe that young infants express love, rage, and fear as completely developed emotions, they do separate neonatal expressions into more than just undifferentiated excitement.

Table 5.2
Emergence of Infant Emotional Expressions

Emotional Expressions	Approximate Emergence
Interest	Present at Birth
Neonatal Smile (a Spontaneous Half Smile)	
Startle Response	
Distress (in Response to Pain)	
Disgust (in Response to Unpleasant Smell or Taste)	
Social Smile	4 to 6 weeks
Anger	3 to 4 months
Surprise	
Joy	
Wariness	
Sadness	
Fear	5 to 7 months
Shame	6 to 8 months
Shyness	
Self-Awareness	
Contempt	Second Year of Life
Anxiety	
Guilt	

Source: Data from R. J. Trotter, "Baby Face" in *Psychology Today,* 20, (8), 56–62, 1983. From L. A. Sroufe, "Socioemotional Development" in *Handbook of Infant Development,* 1979, edited by J. Osofsky, Wiley & Sons, NY. From C. E. Izard, "On the Ontogenesis of Emotions and Emotion-Cognition Relationships in Infancy" in *The Development of Affect,* 1978, edited by M. Lee and L. Rosenblum, Plenum Publishing, NY.

Mothers believe that their 1-month-olds can express a wide range of emotions. In one study, 99 percent thought that their infants could express interest, and 95 percent thought that they could express joy. In addition, 74 percent thought their infants capable of surprise, while the percentages were 58 for fear and 34 for sadness (Campos, Barrett, Lamb, Goldsmith, & Stenberg, 1983).

In another study, a majority of mothers thought that their infants had displayed 6 of 11 different emotions during the first 3 months (see the table). By the end of the first year, most mothers thought that their infants had displayed all but three of the emotions—disgust, contempt, and guilt (Johnson, Emde, & Pannabecker, 1982).

Beliefs about infants' emotions affect how parents and other adults respond to babies. For example, infants who smile a lot are picked up and held more often. Of course, influence is a two-way street. The emotional characteristics of caretakers interact with the emotional characteristics of infants. Mothers with high levels of anger and punitiveness have more negative effects on irritable 3-month-olds than mothers with less irritable natures. The combination of irritable child and irritable mother means more anger, less compliance, and less confidence as a 2-year-old toddler (Crockenberg, 1987).

Effective parents pay attention to cues in their infants' emotional expressions—especially direction of gaze—and modify their behavior to accommodate the babies' moods (Papousek, & Papousek, 1987; Tronick 1989). Mutually coordinated parent-infant emotional communication (*emotional synchronicity*) is associated with positive development. Depressed or indifferent parents exhibit poorly timed affective displays or provide negative messages to infants. These babies develop high levels of negative affect (Tronick, 1989).

Parents' Perceptions of Infant Emotions During First 3 Months	
Emotions	**Percentage of Parents Who Think Emotion Is Exhibited by Infant**
Interest	99%
Joy	95%
Anger	84%
Surprise	74%
Distress	68%
Fear	58%
Sadness	34%
Disgust	22%
Contempt	16%
Shyness	9%
Guilt	0%

From W. F. Johnson, "Maternal Perception of Infant Emotion From Birth Through 18 Months" in *Infant Behavior and Development,* 5, 313–322, Table 1, p. 316, 1982. Copyright © Ablex Publishing Corporation, Norwood, NJ.

At any rate, during the first 6 months of life, infants are already able to display a wide range of emotions. In one study, infants from 5 to 9 months old accurately displayed joy or surprise to a jack-in-the-box toy, sadness or anger to injections from a doctor, and fear to being approached by a stranger (Izard, Huebner, Resser, McGinness, & Dougherty, 1980). Infants from 10 to 12 months old exhibited happiness during peek-a-boo games, surprise to both a toy-switch task and a vanishing-object task, and fear to both the visual cliff and stranger approach situations (Hiatt, Campos, & Emde, 1979).

Infant Interpretations of Others' Emotional Expressions

How well do parents and infants understand each other, and how does emotional expression interpretation affect parent-child interaction? The "Exploring the Parent/Child Relationship" feature describes parents' interpretations of infant emotion. Just as importantly, however, infants early on make differential responses to adult emotional displays. Although recognition of facial expressions improves slowly over the first 2 years and is quite rudimentary, even young

Much earlier than the arrival of language, infants add emotions like fear, anger, shyness, and joy to their capabilities.

Table 5.3
Ten-Week-Old Infants' Reactions to
Emotions Displayed by Their Mothers

Emotion Displayed by Mothers/Babies' Reactions	
Happiness	Infants initially reacted with joy. Over four presentations, infants became less expressive of joy or happiness and displayed more interest. Infants faced forward toward their mothers during this emotion.
Anger	Infants increased their physical movement. Over four presentations, infant interest decreased. Infants often looked toward the side during this emotion.
Sadness	Infants predominantly responded with "mouthing" behaviors, such as lip and tongue sucking and pushing the lips in and out. These behaviors probably were self-soothing ones. Infants tended to gaze downward during these sessions.

From C. A. Malatesta and C. E. Izard, "The Ontogenesis of Human Social Signals" from "Biological Imperative to Symbol Utilization" in *The Psychobiology of Affective Development,* 1984 edited by N. A. Fox and R. J. Davidson. Copyright © 1984 Lawrence Erlbaum Associates, Hillside, NJ.

Table 5.4
Effects of Mothers' Expression on 1-Year-Old Infants'
Behavior on the Visual Cliff Apparatus

Mother's Expression	Percentage of Infants Crossing Deep End of Visual Cliff
Interest	73%
Sadness	33
Anger	11
Fear	0

Source: Data from J. F. Score, et al., "Maternal Emotional Signaling: Its Effects on the Visual Cliff Behavior of 1-Year-Olds," in *Developmental Psychology,* 21, 195–200, 1985.

infants can perceptually discriminate between two faces with different expressive content. This discrimination exists even though infants under 4 months probably lack visual skills to really recognize facial expressions and to examine both internal and external facial features (Nelson, 1987).

Ten-week-olds exhibit different reactions when their mothers display various facial expressions. As shown in Table 5.3, the emotions of happiness, anger, and sadness all produce distinctive responses from babies. A happy display by the mother is followed by the infant's direct gaze at the mother; this response allows further infant perception of the happy maternal expression and also reinforces the mother for her positive expression. On the other hand, a baby avoids maternal anger expressions by looking away and tries self-soothing in response to maternal sad expressions (Malatesta & Izard, 1984). Other studies (e.g., Weinberg, 1989) have found the same pattern of gaze direction and emotions in normal parent-infant interactions. Are there parallels for how adults respond to these same emotional facial displays?

In addition to having the capacity to distinguish among several emotional expressions displayed by adults, infants appear to use this information to guide their behavior. A visual cliff study in which mothers were stationed at the deep side of the apparatus found that maternal expression influenced infants' willingness to cross the deep end (Sorce, Emde, Campos, & Klinnert, 1985). As shown in Table 5.4, mothers asked to pose with an expression of interest influenced the majority of the babies to cross the deep side. A minority of babies made the crossing when mothers posed with angry or sad expressions; no infants crossed when their mothers looked fearful. In other words, infants can use the positive emotional expressions of significant others to override their own reluctance to cross the deep end of the visual cliff.

Emotional Development Theories

Sroufe's Theory

Sroufe's theory of emotional development states that neonates have precursors of at least three emotional dimensions: wariness-fear, rage-anger, and pleasure-joy. According to Sroufe (1979), what changes with time is that infants improve their cognitive level, develop systems to express emotions (e.g., become biologically capable of laughter), and develop new coping capacities (e.g., develop locomotion). Growth in these three areas allows infants to develop more complex emotions.

Sroufe also stated that true emotions require a differentiated sense of the self, which develops at approximately 9 months. At 4 months, wariness appears, and soon after, fear, but anxiety does not occur until approximately 12 months, and shame emerges around 18 months.

Izard's Theory

Izard (1978) proposed that newborns have several quite discrete emotions, such as interest, disgust, distress, and startle, that are based on specific facial displays. Izard also suggested that more complex emotions develop along with perceptual, cognitive, and motor developmental changes but that these developmental changes are not the cause of more complex emotions. Rather, emotions emerge as they become adaptive in living.

According to Izard, joy emerges sometime during the first 3 months, as infants develop the capacity to discriminate social from nonsocial objects. By 4 months, infants also display anger and surprise. During the second half of the first year, according to Izard, fear and shyness emerge. The emergence of fear becomes important in facilitating the attachment system, and shyness is a result of the development of the sense of self.

Development of Fear

Emergence of Fear

When Charles Darwin's son turned 2 1/4 years old, he suddenly developed a strong fear toward zoo animals. The change in his son's emotions led Darwin (1877) to suggest

From eight months on, infants often exhibit symptoms of stranger anxiety, such as this classic clinging behavior.

that unlearned prepotent fears are particular patterns of fear that occur in sequence at certain ages, regardless of experiences.

For example, human infants show little fear before 6 months, when height fear emerges (around the age when crawling begins). Height fear often increases when walking develops. Most infants develop fears of separation and of strange adults sometime between 8 and 22 months. Fear of strange children occurs later, and fear of animals and the dark still later. Similar age of emergence occurs cross culturally and with little influence from style of child-rearing (Marks, 1987).

Fear as a Stable Trait

Aspects of fear appear to be fairly stable, although some ethnic differences may exist. For example, on average, Chinese-American newborns are calmer, less emotional, and more easily placated than are European-American newborns. The Chinese-American babies remain more passive when a cloth is placed over their face; they exhibit less activity, vocalization, and irritability. Between 12 and 29 months, these same babies are more wary and inhibited around unfamiliar peers, and they smile and vocalize less to human masks (Marks, 1987).

Other studies have found that, throughout infancy, babies show consistent levels of timidity to novel toys and to social situations (Jacklin, Maccoby, & Doering, 1983;

Kagan, 1982b). These individual differences in fearfulness seem to persist from infancy into the school years. One study found fairly consistent levels of fearfulness from 1 month to 8 1/2 years, especially for boys (Bronson, 1969).

In another study, 3-year-olds who were extremely inhibited were easily dominated by peers. By first grade, these youngsters typically withdrew from social interactions, avoided dangerous activities, had low aggressiveness levels, and usually conformed to parental standards. From ages 6 to 10, they tended to be socially timid and avoided sports. The fearful boys became adolescents who avoided masculine activities and adults who infrequently chose masculine activities (Marks, 1987).

Stranger Fear

At 3 to 4 months of age, infants initially smile at a stranger and then sometimes stare at the stranger for up to half a minute. After staring, these infants often frown, breathe heavily, and start to cry. By 6 1/2 months, all infants are aware of strangers; three fourths seem wary, and half get noticeably upset. Over the next few months, gaze avoidance is a common response to strangers (Bronson, 1972).

Stranger fear is a common response by infants from 6 months to 2 years of age, regardless of culture (Marks, 1987). During this time period, infants are scared of strange adults but show little fear of infant strangers and children strangers (Trotter, 1987b). In contrast, infants do not fear their mother acting strangely. For example, they do not seem scared if their mother crawls on the floor, wears a mask, or walks like a penguin (Sroufe, 1974). Therefore, these infants fear strange humans rather than novel stimuli or strange behavior from a familiar person.

During this same time period, infants tend to cry when their usual caretaker physically departs. This **separation anxiety** peaks at from 9 to 13 months of age and gradually disappears at around 30 months. During prolonged separation, the typical course of infant response is to protest, detach, and exhibit despair (Marks, 1987).

guided review

1. The three basic cries are called the _____ cry, the _____ cry, and the _____ cry.
2. Strategies such as systematic awakening, adjusting daily schedules, and systematic ignoring can reduce nighttime crying; an effective way to reduce daytime crying is to increase the amount of time the infant is _____.
3. Some theorists, like Darwin, believe that facial patterns evolved from _____ adaptive behaviors—for example, that disgust is rooted in the muscular configuration of being about to _____; as such, emotional expressions are viewed as being _____ to all cultures.
4. The emotions that emerge in the third to fourth month are _____, _____, _____, _____, and _____, with fear developing a couple of months later.
5. Shame, shyness, and self-awareness develop in the sixth through eighth months, while _____, _____, and _____ are emotional expressions that do not emerge until the second year.

6. When a mother's expression is _____, the infant gazes directly at her, but the infant looks away when the mother appears _____ and tries self-soothing if the mother looks _____.

7. Sroufe feels that true emotions require a differentiated sense of the _____, which develops at about 9 months.

8. In Izard's theory of emotional development, _____ develops when infants can differentiate between social and nonsocial objects, the emergence of fear facilitates the _____ process, and shyness is a result of the development of a sense of self.

9. On average, _____ babies are calmer, less emotional, and more easily placated than European-American newborns.

10. From 6 months to 2 years, _____ fear is a common response by infants, regardless of culture, and this response is directed more at adults than at children; during this time, _____ also occurs, and infants cry when their usual caretaker physically departs.

answers

1. hunger; pain; anger [LO-1]. **2.** carried (or: held) [LO-1]. **3.** biologically; vomit; universal [LO-3]. **4.** anger; surprise; joy; wariness; sadness [LO-3]. **5.** contempt; anxiety; guilt [LO-3]. **6.** happy; angry; sad [LO-3]. **7.** self [LO-4]. **8.** joy; attachment [LO-4]. **9.** Chinese-American [LO-5]. **10.** stranger; separation anxiety [LO-5].

Temperament

If motivation is the "why" of behavior and abilities are the "what" of behavior, then **temperament** is the "how" of behavior. Temperament, a set of inborn personality traits, appears early in life and creates individual differences in arousal, primary emotions, activity level, and persistence. These characteristics seem to have more stability than other aspects of the personality (Goldsmith et al., 1987).

Temperament Classifications

Temperament has been classified in many ways. Goldsmith et al. (1987) divided aspects of temperament into activity, reactivity, emotionality, and sociability. Activity aspects deal with intensity, vigor, pace of movement, speech, and thought. Reactivity aspects are approach-withdrawal tendencies and thresholds for response, attention, interest, and persistence. Emotionality aspects involve crying, soothability, frustration, laughing, smiling, and expressions of anger, sadness, fear, joy, pleasure, disgust, and surprise. Sociability aspects are preferences for being with others and sharing.

Thomas, Chess, and Birch (1968) proposed nine areas of temperament, which can be measured by the Baby Temperament Scales (Huitt & Ashton, 1982):

1. Activity level—High activity level may be exhibited by kicking and splashing during bathing and squirming during diapering.

2. Rhythmicity of biological functions—High rhythmicity is shown by regular sleeping, eating, and toileting habits.

3. Adaptability—Highly adaptable infants can adjust to new routines in feeding, to visiting unfamiliar homes,

to interruptions to change diapers or clothing, and to sleeping in unfamiliar cribs.

4. Approach—High approach is shown by interest in visiting places, examining new toys, and trying new foods.

5. Sensory threshold—Sensory threshold temperament is shown by reactions to loud noises, food temperatures, and dirty diapers.

6. Intensity of mood expression—High levels may result in loud crying when restless, or squealing and laughing during play.

7. Predominant quality of mood—Babies differ in how much they smile and laugh or in how fussy they are.

8. Persistence or attention span—This quality is shown in ability to play by oneself for half an hour, in wanting to continue peek-a-boo games, or in enjoying a favorite food for some time.

9. Distractibility—Distractible infants can be settled by distraction with toys, soon forget that you have removed an item of interest, and will play with a toy for awhile when hungry.

These nine aspects are grouped into three clusters, and babies fitting these clusters are labeled easy, difficult, and slow-to-warm-up babies (Thomas, et al., 1968).

Easy, Difficult, and Slow-To-Warm-Up Babies

So Who Doesn't Want an Easy Baby?

The basic descriptions of easy, difficult, and slow-to-warm-up babies are provided in Table 5.5. As you can see, some babies do not fit neatly into any cluster, but of babies who can be categorized, easy babies are the most common. Easy babies are those that keep regular sleeping and eating schedules; adapt fairly readily to new schedules, activities, and people; and approach people and the environment with positive emotions. These are the babies that make parenthood look easy.

About 15 percent of babies show some irregularity, a withdrawal pattern, and initial negative responses to new situations and people but gradually warm up to the surroundings. Parents may feel especially competent with slow-to-warm-up infants because nurturing attempts seem to help their babies be comfortable. These are the babies that make parents seem effective.

The Difficult Baby

On the other hand, about 1 in 10 babies is labeled difficult and reacts strongly and negatively to novelty in the environment. Difficult babies have irregular sleeping and eating schedules and exhibit long periods of intense and negative emotions. These infants are more fearful of strangers than easygoing infants (Berberian & Snyder, 1982), they have more injuries requiring stitches (Carey, 1970), they require more care during the night (Keener, Zeanah, & Anders, 1988), and they have more difficulty adjusting to later-born siblings (Dunn, Kendrick, & Mac-Namee, 1981).

Table 5.5
Three Temperament Styles

Easy Child	Difficult Child	Slow-To-Warm-Up Child
40% of babies	*10% of babies*	*15% of babies*
• Regularity of biology	• Irregular biology	• Irregular biology but not as intense a reaction as difficult child
• Positive approach to new situations and people	• Negative withdrawal reaction to new situations and people	• Withdraws quietly or with mild fussing
• Regular sleeping and eating schedules	• Irregular sleeping and eating schedules	• More regular in sleeping and eating schedules than difficult baby
• Willingness to try new foods	• Accepts new foods slowly	• Mildly negative initial reaction to novel stimuli, such as new food, place, school, person
• Smiles at strangers	• Suspicious of strangers	• Slowly warms up to strangers
• Adapts to new school	• Hard adaptation to new school	• Gradually develops liking and interest for new stimuli, experiences, and people after repeated and unpressured exposure
• Minimal fussing to most frustrations	• Frustration leads to tantrums	• Mildly intense reactions that can be positive or negative
• Fast adaptation to new routines	• Difficulty adjusting to new routines	
• Mild to moderate mood intensity, and usually positive	• Frequent crying periods and also laughs loudly	
	• Intense moods that are frequently negative	

Source: Data from S. Chess and A. Thomas, *Know Your Child,* 1987, Basic Books, New York, NY. From H. H. Goldsmith et al., "Roundtable: What is Temperament? Four Approaches" in *Child Development,* 58, 505–529, 1987.

Difficult babies are not the result of parental personality, home environment, or parent-child interactions. In other words, parents do *not* create the difficult baby patterns (Chess & Thomas, 1987; Daniels, Plomin, & Greenhalgh, 1984). Finding parenting strategies that work with difficult babies is important because difficult temperaments are correlated with childhood and early adulthood problems (Thomas, Chess, & Korn, 1982).

However, it is hard for parents of difficult babies to do good parenting because the tendency is to interact less with these babies. One study found that even hospital nurses paid less attention to 2-day-old difficult babies than they did to other infants (Breitmayer & Riccuiti, 1983). Another study found that babies who were labeled as difficult received less contact from their mothers than did other babies at 10 months of age (Dunn, 1975). Similar results were found among Japanese mothers (Miyake, Chen, & Campos, 1985).

Perhaps the first step in helping parents to deal with difficult babies is to change the label to something less judgmental—"challenging" babies or "intense" infants might be preferable. The second step is to reassure parents that they did not cause their baby's irregular temperament but can learn strategies to alleviate intense responses. Finally, these parents have to learn to live with the stares they may get from others when their child has a public temper tantrum.

Parenting Babies With Different Temperaments

Different Timetables
All parents, not just those with difficult infants, can become better parents by learning how to adjust and adapt to their infants' temperaments. They must realize, however,

that each dimension of temperamental variability has a different developmental time course.

At birth, parents notice differences in distress responses. From 2 to 3 months of age, individual differences in positive emotions become quite noticeable. From 4 to 6 months, approach and avoidance responses emerge as the result of continuing brain development. From 6 months on, parents are likely to notice an increase in the child's ability to withhold or inhibit responses (Goldsmith et al., 1987).

In addition, the advantages and disadvantages of a particular temperament can change as a child gets older. Chess and Thomas (1987, p. 37) wrote,

> *The specific effect the child's temperament has on a child's behavior and on her parents will also vary from one age period to another. High distractibility may be an advantage in a young child, making it easier for parents to divert her from potentially dangerous activities. At a later age, however, this same distractibility may make her forget prearranged appointments or activities, as she gets diverted on the way home or on the way downstairs to breakfast.*

A Few Parenting Guidelines
In the 1950s, there was an attitude of *mal de mere,* or scapegoating the mother for the child's behavior. Today, psychologists recognize that children's individual differences are an important component of the parent-child interaction. As such, parents need to adjust their parenting to match their child's unique makeup (Chess & Thomas, 1987).

For example, parents who have high activity level infants should hold their infants firmly. When they take these children on long trips, parents should minimize discomfort by making frequent stops. When these children are taken to

Parents learn to copy and modify their child's temperament.

concerts or movies, parents should sit near the back so that it is convenient to leave the audience if necessary.

Parents of children who are high in irregularity find that their young children are unpredictable about naps and nighttime sleeping. Yet, they need to respond with a combination of consistency and patience.

Parents of children who are high in withdrawal or who have low adaptability need to give their children periods of adjustment to change, quiet exposure to new events, and reassurance with each change. These parents also need to persist quietly, in spite of children's protests, because exposing their youngsters to new experiences is important.

Long-Term Effects of Temperament

Effects of Temperament on Later Personality
Although it affects behavior most during infancy, temperament has lifelong influences. In later development, temperament's largest role is in behaviors in novel situations (Goldsmith et al., 1987). When confronted with a new situation, how do you characteristically react? If you can recognize a pattern to your responses, you can see the effect of temperament.

Shyness
One long-term effect of temperament on personality is **shyness,** influenced by biological tendencies toward *behavioral inhibition*. Ten to fifteen percent of youngsters exhibit

unusually high heart rates, pupil dilation, salivary cortisol levels, and norepinephrine in response to mild mental stress. These youngsters are overly cautious in unfamiliar situations and shy around strangers. They are hypervigilant and have "stage fright" (Asher, 1987). Of high behaviorally inhibited infants, 40 percent become less inhibited by 5 1/2 years of age, and 10 percent become more timid. The best parenting strategy seems to be to protect these youngsters from high stress but to push them gently into new experiences (Asher, 1987).

guided review

11. According to Goldsmith et al. (1987), _____ is a fairly stable, inborn style of activity, reactivity, emotionality, and sociability.
12. Thomas, Chess, and Birch described three types of temperaments in infants, with the most common being the _____ baby, a second type being the _____ baby, and the most challenging temperament being the _____ baby.
13. Among newborns, temperament differences are first noticed by parents in differences in _____ responses; several months later, individual differences in _____ emotions are quite noticeable; at 4 to 6 months, temperament influences approach-avoidance responses, and later on, differences are noticeable in ability to _____ responses.
14. Biological tendencies toward behavioral inhibition affect the personality style of _____.

answers

11. temperament [LO-6]. 12. "easy"; "slow-to-warm-up"; "difficult" [LO-6]. 13. distress; positive; inhibit (or: withhold) [LO-6]. 14. shyness [LO-6].

Personality

Throughout this book, you will view personality development through various psychological perspectives, but in this chapter, the focus will be on the psychodynamic perspectives of Sigmund Freud and Erik Erikson.

Freud's First Two Psychosexual Stages
Sigmund Freud (1856–1939), a European medical doctor specializing in neurology, is an appropriate theorist for this chapter because his psychoanalytic theory emphasizes the importance of the first few years of life on adult personality. Today, few psychologists believe the Freudian position that the basic adult personality is formed by the age of 6, but they do believe that early childhood has significant impact on overall development. Freud was instrumental in getting modern psychologists to attend to infancy and early childhood. Refer to Appendix A for a summary of the main points of Freudian psychoanalytic theory.

Freud thought that personality development occurred in five **psychosexual stages,** which he named for the region of the body in which libido (the pleasure-seeking

Table 5.6
Freud's First Two Psychosexual Stages of Personality Development

Stage	Age	Source of Pleasure	Possible Personality Traits If Fixations Occur
Oral	0 to 1 year	Sucking, biting, chewing	Dependent, gullible, generous, argumentative, sarcastic
Anal	1 to 3 years	Elimination and retention of feces	Excessively shy, clean, shameful, impulsive, stingy, stubborn, hostile, aggressive

Source: Jensen, L. C., & Kingston, M. (1986). *Parenting* (Table 3.1, p. 61). New York: Holt, Rinehart & Winston.

drive) is most expressed. The first two psychosexual stages—the **oral stage** and the **anal stage**—take place during infancy (see Table 5.6)

Oral Stage

During the first year of life, the mouth is the major *erogenous zone,* the body area of most pleasure. The major pleasurable activities are sucking and biting. Freud believed that, to achieve healthy personality development, infants must receive the proper amount of gratification. Too much gratification or too little gratification results in *fixations,* or permanent influences on personality.

Therefore, a person fixated in the oral stage might become a gullible person—that is, a person who is willing to swallow anything he or she is told. Or, if a baby gets the wrong amount of biting pleasure, the baby may become sarcastic, argumentative, or a member of a debate team.

Anal Stage

At the end of the first year, the baby enters the anal stage, in which urination and bowel movements become the primary sources of pleasure. Over the next 2 years, pleasure in bathroom behaviors, a new need for autonomy, and parental expectations for toilet training interact to influence personality development.

Freud believed that parents who strictly enforced early toilet training made their infants so anxious that they became constipated and "held back" on their bowel movements. He believed that these babies grew up having *anal retentive personalities,* with the characteristics of being stingy, obsessively tidy, and obstinate. On the other hand, according to Freud, parents who encouraged their infant's toilet training through affection and rewards taught their children to feel creative and to value their own productions, resulting in artistic children.

Determining whether Freud was right about the effects of the oral and anal stages is difficult because good research on his ideas is impossible. His theory is also frustrating because, while it allows individuals to know as adults if they have been fixated at different stages, it fails to tell parents what is the right amount of gratification to avoid fixation. Freudian theory seems to scapegoat mothers for their children's faults.

successful study tip

Successful Study Tip: Freud's Psychosexual Stages

Which of the following approaches works best to help you remember Freud's five stages:

1. Create an acrostic out of the initial letters of Oral, Anal, Phallic, Latent, and Genital: Only a Psychologist Looks Good.
2. Use meaningful phrases for each of the stages:
   "Babies like to eat in the oral stage."
   "Toilet training often coincides with the anal stage."
   "Preschoolers develop gender identity in the phallic stage."
   "The early school years are the latent stage."
   "Adolescence and puberty coincide with the genital stage."

Make a note to review this "Successful Study Tip" when the phallic, latent, and genital stages are discussed in later chapters.

Erikson's First Two Psychosocial Stages

Erik Erikson (1963) believed that his psychosocial theory was a compatible extension of Freud's psychoanalytic theory. Whereas Freud emphasized conflicts arising from biological needs, Erikson emphasized conflicts arising from social interactions. Like Freud, Erikson posed development in stages, but his **psychosocial stages** provide for important crises throughout the lifespan, rather than only early childhood.

Another important difference is that Erikson's theory provides more flexibility for correcting early problems through later supportive interactions. While Erikson was learning psychoanalysis, he found himself asking, "If we can know what can go wrong in each stage, can we say what should have gone and can go right?" (Erikson, 1987a). Perhaps because he did not develop his theory from patients as Freud did, but rather engaged in longitudinal and cross-cultural studies of "normal" children and developed biographies of great individuals, Erikson spoke more about healthy personality development than Freud. Turn to Appendix A following Chapter 1 for a summary of Erikson's theory.

Two of Erikson's eight psychosocial stages occur during infancy. Table 5.7 presents information about these first two stages.

Table 5.7
Erikson's First Two Psychosocial Stages

First Stage: Basic Trust Versus Basic Mistrust

	Trust	Mistrust
Characteristics	Feeling of inner goodness, reliance on others to provide effortless feeding and sleeping, trust in one's ability to cope, a sense that the world is "okay"	Feelings of anxiety, helpless rage and pain; feeling deprived or abandoned; dissatisfaction; depression or hopelessness
Adult behaviors contributing to the sense	Consistent caregiving; sensitive attention to baby's needs; solid, trustworthy approach to parenting	Inconsistent, neglectful caregiving; delaying gratification; withdrawing when baby needs attention from caregivers

Second Stage: Autonomy Versus Shame and Doubt

	Autonomy	Shame	Doubt
Characteristics	Sense of inner goodness, pride, and self-control; confidence	Sense of foolish exposure; sense of being too visible, of wanting to withdraw from sight	Sense of inner badness, of wanting to look back or behind
Adult behaviors contributing to the sense	Encouragement to do and try things independently	Suppressing self-expression, punishing with shame, overcontrolling	Critical of child's self-help attempts, overprotective

From L. C. Jensen and M. Kingston, *Parenting,* Table 3.1, p. 61, 1986.

Erik Erikson proposed eight psychosocial stages in a lifetime. Two of these stages, trust versus mistrust and autonomy versus shame and doubt, occur during infancy.

Basic Trust Versus Basic Mistrust

The first crisis of infancy is **basic trust versus basis mistrust,** which Erikson believed was learned mainly from maternal care. If parents provide good nurturant care and a sense of safety, infants develop a sense of the world's goodness and opportunities, an optimism about life's possibilities, and hope, the first psychosocial strength. Infancy, however, also must contain experiences that contribute to some development of mistrust. As Erikson put it:

> *Unavoidable pain and delay of satisfaction, however, and inexorable weaning make this stage also prototypical for a sense of abandonment and helpless rage. (Erikson & Erikson, 1987)*

Neglected and abused infants have many experiences that lead to the development of basic mistrust, and the resulting pessimism and hopelessness can lead to a life of isolation, helplessness, depression, and destructiveness. However, Erikson suggested that positive experiences after infancy may help individuals to resolve unhappy earlier crises. A kind and supportive day-care worker may be able to undo some of the damage caused by inappropriate infancy care.

Autonomy Versus Shame and Doubt

Just as the first psychosocial stage is parallel to Freud's oral stage, Erikson's second stage—**autonomy versus shame and doubt**—corresponds to Freud's anal stage. This second psychosocial stage is influenced by the toddler's muscular maturation, locomotor capabilities, beginning verbalizations, and ability to divide the world into categories, such as "yes and no," "good and bad," "right and wrong," and "yours and mine." All of these new abilities set the stage for the crisis of autonomy versus loss of self-control and self-esteem, resulting in shame or doubt.

Successful Study Tip: Erikson's Psychosocial Stages

Erikson's stages are complex, with several terms to remember. Try creating a vivid visual image to help you organize the stages. Picture yourself building a block wall. On the foundation, see the words "basic trust versus basic mistrust." Mentally lay the next layer of blocks with the words "autonomy versus shame and doubt." In succeeding chapters, as you learn about more of Erikson's stages, mentally visualize adding new layers to your wall.

Table 5.8
Havighurst's Nine Developmental Tasks for Infancy and Early Childhood

1. Reaching physiological stability
2. Consuming solid foods
3. Learning to talk
4. Learning to walk
5. Forming simple concepts of social and physical reality
6. Building emotional relationships with parents, siblings, and other persons
7. Controlling defecation and urination
8. Learning to distinguish right from wrong and developing a conscience
9. Learning sex differences and sexual modesty

From *Developmental Tasks and Education*, 3d edition by Robert J. Havighurst. Copyright © 1972 by Longman Publishing Group.

Toilet training is one developmental task during this stage that contributes to the toddler's sense of self-control, and other early developmental tasks are provided in Table 5.8 (Havighurst, 1972). All of these tasks provide an opportunity to develop self-control. Toddlers who have a sense that they can do things independently and who feel good about themselves build a confidence in their free will.

However, parents who overcontrol toddlers' behavior, suppress toddlers' self-expression, and use shame teach their children to feel foolishly exposed and conscious of being looked at disapprovingly. Overprotective parents and those critical of children's self-help attempts can develop a lasting sense of doubt in their children.

A Sense of Self

To start to develop a sense of **self,** the infant must be capable of separating self from other people and the environment. While this task begins in infancy, the development of a sense of self is a complex and lifelong task (Kohut, 1977).

Origins of the Self

When in infancy does the origin of self occur? Anna Freud (1965) thought that self-differentiation first developed after the fourth month, when object constancy abilities allowed the primary caretaker to be perceived as an independent person. Chess and Thomas (1987) suggested that self-differentiation occurs at least by the third month, as evidenced by how young infants gaze at their own hands, babble sounds repeatedly, and have expectations for how people should behave. Both Mahler (1968) and Stern (1985) also have proposed contrasting theories about the origin of the self.

Mahler's Theory of Separation-Individuation

According to Mahler's **theory of separation-individuation,** three distinct stages occur during the first 4 years of life. The first stage, the *autistic phase,* occurs during the first 2 months. During this phase, infants can only distinguish between tension and relief, pain and pleasure, and good and bad feelings. Mothers become associated with tension reduction. The task of the autistic phase is for infants to learn to distinguish self-regulated tension reduction.

From the second to fifth month, according to Mahler, infants are in the *symbiotic phase,* marked by rudimentary affective (emotional) exchanges. Connections made between intrapsychic processes and externally

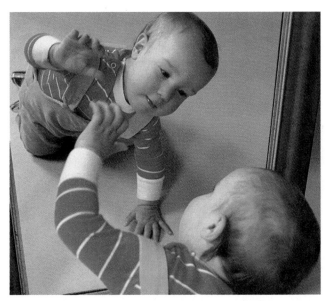

The ability to recognize one's image emerges gradually.

observed characteristics affect all subsequent social relationships and memory organization.

Mahler's third, and longest, stage is called *separation-individuation phase* and lasts past the third birthday. According to Mahler, this stage involves a "hatching out" of the self or a second birth process—the birth of the psychological self.

Stern's Developing Sense of Self

By contrast, Stern (1985) suggested that there is not symbiotic or undifferentiated phase of life since infants are biologically predesigned to distinguish between themselves and others. Instead, he proposed four accumulative stages, summarized in Table 5.9. In Stern's model, infants first have separate, unrelated experiences that they learn to integrate and organize. Next, they come to see themselves as having control over their actions and as

Exploring Cultural Diversity: Racial Identity

What is your racial identity? What do you label yourself, and what does your label mean to you? How did you learn what your label meant, and what influences your feelings about your racial identity? If you are a European American, you might experience different feelings if you say that you are White, Caucasian, or a honkie. You have also learned that this racial identity entitles you to consider yourself a majority American and that persons of your race have experienced less prejudice, been presented with more opportunities, and have more economic and political power than other American racial groups. Whatever your racial identity, that identity influences the opportunities, barriers, obligations, and self-esteem that you experience.

The United States may be referred to as the "melting pot," but many racial/ethnic groups have retained their identity within the larger culture. Your own racial identity may have changed over the years due to societal changes outside of you and to your own personal changes as you have grown older. For example, before the 1960s, most Americans with African ancestry referred to themselves as Negroes. In the 1960s, young Negroes led the way to establishing a new racial identity label by using Black American. This label switch helped to overcome negative stereotypes from other races and to build more positive images within the race. "Black Pride" and "Black Power" became popular statements of racial identity. However, in this struggle to gain a more positive racial identity, some misunderstandings occurred between younger and older

African Americans. Some younger individuals blamed their elders for "putting up" with the earlier stereotypes. Older individuals sometimes were upset with the militant nature of the Black Pride movement or thought that their offspring were expecting changes too fast.

Interestingly, Black leader Jesse Jackson has suggested that Blacks begin to use the term *African American* instead of *Black American* because *African American* allows his race to incorporate a historical identity, rather than a racial identity based solely on skin color. What advantages and disadvantages do you see for the term *African American?*

Although examples of racial identity differ by one's racial background, each individual must deal with circumstances based on race. In some families, direct messages are given about one's own race and other races. In other families, children learn racial identity by how family members interact with their own and other races. Racial identity training begins in infancy but is influenced during the entire lifespan—by peer groups, by school teachers, by identity issues in adolescence, and by adult career and political opportunities. Parent-child interactions involving racial identity include the following:

- Some adults that struggled as young people to have racial equality fail to teach their children about their struggles. Therefore, their children do not understand their racial history.
- Some families who adopt outside of their race may fail to provide the adopted children with a rich cultural

racial history. Adopted children benefit from interaction with both their adoptive families' culture and their biological racial culture.
- Parents who have not accepted their own racial identity may make their children feel rejected or unloved by the parents' devaluation of their race.
- Children may not be taught how to deal with teachers, friends, or strangers who devalue them because of skin color or other racial group characteristics.
- Parents may fail to help children learn to value other ethnic backgrounds while feeling proud of their own racial identity.

Whatever your racial background, race influences how you experience the world. Whether or not parents strategically think about what they want to tell their children about race, the messages are there. They begin early and continue for one's entire life. Emphasizing the importance of one's racial identity without denying the contributions of other racial groups is difficult. Parents need to be able to build pride in racial identity while still promoting universal characteristics of humankind. Children benefit from (1) a positive image of their own race and (2) exposure to many people from diverse cultural, ethnic, and racial backgrounds.

Sources: We thank Janet E. Helms, Ph.D. from the University of Maryland for personal communication on the topic of racial identity (1988). Helms, J. E. (1990). *Black and white racial identity: Theory, research, and practice.* New York: Greenwood Press.

---

being capable of causing events. Third, they realize that they have subjective experiences that potentially can be shared with others. Finally, they develop language and symbolic actions that allow the sharing of the self.

All four stages are present in the first 2 years, but additional skills in the second and third years increase the sense of self. These additional skills include the abilities to use internal-state words in descriptions, to use personal pronouns, to engage in symbolic play, and to exhibit increased memory for locations (Bretherton & Beeghly, 1982; Chess & Thomas, 1987; Kagan, 1982a).

Self-Recognition

One aspect of a sense of self is **self-recognition,** the ability to recognize one's image, which emerges gradually. When rouge is placed on the noses of 15-month-olds and

the infants placed in front of a mirror, only 20 percent wipe their noses to try to remove the rouge. By 18 months, wiping has become the typical response (Lewis & Brooks-Gunn, 1979). Interestingly, chimpanzees and orangutans seem to be the only animal species that learn to react to mirror images as humans do. More typically, fish, birds, and mammals react aggressively to a mirror image, as if attacking another being (Brooks-Gunn & Lewis, 1984; Gallup, 1970).

By studying self-recognition in a variety of ways, researchers have shown that self-recognition develops gradually (Bertenthal & Fischer, 1978):

- A 6-month-old infant placed in front of a mirror will simultaneously look at and touch some part of the mirror

Table 5.9
Stern's Four Stages to the Development of the Self

Stage 1: Emergent Self (First 2 Months)—Infants have separate, unrelated experiences, but also begin to integrate and organize these individual experiences.

Stage 2: Core Self (2 to 6 Months)—Infants begin to form a sense of control over their own actions and to know that actions have consequences.

Stage 3: Subjective Self (7 to 15 Months)—Infants come to realize that inner subjective experiences can potentially be shared with others.

Stage 4: Verbal Self (After 15 Months)—Infants are involved in the development of language, and they have the capacity to engage in symbolic action, such as in pretend play.

From "Four Stages to the Development of the Self" from *The Interpersonal World of the Infant* by Daniel N. Stern. Copyright © 1987 by Basic Books, Inc. Reprinted by Permission of Basic Books, Inc.

image. The infant is capable of coordinating reaching with visual perception.

- An 8-month-old infant suited in a specially designed vest that holds a hat above the head and placed before a mirror will look at the mirror image of the hat and at the real hat and try to grab it. The infant is capable of coordinating reaching with both mirror image and own body movements.

- A 16-month-old infant is placed in front of a mirror. When a toy is lowered from the ceiling behind the infant, the infant looks at the toy's image and turns directly toward the real toy. The infant can coordinate body movements with mirror images of self and of the toy.

- A 2-year-old infant is placed in front of a mirror. When the baby's mother points at the infant's mirror image and asks, "Who's that?" the infant states his or her name or says "me." The infant is able to coordinate mirror image with mother's pointing, mother's vocalization, and own proper vocal response.

With self-recognition, infants also become aware of their racial identity. This topic is examined in the "Exploring Cultural Diversity" feature.

guided review

15. In Freud's view of personality development, the first of five _____ stages is called the _____ stage, and possible personality traits that result from _____ include being dependent, gullible, generous, argumentative, and sarcastic.

16. During the second year, the primary _____ zone moves from the mouth's oral activities to the activities of urination and bowel movements, so Freud's second psychosexual stage is called the _____ stage.

17. Erikson sees his _____ theory as a compatible extension to Freud's _____ theory, with emphasis on _____ rather than biological conflicts and on crises throughout the lifespan rather than just early childhood.

18. Erikson's first psychosocial stage involves the crisis of _____ versus _____, and the second stage involves the crisis of _____ versus _____ and _____.

19. In Mahler's theory of separation-individuation, the initial _____ phase is followed by the _____ phase and the third and longest phase of separation-individuation, during which the _____ self is born.

20. In Stern's third and fourth stages of the developing self, the _____ self is when infants realize that inner experiences can be shared with others, and the _____ self is when infants can use language and pretend play.

21. When infants with rouge on their noses wipe their noses when looking in a mirror, it is an indication that they have _____.

22. Parents should build pride in _____ while still promoting universal characteristics of humankind, and this can be achieved by providing a positive image of one's own race and providing exposure to diverse peoples.

answers

15. psychosexual; oral; fixations [LO-7]. 16. erogenous; anal [LO-7]. 17. psychosocial; psychoanalytic; social [LO-8]. 18. basic trust; basic mistrust; autonomy; shame; doubt [LO-9]. 19. autistic; symbiotic; psychological [LO-10]. 20. subjective; verbal [LO-10]. 21. self-recognition [LO-10]. 22. racial identity [LO-11].

Attachment

What is Attachment?

Attachment is a relatively enduring emotional tie to a specific person. In infancy, attachment is most likely to the mother, father, or other primary caregivers. Attachment develops gradually over time and is established when infants and young children show distress when separated from their significant person and actively seek to be near the caregiver when physical reunion occurs.

Attachment Theory

Early theorists (e.g., Dollard & Miller, 1950; Freud, 1940) believed that mother-infant attachment occurred because mothers repeatedly satisfied infants' biological needs, resulting in the maternal presence itself becoming rewarding. Today, theorists propose biological, behavioral, and psychodynamic attachment theories.

Bowlby's Biological Attachment Theory

In his **biological attachment theory,** John Bowlby (1958, 1969, 1973, 1981) proposed that infants have a biologically based predisposition for social interchange, which in the first few months of life becomes "focused" on one specific adult, usually the mother. The primary relationship becomes the prototype for all future relationships.

According to Bowlby (1969), four basic behavioral functions are biologically prewired for development in infancy. Briefly, these functions are:

1. *Attachment system.* This system directs proximity seeking to achieve protection and care.
2. *Fear-Wariness system.* This system directs avoidance of people, situations, or events that are potentially harmful.
3. *Affiliation system.* This system provides the impetus for playful social interaction.
4. *Exploration system.* This system leads to exploration of nonsocial environments.

These systems influence each other. Over time, according to Bowlby, the attachment system allows infants to prefer one individual's company and care, and this preference is accentuated by the fear-wariness system, which encourages infants to avoid strangers. Good attachment aids both the affiliation and exploration systems.

Schaffer and Emerson's Four Attachment Stages

Schaffer and Emerson (1964) suggested that the attachment process develops in four stages. Over the first 6 weeks of life, neonates are in the *asocial stage* and exhibit similar responses to both social and nonsocial stimuli. By 6 weeks, however, infants are showing a preference for smiling faces and other social stimuli over nonsocial stimuli.

Between 6 weeks and 6 months of age, infants are in the *indiscriminate attachment stage.* During this time period, infants prefer to be with humans than to be alone, but they like being around both strange and familiar persons. However, during the third stage of *specific attachments,* infants become attached to a particular individual, usually the mother, and protest being separated from her even if other persons are nearby. Fear of strangers grows during this third stage.

Schaffer and Emerson's final stage is *multiple attachments,* in which infants begin to form attachments with other familiar adults, such as fathers, siblings, babysitters, and grandparents. This stage may begin within weeks of the third stage; by 18 months, multiple attachments are typical.

Mahler's Separation-Individuation Phase

Earlier in the chapter, you read about infants' developing sense of self according to Mahler's (1968) theory of separation-individuation. The third phase of Mahler's theory—the separation-individuation phase—sheds light on the attachment process. During the first subphase of *differentiation* (5 to 10 months of age), infants develop a preference to be around their mothers yet do not exhibit intense stranger distress.

From 10 to 16 months, infants in the second subphase—*practicing*—become capable of locomotion. Attachment in this phase becomes much stronger and plays a role in keeping mobile babies relatively safe. From 15 to 22 months, infants in the *rapprochement* subphase are even less tolerant of their mothers' absences. Finally, from about 2 years on, infants in the fourth subphase exhibit the *begin-*

nings of emotional object constancy. During this time, infants are better able to tolerate separation yet greet their mothers positively on return.

While each of these attachment theories is somewhat different in emphasis and terminology, they share common features: (1) Infants first learn to prefer social to nonsocial stimuli; (2) then they learn a specific attachment; (3) specific attachment grows, as does stranger anxiety; and finally, (4) toddlers build other attachments.

Individual Differences in Attachment

Mary Ainsworth devised the stranger situation procedure to assess security of attachment between mother and infant (e.g., Ainsworth & Wittig, 1969; Ainsworth, Blehar, Waters, & Wall, 1978). In this procedure, babies are left in a playroom with their mothers. Researchers observe infant behavior in (1) playing with available toys, (2) getting used to a stranger, (3) dealing with the stranger when the mother leaves the room, and (4) responding to the mother when the mother reenters the room. Ainsworth and other researchers found three major patterns of attachment, which are described in Table 5.10.

Securely Attached Babies

Securely attached infants are able to leave their mothers and play with toys, although sometimes they choose to share the toys with their mothers. These infants also gradually warm up to the stranger. Many securely attached infants do not become upset when their mothers leave, and they remain behind for a few minutes with the stranger. They show more distress when left alone. Securely attached infants, whether or not distressed by maternal separation, exhibit positive behaviors toward their mothers when reunited with them (Sroufe, 1978).

Avoidant and Resistant Babies

Anxiously attached-avoidant infants play with toys while their mothers are in the room, interact with the stranger, and do not cry when their mothers leave the room. During reunion with their mothers, avoidant babies casually greet their mothers or turn away from them (Sroufe, 1978).

On the other hand, **ambivalent attached-resistant infants** engage in little exploration of the toys, even when their mothers are present. They are fearful of the stranger, show distress when their mothers depart, and remain upset when their mothers return. During reunion, resistant infants cry and pout and also push their mothers away (Sroufe, 1978).

Impact of Attachment

On Parent-Child Relationship

Maternal characteristics that affect attachment patterns are presented in Table 5.10. In addition, male babies are more vulnerable to caretaking differences, while female babies are more influenced by maternal personality (Egeland & Farber, 1984).

Table 5.10
Security of Attachment in Strange Situations

1. Securely Attached Infants

These infants seek proximity and contact when their mothers return to the room.

About 65 to 70 percent of American infants are securely attached.

Mothers of these infants are more affectionate, use more physical contact and more face-to-face interaction, are less intrusive, and are better at soothing their infants.

When these infants are 5 years old, they are less ego-controlled, more empathic, more dominant, more purposive, more achievement-oriented, and more independent than resistant children (see number 3).

2. Anxiously Attached-Avoidant Infants

These infants avoid their mothers when the mothers return. They fail to cling when held; they treat strangers at least as positively as their mothers.

"Baby fears what he or she wants."

About 20 to 25 percent of American infants, and a higher percentage of German babies, are anxiously attached-avoidant.

Mothers of these infants show controlled anger toward and rejection of the infants.

3. Ambivalently Attached-Resistant Infants

During reunions with their mothers, these infants resist interaction by hitting, pushing, or crying, yet they also seek contact and proximity with their mothers.

"Baby fears he or she will not get enough of what is wanted."

About 10 percent of American babies and a somewhat higher percentage of Japanese and Israeli babies are ambivalently attached-resistant.

Mothers of these infants tend to be insensitive and inept but not rejecting of infants.

Source: Data from M. D. S. Ainsworth, et al., *Patterns of Attachment*, 1978, Lawrence Erlbaum & Associates, Hillside NJ. From M. H. van Ijzendoorn, and P. M. Kroonenberg, "Cross-Cultural Patterns of Attachment: A Meta-Analysis of the Strange Situation" in *Child Development*, 59, 147–156, 1988. From D. Oppenheim, et al., "Infant-Adult Attachments on the Kibbutz and Their Relation to Socioemotional Development 4 Years Later" in *Developmental Psychology*, 24, 427–433, 1988.

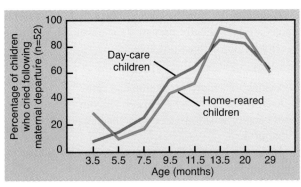

Figure 5.1
In this study of U.S. children in which day care and home-reared children were left alone by their mothers in an unfamiliar room, the percentage of children who cried when their mothers left was highest at about 13 months.

to the mother, only securely attached to the father, and insecurely attached to both parents (Main & Weston, 1981).

Also, parental care versus day care during infancy does not necessarily affect the quality of attachment with mothers. Figure 5.1 shows the expected increase from 7 to 13 months in infants' distress levels during maternal separation, and the curves for day-care children and home-care children are similar. However, when infants receive more than 20 hr of nonmaternal care per week, they are at heightened risk to be insecurely attached (avoidant or resistant) with their mothers. Infants with much nonmaternal care are likely to be insecurely attached when the following conditions are also present: (1) infants are boys, (2) infants have "difficult" temperaments, (3) mothers are dissatisfied with their marriages, and (4) mothers have high levels of maternal separation anxiety (Belsky & Rovine, 1988; McBride & Belsky, 1988).

On Peer Relationships
Securely attached infants have better peer relations in early childhood (van Pancake, 1985). As shown in Table 5.11 quality of attachment at 15 months affects peer competence during the preschool years.

On Personality
As also shown in Table 5.11, securely attached 15–month-olds have stronger ego strength in the preschool years. Other long-lasting effects associated with attachment pattern include (Matas, Arend, & Sroufe, 1978; Oppenheim, Sagin, & Lamb, 1988; Thompson & Lamb, 1986):

- Securely attached 18–month-olds are more capable of using tools and solving simple problems at 24 months. They also have lower frustration levels and seem happier than other infants.
- Securely attached infants are more empathic, achievement-oriented, dominant, purposive, and independent and less ego controlled than others at age 5.
- The combination of insecure attachment and high environmental stress predisposes males to psychopathology.

Although most attachment research involves the mother-infant relationship, many babies also form attachments to their fathers during the first 9 months. Infants develop different attachment patterns with their mothers and fathers. With mothers, infants are more likely to be held and soothed. Mothers tend to play traditional games with infants. In contrast, fathers are more likely to initiate unusual, unpredictable games and to engage in playful physical stimulation (Lamb, 1981). You are more likely to see a dad than a mom gently throw a baby in the air and catch her.

The quality of attachment to one parent cannot be predicted from the quality of attachment to the other parent. In one study, almost equal numbers of babies were likely to be securely attached to both parents, only securely attached

Table 5.11
Attachment at 15 Months and Personality in Preschool

Emergence of Peer Competence

Securely Attached	Insecurely Attached
Is sympathetic to peers' distress	Is a spectator in social activities
Is a peer leader	Is hesitant with other children
Is sought by other children for company	Withdraws from excitement and commotion
Attracts attention	Hesitates to engage others
Suggests activities	Is socially withdrawn
	Is a listener but not full participant

Emergence of Ego Strength

Securely Attached	Insecurely Attached
Forcefully goes after what is wanted	Is unaware, turned off, and "spaced out"
Likes to learn new intellectual skills	Is not curious about the new
Is self-directed	

Table from *Human Nature Magazine,* October 1978, copyright © 1978, by Human Nature, Inc. reprinted by permission of publisher.

- Securely attached infants become more sociable, compliant, persistent, and enthusiastic children.
- The majority of maternally abused or neglected children were insecurely attached infants.

Ideas about attachment reinforce the importance of Erikson's first psychosocial stage of basic trust versus basic mistrust. Infants who trust their mother and father more easily build personal and interpersonal competencies. The effects of infancy attachment of adolescent and adult behavior is more difficult to assess. Some psychologists believe that the infancy attachment pattern plays little role in later development. Others—especially those from a psychodynamic perspective—believe that insecure attachment contributes to such problems as eating disorders and running away from home in adolescence.

guided review

23. _____ is a relatively enduring emotional tie to a specific person.
24. Bowlby's _____ theory emphasizes that biological prewiring aids the development of attachment, fearfulness, affiliation, and exploration.
25. In Schaffer and Emerson's attachment process, fear of strangers grows during the third stage, called the stage of _____.

26. In Mahler's separation-individuation phase, the four subphases are _____, during which infants develop a preference for their mothers and a fear of strangers; _____, which is influenced by locomotion; _____, which is characterized by the least tolerance toward the mother's absences; and finally, the beginnings of emotional object constancy.
27. Ainsworth studied individual differences in attachment, using the _____ procedure, and found three major patterns of attachment: _____, _____, and _____.
28. _____ attached infants have better peer relations and greater ego strength.

answers

23. Attachment [LO-12]. **24.** biological attachment [LO-12]. **25.** specific attachments [LO-12]. **26.** differentiation; practicing, rapprochement and beginnings of emotional object constancy [LO-12]. **27.** stranger situation; securely attached; anxiously attached-avoidant; ambivalently attached-resistant [LO-13]. **28.** Securely [LO-14].

Parenting Infants

The Transition to Parenthood

The arrival of an infant into the family unit may be a joyous occasion, but for many parents, the *transition to parenthood* also involves uncertainty, considerable stress, and conflict among family members (LaRossa & LaRossa, 1981). In one study, nearly half of parents indicated concern about handling parent-child situations during the first year (Sollie & Miller, 1980).

Four general areas of problems are especially evident with new parents (Sollie & Miller, 1980). First, they have to deal with significant restrictions on their time and spending. Before becoming parents, a couple's lifestyle may have included freedom to travel and entertain spontaneously, and now more planning, such as finding babysitters, is involved. Significant adjustments regarding career opportunities also may be required. Second, the relationship between the mother and father may be strained because they have less time to spend together and need to adjust to each other's expectations about parenting. Third, new parents experience emotional costs as they juggle new responsibilities and come to terms with their doubts about their competence as parents. Finally, and perhaps most notable, the transition to parenting is physically demanding, and new parents lose sleep and have heavier work loads.

Adoptive Parents

For most parents, the parenting process began with a personal experience of pregnancy and childbirth. However, for some adults, parenting begins with the adoption process, which is often lengthy and exhausting. Adults choose to adopt for a number of reasons, including infertility, the need to adopt a relative, and wanting to provide a home for a child. Some **adoptive parents** adopt babies, but others adopt much older children. For most adoptive parents, the experience is rewarding.

Adoptions have occurred throughout history. Early cultures in Babylon, Egypt, Greece, and Rome used adoption to continue family lineage. Until recently, modern adoptions usually consisted of matching characteristics of the biological parents with characteristics of the adoptive family, but the current trend is toward less matching (Schaffer & Kral, 1988). More families are adopting special-needs children or children who come from different racial/ethnic backgrounds. When children come from different cultural backgrounds than the adoptive family, many adopting parents find it useful to become familiar with the cultural traditions of the biological parents. Parents who choose to adopt children with backgrounds quite different from themselves tend to have higher occupational levels, more education, politically liberal positions, and less extended family affiliations (Schaffer & Kral, 1988).

Adoptions are actually quite common. About one in five persons has a family member who is adopted, and non-relative adoptions make up just under 5 percent of all live births (Schaffer & Kral, 1988).

How do adopted children deal with having been adopted? Few children under the age of 6 can differentiate between adoption and birth. Yet, during these early years, adoptive parents can set a tone that helps their children later feel good about the circumstances of their birth and adoption. Young children may think that they were given up because they were naughty, and realistic beliefs might not be developed until middle adolescence (Brodzinsky, Singer, & Braff, 1984).

Modern Parenting

Today's parents have a variety of resources for learning how to be good parents. The most commonly used resources are pediatricians and family doctors, who help with a variety of issues, including infant physical health (such as nutrition), use of car restraints, parent-infant communication, and general safety issues (McKim, 1987; Tellerman & Medio, 1988). Medical and psychological experts have flooded the market with "how to raise your infant" books, and some of them are quite good. Grocery and department store shelves are lined with products of all sorts to aid parenting.

While most psychological research is based on chronological age, evidence suggests that mothers are more likely to base their parenting on their baby's developmental status. This, of course, is an appropriate decision since mothers generally know how to handle their own infants better than authors of child psychology books. As one psychologist put it, "With respect to their own child, mothers can well be expected to be better experts than developmental psychologists" (Heckhausen, 1987, p. 224).

Historically, parents were enforcers who taught their young to obey and to respect authority. Children were told to "Be seen but not heard." Of course, parents in earlier times loved their children, but Sigmund Freud was largely responsible for focusing mass attention on the value of mother love in personality development. Other psychologists echoed Freud's sentiment. John Bowlby (1951, p. 289), for example, stated that "Mother love in infancy and childhood is as important for mental health as are vitamins and proteins for physical health."

Early developmental research also supported the importance of maternal love in development. For example, William Goldfarb (1947) followed the development through childhood of infants who spent time with their mothers and then had to be in a foster home, with infants who spent at least 2 years in an institution (the Hebrew Home for Infants) and then in a foster home. Despite the institution's high standards, the institutionalized infants were more aggressive, distractible, and impulsive. In the school years, they had fewer social activities, more easily broken relationships, and lower intellectual levels.

Parent-Child Communication

"Oh, What a Beautiful Baby"

Society tends to have a "beautiful is good" bias for adults, and attractive people are viewed as more intelligent, friendly, and honest. Surprisingly, this bias exists even during the first year of life. Physically attractive infants are judged to be more likeable, smarter, and less troublesome to their parents. The bias seem to affect adult ratings of infants across ethnic groups, including African Americans, European Americans, and Mexican Americans (Stephan & Langlois, 1984). How might this bias affect parenting behaviors and expectations?

Hopefully, the parenting experience allows adults to move away from stereotyped expectations, to evaluate their own offspring more objectively, and to act according to individual needs. One indication that this occurs comes from a study in which adults viewed videotapes of 9-, 15-, and 21-month-olds and rated them for meaningful acts and intentional communications. Parents seemed to be more consistent than nonparents in this rating task (Adamson, Bakeman, Smith, & Walters, 1987).

Mother Versus Father Communication

When mothers are trying to get their babies to play with a new toy, they use five motivating strategies. First, they draw attention to the toy by showing the object or by saying, "Look." Second, they encourage manipulation of the toy by giving it to the infant and verbally encouraging the infant to "Come and play with this." Third, mothers sometimes encourage infant behavior by modeling play with the toy and by saying something like, "Watch mommy play with this." Fourth, mothers might offer explicit verbal encouragement, such as "You do it now," to get the baby to play. The final strategy is to remain neutral and let the infant explore the toy when ready (Heckhausen, 1987).

Fathers, of course, use the same strategies. In fact, fathers can do anything that mothers do, except lactate. Many fathers are involved with bottle-feeding, diaper changing, bathing, soothing, playing, and parent-infant communication (Lamb, 1981). However, fathers tend to be less involved in caregiving than mothers. Fathers are more likely to be actively involved with firstborns than later-borns, and with sons than daughters (Belsky, Gilstrap, & Rovine,

Table 5.12
Play Materials and Social Activity

Toy Situation	Infant Social Activity	Games to Play
Absence of play materials	Distant social signals: • Vocalizing • Smiling • Gesturing • Visually regarding	Name games, singing, fingerplays, pat-a-cake, peek-a-boo
	Physical contact: • Touching	Body part games
Fine motor play materials: • Cubes and containers • Shape sorters • Popbeads	Direct involvement in play: • Taking • Showing • Exchanging • Side-by-side playing • Duplicating action	Filling and dumping, building, in-and-out games, "trade" games
Social/language play materials: • Phones • Books • Hats • Dolls	Direct involvement in peer play: • Offering • Accepting • Exchanging • Duplicating action	Phone play, "reading," dress-up, doll play
Gross motor play materials: • Large balls • Rocking boat • Climbing steps • Tunnels	Direct involvement in peer play: • Ball-rolling • Chasing • Leading • Following	Roll and chase, follow-the-leader, peek-a-boo, "Row, Row, Row Your Boat"

Reprinted by permission of Ryan L. Geismar and the Association for Childhood Education International, 11141 Georgia Avenue, Suite 200, Wheaton, MD. Copyright © 1986 by the Association.

Playing with one's young children makes parenthood a more enriching experience.

1984). Fathers today, more than ever before, give themselves permission to be actively involved in parenting, and future generations will probably find even fewer gender differences in the parenting of infants.

Still, mothers and fathers have unique styles of parent-infant interaction. Studies of how parents play with babies show definite differences between mother-infant and father-infant playing (Brazelton, Yogman, Als, & Tronick, 1979; Park & Tinsley, 1981). Compared to mothers, when fathers play with babies, they are:

• Noisier and evoke more laughing and crying
• More likely to use big gestures, physical movement, surprise elements, and excitement
• More likely to swing toddlers, engage in "crawling chases," move infants' limbs, tickle stomachs, and "turn babies into airplanes"
• Less likely to read and to play quietly with toy objects
• Less likely to talk and sing soothingly
• Less likely to play during caretaking routines, such as diapering and bathing
• Less likely to use verbal interaction

In every culture, mothers are expected to be routinely involved with the parenting of infants, and fathers are more likely to choose their level and type of involvement. Therefore, finding the antecedents of fathering styles is easier than it is of mothering styles. Sixty-eight Israeli first-time fathers were interviewed during the third trimester and again when the infants were 9 months old. Fathers who were active caregivers were high in autonomy, sensitivity, perception, and openness to experience, and viewed fatherhood as a self-enriching experience. Playful fathers scored high on affiliation and on viewing fatherhood as a self-enriching experience (Levy-Shiff & Israelashvili, 1988).

Toys, Books, and Playmates

Toys for the First Two Years

As shown in Table 5.12, simple toy materials can suffice during infancy. Parents can, of course, spend lots of money on store-bought infant toys, but babies are as amused and informed by simple, inexpensive items as by expensive items. Parents should concern themselves with three major aspects of toys: (1) safety (e.g., avoiding very small items that can be swallowed and sharp items that can injure), (2) age-appropriateness, and (3) variety of materials and colors.

During the first 2 months, babies favorite play activities include (Sutton-Smith, 1986):

- Imitating the baby's noises, engaging in baby talk, and singing
- Making funny clown faces for the baby
- Moving the baby's legs in a bicycling action
- Sticking one's tongue out at the baby
- Dancing with the baby in one's arms
- Moving one's fingers in the baby's mouth
- Playful nibbling of the baby's fingers and toes

Young infants enjoy plastic rings, bells, balls, and being able to see mirrors and checkered patterns. A good play object is a colorful visual mobile that is placed to the baby's far right, the direction infants look in most of the time (Sutton-Smith, 1986; White, 1985).

From 3 months of age on, infants engage in a trial-and-error learning about objects (Gibson, J. T., 1988). Between 3 and 6 months, babies are synthesizers because they are learning to coordinate their own movements and senses (Sutton-Smith, 1986). Therefore, toys during these 3 months are often built like hands, fingers, feet, and toes—that is, they are soft and malleable, have multiple parts, and are safe to insert in the mouth. During this time period, infants repeat play actions as they learn about the stability of the world.

From 7 to 12 months of age, infants discover that objects are also tools of inquiry. They become interested in how toy objects respond when they are dropped, thrown, banged, pulled, swung, turned, taken apart, and put together (Sutton-Smith, 1986). Infants of this age enjoy containers that can be nested and stacked. At first, they use trial-and-error and forcing actions with nesting cups, but late in toddlerhood, they develop a strategy for nesting the objects (DeLoache, Sugarman, & Brown, 1985).

Also during the later part of the first year, infants become very interested in simple social games. These games, such as "pat-a-cake," "peek-a-boo," "I'm gonna get you,"

"So big," "Tell-me-a-story," and "walking fingers" or "creepie crawlies," are fairly universal (Trotter, 1987a). Toddlers also enjoy these social games, but they also begin to do more mental and symbolic experimenting. By 2 years of age, they have begun pretend playing. For example, they may take a favorite stuffed animal, place it in a box or on the bed, and say goodnight to it (Gibson, J. T., 1988).

Introducing Infants to Arts and Literature

Infants love to explore colors and shapes, and placing simple pictures, photos, posters, and mobiles in their rooms is a good introduction to art. Toddlers can be introduced to actual art experiences, too. For example, they love modeling clay, although at first they are more intrigued with how clay feels and how they can make it move than they are in making objects. Toddlers also enjoy scribbling with crayons or finger paint on large pieces of paper (Rossi, 1988).

Babies can be introduced to children's books at a young age. Nowadays, there is "baby lit" for infants as young as 2 months. An early introduction to books:

- Helps infants to focus their eyes
- Helps infants to recognize familiar and new objects
- Aids language comprehension
- Reinforces concepts about objects, people, events, and routines
- Builds sensory awareness
- Provides opportunities for physical closeness with caretakers (Dinsmore, 1988)

From 5 to 9 months of age, infants want to handle books just like other play objects—that is, they want to place the book's edge in their mouths and to pull and twist books. These young infants often babble along with the storyteller or pat the pages. From 10 months on, they become more interested in looking at the book and pointing to the pictures. Sometimes, they try turning the pages, although they usually end up turning a few pages at a time. As they begin to talk, infants often try to say some of the words in the story.

Toddlers become even more interested in books, especially the pictures. From age 2 on, interest in the plot and story line usually grows as well (Dinsmore, 1988).

An early introduction to books may lead to a lifelong love of reading and hearing stories. Parents often build storytelling into special daily rituals during a quiet time of day or perhaps before bedtime.

Playmates

About 40 percent of American infants from 6 to 12 months of age, have contact with other babies weekly (Geismar-Ryan, 1986). However, early contact with peers is different from that of older children. During the first year, infants are incapable of playing with toys and interacting with peers at the same time. However, by the second year, toddlers show some ability to coordinate play materials and social play (Geismar-Ryan, 1986).

Although research in peer encounters among children under age 2 is not abundant, several generalizations can be made (Bridges, 1933; Geismar-Ryan, 1986; Maudry & Nekula, 1939; Vandell, Owen, Wilson, & Henderson, 1988): (1) babies as young as 6 months do direct some behavior toward each other, (2) babies become increasingly social throughout infancy, (3) peer play behavior has a fairly predictable order of appearance, and (4) securely attached infants are more interactive than are insecurely attached infants. Among toddlers, when there is peer contact in a toyless setting, peer interaction is conducted with gesturing. When peer contact is initiated in a setting with toys, most toddlers interact by offering and taking toys (Weinraub, Brooks, & Lewis, 1977). Peer play, like moral development, is rudimentary during infancy, but the foundation is set for more complex development ahead, as you will see in the chapters to come.

guided review

29. Although proclaimed as a joyous occasion, the transition to _____ is a period of uncertainty, considerable stress, and conflict.
30. _____ occurs for many reasons, including infertility, the need to adopt a relative, and wanting to provide a home for a child.
31. The resource most commonly used by parents is that of their _____.
32. Most parents do a good job of basing their parenting on the child's _____, rather than on the child's chronological age.
33. Society's _____ bias starts early, as physically attractive infants are judged as more likeable, smarter, and less troublesome.
34. When parents play with infants, _____ are more likely to be noisy, physical, and unpredictable, while _____ are more likely to read, play quietly, and be verbal.
35. Good infant toys are _____, _____, and use a variety of materials and colors.
36. Young infants treat books like other play objects, but from 10 months of age on, they become more interested in _____, and around 2 years of age have a growing interest in the _____.

answers

29. parenthood [LO-15]. 30. Adoption [LO-15]. 31. medical doctor (or: pediatrician; family doctor) [LO-15]. 32. developmental status [LO-15]. 33. "beautiful is good" [LO-16]. 34. fathers; mothers [LO-16]. 35. safe (or: harmless); age-appropriate [LO-17]. 36. looking at pictures; plot (or: story line) [LO-17].

Exploring Human Development

1. Tape-record some infant cries. Have parents and nonparents judge whether the baby is hungry, wet, or distressed. Compare how the two groups do in terms of accuracy.
2. Put together a short booklet on how parents of "difficult" versus "slow-to-warm-up" babies can best work with their infants and toddlers.
3. Interview five persons who became first-time parents within the last 2 years and five persons who have been parents for several years. Ask them questions related to the parenthood transition. Do the two groups provide similar responses? If not, why not?
4. Interview three or more parents who have adopted children. Ask them about the decision-making process to decide to attempt adoption, the adoption process itself, concerns they have about dealing with their children's questions about being adopted, and recommendations they would make to other adults considering adoption. If possible, also interview a caseworker who does home studies for prospective adoptive parents.
5. Visit a toy store, and study the infant toy sections. What toys are available? What toys seem to be appropriate and safe for infants? Which toys could be inexpensively replicated using household items?

Discussing Human Development

1. Have a group discussion about childhood fears. When possible, ask older family members to recall other fears from infancy and early childhood. What kinds of fears were common? Unusual? How long did they last? Are any fears especially persistent?
2. Using your earliest memories, compare your childhood experiences and your resultant adult personality with the ideas in Sigmund Freud's psychoanalytic theory and Erik Erikson's psychosocial theory. Which theory is most useful?
3. Infants not only become attached to other humans but to stuffed animals and other objects as well. What kinds of attachment objects did you and other class members have as toddlers? What can you remember about these objects (e.g., special names, how often you used the objects, the circumstances under which the object was given up)? As adults, do you have any "attachment objects"? Are there similarities between a toddler's security blanket and an adult's lucky charm, for example?
4. How much of personality do you believe is biologically influenced versus learned? What reasons do you have for your position?
5. How do you think the transition to parenthood differs for: young versus older parents, married versus single parents, low-income versus moderate- or high-income parents, dual-career versus single-career parents? Could society make the transition to parenthood easier? How?
6. When do you think parents should begin reading books to their offspring? What kinds of topics, pictures, and values would you want to find in children's books?

Reading More About Human Development

Chess, S., & Thomas, A. (1987). *Know your child.* New York: Basic Books.

Damon, W. (1988). *The moral child: Nurturing children's natural moral growth.* New York: Free Press.

Greenspan, S., & Greenspan, N. T. (1985). *First feelings: Milestones in the emotional development of your baby and child.* New York: Viking.

Jensen, L. C., & Kingston, M. (1986). *Parenting.* New York: Holt, Rinehart & Winston.

Stern, D. J. (1985). *The interpersonal world of the infant*. New York: Basic Books.

White, B. L. (1986). *The first three years of life* (rev. ed.). New York: Prentice-Hall.

Summary

I. Emotional development
  A. Two important ways in which infants communicate are by crying and by smiling.
    1. The three basic normal cries are the hunger cry, the pain cry, and the angry cry, and two important abnormal cries are the malnourished cry and the asphyxiated cry.
    2. Parents of infants are quite skilled at distinguishing the various cry patterns and providing appropriate caretaking responses.
    3. Nighttime crying can be effectively reduced by a scheduled awakenings procedure, a systematic ignoring procedure, or by consistent behavior patterns during the daytime schedule.
    4. Infants learn self-directed regulatory behaviors, such as looking away or engaging in thumb sucking, for negative moods.
    5. Social smiles develop between the fourth and sixth weeks initially to vocalization and later to faces.
  B. Facial expressions develop over the course of infancy, with much similarity across various cultures.
    1. Charles Darwin proposed that the basic emotions were biologically determined.
    2. Neonatal emotional expressions include interest, a half smile, the startle response, distress, and disgust.
    3. By 4 months of age, infants exhibit the emotional expressions of anger, surprise, joy, wariness, and sadness. These emotions are followed shortly thereafter by fear, shame, shyness, and self-awareness.
    4. The emotional expressions of contempt, anxiety, and guilt do not develop until the second year.
    5. Infants can discriminate between facial expressions of others.
    6. Parents tend to overestimate the number of emotional expressions made by their infants.
    7. Emotional synchronicity between parent and infant is associated with positive development.
    8. Maternal emotional expressions influence infant willingness to cross the deep end of the visual cliff.
  C. Sroufe and Izard have each proposed theories of emotional development.
    1. According to Sroufe, neonates have three emotional dimensions (wariness-fear, rage-anger, and pleasure-joy) that are modified by improving cognitive level, growing coping capabilities, and developing systems to express emotions.
    2. According to Izard, initial emotions are based on specific facial displays, with further emotions developing to allow discrimination of social and nonsocial objects, to facilitate attachment, and as a response to the development of a sense of self.

D. The development of fears seems to occur in sequence at certain ages, regardless of experiences.
    1. Fear of heights tends to emerge around 6 months, when infants are beginning to crawl.
    2. Fear appears to be a fairly stable trait, with possible ethnic differences.
    3. Individual differences in fearfulness seem to persist from infancy into the school years, and may affect peer relationships and result in avoidance of danger or sports and conformity to parental standards.
    4. Regardless of culture, stranger fear is common from ages 6 months to 2 years, and separation anxiety peaks from 9 to 13 months of age and gradually disappears around 30 months.

II. Temperament
  A. Temperament is an inborn set of traits dealing with arousal, primary emotions, activity level, and persistence.
    1. The individual differences of temperament are fairly stable.
    2. According to Goldsmith et al., the four major aspects of temperament are activity, reactivity, emotionality, and sociability.
    3. Thomas, Chess, and Birch proposed that temperament could be measured in nine main areas.
  B. Thomas, Chess, and Birch group temperament aspects into three types of temperament style called easy, difficult, and slow-to-warm-up babies.
    1. The most common temperament is the "easy baby," who exhibits regular sleeping and eating schedules, adapts well to new routines and people, and approaches both people and the environment with positive emotions.
    2. "Slow-to-warm-up" babies exhibit some irregularity, a withdrawal pattern, and initial negative responses to new surroundings.
    3. "Difficult" or "challenging" babies have more irregular sleeping and eating patterns; longer periods of intense, negative emotions; and more fearfulness of strangers.
  C. Temperament is an important factor in determining appropriate parenting behaviors.
    1. Temperament is noticeable in distress responses in young infants, in amount of positive emotions in 2- and 3-month-olds, and in avoidance responses around the fourth month.
    2. Children's temperament and other characteristics are important components of parent-child interaction.
    3. Each temperament requires different parental responses.
  D. Temperament has long-term effects on personality.
    1. Although its biggest effects are in infancy, temperament has lifelong influences, especially in novel situations.
    2. Shyness is affected by biological tendencies toward behavioral inhibition.
    3. The best parenting strategy for shy children is to provide some protection while gently pushing the children toward new experiences.

III. Personality
  A. Sigmund Freud's psychoanalytic theory emphasizes the importance of the first few years of life on adult personality.
      1. Freud's work helped to get other scientists interested in the influences of infancy and early childhood.
      2. Psychosexual stages are named for the region of the body in which the libido is most expressed during that age.
      3. The oral stage occurs during the first year of life, when the major pleasurable activities are sucking and biting.
      4. Too much gratification or too little gratification results in fixations, or permanent influences on personality.
      5. Fixations in the oral stage may result in the personality traits of being gullible, sarcastic, and argumentative.
      6. The anal stage occurs during the second year of life, when the most pleasurable activities are urination and bowel movements.
      7. Personality characteristics that may develop from fixations in the anal stage include stinginess, obsessive neatness, and obstinacy.
  B. Erik Erikson proposed his psychosocial theory as a compatible extension of Freud's psychoanalytic theory.
      1. Freud emphasized biological conflicts, whereas Erikson emphasized social conflicts.
      2. Freud emphasized the stages of childhood, whereas Erikson emphasized lifelong stages.
      3. Erikson dealt more with healthy personality development than did Freud.
      4. The first psychosocial stage involves the crisis of basic trust versus basic mistrust, which Erikson believed was learned mainly from maternal care.
      5. Erikson's second stage—autonomy versus shame and doubt—corresponds to Freud's anal stage.
  C. During infancy, individuals begin to develop a sense of self.
      1. According to Mahler's theory of separation-individuation, the self develops in three stages over the first 4 years of life: the autistic phase, the symbiotic phase, and the separation-individuation phase.
      2. However, Stern suggested that infants are biologically predesigned to distinguish between themselves and others and that the development of the self progresses from emergent self to core self, to subjective self, and finally to verbal self over the first 2 years of life.
      3. One aspect of a sense of self is self-recognition, the ability to recognize one's own image, something accomplished only by humans, chimpanzees, and orangutans.
      4. Another important aspect of self is one's racial identity.
IV. Attachment
  A. Attachment is a relatively enduring emotional tie to a specific person.
      1. Attachment is most likely to the mother, father, or other primary caregiver.
      2. Attachment develops gradually.
  B. Attachment theories try to explain how and why attachment develops.
      1. In his biological attachment theory, Bowlby suggested that biological prewiring aids the development of attachment, fearfulness, affiliation, and exploration.
      2. Schaffer and Emerson proposed four attachment stages, in which infants move from being asocial to having indiscriminate attachments, specific attachments, and finally, multiple attachments.
      3. The third phase of Mahler's theory of separation-individuation is important in the attachment stage; its four subphases are differentiation, practicing, rapprochement, and beginnings of emotional object constancy.
      4. All three theories have infants learning to prefer social to nonsocial stimuli, learning a specific attachment that contributes to stranger anxiety, and then building other attachments.
  C. Mary Ainsworth pioneered research in individual differences in attachment, using *the stranger situation procedure*.
      1. Securely attached infants have positive behaviors toward mothers but can leave their mothers and gradually warm up to a stranger.
      2. Anxiously attached-avoidant babies do not cry when their mothers depart, interact with strangers, and avoid a reunion with their mothers.
      3. Ambivalent attached-resistant infants are fearful of exploration even when their mothers are present, are distressed when their mothers depart, and remain upset when their mothers return.
  D. Type of attachment affects both parental and peer relationships and influences personality characteristics.
      1. Affectionate mothers who are good at soothing and being nonintrusive are associated with securely attached infants; anxiously attached-avoidant infants often have mothers who show controlled anger or rejection toward them, while ambivalently attached-resistant infants often have insensitive, inept mothers.
      2. Infants develop different attachment patterns with their mothers and their fathers.
      3. Fathers engage in more unusual, unpredictable games and physical stimulation with their infants.
      4. Use of day care does not necessarily affect attachment with mothers, especially when day care is not more than 20 hr per week.
      5. Nonmaternal care produces more insecurely attached infants for boys with "difficult" temperaments and mothers with high levels of maternal separation anxiety.
      6. Securely attached infants have better peer relations in early childhood.
      7. Securely attached infants have stronger ego strength in the preschool years and also are less frustrated and more achievement-oriented, sociable, and enthusiastic.
V. Parenting infants
  A. The transition to parenting is important for both mothers and fathers.
      1. The transition to parenthood includes uncertainty, stress, and conflict, as well as joy.

2. Parenting affects a couple's lifestyle and freedom, career opportunities, mother-and-father relationships, emotionality, work loads, and self-confidence.

3. One special transition to parenthood involves adoption of a baby or child.

4. The most commonly used parenting resources are medical doctors, and growing in use are psychologically based parenting books.

5. Most parents make the good choice of basing decisions on developmental status rather than chronological age.

6. In contrast to current views, earlier generations placed more emphasis on obedience and respect and less on parental love.

B. An important aspect of parenting is the quality of communication between the parent and infant.

1. The "beautiful is good" bias exists even for infants, as physically attractive infants are rated as more likeable, smarter, and less troublesome.

2. Parents are better than nonparents at rating infants' meaningful acts and intentional communications.

3. Mothers and fathers use similar behaviors and communications with infants, except that fathers cannot lactate and they generally do less caregiving.

4. Fathers are more actively involved with firstborns than later-borns, and with sons than daughters.

5. When playing with their infants, fathers are noisier, use more physical movements and surprise elements, and engage in less reading, quiet play, and verbal interaction.

C. Parents provide the first toys and books during infancy.

1. Infant toys can be simple or expensive, but three qualities are essential: (1) safety, (2) age-appropriateness, and (3) variety of materials and colors.

2. Infant toys can build fine and gross motor abilities, social abilities, and language abilities.

3. An infant's first art experience may be exploring colors and shapes and a variety of pictures; toddlers can enjoy actual art experiences, such as modeling clay, using crayons, or finger painting.

4. Infants introduced to children's books are aided in developing visual abilities, recognizing objects, comprehending language, and developing an interest in reading.

5. During the second year, toddlers begin to show some ability to coordinate play materials and to have social play with peers.

Chapter Review Test

1. Little Ben is engaging in the basic cry of rhythmic and repetitive vocalization. Since Ben's mother is good at interpreting the language of cries, which of the following will she do to meet Ben's immediate need?
   a. Check to see if a sharp object or tight clothing is creating pain.
   b. Get Ben's bottle of formula because Ben seems to be hungry.

c. Comfort him because he is angry at having been left with a stranger.
d. Ignore the crying because a rhythmic, repeated pattern only indicates that Ben is practicing vocalization and exercising his lungs.

2. Baby Florence does a lot of daytime crying. Which of the following might reduce this crying?
   a. Carry her more.
   b. Feed her less.
   c. Do scheduled awakenings during the night.
   d. Pay less attention.

3. Social smiles make their first appearance
   a. shortly after birth.
   b. at about 1 week.
   c. at about 1 month.
   d. at about 3 months.

4. The basic emotional expressions appear to be
   a. culture specific.
   b. completely learned.
   c. present from birth on.
   d. universal.

5. Which of the following emotions is usually the *last* to emerge?
   a. guilt
   b. anger
   c. shame
   d. surprise

6. According to Sroufe's theory of emotional development, although wariness and fear develop in the first 6 months of life, anxiety and shame do not appear in the first year because _____ must first be present.
   a. object permanence
   b. negative experiences
   c. attachment
   d. a sense of self

7. Which of the following statements about fear is *incorrect*?
   a. From about 6 months to 2 years old, infants often exhibit stranger fear but seldom fear their mother acting strangely.
   b. The order of fear emergence for height, strangers, animals, and the dark varies considerably across cultures.
   c. Prolonged separation from one's usual caretaker produces a response pattern in infants of protesting, detaching, and despairing.
   d. Individual differences in fearfulness seem to persist from infancy into the school years.

8. The aspects of temperament that have to do with one's approach-withdrawal tendencies and one's thresholds for response, attention, interest, and persistence are called
   a. emotionality.
   b. activity.
   c. reactivity.
   d. sociability.

9. Which temperament style leads to less parent-infant interaction?
   a. "difficult"
   b. "easy"
   c. "slow-to-warm-up"
   d. No parent-infant interaction differences have been found to be attributable to temperament.

10. According to Freud's psychoanalytic theory, fixations
    a. result from too little gratification.
    b. result from too much gratification.
    c. are permanent influences on personality.
    d. all of the above.
11. Freud is to _____ as Erikson is to _____.
    a. conflict; harmony
    b. lifespan; childhood
    c. biological; social
    d. flexibility; rigidity
12. According to Erikson's psychosocial theory, which adult behavioral pattern is most associated with a child learning self-doubt?
    a. inconsistent, neglectful caregiving
    b. criticism of self-help attempts and overprotectionism
    c. suppression of self-expression and overcontrolling
    d. encouragement of independent attempts and sensitive attention
13. According to Daniel Stern, from 2 to 6 months of age, the _____ self is forming a sense of control over actions and learning that actions have consequences.
    a. core
    b. emergent
    c. subjective
    d. verbal
14. Which of the following statements about the formation of racial identity is accurate?
    a. Racial identity is formed over the entire lifespan.
    b. Children can benefit from adults relating their own racial history.
    c. Besides acquiring a positive image of their own race, children benefit from being exposed to many people from diverse cultural, ethnic, and racial backgrounds.
    d. All of the above are correct.
15. Which of the following is *not* one of the four basic behavioral functions that Bowlby suggested are biologically prewired for development in infancy?
    a. attachment
    b. affiliation
    c. exploration
    d. esteem
16. Which of the following is typical of the ambivalent attached-resistant infant?
    a. does not cry when mother departs room
    b. cries, pouts, and pushes mother away during reunion
    c. interacts with stranger
    d. all of the above
17. You are a counselor holding group sessions for new parents. Which of the following are you *least likely* to hear at one of the sessions?

    a. "It just seems so hard to get out anymore. Outside of these counseling sessions, we just don't seem to go anywhere. I'd love it if we could just get to a restaurant or something."
    b. "Sometimes, I feel like I know my husband less now than before we became parents—it's surprising how much we differ on how to take care of our infant. It's another whole set of adjustments to make."
    c. "Gee, I never expected such an increase in work load! I can only think of two bonuses of being a new parent: I get to catch up on my sleep, and I get to spend more time than usual with my wife."
    d. "Oh boy, did I ever underestimate the effects this baby would have on my career and on our finances."
18. Fathers are more likely to be involved with their _____ than their other children.
    a. youngest child
    b. daughters
    c. sons
    d. No differences have been found.
19. Which of the following is more typical of mothers than fathers when playing with their infants?
    a. evoking laughter
    b. reading and verbal interaction
    c. using gestures and surprise elements
    d. all of the above
20. Which of the following statements is correct?
    a. Young infants treat books like objects; then around age 1, they are quite interested in the pictures; and toward the end of infancy, they may develop an interest in plot.
    b. Simple social games, such as "peek-a-boo," "pat-a-cake," and "creepie crawlies," usually do not develop before a child's first birthday.
    c. Ability to coordinate play materials and social play does not emerge during the infancy period.
    d. All of the above are correct.

Answers

1. B [LO-1].	8. C [LO-6].	15. D [LO-12].
2. A [LO-1].	9. A [LO-6].	16. B [LO-13, 14].
3. C [LO-2].	10. D [LO-7].	17. C [LO-15].
4. D [LO-3].	11. C [LO-8].	18. C [LO-16].
5. A [LO-3].	12. B [LO-9].	19. B [LO-16].
6. D [LO-4].	13. A [LO-10].	20. A [LO-17, 18].
7. B [LO-5].	14. D [LO-11].	

chapter 6

Physical and Cognitive Development in Preschoolers

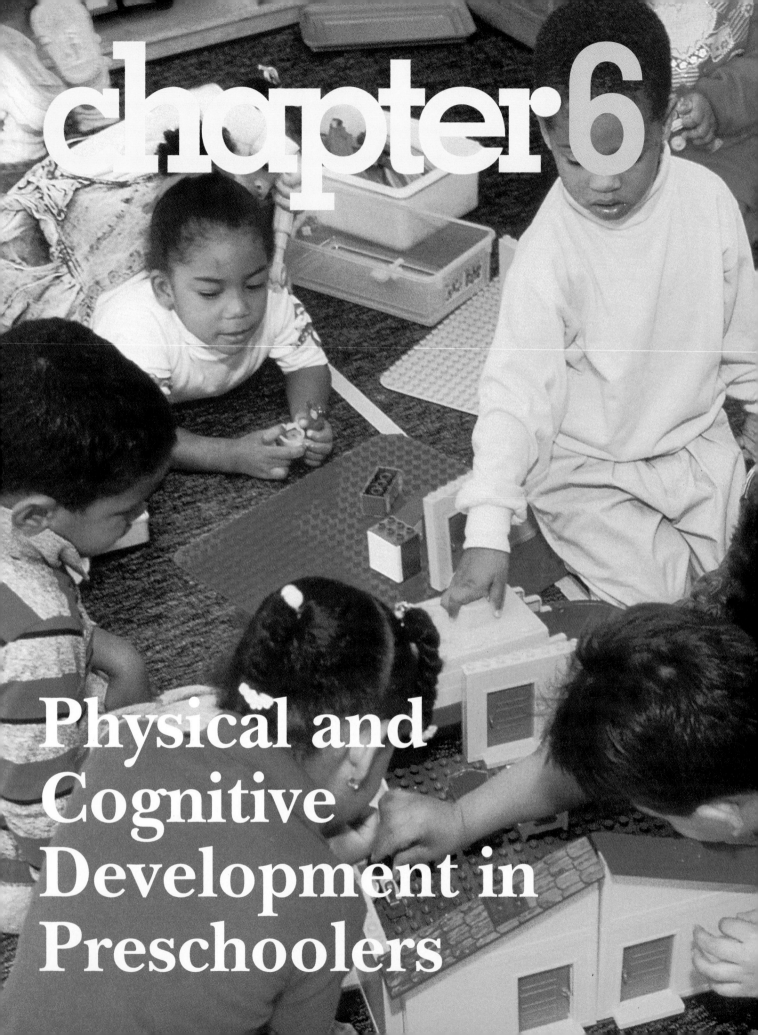

Learning Objectives

1. Describe physical development in the preschool years.
2. Compare and contrast preschoolers' gross motor skills and fine motor skills.
3. Explain the visual limitations of preschoolers, and provide examples of how this affects their abilities on perceptual tasks.
4. Compare the sleep needs of preschoolers with those of younger and older individuals.
5. Define the common sleep disorders of preschoolers.
6. Describe the nutritional needs of preschoolers and their typical eating habits.
7. Discuss health concerns and accident prevention during the preschool years.
8. Summarize the memory capabilities of preschool children.
9. List the main features of Piaget's preoperational stage of cognitive development, and explain the characteristic limitations.
10. Describe language development in young children.
11. Compare and contrast articulation speech disorders and dysrhythmia speech disorders.
12. Summarize the traditional approach to intelligence assessment, and describe the tests most commonly used for children.
13. Discuss the newer methods of intelligence assessment that are being developed and how they are improvements over traditional methods.
14. Compare and contrast organic retardation and familial retardation.
15. Summarize the effects of television on young children.
16. Discuss the major purposes served by toys.
17. Summarize the effects of day care on young children, and explain the different effects on socioeconomic disadvantaged children compared to others.

Early childhood, the years from age 2 through age 5, are exciting years of growth. Through repeated interaction with the world, preschoolers develop efficient physical abilities to move about the world, as well as memory and thinking capabilities to reason about the world. Preschoolers are greatly influenced by their family members and by the environment about them, and they enthusiastically engage in the most important work of childhood—play.

Exploring Your Own Development

What do you remember about your preschool years? If you are typical, your earliest memories are from the time you were about 3 1/2 years old. Some individuals, however, have memories from the age of 1 year, and others cannot remember anything before the age of 5. Some of your earliest memories may even be for events that did not actually occur! Most likely, your earliest memories are visual. Your memories of facts and historical events probably start at a later time period (Henri & Henri, 1898). Some of the most vivid memories might be based on stories about your childhood that have been repeated many times by family members or that are based on childhood photographs.

Take a few moments to write down the early memories of your childhood. What reasons can you give for why these events are recalled, while other events from your early childhood are not? Try to verify the accuracy of your memories by checking with other family members. Perhaps as you read in this chapter about the physical and cognitive development of preschoolers, you will remember even more about your early childhood.

Preschoolers' Physical Development

Physical Growth

Preschool youngsters experience greater growth in their legs than in their head and trunk regions. They also develop greater abdominal muscle strength so that, by 4 years of age, most preschoolers have lost much of their "potbelly appearance." Weight gain is about 5 to 7 lb a year, an average that continues up until the age of 9 or 10. Preschoolers experience more growth in their muscles than in their bones, and the amount of fat tissue decreases. Overall, appearance changes dramatically during these years, as preschoolers move from an infant's physical shape toward more adult features.

Motor Development

Preschoolers make rapid gains in control of body movements and motor skills. Table 6.1 shows some of the abilities that develop from ages 3 to 5.

Developing Gross Motor Skills

Young children usually glory in their new abilities at play and in activities involving grooming and household tasks. They like helping in such chores as dusting and setting the table, although, as expected, their actual accomplishments are rough and incomplete. Preschoolers also enjoy early attempts at art, block building, and playground play. Parents should encourage their young children's attempt to try new physical activities, while keeping the play and work environments as safe as possible.

Preschoolers continually test the limits of their physical abilities. They want to know how far they can walk, how fast they can run, how long they can jump, and whether they can master the monkey bars and sliding board at the neighborhood playground. Through achievements and mishaps, they learn better balance, how to compensate for limitations created by size, and how to express emotions and thoughts through bodily action (Leach, 1982).

Developing Fine Motor Skills

Preschool children develop fine motor skills through construction play and endless varieties of artwork. Young children enjoy the free-form painting allowed by finger painting and the more detailed work associated with crayons and pencils. Typically, 3-year-olds can draw fairly good horizontal lines and circles. Over the next year, they learn to draw squares and rectangles. Average 5-year-olds can draw triangles. Many preschoolers learn to write several letters of the alphabet, especially the letters that appear in their first names.

Handedness

When children first enter the preschool years, half of them are inconsistent in their preferred hand for such tasks as drawing and carrying objects (Gottfried & Bathurst, 1983; Hardyck & Petrinovich, 1977). Handedness is usually established by the fourth year (Schuster & Ashburn, 1986). Among 512 4-year-olds, only 23 children lacked a strong hand preference, and another 41 children were left-handed. Both left- and right-handed 4-year-olds score equally on motor skills assessments, but children with no definite hand preference have lower scores (Tan, 1985). Some research findings suggest that handedness is largely determined by genes. For example, hand preference of adopted preschoolers correlate more with hand preference of biological parents than with that of adopted parents (Carter-Saltzman, 1980).

Sensory and Perceptual Development

Preschoolers' sensory systems are also developing. For example, preschoolers' taste buds become more sensitive; as a result, their likes and dislikes for certain foods become more intense. Prschoolers' eyes are more capable of depth perception, but since development is still incomplete, preschoolers may still exhibit poor hand-eye coordination. This shortcoming may contribute to falls and tumbles and to the quality of their artwork (Schuster & Ashburn, 1986).

Table 6.1

Gross and Fine Motor Skills of Preschool Children

Age	Gross Motor Skills	Fine Motor Skills
3 years	Can ride a tricycle, jump from a low step, throw a large ball, go to the toilet unassisted, take own clothes off, go up stairs unattended	Can string large beads on a shoelace, copy a circle, brush teeth somewhat by self, use blunt scissors
4 years	Can jump and hop well, walk backward, kick a large ball, catch a large ball	Can use scissors to cut out a picture, button clothes, copy a square
5 years	Can jump rope, skip, catch a small ball, do a running jump, descend stairs by self	Can copy a triangle, eat with a fork, print his or her name

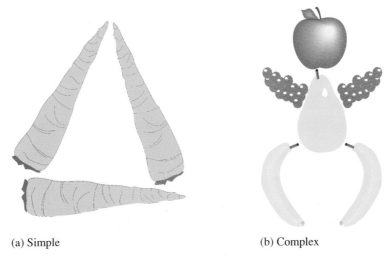

(a) Simple   (b) Complex

Figure 6.1
Simple and complex part/whole identification pictures. Young children can point out the part/whole aspects of simple figures, such as the carrot triangle (a), but are less successful in identifying both the individual fruits and the whole person in the fruit person (b).

Visual Scanning Ability

During the preschool and following years, all preschoolers become more efficient in visual scanning of the environment. In one study, children ages 4 to 10 were asked to study two objects to decide if they were "the same" or "different." Children who were 4 or 5 did an unsystematic, scattered visual scan that led to high error rates. By age 6 1/2, children were able to scan systematically and more slowly and successfully compared the two objects' various features. These children did much better than the preschoolers, though not as well as the oldest subjects in this study (Vurpillot, 1968, 1976).

Young preschoolers' inefficient visual scanning translates into inefficient redundant explorations of the environment. In one study, preschool children looked for an "Oscar the Grouch" toy that had been hidden in one of eight trash cans in a room. Preschoolers often failed to look into each of the trash cans and were likely to look into some cans more than once. As with visual scanning, environmental exploration becomes more efficient throughout the preschool years. For example, 4-year-olds were more accomplished at locating "Oscar the Grouch" than were the 2 1/2-year-old children in the study (Wellman, Somerville, Revelle, Haake, & Sophian, 1984).

Other Perceptual Limitations

Another visual limitation of preschoolers is that they have difficulty perceiving an object in more than one way. Illusions in which one picture can be seen as two objects at the same time (i.e., reversible picture illusions) are quite difficult for preschool children. Five-year-olds probably will see only one of the figures. At 7 years of age, they probably will see both objects, with help from older individuals. By age 10, most children do as well as adults in seeing both objects in reversible pictures (Elkind, 1975, 1978). Basically, small children are unable to study all aspects of a picture at the same time. They see the dominant picture first, which makes them unable to pick out the other figure.

Young children also have difficulty seeing both the parts and the whole of pictures at the same time, and are more likely to notice the whole than the parts (Ames, Metraux, Roedell, & Walker; Werner, 1948). Preschoolers' ability to identify and describe part and whole pictures varies by the simplicity or complexity of the picture. Figure 6.1 shows a simple part/whole picture of a carrot triangle and a complex part/whole picture of a fruit person. Many 3-year-olds are able to distinguish both the carrots and the triangle of the simple picture, but most are unable to name both the person and the individual fruits in the more complex picture. Difficulty of perceptual tasks involving part/whole identification plays a major role in whether young preschoolers can do the task successfully (Prather & Bacon, 1986).

These visual limitations, along with a short attention span, mean that preschoolers may have difficulty in a wide range of perceptual tasks. For example, in comparison to school-age children, preschoolers:

- May find it difficult to find animals that are camouflaged, such as a deer in the woods or a white-haired rabbit in a snowbank
- May overlook small objects, such as eggs, during an Easter egg hunt because of inefficient scanning
- May have more difficulty locating lost items in their rooms because they do redundant and scattered searches
- May find it very difficult to differentiate letters of the alphabet that share features, such as *b* and *d* or *O* and *Q*
- May have difficulty remembering the names of people who are about the same age and height because they have not scanned enough features
- May put on two socks that are similar but not identical because they did not attend to the distinct details
- May mistake a red car for their family's red car because they judge similarity only on one dominant characteristic

Already at this young age, sleep needs are decreasing. As she gets older, both REM sleep and total number of sleep hours will get lower.

Developing abilities and additional experiences with perception and cognitions help young children to overcome these shortcomings within a few years.

Sleep Patterns

As toddlers, children need an average of 12 hr sleep each night and also a nap period during the day. As preschoolers, children average 11 to 12 hr of sleep daily. Preschoolers' sleep needs vary, however, from 8 to 14 hr, so parents may experience much variation in the sleep needs of offspring (Hartmann, Baekeland, & Zwilling, 1972; Schuster & Ashburn, 1986).

Sleep Cycles

Throughout the night, people go through several sleep cycles that consist of stages marked by distinct EEG brainwave readings. Adults take from 80 to 110 min to complete a single cycle, but children's sleep cycles are typically 50 to 60 min long. Along with this difference in cycle length, preschoolers spend more time in **REM sleep,** or dreaming sleep, than adults and less time in REM sleep than they did as infants (Roffwarg, Muzio, & Dement, 1966).

In one longitudinal study, 42 children's dream patterns were followed for nine nights per year from age 3 to 15. Children's dreams tended to follow their conscious thought abilities: Preschool children had simple dreams about themselves in concrete situations and rarely had dreams of fantastic characters or abstract situations. Older children had longer concrete stories, and adolescents' dreams were more likely to be abstract (Foulkes, 1982).

Although some preschoolers are difficult at bedtime, most are more amenable to sleep than they were as toddlers. Parents can increase the likelihood of a smooth transition at bedtime by establishing a regular bedtime routine and a fairly consistent bedtime, and by spending the time before sleep in a quieting and comforting activity, such as reading aloud (Leach, 1982; Schuster & Ashburn, 1986).

Sleep Disturbances

Some sleep disturbances are more common in the preschool and school-age years than in later years. **Nightmares,** disturbing dreams that occur during the REM stage of sleep,

are most common among children 4 1/2 to 5 1/2 years of age. Young children are also subjected to **night terrors,** experiences of strong panic during sleep. Night terrors tend to occur during a non-REM stage of the sleep cycle. While youngsters who awaken during a nightmare are likely to remember vivid images, youngsters awakening from a night terror cannot recall the source of the panic. Young children may also sleepwalk, another non-REM stage activity (Anders, Caraskadon, & Dement, 1980; Hartman, 1981). Young children who experience any of these three sleep disturbances are usually quickly reassured and able to go back to sleep.

Nutrition During the Preschool Years

Preschool children eat the same foods as other family members, but since their stomachs are still small, they eat scaled-down versions. Nutritional needs during this active time of life mean that preschoolers need snacks—preferably in mid-morning and again in midafternoon—to help reach their daily caloric need of 1,300 to 2,300 cal. Parents should provide a variety of foods to meet children's nutrient needs. The most common nutrient shortfalls during the preschool years are calcium, iron, vitamin C, and vitamin A (Gardner, 1982; Leach, 1982).

Three-year-old preschoolers often are more interested in activities other than eating. Therefore, parents should provide sufficient time for their children to finish eating—often 30 to 40 min. One behavior displayed by many preschoolers is food rituals. For example, Jake may only want to eat cereal from his special red cereal bowl, and Kathy may only want to drink her milk if she can use a straw (Schuster & Ashburn, 1986).

Over the next 2 years, preschoolers often display a more erratic approach to their foods. Four- and 5-year-old children, for example, may suddenly stop eating something that was previously a favorite food. They may no longer like the food's color or texture (Fallon, Rozin, & Pliner, 1984). Other children want the same favorite foods served repeatedly and become fussy eaters of other items. Although some of these preferences are the children's idiosyncrasies, many preschoolers are the most picky about foods that also are rejected by other family members (Gardner, 1982).

Preschoolers and Health, Illness, and Injury

Dealing With Infectious Illnesses

Babies receive a natural immunity from their mothers for many infectious diseases, but this natural immunity lasts only about a year. Therefore, in early childhood and during the school years, children tend to get infectious diseases if exposed to someone with the disease.

Some contagious diseases can be prevented through immunization. In immunizations, children are given "germs" in a very weakened or killed form; these "germs" cause the children's bodies to produce antibodies. Early immunizations can prevent diphtheria, pertussis (whooping cough), tetanus, poliomyelitis, measles, rubella (German measles), and mumps. Another contagious disease, smallpox, has been eradicated because of immunization, and routine vaccination is no longer recommended (Leach, 1982).

Vaccinations have reduced the incidence of many serious childhood diseases. Between 1977 and 1982, for example, cases of rubella dropped from over 20,000 to only 2,300. Likewise, measles dropped from over 57,000 cases to just over 1,700 cases in the same 5-year period (Bumpers, 1984).

The low incidences of these diseases may have lulled parents into a false sense of security, however. Beginning in the early 1980s, as many as one third of American children were not receiving immunizations. The result has been an increase in the number of cases of measles and other childhood diseases, such as whooping cough. This underscores the needs to continue public health education programs to encourage immunizations and to provide these services to families who cannot afford them.

Children with stressful lives usually experience more illness, especially illnesses that affect the stomach and respiratory systems. A move to a new home, parental career changes or loss of job, parental conflict with each other or with in-laws, a change in the family's financial situation, legal problems, or a mother's pregnancy can increase young children's health problems (Beautrais, Fergusson, & Shannon, 1982).

Reducing Preschoolers' Accidents

All preschoolers have minor accidents. Young children who seem "accident-prone" may be more distracted by worries, more careless, less well coordinated, or especially fearful in comparison to their peers. Actually, "accident-prone" children are not more likely than other children to have serious injuries, just more mild and moderate-level injuries (Rivara & Mueller, 1987). While minor accidents are an inescapable part of these years, they are survivable. Serious injuries, however, are the leading cause of death among preschoolers in the United States, especially accidents involving motor vehicles (passenger and pedestrian), drownings, fires, suffocations, falls, poisonings, and firearms (Rivara & Mueller, 1987).

Children can benefit from behavioral approaches to injury prevention, using techniques of modeling, skills development, guided practice, and rewards and punishments (Roberts, Fanurik, & Layfield, 1987). All young children can benefit from car safety devices (Decker, Dewey, Hutcheson, & Shafner, 1984; Roberts & Turner, 1984). Professionals estimate that regular use of car seats, booster seats, and seat belts would reduce motor vehicle injuries and deaths to children by 70 to 90 percent (Roberts et al., 1987). In one study, parents were rewarded with lottery tickets if their preschool children arrived properly buckled in at their day-care center. These rewards to parents produced a large increase in the use of safety devices (from 49 to 80 percent at one center and from 11 to 64 percent at another center). Even when the rewards were no longer provided, safety device use stayed above initial levels (Roberts & Turner, 1986).

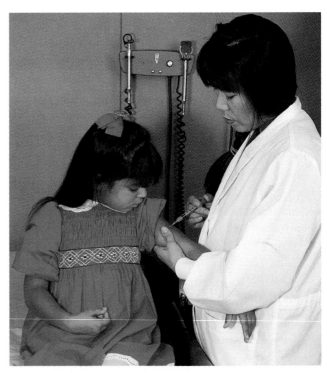

Many childhood diseases can be prevented through immunization. However, about a third of American children are not receiving this preventative treatment. Current social policy is trying to increase the availability and use of low-cost immunizations.

Accidents and injuries are unavoidable during childhood. But by practicing fire drills, installing smoke detectors, regularly using seat belts, securing medicines and household cleaning products, using child-proof medicine containers, and setting the hot water heater at a safe level, parents can build safer environments to reduce the likelihood of serious injuries.

guided review

1. The majority of physical growth in the preschool years is in the _____ region, with a weight gain of _____ lb each year.
2. The typical _____-year-old can ride a tricycle, throw a large ball, go up stairs unattended, string large beads on a shoelace, and copy a circle, while the typical _____-year-old can skip, do a running jump, descend stairs unattended, copy a triangle, and print his or her name.
3. When "Oscar the Grouch" is hidden in one of eight trash cans, preschool children do an inefficient search, due to limitations in _____ ability.
4. Compared to older individuals, preschoolers have _____ sleep cycles and more _____ sleep.
5. Of the sleep disturbances, _____ occur during the REM stage of sleeping, but _____ and _____ occur during non-REM stages.
6. Compared to adults, preschoolers need _____ meals but need to eat _____ often.
7. Due to an increase in infectious diseases in the preschool years, _____ are an important health prevention measure, and because _____ are the leading cause of death in this time period, such precautions as car seats and smoke alarms are important.

8. Research findings show that _____ approaches to injury prevention can modify both children's and parents' behavior and result in fewer injuries and deaths.

Cognitive Development and Preschoolers

Memory Capabilities of Preschool Children

What are the memory capabilities of preschool children? How do these memory capabilities change during the preschool years? How do preschoolers' abilities differ from those of older children? Two-year-olds have functional memory capacities, and on a yes-no recognition task, they can recognize at least a dozen pictures or toys (Perlmutter, 1986). Although 2-year-olds can remember persons and objects, they have little ability to remember events and can only remember single segments, such as getting a present at a party (Brown, Branford, Ferrara, & Campione, 1983). Older preschool children do better remembering events, especially those events that were unusual or highly emotional (Hurlock & Schwartz, 1932).

Memory abilities and language capabilities go hand in hand—just as recall of objects and persons dominates until age 2 1/2, the majority of the first 50 words in a child's vocabulary are object and person names (Nelson & Ross, 1980). By age 3, recall of events exceeds that of objects and persons (Nelson & Ross, 1980). Most 4-year-olds can remember both details and sequence of events. For this reason, children now may protest when an adult, reading a favorite story, tries to skip a page or change some of the wording (Brown et al., 1983).

Other memory research findings suggest that:

- Preschoolers can learn lists of words that are meaningful to them faster than other word lists. When appropriate words are chosen, preschoolers may learn words at rates similar to school-age children (Richman, Niden, & Pittman, 1976). Preschoolers recall more of lists with related words than lists with unrelated words (Perlmutter, 1986).
- Although school-age children have larger memory spans than younger children, younger children often have better visual memory for pictures than do older children (Elkind, 1981a).
- Preschoolers perform better when they expect to be tested than when they do not have this expectation. Preschoolers who rehearse words recall more than children who do not rehearse (Perlmutter, 1986; Weissberg & Paris, 1986).
- Four-year-olds and 5-years-olds can remember the order of items on supermarket shelves and the order of a series of pictures they are shown (Brown et al., 1983).
- The forgetting rates of 3- and 4-year-olds are nearly identical to those of older children (Perlmutter, 1986).

In other words, preschoolers have developed some of the same memory strategies as older individuals. The abilities to learn related lists, to rehearse, and to take advantage of knowing a test will increase in the school years and into adulthood, but the memory abilities of preschool children are quite remarkable. For example, the average 5-year-old child has learned how to use and remember several thousand words (Perlmutter, 1986).

Metamemory

Metamemory—knowing about one's memory strategies and whether particular information is held in one's memory—improves during the preschool years. One study compared the memory strategies used by younger and older preschoolers who were asked to remember five items and to buy these items in the nursery school's playstore (Isotoma, 1975). Three-year-olds barely waited for the items to be said and then rushed to the playstore and bought items, some of which were not on the given list. Four-year-olds listened more attentively and then hurried to buy the five items before they forgot which items to buy. The 5-year-olds, however, listened attentively and actively rehearsed the items. If they forgot an item, they usually asked the adult to repeat the list. Thus, during the preschool years, children learn to make more efficient use of memory strategies.

Development of Scripts

Preschoolers like to have **scripts,** or descriptions of appropriate sequences of events in specific situations. For example, 4-year-olds may ask questions about birthday parties before they go off to a party. Having scripts about events helps young children to know what to expect and how to act, and even aids them in forming memories about the event. Five-year-olds may repeatedly ask, "What is kindergarten going to be like?" "What will happen on the first day?" "What kinds of things will I do in school?" and so on. Their lack of previous experience with school means that they rely heavily on answers that parents and older siblings give to these questions to form scripts about a new experience. Sometimes, children form scripts by asking about people's memories of their childhood. Florence and Benjamin, for example, help themselves to understand what Christmas will be like by asking such questions such as, "What did Santa Claus put in Aunt Jan's stocking when she was little?"

Four-year-olds are good at scripts, and if asked to describe a familiar daily event, such as "What do you do while you're at day care?", they relate events as adults would (Nelson, 1978). However, children may also develop faulty scripts based on misperceptions, combining events from separate settings, and limitations of their thinking processes. For example, here is one 3-year-old's script about how to milk a cow:

> *There's this big brown cow with the red eyes and wet tongue, and he has a balloon under him full of nipples. The man gets a pail of milk and a fire hose, and they put the fire hose on one of the nipples, and put the other end in the milk pail—and then they turn on this machine and fill the cow full of milk. (Linkletter, 1961)*

Preschoolers are more rigid than adults in wanting to adhere exactly to scripts (Wimmer, 1979). When their parents modify mealtime procedures or bedtime rituals, they may get very upset because "That's not the way it's done." They may get confused when an activity that is usually done in one setting is done in a modified way in a different setting. For example, a 4-year-old girl in a church for the first time whispered when the congregation knelt, "Mommy, what are they doing now?" Her mother responded, "Shhh, they're getting ready to say their prayers." The surprised child yelled, "What? With all their clothes on?" (Linkletter, 1961). Obviously, her script called for praying to occur at bedtime in pajamas.

Preschoolers, it seems, would wish the world to be a bit more predictable. For example, they may object when pancakes are served for supper rather than for breakfast. Or, when they know their gender with certainty, they may want to do only activities that fit their gender and reject some activities that they used to enjoy. Parents must learn to deal with preschoolers' rigidity in a variety of ways.

Piaget's Preoperational Stage of Thought

Around age 2, children leave the sensorimotor stage of cognitive development and enter what Jean Piaget called the **preoperational stage** of thinking, a stage that lasts until they are about 7 years old. The stage begins when children are able to use symbols—that is, they can use one thing to represent another (Mandler, 1983). For example, preschool children can use sand to make cakes, to build towers, or as fairy dust to make toys magical. Over the preschool years, children become more adept at using the symbolism of language, numbers, and play.

Preschoolers bring forward into the preoperational stage the hard-earned abilities of the sensorimotor stage, such as believing in the permanence of objects and the world. Although the new entrants into this stage can deal with object permanence, language, symbolism, and imitation, they have numerous shortcomings and errors in their thinking about objects and events. Over the 5 years in this stage, children learn from their play and other activities to overcome the basic faults in their thinking.

Piaget's theory (1952b, 1954, 1962) has held up well, although the way Piaget designed tasks and asked children questions sometimes led him to underestimate the abilities of small children (Brown, 1988; Brown & Desforges, 1979; Siegel, 1978). To avoid underestimating the complexity of young children's cognitive reasoning, researchers have

Young children develop scripts for the holidays. They have set expectations, for example, about birthday parties. They know there should be games, presents, silly hats, ice cream, and cake.

found that they should use familiar situations, remove task distractors, and use simple language. "Under certain circumstances," young children do better than Piaget himself believed, but preschool children do think in a qualitatively different way from infants and also from older children and adults (Boden, 1979; Brown et al., 1983).

Transductive Reasoning

Preschool children primarily use **transductive reasoning,** which is reasoning from particular to particular (Phillips, 1975). Unlike adults, preschoolers are incapable of **inductive** (reasoning from specifics to reach general conclusions) and **deductive** (reasoning from general ideas to reach specific conclusions) thinking. Being limited to transductive reasoning means that preschoolers make many erroneous conclusions about the world. They may, for example, reason that, since hot water in the sink is used to wash dishes, hot water in the sink always means dishes are going to be washed. Or, young children who typically have pancakes for breakfast may get confused that bedtime comes so soon after pancakes are served for an evening meal. Preschool children overgeneralize the connection between one known specific and an event. Of course, adults often make similar errors, but they have the skills to reflect on and logically readjust their conclusions, while preschoolers are more limited in dealing with their errors.

Transductive reasoning leads children to assume that causality is related to the closeness of events. When one event follows another, they reason that the first event causes the second. Therefore, Naomi might conclude that alarm clocks make the sun come up. Or, if the letter carrier usually delivers mail shortly before his sister returns from school, Joshua may think that the postal worker determines when school is dismissed.

Challenging Tasks for Preschoolers

Some tasks are particularly hard for preschoolers, but these are also the tasks that preschoolers must learn before entering Piaget's third stage—the concrete operations stage. These tasks include classification, statements of comparisons, seriation, and conservation problems.

During the preoperational stage, children play with small items to learn about the concept of number and amounts. When these M&Ms are equally spaced, this little girl can easily tell when they have the same number. But will she be fooled when the experimenter spreads the M&Ms in one line farther apart?

Classifications involves the ability to place similar objects into groups. At the beginning of the preoperational stage, children are unsuccessful in grouping tasks. Given blocks that vary in both shapes and colors, young children will start grouping on one factor and switch to another factor in midstream. Thus, Kristen's first group of blocks might consist of a green circle, a yellow circle, and a green square, a group with no overriding common factor. Later in the preoperational stage, Kristen is able to sort on the basis of one factor (either shape or color) but is not yet able to do multiple classification (use both shape and color to form groups).

Another aspect of classification—dealing with subordinate and superordinate classes—also creates difficulty for small children. These tasks pose questions in the form of "Are there more of X or more of Y?" For example, if young children are shown some glass beads, and some of these glass beads are blue and others are red, the children are likely to give an incorrect answer to the question "Are there more blue beads or more glass beads?" Likewise, when 3-year-old Patrick is viewing a spring garden of daffodils, tulips, and hyacinths, he may answer "Daffodils" if asked, "Are there more daffodils or more flowers?" Piaget believed that first-graders still find these tasks difficult.

Ability to deal with subordinate and superordinate classes, however, is greatly affected by familiarity of task materials and how questions are posed to children. Six-year-olds were shown three black toy cows and one white toy cow that were laid on their sides to indicate sleeping. When the children were asked a question like Piaget would have phrased it—"Are there more black cows or more cows?"—only 3 of 12 children answered correctly. However, 11 out of 20 children in the other condition answered correctly the question, "Are there more black cows or more sleeping cows?" Rather than being unable to do any subordinate-superordinate reasoning, young children's abilities are greatly influenced by specific wording that can aid or hinder understanding of the task (Donaldson, 1978).

Seriation is the ability to order items according to size, a challenging task for young children. Piaget asked preschoolers to put 10 sticks in order of their size and found that they could not do this task without errors. However, more recently, researchers found that 75 percent of 3- and 4-year-olds can complete this task if 4 sticks are used instead of 10. Once the 4 sticks are in correct order, the majority of preschoolers can add more sticks at their correct location (Koslowski, 1980).

A final type of task that preoperational children cannot solve involves **conservation.** Conservation problems require an understanding that quantities remain the same even when appearances change. Conservation tasks include conservation of numbers, amounts, and volume. Piaget (1952a) showed 4- and 5-year-old children two rows of candies that each contained six pieces. When these pieces were aligned, the children generally could tell that the rows contained equal numbers of candies. Then Piaget pushed one row of candies closer together and, from the other row, removed one candy and moved the remaining candies farther apart. Children were told that they could eat one piece of candy from the row that contained more candies. Typically, they chose their piece of candy from the longer line that actually had fewer candies. The length of lines was enough to keep young children from having conservation of numbers. Most recent research concludes with Piaget that young children of 3 or 4 years do not understand conservation of number, while children of 6 or 7 years do grasp this concept (Halford & Boyle, 1985).

A more difficult conservation task is conservation of mass, or amount. Some second-graders still do not consistently conserve amount. In one type of task, young children are presented with two balls of clay that they judge as being identical in amount. While they watch, one of the balls is transformed into a coil or snakelike shape. Five-year-olds typically will state that the coil has more clay than the ball.

In a more complex task, children watch as the experimenter puts liquid into two identical glasses. After children state that the two glasses have equal amounts, the liquid in one glass is poured into a taller, thinner glass. When children now compare the two filled glasses, many 6-year-olds state that the taller glass contains more liquid. Failure to conserve volume consistently can be seen in everyday examples of preschoolers' lives. Young children may want more of a desired beverage if it is in a short, squat glass than if the same amount of beverage is poured into a tall, thin glass.

Characteristic Limitations of Preschoolers' Thinking

Research observations with preoperational children have concentrated on the following characteristic limitations of preschoolers' thinking: realism, appearance versus reality, animism, artificialism, transformations, centering, irreversibility, and egocentrism. Also, it takes several years before children understand the concept of money.

Realism

Piaget (1929) and others (e.g., Keil, 1979) suggested that young children believed that everything has physical existence—that even ideas and dreams are physical things. Children are adualistic—that is, they do not separate the world into mental and physical, or into objective and subjective. Childhood **realism** means that young children attribute real physical properties to mental phenomena. In other words, they might believe that dreams are external, objective events, or they might not be able to distinguish between a thought of an event and the event itself—for example, they might believe that thinking about hurting someone is actually hurting someone.

Recent research looked at whether preschoolers understood the distinctions between mental and real phenomena (Wellman & Estes, 1986). These distinctions are:

1. Real entities allow behavioral and sensory contact, while mental entities do not. Therefore, physical objects can be touched and seen, but mental phenomena can only be experienced by the senses during a dream state.
2. Only real entities have public existence—that is, they can be experienced by other people.
3. Physical phenemena have consistent existence, while mental phenomena have temporal and spatial inconsistency.

Children from 3 to 5 years old were asked about characteristics of real and imagined cookies by showing a drawing of a child and telling the subjects: "See this boy. He likes cookies very much. Right now he is hungry, so he is thinking about a cookie." The children were then shown a second drawing and told: "This boy likes cookies, too. Right now, he is hungry, so his mother gave him a cookie." Children were asked to point out which of the boys (or both) could: (1) see the cookie, (2) not touch the cookie, (3) eat the cookie, (4) let a friend eat the cookie, or (5) save the cookie and eat it tomorrow. The results of the study showed that even the majority of the 3-year-olds (72 percent) could correctly answer these questions, although the 5-year-olds had a higher level of correct responses (92 percent).

These research results contradict the belief that young children fail to distinguish between internal mental phenomena and objective reality. Young children do not believe that dreamed and imagined figures can be seen in a sensory-perceptual sense. Piaget's findings may be due to asking children about mental activities, rather than mental objects. Children have more difficulty perceiving, remembering, and understanding events than objects, and this difficulty seems to be true of mental activity, as well as of physical activity (Wellman & Estes, 1986).

Appearance Versus Reality

Preschool children are perception-bound—that is, they have trouble going beyond visual information. For preschool-age children "Seeing is believing." For example, 3-year-olds were shown a red toy car that was then covered by a green filter so that the car now appeared black. Next, the children were handed the car without the filter, followed by placing the car behind the green filter again. When asked what color the car really was, the 3-year-olds were fooled and answered "black." Young children who viewed milk under a green light also tended to conclude that the milk was really green instead of white (Flavell, 1986). Likewise, when young children view small objects under a magnifying glass, they call the objects big. Even having hands-on experience with pseudo-objects may not prevent children from being fooled by the objects' appearance.

Animism

Animism is the belief that inanimate objects have a consciousness and are alive. Animism seems to be a common belief among 3-year-olds but is less evident by the age of 5 (Bullock, 1985). Three-year-olds may believe that a lost item is hiding or that the sidewalk deliberately tripped them when they fell. Young Annie may hit a chair for getting in her way or scold her shoelace for becoming untied. Linkletter (1961) told the following story: A 3-year-old child said, "Look at this! I pulled this cornstalk up all by myself!" Her parent responded, "My, aren't you strong." The child replied, "I sure am. The whole world had hold of the other end." Even adults may sometimes continue bits of animistic thinking. For example, many adults name their cars and boats, kick uncooperative vending machines, and talk back to their television sets and radios.

Artificialism

Artificialism is the belief that human beings cause natural phenomena. Young children may believe that all lakes were dug by people using machines or that people planted every tree in a forest. Belief in artificialism may result in some children asking parents to stop the rain for a picnic or to turn down the volume of thunder.

Transformations

Preschoolers have much trouble in understanding **transformations,** the transitions from one event to another. They can usually point out the beginnings and ends of events but are unable to understand and remember the sequence of events in-between. Difficulty with transformations is one reason why preschoolers are unable to conserve numbers and amounts.

Because of transformation problems, children may combine parts of different stories, events, or understandings into an explanation that does not make complete sense

A child with artificialism believes that people planted each tree that makes up Cathedral Grove on Vancouver Island, British Columbia.

to adults. Note the preschooler's confused thinking in the following exchange: A mother asked her son, "Why can't you behave like Sally next door?" He responded, "Because she's a doctor's kid." The mother asked, "What's that got to do with it?" The son replied, "The doctor always keeps the best babies for himself" (Linkletter, 1961). Obviously, the child understood that doctors have something to do with newborns, but the sequence and details of involved events are unknown.

Centering

Centering is paying attention to only one factor or dimension at a time. For example, in the conservation of volume task in which young children fail to realize that the different-shaped glasses contain the same amount of beverage, the children are paying attention to only one dimension (height) and are not able to consider the three dimensions needed to comprehend volume.

In one situation, a school-age boy used his 3-year-old brother's centering limitation to resolve a problem. The boy's little brother insisted on getting vanilla ice cream, and the ice-cream stand was out of vanilla. Finally, the older boy bought his brother a strawberry cone and handed it to him, saying, "Here you are—pink vanilla!" (Linkletter, 1961). The younger boy focused on the word *vanilla* and ignored the inconsistency of the color pink.

Irreversibility

Irreversibility is the inability to begin at the end of an operation and get back to the start. For example, irreversibility could keep you from using the information that $* + \$ = \#$ to figure out the answer to $\# - \$ = \_\_\_\_\_$. Irreversibility also can keep young children from realizing that their siblings also have siblings—namely, themselves—as the following exchange demonstrates:

> "Michelle, do you have a brother?"
> "Yes, Johnny!"
> "Well, does your brother Johnny have a sister?"
> "No."

Egocentrism

Young children's thinking is characterized by **egocentrism,** or difficulty in understanding another's point of view and the belief that other people experience the environment identical to oneself. One characteristic of egocentric thinking is the belief that the world revolves around onself. Here are some everyday examples of egocentric behavior by preschoolers:

- Small children may point out items to their grandmothers, even though they are speaking to their grandmothers on the telephone.
- Small children may be very easy to locate during a game of hide-and-seek because they do not hide themselves completely behind an object. Once their faces are hidden and they are unable to see others, they assume that others can no longer see them.
- Young children may think that they can play ball with God because, when they throw the ball up into the air, God throws it back to them.
- Preschool children may believe that the sun follows them around, that the birds sing just for them in the morning, or that the ocean makes waves just so they can have fun jumping in them.
- If preschoolers notice that their parents look sad, they may offer them their teddy bears or chocolate chip cookies because those are things that can comfort the children when they are feeling badly themselves. If it works for them, it should work for their mom or dad.

Research indicates that, in some settings, young children display high levels of nonegocentric behavior (Flavell, 1977). In one study, 2- and 3-year-olds were given hollow cubes with a picture inside. The children were asked to show the picture to another person, and nearly all of these very young children turned the cube so that the other person could actually see the picture (Flavell, & Flavell, Lempers, 1977). In a different study with 2- and 3-year-olds, the children understood that, when a card with different pictures on each side is placed between two persons, each person gets to see a different picture (Masangkay et al., 1974).

Other research indicates that preschoolers do understand different sides of objects, and can, for example, think about the different sides of such items as houses or trucks (Flavell, Flavell, Green, & Wilcox, 1981). In a simplification of Piaget's three mountain task, depicted in Figure 6.2, Borke (1975) used a Muppet character ("Sesame Street's" Grover) in a car and familiar objects to study children's abilities to depict scenes from another's perspective. In this study, 3- and 4-year-old children saw Grover drive a car around a fire engine and stop at various spots to look at the fire engine. When the car was parked, the children were asked to turn a turntable with a duplicate fire engine

(a)

(b)

Figure 6.2

Task materials used to test egocentric thinking in preschoolers. (a) With familiar toys, such as a fire engine, most 3- and 4-year-old children can correctly identify Grover's point of view. (b) Fewer 4-year-olds and fewer than 50 percent of 3-year-olds can identify Grover's point of view with the unfamiliar mountain scene. (This figure is similar to the scene appearing in Borke's test.)

Source: Mountain Scene from H. Borke, "Piaget's Mountain Revisited" in *Developmental Psychology,* Vol. 11, p. 240–243, 1975.

on it until the fire engine matched what Grover could see. Children were able to correctly predict Grover's view over 80 percent of the time when a fire engine or other familiar objects (e.g., a boat, farm animals) were used. However, Piaget's initial task of three mountains was more difficult for the young children, with correct response rates of only 42 percent for 3-year-olds and only 67 percent for 4-year-olds.

While young children may think more egocentrically than adults, adults use an egocentric perspective surprisingly often. Egocentric thinking is exhibited when adults fail to understand individuals from different ethnic, age, or gender backgrounds; when adults say "Why me?" when something bad happens to them; and whenever they believe they can influence chance events like slot machines or timed events like traffic lights by talking, cursing, or rituals. The common beliefs in superstitions and magical thinking also reflect egocentric ways of thought.

Remembering the Limiting Characteristics of the Preoperational Stage

First, remember the different limitations of the preoperational stage by using the following silly phrase as a clue to their initial letters: I TRACE AT A.

Then learn the briefest of definitions to remind you what the limitations are. For example:

I—Irreversibility	Can't get back to the start.
T—Transductive	Specific ⟶ Specific
R—Realism	Dreams and thoughts are real.
A—Appearance versus Reality	"Seeing is believing."
C—Centering	One aspect at a time
E—Egocentrism	My view, my way
A—Animism	Objects live.
T—Transformations	Lost in the process
A—Artificialism	Humans make nature.

Table 6.2
Stages in the Development of the Concept of Money and Money's Value

Stage	Characteristics
1	Child has only vague awareness that money is involved in the buying and selling process.
2	Child knows that bought items must be paid for, but child believes that all money denominations are equal.
3	Child understands that money denominations differ in value, but child does not understand the rules.
4	Child understands that items cost different amounts and that, to buy something, one must have enough money.
5	Child understands money's value and the relationship of money to the cost of different items.
6	Child understands the process of getting change from a purchase.

From A. E. Berti and A. S. Bombi, "The Development of the Concept of Money and Its Value: A Longitudinal Study" in *Child Development,* 52, 1179–1182, 1981. Copyright © The Society For Research In Child Development, Inc., at University of Chicago Press, Chicago, IL.

Understanding the Concept of Money

One of Piaget's important contributions was his emphasis on children making gradual progress in understanding aspects of the world. Frequent interaction with materials allows children to learn more about the materials' properties.

Although children are exposed to money and shopping early in life, it takes them several years to understand the rules of the monetary world. For example, young preschoolers can be easily confused about money and may eagerly trade away dimes for bigger nickels. Parents have become frustrated trying to explain the workings of a bank's automatic money machine to a young child. Young

Table 6.3
Normal Speech and Language Development in the Preschool Years

Age	Normal Development
2 years	Has 270-word vocabulary; uses 25 phonemes; averages three-word sentences; starts using pronouns, adjectives, and adverbs; can say vowels correctly
2.5 years	Has 425-word vocabulary; uses 27 phonemes; speaks an average of 140 words per hour; can repeat two digits from memory; often announces intentions before action; begins asking questions
3 years	Has 900-word vocabulary; averages four-word sentences; averages 15,000 spoken words daily; can repeat three digits from memory; starts using plurals and prepositions; states toilet needs aloud
3.5 years	Has 1,200-word vocabulary; can say a nursery rhyme; 7 percent of sentences either compound or complex; can relate activities in correct order
4 years	Has 1,540-word vocabulary; averages five-word sentences; can count to three; can repeat nine-word sentences from memory; can repeat four digits from memory; may ask 500 questions daily
4.5 years	Has 1,800-word vocabulary; averages over five-word sentences; can count to 20; averages 230 words per hour
5 years	Has 2,200-word vocabulary; averages six-word sentences; can repeat five digits from memory; defines most words in terms of their uses

Source: Data from H. K. Silver, "Growth and Development" in *Current Pediatric Diagnosis & Treatment,* 1987, edited by C. H. Kemp, et al. From C. D. Weiss and H. S. Lillywhite, *Communication Disorders: A Handbook for Prevention and Early Intervention,* 1976, Mosby, St. Louis, MO.

children may, for example, not realize that this wondrous machine does not provide the family with an endless supply of paper money. Table 6.2 shows six stages that researchers believe children pass through on their way to understanding money.

In one study, 3-year-olds tended to be in Stage 1 and only possessed a vague awareness that money is necessary to buy items. When reexamined 1 year later, nearly half of these children had progressed to Stage 2 and a fourth of the children had advanced to Stage 3. Although there is much variation among children, most will not reach Stage 6 until they are 7 (Berti & Bombi, 1981).

Language Development During the Preschool Years

Normal Speech and Language Development

Before the preschool years, children's language development has already progressed from prespeech (e.g., cooing, babbling) and holophrases (sentencelike words) to two-word sentences. Young preschool children are already capable of multiple-word sentences, and over the next 3 years, they show rapid progress to adultlike language structures. The typical course of speech and language development is summarized in Table 6.3.

Preschool children love to look at picture books and to have stories read to them. Psychologists believe that reading aloud to young children builds good parent-child communication and is helpful in developing the necessary skills for children to learn to read on their own.

The ability to read seems to develop in three distinct stages (Gibson & Levin, 1975). When parents make a regular practice of reading stories to their preschoolers, they facilitate their children's movement from one stage to another. In the first stage, preschoolers realize that spoken words can be represented in print—that is, that parents do not make up a story to accompany the pictures in the books but instead take the story itself from markings on the pages. Once preschoolers have made this association, they enter the second stage, in which they learn that the markings represent words. Children in this stage often try to match the spoken word to the page's markings. These attempts can be fraught with errors, such as children believing that each letter, rather than group of letters, is the equivalent of a word (Smith, 1977). By the time children are in the third and final stage of prereading, they are able to recognize letters and some of the sounds that make up words, and some youngsters even try to figure out unfamiliar words by sounding out their components.

Children whose parents read to them have more practice in reading readiness skills, such as recognizing various letters, understanding letter order, matching and blending sounds, and perceiving differences in how words look (Venesky, 1975). They learn that reading is an enjoyable task to share, and they have parents who model reading and reading enjoyment.

Reading aloud to children can be begun in infancy or during the preschool years and continued through all the school years. In the preschool years, this activity tends to promote children's desire to read, while in older children, it promotes children's reading skills. Children of all ages enjoy listening to books that are too difficult for them to read alone, and parents can choose books that broaden their children's interests and knowledge (Kimmel & Segel, 1983).

What kinds of books should parents read to their young children? Very young children like books with lots of pictures

that they can view while parents read the story. Preschool children seem to prefer stories that are in verse rather than in prose (Hayes, Chemelski, & Palmer, 1982), and nursery rhymes and other rhyming stories may help in building phonological skills (familiarity with component sounds in words). Research findings suggest a strong relationship between knowledge of nursery rhymes and acquisition of phonological skills: Knowlege of nursery rhymes at age 3 predicted rhyme detection skills at age 4 (Maclean, Bryant, & Bradley, 1987). On the other hand, young children remember more about stories told in prose than in rhyme (Hayes et al., 1982). To build attention span, memory abilities, and phonological skills, parents should read a variety of rhyming and prose stories to their children.

Parents might wish to consider the gender-role stereotypes presented in books and be careful about how they refer to storybook characters by gender. In research with preschool children, children who were read gender-stereotypic children's books usually played with gender-typed toys after the story. However, children who were read nonstereotypic children's books more often chose nonstereotypic toys (Ashton, 1983). Some book publishers have tried to reduce sexism in books by making more storybook characters of indeterminate gender. However, when mothers read stories to their preschoolers, the mothers use masculine pronouns 95

percent of the time when referring to these indeterminate gender characters (DeLoache, Cassidy, & Carpenter, 1987). Since preschoolers are very interested in what boys and girls are able and allowed to do, this behavior by parents may lead children to have limited expectations for girls' behaviors.

In addition to reading books that their children find enjoyable and have picked out for themselves, parents may wish to locate award-winning children's books to assure high quality. Librarians are also excellent references in choosing good children's books. Once children can read for themselves, they tend to prefer to read books that were once read to them, rather than to choose other books (McCormick, 1977).

Once a storybook is chosen, parents can make the storytime more enjoyable by creating a pleasant, warm atmosphere and comfortable physical setting in which reading is done with some consistency. Many parents find that young children especially like to be read to each night just before bedtime. Storytelling occasions are times when parents can become "hams" and create a mood by reading dramatically, modifying volume and pace of speech to fit the story's action and changing voice for the various characters (Kimmel & Segel, 1983). When reading aloud to children, adults should throw out their

When parents read to children, the children know that reading is fun and important. It helps make learning to read something they want to do.

inhibitions and self-consciousness and read for the children's entertainment and pleasure.

Parents can also help children to relate printed words with meanings by pointing out printed words in the environment (McGee, 1986). Many parents of preschoolers have been surprised to see their children call out letters on the television screen during "Sesame Street" or to hear their children identify "McDonald's" while pointing to the appropriate sign at the restaurant. Young children may correctly point out the letter *M* on a package of "M&Ms" or be able to differentiate the *M* and the *S* on the cover of "Ms." magazine. One study found that 3- to 6-year-olds could recognize more words on food labels than they could in books (Jones & Hendrickson, 1970). Another study found that more than half of 4- to 6-year-olds could correctly identify some of the words contained in photographs of natural settings (Ylisto, 1967). This recognition of letters and words in the environment can help young children to learn correspondence between printed and spoken words (Heibert, 1978).

Parents can help children to prepare for reading acquisition by using words that naturally occur in the environment. For example, while preparing lunch, parents can casually point out the word *soup* on a soup can or *milk* on the milk carton. When children express interest in printed words on food labels or in magazines, parents can tell their children what the words are while pointing to each word. Parents and preschool teachers can encourage youngsters to find words in their environment and to incorporate these words into play/learning. Even youngsters who have not expressed much interest in words in books often are excited to discover what the words in their environment mean (McGee, 1986).

In a more active strategy, parents or teachers can create play kits that include print materials. For example, a restaurant play kit could include play dishes, play food, order pads, play money, and menus.

In this way, young children interact with print materials in meaningful situations (McGee, 1983). Another suggested activity is to use food packages and coupons to encourage preschool children to find two identical food packages, to match the correct coupon to the food item, and to find particular letters on the different food items (Tompkins, 1984). These types of activities provide reading variety, encourage children to explore words in their environment, and build reading interest during play.

Reading to preschoolers is beneficial in increasing language development. After daily book-reading for a 3-month period, both 2- and 3-year-olds scored higher than children in control groups on listening vocabularies, speaking vocabularies, and average sentence length (Burroughs, 1972; McCormick, 1977). Studies done several years apart found a positive relationship between being read to and success in first-grade reading (Almy, 1949; Durkin, 1966).

By age 5, children can use language in seven different ways (Dale, 1976):

1. In an instrumental way—that is, to express needs and accomplish tasks:
   "I want a cookie." "Gimme the red crayon."
2. In a regulatory way, to control their own behavior and to influence the behavior of others:
   "No, don't." "Let's go now."
3. In an interactional way, to build and organize relationships:
   "Play game." "Let's pretend to be elephants."
4. In a personal way, to learn about themselves:
   "Happy." "I'm sleepy."
5. In a heuristic way, to ask questions about the world:
   "Why does the sun shine?" "Why do stars twinkle?"
6. In imaginative ways that encourage pretend and fantasy games:
   "You be the mommy, and I'll be the daddy." "I'm a princess, Daddy."
7. To symbolize aspects of reality:
   "I'm sad, Daddy. Are you sad, too?"

Preschool children want to use language correctly. For example, preschoolers who are shown an unusual shape and told that the shape is a "wug" and who then are shown two of the shapes will answer that there are now "two wugs," demonstrating that they are able to figure out the general rule of plurals (Berko, 1958). Often, the errors preschoolers make occur when they generalize a grammatical rule to a situation requiring an exception (e.g., say "deers" for the plural of "deer").

Five-year-old children's use of language can easily be confused by irrelevant detail. In one study, children were shown a large doll and asked, "Is this doll easy to see or hard to see?" The 5-year-olds correctly answered, "Easy to see." When a blindfold was placed on the doll and the children were asked the same question, however, 78 percent of the 5-year-olds incorrectly answered, "Hard to see." From 5-year-olds to 7-year-olds, the percentage of correct answers rose from 22 to 86 (Chomsky, 1969).

Young children already understand the genders of pronouns. Children who were given a gender-neutral description of a fictitious "wudgemaker" heard repeated references to the wudgemaker as "he," "they," "he or she," or "she." When the children were later asked to rate how well women could do a wudgemaker's job, ratings varied by which pronoun the children had heard. Women got the lowest ratings when the children had heard "he," intermediate ratings when the children had heard "they" or "he or she," and the highest ratings when the children had heard "she" (Hyde, 1984).

This speech therapist is working with a four-year-old girl with a phonological disorder, a severe mispronunciation of sounds. Her mother listens in so that she can properly encourage later practice.

Speech and Language Disorders

Children who do not use words by age 2 have **delayed language development** (Silver, 1987). One possible cause is hypoacusis, or hearing loss. Children with hearing loss often have poorer articulation of the sounds *b, f,* and *u,* and may pronounce *d* instead of *g, y* instead of *l,* and *w* instead of *r.* Another contributing factor can be central nervous system dysfunction, especially mental retardation. Other associates of developmental delay of language include maternal deprivation, infantile autism, bilingualism, and a socially disadvantaged background.

Articulation disorders include omissions, distortions, substitutions, and additions (Silver, 1987). They can be caused by anatomical factors, such as cerebrum defects, cleft palate problems, or facial muscles. Other articulation problems occur when children copy cultural patterns or speech disorders of others.

Approximately 4 percent of youngsters have dysrhythmia, the lack of normal language fluency. In one type of dysrhythmia, **stuttering,** children's speech rhythm and fluency are disturbed by periodic blocking, repetition, or prolongation of sounds and words. Most stutterers begin to stutter before age 5, and stuttering is more common in boys than in girls. The early onset may mean that biological factors are involved, but stuttering also can be influenced by family members. Anxious parents who focus on their children's speaking errors increase self-consciousness, which then leads to more stuttering. A second dysrhythmia problem is **cluttering,** or rapid, nervous speech marked by omission of syllables (Silver, 1987).

9. Two-year-olds have memory for people and objects but little ability to remember _____; this ability, however, develops during the preschool years.
10. _____ is knowing about one's memory strategies and whether particular information is held in one's memory.
11. Having _____ about events helps young children to know what to expect, how to act, and what is important to remember.
12. Around age 2, children leave Piaget's _____ stage and enter the _____ stage.
13. Preschool children primarily use _____ reasoning (reasoning from particular to particular) and are not capable of reasoning from specifics to general conclusions (called _____ reasoning) or from general ideas to specific conclusions (called _____ reasoning).
14. _____ involves the ability to place similar objects into groups, and _____ is the ability to order items according to size.
15. From earliest to last, children learn to conserve _____, then _____, and finally _____.
16. _____ is the belief that thoughts and dreams are physical things, while _____ is the belief that inanimate objects are alive, and _____ is the belief that humans create natural phenomena.
17. Conservation tasks are difficult because young children have trouble with _____ (the sequence of events between the beginning and the end) and with _____ (focusing on only one dimension at a time).
18. The preschooler's difficulty in understanding another's point of view is called _____.
19. Most 2-year-olds know 270 words and average 3-word sentences; by age 5, the average vocabulary is _____ words, and the average number of words in a sentence is _____.
20. Children are considered to have delayed development of language if they do not use words by age _____; other speech disorders include _____ disorders, such as omissions and distortions of sounds, and _____ disorders, including stuttering and cluttering.

answers

9. events [LO-8]. 10. Metamemory [LO-8]. 11. scripts [LO-8].
12. sensorimotor; preoperational [LO-9]. 13. transductive; inductive; deductive [LO-9]. 14. Classification; seriation [LO-9]. 15. numbers; amounts (or: mass); volume [LO-9].
16. Realism; animism; artificialism [LO-9]. 17. transformations; centering [LO-9]. 18. egocentrism [LO-9]. 19. 2,200; six [LO-10]. 20. 2; articulation; dysrhythmia [LO-11].

Assessing Intelligence in Preschoolers

Traditional Approaches to IQ Measurement

The modern history of intelligence assessment began in 1904 in France, when Binet and Simon developed tests to distinguish bright from below-average schoolchildren. By 1911, they had a version that could be used with children ages 3 to 15.

Five years later, Lewis Terman at Stanford University adapted the Binet-Simon tests to American children. Terman converted scores from the individual subtests to a single number for intelligence, using the **IQ (intelligence quotient)** formula IQ = MA/CA × 100. In this formula, MA stands for **mental age,** or the average cognitive capabilities of an individual at a given age. CA stands for chronological age, the child's age in years and months. The test was constructed so that the average IQ was 100 (with a range of average from 90 to 110).

---

successful study tip

Rembering the IQ Formula

With regard to the IQ formula (MA/CA × 100), the most common error for beginning students is forgetting which term goes in the numerator and which goes in the denominator. Try the following phrase to help keep them straight!

MA IS ON TOP OF THINGS!

Children who can accomplish more than other children their ages receive MAs larger than their CAs. For example, if 3-year-old Sammy performs as well as the typical 4-year-old, his IQ is 4/3 × 100 or 133. Children with below-average intelligence receive MAs smaller than their CAs. If 5-year-old Chris performs as a typical 4-year-old, the resultant IQ score is only 80 (i.e., 4/5 × 100).

Research using the major intelligence tests (Stanford-Binet, Wechsler) has shown that IQ scores obtained when children are preschoolers are related to IQ scores at ages 10 and 18, but only weakly. IQ scores obtained at age 6 or older correlate much better with later IQ scores than do scores of preschoolers, suggesting that more accurate predictions of IQ are obtained in elementary school (Honzik, McFarlane, & Allen, 1948). Between the ages of 2 1/2 and 17, individuals' IQ scores vary more than 28 points, with one of three children's scores changing at least 30 points and one of seven children's scores changing at least 40 points (McCall, Applebaum, & Hogarty, 1973).

Overall, intelligence tests are better used to assess strong and weak points in children's thinking and interacting with the world than to rank children in terms of their general intellectual functioning.

Stanford-Binet Intelligence Scale

Terman revised the Stanford-Binet Intelligence Scale in 1937, and further revisions were done in 1960, 1972, and 1985. The last three revisions were needed to modernize some of the items, to simplify the score scheme, and to readapt the norms. The 1985 revision also changed from providing only a full IQ score per subject to providing analysis in four separate areas (short-term memory, abstract/visual reasoning, verbal reasoning, and quantitative reasoning) (Thorndike, Hagen, & Sattler, 1985).

The tasks on the Stanford-Binet are arranged by age level. That is, the tasks of the subtest for each age level consist of those items that a majority of children of that age could pass but that could not be passed by most younger children. For example, most 3-year-olds can draw a circle, but this task is too hard for 2-year-olds. Therefore, one of the items at the 3-year-old level is drawing a circle.

In contrast to the subtests for older children and adults, the tasks for preschool children are mostly nonverbal and ones that children enjoy. Four-year-olds, for example, are asked to name objects from memory, to distinguish between geometric forms, to name objects in pictures, and to define simple words, such as *orange* and *hat*. The Stanford-Binet Intelligence Scale can be used from age 2 on, but stability of scores is better after age 6.

Wechsler Preschool and Primary Scale of Intelligence

In 1939, David Wechsler developed his first widely used intelligence test, the Wechsler Bellevue Intelligence Scale, which became the Wechsler Adult Intelligence Test (WAIS) in 1955. He then developed the Wechsler Intelligence Scale for Children (WISC) for ages 6 to 17 and the Wechsler Preschool and Primary Scale of Intelligence (WPPSI) for ages 4 to 6 1/2. The WPPSI contains performance items, such as matching tasks and puzzles, and also verbal tasks, such as defining *shoe* and *ear* (pointing to the correct object counts). The WPPSI gives a composite IQ, a performance IQ, and a verbal IQ. Scores on WPPSI correlate weakly with IQs earned later on the WISC and WAIS.

Kaufman Assessment Battery for Children

The Kaufman Assessment Battery for Children (K-ABC) can be used with children ages 2 1/2 to over 12. Unlike the previously discussed tests, the norms for the K-ABC include a significant number of children with disabilities and minority children. This test tries to rely less on language background than the other two intelligence tests, while maintaining a wide range of testing materials (Kaufman & Kaufman, 1983).

Gesell Preschool Test

The Gesell Preschool Test can be used with children ages 2 1/2 to 6. This test measures development in four different areas: motor skills, language, adaptiveness, and personal-social development. Example tasks assess hand-eye coordination, visual perception, vocabulary, ability to follow directions, and attention span. Children's scores on this test

Young children who get to explore with materials similar to those that are found in intelligence tests are more likely to perform well on the tests.

might be predicted by an infant's attention to novel versus previously viewed individual stimuli or by heart-rate responses to repetitive versus novel stimuli (O'Connor, Cohen, & Parmelee, 1984; Rose & Wallace, 1985). Other studies look at brain-wave patterns during various perceptual or cognitive tasks. Certain patterns, for example, may be indicative of reading problems.

New Range of Intelligence

Traditional intelligence tests have focused largely on verbal, spatial ability, and mathematical tasks. Some psychologists believe that intelligence has been too narrowly defined and should include other components, such as musical ability, social skills, bodily skills, self-knowledge, and ability to deal with novelty (Gardner, 1983; Sternberg, 1984, 1985). A broad approach may help to detect youngsters with strong abilities in such areas as art and music, as well as in the more traditional academic areas.

New Emphasis on Use of Intelligence Assessment

The traditional use of intelligence test scores has been to classify children. Now, however, many psychologists suggest that the emphasis should be on detecting strengths and weaknesses, cognitive styles, and cognitive errors. Proponents of this trend believe in **cognitive modifiability,** the ability to change mental structures and contents. Cognitive deficiencies that can be modified through specially defined learning experiences include impulsiveness, failure to make comparisons, inadequate spatial orientation, not recognizing significant aspects of problems, and difficulty in making connections between different events or relationships (Feuerstein, 1980). Parents can use this emphasis on detection and correction of cognitive errors to help preschoolers to prepare for the school experience.

Intellectual Retardation

An appropriate use of intelligence assessment in the preschool years is to detect youngsters with below-average intelligence. Approximately one fourth of intellectual retardation is **organic retardation** (genetically or biologically caused). Examples include microcephaly (caused by a recessive genetic trait), Down syndrome (caused by an extra chromosome), cretinism (caused by thyroid deficiency), and phenylketonuria (caused by an enzyme deficiency). Of these examples, cretinism, hydrocephaly, and phenylketonuria can be treated if detected early. Without early intervention, however, these three are associated with severe or profound retardation in which IQs are 35 or lower.

Familial retardation is all retardation for which no known biological cause can be identified. Possible causes include impoverished environment, poor nutrition, deficient emotional support, and inadequate medical care. Many cases of familial retardation are mild retardation (IQs from 50 to 70), and early nutritional care, educational enrichment programs for infants and preschoolers, and family training could significantly improve the intellectual ability of many.

are given as a **developmental quotient (DQ).** Children who score a DQ of 100 can pass all the tasks appropriate for their age. Children whose development is accelerated receive DQs over 100; children who are developmentally behind receive DQs under 100. This test can be used to assess children for placement into kindergarten (Ames, Gillespie, Haines, & Ilg, 1980).

System of Multicultural Pluralistic Assessment

The System of Multicultural Pluralistic Assessment (SOMPA) can be used with children who are at least 5 years old. This test not only assesses verbal and nonverbal intelligence—it pinpoints factors that affect intelligence and school performance. Parts of this assessment package look at children's physical health, social adjustment to school, and social and economic background (Mercer & Lewis, 1978).

New Approaches to Intelligence Assessment

New Predictors of Intelligence

One of the trends in intelligence assessment is to explore new possible markers of intellectual potential. For example, studies with infants have suggested that later intelligence

Special Effects on Cognitive and Intellectual Development of Preschoolers

Effects of Television on Preschoolers

What do children do more than anything except sleep? What activity has changed American lives more than any other during the 20th century? For what activity do the majority of Americans rearrange their sleeping patterns, mealtimes, and social lives? The answer is television watching. Television sets are turned on an average of more than 7 hr a day, and preschoolers average over 2 1/2 hr of daily viewing. By age 3, most children can name their favorite television shows (Johnson, 1967; Liebert, Sprafken, & Davidson, 1982; Nielsen, 1985; Steinberg, 1980).

While preschoolers are eager consumers of television shows, their perceptual and cognitive abilities in interpreting television are different from those of older children and adults. Even with their limitations, however, they are affected by television commercials, television violence, and prosocial and educational programming.

Limited Viewing Skills of Preschoolers

Preschoolers do learn from television shows. In fact, 5-year-olds learn more from films and television than they do from still pictures because their attention is held better by the movement (Greenfield, 1984). For preschoolers, the action itself and the show's sound effects are better attention-holders than is the show's dialogue. By age 8, action, sound effects, and dialogue are equal in their ability to hold children's attention (Watkins, Huston-Stein, & Wright, 1980).

Camera techniques fool preoperational stage children because the children have trouble following transformations—they see the beginning state and the end state, but have trouble following the process in-between. Therefore, they find putting the pieces together properly difficult. Illustrating this difficulty are the results of a study by Sparks and Cantor, in which preschoolers (ages 3 to 5) were compared with school-age children (ages 9 to 11) on their comprehension of the television show "The Incredible Hulk" (Greenfield, 1984). Even though the series visually features the transformation of David Banner into the Incredible Hulk, the younger children thought that David Banner and the Incredible Hulk were two separate persons. The older children knew that it was David Banner who transformed into the Incredible Hulk.

Young children often believe that television presents reality. The youngest children may even believe that television events are actually occurring inside the television set (Liebert et al., 1982). Children understand that books are fictional at an earlier age than they realize that television is fictional (Greenfield, 1984). Children from lower socioeconomic status are more likely to believe that television represents realism (Greenfield, 1984). Parents can successfully discuss with their preschoolers that cartoons are make-believe, and slightly older children can be convincingly told that television dramas are only stories (Liebert et al., 1982). Meanwhile, the common distortions of reality on television shows may influence children's views of the world. As early as age 3, children who are heavy television watchers are found to have more stereotyped views of sex roles than do light television watchers (Greenfield, 1984).

Effects of Television Commercials

Most children under age 7 do not distinguish between a show's program and its commercials. In fact, preschoolers prefer the commercials because of their attention-getting uses of visual effects, action, repetition, quick pacing, and catchy jingles (Zuckerman, Ziegler, & Stevenson, 1978). Kindergartners were shown an animated program and a live-format program containing commercials. At various times, the videotapes were stopped, and the children were asked to identify whether they were just seeing "a part of the show" or a "commercial." The children correctly identified commercials only 53 percent of the time (Palmer & McDowell, 1979).

Preschool children believe that commercials always tell the truth. Even among children ages 5 to 7, more than one third believe that commercials are truthful (Ward,

Reale, & Levinson, 1972). In reality, toys that have to be purchased separately are advertised together, and children's programming is likely to be sponsored by manufacturers of sugared cereals, candy, and snack foods (Liebert et al., 1982). Even without full comprehension, trusting preschoolers try to get their parents to buy games, toys, and food products that have been heavily advertised on television programs. Preschoolers make more attempts to influence their parents' purchases, but school-age children are more successful in getting their parents to make purchases (Ward & Wackman, 1972).

Commercials provide another source of information about appropriate behaviors for boys and girls. Many toy advertisements are directed specifically at boys or girls. Overall, ads meant for girls have more fades, dissolves, and background music. Ads directed at boys have more toy action, frequent cuts, sound effects, and loud music. In one study, researchers made advertisements for toys that were abstract shapes, and young children were asked to decide which toys were for girls and which were for boys. The children defined shapes that were advertised with dissolves, fades, and background music as toys for girls, while they decided that shapes that were advertised with much action, louder sounds and music, and more frequent cuts were toys for boys (Greenfield, 1984).

Television and Violence

Another message that young children receive in commercials is that combat and toy weapons are important and that fighting is a natural and inevitable way to solve disputes. American manufacturers and advertisers emphasize war toys more than their European counterparts, who emphasize educational toys (Adams & Fuchs, 1986). Young children are incapable of understanding the tragedies of wars and are easily attracted to the adventure and action potential of war toys.

Since the early 1960s, when Albert Bandura wrote the 1963 *Look* article "What TV Violence Can Do to Your Child," television violence has been the focus of much scientific research and public debate. On the whole, research findings confirm that both young children and older persons are affected negatively by violent television programming. Bandura's best-known study (1965) used a filmed adult model interacting with an inflated Bobo doll. Children who saw the adult model punch, hit, and kick the doll were more likely to act aggressively toward the doll themselves, especially if they viewed the aggressive adult receiving a reinforcer. The modeling effect was almost as strong when the model was an animated character, Herman the cat (Bandura, Ross, & Ross, 1963).

In another study of television violence, 87 preschoolers, ages 4 to 5 1/2, were placed in four different classes that met for 2 1/2 hr three times a week over a 9-week period. During these sessions, three groups watched television shows that were either aggressive (e.g., "Batman," "Superman"), prosocial (e.g., "Mister Rogers' Neighborhood"), or neutral in nature. After viewing the television programs,

Television teaches values and behaviors. While many shows emphasize violence, others, like Fred Rogers' "Mr. Rogers' Neighborhood," teach prosocial values and provide needed information about the world.

children were observed for three 5-min sessions during free play. Those who watched the aggressive shows were more aggressive in interpersonal situations during free play. The effect was especially dramatic for those young children who had initially scored in the top half of aggression level (Stein & Friedrich, 1972).

In a 1-year long longitudinal study, researchers studied 3- and 4-year-olds and found a significant relationship between their action-adventure television viewing and their amount of aggressive behavior. The study suggested that television violence leads to more aggressive behavior, rather than that aggressive children decide to watch more violent television (Singer & Singer, 1980). Other studies found that heavy viewing of aggression on television leads to a belief in a more violent and dangerous world (Berkowitz, 1984; Singer, Singer, & Rapaczynski, 1984).

Other Modeled Behaviors

If television violence can teach children how to be violent and can actually increase their aggressive behavior, can children learn other behaviors and values from television? Stein and Friedrich (1972) found that preschoolers who view prosocial programming increase prosocial behaviors. In fact, analyses of both adult programming and children's programming have found that prosocial acts (e.g., altruism, sympathy, control of aggressive impulses, and resistance to tempatation) are frequently used in story lines. Television can also affect attitudes toward individuals of other races. Children who watched "Sesame Street" for 2 years had more positive attitudes toward children of other races (Bogatz & Ball, 1971). In addition, children may choose to model specific positive behaviors of popular television characters. The day after Fonzie (from "Happy Days") got a library card, five times more children than usual applied for their own library cards (Singer, 1982).

Effects of Toys on Preschoolers

Beginning in the preschool years, toys become major factors in children's lives. Each year in the United States,

Table 6.4		
Solitary Toys and Social Toys for Young Children		
Age Group	Typical Solitary Toys	Typical Social Toys
0 to 3 years	Rattles, mobiles, beads, squeak toys, tricycles, push-pull toys, stacking or nesting toys, hobbyhorses, sandbox toys, blocks, stuffed animals, construction toys, clay, crayons	Peekaboo toys, pets, books, pictures, wading pools, dress-up clothes
3 to 6 years	Toy soldiers, cars, phones, boats, radios, coloring books	Puppets and theaters, phonographs, sleds, wagons, race-car layouts

Source: Data from B. Sutton-Smith, *Toys as Culture,* 1986, Gardner Press, NY.

250,000 tons of plastics and 200,000 tons of metal are used by over 800 companies to produce about 150,000 different toy products (Sutton-Smith, 1986). Why do adults give toys to children? What purposes do toys serve?

Purposes of Toys

Toys teach young children about societal expectations for their behavior. First, preschoolers learn that people give toys as symbols of love and friendship. A parent's act of giving a toy to a child is meant to increase the bond between parent and child, and toys given or shared by others are used to build interpersonal friendships. As they get older, preschoolers learn that receiving toys represents an obligation to either exchange gifts or to return appreciation. Thus, toys can be used to teach about interpersonal relationships and obligations (Sutton-Smith, 1986).

Second, children are often given toys to increase their ability to play by themselves. Interesting toys allow children to build their skill in occupying themselves and also get them to place fewer demands on parents' time. American society highly values being by oneself, and solitary toys build children's ability to be self-absorbed, independent achievers (Sutton-Smith, 1986).

Third, as shown in Table 6.4, not all toys encourage children to play by themselves, and some toys actually encourage group interaction. A preschooler's toys have been shown to actually influence the amount of interaction with others. Children with solitary toys (e.g., crayons, tinkertoys, jigsaw puzzles, clay) only spent 16 percent of playtime interacting with other children. However, young children given sociable toys (e.g., pickup sticks, playing cards, games) played with others 78 percent of the time (Quilitch & Risely, 1973).

Fourth, some toys help to prepare children for school skills, such as reading. Gifted children and early readers have a significant preference for books, alphabet cards, and educational toys and are least likely to enjoy cars, trucks, and dolls (Benbow, 1986; Thomas, 1984). These studies do not indicate which came first—the parents buying books and educational toys for children or the children's preferences for these types of materials. Yet, the findings suggest that parents may wish to include books and similar materials among a young child's playthings.

Overall, the best suggestion for parents and others involved with the rearing of preschool-age children is to provide a variety of toys and play materials and to encourage children to experiment and express themselves in fantasy, constructive, dramatic, intellectual, and artistic play. Moreover, children can become skilled in learning both to play by themselves and to play with other children, although the effects of toys seem to be that children play more with the objects than with others (Eckerman & Whatley, 1977). Sometimes, to inspire a vivid imagination and good people relationships, parents should encourage children to play freely, without toy objects.

Boy Toys and Girl Toys

Young children use toys in learning gender-role appropriate behavior. Increasingly, from the age of 3 on, both boys and girls learn to avoid toys that are inappropriate for their gender and to spend more time with gender-appropriate toys (Benbow, 1986; Giddings & Halverson, 1981; Hartup & Moore, 1963; Krenzke, 1981). Most studies suggest that boys are more likely to avoid feminine-typed toys than girls are to avoid masculine-typed toys (Blomberg, 1981; DiLeo, Moely, & Sulzer, 1979).

Both parents and children agree on what toys are for boys, for girls, and for both (DeLucia, 1963). Typical boy toys include erector sets, planes, racing cars, footballs, tool sets, and dump trucks. Cleaning sets, dishes, jump ropes, dolls and doll clothes, sewing machines, cosmetics, and doll buggies are considered girl toys. Toys that are seen as appropriate for both boys and girls during the play years are rockinghorses, chalkboards, wading pools, banjos, telephones, teddy bears, and roller skates. Studies indicate that preschool girls enjoy and engage more in constructive art play and dolls than preschool boys do, while boys exhibit more play with and are more interested in construction toys, electronic toys, cars and trucks, and blocks (Benbow, 1986; Krenzke, 1981).

Gender-typing of toys increases the likelihood that boys and girls will develop different playing habits. In addition, these different play patterns may result in males developing superior spatial skills and science and mathematics achievement (Tracy, 1987).

Parents should consider whether they want to enhance or reduce differences in the play patterns of boys and girls. While androgynous young children are more likely to play with a wide range of typical boy and girl toys (Adubato, 1984), all young children's play is affected by the type of toys available. Boys and girls who are given vehicles with which to play tend to construct similar play scenes, and boys and girls who are given doll furniture with which to play also play similarly (Karpoe & Olney, 1983). Play seems to be affected more by the toys available than by the child's gender.

The long-term research findings about Head Start suggest it should be expanded to reach all socioeconomically disadvantaged children.

Effects of Child Care

Over the last two decades, the number of preschool children with employed mothers has grown rapidly, and experts estimate that, by 1995, two thirds of children under age 6 will have employed mothers (Hofferth & Phillips, 1987). This employment trend means that most preschool children will spend some time in child-care arrangements other than being cared for by a parent at home. **Child care** is the overall term for educational and day-care services for children younger than kindergarten age. This term has come to be preferred as the distinctions between **preschool** (educationally oriented care) and **day care** (physical-nurturing care) have become blurred (Howes, 1988).

Infants of employed mothers are most likely to be cared for by relatives or by the mother herself (Klein, 1985), but as children reach preschool age, an increasing percentage spend part of their week in formal child-care arrangements. In the 1980s, preschoolers in child care were cared for 32 percent of the time by relatives, 30 percent of the time by group programs, and 25 percent of the time by family day-care homes (Hofferth & Phillips, 1987). Some parents work different shifts and alternate in child-care responsibilities (Presser, 1988). Up to 500,000 preschoolers spend some time looking after themselves (Watson et al., 1984). By contrast, consider the use of older siblings to provide child care in the two societies featured in the "Exploring Cultural Diversity" feature.

Although most parents have found satisfactory child care, one fourth of parents would like to find different arrangements (Hofferth & Phillips, 1987). If they had better access to quality child care for their preschoolers, 17 percent of mothers who are not working would look for work, and 16 percent of employed mothers would increase their work hours (Presser & Baldwin, 1980).

Types of Child-Care Facilities

Currently, about 1.75 million family day-care homes are in operation. About 94 percent of these homes operate without a license, a factor that may change in the future. People who run a day-care center in their homes often have a wide age range of children under their care (Hofferth & Phillips, 1987).

The number of child-care centers is growing rapidly in the United States. In 1976, there were 18,307 licensed child-care centers, with a total capacity of 1.01 million. One decade later, there were 62,989 centers, with a total capacity of 2.1 million. Growth in licensed child-care centers should continue at a fast pace for many years (Hofferth & Phillips, 1987).

Parents need to explore the different approaches that these child-care centers take. For example, in the 1890s, Maria Montessori developed a preschool program based on children's development and interests, and today, many communities offer American **Montessori school** programs. Preschoolers individually work on such tasks as putting buttons through buttonholes, matching sizes and shapes, and tying shoelaces, moving to increasingly harder tasks as earlier tasks are mastered. Individual pacing of accomplishments and positive reinforcement are emphasized. While the tasks emphasize motor, sensory, and language development, the Montessori method fosters patience, self-control, cooperation, and responsibility (Spock, 1985).

Advantages and Disadvantages of Child Care

Is child care better or worse than parental care in the home? How are young children affected by spending a significant amount of their waking hours outside of the home with other children? Does the growth in nonparental care have detrimental effects on young children, or does it promote desirable characteristics? Overall, either adequate mother care or adequate child care seems to provide a good enough environment, and socioeconomically disadvantaged children benefit the most from participation in a well-run preschool center (Scarr, 1984).

Socioeconomically disadvantaged children who attend early intervention child-care programs tend to do better in school than their counterparts who were not enrolled (Lazar, Darlington, Murrar, Roysce, & Snipper, 1982; McCartney, Scarr, Phillips, & Grajek, 1985). The best-known and most researched compensatory education program is **Head Start,** which began in 1965. In its first 20 years, Head Start served over 8 million poverty-level youngsters. Head Start graduates made substantial gains in language and intellectual development, and when they attended schools, were less likely to be absent from classes and more likely to keep up with their appropriate grade level (Collins & Deloria, 1983; Miller & Bizzell, 1983). In fact, 19-year-olds who were in Head Start programs had better high

American older siblings often complain that they grew up being "stuck" with the most responsibility and that they were often forced to allow their younger siblings to tag along. Actually, older siblings in many societies have much more sibling responsibility than the great majority of American firstborns. How would you have liked being raised in either of the following sibling-care societies?

The Mandinka of Senegal

Seventy-one Mandinka children of Senegal were interviewed and observed in 1980 to 1982 for their roles in *dingh mutala,* or child-holding (Wittemore & Beverly, 1989). Mandinkas believe that the sibling caretaker learns how to deal with the demands of another's will. The toddler being cared for learns to relinquish his or her mother, allowing her to return to a productive farming role or to deal with another pregnancy.

The goal of the child's caregiver is to keep the infant content, which is basically defined in terms of quietness. Therefore, children tend to hold the baby until it sleeps, provide playful distraction, or offer physical comfort. Infants who continue to cry are considered contrary and often verbally threatened ("If I hit you . . .") or given mock blows with a hand or reed. Young children may be threatened with such lines as, *"Kangkurangho a be y kono so"* ("The bush spirit will disembowel you") or "The *tubaabo* (white man) will haul you away."

At times, threats are followed by a series of hits to the back. Whether or not actual physical punishment occurs does not seem to relate to the child's intentions, the nature of the misbehavior, or even the amount of misbehavior. The randomness of these actions should render them ineffective, according to behavioral theory, which emphasizes the consistent use of punishment. However, the practices are consistent with the Mandinka's belief that bad times are random and unexpected, and children learn this by the way threats are proposed and carried out.

Young Mandinka children's behavior is also controlled by *manené,* the promise of rewards ("I'll give you some candy"). The child caregiver often promises treats without means or intentions of providing them. Deception via promises by both older sibling and women caregivers is quite common. Erikson's theory would suggest that the children should develop mistrust of their caregivers. Behaviorists would suggest that not providing the actual reward would lead to a decrease in desirable behaviors. Yet, neither outcome occurs in Mandinka. At times, older siblings do provide treats. Moreover, village elders often provide treats for children to share with each other. Young children learn that, eventually, the manené is provided (i.e., in the long run, rewards are provided for correct behavior.)

The Kwaráae of Malaita in the Solomon Islands

A different style of sibling child care is seen among the Kwaráae of Malaita in the Solomon Islands, who were studied in 1981 and 1984 (Watson-Gegeo & Gegeo, 1989). One initial difference is that this society uses classificatory kinship, in which paternal uncles are considered fathers, maternal aunts are considered mothers, and all of their children are considered siblings. Classificatory siblings are treated like biological siblings in lifelong relationships.

Young children learn that they are as responsible for their siblings' welfare and possessions as they are for their own. This culture emphasizes the importance of sharing and of being responsible. When 6-month-old infants are given food, they are told and (helped) to share this with all their siblings. By 18 months, children share without hesitation if asked, and by age 3, they automatically share without prompting. This sharing is incorporated into other activities, including nurturing babies.

As in all community activities, relationship and work roles are governed by seniority. Parents supervise older children, who supervise younger siblings. Young children are quite aware of which siblings were born before and after them. The oldest son is the head of the sibling group throughout life. The oldest daughter is very important in the household and is considered a second mother.

At 3 years of age, a child may help with gardening, cooking, washing dishes, sweeping, and carrying firewood. This young child also babysits under a parent or older sibling's supervision. At age 7, the child may have full responsibility for an infant for up to 3 hr at a time. By age 11, a child can run a household or care for an infant all day long.

Besides modeling sharing, politeness, and responsibility, adults also use induction (providing reasons) to improve the behavior of their children. In the evenings, parents may instruct children about the Kwaráae traditions and gently correct behavioral problems. Instruction emphasizes strengthening sibling ties, social over individual needs, the importance of sibling care, and how individual achievement is a success for all. As a result, this culture has very little sibling rivalry.

The cultures described here are but two examples of sibling-care societies. The way siblings care for their sisters and brothers is unique to each society because siblings do their caretaking in ways consistent with the values and needs of their society.

Sources: Watson-Gegeo, K. A., & Gegeo, D. W. (1989). The role of sibling interaction in child socialization. In P. Goldring, Zukøw (Ed.), *Sibling interaction across cultures: Theoretical and methodological issues* (pp. 54–72). New York: Springer-Verlag. Wittemore, R.D., & Beverly, E. (1989). Trust in the Mandinka way: The cultural context of sibling care. In P. Goldring Zukow (Ed.), *Sibling interaction across cultures: Theoretical and methodological issues* (pp. 24–49). New York: Springer-Verlag.

Table 6.5
Differences Among 19-Year-Olds Who Were Enrolled in Head Start Programs and Who Were Not Enrolled in These Programs

	Head Start Experience	No Head Start Experience
High School Graduation	62%	49%
Employed	59%	32%
College	38%	21%

From Robert Marquand, "Nailing Down the Numbers on U. S. Students and Schools" in *The Christian Science Monitor*, 18, October 16, 1987. Copyright © 1987 University Microfils International, Louisville, KY.

school graduation rates, employment rates, and college attendance rates than their peers who were not in these programs (Marquand, 1987). These differences are summarized in Table 6.5. Day-care intervention programs also help socioeconomically depressed infants to develop better communication abilities (O'Connell & Farran, 1982).

A recent longitudinal study found that early child-care patterns still impact school behaviors after 3 years in elementary school (Howes, 1988). For both boys and girls, stable and high-quality early child care and better parental educational background are associated with good school adjustment. Maternal employment patterns and marital status are shown to be minimal factors in children's adjustment to school. In another study, young children who had quality care with much caregiver-child verbal interaction showed greater social development than children in other child-care situations (Phillips, McCartney, & Scarr, 1987).

The benefits of child care are less obvious for middle-class preschoolers. Good child-care programs may benefit cognitive development (Howes, 1988), but cognitively oriented child-care centers may produce some negative social behaviors, such as an increase in aggressiveness and resistance to adult requests during the early school years (Haskins, 1985). Aggressive behavior is explored further in Chapter 7, along with many other aspects of the psychosocial development of preschoolers.

guided review

29. After sleep, the most frequent activity of children is _____.
30. Youngsters who are heavy television watchers have _____ gender stereotypes and aggression.
31. Ads meant for _____ have more fades, dissolves, and background music, while ads directed at _____ have more action, frequent cuts, sound effects, and loud music.
32. _____ teach about interpersonal relationships and obligations and increase a child's ability to play alone or to interact with others.
33. Typical _____ toys for preschoolers are toy soldiers, boats and cars, coloring books, and toy phones, while puppets, wagons, sleds, and race-car layouts are typical _____ toys.

34. From about the age of _____ years, children increasingly avoid toys that are considered gender inappropriate, and this is especially true for _____.
35. _____ is the overall term for educational and day-care services, some of which are _____ (educationally oriented care), and others are _____ (physical-nurturing care).
36. Cultures that have older siblings providing child care for younger siblings are called _____ societies, and two diverse examples are the _____ of Senegal and the _____ of Malaita.
37. One specific preschool program is that of the American _____ school program, in which preschoolers individually work on learning tasks, progressing to increasingly harder tasks with accomplishments positively reinforced.
38. The best-known and most researched compensatory education program is _____, which started in 1965.

answers

29. watching television [LO-15]. 30. more (or: stronger) [LO-15]. 31. girls; boys [LO-15]. 32. Toys [LO-16]. 33. solitary; social [LO-16]. 34. 3; boys [LO-16]. 35. Child care; preschool; day care [LO-17]. 36. sibling-care; Mandinka; Kwaráae [LO-17]. 37. Montessori [LO-17]. 38. Head Start [LO-17].

Exploring Human Development

1. Visit a child-care center, and observe both the gross and fine motor skills of preschoolers. What physical and motor differences do you notice when you compare 2- and 3-year-olds with 4- and 5-year-olds?
2. Create a short picture-story book that would help a young child to cope with a medical situation, such as a visit to a doctor or dentist or a stay in the hospital. What elements did you want to emphasize in your story? How did you develop the story so that it would be understandable by a preoperational stage child?
3. Replicate the experiment in which 5-, 7-, and 10-year-olds are asked if a large doll is "easy or hard to see" both before and after the doll is blindfolded. Why are young children confused on this task?
4. Have classmates recall their earliest memories. What kinds of events do people tend to remember? Do these early memories seem to fit Freud's concept that people remember trivial things to help represss important early memories? Do men and women remember similar memories? Are there generational differences?
5. Analyze the preschool toys being sold in a toystore. Are different toys designed for boys and girls? Are more solitary or social toys offered? What values do the toys reflect? Are today's toys for preschoolers similar to the ones you had as a preschooler?

Discussing Human Development

1. What parental attitudes and behaviors might contribute to young children's positive body image and confidence in motor skills? What parental attitudes and behaviors would detract in these areas?

2. What scripts can you remember were important for you to know when you were a small child? Did you have scripts for birthday parties, the holidays, family picnics, the first day of kindergarten, and visiting grandparents? What purposes did such scripts serve for you?

3. How would you explain money machines and credit cards to preschoolers? What difficulties would they have in understanding these items?

4. In earlier times, developmental psychologists were most interested in motor and emotional development in the play years. Now the emphasis seems to be on cognitive development. Are psychologists reflecting societal trends? Influencing societal trends? Do you approve of the current emphasis on cognitive development? Why? Speculate about the next big research emphasis in child psychology.

5. How do you think the trend toward using more child care will affect society? What characteristics are more encouraged and discouraged in children in a child-care situation in comparison to children who are raised entirely at home? How would you change child care to maximize positive aspects and minimize negative aspects?

Reading More About Human Development

Kimmel, M.M., & Segel, E. (1983). *For reading out loud!* New York: Delacorte.

Liebert, R.M., Neale, J.M., & Davidson, E.S. (1973). *The early window: Effects of television on children and youth.* Elmsford, NY: Pergamon.

Piaget, J. (1987). *Possibility and necessity* (Helga Feider, Trans.). Minneapolis, MN: University of Minnesota Press.

Scarr, S. (1984). *Mother care/other care.* New York: Basic Books.

Sutton-Smith, B. (1986). *Toys as culture.* New York: Gardner Press.

Summary

I. Preschoolers' physical development
A. Appearance changes dramatically during the preschool years.
1. More growth occurs in the legs than in the head and trunk regions.
2. Average annual weight gain is 5 to 7 lb.
3. More growth occurs in the muscles than in the bones.
B. Preschoolers make rapid gains in control of body movements and motor skills.
1. Motor abilities are a source of pride in both play and in helping with chores.
2. Young children often test the limits of their physical abilities.
3. Fine motor skills are developed through construction play and artwork, as well as by learning to draw letters and shapes.
4. Handedness is usually established by the fourth year.
C. The sensory systems improve during the preschool years, as taste buds become more sensitive and depth perception gets better.
1. Preschoolers have unsystematic, scattered, visual scanning abilities.
2. Inefficient visual scanning translates into inefficient and redundant explorations of the environment.
3. Two important visual limitations of young children are (1) having difficulty in perceiving an object in more than one way, as in reversible picture illusions, and (2) not being able to view the parts and the whole of pictures at the same time.
4. Visual limitations and a short attention span create difficulty with a wide range of perceptual tasks, such as exact matching of socks or searching for lost items or for Easter eggs.
D. The daily sleep needs of preschoolers vary from 8 to 14 hr.
1. Compared to adults, children have shorter sleep cycles (50 min compared to 90 min) and spend more time in REM sleep.
2. Typical dreams of preschoolers are concrete, rather than fantastic or abstract in content.
3. Nightmares, night terrors, and sleepwalking are fairly common during the preschool years.
E. Preschool children can eat the same foods as adults but need smaller meals and nutritional snacks.
1. Daily caloric needs of preschoolers range from 1,300 to 2,300 cal.
2. The most common nutritional deficiencies in the preschool years are calcium, iron, vitamin C, and vitamin A.
3. Preschoolers take longer to eat their meals and may insist on food rituals.
F. The preschool years bring many concerns about health, illness, and injury.
1. Preschoolers get a high rate of contagious, infectious diseases, and immunizations are important in prevention.
2. Children with stressful lives usually experience more illnesses, especially those affecting the digestive and respiratory systems.
3. All preschoolers have minor accidents, and serious injuries are the leading cause of death among preschoolers in the United States.
4. Regular use of car seats, booster seats, and seat belts would significantly reduce motor vehicle injuries and deaths to children, and other safety measures, such as fire drills and having smoke detectors, would reduce other accidents.
II. Cognitive development and preschoolers
A. Research findings help us to understand the memory capabilities of preschool children.
1. Young preschoolers can do well at recognizing pictures or toys, but only older preschoolers can really remember events.
2. Memory abilities are related to language capabilities.
3. Compared to older children, young children have shorter memory spans, better visual memories, and identical forgetting rates.
4. Metamemory improves during the preschool years.
5. Preschoolers like to have scripts (descriptions of appropriate sequences of events in specific situations) and often ask questions to form such scripts.

6. Preschoolers develop rigid scripts and have trouble allowing modifications to rituals or applying scripts to novel situations.

B. During the preschool years, children leave Piaget's sensorimotor stage of cognitive development and enter the preoperational stage until they are about 7.

1. This stage is a time of being able to use symbols, which allows pretend play, improved language abilities, and use of numbers.

2. Piaget's ideas are sound, but at times, he underestimated children's abilities.

3. Preschool children primarily use transductive reasoning (reasoning from particular to particular) and are incapable of both inductive and deductive reasoning.

4. Due to transductive reasoning, young children overgeneralize the connection between one known specific and an event and overassume that causality is related to the closeness of events.

5. Tasks that are learned by the end of this stage of cognitive development include classification, seriation, statements of comparisons, and conservation tasks.

6. During the preoperational stage, children learn to sort on the basis of one factor but have difficulty accomplishing multiple classification.

7. Dealing with subordinate and superordinate classes is difficult and greatly affected by familiarity of task materials and specific wording of questions.

8. Conservation of numbers is learned before conservation of mass (amounts), which is learned before conservation of volume.

C. Preschooler thinking has several characteristic limitations.

1. Realism is when children attribute physical properties to mental phenomena, such as not differentiating between a thought of an event and the event itself.

2. Preschoolers have trouble distinguishing between appearance and reality, often not getting beyond visual information.

3. Animism is the belief that inanimate objects have a consciousness and are alive—for example, believing that a lost item is hiding.

4. Artificialism is the belief that human beings cause natural phenomena—for example, believing that people planted every tree in a forest.

5. Preschoolers have much trouble in understanding transformations, the transitions from one event to another.

6. Centering is paying attention to only one factor or dimension at a time.

7. Irreversibility is the inability to begin at the end of an operation and get back to the start.

8. Egocentrism is having difficulty in understanding another's point of view and the belief that others experience an identical environment to oneself.

9. It takes several years for children to understand the concept of money.

D. Young preschool children are already capable of multiple-word sentences, and over the next 3 years, they show rapid progress to adultlike language structures.

1. By the age of 5, children can use language in seven different ways.

2. A common grammatical error is using a general rule when an exception should be made.

3. Preschoolers understand the genders of pronouns.

4. Children who do not use words by age 2 have delayed language development.

5. Articulation disorders include omissions, distortions, substitutions, and additions.

6. About 4 percent of preschoolers have dysrhythmia, such as stuttering or cluttering.

7. Young children reap many benefits from being read stories by their caretakers.

III. Assessing intelligence in preschoolers

A. Traditional approaches to IQ measurement began in 1904 and are still used.

1. IQ stands for intelligence quotient, which used to be determined by the formula $IQ = MA/CA \times 100$.

2. The best use of intelligence tests is to assess an individual's strong and weak points in thinking, rather than to rank children in terms of general intellectual functioning.

3. Terman's Stanford-Binet Intelligence Scale was last revised in 1985, at which time analysis in short-term memory, abstract/visual reasoning, verbal reasoning, and quantitative reasoning was added to the full IQ score.

4. David Wechsler's WPPSI can be used for ages 4 to 6 1/2, with the WISC being used with older children.

5. Other traditional assessment tests include the Kaufman Assessment Battery for Children, the Gesell Preschool Test, and the System of Multicultural Pluralistic Assessment.

B. Recently, researchers have been looking at new possible markers of intellectual potential.

1. Examples of newer approaches include attention to novel versus repetitive stimuli and brain-wave patterns during cognitive tasks.

2. Another trend is to focus on other components, such as musical ability, social skills, and self-knowledge, instead of only on verbal, spatial ability, and mathematical tasks.

3. Another important trend is the belief in cognitive modifiability.

C. An appropriate use of intelligence assessment is to detect below-average intelligence, or intellectual retardation.

1. One fourth of intellectual retardation is organic retardation, such as Down syndrome, phenylketonuria, and cretinism.

2. Cretinism, hydrocephaly, and phenylketonuria can be treated with early detection; otherwise, these and other forms of organic retardation are associated with severe or profound retardation.

3. Familial retardation is all retardation for which no known biological cause can be identified; many cases of familial retardation are mild retardation.

IV. Special effects on cognitive and intellectual development
   A. Next to sleeping, the most time-consuming activity of young children is watching television.
      1. Preschoolers average 2 1/2 hours of daily television watching and can usually name favorite shows by age 3.
      2. Television action and sound effects hold preschoolers' attention more than the dialogue.
      3. Preschoolers have difficulty following the transformations in television shows.
      4. Preschoolers often believe that television represents reality.
      5. Children who watch the most television have the strongest gender stereotypes.
      6. Most preschoolers are attracted more to commercials than to television programs, and young children believe that commercials always tell the truth.
      7. Television can teach aggressive behaviors or prosocial behaviors, depending on the content of watched shows.
      8. There is a significant relationship between action-adventure television viewing and amount of aggressive behavior and also with belief in a violent world.
   B. Beginning in the preschool years, toys become major factors in the lives of children.
      1. Toys teach children about social expectations, with some toys encouraging independent play and others encouraging group interaction.
      2. Both parents and children agree on what toys are for boys, for girls, and for both.
      3. Some toys help to prepare children for school skills.
   C. Due to increasing numbers of dual-career families and employed single-parent families, use of child care is growing.
      1. Preschool is educationally oriented, and day care is physical-nurturing care, although the distinctions between the two types of child care are blurring.
      2. Although most parents have found satisfactory child care, about one fourth would like to find different arrangements.
      3. Some cultures are sibling-care societies in which older siblings are responsible for rearing younger siblings.
      4. Child-care facilities vary from day-care homes to Montessori school programs.
      5. In general, either adequate mother care or adequate child care seems to provide a good enough environment.
      6. Socioeconomically disadvantaged children benefit the most from participation in a well-run preschool center.
      7. Participation in Head Start programs is associated with higher high school graduation rates, employment rates, and college attendance rates than peers who were not in these programs.

1. Which of the following accurately describes preschool physical development?
   a. The "potbelly appearance" of young children peaks around age 5.
   b. The greatest amount of growth occurs in the trunk area and the least in the head.
   c. The average annual weight gain is 5 to 7 lb.
   d. Bone tissue grows more than fat or muscle tissue.
2. Which of the following shapes would be the last that a preschooler could copy?
   a. triangle
   b. circle
   c. square
   d. rectangle
3. Which of the following is typical of preschoolers' visual abilities?
   a. inefficient visual scanning ability
   b. poor hand-eye coordination
   c. difficulty seeing both the parts and the whole of pictures at the same time
   d. all of the above
4. Compared to older individuals, the sleep of preschoolers involves
   a. longer sleep cycles.
   b. about the same number of total hours.
   c. more REM sleep.
   d. fewer nightmares and night terrors but more sleepwalking.
5. Which of the following is *not* one of the most common nutrient shortfalls during the preschool years?
   a. iron
   b. vitamin E
   c. calcium
   d. vitamin C
6. The leading cause of deaths among preschoolers is
   a. serious injuries.
   b. infectious diseases.
   c. genetic disorders.
   d. homicides.
7. Which of the following memory capabilities is weakest in young preschool children?
   a. visual
   b. events
   c. objects
   d. people
8. Metamemory refers to
   a. a measure of memory abilities similar to intelligence assessment.
   b. having a memory capability that is much above average.
   c. knowing whether particular information is held in one's memory.
   d. memory of events that happened prior to the age of 6.
9. Which of the following is an example of a script?
   a. the pretend play of two children telling a fairy tale with puppets
   b. using efficient visual-scanning techniques while searching for hidden Easter eggs

c. Being able to sort items by shape and color and group appropriate items together

d. A young child making inquiries about what a birthday party is like and what one should do while at a birthday party

10. Preschool children use which of the following types of reasoning?
    a. deductive
    b. inductive
    c. transductive
    d. all of the above

11. Being able to place items in order of their size is called
    a. classification.
    b. seriation.
    c. conservation.
    d. both classification and seriation.

12. A small child's belief that a sidewalk deliberately tripped her is an example of
    a. animism.
    b. realism.
    c. artificialism.
    d. centering.

13. If Jan can correctly answer that she has a brother Bob but fails to see that Bob has a sister Jan, she is exhibiting the thinking limitation called
    a. egocentrism.
    b. centering.
    c. realism.
    d. irreversibility.

14. Which of the following would be the last money concept acquired by children?
    a. understanding that different items cost different amounts of money
    b. knowing that one must pay for items that are bought
    c. understanding the process of getting change
    d. knowing that one must have enough money to buy an object

15. Which of the following is(are) dysrhythmic speech disorder(s)?
    a. stuttering and cluttering
    b. omissions and substitutions
    c. delayed language devlopment
    d. all of the above

16. Which of the following intelligence tests was the first to be developed?
    a. Wechsler Intelligence Scales
    b. Stanford-Binet Intelligence Scale
    c. Kaufman Assessment Battery for Children
    d. Gesell Preschool Test

17. Compared to familial retardation, organic retardation is
    a. more severe.
    b. less common.
    c. attributed to biological or genetic causes.
    d. all of the above.

18. Which of the following is least effective in holding preschoolers' attention during a television show?
    a. sound effects
    b. dialogue
    c. action
    d. repetition

19. Which of the following toys do parents and children label as a toy for both boys and girls?
    a. toy telephones
    b. jump ropes
    c. erector sets
    d. dolls

20. Which child-care program emphasizes preschoolers individually working on tasks that emphasize motor, sensory, and language development, with individual pacing toward harder tasks as progress occurs?
    a. dingh mutala
    b. Head Start
    c. Montessori school
    d. family day-care homes

Answers

1. C [LO-1].
2. A [LO-2].
3. D [LO-3].
4. C [LO-4,5].
5. B [LO-6].
6. A [LO-7].
7. B [LO-8].
8. C [LO-8].
9. D [LO-8].
10. C [LO-9].
11. B [LO-9].
12. A [LO-9].
13. D [LO-9].
14. C [LO-9].
15. A [LO-11].
16. B [LO-12].
17. D [LO-14].
18. B [LO-15].
19. A [LO-16].
20. C [LO-17].

chapter·7

Psychosocial Development in Preschoolers

Learning Objectives

1. Explain the essential features of Freud's phallic stage, including the Oedipus complex, castration anxiety, the Electra complex, and penis envy.
2. Explain Erikson's third psychosocial stage—initiative versus guilt—and its resolution.
3. Describe Adler's concepts of birth order and sibling rivalry.
4. Describe and evaluate Bandura's social-learning theory approach to personality development.
5. Identify the major features of Maslow's metamotivational theory of personality development.
6. List suggestions for reducing children's aggressive behaviors.
7. Distinguish between prosocial and altruistic behaviors, and discuss factors that encourage the development of prosocial behaviors.
8. Define and give examples of sex differences, gender differences, gender roles, and gender stereotypes.
9. Contrast the major theoretical explanations of gender-typing, including psychoanalytic, social-learning, cognitive-developmental, and gender-schema theories.
10. Define androgynous behavior, and discuss the pros and cons of promoting greater androgyny in society.
11. Describe the characteristics of Baumrind's four styles of parenting and the developmental outcomes resulting from each style.
12. Explain the effects of different discipline approaches as described by Hoffman.
13. Identify correlates and causes of child abuse.
14. List types of nonsocial and social play.
15. Describe the important features of functional, constructive, dramatic, and games-with-rules play.
16. List the factors that are important in forming friendships, including the role of parents.

In this chapter, you will learn about the personality and emotional development of preschoolers, the process of gender identification in preschoolers, and how preschoolers interact with parents, playmates, grandparents, and other persons. These years are, indeed, active, busy, and productive.

Exploring Your Own Development

The theories of personality development discussed in this chapter provide you with an opportunity to compare the theorists' ideas with your own experiences. For example, as you read about Adler's views regarding the influence of birth order and family atmosphere on personality, decide if these concepts help you to understand your own development and that of other family members. Do these ideas make sense in light of your own experiences? Regardless of your birth order, do you have any of the characteristics of a firstborn or last-born sibling? If so, do Adler's or any of the other theorists' ideas help you to understand why you have these characteristics?

When you read about gender identification and gender-role development, reflect on your own childhood experiences. How stereotypical were the gender roles in your home? Were there chores that were definitely "women's work," while others were "men's work"? Were you allowed to play with any type of toy? Or were there "boys' toys" and "girls' toys"? How did your parents decorate your room as a preschooler? Was it highly masculine, highly feminine, or neither? How did your playmates react to your favorite doll? Was their reaction different if you were a boy than if you were a girl? Did your grandparents, baby-sitters, or day-care providers give you different messages from those of your parents about appropriate gender-role behavior? If you are a parent or plan to be one in the future, what, if anything, will you do differently with regard to your child's gender-role development from the way you were raised?

Theories of Personality Development

Developmental theorists view the preschool years as important in lifelong personality development. The ideas in this section provide diverse frameworks for examining other topics of development, including gender roles (this chapter), sexual orientation (Chapter 10), and moral development (Chapter 8).

Sigmund Freud's Psychoanalytic Theory

In Chapter 5, you learned about Sigmund Freud's first two stages of psychosexual development—the oral and anal stages. Freud believed that preschool children are in the **phallic stage.** According to Freud, although preschoolers still experience pleasurable sensations in the mouth and anal regions, by age 3, the primary source of gratification is the genital area, and all preschoolers discover and play with their genitals.

The Victorian Era

In the Victorian era in which Freud lived (1856–1939), sexual expression was repressed. For example, in polite society, no one would request a chicken *breast,* male- and female-authored books were kept on separate shelves, parts of the Bible were not read because they were too sexually explicit, adults did not disrobe for sex, and women were considered sexually neutral and without orgasmic capacity. Moreover, people (including medical doctors) believed that masturbation led to physical illnesses, mental illnesses, and even death. Thus, during the Victorian era, children caught masturbating were usually punished and threatened with "keep doing that and I'll cut it off."

Within this cultural context, Freud (1905) proposed that, during the phallic stage, all children form sexual attachments with their opposite-sex parents, experience internal conflict about these attachments, and resolve their conflict through gender-role identification with same-sex parents. The process is described differently for boys and girls, with boys experiencing the Oedipus complex and girls experiencing the Electra complex. Freud believed that neither boys nor girls really wish to be sexual with their parents and that children successfully resolve their sexual attachments unless parents act seductively toward their children (Bettelheim, 1983).

Most students today do not accept Freud's ideas or understand the basis for his beliefs. However, given the Victorian era during which Freud lived, it is not surprising that some of his ideas do not "fit" the current times.

The Oedipus Complex

According to Freud, the **Oedipus complex** is a universal experience for preschool-age boys. In fact, according to Freudians, when boys are reared entirely by their mothers, they find some adult male (e.g., an uncle, mother's boyfriend, next-door neighbor) with whom they can reenact the principal characteristics of the Oedipus complex. Freudians believe that such comments as, "When I grow up, I want to marry you, Mommy!" and "Do you love me more than Daddy?" are evidence that preschool boys fall in love with their mothers. Boys also are said to feel a rivalry with their fathers and compete with them to get their mothers' attention. Little boys are supposedly pleased when fathers go off on business trips or have to stay late at work because these situations allow them to have more time alone with mothers. According to Freudians, however, this pleasure is accompanied by the fear that their fathers will figure out that they would like to "dispose of Dad" or "be more powerful and important than Dad."

Rivalry with fathers is especially unsettling, say Freudians, because boys begin to think about their fathers' responses to the rivalry in terms of the warnings they have been given about masturbation ("I'll cut it off"). Therefore, young boys develop **castration anxiety,** anxiety that, if they directly compete with their fathers for their mothers' affections, their strong fathers will punish them by cutting off their penises. According to Freudians, young boys conclude that this punishment is too severe, so they block their sexual love for their mothers and learn to identify with the strength of their fathers, thereby resolving their Oedipus complexes.

Freudians believe that successful resolution of the Oedipus complex results in identification with the male gender role. On the other hand, they maintain that unresolved Oedipus complexes can result in weak superegos, feminine personality and behavior, overidentification with mothers, and male homosexuality. Although the concept of the Oedipus complex is not widely endorsed today, many people mistakenly continue to believe that male homosexuals come from families with dominant mothers and passive fathers—a stereotype developed from this aspect of Freudian theory.

The Electra Complex

Freudians believe that a similar conflict arises for preschool-age girls. In the Freudian **Electra complex,** young girls are in love with their mothers, their primary caregiver. However, little girls come to realize that they do not have penises and believe that their jealous mothers betrayed them and removed their penises. Therefore, little girls block their feelings toward their mothers and fall in love with their fathers. The love for their fathers, however, is tainted by **penis envy,** the longing for the return of their penises and envy toward their fathers' penises. Young girls, according to Freudians, hope that their fathers will replace their penises; when this does not occur, they block their sexual feelings for their fathers and, out of weakness, start to identify with their mothers.

Unlike the Oedipus complex, the Electra complex cannot be fully resolved because young girls are not given the penises they desire. Freud believed that boys come to feel internally strong as they identify with their fathers but that girls feel a weak and incomplete identification with their mothers. Coming to terms with the Electra complex means that girls must learn to identify with the passive female gender role. Freud believed that every girl needs to get married and give birth to a son to best resolve the Electra complex. According to Freud, less successfully resolved Electra complexes result in weak female superegos, women attempting to be superior to men (Freud viewed females as biologically inferior and said that "Anatomy is destiny"), masculine personality and behavior, and lesbianism.

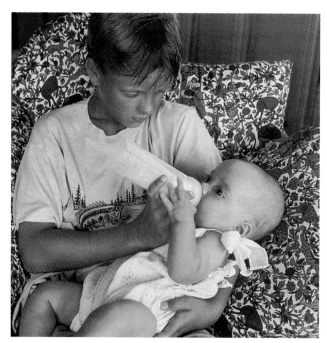

Horney believed that all persons need to be creative and productive, and females have the advantage of having the option of biological creativity through giving birth. Horney believed that males envied women's procreation abilities and resolved this envy by belittling female accomplishments. Fortunately, more boys are being taught to partake in nurturing young children.

successful study tip

Freud's Phallic Stage

Important aspects of Freud's phallic stage include:

When: 3 to 6 years old

Process: Phallic stage is when the genitals are the primary source of gratification.

Boys: Oedipus complex
Block love for mother and identify with father
Castration anxiety involved

Girls: Electra complex
Block love for mother, love father, and then realign with mother
Penis envy involved

Outcomes: Results in gender-role identification (strength for boys; weakness for girls)
Has impact on personality characteristics
Determines sexual preference
Affects strength of superego

Womb Envy

Karen Horney (1967), the first feminist psychologist, disliked Freud's emphasis on penis envy. She counterproposed that little boys experience womb envy when they realize that only girls can biologically create a baby. According to Horney, little boys repress their jealous feelings of womb envy and learn to deny the importance of motherhood, demand to be treated as superior to females, and disparage women by belittling their achievements, denying them equal rights, and perceiving "feminine" in negative, weak terms. Horney believed that both men and women need to be creative and productive, but that men satisfy this need in the external world of work, while women may be creative and productive in work or biologically in procreation.

The Superego

According to Freud, beginning in the toddler years, the **superego**—the moral arm of the personality—emerges within the personality as an abstract representation of society's rules and values, especially as taught and modeled by parents. The superego can get individuals to forsake personal pleasure through the weapons of guilt and pride. The superego's conscience uses guilt to punish and control behavior. Guilt is first exhibited in the early preschool years. The superego's ego-ideal rewards with pride when one strives to be the best one can be. Children often identify with strong, wise, and nobel superheroes, thereby incorporating their ego-ideal into their play activities.

Ego Defense Mechanisms

According to Freud, people fail to live their ideal lives and must endure frustrating disappointments. People use ego defense mechanisms to deny and distort aspects of their lives so that they can more easily deal with ordinary day-to-day living (Freud 1959a, 1959b). The fundamental defense mechanism is repression, or motivated forgetting. In repression, disturbing thoughts and events are kept from conscious awareness; people forget more about distressing events than about pleasurable events.

Freudians believe that other defense mechanisms involve repressing some aspect of reality and distorting other aspects. For example, in rationalization, people repress the real reasons for their behavior and justify the way they act with false reasons. An investigation of denial (adamant refusal to perceive unpleasant reality), projection (perceiving one's own characteristics as belonging to another and not to oneself), and identification (perceiving another's characteristics as belonging to oneself) found age differences in emergence and usage (see Table 7.1). Denial is a primitive defense that infants and preschoolers often use because they cannot physically remove themselves from unpleasant situations. Soon, however, increased social skills and cognitive abilities contribute to a reduction in denial and an increased use of projection (Cramer, 1987).

Erik Erikson's Third Psychosocial Stage

Erik Erikson (1963, 1972) believed that, during the preschool years, children face their third psychosocial crisis, **initiative versus guilt.** Erikson's central issue during these years is compatible with Freud's superego development. In contrast to the more limited concepts of the Oedipus and Electra complexes, however, Erikson suggested that preschoolers exhibit an early "generational complex," in which they have an elementary awareness of generations, growth, and death.

Table 7.1
Development of Defense Mechanisms: Use of Denial, Projection, and Identification by Various Age Groups

Age Group	Mechanism Most Commonly Used	Mechanism Least Commonly Used
Preschoolers	Denial	Identification
School-Age Children	Projection	Denial
Adolescents	Identification	Denial

Source: Data from P. Cramer, "The Development of Defense Mechanisms" in *Journal of Personality*, 55, 397–630, 1987.

During Erikson's third psychosocial stage, preschoolers learn to take initiative and to be goal-oriented. They usually play active roles in the environment, are open to new learning, and exhibit extraordinary attempts to master skills and tasks. Ideally, they are able to combine spontaneous enjoyment and responsibility. Parents who give children opportunities to plan their own activities, yet who also provide helpful guidance and firm limits, help their children to successfully resolve this stage. According to Erikson, the virtue gained from successful completion of this stage is *purpose,* the ability to be future-oriented and to focus efforts on attainable goals.

Some preschoolers do not successfully resolve this stage and experience much guilt. These preschoolers experience anxiety about their own behavior, evaluate their behavior and themselves as bad, and are fearful of doing wrong things. They overcontrol and constrict their own activities. According to Erikson, parents who inhibit their children's initiations of activities, who ridicule and criticize their children's efforts, and who often use punishment and discouragement may keep their children from happily resolving this stage. Children who failed to resolve Erikson's earlier psychosocial crises of basic trust versus basic mistrust and autonomy versus shame and doubt also have increased problems resolving the third stage.

Sometimes, children in Erikson's third stage attempt to act grown up and try to handle responsibilities beyond their capacities. At other times, they take on projects and goals that are in conflict with sibling and parental wishes. Parents need to help their youngsters to choose reasonable activities for their age and to respect the rights and privileges of the rest of the family. Another challenge during this stage is preschoolers' love of the word *why.* Just as toddlers' favorite word *no* was a central expression of the autonomy versus shame and doubt stage, the word *why* illustrates the need for young children to be able to master their surroundings.

According to Erikson, if this psychosocial stage is not resolved during the preschool years, it may still be resolved in later years. He also believed that, until this stage is successfully resolved, excessive guilt adds difficulty to one's life and that, on a long-term basis, guilt contributes to inhibited impulses, self-righteous intolerance, anxieties and fears, psychosomatic illness, and impotence.

Erikson's Third Psychosocial Stage

To remember the initiative versus guilt psychosocial crisis, form a vivid image of a preschooler exhibiting initiative (purposefulness) and another preschooler exhibiting guilt (anxiety and fear).

Alfred Adler's Individual Psychology

Although the work of Alfred Adler (1929, 1931, 1946) was influenced by Sigmund Freud, Adler's theory of individual psychology has quite a different flavor (see Appendix A). Freud emphasized the past (especially early childhood), while Adler emphasized the future. For Freud, aspects of the unconscious were the greatest influence, while Adler emphasized conscious memories, intentions, and goals. Freud believed that the central drive in life is the sex drive, while Adler believed that life is centered around the power drive, or the drive for superiority. Several of Adler's concepts, including the family constellation, birth order, sibling rivalry, and family atmosphere, provide useful insights about the personality development of preschoolers.

Family Constellation

According to Adler, by the preschool years, children become aware of their family constellation, their family's structure. Your family constellation represents your position within the family in terms of presence or absence of parents and your birth order among siblings. Think about how different your life might be if you came from a much smaller or larger family. People are influenced by how many siblings they have, the genders and ages of those siblings, and the spacing of ages among siblings. During the preschool years, the family constellation may change as a new sibling enters the family.

Birth Order

Adler believed that **birth order** of siblings influences lifestyle. A preschooler born into a family that already has one child has a built-in playmate, rival, and supporter. A preschooler who is the oldest child must learn different ways to cope as parents have additional children. Birth-order position does not lock individuals into a specific

Table 7.2
Effects of Birth Order

The Oldest Child: The firstborn child has a time period of undivided attention from parents, which ends when another sibling is born (the "dethronement"). This child is likely to be adult-oriented and often attempts to gain favor with parents (and other adults) by conforming to parental values, being very responsible, and achieving at home, school, and work. Frequently, the oldest child is conservative, dislikes change, prefers authority, is ambitious, and prefers adults to children.

The Middle Child: This child is born with an older sibling who is a "pacesetter" for behaviors. Often, a middle child tries to overtake the first child but typically attempts achievements in areas in which the oldest child is not strongly developed. The middle child is likely to be more sociable than the oldest child, is more in tune with injustices and unfairness, and may sometimes feel like he or she has "no place" within the family. This child also feels "dethroned" when another child is born into the family.

The Youngest Child: This child has one or more "pacesetters" but does not experience "dethronement." The child may be powerful in the family because both parents and older siblings may do things for and with the child. On the other hand, other family members may not take this child as seriously because of age and size. Because the parents have less time for the youngest child (time is divided among all the children) and because the parents are more relaxed about their parenting role, the youngest child often has the most lax rules and discipline; there is a risk of being spoiled.

The Single Child: The single child may reflect characteristics of either the oldest or youngest child; the single child may be either modeling adult competence or be helpless and irresponsible for some time. Most likely, the single child works better with adults than with children. Sometimes, the single child is a loner.

Source: Material summarized from Eckstein, D., Baruth, L., & Mahrer, D. (1982). *Life style: What it is and how to do it* (2nd ed). Dubuque, IA: Kendall/Hunt.

lifestyle; rather, it provides general situations that shape the way lives are lived. Typical birth-order effects are summarized in Table 7.2.

Consider additional influences on birth order: Are your siblings brothers and/or sisters? Are they closely spaced in age or far apart? Are there half-siblings that entered your life as children rather than as infants? Adler believed that siblings who were more than 5 years apart formed subfamilies and that the birth-order effect partially started over. Therefore, if Pamela is 15 years old, Mary is 13 years old, Donald is 11 years old, Shellie is 4 years old, and Frank is 2 years old, Pamela, Mary, and Donald form one subfamily, and Shellie and Frank form another subfamily. In some ways, both Pamela and Shellie have characteristics of the oldest child, and both Donald and Frank have characteristics of the youngest child.

Analyzing the preceding family on the basis of gender reveals that Pamela is the oldest female sibling, Donald is the oldest male sibling, Shellie is the youngest female sibling, and Frank is the youngest male sibling. The effect of birth order by gender can be magnified if parents treat boys and girls differently.

Obviously, birth-order effects can become quite complex, depending on what factors are considered. Children may experience more than one birth-order effect. This

Older siblings often take on the roles of protector, caretaker, mentor, and teacher for their younger siblings. Dance steps are just one of many things an older sister instructs a younger sister about.

complexity makes research difficult and research findings less impressive, but also represents how most individuals experience their childhood family life.

Sibling Rivalry

According to Adler, preschoolers with siblings experience **sibling rivalry,** the competition between siblings for the affection and approval of their parents. Sibling rivalry is a healthy source of appropriate levels of inferiority feelings, leading to attempts to improve oneself. Two siblings close in age are likely to experience the most sibling rivalry, and they often deal with the intense competition by choosing to excel in different activities (e.g., one may achieve in school and the other excel in athletics).

Family Atmosphere

Adler also proposed that family atmosphere—the quality of emotional relationships among family members—influences the preschooler's personality development. Parents set the tone that helps to determine whether children learn to act actively versus passively, and constructively versus destructively.

Children reared in a neglected atmosphere feel unwanted and rejected. These children experience much parental anger and punishment, do not have basic nurturing needs met, and face the severe consequences of emotional, verbal, physical, and/or sexual abuse. Children in these homes have increased feelings of inferiority and often learn to withdraw from new experiences and people. As they grow older, they may continue to display resistance to life situations, feel like they have no place in the social order, and doubt that they can have constructive lives. Some neglected children remain overwhelmed with an inferiority

complex, or they may exhibit a superiority complex, an overcompensation pattern in which individuals exaggerate self-importance to hide intense feelings of inferiority.

Children from spoiled atmospheres seem to "have it made," since they are pampered and protected from ordinary frustrations of life. However, spoiled children remain dependent on their parents and fail to develop social feelings and usefulness within society. As adults, they dislike and display hostility toward order; they often demand undue attention and regard. Underneath it all, spoiled children doubt themselves. They come to believe that their parents overprotected them because they could not protect themselves. Spoiled individuals remain uncertain about their abilities and stamina because their potential has never been tested. In an abundant, materialistic society, many children can grow up with some of the characteristics that describe spoiled children.

The theories of Freud, Erikson, and Adler are similar in that they assume that preschoolers are influenced by a developing set of psychodynamic forces within them that begin to regulate their behavior and determine who they are. The remaining two theories discussed in this section represent distinctly different pictures of personality development in the preschool years.

Albert Bandura's Social-Learning Theory

Albert Bandura's social-learning theory explains personality development in terms of learned behavior within a social context (see Appendix A). Bandura's concepts are used to understand socialization processes—for example, gender-role identification, moral development, and parenting discipline styles. According to Bandura's concept of reciprocal determinism, children actively shape the environments that influence their behavior and personality (Bandura, 1977, 1978). They also learn by observing and imitating others. For example, preschoolers may learn to put on shoes and buckle them by observing older children performing this task. To model someone's behavior, individuals must be capable of performing the necessary responses and must have the opportunity to do these actions. For example, a preschooler may admire an older sibling's artwork and want to make a similar picture. However, the artistic results are different because the younger child does not have sufficient fine motor control.

Abraham Maslow's Metamotivational Theory

Abraham Maslow (1968, 1970) was a humanistic psychologist who believed that individuals play active roles in their own development (see Appendix A). His theory, called metamotivational theory, emphasizes that people strive to grow beyond their present condition toward fulfilling their potential. According to Maslow's theory, preschoolers whose basic biological and safety needs are not met will not strive to reach higher personal growth needs. Hungry preschoolers are unable to turn their attentions to love, self-esteem, and personal fulfillment. Preschoolers who have

Children seem to naturally try out new experiences including swinging upside down until one is dizzy. Balancing children's appetite for new experiences and challenges is the parents' emphasis on safety.

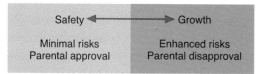

Safety ←	→ Growth
Minimal risks Parental approval	Enhanced risks Parental disapproval

Figure 7.1

The pull toward growth and safety.

From A. H. Maslow, *Toward a Psychology of Being,* 2nd edition, p. 47, 1968. Copyright © 1968 Van Nostrand Reinhold, New York, NY.

basic biological needs met but who are unsafe because of physical and sexual abuse or who feel unloved because of emotional or verbal abuse cannot feel good about themselves and their efforts.

Maslow believed that human beings are born with the innate need to grow in positive ways. As shown in Figure 7.1, young children learn to balance inner tendencies toward growth with the need to receive parental approval by seeking safety. Preschoolers want to explore and experience everything and have only vague awareness of the dangers involved in limitless exploration. Parents, on the other hand, are aware that children can fall if they climb, can get hit by a car if they cross the road, and can consume poisons or be hurt if not monitored. Because children desire parental approval, most of them learn to internalize parents' restricting rules. Moreover, they may repress some of their own growth needs and accept parental values and activities *instead of* developing their own standards and goals.

When children stop relying on their own visions of what their lives should be, they may feel empty, unsatisfied, and unfulfilled. As adults, they may need to stop listening to their parents' "voices" and get back to their own "game plan" that was misplaced in early or middle childhood. Maslow believed that, if basic needs are met and if people are encouraged to trust themselves, they will have high self-esteem and work on the process of self-actualization, living to one's fullest potential.

Aggressive and Prosocial Behaviors of Preschoolers

Aggression

Preschooler Aggression

Parents notice a drop in temper tantrums over the preschool years; however, the amount of aggressive behavior—actions intended to hurt or dominate someone—increases. At age 2 and 3, youngsters tend to kick and hit; by kindergarten, children are more likely to tease, taunt, and call names. Children older than 3 exhibit a sharp increase in acting aggressively after becoming frustrated or after being attacked. Preschoolers' aggressiveness increases after parents have been angry at them (Shaffer, 1988).

Longitudinal studies find that the aggressiveness levels of preschoolers are predictive of physical and verbal aggressiveness levels among school-age children, which, in turn, are predictive of adult aggression levels (Emmerich, 1966; Huesmann, Eron, Lefkwitz, & Walder, 1984; Olweus, 1982). Although influenced by environmental factors, especially parenting style, aggression levels exhibit stability over the years.

Preschoolers exhibit gender differences in aggression: Boys express more physical and verbal aggression. Aggressive acts are more common in boy-boy pairs than in either boy-girl or girl-girl pairs (Maccoby & Jacklin, 1980). Many psychologists believe that this gender difference is biological but that social factors enhance the differences.

Table 7.3
Reinforcements of Aggressive Behaviors

1. **Instrumental Value:** Aggression is reinforcing when it successfully helps in reaching a goal. Examples: A child may increase aggressive behavior if the child is successful in taking attractive toys from playmates by hitting or threatening them.

2. **Social Approval:** Aggression may be socially rewarded when other people approve of the aggressive acts. Examples: Young children may be encouraged to act aggressively in their early attempts at team sports. Parents may express pride that their child is able to control the behavior of other children in the neighborhood.

3. **Self-Protection:** Aggression is reinforcing when it serves to discourage attacks from others. Examples: A child may act more aggressive to keep another child from stealing his or her allowance. A child may fight back when teased by an older sibling.

4. **Intrinsic Reward:** Aggression may be present because individuals enjoy hurting others. Examples: A child may feel powerful using aggressive language. A child may take pleasure from seeing another child express intimidation.

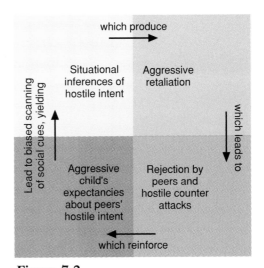

Figure 7.2
A social-cognitive model of the aggressive child's social information-processing biases and the behavioral consequences.
Source: Shaffer, D.R. 1988. *Social and personality development.* 2nd ed. Pacific Grove, CA: Brooks, Cole. p. 248.

Parents refer to newborn males and females with different adjectives and nicknames. They engage in more physical, roughhousing with their sons, buy more aggressive toys for their sons, and have different attitudes ("Be ladylike," "Boys will be boys") about what little boys and girls should be like (Shaffer, 1988).

A recent study highlighted the effects of differential attitudes (Condry & Ross, 1985). A videotape of two preschoolers dressed in snowsuits and playing aggressively in the snow (e.g., hurling snowballs, jumping on each other) was shown. Viewers interpreted the play as friendly if the preschoolers were believed to be two boys, but as aggressive if the preschoolers were believed to be two girls.

Theories of Aggression
Some theorists consider aggression biologically innate. Freud proposed that human beings are heavily influenced by a death instinct, which he called Thanatos. According to Freud, aggressive energy builds up until it is discharged through some form of destructive behavior or, alternatively, through catharsis, the vicarious release via playful, symbolic aggression. Thus, according to their theory, children playing with toy guns are reducing their aggression levels through catharsis.

Konrad Lorenz (1966) also thought that aggression was innate, that to aid survival, humans have a fighting instinct triggered by environmental cues. Sociobiologists have proposed that aggression is a built-in survival advantage: Aggressive persons increase their chances of survival and of attracting and protecting the most desirable mates.

Most psychologists, however, believe that aggression is a learned phenomenon. Originally proposed in the 1930s, the frustration-aggression hypothesis stated that frustration (the blocking of goal-directed behavior) always led to some

kind of aggression (Dollard, Doob, Miller, Mowrer, & Sears, 1939). Berkowitz (1965, 1974) revised this hypothesis significantly. First, he observed that frustration does not always lead to aggression, although frustration increases the potential for aggression. Second, Berkowitz suggested that the presence of "aggressive cues" (e.g., toy guns) may increase aggressive acts even without frustration. Third, according to Berkowitz, persons may act aggressively when (1) not frustrated (e.g., aggression is a means to an end) and (2) aggressive cues are not present. Preschoolers have been known to exhibit more aggression after their behaviors have been restrained by their parents and after their parents have punished them. These observations are consistent with Berkowitz's revised frustration-aggression hypothesis.

Bandura (1973) emphasized the role of observational learning and reinforcement in aggression. According to Bandura, youngsters act more aggressively when they view others—especially competent, attractive models who are reinforced—acting aggressively. Aggression itself can be reinforced in several ways, as listed in Table 7.3. Because social learning theorists emphasize that aggression is learned behavior, they are optimistic that aggression can be reduced or modified.

The information-processing theory emphasizes the role of previously remembered experiences and styles of information processing (Dodge, 1986). The paradigm of this theory is illustrated in Figure 7.2: Individual differences in aggression are attributed to expectancies about others' hostile intentions, which are based on remembered negative interactions with peers. A preschooler who has been the victim of other children's cruel behavior might overanticipate hostility in other situations. Once this child expects hostility, he or she might initiate aggression to become an aggressor instead of a victim. This initiation of aggression, however, provokes retaliatory aggression from others.

Reducing Aggression

How can aggression be controlled and reduced in preschoolers and other children? Possible ways to decrease aggression are:

1. Find appropriate ways for children to express anger and frustration.
2. Use time-out procedures, in which aggressively acting children are temporarily removed from the arena of interaction.
3. Ignore aggressive behaviors and reinforce behaviors that are not aggressive. Use the incompatible response technique (have two aggressive children cooperate in helping you move a bench), selectively rewarding prosocial behaviors while extinguishing aggressive acts (Brown & Eliot, 1965).
4. Model nonaggressive and prosocial behavior to children. Parents especially can lessen their own aggressive, punitive behaviors and substitute warm, reasoning, and helpful behaviors. Reduce children's exposure to aggressive models (e.g., television violence).
5. Discuss with children the differences between fantasized and real aggression and between harmful aggression and helpful assertion.
6. Provide nonaggressive environments for children. Larger play spaces may reduce fighting and shoving behaviors. Adequate play materials reduce arguments about supplies. Eliminate toys that elicit aggressive responses (e.g., guns, toy soldiers).
7. Teach children that empathy can help them to inhibit aggressive behaviors toward others.

Prosocial Behaviors

Preschooler Prosocial Behavior

Prosocial behaviors are behaviors that benefit other people and include sharing, rescuing, comforting, cooperating, complimenting, and helping behaviors. Prosocial behaviors become **altruistic behaviors** when the behaviors are *intentionally* done for the benefit of others. Intention is difficult to determine. For example, if a preschool girl helps to feed her baby brother, is it her intention to help her hungry sibling, or to receive parental approval? Because of the difficulties involved in ascertaining motives, psychologists study prosocial behaviors, rather than altruistic behaviors.

Among preschoolers, spontaneous sharing of prized possessions is relatively uncommon. During the preschool years, prosocial behaviors increase, but aggressive acts outnumber prosocial behaviors (Yarrow & Waxler, 1976). Preschoolers actually exhibit more prosocial behaviors in their pretend play than they do in real situations (Bar-Tal, Raviv, & Goldberg, 1982)! Most preschoolers will share toys and food items when told to do so by an adult (Levitt, Weber, Clark, & McDonnell, 1985).

One study of preschooler prosocial behavior looked at how preschoolers, ages 2 to 6, interact with a 6- to 8-month-old baby. With no adult encouragement, almost all of the chil-

Whether due to genetic programming, messages from the superego, or modeling effects, preschoolers often engage in sharing and helpful behaviors.

dren looked at the baby, more than 50 percent of them bent down to the infant's level, about 33 percent of them smiled at the baby and offered a toy object, and 15 percent touched the baby. When mothers became involved, more than 80 percent of the children approached the baby, smiled, and offered toys, and 33 percent touched the baby. Boys were more caring about male infants, and girls were more caring about female infants. Until the age of 5, boys showed as much interest in the infants as girls did; among school-age children, boys exhibited much less interest, and girls exhibited much more interest (Melson & Fogel, 1988).

Theories of Prosocial Behavior

Sociobiologists have proposed that human beings are genetically programmed for prosocial behavior because behavior on the behalf of others has survival advantages. If people help others, other people are more likely to help them back; reciprocal assistance increases likelihood of survival and the possibility that one's genes can be passed on to the next generation. Indeed, people are more helpful to close relatives than to distant relatives and strangers, perhaps because close relatives are the most likely to return the help (Campbell, 1965; Eberhard, 1975).

According to psychoanalytic theory, the superego's conscience and ego-ideal encourage prosocial behavior. Children feel pride when they act altruistically; they feel guilty when they fail to act altruistically.

According to social-learning theory, people are more likely to act altruistically if they observe altruistic models and feel empathic toward the victim. If a child feels the other person's distress, helping the other person helps to alleviate internal negative emotions (Maccoby, 1980). As children get older, cognitive skills allow them to better understand the other person's predicament and to know what would be useful; therefore, prosocial behaviors increase after age 7 (Eisenberg, Lennon, & Roth, 1983).

Increasing Prosocial Behavior

The following techniques increase and encourage prosocial behaviors:

1. Reduce emphasis on competition and winning.
2. Emphasize cooperation; set group, rather than individual, goals.
3. Model warm, cordial, prosocial behaviors.
4. Use fewer harsh, physical punishments, and provide reasons for discipline. Empathy training, in which parents point out the effects that the child's behaviors have on others' feelings, is useful in building prosocial behaviors (Maccoby, 1980).
5. Have children watch prosocial television shows (e.g., "Mister Rogers' Neighborhood" instead of aggressive television shows.

Gender Identification in Preschoolers

Gender Roles

An understanding of the process of gender identification begins with some basic definitions: **Sex differences** are physical differences between males and females. **Gender differences** are psychological and behavioral differences between males and females that may or may not be of biological origin. **Gender roles** are culturally defined behaviors, attitudes, skills, and interests that a society considers appropriate for males and females. Some traditional female gender roles are nurturance, cooperation, and dependence, while traditional male gender roles include aggression, competition, and independence. **Gender-typing** occurs when children acquire the appropriate gender role (i.e., they identify with the appropriate role for their gender). Sometimes, gender-typing leads to **gender stereotypes,** exaggerated generalizations about male or female behavior (Pillard & Weinrich, 1987).

Gender identity—knowing you are a female or a male—is one of the earliest concepts children understand;

Preschoolers can identify which toys are "for boys" and which toys are "for girls."

by age 2, children can identify their gender, and by age 3, they understand **gender constancy** (the awareness that their sex will always remain the same).

One of the first tasks of preschool children is to learn that they have gender constancy. Researchers can assess whether preschoolers have developed gender constancy by asking a series of questions, such as "If Sally really *wants to be* a boy, can she be?" "If Sally *played with trucks and did boy things,* what would she be? Would she be a girl, or would she be a boy?" "If Sally *puts on boy clothes* like this, what would she be? Would she be a girl, or would she be a boy?" "If Sally has her *hair cut short* like this, what would she be? Would she be a girl, or would she be a boy?" "If Sally has her *hair cut short* like this and *wears boy clothes* like this, what would she be? Would she be a girl, or would she be a boy?" (Emmerich, Goldman, Kirsh, & Sharabany, 1976).

During the rest of the preschool years, children learn more about gender-appropriate objects and activities and begin to seek out appropriate ways to express their gender. By age 6, children are very conforming to societal expectations based on gender. They especially model same-sex adults perceived as competent, powerful, and prestigious so that they can do their roles correctly (Kohlberg & Ullman, 1974).

Gender-Typing: Acquiring Gender Roles

Gender-typing occurs early in the preschool years. Two- and three-year-olds already know about gender roles—when given paper dolls named Lisa and Michael, they make judgments about which doll would be more likely to say or do something (see Table 7.4) (Kuhn, Nash, & Brucken, 1978). By age 3, children know which toys are for boys and which are for girls, and they can tell which tools, appliances, clothing, and activities belong to daddies and which to mommies (Pogrebin, 1980).

Preschoolers modify their behaviors and their aspirations to be consistent with gender roles. In one study, although equal numbers of boys and girls were in a zoo, the majority of those who rode elephants, fed animals, and

Table 7.4
Gender-Role Concepts Held by 2- and 3-Year-Olds

	Girls More Likely to—	Boys More Likely to—
Boys thought:	Cry, be slow, cook dinner	Be loud, be naughty, become a doctor or a governor
Girls thought:	Look nice, give kisses, take care of babies, say "I can't do it best"	Fight, be mean
Both boys and girls thought:	Play with dolls, help mother, talk a lot, never hit, clean house, say "I need some help," become a nurse	Help father, become a boss, say "I can hit you," mow the grass
Boys and girls thought there were no gender differences in:	Playing ball, playing house, running fast, saying "I can do it," washing the car, washing dishes, being smart, being a leader, being kind, being neat, being messy, being dirty	

From D. Kuhn, "Sex Role Concepts of Two- and-Three-Year-Olds" in *Child Development*, 49, 445–451, 1978. Copyright © The Society For Research In Child Development, Inc., at University of Chicago Press, Chicago, IL.

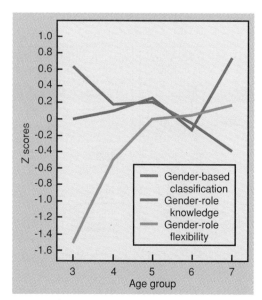

Figure 7.3
Changes in the preschool years in children's gender-role knowledge, gender-role flexibility, and gender-based classification. Z scores are a way to transform data from different groups to a standard scale.
Source: Serbin, L.A. & Sprafkin, C. 1986. The salience of gender and the process of sex typing in three- to seven-year-old children. *Child Development, 57*, p. 1195.

climbed the embankment were boys (Ginsberg & Miller, 1982). Five-year-olds believe that boys are better at physical activities and that these activities are more appropriate for boys.

In a study of potential adult occupations, kindergarten students were influenced by societal concepts of female and male careers. Boys picked fireman, policeman, and factory worker as the top three potential careers. Girls chose nurse, teacher, and cheerleader most often. Interestingly, 5-year-old girls named more nontraditional potential occupations than did boys. Among their nontraditional choices were head of an office, factory worker, doctor, firefighter, postal worker, and police officer. Older children in the study were less influenced by gender stereotyping and listed a wider range of occupations (Archer, 1984).

As shown in Figure 7.3, during the preschool years, children gain in gender-role knowledge. As they get older, youngsters decline in their rigid gender-based classifying. However, how much young children know about gender roles does not predict the amount of gender-typing in their own behaviors and attitudes (Serbin & Sprafkin, 1986).

Gender-Role Transgressions
Parents put more emphasis on male gender-role characteristics, and they put more pressure on boys than on girls to act according to gender-role expectations. Both boys and girls learn the male gender-role stereotypes earlier than the female ones (Pogrebin, 1980), and stronger commitment exists for male gender-role expectations. Both boys and girls believe that female gender-typed appearance is more important than female gender-typed activities. While males believe that engaging in masculine activities is important,

young boys believe that it is a more serious offense to have cross-gender appearance than to engage in cross-gender activities (Smetana, 1986). Not surprisingly, then, a 2-year-old boy would be more likely to agree to play house than to wear a skirt.

Theoretical Explanations for Gender Identification

Psychoanalytic Theory
According to Freudian theory, gender-role identification occurs between the ages of 3 and 5 through the Oedipus and Electra complexes. Boys are believed to be largely motivated by fear of castration, and girls by fear of loss of love and feelings of inferiority because they have no penis (Bronfenbrenner, 1960). According to psychoanalytic theory, the female role is passive, nurturant, masochistic, affectionate, and maternal, and females need the approval of others and want to please others. The male role is viewed as active, worldly, aggressive, punitive, individualistic, and independent, and males are seen as needing to perform in the world (Pogrebin, 1980). Many objections have been raised about these aspects of psychoanalytic theory; one major objection is that gender identity seems to be fairly set by age 2, rather than by age 3 to 5, as proposed by Freud (Money & Ehrehardt, 1972).

Social-Learning Theory
According to social-learning theorists, appropriate gender roles are learned by modeling same-sex individuals (e.g., parents, peers, culture heroes) and by reinforcement (Bandura, Ross, & Ross, 1963). In play, girls practice how to be

Calvin and Hobbes   by Bill Watterson

mommies and nurses, and boys practice how to be daddies and doctors. Social-learning theorists emphasize that gender socialization is *not* biological but is learned from others, although the learning process is not always conscious and intentional (Mischel, 1966).

Modeled and reinforced gender roles produce similar characteristics, as predicted by psychoanalytic theory: Females raise children, keep house, are nurturant, comforting, passive, and cautious, and yet are critical and attention seeking. Males go to work, make money, are task-oriented, have minimal child-rearing responsibilities, and are active, angry, impulsive, and demanding (Pogrebin, 1980).

Cognitive-Developmental Theory
According to cognitive-developmental theory, children categorize their gender identity based on physical cues. Then, throughout childhood, they consciously seek out and process information about males and females based on both physical and social reality and adopt those behaviors they see as consistent with their views of themselves as males and females. Compared to other theories, cognitive-developmental theory has children playing a very active role in their own gender-role socialization. Children want to act the right gender role because they come to believe that conforming to the proper role pattern is morally right (Kohlberg, 1966).

Gender-Schema Theory
Gender-schema theory contains elements of the cognitive-developmental and social-learning theories (Bem 1983, 1985). A **gender schema,** like other cognitive schemata, is a mental structure that you use to process information about your gender and to organize your behaviors related to gender. As with cognitive-developmental theory, the gender schema you form is first based on your gender identity. Your schema or concept of what it means to be male or female is influenced by your observations of how others act and by the feedback you receive from others regarding the appropriateness of your gender-related behaviors (ideas emphasized by social-learning theorists). Unlike cognitive-developmental theory, which emphasizes the achievement

of gender constancy as the essential factor in gender-role development, gender-schema theory emphasizes both cognitive and social factors. Therefore, as children become aware from society of how they are to conduct themselves as girls and boys, they modify their gender schemata to maintain consistent views of themselves as males or females. Thus, gender-schema theory predicts that, as society's gender schemata (society's gender-role expectations) change, the gender schemata of individuals also change.

Traditional Roles Versus Androgyny
Although many adults remain bound in traditional gender roles, people may choose to move beyond differentiated gender roles and to adopt lifestyles that incorporate the best of traditional male and female roles. Although individuals are not considered capable of gender-role transcendence before age 11 or 12, structuring a gender-free environment for young children and encouraging them to reach their fullest potential may help to reach this stage (Rebecca, Hefner, & Olesansky, 1976). Persons who no longer act entirely from the perspective of traditional roles but rather are able to express positive qualities of both genders are called **androgynous.**

Traditional Roles
Traditional gender roles are reinforced by societal institutions (e.g., church, family, military, schools, and workplace), accentuated by sex-segregated activities (e.g., mother-daughter hairstyles and father-son teams), and strengthened by such reinforcements as praise and punishment and by instructions to act like a same-sex individual (Pogrebin, 1980). Traditional female gender-role characteristics include: child caretaker, housekeeper, love-giver, one who acts in the religious sphere, behind-the-scenes influencer, and being submissive, subordinate, obedient, dependent, sympathetic, and deferential. Traditional male gender-role characteristics include: breadwinner, producer, disciplinarian, one who acts in the secular sphere, being responsible for standards, commanding respect, and being dominant, authoritarian, demanding, and autonomous.

(a)

(b)

(c)

(d)

In sex-segragated families, girls do inside cleaning chores like washing dishes and boys do outside chores such as raking. In androgynous families, the chores are more varied and not linked to one's sex. Girls might mow the lawn and boys might help with the cooking.

Pogrebin (1980) suggested that homes that emphasize traditional gender roles are not entirely consistent:

> *In such homes, children get discordant messages. They see women as manipulators who must act weak but be strong enough to hold a job and then come home and do all the child care and housework in order to "retain their femininity" and protect Dad's ego. They see fathers trained to link their maleness to their job, who play the strongman-provider, but who are vulnerable to unemployment or a wife's earning power. These rigid gender roles teach posturing and pretense, not identity. (p. 307)*

Androgyny

Traditional gender roles emphasize the differences between boys and girls, when in reality, males and females are more alike than they are different. Male-female differences are not as universal, consistent, and dramatic as many have assumed, as indicated by differences in gender schemata (role expectations) across cultures. For example, consider the differences in gender-role expectations in Sweden and the United States, as presented in the "Exploring Cultural Diversity" feature. If these differences are learned in cultural contexts, instead of being innate, individuals may choose the male-female qualities that seem appropriate for them (Hare-Mustin & Marecek, 1988). In fact, androgyny seems to be an adaptive lifestyle (Huston, 1983).

In 1968, Sweden set out to legally establish *jamstalldhet,* equality between the sexes. Although full equality has not yet been achieved (e.g., gender differences still exist in wages and in division of household labor), most Swedes accept the goal of jamstalldhet and are involved in both active parenthood and gainful employment.

Lifetime Gender-Role Expectations

Research conducted in both Sweden and the United States examined gender-role expectations (Intons-Peterson, 1988). One research strategy was to compare lifetime gender-role expectations. In other words, how do gender-role expectations for children compare to the expectations for adults? Swedish subjects were found to have significant differences for gender-role expectations of girls and boys, but similar expectations for adult females and males. Gender roles for girls emphasize interpersonal matters, and gender roles for boys emphasize instrumental matters. As adults, Swedes are expected to broaden their gender roles to embrace both interpersonal and instrumental concepts.

On the other hand, the gender-role expectations for American males were found to be fairly consistent throughout their lifetimes. As children and as adults, American males are expected to emphasize instrumental characteristics. American girls are given the most latitude—they are encouraged to develop both interpersonal and instrumental aspects. However, as adults, American females are expected to relinquish some of their instrumental characteristics.

Most Typical Characteristics of Men and Women

Another method used to compare Swedish and American gender concepts was to ask individuals in each country to list traits that are most typical of the men and women in their nation—in other words, to define their *national image* (Intons-Peterson, 1988). The most typical characteristics of Swedish women are trying to do one's best, being kind and nice, never giving up, being friendly, and being sincere. Typical traits ascribed to American women are affectionate, warm, friendly, self-confident, and feeling good about themselves. Traits that were given as typical of Swedish men are being kind and nice, being gentle, being helpful, trying to do one's best, and never giving up. American men's typical traits are trying to do one's best, feeling good about one's self, being self-confident, being hardworking, and being loyal. As with the women, males in these two countries are described with different traits.

Thus, American women are described with different traits than Swedish women, and American men are described with different traits than Swedish men. However, Swedish men and women are described more similarly than are American men and women. A fairly consistent Swedish national image exists for both men and women that is a combination of interpersonal and instrumental characteristics. On the other hand, American men and American women have largely different images, with women being described in interpersonal terms and men being described in instrumental terms. These cultural differences in gender concepts may have occurred since Sweden's 1968 decision to establish jamstalldhet, or traditional Swedish traits may have made jamstalldhet a more reasonable goal in that nation (Intons-Peterson, 1988).

Joseph Pleck (1975) proposed a three-step **phased freedom** process by which persons move into androgyny:

1. **Amorphous.** This initial stage occurs when young children are confused about gender identity and gender-role concepts.
2. **Conformist.** During this stage, children learn gender roles and make themselves fit these roles. Some adults choose to remain in this stage.
3. **Transcendent.** Some individuals choose to transcend gender roles and to develop psychological autonomy.

Pleck believed that role dichotomies are dysfunctional and that the happiest people allow themselves to outgrow role rigidity.

Although children acknowledge and deal with gender roles, in her book *Growing Up Free* (1980), Pogrebin proposed that parents can work toward raising gender-free kids by using gender-free colors, providing a full range of toys, encouraging a variety of activities, varying chores regardless of child's sex, giving boys and girls equal allowances, emphasizing safe independence skills, giving nonsexist compliments, and being nurturing and worthy models.

guided review

8. _____ are physical differences between men and women, _____ are psychological and behavioral differences between women and men that may or may not be of biological origin, and _____ are exaggerated generalizations about male and female behavior.
9. Freud's explanation of gender-typing involved the _____ and _____ for boys and the _____ and _____ for girls.
10. _____ theory blends ideas from _____ theory (by emphasizing gender identity) and _____ theory (by emphasizing society's influence).
11. People who are able to express the positive qualities of both genders are called _____.

answers

8. Sex differences; gender differences; gender stereotypes [LO-8]. 9. Oedipus complex; castration anxiety; Electra complex; penis envy [LO-9]. 10. Gender-schema; cognitive-developmental; social-learning [LO-9]. 11. androgynous [LO-10].

Parenting Preschoolers

Parenting Styles

Parental Involvement

How would you describe your parents' parenting style? What were their major guidelines and values in raising children? What is (or would be) your parenting style in terms of interaction, availability, and responsibility? Interaction is direct contact through caretaking and shared activities. Availability is potential interaction availability, such as the child playing in one room, while the parent does dishes in the next room. Most studies suggest that at-home mothers and working mothers have about the same amount of daily interaction with their children but that at-home mothers are more available (Grossman, Pollack, & Golding, 1988; Lamb, Pleck, Charnov, & Levine, 1987).

Responsibility involves being in charge of arranging for or carrying out the children's needs. Today, fathers and mothers spend nearly the same amount of time interacting with their children, but fathers let mothers take charge in child-care tasks. In a study of 160 fathers, 113 were responsible for 0 of 11 child-care tasks, 35 were responsible for 1 task, and 12 were responsible for 2 to 3 tasks (Lamb et al., 1987).

Availability represents a low level of involvement, but availability does provide children with a stabilizing presence. Even though the caretaker may be dusting while the child is building with blocks nearby, the physical closeness is reassuring and pleasurable to the preschool child. The level of involvement goes up when the parent or caretaker enters into the children's experience for a time or if a shared project is initiated.

When parents or other adults actually interact with the children, six patterns of adult-child interaction can exist: (1) physical intimacy (e.g., lap-sitting, hugging), (2) spontaneous and informal conversation, (3) praise, (4) assistance, (5) structured turn-taking, and (6) understanding and following rules (involves both rule implementation and conflict resolution). All of these interactions contribute to parenting quality (Klass, 1987).

Baumrind's Styles of Parenting

Diana Baumrind (1968, 1971) proposed four types of parenting styles: **authoritarian** (autocratic), **permissive, authoritative** (democratic), and **rejecting-neglecting** (laissez-faire). Characteristics and effects of these styles are summarized in Table 7.5.

Notice that the authoritarian parent, who is power-oriented, unresponsive to children's views, demanding, and authority-oriented, is the opposite of the permissive parent, who is nonpowerful, responsive to children's views, undemanding, and nonauthoritative. What kinds of children develop from these two different styles?

Authoritarian children learn to obey and to not question authority. As a result, they often have low creativity and low initiative. Many of them are polite, well-behaved, and obedient. As they get older, they tend to either be traditionalists who respect authority, work, and the current so-

cial order, or they tend to rebel and break away from the family mold (Baumrind, 1968). Many children with permissive parents seem to be difficult and somewhat unruly during childhood. However, these same children are likely to develop into cooperative, caring adults (McClelland, Constantian, Regalado, & Stone, 1978).

The rejecting-neglecting parenting style seems to be the worst of all worlds. Parents are unresponsive, undemanding, and nonaffirming. The laissez-faire ("let it be") approach comes across as indifferent, noncaring, no-bother childcare. Children often feel lost and unloved in this family atmosphere.

Perhaps the best parenting style is the authoritative or democratic approach. Authoritative parents are power-oriented and demanding like authoritarian parents, but they are also responsive like permissive parents. In addition, authoritative parents emphasize reasoning and explain their rules and enforcement to their children (Baumrind, 1968).

Authoritative parents are really authoritative-reciprocal because they allow their children to participate in their own development. Although similar to authoritarian parents in expecting mature behavior and in firm enforcement of rules, they differ in three important ways: (1) they encourage their children's individuality; (2) they allow two-way communication with their children (e.g., children can present reasons for why their parents should change their bedtime to 30 min. later); and (3) they respect their children's rights (Baumrind, 1971).

The authoritative parenting style is the most difficult style to consistently maintain. Parents must take the time to figure out their reasons for their parenting decisions and also must be willing to explain the reasons to their children.

Of course, there are actually more than four styles of parenting. Parents may combine aspects from the different styles. Others may shift from one style to another as children get older. For example, some parents may be authoritarian with small children, become more authoritative with school-age and early adolescent children, and end up permissive when they decide that their children can make healthy choices for themselves. Although the rejecting-neglecting style should be avoided, all other styles are capable of producing good results. Good parenting is not just type of parenting, nature of rules, and type of punishment; good parenting is all about good involvement between parent and child (Maccoby & Martin, 1983).

Disciplining Children

Hoffman's Discipline Styles

How do parents guide their children and enforce their rules? Martin Hoffman (1984) suggested that parents use three major types of discipline: **power-assertion, love-withdrawal,** and **induction.** In power-assertive discipline, parents use their overwhelming power to control the situation. Because parents are larger and stronger than their children, all parents use power-assertion sometimes. Examples include bodily removal of children from a situation, shouting and yelling at them, threatening children,

Table 7.5
Four Parenting Styles

Authoritarian (Traditional, Autocratic):	Permissive (Nurturing, Child-Centered):	Rejecting-Neglecting (Laissez-Faire, Abusive):	Authoritative (Democratic):
Unresponsive and Demanding Power and Authority	*Responsive and Undemanding Nonpower and Affirming*	*Unresponsive and Undemanding Nonpower and Noninvolvement*	*Responsive and Demanding Power and Reason*
Parent adheres to a set standard of conduct (often theologically motivated).	Parent is nonpunitive, accepting, and affirming toward child's desires, impulses, and behaviors.	Parent seems indifferent to children.	Parent directs child, but in rational, issue-oriented manner.
Parent has control over the child.	Parent includes child in policy decisions.	Parent spends little time with children.	Parent provides verbal reasoning with give-and-take.
Parent expects obedience (without questioning).	Parent is a resource rather than a controller.	Parent makes little effort to parent.	Parental values: Expressive and instrumental attributes, self-will, self-discipline.
Parent uses punitive, forceful measures to curb children's self-will.	Parent expects child to regulate own behavior.	Parent does not deal with the aspects of parenting that are inconvenient.	Parent has firm control but keeps child's individuality in mind.
Parental values: Respect for authority, work, preservation of order, and traditional structure.	Parental rights are low.	Effects on children: Low self-esteem, confusion, guilt about not being worthy of love, may act out in attempts to get parental attention, inconsistent.	Parent affirms child's present personality while setting future standards.
Parental needs come first.	Parent condones all that the children do.	Parent is at high risk for child abuse.	Parent allows children to choose among permitted alternatives and to learn from the consequences.
Effects on children: Want to be told what to do, distrust their feelings, low creativity, compliant and withdrawing or defiant and rebellious, lack of sense of personal control and responsibility over own life.	Children may be confused, insecure, dependent, angry.		Effects on children: Cooperate, respect rules, self-disciplined and respectful, understand cause-and-effect, self-determination.
Parent is at high risk for child abuse.	Effects on children: Have difficulty with limits (while craving them), may take care of parents instead of being taken care of by them, prematurely on their own, do whatever they wish without social responsibility.		Parent must invest much effort to do this consistently.

Source: Data from D. Baumrind, "Authoritarian Versus Authoritative Parental Control" in *Adolescence*, 3, 255–272, 1968. From D. Baumrind, "Current Patterns of Parental Authority" in *Developmental Psychology Monographs*, 4, (1, pt 2), 1971. From E. E. Maccoby and J. A. Martin, "Socialization in the Context of the Family: Parent-Child Interaction" in *Handbook of Child Psychology: Vol. 4, Socialization, Personality, and Social Development,* 1983, edited by P. H. Mussen, John Wiley & Sons, NY. From L. Hart, *The Winning Family: Increasing Self-Esteem in Your Children and Yourself,* 1987, Dodd, Mead & Company, NY.

ordering children to do or stop doing something, and physical punishment. Power-assertion is based largely on children's fear of punishment (Hoffman, 1984). Parents who rely mostly on this style produce self-centered children who are intent on avoiding punishment (Brody & Shaffer, 1982).

Love-withdrawal discipline is based on children's fear of losing parental emotional support, approval, and affection. Love-withdrawal discipline occurs when parents physically, verbally, or emotionally withdraw from their children, when they tell their children that they dislike them, and when they threaten to leave their children (Hoffman, 1984). Children whose parents use these techniques often learn to repress their emotions and to administer self-punishment by not loving themselves when they disapprove of their own behavior (Hoffman & Saltzstein, 1967).

Inductive discipline is the "teaching style" and involves directing attention to children's reasoning, pride, concern for others, and desire to be mature. Parents also inform their children about harmful consequences of behaviors. Children raised by inductive discipline are the most likely to internalize their parents' standards and to develop high levels of prosocial behavior (Hoffman, 1984). Japanese mothers use inductive style almost exclusively—"How do you think it makes (me/the owner) feel when you do that?" (Bettelheim, 1985).

Parents who use the inductive style of discipline can use two kinds of reasons: person-oriented and position-oriented. A person-oriented reason might be: "Please put your shoes on before you go out to play; I'm concerned that there may be broken glass at the playground." A position-oriented reason might be: "Please put your shoes on before you go out to play; good girls don't play outdoors in their bare feet." More boys than girls are given position-oriented reasons (remember, more pressure is put on boys to conform to gender roles). Also, same-sex parents use more person-oriented appeals, and opposite-sex parents use more position-oriented appeals (Pogrebin, 1980).

Again, parents can use all three discipline styles, and do. Some parents start with power-assertion and move to induction; others move from love-withdrawal to induction (Hoffman, 1984). Authoritarian parents use mostly

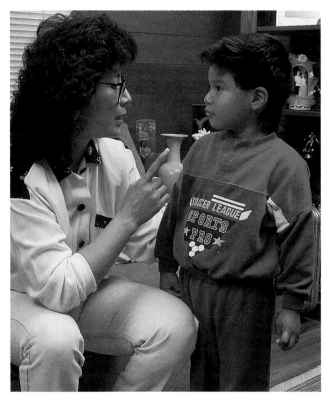

Inductive discipline involves active instruction of the child by the parent.

power-assertion; rejecting-neglecting parents use no discipline and sporadic power-assertion. Authoritative parents use both power-assertion and induction. Permissive parents use largely inductive style (Maccoby & Martin, 1983).

Discipline Versus Physical Punishment

Discipline involves guidance and teaching. Physical punishment involves enforcement and correction. Some parents believe that discipline equals physical punishment, citing the biblical passage "Spare the rod and spoil the child." But biblical shepherds did not use their rods to hit the sheep; they used them to guide sheep in the correct direction (Hart, 1987).

Physical punishment is common in the United States. Eighty-one percent of parents use corporal punishment. Six out of ten parents spank or hit their children at least once a week. Boys are spanked three times more often than girls (Pogrebin, 1980).

While physical punishment has the goal of reducing undesirable behavior, it fails to teach children what to do. To be effective, parents should pair punishment with reasons, constructive alternatives, and good parental examples. Parents should realize that physical punishment may teach their children to associate parents with anger and fear. Children may also learn that physical aggression can get you what you want. Some children who are often physically punished learn to obey their parents but to act aggressively toward their peers. Another unfortunate aspect of physical punishment is that children often devote their energies to avoiding getting caught and become quite devious (Bettelheim, 1985; Brody & Shaffer, 1982; Walters & Grusec, 1977).

Physical punishment is most effective when it is intense (while effective, it is not humane), when it is administered immediately after the violation ("Wait until your father gets home" is a poor idea), and when discipline rules are consistent.

Many parents use physical punishment poorly and underestimate its drawbacks on children's behavior. When physical punishment is severe and misused, children are abused.

Child Abuse

Historical View

Child abuse is not new; only widespread awareness of child abuse and societal involvement to help reduce abuse is new. Traditionally, harsh discipline was culturally sanctioned to cure unruly behavior, to discipline children, and to expel evil spirits. In the early 1600s, Massachusetts even passed a "Stubborn Child Act" that allowed parents to have rebellious or stubborn children put to death (Wolfe, 1987).

Intervention in child abuse is a 20th-century phenomenon. The first American child to be helped was aided by the Society for the Prevention of Cruelty to Animals because no organization existed for preventing cruelty to children. The first legal intervention came in the 1930s when the Social Security Act was passed and child protection became a public responsibility. Yet, attention to child abuse remained low. The term battered child syndrome was not used until the 1960s (Wolfe, 1987).

Data collected from 1976 to 1982 on reported child abuse cases suggested that 64 percent experienced significant neglect, 25 percent had physical injuries (e.g., brain damage and skull fractures, hematomas, bone fractures, sprains, poisonings, burns, cuts, bruises, welts, twisting), 17 percent were emotionally abused, and 7 percent were sexually abused. Other data suggested that nearly two thirds of maltreated children had insufficient necessities of life and parental disinterest. Nearly half of neglect reports involved suspicion of other forms of abuse (Wolfe, 1987).

Characteristics of Abused Children and Their Parents

Neglect of children often begins before the preschool years; neglect declines among older children, perhaps because they can partially manage self-care. Physical abuse increases in the preschool years and actually peaks during the adolescent years. Sexual and emotional abuse occurs from infancy on, though many experts believe that these forms are most common among school-age children and adolescents. The victims of sexual abuse by family members are mostly girls (85 percent), but other forms of abuse occur about equally to girls and boys.

Psychological characteristics of abusive parents are provided in Table 7.6. A factor not mentioned in Table 7.6 is that many abusive parents started families at a younger age than the general population. Teenage parents may become more frustrated by their children, due to fewer life experiences, less financial resources, and more unrealistic expectations about their offspring. Natural parents are often the perpetrators of abuse, but in cases of sexual abuse and

Table 7.6
Psychological Characteristics of Abusive Parents

The following characteristics of abusive parents were found in studies from 1978 to 1986. Each study used matched control groups to compare responses of abusive parents to nonabusive parents from similar backgrounds.

I. Behavioral Dimension
   - Isolation from family and friends
   - Less communication and less child stimulation
   - Disproportionate rate of negative to positive interactions with other family members
   - Failure to match disciplinary methods to child's transgression; intrusive; inconsistent

II. Cognitive-Emotional Dimension
   - Self-described as unhappy, rigid, distressed
   - More self-expressed anger
   - Child's behavior perceived as stressful
   - Low frustration tolerance—that is, greater emotional (psychophysiological) reactivity to child provocation
   - Inappropriate expectations of child: disregard for child's needs and abilities—for example, belief that child intentionally annoys parent
   - Greater perceived life stress
   - Flattened affect during parent-child interactions

III. Other Findings Related to Psychological Functioning
   - More physical health problems

IV. Empirical Findings That Did *Not* Differ From Controls
   - Amount of stressful life events
   - Self-expressed emotional needs—for example, feeling unloved, dependency, emotional problems, or personal adjustment
   - Denial of problems

From D. A. Wolfe, *Child Abuse: Implications for Child Development and Psychopathology*, p. 72, 1987. Copyright © 1987. Reprinted by permission of Sage Publications, Inc.

physical abuse, stepparents and foster parents have higher rates than do biological parents (Wolfe, 1987). Contrary to stereotypes, most abused children do not grow up to be abusive parents (Zigler, Rubin, & Kaufman, 1988).

Parents who are unprepared for parenting and who have unrealistic expectations are at risk for emotional abuse and neglect. These "uninvolved" parents may expect children to meet their own needs. Parents who are in favor of corporal punishment and the authoritarian style of parenting may make poor judgments about discipline versus abuse. Not all abusing parents are alike. For all parents, learning good communication with their children can help relationships.

Parent-Child Communication

Children often misbehave and seek inappropriate attention to communicate needs to their parents (Dreikurs & Soltz, 1964). When children feel unworthy or ignored by their family, they often try to force attention from others by cute or annoying behaviors. If these mildly irritating behaviors fail to get their needs met, children may next try to seek power by stubbornness or rebelliousness. Again, if parents fail to respond to their children's attempts to get attention and support, they may try even more extreme behaviors, such as hurting others.

When children feel valued and loved within the family setting, they reduce inappropriate behaviors and increase their cooperative and positive interactions. If parents fail to deal with the real issues, the children may eventually give up and become passive and noninteracting. These children feel many negative emotions and have low self-esteem, but parents may interpret the quietness as good behavior.

Just as parents are influencing their children's behaviors, children are shaping their parents' behavior, and the children often do a better job! For example: The parent asks the child to pick up the toys that are strewn across the room. Instead of complying with the parent's request, the child delays in the task and whines and complains. The parent repeats the request several times, only to hear increased whining and complaining and the vague promise to "get it done soon." Eventually, the parent stops requesting the cleanup, and the child stops whining.

In the preceding scenario, the parent has been *negatively reinforced* by the child—it feels good to the parent to have the child stop whining, so the parent learns to pick up the toys rather than to get the child to do this chore (Patterson, 1980). Parents are often unaware of the controlling factors in these situations. Learning about this *reinforcement trap* helps them to overcome it. With practice, parents learn to give more definite and more specific requests to their children and to extinguish the whining behaviors. Effective behavior shaping is an important part of parent-child communication.

guided review

12. Match the parenting style with the appropriate characteristics:
    A. Authoritarian   _____ Unresponsive; undemanding
    B. Permissive   _____ Unresponsive; demanding
    C. Authoritative   _____ Responsive; undemanding
    D. Rejecting/   _____ Responsive; demanding
        neglecting
13. Parents who rely on the discipline style of _____ are most likely to have children who internalize their parents' values, while children who experience the _____ style are most likely to try to avoid punishment.
14. _____ has several undesirable consequences: Children may learn to fear their parents, and they may become more devious and aggressive themselves.
15. The characteristics of abusive parents can be categorized along the _____ and _____ dimensions.

answers

12. D, A, B, C, [LO-11]. **13.** induction; power-assertion [LO-12]. **14.** Physical punishment [LO-12]. **15.** behavioral; cognitive-emotional [LO-13].

Play and Playmates

The Importance of Play

Play has been defined as the serious work of children and seems to be necessary for healthy development. In playing, children learn to combine freedom with personally imposed rules in activities that have no goals outside of the activity itself (Bettelheim, 1987; Isenberg & Quisenberry, 1988). Young children engage in play; older children engage in games. Play involves freewheeling fantasy, while games have externally imposed rules, usually are competitive, and have winners and losers (Bettelheim, 1987).

Purposes of Play

One purpose of play is that children are able to work through and be in control of psychological difficulties of the past and present. This purpose of play is helpful with children during counseling (and is called, appropriately, play therapy). Children use play to be able to handle future scenarios, such as rehearsing for a birthday party or the start of kindergarten (Bettelheim, 1987; Rosenthal, 1988). Sometimes, children practice in play the behaviors that will later become their everyday behavior; play helps to hone the skill before it is widely used.

Play builds a number of specific skills. The physical activity of play, for example, helps young children to develop and improve their motor skills. Imaginary and fantasy play is a beginning step toward the development of abstract thinking and allows the child to develop personal myths. All play helps children to persevere and to build attention skills (Bettelheim, 1987; Isenberg & Quisenberry, 1988).

Moreover, play is important in social-emotional development. Children use play to understand, express, share, and control emotional experiences. Some experts believe that play allows children to symbolically get rid of aggression and to learn to control aggressive urges (Bettelheim, 1987). Moreover, during play, preschoolers form their first friendships and build social skills. Playing with others allows a fairly safe environment in which children can compare their own behaviors and skills with those of other children (Isenberg & Quisenberry, 1988).

Play Trends

Play is a universal phenomenon—children in all cultures play, except in the few cultures that make young children work and do chores instead of play (Whiting & Whiting, 1975). Play socializes and educates youngsters, and play activities should not be viewed as frivolous. In fact, gifted preschoolers engage in more physical, cognitive, and social play than other preschoolers (Barnett & Fiscella, 1985). However, over the last 60 years, the trend has been toward less playing, especially social play (Barnes, 1971; Isenberg & Quisenberry, 1988).

Preschool children, like older children, have more same-sex than opposite-sex playmates (Jacklin & Maccoby, 1978). Two-year-old boys start playing "like the boys," but even 3-year-old girls play both "like the boys" and "like the girls" (Blakemore, LaRue, & Olejnik, 1979). Parents affect these gender differences. For example, fathers allow girls a wide range of play but restrict their boys from playing like girls (Snow, Jacklin, & Maccoby, 1983).

Styles of Play

Nonsocial and Social Play

In the 1920s, Mildred Parten (1932) studied 2- to 5-year-olds at play. From her observations, she divided play into nonsocial play and social play. Children who were 2 or 3 engaged in four types of nonsocial play: (1) unoccupied play (vacant time spent observing some event or object), (2) onlooker play (watching other children play but not joining in except perhaps to ask questions or to make suggestions), (3) solitary independent play (playing by oneself without play interaction with others), and (4) parallel play (playing by oneself but by other children who are also playing).

Parten found that older preschoolers engaged in some social play. In associative play, children play with other children in a common activity. The children share play materials and influence each other's play activities. However, associative play involves no division of labor and no unified goal. Children do all aspects of planning, and each plays as he or she wishes. Cooperative play is more organized and has a goal—for example, to make a product, follow a joint process, divide responsibilities, or organize a game. This type of play becomes common in the middle school years.

> ### successful study tip
>
> #### Parten's Types of Social and Nonsocial Play
>
> Mildred Parten described four types of nonsocial play, which can be cued with the word soup (S for solitary; O for onlooker; U for unoccupied; and P for parallel). She also described two types of social play, which can be cued by remembering A.C. (A for associative; C for cooperative). The letters A.C. can be remembered for their other usage as an abbreviation for "alternating current."

Social play is now less common among young children than it was when Parten did her original study (Barnes, 1971). Four developments have influenced this trend: (1) television, (2) solitary and educational toys, (3) growing use of computers by children, and (4) families with fewer siblings for "convenient" social playing (Barnes, 1971).

Functional Play

Four types of play—functional, constructive, dramatic, and games-with-rules—are described in Table 7.7. The table is hierarchical—that is, functional play is the first to appear, and games-with-rules is the last to appear (Rubin, 1977; Smilansky, 1968). Functional play is the most common

Table 7.7
Types of Play

Name	Description	Example
Functional (Sensorimotor)	Simple, repetitive, muscular activities (with or without objects)	Rolling ball; pulling toy; playing pat-a-cake
Constructive	Manipulation of objects to build or create something	Using blocks, legos, tinkertoys, clay
Dramatic (pretend or fantasy)	Using imaginary situations or characters; may be simple or elaborate	Playing careers; using puppets or costumes
Games-with-rules	Activities involving rules, structure, and a goal	Playing hopscotch, tag, softball, card games, marbles, darts

From S. Smilansky, *The Effects of Sociodramatic Play on Disadvantaged Preschool Children*, 1968. Reprinted by permission of Sara Smilansky. Source: from K. H. Rubin, "The Social and Cognitive Value of Preschool Toys and Activities" in *Canadian Journal of Behavioral Science*, 9, 382–385, 1977.

play for the first 3 years of life and is more common among boys than girls (Christie & Johnsen, 1987; Rubin, Fein, & Vandenberg, 1983).

The amount of nonsocial or solitary play seems to remain constant at all age levels, but as children become older, they engage in less solitary-functional play and in more solitary-constructive and solitary-dramatic play. The cognitive characteristics in solitary play mature with age (Christie & Johnsen, 1987).

Constructive Play

Constructive play begins about age 2 and, between the ages of 4 and 6, is the most common play. Girls engage in more constructive play, especially social-constructive play, than boys (Christie & Johnsen, 1987; Rubin et al., 1983).

At day-care centers, preschoolers spend about half of their playtime in constructive play; at home, they engage in constructive play less than a fifth of the time. This difference is probably due to the type of materials and toys available in day-care centers versus homes (Christie & Johnsen, 1987; Rubin et al., 1983).

Constructive play aids problem solving by increasing flexibility, consolidating learning, encouraging elaboration, and enhancing creativity. As children become older, they shift from emphasizing the means of constructive play to emphasizing the ends. This shift is shown by their constructive play becoming less playlike and more craft-oriented (Christie & Johnsen, 1987).

Dramatic Play

Dramatic play, also called pretend play or fantasy play, also begins around the age of 2. Pretend play increases during the preschool years, and interactive pretend play increases until age 6 or 7, with solitary pretend play decreasing (Rubin et al., 1983). Sociodramatic play—make-believe play about social situations—is common around the age of

4 or 5. Sociodramatic play occurs when children set up a social setting, such as: "I'm the mommy. You be the daddy. We're playing house."

Dramatic play allows learning through role-play, permits children to rehearse problems in a no-failure situation, and lets children feel more powerful and competent by taking on the roles of parents, workers, and even superheroes. Preschool children can use fantasy play to handle feelings of helplessness, frustration, and anger (Rosenthal, 1988).

Fantasy and daydreaming are healthy unless children exclude the real world, and that rarely occurs (Rosenthal, 1988). In fact, Bettelheim (1987) expressed concern that modern children do not get enough fantasy time. He used the German word *Spielraum,* which means "free scope, plenty of room," to indicate that children need time and space to let their ideas run wild. Bettelheim believed that some youngsters have too many scheduled activities and not enough daydreaming time:

> *The biographies of creative people of the past are full of accounts of long hours they spent sitting by the river as teenagers, thinking their own thoughts, roaming through the woods with their faithful dogs, or dreaming their own dreams. But who today has the leisure and the opportunities for this? If a youngster tries it, as likely as not his parents will fret that he is not using his time constructively, that he is daydreaming when he should be tackling the serious business of life. However, developing an inner life, including fantasies and daydreams, is one of the most constructive things a growing child can do. (p. 37)*

Many preschoolers—perhaps the majority of them—have imaginary playmates. Children with imaginary playmates tend to be less aggressive and better able to concentrate. The more vivid the imaginary playmates, the more likely the children are to have high intelligence (Pines, 1978; Rosenthal, 1988).

successful study tip

Types of Play

Use the first letter of each word in the sentence "Farmers Can Dig Gardens" to help recall the four types of play. (*F* is for functional [sensorimotor]; *C* is for constructive; *D* is for dramatic [pretend, fantasy]; *G* is for games-with-rules.)

Parents and Play

Parents influence how children play, how children value their play, and how good the playing makes the children feel. At times, parents can make their children feel inferior and incapable of good play. According to Bettelheim (1987):

> *Some parents . . . are not satisfied with the way their child plays. So they start telling him how he ought to use a toy; and if he continues to suit his own fancy,*

Parents influence the number of relationships and the kinds of relationships their children have with their peers. First, parental values influence children's friendships. Second, concrete behaviors, such as inviting friends over to the house, have an impact on developing friendships.

Parents' values along four dimensions influence their children's friendships (Rubin & Sloman, 1984):

1. Parents vary in how important they believe peer relationships are for their preschoolers. Few parents believe that friends are not important to 4-year-olds. Most believe that peer relationships help to build social skills, independence, and general well-being.

2. Parents have opinions about what friends are beneficial to their children. Most parents prefer their young children's friends to be from similar social and value backgrounds, although some parents prefer exposure to a wide variety of backgrounds. Most want their children to play with both boys and girls but believe that same-sex friendships are the most important. Parents believe that preschoolers' playmates are most successful when similar in age, yet recognize that older children teach their children skills and that younger children encourage nurturance from their older children.

3. Parents differ on how they think children's friendships are best structured. Some believe that young children play best in exclusive play (playing with one or two children at a time), and others prefer inclusive play (playing with several children). Another value difference is whether play contacts should be spontaneous (e.g., happen to be outside playing at the same time) or scheduled (e.g., calling and inviting the child over to play).

4. Parents differ on whether they should direct or control their young children's social lives.

All parents act as social directors through a number of unavoidable decisions (Rubin & Sloman, 1984). Childhood friendships are influenced by how parents *set the stage*. In other words, playmates are partly determined by choice of neighborhood, whether children are in day care, and parents' social contacts. All parents serve as *models of social relationships* for children: Many bullies come from homes in which the father acts like a bully with the children; many above-average nurturing children learn to nurture from their parents. In addition, all parents *provide a home base;* secure parent-child relationships help children to feel more secure in their first friendships.

Parents who actively take on the role of social director are more likely to *arrange social contacts* by scheduling playmate visits, enrolling children in organized activities, and chauffeuring their children. Active social directors provide more *coaching* or advice on who their children should have as friends and how they should conduct themselves.

Outgoing, uninhibited children will probably make friends, regardless of their parents' efforts. Shy, inhibited children may benefit more from active encouragement and scheduling. Overly intrusive parents, however, may actually retard their children's abilities to initiate and control friendships. Laissez-faire parents may either provide their children with productive freedom or leave their children floundering without guidelines. Parents need to assess their own reasons for their behavior (e.g., are they helping the child or building their own self-esteem?) and their children's needs (e.g., does my child have trouble making friends and is there a helpful way to assist?).

---

they "correct" him, wanting him to use the toy in accordance with its intended purpose or the way they think it ought to be played with. If they insist on such guidance, the child's interest in the toy—and to some extent also in play in general—is apt to wane, because the project has become his parents' and is no longer his own. (pp. 36–37)

How can parents help their children to play well? Sometimes, parents should have benign neglect toward their children's fantasy play. As long as children are given time to create make-believe, they will (Rosenthal, 1988). In fact, rewarding certain play activities seems to reduce rather than increase those particular play activities. Since play is intrinsically rewarding, providing small extrinsic rewards, such as praise and money, makes children focus on the extrinsic reward and forget how rewarding the activity itself is (Lepper, Greene, & Nisbett, 1973).

On the other hand, parents can participate in their children's play. Mother-child dyads are especially likely to include instructive play (Stevenson, Leavitt, Thompson, & Roach, 1988). When parents allow themselves to become engrossed in their children's play, they are telling their children that their play is important (Bettelheim, 1987).

Games-With-Rules Play

Dramatic play gradually declines and is replaced by games-with-rules play (Rubin, Fein, & Vandenberg, 1983). Preschoolers play games with such simple rules as taking turns. The more social and complex rule-determined play of school-age children reflects changes in their cognitive abilities (Piaget, 1951). As children mature, games-with-rules play gives them practice in following complex rules, cooperating in large and small groups, and dealing with winning and losing (Kamii & deVries, 1980). The role of games-with-rules play in later childhood is explored further in Chapter 9.

Although they spend more time interacting with adults, spending time with other children is important to preschoolers.

Peer-Group Interactions

Preschoolers do not just play with their parents and siblings; they develop playmates. Friendship is an important concept from the age of 3 (Rubin & Sloman, 1984), and young children initiate friendships by directly asking for friendship or by sharing a toy (Hartup, 1983). Parents often try to influence who their children have as friends and how they play, the topic of the "Exploring the Parent/Child Relationship" feature.

Factors Involved in Friendships

Four factors are important in young children making friends. From high to low in importance, these factors are: (1) liking and engaging in common activities, (2) liking each other, (3) propinquity (nearness), and (4) physical characteristics of the children (Furman & Bierman, 1983).

Amount of Interaction with Peers

While friends are important, preschool children have more adults than peers in their social network. They have more contact with nonrelatives than with relatives, and more contact with females than with males. Thirty-five percent of 3-year-olds have daily contact with peers, while this percentage grows to 55 percent by age 6 (Feiring & Lewis, 1987).

Preschoolers are more prosocial and more playful with peers than they are with siblings (Abramovitch, Carter, Pepler, & Stanhope, 1986). Since boys are socialized away from the family earlier, boys move toward greater peer contact earlier than girls, and boys are more likely to play in larger groups than girls (Feiring & Lewis, 1987).

Benefits of Early Friendships

Friendships serve many purposes besides increasing pleasure and fun. Young children are more willing to explore new environments with peers than alone (Schwartz, 1972).

Peers help young children to pick up social skills and to learn to deal with equals (Hartup, 1983). Friends also are handy sources for social comparisons so that young children can decide what aspects about themselves are likeable and favorable and which need to be changed (Rubin, 1980). Peer interactions grow in importance throughout the childhood and adolescent years.

Exploring Human Development

1. Assess your family constellation. If possible, have your siblings do the same thing, and discuss your responses together.
2. Create a short survey to give to several students to assess whether people believe that aggression and prosocial behaviors are innate or learned.
3. Interview children of different ages to assess their views of how boys and girls are the same or different. Also ask them about how mommies and daddies are alike and different.
4. Visit the homes of several preschoolers. observe the preschoolers' rooms, and note the degree to which gender-role stereotypes are present. What colors predominate? What types of toys do you see? Interview a parent of the preschooler on his or her views regarding the importance of gender-typing and the concept of androgyny.
5. Visit a playground, and observe the various play styles and types of play exhibited by the children playing there. Interview the parents of the children about their children's friends and how involved the parents are in choosing friends for their children.

Discussing Human Development

1. Which aspects of the various theories discussed in this chapter did you prefer or not prefer? Why?
2. Under what circumstances do you think parents should actively try to modify their preschool children's: aggression levels, prosocial behaviors, gender-deviant behaviors, play patterns, choice of friends? On what do you base your decisions? How might you program these modifications?

3. What are your opinions about use of physical punishment with preschool children? In Sweden, it is illegal for parents to spank their children. Would you like to have a similar law in the United States? Why or why not?
4. Which type of parenting style do you prefer? Did your parents use this style?
5. What were your favorite play activities in the preschool years? How did your preferences change as you grew older?

Reading More About Human Development

Hall, E. (1986). *Growing and changing: What the experts say.* New York: Random House.

Hart, L. (1987). *The winning family: Increasing self-esteem in your children and yourself.* New York: Dodd, Mead.

Summary

I. Theories of personality development
   A. Freud's third stage—the phallic stage, in which the primary source of gratification is the genital area—occurs during the preschool years.
      1. Freud's ideas about the genital stage were influenced by the sexual repression of the Victorian era.
      2. The Oedipus complex is Freud's explanation for how boys resolve internal conflicts about sexual attachments with their mothers through gender identification with their fathers.
      3. The Electra complex is Freud's explanation for how girls come to identify with the female gender role.
      4. Karen Horney, who disliked Freud's emphasis on penis envy, proposed that little boys experience womb envy.
      5. The superego, with its components of the conscience and the ego ideal, continues to develop during the preschool years.
      6. Preschoolers most commonly use denial as an ego defense mechanism.
   B. Erik Erikson's third psychosocial stage is initiative versus guilt.
      1. Preschoolers learn to take initiative and to be goal-oriented.
      2. Failure to resolve this stage causes preschoolers to experience anxiety in the form of guilt.
   C. Unlike Freud, Alfred Adler in his individual psychology emphasized the future.
      1. Preschoolers become aware of their family constellation, including the effects of their birth order.
      2. Adler proposed that preschoolers experience sibling rivalry, in which they compete with their siblings for their parents' approval and affection.
      3. Adler recognized that family atmosphere—the emotional relationships among family members—also influenced the preschooler's personality development.
   D. Albert Bandura's social learning theory explains personality development in terms of learned behavior within a social context.
      1. Reciprocal determinism is the concept that children actively shape the environments that influence their development.
      2. Modeling, observation, and imitation are important aspects of how a preschooler is influenced by others.
   E. Abraham Maslow's metamotivational theory proposes that people strive to grow beyond their present condition toward fulfilling their potential.
      1. Preschoolers need to have their biological and safety needs met in order to reach their higher personal growth needs.
      2. Children have to learn to balance tendencies toward growth, which involve taking risks, with the need to receive parental approval by seeking safety.

II. Aggressive and prosocial behaviors of preschoolers
   A. Aggressive behavior tends to increase during the preschool years.
      1. Aggressiveness levels in preschoolers are predictive of aggressiveness in later childhood and adulthood.
      2. Boys exhibit more physical and verbal aggression than girls.
      3. Theories of aggression include Freud's view that children release aggressive energy in their play, Lorenz's view that aggression is innate and triggered by environmental cues, and Bandura's theory that aggression is learned by observing others acting aggressively.
      4. Aggressive behavior among preschoolers can be controlled or reduced in a number of ways, including modeling nonaggressive, prosocial behaviors.
   B. Prosocial behaviors benefit other people, and altruistic behaviors are intentionally done for the benefit of others.
      1. Preschoolers increase their prosocial behaviors but are more aggressive than prosocial.
      2. Sociobiologists believe that prosocial behaviors are genetically programmed.
      3. Prosocial behavior is encouraged by the child's conscience and ego-ideal, according to psychoanalytic theory.
      4. Social-learning theory predicts more prosocial behavior when children observe models acting prosocially.
      5. One way to encourage prosocial behaviors is to reduce competitiveness while emphasizing cooperation.

III. Gender identification in preschoolers
   A. Gender roles are the culturally derived roles considered appropriate for males and females.
      1. Sex differences are physical differences, while gender differences are psychological and behavioral differences.
      2. Gender stereotypes are exaggerated generalizations about male and female behaviors.

3. Preschoolers have gender identity (awareness of being female or male) and acquire gender constancy (the awareness that they will always be either female or male).
4. Gender-typing occurs when children acquire the appropriate gender role.
5. Parents emphasize male gender-role characteristics and put more pressure on boys than girls to act according to gender-role expectations.

B. Four major theoretical positions may be used to explain gender-role identification.
1. Psychoanalytic theory accounts for gender-role acquisition through the Oedipus complex for boys and the Electra complex for girls.
2. Social-learning theory emphasizes the modeling of and reinforcement of same-sex behavior.
3. Cognitive-developmental theory stresses children's active roles in processing information based on their gender identities.
4. Gender-schema theory proposes that children create a gender schema in light of society's gender views and use it to process information and to organize behavior related to gender.

C. Traditional gender roles emphasize the distinct roles of males and females, while androgynous gender roles incorporate the positive qualities of both genders.
1. Traditional female roles include child-rearing, housekeeping, obedience, and dependence.
2. Traditional male roles include breadwinning, disciplining, domineering, and independence.
3. Cultural variations in gender roles suggest that gender roles are learned in a cultural context and, therefore, that individuals can adopt androgynous gender roles.

IV. Parenting preschoolers
A. Parents vary in their parenting styles, including in how much direct contact they have with their children, how available they are, and how much responsibility they take for their children.
1. Baumrind proposed four types of parenting styles.
2. Authoritarian parents are traditional, autocratic, demanding, and unresponsive.
3. Permissive parents are nurturing, child-centered, and undemanding.
4. Rejecting-neglecting parents are laissez-faire, abusive, unresponsive, undemanding, and uninvolved with their children.
5. Authoritative parents are democratic, responsive, and demanding, and know how to reason with their children.

B. Hoffman proposed that parents use three major types of discipline.
1. Power-assertion involves parents using their greater power to control the situation.
2. Love-withdrawal is based on children's fear of losing parental emotional support and approval.
3. Induction focuses on reasoning with the child while directing the child's attention to the consequences of his or her actions.

4. Discipline involves guidance and teaching, while physical punishment involves enforcement and correction.
5. Physical punishment is most effective when it is intense, immediate, and consistent.

C. While child abuse has occurred across the centuries, intervention in child abuse cases only began in the 20th century.
1. Abusive parents can be characterized along behavioral and cognitive-emotional dimensions but do not experience more stressful life events than nonabusive parents.
2. Contrary to a widely accepted notion, most abused children do not grow up to become abusive parents.

D. Parent-child communication patterns influence preschoolers' behavior patterns.
1. Misbehavior may be an attempt by children to communicate needs for attention to their parents.
2. Children who feel unworthy or ignored may act out in increasingly severe ways.
3. Parents who communicate their approval and love to their children have children who are more cooperative and positive in their interactions.
4. Just as parents may inadvertently reinforce misbehavior in their children, children may negatively reinforce their parents by stopping their whining when parents do things for them.

V. Play and playmates
A. Play fulfills many important purposes in the lives of preschoolers.
1. Play builds physical skills while allowing children to work through past difficulties, to prepare for future events, and to build social-emotional skills.
2. The trend over the last 60 years has been toward less play, especially social play.
3. Preschoolers, like older children, have more same-sex than opposite-sex playmates.

B. As children move through the preschool years, their style of play changes.
1. Two- and three-year-olds engage in four types of nonsocial play: unoccupied, onlooker, solitary independent, and parallel play.
2. Older preschoolers engage in social play, which includes associative play with other children in a common activity and cooperative play (more organized, goal-oriented play).
3. The play of preschoolers may also be characterized as functional (rolling a ball), constructive (building with blocks), dramatic (play acting), and games-with-rules (playing hide-and-seek).

C. Parents influence how their children play in many ways.
1. Parents can be overinvolved in their children's play, making the child feel inferior or incapable of playing well.
2. Parents who reward play activities may actually reduce the amount of play in which their children engage.
3. Occasional playing with children for the sake of enjoying playing can indicate to children that the parent thinks that the child's play is important.

D. Peer-group interactions become more important during the preschool years.
1. Parents are influential in the number and kinds of relationships that preschoolers have with each other.
2. Preschoolers think that liking and doing the same activities are the most important factors in determining with whom they become friends.
3. Preschoolers derive many benefits from having friends, including social skills and the opportunity for social comparisons.

Chapter Review Test

1. Freud believed that, during the phallic stage, young children form sexual attachments with
   a. their mothers.
   b. their friends.
   c. their opposite-sex parents.
   d. their siblings.
2. According to Freud, young boys' rivalry with their fathers results in their experience of
   a. castration anxiety.
   b. penis envy.
   c. overidentification with their mothers.
   d. all of the above.
3. The fundamental ego defense mechanism is
   a. projection.
   b. denial.
   c. identification.
   d. repression.
4. Children who do not successfully resolve Erikson's third psychosocial stage experience much
   a. guilt.
   b. shame.
   c. loneliness.
   d. distrust.
5. Freud is to _____ as Adler is to _____ .
   a. sex drive; sex drive
   b. power drive; power drive
   c. power drive; sex drive
   d. sex drive; power drive
6. Which of the following children best fits Adler's description of the typical oldest child's position in a family?
   a. Rumi experienced the most lax rules and discipline in her family and is viewed by her siblings as a bit spoiled. She is valued for her humor, but often wishes that her family would take her ideas and goals more seriously.
   b. Susan is more conservative than her siblings. While she has ambitious career plans, she hopes not to have to make too many major changes in her life. Often, she is the one her siblings ask for advice.
   c. Teddie is the most sociable sibling and often is out of the house with an assortment of friends. Teddie believes strongly in a variety of political issues and devotes some time to ecological and homelessness issues.
   d. Barry is very comfortable spending time by himself. Indeed, when not by himself, he prefers the company of older individuals, rather than friends his age. Barry is quite competent in academic matters but hardly ever takes the initiative to help out around the house.

7. Which term is Bandura's concept for how children actively shape the environments that, in turn, influence their behavior and personality?
   a. induction
   b. reciprocal determinism
   c. metamotivation
   d. prosocial behaviors
8. According to Maslow's ideas, which is the correct pairing regarding a child's struggle between safety versus growth choices?
   a. safety—parental approval
   b. growth—minimal risks
   c. growth—parental approval
   d. safety—developing own standards and goals
9. Which of the following statements is true about preschooler aggression?
   a. The most typical aggressive behavior exhibited by 5-year-olds is kicking and hitting.
   b. Preschooler aggression levels do not predict aggression levels at older ages.
   c. A snowball fight was viewed as more aggressive when thought to be girls at play than when thought to be boys.
   d. Boys and girls express equivalent amounts of both physical and verbal aggression.
10. Altruistic behaviors are prosocial behaviors that are
    a. done accidentally.
    b. executed for selfish reasons.
    c. done intentionally to benefit others.
    d. observed by other people.
11. Sex differences are _____ differences between males and females.
    a. behavioral
    b. cultural
    c. psychological
    d. biological
12. Which of the following is the first gender concept that children acquire?
    a. gender identity
    b. gender-typing
    c. gender constancy
    d. All three concepts are acquired around the same age.
13. Which theoretical explanation of gender concepts emphasizes modeling?
    a. cognitive-developmental theory
    b. social-learning theory
    c. psychoanalytic theory
    d. gender-schema theory
14. During which of Joseph Pleck's three-step phased freedom process would individuals move into androgyny?
    a. amorphous
    b. conformist
    c. transcendent
    d. jamstalldhet
15. Which of the following is *not* descriptive of Diana Baumrind's authoritarian parenting style?
    a. Parental needs come first.
    b. Obedience without questioning is expected.
    c. Child is expected to regulate own behavior.
    d. Parents value order, tradition, and authority.

16. Which of the following is associated with the inductive style of discipline?
    a. based on children's fear of punishment
    b. results in repression of emotions and self-punishment
    c. based on children's fear of losing support and approval
    d. involves teaching reasons and consequences

17. Which type of discipline do authoritarian parents use the most?
    a. induction
    b. love-withdrawal
    c. power-assertion
    d. laissez-faire

18. Which type of child abuse seems to be the most common?
    a. emotional abuse
    b. neglect
    c. physical injuries
    d. sexual abuse

19. Which of the following types of play did Mildred Parten include as social play?
    a. parallel
    b. associative
    c. onlooker
    d. all of the above

20. Which of the following is an example of functional play?
    a. a card game
    b. playing with puppets
    c. building a castle with Legos
    d. rolling a ball

Answers

1. C [LO-1].	8. A [LO-5].	15. C [LO-11].
2. A [LO-1].	9. C [LO-6].	16. D [LO-12].
3. D [LO-1].	10. C [LO-7].	17. C [LO-11, 12].
4. A [LO-2].	11. D [LO-8].	18. B [LO-13].
5. D [LO-3].	12. A [LO-8].	19. B [LO-14].
6. B [LO-3].	13. B [LO-9].	20. D [LO-15].
7. B [LO-4].	14. C [LO-10].	

chapter 8

Physical and Cognitive Development from Ages Six to Twelve

Key Terms

Ossification
Operational thinking
Stage of concrete operations
Cognitive style
Metamemory
Episodic memory
Metalinguistic awareness
Morality of constraint
Morality of cooperation
Immanent justice
Belief in a just world
Preconventional morality
Conventional morality
Postconventional morality
Morality of rights
Morality of caring
Morality of justice
Fluid abilities
Crystallized abilities
Need for achievement (nAch)
Autonomous motivation
Social comparison motivation
Integrated motivation

Learning Objectives

1. Describe the typical patterns of physical and motor development for boys and girls ages 6 to 12.
2. Discuss the relationship between physical fitness and risk for illness in school-age children.
3. Describe the health status and common illnesses and injuries of school-age children.
4. Explain the general characteristics of operational thinking and the specific characteristics of the stage of concrete operations.
5. Identify different principles of conservation, and explain how these principles develop.
6. Compare and contrast the cognitive styles of impulsive and reflective, and field-dependent and field-independent.
7. Explain memory strategies typically used by school-age children.
8. Describe how changes in metalinguistic awareness are exhibited in school-age children's use of language to plan ahead and to understand humor.
9. Identify the major features of Piaget's, Kohlberg's, and Gilligan's theories of moral development.
10. Compare and contrast Piaget's, Kohlberg's, and Gilligan's views of moral development.
11. Summarize the approaches of Cattell, Gardner, Sternberg, and Feuerstein to the concept of intelligence.
12. Discuss Veroff's three-stage developmental theory of achievement motivation.
13. Describe the five components in expectancy-value theory that influence individuals' achievement needs.
14. List the characteristics of excellent schools.
15. Explain the relationship between parental involvement and student achievement.

Children from ages 6 to 12 experience many changes in physical and cognitive development. They have more control over their bodies, can deal with more complex knowledge and processes, and are more aware of themselves as active and unique participants in the world. During these few years, children are heavily influenced by their families but increasingly learn from and share with their friends and participate in other arenas, such as schools, churches, and organizations. School-age children at age 6 are quite different from school-age children at age 12.

Exploring Your Own Development

What were you like at age 6? Did you feel secure in your physical abilities? What types of play and games did you enjoy—hide-and-seek, tag, chasing fireflies? Compared to your first-grade classmates, were you tall or short, shy or outgoing, serious or fun-loving? What memories do you have about family get-togethers and holidays? Who were your friends, and what did you do with them? Do you remember your sixth year as pleasant or unpleasant? What were the best and worst aspects of being 6?

Move your memories ahead through these years until you get to age 12. What were you like? How had you changed physically? Were you one of the more physically mature members of the sixth grade? What kinds of games and activities did you enjoy in sixth grade—videogames, organized sports, art, drama? What was happening in your family and among your friends? Was your sixth grade in an elementary school or middle school, and how did this placement affect you? Did you date or beg your parents to let you date? How did you relate to your parents and siblings? What did you worry about—looks, grades, popularity, clothes, politics? Do you remember your 12th year as being pleasant or unpleasant? What were the best and worst aspects of being 12?

Compare what psychologists say about the school years (or middle childhood) with your own experiences. Observe both the general trends from middle childhood to late childhood (or preadolescence) and how you and other individuals actually experienced these times.

Physical Development in Middle and Late Childhood

Patterns of Physical Growth

During the first few years of the time period from age 6 to age 12, children gain an average of 7 lb and 2 or more inches a year. During these years, average body weight doubles. Up until age 10, boys and girls have approximately the same average height. Then girls start a growth spurt that boys do not usually experience until age 12 or 13. Therefore, in the fifth through seventh grades, many girls are taller than most of the boys. Of course, most children do not match the average, and school classrooms contain a wide variety of heights and shapes.

An important environmental factor influencing growth is adequate nourishment. Advances in good nutrition have led to earlier increases in height, a development called the secular trend in height. Other growth factors involve complex hormonal processes; growth hormones and thyroid hormones (and gonadal steroids during adolescence) modulate bone growth and maturation. Growth slows progressively during childhood, increases again in puberty, and ends by age 20 (Tanner & Davies, 1985).

Internally, many important physical changes are also occurring. Heart weight increases 5-fold, and lung weight increases 10-fold. As a result of the increased size and capacity, both heart and respiration rates are lowered. By the end of the middle years, the brain has reached full size and weight but has not achieved full functioning.

The skeletal and muscular systems are also changing during the school years. In the preschool years, bones are mostly pliable cartilage. During the school years, calcium and phosphorus deposited in the cartilage harden the bones; this **ossification** process is not completed until the young adult years. Skeletal growth is uneven during these years, and many youngsters go through an awkward, clumsy stage in which they trip over their feet, which grow more rapidly than other body parts. The muscles become better attached to the bones and increase significantly in mass. At times, the developing muscles may not keep up with skeletal growth, and the muscles may ache as a result.

Physical Abilities and Fitness

Motor Skills

By age 6, almost all children can skip well, and by age 7, most can do jumping jacks accurately and balance on one foot while blindfolded (Cratty, 1970). Schoolchildren enjoy running, utilizing playground equipment, and becoming skilled in such sports as softball and badminton as they gain in physical strength, agility, and energy.

Fine motor skills also improve. School-age children can handle tools and instruments precisely by the end of this period. With the acquisition of improved fine motor skills, children often enjoy learning to sew, draw, build, cook, and construct. They may start to play a musical instrument, put together a collection of airplane models, or enjoy building elaborate buildings with Legos.

Lack of Physical Fitness

Not all school-age children have good physical abilities and physical fitness, however, and physically unfit children are likely to grow up into physically unfit adults. The physical fitness of boys at ages 10 and 11 was compared with their

One major contributing factor to children's poor physical fitness is the number of hours spent in front of the television instead of active play.

physical fitness in their early 20s. Physically fit adults usually had better childhood physical fitness test scores than did physically inactive adults (Dennison, Straus, Melits, & Charney, 1988).

The seriousness of poor physical fitness among children ages 7 to 12 is evident from statistics that 41 percent of children have high cholesterol, 28 percent have above-normal blood pressure, and 98 percent have at least one risk factor for coronary heart disease (Reif, 1985). Obesity, one risk factor, is common among schoolchildren for several reasons: more fat and sugar in the diet, less physical activity due to television and video games, and overeating to control stress created by school and home pressures.

A recent cholesterol study of 2,446 subjects between the ages of 8 and 18, who were reexamined in their 20s, concluded that elevated cholesterol levels during childhood are associated with elevated levels in adulthood. Of the subjects who were above the 90th percentile as children, 43 percent were in the top 10 percent as adults, and 81 percent were in the top half. Although other factors, such as obesity, oral contraceptive use, and cigarette smoking, influence adult cholesterol levels, from 25 to 50 percent of adult cholesterol variability is probably explained by childhood cholesterol levels (Dennison et al., 1988).

Table 8.1 summarizes the cardiovascular disease risk factors that can appear in children. Children with Type A behavior exhibit other physical symptoms—stress, muscle tension, sleep disturbance, headaches, and sore throats—in addition to cardiovascular symptoms. Type A children have lower self-esteem and feel less secure. Type A behaviors include anger, hostility, impatience, competitiveness, achievement anxiety, and striving. Parents of high Type A children are more likely to compare their children to others and thereby condition them to overreact to competition, to fear failures and temporary setbacks, and to be very high in

achievement orientation. Children often model Type A behaviors from their parents. Eighty percent of high Type A boys have high Type A dads, while only 30 percent of low Type A boys have high Type A dads (Eagleston et al., 1986).

Children repeatedly exposed to the tobacco smoke of other persons run increased health risks. As involuntary or passive smokers, they have above-average respiratory symptoms and more lower respiratory tract infections. Their lung growth is slowed down, and they have decreased pulmonary function. Passive smoke exposure predisposes children to chronic obstructive lung disease, lung cancer, and ischemic heart disease (Committee on Environmental Hazards, 1986).

Parents who wish to modify cardiovascular and respiratory risk factors can increase family exercise activities; reduce children's television watching hours and video game playing time; quit smoking; change diet to decrease fat and sugar and increase oatmeal, fruits, and vegetables; and decrease messages that add to children's worries and aggressive competitiveness (Kowalski, 1988). In addition, parents can encourage schools to include more physical education, with the emphasis on helping children of all abilities and fitness to enjoy physical tasks.

Physical Health Care, Illness, and Injuries

Health Care

Ideally, school-age children have regular medical, visual, and dental checkups. However, unlike most industrialized nations, the United States has no national health insurance program, and families vary in their ability to provide good preventive care. Compared to their peers, children in poverty-level families are less likely to receive routine preventive care. Low-income families on Medicaid receive more routine preventive medical care than do other low-income families (Newacheck & Halfon, 1988).

Illnesses

Typically, children during the school years experience four to six illnesses per year (adults average four). The most common illnesses among children are respiratory illnesses, including the fastest growing serious illness—asthma (Parmelee, 1986). In the 1970s, asthma in children increased by 50 percent, and deaths increased by 23 percent. Fifteen percent of all chronically ill children have asthma. During asthma attacks, the breathing airways become blocked and cause wheezing and breathlessness. Asthma attacks can be triggered by pollen, animal dander, specific foods, cigarette smoke, exertion in cold air, and stress (Berkman, 1987; Hurley, 1987).

At age 6, many children think of illness as punishment for bad behaviors, and being sick may be accompanied by guilt, lower self-esteem, and anxiety. This faulty cause-and-effect reasoning is especially troublesome when a young child has an extended illness. As the child gets older, however, illnesses are understood more realistically: Usually, diseases are reversible, they are not sent as punishments, and diseases often are preventable by proper care. Most 12-year-olds have stable health beliefs, comparable in content and structure to adult beliefs (Lau & Klepper, 1988).

Usually, children's illnesses are only thought about in negative terms—the pain and discomfort of the illness, time lost from school, and medical expenses. However, non-life-threatening illnesses of short duration can have beneficial effects. The lack of energy, the mood changes while sick, and the physical distress can result in more awareness of the physical self and the process of change and recovery (Parmelee, 1986).

Injuries

As children expand their physical activities, risk for injuries increases. In 1985, about 12,000 injuries and 18 fatalities were linked to toys with small parts that could be swallowed. About 450 deaths and 165,000 serious injuries of children are attributed to off-road bikes or all-terrain vehicles (Waldman, 1988). Five recreational toys account for most children's injuries requiring emergency-room care: skateboards, roller skates, bicycles, dirt bikes, and all-terrain vehicles (Consumer Product Safety Commission Product Summary Report, 1988).

Although children enjoy organized sports, thousands of participants are injured each year. Safety equipment, proper instruction and level of play, and deemphasizing winning can help reduce the number of injuries.

Table 8.2
Approximate Numbers of Children With Disabilities (Ages 5 to 18) in the United States (1985)

Disability	Number of Children
Speech Impairments	1,650,000 to 2,200,000
Emotional Disturbances	1,100,000 to 1,650,000
Learning Disabilities	1,100,000 to 1,650,000
Mental Retardation	1,100,000 to 1,650,000
Hearing Impairments	275,000 to 385,000
Multiple Disabilities	275,000 to 385,000
Orthopedic and Health Impairments	275,000
Visual Impairments	55,000
Total	5,830,000 to 8,250,000

Reprinted with the permission of Merrill, an imprint of Macmillan Publishing Company from *The Exceptional Student in the Regular Classroom,* Third edition by Bill R. Gearhart and Mel W. Weishahn. Copyright © 1986 by Merrill Publishing Company.

Another common source of childhood injuries is organized sports. A study of over 5,000 boys participating in youth football found that about 5 percent experience a significant injury, resulting in at least 1 week of restriction (16 percent for high school teams; 27 percent for college teams). Fractures are the most common injuries, and upper extremities—especially hands and wrists—are the most common injury locations (Goldberg, Rosenthal, Robertson, & Nicholas, 1988).

Physical and Cognitive Disabilities

Several million U.S. children must learn to cope with long-term physical or cognitive disabilities (see Table 8.2). Three of 100 children are born with major defects (Adler, 1987), and about 2 percent of all children have severe chronic illnesses (Hurley, 1986).

Family members are sometimes overwhelmed with coping and adjusting to the needs of a child with a disability. However, recent studies suggest that families with children with disabilities typically cope well. In fact, most of these families are very similar to families without children with disabilities. Marital satisfaction and divorce rates are similar for both family groups. The results of recent studies differ from earlier studies because assisting services are now more accessible, and less stigma is placed on the child with the disability and the child's family (Widerstrom & Dudley-Marling, 1986).

Cognitive Development in Middle and Late Childhood

What are the cognitive capabilities of school-age children? At what ages can children understand numbers? How do thinking capabilities influence children's preferences for games, their ideas of morality, and their senses of humor? During the school years, children overcome basic thinking limitations and learn to do **operational thinking,** which involves symbols and mental activities. They can get beyond one main characteristic of a situation and consider many aspects at once, allowing true logical thinking (Piaget, 1970). The tremendous growth in cognitive abilities during this time period is evident in children's school tasks, expanding knowledge base, increased memory and memory organization, and in improved judgments, problem-solving strategies, language use, and creativity.

Parents' Overestimation of Cognitive Abilities

Parents, however, often overestimate the growth in their school-age children's capacity to reason and are fairly unaware of remaining cognitive limitations. In fact, parents of school-age children are six times more likely to overestimate their children's abilities as to underestimate them and sometimes overestimate capabilities by several years. Parents also overestimate their children's performance on both memory recall tests and intelligence tests (Miller, 1988).

Parents' misconceptions about their children's thinking abilities can be frustrating to both parents and their offspring. Parents might provide the wrong kinds of assistance with schoolwork, have unrealistic expectations about

problem-solving performance, or expect children to make more mature daily judgments than they can make. When parents have realistic information about children's cognitive abilities, they can more appropriately answer children's questions, provide toys and games that challenge but do not frustrate their children, understand their children's ideas about right and wrong, and work better with their children's school system. Most teachers understand and take into account the basic characteristics of children's cognitive development, though they may have difficulty constructing classes that can deal with the great individual differences.

Piaget's Stage of Concrete Operations

When Joey was 4, he could turn a pencil into a pretend airplane and enjoyed moving it up and down in the air. At 8, Joey prefers to construct an airplane from Legos and to build runways and airports out of blocks, construction paper, and cardboard boxes. Joey can occupy himself for long periods of time as he elaborates on his airport system. Compared to his earlier pretend airplane play, Joey's play at 8 is more complex, more thought out, and a reflection of more advanced cognitive capabilities.

Joey is well into Jean Piaget's **stage of concrete operations,** in which children can make mental representations of objects and events and then figure out how to turn them into physical representations. Children in this stage can think logically, use symbols, and manipulate materials more accurately, new abilities that are summarized in Table 8.3. Children start to learn these abilities around age 5 to 7, and many are quite proficient at all of these abilities by age 11 or 12. Growth in cognitive abilities involves learning relationships among objects, space, and time gradually, rather than experiencing a sudden shift from "no or wrong knowledge and understanding" to "full, correct knowledge and understanding."

Dealing With Numbers

Preschoolers often make appropriate decisions based on numbers in simple tasks. If Cara is hungry for ice cream, she will choose the cone with two dips over the cone with just one dip. However, as numbers get bigger and questions become more complex, Cara is liable to make many errors in number judgments. Although Cara enjoys counting and can count to 10 quite well, she does not fully understand how numbers work, and numbers without objects are often confusing. For example, Cara can understand that six apples are more than five apples, but she cannot really understand that six is larger than five. Sometimes, Cara and even her first-grade sister Danielle make judgments about numbers that seem inconsistent with their counting—for example, they can forget which number is bigger, something that Cara does much more often than Danielle. Both girls make errors because they forget the results of counting. Typical of children her age, 6-year-old Danielle is much better than Cara in judging the number of objects when length cues are inconsistent—Danielle has acquired conservation of number (Cowan, 1987).

Table 8.3
Abilities of the Concrete Operations Stage

Ability	Explanation
Classification	The ability to sort objects into related subgroups based on such characteristics as color, size, shape, and function
Seriation	The ability to order a group of objects in succession, such as from smallest to largest, tallest to shortest, first to last, and most important to least important
Numbering	The ability to count and compare discrete quantities; knowledge that the number of objects remains the same even when the objects are rearranged in space
Reversibility	The ability to make a change in form and know how to get back to the original condition via physical or mental reversal of the change
Conservation	The ability to understand that any material characteristic remains unchanged even when internal changes occur; learned at different rates for different aspects of a material:
Of numbers	The ability to understand that the number of objects remains the same, even when the objects are rearranged in space
Of quantity	The ability to understand that the amount of a material is not increased or decreased when the material's shape or form is changed
Of length	The ability to understand that the length of an object remains the same, regardless of how the object is altered in space (e.g., a line is the same from end to end when it is changed from a straight to a curved line)
Of area	The ability to understand that the total amount of surface covered by a set of plane figures remains the same, even when the position of the figures is changed
Of weight	The ability to understand that the heaviness of an object does not change when the object's shape changes
Of volume	The ability to understand that the space occupied by an object stays the same when the object's shape is modified
Physical causality	The tendency to look for physical causes of events, rather than believing in magic-based psychological causes
Rule orientation	The ability to use established or agreed-upon guidelines and regulations to decide behavior, rather than egocentric wishes
Spatial awareness	The ability to know one's location in geographical distances
Time consciousness	The ability to distinguish the present from the past and the future

In a typical experiment, Piaget lined up eight checkers directly across from eight other checkers. Young children then stated that the two lines had the same number. Then Piaget would move the checkers in one line farther apart. Although the number of checkers in both lines were still the same, preschoolers often said that the longer line had more checkers. Piaget found that number conservation

An important task for children is to learn how the world works by reliable rules. This task is accomplished in the replication of many experiences during play and learning.

is usually achieved between the ages of 5 and 7. Some researchers believe that younger children can exhibit conservation of number, but that when the children are asked to justify their answers, they change their correct judgments to nonconservational answers (Bovet, Parrat-Dayan, & Kamii, 1986).

Other Conservation Tasks

All conservation tasks involve knowing that changes in external appearance do not change the material aspects of an object. Ability to conserve involves decentering, more exhaustive encoding, reversibility, and improved cognitive strategies (Flavell, 1985). Number conservation is the first conservation principle acquired because judging discrete quantities, such as checkers and coins, is easier than conserving continuous quantities, such as water (Siegler, 1981).

The types of conservation are listed in Table 8.3 in the most typical order of acquisition. Conservation of quantity and conservation of length are usually understood around age 7 or 8, and conservation of area is accomplished about a year later. Most 9- and 10-year-olds have acquired conservation of weight. Finally, conservation of volume is understood around the age of 12 to 14.

The presence or absence of conservation in children is highly dependent on situational cues and on the children's reading of the experimenter's intentions (Rose & Blank, 1974; Winer, Hemphill, & Craig, 1988). In a typical conservation of quantity experiment, children first judge that two identical glasses have the same amount of water. Then the liquid from one glass is poured into a taller, skinnier glass. Children under 7 years old are most likely to say

Table 8.4
Results of Children's Judgments of Weight Conservation Based on Misleading and Nonmisleading Questions

Subject Groups	Failed to Conserve Three to Four Questions	Correct on at Least Three Questions
Misleading Questions	69% (27 of 39)	21% (8 of 39)
Nonmisleading Questions	22% (9 of 41)	51% (21 of 41)

Source: Data from G. A. Winer, et al., "The Effect of Misleading Questions in Promoting Nonconservation Responses in Children and Adults" in *Developmental Psychology*, 24, 197–202, 1988.

that there is more water in the taller glass. Young children center on the one aspect of height of water line and ignore the narrowed width. However, 6-year-olds do better than expected if they are not asked about quantity before the manipulation of pouring the water into the other glass (Rose & Blank, 1974) or if they are allowed to pour the water themselves (Siegler, 1986).

Forced-choice misleading questions asked by experimenters promote nonconservation response in children, and in adults as well. For example, many adults answer the following questions wrong because of the questions' wording: "Who is a psychologist, Piaget or Skinner?" or "When do you weigh more—when you are standing up or sitting?" (Winer et al., 1988). When asked to choose between two correct answers, some adults do not answer, "Both." Children are even more misled by such wording.

In one study, third- and sixth-graders were asked misleading forced-choice questions: "When do you weigh the most—when you are walking or running?" "when you make your muscles tight or relax them?" "when you are standing or crouching?" "when you are hot or cold?" Others were asked the same questions, but added to each question was "or do you weigh the same?" As shown in Table 8.4, misleading questions produced three times the rate of subjects getting none or only one correct answer. Misleading questions reduced the number getting three or four correct answers by more than half.

Education also influences the ability to learn conservation. Cross-cultural research done in Senegal indicated that exposure to education was a major determinant of whether 11- and 12-year-olds were capable of conserving liquid quantity (Greenfield, 1966).

Other Aspects of the Concrete Operations Stage
Egocentrism is the inability to perceive another's perspective. Piaget believed that children under age 8 or 9 would fail at a task in which they were asked to draw a picture from another person's view. In fact, however, under the following conditions, 6-year-olds can draw the other's view: (1) if the object array is quite simple, (2) if the other person's view is drawn first and the child's own view second, and (3) if the child is allowed to view the array from the

other position (Moore, Williams, & Gorczynska, 1987). Performance on Piagetian tasks varies with small details of the task and questions.

The Piagetian belief that much of the thinking during the middle childhood years is reality-bound appears to be correct. For example, Piaget asked children, "Where would you put a third eye?" All 9-year-olds placed the third eye above and between where their eyes were. However, 11- and 12-year-olds were less restricted and thought more creatively about objects that have never existed or events that could never happen. These sixth-graders gave such answers as putting the extra eye on the palm of the hand to allow vision around corners or on the back of the head to allow vision in all directions (Piaget, 1970). These children had accomplished the tasks of the concrete operations stage and were about to enter the fourth stage of cognitive development, the formal operations stage.

Cognitive Style

Cognitive styles are stable preferences for organizing perceptions and information. For example, people differ in preferred cognitive tempo, or general approach to problem solving. Some children are impulsive and respond to problems rapidly, without much consideration for accuracy. Others are more reflective and consider alternative solutions before answering problems (Kagan, 1965). Reflective children do better on creativity, reading tasks, reasoning tasks, and recognition memory tests, while impulsive children excel at broad analysis (Fuqua, Bartsch, & Phye, 1975). Reflective children deal with people in direct and assertive ways; impulsive children prefer passive, yielding approaches (Peters & Bernfeld, 1983).

Other cognitive styles include the perceptual styles of field-independence and field-dependence. Persons high in field-independence perceive items as separate from their backgrounds and are likely to analyze elements in a scene. Persons high in field-dependence look at scenes as a whole, rather than analyzing their parts. Field-dependent persons are more likely to be characterized as warm, considerate, and accommodating; field-independent persons are described as cold, distant, and manipulating. Field-independent persons like such school subjects as math, biology, and the physical sciences; field-dependent persons prefer the humanities and social sciences (Witkin & Goodenough, 1981).

Memory Development

Memory Capacity
One way to conceptualize memory is to think in terms of three different types of memory. The first memory is called sensory memory and consists of a brief awareness of images. Sensory memory lasts less than 1 sec. The second memory is the working memory, or short-term memory (STM). STM consists of all information that is currently being used. Finally, the third memory, called the long-term memory, is a relatively permanent memory with unlimited capacity.

(a) Simple (b) Complex

Figure 8.1

Examples of pictures in both (a) simple and (b) complex form.

Source: Pexdek, K. 1987. Memory for pictures: A life-span study of the role of visual detail. *Child Development, 58,* 807–815. Fig. 1, p. 810.

As adults, most individuals can remember five to nine "chunks" of information in their STMs. For example, the average adult can recall a string of six or seven digits in reverse order. On the other hand, the average 5- or 6-year-old can only remember two digits in reverse order. Most 13-year-olds can recall six digits in reverse order. Therefore, the STM's capacity seems to increase rapidly during the school years (Miller, 1956). An alternative explanation is that the STM's total capacity does not increase with age but that, as mental operations become more automatic, more of the STM is available for "storage space" as less is needed for "operating space" (Case, 1984).

Children's visual memory also improves with age. Throughout the middle childhood years, children improve in their ability to recognize large numbers of pictures, in their face-recognition memory, and in their recall and recognition of visual objects (Pezdek, 1987). Both children and adults do well at distinguishing "old" pictures (i.e., seen before) and "new" pictures (i.e., never viewed before).

A more difficult task is to detect changes—either additions or deletions—to a picture. Figure 8.1 illustrates representative stimuli used in one such visual memory experiment in which 7- and 9-year-olds were compared with young and old adults on their memory for whether changes had been made to either simple or complex pictures. Regardless of subject age, recognition accuracy was better for simple pictures than for complex pictures. That is, all sub-

jects found it easier to tell when additions were made to simple pictures than when deletions were made to more complex pictures (Pezdek, 1987).

Metamemory

Metamemory is the knowledge of the processes of memory and develops in the middle childhood years. First-graders can tell several aspects about how memory works: They know that people remember better if they study longer. They realize that people forget items as time goes by. They know that relearning is easier and takes less time than does initial learning. They even understand that external cues can help them to remember things (Kreutzer, Leonard, & Flavell, 1975).

Older elementary school students know that some people remember more than others do, and they can identify which students have better memories. They also know that some things are easier to remember than other things. The older students actively use more remembering strategies (Kreutzer, et al., 1975; Schneider, Korkel, & Weinert, 1987). More intelligent third- and fifth-graders knew more about how their memories worked than did other classmates. By fifth grade, desire to succeed on memory tests had a significant influence on memory performance (Schneider et al., 1987).

Strategies for Remembering

As metamemory improves with age, schoolchildren use more organized strategies for remembering. For example, objects can be presented to subjects in an organized or unorganized fashion, as shown in Figure 8.2. Schoolchildren recall more objects in pictures organized for meaningfulness, but the difference in recalling the objects is greater for fifth-graders than for third-graders, who, in turn, are aided more by the organized picture than are first-graders (Mandler & Robinson, 1977).

Memory strategies that improve as children get older include verbal rehearsal, visual imagery, and clustering. Only about 10 percent of 5-year-olds use verbal rehearsal to help recall pictures, but 60 percent of 7-year-olds and 85 percent of 10-year-olds use it. Verbal rehearsal becomes more complex and efficient as children get older. When learning a list of words, most 7-year-olds repeat a single word at a time (e.g., repeating *swan, swan, swan, swan; fish, fish, fish, fish),* but somewhat older children may rehearse several words simultaneously, (e.g., repeating *swan, fish, rose, tree; swan, fish, rose, tree)* (Kail, 1984).

Middle childhood subjects can use visual imagery to improve recall. Children 6 to 11 years of age were asked to learn some sentences. Half of the subjects were instructed to construct visual images of the sentences. For all ages, those who were asked to use visual imagery did better than the other subjects their age, although the effect was more dramatic among the older subjects (Pressley, Cariglia-Bull, & Deane, 1987).

Clustering, the organization of lists by meaning, is usually not used before the age of 10 or 11. Given the list *tree, spoon, cheese, bush, fork, milk, shrub, knife, cream, yogurt, fern, napkin,* older children, but not younger

(a) Organized

(b) Unorganized

Figure 8.2

Examples of (a) an organized and (b) an unorganized version of a picture.

Based on: Mandler, J. M., & Robinson, C. A. 1977. Developmental changes in picture recognition. *Journal of Experimental Child Psychology, 3*, 386–396.

children, are likely to reorganize the list into *tree, bush, shrub, fern; spoon, fork, knife, napkin; cheese, milk, cream, yogurt.* Older children use meaningful categories that help in retrieving words on the list.

The Context of Memory Development

Family experiences and personal beliefs may influence how and what you remember, both in factual knowledge and in personal memories. What kinds of things and events do you remember about your childhood? Why were these aspects remembered and others forgotten?

One unique study looked at how parents use photo albums to help teach young children to do elaborate rememberings and at how children themselves learn to use photo

cues as mnemonic devices (Edwards & Middleton, 1988). Parents use family photographs to teach children about memorable events from the past, how to infer information from details in the picture, and how to reconstruct a reasonable version of what the photograph depicts.

For example, 6-year-old Teddy is looking at a picture of a family picnic. His mother says, "Oh, look at how bright the picture is. It must have been sunny that day. And look, there's Grandpa. He looks like he's telling one of his stories again. Do you suppose it's a fishin' story, Teddy?" Teddy replies, "Yeah. And we must be going to eat a lot at the picnic." Mom points out, "Well, some of the food is missing. See how empty this casserole is. I think this picture was taken right after eating. See, doesn't Aunt Mary look

Table 8.5
Story Characters' Gender Stereotype-Consistent and
Stereotype-Inconsistent Traits and Behaviors

	Male Character	Female Character
Stereotype-Consistent	Plays drums	Plays with dolls
	Tough	Dresses up
	Dirty	Does housework
	Daring	Hugs babies
Stereotype-Inconsistent	Sews	Strong
	Picks flowers	Uses tools
	Gentle	Helps Dad
	Cooks	Fights

From A. R. Nesdale and K. McLaughlin, "Effects of Sex Stereotypes on Young Children's Memories, Predictions, and Liking" in *British Journal of Developmental Psychology,* 5, 231–241, table 1, p. 235, 1987. Copyright © British Psychological Society, Leicester, England.

Children learn about language through daily experiences and during formal schooling.

satisfied and full? You remember Aunt Mary, don't you? We visited her at the seashore last summer. . . ." By pointing out details in the picture and by elaborating memories, the mother is teaching her son how to infer information from available evidence and how to build and remember **episodic memory,** memories set within a context of time.

Children's memories are influenced by what they are told to expect and anticipate in the situation (Nesdale & McLaughlin, 1987). For example, children remember more information about characters when the information is consistent with advance descriptions. Ten-year-olds were told about Stephen and Wendy in a 440-word story. Both Stephen and Wendy had four behaviors or traits that were consistent with gender-role stereotypes and four that were inconsistent (see Table 8.5). Children who were told in advance that Stephen was like most boys and that Wendy was like most girls remembered much of the stereotype-consistent descriptions. Children given the opposite advance description tended to remember most stereotype-inconsistent descriptions.

Language Development

Communication Competence

Around the age of 5, **metalinguistic awareness**—an intuitive awareness of how language works—emerges and grows rapidly. Language skills improve during the school years because children can now think about what has been said to them, can apply general rules about grammar, and have learned more precise meanings of words.

If first-graders are given incomplete directions for playing a game, they start to play the game and then ask what to do when they reach an instructional gap. On the other hand, many third-graders are sophisticated enough in their communication skills to judge that the directions are incomplete before starting the game, and they ask for more

directions before the play commences (Markman, 1977). In both thinking and language, third-graders have ability to anticipate, to follow an entire story or sequence, and to know when to ask for clarification.

During the school years, children grow in their understanding of syntax, the underlying grammatical rules that specify the order and function of words within sentences. Children may overgeneralize the general rules of grammar until they learn the exceptions to the rules. Therefore, first- and second-graders are more likely than preschoolers to use incorrect words based on standard grammatical rules (e.g., "helded" and "goed").

The vocabulary of school-age children is quite large and functional, and the children are aware of many meanings. Yet, the precise differences between similar words may remain elusive during the early school years. Children may think that *ask* and *tell* are synonyms. If Mother sends Helen to ask the guests if they want something to drink, Helen may announce, "You are going to have a drink now." Likewise, children may confuse such words as *heavy* and *strong*. Helen may tell her friend that the box she is carrying is "strong" when she actually means that the box is "heavy."

Metaphors

Metaphors are often misunderstood by young school-age children, primarily because children are limited to concrete images and have trouble extracting abstract meanings. "A rolling stone gathers no moss" forms a vivid image of a stone gathering momentum as it rolls downhill, but the second, abstract meaning is beyond a child's reasoning.

Children find it difficult to switch from one meaning of a word to a second meaning. An additional difficulty is adjusting from using a word to describe an object and then using the same word to describe a person. For example, a 7-year-old has difficulty switching from "Sugar is sweet," to

"She is a sweet little girl." Even more challenging is the switch from "Boy, that bruised spot really smarts," to "That scientist is smart." While 7- and 8-year-olds are beginning to comprehend these language transfers, the transfers are not fully understood until age 10 or 11. Most children therefore do not accurately explain metaphors until age 10 or 11.

Humor

School-age children's growth in communication competence and awareness is also reflected in their humor at various ages. During the late preschool years, for example, children find the most humor in body sounds and body contortions. They may laugh at jokes because others laugh, but preschoolers do not understand most jokes and riddles (Tamashiro, 1979). Between the ages of 6 and 8, children begin to truly appreciate jokes (Whitt & Prentice, 1977). The earliest jokes that are understood are those based on phonological ambiguities, or sound similarities, such as those found in "knock-knock" jokes (deVilliers & deVilliers, 1979). Therefore, a 5-year-old might like the joke: "Knock Knock," "Who's there?" "Esther," "Esther, who?" "Esther a doctor in the house?"

From first to third grade, youngsters enjoy reality riddles, or jokes based on conceptual tricks. For example, "How many balls of string would it take to reach the moon?" "One, but it would have to be a big one" gets its humor from assumptions made about the size of balls of string.

At every age, humorous jokes are those that provide a moderate amount of intellectual challenge (Pinderhughes & Zigler, 1985). A child who understands the use of pronouns is therefore capable of enjoying Peewee Herman's response to "You're an idiot" with his mocking comeback: "I know you are, but what am I?" Likewise, the correct use of personal pronouns allows a child to find this joke funny: "Call me a taxi." "You're a taxi."

From the ages of 7 or 8 until 9 to 11, children prefer jokes based on lexical ambiguities, or plays on words and word meanings (Yalisove, 1978). Children find the following riddles humorous; adults usually just moan:

> *"If April showers bring May flowers, what do May flowers bring?" "Pilgrims."*
> *"What has eyes but cannot see?" "A potato."*
> *"Why was the cookie crying?" "Because his mother was a wafer so long."*
> *"What's the tallest building in New York City?"*
> *"The public library because it has the most stories."*
> *"How do you stop a bull from charging?" "Take away his credit card!"*

Most second-graders enjoy jokes based on lexical ambiguities, but these jokes are usually too difficult for first-graders. In one study, children were asked to pick which of two answers was funnier. For example, "Why did the man tiptoe past the medicine cabinet?" Choice 1: "Because he did not want to wake up the sleeping pills." Choice 2: "Because he dropped a glass and didn't want to cut his foot."

First-graders are just as likely to pick Choice 2 as Choice 1. The majority of second-graders choose the first answer (McGhee, 1979).

By age 11 or 12, children begin to appreciate absurdity riddles, which derive their humor from syntactical ambiguity (e.g., "Tell me how long cows should be milked." "The same way as short cows." "What animal can jump higher than the moon?" "Every animal—the moon does not jump."), and riddles that ask absurd questions yet have a logical answer ("How can you tell if the elephant has been in the refrigerator?" "From the footprints in the Jell-O.").

As children enter the formal operational stage of cognitive development, they can relate to humor that involves self-referential statements (e.g., "Does this sentence remind you of Christmas?" "When you're not reading it, this sentence is in German.") or complex knowledge of words, people, history, culture, or politics (e.g., "Did you hear that there's a move to replace white rats in research with lawyers? It seems that there are three advantages to using lawyers. First, there are more of them. Second, students don't get as attached to them. And finally, there are some things that white rats refuse to do.").

Although psychologists have some understanding of the developmental changes in humor preferences, there is less agreement about the purposes of humor. Most psychologists agree that people use humor to help reinterpret situations and to help control such emotions as anger, anxiety, and depression. Some psychologists suggest that humor is a way to express superiority—either over situations or over other people. Indeed, some humor is done at the expense of others. Sigmund Freud believed that there was a "joke facade" that let people hide their aggression toward other persons and their embarrassment over sexual or destructive drives (Wolfenstein, 1954).

Moral Development

How do children learn right from wrong behavior? What roles do societal values, such emotions as guilt and pride, and cognitive reasoning play in the learning of moral values? Does moral reasoning influence moral behavior more than modeling, parental sanctions, and peer conformity?

How do concepts about morality and moral behavior change as individuals get older? Moral development is an important topic during the school years because parents and school authorities expect good conduct and because cognitive development during these years significantly influences children's moral judgment.

Historical Views

The three major psychological approaches to moral development are societalism, emotivism, and cognitive primacy (Gibbs & Schell, 1985). Societalism suggests that morality consists of the conformity of the individual to society. Sociologist Emile Durkheim (1961), who wrote from this position back in 1925, believed that moral socialization was the "cultural impression upon the child."

Emotivism emphasizes that morality is a matter of feeling. Like societalism, emotivism suggests that morality begins with external sanctions on conduct, but it also proposes that these external sanctions are replaced by internal feelings of right and wrong. Freud (1961) wrote from this approach at the same time that Durkheim was writing about societalism. According to Freud, parents provide the vehicle by which society teaches morality to children; the superego develops as an internal representation of parental-societal values and employs both guilt and pride to enforce the individual's adherence to these values.

In Europe, Jean Piaget began to expound on the third approach to moral development—cognitive primacy—in 1932. He stressed emphasizing cognitive understanding learned through dealing with social conflicts (Piaget, 1932). About a quarter of a century later, American Lawrence Kohlberg (1958) based his elaborate theory of moral development on moral reasoning.

Although cognitive approaches to moral development currently dominate, other theories exist. Learning theories emphasize that moral behavior is learned by the use of rewards and punishments, imitation of models, and generalized expectancies about the consequences of behaviors. Modern psychoanalytic theorists emphasize parental identification, the formation of the superego and conscience, and the experience of guilt.

Piaget's Theory of Moral Development

Piaget dealt with rules—both how individuals practice rules and their awareness of the rules (Onuf, 1987). As shown in Table 8.6, understanding the rules does not mean automatic adherence to the rules. Although 6-year-old Tammy believes that rules come from God and therefore cannot be changed, her remaining cognitive limitations mean that she breaks rules often. Although her 9-year-old sister Jackie knows that rules can be modified, she adheres rigorously to rules during play, school, and family activities.

During the beginning school years, children confuse intentions and commitments. Although they can differentiate the moral distinction between intentional lies and unintentional misinformation, they are likely to overgeneralize commitment and judge some unintentional situations quite severely (Mant & Perner, 1988). They do poorly at understanding the differences between "I promise," "I intend to," "I hope to," and "I expect to." Thus, 7-year-old Joey may not appreciate the difference between "I promise to take you shopping this afternoon" and "I expect to be able to take you shopping this afternoon," and Joey may become morally outraged when expectations do not become reality. Both a broken promise and a broken expectation are met with an intense "That's not fair!" or "But you said. . . ." Around age 9 or 10, children can understand the difference between expectations and commitments.

The confusion about what is a commitment may also make young children hesitate about talking about what they expect to do in the future. Six-year-old Jeff may feel as if he has lied to his family if he says he would like to be a surgeon and then a few days later decides he would rather be an auto mechanic (Stern & Stern, 1931). Around age 8,

Table 8.6
Piaget's Ideas of Children's Understanding of Rules and Use of Rules

Average Age	Child's Beliefs About Rules	Adherence to Rules
Before age 3	Child does not understand rules.	Rules are not part of play.
Age 3 to 7 or 8	Child believes that rules come from authority (e.g., the president of the United States, God, parents, teachers) and cannot be changed.	Child breaks and changes rules because of cognitive limitations.
Age 7 or 8 to 11 or 12	Child believes that rules have social nature and could be changed.	Child adheres to rules rather rigidly.
After age 11 or 12	Child has good understanding of rules.	Child understands that rules can be changed by mutual consent.

Based on J. Piaget, *The Child's Conception of the World*, 1951. Copyright © 1951 Routledge and Kegen Paul, London, England.

children can differentiate between lies, jokes, and fantasies and make appropriate moral judgments (Leekam, 1988).

Basically, Piaget (1932) presented two stages of moral reasoning—the **morality of constraint** and the **morality of cooperation**—to explain developmental changes in moral judgments. The morality of constraint is a rigid morality in which behaviors are judged as either totally right or totally wrong and in which children believe that everyone agrees on what behaviors are right and wrong. Rules are seen as sacred and unchangeable, adult authority is supposed to be respected and obeyed, and violations of standards are expected to be severely punished.

Children in this first stage of morality of constraint do not judge the morality of behavior on the basis of intentions; they judge behaviors in terms of behavioral consequences. Six-year-old Samuel cannot understand why his parents got so upset when he played farther from home than he was supposed to since nothing bad happened to him. His twin sister Rebecca was surprised when her parents did not punish her when she accidentally broke a vase while trying to help her mother.

During this first stage, children strongly believe in the concept of **immanent justice,** the belief that every misdeed *will be* followed by a misfortune that serves as a punishment from God. They believe that bad events or consequences are experienced because they have previously misbehaved. Therefore, first- and second-graders may believe that illness is a punishment for misbehaving. Belief in immanent justice may lead to beliefs that pets die because of childhood misbehavior or that Mom goes on a 3-day business trip to punish her children.

The belief in immanent justice exists because children confuse moral law and physical law; the confusion between the types of laws does not entirely disappear in

Jean Piaget's stages of morality are compatible with his cognitive stages.

Table 8.7
Kohlberg's Stages of Moral Development

Stage	What Is Considered Right
1. Obedience and punishment orientation (Level I: Preconventional morality)	Avoiding breaking rules backed by punishment; obedience for obedience's sake; avoiding physical damage to property and people
2. Instrumental purpose and exchange (Level I: Preconventional morality)	Following rules in one's immediate personal interest; behaving to meet one's own interests and allowing others to do the same; making equal exchanges, or fair and good deals
3. Interpersonal orientation and conformity (Level II: Conventional morality)	Living up to what is expected by both people close to you and by people in general; being good is an important goal
4. Social accord and system maintenance (Level II: Conventional morality)	Fulfilling duties; upholding laws in all but extreme circumstances; also involves contributing to society and valued groups
5. Social contract, utility, individual rights (Level III: Postconventional morality)	Having awareness that people have a variety of values and that rules are relative; rules should usually be upheld because laws represent social contracts; some values (e.g., life and freedom) are upheld regardless of majority opinion
6. Universal ethical principles (Level III: Postconventional morality)	Following self-chosen ethical principles; following laws that are based on these principles and violating those laws that do not; belief in equality of human rights, respect for all persons' dignity, and doing right because of a personal commitment to universal moral principles

Table 8.7 "Stages of Moral Development" from *Essays on Moral Development, Vol. 1: The Philosophy of Moral Develoment* by Lawrence Kohlberg. Copyright © 1981 by Lawrence Kohlberg. Reprinted by permission of HarperCollins, Publishers, Inc.

adults. As adults, remnants of immanent justice are displayed in a **belief in a just world,** the belief that, sooner or later, there will be justice—good things will happen to good people, and bad things will happen to bad people. Although adults can name instances in which good behavior was punished, good people died young, and bad behaviors were rewarded, many people prefer to believe that, overall, justice prevails.

During the school-age years, children move from the rigid moral concepts of constraint to the second, more flexible stage of the morality of cooperation. Children enter this second stage when they are sufficiently versed in the skills of the concrete operations stage.

In the morality of cooperation stage, children begin to judge behaviors more in terms of intentions rather than merely by consequences. They are able to view situations from others' points of view and know that a variety of possible viewpoints exist. They can comprehend that rules are made by people and that people can change rules. When it comes to punishment, these children favor milder punishment and compensation for the victim.

Because older schoolchildren consider intentions in addition to consequences, they compare situations quite differently from their younger friends. Bobby, who steals some fresh fruit to feed his friend who has been without food for 2 days, is judged less harshly than Larry, who steals a pretty ribbon to impress his girlfriend Peggy. Children in the first stage of morality of constraint, however, typically judge Bobby more severely because the fruit cost more than the ribbon that Larry took.

Maturity of moral thought may vary with the context. As predicted by Piaget, older school-age children use more than one dimension of moral reasoning. Nine- and 10-year-olds typically behave in stereotypical fashion without even considering morality. Their behavior merely reflects things "as they naturally are." They also employ social rituals that are negotiable and mutually agreed-upon. For example, they agree that the appropriate ways to deal with bullies are: (1) retaliation, (2) avoidance, and (3) negotiation. At other times, they deal with their distress at exaggerated punishment situations, their tolerance of morally ambiguous situations, and their evaluation of their own moral experience. Mature, flexible moral reasoning develops slowly over several years (Skrimshire, 1987).

Kohlberg's Theory of Moral Reasoning
Building on Piaget's concepts of morality, Kohlberg (1981, 1984, 1986) developed a theory of moral reasoning with six stages. Kohlberg believed that moral reasoning guides moral behavior and that individuals progress through six stages in a set sequence. These six stages, which are described in Table 8.7, are divided into three levels of two

Kohlberg viewed his six stages as representing a universal order in moral-reasoning development. Not all researchers, however, believe in an invariant sequence of the stages. In a survey of 38 cross-sectional and 7 longitudinal studies in 27 countries, good support was found for the universality of the first four stages, but Stage 5 was extremely rare in all cultures (Snarey, 1985, 1987).

Some critics suggest that Kohlberg's theory is culturally biased because post-conventional morality is present only in western, industrialized societies (Edwards, 1982; Snarey, 1985). Kohlberg's theory does not seem to do justice to cultures that emphasize harmony and amity within the

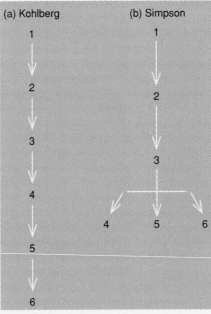

(a) Kohlberg's ordering of the six stages of moral development. (b) Simpson's ordering of the six stages.

community. For example, the Maisin people of Papua New Guinea have a concept of *marawa wawe,* a state of being in harmony with others. Likewise, Confucian morality of the Chinese emphasizes *ho,* or harmony achieved by empathy, concern for the welfare of others, and mutual benevolence, and *jen,* a moral person who correctly interprets the environment and acts to maintain harmony in the external world (Boyes & Walker, 1988). Even in the United States, some believe that only the first three stages are in a set develop.mental order and that the last three stages may represent differences in ideology (Simpson, 1987). This approach is illustrated in the figure.

stages each. It might be helpful to think of Stages 1, 3, and 5 as levels of development in the practice of rules, while Stages 2, 4, and 6 represent lagging levels of consciousness about rule practices (Onuf, 1987).

Before age 9 or 10, most children display **preconventional morality** (Level I). During this level of morality, children make moral judgments based on self-interest—either to avoid punishment or to receive rewards.

During preadolescence (ages 10 to 13), children develop **conventional morality** and seek approval by upholding society's standards. In Stage 3, morality is achieved by "being a good boy or girl"—wanting the approval of teachers and parents. Instead of operating solely for self-interests, children think about being fair to others and pleasing others. During this stage, children try to live by the Golden Rule of "Do unto others as you would have them do unto you." In Stage 4, morality is achieved by abiding by laws and doing one's duty. Kohlberg believed that this law-and-order stage of moral reasoning was the most advanced stage reached by the majority of adults.

According to Kohlberg, school-age children do not reach the third level of moral reasoning—**postconventional morality** or morality of autonomous moral principles. Kohlberg believed that this level is typically reached in young adulthood or later, or never. The stages in this level represent concerns for the welfare of society and for universal moral principles. Some have suggested that this level be labeled maker-of-society because it is a rule-making perspective representing persons who are fully conscious of

the implications of remaking and creating society by making commitments (Onuf, 1987).

successful study tip

Kohlberg's Six Stages of Moral Reasoning

The key to remembering Kohlberg's six stages is to use brief definitions of each stage:

1. Punishments and obedience
2. Rewards and satisfaction
3. Goodness and approval
4. System-maintenance and duty
5. Social contract and welfare
6. Universal ethical principles

Then use the first letter of one of the key words in each definition to form a six-letter nonsense word to help recall—in this case, PRAD—SU.

Kohlberg (1969) tested his moral development theory by postulating moral dilemmas and asking people what they would do and for what reasons. Kohlberg was more interested in the moral reasoning than the behavioral choice. One such moral dilemma involved Heinz, who did not have $2,000 to pay the pharmacist for medications that would keep his wife from dying. The pharmacist would not allow Heinz to have the drugs without paying first. Subjects were asked what Heinz should do—that is, they were asked whether Heinz should steal the drugs in order to have his

Table 8.8
Gilligan's Female Stages of Moral Reasoning

Level 1: *The Orientation Toward Self-Interest*
 Pragmatic and egocentric preoccupation with self-interest and survival
 Obey restrictions imposed by society
 Make decisions that are best for self under the circumstances

First Transition: *From Selfishness to Responsibility*
 Awareness of difference between one's wants and what one ought to do
 Emerging concern for others

Level 2: *Identification of Goodness With Responsibility for Others*
 Emergence of a societal perspective
 Overriding sense of responsibility for others
 Capacity for self-sacrifice (subordination)
 Pleasing or caring for others (pleasing at any price, fear of abandonment)

Second Transition: *From Conformity to a New Inner Judgment*
 Questioning own values
 Remaining true to self without hurting others
 Acknowledging self and values

Level 3: *Focusing on the Dynamics Between Self and Others*
 A universal perspective
 Minimize hurt for others and self
 Decision making still involves interpersonal connectedness

From R. E. Muuss, "Carol Gilligan's Theory of Sex Differences in the Development of Moral Reasoning During Adolescence" in *Adolescence*, 23, 229–243, 1988. Copyright © 1988 Libra Publishers, Inc., San Diego, CA.

Surrounded by some of the students she interviewed about their development process is Carol Gilligan who has pointed out the importance of caring and relationships in the lives of females.

wife live. Some subjects at all six stages opted to have Heinz steal the medicines, while others in each of the stages argued that it would be wrong to take the drugs.

For example, a Stage 1 subject might argue against stealing the medicines by saying, "Heinz should not steal the drugs because stealing is a bad crime, and he might damage property, too." A Stage 3 person might argue that Heinz should take the medicines because "A good husband would do that out of love for his wife—it would be bad if Heinz did not love her enough to save her life." A Stage 6 person might decide to steal the drugs because "Heinz is in a situation that forces him to choose between stealing and letting his wife die. He has to act in terms of the principle of preserving and respecting life."

People do not operate out of only one stage—moral judgments often take place within networks of relationships with inadequate information and with pressured deadlines. "Under the pressure of circumstances, even highly moral thinkers could not live up to their ideal moral selves" (Linn, 1987, p. 193). People most often use lower modes of moral justification in situations that invoke self-interests (Linn, 1987).

Critics have questioned several aspects of Kohlberg's theory. The "Exploring Cultural Diversity" feature examines the issue of cultural bias in Kohlberg's stages.

Some critics suggested that Kohlberg's faith in Level III, postconventional morality, was unjustified (Gibbs & Schnell, 1985). While Kohlberg believed that the achievement of universal ethical principles was the most mature and positive level of moral reasoning, its ideological individualism could be viewed as having anarchistic implications. Society is preserved because the majority of citizens choose to obey the laws and maintain the system.

In his later works, Kohlberg acknowledged that his model only looked at justice reasoning. He suggested that mature moral reasoning also involved sensitivity to complex human emotions and situations and personal experiences in responsibility, moral conflict, and choices (Kohlberg, Levine, & Hewer, 1983; Skrimshire, 1987). Carol Gilligan (1982, 1984) suggested that Kohlberg's theory is gender biased because of its emphasis on a justice morality and its neglect of a morality based on caring. From a justice viewpoint, females tend to be labeled as less morally developed because more females are in Stage 3 and more males are in Stage 4 (Muuss, 1988).

Gilligan's Moralities of Caring and Justice
Gilligan suggested that men tend to organize social relationships in hierarchical order and use a **morality of rights.** However, women tend to place more emphasis on interpersonal connectedness as shown by care, sensitivity, and responsibility (Gilligan, 1982, 1984; Muuss, 1988). Table 8.8 summarizes Carol Gilligan's female stages of moral reasoning.

Exploring the Parent/Child Relationship: Parental Influence on Moral Development

More than 90 percent of adult Americans believe that morals have declined because parents fail to take responsibility for their children and instruct them with decent moral standards (Bowen, 1987). Are parents an important influence on their children's morality? The answer is "yes." For example, style of discipline is linked to moral orientation.

Martin Hoffman's (1983) discipline styles of power-assertion, love-withdrawal, and induction are described in Chapter 7.

These parental discipline styles apparently influence moral orientation. Parents who rely heavily on frequent power-assertive discipline have offspring whose moral orientation is based on fear of external detection and punishment. Parents who frequently use induction techniques have offspring with internal moral orientations. Induction techniques help to build a child's conscience; conscience strength plays a role in the transition from Kohlberg's Stage 2 to Stage 3 reasoning and an even bigger role

in the transition from Stage 3 to Stage 4 (Hart, 1988).

Parental identification and involvement also influence moral reasoning development during all stages of life—childhood, adolescence, and adulthood. In one study, boys who had fathers with whom they strongly identified and who also encouraged democratic discussions in the family had the most advanced moral development (Hart, 1988).

Table 8.9
Justice and Caring Orientations in Moral Reasoning in Six Studies

	Care Orientation			Justice Orientation		
	Included	*Preferred*	*Excluded*	*Included*	*Preferred*	*Excluded*
Women	92%	62%	8%	77%	38%	23%
Men	62%	7%	38%	100%	93%	0%

Source: Based on C. Gilligan, *Remapping the Moral Domain in Personality Research and Assessment,* 1984. Invited address given at the American Psychological Association Convention in Toronto. Cited in R. E. Muuss, "Carol Gilligan's Theory of Sex Differences in the Development of Moral Reasoning During Adolescence" in *Adolescence,* 23, 229–243, 1988.

According to Gilligan (1982), a theory of moral reasoning should encompass the two complementary orientations of justice and care, since both are important parts of the human potential. Yet, even before Kohlberg, the **morality of caring** was seen as less mature and as inferior to the **morality of justice.** Back in 1925, Freud wrote,

> *Their [women's] superego is never so inexorable, so impersonal, so independent of its emotional origins as we require it to be in men . . . that they show less sense of justice than men, that they are less ready to submit it to the great exigencies of life, that they are more often influenced in their judgment by feelings of affection or hostility. (Freud, 1961, pp. 257–258)*

As summarized in Table 8.9, most women and men use both the justice and caring orientations in their moral reasoning. A majority (65 percent) rely heavily on only one of the two orientations. Males strongly prefer a justice orientation; females prefer a caring orientation, but the preference is less one-sided. Other studies (e.g., Arnold, & Burkhart, Gibbs, 1984; Gilligan & Attanucci, 1988; Walker, 1984) also suggest that the majority use both orientations in their reasoning; only some studies find significant gender differences in moral reasoning.

Along with cultural influences, such as the schools, the government, and religious organizations, parents play a major role in the development of morality. Parental

guided review

4. In Piaget's third stage—the stage of _____—children come to rely on _____ thinking and to master principles of _____.
5. In conservation of _____, children understand that the number of objects in a group does not change when the arrangement of the group is changed.
6. Children develop preferences, called _____, for organizing perceptions and information.
7. With the emergence of _____ around age 5, children can think about what has been said to them.
8. According to Piaget, during the years from 6 to 12, children move from a morality of _____ to a morality of _____.
9. Kohlberg proposed that moral _____ guides moral _____ and that individuals may progress through _____ stages in a set sequence.
10. Gilligan criticized Kohlberg's theory for its emphasis on morality based on _____, while neglecting morality based on _____.

answers

4. concrete operations; operational; conservation [LO-4].
5. number [LO-5]. 6. cognitive styles [LO-6]. 7. metalinguistic awareness [LO-8]. 8. constraint; cooperation [LO-9].
9. reasoning; behavior; six [LO-9]. 10. justice; caring [LO-10].

influence on moral development is the topic of the "Exploring the Parent/Child Relationship" feature.

Schools and Achievement in Middle and Late Childhood

When children begin school, two closely related concepts become important: intelligence and achievement. As you will read in the sections that follow, psychologists are proposing changes away from the traditional views of intelligence as measured by IQ tests, while parents and school officials continue to focus on the achievement levels of their children and students.

Intelligence

Information-Processing Views of Intelligence

How would you define intelligence? Most people believe that, by school age, intelligence is becoming less perceptual-motor and more cognitive in nature (Siegler & Richards, 1982). Views of intelligence include the ability to do abstract thinking, to learn from experience, to increase one's capacity for processing information, and to make good responses in one's environment. Robert Sternberg (1984, 1985, 1988) emphasized that intelligence is skill at coping with novel tasks and learning to "automatize" information processing. Children who can master complex tasks and learn information fairly quickly are good automatizers.

Raymond Cattell (1971) proposed that intelligence be divided into fluid and crystallized abilities. **Fluid abilities** involve general, innately determined aspects of thinking that relate to speed, flexibility, adaptation to novel situations, and abstract reasoning. Steven has good fluid abilities because he can perceive relationships quickly and is good at solving a variety of problem tasks. **Crystallized abilities** are related to experiences, learning, and culture. These abilities are general information and knowledge, vocabulary, logical reasoning, and mechanical knowledge. Crystallized intelligence remains constant or increases as individuals get older; fluid intelligence improves during childhood and decreases during older adulthood.

Intelligence has traditionally been measured in the areas of verbal, mathematical, and spatial abilities. Howard Gardner (1983) suggested that there are multiple intelligences and proposed seven major intellectual components: verbal, mathematical, spatial abilities, musical ability, bodily skills, social skills, and self-knowledge. Gardner also believed that each culture should measure intelligence according to the abilities and skills important for survival and success. Therefore, an intelligence test in the 19th century would have best featured items about farming and canning, while a test for the 1990s might best feature adaptability to computers.

Robert Sternberg's (1984, 1985, 1988) triarchic theory emphasizes (1) the ability to adapt to or improve on one's environment; (2) the components of information processing—from planning, monitoring, and selecting, to performance and knowledge acquisition; and (3) the ability to deal with novel tasks and to automatize a performance strategy for a type of task.

Table 8.10
Common Cognitive Deficiencies

Impulsiveness. Impulsive individuals often approach problem-solving tasks in a trial-and-error fashion. They often try to answer questions before they understand what question was asked. They have not yet learned to use a deliberate plan or strategy, rather than chance approaches.

Inability to Recognize Problems. Individuals with this cognitive deficiency fail to perceive significant characteristics of problems. They often fail to notice inconsistencies and discrepancies in situations and problems. They have trouble knowing which information pieces are more important than others.

Episodic Grasp of Reality. Individuals with episodic grasp of reality have difficulty making connections between different events, putting items in context, and perceiving relationships.

Failure to Make Comparisons. Persons with this cognitive deficiency have trouble knowing how objects and people are alike and how they are different.

Inadequate Spatial Orientation. Persons with this difficulty cannot orient themselves, solve spatial problems, or use maps well.

General Passiveness. Passive individuals do not work on problems or do not think about them. They receive information passively and fail to actively generate relevant information.

From Reuven Feuerstein, *Instrumental Enrichment: An Intervention Program,* 1980. Reprinted by permission of the author.

Testing Intelligence

Many intelligence tests measure verbal reasoning, mathematical skills, and spatial abilities almost exclusively. Intelligence tests of the future will probably be influenced by the information-processing theories mentioned in the previous section and include a wider variety of tasks. Another advance in assessment comes from neuropsychological tests that help to determine level and pattern of performance, right-left brain differences, and specific concerns with neuropathology. Finally, future tests will emphasize how to modify and improve intellectual abilities, rather than peg a person's lifetime potential.

Modifying Intelligence

Reuven Feuerstein (1980) suggested that people have cognitive modifiability, the ability to change mental structures and contents. According to Feuerstein, people can be taught to eliminate specific flaws in their thinking by using mediated learning experiences (specially designed learning tasks to help correct thinking patterns).

Feuerstein (1980) identified several cognitive deficiencies (see Table 8.10). Both children and adults can learn how to reduce these deficiencies. If any of these cognitive deficiencies seems familiar, you can still learn to correct them. Read about thinking strategies and try to apply them in problem solving. Practice making comparisons and solving spatial orientation problems. Some colleges offer thinking skills courses that may assist you.

Achievement

What Is Achievement?

Need for achievement (nAch) involves the motivation for accomplishing difficult tasks, competing to do more than others, and working toward a standard of excellence (McClelland, 1984). Many different behavioral styles can be used to gain achievements: Some individuals attain achievement through their own individual efforts, some through their personality qualities, and some by aiding achievement efforts of others (Lipman-Blumen, Handley-Isakin, & Leavitt, 1983).

Although researchers have measured nAch primarily in school and vocational settings, it can be measured in any performance area (Spence & Helmreich, 1983). For example, some school-age children show high nAch by earning proficiency badges in scouting, by pitching well in Little League games, or by learning to draw well. How did you express your nAch in your school years?

Veroff (see Chafel, 1988) developed a three-stage theory of achievement motivation. The first stage is **autonomous motivation,** in which children orient themselves to internal, self-generated norms. Around age 6, children engage in **social comparison** and direct themselves according to social norms. Around age 10 to 12, children can experience **integrated motivation** and draw upon both autonomous and normative motivations. Veroff hypothesized that boys are higher in autonomous motivation and that girls place more emphasis on social comparison. As a result, boys who do not move through the three stages well are especially vulnerable to impulsive achievement motivation, and girls are more vulnerable to fear of success and fear of failure problems.

---

successful study tip

Veroff's Three-Stage Development of Need for Achievement

The order of stages in Veroff's theory can be remembered with the phrase:

AS I ACHIEVE

Use "AS I" to remember the order: (1) Autonomous motivation, (2) Social comparison motivation, and (3) Integrated motivation.

According to the expectancy-value theory, five components influence an individual's achievement needs (Atkinson, 1974). One component is the need to approach success, or the hope for success. Jerry is expressing this component when he spends hours trying to improve his pitching aim by throwing his baseball repeatedly at a target.

A second component is the need to avoid failure, or the fear of failure. Sometimes, instead of positively striving for success, individuals work under the anxiety of threats of failure. Bert practices the piano because he fears his teacher will be disappointed with his performance and because his parents have told him that his lessons are expensive and should not be wasted. Bert actually plays as well as Irene, who enjoys practicing because she hopes to improve her skills, but Bert experiences high levels of stress about piano playing, and Irene does not. Bert may decide to quit taking piano lessons because he is too critical of his own performance and because he feels he is disappointing his teacher and parents.

A third aspect of achievement is expectancy, one's belief in the likelihood of success or failure with an achievement goal. Although Carol is quite intelligent, her family rarely reinforces her abilities. They often correct her mistakes by telling her, "Why are you so stupid?" or "Now that was really dumb." Although Carol would like to bring home good grades, she rarely performs well in her classes because she does not expect that she is capable of grades higher than Cs.

Related to this component of expectancy is delay of gratification, the ability to give up immediate, small rewards in favor of later, larger rewards. Children who develop the ability to delay gratification are likely as adolescents to be able to persist at efforts to plan ahead, and to set high standards (Mischel, 1984). Children with parents who fairly consistently live up to their promises learn more easily to rely on deferred reinforcers.

A fourth component of achievement is incentive value of success or failure. Incentive value involves the individual's estimate of the achievement's worth. Donna exhibits high reading achievement because she has learned that reading is an important task: She enjoys her parents reading to her and someday will read to her children; she sees her parents reading the newspaper and discussing the articles; and she is often treated to visits to the library to get new books to read.

The last component of achievement is the tendency to seek extrinsic rewards, such as money, grades, awards, and praise. Matthew showed little interest in learning his spelling words until his teacher started to reward high performance with stickers.

Intrinsic Versus Extrinsic Motivation

While it might seem that an endless supply of stickers is all that is needed to build high nAch among schoolchildren, such a strategy actually lowers achievement. According to the theory of intrinsic motivation, when activity is performed for externally based reasons (e.g., money, fear of punishment, approval from others, stickers), individuals shift from an internal control over performance to an external control. Extrinsic rewards can therefore decrease self-determination and interest in activities (Deci & Ryan, 1985). For example, Barbara used to enjoy riding horses more than anything else. After awhile, Barbara was good enough to compete in riding competitions. After she and her horse had won a few ribbons and trophies, Barbara found that she was only enjoying riding competitions and was not enjoying leisurely riding.

The use of extrinsic rewards, like grades or written compliments, can help build new skills and provide feedback to let students know they are learning correctly, but their overuse can result in lower intrinsic motivation.

Numerous studies have found that grades and other tangible rewards can lead to (1) decreased creativity, (2) a preference for less challenging and simpler versions of a given target activity, and (3) a preference for easier versions even when extrinsic rewards are over (Boggiano, Main, & Katz, 1988). Even verbal positive feedback (e.g., "Excellent, you should keep up the good work") can reduce intrinsic motivation (Ryan, 1982). Children with high artistic interests were placed in one of three conditions: no reward, expected reward, and unexpected reward (no knowledge of reward while working) for doing artwork. In subsequent opportunities, students in the expected-reward condition exhibited lower interest in doing art than did others (Lepper, Greene, & Nisbett, 1973).

Can extrinsic rewards be used to benefit achievement levels and not detract from intrinsic motivation? Extrinsic rewards help to build interest and mastery in areas in which individuals do not currently have nAch. Extrinsic rewards can be used to convey information about performance excellence, rather than becoming the focal point of the situation. The best use of external rewards is when the rewards are fairly small and are used to reward good performance and not just performance (Deci & Ryan, 1985).

Parents of High-Achievement-Oriented Children

At least 20 percent of high-ability children seriously underestimate their abilities. As a result, these children adopt lower standards and expectancies for success. The biggest predictors of whether highly competent children seriously underestimate their abilities are their parents' appraisals of their abilities. That is, parents' high expectancies for their children predict children's self-concepts about their abilities (Boggiano, Main, & Katz, 1988; Phillips, 1984, 1987).

Of course, some parents carry expectancies about their children's achievements to an unhealthy extreme—they push their children too far and too fast. Excessive parental pressure on kids or situations in which parents interpret children's success as parents' success can lead to "burned-out" kids who suffer stress disorders, psychosomatic illnesses, and long-term personality problems (Elkind, 1987b).

Parents of adjusted, high-achieving, and talented children introduce their children to areas of interest, such as sports, music, the arts, or science, with enthusiasm and romanticism, rather than with intense competition and pressure for top performance. These parents do, however, model the work ethic themselves, and their children learn from their parents' examples that working and performing duties are important in addition to leisure and pleasurable activities (Bloom, 1984).

In general, parents of high-need-achieving children emphasize independence training, expect early self-reliance and quality performance, and show their children an abundance of warmth and affection (McClelland, Atkinson, Clark, & Lowell, 1953; Rosen & D'Andrade, 1959; Winterbottom, 1958). Achievement is hurt when parents punish failures, respond neutrally to successes, or tell their children exactly how to accomplish their tasks (Rosen & D'Andrade, 1959; Teeven & McGhee, 1972).

Children who develop high intrinsic motivation have higher perceptions of competence and greater self-determination. This pattern is influenced by family behavior and also by the school system. Children who have such a foundation from their family start out in school-related activities with more interest, have higher preference for challenging lessons, and exhibit better ability to resist evaluative pressures (Boggiano, Main, & Katz, 1988). These children are more likely to enjoy school and to feel successful in the classroom.

Schools

What Should Schools Teach?

Few people disagree that schoolchildren should learn basic skills in reading, mathematics, and other fundamental content areas. Typical abilities for children ages 6 to 12 are shown in Table 8.11. These are what parents expect their children to learn at school. However, less agreement exists over the role that schools should play in teaching values, sex education, and home living skills.

Reading has been taught by a variety of techniques—from memorizing each new word to use of phonetics. Often, young children use analogies, or rhyming words, to read new words (e.g., using *beak* to read *peak*). By age 7, children often use these rhyming words to help themselves learn how to spell correctly (Goswami, 1988). One current proposal for teaching reading is that teachers use a natural process to teach reading. Proponents believe that a natural technique is needed because the artificial nature of phonics results in some children not reading well and not enjoying what reading they do (Tovey, Johnson, & Szporer, 1988). The three phases of this system are presented in Table 8.12. What do you think are the advantages and disadvantages of this system, compared to how you were taught to read?

Table 8.11
Average Learning Activities From Ages 6 to 12

6 to 7	Copies a triangle. Defines words by use ("What is an orange?" "Something to eat."). Knows if morning or afternoon. Draws a person with 12 details. Reads several one-syllable printed words (*my, dog, see, boy*). Uses pencil for printing name.
7 to 8	Counts by 2s and 5s. Ties shoes. Copies a diamond. Knows what day of the week it is (not date or year). Can read: "Muff is a little yellow kitten. She drinks milk. She sleeps on a chair. She does not like to get wet." Can do the following arithmetic: $7 + 4 =$ $\quad$ $6 + 7 =$ $\quad$ $6 - 4 =$ $\quad$ $8 - 3 =$ No evidence of sound substitution in speech (e.g., *fr* for *thr*). Adds and subtracts one-digit numbers. Draws a person with 16 details.
8 to 9	Defines words better than by use. ("What is an orange?" "A fruit."). Can give an appropriate answer to the following: $\quad$ "What is the thing for you to do if . . . $\quad\quad\quad$ . . . you've broken something that belongs to someone else?" $\quad\quad\quad$ . . . a playmate hits you without meaning to do so?" Can read: "A little black dog ran away from home. He played with two big dogs. They ran away from him. It began to rain. He went under a tree. He wanted to go home, but he did not know the way. He saw a boy he knew. The boy took him home." Can do the following arithmetic: $67 + 4 =$ $\quad$ $45 + 16 + 27 =$ $\quad$ $14 - 8 =$ $\quad$ $84 - 36 =$ Is learning borrowing and carrying processes in addition and subtraction.
9 to 10	Knows the month, day, and year. Names the months in order (15 sec, one error). Makes a sentence with either of these two sets of three words in it (can use words orally in proper context): $\quad$ 1. work . . . money . . . men $\quad$ 2. boy . . . river . . . ball Can read: "Six boys put up a tent by the side of a river. They took things to eat with them. When the sun went down, they went into the tent to sleep. In the night, a cow came and began to eat grass around the tent. The boys were afraid. They thought it was a bear." Can comprehend and answer question: "What was the cow doing?" Can do the following arithmetic: $5,204 - 530 =$ $\quad$ $23 \times 3 =$ $\quad$ $837 \times 7 =$ Is learning simple multiplication.
10 to 12	Can read: "In 1807, Robert Fulton took the first long trip in a steamboat. He went one hundred and fifty miles up the Hudson River. The boat went five miles an hour. This was faster than a steamboat had ever gone before. Crowds gathered on both banks of the river to see this new kind of boat. They were afraid that its noise and splashing would drive away all the fish." Can comprehend and answer question: "What was the trip made on?" Can write the sentence: "The fishermen did not like the boat." Can do the following arithmetic: 420×29 $\quad$ $9\overline{)72}$ $\quad$ $31\overline{)62}$ Can do multiplication and simple division.

Reproduced by permission of *Pediatrics*, Vol. 31, page 499. Copyright © 1963 American Academy of Pediatrics, Elk Grove Villiage, IL.

Early mathematics instruction needs to include activities that facilitate children's understanding of numbers. Most children entering school can make relative number judgments, accomplish pattern recognition for small numbers, count, and do simple adding and subtraction. Children can count, add, and subtract before they have complete ability to conserve numbers, and they can experience some linear measurement success before they have completely acquired the ability to conserve length. What young children need

most in mathematics instruction is to be able to deal with one aspect of a problem at a time. Teachers can also help children by introducing new material in ways that relate the new aspects to what students already know and have experienced (Young-Loveridge, 1987).

Children may fail at mathematics tasks if they do not understand the language used in presenting the task. Word problems, for example, are often difficult for third-graders because they make figuring out the proper problem-solving

Table 8.12	
Three Phases of Learning to Read	

Phase I: Dictating Stories

Children tell stories, which are then written down. They do **echo-reading,** in which the finger points out the print while reading the stories. Children write and tape stories each day.

Phase II: Identifying Phrases and Sentences

Children listen to their stories at least once each day. They learn to point out which story is which ("That's the one with the monster" and "That's the one about going fishing with Mother"). Children indicate which phrases they would like to learn; they learn to recognize phrases they have already learned.

Phase III: Transition to Books Authored by Others

Now children write stories for children to read and also enjoy stories written by the teacher and older children. Children are also introduced to books written by authors. Reading to children continues to be a frequent activity.

Reprinted by permission of D. R. Tovey, et al., and the Association for Childhood Education International, 11141 Georgia Avenue, Suite 200, Wheaton, MD. Copyright © 1988 by the Association.

Table 8.13

Examples of Consistent and Inconsistent Language in Mathematical Word Problems

Consistent Language	Inconsistent Language
Addition:	*Addition:*
Joe has 3 marbles. Tom has 5 more marbles than Joe. How many marbles does Tom have?	Joe has 3 marbles. He has 5 marbles less than Tom. How many marbles does Tom have?
Subtraction:	*Subtraction:*
Joe has 8 marbles. Tom has 5 less marbles than Joe. How many marbles does Tom have?	Joe has 8 marbles. He has 5 more marbles than Tom. How many marbles does Tom have?

From A. B. Lewis and R. E. Mayer, "Students' Miscomprehension of Relational Statements in Arithmetic Word Problems," Table 1, 1987 in *Journal of Educational Psychology,* 79, 363–371. Copyright © 1987 American Psychological Association. Reprinted by permission..

strategy more difficult. By sixth grade, word problems cause fewer difficulties (Morales, Shute, & Pellegrino, 1985; Young-Loveridge, 1987).

Addition word problems that use the word *less* are more difficult than those that use the word *more;* likewise, *subtraction* word problems that use the word *more* are more difficult than those that use the word *less.* In other words, mathematical word problems with consistent language are easier than word problems with inconsistent language (Lewis & Mayer, 1987). Examples of different language problems are presented in Table 8.13.

How Should Schools Teach?

Schools that perform well have pleasant environments, emphasize academic subjects, provide special and remedial programs, have good discipline, and have student participation. Teachers in these schools emphasize student and school successes, rather than shortcomings; are well-prepared and make good use of school time; assign homework; spend time with the whole class, rather than just a few students; and work with other school staff members on curriculum and discipline goals. Factors that do not determine a school's performance include the school's financial resources, class size, student-teacher ratio, and social and ethnic mixes (Rutter, Maugham, Mortimer, & Ouston, 1979).

Benjamin Bloom (1984) suggested that schools overemphasize rote learning and learning by drills, competition among schools, and passive learning methods, such as lectures. Bloom would utilize tutoring methods and mastery learning. Tutoring allows 90 percent of students to achieve what only 20 percent of students are able to accomplish in conventional classes (Chance, 1987). Low-achieving students who are given opportunities to tutor younger children improve in motivation and performance (Feldman, Devin-Sheehan, & Allen, 1976). Yet, school systems cannot afford the student-teacher ratios required of tutoring methods. In-

stead, in mastery learning teachers instruct students on how to analyze problems and how to use systematic thinking. Tests determine what kinds of thinking errors remain, and this material is retaught until the ideas and concepts are understood. Bloom claimed that, with this system, 70 percent of students can match the performance of the top 20 percent of students in conventional classrooms (Chance, 1987).

Teachers' Expectations and Performance

Looking back on your first school years, you probably have several memories about specific teachers. Teachers are very important people to school-age children. Teachers can help to ignite lifelong interests in reading or science or art. Sometimes, special teachers are able to help children from dysfunctional homes to have more balanced lives because the teachers model good qualities and share kindness, concern, and affection with their students. However, some teachers fall prey to societal stereotypes and treat students unfairly. Teachers often have lower expectations for children from low-income families (Minuchin & Shapiro, 1985), and some may even place students into "ability groups" based on superficial characteristics, such as physical attractiveness, grooming, clothing quality, and English usage (Rist, 1970).

Teacher expectations can be based on gender, too. In one study of 63 female student teachers, 65 percent already preferred female students because they thought that females would be more conforming, quiet, controllable, practical, responsible, timid, and passive. The 35 percent who preferred male students expected them to be more outgoing, aggressive, abstract, and leadership-oriented (Payne & Manning, 1984).

Teachers dispense rewards to students. Remember the theory of intrinsic motivation discussed earlier in this chapter? Teachers can use comments, stickers, and good-worker awards to increase learning, but these same rewards

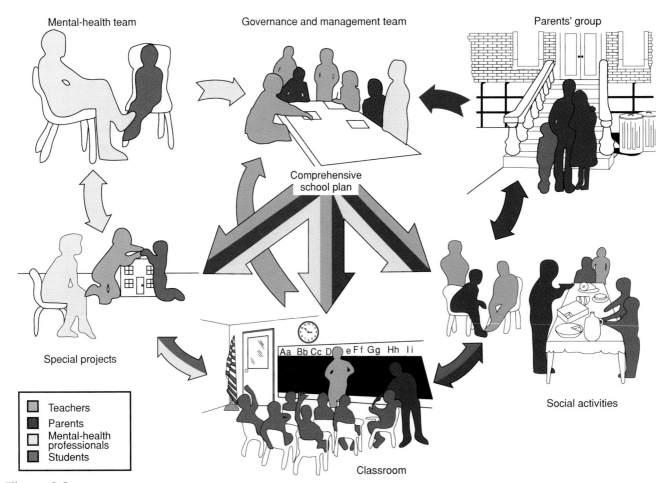

Mental-health team

Governance and management team

Parents' group

Comprehensive school plan

Special projects

Teachers
Parents
Mental-health professionals
Students

Classroom

Social activities

Figure 8.3

Schematic of the school-intervention program in New Haven, Connecticut, showing its key components and the relations among them. A governance and management team, consisting of the principal, parents, teachers, and a mental-health worker, develops a comprehensive school plan covering academics, social activities, and special programs, such as a Discovery Room for children who have lost interest in learning. Social activities, such as potluck suppers, teach children social skills and enable parents to meet teachers. Some parents become teachers' aides. The mental-health team assigns a member to work with a child who is having difficulty. It also tries to prevent behavior problems by recommending changes in school procedures. By reducing behavior problems and improving relations with parents, the program creates a school climate conducive to learning.

Source: Comer, J. P. 1988. Educating poor minority children. *Scientific American, 259,* p. 45.

can give children the message that learning is not enjoyable or worthwhile (Cannella, 1986). Some students—younger students, low-ability students, students from lower socioeconomic families, introverts, and students with external locus of control—seem to benefit more from praise for good performance than other students. Therefore, "identical statements made by the same teacher under the same circumstances produce different results for different students" (Cannella, 1986, p. 298). Overall, in high-praise classrooms, the teacher is viewed as the authority; in low-praise classrooms, students are more likely to share ideas, to be more persistent in tasks, and to exhibit more self-confidence (Cannella, 1986).

Teachers use punishment in the classrooms, which may include loss of privileges, detentions, extra assignments, verbal admonishments, time-outs, spankings, and suspensions. Among the most controversial are corporal punishment (e.g., spanking) and suspensions. One of the problems with corporal punishment is that children who are

frequently spanked tend to become highly resentful and distrustful of authority. Some become very hostile; others become conspicuously quieter, less articulate, more sullen, and nervous (Gilmartin, 1979). The most common behavioral problems that lead to student suspensions are physical violence (30 percent) and verbal abuse to school personnel (42 percent). One problem with suspensions is that parents often think that the schools are being unreasonable. Only 30 percent of parents believe that their children's suspensions were justified; more than 60 percent believe that the school is primarily to blame. Over one-third of the children who are suspended from school exhibit severe behavioral problems into adulthood (Nicol, Wilcox, & Hibbert, 1985).

Parental Influences on School Performance

One influence that parents have on their children's school performance is on children's reading abilities. Parents who read to their children 8 or more min a day at least four times a week and who ask their children lots of questions

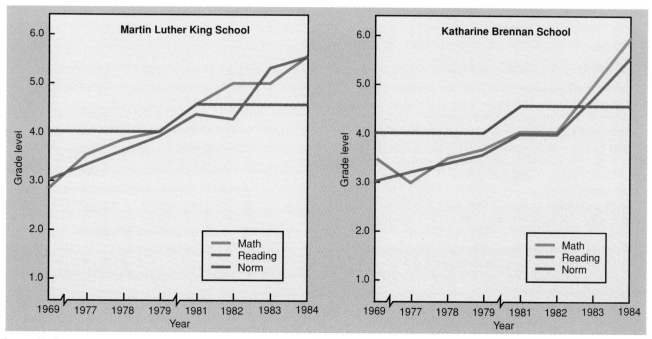

Figure 8.4

Gains in achievement-test scores (Iowa Test of Basic Skills) of fourth-graders at two New Haven, Connecticut schools in Yale University's Child Study Center's intervention program from 1969 through 1984.

Source: Comer, R. J. 1988. Educating poor minority children. *Scientific American, 259*, p. 47.

about the reading have children with bigger listening and speaking vocabularies, better letter recognition abilities, longer spoken sentence lengths, better comprehension skills, and higher interest in reading (Becher, 1985).

Unfortunately, many parents have little contact with their children's schools and teachers. One study highlighted the importance of parental involvement with the schools (Conner, 1988). When administrators, teachers, counselors, and parents work together, even schools in poor neighborhoods can achieve academic excellence. Problems (whether academic or behavioral) are seen as challenges that can be handled, and children are never labeled as "the problem." Instead, behavioral problems are reduced and often prevented by changing school procedures, improving relations with parents, and developing an environment conducive to learning.

In one school-intervention program, a comprehensive school plan, shown in Figure 8.3, was developed to help parents who felt out of the educational mainstream to feel comfortable in their children's school setting. Many educators fail to appreciate the number of parents who feel uncomfortable in school and library settings; to these parents, schools are places of failure and disenfranchisement. Only by changing these perceptions can parents work well with teachers and educational administrators.

Some of the specific changes that schools in this school-intervention program made were: (1) The principals shared their power with staff and parents and reached more decisions by consensus; (2) parents were encouraged to work as classroom assistants, and some of them were hired

at minimum wage for their help; and (3) parents and staff co-sponsored social activities, such as potluck suppers, graduation ceremonies, and book fairs. These types of reforms have worked so well that the two initial pilot schools have 92 percent of the parents visiting the schools at least 10 times a year. Academically, these two schools have made steady gains, so that now they are among the best in the city (Comer, 1988). The changes in academic achievement are illustrated in Figure 8.4. Schools of all types could probably benefit from the changes made in this intervention program.

guided review

11. Current views of intelligence include Sternberg's three-factor _____ theory, Gardner's idea of _____ intelligence, and Feuerstein's concept of cognitive _____.
12. Verhoff hypothesized that boys are higher in _____ motivation, while girls place more emphasis on _____.
13. List at least four characteristics of schools that are effective in promoting higher student achievement.

answers

11. triarchic; multiple; modifiability, [LO-11]. 12. autonomous; social comparison, [LO-12]. 13. Pleasant environments, an emphasis on academic subjects, provision of special and remedial programs, good discipline, and student participation [LO-14].

Exploring Human Development

1. Go to a busy children's playground and estimate children's ages. Ask the children to verify their ages. How did you do? What assumptions did you make? Turn this into an experiment by having students in the class bring in an assortment of school-age children's photographs. Have several people guess ages. What factors produced the most errors?
2. Try duplicating some of Piaget's concrete operations stage experiments with first- and third-graders. Write up your observations.
3. Borrow a children's riddle book from a library. Choose different types of jokes from the book, and try them out on children ages 6 to 12. Did you find an age pattern?
4. Create some moral dilemma situations, and ask children to solve them. Rate the responses according to Piaget, Kohlberg, and Gilligan. What are your conclusions about moral development?
5. Obtain permission to observe elementary school classrooms. Compare these classes to your elementary school experience.

Discussing Human Development

1. Children vary in physical size. What are the advantages and disadvantages of being one of the largest children in a class? The smallest? Do you think there are long-term implications?
2. Imagine yourself as the head of a physical education program interested in helping children to maintain or achieve good physical fitness. What types of programs would you initiate in the elementary schools? How often would children have physical education? How would you get physically inactive children and physically inept children to participate more fully?
3. Discuss the impact of concrete operations thinking on children's interpretations of holiday customs (e.g., Santa's existence), death, vacations, politics, and movie plots.
4. Do you think that school-age children should be taught remembering strategies and thinking strategies? Why?
5. Does your own moral development fit into the theories presented in this chapter? How do you view your typical moral reasoning now?

Reading More About Human Development

Elkind, D. (1981). *The hurried child: Growing up too fast too soon.* Reading, MA: Addison-Wesley.

Gardner, H. (1983). *Frames of mind: The theory of multiple intelligences.* New York: Basic Books.

Gilligan, C. (1982). *In a different voice: Psychological theory and women's development.* Cambridge, MA: Harvard University Press.

Rutter, M., Maugham, B., Mortimer, P., & Ouston, J. (1979). *Fifteen thousand hours.* London: Open Books.

Siegler, R. S. (1986). *Children's thinking.* Englewood Cliffs, NJ: Prentice-Hall.

Sternberg, R. J. (1988). *Intelligence applied.* San Diego: Harcourt Brace.

Summary

I. Physical development in middle and late childhood
   A. During the years from ages 6 to 12, children grow somewhat steadily, gaining an average of 7 lb and 2 or more inches per year.
      1. Boys and girls exhibit the same growth pattern until about age 10, when girls begin a prepubertal growth spurt.
      2. Better nutrition has led to earlier increases in height, a development called the secular trend in height.
      3. During the school years, ossification of cartilage into bone continues, often with uneven skeletal growth, which results in temporary clumsiness.
   B. School-age children enjoy using their increasing physical abilities in new games and activities.
      1. Both fine and gross motor skills continue to improve.
      2. The lack of physical fitness among school-age children is an important concern, as indicated by the 98 percent of school-age children who have at least one risk factor for coronary heart disease.
      3. To modify their children's risk factor for heart disease, parents can increase family exercise activities, improve the nutritional quality of children's diets, and encourage schools to emphasize physical fitness.
   C. Physical health care, illness, and injuries influence school-age children's physical development.
      1. Ideally, school-age children should have regular medical, visual, and dental checkups, but many fall short of this ideal because of socioeconomic factors.
      2. School-age children typically have from four to six illnesses per year, with respiratory illnesses the most common.
      3. Children's injuries are most often associated with their recreational toys (e.g., skateboards, roller skates, and bicycles) and organized sports.
      4. A small percentage of children must learn to cope with long-term physical or cognitive disabilities.
II. Cognitive development in middle and late childhood
   A. The increase in cognitive skills during the school years may mislead parents to overestimate their children's reasoning abilities.
   B. During Piaget's stage of concrete operations, children become operational thinkers, meaning that they can get beyond one main characteristic of a situation and consider many aspects at once.
      1. During the concrete operations stage, children acquire the abilities to classify, seriate, number, reverse operations, and conserve physical properties of objects.
      2. In the concrete operations stage, school-age children begin to look for physical causes of events, to establish rules to guide behavior, and to expand their spatial awareness and time consciousness.

C. Cognitive styles include cognitive tempo (impulsive and reflective) and field-dependence/independence.

D. Memory development continues in school-age children, with rapid increases in short-term memory.

    1. Metamemory, knowledge of one's memory processes, develops in the middle childhood years.

    2. School-age children can take advantage of a variety of strategies for remembering, such as verbal rehearsal, visual imagery, and clustering.

    3. The contexts of time, personal beliefs, and family experiences influence episodic memory (memories of past personal events), as well as memory for factual knowledge.

E. Language skills, including learning more precise meanings of words, applying rules of grammar, and remembering what has been said, improve during the school years.

    1. Metalinguistic awareness—awareness of how language works—is a major development during the school years.

    2. Children do not fully understand metaphors until nearly age 10 or 11.

    3. Children's understanding of humor reflects their advancing language competence; they move from humor based on similar-sounding words to humor based on ambiguities of meaning.

F. How children reason about the right and wrong thing to do (moral development) changes significantly during the school years.

    1. Three major psychological approaches to moral development are societalism, emotivism, and cognitive primacy.

    2. Societalism involves conforming to society's morality, while emotivism focuses on internal feelings of right and wrong.

    3. Piaget advocated cognitive primacy— understanding learned from experience.

    4. Piaget proposed two stages of moral reasoning— the morality of constraint and the morality of cooperation.

    5. Kohlberg expanded upon Piaget's ideas and proposed six stages of moral reasoning, believing that moral reasoning guides moral behavior.

    6. Kohlberg's theory has been criticized for its hierarchical, invariant sequence of stages and gender bias.

    7. Gilligan maintained that men and women are socialized into different cognitive schemes for making moral judgments and proposed moralities of caring and justice to explain these gender differences.

III. Schools and achievement in middle and late childhood

A. Traditional views of intelligence are undergoing revision.

    1. Sternberg emphasized intelligence as coping with novel tasks and learning to automatize information processing.

    2. Cattell proposed that intelligence be divided into fluid and crystallized abilities.

    3. Gardner suggested that people possess multiple intelligences with seven major intellectual components.

    4. Future intelligence tests will probably include a wider variety of tasks and will emphasize how to modify and improve intellectual abilities.

    5. Feuerstein suggested that intellectual abilities can be enhanced (cognitive modifiability).

B. School-age children exhibit need for achievement (the motivation to accomplish tasks, compete with others, and work toward self-imposed standards).

    1. Children start with autonomous motivation, then begin to engage in social comparison, and around age 10 to 12, experience integrated motivation.

    2. According to expectancy-value theory, children's and adults' achievement needs are influenced by five different factors, including hope for success and the need to avoid failure.

    3. Providing external incentives for intrinsically motivated activities actually lowers school-age children's achievement motivation.

    4. Parental expectations are an important factor in children's levels of achievement motivation.

C. Schools become an important aspect of children's lives between the ages of 6 and 12.

    1. Most parents have similar expectations for the basic skills that schools should teach but disagree on the role of schools in teaching sex education and values.

    2. Characteristics of successful schools include pleasant environments, emphasis on academics, programming for special needs, good discipline, and student participation.

    3. Successful teachers emphasize student and school successes, are well-prepared, make good use of time, assign homework, and work with the whole class.

    4. Teachers influence their students both positively and negatively, especially through their expectations based on gender and socioeconomic standing and their use of rewards and punishments.

    5. Parents also influence their children's school performance by the behaviors they model, such as reading, and their expectations.

    6. Parents can become more involved in their children's education through school-intervention programs that emphasize administrators, teachers, counselors, and parents working together.

Chapter Review Test

1. Which of the following statements accurately describes physical growth from ages 6 to 12?

    a. Up until age 10, boys are ahead of girls in physical growth but then girls move ahead of boys.

    b. A gender difference in physical growth does not exist until age 10, when girls experience a growth spurt before boys.

    c. A gender difference in physical growth does not exist until age 10, when boys experience a growth spurt before girls.

    d. Up until age 10, girls are ahead of boys in physical growth, but then boys move ahead of girls.

2. The secular trend is largely attributable to
   a. improved nutrition.
   b. medical interventions.
   c. the changing role of religion in children's lives.
   d. survival of the fittest.
3. Which of the following is a factor in the growing rate of obesity among schoolchildren?
   a. too much fat and sugar in their diet
   b. less physical activity due to television and videogames
   c. overeating to control stress caused by school and home pressures
   d. all of the above
4. The most common illnesses among school-age children are
   a. digestive illnesses.
   b. endocrine disorders.
   c. respiratory illnesses.
   d. mental disorders.
5. Which of the following disabilities is most common among children?
   a. speech impairment
   b. mental disabilities
   c. hearing impairment
   d. visual impairment
6. _____ is the ability to order a group of objects in succession, such as from shortest to tallest, largest to smallest, or first to last.
   a. Seriation
   b. Classification
   c. Numbering
   d. Rule orientation
7. Of the following types of conservation, which would typically be acquired last?
   a. conservation of length
   b. conservation of quantity
   c. conservation of volume
   d. conservation of weight
8. Which of the following is an ability crucial in achieving conservation?
   a. decentering
   b. reversibility
   c. more exhaustive encoding and improved cognitive strategies
   d. all of the above
9. Impulsive children are better at _____ than are reflective children.
   a. reading tasks
   b. broad analysis
   c. creativity
   d. all of the above
10. Ira, Ida, Irene, and Ito have a field-independent style, while Darla, Don, Diane, and Danny have a field-dependent style. Which of the following is likely to be the correct pairing of their favorite school subjects?
    a. Ira likes history, and Darla likes math.
    b. Ida likes geography, and Don likes biology.
    c. Irene likes biology, and Diane likes social studies.
    d. Ito likes math, and Danny likes earth science.
11. Which of the following is a correct statement about schoolchildren's metamemory?
    a. First-graders do not yet realize that people forget items as time passes.
    b. During the school years, children use more organized strategies for remembering.
    c. Clustering and visual imagery strategies are not adopted before adolescence.
    d. All of the above are correct.
12. Humor based on _____ cannot be appreciated until the age of 11 or 12.
    a. conceptual ambiguities
    b. lexical ambiguities
    c. phonological ambiguities
    d. syntactical ambiguities
13. Which of the following is *not* typical of Piaget's morality of constraint stage?
    a. low belief in use of punishments
    b. immanent justice
    c. unchangeable rules
    d. obedience to authority
14. Kohlberg's conventional morality is based on
    a. social approval and duty.
    b. avoiding punishment and receiving rewards.
    c. self-chosen ethical principles.
    d. social contracts.
15. Comparisons of theories of moral development indicate that Kohlberg emphasized _____, while Gilligan emphasized _____.
    a. reasoning; emotions
    b. justice; caring
    c. self-interest; society's needs
    d. social development; cognitive development
16. Which of the following psychologists proposed that intelligence could be divided into fluid and crystallized abilities?
    a. Robert Sternberg
    b. Howard Gardner
    c. Reuven Feuerstein
    d. Raymond Cattell

17. According to Veroff's three-stage developmental theory of achievement, boys are more vulnerable than girls to problems involving
    a. social comparison.
    b. fear of success and fear of failure.
    c. impulsive achievement motivation.
    d. all of the above.

18. Which of the following is *not* one of the five components in Atkinson's expectancy-value theory that influence individual achievement needs?
    a. hope for success
    b. need to avoid failure
    c. fear of success
    d. incentive value of success or failure

19. Benjamin Bloom thought that schools needed to rely more on
    a. student tutoring and rote learning.
    b. mastery learning and student tutoring.
    c. rote and mastery learning.
    d. student tutoring and rote and mastery learning.

20. Which of the following parental behaviors positively influences children's school performance?
    a. reading to one's children
    b. helping with classroom learning activities and interacting with the teacher
    c. taking part in school social activities
    d. all of the above

Answers

1. B [LO-1].	8. D [LO-5].	15. B [LO-10].
2. A [LO-1].	9. B [LO-6].	16. D [LO-11].
3. D [LO-2].	10. C [LO-6].	17. C [LO-12].
4. C [LO-3].	11. B [LO-7].	18. C [LO-13].
5. A [LO-3].	12. D [LO-8].	19. B [LO-14].
6. A [LO-4].	13. A [LO-9].	20. D [LO-15].
7. C [LO-5].	14. A [LO-9].	

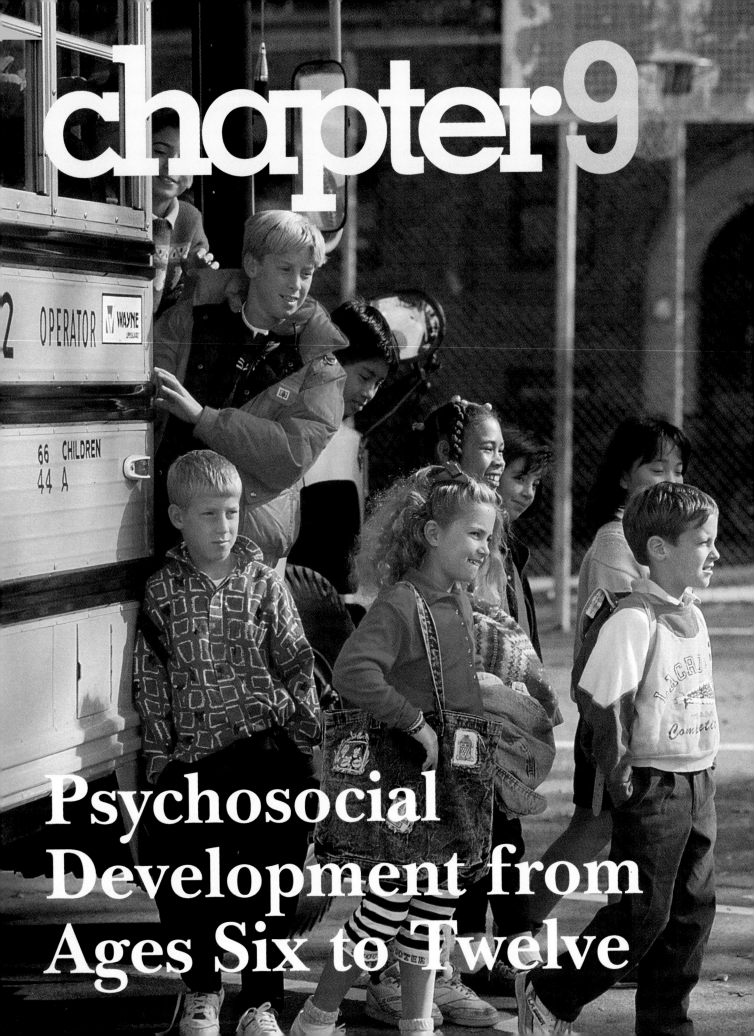

chapter 9

Psychosocial Development from Ages Six to Twelve

Learning Objectives

1. Describe Freud's and Erikson's fourth stages of personality development.
2. Relate Gordon's ideas about parent effectiveness training (PET) to Rogers's self theory.
3. Describe the course of emotional development from ages 6 to 12, including the development of the ability to distinguish apparent from real emotions.
4. Distinguish between the experience of sadness and depression in school-age children.
5. Describe the characteristics, methods of treatment, and probable outcomes for attention-deficit disorder with hyperactivity (ADDH).
6. Explain the various coping strategies resulting from the combination of coping functions, modes, and types of focus.
7. Compare and contrast repressors and sensitizers, and helpless and mastery-oriented children.
8. Discuss the long-term effects of childhood shyness in adulthood and the different patterns of effects for shy males and females.
9. Identify factors associated with resilient children.
10. Describe and contrast five levels of parental acceptance.
11. Define and identify characteristics of dual-career and dual-earner families.
12. Discuss the pros and cons of latchkey kids.
13. Explain the short-term and long-term effects of parental divorce on children.
14. Make recommendations for counteracting the detrimental effects of parental divorce.
15. Distinguish among three types of dysfunctional family triangles.
16. Explain the concept of parentification.
17. Describe the nature of play in later childhood.
18. Identify Piaget's three stages of development in understanding games and the rules of games.
19. Describe the types of friendships that children develop between the ages of 6 and 12.
20. Compare and contrast characteristics of accepted, neglected, and rejected children.

The physical, cognitive, and moral development of school-age children that you learned about in Chapter 8 is accompanied by changes in personality, as well as emotional and social development.

Exploring Your Own Development

Which of the following values would you most want your children to have? Rank them from most important (1) to least important (7).

_____ Social mindedness
_____ Strict obedience
_____ Loyalty to church
_____ Tolerance
_____ Patriotism
_____ Good manners
_____ Independence

In the 1920s, Helen and Robert Lynd asked 141 mothers of Muncie, Indiana, to identify the traits they considered the most important for their children to possess. The top three choices were "loyalty to church," "strict obedience," and "good manners," which all emphasize conformity (Remley, 1988). This study was replicated in the late 1970s by Theodore Caplow, Howard Bahr, and Bruce Chadwick, who found the top-ranking traits to be quite different. Mothers now emphasized "independence" and "tolerance," or qualities linked to autonomy (Remley, 1988).

Surveys by the National Opinion Research Center at the University of Chicago found the same shift between the years 1964 and 1986. Since 1964, fewer parents are emphasizing conformity, obedience to parents, cleanliness, and fitting one's gender role, and more parents are emphasizing autonomy, independence, and having good sense and judgment. Surveys done in Germany, Japan, Italy, and England all reveal the same tendencies (Remley, 1988).

Which values did your parents emphasize? What changes in societies have led to these preference changes? Educational changes, political events, technological complexities, and changes within families have contributed to parents' current value preferences and also influence most aspects of psychosocial development between the ages of 6 and 12.

Personality Development in Middle and Late Childhood

Freud's Latency Stage

Sigmund Freud (1905) placed 6- to 12-year-old children in the fourth of his five psychosexual stages of personality development—the **latency stage.** This stage was not considered as important as the first three stages. According to Freud, during the latency stage, the id is temporarily suppressed, resulting in minimization of sexual and aggressive conflicts (see Appendix A). Therefore, during the 6 years from ages 6 to 12, children are able to concentrate on cognitive development and on building relationships with their peers.

Erikson's Industry Versus Inferiority Stage

Erik Erikson (1963) placed more importance on personality development during the school years than did Freud. According to Erikson, during the years from ages 5 to 12, children are in the fourth psychosocial stage—**industry versus inferiority.** Children who have had healthy resolutions of the first three psychosocial stages are more likely to develop industry.

Erikson theorized that, during this period, the critical conflict for children is whether they experience a sense of accomplishment or whether they feel inferior in task performance. During the school years, play is taken more seriously. Younger children start and switch their play strategies on a whim, but school-age children want to learn the correct way to work on a play project and carry it through to its conclusion. Often, school-age children begin hobbies or start collections to help feel industrious. Participation in such organizations as the Boy Scouts and youth groups can help them to experience mastery.

According to Erikson, children face the critical conflict of industry versus inferiority in every domain in which they participate. In school, children with teachers who help each student experience successes are more likely to resolve this stage positively. At home, children often become very involved in industrious tasks, such as helping with the cooking, mowing the lawn, and washing the car, and take pride in their new accomplishments.

Children get a sense of whether they are gaining mastery by comparing themselves to peers. They brag about being able to roller-skate better than their friends, about being the best readers in the class, and about being able to draw better than others. Brothers and sisters also provide points of comparison, and at times, the heavy sibling rivalry leads to major quarrels. Children who resolve the fourth psychosocial stage in positive ways gain the virtue of competence.

successful study tip

Erikson's Fourth Stage

To remember Erikson's fourth stage, imagine a teeter-totter with industry on one end of the board and inferiority on the other end. Visualize the virtue of competence weighing down the industry side.

Rogers's Self Theory

Carl Rogers (1951, 1961) in his humanistic **self theory** (see Appendix A) added another perspective for understanding children's personality development from ages 6 to 12. Rogers assumed that all people possess an actualizing tendency that directs them to grow in positive ways as long as they are in supportive circumstances.

According to Rogers, all infants begin by trusting themselves and choosing to grow in life. For young children, growth choices are satisfying, bring pleasure, and feel good. However, as shown in Figure 9.1, important people in children's lives often try to get children to pick safety choices over growth choices. Young children know the attractive side of growth choices but overlook and do not understand the dangers involved with risking growth. Adults, especially parents, are aware of potential dangers and get children to pay more attention to safety than growth.

Most children learn to emphasize safety because gaining the approval of others is powerful and seductive. Not only do people give up their growth choices for safety choices, they make other choices based on what other people want them to do. Candice takes boring ballet lessons because her mother thinks she looks adorable in a tutu. Roseanne likes soccer but went out for the baseball team because her father loves baseball. Although John loves to help his mother cook, he hardly ever helps her anymore because his uncle told him that he would become a "momma's boy." With time, original interests, abilities, and goals may be repressed and forgotten. According to Rogers, many children (and adults) should relearn how to take moderate growth risks over safety to have more fulfilling lives.

Rogers also suggested that people have a concept of their real self that is composed of their experiences, awarenesses, and self-expressions. People have another image of their ideal self, the person they would most like to be. Six-year-old Louise can fairly accurately describe herself, but when she is thinking about her ideal self, Louise becomes a combination of a beautiful Snow White and a brilliant doctor. As Louise gets older, her real self may be a good student, while her ideal self is a very good student.

According to Rogers and other humanists, self-concepts improve by setting a positive environment. In such an environment, positive feedback to children allows them to drop self-concealing roles, aids in decision making, encourages living for one's own goals rather than someone else's, and results in people feeling self-fulfillment. As shown in Figure 9.2, supportive comments to children allow them to view themselves positively. As a result, they are more trusting and open to new experiences, more accepting of others, better able to set and achieve realistic goals, and not threatened by accurate assessments of themselves (Jensen & Kingston, 1986).

Gordon's Parent Effectiveness Training

One way to achieve a more positive environment for the development of healthy self-concepts in school-age children is to use techniques from Thomas Gordon's (1980)

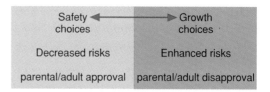

Figure 9.1

The basic human dilemma of safety and growth.

Adapted from: Maslow, A. H. 1968. *Toward a psychology of being.* 2nd ed. NY: D. Van Nostrand Co. p. 47.

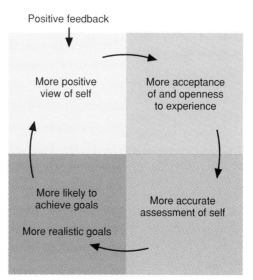

Figure 9.2

The self-concept circle.

Source: Data from L. D. Jensen and M. Kingston, *Parenting,* Fig. 4.1, p. 106, 1986, Holt, Rinehart and Winston.

parent effectiveness training (PET) program. PET, based on the ideas of Rogers and humanistic psychologists, begins with the assumption that parents are human and therefore will make some parenting mistakes. Parents must extend this assumption to children—children are going to make mistakes, too. However, children will do best when parents are accepting of most of the children's behaviors. Some unruly and deliberate behaviors are unacceptable and need to be eliminated; Janet's parents, for example, did not need to be accepting of her drawing ink pictures on the living room wall. But other behaviors are normal errors; Bobby did not wet his bed on purpose, and Betty was trying to be helpful when she broke a dish she was drying.

According to Gordon, parents need to be as consistent as possible in their expectations. Harry was very confused when he was expected to have good table manners at Grandma's house but no one seemed to care if he had good table manners at home.

Gordon also suggested that parents be genuine with their children. Children not only hear what their parents tell them to do, they also see how parents conduct their own lives. Lorraine's parents continually tell her that she better not use drugs when she gets older, yet her father has a double martini each night when he gets home from work and her mother has had a prescription for tranquilizers for several years now.

According to Gordon, effective parents need to do more than provide a supportive environment. They also need to actively listen, share feelings, use "I" messages, and negotiate. Active listening, paying close attention to what children say with a nonjudgmental attitude of acceptance, is important because it allows children to feel that their verbal messages are important to their parents. Unlike warnings, criticisms, advisements, and judgments, active listening is done *with* the child not *to* the child. Active listening helps children to think about their problems and to develop possible solutions.

Sharing feelings allows children to learn more about the impact they have on other people. Many families yell their emotions or moralize about their feelings. Family members do better when they express their emotions and listen to others' emotions. Gordon suggested that "I" messages are better than "You" messages for sharing feelings. Which is easier to pay attention to: "You are climbing this tree just to give me a heart attack. Why are you doing this to me?" or "I worry so much when you climb so high in that tree. I would prefer that you not go beyond the second branch." Parents should also use "I" messages to express positive statements, such as "I'm so glad to see how nice your bedroom looks."

Gordon proposed that parents can negotiate conflict situations with their children with a six-step "no-lose" method: (1) identify and define the conflict, (2) generate possible solutions without judging their quality, (3) evaluate the alternative solutions, (4) choose the most acceptable solution, (5) figure out how to implement the solution, and (6) evaluate the solution.

---

guided review

1. Freud's fourth psychosexual stage is the _____ stage, a less important stage in which the _____ is temporarily suppressed.
2. In Erikson's fourth psychosocial stage, _____ versus _____, children who positively resolve this stage acquire the virtue of _____.
3. According to Rogers, parents and other adults often overencourage children to make _____ choices when learning to make moderate _____ choices would lead to more fulfilling lives.
4. Gordon believes that _____ parents provide _____ environments, practice _____ listening, share their feelings, and use _____ messages.

answers

1. latency; id [LO-1]. 2. industry; inferiority; competence [LO-1]. 3. safety; growth [LO-2]. 4. effective; supportive; active; "I" [LO-2].

Emotional Development and Disturbances in Middle and Late Childhood

Patterns of Emotional Development From Ages 6 to 12

Knowledge About Emotions

During the school years, children become more aware of and more accurate in expressing their own emotions, better understand the meaning of others' emotional displays, and learn how to judge others' emotions. As ability in this area grows, children become more adept at displaying "proper" emotions in social settings and in telling effective "little white lies." Their growth in emotional knowledge also allows them to better empathize with others and to respond more appropriately to others' needs.

In a study of English and Dutch children, researchers found that knowing which emotions are triggered by various situations improves from age 5 into the early adolescent years. Five-year-olds can fairly accurately describe specific situations for the emotions that have distinct facial displays—afraid, happy, sad, and angry. By age 7, most children exhibit some accuracy even for emotions without distinctive facial or behavioral display, such as pride, jealousy, gratefulness, worry, guilt, and excitement. A second study of children in an isolated Himalayan village produced similar results, suggesting that all children first learn about the basic emotions and then learn each additional emotion, not gradually over time, but abruptly, in an all-or-none fashion (Harris, Olthof, Terwogt, & Hardman, 1987).

Another way to test children's knowledge about emotions is to provide them with a situation and have them infer the cause of an emotion displayed in that situation. Nine-year-olds were asked to infer from a teacher's emotion toward a failing student the reason for the student's failure. When the teacher was angry or surprised, the subjects thought that the student had not put much effort into schoolwork. When the teacher expressed guilt feelings, they attributed the student's failure to poor teaching. When the teacher felt pity, the subjects thought that the student failed because of low ability (Weiner, Graham, Stern, & Lawson, 1982). However, 5-year-olds did not make the connection between pity and low ability, although they were able to attribute a teacher's anger to lack of effort on the failing student's part. Evidently, pity is not paired with ability level until middle childhood, perhaps because the children do not yet understand that low ability is a fairly stable cause for failure (Weiner et al., 1982).

Accuracy in judging complex, socially oriented emotions improves greatly during the school years. Children from ages 5 to 11 were asked to report events that made them feel proud and that made them feel embarrassed. All ages understood that pride was determined mainly by their own behavior and characteristics. The youngest subjects had a less firm grasp of their own role in embarrassment.

Children may experience sadness and depression for many reasons, such as viewing their abilities and appearance as inferior to their schoolmates.

All age groups seemed to realize that the presence of other people contributed to feelings of embarrassment and pride (Seidner, Stipek, & Fesbach, 1988). Like other emotions, accurate knowledge about embarrassment and pride is fine-tuned over the years.

Real Versus Apparent Emotions

Some emotions are really experienced, and others are apparent emotions—emotions that people display toward others. School-age children understand the differences between real and apparent emotions (Harris, Donnelly, Guz, & Pitt-Watson, 1986). About half can relate strategies for hiding feelings by outwardly displaying a change in facial, verbal, or behavioral expression (Carroll & Steward, 1984; Harris, Olthof, & Terwogt, 1981). One study compared 1st- through 10th-graders on their understanding of emotion display rules (Gnepp & Hess, 1986). Understanding improved from 1st through 5th grade, and improved only a little from 5th through 10th grade.

School-age children understand how to adjust verbal aspects of emotions more than how to adjust facial aspects when they wish to publicly portray an emotion that is different than what is truly felt. Children may have better understanding of verbal display rules because parents emphasize regulating their children's speech more than they do facial appearance. Also, more subtle skills may be required to successfully regulate facial characteristics than to regulate words and tone.

Depression in Childhood

Sadness

The root of depression is sadness. Children and adults feel sad when they think about "losses." Some losses involve material goods, such as Lyla losing her lunch money. Others concern interpersonal losses, such as Cynthia's loss of a friendship after fighting with Sharon on the playground. A third type of loss is not getting something that one expected. Joanne may feel sad on Christmas morning, even if she received wonderful gifts, because she expected more. Losses may even involve pending future losses—Tommy knows that his best friend is moving away next summer and often feels that loss now, even though the actual loss is still months away. Other losses are hypothetical: Joyce worries that her report card will have lower grades, even though her grades are really as good as ever.

Losses involving lowered self-respect, self-worth, and self-confidence are especially likely to lead to the experience of sadness. Self-deprecating remarks increase during the school years, as children become more aware of personal shortcomings and are in situations in which they feel evaluated and compared to others. Seven-year-olds experience more self-deprecatory sadness than 5-year-olds, with the younger children viewing themselves more positively, not perceiving sadness as part of their emotional disposition, and denying sad experiences (Glasberg & Aboud, 1982).

As children age, they change their ideas about what causes their sadness. Young children are more likely to attribute their sadness to other family members than are 7- to 9-year-olds. Children older than 9 are even less likely to believe that family members caused their sadness. As children get older, they increasingly attribute sadness to themselves, rather than to family members (Covell & Abramovitch, 1987). As shown in Figure 9.3, this attributional change also occurs with other emotions, such as happiness and anger.

Depression

Depressed children have the same symptoms as depressed adults. Polly is a seriously depressed 10-year-old, who is often sad and angry with a strong tendency to direct her hostility toward herself. Polly explains negative events as resulting from her own shortcomings and ineptness. Her negative self-image is long-lasting, and she sees herself as a failure in many areas (Blumberg & Izard, 1985).

Although adults often remember childhood as a wonderful time of innocence and joy, childhood also can be filled with unpleasant experiences and feelings. Children may experience high levels of depression due to experiencing parental divorce, living in a dysfunctional family, or being abused. Children may also get depressed about school situations and friendship problems.

Young children can get depressed, but depression increases with age because children become more aware of how they are evaluated by others. Depression especially increases from the age of 11 on, as children enter Piaget's last

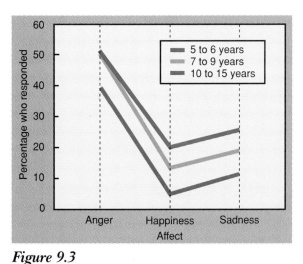

Figure 9.3

Children's attributions of their own anger, happiness, and sadness to their families.

Source: Data from K. Covell and R. Abramovitch, "Understanding Emotion in the Family: Children's and Parent's Attributions of Happiness, Sadness, and Anger" in *Child Development*, 58, 985–991, 1987.

stage of cognitive development and become capable of abstract thinking, including "if-then-therefore" thinking. An 11-year-old whose mother has died of cancer may engage in such depressing thoughts as, "IF only I had been kinder to my mother, THEN she wouldn't have suffered so much; THEREFORE, I am a terrible person." Children are as likely as adults to be unrealistic in their thinking—expecting perfection from themselves, overjudging people's critical remarks, and overestimating the impact they could have had.

Because children may worry and become depressed about different things than adults, they sometimes find that their sad thoughts are not taken seriously by their parents, teachers, and other adults. Children who try to share their concerns are often told that they are worrying about trivial things or that they are sad about something they should be able to handle easily. Such dismissals only add to the depressed feelings. When sad, depressive thoughts include a sense of hopelessness, children may begin to think of suicide as a solution to their despair.

Suicidal Feelings

Although young children sometimes kill themselves, the big increase in suicide attempts comes around the age of 11 (Kienhorst, Wolters, Diekstra, & Otte, 1987). Around this age, children experience increased cognitive abilities that can lead to more depression and also are faced with the ambivalent world of the preadolescent, family pressures, and academic competition. Most children who try to kill themselves have had many stressful events in their childhood and live in problematic environments (Kienhorst et al., 1987; Spencer, 1979).

Suicidal children often witness or personally experience domestic violence, have suicidal family members, and have experienced personal failures. They are often unrealistic about suicide because they do not understand the finality of death. These children may focus on killing themselves to

make a parent or a friend feel bad and may even fantasize about being at their own funeral to view with satisfaction survivors' grief and guilt. In contrast to suicide attempts by older individuals, children's suicide attempts often involve hideous, painful methods, such as stabbing themselves in the chest with scissors, repeatedly smashing their heads against a wall, or mutilating their genitals (Spencer, 1979).

Suicidal thoughts in children should be taken seriously, and depressed children should receive help from capable adults, such as a school counselor or a therapist. Children can be helped to feel better about themselves, to think more realistically and more kindly about their own abilities and opportunities, and to learn skills that bring about more successes at home and at school.

Hyperactivity and Acting-Out Behavior

Hyperactivity

Children with attention-deficit disorder with hyperactivity (ADDH) are excessively active, although not all very active children are hyperactive. Hyperactive children also have symptoms in the areas of inattentiveness, impulsivity, and overactivity (American Psychiatric Association, 1980).

Charlie was diagnosed when his first-grade teacher noticed that Charlie fidgeted almost constantly, had trouble sitting still, often got up and wandered around the classroom, and required more supervision than other students. Charlie was easily distracted from classroom activities, was unable to wait for his turn to speak in class, could not organize his work well, and usually did not finish school projects. He was also quite impulsive and tended to act before thinking.

Charlie's parents were a little surprised that he was hyperactive. Although they saw Charlie as "always on the go" and knew that he did not even settle down while sleeping, they had not witnessed the behavioral problems that his teacher discussed with them. Charlie's teacher told his parents that hyperactive behavior is more common and more noticeable in school than at home because classrooms require stricter conduct, more sustained attention, and frequent and varied interactions in group settings, requirements that are hard for hyperactive children.

Like many experts, Charlie's teacher was unsure whether Charlie's aggressive behaviors and general disobedience were a part of his hyperactivity or whether the misbehavior was caused by social difficulties resulting from the hyperactivity. Nor could a specialist pinpoint the cause of Charlie's hyperactivity. Experts have proposed a variety of causes: prenatal influences (e.g., premature birth, anoxia), genetics, food allergies, hormones, and environmental factors.

Regardless of cause, Charlie's teacher, the specialist, and his parents are working out procedures that will help Charlie to reduce his hyperactive behaviors. They are experimenting with Charlie's diet, utilizing behavior modification training, and considering using stimulant drugs. Although adults usually become more behaviorally active

Children who misbehave often at school are often labeled obnoxious, stubborn, hurtful, or inferior. Still, misbehavior may allow children to reach their goals of attention, power, revenge, and assuming inferiority.

Table 9.1
Basic Goals of Misbehavior

Goal	Parent's Reaction	Inappropriate Parental Reaction
Attention	Annoyance	Reprimanding or Coaxing
Power	Anger	Giving in or Exerting Own Power
Revenge	Hurt	Trying to Get Even
Assuming Inadequacy	Despair	Punishment, Ignoring

From L. C. Jensen and M. Kingston, *Parenting*, Table 9.1, p. 231, 1986. Reprinted by permission of Larry C. Jensen.

with stimulants, hyperactive children are slowed down and calmed with these drugs. Charlie may be given Ritalin (methylphenidate hydrochloride)—one of the most commonly used stimulants with hyperactive children—to reduce his disruptive behaviors and to improve his attentiveness. Fortunately, Charlie will probably outgrow his hyperactivity during adolescence. Because he is receiving treatment now, by the time Charlie outgrows hyperactivity, he will have a minimum of negative long-term effects (Fine, 1980).

Acting-Out Behaviors

Usually, acting-out behaviors are not due to a physical condition, such as hyperactivity. Acting out can be the result of poor parenting techniques, such as rewarding temper tantrums, loud behavior, and showing off with parental attention or concrete rewards. Other acting-out behaviors result from children acting out crises and stressful situations in their lives. For example, many parents who are experiencing marital conflict find that their children respond to the tension by increasing their inappropriate and disruptive behaviors.

Children who do not have their needs met when they are well behaved and well adjusted often use misbehavior to reach their goals. Misbehavior can help children to reach four different goals: attention, power, revenge, and assuming inadequacy (Dreikurs, 1972). These basic goals, typical parental reactions, and inappropriate parenting responses are summarized in Table 9.1. Children who fre-

quently use attention-seeking misbehaviors often are labeled obnoxious, annoying, charming, or lazy, depending on their style of attention seeking. Children using the power goal are likely to be labeled as rebellious or stubborn. Children using the goal of revenge to misbehave are seen as vengeful, hurtful, and teasing. Children often begin with one or more of these styles. If they still fail to feel a sense of belonging and importance, they may become helpless and assume inadequacy, and consequently are labeled losers, loners, and hopeless (Dreikurs, 1972; Jensen & Kingston, 1986).

Childhood Aggression

Aggressive behaviors increase when children see other children and adults engaging in aggression, especially when these aggressive models are rewarded for their actions. Children who are rewarded for aggression are likely to be more aggressive in the future. Horace acts aggressive because his father is proud that his son can win fights and because Horace likes the money that kids give him so he won't beat them up.

Children who are more aggressive than their peers believe that enacting aggressive responses is relatively easy compared to inhibiting contemplated aggression. These aggression-prone children are also likely to believe that aggression produces desirable results. Boys are less likely than girls to express concern about the suffering of victims or about possible punishment (Perry, Perry, and Rasmussen, 1986).

Fortunately, children can be taught skills that reduce their aggressive acts. In one study, second- and third-graders were taught assertiveness social-skills over six hour-long sessions (Tanner & Holliman, 1988). The treatment successfully reduced physical aggression during transportation and play, increased cooperation during play periods, and improved general classroom behavior. Unfortunately, many ill-tempered, hostile children are not in programs that help them to gain control over their aggressive behaviors. Researchers who did a follow-up study from data collected in the Berkeley Guidance Study in the early 1950s found that ill-tempered school-age children (children who "move against the world") typically persist in this pattern into their 30s (Caspi, Elder, & Bem, 1987).

Childhood Stress

Coping Strategies

Coping is making effortful or purposeful responses to stress in order to manage external and internal demands that individuals view as taxing. Even 6-year-olds are aware of their stress and coping responses and can report on events that are stressful (Band & Weisz, 1988). They are able to generate alternative solutions to stressful social settings, but until they are 8 to 10 years old, cannot articulate each step of their solutions (Compas, 1987).

Children can use either primary coping or secondary coping to combat stress. In primary coping, children try to directly influence conditions or events. In secondary coping, children try to make self-adjustments to better fit the situation. Most 6-year-olds do more primary coping than secondary coping. Secondary coping increases with age, although primary coping remains predominant in familiar situations. Secondary coping probably develops more slowly than primary coping because it requires higher cognitive skills (concrete operations) and because use of secondary coping is more hidden from view and therefore harder to learn from others (Band & Weisz, 1988).

During the school years, individuals learn a variety of coping strategies. The two major coping functions involve problem solving and regulating emotions (Lazarus & Folkman, 1984). How do you usually cope with stress—do you find a solution, or do you manage your emotional reactions? Children learn one preference over the other.

Each coping function can have one of three focuses: Individuals can focus their attention on (1) the self (e.g., "I am not a failure"), (2) the environment (e.g., "The spelling test won't really be that bad"), or (3) other people ("Perhaps my mom can help me with this one") (Wertlieb, Weigel, & Feldstein, 1987).

In addition, with each coping function and focus, there are five modes with which to work: (1) Information seeking is trying to increase knowledge about the stressful situation; (2) support seeking involves trying to elicit the assistance of others; (3) direct action refers to directly acting on the stressful situation; (4) inhibition of action is coping by preventing or containing the limiting behavior or impulses; and (5) intrapsychic mode involves cognitive processes used to regulate emotions (Wertlieb et al., 1987). The 30 possible coping strategies resulting from choice of function, focus, and mode are summarized in Figure 9.4.

Ted, Bart, and Daniel use different coping strategies when they are chosen last for the school's baseball game. Ted uses coping strategy IA-IIA-IIIC when he decides to practice his batting skills so that he will be chosen earlier in the future. Bart uses IB-IIA-IIID when he tells himself that he really did not want to play baseball anyway. Daniel uses strategy IA-IIB-IIIC when he stays inside during recess, rather than be chosen last.

In a study of 187 school-age children, all 30 coping strategies were used, but the most prevalent strategies were those with a problem-solving function, a focus on the self, and a direct-action mode. Older school-age children used more intrapsychic coping than did younger children; support-seeking and inhibition-of-action modes also increased with age. Girls reported a greater relative proportion of environment-focused coping; boys used more self-focused coping. For girls, self-focused coping was used more with emotion regulation, and environmental focus was used more with problem solving (Wertlieb et al., 1987).

Repressors and Sensitizers

One personality style that influences how individuals cope is the dimension of **repression-sensitization** (Byrne, 1964; Krohne & Rogner, 1982). Children and adults in the middle of this continuum adapt better than individuals at either extreme (see Figure 9.5). Repressors are individuals who tend to neglect or avoid information in threatening situations; sensitizers are individuals who focus their attention on situational cues that indicate possible danger. Are you a repressor or a sensitizer?

Sensitizers use coping styles called "monitoring"—strategies that alert them to potentially negative aspects of an experience. Repressors use coping styles called "blunting," which allow them to distract themselves from sources of danger (Miller & Green, 1984).

Coping and Mastery

In achievement settings, some children are "helpless," and some are "mastery-oriented." **Helpless children** have high levels of discouragement, low levels of effort, and deteriorating performance over time. When they experience failure, they blame their lack of ability, yet they do not often attribute successes to their ability. **Mastery-oriented children** display sustained levels of high motivation, exhibit good concentration, and persist in problem-solving attempts. They usually credit successes to their ability level, and they attribute failures to insufficient effort and try to find alternative solutions (Compas, 1987).

Mastery-oriented children are likely to have an internal locus of control in most settings. That is, they believe that they control their own destiny, make their own decisions, and influence the reinforcements in their own lives. Helpless children are likely to have an external locus of control and to believe that reinforcements are not under personal control. For them, situational outcomes are due to luck, chance, fate, or the actions of other people (Swick & Graves, 1986).

Children with a strong internal locus of control orientation are likely to have parents who are strong, warm, reliable, and affectionate. These children frequently experience their ability to control circumstances in their lives (Swick & Graves, 1986). Throughout the school years, children learn mastery in many areas, from making friends to learning to read; thus, it is not surprising that, from ages 8 to 12, most children become more internal, as shown in Figure 9.6 (Sherman, 1984). However, 13-year-olds are more external than internal; perhaps, children entering adolescence feel less self-control than children in the more predictable school years.

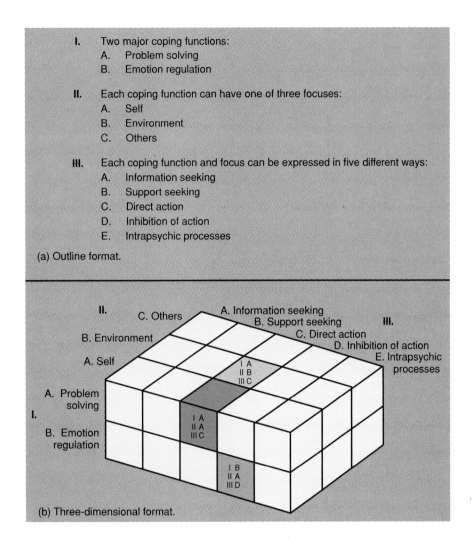

Figure 9.4

Thirty coping choices. (a) Outline format. (b) Three-dimensional format. The combination of two major coping functions (IA and IB) with three focuses (IIA, IIB, and IIC) and five ways of expression (IIIA, IIIB, IIIC, IIID, and IIIE) yields 30 different coping choices, as illustrated by this 2 by 3 by 5 matrix. A school-age child faced with the situation of not being chosen for a team at recess could choose to cope in several ways:

1. Improve his or her skills (cube IA-IIA-IIIC)
2. Tell self that he or she didn't want to play (cube IB-IIA-IIID)
3. Stay inside at recess (cube IA-IIB-IIIC)

Adapted from: Wertlieb, D., Weigel, C., & Feldstein, M. 1987. Measuring children's coping. *American Journal of Orthopsychiatry, 57,* 548–560.

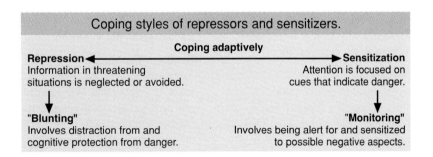

Figure 9.5

Coping styles of repressors and sensitizers.

Source: Adapted from B. E. Compas, "Coping with Stress During Childhood and Adolescence" in *Psychological Bulletin,* 101:393–403, 1987. American Psychological Association.

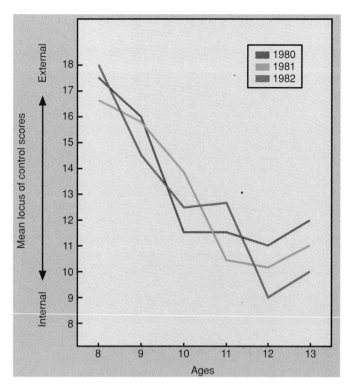

Figure 9.6

Mean locus of control scores by chronological age groups.

Source: Fig. 1 (p. 346) from Sherman, L. W. 1984. Development of children's perceptions of internal locus of control: A cross-sectional and longitudinal analysis. *Journal of Personality, 52,* 338–354.

Children with external locus of control have poorer academic skills and more social adjustment problems; individuals who do not believe that their own efforts "pay off" often remain deficient in important skills. High internal locus of control beliefs are associated with being more task-oriented, achievement-oriented, and goal-oriented. Internal individuals act independently of others and resist manipulation by analyzing the components of a situation. Compared to external peers, they are more able to delay gratification (Swick & Graves, 1986).

Vulnerable and Resilient Children

Some children cope better than others under similar circumstances. What factors predispose children to be vulnerable to stress, and what factors help others to become **resilient children** and to survive tough circumstances?

Shyness: One Type of Vulnerability

Shyness, the tendency to "move away from the world," is a type of vulnerability. Shy children are less friendly and social and are more reserved, somber, and withdrawn. They underestimate their performance and exaggerate evidence of poor achievement.

Although most children are shy initially in novel situations and many go through a shy phase during part of their childhood, some children exhibit persistent and strong shyness. As shy children avoid peers, adults, and social settings, they become deficient in age-appropriate social skills and knowledge. These deficiencies make it increasingly difficult to take the initiative to overcome shyness. There-

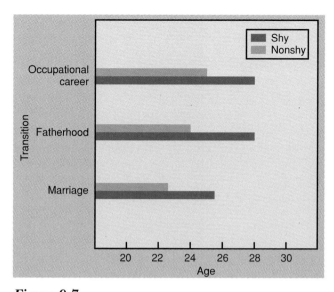

Figure 9.7

Timing of life transitions in males as a function of shyness in late childhood.

Source: Fig. 1 from Caspi, A., Elder, Jr., G. H., & Bem, D. J. 1988. Moving away from the world: Life-course patterns of shy children. *Developmental Psychology, 24,* 824–831.

fore, intense shyness during the school years may alter a person's life course. Shyness during late childhood does indeed affect marriage, parenthood, and career patterns (Caspi, Elder, & Bem, 1988).

Figure 9.7 illustrates how shyness in males alters the timing of life transitions in the young adult years. Boys who are reluctant to enter social settings are likely to become men who are reluctant to become involved in the social settings that lead to marriage, fatherhood, and career stability and achievement. While shy men do experience successes in these areas, they are "off-time" in their transitions.

Girls who are shy in late childhood exhibit a different adult pattern. Shy females do not delay the start of married life or parenthood, but their career patterns, compared to nonshy females, are altered. More shy females become traditional homemakers and are highly feminine. In one study, over half of the shy females had no work history or terminated employment at marriage or first childbirth; about a third of the nonshy females had this abbreviated career pattern (Caspi et al., 1988).

Resilient Children

Protective factors are those aspects of personality, environment, or events that help children to be resilient when they are in psychologically unhealthy situations. Three broad factors characterize invulnerable or resilient children: (1) resilient children have strong temperaments, high self-esteem, internal locus of control, and high autonomy drive; (2) resilient children have supportive family environments, characterized by parental warmth, closeness, cohesiveness, and order; and (3) resilient children have individuals or agencies that provide support systems, coping skills, and positive role models. The more of these characteristics that are present, the more children are able to cope with difficult circumstances.

5. School-age children understand the difference between _____ emotions (emotions that people display toward others) and _____ emotions (the actual emotions that people experience).
6. True or false: As children become older, they increasingly attribute the causes of their sadness and other emotional states to themselves, rather than to family members.
7. _____ is making effortful or purposeful responses to stress in order to manage demands that are placed on the individual.
8. _____ children tend to have an _____ locus of control, believing that they are in control of what happens to them, while _____ children tend to have an _____ locus of control, believing that they are at the mercy of others' actions and the forces of luck and fate.
9. _____ children have high self-esteem, supportive families, and positive role models.

answers

5. apparent; real [LO-3]. 6. True [LO-4]. 7. Coping [LO-6]. 8. Mastery-oriented; internal; helpless; external [LO-7]. 9. Resilient [LO-9].

Parenting and the Family

Family Patterns

Expectant parents often overestimate the effects that they will have on their offspring. Children are not permanently marked by every action their parents take, and they often turn out quite differently than the parents themselves. In fact, all children develop some characteristics and talents that seem untraceable to their parents or to their parents' behaviors. Letty Cottin Pogrebin (1988) expressed this aspect well:

> This is about not taking credit for one's children. This is about acknowledging that your child, biological or adopted, is a Separate Person, whose development in many areas may have nothing to do with you. Regardless of nature and nurture, regardless of the long line of athletes, artists, or preachers in your family, regardless of years of loving exposure to your politics, your music, or your work, your children are likely to break out in unidentifiable talents all their own. (p. 94)

Sooner or later, parents realize that their children's outcomes are not totally under the parent's control.

Parenting Styles

On the other hand, parenting style does affect a child's adult personality. A recent longitudinal study by Eric Dubow followed nearly 400 people from the age of 8 to the age of 30 and explored the long-term effects of the authoritarian, authoritative, and permissive/laissez-faire parenting styles. The 30-year-olds who had supportive, accepting parents were more self-aware and gave themselves construc-

tive criticism, formulated long-term goals, and cherished interpersonal relationships. The 30-year-olds who had critical, harsh, authoritarian parents were more likely to be self-absorbed adults with higher levels of impulsiveness, violence and substance abuse. Boys who had high levels of nonaggressiveness and girls who had high levels of altruism and sharing behaviors became the most self-reliant adults (Dubow, Huesmann, & Eron, 1987).

Parental Acceptance

Parental acceptance—the parent's responsiveness to the child's needs—also predicts children's behaviors. Table 9.2 defines five levels of parental acceptance: (1) enemies hurting, (2) opponents contending, (3) business partners bargaining, (4) allies facilitating, and (5) companions harmonizing. In a study of 24 first- and second-graders and their mothers and the effects of maternal acceptance, the higher the level of maternal acceptance, the better the adaptation to and performance in school and the fewer the externalized problem behaviors (Rothbaum, 1988). Children who feel valued and accepted by parents can transfer that strong foundation to the school environment.

Androgynous Parents

One recent change in parenting has been an increase in **androgynous parents,** parents who do not rigidly adhere to traditional mother and father roles. While androgynous adults are more personally competent, internally directed, and higher in self-esteem, they do not possess more parenting skills than gender-typed parents. Androgynous parents are neither authoritarian nor authoritative; they tend to be **child-centered parents.** Child-centered parents are responsive to their children but less demanding than authoritative parents (Baumrind, 1982).

Family Members

The families of school-age children vary in number of siblings, age of parents, presence of parents, and styles of interactions—so many variables, in fact, that everyone grows up in a unique environment. In the sections that follow, three types of family situations are featured: dual-career families, families that experience a divorce, and dysfunctional families.

Working Parents

Dual-Career Families

Which is the more typical family: The Smiths, who have two children, a mother who is a full-time homemaker, and a father who is the single income provider; or the Joneses, who have two children, and both the mother and father have careers. The Joneses are the more common pattern these days, and this trend is expected to grow (Sekaron, 1986).

Some researchers distinguish between dual-career families and dual-earner families. In dual-earner families, both husband and wife work for pay, but their jobs do not require much personal commitment or updating of professional knowledge. In dual-career families, both husband and wife are personally committed to careers that require current, professional knowledge. In a minority of families,

Table 9.2
Five Levels of Parental Acceptance

Note: Levels of parental acceptance measure the parent's responsiveness to the child's needs. All examples involve a situation in which child and mother have been asked to draw a picture of something they do together and are now discussing what they will draw.

Level 1: Enemies Hurting

Definition: Parent's behavior involves gross neglect or abuse of the child's needs.

Example: When the experimenter leaves the room, mother turns to child and asks in annoyed tone, "So, what do *you* want to do? You don't like the Cub Scout deal, huh? Or the movies? . . . Well?" Child responds defensively that it would be a lot of drawing. She challenges him, "What do you mean, 'that would be a lot of drawing?'" Child turns away in frustration, and parent says with disgust, "So what do *you* want to do if you think my ideas are so lousy?"

Level 2: Opponents Contending

Definition: Parent adopts negative or cold behavior, with the assumption that one party will win and have its needs met and the other party will lose.

Example: When the experimenter leaves the room, child turns to mother expectantly, but mother does not look at child. Child then asks, "What do we draw?" Mother throws question back to child in disengaged manner: "What do you want to do?" He suggests, hopefully, "We could draw a picture of Atari," and laughs nervously. She does not respond or return his laugh; he then adds, "No, let's do something else, O.K.?" Mother does not respond immediately, then says, "I don't care."

Level 3: Business Partners Bargaining

Definition: Parent partially meets child's needs in exchange for child's willingness to meet parent's needs, and there is a sense that both parties' needs can be partially met, but there is tension along the way.

Example: As soon as the experimenter leaves the room, mother looks at child and asks, "What do we want to do in the drawing?" Child responds, "We could . . . ," and shows her his idea by tracing it on the paper with his finger. She watches him, pauses briefly, "Hmm . . . ," then changes tack and says with excitement: "Know what I was thinking? . . . . You decide because it doesn't matter to me . . . but I was thinking about the time we went sledding."

Level 4: Allies Facilitating

Definition: Parent helps child in developing behaviors that he or she can eventually use to meet his or her needs effectively, but there is no fluid integration of parent and child needs.

Example: When the experimenter leaves the room, mother turns to child and asks, "What should we draw? . . . . What do we do together?" Child offers, "Bowl." She repeats, "Bowl. We haven't done that in a while! . . . . Yeah, we could do that," and she smiles at child.

Level 5: Companions Harmonizing

Definition: Parent and child work together in meeting needs, with their major concern being the strengthening of their relationship.

Example: When the experimenter leaves the room, child looks as if he is thinking hard. Mother watches him intently and sprinkles several comments into the silence: "What do you think is best to draw? (pause) We were talking about some things on the way over." Child mentions going bowling. Mother responds in a positive tone, "Bowling, yes," and waits for child to continue. "Going to eat." She agrees, "Going out to eat, yeah, we enjoy doing that. (pause) And remember you mentioned summer nights . . ." Child responds: "Go out for a walk." Parent smiles and again validates his idea by repeating it warmly and enthusiastically.

Reprinted from "Maternal Acceptance and Child Functioning" in *Merrill-Palmer Quarterly,* 34, 163–184, 1988 by Fred Rothbaum by permission of Wayne State University Press and the author. Copyright © 1988 Wayne State University Press.

the husband and wife are coordinated couples, who work in allied occupations, or complementary couples, who specialize in different areas that complement each other, such as an industrial psychologist and a statistician (Sekaron, 1986).

The major rewards of dual-career families are that both husband and wife (1) have careers, allowing self-expression and a sense of accomplishment; (2) experience increased collegiality; and (3) feel competent. However, dual-career families have additional stresses over the more traditional single-earner family: The husband and wife may suffer from role overload and identity dilemmas (e.g., women who try to be "Supermoms" are often physically and mentally exhausted). They also may have more difficulty in deciding when to have children, in keeping their careers steadily advancing, and in handling two sets of social networks (Sekaron, 1986).

In dual-career families, one usually unavoidable question is what to do with the children when the parents are at work. Young children are cared for by family members, baby-sitters, nannies, or day-care centers. As children get older, they are often in self-care arrangements and are known as latchkey kids.

Latchkey Kids

In the United States, over 2 million school-age children are latchkey kids, children who take care of themselves after school. Ninety percent are at least 9 years old, and most of them are from well-educated, middle-to-upper-class families (Chollar, 1987). Approximately 15 percent of self-care children spend some time alone in the morning, 76 percent are alone in the afternoons after school, and only 9 percent are alone after 6 P.M. (Cole & Rodman, 1987). On average, school-age children are alone for less than 2 hr per day (Chollar, 1987; Landers, 1988).

Dual-career couples with small children must make childcare arrangements. Diverse solutions include relative to non-relative care in the couple's home, child care in a home-setting, large day-care setting, and child care at the workplace.

In appropriate settings, latchkey children do not seem to suffer many negative results—at worst, some studies have found that unsupervised youngsters become scared or use the television set for companionship (Galambos & Garbarino, 1983; Long & Long, 1982). Self-care children and children who have a parent available when they get home from school are similar on self-esteem, locus of control, and teachers' ratings of social adjustment (Cole & Rodman, 1987).

In fact, several studies have found some positive aspects to self-care. Self-care children take on early responsibilities, become more independent and self-reliant, and are more resourceful than peers who are constantly supervised. Latchkey kids also hold fewer gender-role stereotypes than children with a traditional mother at home. Self-care children rank higher than their peers in knowledge and ability to take care of themselves (Robinson, Rowland, & Coleman, 1986).

Some parents, however, leave fairly young children to take care of themselves. At least 230,000 children younger than age 8 are left alone or with someone younger than 13 for several hours a day (Landers, 1988). Children should be at least 8 before staying home alone (Cole & Rodman, 1987). Even then, not all 8-year-olds are capable of adequate self-care. Table 9.3 provides guidelines for assessing whether a child is ready for self-care responsibilities.

Most parents use self-care well. Fewer than 2 percent of 5-year-olds are placed in self-care settings, while nearly 16 percent of 13-year-olds are in self-care situations (Lan-

Table 9.3
Assessing Individual Readiness for Self-Care

The following guidelines represent minimum standards for evaluating whether children are ready for self-care:

Physical

1. The child is capable of controlling his or her body adequately so that injury is unlikely while moving around the house.
2. The child is able to manipulate locks and doors so that he or she is not locked in or out of the house.
3. The child can and does operate accessible household equipment safely. The child can safely operate such items as the stove, blender, microwave oven, and vacuum cleaner.

Emotional

1. The child can comfortably tolerate separations from adults without much loneliness or fear.
2. The child does not exhibit many withdrawn, hostile, or self-destructive behaviors.
3. The child is capable of handling both usual and unexpected situations well without excessive fear or distress.
4. The child can and does follow important rules well.

Cognitive

1. The child is able to understand and remember both oral and written instructions.
2. The child exhibits good, logical, problem-solving skills.
3. The child can read and write well enough to take telephone messages.

Social

1. The child knows how to solicit help from friends and neighbors when appropriate.
2. The child understands the functions of police, fire fighters, rescue squads, and other community resources and is willing to call on them when appropriate.
3. The child should be able to maintain friendships with children and adults.

Parental Responsibilities in Self-Care

1. Parents will maintain communication and supervision of their children even when they are not physically present.
2. Parents will be available for emergencies or will designate other adults to handle emergencies.
3. Parents will be stable enough to provide emotional security for their children.
4. Parents will train children in any special issues (e.g., when to answer the door, getting homework done) that may arise in self-care.

From C. Cole and H. Rodman, "When School-Age Children Care For Themselves: Issues for Family Life Educators and Parents" in *Family Relations,* 36, 92–96, 1987. Copyright © 1987 by the National Council on Family Relations, 3989 Central Ave. NE, Suite 550, Minneapolis, MN 55421. Reprinted by permission.

ders, 1988). In the near future, children in self-care arrangements may grow by several million, so findings that children do not suffer from the experience are important. Contrary to initial fears, most latchkey kids are capable of periods of self-care and grow from the experience. Over 89 percent of parents using self-care arrangements are satisfied with the arrangements (Robinson et al., 1986).

Children and Parental Divorce

Each year about 1 million U.S. children experience parental divorce; about one in three experiences parental divorce during the childhood years (Fine, 1987; Kalter, 1987). This growing trend influences children's lifestyle and development. In 1970, 12 percent of individuals under age 18 lived in single-parent households. By 1984, 25 percent of children (60 percent of African-American children) were in single-parent households. Others have experienced parental divorce and are now in reconstituted families, also called blended families or stepfamilies (Demo & Acock, 1988).

What are the typical effects of parental separation and divorce on children? Children experience negative short-term effects in social adjustment, emotional well-being, and academic performance. Research findings are less consistent on long-term effects, but a sizeable minority experiences a lasting negative impact. Adults who experienced divorce as children have higher divorce rates themselves, more work-related problems, and higher emotional distress (Kalter, 1987).

Short-Term Effects of Parental Divorce

Children whose parents divorce experience an increase in four emotions: guilt, fear, anger, and depression (Freeman, 1985). Lillian feels guilty because she sees herself as the cause of her parents' divorce. Lee experiences high levels of fear and anxiety, feels abandoned and unloved, and has had a lot of nightmares lately. Frank is angry at his parents. Like Lee's anxiety, Frank's anger is provoked by feelings of abandonment and rejection. Nancy has been depressed since her parents separated. She has been apathetic, does not seem to enjoy her toys, has withdrawn from her friends, and is exhibiting poor concentration in classes. Lillian, Lee, Frank, and Nancy sometimes lie to others and themselves about the divorce by clinging to unrealistic hopes of reconciliation. At times, they try to compensate for nonresident parents and take over roles those parents used to play. They have more psychosomatic symptoms (stress-related ailments) than their peers from intact families (Freeman, 1985).

When nonresident parents (noncustodial parents, or parents absent from the home) are fairly uninvolved with their children, children's self-worth goes down and they feel helpless. Some children turn this helplessness into hurtfulness-power. Aggressive behavior and feelings of abandonment may increase when resident parents become emotionally involved in work and new social relations (Kalter, 1987).

Children of parental divorce may act more aggressive than other children because many have witnessed a high level of interparent hostility. Children often find themselves in the role of protecting the attacked parent or of identifying with the attacking parent, and they learn to model the behavior (Kalter, 1987).

Parental separation and divorce may cause problems with children achieving emotional separation. The type of dysfunctional emotions and behaviors varies with the age of the children at the time of separation: Preschoolers experience increased separation anxiety and regressive behaviors, school-age children are most likely to exhibit an increase in dependency, while adolescents are likely to express their problems in acting-out behaviors and intense conflicts with parents (Kalter, 1987). This variety of emotions and behaviors stems from the newly acquired skills of each age group: Most preschoolers have just learned to feel comfortable being away from their parents for short periods of time, most school-age children are enjoying their newfound independence, and adolescents have just achieved cognitive and problem-solving skills that allow them to work out their problems. Parental divorce seems to temporarily disrupt these new skills, and children act in ways that seem less mature. Either the divorce is so stressful that it interferes with mature behaviors, or these behaviors allow children to symbolically express to their parents their frustrations and fears about their parents' divorce.

Long-Term Effects of Parental Divorce

Parental divorce often affects gender identity in children, and these children may have difficulty learning to feel worthwhile within their gender roles. Boys experience more adverse effects than girls in this area (Demo & Acock, 1988; Freeman, 1985; Hetherington, Cox, & Cox, 1985). Boys who have experienced parental divorce often have lowered academic performance, less impulse control, and inhibited assertiveness. Their relationships with their parents are quite changed, with ties to fathers weakened. Although most boys live with their mothers, many of them do not view their mothers as authority figures and may feel aggressive or sexual toward their mothers (Kalter, 1987).

Girls experience the most difficulties with divorce when the separation occurs during preadolescence. Their self-esteem is lowered, and the girls engage in more precocious sexual activity and delinquent behavior, including running away (Kalter, 1987; Kalter, Riemes, Brickman, & Chen, 1985). A more typical adjustment for girls is an increase in androgynous behavior. Both boys and girls tend to take on more domestic responsibilities than their peers in intact families (Demo & Acock, 1988).

In one Australian study, 18- to 34-year-olds who had experienced parental divorce as children were compared with peers who had experienced parental death or who were in intact families. Researchers found that adults who had experienced their parents' divorce had more negative attitudes toward their family than the two comparison groups. However, all three groups held similar attitudes about the advantages and disadvantages of the lifestyles of marriage, living together, and singlehood. The survivors of the parental divorce group valued marriages as much but were more likely to be aware of the limitations of marriage. In other words, this group held the most complex views about marriage (Amato, 1988).

Two longitudinal research studies provide insights about how individuals adapt to parental divorce over time. In one study, subjects were assessed 6 years after the initial study (Hetherington et al., 1985). In the original study, 24 boys and 24 girls, ages 4 to 6, from European-American, middle-class backgrounds and in their mothers' custody were compared to children from intact homes. The researchers concluded that children's behaviors were more disturbed during the first year of divorce but improved during the next year (Hetherington, Cox, & Cox, 1979). Six years later, one of the major factors in adjustment was whether the custodial mother had remarried. When remarriage occurred, boys had some decrease in problems, but problems with girls increased.

In the other study, 38 subjects were assessed 10 years after their parents separated when the subjects were 6 to 8 years old (Wallerstein, 1987). In the initial study, the children were found to be preoccupied with issues of loss and separation and to be experiencing intense anxiety that interfered with both school and competitive play. The children often displayed anger toward or fear of their custodian mother, while longing for and romanticizing their absent fathers, even if they had not had good father-child relationships prior to the divorce. When studied 10 years later, custody was still held almost exclusively by mothers, but several subjects had spent at least one extended time period with their fathers. During adolescence, more than 40 percent had left to live with their fathers; most stayed 1 year and then returned to their mother's residence. Over a third of the sample had visited their father regularly during the decade; most of the rest had irregular visits or visits only during school vacations. Other findings in this study included:

- Eighty-nine percent of the subjects had remained in school. Half were doing well academically, a fourth had an average grade point average, and a fourth were doing poorly.
- Three fourths of the subjects had part-time jobs.
- About 25 percent of the females and 30 percent of the males thought that they had adequate father-child relationships; over 50 percent felt intense rejection.
- Many fathers were not helping with college expenses, especially in comparison to fathers in intact homes.
- Many of the subjects experienced profound unhappiness with their current relationships and had numerous fears about future relationships.
- Compared to other peers, the girls in this study had a high number of abortions and made a number of suicide attempts.

Wallerstein's (1987) study showed that divorce had been a central experience to this group of subjects, and experiencing parental divorce at 6 to 8 years of age resulted in less adjustment than if parents had divorced when the children were preschoolers. In fact, school-age children may have the hardest time of all age groups in adjusting to their parents' divorces. Adolescents tend to adjust better because they are more likely to discuss their reactions with friends (Demo & Acock, 1988).

Non-custodial parents may only see their children on alternate weekends. As such, parents sometimes feel a lot of pressure to fill their parent-child time with special activities. Currently, 85 percent of single parent households are with mothers and 15 percent are with fathers.

Counteracting Detrimental Effects of Parental Divorce

The following factors seem to help children to adjust to parental divorce (Demo & Acock, 1988; Fine, 1987; Hetherington et al., 1985; Seltzer & Bianchi, 1988):

- Children should be informed about the separation and divorce. They need reassurance that their parents love them and that they did not cause the divorce. They should be told that parents are not going to reverse their decision to divorce.
- Children adjust better when the divorced parents can treat each other with mutual respect and see each other as co-parents. At the very least, parents should try to avoid battling around their children and forcing their children to take sides.
- Extended family assistance can be beneficial if other family members have constructive attitudes.
- Decisions involving children should consider their age and emotions.
- Children need parents to retain limits on the children's behavior. In other words, parents should not abandon their role of parenting. Children's lives should be kept as consistent as possible.
- Short-term counseling for children during the separation and divorce can often provide a safe relationship for expressing fears and anger. A children's support group is another possibility.
- Stepparents need to develop a relationship with stepchildren before disciplining them; stepparents do best when they start out supporting the biological parents' decisions.
- Nonresident parents must make special efforts to retain regular contact with the children over the years. Some absent parents see their children less frequently as the children get older or after the resident parent remarries. Children who have frequent contact with noncustodial parents tend to adjust better.

Children in Dysfunctional Families

No family is perfect, and all children deal with some family conflict, unfair situations, and inconsistency, but children suffer when families have major dysfunctions. Families may be dysfunctional in many ways—marital conflict, hostile divorces, parental abuse, alcoholism, and drug abuse. Some children in dysfunctional families receive help in coping with their problems, but others find that family dysfunctions leave problems that last into adulthood. The popularity and usefulness of Adult Children of Alcoholics support groups attest to the importance of working out unresolved problems from dysfunctional families.

Family Scripts

Within the family, individuals learn what roles are expected of them, how to play the roles, and how to think within those roles. In healthy families, children learn many diverse roles that help them to feel good about themselves, their relationships, and their place in the world and that build self-confidence and self-worth. But in unhealthy, dysfunctional families, children learn unbalanced, extreme, and limited roles that "catch" them in unrewarding, unfulfilling, demeaning roles. Roles learned in families are repeated with variations in other relationships and settings.

As individuals learn scripts, or rules about operating in different settings, they become more efficient in their roles but lose awareness of other ways of acting. Thus, as scripts are learned well, other options become less likely (Tomkins, 1987). Dysfunctional families often insist on rigidity to certain scripts to survive family problems.

Family Triangles

Family triangles exist when parents confuse marital issues by developing a serious conflict with one or more of their children (see Table 9.4). Instead of dealing with spousal concerns, parents transfer their attention to the child, and the central issue becomes how to parent the child (Guerin, Fay, Burden, & Kautto, 1987). When used for emotional support or as the target problem, children are placed in an unhealthy relationship with their parents.

Theodore is part of a child-as-refuge triangle. As Theodore's parents grew more emotionally distant from each other, Theodore's mother put her time and emotional energy into her children. She became especially close to Theodore and would confide to him her negative feelings about his father. Theodore's father became resentful of his son's close relationship with his wife. Rather than taking responsibility for his own emotional distancing from his wife, the father told himself that Theodore was responsible for his poor marital relationship.

June is the victim of a target-child triangle. When June's father looks at June, he is reminded of his wife. His wife had an affair, and although the affair ended a few years ago, the two of them have never really resolved the emotional hurts, and June's father feels much anger toward his wife. Now that June is a preadolescent, the father assumes that June is just like her mother and starts accusing her of wanting to have sex with boyfriends. Although June

---

Table 9.4
Triangles With the Children

Triangles formed with children serve two major functions: (1) They cover up marital conflict, and (2) they allow parenting to become the issue around which marital conflict is organized. The three main versions are:

1. *The Child-as-Refuge Triangle:* In this version, one parent is overly close to and overinvolved with one or more of the children; the other parent is distant with the child/children. The child is a substitute emotional support to one parent and a threat to the other.

2. *The Target-Child Triangle:* A target child feels caught between his or her parents. While the child is special to one parent, the other parent directs anger at the child.

3. *The Tug-of-War Triangle:* In this triangle, both parents attempt to be closer to and more influential with the child than the other parent.

"Triangle With The Children" Table from *The Evaluation and Treatment of Marital Conflict: A Four-Stage Approach* by Philip J. Guerin, Jr., Leo F. Fay, and Susan L. Burden. Copyright © 1987 by Basic Books, Inc. Reprinted by permission of Basic Books, Inc., a division of HarperCollins, Publishers, Inc.

---

has no intention of engaging in early sexual activity, she gets fed up with the continual accusations and angrily decides that she might as well "sleep around." At this point, her parents put on a united front of concern to deal with the troublemaking daughter and to temporarily cover up their dysfunctional relationship.

Eddie is caught in the third type of family triangle—the tug-of-war triangle. In this kind of triangle, both parents try to be closer to and more influential with the children. Eddie's parents are divorced, and both his mother and father are trying to buy their way into being the more important parent. Eddie feels caught between two parents who battle with each other through gifts, vacations, and new clothes that they buy for their son. Deep down, Eddie feels unloved and used as a pawn. Eddie's parents, however, do not recognize that they are expressing hostility toward their former spouses and pretend that they are doing their best parenting for Eddie.

Parentification

Children in dysfunctional families commonly experience **parentification,** in which children or adolescents are assigned roles and responsibilities that are normally reserved for parents (Mika, Bergner, & Baum, 1987). Table 9.5 shows sample items used to assess the degree of parentification.

Typical parentification roles include extensive caring for younger siblings, assuming household responsibilities (e.g., cleaning, cooking, and laundry), and taking on emotional relationships with a parent (e.g., confidant, adviser, and peacemaker). In some family situations, parentification patterns are implemented well, with the needs and capabilities of the children kept in mind (e.g., most latchkey kids are given reasonable responsibilities). However, parentification becomes problematic when children are overburdened, are given responsibilities beyond their developmental capabilities, receive mixed messages about whether they

Exploring Cultural Diversity: Sibling Caretaking Societies

Some nonwestern societies are sibling caretaking societies in which parents, other adults, and older children together take care of younger children. In these societies, child-care skills may be learned from age 5 on without negative effects of parentification. One advantage of such societies is that new parents have already practiced child-care skills. These societies handle sibling caretaking well because only some parenting functions are given to the older siblings.

Parenting can be separated into five major functions: (1) safety and protection, (2) shelter and food provision, (3) the teaching of culture and conduct, (4) direct childcare (e.g., feeding, carrying, bathing, dressing), and (5) emotional support and comfort. Siblings in sibling caretaking societies are usually assigned tasks in the fourth and fifth function areas first. The third function is primarily the mother's responsibility, and the first two functions are usually shared by both parents (Weisner, 1987).

These parenting functions are also present among families in the United States and other western nations, but the degree to which they occur varies widely. In addition, using these functions to encourage sibling learning of skills needed for future parenting is highly inconsistent. In fact, in the United States, students often are taught these skills in family-life classes in high school.

What are the advantages in both approaches? What drawbacks do you see?

Table 9.5
Sample Items from a Parentification Scale

Items Regarding Spousal Role Vis-à-vis Parents

1. My parent(s) asked for my advice when making a decision about my siblings' misbehavior.
2. My parent(s) shared intimate secrets (e.g., concerning relationships and/or sexual issues) with me.
3. My parent(s) discussed their financial issues and problems with me.
4. One parent would come to me to discuss the other parent.

Items Regarding Parental Role Vis-à-vis Parents

1. I was the mediator or "go-between" when a conflict arose between my parents.
2. I consoled one or both of my parents when they were distressed.
3. My parent(s) at times became physically ill, and I was responsible for taking care of them.
4. I restored peace if conflicts developed between my parents.

Items Regarding Parental Role Vis-á-vis Siblings

1. I baby-sat for my younger sibling(s).
2. When one of my sibling(s) had a personal concern, they came to me for advice.
3. I was responsible for deciding what action to take if one of my sibling(s) misbehaved, even when my parent(s) were present.
4. I would decide what time my sibling(s) went to bed for the evening, even when my parent(s) were home.

Nonspecific Items Regarding Adult Role Taking

1. I did the laundry for members of my family.
2. I made dinner for members of my family.
3. I cleaned house for my family.
4. I did the dishes for members of my family.

From P. Mika, et al., "The Development of a Scale for the Assessment of Parentification" in *Family Therapy*, 14, 229–235, pp. 232 & 233, 1987. Copyright +© Libra Publishers, Inc., San Diego, CA.

are to carry out these responsibilities, or are assigned these roles excessively (Mika et al., 1987). Healthy and unhealthy parentification are contrasted in the following two examples:

Judy helped extensively in raising her younger siblings while her mother recovered from a lengthy illness. Her father made certain that Judy had time to herself and time with her friends. On weekends, Judy's grandmother often came over to the house so that Judy did not have to spend her entire weekend playing mother. When Judy's mother got better, Judy's responsibilities were reduced significantly. Since Judy's father made certain that Judy was not overburdened while watching her brothers and sisters, this parentification was not problematic.

On the other hand, Wally is stuck in a parenting role because his mother is dead and his father gets drunk. Wally must make decisions about what his younger brothers Hugh and Whitey can eat for breakfast and dinner, when the three of them can play, and when they should study or clean house. Although Wally does fairly well in running the home without direction, his father sometimes beats him for the decisions he makes.

In some divorced families, boys become overinvolved with family decisions and experience pressure to be the "man of the house." Some boys see themselves as the confidant and caretaker of their mother and try to be in control of the home, and some mothers abdicate control to their sons (Kalter, 1987). Clarence, the oldest son, often tried to make the decisions around the house and bossed his younger siblings around. He felt little pressure to obey his mother's views because he saw himself as in charge of the family now that his father was not around.

The "Exploring Cultural Diversity" feature describes how some cultures handle childcare without the negative effects of parentification.

The "Hurried Child"

David Elkind (1981) used the term **the "hurried child"** to denote a modern style of raising children. Parents often push children into early education, schedule their free time with organized activities, and have them take care of themselves as "latchkey" children. Television and movie topics introduce children to swearwords, drugs, and sex. School-age children are aware of more such topics today than most adolescents were familiar with just a couple of decades ago.

This "hurried" timetable may have some advantages, since children today will exist in a very complex world requiring diverse knowledge, but "hurrying" childhood also has heavy costs. Children today suffer from academic burnout, high levels of stress and depression, and greater fears about the future. And while children are "hurried" through the school years, modern society also prolongs adolescence and makes these "hurried children" wait a long time for adulthood.

Children and adolescents are often placed in situations in which their cognitive and moral development have not and cannot keep up with the behavioral choices they are asked to make. The cost is high for society and for the children. We will continue to explore these and other issues as we move into the teen years in Chapters 10 and 11.

guided review

10. _____, the parent's responsiveness to the child's needs, is related to school achievement and behavior problems: Higher levels are associated with better school performance and fewer behavior problems.
11. True of false: Contrary to initial fears, most latchkey kids are capable of periods of self-care and grow from the experience.
12. Regarding the impact of divorce on children, most children experience _____ short-term effects, while some experience long-lasting negative impact.
13. One aspect of dysfunctional families is the formation of _____, situations in which marital conflicts are transferred to children and parenting.
14. In _____, children or adolescents are assigned roles that are normally reserved for parents.

answers

10. Parental acceptance [LO-10]. **11.** True [LO-12].
12. negative [LO-13]. **13.** family triangles [LO-15].
14. parentification [LO-16].

Play, Peers, and Friendship, Ages 6 to 12

The Role of Play in Later Childhood

One change in play during the school years is that school-age children enjoy games. Participation in games involves playing according to agreed-upon, often externally imposed rules. Before the school years, play involves personally imposed rules, freewheeling fantasy, and relatively goal-free activity. School-age children, however, prefer the more complex nature of games (Bettelheim, 1987).

According to Piaget, games are learned in three stages. In the first stage, rules are considered arbitrary in nature. In other words, children in this stage engage in games just like they engage in regular play. In the second stage, rules are considered absolute. Children in this stage do not want to adjust a rule or shorten a game because "that's not the way it's done." In the third stage, children view rules as agreed-upon standards. A game's rules can be modified if all the players agree to the changes and if the modifications are logical (Bettelheim, 1987). Consider the suggestions on how family members can play games together presented in the "Exploring the Parent/Child Relationship" feature.

As school-age children grow older, they are better able to describe the games they play. Eighth-graders are much superior to fourth-graders in providing complete descriptions of their favorite games. When introduced to a new game, eighth-graders are able to ask questions that facilitate learning the object and rules of the novel game. However, most fourth-graders are unable to generate good questions of inquiry that aid in understanding the new game (Worth, 1988).

Also, as children get older, they enjoy more complex games and other play activities. For example, second-grade boys and girls prefer tag, kickball, jump rope, and hopscotch, but their fifth-grade counterparts prefer organized sports, such as football and soccer. Boys tend to play more complex games than do girls (Borman & Kurdek, 1987).

Nowadays, video games are popular with school-age children and teens. Over 90 percent have played video games (Schutte, Malouff, Post-Gorden, & Rodasta, 1988). Advocates believe that video games teach game skills and hand-eye coordination and that they provide the ideal combination of learning and entertainment. Video-game familiarity is correlated with participation in other social activities and with ability to use microcomputers (Lin & Lepper, 1987).

Opponents argue that video-game playing reduces time spent on homework, family activities, and active play with friends. Teachers perceive children who spend much time playing video games as impulsive individuals who get lower academic grades. Opponents of video games also argue that the majority of games are based on violent themes, which children then model in their play and social interactions (Lin & Lepper, 1987). The content of video games does influence later play activity. In one study, children played either a violent karate video game or a nonviolent jungle-vine-swinging video game. During free play, those children who had played the karate game engaged in more aggresive play, while those children who had played the jungle-vine-swinging game were more likely to play with a jungle swing toy (Schutte et al., 1988).

Peers, Friendship, and Popularity

During middle childhood, friendships and peer groups grow in importance. Children spend more time outside of their immediate family and increase their interaction with

Parents of three school-age children of varying ages may find themselves in an interesting predicament when playing a game such as Parcheesi. Their first-grade child may not understand how to play the game correctly and may move his piece when it is not his turn or move in the wrong direction. Their third-grade child may become angry at her younger brother because "He's not playing right" and "He's cheating!" Their sixth-grader may want to try out a new version of Parcheesi that he has thought up, but his younger sister insists that "The game is not played that way."

Parents who recognize the cognitive limitations and strengths of their children can develop strategies for successful family game playing. Note how the three children in the preceding paragraph represent different stages of game playing: (1) not understanding the rules, (2) absolute rules, and (3) agreed-upon rules. How is each influenced in this social activity by their progress in cognitive development?

Young school-age children play a limited number of games successfully (e.g., Candy Land, Chutes and Ladders). From time to time, the oldest and middle children may be willing to play some simple games for the youngest child's benefit. Older children will be more willing to play games preferred by children closer to their age (e.g., Parcheesi, Rummy, Battleship), but these games may be too frustrating for the youngest children to play for long periods or without cheating. When older children tolerate younger children's quitting, complaining, or cheating, the younger children may learn to play better. However, if older children do not want to tolerate this behavior, one solution is to pair the younger children with older players. In this way, the younger children believe that winning is a possibility, and the older children can serve as game tutors. Sometimes, older children develop other strategies that help younger children to cope with games that tax their cognitive limits. They may allow younger children to compensate by taking an extra turn or suggest that different games be chosen for awhile (Bettelheim 1987).

Parents often take following through on a game and sticking to rules too seriously because they think that this strategy will help their children to build more self-control and perseverance. However, children who are forced to finish games when they are frustrated, who are never allowed to "break the rules" to increase their chances of winning, and who are supposed to be able to "take" losing even though their inexperience with the game makes it likely that they will lose may end up with less self-control and more frustration than children whose parents are more lenient in enforcing game rules (Bettelheim (1987).

For children, games represent a serious undertaking that tests ability, competence, and self-esteem. Therefore, many children go through a stage when they feel that they cannot afford to lose. During this stage, children may often ask, "Can we start over?" or "Can I take an extra turn?" or they may even want to take extra spaces or points. Perhaps letting young children take small advantages during games will let the children enjoy the games. Starting games over may allow them to build skills in playing the first part of the game and eventually increase their ability to use a winning strategy (Bettelheim 1987).

Older children are most challenged by complex games (e.g., Monopoly, Dungeons and Dragons) that may be too difficult for children under the age of 10. These games may best be played with peers or with adult family members, rather than the entire family unit.

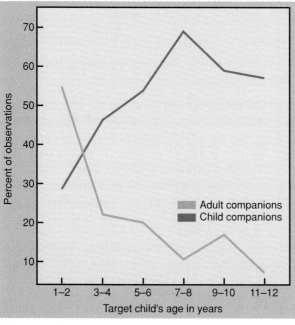

Figure 9.8
Developmental changes in children's companionship with adults and other children.

Based on: Ellis, S., Rogoff, B., & Cromer, C. C. 1981. Age segregation in children's social interactions. *Developmental Psychology, 17*, 399–407.

peers. By adolescence, friends are as important a reference group as parents were earlier. As shown in Figure 9.8, throughout childhood, children increase their time with other children and decrease time with adults (Ellis, Rogoff, & Cromer, 1981). Children play with both genders but do more with same-sex companions. They also spend more time playing with children who are more than a year different in age than with age mates (Barker & Wright, 1955; Ellis et al., 1981).

During childhood then, children learn about forming friendships, relating to children of various ages, developing peer norms, and being able to resist peer norms. For many individuals, the middle childhood years also represent their first participation in organized groups, such as Girl Scouts, Little League, and neighborhood clubhouses. Throughout these years, qualities of friendship change significantly.

Stages of Friendship

Just as children evolve in cognitive development, in moral reasoning, and in personality development, children's friendships evolve into more mature forms during the school years. Until children are of school age, friends are convenient, momentary playmates who provide toys. During the school years, friendships move from relationships based on "what a friend can do for me"; to cooperative

Table 9.6
Stages of Friendship

Stage	Description
Stage 0: Momentary playmateship (ages 3 to 7)	In this undifferentiated level of friendship, children's egocentricity keeps them from considering their playmates' points of view. Young children think only about what they get from the relationship. Friendships are defined on the basis of proximity, material attributes, and physical attributes.
Stage 1: One-way assistance (ages 4 to 9)	In this unilateral level of friendship, friends are those who do what one requests them to do.
Stage 2: Two-way cooperation (ages 6 to 12)	In this reciprocal level of friendship, friendship involves give-and-take aspects. The relationship still involves separate self-interests, rather than common, mutual interests. Friendships retain a "fair-weather" aspect or a "convenience" aspect.
Stage 3: Mutual sharing (ages 9 to 15)	In this stage, friendships are viewed as intimate and shared relationships. Friendship involves a systematic, committed relationship that means more than doing things for each other. Friends often demand loyalty and exclusivity during this stage. Girls frequently have several close friendships that are deeply developed, while boys develop many friendships but keep them less intimate.
Stage 4: Autonomous interdependence (ages 12 and up)	Around age 12, children develop friendships that involve interdependence. Children are able to respect their friends' needs for both dependency and autonomy.

From R. L. Selman and A. P. Selman, "Children's Ideas About Friendship: A New Theory" in *Psychology Today,* 71–80, 114, October 1979. Copyright © 1979 Sussex Publishers, Inc.

friendships; to shared, mutual friendships; and finally, around age 12, to autonomous, interdependent friendships (Selman & Selman, 1979). The developmental stages are summarized in Table 9.6.

Notice that the stages in Table 9.6 overlap by ages. Therefore, 6-year-old Martha may have some friendships based on Stage 0, momentary playmateship, such as playing with a cousin only when together at family celebrations, yet have the majority of her friendships based on Stage 1, one-way assistance. In her Stage 1 friendships, Martha describes good friends in terms of what her friends can do for her. For example, Judy is her friend because she lets Martha play with her Barbie doll, and Kenny is her friend because he went to the movies with her. Sally is no longer her friend because she would not loan her a book, and Bobby can be her friend if he lets her play with his sandbox tools. Martha is just starting to view friendships in terms of their reciprocal nature, a characteristic of Stage 2. Martha says that Bonnie is her very best friend because they like to do things for each other.

Four years from now, at age 10, most of Martha's friendships will be reciprocal in nature, but some of her friendships will be defined in terms of being intimate, shared, and mutually desirable. These Stage 3 friendships are characterized as **mutual friendships.** At age 10, Martha expects loyalty from her friends. Martha and her

friends call each other by nicknames that help separate "us" from "them" (Harre, 1980). Unlike 6-year-old Martha, 10-year-old Martha expects her best friends to remain the same persons for a long time. Therefore, Martha feels a little threatened and jealous when her best friend Cynthia plays with Jenny instead of her.

At age 10, Martha plays with and spends time with Cynthia, Bonnie, Gloria, and Whitney more than any others. However, 10-year-old Owen plays with a greater number of boys and does not become as close to each of his friends as Martha does with hers. Martha and Owen are exhibiting typical gender differences (Selman & Selman, 1979). The source of these differences may include how parents encourage children to play; for example, at all ages, boys are allowed to play farther from home than are girls (Block, 1979; Huston, Carpenter, & Atwater, 1986). Therefore, boys come into contact with more potential friends than do girls. Also, boys may be more encouraged to participate in large-group sports, such as baseball, thereby increasing their contacts with friends.

Within a couple of years, both Martha and Owen will be capable of Stage 4, **interdependent friendships,** in which they can make commitments to their friends and yet allow their friends to be autonomous. These characteristics describe most adult friendships, too.

successful study tip

Stages of Friendship

Use this acronym to cue the meaning and order of the five stages of friendship proposed by Selman and Selman:

MORMI

In this acronym, M = Momentary playmates
O = One-way friendships
R = Reciprocal friendships
M = Mutual friendships
I = Interdependent friendships

One of the significant changes in maturing friendships is the switch from competition with friends to cooperation. In one study, pairs of fourth-graders and eighth-graders worked on a task in which they could compete or cooperate. The fourth-graders were more likely to compete with friends than with nonfriends, even though this decision would maximize their own personal outcomes at the expense of their friends. By contrast, eighth-graders were more likely to compete with nonfriends and cooperate with friends. By eighth grade, friendships tend to emphasize equality and interdependence (Berndt, Hawkins, & Hoyle, 1986).

This model of friendship development is consistent with Piaget's stages of cognitive development. Six-year-old Martha is still struggling with the cognitive limitations of egocentrism and irreversibility, and these cognitive limitations are reflected in her viewing friends in terms of what they can do for her, rather than what they can do for each other. As these cognitive limitations are overcome, friendships become less egocentric and more reciprocal in nature.

Table 9.7
Characteristics of Accepted, Rejected, and Neglected Children

Accepted children	Accepted children distribute more positive reinforcers to other children and also receive more positive reinforcers. Accepted children communicate better and cooperate more with their peers. These children are viewed as having more leadership skills and as being more willing to share with peers. They are viewed by their peers as being more trustworthy. They have greater social mobility. Accepted children also generate multiple, effective solutions to interpersonal problems.
Rejected children	Rejected children have more behavioral problems than do other children. They also display more physical and verbal aggression. Rejected children get more off-task (not doing what they are asked to do) in both the classroom and on the playground than do other children. Rejected children without a best friend are less trusting than popular, average, or neglected children. They tend not to follow either adult rules or peer rules.
Neglected children	Neglected children show the least amount of aggressive behavior. They are characterized by others as passive, withdrawn, timid, and shy. These children rarely make it onto "most liked" lists, and they are the "invisible children."

Source: Data from S. L. Bichard, et al., "Friendship Understanding in Socially Accepted, Rejected, and Neglected Children" in *Merrill-Palmer Quarterly,* 34, 33–46, 1988. From C. A. Buzzelli, "The Development of Trust in Children's Relations With Peers" in *Child Study Journals,* 18, 33–46, 1988. From J. D. Coie, et al., "Dimensions and Types of Social Status: A Cross-Age Perspective", in *Developmental Psychology,* 18, 557–570, 1982. From W. Furman and J. C. Masters, "Peer Interactions, Sociometric Status, and Resistance to Deviation in Young Children" in *Developmental Psychology,* 16, 229–236, 1989.

Until then, however, "best friends" and "worst enemies" may shift frequently for children. Sometimes, big fights result in friendships ending for awhile. Parents can help their children to deal with terminated friendships by acknowledging their children's hurt feelings and sadness. Parents might also suggest that their children talk to former friends about the reasons for breaking up and about whether anything can be remedied. Parents should avoid downgrading ex-friends; after all, today's ex-friends may be tomorrow's "bosom buddies." Finally, parents can encourage the formation of new friendships (Lansky, 1985).

Accepted, Neglected, and Rejected Children

Not all children find it easy to form and keep friends. Between 15 and 30 percent of elementary schoolchildren have poor peer relationships (Bichard, Alden, & Walker, 1988) and can be classified as **rejected children** (peers actively dislike them) or **neglected children** (peers ignore them). Characteristics of accepted, rejected, and neglected children are given in Table 9.7.

Boys are more likely than girls to be actively rejected by their peers (Schwartzberg, 1988b). One type of rejected child is the intolerable classroom bully who bosses, insults,

threatens, and uses much physical aggression. Bullies derive satisfaction from harming others in both psychological and physical ways. Joey, a typical bully, picks on weaker or younger children, rather than on boys his own size and strength (Roberts, 1988; Schwartzberg, 1988b).

Bullies often have parents who do not pay much attention to them and who use harsh, physical punishment. Bullies learn at home that aggression works because the aggressor gets his or her own way (Roberts, 1988). Some highly aggressive children do have friends, but these friends are also highly aggressive (Cairns, Cairns, Neckerman, Gest, & Gariepy, 1988).

Like the bullies themselves, the victims of bullies also tend to be rejected children. About 10 percent of children in the third through sixth grades are extremely victimized by their peers. These victims have low peer acceptance and high peer rejection (Perry, Kusel, & Perry, 1988).

On the other hand, neglected children tend to be "invisible children" who rarely make it onto either "most liked" or "least liked" lists. They have little impact on anyone. Few of the children in this group have nicknames because others think that these children are too unimportant to spend time creating a nickname for them (Harre, 1980). Sometimes, neglected children who are placed in a new setting with new playmates can break out of their usual withdrawn social pattern (Coie & Dodge, 1983; Schwartzberg, 1988b).

Accepted children are viewed as friendlier, less aggressive, more compliant, and more supportive than other children, and these children also behave differently from others when placed in a new play group. They are superior at initiating social interactions and at paying attention to others' needs. They slowly work their way into the group, rather than forcing themselves on others (Coie, Dodge, & Coppotelli, 1982). These socially competent children turn rough-and-tumble play into games-with-rules play, while rejected children who engage in rough-and-tumble play progress into aggression (Pelligrini, 1988).

Social interaction skills, rather than ability levels, best predict popularity during the school years. In fact, school-age children are poor predictors of their own or peers' cognitive abilities, but do well at evaluating peers' social attributes (Miller, Harris, & Blumberg, 1988).

While popular or accepted children are those whose names often appear on "most liked" lists and rarely on "least liked" lists, some children appear on both lists. Labeled controversial children, these "loved-and-hated" individuals have the characteristics of both popular and unpopular children. At times, they are organized and task oriented, but at other times, they are disruptive and combative (Schwartzberg, 1988b).

Do rejected and neglected children remain rejected and neglected? Within 5 years, about a third of rejected children become average in popularity, a third become relatively invisible, and a third remain rejected. Of the invisible, neglected children, about a fourth stay neglected, but most of the rest become accepted. In fact, nearly a fourth of neglected children are considered popular 5 years later

School-aged children value their friendships and like to play with their friends, engage in games and sports, go places with them, and have sleep overs. At this age, boys tend have mostly boy friends and girls have mostly girl friends.

(Coie & Dodge, 1983). Children who continue to have poor peer relations are more likely to have severe emotional disturbances as young adults, to have poor military records, to be delinquent as adolescents, and to seek treatment for psychological problems later on (Cowen, Pederson, Babigan, Izzo, & Trost, 1973; Roff, Sells, & Golden, 1972).

Helping Children to Make Friends

Although such characteristics as being attractive, having a common name, being athletic, and being a later-born child have all been shown to be associated with popularity (Mc-David & Harari, 1966), adults can intervene to help all children make friends more easily. The first step is to see if children are having trouble making friends.

Virginia has been showing several signs of having trouble making friends: She has tried to buy friends by giving them her lunch money and by giving away toys. At other times, she has been showing off with her friends and has tried to be the most daring, most boisterous, noisiest, and even most obscene. On top of this, Virginia sometimes alienates her peers by demanding that they be perfect, by insisting on being the leader, and by cruelly teasing them (Lansky, 1985). Virginia needs to learn better ways to get the attention of her peer group. The following tips can help Virginia and other children make friends (Lansky, 1985):

1. Ask children to say hello to one unknown schoolmate each day.
2. Give instructions on eye contact, smiling, and beginning conversations.
3. Meet parents who have children the same age. The children will usually play together while the parents talk.
4. Acknowledge that verbal insults and slights hurt feelings. As maturity permits, encourage children to avoid using verbal comments to revenge their own hurts.
5. Tell or discuss with children any rules you want them to follow—for example, under what conditions they may bring friends home.

6. Peer conformity is important. Children need permission to be part of some of the trends. Participating in "in" fashions and activities allows children to fit in. Most trends will pass, and most of the time, peers will serve as good role models.
7. Let children use parents as the reason they cannot "go along with the crowd." Praise children when they resist poor peer pressure.

guided review

15. According to Piaget, children's understanding of games passes through three stages in which rules for playing are first viewed as _____, then as _____, and finally as _____.
16. Between the ages of 6 and 12, friendships move from the stage of _____, in which friends are described in terms of what they can do for a child, to _____ friendships, in which children can make commitments to their friends and yet allow their friends to be autonomous.
17. _____ children are ignored by other children, whereas _____ children are actively disliked by their peers.

answers

15. arbitrary; absolute; agreed-upon [LO-18]. 16. one-way assistance; interdependent [LO-19]. 17. Neglected; rejected [LO-20].

Exploring Human Development

1. Have two school-age children draw pictures of their families. Ask them questions about their drawings. Write a report based on what they drew and talked about. How were the children similar and different?
2. Visit a large toy store. Observe what toys and games are stocked for lower elementary schoolchildren and upper elementary schoolchildren. Do the toys and games match children's cognitive development? Do the toys reflect Erikson's industry versus inferiority psychosocial stage? Are toys advertised specifically for boys and girls? What themes seem to be most prevalent?
3. Observe a Little League game or a group of children engaged in team play on a neighborhood playground. How are the rules of the game decided? Are the rules formal or informal? How are disagreements handled? Are any allowances made for differences in children's ages and abilities?
4. Write stories about family rituals and traditions during your childhood. You might write about holiday celebrations, family vacations, family crises, a death in the family, or your responsibilities in the home. Share a few stories with classmates.
5. Visit a school library or the children's section in a public library. Ask a librarian what kinds of books and authors are currently popular with schoolchildren. Browse through some of these books. Why are these particular books popular? What kinds of families are in the books? What kinds of social issues? Do any of the books deal with the "hurried child" syndrome?

1. Given your memories of your childhood, which personality theory do you prefer: Freud's latency stage, Erikson's industry versus inferiority psychosocial stage, or Rogers's self theory? Why?

2. What aspects of parent effectiveness training (PET) do you like? Are there aspects that you do not like or that you doubt would be effective? Are there aspects that could be utilized with adults?

3. Do you believe that children today are experiencing more, less, or the same amount of depression and stress as previous generations? Why? What can be done to help depressed and highly stressed children? What could be done by families? Schools? Churches? Television programmers?

4. What values do you think are most important for parents to teach their children? Why? What values do you think will be most important for children to have in the 21st century?

5. What are your reactions to the "latchkey kid" phenomenon? Do you believe that most schoolchildren can handle self-care for a couple of hours each day? What kinds of commercial services and products could arise to help latchkey kids thrive?

Reading More About Human Development

Anthony, E. J., & Cohler, B. J. (1987). *The invulnerable child.* New York: Guilford.

Dreikurs, R. (1972). *The challenge of child training.* New York: Hawthorn.

Garmezy, N., & Rutter, M. (Eds.). (1983). *Stress, coping, and development in children.* New York: McGraw-Hill.

Gordon, T. (1980). *Parent effectiveness training* (2nd ed.). New York: Peter H. Wyden.

Hotaling, G. T. (1988). *Family abuse and its consequences.* New York: Sage.

Jensen, L. C., & Kingston, M. (1986). *Parenting.* New York: Holt, Rinehart & Winston.

Summary

I. Personality development in middle and late childhood
   A. During Freud's latency stage, the id is temporarily suppressed, resulting in minimization of sexual and aggressive conflicts.
   B. Erikson's industry versus inferiority psychosocial stage places more emphasis on personality development in school-age children than does Freud's latency stage.
      1. The critical crisis of the industry versus inferiority stage is balancing experiences of accomplishment against feelings of inferiority such that the child is left with the sense that he or she is competent (the virtue for this fourth psychosocial stage).
      2. At home or at school, children gain a sense of their own competence in feedback from parents and teachers and by comparing their accomplishments with siblings and peers.
   C. Rogers's self theory distinguishes between the real self that children experience being and the ideal self that they would like to be.
      1. Children have an actualizing tendency that intrinsically prompts them to grow in positive ways when they are in supportive environments.
      2. Parents and adults generally urge children to avoid risks and try to minimize dangers for children, conditions that encourage children to make safety choices over growth choices.
   D. Gordon's parent effectiveness training is a parent education program based on humanistic assumptions.
      1. PET guidelines include teaching parents to be consistent and genuine with their children.
      2. Gordon also suggested that parents actively listen, share feelings, use "I" messages, and negotiate with their children.

II. Emotional development and disturbances in middle and late childhood
   A. During the school years, children become more aware of and more accurate in expressing their own emotions.
      1. Children become more adept at telling "little white lies."
      2. Children improve at knowing which emotion goes with which situation.
      3. Accuracy in judging complex, socially oriented emotions, such as pride and embarrassment, improves greatly during the school years.
      4. School-age children understand the difference between real and apparent emotions and have greater difficulty regulating the facial displays for apparent emotions than the verbal displays.
   B. Depression in childhood arises from feelings of sadness experienced as the result of losses.
      1. Younger children are likely to attribute their sadness to family members, while older children are likely to attribute their sadness to themselves.
      2. Depressed children have the same symptoms as depressed adults, including sadness, hostility, and negative self-image.
      3. Older children are more likely to experience depression—in part, as the result of their advancing cognitive abilities.
      4. Depression can lead to suicidal feelings and suicide attempts, with suicide attempts increasing substantially after age 11.
      5. Suicidal feelings in children should be taken seriously, and depressed children should receive help from counselors or therapists.
   C. Hyperactivity and acting-out behavior are two other childhood disturbances.
      1. The primary symptoms of hyperactivity or attention-deficit disorder with hyperactivity are inattentiveness, impulsiveness, and overactivity.
      2. Though sometimes difficult to diagnose, hyperactivity can be treated with dietary changes, behavior modification techniques, and drug therapy.
      3. Unlike hyperactivity, acting-out behaviors usually are not due to a physical condition and may result from ineffective parenting techniques.
      4. Children may act out to gain attention, to assert power, to seek revenge, or to appear to be inadequate.

5. Childhood aggression increases when aggressive behavior is both modeled and rewarded.

6. Children can be taught skills that reduce their aggressive behavior.

D. Everyone, including children, experiences stress.

1. Children cope with stress by trying to change conditions or events (primary coping) or by trying to change themselves (secondary coping).

2. Two broad coping strategies that children acquire during the school years are problem solving and regulating emotions.

3. Children combine these two broad strategies with other factors to yield 30 different coping strategies.

4. Extreme reactions to stress include repression (underreacting) and sensitization (overreacting).

5. Children who are mastery-oriented are likely to have an internal locus of control and to feel that they can manage stressful situations, while "helpless" children have an external locus of control and are likely to believe that stressful events are beyond their control.

E. Some children appear to be vulnerable to stress, while others appear to be resilient.

1. Shyness in children is one type of vulnerability, and if it persists, may alter the individual's life course.

2. Resilient children are characterized by high self-esteem, internal locus of control, and supportive family environments, and usually have individuals or agencies that provide support systems, coping skills, and positive role models.

III. Parenting and the family

A. Parents often overestimate the effects they have on their children; children are not permanently marked by every action their parents take.

1. Supportive, accepting parents do influence their children to become more self-aware and self-reliant adults.

2. Parental acceptance—the parent's responsiveness to the child's needs—is a key factor, with higher acceptance resulting in better school performance.

3. Androgynous parents tend to be child-centered and responsive to their children, but are less demanding than authoritative parents.

4. The families of school-age children involve so many variables, such as number of siblings, age of parents, and styles of interaction, that everyone grows up in a unique environment.

B. Dual-career families, in which both parents work outside the home, are a common family pattern.

1. Dual careers provide several rewards, such as both parents experiencing feelings of competence.

2. Dual careers also result in additional stressors, such as role overload, identity dilemmas, and child care.

3. Latchkey children (children left in their own care) usually come from dual-career or single-parent families and do not appear to suffer many negative effects; in fact, several studies have found some positive aspects of self-care.

C. Each year, about 1 million children experience parental divorce, and many will eventually become part of a reconstituted or blended family when one or both of their parents remarries.

1. The short-term effects of parental divorce include increased feelings of guilt, fear, anger, and depression and may also include lowered self-esteem and higher levels of aggressiveness.

2. After parental divorce, school-age children are most likely to exhibit an increase in dependency, while adolescents are more likely to express their problems in intense conflicts with parents and in acting-out behaviors.

3. The long-term effects of parental divorce for boys often include lower academic performance, less impulse control, and inhibited assertiveness.

4. Girls experience the most difficulties when the divorce occurs during their preadolescent years.

5. Both boys and girls who have experienced parental divorce tend to take on more household responsibilities than children from nondivorced families.

6. Longitudinal studies suggest that the impact of divorce is greatest for children who are of school age at the time of the divorce, with remarriage somewhat decreasing problems for boys while increasing problems for girls.

7. Children's adjustment to divorce is facilitated by assurance that they are not the cause of the divorce, by both parents maintaining contact with the children, and at times, by short-term counseling.

D. Families may become dysfunctional in many ways, and for some children, the effects of living in a dysfunctional family may last into adulthood.

1. Children in dysfunctional families may learn limiting roles that cause problems for them, both as children and as adults, in other relationships.

2. Family triangles exist when children are drawn into marital conflicts between parents.

3. Parentification occurs when children take on roles normally reserved for parents, including child care, household duties, and being a parental adviser and confidant.

4. In sibling caretaking societies, children learn parenting skills without the negative effects of parentification.

E. Elkind uses the term the "hurried child" to denote children who are pushed through childhood by their parents.

1. Hurried children experience adult activities and situations (e.g., sexual scenes in movies and on television) before they may be cognitively or emotionally ready.

2. Hurried children may suffer from academic burnout, high stress levels, and greater anxiety about the future.

IV. Play, peers, and friendship, ages 6 to 12

A. Play continues to be an important aspect of school-age children's lives.

1. Games become a preferred type of play, and parents may need to mediate when children of different ages attempt to play games together.

2. Video games have positive aspects, such as learning computer skills, and negative aspects, such as taking time away from other important activities and the often violent, aggressive themes of the games.

B. Throughout childhood, children increase the time they spend with peers and decrease the time they spend with adults.

1. Children move through five overlapping stages of friendship that are consistent with Piaget's stages of cognitive development.

2. Between 15 and 30 percent of school-age children can be classified as rejected (disliked by others) or neglected (ignored by others).

3. Boys are more likely than girls to be rejected, in part because of boys' greater aggressiveness, resulting in some boys becoming bullies.

4. Neglected children are passive, withdrawn, timid, and shy.

5. Over time, about a third of rejected children become accepted, but those who continue to have poor peer relations are more likely to have emotional problems as young adults.

6. Adults can intervene to help children make friends by identifying rejected/neglected children and helping them to develop better social skills.

Chapter Review Test

1. Corresponding to Freud's latency stage is Erikson's stage of
   a. generativity versus stagnation.
   b. identity versus role confusion.
   c. industry versus inferiority.
   d. initiative versus guilt.

2. According to Rogers's self theory, parents and other important adults influence children to choose _____ over _____ .
   a. education; ignorance
   b. safety; growth
   c. morality; selfishness
   d. self-actualization; peer influence

3. Which of the following is *not* emphasized in Gordon's parent effectiveness training (PET)?
   a. Parents need to establish themselves firmly as the authority that children must obey.
   b. "I" messages are more effective communication than are "you" messages when parents and children express emotions.
   c. Parents can negotiate conflicts with their children, using a six-step "no-lose" method.
   d. Parents need to be fairly consistent in their expectations about their children's behaviors.

4. Schoolchildren improve in their emotional development in that they
   a. can better empathize with others and realize how to meet others' needs.
   b. are much improved in judging other people's emotions.
   c. are now able to display the appropriate emotions that allow them to get away with "little white lies."
   d. all of the above

5. Which of the following statements is true about sadness and depression?
   a. Depression occurs at the same rate for preschoolers and schoolchildren, suggesting that genetics and biological explanations are most likely.
   b. Schoolchildren are more likely than younger children to blame others for their sadness.
   c. Depressed children have the same symptoms as depressed adults.
   d. Counseling depressed children does little good before the child is about 13 years old, or well into Piaget's last stage of cognitive development.

6. Ritalin is one of the most commonly used stimulants to treat
   a. childhood depression.
   b. children's phobias.
   c. attention-deficit disorder with hyperactivity.
   d. chronic bed-wetting in children older than age 7.

7. Which of the following statements is correct about coping strategies?
   a. As children get older, they use more secondary coping strategies.
   b. Choice of function, focus, and mode results in nearly 20 different specific coping strategies.
   c. Secondary coping is predominant in familiar situations, and primary coping is predominant in novel situations.
   d. All of the above are correct.

8. Which of the following is *incorrectly* paired?
   a. repressor/distraction from danger
   b. mastery-oriented/external locus of control
   c. sensitizer/monitoring
   d. helpless/deteriorating performance

9. Childhood shyness
   a. influences marriage, parenthood, and career patterns.
   b. is associated with deficiencies in age-appropriate social skills and knowledge.
   c. includes underestimating one's performance and exaggerating one's failures.
   d. all of the above.

10. Which of the following is *not* associated with resilient children?
    a. strong temperament
    b. external locus of control
    c. high self-esteem
    d. autonomy

11. What do the levels of parental acceptance measure?
    a. The parent's responsiveness to the child's needs
    b. The child's emotional acceptance of the parent
    c. The amount of misbehavior by a child that a parent can tolerate
    d. The ability of a parent to accept child-rearing advice

12. What is the difference between dual-career families and dual-earner families?
    a. Nothing, the terms are synonymous.
    b. the degree of personal and professional commitment parents exhibit to their work
    c. the number of hours children spend in the home versus in child care
    d. whether or not the parents' work hours require the use of day-care facilities

13. The majority of school-age latchkey children spend _____ alone.
    a. time in the morning
    b. time in the afternoon
    c. time after 6 P.M.
    d. at least 2 hr
14. When parents are going through a divorce, school-age children are most likely to display an increase in their _____ behaviors.
    a. acting-out
    b. separation anxiety
    c. parent-child conflict
    d. dependency
15. Which of the following is good advice for reducing the detrimental effects of divorce on children?
    a. It is best to let children gradually figure out on their own that parents are separating and divorcing.
    b. In the long run, children make the best adjustment if the nonresident parent gradually reduces frequency of contact.
    c. Divorcing parents should try to avoid battling around their children and should not ask children to take sides.
    d. All of the above are correct.
16. Which of the following children is part of a tug-of-war triangle?
    a. George's divorced parents keep trying to outdo each other with his Christmas and birthday presents so that George will choose them for the special parent.
    b. Janna's mother feels emotionally alienated from her husband, so she turns to Janna for discussing Dad's aloofness and drinking and for doing fun things together "almost like sisters."
    c. Miyoko's father is always accusing her of things she hasn't done, such as smoking pot or having sex with her boyfriend. She gets fed up with the accusations and runs away. Her estranged parents work together to try to bring her home.

    d. Spencer often tells his parents off, telling them that their politics are stupid and that they have all the wrong values. He sermonizes that he will never grow to be as boring, dull, or selfish as they have.
17. Which of the following is a typical parentification role?
    a. assuming household responsibilities
    b. caring for younger siblings
    c. taking on emotional relationships with a parent
    d. all of the above
18. Which of the following is more true of play among school-age children than among younger children?
    a. goal-free activity
    b. freewheeling fantasy
    c. externally imposed rules
    d. personally imposed rules
19. According to Piaget, in the second stage of learning games, children
    a. consider game rules to be absolute.
    b. view game rules as agreed-upon standards.
    c. see rules as arbitrary in nature.
    d. enjoy breaking the rules and getting by with cheating.
20. Which of the following stages of friendship has not yet appeared for 9-year-old Keri?
    a. mutual sharing
    b. one-way assistance
    c. two-way cooperation
    d. autonomous interdependence

Answers

1. C [LO-1].	8. B [LO-7].	15. C [LO-14].
2. B [LO-2].	9. D [LO-8].	16. A [LO-15].
3. A [LO-2].	10. B [LO-9].	17. D [LO-16].
4. D [LO-3].	11. A [LO-10].	18. C [LO-17, 18].
5. C [LO-4].	12. B [LO-11].	19. A [LO-18].
6. C [LO-5].	13. B [LO-12].	20. D [LO-19].
7. A [LO-6].	14. D [LO-13].	

chapter10

Physical and Cognitive Development in Adolescence

Key Terms

Larche
Pubarche
Menarche
Nocturnal emissions
Pubescence
Puberty
Pubertal timing
Formal operations
Postformal operations
Adolescent egocentrism
Personal fable
Imaginary audience
Bulimia (Bulimarexia)
Sexually transmitted
  diseases (STDs)
Sexual orientation
Gestational neurohormonal
  theory
"Sissy boy" syndrome
Erotophobia
Erotophilia

Learning Objectives

1. Describe the general growth patterns of preteens and teens.
2. Define puberty and the related terms of *pubescence, menarche,* and *pubarche.*
3. Compare and contrast the short- and long-term effects of early and late maturation.
4. List the general characteristics of Piaget's formal operations stage.
5. Explain Elkind's concepts of adolescent egocentrism, personal fable, and imaginary audience.
6. Discuss the impact of schooling on the lives of teenagers.
7. Identify the defining characteristics of obesity, anorexia nervosa, binge-eating, and bulimia.
8. Discuss causal factors for eating disorders.
9. Identify the drug most frequently used and abused by adolescents, and discuss factors generally associated with drug use and abuse in adolescents.
10. Give examples of at least four sexually transmitted diseases (STDs).
11. Discuss the impact of educational programs about AIDS and other STDs on adolescents' knowledge and behaviors.
12. Compare and contrast the sexual orientation characteristics of heterosexual, homosexual, and bisexual males and females.
13. Explain the gestational neurohormonal theory of gender determination and sexual orientation.
14. Relate the concept of erotophobia to teenage sexual attitudes and behaviors.
15. Identify factors that contribute to sexually active adolescents' nonuse of contraceptives.
16. Describe characteristics associated with school-age pregnancies.
17. Discuss the short- and long-term consequences of pregnancy for adolescent mothers and fathers.

The teen years are a time of tremendous growth and experience, and adolescents have more diverse experiences than do younger individuals. In infancy, the physical growth and development that allows individuals to take their first steps may be only a few months apart; during adolescence, physical growth and maturity may be several years apart in different individuals. Abstract thinking abilities may develop as early as age 11 or later than age 14. Some teenagers are very active in school, while others drop out. Some adolescents have fairly good relationships with their parents, and others have parent-child relationships that are full of turmoil.

Exploring Your Own Development

Currently, there are over 40 million teenagers in the United States—and this population will grow to 54 million by the 21st century (McAnarney & Greydanus, 1987). Each adolescent forms a unique life pattern that defies psychologists' efforts to describe and understand. Yet, despite the limitations, the research findings and theoretical positions presented in this chapter should help you to understand your own adolescent experiences and should provide insights about current and future teenagers.

Physical and cognitive development are the major topics in this chapter. Much of physical development unfolds biologically at its own pace; cognitive development has both maturational and chronological factors. As Petersen (1988) wrote:

> Beginning puberty is a major developmental milestone of adolescence, considered by many as the developmental change that signals one's transition into adolescence from childhood. . . . It is probably not appropriate, however, to consider pubertal development as the sole developmental marker in adolescence because of the strong organization of the period accomplished by the school in our society. This largely age-graded institution emphasizes the importance of chronological age, regardless of any other developmental status. (pp. 585–586)

How many of your memories of your teen years are tied to your school experiences? Do you identify events by "when I was a sophomore" and "when I was a junior"? How have 15- and 16-year-olds changed from when you were that age?

Physical Development in Adolescence

Patterns of Growth in Preteens and Teens

A visit to a sixth- or seventh-grade classroom reveals children of varying physical maturity. Many of the girls are taller and more developed than the boys. A high school graduation ceremony also reveals startling differences, especially among males. Parading across the stage to receive their diplomas is a variety of shapes and sizes, from fully mature to still developing.

The Order of Physical Changes

Although the rate of maturation varies, the order of physical changes is fairly inflexible. In girls, **larche** (budding of breasts) is followed by **pubarche** (pubic hair growth), the growth spurt, and finally **menarche** (the first menstrual period) (McAnarney & Greydanus, 1987; Watson, 1978). For 99 percent of girls, menarche comes *after* the period of greatest acceleration in height growth (Eveleth, 1986). In boys, the typical order of changes is early testicular growth, pubarche, further testicular growth, penile growth, **nocturnal emissions** (ejaculations during sleep), growth spurt, voice change, and hair growth (McAnarney & Greydanus, 1987; Watson, 1978).

These physical changes in girls and boys take 2 or more years, and this time period of sexual maturation is called **pubescence.** Pubescence is more closely related to bone maturation than to chronological age, but this time period begins around age 10 (with a range from ages 7 to 14) for girls and around age 12 (with a range from ages 9 to 16) for boys (Watson, 1978). The end of pubescence, when individuals are capable of producing mature sex cells (eggs and sperm), is called **puberty.**

Although pubescence is a biologically determined time period that adolescents cannot will into an earlier or later schedule, **pubertal timing** (the rate of maturation) affects pubertal status (interpersonal status and life experiences influenced by physical maturation) (Petersen, 1988). Therefore, early adolescents are especially concerned with maturation and body image.

Body Image

Body image is a person's mental representation of his or her physical body and includes the sensations, feelings, and attitudes that a person has toward his or her body (Hutchinson, 1982). Table 10.1 summarizes some of the research findings about body image. Do you agree with these findings? How has your body image changed since early adolescence? Do you still hold the same values and preferences in evaluating the bodies of others? Do you still worry about how others evaluate your physical features? How has your impression about your physical appearance influenced your attitudes, behaviors, and interactions with others?

Although few adults are as self-conscious about their bodies as they were during pubescence, most adults continue to worry about their personal appearance. Two thirds of all U.S. adults try to figure out other people's reactions to them and often glance at themselves in mirrors and window reflections. Ninety-six percent would like to change something about their personal appearance (Harris, 1987). How about you? What features would you like to change? Compare your responses to those of other adults, as summarized in Figure 10.1.

Table 10.1
Research Findings About Adolescents' Body Images

- A study of 6,500 adolescents found that more adolescents put their body image down than have inflated estimates. Males are likely to think that they are too thin, and females are likely to think that they are too fat (Levinson, Powell, & Steelman, 1986).

- Overweight adolescents often have significant body image distortion (Stein, 1987).

- Anorexic individuals tend to overestimate their body size (Boskind-White & White, 1987).

- Parental assessments of their teenagers' bodies are the most powerful predictor of teens' (especially females') evaluations of their body image (Levinson et al., 1986).

- In assessing their own physical attractiveness, adolescent males believe that upper body strength is most important; adolescent females believe that weight is most important (Franzoi & Herzog, 1987).

- Males are more likely than females to have positive attitudes toward their bodies (Franzoi & Herzog, 1987).

- In judging male body image, both males and females rate as important (but females think they are more important): buttocks, eyes, legs, and health. Females also consider body scent and physical stamina (Franzoi & Herzog, 1987).

- In judging female body image, males but not females consider: sex drive, sex organs, and sex activities (Franzoi & Herzog, 1987).

- For most teenagers, appearance is as large a motivating factor in eating habits as is concern with health (Hayes & Ross, 1987).

- Teenage boys worry most about facial features, complexion, weight, and penis size (Clifford, 1971).

- Teenage girls worry most about facial features, complexion, breasts, buttocks, legs, knees, and feet (Clifford, 1971).

- Teenage boys seek in girls (in order) good looks, good body, friendliness, and intelligence (Hass, 1979).

- Teenage girls seek in boys (in order) intelligence, good looks, good body, and good conversation skills (Hass, 1979).

- Physical attractiveness is related to teenage achievement and psychological well-being (Umberson & Hughes, 1987).

- Early adolescents are the most concerned with body image. In one study, subjects were blindfolded and asked to touch an upside down mask of their own face. Young adolescents recognized themselves faster than either older adolescents or adults (Collins & LaGanza, 1982).

Puberty

Although pubescence is viewed as a 2-year period, the roots of sexual maturity begin much earlier. The mechanisms that control pubertal change develop prenatally, and pubertal hormones begin increasing around age 7, although somatic changes do not come until 4 or 5 years later. These somatic changes do not come smoothly, and early adolescents experience extreme asynchrony, which contributes to awkwardness and clumsiness (Petersen, 1988). For example, feet usually grow faster than the arms and legs, and many preadolescents trip over their own feet and every object within reach.

Women	Men
1. Weight (78%)	1. Weight (56%)
2. Waistline (70%)	2. Waistline (49%)
3. Aging (48%)	3. Muscles (39%)
4. Thighs (46%)	4. Hair (36%)
5. Teeth (37%)	5. Teeth (36%)
6. Hair (35%)	6. Height (34%)
7. Height (28%)	7. Aging (27%)
8. Muscles (19%)	8. Thighs (9%)

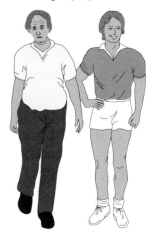

Figure 10.1
Physical features that men and women would like to change.
Source: Data from L. Harris, *Inside America*, 4, 1987. Vintage. New York.

Hormones and Puberty

Scientists are interested in the hormonal processes involved in puberty, and studies in this area are often quite creative. For example, some researchers compared hormones in adolescent boys of normal stature with pygmy adolescent boys (Merimee, Zapf, Hewlett, & Cavalli-Sforza, 1987). The researchers found that both groups of boys had normal growth hormone and testosterone levels. However, pygmy adolescent boys had only a third of the normal level of IGF 1 (an insulin-like growth factor). IGF 1 may be the principal factor responsible for normal pubertal growth. Without IGF 1, testosterone seems incapable of stimulating much growth.

Hormone levels may affect adjustment; the most competent adjustment during adolescence is associated with higher sex steroids (testosterone and estradiol) and lower adrenal androgen levels. This relationship is found for both males and females, although the relationship is stronger for males (Nottelman et al., 1985). Higher estradiol and androstenedione levels are associated with increased aggressive behaviors for girls (Inoff-Germain et al., 1988).

Menarche

Menarche, a female's first menstruation, is triggered by a complex hormonal sequence controlled by the hypothalamus and the amount of body fat. On average, at menarche, girls are 55 percent water and 24 percent body fat. An additional 10 lb (4.5 kg) of fat is typically added by age 18. At age 18, an average of 28 percent of the female body weight is fat, while men's average percentage of fat is only 13 (Frisch, 1987). This higher percentage of body fat for females is normal and desirable—the extra body fat helps to provide the extra energy needed for pregnancy and breast-feeding.

Better nutrition and health care have resulted in today's girls meeting the appropriate body fat percentage sooner. Therefore, menarche now occurs at younger ages than it did previously. This downward trend in average age of menarche is another example of a secular trend (a secular trend in height was discussed in Chapter 8). Aspects of this secular trend are listed in Table 10.2. One result of the secular trend is that ovulation begins at younger ages, thereby increasing the risk of pregnancy in adolescence.

The complex chain of events controlling the menstrual cycle begins with GnRH, or gonadotropin-releasing hormone. GnRH stimulates the pituitary gland, which, in turn, releases FSH (follicle-stimulating hormone) and LH (luteinizing hormone). FSH triggers the growth of an ovarian follicle, while LH causes the release of an egg from a follicle. Meanwhile, the resultant decline in GnRH stimulates estrogen production, which leads to growth of the uterine lining. After ovulation, the follicle secretes progesterone. The progesterone readies the uterus for implantation of the egg. If a fertilized egg is not implanted, both progesterone and estrogen levels decrease, and these hormonal changes lead to menses (Frisch, 1987).

successful study tip

The Menstrual Cycle

The menstrual cycle is complex, and charting the chain of events that leads to it will help you to learn it. As you chart the chain of events, audibly tell yourself what is happening. For example:

GnRH → stimulates pituitary gland → which releases (1) FSH (follicle growth) and (2) LH (egg release) → A decline in GnRH → stimulates estrogen production → which leads to growth of uterine lining → Ovulation → triggers release of progesterone → which readies uterus for implantation → If no implantation, → menses

Effects of Early and Late Maturation

Puberty is more than a physical event. Individuals going through these biological changes evaluate themselves differently and often revise their current relationships. For example, pubertal maturation is associated with distancing between parents and their children. Both boys and girls have increased conflict with their mothers and feel less close to their fathers. Girls' level of conflict with their fathers increases notably. Boys tend to experience the most increase in emotional and behavioral autonomy (Steinberg, 1988).

Pubertal change is most stressful when the young adolescent feels different from peers and when the changes are not seen as desirable (Petersen, 1988). Most early-maturing boys have enhanced body image and improved moods; however, most early-maturing girls have decreased feelings of attractiveness (Blyth, Bulcroft, & Simmons,

Table 10.2
Facts About the Secular Trend and Menarche

- Average height has increased about 5 cm in the 20th century. Average foot size has increased about one size (Roche, 1979).

- In 1840, average menarche occurred when females were 17 years old. Now, the average age is under 13 years (Malina, 1979).

- Male puberty is also 4 to 5 years earlier than in previous centuries. For example, in Bach's time (mid-1700s), choirboys' voices "cracked" around the age of 18; the average age now is about 13 (Rose, 1988).

- From 1890 to about 1970 the average age of menarche decrease 3 months per 10 years; the average age is no longer dropping (Vaughn, McKay, & Behrman, 1984).

- Climate has little effect on sexual development; Eskimos and Brazilians have about the same menarche timing (McAnarney & Greydanus, 1987).

- Women must have a certain percentage of fat stored before menarche—enough to meet the energy requirements of pregnancy and 3 months of lactation. Therefore, the secular trend is largely due to better nutrition and better medical care. Puberty is delayed wherever nutrition is poorer (Frisch, 1988; Leon, 1987; Malina, 1979).

- Young female ballet dancers and athletes often have later menarche than other adolescent females because they have a smaller percentage of body fat (Eveleth, 1986).

- For the first year or two after menarche, ovulation and periods may be irregular. About 45 percent are anovulary or abnormal during the first year. By age 23, most females (97 percent) experience normal menstrual cycles (Eveleth, 1986; McAnarney & Greydanus, 1987).

- In any population, 95 percent of females have menarche within ±3 years of the average age of menarche (Eveleth, 1986).

- Today, adolescent females have more positive attitudes toward menstruation than did previous generations (Henton, 1961).

- Twins have a later menarche average (Frisch, 1988).

- Both early and late maturers have the same average weight—47 kg or 103 lb—at menarche (Frisch, 1988).

1981; Crockett & Petersen, 1987). This sex difference is due to early-maturing males feeling more positive about their body changes than females. Adolescent males want to be strong, muscular, and athletic; early-maturing males excel in these areas. However, adolescent females want to be thin, and early-maturing females experience earlier weight gain than do other females (Petersen, 1988).

Early-maturing females have more behavioral problems (e.g., skipping classes) than late-maturing females. Early-maturing females are more likely to be independent and to become involved in opposite-sex relationships (Blyth et al., 1981). A longitudinal Swedish study begun in 1965 and currently studying subjects in their young adult years, found a 6-year spread in girls' maturation. As summarized in Table 10.3, early-maturing girls had more problems and even committed more criminal offenses up to the age of 26 (Magnusson, Stattin, & Allen, 1986).

Females with early menarche have accelerated growth curves, but the growth period is briefer. On the average, girls who mature later grow taller (McAnarney &

The growth spurt occurs at different ages for children, and since girls have their spurt earlier than boys, for a while some girls tower over their male peers.

Table 10.3
Percentage of Girls in Different Menarche Groups Reporting Frequent Norm Breaking at 14½ Years Old

	Age of Menarche			
	11	**11 to 12**	**12 to 13**	**13**
Home				
Ignore Parents' Prohibitions	16.7%	7.1%	2.8%	3.6%
Stay Out Late Without Permission	27.1	12.2	5.6	4.5
School				
Cheat on an Exam	17.0	5.1	5.1	7.3
Play Truant	39.6	14.3	5.6	7.1
Leisure Time				
Smoke Hashish	12.0	4.1	1.1	0.9
Get Drunk	35.4	20.0	7.9	6.3
Loiter in Town Every Evening	20.8	9.1	8.5	3.6
Pilfer From a Shop	14.6	5.2	4.5	1.8

From Magnusson, et al., "Differential Maturation Among Girls and its Relations to Social Adjustment: A Longitudinal Perspective," Table II, in *Life-Span Development and Behavior,* Vol. 7, p. 145, 1986. Copyright © 1986 Lawrence Erlbaum Associates, Hillsdale, NJ.

Greydanus, 1987). As a result, by 10th grade, late-maturing girls have more positive body images than do early-developing females—after all, the late maturers are more likely to achieve the tall and slim ideal (Blyth et al., 1981). Overall, both male and female late maturers have better psychological adjustment (Petersen & Crockett, 1985).

Because girls today have a more positive attitude about menarche than girls of earlier generations, females spend more time worrying about reaching puberty later

than their friends than they worry about being earlier than their friends (Ruble & Brooks-Gunn, 1982). Attractive girls are more anxious about pubescence than are less attractive girls (Zakin, Blyth, & Simmons, 1984).

Puberty may be especially difficult if prospective careers (e.g., dancer, runner, wrestler) require a certain body type, and puberty brings about a different body type (Zakin et al., 1984). Dissatisfaction with body size, for example, may lead to eating disorders (Petersen, 1988).

guided review

1. During adolescence, the pattern of physical changes in girls is _____ (budding of breasts), followed by _____ (pubic hair growth), the _____ spurt, and finally _____ (the first menstrual period). In boys, the typical order of changes is early _____ growth, _____, further testicular growth, _____ growth, _____ (ejaculations during sleep), growth spurt, voice change, and hair growth.
2. _____ is a person's mental representation of his or her physical body.
3. The _____ trend in menarche is largely due to improved nutrition and health care resulting in adolescent girls today attaining the appropriate body _____ composition necessary to trigger the events causing sexual maturation.
4. Most _____ boys have enhanced body images, while _____ girls are more likely to have decreased feelings of attractiveness. Late-maturing girls, on the other hand, are likely to have more positive body images than early-maturing girls.

answers

1. larche; pubarche; growth; menarche; testicular; pubarche; penile; nocturnal emissions {LO-1, 2}. **2.** Body image [LO-1]. **3.** secular; fat [LO-2]. **4.** early-maturing; early-maturing [LO-3].

Cognitive Development in Adolescence

Piaget's Stage of Formal Operations

During early adolescence, many teenagers enter Piaget's fourth stage of cognitive development, the stage of **formal operations.** Piaget believed that many individuals make this transition between the ages of 11 and 14 (Inhelder & Piaget, 1958).

Characteristics of the Formal Operations Stage

The formal operations stage is characterized by the hypothetico-deductive method of problem solving, efficient convergent problem solving, and the ability to do abstract thinking (Wagner, 1987). Figure 10.2 gives examples of tasks that individuals in the formal operations stage are more skilled at than are those still in Piaget's third stage. Adolescents in the fourth stage become skilled in scientific experimentation, understanding metaphors, using contrary-to-fact reasoning, and thinking about ideal situations (Siegler, 1981).

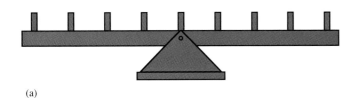

(a)

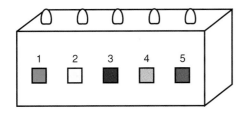

(b)

1	2	3	4	5	6
7	8	9	10	11	12
13	14	15	16	17	18
19	20	21	22	23	24
25	26	27	28	29	30
31	32	33	34	35	36
37	38	39	40	41	42

(c)

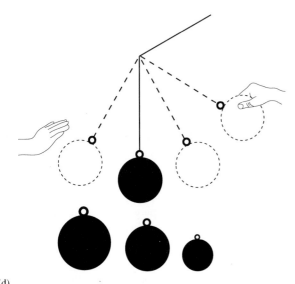

(d)

Figure 10.2

Typical tasks to measure formal operations ability. (a) Balancing scale. (b) Combinatorial task. (c) Which square is it task. (d) Pendulum problem.

Table 10.4
Formal and Postformal Thought

Piagetian Stage	Overriding Conceptualization	Tiers of Thought
Formal Operational	Analysis	Hypothetico-Deductive; Empirical Verification
Postoperational	Synthesis	Relativism Dialectical Synthesis

From D. A. Kramer, "Post-Formal Operations? A Need for Further Conceptualization" in *Human Development,* 26, Table 1, p. 96, 1983. Reprinted with permission from Aldex Publishing Corporation.

They are able "to think beyond the present, as the empirical world comes to be viewed as only one of an infinite number of possibilities" (Wagner, 1987, p. 23). Adolescents can take this new ability in many directions—from fascination with science fiction novels or such games as Dungeons and Dragons, to involvement in political campaigns or specific social causes.

Postformal Operations Stage

Some psychologists have proposed an additional stage to cognitive development—the **postformal operations** stage. These researchers believe that the formal operations stage is characterized by convergent problem solving but that a more advanced style of thinking is divergent thinking. Formal operations allows good problem *solving;* postformal operations allows good problem *finding.*

Table 10.4 summarizes the major features of both formal and postformal thought. The postformal operations stage features: (1) the realization that knowledge is relative and nonabsolute in nature, (2) the acceptance of contradiction, and (3) skilled integration of contradictions into an overriding whole view or goal (Kramer, 1983). Some sophisticated humor is based on the joining together of nonagreeing elements, such as the bumper sticker that announces "Another ho-hum day in paradise." Adolescents may develop what appears to be an odd sense of humor as they learn to deal with the world's inconsistent elements.

Elkind's Concept of Adolescent Egocentrism

Aspects of Adolescent Egocentrism

David Elkind (Elkind, 1978; Elkind & Bowen, 1979) proposed that adolescents experience their own version of egocentrism, an inability to think beyond their own perspectives. In **adolescent egocentrism,** teenagers fail to differentiate between what is important to themselves and what is important to others. They often think that others share their same thoughts and preoccupations. Therefore, they often fail to distinguish between what is unique and universal—that is, a new, exciting experience (e.g., falling in love) for the self is assumed to be unique for humankind (e.g., "No one has even loved like this before").

What causes adolescent egocentrism? The cognitive abilities associated with the formal operations stage allow so many new ideas and ways to process information that teenagers may become preoccupied with their own world and not pay much attention to the needs of others. Since these formal operations cognitive skills are new, however, adolescents make several errors when they use these sophisticated ways of thinking. In addition, the physical, emotional, and social changes that occur in adolescence force teenagers to deal with themselves, instead of with the world view of others (deRosenroll, 1987).

Most of the physical, emotional, and social changes of adolescence occur in the early adolescent years, and self-consciousness and egocentric behavior form a curvilinear relationship from childhood to adulthood. Self-consciousness dramatically increases in early adolescence and then gradually declines from middle adolescence through late adolescence (deRosenroll, 1987). Egocentrism peaks around age 15 or 16 (Elkind, 1978).

Actually, attitudes toward the self (the individual as known to the individual) can be influenced by four dimensions (Simmons, Rosenberg, & Rosenberg, 1973):

1. **Self-consciousness**—the prominence one ascribes to oneself in others' perceptions
2. **Stability**—The consistency of one's self-image
3. **Self-esteem**—One's general self-attitude of worth
4. **Perceived self**—How one imagines others see him or her

In all areas, self-image disturbances are greater for early teens (12 to 14) than for children (8 to 11) and older adolescents. Many early adolescents are highly critical of themselves (Simmons et al., 1973).

Not only does adolescent egocentrism make teenagers self-conscious and self-critical; it also tends to make them overly conscious and extremely critical of others, especially parents (deRosenroll, 1987). No wonder many parents believe that the early adolescent years are the most difficult and least rewarding part of child-rearing.

Elkind (1978) emphasized two ways in which adolescents are affected by their low skills in differentiating their own viewpoints from those of others: personal fable and imaginary audience.

Personal Fable

Adolescents develop a **personal fable** because their new thinking abilities make them feel special, unique, and eternal. The personal fable contributes to a sense of personal strength and comfort, but also can lead to an inappropriate sense of indestructibility.

Personal fable contributes to high risk-taking behaviors and lack of safety precautions because teenagers believe that their uniqueness will magically protect from negative outcomes: *Only other people* die if they drive after consuming alcohol, only other people get hooked on drugs or cigarettes, and only other people get pregnant if they have sex without contraceptives. *Even if* engaging in potentially dangerous behaviors, adolescents often feel safe, om-

Younger children get higher scores on video games when observed while teenagers do better when they think they are not being observed.

nipotent, and indestructible. As individuals get older, they fall prey to the personal fable less often, but few individuals completely outgrow the idea that "Despite the odds, I'll make it" or "That can't happen to me."

The personal fable also has an endearing side. As teenagers consider political and social issues, they may come to believe that their generation can do better than all previous generations, that it is up to them to end poverty, bring about world peace, and make the environment safe again. This idealism has played roles in changing people's lives: Some adolescents have marched for civil rights or to end wars; others have joined the Peace Corps to make a difference.

Imaginary Audience

The **imaginary audience** involves self-consciousness and an exaggerated sense of how often an individual is at the center of others' thoughts. Adolescents believe that they are usually the target of others' attention and criticism (Elkind, 1978). Therefore, they may spend inordinate amounts of time adjusting their physical appearance to please the "audience." Or they may become very embarrassed over a minor blunder that hardly anyone even noticed (because they believe everybody noticed). Parents often find that teenagers respond dramatically to minor criticism because the comment validates the scrutinizing attention of their imaginary audience. Although the imaginary audience usually increases feelings of being ill-at-ease, adolescents occasionally glory in the imaginary spotlight of attention.

As with the personal fable, the imaginary audience is not entirely outgrown. From time to time, you may still feel very self-conscious because you cognitively overestimate how much you are being observed and judged by others. Still, the imaginary audience exerts its strongest effects in early adolescence. Researchers comparing 4th- through 12th-graders on imaginary audience scale scores found that 8th-graders received the highest scores of all (Elkind & Bowen, 1979). In another study investigating self-consciousness aspects of the imaginary audience, video-game players were observed either covertly or overtly.

Subjects under age 12 and less self-conscious improved their scores when overtly observed, but subjects over age 12 and more self-conscious scored better when the observer was hidden rather than overt (Tice, Buder, & Baumeister, 1985).

The Impact of Schooling

How Cognitive Abilities Affect School

As individuals enter the formal operations stage of cognitive development, their school abilities are greatly modified. Until this stage of thinking, science class is limited to learning facts and doing rote observations and experiments. How, students can engage in abstract thinking and theoretical reasoning about science. Rather than just doing experiments, students can now figure out formulas and why the experiments work (Lovell & Shayer, 1978). Likewise, algebra becomes possible. Composition papers are likely to include better reasoning, more logical organization, and more sophisticated comparisons.

On the other hand, chronological age is not a good predictor of when formal operations thinking is possible. Some adolescents experience failures in school because they are scheduled for algebra class before their cognitive abilities have matured. In fact, some researchers believe that the majority of high school students have not completely reached formal operational thought and suffer if most of their instruction is hypothetical in nature, rather than filled with concrete or personal examples (Cowan, 1978).

How School Affects Cognitive Abilities

Schooling influences cognitive abilities. Formally educated people understand more about general rules and apply them better; they can verbalize their behavior better and are better at applying cognitive skills to new situations; they also do better on memory tasks (Nerlove & Snipper, 1981; Rogoff, 1981; Scribner & Cole, 1973). Even though schools might not specifically teach thinking and memory skills, school tasks improve these skills and help individuals to generalize their usefulness to novel situations.

School Building Transitions

When you were in the kindergarten to 12th grade school system, at what grades did you change school buildings? Some individuals went to schools that put only a couple of grades in one building, and others were in schools that kept six or more grades in one building. What effects did these different building transitions have on your personality and self-evaluations? What do you think would be the optimal grade groupings within school buildings? Why?

Researchers compared the effects of kindergarten-through-sixth (K–6) and kindergarten-through eighth (K–8) schools on the transition into adolescence (Simmons & Blyth, 1987). They concluded that joint pubertal changes and school changes for seventh-graders were associated with negative effects:

> *Short- and longer-term negative effects were associated with an early transition in Grade 7 into a large, impersonal junior high school. Children who remained in an intimate K–8 school 2 more years before moving into a large senior high did not evidence these negative effects. In addition, early pubertal development for girls, extremely early pubertal development for boys, early independence from parental supervision and chaperonage, and early dating all had problematic aspects. (p. xii)*

Figure 10.3 shows the differences between K–6 and K–8 school systems. As you can see, K–8 systems produce higher levels of participation and self-esteem for grades 6 through 10. The differences are stronger for girls than for boys (Simmons & Blyth, 1987).

The negative effects of the K–6 system seem to be largely due to the burden of cumulative life changes. All seventh-graders are dealing with biological, cognitive, family, and social changes, but K–6 students are also dealing with school transitions, while those in K–8 can delay this transition to a more settled time. In addition, K–8 seventh-graders may be benefiting from a "top dog" effect—that is, the positive aspects of being among the older students in the school when little else seems to be under control. Meanwhile, in the K–6 system, seventh-graders must add a school transition and being the "bottom dog" (youngest students in the school) to all the other changes going on (Simmons & Blyth, 1987).

How Much School?

Many adolescents decide to drop out of the school system. Some are illiterate and have experienced years of low performance and failures. Others leave because of economic pressures or because of pregnancy. Some dropouts are academically gifted and are bored by high school, or they believe that they can achieve more in a different setting. Alternatives to traditional high school (individualized instruction, alternate hours, tutoring, GEDs [general equivalency diplomas]) help with some of these issues. Other individuals decide to continue their education beyond the high school years, either in a vocational training school or a college. One of the tasks for these students is choosing the right school and appropriate career. The exploration of options can be both exhilarating and scary for the adolescent (Elkind, 1988).

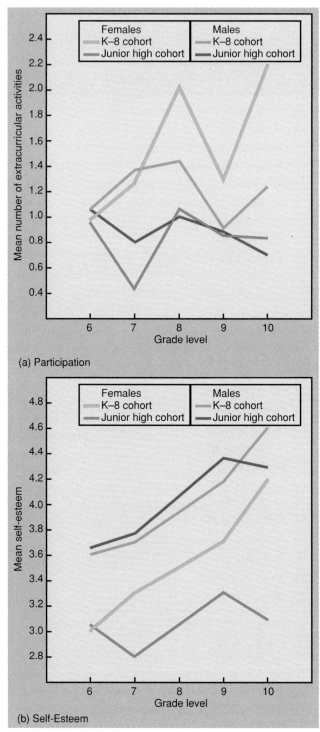

(a) Participation

(b) Self-Esteem

Figure 10.3

Differences in (a) participation and (b) self-esteem for adolescents in K–6 and K–8 school systems.

Source: Data from R. G. Simmons and D. A. Blyth, *Moving Into Adolescence: The Impact of Pubertal Change and School Context,* fig. 7.3, page 220 and fig. 8.1, page 234, 1984, Aldene deGruyter, New York.

5. Piaget's _____ operations stage of cognitive development is characterized by significant increases in the ability to do _____ thinking, with major advances in _____ reasoning and _____ problem solving.
6. By contrast, the _____ operations stage is characterized by _____ and _____ thinking.
7. Elkind proposed that in _____, teenagers again experience the inability to assume a perspective other than their own.
8. The _____ involves feelings of uniqueness and invulnerability, while the _____ involves feelings of self-consciousness and exaggerated attention from others.
9. List three ways in which schooling positively influences cognitive development.
   1.
   2.
   3.

answers

5. formal; abstract; hypothetico-deductive; convergent [LO-4]. 6. postformal; problem finding; divergent [LO-4]. 7. adolescent egocentrism [LO-5]. 8. personal fable; imaginary audience [LO-5]. 9. Possibilities include: better verbal skills, better memory skills, better application of cognitive skills to new situations, better understanding of general rules and their application [LO-6].

Health Concerns in the Teen Years

General Health Concerns

Over 90 percent of high school students rate their health as either excellent or good (Sobal, Klein, Graham, & Black, 1988). Yet, many adolescents deal with illness, disabilities, and health-risking behaviors, as the following list suggests (McAnarney & Greydanus, 1987):

Five million (12 percent) adolescents have chronic illnesses or disabilities.

Over 1 million adolescents have epilepsy.

Over 100,000 individuals under the age of 20 have diabetes.

The most common reason for school absenteeism is asthma.

The average 15-year-old has had 10 "diseased" teeth.

Over 80 percent have to deal with some degree of acne vulgaris.

Sixteen of every 100,000 teenagers have cancer.

At least 5,000 adolescents die by suicide each year, and 250,000 to 1 million attempt suicide.

About 5,000 teenagers are murdered annually.

Over 25,000 adolescents die in accidents each year.

Over 10 percent of teenagers smoke at least 10 cigarettes a day.

Teenagers get pregnant over 1 million times each year. About 600,000 give birth to babies, and about 400,000 choose abortions. About 30,000 pregnancies occur to girls under the age of 14.

Teenagers have millions of cases of sexually transmitted diseases per year. Teenagers get at least one fourth of all gonorrhea.

More than 1 million female adolescents have had pelvic inflammatory diseases.

More than 1 in 10 teenagers will become infertile because of sexually transmitted diseases.

Among early adolescents (seventh- and eighth-graders), 35 percent often think about their own health, 55 percent sometimes think about it, and the other 10 percent rarely concern themselves. Early adolescents' highest concerns are dental health, friendships, nutrition, and sex. Their lowest concerns are smoking, birth control, pregnancy, and homosexuality. Even among the lowest concerns, from 15 to 23 percent of the students were very concerned about the issue. Overall, girls have more health concerns than boys. Girls are more concerned than boys about menstruation, pregnancy, birth control, being overweight, dieting, child abuse, stomach pain, nervousness, depression, acne, and headaches. Boys are more concerned than girls on only two issues—sports injuries and sex—and would most like to have class health presentations on sex (Sobal, 1987).

High school students are more concerned than junior high students with their health. About 8 percent of middle adolescents still do not concern themselves with their health, but 61 percent think about their health often (Sobal et al., 1988). The top health concerns of 831 high school students and their teachers are summarized in Table 10.5. Late adolescents (college freshmen) would like additional health knowledge in the following areas: stress control, rape prevention, suicide prevention, safety, and prevention and care of minor illness (Vinal et al., 1986).

Adolescents are more likely to assess their physical health as high when their school achievements are high, when they participate in sports and other exercise, and when they are not depressed (Mechanic & Hansell, 1987).

Eating Disorders

Why So Prevalent Among Teens?

Eating disorders affect many adolescents, especially females. Teenagers are vulnerable because they become pre-occupied with analyzing their bodies as they are undergoing revolutionary changes. Careful scrutiny in mirrors reveals many imperfections that teenagers want to overcome. Many girls entering adolescence find it hard to appreciate the attractiveness of their new curves because they misinterpret the curves as "getting fat." Only 20 percent are overweight, yet about half perceive themselves as overweight (Tiggemann & Rothblum, 1988). Teenagers who are self-critical about their physical aspects, thinking abilities, social graces, fashion tastes, achievements, and communication skills may decide that improving their bodies is the area to "tackle" first.

Add to the individual's preoccupation the cultural preoccupation with thinness. Many teenagers find it hard to believe that, in the 19th century, popular sex-symbol singer

Table 10.5
Top Health Concerns of High School Students and as Perceived by Their Teachers

Health Concerns According to Students:

1. Schoolwork (81.1%)
2. Dental (75.1%)
3. Abuse (72.6%)
4. Venereal Disease (66.9%)
5. Acne (66.8%)
6. Sex (66.7%)
7. Adults (63.9%)
8. Pregnancy (57.7%)
9. Friends (57.3%)
10. Drugs (54.8%)
11. Headache (54.5%)
12. Overweight (54.0%)

Students' Health Concerns as Perceived by Their Teachers:

1. Sex (78.8%)
2. Friends (73.3%)
3. Acne (63.6%)
4. Discrimination (61.5%)
5. Pregnancy (53.5%)
6. Overweight (50.4%)
7. Drugs (48.3%)
8. Depression (45.4%)
9. Venereal Disease (44.8%)
10. Abuse (42.0%)
11. Birth Control (41.5%)
12. Headache (40.0%)

From J. Sobal, et al., "Health Concerns of High School Students and Teachers' Beliefs About Student Health Concerns." Reproduced by permission of *Pediatrics,* Vol. 81, p. 220, Table 2, 1988.

Lillian Russell weighed about 200 lb, or that 5-ft, 5-inch Marilyn Monroe weighed 135 lb. Today's models and actresses tend to be thin, thin, thin. Supermodel Twiggy of the 1960s may best symbolize this movement—her measurements were 31–22–32 (Boskind-White & White, 1987). Miss America beauty contestants have averaged 10 to 15 percent below the average weight for women of equal height. Sixty-nine percent of female television characters are thin (Stake & Lauer, 1987).

Obesity

Obesity is defined as having (1) body weight at least 20 percent above the upper limit for one's height, and (2) body fat at least 25 percent of a male's body weight or 30 percent of a female's body weight. Adolescents are a significant proportion of the 45 million obese Americans (Stein, 1987), and overweight adolescents suffer both physical and social

Table 10.6 Comparison of Eating Habits Between Thais and Americans		
Eating Habit	**Percentage of Thais With Habit (N=221)**	**Percentage of Americans With Habit (N=243)**
1. Eating Between Meals	88%	81%
2. Eating When Not Hungry	89	76
3. Influenced by Sight or Smell	90	69
4. Inclined to Overeat	72	66
5. Finishing Food on Plate Even If Not Hungry	63	45
6. Using Food as a Reward	25	74
7. Rate of Eating: Fast	36	26
Average	56	63
Slow	8	21

From J. F. Schumaker, et al., "Eating Behavior Among Thais and Americans" in *The Journal of Psychology,* 119, Table 1, p. 472, 1986. Reprinted with permission of the Helen Dwight Reid Educational Foundation. Published by Heldref Publications, 1319 Eighteenth St., N.W., Washington, DC. 20036-1802. Copyright © 1986.

negative consequences. Although both obese boys and girls are devalued, the negative effects are stronger for females. Average-weight subjects rate the ideal man as slightly above normal weight and the ideal woman as slightly below normal weight (Stake & Lauer, 1987).

Overweight adolescent females date less, are the least likely to attract upwardly mobile men for marriage, and are rated low in likability by others (Bray, 1986; Stake & Lauer, 1987). Being fat leads to more body self-consciousness and fewer social activities (Tiggemann & Rothblum, 1988). Not surprisingly, overweight teenagers often have below-average self-esteem (Davis, Wheeler, & Willy, 1987). Which came first—the weight or the self-depreciation?

Extra weight poses a significant health risk, even for adolescents. In a study of 36 obese adolescents, 97 percent had at least four of eight risk factors for coronary heart disease. This same study found that a 20-week exercise and diet program reduced the risk factors much more than just dieting alone (Becque, Katch, Rocchini, Marks, & Moorehead, 1988).

One common assumption has been that overweight people eat differently and more poorly than do others. Yet, a study comparing the eating habits of Americans and Thais (who are much thinner) found that the Americans had better eating habits (see Table 10.6). In addition, the obese subjects in the American sample had better eating habits than normal-weight subjects, except for eating too quickly (Schumaker, Small, & Ward, 1985).

Most researchers believe that being overweight involves a number of factors in addition to eating style and food choices. Recent evidence suggests that obesity problems are also influenced by genetics (Price, Cadoret, Stunkard, & Troughton, 1987), exercise habits, and attitudes about food's role in life.

Dieting alone usually fails to help obese individuals lose fat. The first weight loss is glycogen, which is stored

Often adolescents who are thin view themselves as overweight. A distorted body image is associated with the eating disorder of anorexia nervosa and bulimia.

in the muscles and liver, and not fat. The body soon readjusts to the lower number of calories and slows the metabolic rate. A combination of more nutritious eating and regular exercise has more success, but this change in lifestyle is difficult in the pizza-ice-cream-and-television world of many adolescents.

Anorexia Nervosa

Anorexia nervosa is an eating disorder in which individuals—mostly, female adolescents—diet and exercise until their body weight is significantly below normal, which creates serious, life-threatening health risks. Individuals who believe that "You can never be too rich or too thin" and people pursuing careers requiring strict body weight (acting, dancing, modeling, gymnastics) are at increased risk for anorexia (Striegel-Moore, Silberstein, & Rodin, 1986).

Although anorexics look very thin and unhealthy to others, they usually have a disturbed body image and view themselves as overweight (Striegel-Moore et al., 1986). Perhaps adolescent girls who have anorexia are trying to keep their prepubertal looks and avoid growing up—they want to be their parents' "good little girl." An opposing viewpoint is that society equates weight-loss efforts with a sign of maturity—that is, dieting is a metaphor for growing up and becoming independent (Striegel-Moore et al., 1986). Table 10.7 lists factors that contribute to the incidence of anorexia nervosa.

Although anorexics come from a variety of backgrounds and exhibit a wide range of personality characteristics, some researchers and therapists believe that middle-class

1. Psychological consequences of starvation: Inability to experience pleasure, restricted affect, preoccupation with thoughts of food, accentuation of preexisting personality features, decreased mental concentration, social isolation

2. Central dynamic conflict: The purpose anorexia nervosa serves in the individual's life

3. Cardinal symptoms of anorexia nervosa: Fear of fatness, pursuit of thinness, severe perceptual distortion

4. Predisposing personality features: Obsessional, histrionic, borderline

5. Consequences of chronic illness: Prolonged dependence; immaturity; change in, or lack of progression in, social role

6. Associated psychiatric syndromes: Depressive illness, obsessive-compulsive disorders, alcoholism

7. Misbeliefs learned from family, peers, and society that thinness leads to happiness and effectiveness

adolescent and young adult females who are strongly oriented toward academic achievement and traditional lifestyles are most vulnerable to this eating disorder. These "good children" are eager to comply, achieve, and receive approval, but feel isolated, lonely, and imperfect, and have low self-esteem (Boskind-White & White, 1987).

Almost all female anorexics experience amenorrhea (absence of menstruation) because their body fat percentage is too low. They have intense hunger pangs and other signs of hunger, but they either ignore them or use them as positive reinforcers for doing well on their diet. Anorexics wear several layers of clothes, both to reduce negative comments from others and to compensate for their thermoregulation disorder (inability to maintain normal body temperature). They suffer from bone marrow hypoplasia, which results in anemia, constipation, kidney problems, and various cardiovascular disorders, including postural hypotension and bradycardia. When the body has no fat to metabolize, it metabolizes heart muscle, increasing the anorexic's risk of heart attack (Palla & Litt, 1988).

Professional help is recommended because professionals are aware of the life-threatening risks to anorexics if refeeding occurs too quickly (Palla & Litt, 1988). Treatment programs can educate individuals to think differently about food and weight, and adolescents enjoy the shared support of other anorexics. In one study, over a period of 24 months, 29 percent of anorexic patients improved significantly in weight and health (Yager, Landsverk, & Edelstein, 1987).

Binge-Eating

Another eating disorder that teenagers may acquire is binge-eating, the obsession and craving for food accompanied by obsessive eating. Binge-eaters may be overweight, normal weight, or underweight, depending on how often they binge and what behaviors (e.g., exercise, dieting) they engage in between binges. About 10 percent of the American population and 18 percent of females ages 13 to 30 have been bingers at some point (Pope & Hudson, 1984). More homosexual men than heterosexual men have binge-eating problems (Yager, Kurtzman, Landsverk, & Wiesmeier, 1988).

Like anorexics, bingers are likely to agree with such statements as, "Attractiveness increases the likelihood of professional success," and "What is fat is bad, what is thin is beautiful, and what is beautiful is good" (Striegel-Moore et al., 1986). Women who engage in eating binges estimate lower body weights for their ideal body weight than do nonbingers (Williamson, Kelley, Davis, Ruggiero, Blovin, 1985). Also, binge-eaters tend to be more depressed than nonbingers (Krueger & Bornstein, 1987).

Bulimia

Bulimia, also called **bulimarexia,** binge-purge syndrome, and dietary chaos syndrome (Boskind-White & White, 1987), is an eating disorder in which individuals binge-eat from 1,000 to 10,000 cal and then use fasting, self-induced vomiting, laxatives, and diuretics to purge themselves of feelings of being bloated, nauseous, and physically sick. Some bulimics consume huge amounts of fruits to purposely cause diarrhea (Muus, 1986; Striegel-Moore et al., 1986). Table 10.8 shows the behaviors that bulimics use to counteract binge-eating, as well as some of the serious medical complications associated with bulimia.

Bulimics want thin, noncurvaceous bodies because this represents fashionable slimness and because they believe that curvaceous figures represent less intelligence (Silverstein & Perdue, 1988). Like anorexics, bulimics often come from upwardly mobile families with very high expectations and low structure. The fathers are preoccupied with work, the mothers are overinvolved in their daughters' lives, siblings engage in intense competition, and males have more power than females (Boskind-White & White, 1987; Powers, Schulman, Gleghorn, & Prange, 1987; Schwartz, 1987). Eating disorders may serve to divert attention from unacknowledged conflicts within families (Erens, 1985).

Drug Use and Abuse

Prevalence of Drug Use

Only 11 percent of 9- to 13-year-olds, but 42 percent of 14- to 17-year-olds, use drugs frequently (Coombs & Landsverk, 1988). As shown in Figure 10.4, drug use is prevalent among high school students. Drug use among young people peaked at the end of the 1970s, but despite a downward trend in the 1980s, many young people currently use drugs both experimentally and regularly (Johnston, O'Malley, & Bachman, 1987).

Alcohol

A survey of 650 junior and senior high school students found that 83 percent had drunk some alcohol and that 57 percent had had their first drink by age 12 (Gibbons, Wylie,

Table 10.8
Characteristics of Bulimics and
Typical Medical Complications

Symptoms of Bulimics

1. Have intense fear of obesity (92.7%)

2. Consume high-calorie foods during binges (92.7%)

3. Feel fat although underweight (84.0%)

4. Have sought help for binge-eating (56.3%)

5. Binge-eat several times a week (54.2%)

6. Have a marked history of amenorrhea (48.0%)

7. Engage in the following behaviors to counteract binge-eating:

   a. Fasting (90.7%)

   b. Self-induced vomiting (85.2%)

   c. Excessive exercise (75.5%)

   d. Diet pills (75.5%)

   e. Laxatives (56.3%)

   f. Diuretics (32.1%)

Typical Medical Complications of Bulimics

1. Postural hypotension (83%)

2. Bradycardia (92% less than 60 per minute; 25% less than 40 per minute)

3. Renal changes

4. Thermoregulation disorder (83% under 36.3∞ C; 17% under 35.5∞ C.)

5. Constipation (about 33%; especially with laxative use)

6. Gastric dilation

7. Esophagitis (burning pain, at times radiating to the jaw or down one or both arms)

8. Involuntary vomiting

9. Loss of gag reflex

10. Electrolyte imbalances (especially after vomiting, if "water loaded," or if laxatives, diuretics, or ipecac have been abused)

11. Enamel erosion and dental caries

12. Fluid retention and malabsorption syndromes

13. Endocrine abnormalities

14. Bleeding tendency

Source: Data from P. S. Powers, et al., "Perceptual and Cognitive Abnormalities in Bulimia" in *American Journal of Psychiatry,* 144, 1456–1460, 1987. From B. Palla and I. F. Litt, "Medical Complications of Eating Disorders in Adolescents" in *Pediatrics,* 81, 613–623, 1988. From J. E. Mitchell, "Bulimia: Medical and Physiological Aspects," in *Handbook of Eating Disorders,* p. 341, Table 18.2, 1986, edited by K. D. Brownell and J. P. Foreyt, Basic Books, New York, NY.

Echterling, & French, 1986). Over 90 percent of high school seniors have tried alcohol. More males than females drink frequently, but this sex difference has been declining over the last decade. Another study found that approximately 65 percent of 1986 high school seniors used alcohol at least monthly, 5 percent used alcohol daily, and 37 percent had had five or more drinks on at least one occasion in the previous 2 weeks (Johnston et al., 1987).

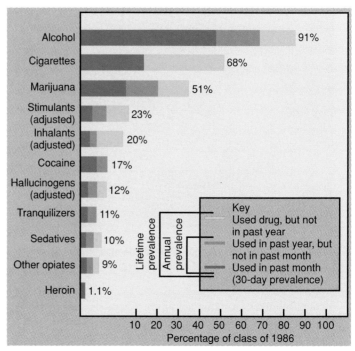

Figure 10.4
Prevalence and recency of drug use in high school seniors, class of 1986.
Source: Data from L. D. Johnson, et al., *National Trends in Drug Use and Related Factors Among American High School Students and Young Adults,* 1975–1986, fig. 2, p. 30, 1987. National Institute on Drug Abuse, Rockville, MD.

Obviously, many teenagers are already problematic, heavy drinkers, and the number of alcohol treatment programs for young people increased during the 1980s. Societal concerns also led to the raising of the drinking age from 18 to 21. This change in legal drinking age already is credited with reductions in road accidents and other risk-taking behaviors among adolescents (Newman, 1987).

Although adolescents are affected by drug education programs that advise abstaining from alcohol and other drugs, other influences promote alcohol use among the young. Each year, more than 5,000 beer commercials are shown on network television. The typical teenager is exposed to nearly a thousand beer, wine, and liquor ads through television and print media each year. The drinkers in these ads are physically attractive, adventurous, affluent, sophisticated, and successful. Alcohol is associated with sports figures, entertainment celebrities, and sensuous personalities (Atkin, Hocking, & Block, 1984).

Even more powerful than exposure to alcohol advertising, however, is peer influence on alcohol drinking. Males are more influenced by their peers than are females; older adolescents are more influenced by their peers than are early adolescents (Atkin et al., 1984). Research suggests that, while drinking friends influence teenagers' decisions to drink, teenagers who drink start to make new friends with teens who drink (Fisher & Bauman, 1988). Peers are very important in the adolescent years, and one difficulty with giving up frequent drinking is the feeling of being different from friends. In addition, the exdrinker no longer feels comfortable in drinking situations. Giving up

Many teenagers drink alcohol at times, and some drive while intoxicated. Faulty thinking may lead them to mistakenly believe that bad consequences will not happen to them because of these poor choices.

alcohol involves changing activities, situations, and friendships (Fingarette, 1988). Parents and religious background have relatively little effect on adolescents' decisions regarding drinking (Atkin et al., 1984).

Many teenagers who drink alcohol also use other drugs, a combination that can create huge problems (see Table 10.9). The combination of cigarette smoking and alcohol is associated with long-term health risks. Drinking alcohol appears to increase the absorption of cancer-causing tobacco chemicals in the body. As a result, those who combine drinking and smoking have higher incidences of mouth and throat cancers (Parker, 1985).

Cigarettes

Among adolescents, cigarette smoking is second only to alcohol as the most common drug: About two thirds of high school seniors have tried smoking cigarettes. About 20 percent of high school seniors smoke cigarettes daily (Johnston et al., 1987). Occasional cigarette use is more common among females than among males, but regular use is more common among males. More female adolescents smoke half a pack a day, and more male adolescents smoke a pack a day (Boyle & Offord, 1986; Johnston et al., 1987). Most people who ever smoke start smoking at a young age: 95 percent of smokers start before age 20, with grades 6 through 10 being the most vulnerable years (Benderly, 1987).

As with alcohol, peer influence is a strong predictor of cigarette smoking (Castro, Maddahian, Newomb, & Bentler, 1987). Friends influence the decision to begin smoking, and after that, smokers often choose friends who smoke. Especially now, smokers may align themselves to maintain support for their cigarette habit in a society that is more strongly discouraging smoking (Fisher & Bauman, 1988).

Children and adolescents agree that smoking hurts the body. Two thirds say that they "hate" smoking. However, young people also overestimate the number of peers who smoke (Benderly, 1987). Their misperceptions in this area may add pressure to "be like the others" and smoke. In fact, those who begin smoking are the most likely to overestimate cigarette usage (Collins et al., 1987).

Table 10.9
The Effects of Mixing Alcohol and Drugs

Drug Class/Trade Name(s)	Effects of Alcohol
Antialcohol Antabuse	Severe reactions to even small amounts: headache, nausea, blurred vision, convulsions, rapid drop in blood pressure, coma, possible death.
Antibiotics Penicillin, Cyantin	Reduces therapeutic effectiveness.
Antidepressants Elavil, Sinequan, Tofranil, Nardil, Marplan	Increased central nervous system depression, blood pressure changes. Combination use of alcohol with monoamine-oxidase inhibitors can trigger massive increases in blood pressure, even brain hemorrhage and death.
Antihistamines Allerest, Dristan	Drowsiness and central nervous system depression. Impairs driving ability.
Aspirin Bayer, Alka-Seltzer	Irritates stomach lining. May cause gastrointestinal discomfort, bleeding.
Depressants Valium, Ativan, Placidyl, Amytal	Dangerous central nervous system depression, loss of coordination, coma. High risk of overdose and death.
Narcotics Heroin, Codeine, Darvon	Serious central nervous system depression. Possible respiratory arrest and death.
Stimulants Caffeine, Cocaine	"Masks" depressant action of alcohol. May increase blood pressure, physical tension.

From C. Parker, *Alcohol: Simple Facts About Combinations With Other Drugs,* 1987. Copyright © 1987 Do it Now Foundation, Tempe, AZ. Used with permission.

Marijuana

Marijuana use among high school seniors has been declining since 1979, suggesting that realistic education about the hazards of drugs has had some effects (Bachman, Johnston, O'Malley, & Humphrey, 1988). Yet, slightly over half of high school seniors have tried "pot," with 39 percent using it during their senior year. About 1 in 25 seniors smokes marijuana daily (Johnston et al., 1987).

Marijuana use decreases among adolescents who perceive the risks to be high and who believe that others disapprove of smoking "pot" (Bachman et al., 1988). Only recently has marijuana been considered a serious health problem, as opposed to a moral or political problem (Silber, 1987), and this change in emphasis may make marijuana less appealing among young people. Marijuana poses increased health risks since the drug itself has been getting stronger over the years (National Institute on Drug Abuse, 1984).

Cocaine

About 17 percent of high school seniors have tried cocaine, and this figure climbs to 40 percent by age 27 (Johnston et al., 1987). About 4 percent of high school seniors have tried "crack," which is a form of cocaine that is processed with baking soda and water. Compared to older cocaine users, adolescents who use cocaine (National Institute on Drug Abuse, 1986):

- Have a higher incidence of cocaine-related brain seizures, make more suicide attempts, and engage in more violent behavior.
- Exhibit marked behavioral changes and retarded psychosocial maturation.
- Are less successful in compensating for cocaine-caused dysfunctions.
- Deteriorate in functioning in an average of 1 1/2 years, as opposed to 4 years in adults.

The average young user spends about $100 a week and is from a family whose annual earnings are over $25,000. Most adolescents who use cocaine snort the drug, but about 10 percent freebase (smoke), and 2 percent inject it. Most use other drugs, especially marijuana (92 percent), alcohol (85 percent), and sedatives (64 percent) (National Institute on Drug Abuse, 1986).

Factors Associated With Drug Usage

Which adolescents use drugs? A group of researchers concluded that "the kinds of young people most 'at risk' tend to remain much the same, while the kinds and amounts of substances used shift somewhat from year to year" (Bachman, et al., 1988, p. 93). Some studies suggest that both female and male adolescents with masculine identities have relatively low rates of alcohol and drug abuse, while those who do not identify with masculine characteristics are at a greater risk of developing alcohol and drug problems (Horwitz & White, 1987).

Genetics plays a modest role in alcohol and chemical dependency. Although sons who have at least one alcoholic parent are three times more likely to become alcoholic than sons with nonalcoholic parents, more than four of five sons with an alcoholic parent do not develop a drinking problem (Fingarette, 1988).

Adolescents who regularly use drugs and alcohol tend to be disinterested in both social and educational activities and to have increased school truancy and dropout rates, low grades, heavy job commitments, and high home conflict (Bachman et al., 1988; Mensch & Kandel, 1988; Miller, J. D., 1981; Scarpitti & Datesman, 1980). Drug use in girls is higher for those from unstructured and laissez-faire homes in which there is little pressure to achieve (Block, Block, & Keyes, 1988).

Personality characteristics of adolescents who use drugs are different from those of adolescents who abstain or who are minimally involved. Specifically, alcohol misusers have more negative feelings about themselves and are less responsible, more immature, more impulsive, less concerned with social norms, self-centered, low in trust, stubborn, very expressive, and more adventurous and rebellious (Mayer, 1988).

While a major factor in adolescent drug usage is peer influence (e.g., Castro et al., 1987; Fisher & Bauman, 1988), family factors are also important. Adolescent drug users often are dealing with the absence of one or both parents, parents who use children as scapegoats, parents who use drugs themselves, parents who are inconsistent or often in conflict, poor parent-child communication, or harsh discipline. Drug *abusers* come from laissez-faire or authoritarian-type families; drug *users* are more likely to come from democratic-type families (Coombs & Landsverk, 1988; Jurich, Polson, Jurich, & Bates, 1985). Family size, birth order, religion, social class, and maturity level are not major influences (Mayer, 1988).

Sexually Transmitted Diseases

Sexually active teenagers are a high-risk group for **sexually transmitted diseases (STDs)**. Some STDs can be contracted by general poor health, lack of hygiene, and low resistance, but all genital infections labeled STDs can be contracted by sexual contact with an already infected person. Information about sexually transmitted diseases is summarized in Table 10.10.

Lowering STD Risks

Besides abstinence, risk for STDs can be lowered by taking the following precautions (Planned Parenthood of Mid-Iowa, 1987):

- Limit your sexual partners. If sexual contact is limited to one partner who is limiting contact to just you, risk for STDs is greatly reduced. Know and communicate with your partner about health issues. Look for signs of infection (e.g., sores, rashes, discharges) before sexual intercourse.
- Washing the genitals with soap and water both before and immediately after sexual contact washes away some germs. Urinating immediately after contact also removes some germs.
- Use a condom and spermicide combination, one of the best preventive measures against a variety of STDs, including AIDS.
- Sexually active persons should include STD checkups in physical exams (especially for chlamydia, gonorrhea, and AIDS). If you have an infection, tell your current and previous partners. All potentially infected individuals need to be treated.
- Know about STDs. Many do not realize that they can have more than one STD at a time or that they can be reinfected with the same STD.

AIDS

The following statistics point out the severity of AIDS (acquired immune deficiency syndrome), a deadly viral disease unnamed until 1981 and unknown prior to 1978 (Jacobs & Kerrins, 1987; Macklin, 1988; Raper & Aldridge, 1988; Rotherberg et al., 1987; Urwin, 1988):

- A study of 5,833 New Yorkers with AIDS diagnosed before 1986 (90.5 percent males; 9.5 percent females) found that 67 percent were already dead. Only 4 percent survived more than 3 years and slightly more than 1 percent survived more than 4 years. The longest anyone had survived was 8.9 years.

Table 10.10
Sexually Transmitted Diseases

Disease	Cause or Organism	How It Is Spread	How Long Before Symptoms Appear (This is only a close guess. Often, this time is hard to know. Times given are a general guide only.)	Symptoms to Look For	Possible Complications	How It Is Diagnosed	
Gonorrhea (G. C., the "clap," "drip")	A bacteria called Neisseria gonorrhoeae	Spread by close contact of a sexual nature.	2 to 10 days. Can be up to 30 days. It is difficult in a woman because she may have it for awhile before symptoms appear.	Most men have a drip from the penis, but a few men have no signs. Most women have no signs, but some may have a discharge. In later stages, women can have low abdominal pain. She can have a sore throat or anus, but it is less common.	In women: Pelvic inflammatory disease (P.I.D.) In men: Blocking of the urethra, problems with erection. Both men and women: Sterility, arthritis, heart problems, blindness. In pregnancy: Early labor, baby born dead, baby born with serious eye infection.	Tests are done on discharge from inside the penis, vagina, throat or anus. Depending on what part of the body is infected and on tests available, testing can be immediate or take up to 1 or 2 weeks for results.	
Herpes (herpes simplex II, genital herpes)	A virus called herpes simplex virus (HSV)	Spread by sexual contact.	4 to 5 days and as long as 2 weeks.	Often, there are no symptoms. If there are symptoms they will be areas of tiny blisters on the sex organs. These break open to form many small, very painful open sores. The symptoms often recur at irregular intervals.	In women: Painful urination, unable to urinate; if pregnant, can pass it on to newborn. In newborn: Eye problems, mental retardation, death.	Tests are done on the discharge from the sores or on scrapings from the sores. Blood tests. Sometimes herpes can be diagnosed by the examiner just by looking at the blisters or sores.	
Syphilis (syph, pox, bad blood, loues)	A spirochete called Treponema pallidum	Spread by sexual contact with the first sore, or with the rash later.	First stage: 10 to 90 days. Second stage: 6 weeks to 6 months later. Later stage: 10 to 20 years later.	First stage: Single, painless sore at point of contact, usually the genital organs. Second stage: "Flu-like" symptoms, rash. These symptoms may be recurring. Late stage: Problems with brain, heart, nervous system, eyes, etc.	A pregnant woman can pass the disease to her newborn. A newborn can have various birth defects or be born dead. Damage to heart, brain, and eyes.	Blood test. Microscopic exam of discharge from the open sores.	
AIDS, (acquired immune deficiency syndrome)	A virus called human T-lymphotrophic virus-type III (HTLV III) or human immunodeficiency virus (HIV)	Virus spread in body fluids, such as semen, vaginal secretion, and blood. Virus must come in contact with new person's blood through intercourse, sharing needles, blood transfusions (rare now), giving birth.	Unknown for sure. Antibodies may show up in a blood test 2 weeks to 3 to 6 months after infection with the virus. Symptoms of AIDS can show up in 6 months to 10 years. May never show symptoms, but could potentially pass it on to a sexual partner.	No symptoms at all in early stages. General "flu-like" symptoms in high-risk groups, such as: anyone with multiple sex partners or with a single partner who has multiple sex partners,homosexual men, "mainline" drug users, anyone with a blood transfusion before mid-1985, infants born to infected mothers.	The patient's body is unable to fight off other infections in lungs, blood cells, liver, brain, intestines,skin, etc. Secondary infections go unchecked and can eventually lead to death.	Usually diagnosed from signs and symptoms of the secondary disease. Presence of antibody in blood reinforces suspicion. Absolute diagnosis only with difficult, expensive tests.	
Chlamydia (nongonococcal urethritis or NGU)	A bacteria called Chlamydia trachomatis	Spread by sexual contact.	Usually about 1 to 3 weeks in men. It is unknown in women because symptoms can be vague, appearing at anytime or not at all.	In men, usually there is a discharge from the penis and burning when urinating. In women, there may be discharge from the vagina and burning when urinating. May have low abdominal pain and pain with intercourse. May have no symptoms at all.	Infection of bladder and urethra in both men and women, uterus and/or tubes (pelvic infection), anus, and sometimes eyes. Possible sterility in infected women. Pneumonia in newborn infants.	Often, diagnosed by ruling out all other sexually transmitted diseases. There are tests that can be done on the discharge taken from from vagina or penis, but they are expensive.	

Disease	Cause	How Spread	Incubation	Symptoms	Complications	Diagnosis
Yeast (candidiasis, monilial vaginal infection)	A fungus called Candida albicans	Some yeast cells are normally found in the mouth, intestines, and vagina. When there is an overgrowth of yeast, there can be symptoms. It can be passed back and forth sexually, too.	Unknown since some yeast are present normally.	White, cottage-cheese-like discharge from the vagina. Vaginal itching and burning.	Women can get bacterial infections on top of the irritation caused by yeast. If a pregnant woman has an infection while giving birth, the newborn can have a mouth infection called Thrush.	Some of the vaginal discharge is put under a microscope for evaluation. If this doesn't work, some of the discharge can be put on a culture medium, and if yeast is present, it will grow.
Gardnerella (bacterial vaginosis, bacterial vaginitis, nonspecific vaginitis)	A group of bacteria called Gardnerella vaginalis, Mobiluncus, and others (In the past, it has been called Hemophilus vaginalis or Corynebacterium vaginale)	Spread by sexual contact.	Unknown. The onset can be so gradual and vague that pinpointing it is impossible.	Many men and women do not have any symptoms. In women, heavy, chalk-like vaginal discharge that often has a bad odor; burning and pain in vagina and urinary tract can occur. In men, it may cause burning and pain on urination.	None.	Vaginal discharge is checked under a microscope.
Trich (trichomoniasis, trichomonas vaginitis)	A tiny protozoan called Trichomonas vaginalis	Spread by sexual contact.	Anywhere from 4 to 7 days to 3 to 4 weeks.	In women, there can be frothy, yellowish vaginal discharge that may smell bad, and itching and burning. Some women may have no symptoms. Most men have no symptoms, but may have discharge from penis and itching and burning.	None.	Vaginal discharge is checked under a microscope.
Venereal warts (genital warts, condyloma accuminata)	A virus called Human papilloma-virus (HPV)	Spread by sexual contact.	Normally, from 1 month to about 8 months. Occasionally, it may even be several years after infection.	There may be a few or many wartlike growths on the genital areas and/or around the anus. It's rarely found in the throat. It can cause itching. It can be found in the woman and/or the man.	The warts can spread enough and become so big that they block off the opening of the vagina, the anus, or the throat. Possibility of venereal warts becoming cancerous is under study.	A diagnosis is made from the appearance of the wartlike growths. If there are warts on the cervix, they may be found on the Pap smear.
Pubic lice (pediculosis pubis, "crabs," "cooties")	A louse called Pithirus pubis	Spread by sexual contact. Can also be "caught" from infected clothes or bedding.	About 4 to 5 weeks.	There is severe itching in the pubic area or around the anus. The lice and their eggs (nits) can be seen attached to hairs. There may be tiny dark spots on underwear.	None.	Finding the symptoms noted upon examination.
Scabies	An itch mite called Sarcoptes scabiei	Spread by sexual contact. Can also be "caught" from infected clothes or bedding.	Several days to several weeks.	There are small red areas of the skin between the fingers, creases of wrists, underarms, waist, thighs. These red spots are usually in a line. They itch severely, worse at night.	None.	Diagnosed by observing the symptoms noted. It can be confused with other rashes. It can be confirmed by scraping one of the red spots, studying it under a microscope and finding the mite.

Reprinted by permission of Family Planning Council of Iowa, Des Moines, Iowa.

Table 10.11
Ways in Which Children Acquire AIDS

1. In-utero transmission. About half of the time, an HIV-infected mother passes on her infection to the unborn fetus.

2. Trauma during vaginal delivery, when blood can be directly exchanged between an HIV-infected mother and infant.

3. Breast-feeding from an HIV-infected mother.

4. Sexual abuse by an HIV-infected person.

5. HIV-contaminated needle injections by someone to a child.

Sources: From J. Raper and J. Aldridge, "What Every Teacher Should Know About . . . AIDS," in *Childhood Education,* pp. 146–149, Table 1, p. 147, February, 1988. From E. D. Macklin, "AIDS: Implications for Families" in *Family Relations,* 37, 141–149.

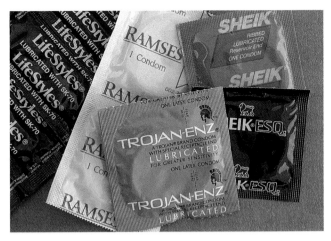

Although some adults believe that providing adolescents with condoms encourages permissive sexuality, the majority of adults approve because it means fewer pregnancies and less transmission of diseases, including AIDS.

- As of 18 January 1988, 51,361 cases of AIDS had been reported to the Centers for Disease Control, and 56 percent had already died.
- One percent of AIDS cases are individuals under age 15 (see Table 10.11). This percentage will increase as more females of childbearing age pass the HIV virus on to their newborns.
- Twelve thousand persons were affected by blood transfusions prior to 1985. At least 70 percent of hemophiliacs are infected with the HIV virus.
- Of the first 49,342 cases of AIDS (those reported by December 1987), 632 were persons under age 5; 104 were persons ages 5 to 12; and 201 were persons ages 13 to 19. Eighty-one percent of children under age 13 who were diagnosed more than 2 years ago have died.
- Sixty to seventy percent of intravenous drug users in New York City are infected.
- More than 1 million Americans are infected with HIV, and experts expect that 179,000 people will die of AIDS by the end of 1991.

HIV, the precursor of AIDS, is a retrovirus—that is, it enters a cell and reprograms the cell's DNA so that the cell reproduces the virus. Because of this, once an individual is infected with HIV, the infection is lifelong. Estimates indicate that 25 to 50 percent of HIV-positive individuals progress to AIDS within 5 to 10 years of the initial infection. AIDS itself is usually fatal within 2 years, and 80 percent die within 3 years. AIDS leads to several fatal disorders, including pneumocystis cannii and Kaposi's sarcoma, both of which were fairly rare and curable before AIDS (Jacobs & Kerrins, 1987; Macklin, 1988). Besides physical symptoms, AIDS has several psychiatric symptoms— memory loss, hallucinations, impaired concentration, anxiety, confusion, and depression (Maloney, 1988).

An individual with HIV can infect others—by blood through needles and transfusions or by sexual behaviors that allow semen or vaginal fluids to enter another's mucous membranes or blood system. There is a slight risk of becoming HIV-positive from tattoos, ear piercing, or becoming "blood brothers/sisters" (if infected needles were used), by vomiting on an open wound, or from bites that draw blood. HIV is not transmitted by air, water, food, sneezes, coughs, insect bites, drinking glasses, hugs, handshakes, or tears (Macklin, 1988; Marzollo, 1988).

Despite the grim facts, AIDS has had no effect on how 92 percent of the population lead their lives (Smilgis, 1987). Among sexually active college students, 46 percent say that AIDS has no effect on their sexual activity, while 50 percent claim that they are now more selective in their partners. Of sexually nonactive students, 15 percent say that concern about AIDS is the principal reason why they are not sexually active (Carroll, 1988).

In a study of high school and college students, the majority were not taking any precautions to protect themselves from HIV. The students averaged 17 years of age when they had their first vaginal intercourse (the range was 11 to 24 years), and they averaged two sexual partners each year (an average student had 10 to 12 sexual partners by college graduation). Although these students were informed about AIDS transmission (they averaged 15 correct out of 19 answers), they had little concern about contracting AIDS. Seventy percent thought that their risk of contracting AIDS was "very unlikely" or "unlikely." Eighty percent worried not at all or only a little about contracting AIDS from their own sexual practice. Yet, 66 percent of the students never used condoms, and only 13 percent always used condoms. Condom use was not predictable by number of sex partners, a sex education course, or religious background. Condom use was, however, related to consistent use of car seat belts—those who buckle up for safety tend to practice safer sex (Baldwin & Baldwin, 1988).

The great majority of adolescents (90 percent) are well informed about the AIDS virus, but only one third of the adolescents surveyed report that they have changed any of their drug- or sex-related behaviors in response to the information they possess about AIDS (Roscoe & Kruger, 1990). In part, the personal fable of adolescents may explain this discrepancy. Clearly, however, specific behavior change programs are needed in addition to the current educational efforts used with teens.

guided review

10. A major area of health concern among adolescents is _____ disorders, including _____ (being greatly overweight), _____ (excessive dieting and/or exercise), and _____ (binging with purging or exercise).
11. In spite of declines, _____ use and abuse continues to be a major health concern, especially for the most abused drug, _____.
12. _____ influence is a major factor in adolescent drug use, but _____ factors, such as harsh discipline, parental conflict, and poor communication, also are influential.
13. True or false: Teens are generally well informed about the AIDS virus and other STDs and about how to protect themselves.
14. True or false: Educational programs about AIDS have been successful in getting most adolescents to engage in protective sexual and drug-use behaviors.

answers

10. eating; obesity; anorexia nervosa; bulimia [LO-7].
11. drug; alcohol [LO-9]. 12. Peer; family [LO-9]. 13. True [LO-10,11]. 14. False [LO-10].

Adolescent Sexuality

Concerns about STDs are only a small part of adolescent sexuality. Teenagers also must deal with sexual orientation and values regarding sexual behaviors and lifestyles, experiment with sexual behavior choices, and if sexually active, handle contraceptives and, possibly, pregnancy.

Sexual Orientation

Although sexuality has been a part of the growing child, it takes on a more urgent and enhanced role during adolescence. One issue that each teenager faces is **sexual orientation.** *Sexual orientation* is a more accurate term than *sexual preference* because the word *preference* implies voluntary

choice. As the prominent researcher John Money stated, *"Sexual preference* is a moral and political term. The concept of voluntary choice is as much in error here as in its application to handedness, or native language" (Bales, 1986, p. 18).

Although sex research pioneer Alfred Kinsey proposed that sexual orientation falls along a continuum, most individuals use three labels for sexual orientation: (1) heterosexual (sexual attraction to members of the opposite gender), (2) homosexual (sexual attraction to members of the same gender), and (3) bisexual (sexual attraction to members of both genders). Most explanations of sexual orientation start with heterosexuality as a given and try to explain why some individuals deviate from it. Most explanations of homosexuality deal only with male homosexuality because of a general male bias and because there are more male homosexuals than lesbians (female homosexuals) (Diamant, 1987; Ellis & Ames, 1987).

Experiential and Social Explanations
Much of the psychological research on sexual orientation has centered on possible causes of a homosexual orientation (Diamant, 1987; Ellis & Ames, 1987). Some theories have suggested that homosexuality develops out of early experiences, family characteristics, and societal values. For example, Sigmund Freud believed that homosexuality developed out of an unresolved Oedipus complex involving a romantic triad with a dominant mother, weak father, and the mother's favorite son. Freud's influence can be seen in Fenichel's 1945 proposal that homosexual males repress, rather than cease, sexual arousal for women due to overidentification with the mother or disapproval of the mother. Other analysts have suggested that lesbians are women who cling to their early hope of getting a penis (Diamant, 1987) and that seduction in early childhood by an older same-sex sibling or playmate is a major cause of homosexuality (Ellis & Ames, 1987).

Despite a widespread cultural belief that parents influence sexual orientation, research findings do not support this position. The Kinsey Institute had 5-hr interviews with 686 male homosexuals and 293 lesbians. From the interview data, the researchers concluded that neither closeness to the mother nor seductive or negative mother-son relationships cause homosexuality. About half of the homosexual males had less favorable relationships with their fathers, but the poorer relationships were a consequence of a homosexual orientation and not the cause. Most lesbians had good relationships with their mothers, but only a minority felt very close to their fathers (Bell & Weinberg, 1981).

Many other psychological explanations for sexual orientation have been proposed (see Diamant, 1987; Ellis & Ames, 1987), including:

- Homosexuals come from unhappy, broken homes with inadequate parental models and poor same-sex role models.
- Boys experience heavy demands to be "masculine." Boys who feel inadequate may take refuge in female roles.

- Sexual orientation is decided by reinforcers and punishers—one's orientation depends on which early experiences are pleasurable and which are distasteful.
- Early-maturing males are more likely to become homosexuals because they experience sexual arousal at the time when most activity is done in same-gender groups.
- Adler proposed that homosexuality is a neurotic lifestyle that compensates for inferior feelings.
- Jung believed that homosexuality is due to projections of the archetypes anima (femininity) and animus (masculinity).

None of these theories receives much research support. Biological explanations seem to have more credibility, yet only one quarter of American adults believe that innate factors cause homosexuality. The majority attribute homosexuality to childhood or adolescent experiences (Ellis & Ames, 1987).

Biological Explanations
Biological explanations for homosexuality also have a long tradition (Ellis & Ames, 1987). Early in the 20th century, Von Krafft-Ebbing and Havelock Ellis both concluded that homosexuality was inborn because they could not locate any social experiences common to homosexuals and because other species exhibited homosexual behaviors. By the 1920s, hormonal imbalances were proposed as the cause of homosexual orientation. However, treating male homosexuals with testosterone did not alter orientation. By the 1940s, genetic factors and brain functioning were proposed causes. Finally, in the late 1960s, hormonal levels were proposed again, but this time, the theorists proposed that prenatal hormone levels were responsible. Ellis and Ames (1987) stated that:

> *Scientific evidence supports the view that hormonal and neurological variables, operating during gestation, are the main determinants of sexual orientation. This does not deny the involvement of experiential and social variables, at least in the case of individuals who were exposed to intermediate levels of the requisite hormonal regimens, but it does imply that very unusual postnatal experiences would be required to overcome strong predispositions toward either heterosexuality or homosexuality.* (p. 235)

The rather complex theory of prenatal hormones causing sexual orientation is called **gestational neurohormonal theory** (Ellis & Ames, 1987). According to this theory, sexual orientation is determined by essentially the same process in all mammalian species. In humans, the crucial timing of sexual orientation is from the middle of the second month to the middle of the fifth month of gestation (the next 2 months also influence gender-typical behavior—that is, whether the individual acts masculine or feminine). According to this theory, learning appears to only alter how, when, and where the biological sexual orientation is expressed.

Sexual Orientation and Gender-Role Characteristics
Researchers have identified a **"sissy boy" syndrome** that involves boys wishing to become members of the opposite sex and liking feminine clothing, toys, activities, and female fantasy roles. These boys like to play with girls instead of boys and exhibit effeminate mannerisms. They avoid masculine stereotypical activities and have aversion toward rough-and-tumble play. Boys who fit these characteristics at age 7 are 75 percent of the time bisexual or homosexual in sexual fantasies and/or behaviors as adults (Green, 1987; Roberts, Green, Williams, & Goodman, 1987). The gestational neurohormonal theory suggests that the "sissy boy" syndrome is a related but not identical process to the homosexual orientation. Therefore, although the majority of "sissy boys" are homosexual, many male homosexuals are masculine-typed in behaviors (Ellis & Ames, 1987).

The gender-typical behaviors of lesbians are associated with the pattern of acknowledging their lesbian orientation. Women who establish their lesbian identities during adolescence are more likely to be androgynous or masculine (86 percent), and those who establish their lesbian identities after age 20 are more likely to be feminine or androgynous (79 percent) (Vance & Green, 1984).

Regardless of homosexuals' gender-typical behavior, they live varied lives. The over 23 million homosexuals in the United States have approximately 14 million offspring. About 20 percent of male homosexuals have been or are married to women (Bozett, 1987). Homosexuals are in every kind of profession—from professional sports, medicine, and law, to the more stereotypical professions of dance, hair styling, and entertainment.

Despite the many advances in understanding of gender orientation, many adolescents (as well as adults) remain woefully ignorant with regard to understanding their own sexuality and that of others at a time when many of them become sexually active.

successful study tip

Useful Word Roots

Phobia = Fear of
Philia = Love of
Eroto = Sexual
Hetero = Different
Homo = Same
Bi = Two

The preceding are useful word roots for words in this chapter and in other settings. For example, you can figure out that *erotophobia* is fear of sexuality, that *homophobia* is fear of homosexuals, and that *bisexual* is a sexual orientation involving attraction toward two genders.

Adolescence is a time period of exploring sexual beliefs and experimenting with sexual behaviors and intimate relationships.

Sexual Attitudes and Behaviors of Teens

Sexual Attitudes

A sizable number of adolescents who are sexually active have some **erotophobia** (avoidance or distaste for sexuality) and feel significant anxiety and guilt about their sexual decisions (Chilman, 1986). Individuals who score high on erotophobia avoid learning about sexuality and discourage sex education, feel guilty about sexual fantasy behavior, avoid sex-related health care, are less likely to use contraceptives, and are not sexually active during pregnancy (Fisher, Byrne, White, & Kelley, 1988). A contrasting sexual attitude is **erotophilia** (literally, love of sexual arousal), which is more typical of those who view sexual behavior as pleasurable. Sexual attitudes can be placed on an erotophobia-erotophilia continuum with placement based on the individual's exposure to sex-related restrictiveness and punishment during childhood and adolescence.

Changes in Sexual Attitudes

Adolescents also have attitudes about important sexuality issues, and these issues and attitudes change as society changes. In 1974, the greatest concern was about cohabitation—living together as a couple without being married. In 1985, young people were most concerned about date rape, other sexual violence, and AIDS (Spees, 1987).

Overall, adolescents' sexual attitudes have become more permissive over the last 60 years, with the major shift in permissiveness coming between 1965 and 1980 (see

Table 10.12
Sexual Attitudes Among Late-Adolescent College Students From 1965 to 1980

		Percent Strongly Agreeing	
	Year	*Males*	*Females*
"Premarital intercourse is immoral."	1965	33%	70%
	1970	14	34
	1975	20	21
	1980	17	25
"A man who has sexual intercourse with a great number of women is immoral."	1965	35	56
	1970	15	22
	1975	20	30
	1980	27	39
"A woman who has sexual intercourse with a great many men is immoral."	1965	42	91
	1970	33	54
	1975	29	41
	1980	42	50

From I. E. Robinson and D. Jedlicka, "Change in Sexual Behavior of College Students from 1965 to 1980: A Research Note" in *Journal of Marriage and the Family*, 44, 237–240. Copyrighted by the National Council of Family Relations, 3989 Central Ave. NE, Suite 550, Minneapolis, MN 55421. Reprinted by permission.

Table 10.12) (Chilman, 1986; Robinson & Jedlicka, 1982). Females especially became more permissive during those 15 years. Another trend is that there are fewer gender differences in 1980 than in 1965. A third trend seems to be a slight move toward more conservative attitudes between 1975 and 1980, especially with regard to women's sexual activities (Robinson & Jedlicka, 1982). Spees (1987) found that college students' sexual attitudes became somewhat more conservative from 1974 to 1985 but noted that the sexual behaviors of college students were not affected.

Overall, however, most adolescents hold fairly permissive sexual attitudes, a trend that may be largely due to changes in attitudes about women's roles and to more sex-role equality and equity (Chilman, 1986). Another factor is the increasing length of maidenhood (the time interval from menarche to a wedding). Currently, the median menarche age is 12.8 years, and the median wedding age is 20.6 years; therefore, the average length of maidenhood for American females is about 8 years. In preindustrial societies, maidenhood is usually less than 3 years. In some societies, girls become wives even before menarche (Whiting, Burbank, & Ratner, 1986). As maidenhood lengthens in years, sexual restrictiveness becomes more difficult to justify and to enforce.

Sexual attitudes are influenced by other factors, too. Hispanic-American adolescents are more influenced by their parents, peers, and religious authorities than are other American teens. Hispanic-American teens are more concerned with pregnancy issues, and Hispanic-American males are more likely than other males to believe that intimacy is important before becoming sexually active (Juhasz & Sonnenshein-Schneider, 1987).

As shown in the table, adults believe that parents have significant rights in regulating the sexual activities of their sons and daughters. The majority believe that parents should be actively involved in their children's sex education. But are parents involved? Mothers are more likely to discuss sex with their children than are fathers, and mothers discuss more with daughters than with sons (Furstenberg, Heceg-Baron, Shea, & Webb, 1986). Parents who do talk with their children about sex tend to have this discussion just after the child's 10th birthday, although a third wait until after puberty (Harris, 1987).

Adult Beliefs About Parental Rights Regarding Teen Sexuality

- Eighty-four percent think that parents have the right to make their 15-year-old son keep his bedroom door open when his girlfriend is in the room; 70 percent believe that a 16-year-old female should be able to obtain birth control information from her family physician without her parents' permission.

- Sixty percent support parents' right to tell a pharmacist to stop selling contraceptives to their 15-year-old son.

- Seventy-one percent say that parents should not allow their 13-year-old son to read sexy, best-selling novels.

- Seventeen percent think that parents have the right to read their 13-year-old's love poems to his girlfriend without their son's permission.

- Seventy-one percent believe that parents had the right to keep their 14-year-old daughter from going to school braless.

- Ninety percent agree with parents who would not let their 15-year-old daughter make a weekend visit to a college to see a guy she has dated twice.

Source: Adapted from Borhnstedt, G. W., Freeman, H. E., & Smith, T. (1981). Adult perspectives on children's autonomy. *Public Opinion Quarterly, 4,* 443–462.

The lack of good parent-child communication is illustrated by the statistics that, among mothers of seventh-grade girls, 20 percent of the mothers have not told their daughters about menstruation, 50 percent have not told their daughters about the male role in reproduction, and 68 percent have not told their daughters about birth control (Hamburg, 1986).

Parent-child communication about sex influences later onset of first sexual intercourse and increases the likelihood that adolescents will effectively use contraceptives (Furstenberg et al., 1986). Parents who discuss sexuality with their children help them to make better behavioral choices and to avoid pregnancy. Today, with the prevalence of AIDS and other sexually transmitted diseases, discussing sex with one's children might even save their lives.

Whether or not parents discuss sexual issues, their attitudes and behaviors influence their adolescent children's sexuality. Adolescents with liberal, approving parents are somewhat more likely to be sexually active and are more likely to use contraceptives (Baker, Thalberg, & Morrison, 1988). Parents also affect their daughters' romantic relationships, with mothers mostly influencing the intimacy components and fathers mostly influencing passion and commitment components (Georgaklis, 1987). Even parental marital status affects adolescent sexual behaviors: Daughters are more likely to be sexually active if in a mother-only household (i.e., no father present), and sons are more likely to be sexually active if in a two-parent household that is undergoing disruption (i.e., losing a father) (Newcomer & Udry, 1987).

Since parents are going to have some effect on their offsprings' sexuality, they should try to have some *direct* influence via discussion. For parents who are ambivalent or nervous about such discussions, materials from the public library or from such organizations as Planned Parenthood may help. Reading materials together and discussing them can be very helpful. Encouraging children to ask questions is also beneficial.

Gender Differences in Sexual Attitudes

Although some studies find little gender difference in sexual attitudes (e.g., Meikle, Peitchinis, & Pearce, 1985), the majority find gender differences that can be summarized as adolescent males being moderately permissive and adolescent females being moderately conservative (Hendrick & Hendrick, 1987; Hendrick, Hendrick, Foote, & Slapion-Foote, 1985). In one study, over 800 subjects were assessed on 102 items, and gender differences were found on 73 of the items (Hendrick et al., 1985). Most of the difference in what adolescent boys and girls consider proper sexual behavior occurs in the early stages of dating; as relationships involve more commitment, there is more agreement on what is appropriate (Roche, 1986).

The double standard (evaluating female sexual behaviors as more negative than male sexual behaviors) still exists to a degree. The double standard is stronger in judging adolescents than in judging adults, and in judging casual relationships than in judging committed relationships (Sprecher, McKinney, & Orbach, 1987).

Sex Education

As discussed in the "Exploring the Parent/Child Relationship" feature, many parents do not know how to or simply do not discuss sexual topics with their adolescents. However, in 1986, 86 percent of all American adults were in favor of sex education in the schools (Harris, 1987; Leo, 1986).

Friends—not schools—are the most common source of sex education—and misinformation (see Table 10.13). The amount of misinformation from peers (or lack of accurate information from mothers) was evident in one study, in which only a third of teenage girls knew the time of greatest pregnancy risk during the menstrual cycle (Zelnick & Kantner, 1977).

Table 10.13
Initial Sources of Sex Information

Source	Information Regarding								
	Abortion	*Conception*	*Contraception*	*Homosexuality*	*Intercourse*	*Masturbation*	*Menstruation*	*Petting*	*STDs*
Peers	20%	27%	43%	51%	40%	36%	22%	60%	28%
Literature	32	3	24	19	15	25	11	10	21
Mother	22	49	13	8	24	11	42	4	9
Schools	24	16	17	16	8	18	16	9	37
Experience	1	1	1	2	8	8	8	14	1
Father	1	1	2	4	1	1	1	2	2
Other	0	3	0	0	4	1	1	1	2

From H. D. Thornburg, "Sources of Sex Education Among Early Adolescents" in *Journal of Early Adolescence*, 1, 171–184. © 1981 Reprinted by permission of Sage Publications, Inc.

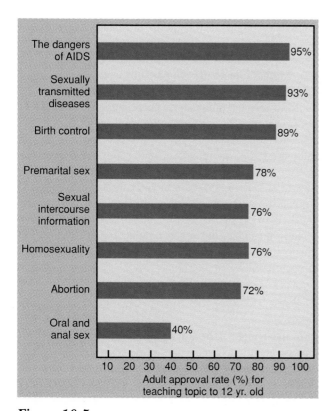

Figure 10.5
What adults believe sex-education courses should teach 12-year-olds.

Source: Data from a Poll by Yankelovich, Clancy, and Shulman in J. Leo, "Sex and Schools," in *Time*, 54–63, November 24, 1986.

Adults who want sex education in the public schools want the schools to teach a wide range of topics. Figure 10.5 illustrates adult approval rates for teaching different topics to 12-year-olds. Although adults believe that schools should include sex education courses, they also believe that parents need to be more involved in the sex education of their children (Leo, 1986).

Sexual Intercourse
Sexual activity among teenagers has been increasing since the 1940s. From 1971 to 1982, teenagers who were engaging in sexual intercourse climbed from 28 to 43 percent. By age 19, 8 in 10 men and 7 in 10 women have experienced intercourse (Alan Guttmacher Institute, 1985). The most common place for intercourse is in the parents' home when they are away (Chilman, 1986). Eleven- to fifteen-year-olds who engage in risk-taking behaviors (e.g., fancy bicycle tricks, getting drunk, taking dares) are the most likely to be thinking of engaging in sexual intercourse (Schwartz, 1988).

African-American and European-American teenagers have different patterns of sexual activity. The majority of European-American teen couples progress from kissing to necking to light petting to heavy petting and then to intercourse. African-American teen couples are more likely to go from kissing and necking right to intercourse. Partly due to this pattern difference, African-American teenagers tend to be sexually active at earlier ages. Among 12- to 15-year-olds, only 29 percent of European-American males and 11 percent of European-American females are nonvirgins;

among African-American teenagers, 76 percent of the males and 40 percent of the females are nonvirgins (Smith & Udry, 1985).

Coercive Sex

Sexual behaviors among adolescents fall on a continuum, with caring premarital sexual expression at one pole and coerced sexual expression at the other (Christopher, 1988). Many teenagers, especially females, are pressured into sexual behaviors. A variety of studies have found that from 12 to 43 percent of females have submitted to sexual intercourse because of pressure from their dating partner (Christopher, 1988; Kanin & Parcell, 1977; Koss & Oros, 1982):

- One third of women have submitted to intercourse because they felt that the man was so aroused that he would not be able to stop.
- Twelve percent of women have submitted to intercourse because their dating partner threatened or used violence.
- Twenty percent of females engaged in intercourse when the man said things that proved to be untrue, such as saying they were in love or that they would continue the relationship if they had sex.

One of the more complete studies of coercive sex surveyed 275 single women about the frequency of different types of sexual pressure (Christopher, 1988). When pressure was broadly defined (e.g., persistent physical attempts, verbal promises, verbal threats, physical force), 95 percent of women reported that they had been pressured into at least one sexual behavior. The most common forms of pressure from males were persistent physical attempts and making positive verbal statements that were untrue. Over half of the women had been coerced into prolonged kissing, having their breasts fondled, fondling the male's genitals, and having oral contact with male genitals. Forty-three percent felt coerced into having sexual intercourse.

The women's responses to being pressured into sexual behavior were overwhelmingly negative. When pressure was exerted during casual dating, most of the women reacted with screaming and fighting. When pressure was exerted during a serious dating relationship, women tended to respond by quarreling, crying, being verbally abusive, and feeling disillusioned. Most women in serious relationships gave into the pressure to keep the dating relationship going (Christopher, 1988).

A study of 190 college males found that 15 percent had forced intercourse on a woman at least once or twice. Twelve percent also admitted to physically restraining a woman to gain sexual advantage. College males admitted that they most commonly used verbal persuasion (70 percent) or ignored women's protests to stop (35 percent). Sexually coercive males had a value system in which females were perceived as adversaries (Rapaport & Burkhart, 1984).

Adolescent Contraceptive Practice

Although many adolescents are comfortable with having sex, they are not comfortable enough with themselves, their partners, and their sexuality to plan ahead and use contraceptives (birth control). Only 14 percent of adolescent girls use contraceptives the first time they are sexually active (Stark, E., 1986). Two thirds of sexually active teenagers do not use contraceptives responsibly (Mullins, 1987).

Adolescents receive mixed messages about being sexually active and being permitted to get contraceptives. In addition, effective use of contraceptives requires advanced planning, open communication with the sexual partner, comfortableness in touching their own genitalia, and behavioral consistency (Gruber & Chambers, 1987). The advantages and disadvantages of the different contraceptive methods for adolescents are summarized in Table 10.14.

Knowledge about contraceptive use can be quite limited, and teenagers have been known to engage in such ineffective behaviors as pricking a hole in the end of a condom for fear that it could explode during ejaculation or substituting grape jelly for spermicidal jelly. Teenagers often have unrealistic beliefs about contraceptives being unsafe and misconceptions about the risk of pregnancy (Gruber & Chambers, 1987). Despite the inaccuracy of knowledge about contraceptives, only a third have discussed contraceptives with parents (Mullins, 1987). In fact, fear that family members will find out about contraceptive use is a major barrier to teenagers using them (Polit-O'Hara & Kahn, 1985). Parental values, especially the mother's, are most predictive of whether birth control will be used (Baker et al., 1988). Mothers generally support birth control once their daughters are sexually active (Furstenberg et al., 1986).

Most teenage pregnancies occur in the first months of becoming sexually active (Zabin, Kantner, & Zelnick, 1979), and contraceptives are usually not used for several months after first intercourse. Contraceptive use often begins after a pregnancy scare (Polit-O'Hara & Kahn, 1985; Schwartz & Darabi, 1986). Teenagers in stable, committed relationships with good communication patterns are the most likely to use contraceptives (Milan & Kilmann, 1987). For many teenagers, however, contraceptive use does not begin in time. Often in American society, "Children are having children."

Teenage Pregnancy

Incidence

Within the United States, 1 in 10 adolescent females becomes pregnant each year, and 45 percent of them choose to have an abortion. Teenagers undergo 30 percent of all abortions in the United States (Stark, E., 1986). Some experts prefer the term *school-age pregnancy* over *teenage pregnancy* because the issues for younger adolescents are different than for 18- and 19-year-olds. In fact, the rate of pregnancy is going down for 18- and 19-year-olds and is

Table 10.14
Developmental Advantages and Disadvantages of Some Common Contraceptive Methods for the Adolescent Age Group

Method	Developmental Advantages	Developmental Disadvantages
Barrier condom	Little planning is needed (short term) Is nonprescription Can be kept available easily Is inconspicuous Is only method that allows male to take major responsibility Provides some STD protection	Discourages use of more effective methods Requires consistency of use
Sponge	Is nonprescription Is inconspicuous Can be kept available easily Little planning is needed (short term) Can be inserted 24 hrs prior to intercourse	Discourages use of more effective methods Requires consistency of use Requires touching genitals
Diaphragm	Encourages partner communication	Is messy and conspicuous Requires consistency of use Demands highest level of comfort with body Repeated sexual activity requires additional spermicide to be inserted Requires prescription and doctor visit
Oral contraceptives	Separates contraception from act of intercourse No communication with partner is necessary	Requires prescription and doctor visit Long-term planning is needed to maintain supplies Must be used whether or not sexually active

From E. Gruber and C. V. Chambers, "Cognitive Development and Adolescent Contraception: Integrating Theory and Practice" *Adolescence,* 22, Table 1, p. 667, 1987. Copyright © 1987 Libra Publishers, Inc., San Diego, CA.

Although many nations have a high rate of adolescents who are sexually active, only the United States has an exceptionally high rate of teen pregnancies.

going up for 11- to 15-year-olds (Hamburg, 1986). Thirty thousand girls *under* the age of 15 give birth annually (Stark, E., 1986).

Among sexually active early adolescents, 1 in 10 becomes pregnant during their first month of sexual activity, and 1 in 5 becomes pregnant within 6 months (Zabin et al., 1979). These statistics are not surprising given that only 14 percent of teen girls use contraceptives the first time they have intercourse. However, more surprising sta-

tistics are that 17 percent of teen mothers experience a second pregnancy within 1 year of giving birth, and half are pregnant again within 36 months (Blinn, 1987). Factors associated with a second adolescent pregnancy are: (1) mother was below age 16 at the time of the first birth; (2) mother is of African-American or Hispanic-American heritage; (3) mother wanted the first pregnancy; and (4) mother is from a lower socioeconomic status (Blinn, 1987).

Factors Associated with Teenage Pregnancies
The "teen mom epidemic" exploded in the 1970s, when the number of sexually active teens in the United States increased by two thirds (Stark, E., 1986). However, the epidemic has not been worldwide: Statistics from other industrialized countries are presented in the "Exploring Cultural Diversity" feature.

Behavioral Options of Pregnant Adolescents
When adolescent girls become pregnant, they must decide whether to give birth to the baby. In one study sexually active teens were asked about what they would do *if* they got pregnant. Their values about abortion, their mothers' attitudes about abortion, and their closeness to their boyfriends were factors (Brazzell & Acock, 1988).

For those who choose to give birth, lifestyle options are most influenced by the biological father and by the girl's parents. About one third of pregnant teens marry the father (Stark, E., 1986). Fewer than 40 percent of teen mothers had adolescent partners; however, 97 percent of teen fathers had adolescent partners (Elster & Lamb, 1986). Of those teen males who marry before age 16, most get divorced. The boy's age at the birth of his first child is also inversely related to the amount of schooling he achieves (Elster & Lamb, 1986).

Many adolescent mothers live with parents (some adolescent couples live with his parents); these girls are bound into the parent and child roles simultaneously.

Among other industrialized countries (see the figure), the rates of adolescent sexual activity are as high as those in United States, but without the same high rates of pregnancy (Hanson, Myers, & Ginsburg, 1987; Jones et al., 1986; Theirot & Bruce, 1988). Many factors may contribute to the higher pregnancy rates in the United States. American ambivalence about the morality of adolescent sexual activity is one factor. The mixed attitudes encourage teenagers to deny that they are sexually active, and therefore, they do not plan effective birth-control methods (Hamburg, 1986).

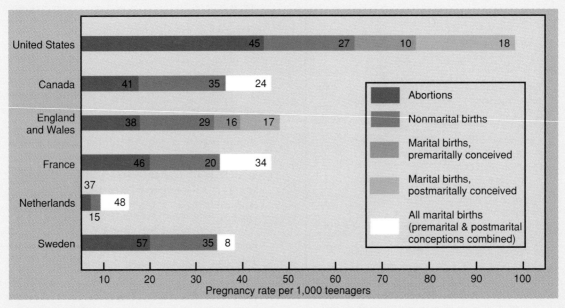

Box Fig. 10.1

Percentage distribution of teenage pregnancies and pregnancy rates among the five categories in six industrialized countries. For example, 45 percent of all pregnancies among 15- to 19-year-olds in the United States in 1981 ended in abortion; 27 percent ended with birth outside of marriage; 10 percent were conceived premaritally but ended with birth after marriage; and 18 percent were conceived and born after marriage. For Canada, France, the Netherlands, and Sweden, the premarital and postmarital data were not available.

Source: Data from E. F. Jones, et al., *Teenage Pregnancy in Industrialized Countries,* fig. 9.1, 1986. Yale University Press, New Haven.

They are someone's child trying to rear a child. Often, grandparents do child-rearing under these circumstances (Land, 1987).

The Long-Term Picture

Adolescent mothers are a diverse group. One subset of adolescent mothers is problem-prone: They use more drugs and alcohol and have lower school achievement. This group has the highest risk for both mother and child of physical and medical problems. A subset with competent coping skills consists of adolescents who were older at the time of pregnancy. They have better parenting skills and are less punitive with their children than their younger counterparts. All adolescent mothers do better parenting if they know about infant and child development (Hamburg, 1986; Reis & Herz, 1987). For most young mothers, attitudes toward parenthood become more positive over time, especially if they have supportive families. Most teen dads have at least weekly contact with their children, although teen moms think that the fathers should be more involved (Martin & Baenen, 1987).

Although the teen years are not the best years physically or psychologically to become parents, the long-term picture suggests that many young parents cope successfully with circumstances. A longitudinal study that followed teen moms into their early 20s did not find an overwhelmingly negative picture—early pregnancy did not inevitably lead to deprivation and poverty. In fact, many young mothers benefited from their children being old enough to take on some household responsibilities when the mothers reentered the work force (Furstenberg, 1976). Another study compared the children of mothers who were 15 to 17, 18 to 19, or 20 to 24 at the birth of their first child. The children

15. The _____ theory of sexual orientation attributes _____, _____, and _____ orientations to hormonal influences on the nervous system early in prenatal development.

16. Sexually active adolescents with _____ (avoidance of or distaste for sexuality) attitudes feel significant guilt about their behavior and are likely to avoid sex-related health care and to not use contraceptives.

17. True or false: While the sexual attitudes of teenagers have become more permissive over the last several decades, rates of adolescent sexual activity have remained relatively constant.

18. Even with effective education and access, many sexually active teenagers fail to use contraceptives
    A. because contraceptive use means that the teen planned on having sex.
    B. because of poor communication (teens have sex but don't talk about it).
    C. for fear that family members will find out.
    D. all of the above.

19. Among sexually active teenage girls, _____ percent become pregnant during the first month they are sexually active, and _____ percent become pregnant within the first 6 months of activity. Furthermore, among those who become pregnant as teens, _____ percent are pregnant with a second child within 36 months.

answers

15. gestational neurohormonal; heterosexual; homosexual; bisexual [LO-12,13]. **16.** erotophobic [LO-14]. **17.** False [LO-14]. **18.** D [LO-15]. **19.** 10; 20; 50 [LO-16].

did not differ in behavioral or emotional functioning based on maternal age; the children did benefit when their mothers had more education (Kinard & Reinherz, 1984).

In Chapter 11, we examine the psychosocial development of adolescence, development that goes hand in hand with the physical and cognitive changes of the teen years and that is intertwined with the same issues and problems discussed in this chapter.

Exploring Human Development

1. Interview junior high school teachers about how they deal with the diversity of cognitive abilities (e.g., some students in the formal operations stage, some not) within their classes.

2. Have class members bring in photos from the time they were age 12 until they were age 18, and compare the different rates of physical maturation. Discuss the different feelings and attitudes that class members had about their pubertal timing.

3. Visit an eating disorders clinic and a chemical dependency clinic that deals primarily with adolescents. What are the features of the treatment programs? What aspects are designed especially for adolescents?

4. Collect pictures from adolescents' women's, and men's magazines, and discuss what these pictures emphasize in terms of body image and sexuality.

Discussing Human Development

1. What examples of the personal fable and imaginary audience do you and other class members remember from your own adolescence? How is remembering these incidents different from the actual experience?

2. If you were a junior high or senior high teacher, how might you accommodate the differences in students who are in the concrete operations stage versus those who are in the formal operations stage?

3. When would you start sex education in the public schools? What would you teach to 8-year-olds, 12-year-olds, and 16-year-olds?

4. What do you think that parents should tell their children about drugs? About sexuality? Why? How much should parents regulate behavior in these areas? How should these regulations be enforced?

5. What factors do you think account for the high rate of teenage pregnancy in the United States, compared with the rates in other industrialized countries in which adolescents are sexually active? How would you reduce the number of school-age pregnancies?

Reading More About Human Development

Elkind, D. (1984). *All grown up and no place to go: Teenagers in crisis.* Reading, MA: Addison-Wesley.

Hatfield, E., & Sprecher, S. (1986). *Mirror, mirror . . . The importance of looks in everyday life.* Albany, NY: State University of New York Press.

Rose, K. J. (1988). *The body in time.* New York: Wiley.

Schwartz, H. (1986). *Never satisfied: A cultural history of diets, fantasies, and fat.* New York: Free Press.

Summary

I. Physical development in adolescence
   A. The order of physical growth in preadolescent and adolescent youth is fairly inflexible, with only the timing between males and females and individuals' rates of development varying greatly.
      1. The order for girls is larche (budding of breasts), pubarche (pubic hair growth), growth spurt, and menarche (first menstrual period), and begins at about 10 years of age (approximately 2 years before boys).
      2. The order for boys is early testicular growth, pubarche, further testicular growth, penile growth, nocturnal emissions, growth spurt, voice change, and hair growth, and begins at about 12 years of age.
   B. Puberty is achieved when adolescents become capable of producing mature sex cells.
      1. The time period of sexual maturation is called pubescence and ends when puberty occurs.
      2. Early adolescents are especially concerned about maturation and body image because pubertal timing (the rate of maturation) varies greatly among individuals.

3. In adolescent boys, sexual maturation and growth involves the presence of testosterone and IGF 1 (an insulin-like growth factor).
    4. In adolescent girls, menarche occurs as the result of a complex hormonal sequence controlled by the hypothalamus and the proportion of body fat.
C. The effects of early and late maturation are different for adolescent boys and girls.
    1. Pubertal changes are most stressful when adolescents feel different from their peers and when the changes are not seen as desirable.
    2. Early-maturing males generally experience positive effects, including an enhanced body image, while early-maturing females have decreased feelings of attractiveness and have more behavioral problems than later-maturing females.
    3. Late-maturing girls are likely to have more positive body images, and both late-maturing males and females generally have better psychological adjustment.

II. Cognitive development in adolescence
A. Piaget's stage of formal operations is characterized by significant increases in the ability to do abstract thinking, with major advances in hypothetico-deductive reasoning and convergent problem solving.
    1. Adolescents become skilled in scientific experimentation, understanding metaphors, using contrary-to-fact reasoning, and thinking about ideal situations.
    2. A postformal operations stage has been proposed in which divergent thinking and problem finding are characteristic.
B. Elkind proposed that adolescent egocentrism is adolescents' inability to think beyond their own perspectives.
    1. The beginnings of pubescence and formal operations are accompanied by a large increase in self-consciousness that gradually declines through late adolescence.
    2. Adolescents develop a personal fable because their new thinking abilities make them feel special, unique, and eternal.
    3. The imaginary audience involves self-consciousness and an exaggerated sense of the adolescent's prominence in others' thoughts.
C. The adolescent's developing cognitive abilities affect school experiences.
    1. Adolescents do not all acquire formal operations abilities at the same rate, but schools often schedule students as if they do.
    2. Schooling generally improves students' verbal and other cognitive skills.
    3. Transitions from grade school, to middle school or junior high, and to high school have different effects.

III. Health concerns in the teen years
A. General health concerns are greater among adolescent females than males.
    1. Over 90 percent of high school students rate their health as either excellent or good.
    2. The health concerns of early adolescents are different from those of older adolescents.

B. Eating disorders are a major health problem for adolescents because they become preoccupied with analyzing their bodies.
    1. Cultural preoccupation with thin body images is also a contributing factor to eating disorders.
    2. The health risks of obesity are significant for both adolescent boys and girls, but the negative social effects of obesity are greater for girls.
    3. Anorexia nervosa occurs mostly among adolescent girls and is a life-threatening health risk.
    4. Binge-eating and bulimia (binge-purge syndrome) also have serious medical complications.
C. Despite declines in drug use among adolescents since the late 1970s, drug abuse is still a major health problem.
    1. Drug education programs and increases in the legal age for drinking have been effective in decreasing drug use.
    2. Peer pressure, however, is still a major contributing factor for alcohol consumption, the most frequently abused drug among adolescents.
    3. Cigarette smoking is second only to alcohol as the most frequently abused drug among teens and is greatly influenced by peer pressure.
    4. Adolescent drug use leads to different personality profiles from those of nonusers.
D. Sexually active teenagers are a high-risk group for sexually transmitted diseases (STDs).
    1. Gonorrhea, herpes, syphilis, AIDS, and chlamydia are commonly occurring STDs.
    2. Besides abstinence, the risk of contracting STDs can be reduced by awareness and practice of basic health precautions.
    3. HIV-positive status is the precursor to the appearance of AIDS (acquired immune deficiency syndrome) and results from body fluid contact with an infected individual.
    4. The personal fable of adolescents may explain why, when the great majority of adolescents are well informed about AIDS, only a third have changed their risk behavior in response to the information they possess.

IV. Adolescent sexuality
A. Sexual orientation is one of many sexuality issues faced by adolescents.
    1. Although sexual orientation falls along a continuum, most people identify categories: heterosexual, homosexual, and bisexual.
    2. The majority of Americans attribute homosexuality to childhood or adolescent experiences, despite research evidence that strongly points to biological explanations.
    3. The gestational neurohormonal theory maintains that sexual orientation is primarily determined during the first half of prenatal development.
    4. Although many males who exhibit female gender-role characteristics as boys (the "sissy boy" syndrome) display a homosexual orientation as adults, other male homosexuals exhibit masculine, male-appropriate gender behaviors, and lesbians also exhibit diversity in gender-role characteristics.

B. The sexual attitudes and behaviors of teens have changed over the years.

    1. Individuals who score high on erotophobia (avoidance of or distaste for sexuality) avoid learning about sexuality and are less likely to use contraceptives.

    2. Sexual attitudes of adolescents have become more permissive over the last 60 years.

    3. Gender differences include adolescent males being more permissive and adolescent girls being more conservative in their attitudes, with a double standard also present.

    4. Although a majority of Americans are in favor of sex education in the schools, friends remain the main source of information (and misinformation).

    5. Sexual activity among teenagers has been increasing since the 1940s, with different ethnic groups exhibiting differing patterns of activity.

    6. When pressure for sex is broadly defined, 95 percent of all women report having been pressured into at least one experience.

    7. Teenagers in stable, committed relationships with good communication patterns are the most likely to use contraceptives, but two thirds of sexually active teens do not use contraceptives responsibly.

C. *School-age pregnancy* may be a more appropriate term than *teenage pregnancy* for the 1 in 10 adolescent females who become pregnant each year.

    1. The pregnancy rate has been declining for 18- and 19-year-olds, but increasing for 11- to 15-year-olds.

    2. In the 1970s in the United States, but not as dramatically elsewhere in the world, sexual activity among teens and also teen pregnancies increased greatly.

    3. The options for pregnant teens (marriage, adoption, abortion, etc.) are influenced by many factors (age of father, closeness to father, attitudes about abortion, and availability of caregivers).

    4. Pregnant teenagers are a diverse group in which those with other such problematic factors as alcohol abuse and low school achievement are at greater risk for long-term problems than those who are older and have more education; overall, however, many young parents cope successfully.

Chapter Review Test

1. Of the following physical changes, which would females experience first?
  a. growth spurt
  b. larche
  c. menarche
  d. pubarche

2. Of the following choices, which would males experience last during pubescence?
  a. nocturnal emissions
  b. penile and testicular growth
  c. pubarche
  d. voice change

3. Which of the following would be experienced by both males and females during pubescence?
  a. larche
  b. menarche
  c. nocturnal emissions
  d. pubarche

4. Puberty is reached when
  a. the growth spurt is finished.
  b. females experience menarche and males experience a nocturnal emission.
  c. mature sperm and eggs are produced.
  d. all of the above.

5. Female adolescents have a higher percentage of body fat than teenage males because the females
  a. need the extra body fat for energy during pregnancy and lactation.
  b. get less exercise than males—their schools have fewer sports programs for them.
  c. see a rounded body image as the female ideal.
  d. eat more fatty and sugary foods than do the males.

6. The positive effects of maturational timing seem to be experienced by which of the following groups of teenagers?
  a. early-maturing females
  b. late-maturing females
  c. early-maturing males
  d. both early-maturing males and late-maturing females

7. Which of the following characteristics is more typical of the post formal operations stage than of the formal operations stage?
  a. convergent thinking
  b. good problem finding
  c. hypothetico-deductive method
  d. abstract thinking

8. Which of the following is an example of a personal fable?
  a. Even though Sylvia is sexually active and occasionally fails to use birth control, she firmly believes that she will not get pregnant.
  b. Dennis often criticizes his parents' behavior on everything—from how they drive to their musical preferences and clothing styles.
  c. Heather is dreading going to school tomorrow because she just knows everyone will laugh at the zit on her face.
  d. Robert is enthusiastic about the things he is learning in his algebra class; for him, solving algebraic equations is a challenge.

9. Researchers have found that the influence of an imaginary audience is highest around _____ grade.
  a. 6th
  b. 8th
  c. 10th
  d. 12th

10. Which of the following is associated with adolescent egocentrism?
  a. self-consciousness
  b. self-criticism
  c. criticism of parents
  d. all of the above

11. Which of the following is a good suggestion for improving instruction to high school students?
    a. Use many concrete examples, since many students are not yet capable of formal operational thinking.
    b. Use fewer personal examples so that students who cannot yet do abstract thinking do not suffer.
    c. Use mostly hypothetical problems to take advantage of students' formal operations skills.
    d. Because of adolescent egocentrism, avoid personal examples that would result in self-consciousness.

12. Which of the following statements is correct?
    a. During adolescence, obesity has negative social consequences but is not yet associated with physical concerns.
    b. Bulimia is associated with fewer medical complications than either binge-eating or obesity.
    c. Female anorexics typically experience problems with amenorrhea and thermoregulation, among other complications.
    d. Binge-eaters tend to estimate higher body weights for their ideal body weight than do nonbingers.

13. Which of the following STDs cannot be successfully treated?
    a. syphilis
    b. genital herpes
    c. gonorrhea
    d. chlamydia

14. Which of the following is associated with AIDS?
    a. Kaposi's sarcoma
    b. depression and anxiety
    c. memory loss and confusion
    d. all of the above

15. Which of the following explanations of homosexuality seems to have the most research support?
    a. Homosexuality results from an unresolved Oedipus complex involving a dominant mother and a weak father.
    b. Early-maturing males are more likely to become homosexuals.
    c. Homosexual orientation appears to be innate and biologically determined.
    d. Homosexuality is a neurotic lifestyle that compensates for inferior feelings.

16. According to the gestational neurohormonal theory, one's sexual orientation is determined
    a. during the last 3 months of pregnancy.
    b. between the second and fifth months of gestation.
    c. after the determination of gender-typical behavior.
    d. within the embryonic period.

17. Which of the following is *not* typical of erotophobic individuals?
    a. consistently uses contraceptives
    b. discourage sex education
    c. avoid sex-related health care
    d. feel guilty about sexual fantasy behavior

18. What portion of sexually active teenagers use contraceptives responsibly?
    a. one fourth
    b. one third
    c. one half
    d. two thirds

19. Which of the following is *not* an accurate statement concerning school-age pregnancies?
    a. The rate of pregnancy is going up for American girls ages 11 through 19.
    b. Half of teen mothers experience a second pregnancy within 36 months.
    c. Most teenage pregnancies occur in the first months of becoming sexually active.
    d. Other industrialized countries also have high rates of adolescent sexual activity, but the United States is unique in having a high school-age pregnancy rate.

20. Which of the following statements about the consequences of pregnancy for adolescent mothers and fathers is accurate?
    a. The majority of school-age mothers and their children live their lives in poverty.
    b. Most school-age mothers' attitudes toward parenthood become less positive over time.
    c. Most school-age pregnancies do not lead to a marriage between the expectant mother and the biological father.
    d. Children born to mothers younger than 16 have more dysfunctional behaviors and emotions than children born to mothers who are older.

Answers

1. B [LO-1,2].	8. A [LO-5].	15. C [LO-12].
2. D [LO-1,2].	9. B [LO-5].	16. B [LO-13].
3. D [LO-2].	10. D [LO-5].	17. A [LO-14].
4. C [LO-2].	11. A [LO-6].	18. B [LO-15].
5. A [LO-2].	12. C [LO-7,8].	19. A [LO-16].
6. D [LO-3].	13. B [LO-10].	20. C [LO-17].
7. B [LO-4].	14. D [LO-11].	

chapter11

Psychosocial Development in Adolescence

Key Terms

Genital stage
Ego identity versus role
  confusion
Identity
Identity crises
Fidelity
Role repudiation
Negative identity
Sincerity
Authenticity
Identity diffusion
Identity foreclosure
Radical departers
Identity moratorium
Identity achievement
Identity panic
Rites of passage
Propinquity
Complementarity of needs
Reinforcement-affect model
Gain-loss theory
Exchange theory
Equity theory
Communal relationships
Fantasy stage
Tentative stage
Realistic stage
Self-concept theory
Career adaptability
Career maturity
Pioneer careers

Learning Objectives

1. Evaluate Hall's view of adolescence as a time of turmoil.
2. Explain Freud's genital stage of psychosexual development.
3. Compare and contrast Erikson's concepts of ego identity versus role confusion, fidelity versus role repudiation, and sincerity versus authenticity.
4. Describe Marcia's four identity statuses in terms of the dimensions of commitment and crisis.
5. Identify modern rites of passage in American culture.
6. Describe how teenagers typically spend their time.
7. Evaluate the idea of adolescent rebellion against parents in terms of the normal patterns of parent/teenager interactions.
8. Discuss adolescents' relationships with their peers, including friendships, conformity, cliques, and crowds.
9. Discuss teenage gender differences in dating patterns and preferences.
10. Explain the five factors that are primarily responsible for interpersonal attraction.
11. Describe the reinforcement-affect model, gain-loss theory, exchange theory, and equity theory, and apply them as explanations for initiating and maintaining relationships.
12. Identify different patterns of work experience among teens.
13. Compare and contrast Ginzberg's fantasy, tentative, and realistic stages of career decision making.
14. Describe Super's approach to career development.

The biological and cognitive changes during the teen years have an impact on personality development and modify relationships with parents and peers. More than ever before, adolescents become involved with questions of their self-identity and purpose and seriously explore the arenas of work and relationships. Psychosocial development in adolescents is massive, challenging, and individualized.

Exploring Your Own Development

"Who am I?" "Why am I?" "What is the purpose of life?" "Is there any meaning to my existence?" "Is life a meaningless farce?" "What should I do with a life that is only going to end soon in death?" "Why am I separate from nature?" "Why me?" "Why was I born?" "What difference does anything make?" Questions like these provide the makings of existential crises. As individuals enter adolescence, they are able, for the first time, to deal with philosophical issues of existence. They often delight in their new cognitive skills, but from time to time may suffer from existential depression and anxiety because some of the issues with which they wrestle are unanswerable.

Existential anxiety is when individuals feel alienation—separation from important aspects of existence, such as family, society, and God. Fromm (1947) postulated that aloneness is inevitable because of human awareness that people are different from animals and the rest of nature, that all of us are separate and temporary beings, and that true knowledge of existence is never completely accessible. Limitations of the self and the certainty of death may lead to the expression of dread—overwhelming and long-lasting fear.

Sometimes, the loneliness and anxiety of alienation drive people to look for "quick fixes," such as trying to bond with others by conforming—thinking alike, dressing alike, and behaving alike. Since alienation is first felt during adolescence, teenagers do a lot of conforming.

The best way to get over feelings of alienation, however, is to become authentic, or self-actualized. To do this, individuals must sidestep the usual ruts and try new experiences. Commitment to action is critical because ideas are empty unless they are acted upon. Perhaps this is why many teenagers like taking risks, being involved with the creative arts or drama, learning new jobs, and thinking about new ideas.

Another part of authenticity is taking responsibility for one's own life. Individuals are their own victims, not the victims of parents, schools, and society. Often, teenagers blame the circumstances of their lives, rather than their own decisions and actions, for how their lives are progressing. Existentialists believe that only *dasein,* the particular setting and circumstances of one's birth, is beyond individual choice. The starting point cannot be chosen, but healthy individuals choose all circumstances from that point on.

People who blame dasein (e.g., "My problems are caused by poverty, poor parenting, lousy teachers . . .") avoid working on self-improvement and on building strong identities. They are more likely to feel anonymous, or "like a nobody." Anonymity can be counteracted by passionate acts, behaviors in which people are completely involved. Adolescents often find passion in volunteer work.

Within the confines of one's destiny with death are numerous opportunities for freedom, personal growth, and acting on values. To get lost in the limitations, the potential dangers, and the lack of perfect solutions and to avoid responsibility for personal existence is to experience existential crises. Teenagers and adults may experience these at various times. Working through the dilemmas and fears results in renewal and growth.

Did you recognize any of your own adolescent experiences and feelings in the preceding paragraphs on existential ideas in adolescence? You will undoubtedly recall many more feelings and experiences of your teen years as you proceed through this chapter.

Personality Development in Teenagers

Adolescents in Turmoil

G. Stanley Hall's Stormy, Stressful Adolescents

The study of adolescence began with the work of psychologist G. Stanley Hall (1904), who saw the adolescent period as a time of emotional upheaval resulting from rapid biological changes, the beginning of mature sexuality, maturing thoughts, increased peer influence, and growing adult responsibilities. Hall believed that typical teenagers experience stressful, stormy turmoil and erratic emotional development. The emotional distress of adolescence is like a period of rebirth and has the potential for renewal (fresh ideas, altruistic acts, and idealistic revolutions) or destruction (delinquency, alienation from society, and self-destructiveness) (Eisenberg, 1965).

Hall's need to have a separate adolescent life stage of confused, tormented youths is an outgrowth of the Zeitgeist of the 19th century's Industrial Revolution. During this period, the massive changes in workplace, haphazard urbanization, increasing separation of the classes, and use of children in factories resulted in unsupervised working-class youths. Two images of the teenage years emerged: (1) youth as a transitional period, and (2) youth as violent and delinquent (Hebdige, 1984). Hall's descriptions of adolescents combined these two images.

Freud's Genital Stage

Like G. Stanley Hall, Freud's psychoanalytic theory describes adolescence as years of inescapable stresses and turmoil. For Sigmund Freud, the source of the conflict was that teenagers had strong, maturing sex drives that they wished to express, while traditional adult society prohibited this expression. According to Freud, because of these undeniable

According to Freud, adolescents are in the genital psychosexual stage. During this stage there is a switch from a narcissistic sex drive to an interpersonal sex drive.

instinctual sex drives, all teenagers were in conflict, regardless of parenting and cultural background, but that individuals with healthy family and cultural backgrounds were better able to survive these stressful years. Psychoanalytic theory puts teenagers in a no-win situation—the basic assumption is that adolescents cannot function well. Freudians believe that seemingly unruffled teenagers are actually overrepressed and prone to depression and phobias. As Anna Freud concluded, "To be normal during the adolescent period is by itself abnormal" (Freud, 1958, p. 275).

Upon entering adolescence, individuals leave Freud's fourth psychosexual stage—the latency stage—a period of emotional and biological equilibrium. They enter Freud's **genital stage,** and initially, equilibrium is disrupted by instinctual sexual impulses. This disruption is exhibited in rebellious or even deviant behavior, mood swings, and inconsistent thought and action (Blos, 1962; Offer & Offer, 1975). As one Freudian analyst wrote, "Adolescence is the only period in human life during which ego regression and drive regression constitute an obligatory component of normal development" (Blos, 1967, p. 172). This ego regression and disruption of equilibrium has even been compared to an acute schizophrenic reaction (Offer & Sabshin, 1984). According to Freudians, the positive side of this process is that, when adolescents reexperience their past conflicts, they have a second chance to resolve them (Blos, 1962). Unresolved fixations, or problems, from the first three psychosexual stages are expressed in adolescent and adult personality (Engler, 1985).

Freudians believe that the major change during the genital stage is the switch from a narcissistic sexual drive, in which individuals obtain gratification from their own bodies, to a mature, interpersonal sexual drive. In this process, teenagers may first experience an increase in masturbation, followed by a transitional homosexual phase, as exemplified by hero worship of a same-sex adult or a very close same-sex friendship. The temporary homosexual phase helps young adolescents to become less dependent on their parents. According to Freudians, by the end of adolescence, most individuals are expressing their sex drives primarily in genital, reproductive activity with persons of the opposite sex in socially acceptable ways (Engler, 1985; Freud, 1953).

Many Paths of Adolescence—Smooth, Sometimes Rocky, and Rough

Since Hall, many people have viewed adolescence as a stage of life filled with storminess and stressful experiences. For example, in 1959, Abrams wrote in *The Teenager Consumer,* "Generational differences are now replacing class differences as the primary source of social conflicts in our society." The 1960s saw the popularization of the term *generation gap* as an explanation for the political protests and demonstrations of the decade. Popular magazines continue to feature articles about the commonality of adolescent rage and conflict, such as a recent article in *Ladies' Home Journal* called "Teen Rage" (Salvatore, 1987) that begins, "Whether it's drug abuse, violence, or suicide, rage is key to the most destructive problems in so many teenagers' lives today. Why are adolescents so angry—and what can be done about it?" (p. 95). Articles, movies, and television shows popularize the image of the out-of-control, conflicted, and confused teenager. But is this image accurate? Is adolescence an emotional purgatory before the stability of adulthood?

For most teenagers, adolescence is not nearly as tormented and out of control as Hall suggested. In one longitudinal study of adolescent males, only 21 percent had substantial turmoil during the teen years (Offer & Offer, 1975). Likewise, in a New York longitudinal study, about three fourths of the subjects were free of a turbulent adolescence, and only one fourth had significantly distressful experiences (Chess & Thomas, 1984, 1987). A survey of all large-scale empirical studies of teenagers concluded that normal adolescence was not characterized by disturbance, stress, and upheaval (Rutter, 1979).

While normal adolescence may not be full of turmoil, personality development in adolescence may not follow a universal set of characteristics. Assuming that adolescents around the world are alike in their development minimizes the effects of culture and place. Differences in the personality structures of adolescents in different cultures and places is the focus of the "Exploring Cultural Diversity" feature.

One of the first scientists to question Hall's and Freud's concept of tormented adolescence was anthropologist Margaret Mead (1928), who noted that, in some cultures, adolescence is an easy transition between childhood and adulthood. Specifically, her observations of female teenagers in Samoa in the South Pacific found a peaceful adolescent period. Mead concluded that the nature of adolescent transition to adulthood depends on how a culture handles adolescence.

Even in the United States, most researchers now conclude that Hall and Freud exaggerated the amount of conflict and turmoil experienced by adolescents. Offer and Sabshin (1984) concluded:

> As far as we know, almost every researcher who has studied a representative sample of normal teenagers has come to the conclusion that, by and large, good coping and smooth transition into adulthood are much more typical than the opposite. Among middle-class high school students, 80 percent can, in general, be described as normal, free of symptoms, and without turmoil. (p. 101)

While some individuals experience classic adolescent turmoil, three major developmental growth patterns exist: (1) continuous growth (smooth), (2) surgent growth (sometimes rocky), and (3) tumultuous growth (rough) (Offer & Offer, 1975). Tumultuous growth seems to be more common in the fearful expectations of parents and other adults than in adolescent reality (Offer & Sabshin, 1984).

Erik Erikson's Ego Identity Versus Role Confusion

Adolescents' Search for Identity

Erik Erikson's (1959, 1968, 1981, 1982) fifth psychosocial stage—**ego identity versus role confusion**—also features conflict, but conflict that focuses more on adolescent-society interaction than on the youth's biological and sexual conflicts (Offer & Sabshin, 1984). According to Erikson, psychosocial **identity,** or the sense of knowing oneself, depends on developing an integrated internal self that can operate compatibly with external roles. Identity involves the integration of earlier identifications and ideology so that the individual has a sense of the self being continuous across the lifetime (Erikson & Erikson, 1987).

As summarized in Table 11.1, Erikson believed that the goal of adolescence is establishing personal identity and having this chosen identity confirmed by others. During adolescence, then, teenagers develop a unique, integrated, and continuous identity, and use this growth in identity to develop a new role within their families and peer groups, and to increase and expand their experiences and responsibilities in the larger community. This is a long process, involving all of the adolescent years and, for many individuals, part of adulthood.

Identity Crises

According to Erikson, progress toward a psychosocial identity is achieved through **identity crises**—crucial, inescapable turning points of development during which individuals confront aspects of themselves. Identity crises can lead to complementary blending of an individual's energies or, unfortunately, to prolonged identity confusion, in which individuals regress or stay in unsatisfactory ruts. Successfully completed identity crises result in possessing the strength of **fidelity,** a combination of loyalty and competence. Fidelity creates enthusiasm for values, faith, and ideologies in youth. Failure to resolve identity crises leads to **role repudiation,** in which roles and values are seen as alien to oneself. Role repudiation can be exhibited as diffidence, defiance, or a **negative identity.** In negative identities, adolescents choose to adopt identities that are the opposite of expectations, such as a minister's child using drugs or a high school teacher's child dropping out before graduation (Erikson, 1982; Erikson & Erikson, 1987). Failures to resolve identity crises in favorable ways may be only temporary. Erikson said, "But worse can ultimately lead to better: Extraordinary individuals, in repeated crises, create the identity elements of the future" (Erikson & Erikson, 1987).

In some ways, teenagers are given the task of putting together a picture of their individual identity from hundreds of jigsaw pieces that each represent an aspect of

Table 11.1
Erikson's Fifth Psychosocial Stage: Ego Identity Versus Role Confusion

Identity—Identity is the sense of knowing yourself. It includes congruence between your view of yourself and how you are viewed by others. It involves a sense of continuity between your past, your current identity, and your future life plans and goals.

Identity is fostered by opportunities that allow you to participate in activities that match abilities and knowledge. Identity is also encouraged when other people see you in ways that are consistent with your beliefs about yourself.

Role Confusion (Role Diffusion)—Role confusion occurs when you fail to develop a personal identity. Role confusion is characterized by feelings of aimlessness and purposelessness and by doubts about career identity and sexual identity. Individuals with role confusion may withdraw from activities, act in rebellious or delinquent ways, or become suicidal.

Role confusion is more likely when an individual receives too little attention or gets feedback about inadequacies. Overidentification with cliques or hero figures and low interaction with opposite-sex friends also are associated with role confusion.

Basic Strength—Fidelity   **Basic Antipathy—Role Repudiation**

Ambivalent, androgynous musical and acting stars are often preferred by young adolescents who themselves are struggling with issues of maturity and gender roles.

themselves. Some youth work relentlessly on this puzzle until it is completed, some work on it in spurts, and some decide to put the puzzle away until a later date. Some aspects of this self-identity puzzle are worked on and put together before other aspects. For many, the physical aspects of the puzzle receive the most attention in the early adolescent years. Other aspects that follow include the quest for autonomy and the need to develop an authentic self.

According to Tanner Staging, early adolescents (10 to 14 years old) feel ambivalent toward having independent identities and therefore focus primarily on physical identities. Middle adolescence (15 to 16 years old) is the most difficult phase for most teenagers because they turn some of the focus away from physical identity and toward gaining independence from their families. Other problems for middle adolescents result from emotions created from increased verbal and cognitive skills that allow "thinking about thoughts." Some teenagers experience their first existential crises, which are discussed at the beginning of this chapter. For most adolescents, late adolescence (17 to 20 years) involves some security and comfort about the personal and sexual identity that has been developing (McAnarney & Greydanus, 1987). Typically, self-consciousness declines, self-images become more stable, and self-esteem grows through the adolescent years (Chiam, 1987).

Physical Aspects of the Search for Identity
Young adolescents focus primarily on their bodies and physical appearance because puberty has changed their appearance and bodily processes so much that they are forced to become body-oriented. Teenagers are both proud and embarrassed by their new bodies, so they may alternate between phases of showing off and being shy and humiliated by their physical aspects.

Due to the imaginary audience, adolescents may feel like they are on display and that everyone is preoccupied with observing and critiquing them. As a result, many teenagers spend numerous hours in front of mirrors, experimenting with the tiniest detail of appearance and trying different clothing, makeup, hairdo, and accessories styles so that others will approve of them. Styles developed by each adolescent generation—from the Roaring Twenties, to hippies, to punk, and beyond—may allow teenagers to magically develop a quick identity separate from both children and adults. Thus, appearance can give a symbolic sense of personal, authentic identity. Moreover, it can turn fear produced from the sense of an imaginary audience into a pleasurable exhibitionism: "It translates the fact of being under scrutiny into the pleasure of being watched. Its outrageous displays are also a kind of concealment: a hiding in the light" (Hebdige, 1984, p. 194).

Like proponents of the psychoanalytic view, Erikson (1968) believed that part of this psychosocial stage is accepting one's sexual identity and gender identity. In sexual polarization versus bisexual confusion, adolescents move from diffuse sexuality and sexual fantasy to seeing themselves as mature females and males. In an attempt to achieve sexual identity, most early adolescents adhere fairly closely to gender roles and conform to behaviors and appearances encouraged by society. By late adolescence, many teenagers allow themselves more flexibility in gender roles. Some younger adolescents who are ambivalent about maturing and who are also trying to resist the rigidity of traditional sex roles may find themselves choosing such rock idols as Mick Jagger and Michael Jackson, who represent ambivalent, androgynous sensuality (Rubenstein, 1984).

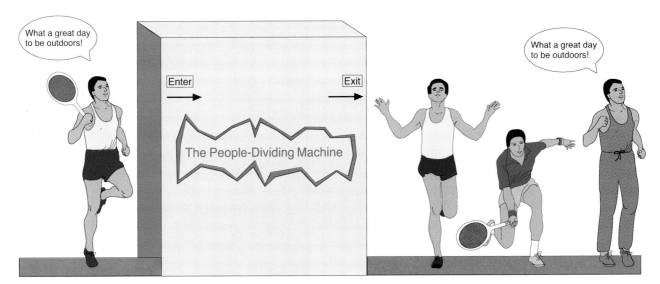

Figure 11.1
The people-dividing machine.

Erikson believed that male and female identity were different since identity was "anchored in physiological givens" (Erikson, 1968; Erikson & Erikson, 1987). According to Erikson, women have inner-bodily space because of their capabilities to bear offspring. He suggested that an important aspect of female identity is the female's attention to selecting and attracting an appropriate mate. Erikson also believed that maternal orientation and female values are important and should influence both work and citizenship, but that instead, societies tend to exploit nurturant, caring aspects and delegate women to confining roles. Some psychologists believe that Erikson's position emphasizes women's biological creativity, while others criticize his emphasis on male and female differences.

Autonomy Aspects of the Search for Identity
An important aspect of identity is autonomy, which involves becoming less dependent on parents. Adolescents who are somewhat autonomous from parents agree with such statements as, "It's better for kids to go to their best friend than to their parents for advice on some things," "There are some things about me that my parents don't know," and "My parents would be surprised to know what I'm like when I'm not with them" (Steinberg & Silverberg, 1986). From fifth grade on, youngsters become less dependent on parents, feel more like separate beings from parents, and are more likely to perceive parents realistically rather than ideally (Steinberg & Silverberg, 1986).

However, as dependence on parents declines, adolescents become more dependent on peer opinions and support. In fact, those teenagers who are most independent from their parents are most likely to be slavish to the demands of their peer group (Steinberg & Silverberg, 1986). This shift from parental dependency to peer dependency is important in predicting teenage behavioral patterns. While parental attitudes are more important than peer attitudes in elementary school, adolescents' attitudes and behavioral choices are more influenced by their peers. Among sixth-graders, students who smoke tend to have parents who smoke; among eighth-graders, students who smoke are more likely to have friends who smoke than parents who smoke (Krosnick & Judd, 1982). Later in adolescence, most individuals resist peer pressure and feel more comfortable being in control of their own lives. Especially for females, self-reliance and assertiveness is related to ability to resist peer influence (Steinberg & Silverberg, 1986).

An Authentic Self-Identity
Suppose that you were placed in the "people-dividing machine" shown in Figure 11.1. You enter via the door on the left, and this machine divides you into three people, A, B, and C. Person A looks just like you but does not have your thoughts or emotions and is not involved in the same activities you are. Person B looks, thinks, and feels differently than you do, but B is involved in the same activities as you and behaves just like you. Person C does not do what you do and does not look like you. Unlike A and B, however, C shares your thoughts and emotions. Which of these persons—A, B, or C—do you consider to be most like you (Hart, 1988)? Who is the most authentic you?

Young children often base their sense of self on physical aspects, while adolescents are more likely to base their sense of self on psychological aspects. In studies involving the people-dividing machine, only a few fifth-graders choose person A, with most choosing B, and by ninth grade, most choose person C. In one study, 67 percent of ninth-graders and 76 percent of eleventh-graders chose person C, the one with identical thoughts and emotions (Hart, 1988). Children define the self in terms of typical activities and physical capabilities, while young adolescents define the self in terms of relationships in social networks, and older adolescents define themselves in terms of their psychological nature. When asked, "Who are you?" young children emphasize their physical looks and activities, while older adolescents emphasize their personal thoughts, moods, and stable personality characteristics (Damon & Hart, 1982, 1986).

Adolescents wish to be genuine individuals—to be their true selves and freely to express their basic natures. However, what adolescents mean by the "true self" changes during the course of adolescence, and these changes are reflected in their friendships. During the elementary school years, friendships are based on sharing objects and activities, and then move toward being based on similar attitudes and reciprocity. In adolescence, friendships involve the potential for intimacy and expectations of self-revelation. For young adolescents, being "genuine" means honest disclosure of facts that are largely available to others anyway. For older adolescents, genuineness more frequently centers around the honest expression of beliefs and feelings (Ullman, 1987).

This transition from facts to beliefs suggests that adolescents move from emphasizing sincerity to emphasizing authenticity. **Sincerity** focuses on efforts of loyalty and honesty to others, while **authenticity** places internal consistency above cultural roles and expectations (Trilling, 1968). Young adolescents focus on representing the self honestly by reducing differences between themselves and others; older adolescents focus on representing the inner self, even if there are differences from others (Ullman, 1987).

These changes occur, in part, because of the cognitive development during the formal operations stage. The growth of in-depth abstract thinking allows adolescents to make sophisticated observations about authenticity. For example, adolescents make judgments about the sincerity and authenticity of others and may come to believe that most adults are "phonies" (Broughton, 1981). Their own parents are often the targets of these judgments of hypocrisy.

Moreover, adolescents become able to see the possibility of the multiplicity of their own selves, such that their "real selves" can even be hidden from them (Broughton, 1981; Selman, 1980). The prospect of the unknown self may lead high school students to turn to writing poetry, song lyrics, and in diaries as a means of self-expression and self-discovery (Roscoe, Krug, and Schmidt, 1985).

James Marcia's Patterns of Development

James Marcia (1966, 1980) proposed that the development of identity in adolescence and early adulthood involves four identity states that vary according to individuals' experience with crisis and commitment. To Erikson's (1968) two states of identity achievement and identity diffusion (i.e., role confusion), Marcia added identity moratorium and identity foreclosure. According to Marcia, the adolescent and early adulthood experience is quite different for individuals in each of these states.

Identity Diffusion

Individuals in an **identity diffusion** state have little inclination to examine goals and values and have low commitment to career plans and ideology. These adolescents are detached from their parents and feel rejected by them, have low self-esteem, and are usually self-conscious. They drift aimlessly with confusion and emptiness. Although identity diffusion is most common in early adolescence, adult play-

boys and adults who avoid career commitments and long-term relationships are part of this identity status, too. Runaways who leave dysfunctional family settings often are in identity diffusion status, unless they have settled into a negative identity. Identity diffusion represents the least advanced group in terms of achieving identity.

Identity Foreclosure

A somewhat more advanced status is **identity foreclosure,** which describes individuals who have made premature identity decisions. These adolescents have not experienced a crisis period, yet they have high commitment to goals. They often accept parental preferences and choices without challenging their parents' positions and considering alternatives. Compared to the other three statuses, these individuals have high need for social approval. Teens in the foreclosure state can express their values, have made career commitments, and usually have close, positive ties with parents.

Examples of identity foreclosure include offspring who are going into a family-run business, thereby avoiding career exploration, and persons who marry at an early age and quickly settle into established adult roles. These individuals seem to have the smoothest, most secure adolescence, but some of them go through a belated identity crisis in adulthood.

Another variation of identity foreclosure involves individuals who become **radical departers** from their families' values and goals by joining cults, or ideological communes. Most cult members are single and between the ages of 18 and 26, and most come from well-educated, warm, and affluent families. Prior to joining a cult, these individuals are dependent on their parents and noncommitted to relationships and career options. Wanting to achieve an individual identity apart from their parents but feeling too uncertain to work on this process, radical departers find the cult's lifestyle a way to separate without risk of failed decisions. For most joiners, the cult is a temporary lifestyle that aids in developing mature identities. No more than 1 in 500 who are approached to join a cult choose to join; most of these individuals stay in a cult from 6 months to 2 years. Over 90 percent of radical departers leave the cult and return to their middle-class upbringings within 2 years, more emancipated from their families than before the cult experience (Levine, 1984).

Identity Moratorium

Unlike the foreclosers, individuals in the **identity moratorium** group have questioned their goals and values and considered alternatives, but remain doubtful and uncommitted to specific choices. Adolescents in this group are actively searching for identity. This identity status is the least stable, but with time, many of these individuals confirm identity choices. Meanwhile, however, these teenagers may seem to be a contradictory package of attitudes and values. They often have bonds of both love and hate with their parents and toward their peers. Usually, they know more about what they do not like in various situations than about what they do like. Both Erikson and Marcia assumed that this active searching through confusing alternatives is necessary for identity achievement, so identity moratorium is considered a more advanced status than either diffusion or foreclosure.

Identity Achievement

The most advanced of the four identity statuses is **identity achievement.** In this identity status, individuals have a solid, personal identity because they have already experienced a crisis in personal goals, weighed the various alternatives, and made committed choices in values, career, and relationships. These individuals have balanced, realistic feelings toward their parents and others. They have good self-esteem, low self-consciousness, and can perform better than others in stressful situations. In school, identity achievers have the highest grade point averages and the best study habits (Adams, Abraham, & Mankstrom, 1987; Waterman, 1984).

Identity development takes a long time. In early adolescence, many individuals are in identity diffusion. Some older adolescents opt for identity foreclosure, but many are in identity moratorium. Oftentimes, identity achievement is not established until people are in their 20s. Only 16 percent of 20-year-olds are identity-achieved (Cella, DeWolfe, & Fitzgibbon, 1987). The most significant move toward identity achievement comes between the ages of 18 and 21 (Meilman, 1979).

---

successful study tip

Marcia's Identity Statuses

Marcia's four different identity statuses can be differentiated on the basis of whether individuals within a status have dealt with crisis and made a commitment. Use this simple chart to remember each status:

		Committed?	
		Yes	No
Crisis?	Yes	Achievement	Moratorium
	No	Foreclosure	Diffusion

Characteristics Associated with Identity Statuses

As shown in Table 11.2, research findings suggest that males and females in the various identity statuses differ in such characteristics as levels of fear of success, self-esteem, and decision-making style. Some researchers believe that the identity process is somewhat different for males and females, and that for males, the most adaptive identity statuses are achievement and moratorium, while for females, they are achievement and foreclosure (Josselson, 1982).

Events of our time influence our identity formation. For example, the LA riots following the Rodney King trial seem to have increased youth's awareness of racial discrimination in the United States and to have more young people interested in social issues and reform.

Zeitgeist and Identity Formation

Erikson believed that individuals cannot experience identity closure before adolescence because only in adolescence do they have the cognitive skills to explore their experiences and understand the consequences of their decisions. However, Erikson also proposed that how individuals experience identity formation is influenced by their Zeitgeist, or historical time period. He wrote:

> In some young people, in some classes, at some periods in history, the identity crisis will be noiseless; in other people, classes, and periods, the crisis will be clearly marked off as a critical period, a kind of "second birth," either deliberately intensified by collective ritual and indoctrination or spontaneously aggravated by individual conflict. (Schlein, 1987b, p. 679)

Compared to the 1950s, adolescence in the 1960s involved more conflict and intensified experiences because of such societal efforts as the civil rights movement and Vietnam peace movement.

Historical Crisis and Identity Panic

Erikson also proposed that a society can have historical crises when it fails to confirm the positive identities that emerge from young people's struggle with identity achievement. Erikson suggested that changes in technologies, political systems, and cultures may increase the difficulties for adolescents who are trying to assimilate their new identities with society-at-large. The "generation gap" that developed during the 1960s is one example of a historical crisis. The result, according to Erikson, is **identity panic.** He wrote:

> Large-scale irreconcilabilities in this ongoing assimilation result in identity panic that, in turn, aggravates irrational aversions and prejudices and can lead to erratic violence on a large scale or to widespread self-damaging malaise. (Erikson & Erikson, 1987)

Table 11.2
Characteristics Associated With Marcia's Identity Statuses

	Fear of Success		Self-Esteem		Decision-Making Style	
	Males	Females	Males	Females	Males	Females
Diffusion	High	Low	Low	Low	Reflective	Reflective
Foreclosure	High	Low	Low	Mixed	Impulsive	Impulsive
Moratorium	Low	High	High	Low	Reflective	Impulsive
Achievement	Low	High	High	High	———	———

Source: Data from Cella et al., 1987; Waterman, 1984; Adams et al., 1987; and Marcia, 1980.

Erikson also suggested that three types of situations can actually lead to identity vacuum periods because fear and apprehension can aggravate the identity formation process. These situations are: (1) apprehension about discoveries and inventions that can radically transform the world; (2) fears about decline in historical, basic institutions; and (3) concerns about an existential void, lack of spiritual meaning, and insufficient reverence for life (Erikson & Erikson, 1987).

Timing of Identity Formation

Each generation creates a "way of life," or ideology, during the adolescent and young adult periods. The systematized set of ideas and ideals of the group is formed in one of two ways: through an experimental period or through rites or confirmations that transmit the "official rules" of a culture (Erikson & Erikson, 1987). U.S. society uses the experimental period, or psychosocial moratoria. Many American adolescents choose to formulate their identities gradually, while experiencing college, altruistic service, military service, or travel, or, in earlier eras, by traveling to colonies or to the frontier. Adolescence is a slow maturation period during which young people gain a mature identity step-by-step through a variety of symbolic events. Of events listed in Table 11.3, which were part of your growing up experiences, of your rites of passage? What did they symbolize to you?

Some societies choose an abrupt transition from childhood to adulthood by using **rites of passage** (puberty rites), which are often harsh tests of endurance and strength. Adolescents go through ceremonies in which they learn adult practices and knowledge and are dramatically separated from childhood and thrust into adulthood (Brown, 1975; Eliade, 1958; Sommer, 1978). Some rituals involve a separation period from family and members of the opposite sex, during which adolescents must prove their skills in important areas, such as hunting. In other societies, adolescents are assigned adult instructors who teach them what they will need to know for adulthood.

Table 11.3
Markers of Growing Up

Graduating From High School	Getting Married
Going to College	Becoming a Parent
Becoming Pregnant	Getting Driver's License
Getting First Job	Reaching Legal Drinking Age
Taking First Alcoholic Drink	Having First Sexual Experience
Going on First Date	Buying a House
Owning First Car	Graduating From College
Deciding on Career	Defying Parents
Moving Out of Parents' Home	Joining Peace Corps or Similar Service
Being Confirmed	
Participating in High School Athletics	Having First Menstrual Period
Shaving for First Time	Opening a Checking Account
Joining a Fraternity/Sorority	Smoking Cigarettes
Taking Drugs	Getting a Tattoo
Running Away From Home	Reaching Voting Age
Wearing Hose or High Heels	Wearing Makeup
Having Own Fashion Statement	Having Own Music Statement
Achieving in School	Going Steady or Getting Engaged
Changing Relationship With Parents	Making Own Decisions
Buying Lottery Ticket	Going to a Strip Joint
Looking Older	Becoming Financially Self-Sufficient
Joining Military Service	

Important Relationships— Parents and Peers

How Adolescents Spend Their Time

The Activities of Teenagers

Obviously, teenagers spend their waking hours differently than do school-age children. Parents report that their teenagers sometimes want to spend lots of time by themselves, constantly tie up the family phone, and upon returning from outings with friends, report simply that they were doing "nothing" and "just hanging out."

In one study, adolescents were given paging devices so that researchers could assess how they spent their time. Approximately six times a day between 8 A.M. and 11 P.M., the pager would beep and the adolescents would fill out self-report forms on their activities. The researchers analyzed hundreds of these self-report forms and found that approximately 29 percent of the average day is spent productively in attending classes, studying, and working at jobs. Working adolescents average 18 hr a week on the job. About 40 percent of adolescents' time is spent in leisure activities—playing sports or games, doing hobbies, reading books and magazines, listening to music, watching television, and talking. In fact, the number one activity of teenagers is talking, most typically with friends. Thirteen percent of conversations take place over telephones (Larson & Csikszentmihalyi, 1978).

In the Company of Teenagers

Typical teenagers spend about half of all their time with peers, about a third of the time alone, and the rest of the time with family. Of the 52 percent of the time spent with other teenagers, 23 percent is in the classroom. Teenagers actually only spend about 5 percent of their time alone with their parents. Another 8 percent of their time involves parents and siblings, and 2 percent is with parents and friends together. Adolescents who average more time with family members are the most likely to have good school grades and better school attendance.

Adolescents' bedrooms are the most common locations of time spent alone. This time is spent listening to music, reading books, watching television, rehearsing musical instruments, and working out blue moods. Longer than average amounts of solitary time aid in the identity-formation process, lead to the most positive outlook, increase fantasizing and daydreaming, and also enhance self-consciousness (Larson & Csikszentmihalyi, 1978).

During the teen years, adolescents not only are developing their identities; they also are evolving new relationships with their families and friends. Adolescents' cognitive and personality changes affect these relationships, and in turn, these interpersonal relationships influence cognitive and identity development.

Relationships With Parents

Parent–Adolescent Interactions

If you listen to parents talk about their adolescent offspring and then to adolescents talking about their parents, you might conclude that, during this phase of life, parent and child are like oil and vinegar—they just don't mix. Yet, 88 percent of adolescents state that they get along with their parents (Sorenson, 1973), and indeed, most teens believe that their parents are supportive of them (Offer, Ostrov, & Howard, 1981). Yet, as discussed in the "Exploring the Parent/Child Relationship" feature, arguing and bickering between parent and teenager does increase, especially in the early adolescent years.

Parent-adolescent conflict is partly due to adolescents being in the formal operations stage of thinking, which allows teens to anticipate parents' counterarguments to their positions (Clark & Delia, 1976). These new thinking abilities also lead adolescents to conclude that they are special, unique, and powerful (i.e., the personal fable) and idealistic, while their parents are much too pragmatic. They may argue with parents because they are disappointed with how few attempts their parents make to improve the world. The increase in conflict is also partly attributable to adolescents wanting fewer restrictions on their behaviors. Eighty percent of 14- to 16-year-olds want their parents to be less restrictive (Douvan & Adelson, 1966).

Most parents believe that their adolescents become less interested in the parents' opinions, which is true on such behaviors as dating, dressing, and academics. However, parents retain a major share of the influence on value and belief systems, religion, and careers (deVaus, 1983; Hall, 1987). Even though adolescents want to exchange ideas with their parents, they disappointedly express that their parents tend to explain their views much more than they listen to their teens' views (Hunter, 1985a). Parents, in turn, often have become so accustomed to meeting their children's needs, setting the rules and guidelines of their behavior, and protecting them from the world's dangers that they fail to perceive the need to allow their teenagers more autonomy and more input into family decision making.

For Better or For Worse®　　　　　　　　　　by Lynn Johnston

Exploring the Parent/Child Relationship: Bickering and Battling

Most parents and teenagers report an increase in bickering during early adolescence. Parent-adolescent conflict seems to build from puberty until about age 14 or 15. After that, conflict usually declines (Grotevant & Cooper, 1986; Steinberg, 1987a).

Conflict such as nagging, bickering, and squabbling is more common with teenagers than with younger children, making the adolescent years the most challenging parenting years (Garbino & Gilliam, 1980; Pasley & Gecas, 1984). In fact, parents usually feel the least satisfied with the parenting role while their children are teenagers (Steinberg, 1987a).

Usually, parent-adolescent conflict is over "little, everyday things"—for example, phone use, chores, and studying (Richardson, Galambos, Schulenberg, & Petersen, 1984). For early adolescents, the two most conflicting areas with parents are home responsibilities and spending money (Ellis-Schwabe & Thornburg, 1986).

Sons have more conflict with mothers than with fathers. Upon entering adolescence, sons interrupt their mothers more during conversation and defer less to them.

On the other hand, fathers of teenage sons often become more assertive, and their sons defer to them. In middle adolescence, the communication situation improves for all concerned, yet fathers tend to retain the most power in discussions, mothers the least, and sons in-between (Steinberg, 1981).

Daughters also have more bickering with their mothers than with their fathers. Menarche, rather than chronological age, is the best marker for when mother-daughter relationships begin to become strained. Teenage daughters view mothers as less accepting, believe that the family is too strict, and often choose to participate in fewer family activities. With daughters, too, communication improves in later adolescence (Hill, Holmbeck, Marlow, Green, & Lynch, 1985; Steinberg, 1987a).

Why does bickering lessen after age 15? Older adolescents feel more self-confident about reasoning abilities and personal identity. The uneasiness created by belief in an imaginary audience is diminishing. Moreover, many adolescents can use negotiation skills about privileges,

freedoms, and discipline. Early adolescents are novices at reflecting on the morality of their actions and at dealing with the appropriateness and effectiveness of punishment. Therefore, they complain more. By age 16, most can coordinate their own and their parents' perspectives on behavior. This ability results in more understanding and appreciation of their parents' needs and restrictions (Selman, 1980).

While bickering is the norm for most adolescents, some adolescents battle hard with their parents. At least 650,000 adolescents are abused each year. Adolescents make up only 38 percent of the population, but they are the recipients of nearly half of all child abuse. Adolescents who are abused are more likely to be depressed and suicidal, have low self-esteem, and be angry at family and society. Adolescent abuse is also associated with the serious problems of runaways, homeless youth ("throw-away kids"), suicide attempts, delinquency, and prostitution (Burgdorff, 1980; Garbino, 1986; Garbino & Gilliam, 1980; Hall, 1987).

Parenting Patterns

Adolescents have the best odds of successful development when their parents stay involved in their lives. Although this parental support may sometimes be called interfering, babying, and meddling, most teenagers want their parents to be actively involved in their lives. If this active involvement can be infused with the qualities of warmth, support, and authoritativeness, parent-adolescent relationships are likely to be positive (Bell & Bell, 1983; Enright, Lapsley, Drivas, &

Fehr, 1980; Powers, Hauser, Schwartz, Noam, & Jacobson, 1983). Parents who are willing to listen to their teens' feelings and who are willing to deal with disagreements by using compromise encourage teenagers' healthy exploration of alternatives (Cooper, Grotevant, & Condon, 1983).

How do parenting styles influence adolescent attitudes and behavior? Authoritarian parents emphasize their control over their teenagers' behavior. They believe that teens should abide by rules, and they do little to adjust to their children's growing need for autonomy. Some teenagers reared in authoritarian homes are quite content to accept parental rules and internalize the same standards. More likely, though, teenagers with authoritarian parents are conflict-ridden and have difficulty developing their own identity. A minority choose to engage in a "grand rebellion"—acting-out behavior that is totally repulsive to their parents (e.g., drug use, sexual activity, and pregnancy)—to force their way out of their parents' control.

Permissive parents are undemanding and have no rules or inconsistent rules. Many permissive parents expect their teenagers to make all their own decisions. Much as this may sound ideal to teenagers who believe that their parents are overinvolved in their lives, the permissive environment is not associated with positive outcomes. Many adolescents from permissive homes feel rejected and confused, and a sizable portion of them have emotional and behavioral problems. Both the authoritarian and permissive parenting styles are negatively associated with school grades. The third parenting style (authoritative/democratic) is associated with the highest school grades (Dornbusch, Ritter, Leiderman, Roberts, & Fraleigh, 1987).

Democratic (or authoritative) parents provide a flexible environment. Parental rules provide the teenagers with some autonomy, and parents are open to learning from their teens in ways that lead to revision of parental rules. Teenagers from democratic homes are most likely to be socially active, responsible, self-confident, independent, and high in self-esteem (Elder, 1963).

One study compared characteristics of Danish and American adolescents. A higher proportion of Danish adolescents than American adolescents are raised in democratic, discussion-oriented families. Predictably, Danish adolescents measure more independent, less rebellious, and more internalized in behavioral control than their American counterparts (Kandel & Lesser, 1972).

Some parents who begin as authoritarian move toward the democratic style of parenting as their children age. They seem to realize that the needs of their teenage children have modified. Parents who have practiced the democratic style for years, however, have easier times in adjusting to teenagers' needs for independence.

Overall, three general guidelines for parents can help adolescents to achieve healthy independence (Goethals & Klos, 1970):

1. Recognize teenagers as their own persons, with competent attitudes and behaviors that may vary from parents' positions.
2. Be genuinely concerned but not overinvolved with children's lives.
3. Modify house rules and processes to meet adolescents' personal growth.

Relationships with Peers

Friendships

Just as adolescents interact differently with their parents than they did when they were younger, friendships change massively from childhood to adolescence. At age 6 or 7, friends are defined as playmates who can share things and activities; from ages 8 to 11, friends are important because they have similar values; by adolescence, friends add a new dimension to life—friendships have potential for intimacy. Teenagers understand that their friends are unique human beings, that they have their individual reasons for behaviors, and that friends can attempt to achieve mutual understanding (Bigelow, 1977; Youniss, 1980).

The major strength of the psychosocial stage of ego identity versus role confusion is fidelity, and appropriately, adolescents are more loyal to their friends than they were at younger ages. Teenagers want more commitment, intimacy, and self-disclosure with their friends (Youniss, 1980). In childhood, best-friend status may change on a weekly basis, but 80 percent of eighth-graders have a stable best friend, most typically for at least a year. Best friends see each other daily (or at least weekly), and half of eighth-grade boys and four-fifths of eighth-grade girls talk to their best friends nearly daily over the telephone (Crockett, Losoff, & Petersen, 1984). Best friends are especially stable from ages 16 to 19 (Hartup & Sancilio, 1986).

During adolescence, males and females think that friends are important, but the two genders emphasize different aspects of relationships. Females emphasize intimacy, dependency, sensitivity, and empathy; males emphasize skills, achievement, and self-sufficiency (Coleman, 1980). Females are more likely than males to seek advice from friends, share secrets and inner feelings with friends, and want to be friends (Crockett et al., 1984). Fourteen- to sixteen-year-old females rate the most valuable aspects of friendship as loyalty, trustworthiness, reliability, confidence, and emotional support; males rate the most valuable aspects of friendship as congenial companionship and sharing activities. Males in these middle adolescent years value most what females used to value most in early adolescence (ages 11 and 12) (Douvan & Adelson, 1966).

Conformity

Early adolescents have high rates of conformity as they pull away from their parents and turn toward dependency on peers (Steinberg & Silverberg, 1986). Twelve- and thirteen-year-olds conform with their friends more than do 7- and 8-year-olds. Conforming to peer pressure to do antisocial acts peaks by ninth grade (Berndt, 1979; Brown, Clasen, & Eicher, 1986). Older adolescents rely more on their own independent thinking and judgment than on their peers (Berndt, 1979; Constanzo, 1970; Constanzo & Shaw, 1966). Middle-status adolescents conform more than do those who have high status or low status among their peers (Lansbaum & Willis, 1971).

Conformity is common during adolescence, as is readily apparent in fashion, hairstyles, music, and language of teenagers.

Cliques and Crowds

Cliques—close-knit groups of three to nine friends who do activities together—are the dominant peer-group structure. The importance of cliques grows most from sixth to eighth grade. The most popular cliques for boys are those formed on the basis of athletic interests; next in importance is physical appearance, followed by personality characteristics. For girls, the most popular cliques are formed on the basis of physical appearance and, second, personality characteristics. For both genders, academic ability and performance play little role in becoming a member of a prestigious clique (Crockett, et al., 1984).

The other peer grouping of importance is the crowd, a large, broad-ranging group that often is a source of informal contacts, mainly on weekends. Many crowds are made up of several cliques. Crowds often are identifiable by one characteristic. For example, most high school students can identify which of their peers are the "jocks," "nerds," "yuppies," "druggies," and "intellectuals."

Each crowd is perceived to have a certain level of peer status. In a study of over two hundred 7- through 12-graders, the ranking of peer groups (from most to least popular) were: "jocks," "populars," "normals," "druggies/toughs," and "nobodies." Self-esteem was higher for crowd members than for nonmembers, and the higher the ranking of one's crowd, the higher one's self-esteem. Lowest self-esteem levels belonged to individuals who perceived themselves as being crowd members, while peers did not (Brown & Lohr, 1987).

Clique and crowd activity changes during the course of adolescence (Dunphy, 1963). In early adolescence, the most typical peer interactive pattern is a single-sex clique averaging five members who share similar values and interests. By age 14, members of different cliques increase their interaction with each other. By high school, same-sex cliques of two or three members tend to hang out with opposite-sex cliques. Often, crowds averaging 20 persons form on the weekend or during the summer. Crowds gather informally in parks, on street corners, and at shopping malls. A significant number of adolescents visit shopping centers once or twice a week, with most spending 1 to 5 hr there at a time. Moving clusters of teenagers at malls tend to be male-female, but stationary groups are usually same-sex clusters (Anthony, 1985). The final developmental stage of crowds is the disintegration of crowds to form associated groups of couples.

First Loves—Relationships in the Teen Years

The Dating Game

Dating Functions

Dating serves seven major functions (McCabe, 1984; Roscoe, Diana, & Brocks, 1987; Skipper & Nass, 1966):

1. Dating is enjoyable recreation and entertainment.
2. Dating is a socialization process that provides opportunities to interact with and learn about members of the opposite sex.
3. Dating provides companionship with members of the opposite sex.
4. Dating is a means for improving one's status and prestige among one's peer group.
5. Dating allows for sexual experimentation.
6. Dating leads to intimate, meaningful relationships.
7. Dating is a means for courtship and selection of a marriage partner.

Adolescents may date for any and all of these reasons.

The major purposes of dating tend to shift from early to late adolescence. Early and middle adolescents (6th- through 11th-graders) are more likely to cite recreation and status as reasons for dating than are older teens. These choices reflect an egocentric and immediate gratification orientation and fit well with those aspects of cognitive and identity achievement that are worked on in these early years. Later adolescents more often give the reasons of companionship, sexual activity, and mate selection. These choices are compatible with their more advanced sense of identity and their view of dating as a more personally fulfilling interpersonal activity. Older adolescents deal more realistically with the reciprocity of dating situations (Roscoe et al., 1987). Just as older adolescents move away from conformity with peers toward a sense of autonomous self, they move from dating persons who add to their status within the peer group to dating persons who add to their own sense of meaning and pleasure.

Although males and females give many similar reasons for dating, sexual activity and intimacy have different priorities. Males more frequently give sexual activity as a major reason for dating, but females are more likely to cite intimacy as a major reason (Roscoe et al., 1987). This gender difference seems to fit socialization patterns. Many adolescent males are encouraged to be sexually active, and many adolescent females are not. Furthermore, female socialization is more likely to emphasize nurturance, caring, and sharing and lead to wanting intimacy in dating situations.

Selection of Dating Partners

Do adolescents choose dating partners by prestige factors, such as popularity and car ownership? Or do adolescents choose dating partners on the basis of personality characteristics, such as being pleasant, dependable, honest, and affectionate? A 1977 study of high school students found that personality factors are more important than prestige factors (Hansen, 1977).

A more recent study compared early adolescents and later adolescents on their selection of dating partners (Roscoe et al., 1987). According to this study, early adolescents place more emphasis on both approval by others and on superficial features, such as clothing, than do older adolescents. Remember, early adolescence is when independence from parents is partially achieved by conformity with the peer group. Therefore, younger adolescents may date persons who are popular and fashionable to achieve increased status with their peers. This study also found that, compared to younger teens, older adolescents place more emphasis on their dates sharing interests and having future goals. This emphasis is consistent with later adolescents' growing realism about career and life decisions.

Males have only three characteristics of dating partners that they rank more important than do females: being physically attractive, being sexually active, and not being physically disabled. Females, on the other hand, have several characteristics for dates that they rank more important than do males: being confident, being the same age or older, receiving parental approval, having money to spend, being kind and honest, being responsible and dependable, expecting to have a good job, being the same height or taller, having set goals for the future, respecting others, and not drinking alcohol or taking drugs. Males appear

more likely to choose dating partners on the basis of appearance and sexuality, and females are more likely to choose dating partners on the basis of personality and behaviors (Roscoe et al., 1987).

Dating Patterns

Both male and female adolescents feel pressure to conform to perceived (rather than actual) dating behavior norms among their peers (Collins, 1974). Often, this pressure to measure up to make-believe norms means that adolescents make choices in dating, sexual, and drug-taking behaviors that they actually do not wish to make or do not believe that they are ready to do.

For example, adolescents may choose to go steady because they believe that adolescents who have steady dating partners have higher self-esteem than adolescents who are without a steady date. Males who go steady are more highly evaluated than are females, and older adolescents are perceived to be more positively affected by going steady than are younger adolescents (Samet & Kelly, 1987). Older adolescents may feel peer pressure to become heavily involved in a continuing dating relationship. Late adolescents may also be perceiving that intimate relationships may make it easier to satisfactorily complete identity achievement and enter the intimacy stage of young adulthood.

Late adolescents were asked to differentiate intimate and nonintimate relationships. In order of ranking, the top 12 characteristics of intimate relationships are: (1) sharing, (2) physical/sexual interaction, (3) trust/faith, (4) openness, (5) love, (6) caring, (7) acceptance, (8) understanding, (9) mutuality/reciprocity, (10) honesty/sincerity, (11) friendship/companionship, and (12) respect. The first four characteristics are those that teenagers see as most distinguishing between intimate and nonintimate relations (Roscoe, Kennedy, & Pope, 1987).

Adolescents in longer-lasting dating relationships engage in more relationship-maintaining behaviors, evaluate the relationship more favorably, disclose more about themselves to each other, and feel more in love (Berg & McQuinn, 1986). They distribute benefits of the relationship either equally or according to each's needs (Clark & Reis, 1988).

Dating and Sexual Activity

What are teenagers' perceived norms for sexual behaviors on dates? In a survey of 3,600 Canadian high school students ages 15 to 19, subjects were asked what two dating persons who liked each other should allow on a first date. In this sample, 92 percent believed that it is appropriate to hold hands, 82 percent approved of kissing on the first date, and 50 percent felt that it was all right to neck. In addition, 28 percent approved of petting on a first date, and 11 percent approved of sexual intercourse on the first date. More males than females said that it was appropriate first-date behavior to neck (59 to 42 percent), pet (42 to 16 percent), and have intercourse (19 to 3 percent).

The approval rates increase when teenagers are asked about appropriate behavior after a few dates: Now, 97 percent of the males and 94 percent of the females approve of necking; 92 percent of the males and 80 percent of the females approve of petting; and 70 percent of the males and 36 percent of the females approve of sexual intercourse (Bibby & Posterski, 1985). These gender differences in approval rates match both the male emphasis on sexuality of dates and societal attitudes toward male and female sexual activity.

Despite adolescent approval of rather liberal sexual behaviors early on in dating, sexual activity among teenagers still often meets with disapproval, even from people who are just out of adolescence themselves. Sexually active teenage males receive little disapproval, but sexually active teenage females face significant disapproval, especially if they are sexually active in casual relationships (Sprecher, McKinney, & Orbuch, 1987). The double standard has diminished over the years but still affects young females in transitional relationships.

Interpersonal Attraction

Factors of Attraction

Five factors play major roles in attracting people to others and helping relationships to continue: (1) propinquity, (2) physical attractiveness, (3) competence, (4) similarity, and (5) complementarity of needs. **Propinquity,** or physical proximity, is a necessary requirement in forming an initial relationship with someone. Being physically near another increases the likelihood of meeting that individual and being able to interact and get to know that person over time. Thus, adolescent relationships are more likely to involve teens from the same high school, workplace, or church.

A second factor that is especially important in the beginning of relationships is physical attractiveness. In studies of first dates, liking of dating partners is best predicted by the physical attractiveness level of the dates (Brislin & Lewis, 1968; Walster, Aronson, Abrahams, & Rottman, 1966). Overall, beautiful and handsome persons are viewed as having better personalities, more abilities, higher achievement, and better morals than are other persons, even though their personalities and behaviors do not actually differ from others (Dion, Berscheid, & Walster, 1972; Udry & Eckland, 1984). Most people will try harder to please highly attractive persons than they will to please more average-looking persons (Sigall, Page, & Brown, 1971). Males tend to weigh attractiveness of their dating partners more than females do (Buss, 1988).

The last three factors of attraction play the most important roles in long-lasting relationships. One of the factors is competence, or ability. People prefer to be around competent persons. In dating relationships, women place more emphasis on competence in dating partners than do men (Buss, 1988). Perhaps men learn to brag about accomplishments and to demonstrate strength to impress women who are interested in men's competence, education, and earnings potential. Meanwhile, women learn to focus on

The primary factors of interpersonal attraction are propinquity, attractiveness, similarity, competence, and complementarity.

their appearance and use cosmetics, tantalizing clothing, and thin, shapely bodies because males base dating relationships more on physical attractiveness than on female competence (Buss, 1988). This preference may be why female attractiveness correlates with marriage to highly educated men with high incomes but does not correlate with the females' own education, occupation, or income (Udry & Eckland, 1984).

Similarity is another predictor of long-lasting, fulfilling relationships. People like to be around people with similar attitudes, interests, values, and abilities. People who are similar like to do the same activities in sports, music, and recreation, and compatible people find it easier to agree on rewarding ways to spend time together. In discussions, people who are similar support the same positions and validate each other's perceptions of politics, religion, and living styles. People also assume that people with similar attitudes like each other (Backman & Secord, 1959).

While similarity may increase the chance of becoming intimately involved with another person, sometimes, the order is reversed. People who are romantically interested are led to underestimate their dissimilarities and overestimate their similarities—that is, individuals who are romantically involved distort their dating partners' attitudes so that they mistakenly believe that they and their partners hold similar ideas (Gold et al., 1984). However, these misperceptions are usually only temporary. After a few months, some couples break up and legitimately question, "What did I ever think I had in common with that person?"

The final factor of interpersonal attractiveness is **complementarity of needs.** While similarity is important in relationships, people also are attracted to individuals of opposite characteristics when these characteristics fit their needs: A somewhat disorganized person may have a special relationship with an organized person; a shy, introverted person may benefit from an outgoing, unabashed individual. Similarity of values and interests may be the most important factor in long-lasting relationships, but complementarity is also important in relationships lasting over a year (Kerchoff & Davis, 1962).

Factors of Interpersonal Attraction

Remember: C CAPS (*Competence, Complementarity, Attractiveness, Propinquity,* and *Similarity*).

Theories of Interpersonal Attraction

According to the **reinforcement-affect model** of attraction, people like individuals more when the individuals are associated with events that arouse positive feelings (Byrne & Clore, 1970). Adolescents may be more likely to date someone who is in a class that they enjoy and do well in than someone who is in a class in which they are getting a failing grade. This model also suggests that dates in pleasant restaurants or beautiful scenic locations may result in more interpersonal attraction than dates in more routine settings.

A different model—the **gain-loss theory**—predicts that people are more attracted to others who become more positive in their evaluations of them than in people who liked them from the beginning. Also, people are more disappointed in and become less attracted to others who once liked them and who then became more negative in evaluations than to people who disliked them from the start (Aronson & Linder, 1965). Gaining approval is more reinforcing than having approval from the start. Losing approval hurts more than never having approval. Some relationships become very strong even though, initially, the people involved intensely disliked each other. Over time, people in these situations gain in evaluation. Some relationships that begin with an abundance of compliments, gifts, and courtesy become much less interesting as the individuals become their more balanced selves of both positive and negative characteristics. Even though the people involved may be fairly nice, these relationships involve a loss as they move from completely positive to a mixture of mostly positive and some negative interactions.

According to **exchange theory,** relationships are characterized by cost-reward ratios. Emotional, behavioral, and monetary costs in relationships are compared with the various benefits or rewards in these relationships. Relationships are evaluated according to "What's in this for me?" and "What do I have to put up with in this relationship?" Individuals are motivated to maximize the rewards and minimize the costs of relationships, and will choose the best available outcomes (Thibaut & Kelley, 1959). Exchange theory predicts that people stay in unsatisfactory relationships if they believe that better relationships are not available. This theory also predicts that people may sometimes leave satisfactory relationships because they believe that even better relationships (those with more rewards and/or less costs) are available.

Equity theory features the belief that the ratio of each person's inputs relative to their outcomes should be equal (Clark & Reis, 1988). Couples who view their relationships as equitable are more confident about remaining together,

report more satisfaction with their relationships, and like each other more (Hatfield, Traupmann, Sprecher, Utne, and Hay, 1985; Sabatelli & Cecil-Pigo, 1985). Interestingly, in close relationships, women are more upset with receiving more than their share of benefits than men, and men become more upset with receiving less than their share of benefits than women (Hatfield et al., 1985). However, in many intimate relationships, equality, or meeting individual needs, becomes more important than equity (Clark & Reis, 1988).

Actually, many relationships between romantic partners, family members, and good friends may be based mostly on **communal relationships,** in which members feel mutual responsibility for each other's welfare (Mills & Clark, 1982). In communal relationships, people want to show concern for each other and help the other person meet needs. Communal relationships reflect little concern for the exchange theory's ideas of cost-reward analysis or the equity theory's ratio of inputs and outputs.

As you review your adolescent years and your dating relationships, which of the preceding theories helps you to better understand your own experiences?

9. True or false: Early and middle teens are more likely to cite recreation and status as reasons for dating than are older teens.
10. In dating relationships, males are more likely to emphasize _____, while females are more likely to emphasize _____.
11. As factors in interpersonal attraction, _____ refers to being in physical proximity to each other, and _____ refers to having the ability to fulfill each other's needs.
12. In _____ relationships, individuals show little concern for input/output ratios as suggested by _____ theory or cost-reward analyses as suggested by _____ theory.

answers

9. True [LO-9]. **10.** sexual activity; intimacy [LO-9].
11. propinquity; complementarity [LO-10]. **12.** communal; equity; exchange [LO-11].

Career Development and the World of Work

Patterns of Work Experience Among Teens

Who Works?

The majority of adolescents have job experiences. Approximately one of every three 9th- and 10-graders holds a part-time job while going to school (Cole, 1981). By their senior year, three fourths of teenagers hold part-time jobs (Bachman, 1987). These figures represent a big increase in teen employment over the last 50 years. In 1940, for example, only 1 in 25 16-year-old males worked while attending school; 30 years later, the ratio was 1 in 4; and today, it is 1 in 3 (Cole, 1980).

Not only are more teenagers combining school and work, but the average number of hours on the job is also increasing. In 1960, 44 percent of working 16-year-old males spent more than 14 hr per week on the job. By 1970, this figure was up to 56 percent (Cole, 1980). Working high school seniors now average 16 to 20 hr per week on the job (Bachman, 1987).

Job growth in retail and service industries has provided the additional employment opportunities for adolescents. The six most frequent job categories for working teenagers are: (1) food service, (2) retail sales and cashiering, (3) manual labor, (4) clerical work, (5) operative and skilled labor, and (6) cleaning (Cole, 1980). Work in these industries tends to be low skilled, requiring little experience and minimal educational background. The low pay is not a deterrent for teenagers because most of them are supported by their families and are working only for spending money. In addition, employers are usually willing to schedule teenagers' work hours around their school hours (Greenberger & Steinberg, 1986).

What Are the Effects of Working During the Teen Years?

Teenagers who work learn much from the job search procedure, are often better than their nonworking peers at managing demands on their time, and may increase their skills in working with other people (Cole, 1980). Although parents often expect their working teens to exhibit improved cognitive skills and understanding of the business work ethic, researchers find that work does not positively influence these areas (Greenberger & Steinberg, 1986). Even more surprising are the number of negative effects of work on adolescents (Bachman, 1987; Cole, 1980; Greenberger & Steinberg, 1986):

- Teenagers who work feel less involved in school than do their nonworking counterparts. The more hours on the job, the more dissatisfaction the adolescents express with school. Working teenagers are less likely to participate in school activities, such as sports, drama, school newspaper, and band.
- Working is more likely to have a negative effect on school grades than a positive effect. More than one in four working teenagers experiences a decline in grade point average. Working adolescents spend less time on homework than do nonemployed teenagers.
- Students who work many hours had lower educational goals.
- Few working adolescents contribute to their family's finances, and only a minority (less than 20 percent) save any of their money for future goals, such as college. Adolescents who work only for spending money may experience a "premature affluence" that does not realistically prepare them for adulthood. In other words, working in the teen years may encourage self-indulgence.
- Almost half of working seniors believe that their jobs interfere with their social life. About a fourth of them

The most common first job is working in a fast food restaurant.

believe that their jobs interfere with their schoolwork or with their family life.
- Working teens may not get enough time for leisure activities and for solitary, introspective activities.
- Teenagers with jobs are more likely to use alcohol, cigarettes, marijuana, and other drugs, possibly because working teens have more money to spend on alcohol and drugs.
- The types of jobs teenagers hold may contribute to negative attitudes toward employment because, typically, their jobs are repetitive, unsupervised, and nonchallenging. Many employed teenagers develop cynical attitudes about work.
- Some teenagers have developed poor working attitudes and habits. One in eight working adolescents has admitted working under the influence of alcohol or marijuana. Almost one in five has admitted taking goods from employers; one in twenty has admitted taking money from employers.
- Some researchers believe that teenage employment produces pseudomaturity, the attainment of adult roles without psychological maturity. Working during adolescence may result in identity foreclosure rather than identity achievement.

To minimize the negative and maximize the positive effects of working during the teen years, parents might consider restricting their children's work time to 10 hr a week (Cole, 1980). They may also want to require their children to save part of their earnings for college or other expenses. Meaningfully volunteer work may have more benefits than monotonous minimum-wage jobs (Greenberger & Steinberg, 1986).

Another suggestion is that schools should be made more challenging and interesting so that teenagers are not able to work so many hours during their school years:

> Students have been able to fashion academic programs for themselves that are so unchallenging, and schools have become so undemanding, that adolescents are able to invest considerable hours in their jobs without jeopardizing their school performance. (Greenberger & Steinberg, 1986, p. 191)

Making Career Choices

How do adolescents make career choices? For most individuals, career decisions occur over a several-year period spanning from childhood into the adult years. Psychologists have formulated several models to look at the career decision-making process.

Ginzberg's Career Stages

Ginzberg (1984) proposed three developmental stages in the career decision-making process. The first stage, called the **fantasy stage,** lasts until individuals are approximately 11 years old. Persons in the fantasy stage are unrealistic about careers and about their own abilities and interests. If actual career decisions were made during this stage, the world would probably be overpopulated with police officers, ballet dancers, rock stars, cowboys, and fire fighters.

During the **tentative stage,** adolescents begin more serious and realistic exploration, definition, and clarification of possible career options. Adolescents realize the need to adequately assess their interests, abilities, and values and to determine how these aspects of themselves would fit various careers. Table 11.4 compares high school seniors in 1976 and 1986 on their values about work. As you can see, seniors know that they want jobs that match their interests and abilities, and they also value security, salary, and advancement.

At the end of adolescence, most individuals enter Ginzberg's third stage in the career decision-making process—the **realistic stage**—which is further broken down into three substages: exploration, crystallization (selection of a career field), and specification (selection of a specific job). In the exploration substage, the potential career fields have been narrowed, but there is still ambivalence. This substage may be short or quite long. A longitudinal study that started when subjects were adolescents found that 37 percent of the subjects were still making exploratory decisions at age 36 (Phillips, 1982). Persons in the exploratory substage benefit from further clarification of their work situation preferences, using lists such as presented in Table 11.5.

When Ginzberg first proposed his three stages in the 1950s, he saw them as inflexible and irreversible. In his most recent version, Ginzberg not only added flexibility and the potential to reverse decisions, but he stated that ca-

Table 11.4
What High School Seniors Rate as Very Important in a Job

Aspect of Job	Percentage of Seniors Who Rate Aspect of Job as Very Important	
	1976	1986
Interesting to Do	88%	87%
Uses Skills and Abilities	71	72
Good Chance for Advancement and Promotion	57	67
Predictable, Secure Future	62	64
Chance to Earn a Good Deal of Money	47	58
Chance to Make Friends	54	53
Worthwhile to Society	45	41
Chance to Participate in Decision Making	27	33
High Status or Prestige	20	32

From J. G. Bachman, "An Eye on the Future," p. 8, July, 1987 in *Psychology Today.* Reprinted with permission from Psychology Today Magazine Copyright © 1987 Sussex Publishers Inc.

reer choices are also influenced by what economic opportunities are available and by social-role expectations (Ginzberg, 1984; Yost & Corbishley, 1987).

Super's Self-Concept Theory

Donald Super's (1980) **self-concept theory** is similar to Ginzberg's model in that both have people assess their abilities and traits and compare these to what they know about occupations (Yost & Corbishley, 1987). However, Super emphasizes change and flexibility in the many roles that people play throughout life. These role modifications precipitate changes in career choices. That is,

> These roles interweave as well as wax and wane in idiosyncratic yet generalizable fashions that define the occupational tasks individuals must successfully negotiate. (Osipow, 1987, p. 259)

Super proposes five stages (or maxicycles) of career development: (1) growth (up to age 14), (2) exploration (ages 14 to 25), (3) establishment (ages 25 to 45), (4) maintenance (ages 45 to 65), and (5) disengagement (over age 65) (Super, 1980; Yost & Corbishley, 1987). In many ways, the growth and exploration stages relate to Ginzberg's fantasy and tentative stages, and the other three stages proposed by Super relate to Ginzberg's realistic stage. One of the advantages of Super's model is the additional stages during the adult years, which allow more understanding of long-term careers (maintenance stage) and the retirement process (disengagement stage).

Super's theory provides useful concepts of career adaptability and career maturity for individuals in career counseling. **Career adaptability** is adult readiness for career decision making. Some adolescents have this readiness, but more individuals reach readiness in the young adult years. **Career maturity** is the extent to which a person has completed stage-appropriate career developmental

Table 11.5
Exploring Work Situation Preferences

Choose your preferences among the following options:

A. Work Tasks

1. Routine Work (e.g., data coding, filing, assembly-line work)
2. Physical Work (e.g., heavy labor, crafts, gardening)
3. Machine and Tool Work (e.g., computers, cameras, earthmovers)
4. Work With Numbers (e.g., accounting, computer programming)
5. Work With Words (e.g., editing, writing, critiquing)
6. Work With Plants/Animals (e.g., nurturing, healing, research)
7. Work With People (e.g., selling, teaching, advocating)
8. Work With Information (e.g., problem solving, explaining)
9. Clerical Work (e.g., proofreading, filing, copying, sorting)
10. Creative Expression Work (e.g., music, dance, drama)

B. Working Conditions

1. People Relationships (Work with many, a few, alone? Preferred authority structure?)
2. Movement and Time (One location or more? Travel requirements? Work schedule?)
3. Performance Conditions (Self-managed? Supervision expected? Autonomy? Degree of responsibility?)
4. Variety (Predictability of tasks? Location? Hours?)
5. Environment (Calm or bustling? Quiet or noisy? Size? Aesthetic appearance?)
6. Location (Indoors or outdoors? Geographical region? Size of locality? Special preferences or needs?)

C. Benefits

1. Salary Range and Fringe Benefits (What lifestyle do I wish? How many will I support? What benefits are needed/wanted?)
2. Opportunities (Advancement? New skills? People connections?)
3. Job Security (How does security rank against prestige, challenge, possible advancement?)
4. Job Status (How do I want others to view my position? Is prestige more important than salary? Security?)
5. Worth of Work (Does work enhance self? Community? Others?)
6. Personal Rewards From Work (Feel needed? Challenged? Appreciated? Stimulated?)

From E. B. Yost and M. A. Corbishley, *Career Counseling: A psychological Approach,* Exhibit 8, pp. 72–75, 1987. Copyright © 1987 Jossey-Bass Inc., Publishers, San Francisco, CA.

tasks. Career-mature individuals are realistic and consistent, and seek out useful information about careers (Yost & Corbishley, 1987). Through a continuing longitudinal career pattern study begun in 1957, Super found that career maturity generally correlates with self-esteem. In addition, the career maturity level of adolescents is associated with education and career aspirations, self-estimates of ability, and internal locus of control (Osipow, 1987; Super, 1980).

Females and Careers

Both men and women now support women's careers in much greater numbers. Still, because the emphasis on women's careers is fairly recent, many female teenagers do more tentative and limiting career exploration than do male teenagers. Researchers suggest that most women consider a smaller range of careers than do men, and researchers have become interested in what characteristics encourage female adolescents to choose **pioneer careers,** those careers that are still male-dominated (Sandberg, Ehrhardt, Mellins, Ince, & Meyer-Bahlburg, 1987). Female adolescents who intend to choose pioneer careers have higher educational aspirations, less anticipation of marriage within 10 years, and less conformity to feminine characteristics. Pioneering female teenagers are more likely to have working mothers, more male friends, and fewer brothers but an adjacent or older brother, and wish fewer children than female teenagers who plan traditional female careers (Sandberg et al., 1987).

guided review

13. Working high school seniors are most likely to be working at _____ or _____ jobs an average of _____ or more hours per week.
14. Positive outcomes that result from teenage work experience include
    A. better time management
    B. better work ethic
    C. greater identity achievement
    D. all of the above
15. Ginzberg's three developmental stages of career decision making are the _____, _____, and _____ stages.
16. Super's approach to career development, compared to Ginzberg's, provides the additional stages in adulthood of career _____ and career _____.

answers

13. food service; retail clerking; 16 [LO-12]. **14.** A [LO-12].
15. fantasy; tentative; realistic [LO-13]. **16.** maintenance; disengagement [LO-14].

Exploring Human Development

1. Read early writings about adolescence (e.g., works by G. Stanley Hall, Anna Freud). What beliefs about adolescence in these books are still accepted today? What aspects have largely changed?
2. Compare the various magazines on the newsstands that are targeted for adolescent audiences. What kinds of magazines did you find? How do the publishers try to make their magazines appeal to teenagers?
3. Ask adults of various ages, "What event(s) made you realize you were now grown up?" Have them describe the event(s), and then compare your findings with others in the class.
4. With other students, debate the pros and cons of holding jobs during the teen years.
5. Arrange to take a career interest inventory, and compare the test results with your own career decisions.

Discussing Human Development

1. With other students in the class, discuss the best and worst aspects of the adolescent years. How many would like to relive their adolescent years? Why?
2. Do you think that counseling could help most teenagers to do a better or more efficient job of identity achievement?
3. Should teenage boys be socialized to value intimacy more and sexuality less in dating relationships? If this is desirable, how could it be accomplished?
4. How do the various factors of interpersonal attraction (propinquity, physical attractiveness, competence, similarity, and complementarity of needs) affect your friendships?
5. How would you recommend adolescents spend their days? How much time should be allotted to school/studying, working (chores and jobs), leisure activities? How do you justify your decisions?

Reading More About Human Development

Bibby, R. W., & Posterski, D. C. (1985). *The emerging generation: An inside look at Canada's teenagers.* Homewood, IL: Irwin.

Elkind, D. (1984). *All grown up and no place to go.* Reading, MA: Addison-Wesley.

Erikson, E. (1981). *Youth, change, and challenge.* New York: Basic Books.

Greenberger, E., & Steinberg, L. (1986). *When teenagers work: The psychological and social costs of adolescent employment.* New York: Basic Books.

Pogrebin, L. B. (1984). *Family politics; Love and power on an intimate frontier.* New York: McGraw-Hill.

Selman, R. (1980). *The growth of interpersonal understanding.* New York: Academic Press.

Summary

I. Personality development in teenagers
   A. G. Stanley Hall began the study of adolescence and viewed this period of emotional turmoil as stormy and stressful due to all of the changes occurring.
   B. Freud also believed that adolescence was a time of conflict as teenagers strove to achieve mature sexuality during his fifth psychosexual stage, the genital stage.
      1. During the genital stage, adolescents experience the emergence of strong sexual drives.
      2. Resolution of this stage results in the achievement of mature sexual relationships in socially acceptable ways.
   C. Recent studies of adolescents found that the lives of most teenagers are relatively free of stress and upheaval.
      1. Adolescents from diverse cultural backgrounds may develop differing personality structures.
      2. Three personality growth patterns are observed for adolescents: (1) smooth, continuous growth; (2) rocky, surgent growth; and (3) rough, tumultuous growth.
   D. Erikson's fifth psychosocial stage is ego identity versus role confusion.
      1. Ego identity is a sense of knowing oneself and of having that sense confirmed by others.
      2. Role confusion is characterized by feelings of purposelessness and doubts about personal identity.
      3. Erikson believed that experiencing an identity crisis was necessary to develop a stable, enduring identity.
      4. Successful resolution of the identity crisis results in the achievement of the virtue of fidelity.
      5. Failure to resolve the identity crisis may lead to prolonged identity confusion, role repudiation, or a negative identity.
      6. The physical aspects of identity often receive the most attention during the early adolescent years, as adolescents move from a diffuse sexuality to mature male and female identities.
      7. Middle adolescence is marked by quests for autonomy and for establishing independence from family, while becoming more dependent on peers.
      8. As adolescents achieve an authentic self-identity, they move from emphasizing sincerity to emphasizing honest expression of feelings and beliefs.
   E. Marcia emphasized the development of identity involving four identity states that vary according to individuals' experience with crisis and commitment.
      1. Individuals in the state of identity diffusion have neither experienced an identity crisis nor made commitments to mature identities.
      2. Individuals in identity foreclosure make a premature identity commitment without experiencing an identity crisis.

3. Individuals in identity moratorium are experiencing an identity crisis in which they are actively exploring identity issues but have not yet committed themselves to mature identities.

4. Individuals in identity achievement have experienced an identity crisis and have emerged with a mature identity that includes commitments to values, career, and relationships.

F. Identity formation varies with historical (Zeitgeist) and cultural (Ortgeist) experiences.

1. Erikson proposed that societal change across time may make the process of identity formation more difficult.

2. The timing of the process of identity formation also changes from culture to culture.

3. In the United States, identity achievement is a slow and gradual process throughout adolescence and into young adulthood.

4. In other cultures, the transition from childhood to adulthood is abrupt and makes use of rites of passage to confer adult identity on adolescents.

II. Important relationships—Parents and peers

A. Teenagers spend their waking hours in different activities from those of younger children.

1. Teenagers typically spend 40 percent of their waking hours in leisure activities and 29 percent in productive activities.

2. Teenagers typically spend about half their time with peers, a third of their time alone, and the remainder with family.

B. Despite folklore to the contrary, most teenagers get along well with their parents and believe that their parents are supportive of them.

1. Bickering and arguing with parents do increase, especially during the early adolescent years.

2. Peers exert greater influence on such day-to-day activities as dating and clothing choices, but parents remain the major influence on teens' values, beliefs, and careers.

3. Positive relationships and healthy adolescent personality development are most likely when parents are actively involved in their teenagers' lives; provide a warm, supportive family atmosphere; and are authoritative in their parenting style.

4. Authoritarian and permissive parenting styles are less likely to promote healthy development and are negatively associated with school grades.

C. Adolescents experience major changes in friendships and peer relationships.

1. Fidelity is an important factor in adolescent friendships.

2. Adolescent girls emphasize such qualities as intimacy and empathy in friendships, while adolescent boys stress skills and achievement.

3. Peer conformity is high during early adolescence, with less conformity occurring among high-status or low-status peers.

4. Physical appearance is an important factor in the formation of cliques for both adolescent boys and girls, while academic ability is not.

5. Cliques often group together into crowds of somewhat similar characteristics (e.g., the "jocks").

6. Clique and crowd activity changes during the course of adolescence, from single-sex, single-interest cliques, to same-sex cliques being with opposite-sex cliques, to groups of dating couples in later adolescence.

III. First loves—Relationships in the teen years

A. Dating serves seven major functions, ranging from entertainment to selection of a marriage partner.

1. The major purposes of dating change from early to later adolescence, with older adolescents viewing dating as a personally fulfilling activity engaged in for companionship, sexual activity, and mate selection.

2. Males more often emphasize sexual activity as a reason for dating, while females are more likely to stress intimacy.

3. Peer status and being fashionable are more important factors in dating partners for younger adolescents; older adolescents stress similarity of interests and personality factors.

4. Males are more likely to choose dating partners on the basis of appearance and sexuality, while females are more likely to choose on the basis of personality and behaviors.

5. Dating patterns of adolescents more often are influenced by perceived peer dating norms than by the actual dating behaviors of teens.

6. Gender differences in perceived appropriateness of differing degrees of sexual involvement when dating reflect the greater emphasis males place on sexuality in dating and society's double standard that is more approving of sexually active teenage males.

B. Important factors in interpersonal attraction include propinquity, physical attractiveness, competence, similarity, and complementarity of needs.

1. Propinquity (physical proximity) and attractiveness are important factors in the initial formation of relationships.

2. Competence, similarity, and complementarity of needs are important in maintaining long-lasting relationships.

3. The reinforcement-affect model of attraction proposes that people are attracted to individuals who are associated with events that arouse positive feelings.

4. The gain-loss model of attraction predicts that people are more attracted to those for whom their attraction has increased over time.

5. Exchange theory proposes that people are attracted to relationships that have more rewards than costs.

6. Equity theory predicts that people are attracted to relationships in which each partner's inputs and outcomes are relatively equal.

IV. Career development and the world of work
   A. The majority of adolescents have job experiences.
      1. Teen employment has increased over the last 50 years, as has the average number of hours worked per week.
      2. Benefits from working include awareness of job search procedures, better time management, and increased interpersonal skills.
      3. On the negative side, the more hours that teenagers work, the more that school involvement, school achievement, and the teenagers' social lives suffer.
      4. The negative effects of working during the teen years may be limited by restricting the number of hours worked, emphasizing saving for future goals, finding meaningful volunteer experiences, and making schooling more challenging and interesting.
   B. The career decision-making process usually stretches from childhood to adulthood, with the adolescent years playing an important role.
      1. Ginzberg proposed three stages in career decision making: (1) the fantasy stage of childhood; (2) the tentative stage of adolescence, in which individuals become more realistic and serious about career exploration; and (3) the realistic stage at the end of adolescence.
      2. Super's self-concept theory is similar to Ginzberg's in that adolescence is seen as a time of active career exploration, but Super's stages extend through the retirement years.
      3. Even with the recent emphasis on career decision making for women, most women consider a smaller range of career options than do men.
      4. Women who choose pioneer careers (careers in areas traditionally dominated by men) are more likely to have higher educational goals, working mothers, and less conformity to feminine characteristics than women who choose more traditional female careers.

Chapter Review Test

1. Which of the following psychologists is considered the founder of the study of adolescence?
   a. James Marcia
   b. Erik Erikson
   c. G. Stanley Hall
   d. William James

2. Which of the following best represents the proportion of teenagers who have significantly distressful experiences during adolescence?
   a. 1 in 10
   b. 1 in 4
   c. 1 in 2
   d. 2 in 3

3. According to Freud, which of the following is typical of the adolescent experience during the genital stage?
   a. Adolescents reexperience their past conflicts and have a second chance to resolve these fixations from earlier stages.
   b. Adolescents largely switch to a narcissistic sexual drive.
   c. Most adolescents function well, with only a minority dealing with high levels of conflict and stress.
   d. All of the above are correct.

4. Adolescents are in Erikson's fifth psychosocial stage, called
   a. intimacy versus isolation.
   b. ego identity versus role confusion.
   c. autonomy versus shame and doubt.
   d. generativity versus stagnation.

5. The basic strength that can develop in Erikson's fifth psychosocial stage is
   a. achievement.
   b. self-assurance.
   c. compassion.
   d. fidelity.

6. Which aspect of the search for identity is likely to be the earliest focus of an adolescent's attention?
   a. authenticity aspects
   b. autonomy aspects
   c. physical aspects
   d. sincerity aspects

7. _____ is older adolescents' focus on representing their inner self, even if there are differences with others.
   a. Authenticity
   b. Fidelity
   c. Independence
   d. Sincerity

8. Which of the following is associated with teens who experience identity foreclosure?
   a. high need for social approval
   b. radical departers
   c. belated identity crisis in adulthood
   d. all of the above

9. Which of the following individuals is experiencing an identity moratorium?
   a. Laura is exploring which of her favorite school subjects might make a good college major by looking at the types of careers that are associated with each.
   b. Albert seems to be drifting aimlessly and is disinterested in school, work, and family.
   c. Charles suddenly left his family and school and joined a cult that was recruiting members on his campus.
   d. Mary enthusiastically studies her engineering courses and also maintains a high grade point average in courses outside of her major.

10. Which of Marcia's identity statuses is characterized by no commitment and no crisis?
    a. identity achievement
    b. identity diffusion
    c. identity foreclosure
    d. identity moratorium

11. Identity formation in the United States is basically developed by
    a. apprenticeship.
    b. puberty rites.
    c. psychosocial moratoria.
    d. legal guidelines.
12. The number one activity among teenagers is
    a. watching television.
    b. doing homework.
    c. playing sports.
    d. talking with friends.
13. Which of the following statements is correct?
    a. Parent-child bickering is most common in middle adolescence.
    b. Sons have more conflict with their fathers than with their mothers.
    c. Daughters have more conflict with their mothers than with their fathers.
    d. All of the above are correct.
14. Which of the following characteristics do males rate as more important aspects of their dates than females do?
    a. being physically attractive
    b. being confident
    c. being kind and honest
    d. having money to spend
15. Which of the following factors is especially important in the beginning of relationships, rather than in long-lasting relationships?
    a. competence
    b. physical attractiveness
    c. similarity
    d. complementarity of needs
16. Which of the following statements reflects exchange theory?
    a. "We like people we meet in pleasant surroundings and situations."
    b. "We like people when what we put into a relationship and what we get out of a relationship are equal for each person."
    c. "We prefer relationships in which our evaluations improve over time to relationships in which liking was there initially."
    d. "We like relationships in which rewards are high and costs are minimal."

17. Which of the following individuals are you likely to end up preferring?
    a. Linda positively impressed you from the first and has continued to impress you.
    b. Don initially left a negative impression but since then has positively impressed you.
    c. Ron negatively impressed you at first, and little has changed since.
    d. Georgia positively impressed you initially but has not consistently done so.
18. Which of the following statements regarding adolescents who both work and attend school is correct?
    a. Students who work the most hours also have the highest educational goals.
    b. Working teenagers are less likely to use alcohol, cigarettes, marijuana, or other drugs.
    c. Teenagers who work are less likely to participate in school activities, such as sports, drama, and band.
    d. All of the above are correct.
19. Most teenagers are in Ginzberg's _____ stage of career decision making.
    a. tentative
    b. realistic
    c. fantasy
    d. pioneer
20. Most adolescents are in the _____ stage, according to Super's self-concept theory.
    a. establishment
    b. growth
    c. maintenance
    d. exploration

Answers

1. C [LO-1].	8. D [LO-4].	15. B [LO-10].
2. B [LO-1].	9. A [LO-4].	16. D [LO-11].
3. A [LO-2].	10. B [LO-4].	17. B [LO-11].
4. B [LO-3].	11. C [LO-5].	18. C [LO-12].
5. D [LO-3].	12. D [LO-6].	19. A [LO-13].
6. C [LO-3].	13. C [LO-7].	20. D [LO-14].
7. A [LO-3].	14. A [LO-9].	

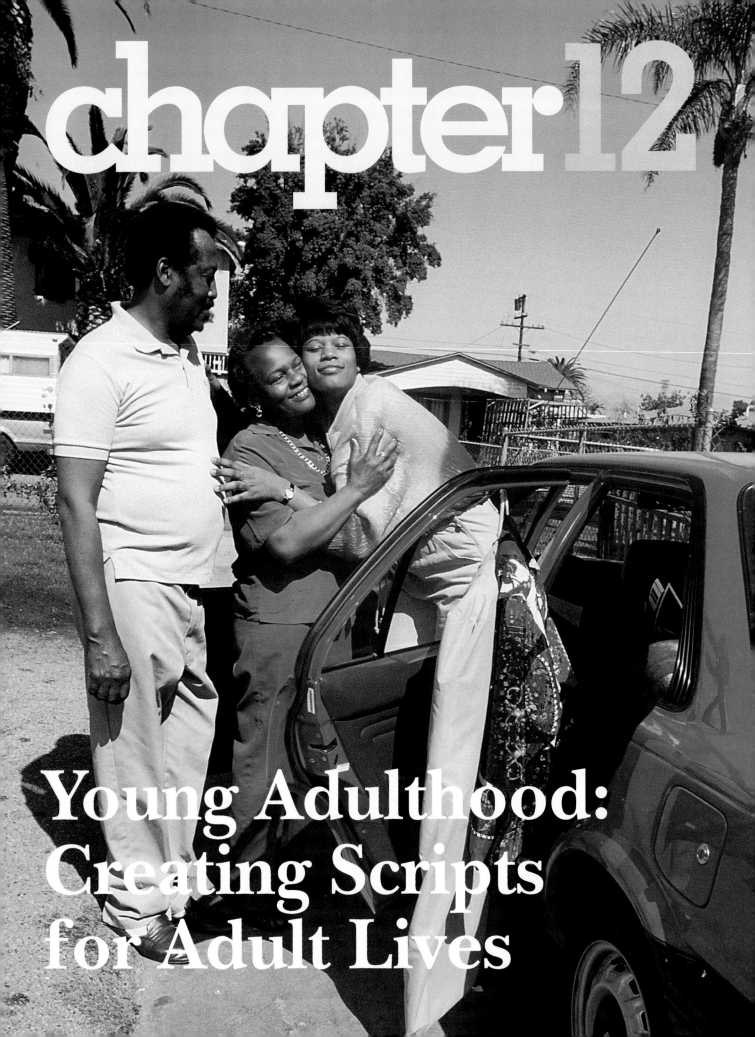

chapter 12

Young Adulthood: Creating Scripts for Adult Lives

Key Terms

Age-graded
Normative, age-graded life event
Life structure
Social clocks
Nonnormative life events
Nuclear family
Extended family
Family of origin
Family of procreation
Blended families
Family life cycle
Love relationships
Friendship
Passion
Caring
Productive love
Occupation
Vocation
Job
Career
Professions
Realistic
Investigative
Artistic
Social
Enterprising
Conventional
Dualism
Relativism
Commitment
Dialectical thinking
Youth

Learning Objectives

1. Explain the predictable life events models of development.
2. Describe the principal features of the predictable life event approaches of Havighurst, Erikson, Levinson, and Gould.
3. Distinguish between normative, age-graded life events and nonnormative life events.
4. Evaluate the predictable life events models of development.
5. Explain the contextual models of development.
6. Describe the principal features of the timing-of-life-events and the systems contextual models.
7. Explain script theory as a model of adult development.
8. Identify and contrast terms describing different kinds of families.
9. Describe and critique family life cycle models.
10. Identify problems associated with nonnormative family scripts.
11. List the three clusters found in love relationships.
12. Describe the four main characteristics of Fromm's productive love.
13. Contrast the characteristics of passionate and companionate love.
14. Distinguish among the six basic love styles identified in the Love Attitudes Scale.
15. Define the following terms: *occupation, vocation, job,* and *career.*
16. Explain Holland's theory of personality types and work environments.
17. Describe the impact of attending college on students' attitudes, values, and intellectual development.
18. Discuss the common features of transitions in adulthood, including those associated with the concept of youth.

Adolescence ends, and adulthood begins. However, the change is rarely abrupt and is more likely to be a series of events that represent a transition to adulthood. Understanding of adult life and of adult development has changed as researchers and theorists have begun to actively explore the longest period of human development—adulthood.

Exploring Your Own Development

Can you pinpoint the day you became an adult? When were you initiated into adulthood? Does suggesting that you can identify a specific day and ceremony when you finally became a grown-up sound strange to you? In some societies, definite rites of passage celebrate the transition from childhood to adulthood. These ceremonies and rituals mark the individual's newly acquired status within the society. Typically, rites of passage are **age-graded,** which means that they occur for all individuals at the same age.

Review the list of events in Table 11.3. Which, if any, of those events marked your transition into adulthood? Can you identify a specific event that marked your entry into adulthood?

In the United States and many other cultures today, the transition from adolescence to adulthood is neither age-graded nor marked by rites of passage. Instead, it is characterized by increasing autonomy and financial independence. For many young people today, adulthood emerges over a period of years, as decisions regarding intimate relationships, parenthood, vocations, and education set the stage for each individual's adult life course.

Models of Adult Development

While each person's adult life course is individual and unique, within a given society, expectations have arisen regarding the likely events of adulthood and the timing of these events. Two types of models—predictable life events models and contextual models—reflect different emphases in understanding the expectations we hold about our own and others' adult development.

Predictable Life Events Models

Several theorists have suggested that adulthood is a series of predictable life events, those events that typically occur during one phase of adulthood or another. For example, while adults of all ages marry, most adults typically marry early in their adult years. Marriage, therefore, is a **normative, age-graded life event.** It is normative in that most people are expected to marry, and it is age-graded because most people marry for the first time as young adults. Marriage becomes a predictable life event of early adulthood when most people in a society behave as expected and marry in their early adult years. Thus, predictable life events models of adult development propose that adult development consists of a series of developmental tasks to complete at different times across the adult years.

Table 12.1
Havighurst's Developmental Tasks for Adulthood

Early Adulthood

Selecting a mate

Learning to live with a marriage partner

Starting a family

Rearing children

Managing a home

Getting started in an occupation

Taking on civic responsibility

Finding a congenial social group

Middle Age

Assisting teenage children to become responsible and happy adults

Achieving adult social and civic responsibility

Reaching and maintaining satisfactory performance in occupational career

Developing adult leisure-time activities

Relating oneself to one's spouse as a person

Accepting and adjusting to the physiological changes of middle age

Adjusting to aging parents

Late Maturity

Adjusting to decreasing physical strength and health

Adjusting to retirement and reduced income

Adjusting to death of spouse

Establishing an explicit affiliation with one's age group

Adopting and adapting social roles in a flexible way

Establishing satisfactory physical living arrangements

Source: Havighurst, R. J. (1972). *Developmental tasks and education* (3rd ed.). New York: D. McCay.

Havighurst's Adult Developmental Tasks
Robert Havighurst (1972) created a set of developmental tasks for each phase of the lifespan. His tasks for the adult years are listed in Table 12.1. Havighurst's approach stresses basic expectations regarding life events for different age groups within a society. To the extent that a majority of people encounter these life events as expected, then Havighurst's list presents a reasonable pattern of adulthood for most people.

While Havighurst's list is useful, it is not predictive for everyone. For example, many middle-aged adults find that they do not have time to develop leisure-time activities. In addition, Havighurst omits important adulthood tasks, such as obtaining further education or vocational training. Despite these problems, Havighurst's list generally reflects many of society's expectations about the predictable pattern of life events in adulthood.

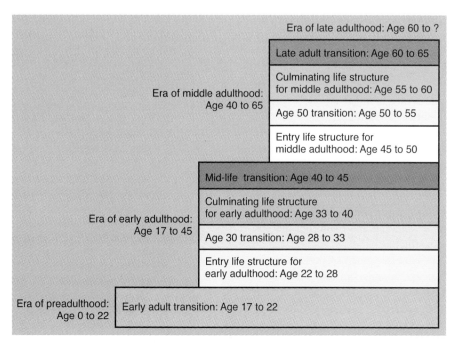

Figure 12.1

Levinson's "seasons" of adult development.

Source: Data from D. J. Levinson, et. al., *The Season's of a Man's Life*, 1978. Alfred A. Knopf, Inc.

Table 12.2
Erikson's Psychosocial Stages of Adulthood

Stage	Age Range	Crisis	Basic Strength
6	18 to 35 years	Intimacy Versus Isolation	Love
7	35 to 60 years	Generativity Versus Stagnation	Will
8	60 and Beyond	Ego Integrity Versus Despair	Wisdom

Source: Data from Erikson, 1968.

Erikson's Psychosocial Stages of Adult Development

Erik Erikson's (1968) psychosocial stage theory (see Appendix A) proposes three predictable crises to be resolved in adulthood (see Table 12.2). Each crisis presents a new opportunity for balancing the needs of the individual with the needs of the larger society. The crisis can be resolved in a positive way, toward a more healthy balance or equilibrium between the poles, or in a negative way, toward a more unhealthy reliance on one extreme or the other. For example, an overcommitment to the next generation during middle adulthood at the expense of one's own needs is just as unhealthy as too much self-absorption.

Each of Erikson's successive stages builds upon the previous ones. Thus, healthy resolution of the previous crises facilitates resolution of the next crisis, while incomplete or negative resolution of a previous stage hinders the satisfactory resolution of the next one. At each stage, not only must the particular crisis of that age be resolved, but

also each of the previously resolved crises must be adapted to the new level of functioning (Erikson, 1980). For example, according to Erikson, adapting an appropriate level of trusting is as much an issue for adults as it is for infants. One's sense of identity is continually modified from adolescence onward.

Erikson's theory reflects this same sense of continual adaptation of previously resolved crises to new life events. The changes over the years in Erikson's ideas are, in part, the result of Erikson's own development. In particular, he expanded and modified his ideas about the crises of adulthood as he moved through the stages of adulthood himself (Erikson, 1985).

Levinson's Seasons of Men's Adult Lives

Daniel Levinson (1978) and his colleagues (Darrow, Klein, Levinson, & McKee, 1976) extensively studied the lives of 40 men between the ages of 35 and 45 and discovered a predictable pattern of periods of transition and change leading to periods (*seasons* in Levinson's terminology) of consolidation and stability (see Figure 12.1).

According to Levinson, adulthood is marked by the development and periodic reformulation of a **life structure** consistent with self-concept (Levinson, 1986). Life structures are the basic patterns or designs of people's lives that shape and are shaped by people's interactions with the world. At any given time in their lives, people's life structures consist of their interests, roles, and goals and reflect their values, hopes, and dreams. Levinson found among his sample that designing their lives around a dream provided men with a sense of direction and that, most often, the dream centered on the men's occupations.

According to Levinson, people have periods, or eras, during which they formulate and consolidate their life structures. These eras are preceded or followed by periods of transition of up to 5 years in length, during which the life structure from the previous era is evaluated and the possibilities for reformulation during the next era are explored. The phases within each era of early, middle, and late adulthood are also separated by briefer periods of evaluating and restructuring. For example, as shown in Figure 12.1, the phases "Entry life structure for middle adulthood" and "Culminating life structure for middle adulthood" are separated by an "Age 50 transition." The result, according to Levinson, is that nearly half of the adult years are spent in some form of transition (evaluating and exploring the possibilities within one's life structure).

Levinson argued that the sequence of periods is universal across differing socioeconomic, cultural, and historical contexts, although data to support his position is scant (Levinson, 1986). He also contended that, with some alterations, his schema is descriptive of the adult development of women. He maintained that the sequence of changes in evolving a life structure is predictable for essentially everyone, while the contents of individual life structures are different from person to person. Thus, the work of Levinson and his colleagues points to the existence of a set of predictable developmental life events for adulthood.

Gould's Theory

Roger Gould (1978, 1980) proposed that the task at each stage of adult development is to eliminate particular irrational ideas carried forward from childhood. For example, according to Gould, during the period from age 16 to 22 (Gould called this the "leaving our parents' world" period), young people must begin to confront irrational ideas—for example, that they will always live with their parents and believe in their parents' world. Gould maintained that, as people move through their young and middle adult years, they must deal with other false assumptions: that their parents will always be able to do for them what they themselves cannot do; that parents can always simplify and control an increasingly complex set of experiences; and that the world is always a good place where people do not die.

Levinson's and Gould's theories of adult development are compatible. Both are notable in that they emphasize that development results from the ongoing interaction between the outer events of one's life and the inner experiences of those events. Levinson depicted this sequence as the development of a life structure in the form of a dream for one's life, which is shaped by the realities of actual life events. Gould also viewed adult development as a repeated cycle of examination of one's inner reality in light of actual experiences. What sets these theories, along with those of Havighurst and Erikson, apart from other theories of adult development is that the experiences described in these theories are normative (expected for most people) and age-graded (different predictable experiences at different ages in adulthood).

Neugarten suggests we are becoming an age-irrelevant society. For example, what is the "right time" to be a college student? The answer is no longer "from 18 years to 22 years." It's anytime you want to be in classes.

Critique of Predictable Life Events Models

The foregoing models of development based on the predictability of adult life events have been criticized with regard to both the normative and age-graded nature of adult development. Bernice Neugarten (1980a), in challenging the age-graded concept of adult development, noted that U.S. society is increasingly age irrelevant. College classrooms are now populated with a much wider age range of people than was the case 25 years ago. Greater numbers of retirees are continuing to work, in part for the social interaction that working brings. Even Erikson believed that each of the preceding crises must be adapted to one's present age, suggesting that adult personality development is an amalgam of recurrent crises, rather than a succession of predictable crises.

Criticizing the normative features of adult development is even easier. An obvious flaw in the normative views of Levinson is that his study examined only the lives of men, and a rather small sample of men at that. In fact, many studies appear to make the tacit assumption that data collected from male subjects reflect human development in general. This assumption has not gone unchallenged (Baruch, Barnett, & Rivers, 1983; Gilligan, 1982; Lauer & Lauer, 1987).

The critics argue that men and women exhibit different patterns of development and react differently to the same factors influencing development. For example, Lauer and Lauer (1988) found that, when the influences of unpredictable life crises were examined, men and women identified the same set of turning points in their lives. However, the frequency of the type of crisis mentioned differed between the 632 men and women in the study. The

Table 12.4
Crucial Events in Achieving Adulthood

Life Event	Women					Men		
	Parents			Nonparents		Parents		Nonparents
	European American	African American	Hispanic American	European American	African American	European American	African American	European American
Becoming a Parent	40.2	34.8	33.3	11.1	14.3	31.6	11.5	5.3
Getting Married	19.8	21.7	21.2	19.9	35.7	15.0	3.8	13.7
Supporting Yourself	13.9	14.1	15.2	34.8	21.4	24.7	46.2	47.4
Getting a Job	8.1	3.3	6.1	9.1	14.3	9.1	7.7	6.3
Finishing School	5.8	8.7	18.2	7.3	0.0	5.6	3.8	5.3
Moving Out of Parental Home	5.1	10.9	3.0	9.8	7.1	7.8	23.1	7.4
Other	7.1	6.5	3.0	8.0	7.1	6.2	3.8	14.8
N	1,113	92	33	287	14	320	26	95

From L. W. Hoffman and J. D. Manis, "The Value of Children in the United States: A New Approach to the Study of Fertility", in *Journal of Marriage and the Family*, 41, 589, 1979. Copyrighted 1979 by the National Council on Family Relations, 3989 Central Ave. NE, Suite 550, Minneapolis, MN 55421. Reprinted by permission.

Table 12.3
Rankings of Unpredictable Life Crises for Men and Women

Women	Men
1. Interpersonal Problems (Divorce, Death, Love Relationships)	1. Crucial Decisions about Education and Careers
2. Social Transitions (Traveling, Moving, Involvement in New Group)	2. Interpersonal Problems (Divorce, Death, Love Relationships)
3. Crucial Decisions About Education and Careers	3. Social Transitions (Traveling, Moving, Involvement in New Group)
4. Meaningful Relationships (Friends, Lovers, Spouse, Children)	4. Personal Problems
5. Personal Problems	5. Meaningful Relationships (Friends, Lovers, Spouse, Children)

From *Watersheds: Mastering Life's Unpredictable Crises* by Robert H. Lauer and Jeanette C. Lauer. Copyright © 1988 by Robert H. Lauer, Ph.D. and Jeanette C. Lauer, Ph.D. By permission of Little, Brown and Company.

major difference, as shown in Table 12.3, is that men were most likely to mention a crucial decision about their education or career as a major turning-point crisis in their lives, a finding that is consistent with Levinson's research with men. Women, however, most frequently cited interpersonal problems, with crucial decisions about education and careers mentioned third most frequently. These findings point out the inadequacy of developmental explanations based on results obtained solely from one gender. If only men or only women had been studied, the same set of five life crises would have been identified, but a potentially misleading pattern of rankings would have been calculated.

Psychologist Carol Gilligan (1982) argued that, in general, women's experiences in adulthood are different from those of men because women have acquired a different set of values. According to Gilligan, instead of seeking competitive success, women view success as achieving cooperation and consensus. Women also value mutuality (establishing interdependence) and preserving relationships more than men.

Generalizing from studies of men is also a problem for other cultural groups. African Americans, Hispanic Americans, Asian/Pacific Island Americans, Native Americans, and others may legitimately ask if the predictable life events in these models are, in fact, predictable, for their cultural groups. For example, when different groups of individuals were asked which event was (or might be) most important in making them feel like an adult, the responses differed considerably among the groups (see Table 12.4). Hoffman and Manis (1979) found that, regardless of ethnic grouping, among women who were mothers, "becoming a parent" was the most important event in making them feel like an adult. This was also true for European-American men who were fathers, but was not true for African-American fathers. "Supporting yourself" was the important factor for African-American fathers, as well as for European-American men and women without children. African-American nonparents regarded marriage as the crucial event in achieving adulthood.

In summary, while helping to organize and differentiate different stages of adulthood, the predictable life events models may both overgeneralize and oversimplify adulthood experiences, which are becoming increasingly less predictable for many adults of all ages. These models are useful for testing individual adult development but are self-limiting by the nature of their social, cultural, and historical contexts.

Contextual Models

In contrast to the normative, age-graded characteristics of predictable life events models, contextual models emphasize the ordering of life events and the sociohistorical factors present when a life event occurs. These models suggest that the experience of adulthood is different for an individual who marries at age 18, has two children by age 22, and enters college at age 32, compared to an individual who enters college at age 18, marries at age 22, and has two children between the ages of 28 and 32. An additional factor influencing the outcome is whether the individuals were 18 in, for example, 1952 or 1972.

Timing-of-Life-Events Model

Bernice Neugarten was among the first psychologists to suggest that age-graded factors were becoming increasingly less important in understanding the developmental changes occurring in contemporary adulthood. Beginning in the 1960s, Neugarten recognized that people are generally aware of **social clocks** (the times when certain life events are expected to occur) and also that more and more people are experiencing those events at unexpected times (**nonnormative life events**) (Neugarten, Moore, & Lowe, 1965). According to Neugarten (1980a), U.S. society has in many ways become less age conscious, diminishing the effects of the social clock. Neugarten's timing-of-life-events model, however, points out that, regardless of whether one feels that he or she is early, late, or on time with respect to the social clock, receiving a college degree at age 22 has social and economic effects that differ from receiving a college degree at age 42 or 62.

Systems Models

The emergence over the past several decades of a global awareness of the interdependence of environmental, social, political, and economic conditions is reflected in models of adult development that emphasize the systems (contexts) in which development occurs. Urie Bronfenbrenner (1979) proposed an ecology of human development, with overlapping systems ranging from the influence of the family to the influence of cultural-political systems. Arnold Sameroff (1982, 1983), reflecting the use of systems theory in computer science, argued for a systems approach to the study of adult development.

The systems approach stresses the linking together of interacting systems on development. Interactions occur within and between systems. For example, the experience of being a parent is influenced by the parent-child or family system. The presence or absence of another person with whom to share parenting is one influence in this system; the role of grandparents is another. The community in which the family lives is another system. Are day-care services available for working parents with young children? Do employers provide parental leave for family illness and emergencies? Larger political systems, in turn, can affect these interactions by enacting state and federal laws pertaining to family needs. Cultural systems influence parent-child interactions. Your grandfathers may have paced the floor in a waiting room when your parents were born, while your father may have been present at your birth and may have even cut your umbilical cord.

Advantages and Disadvantages of Contextual Models

Contextual models recognize the individuality of development while investigating a wider range of developmental influences. While helpful in studying development at any age, they are especially useful in adulthood, which lacks the uniformity of age-graded changes so prevalent in infancy, children, and adolescence. Also, gender differences can be investigated by examining the different contexts (systems) for men and women and the differing interactions within systems for women and men. The advantages of contextual models, however, may become disadvantages if the increased complexity of developmental analyses obscure, rather than clarify, the understanding of our own and others' development in adulthood.

Script Theory

The complexity involved in understanding the development of one person across his or her lifespan becomes even more apparent when the focus is shifted from investigating the influence of past contexts to predicting future life events. At any point in your development, many pathways for future development exist, each with its own set of contexts and life events. Each life event, each choice point, presents a new fork in the road for your development. William Runyon (1982) developed a method for investigating the many possible developmental pathways. For example, if you consider the family context and whether your relationship with your parents was good or poor over a 4-year period, 16 different patterns of development are possible. One pattern would be a good relationship each year. Another pattern would be a poor relationship the first 2 years, followed by 2 years of a good relationship. Runyon investigated the occupational histories of 20,000 American men. He divided their lives into four contexts (family background, level of education, and first and last job), with four possible conditions for each context. This yielded 256 possible life course patterns. Interestingly, Runyon found that 99 of 256 possible patterns did not occur in his sample. Likewise, some patterns occurred frequently, such as those in which the son's education and job level were similar to that of his father.

Runyon's studies suggest that, while many possible life courses exist for each of us, we actually pursue somewhat predictable life courses. Like social clocks, we may have a set of social guidelines, or scripts, that we adopt or alter to enable us to behave in an organized and predictable manner (Tomkins, 1979, 1988). As Tomkins described them, scripts are largely unconscious, culturally determined cognitive plans that individuals use to organize and guide their behavior. Each of us is like a playwright, and our individual development is the play. We act out different roles, following a complex set of scripts. Thus, in adulthood, where development is increasingly nonlinear and governed more by social than biological clocks, we acquire internal

What is your script for being a college student? Do you emphasize class attendance, studying or social activities? How did your script develop?

sets of rules that allow us to make sense of our past, to navigate our present circumstances, and to plot our future life course. For the men in Runyon's study, some patterns (scripts) were unworkable and never were pursued, while other scripts were frequently adopted.

The concept of scripts can be applied across contexts and at different levels of interaction among people. Do you have a script for how to ask for or accept a date with someone? What script(s) are you following as a college student? How similar is your script to the person sitting next to you in class?

Scripts provide a program for action. For that action to occur, the script must be represented cognitively, a context must arise that calls for that script, and the individual must be willing to follow the script (Abelson, 1981). The script defines the situation, identifies the actors, and predicts the sequence of future events. Have you rehearsed the script for your life after college? While scripts share some features with social norms, scripts are our individual adaptations of social norms to the particular set of life events we have experienced and expect to experience.

Script theory is helpful in understanding many areas of adult development and also adds to understanding of gender and ethnic/cultural differences. Continue to examine your own individual scripts as we now look at the contexts of family and career.

Family Scripts

What images come to mind when you consider your family? Your images are individualized and personal. Mistakenly, we sometimes believe that those around us have similar images of their families. Part of our error comes from our inherent egocentrism, which leads us to believe that others share our personal perspectives of the world. We are also influenced by media images of families. In this section, we survey the variety of family contexts present today and examine some of the frequently occurring family scripts.

Family Contexts

Families are as different from one another as are snowflakes. The prototypical family may still be represented by a father who earns the income for the family, a mother who is a homemaker and who has primary responsibility for childcare, and two or more children; however, many of your classmates—if not you yourself—have experienced family settings very different from this prototype. In fact, the myriad of differences can be overwhelming when trying to understand the effects of differing family contexts on development.

A clarification of terms highlights the complexity of current family contexts. The prototypical family is often referred to as the **nuclear family:** a father, a mother, and their children. When those children leave home and begin nuclear families of their own, an **extended family** is created. Extended families may extend across several generations of individuals related by birth and by marriage. Today, the traditional nuclear family is found in fewer than 30 percent of U.S. family units (Lamanna & Reidmann, 1988). Dual-income and single-parent family units are more common today. The extended family unit has changed also. With smaller family units (fewer children) and greater longevity, the extended family extends across more generations today but encompasses approximately the same number of individuals. In addition, the extended family is spread over a much wider geographic area, so that actual contact among extended family members may be less now than during earlier eras.

Your **family of origin** usually refers to your biological parents who raised you and any other siblings. This traditional view assumes an "intact" family of origin. The term loses precision if you were adopted or if your parents divorced when you were young. Regardless of whether one or both parents remarried, if they shared joint custody of you and your siblings, determining what constitutes your family of origin may be more difficult.

As an adult, determining what constitutes your family can be equally difficult. You may remain more or less tied to your family of origin while you establish a family unit of your own, your **family of procreation.**

Families that are not intact—families in which divorce has occurred—were once referred to as "broken" families, as in "He came from a broken home" (i.e., his parents are divorced). The term *broken* seems inappropriate since some intact families are dysfunctional (i.e., "broken") while some families divided by divorce become more functional as a result of the divorce. Substituting less disparaging terms, such as *divided, divorced,* or *split families,* does not necessarily clarify the situation. Many divorced individuals remarry, causing further difficulty in sorting our family ties.

The term **blended families** appears to be a useful way of describing the unit that results when individuals with children from a previous family marry. These reconstituted families are as widely varying in their makeup as are intact families today. The contextual variations within and between differing family units is almost limitless. What about parents who cohabitate? Single parents who never marry? Divorced parents who never remarry? Childless couples?

The Family Life Cycle

Despite its widely varying forms, the family is a major factor in everyone's development throughout their lifetimes. The kinship support system of the family ideally features not only a stable environment for raising children but also a supportive environment for the parents and continued support for adult children. Even when the family system is less than ideal, few cultures have devised a better system for providing the continuous social support that families provide across the lifespan.

Starting in the 1940s, Evelyn Duvall and her colleagues began devising models of the **family life cycle** (Duvall & Hill, 1948). Her original model had four stages, which she eventually expanded to eight (Duvall, 1977). Figure 12.2 illustrates that, as a family unit develops along a traditional pattern, predictable time periods exist for each stage. Interestingly, in the family life cycle depicted of approximately 55 to 60 years in length, the periods of childbearing, child-rearing, and child launching total less time than the couple spends together without children.

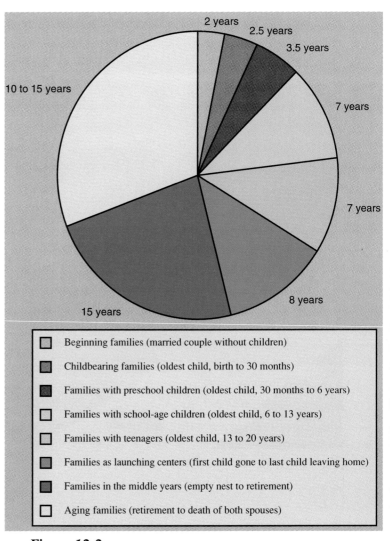

Figure 12.2
Duvall's stages of the family life cycle.
Source: Data from Evelyn Duvall, 1977.

Table 12.5 presents a somewhat revised and updated version of Duvall's stages by Mattessich and Hill (1987), along with data on marital and life satisfaction at each stage. In this model as well, the with-children years are fewer than the without-children years. Noteworthy also is that overall marital satisfaction is greater during the without-children years.

Obviously, these models are based on the assumption of predictable life events and demographic data for traditional prototypical families. As already noted, many fewer families currently fit the traditional format, and thus, the models of the family life cycle are in need of revision (Glick, 1989a).

Hill (1986) proposed a complex model for differing family contexts. He compared the traditional family with other contexts, such as the reconstituted family, remarriage with later childbearing, the premarital pregnant family, the single-parent family, and the childless family. He focused on the expected changes in the roles of various family members and the stresses that accumulated during the transitions between stages.

Table 12.5
Stages of the Family Life Cycle, With Marital and Life Satisfaction at Each Stage (H = Husband; W = Wife)

Stage	Age of Couple	Number of Years in Stage	Major Goal of the Family	Percent Always Satisfied with Marriage		Percent Very Satisfied with Life in General	
				H	W	H	W
Establishment (married, no children)	H 22 to 23 W 20 to 21	1	Adjusting to living as a couple	41%	27%	74%	55%
Childbearing (infants and preschool children)	H 24 to 30 W 22 to 28	6	Developing attachment between parent and child; recognizing and adapting to the needs of infants and young children	22–31	14–17	50–76	61–69
School-Age (one or more children in elementary school)	H 30 to 37 W 28 to 35	7	Adjusting to the expanding world of schoolchildren; encouraging educational achievement	11	14	35	39
Adolescence (one or more teenage children)	H 37 to 44 W 35 to 42	7	Recognizing the adolescent's need for freedom; gradually allowing greater degrees of independence and encouraging the adolescent to behave responsibly	14	18	17	44
Transition (children entering adulthood)	H 44 to 52 W 42 to 50	8	Launching young adults out of the home and into the world; relinquishing the role of parent while maintaining a supportive home base	20	27	9	9
Postparental (parents middle-aged; children no longer at home)	H 52 to 65 W 50 to 64	14	Reestablishing the husband-wife relationship; assuming the role of grandparent	17	27	17	24
Retirement	H 66 until death W 64 until death	3 to 13?	Adjusting to retirement and to aging; coping with death of spouse and living alone	38	42	82	66

From P. Mattessich and R. Hill, *Handbook of Marriage and the Family,* p. 447, 1987, edited by M. B. Sussman and S. K. Steinmetz. Copyright © 1987 Plenum Publishing Corporation, New York, NY.

A number of social changes have intensified the need to accommodate the many nontraditional family forms in family life cycle models. Elinor Macklin (1987) noted that the varied nontraditional family forms are the result of the increased status of American women, improved methods of contraception, increased acceptance of sexuality outside of marriage, and the diminished need for a kinship support system to survive.

A significant factor in altering the family life cycle has been the postponement of marriage. Compared to 1960, the average age for first marriages in the United States in 1988 was 3 years later, at 25.9 years for men and 23.6 years for women (Glick, 1989a). Many young adults appear to be delaying marriage in order to advance their education and their occupational careers. In addition, the marriage delay has been accompanied by large increases in cohabitation (five times as great in 1988 as in 1960) and in the proportion of births to unmarried women (four times as great).

Marriage delay appears to be part of a "deferral syndrome" that is evident in other stages of the family life cycle as well (Teachman, Polonko, & Scanzoni, 1987). Later first marriages coincide with delays in childbearing. Women who obtain more education delay their childbear-ing. This information, combined with knowledge of the high rate of teenage pregnancies and a declining birthrate, led Bloom (1981) to conclude that women were beginning childbearing early, late, or never. Thus, at a time in the past when families were engaged primarily in child-rearing, many of today's families are just beginning to bear children. Or, they are families with teenagers, resulting from early childbearing.

Divorce, remarriage, and single parenting are additional significant social changes that have caused the original models of the family life cycle to become outmoded. These three factors were not addressed in the original models and are closely linked. The rate of divorce has risen, while the rate of remarriage has declined. Together, the two have been accompanied by an increase in the number of single-parent families (more than twice the proportion in 1988, compared to 1960). Six out of seven single-parent families are maintained by women (Glick, 1989a). Ethnic differences are also present: In 1987, 9 percent of European-American families were single-parented, compared to 30 percent for African-American families.

With delays in childbearing come delays in the child-launching stage of the family life cycle. The delay

Exploring the Parent/Child Relationship: Homing Pigeons

When did your parents expect you to leave home? Schnaiberg and Goldenberg (1989) suggested that, among middle-class parents, one result of the traditional family life cycle pattern has been a set of idealized parental expectations for launching young adults from the family nest. These expectations are presented in Box Table 12.1.

Box Table 12.1
Idealized Parental Expectations for Young Adults

Education	Living Arrangements	Family of Procreation
College attendance away from home	Dorms or apartments or fraternity/sorority houses away from home	Early marriage and early childbearing, in a context of a marriage expected to be permanent
Postgraduate or professional training away from home	Neolocal household, normatively and structurally *relatively* independent of kin utilization for utilitarian, instrumental purposes	
Entry-level position in a career expected to lead to upward mobility and, generally, sufficient income to provide independence		

© 1989 by the Society for the Study of Social Problems. Reprinted from *Social Problems,* Vol. 36, No. 3, June 1989, pp. 251–269, by permission.

Underlying these expectations is the belief that parents will make a large but time-limited investment in rearing their children. Thus, when parents have successfully launched their children from the nest, the expectation is that the parents will now have more time and resources to devote to their own developmental needs. However, when economic and other social changes constrict the achievement of independent living for young adults, the expected empty nest may become crowded with incompletely launched young adults (ILYAs). These "homing pigeons" exhibit patterns of behavior quite different from their parents' idealized expectations (see Box Table 12.2).

Box Table 12.2
Typical Constricted Achievement Patterns of ILYAs

Education	Living Arrangements	Family of Procreation
Interrupted, postponed, or intermittent college attendance	Commuting from home daily; sporadic periods of household independence but with heavy reliance on parental home as base and resource pool	Postponement of marriage and/or postponement of childbearing, or a decision to have children despite marital risks
Interrupted, postponed, or intermittent postbaccalaureate attendance	"Home is the place you can always return to," however unwillingly and uncomfortably; unusual living arrangements (neither parental nor independent household of procreation)	Expectations of instability a and high marital pressure
Erratic job patterns, often remote from career path, and with no assurance of future upward mobility or even status maintenance; no assured income level for self-sufficiency		

© 1989 by the Society for the Study of Social Problems. Reprinted from *Social Problems,* Vol. 36, No. 3, June 1989, pp. 251–269, by permission.   *continued*

may coincide with greater economic resources, since parents are further advanced in their occupational careers. At the same time, however, those parents will have fewer years remaining after their children are launched in which to feather their empty nests financially for their retirement.

General economic forces also have shaped the family life cycle. During recent times, rising educational costs, coupled with intermittent periods of inflation and recession, along with higher levels of unemployment and shifting patterns of employment, have caused significant numbers of young adults to return to their parents' empty nest. The phenomenon of "incompletely launched young adults," a term used to describe adult children who have left home and then returned again (Schnaiberg & Goldenberg, 1989), occurs at all socioeconomic levels but has been most noticeable in middle-class families. The "Exploring the Parent/Child Relationship" feature presents one explanation of this phenomenon.

Family life cycle models will continue to be remodeled as families continue to adjust to a changing society. The many current variations in family scripts are an indication of the great adaptability and resiliency of the family in changing times. A lag will always necessarily exist between the present conditions and the models developed to explain them.

Schnaiberg and Goldenberg argued that shifting economic and social conditions have constricted the opportunity structure for young adults. Young adults today have been experiencing an educational/financial squeeze, accompanied by greater competitiveness for career-entry jobs and career advancement. Young adults may perceive the same constriction of opportunity occurring in other areas of their lives, such as marriage and becoming parents themselves. For example, the prevalence of divorce, as well as educational financial factors, may be contributing to postponement of marriage.

ILYAs are caught in a conflict between desiring the benefits of the adult roles of economic independence, marriage, and children (i.e., fulfilling their parents' idealized expectations) and facing rising costs for fulfilling those roles. As Box Table 12.3 illustrates, middle-class parents may have unwittingly contributed to this situation by not only passing on their expectations but also by having a family setting that compares all too favorably with independent living.

Box Table 12.3
Gains From Independent Living at Times of Constricted Opportunity
(ILYAs = Incompletely launched young adults; YAs = Young adults)

Dimension	ILYAs in Supportive Family	Independent, Constricted YAs	Net Gain
1. Material Comfort	Higher	Lower	Strong Negative
2. Economic Security	Higher	Lower	Strong Negative
3. Privacy	Moderate	Higher	Weak Positive
4. Social Freedom	Moderate	Low to High	Negative/Positive
5. Sexual Freedom	Moderate	Higher	Weak Positive
6. Emotional Support	High	Low to High	Negative/None

© 1989 by the Society for the Study of Social Problems. Reprinted from *Social Problems,* Vol. 36, No. 3, June 1989, pp. 251–269, by permission.

Unless societal conditions change quickly, the ILYA phenomenon is likely to remain. Schnaiberg and Goldenberg suggested that two possible outcomes of this phenomenon include: (1) the lowering of expectations by parents in future generations for their children's achievement of independent living and (2) the concomitant raising of the importance of familial satisfaction, as opposed to individual satisfaction.

Single-parent families are usually headed by women. They are also three times more common among African-Americans than among European-Americans.

Nonnormative Scripts

The family unit is a major societal institution that meets important individual needs for belongingness and intimacy, while achieving important societal goals for stability and child-rearing. According to Macklin (1987), two current nonnormative scripts significantly challenge the conceptualization of the family as a "legal, lifelong, sexually exclusive marriage between one man and one woman, with children" (p. 343): cohabitation and gay and lesbian couples.

Cohabitation is a nonnormative script adopted in 1988 by more than 2.5 million couples of the opposite sex (U.S. Bureau of the Census, 1989). Over half of these 5 million individuals had never married. The relationships between cohabiting women and men vary widely, from having a limited commitment to being committed to marrying.

For some individuals, cohabitation has become part of the courtship process and may, in fact, hasten the process for those who eventually marry (Risman, Hill, Rubin, & Peplau, 1981). Among cohabiting couples in the Risman et al. study who did marry, the average elapsed time between first date and marriage was 23 months, compared to 36 months for noncohabiting couples.

For others, cohabitation may be a way to simulate marriage and experience its benefits without legal commitments or entitlements. However, without the legal status, some of the benefits may not occur. Most employers do not recognize cohabiting couples (with or without children) as family units. Therefore, family health benefits, sick leave, paternity leave, and bereavement leave may not be applied to the cohabiting partner and his or her children. Likewise, insurance death benefits and the distribution of the deceased's estate may not include the cohabiting partner unless specific prior arrangements have been made. These legal benefits are among those that help to assure the stability of the family unit and the support of child-rearing.

Many of these same difficulties and others arise when the cohabiting couple are of the same gender. Gay and lesbian couples represent another nonnormative script that is problematic for U.S. society. Not only are many family benefits denied to these couples, they also cannot achieve legal entitlement to the benefits through marriage. In addition, many people still view homosexuality as deviant and disturbed, although the American Psychiatric Association removed it from its list of disorders in 1974. Intolerance from the heterosexual majority increases the difficulties for gay and lesbian couples wanting to establish and maintain stable family units.

These and other variations in family scripts are, as you have seen, the consequences of relatively rapid and great changes in society. In light of these changes and variations, it is important to not lose sight of the great stability of the family. Three fourths of all Americans live in married-couple families, while the majority of the remainder live in single-parent families. Ninety percent of all adults are likely to establish a family unit through marriage at some time in their adulthood. Nearly half of the family units created by first marriages remain intact and are not dissolved by divorce. Between two thirds and three fourths of those family units divided by divorce become reconstituted through remarriage. In light of the predominance of the family in U.S. society, we need "to promote more understanding of the problems faced by families of all types and to give more sympathetic support for the development of coherent relationships among those who live together, as well as for those who by choice or through circumstances are living alone" (Glick, 1989a, p. 129).

The Love Connection

One way to "promote more understanding" and to develop more "coherent relationships" is to better understand that sustaining quality of relationships called love. In this section, we discuss different theoretical views of love and loving.

Categorizing Love Relationships

Love relationships are a special subset of possible interpersonal relationships. Psychologists have looked at love in a variety of ways. One way to categorize complete **love re-**

Love comes in many forms and may emphasize any combination of passion, intimacy, and commitment.

lationships is to view them as consisting of three clusters: **friendship** (acceptance, trust, respect, enjoyment, confidence, understanding, spontaneity, and assistance), **passion** (fascination, sexual desire, and exclusiveness), and **caring** (nurturance, support, and advocation). Some love relationships may have only one or two of the clusters (Davis, 1985).

Erich Fromm (1956) also noted several kinds of love, labeling the most complete and basic love **productive love.** According to Fromm, productive love has four main characteristics: (1) care (expressing concern for the other), (2) responsibility (addressing needs of the other), (3) knowledge (liking to learn about the other), and (4) respect (accepting the other). These four characteristics are important in self-love as well as in all relationships with equals. Parental love has all four aspects, with an increased emphasis on caring. Fromm believed that the best intimate relationships included all four aspects of productive love.

successful study tip

Fromm's Aspects of Genuine Productive Love

The capitalized letters in the word *CRacKeR* cue you to remember Caring, Responsibility, Knowledge and Respect.

Another way to categorize types of love is in terms of passionate love and companionate love. Passionate love involves absorption in the other person, wanting to be with the other, and intense physical arousal and feelings of ecstasy (Berscheid & Walster, 1978). Passionate love usually lasts only 6 to 30 months, and relationships based only on passionate love often end within this time frame (Walster & Walster, 1978). Passionate couples tend to be more exclusive than others; they have fewer friends, disclose less to other people, and value friends' opinions less (Johnson & Leslie, 1982).

Companionate love (conjugal love) involves trust, respect, attachment, appreciation, and loyalty; that is, it features the primary characteristics of good friendships.

Table 12.6
Items Measuring Six Basic Love Styles on the Love Attitudes Scale

1. Eros—Romantic, Passionate Love

1. My lover and I were attracted to each other immediately after we first met.
2. My lover and I have the right physical "chemistry" between us.
3. Our lovemaking is very intense and satisfying.
4. I feel that my lover and I were meant for each other.
5. My lover and I became emotionally involved rather quickly.
6. My lover and I really understand each other.
7. My lover fits my ideal standards of physical beauty/handsomeness.

2. Ludus—Game-Playing Love

1. I try to keep my lover a little uncertain about my commitment to him/her.
2. I believe that what my lover doesn't know about me won't hurt him/her.
3. I have sometimes had to keep two of my lovers from finding out about each other.
4. I can get over love affairs pretty easily and quickly.
5. My lover would get upset if he/she knew of some of the things I've done with other people.
6. When my lover gets too dependent on me, I want to back off a little.
7. I enjoy playing the "game of love" with a number of different partners.

3. Storge—Friendship Love

1. It is hard to say exactly where friendship ends and love begins.
2. Genuine love first requires caring for awhile.
3. I expect to always be friends with the one I love.
4. The best kind of love grows out of a long friendship.
5. Our friendship merged gradually into love over time.
6. Love is really a deep friendship, not a mysterious, mystical emotion.
7. My most satisfying love relationships have developed from good friendships.

4. Pragma—Logical, "Shopping List" Love

1. I consider what a person is going to become in life before I commit myself to him/her.
2. I try to plan my life carefully before choosing a lover.
3. It is best to love someone with a similar background.
4. A main consideration in choosing a lover is how he/she reflects on my family.
5. An important factor in choosing a partner is whether or not he/she will be a good parent.
6. One consideration in choosing a partner is how he/she will reflect on my career.
7. Before getting very involved with anyone, I try to figure out how compatible his/her hereditary background is with mine in case we ever have children.

5. Mania—Possessive, Dependent Love

1. When things aren't right with my lover and me, my stomach gets upset.
2. When my love affairs break up, I get so depressed that I have even thought of suicide.
3. Sometimes, I get so excited about being in love that I can't sleep.
4. When my lover doesn't pay attention to me, I feel sick all over.
5. When I am in love, I have trouble concentrating on anything else.
6. I cannot relax if I suspect that my lover is with someone else.
7. If my lover ignores me for a while, I sometimes do stupid things to get his/her attention back.

6. Agape—All-Giving, Selfless Love

1. I try to always help my lover through difficult times.
2. I would rather suffer myself than let my lover suffer.
3. I cannot be happy unless I place my lover's happiness before my own.
4. I am usually willing to sacrifice my own wishes to let my lover achieve his/hers.
5. Whatever I own is my lover's to use as he/she chooses.
6. When my lover gets angry with me, I still love him/her fully and unconditionally.
7. I would endure all things for the sake of my lover.

From C. Hendrick and S. Hendrick, "A Theory and Method Love" in *Journal of Personality and Social Psychology,* 50, 392–402, 1986. Copyright 1986 by the American Psychological Association. Reprinted by permission. Washington, DC.

Companionate love is characteristic of long-lasting romantic relationships and plays a large role in marriage satisfaction and marriage survival (Berscheid & Walster, 1978).

In a study exploring the concepts of passionate and companionate love, analysis of emotional words and written accounts of loving experiences resulted in characteristics of love being grouped in companionate and passionate clusters (Shaver, Schwartz, Kirson, & O'Connor, 1987). In another study, subjects rated the importance of 68 attributes to the concept of love. Companionate characteristics (e.g., trust, caring, honesty) were viewed as more central than passion and attraction attributes (Fehr, 1987). Companionate aspects may characterize all love, while passionate aspects may be an additional factor in romantic love (Davis & Todd, 1982).

The Love Attitudes Scale

One of the more extensively developed classifications of love is Lee's (1973, 1977) "colors of love" typology, which separated love into six categories: eros, ludus, storge, pragma, mania, and agape. Lee's classification system was used to develop the Love Attitudes Scale presented in Table 12.6 (Hendrick & Hendrick, 1986). Each of Lee's categories seems to measure separate types of love experiences, although agape is somewhat positively correlated with the eros and mania scales. What types of love have you experienced? Which types do you prefer?

Males tend to score higher on the ludus (game-playing love) scale in Table 12.6 than do females. This gender difference fits males' more permissive sexual attitudes. Females tend to score higher on the storge (friendship love), pragma (logical, "shopping list" love), and mania (possessive, dependent love) scales. Females' high scores on the pragma scale reflect their socialization to find competent and practical relationships. Males and females score similarly on the eros (romantic, passionate love) and agape (all-giving, selfless love) scales (Hendrick, Hendrick, Foote, & Slapion-Foote, 1984; Hendrick & Hendrick, 1986).

Individuals who are currently in love score higher on the eros, mania, and agape scales and lower on the ludus scale than do individuals who are not currently in love (Hendrick & Hendrick, 1986). Emotionally intense love shows up in the love styles of eros and mania; agape love is of moderate emotional intensity; ludus, storge, and pragma love styles are low in emotional intensity. Individuals who are high in self-esteem tend to have high eros scores, while individuals who are low in self-esteem are most likely to score high in mania (Hendrick & Hendrick, 1986).

Adult Love Relationships Versus Childhood Attachment

Although various psychologists use different labels for different kinds of love, your personal experiences and observations probably confirm the great variety of loving relationships. How do these love relationships compare to early childhood experiences, such as the bond between parent and child? One new theory of love compares adult love experiences with childhood attachment processes (Hazan & Shaver, 1987; Shaver & Hazan, 1987; Shaver, Hazan, & Bradshaw, 1988). In this viewpoint, romantic love between adults is similar to the affectional bonds between infants and their parents. Satisfying adult love relationships, like infancy attachment, provide a sense of security, contentment, and joy. Dissatisfactory, insecure adult love relationships are also like insecure infancy attachments: they are associated with avoidance, unreciprocated feelings, and anxiety. Of course, adult romantic relationships differ from childhood attachment in that they include equality and sexuality (Clark & Reis, 1988). Adults, however, who do not understand these developmental differences may be more likely to be involved in child molestation or incestual situations.

Loving relationships are assumed to be part of the family scripts discussed earlier in this chapter. We now move on from love and families to look at the scripts that people acquire in the vocational areas of their lives.

Career Scripts

Jobs and Careers

How many jobs have you held? What jobs do you need to finish today? Have you made a career choice? Has anyone accused you of making a career out of being a college student?

The terms *job, vocation, occupation, profession,* and *career* have a variety of meanings in everyday usage. An **occupation** is the principal work activity in which you are employed. A **vocation** is the specific occupational choice you make for which you seek training and employment (in literal terms, a vocation is a calling, as in being called to a life of religious service). A **job** is your specific employment within an occupational area. A **career** is the pursuit of a specific vocation for a number of years. Some researchers make more specific distinctions between jobs and careers (Perlmutter & Hall, 1985), maintaining that jobs, unlike careers, offer limited opportunities for advancement. Likewise, distinctions are sometimes made between vocations, which require limited amounts of training, and **professions,** which require extensive specialization and academic preparation.

Thus, you may currently hold a job that is not your career, while you engage in the occupation of student, which will prepare you for a career. One way to get through this maze of terms is to look at the answers to a few simple questions. For example, your answer to "What do you do?" is your occupation, and your response to "Where do you work?" identifies your job.

The Vocational Choice

Chapter 11 presented Super's views on the occupational life cycle. In this next section, we discuss factors that influence vocational choice.

Holland's Personality Types and Work Environments

John Holland's (1985) theory of personality types and work environments is a structural-interactive approach that assumes that (1) career choice expresses personality, (2) people within an occupation have similar personalities, (3) people within an occupation use similar problem-solving strategies, and (4) career satisfaction and achievement are influenced by the match between personality and work environment (Weinrach, 1984).

Holland proposed six personality types and six corresponding work environments: realistic (R), investigative (I), artistic (A), social (S), enterprising (E), and conventional (C). **Realistic** people are most satisfied in work that is mechanical, technical, manual, or agricultural in nature. Their best skills are in concrete, practical problem solving, and their weaknesses are in interpersonal skills. **Investigative** people are most satisfied with scientific and mathematical areas. They are analytical, introspective, and intellectual, but may be lacking in social and leadership skills. People who are **artistic** like to use creative skills, imagination, and expressiveness, and are viewed as nonconforming and sensitive. They usually are weak at orderly manipulation of facts and data. **Social** people value interpersonal relationships and work in social, educational, and therapeutic arenas. They often lack mechanical and scientific skills. **Enterprising** persons tend to be extraverted, dominant, self-confident, and ambitious, and they thrive in work environments that utilize manipulation and persuasion, such as politics, economics, and business. Enterprising persons are usually low in scientific abilities. Finally, **conventional** individuals prefer work that features systematic organization and manipulation of data. These individuals are practical, conscientious, and conforming. Conventional individuals usually lack artistic skills (Holland, 1985; Yost & Corbishley, 1987).

Holland proposed that some personality types are more similar than others. Arranging the first letters of these types in a hexagon (see the "Successful Study Tip" that follows) in the order R-I-A-S-E-C indicates which categories are most compatible. Thus, A-S, R-C, and R-I are more similar pairings than are R-S, A-C, or I-E. Holland believed that most people have one dominant personality type and one or two lesser types. People with consistent types (i.e., whose types are adjacent letters on the hexagon) are more satisfied with their jobs than are individuals with inconsistent personality types. Inconsistent personality types tend to have lower job achievement, less job satisfaction, and less stable vocational choices (Holland, 1985).

Consistent personality types are likely to increase job satisfaction by altering the work environment, while individuals with inconsistent or undifferentiated personality types are more likely to improve job satisfaction by changing themselves to fit the job (Yost & Corbishley, 1987). One of the difficulties that people face in their careers is that, as they advance in a career field, the types of skills and interests involved may change. In other words, work environment types change intraoccupationally as well as interoccupationally (Zytowski & Hay, 1985). For example,

an art teacher (S-A) may be ill-fitted for advancing into a school administrative position (E-S).

Men and women differ in preferred personality types. Women receive more S-A-C scores, and men receive more R-I-E scores (Weinrach, 1984). Men and women also differ in the amount of significance they attach to personality type matching work environment. Researchers found that women are more likely to choose a career that matches their interests, even if another career option has higher prestige, while men are more likely to choose the career with higher prestige than the career option that better fits their interests (Taylor & Pryor, 1985).

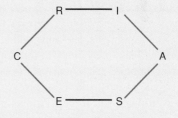

Holland's Personality Types and Work Environments

Remember Holland's six personality types with the word RIASEC, which stands for realistic, investigative, artistic, social, enterprising, and conventional. Also, arranging these six letters in a hexagon shape as shown indicates which categories are most compatible: Those types that are most compatible appear next to each other around the hexagon.

Sex Differences in Career Decisions

Men and women differ in career decisions more than by their personality type preferences and by the emphasis they place on interests versus prestige. The role of work in men's lives has remained fairly consistent and very prominent over the years, but the role of work in women's lives has changed radically over the last 50 years, with the majority of these changes occurring in the last 20 years.

In 1972, about 4 percent of college men expected their future wives to have continuous careers outside the home, and most college women held compatible views (Phillips & Johnson, 1985). The ideal just 20 years ago was for married women to be full-time homemakers or to work after the children were no longer small. In 1972, 1 in 8 high school senior females hoped to be a full-time homemaker by age 30; by 1986, only 1 in 100 wanted this option (Bachman, 1987).

College students' attitude changes about working wives are summarized in Table 12.7. As you can see, both men and women now support women's careers outside the home in much greater numbers. However, because the emphasis on women's career options is fairly recent, many females still tend to be more tentative and limiting in their career exploration than do males. Most women, researchers suggest, consider a smaller range of careers than do men.

Table 12.7
Attitudes of College Students About
Women Working After Marriage

Attitude About Women Working After Marriage	Year		
	1972	1985	(Male/Female)
No work after marriage	12%	2%	(2% / 0%)
Interrupted work option (to rear children)	40	48	(48 / 54)
Minimal career involvement after children	38	9	(9 / 1)
Continuous career involvement	4	33	(33 / 32)
No marriage option		7	(8 / 3)

Reprinted from S. D. Phillips and S. L. Johnson, "Attitudes Toward Work Roles for Women" in *Journal of College Student Personnel*, 26, 334–338, 1985. Copyright © 1985 American Counseling Association. Reprinted with permission. No further reproduction authorized without written permission of American Counseling Association.

The last few decades have seen large increases in the number of women college students and a wider range of college major selections.

Researchers are also investigating what characteristics encourage female adolescents to choose pioneer careers, those careers that are still male-dominated (Sandberg, Ehrhardt, Mellins, Ince, & Meyer-Bahlburg, 1987).

Females who choose pioneer careers tend to have higher educational aspirations, less anticipation of marriage within 10 years, and less conformity to feminine characteristics. Pioneering females are more likely to have working mothers, more male friends, and fewer brothers (but an adjacent or older brother), and to desire fewer children than females who plan traditional female careers (Sandberg et al., 1987).

Because of the massive changes in female employment over the past few decades, future generations will likely create different career patterns than exist now.

The Decision for Further Training or College
Societal changes that are modifying the workplace are also modifying adolescent and adult decisions for vocational training and college education. In the 1980s, for example, more women than men attended college, a major change over previous decades. College is no longer something just for males, just for those from ages 18 to 25, and just for those from at least middle-class backgrounds. These changes allow many more women and men to consider whether to go to college and, if so, when to go.

Although college is available to a wider range of people, parents' attitudes, encouragement, and support still greatly influence the choice to attend college or other training programs. Parental educational and career backgrounds also serve as models for career decisions. College-educated daughters of working mothers have higher career aspirations and achieve more in their work than do college-educated daughters of homemakers (Hoffman, 1979). Likewise, sons are greatly influenced by their fathers' occupations (Conger & Peterson, 1984). For example, a high percentage (44 percent) of doctors' sons choose careers in

medicine, and a high percentage (28 percent) of lawyers' sons choose legal professions (Werts, 1968).

Some individuals choose to go to college because they expect a college degree to enhance their earning power. The supply of college graduates, however, is becoming greater than the number of jobs requiring college training. Although the cost of a college education is rising dramatically, the financial gain of a college degree is diminishing. For example, college graduates outearned high school graduates by 65 percent in 1962, but only by 52 percent in 1982 (Levitan, 1984). Individuals who choose college or further training should do so to meet their interests, capabilities, and future work tasks, and not only to increase their potential earning power.

The College Choice

The Changing College Population
For many, the occupational life cycle includes 1 to 4 or more years of preparation beyond high school. The additional preparation usually is obtained by enrolling in a 2- or 4-year college. More than 50 percent of high school graduates enroll directly in college, but nearly half of those initially enrolling do not graduate within the typical 4-year sequence.

An increasing proportion of the college student population consists of older returning students, while the proportion of traditional 18- to 22-year-old students has declined. Enrollments for returning students ages 25 to 34 increased by 69.8 percent between 1972 and 1982 (Grant, 1984). For returning students 35 and older, the increase in the same time period was over 77 percent. Most college students now are women, and over 1 million of these women are age 35 or older. Saslaw (1981) noted that a majority of these returning women students 35 and older are married and report family incomes of $25,000 or more. Saslaw also reported an increasing number of single-parent women. In either case, these returning women attended class more regularly and got better grades, on the average, than did the traditional direct-from-high-school students.

The Influence of College Attendance

The choice to attend college is often motivated by the desire to seek career development or advancement, greater financial security, and different job/career opportunities. However, college attendance has a much greater impact on attitudes, values, and intellectual development than it does on career-related factors, as indicated by survey results from several hundred thousand college students in the early 1970s (Astin, 1977). The effects are broadly based. College attendance alters students' beliefs about themselves and results in more positive self-concepts, as seen in more favorable self-ratings of students' intellectual capabilities, leadership skills, and peer popularity. In addition, college students become less dogmatic, authoritarian, ethnocentric, and traditional in their gender roles, while they become more interested in world events and more tolerant.

The impact of college attendance on intellectual development has been particularly well documented (Belenky, Clinchy, Goldenberger, & Tarule, 1986; Kitchener & King, 1981; Perry, 1968a, 1968b, 1981; Strange & King, 1981). Perry's views are derived from studies of several hundred male Harvard students, ages 17 to 22. While King has been critical of Perry's depiction of cognitive change across 4 years of college, their views are compatible.

According to Perry, beginning college students typically have a dualistic world view. This **dualism** is represented by the beliefs that all questions have either absolutely right or absolutely wrong answers and that the two different kinds of answers are knowable. Students with this world view prefer information that is absolutely certain, answers that are unequivocal, and situations that do not challenge the rightness (or wrongness) of their views.

College classroom experience brings repeated exposure to the questioning of absolutism; to the presentation of varied, often conflicting, viewpoints; and to the challenge "to think for yourself." According to Perry, the result is a shift from a dualistic to a relativistic world view. This **relativism** results in students coming to believe that few things are simply right or wrong and that any answer can be right or wrong, depending on the situation. Therefore, all viewpoints are equally valid (i.e., everyone has a right to an opinion).

According to Perry, continued college experience brings about **commitment** by the senior year. As students evolve toward commitment, they shift away from emphasizing whether a conclusion or opinion is right or wrong and from considering everyone's right to an opinion. They shift toward weighing the evidence in support of a specific conclusion or opinion. All viewpoints are no longer considered equally valid, and therefore, support of (commitment to) specific positions based on the available evidence is possible. With commitment to specific values and ideas also comes the awareness that commitment brings responsibility.

Perry's ideas were derived from the responses of male students. Although Belenky and her colleagues (1986) did not specifically address the question of intellectual development in college, they attempted to see if similar types of thinking and a similar pattern of progression were present for women. They extensively interviewed 135 women from varied socioeconomic backgrounds and found five categories of world views, but no definite progression from one category to the next. These women's thoughts about experience and knowledge, while similar in some cases to the positions of the men in Perry's study, were clearly distinct from the men's reasoning. Because of methodological differences, exact comparisons of the Perry and Belenky studies are difficult. However, Belenky's results support the distinctions made by Gilligan (1982) between men's and women's moral reasoning. Further investigation of these intriguing findings is definitely needed.

guided review

10. Your _____ is the principal work activity in which you are employed, while your _____ is the occupation you choose to prepare for and for which you seek employment.
11. True or false: Holland proposed that career satisfaction and career achievement are influenced by the match between personality and work environment.
12. When it comes to career choices with conflicts between interests and prestige, more _____ (women, men) are likely to choose the career with higher prestige than the career that better fits their interests.
13. College attendance has which of the following impacts on individuals' attitudes and values?
    A. More positive self-concepts
    B. More tolerant, less authoritarian
    C. Less traditional gender roles
    D. All of the above
14. According to Perry, college attendance causes students to change their world view of _____ (the belief that all questions have either absolutely right or absolutely wrong answers) to a _____ world view, in which everyone has a right to their opinion, and eventually, by senior year, to _____ (the ability to support a specific position based on available evidence).

answers

10. occupation; vocation [LO-15]. 11. True [LO-16]. 12. men [LO-16]. 13. D [LO-17]. 14. dualism; relativistic; commitment [LO-17].

Adulthood Transitions: Continuity and Change

As has been presented thus far in this chapter, the transition to adulthood occurs along the major dimensions of intimacy and love, work and education, and leaving one family setting with the possibility of beginning another. In contrast to childhood and the teen years, once these initial transitions are made, adulthood gives the appearance of stability and continuity. However, adulthood is marked by continual transitions, and change is as much the hallmark of adult development as continuity.

The Dialectics of Adulthood: Continual Change

"The only constant is change." This paradoxical statement represents the type of cognitive development some researchers believe is characteristic of adulthood. The ability to recognize and resolve such self-contradictory statements has been called **dialectical thinking** (Basseches, 1984; Riegel, 1973). In many ways, adult development is dialectical—full of problems, paradoxes, and contradictions waiting to be resolved. For example, getting married resolves some problems but creates others.

"Change in the face of change." Adulthood also can be viewed as a series of overlapping transitions, each producing changes that, in turn, affect the others. Nancy Schlossberg (1978) proposed that "adults continually experience transitions requiring adaptations and reassessments of the self" (p. 421). Some of the transitions and changes are the result of personal deliberate choice (e.g., to go to college, to marry, to change jobs). Some are the result of the actions of others (e.g., the closing of the plant where you work, becoming a grandparent). Some are beyond the actions of self and others (e.g., a parent, spouse, or child dies). The dialectics of adulthood brought about by these continuous changes during continuous transitions result in adaptations that give the appearance of stability and continuity to adult development.

The Concept of Youth

One reaction to the complex set of transitions that appear at the threshold of adulthood has been to prolong the period of adaptation. Kenneth Keniston (1975) termed this extended transitional period the stage of **youth.** The characteristics he described as typical of youth fit best the experiences of being a college student.

Youth emphasize the present while preparing for the future. Youth have been described as focused on occupational preparation, and this focus brings about a second paradoxical characteristic. While youth prepare for the future, they often defer some decisions and activities. They concentrate on fulfilling immediate short-term goals, while postponing other goals until after their career preparation. Finally, because youth have completed the tasks of adolescence but have not fully assumed all responsibilities and commitments of adulthood, they must redefine their relationships with their parents and other important individuals in their lives.

Common Features of Adult Transitions

While Keniston intended the stage of youth to describe the transition from adolescence to adulthood, the characteristics of youth appear to apply to college students of all ages. In addition, the stage of youth may serve as a model for all periods of transition in adulthood. To begin with, attending college is often a choice made by adults whose lives are in transition. People who lose their jobs often go to college for further training. Divorced individuals, especially single-parent women, may react to the transition from being married to not being married by going to college to improve their economic circumstances. Parents often go to college after their children are raised. Thus, the characteristics of youth that coincide with being a college student come to apply to adults whose adaptations to transitions lead them to go to college.

Moreover, adaptations to transitions that do not involve becoming a college student appear to possess two of the main characteristics of youth. Consider the transition that results from the death of a family member. In adapting to this change, people generally focus on the immediate tasks of the present situation (making funeral arrangements), while deferring other tasks for the future ("I'll just have to get through the next few days and weeks before I can think about that"). In the process of adapting to the loss, family members must redefine their relationships with each other and others outside the family circle. The redefining of relationships and the emphasis on the present while deferring to the future may, in fact, be two significant mechanisms for resolving the dialectics of the continual transitions of adult development.

A contextual note: The foregoing discussion makes no distinctions among cultural settings. Keniston's concept of the stage of youth was meant to be descriptive primarily of Western, industrialized societies, where substantial numbers of young adults attend college. His original concept may not apply as well to noncollege and non-Western young adults. However, the key characteristics may still be useful in understanding adult transitions across cultural contexts. The "Exploring Cultural Diversity" feature looks at the leaving home transition for adolescents and young adults in Central and South America.

Reviewing Life While in Transition

Just as each transition requires adaptation to change, each transition is also an opportunity to assess and evaluate past development. We are accustomed to year-end and end-of-decade reviews. People customarily describe what life was like in their 20s or their 30s. However, transitions, other than birthdays and anniversaries, do not usually occur neatly once a year or even once a decade. While some transitions are predictable and others are somewhat under a person's control, many are not. Nonetheless, each transition provides an occasion for reflection and the opportunity to look ahead.

In this chapter, we have created the framework for considering adulthood as a richly contextual developmental era. In the chapters ahead, we explore the complex interplay of the life events of adulthood against the background of physiological and cognitive changes across the adult years. The journey through adulthood, as you already know, can be at the same time fascinating and frightening. Hopefully, the knowledge you gain from the following chapters will decrease your fears and increase your fascination.

If you are like many persons, you may automatically assume that people everywhere grow up, leave their parents' homes, and establish independent adult living in the same manner in which you and your friends do. In Western cultures, leaving home either prior to or at the time of marriage is a common pattern (Goldscheider & Da Vanzo, 1985; Hajnal, 1982). A recent study examined whether this pattern was typical for six Latin American countries (Colombia, Costa Rica, the Dominican Republic, Mexico, Panama, and Peru) and what specific factors influenced when young adults in these countries left home (De Vos, 1989).

Marrying is a major reason for leaving home in all six of these Latin American countries, as is also the case in the United States (Goldscheider and Da Vanzo, 1985) and in Australia (Young, 1977). Over 80 percent of never-married 15- to 29-year-olds from the six Latin American countries live in their parental home, compared to 26 percent or fewer of the married young adults. Age is also related to leaving home in these countries. The number of young adults living in their parents' home steadily declines between the ages of 16 and 30. By approximately age 24, half of the young adults no longer live in their parents' home. The effect of age is not as great as that of marrying in determining when young adults leave home, but it is still important.

Economic factors also influence when young adults leave home in these countries. Earning an income does not appear to be a factor in young adults gaining independence. In fact, those who can contribute economically to the parental household are less likely to leave home. In this regard, male offspring are valued more economically than female offspring. Thus, gender is a factor when young adults of these Latin American countries leave home. Young adult males remain at home longer than females. This effect remains even after taking into account that, at any age, more females tend to be married. Interestingly, and probably contrary to popular opinion, this gender difference also exists in the United States (Goldscheider & Da Vanzo, 1985).

When patterns of young adults living in rural areas are compared to those of young adults living in urban areas, living in an urban area is an important factor in leaving the parental home at an earlier age. This effect is consistent with the economic factors that influence leaving home. Keeping children at home longer may be more economically beneficial in rural areas than in urban areas.

Education plays an interesting role in when young Latin Americans leave home. First, an important difference from the United States is that the majority of Latin American youth do not get more than an eighth-grade education. Those who remain in school beyond eighth grade are more likely to remain at home and more likely to come from higher social strata than those who do not complete a secondary education. Thus, economics is also an underlying factor in this effect. Parents of greater economic means can afford to keep their children at home longer and to assist them in obtaining more education.

Conflicting trends may be emerging from De Vos's data. Young adults in these six Latin American countries are moving from rural to urban areas and are getting more education. According to the present data, the first trend should lead to young adults leaving home at earlier ages, while data consistent with the second trend suggest that young adults will remain at home longer while obtaining more education.

Source: De Vos, S. (1989). Leaving the parental home: Patterns in six Latin American countries. *Journal of Marriage and the Family, 51,* 615–626.

guided review

15. "The only constant is change" is an example of a self-contradictory statement that requires _____ thinking to understand.
16. According to Keniston, _____ is a transitional period in which individuals have completed the tasks of adolescence but have not fully entered adulthood.
17. Adults in transition often share the characteristics of focusing on _____ goals while deferring other activities and of _____ relationships with others.
18. True or false: Gender differences in leaving home (women leave sooner than men) are the same in the United States and Latin American countries.

answers

15. dialectical [LO-18]. 16. youth [LO-18]. 17. short-term; redefining [LO-18]. 18. True [LO-18].

Exploring Human Development

1. Study perceptions of the social clock on your campus by constructing a questionnaire similar to the one used by Neugarten et al. (Neugarten, B. L., Moore, J. W., & Lowe, J. C. [1965]. Age norms, age constraints, and adult socialization. *American Journal of Sociology, 70,* 710–717.). Neugarten and her colleagues asked people for their perceptions of the best ages for a number of significant life events, such as marriage for men, marriage for women, and becoming a grandparent. You may want to edit and/or add to the original list. Share and combine your results with those of your classmates.
2. Plot your own family's life cycle with a pie graph similar to the one in Figure 12.2. Begin with your family of origin. Divide the circle into the eight stages suggested by Duvall, making each sector proportional to the number of years your parents have spent in each stage. If your parents have divorced, create a separate pie graph for each parent. If you have left home and begun your own family life cycle, make a pie graph for the family you are originating. Include the

actual years for the stages you have experienced, and make reasonable estimates of the number of years you will spend in future stages.

3. If you have not already done so, make an appointment with a counselor at your college's career advising center. Explore the services that the center provides. Find out if they use Holland's personality types and work environments model. Consider using the services provided at the center to do some further career exploration. Share the information you obtain with your classmates, with friends needing career counseling, and with other family members who may be considering future career options or career changes.

4. Survey your classmates concerning their reasons for attending college. Do their responses match with the information presented in this chapter?

5. Interview people in transition other than college students. Choose people who recently have become employed or unemployed, married or divorced, new parents or "empty-nesters." Are their responses to their differing situations similar? Do they exhibit the characteristics that Keniston attributed to youth?

Discussing Human Development

1. Examine Havighurst's developmental tasks for adulthood listed in Table 12.1. Which of the tasks have you already accomplished, and which are you currently striving to accomplish? Discuss with your classmates any revisions you would make in the list. Why do you think Havighurst considered "developing adult leisure-time activities as a developmental task of middle age? Has society's collective expectations for age-appropriate predictable life events changed?

2. Review your own past development in terms of the timing of the various major events in your life and their predictability according to society's norms. When have you been "on time," and when have you been "off time" with respect to the social clock? Discuss with your classmates and friends the variability of the social clock. Does the social clock differ for men and women? Do different ethnic groups have differing social clocks? Use the results from activity 1 in "Exploring Human Development" in your discussion.

3. What constitutes a family? Begin by discussing whether children must be present for the living unit to be called a family. If childless couples and parents whose children have left home are not a family unit, then what label would you apply to their situation?

4. Use the plots of your own family life cycles to discuss with your classmates the variations in context that exist for the family unit today. Extend your analysis to past generations in your families to assess how common any of the family context variations have been in the past.

5. What transitions do you anticipate in your future? Discuss with your classmates and friends their expectations about these transitions. Do you share common expectations? Which are you looking forward to (or dreading) most—your first job after finishing college or your retirement from your last job? What experiences have helped you to better handle the transitions that you have experienced?

Reading More About Human Development

Bolles, R. N. (1984). *What color is your parachute? A practical manual for job-hunters and career changers.* Berkeley, CA: Ten Speed Press.

Cherlin, A. J. (Ed.). (1988). *The changing American family and public policy.* Washington, DC: Urban Institute Press.

Gilligan, C. (1982). *In a different voice.* Cambridge, MA: Harvard University Press.

Gould, R. L. (1978). *Transformations.* New York: Simon & Schuster.

Kilpatrick, W. K. (1975). *Identity and intimacy.* New York: Delacorte.

Levinson, D. J. (1978). *The seasons of a man's life.* New York: Knopf.

Summary

I. Models of adult development
   A. Predictable life events are normative, age-graded events that occur throughout adulthood.
      1. Havighurst's set of adult developmental tasks represents one model of predictable life events.
      2. Erikson's three crises of adult psychosocial development comprise another predictable life events model.
      3. Levinson's periods of adult development reflect a series of predictable patterns of stability and change throughout adulthood, during which people develop a life structure.
      4. Gould's approach to predictable life events views adult development as a repeated cycle of evaluations of inner reality with actual experiences.
   B. Both the normative and age-graded aspects of the predictable life events models have been criticized.
      1. American society is increasingly age irrelevant.
      2. Gender differences and cultural diversity are not accounted for in the predictable life events models.
      3. Predictable life events models may overgeneralize and oversimplify the increasingly complex and diverse course of adult development.
   C. Contextual models of adult development emphasize the ordering of life events and the sociohistorical factors present when a life event occurs.
      1. Neugarten's timing-of-life-events model emphasizes the role of social clocks and nonnormative life events.
      2. Bronfenbrenner's systems model proposes overlapping systems—from the family system to cultural-political systems—that interactively influence adult development.
      3. Advantages of contextual models include the recognition of the differing contexts for individuals, genders, and cultural groups, as well as their interconnectedness.
   D. Script theory proposes that individuals use scripts (cognitive plans) to organize and guide their behavior in predictable ways.
      1. Each person follows a complex set of scripts that are largely unconscious and culturally determined.
      2. The script concept can be applied across contexts and at different levels of interaction, making it useful in understanding ethnic cultural and gender differences in adult development.

II. Family scripts
  A. While a protypical family script exists, family contexts are quite diverse.
     1. Specific family contexts include nuclear and extended families and families of origin and procreation.
     2. Because many people divorce and remarry, family contexts also include blended families.
  B. In the family life cycles devised by Duvall and others, more time is spent in the cycle without children than with children.
     1. The family unit is one of the best systems for providing continuous social support across the lifespan.
     2. Overall marital satisfaction is greater during the years when children are not present.
     3. The increasing status of women and the rise of cohabitation, divorce, remarriage, and single parenting, along with the recent trend to marry at older ages, have all contributed to altering the traditional family life cycle.
     4. Parents have expectations about when their children should leave home that may be altered when, due to economic conditions, adult children continue to rely on the support system of the family.
  C. Such nonnormative family scripts as cohabitation and gay and lesbian couples are problematic for societies that maintain more restricted concepts of what constitutes a family.
     1. Cohabitating couples generally do not receive the same economic benefits given to more traditional family units.
     2. Gay and lesbian couples not only do not receive most economic benefits accorded other family units, but they also face discrimination from the heterosexual majority.
     3. The family unit in its great variety of forms remains the predominant living arrangement for adults.
  D. The experience of love and the act of loving can be examined from several theoretical perspectives.
     1. Love relationships consist of three components: friendship, passion, and caring.
     2. Fromm proposed three kinds of love: productive love, consisting of caring, responsibility, knowledge, and respect; passionate love; and companionate love.
     3. Lee classified love into eros, ludus, storge, pragma, mania, and agape love, and devised a Love Attitudes Scale to measure these aspects of love.
     4. Hazan and Shaver compared adult love relationships to the childhood attachment process.
III. Career scripts
  A. Individuals' work scripts vary, depending on how individuals classify their work.
     1. An occupation is the principal work activity of an employed person, while the person's job is his or her specific employment within the occupation.
     2. A vocation is a person's specific occupational choice, while a career is the pursuit of a specific vocation over a number of years.

     3. Professions may be distinguished from vocations by the amount of specialization and academic preparation required.
  B. Holland's theory of personality types and work environments assumes that people's career choices reflect their personalities.
     1. Holland proposed six personality types and corresponding work environments: realistic, investigative, artistic, social, enterprising, and conventional.
     2. Realistic individuals prefer mechanical, technical careers, while investigative types like mathematical and scientific careers.
     3. Artistic types like careers that require the use of creativity and imagination, while social individuals prefer work in social, educational, and therapeutic areas.
     4. Enterprising individuals like politics and business, and conventional types prefer manipulating data and systematic organization.
     5. Women receive more social, artistic, and conventional scores, and men receive more realistic, enterprising, and investigative scores.
     6. Both men's and women's attitudes have grown more favorable to women having careers outside the home.
     7. Since the 1980s, more women than men have been attending college, with parental educational and career backgrounds serving as models for career decisions.
  C. Many individuals choose to attend college, with 50 percent of high school graduates enrolling immediately after high school.
     1. The choice to attend college enhances career development and advancement, earning potential, self-concept, attitudes, and intellectual development.
     2. Perry's studies of male college students' intellectual development suggest that men move from dualism (ideas are either right or wrong) through relativism, to commitment to specific values based on the available evidence.
     3. Women attending college may experience different intellectual development than men.
IV. Adulthood transitions: Continuity and change
  A. The constant change and overlapping transitions of adulthood promote the development of dialectical thinking to deal with the paradoxes and contradictions that arise in the complex lives of adults.
  B. Keniston proposed that some individuals experience an extended transition from adolescence to adulthood that he termed youth.
     1. Youth have completed the tasks of adolescence without having fully assumed the responsibilities and commitments of adulthood.
     2. Youth are typically college students, and they focus on the present while preparing for the future, redefine relationships, and postpone some commitments while fulfilling immediate short-term goals.

C. The stage of youth as described by Keniston may serve as a model for all periods of adult transitions.
   1. Losing a loved one, losing a job, divorcing, and children leaving home are just a few of the transitions in which adults often display the characteristics ascribed to youth.
   2. Keniston's concept of youth was meant to be descriptive of college students in industrialized societies and may not as accurately describe noncollege and nonindustrialized societies.
   3. The leaving-home transition in Latin America is similar to that in the United States in that marrying is the major reason for leaving home, but is different from the United States in the role of economic and educational factors.
D. Each transition in adulthood provides the opportunity to evaluate past development and to contemplate the future.

Chapter Review Test

1. Marriage is
   a. a normative, age-graded life event.
   b. experienced by most adults.
   c. most likely to occur during young adulthood.
   d. all of the above.
2. Robert Havighurst's developmental tasks for early adulthood include all of the following *except*
   a. selecting a mate.
   b. developing adult leisure-time activities.
   c. starting a family and rearing children.
   d. getting started in an occupation.
3. According to Erikson's psychosocial stage theory, what is the basic strength acquired from the sixth stage, which occurs in early adulthood?
   a. fidelity
   b. love
   c. will
   d. wisdom
4. According to Roger Gould, the task at each stage of adult development is to
   a. eliminate specific irrational ideas remaining from childhood.
   b. develop and reformulate one's life structures.
   c. balance the needs of the individual with the needs of the larger society.
   d. achieve healthy resolution of various crises as well as to adapt previously resolved crises to current circumstances.
5. Who referred to adult development as being "age-irrelevant?"
   a. Erik Erikson
   b. Robert Havighurst
   c. Bernice Neugarten
   d. Daniel Levinson

6. Lauer and Lauer found that the major turning-point crisis in the lives of men involved
   a. social transitions, such as moving, or involvement in a different group.
   b. meaningful relationships, including those with a spouse, one's children, and friends.
   c. crucial decisions about education and careers.
   d. interpersonal problems, such as dealing with divorce or somebody's death.
7. Who proposed an ecology of human development?
   a. Urie Bronfenbrenner
   b. Bernice Neugarten
   c. Arnold Sameroff
   d. William Runyon
8. William Runyon's study of four contexts (family background, educational level, first job, last job) in the occupational histories of 20,000 American men found
   a. nearly 250 possible life course patterns.
   b. over one third of the possible life course patterns did not occur at all.
   c. that some life course patterns occurred quite frequently.
   d. all of the above.
9. According to Tomkins, scripts are
   a. less important in adulthood than in childhood.
   b. largely conscious and fairly culture-free.
   c. a set of social guidelines.
   d. all of the above.
10. In a comparison of today's extended families with those of previous generations, today's extended families
    a. include fewer generations.
    b. include fewer individuals.
    c. include more generations.
    d. include more individuals.
11. According to Evelyn Duvall, which family life cycle stage encompasses the most time?
    a. couple without children stage
    b. childbearing stage
    c. child-rearing stage
    d. child-launching stage
12. What does Schnaiberg and Goldenberg's ILYA stand for?
    a. independently living young adults
    b. incompletely launched young adults
    c. isolated, lonely young adults
    d. intimate, loving young adults
13. Which of the following characteristics is *not* part of the friendship cluster of love?
    a. acceptance
    b. respect
    c. understanding
    d. nurturance
14. Which of the following is *not* one of the four aspects of Fromm's productive love?
    a. responsibility
    b. fascination
    c. knowledge
    d. caring

15. Companionate love
    a. is also called conjugal love.
    b. has the primary characteristics of good friendships.
    c. plays a greater role than passionate love in satisfying, long-lasting marriages.
    d. is all of the above.
16. Which comment typifies the ludus love style?
    a. "I try to plan my life carefully before choosing a lover."
    b. "Our friendship merged gradually into love over time."
    c. "I try to keep my lover a little uncertain about my commitment to him/her."
    d. "I would rather suffer myself than let my lover suffer."
17. Agape can best be defined as
    a. all-giving, selfless love.
    b. romantic, passionate love.
    c. possessive, dependent love.
    d. friendship love.
18. A major difference between a job and a career is
    a. number of years of employment.
    b. wages.
    c. extensive specialization and academic preparation.
    d. all of the above.

19. According to John Holland's theory of personality types and work environments, most scientists and mathematicians have a(n) _____ personality type.
    a. realistic
    b. investigative
    c. enterprising
    d. social
20. Which of the following is *least* affected by attending college?
    a. attitudes
    b. values
    c. intellectual development
    d. career-related factors

Answers

1. D [LO-1].	8. D [LO-7].	15. D [LO-13].
2. B [LO-2].	9. C [LO-7].	16. C [LO-14].
3. B [LO-2].	10. C [LO-8].	17. A [LO-14].
4. A [LO-2].	11. A [LO-9].	18. A [LO-15].
5. C [LO-3, 4].	12. B [LO-10].	19. B [LO-16].
6. C [LO-4].	13. D [LO-11].	20. D [LO-17].
7. A [LO-5,6].	14. B [LO-12].	

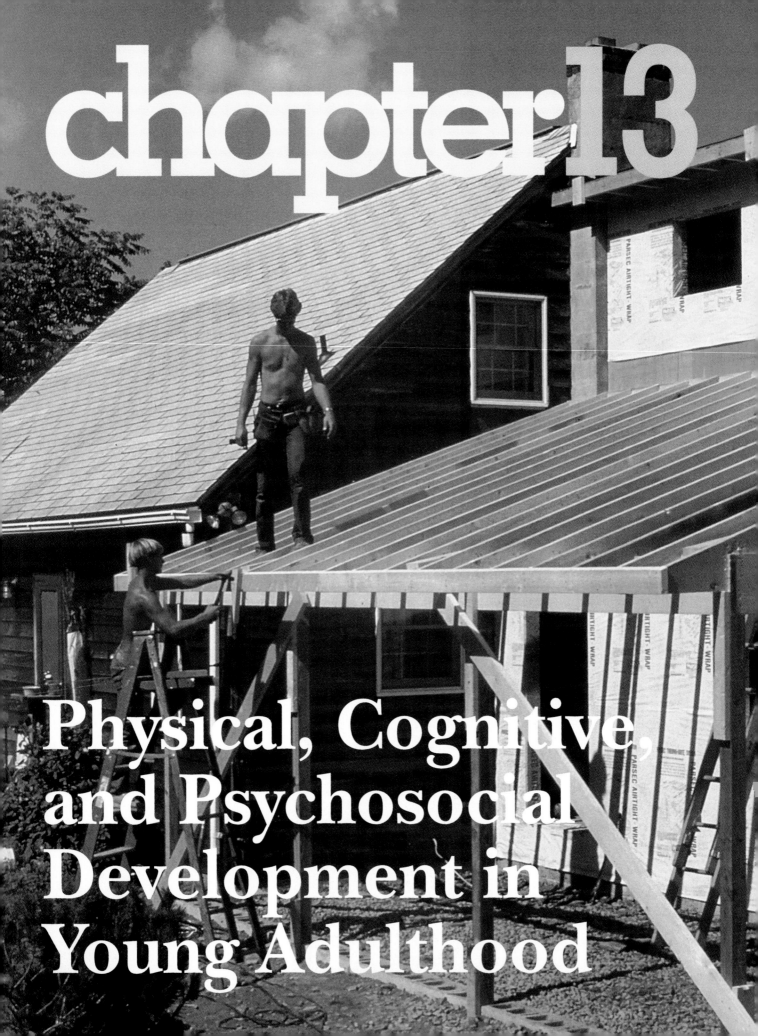

chapter 13

Physical, Cognitive, and Psychosocial Development in Young Adulthood

Learning Objectives

1. Describe the normal physical abilities of young adults and age-related changes.
2. Define sexual scripts and the double standard.
3. Explain the dimensions of instrumentality and expressiveness as they relate to sexual behavior.
4. Compare gender differences in sexual behavior patterns.
5. Identify seven basic health habits.
6. Assess information on diet and nutrition from cross-cultural research as it relates to disease factors.
7. Discuss the relationship between hardiness and stress, including the concepts of disease-prone and physically fit personalities.
8. Describe different kinds of loneliness and irrational beliefs associated with loneliness.
9. List the most frequent problems and mental disorders of young adult men and women.
10. Describe changes in intellectual functioning across the adult years, including the concepts of fluid and crystallized abilities.
11. Discuss factors associated with postformal operational thought.
12. Explain Schaie's, Sternberg's, and Kolb's approaches to adult cognitive abilities.
13. Explain Erikson's sixth stage of intimacy versus isolation, along with various models for the development of intimacy.
14. Contrast gender differences in intimacy, communication patterns, and relationships.
15. Compare the four types of ethnic identification.
16. Discuss factors contributing to a growing acceptance of the single lifestyle.
17. Describe factors associated with mate selection and the decision to marry.
18. Explain the different types of marriages and potential marital power structures.
19. Identify factors involved in the decision to become a parent and in achieving a parental identity.
20. Distinguish between mothers' and fathers' roles with respect to their involvement in and responsibility for child-rearing.
21. Describe gender differences in friendship patterns in adulthood.

Infancy, childhood, and adolescence have an underlying theme of physical growth and the development of new functions. The emphasis on physical growth in the earlier years changes to an emphasis on physical condition in adulthood, as the effects of aging begin to be seen even in early adulthood. In this chapter, we discuss the physical condition of young adults and also examine how the development of new functions continues in adulthood in cognitive and psychosocial areas.

Exploring Your Own Development

The young adult years are marked by choices. As you read in Chapter 12, the timing of these choices sets the stage for further developmental changes in middle and later adulthood. For example, your decision in young adulthood to become or not to become a parent will influence the remainder of your life.

If you have already experienced the young adult years, consider how the lifestyle choices you made then have influenced your later development. Compare your pattern and timing of choices with those of others.

If you are presently in early adulthood, what choices have you already made? Are you married? Are you a parent? Have you decided on a specific career choice? What choices do you anticipate making in the next 5 years? In the next 10 years? How are your pattern and timing choices different from those of other people? Would you want to trade places?

Regardless of your age, scripts play an important role in the choices you make. Do you recognize the scripts you are following in the areas of career development, marriage, and parenthood? How similar are your scripts to those of your parents and grandparents? Are your friends pursuing scripts similar to your own? As you review your scripts while studying this chapter, keep in mind that you can actively choose to rewrite a script at any time.

Physical Condition of Young Adults

Physical Aspects

Typical Functioning

Most young adults reach their peak in physical strength and health and find this period good for physical activity. As shown in Table 13.1, athletes usually have their peak performances during young adulthood.

Although height growth comes to an end during adolescence, other physical growth continues in young adulthood. Throughout the 20s, muscular strength increases. Females experience additional breast and hip growth, and males add growth in their shoulders and upper arms. Typically, adults experience gradual but steady weight gain throughout both young and middle adulthood. For females who have idealized the thin, low-

Table 13.1
Peak Performance of Athletes by Event

Age	Men	Women
18		Swimming
19		
20	Swimming	
21		
22		Running Short Distance
23	Running Short Distance	
24	Jumping; Tennis Running Medium Distance	Running Medium Distance; Tennis
25		
26		
27	Running Long Distance	Running Long Distance
28	Baseball	
29		
30		Golf
31	Golf	
32		

From J. C. Horn, "The Peak Years", table on p. 63 in *Psychology Today,* 1988. Reprinted with permission from Psychology Today Magazine Copyright © 1988 Sussex Publishers, Inc.

weight, adolescent body shape, the normal weight gains and size changes of these years can be distressing. Men and women are about equal in degree of body dissatisfaction, but men are as likely to want to be heavier as thinner, whereas almost all female dissatisfaction is in feeling too heavy (Cash & Brown, 1989; Silberstein, Striegel-Moore, Timko, & Rodin, 1988).

Age-Related Changes

Although physical health and appearance are good for most young adults, the first indications of physical aging become visible. Many first notice aging in their physical appearance during their late 20s, as their skin starts to lose elasticity. Women are more likely than men to be critical of their appearance, and women appear to be more accurate in knowing how their appearance is judged by others (White, 1988).

More importantly, age-related changes are occurring internally. With age, homeostatic adjustments take longer. Some of the internal physical characteristics that begin their gradual decline during the early adulthood years are:

- Speed of neural transmission
- Basal metabolic rate
- Grip strength
- Cardiac output
- Reaction time to light
- Reaction time to sound
- Sexual intercourse frequency
- Brain weight
- Liver weight

Table 13.2
Average Maximum Heart Rate Across Adulthood Years
(in Number of Beats Per Minute)

	Age				
	20s	*30s*	*40s*	*50s*	*60s*
Men	194	189	182	173	162
Women	188	184	178	170	153

Source: From M. L. Pollack, J. H. Wilmore, and S. M. Fox, *Health and Fitness Through Physical Activity*, 1978. John Wiley & Sons, New York, NY.

- Maximum breathing capacity
- Renal plasma flow
- Standard cell water

Until middle adulthood, these declines may go unnoticed because of the **organ reserve,** the part of total physical capacity not normally used. The organ reserve is quite large during young adulthood but is already diminishing. The loss of organ reserve capacity affects ability to adapt to physical stresses in later adulthood.

An example of a typical age-related change is the average maximum heart rate. As shown in Table 13.2, maximum heart rate declines throughout adulthood. Although the amount of change in the earlier half of adulthood does not significantly affect physical activities, the overall loss is quite noticeable by later adulthood.

Which types of physical decline do adults notice? A significant number of young adults acknowledge declines in body shape and energy level and increases in body weight. Declines in eyesight are often cited during the 30s. About 33 percent of men but only 10 percent of women report decline in the condition of their hair during their 30s (White, 1988).

Because aging is associated with declines in attractiveness and performance, adults delay seeing themselves as aging for as long as they can. In young adulthood as well as middle adulthood, the majority of each age group report looking and feeling younger than their age. Moreover, when adults admit that they perceive some physical decline, they usually attribute the decline to stress or lack of exercise, rather than to the aging process (White, 1988).

Adult Sexuality

Sexual Motivations

How and why is sexuality important? For Sigmund Freud, sexuality was the fundamental motivation—motivating all human behavior. Most psychologists give sex a less predominant role. Some emphasize the biological reproduction aspect of sexuality; as such, the sex drive is often presented as a unique primary motive because it is necessary for species survival. Sociobiologists suggest that sexual reproduction provides a way to create biological diversity among individuals and that this diversity helps the species to adapt to environmental changes over time (e.g., Wilson, 1978).

For individuals, however, sexual motivation does not center around reproductive diversity and only occasionally focuses on reproduction itself. Instead, sexual motivation aids individuals in meeting several important needs (Mitchell, 1972): (1) intimacy; (2) belonging and not being alone; (3) power, which can be expressed in domination, manipulation, or satisfying another; (4) submission, or being cared for by a more powerful other; (5) curiosity and playfulness; and (6) passion and ecstasy.

Sexual Scripts

Children learn **sexual scripts** from the attitudes and behaviors of others (Gagnon & Simon, 1987). Both healthy and unhealthy sexual messages in childhood can be incorporated into one's sexual framework and affect adult values and behaviors. Whether learned haphazardly or in a more organized fashion, in a covert or overt manner, sexual scripts affect adult sexual patterns and sexual problems.

Cultural sexual scripts involve the double standard, or male-female differences in sexuality. According to this double standard, males are more sexually active than females, and sexually active females receive more disapproval than sexually active males. Gender-targeted sexual messages account for much of the difference in male and female sexual behavior. However, within each sex, the personality dimensions of **instrumentality** (e.g., independent, assertive, forceful, risk-taking, dominant, aggressive) and **expressiveness** (e.g., warm, tender, affectionate, sympathetic, care-taking, compassionate) are predictive of personal sexual scripts and behaviors (Leary & Snell, 1988).

Sexual Behavior Patterns

Although gender differences in sexual behavior have been decreasing over the last several decades, males still become sexually active earlier, have more sexual partners, have more sexual experiences, and hold more sexually permissive attitudes than do females (Leary & Snell, 1988). Females are more likely to support the double standard, placing more restrictions on female sexuality than do males (Murstein, Chalpin, Heard, & Vyse, 1989).

For both men and women, those high in instrumentality tend to be more sexually active than those low in instrumentality (Leary & Snell, 1988). Individuals who are assertive, independent, and self-confident are more likely to initiate sexual encounters and to question traditional sexual prohibitions. Typically, instrumental individuals have more sexual experience, sexual knowledge, and liberal sexual attitudes than others.

This pattern is quite clear for males—the higher the instrumentality, the more sexually experienced. However, the pattern for females is less straightforward. For women, high instrumentality *and* low expressiveness produce the same pattern as in men. However, being sexually active, early first sexual intercourse, and frequency of sexual activities is high for women with *either* high instrumentality *or* expressiveness orientation, but low for women strong in *both* orientations. Some women (high instrumentality) may be sexually active as active initiators, and others (high

Persons who are assertive, confident, and independent are more likely to have liberal sexual attitudes, have more sexual experience and knowledge, and are more likely to initiate sexual encounters.

expressiveness) may be sexually active as expressive responders (Leary & Snell, 1988).

Over the last few decades, sexual experience has increased among unmarried young adults, and sexual behaviors are now initiated at younger ages (e.g., Earle & Perricone, 1986; Murstein et al., 1989). In addition to the instrumentality-expressiveness dimension, family background influences premarital sexual behaviors among young adults. For example, young female adults from divorced families, stepfamilies, or high-conflict families report significantly more sexual behavior than females from intact families (Kinnaird & Gerrard, 1986).

Unlike its mixed attitudes toward premarital and extramarital sex, society unequivocally approves of marital sex. However, unsatisfactory marital sexual relations can lead to a variety of marital problems. Even good marital sexual relationships are negatively affected as couples become parents; sexual closeness lessens with each birth unless couples actively work at remaining close. Research suggests that marital couples who experience sexual difficulties can satisfactorily resolve their problems through therapy (Whitehead & Mathews, 1986).

Extramarital relationships have been the focus of few research studies. Almost all of these studies have looked at extramarital sex, rather than at intimate extramarital relationships without sexual intercourse. In addition, the studies on extramarital sex focus on covert relationships and ignore situations of co-marital sex, or consensual sex outside of the marital relationship (Thompson, 1983).

Although difficult to estimate, research findings suggest that over half of husbands and nearly half of wives engage in extramarital sex by age 40. Factors associated with extramarital sex include low incidence of marital sex, low marital satisfaction, feelings of marital isolation and powerlessness, perception of extramarital sex opportunities, permissive attitudes toward infidelity and premarital sex, and attitudinal separation of love, sex, and marriage (Thompson, 1983).

Attitudes toward sexuality do not always correspond to sexual behaviors. For example, extramarital sex attitudes are not strongly related to actual behaviors. A cross-cultural study of American and Japanese women found opposite discrepancies in the attitude-behavior relationship. American women were more likely to approve of extramarital sex than to engage in its practice; Japanese women were more likely to engage in extramarital sex than to approve of the behavior (Maykovich, 1976).

Sexual Concerns

Some individuals experience overt and covert sexual abuse during childhood or adolescence (e.g., inappropriate nudity, lingering kisses, fondling of the genitals, involvement with adult masturbation, oral sex, intercourse, suggestive behaviors), and this abuse affects adult sexual relationships. Individuals who were sexually abused may find it hard to trust in adult intimate relationships. Their adult responses are affected by the coping mechanisms they used to survive their earlier abuse; typical coping mechanisms involve resistance, reinterpreting abuse as love, passive compliance, emotional shutdowns, dissociative behaviors, repression, and amnesia (Woititz, 1989).

The effects of sexual abuse are numerous. Short-term effects include low self-esteem; feeling damaged, guilty, shameful, and powerless; fearing additional abuse; distrusting adults; experiencing depression, suicidal thoughts, and anger; losing one's childhood; and having uneven maturing development. Without help and intervention, these short-term effects can become generalized long-term adult effects. Adults who were sexually abused in youth also commonly experience compulsive behaviors and posttraumatic stress disorder. Indeed, early sexual traumas can manifest themselves in numerous ways in adulthood (Woititz, 1989).

Sexual addiction, in which some adults compulsively center their lives around sexuality, is one possible adult pattern response to having been abused. Sexual addiction involves a four-step cycle of (1) preoccupation with sexual thoughts and searching for sexual stimulation, (2) ritualization of sexual behavior to intensify sexual arousal, (3) compulsive sexual behavior, and (4) despair and feelings of powerlessness over the cycle. The key aspects of compulsive sexuality are that it is secretive, is abusive, involves the altering of negative feelings, and results in empty, noncaring relationships (Carnes, 1983). One way to treat sexual addiction is to use the 12-step program first designed for treating alcoholism.

The effects of sexual abuse can be treated. Immediate treatment is preferred, but many adults have improved their sexuality and their interpersonal relationships by dealing with childhood abuse issues as adults (Woititz, 1989).

Health Factors

Health Habits

How many of the seven health habits listed in Table 13.3 do you practice? In the 1960s and 1970s, a pioneer health psychology study of 7,000 adults in Alameda County, California, found that persons who practice these basic habits have better physical health and live longer (Belloc & Breslow, 1972). The earlier that an individual adopts these seven health habits, the more benefits that can be reaped.

Table 13.3
Seven Basic Health Habits

1. Eat breakfast.
2. Eat regular meals, and avoid snacks.
3. Maintain normal body weight.
4. Do not smoke.
5. Drink alcohol moderately or not at all.
6. Sleep regularly 7 to 8 hr a night.
7. Exercise moderately and regularly.

From N. B. Belloc and L. Breslow, "Relationship of Physical Health Status and Health Practices" in *Preventive Medicine*, 1, 1171–1190, 1972. Copyright © 1972 Academic Press Inc., Orlando, FL.

However, several research studies have indicated that adopting a healthy lifestyle at any age has positive results.

Another study investigated the frequency of various health habits among American adults in the mid-1980s (Schoenborn & Cohen, 1986; Thornberry, Wilson, & Golden, 1986). Some conclusions from this research include:

- More than half of adults eat breakfast daily, but about a fourth regularly skip breakfast. Breakfast habits are related to age—young adults are more likely than older adults to skip breakfast. African Americans are less likely to eat breakfast than other adults.
- Many Americans eat snacks—about 4 in 10 snack daily, and another 3 in 10 snack sometimes. Hispanic Americans do the least snacking.
- Over a third of adults (more women than men) are trying to lose weight.
- One in five adults is getting too little sleep on a regular basis. More African Americans average fewer than 6 hr of sleep than other Americans. Some experts believe that prolonged sleep deficiencies lead to a variety of emotional and physical problems.
- About half of women have had a Pap smear test or a breast examination by a health professional within the past year. Most women (87 percent) know how to examine their own breasts for lumps, but only a third conduct the examination at least six times a year.
- Over a third of adults regularly use their seat belts. This survey was conducted in 1985, the year seat belt regulations went into effect. The rate of usage during the first three months of the year was 30 percent but rose to 41 percent by the last 3 months. Laws do have some effect on health habits.
- At least half of adults experience significant levels of stress, and stress levels are quite high during the young adulthood years.
- Fewer than half of adults exercise on a regular basis. More active physical activity levels are associated with both income and education.
- Three in ten adults smoke cigarettes. Cigarette smoking has gradually decreased since the 1964 *Surgeon General's Report on Smoking and Health*. This is evidenced by the statistic that a third of adults are former smokers. More African Americans than European Americans are current smokers, and Hispanic Americans have the lowest proportion of current smokers. Among smokers, however, European Americans tend to smoke more heavily than other ethnic groups. Smoking also varies by age group: More younger than older adults smoke. This is probably not surprising since most people who choose to smoke make this decision during adolescence. Cigarette smoking is inversely related to income.
- Eight percent of adults are classified as heavy drinkers, 19 percent as moderate drinkers, and 24 percent as light drinkers. While 10 percent of adults admit to driving under the influence at least once in the last year, 20 percent of young adults make this admission. Higher numbers of African Americans and Hispanic Americans are lifetime abstainers than are European Americans. In contrast to cigarette smoking, individuals with higher incomes are more likely to drink and to drink heavily.

Modifying Health Habits

A current focus in psychology is health psychology—looking at behaviors, attitudes, and lifestyles that influence physical well-being. Like the longitudinal Alameda-County study mentioned previously that indicated the importance of a few good health habits, research findings from health psychology provide clues for living healthier and longer lives. Research areas include exploring the effects of nutrition, exercise, sleep habits, attitudes, personality characteristics, chemical use, and other factors on health. Studies are varied and include cross-cultural research. The "Exploring Cultural Diversity" feature examines conclusions made from international nutritional studies.

Nutrition

A wide range of nutritional studies make a few basic recommendations for improving the typical American diet: Eat more fruits and vegetables; increase fiber; decrease fat; use meats and sugars sparingly. Table 13.4 provides a quick way to assess your fat- and fiber-eating pattern.

Exercise

The role of exercise in our lives has captured the interest of the American public as well as the health psychologists. Adults give seven major reasons for exercising: (1) attractiveness, (2) body fitness, (3) health, (4) weight, (5) mood, (6) body tone, and (7) enjoyment (Silberstein et al., 1988). Among adults 18 to 30 years old, the most important reason for engaging in exercise and weight control is enhancing attractiveness, followed by the health benefits (Koslow, 1988).

Exercise has immediate effects on increasing energy levels and decreasing feelings of tiredness and tension. When subjects were assigned either a candy bar or a brisk 10-min walk, walking was much more effective in increasing energy and decreasing tension for 2 hr. The sugar consumption at first increased energy and reduced tension, but within an hour, subjects reported increased tiredness and reduced energy (Thayer, 1987).

In the long run, health reasons and increased longevity are the most important benefits of exercise. In a

Exploring Cultural Diversity: International Nutrition Studies and Healthy Eating Habits

Several nutritional studies have compared diet habits and health risks across cultures. Multicultural studies provide support that diet affects cancer rates. A strong correlation exists between dietary fat and breast cancer deaths. Moreover, when persons change cultures and adopt a new diet, cancer rates begin to reflect the diet modifications. For example, the incidence of breast cancer in Japan is quite low; however, among Japanese immigrants to Hawaii and California, the breast cancer incidence is high (as is their fat intake). In addition, as people (e.g., in Italy, Greece, Iceland) increase fat in their diet, the incidence of breast cancer rises (Cohen, 1987).

Multicultural nutritional studies indicate that other dietary aspects are associated with specific cancers. Colon cancers are associated with low fiber intake and simple carbohydrates, as well as fat. Stomach cancers are associated with pickled, salted, and smoked food. Vitamin-A deficiency is associated with esophagus cancer. The Japanese diet, high in salt and pickled foods, is related to higher rates of both stomach cancers and strokes than in the United States (Cohen, 1987; Freudenheim, Graham, Marshall, Haughey, & Wilkinson, 1990; Preventing Early Deaths, 1985).

Another cross-cultural study of special significance—the Cornell-China-Oxford Project on Nutrition, Health, and Environment—began in 1983 in the People's Republic of China (Campbell and Junyao, 1990; Campbell et al., 1990; Vines, 1990). The project uses a unique study design made possible because of the population's limited mobility. More than 90 percent of the over 6,000 adults participating in the study lived in the same region of their birth. This population stability allowed local variations in diet and lifestyles to be studied for their effects on disease and mortality. Locations used in the survey are shown in Box Figure 13.1. Researchers were able to analyze blood and urine samples, obtain information on

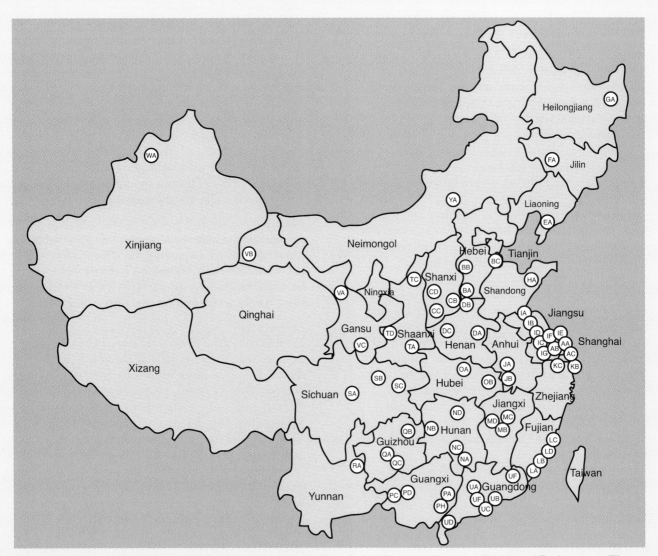

The 130 rural areas in 24 provinces of China used in the Cornell-China-Oxford Project on Nutrition, Health, and Environment. (The locations of the counties surveyed are indicated by circles.)

continued

lifestyle practices, measure 3-day actual food intake for each village, and evaluate the nutrition of major food items in each village.

The typical Chinese diet is notably different from the American diet. For example, average caloric intake is higher for Chinese men than for American men, yet there is less obesity in China. This may be attributable to differences in physical activity levels or to the fact that fat makes up 40 percent of the typical American diet but only 15 percent of the average Chinese diet. Also, the largely vegetarian diet of the Chinese results in much lower blood cholesterol levels, but even with these lower norms, the higher the cholesterol levels, the greater the risk of coronary heart disease. Another basic dietary difference is that Americans average only 10 to 12 g of dietary fiber daily, while the mean intake for the Chinese is 34 g. These high levels of dietary fiber do not hurt trace mineral status.

How do these diet differences affect mortality rates in these two countries? The mortality rates for coronary heart disease, diabetes, colon cancer, lung cancer, and female breast cancer are lower for the Chinese (Campbell, and Junyao 1990; Vines, 1990).

The international nutrition studies come to the same conclusions as American nutritional research: Eat a wide variety of plant foods, minimize intake of animal foods, reduce the amount of fat in the diet, and increase the amount of fiber (Brody, 1990).

Among young adults, enhancing attractiveness is the most important reason for exercising and controlling weight.

longitudinal study of nearly 17,000 Harvard alumni, those who exercised regularly with such activities as walking, stair climbing, and sports had lower mortality rates. Moderate exercise (2,000 kcal per week) was sufficient to bring about dramatic results (Paffenbarger, Hyde, Wing, & Hsien, 1986).

Adults' physical fitness programs should include four basic components (President's Council on Physical Fitness & Sports, 1985): (1) cardiorespiratory endurance, or aerobic exercise; (2) muscular strength; (3) muscular endurance; (4) flexibility. Table 13.5 shows the benefits for several activities.

Hardiness and Stress

Health habits have been shown to affect physical health, but is health affected by personality and attitudes? A meta-analysis of 101 studies on the relationship between personality and five diseases (coronary heart disease, asthma, peptic ulcers, rheumatoid arthritis, and headaches) suggests the presence of a **disease-prone personality.** The characteristics associated with this personality type are depression, anxiety, and to some degree, anger and hostility. Apparently, an imbalanced personality, like an improper diet, increases susceptibility to a variety of illnesses (Friedman & Booth-Kewley, 1987).

Likewise, a particular personality pattern is associated with good health. The person with the **physically fit personality** exhibits optimism, energy, perfectionism, competition, self-confidence, and self-discipline (Hogan, 1989). The keys to **hardiness** are commitment, challenge, and control; lack of these qualities can have negative health effects because they produce psychological stress (Clausen, 1987; Fischman, 1987; Hull, Van Treuren, & Virnelli, 1987). A sense of humor has been shown to alleviate depression and aid good health (Nezu, Nezu, & Blissett, 1988).

Hardy individuals are able to make more positive statements about themselves when under high levels of stress (Allred & Smith, 1989). In other words, hardy individuals do not just have different behaviors than others—they also think differently. Positive, optimistic attitudes seem to aid mental and physical health, even when these attitudes are unrealistically positive. Besides better health, an illusive optimism is associated with increased happiness, contentment, productivity, and creativity (Taylor & Brown, 1988).

In national surveys, adults under the age of 30 express lower levels of psychological well-being and more life dissatisfaction than older adults. They are the most likely to describe their lives as hard, to worry about finances, to feel tied down or trapped, and to be concerned about mental strain. Compared to older adults, young adults express higher levels of dissatisfaction in most arenas—work, education, marriage, family, savings, housing, friends, neighborhood, standards of living, and conditions in the nation (Campbell, 1981). In other words, attitudes pervasive among young adults may be damaging to their physical and mental well-being.

Table 13.4
Fat Versus Fiber Questionnaire—The Balanced Diet. Answer each question and keep a running total of the number of points awarded for each.

Fat

Which type of milk do you drink?		How many times a week do you eat chocolate bars?	
High/full fat	3	Once or twice	1
Medium fat (2%)	2	Occasionally/never	0
Semi-skimmed (1%)	1		
Skimmed/none	0		

Which type of milk do you drink?
- High/full fat — 3
- Medium fat (2%) — 2
- Semi-skimmed (1%) — 1
- Skimmed/none — 0

Do you eat cream or evaporated milk?
- Every day — 3
- Several times a week — 2
- About once a week — 1
- Less than weekly/never — 0

Which do you usually eat?
- Butter or hard margarine — 3
- Soft or polyunsaturated margarine — 2
- Low-fat spread — 1
- Nothing — 0

Do you spread it:
- Thickly — 3
- Medium — 2
- Thinly — 1
- Not at all — 0

Which do you usually use for cooking?
- Lard, meat fat, butter, margarine — 3
- Mixed/blended vegetable oil — 2
- Corn, sunflower, olive, or canola oil — 1

How many times a week do you eat french fries?
- Five or more — 3
- Two to four — 2
- Once — 1
- Occasionally/never — 0

What type of cheese do you eat most of?
- High-fat (cheddar, cream, stilton) — 4
- Medium-fat (Camembert, Edam, spreads) — 3
- Low-fat (cottage, curd) — 1
- Variety — 3

How many times a week do you eat potato chips?
- Six or more — 3
- Three to five — 2
- Once or twice — 1
- Occasionally/never — 0

How many times a week do you eat chocolate bars?
- Six or more — 3
- Three to five — 2
- Once or twice — 1
- Occasionally/never — 0

Do you eat high/medium fat cheese (times per week)?
- Five or more times — 3
- Three to five times — 2
- Once or twice — 1
- Occasionally/never — 0

How much meat fat do you eat?
- All — 4
- Some — 3
- None — 1
- Vegetarian — 0

How many times a week do you eat sausages/meat pies/burgers?
- Six or more — 3
- Three or five — 2
- Once or twice — 1
- Occasionally/never — 0

When cooking bacon or burgers, do you:
- Fry — 3
- Grill with added oil/fat — 2
- Grill with no added fat — 1
- Eat occasionally/never — 0

How many times a week do you eat a whole packet of nuts?
- Six or more — 3
- Three to five — 2
- Once or twice — 1
- Occasionally/never — 0

How many times a week do you eat cream cakes?
- Six or more — 3
- Three to five — 2
- Once or twice — 1
- Occasionally/Never — 0

Fat Total Score _____

Fiber

What kind of bread do you eat?
- Wholemeal — 3
- Brown — 2
- White — 1
- Mixture — 2

How many slices of bread do you eat a day?
- Six or more — 6
- Three to five — 4
- One or two — 2
- None — 0

How many times a week do you eat cereal?
- Six or more — 4
- Three to five — 3
- Once or twice — 2
- Occasionally/never — 0

How many times a week do you eat rice or pasta?
- Six or more — 6
- Three to five — 4
- One or two — 2
- Occasionally/never — 0

How many times a week do you eat boiled/mashed/baked potatoes?
- Six or more — 6
- Three to five — 4
- One or two — 2
- Occasionally/never — 0

Fiber Total Score _____

Interpretation: If your fat total was less than your fiber total, well done. If your fat total was about the same as your fiber total (within one or two points), try to cut down on fat (and add fiber). If your fat total was greater than your fiber total, you need to make changes in your diet.

Table 13.5
Energy Expenditure Requirements, Aerobic Benefits, and Strength, Endurance, and Flexibility Aspects for Various Activities

Activities are listed in ascending order for calorie usage. On selected activities, aerobic benefits are rated from 1A (lowest benefits) to 6A (highest benefits), strength as S or SS, muscle endurance as E or EE, flexibility as F or FF, and fat loss as L or LL, with the single letter representing lower benefits and the double letters representing higher benefits.

Rest and Light Activity (50 to 200 Cal Per Hour)

Lying Down and Sleeping		Standing	
Sitting		Domestic Work	
Driving an Automobile			

Moderate Activity (200 to 350 Cal Per Hour)

Bicycling (5 1/2 mph)		Rowboating (2 1/2 mph)	
Walking (2 1/2 mph)		Calisthenics	2A, S, E, FF
Gardening		Swimming (1/4 mph)	6A, S, EE, FF, LL
Weight Training	2A, SS, EE	Walking (3 3/4 mph)	4A, E, L
Canoeing (2 1/2 mph)		Badminton	
Golf	1A	Horseback Riding (Trotting)	
Lawn Mowing		Square Dancing	
Bowling		Volleyball	
Fencing		Roller Skating	

Vigorous Activity (360 to 900 Cal Per Hour)

Table Tennis		Cross-Country Skiing	6A, S, EE, F, LL
Ditch Digging (Hand Shovel)		Skiing (10 mph)	
Ice skating (10 mph)		Aerobic Dance	5A, S, EE, F, LL
Wood Chopping or Sawing		Squash and Handball	5A, E, LL
Tennis	4A, E, L	Cycling (13 mph)	5A, E, LL
Water Skiing		Scull Rowing, Rowing Machine	5A, S, EE, F, LL
Hill Climbing (100 ft per hr)		Running (10 mph)	6A, EE, F, LL

Source: R. E. Johnson, "Exercise and Weight Control" published in *The President's Council on Physical Fitness and Sports,* August, 1967, by Superintendent of Documents, U.S. Government Printing Office, Washington, D.C. Adapted with permission from the August 1987 issue of *Changing Times Magazine.* Copyright © 1987 The Kiplinger Washington Editors, Inc.

The current interest in the role of personality on health is similar to the popular psychosomatic approach of the 1940s and early 1950s. Both movements have the same promise and potential problems. The temptation is great to overinterpret psychosomatic findings, overemphasize the role of personality on disease, and overgeneralize from a few results to suggest a major trend (Holroyd & Coyne, 1987). For example, many have concluded that couples in which one member has cancer always should openly discuss their cancer concerns to alleviate stress. In actuality, couple concordance (i.e., both want to talk or neither want to talk) about the disease is the important factor. Poor adjustment occurs when one member of the couple wishes to openly discuss the cancer and the other wishes to remain silent (McCarthy, 1990).

The goal of health psychology should be acquiring information that can help people to make better health choices. At times, however, findings are misinterpreted and patients are blamed for becoming sick. Moreover, researchers sometimes wrongly assume simple relationships among variables when complex relationships are more likely. For example, Figure 13.1 illustrates how personality can both influence the onset of illness and choices about health behavior (Holroyd & Coyne, 1987).

Emotions During Young Adulthood
Emotionality is also related to stress. Individuals who are higher than average in emotionality report more stressful life events and more daily hassles than others. When in a stressful situation, high emotionality individuals experience the most symptoms. The relationship between personality and stress reaction even holds when the personality is measured 10 years prior to the stress measures (Aldwin, Levenson, Spiro, & Bosse, 1989).

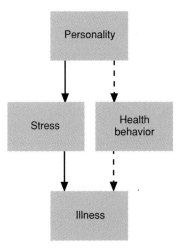

Figure 13.1

Commonly assumed pathways for the influence of personality on health.

Source: Data from K. A. Holroyd and J. Coyne, "Personality and Health in the 1980s: Psychosomatic Medicine Revisited?" in *Journal of Personality, 55*, 359–375, Fig. 1, page 368, June 1987.

Many aspects of life influence a person's sense of positive or negative well-being. Studies that explore emotional style and marital status find that being married is associated with a more favorable well-being than being single; the relationship is stronger for women than for men (Wood, Rhodes, & Whelan, 1989). On the other hand, marital partners of depressed persons are affected by their partners' emotional problems. When the depression is not successfully treated, the healthy partner must deal with more family conflict, more emotional strain, and more isolation from social and recreational activities (Rosenfeld, 1987). Other studies find that perception of having strong control over daily events is associated with greater happiness (e.g., Larson, 1989). A generalized sense of control is important to well-being.

Loneliness is a common experience in late adolescence and young adulthood. Three kinds of loneliness exist: (1) transitional loneliness, lasting several minutes to a few hours; (2) situational loneliness, resulting from important events (e.g., leaving home, ending a relationship) and accompanied by physical or mental problems (e.g., headaches, sleep disturbances); and (3) chronic loneliness, lasting several years and accompanied by the belief that nothing can relieve it. During young adulthood, situational loneliness is fairly common, probably because of the number of developmental tasks typical of this period of life (Roscoe & Skomski, 1989).

Loneliness is associated with several characteristics: low sociability, nonassertiveness, dissatisfaction with life, depression, anxiety, helplessness, external locus of control, suicidal ideation, and lower ratings of personal attractiveness and likability. In behaviors, lonely individuals engage in many solitary activities (e.g., watching television, reading, writing, and studying) whenever they feel "down"; nonlonely individuals talk with others when in a negative

Table 13.6
Ten Basic Irrational Beliefs

1. Demand for Approval. Individuals must have love and approval from everyone.

2. High Self-Expectations. Individuals must be perfect to consider themselves worthwhile.

3. Blame Proneness. Individuals must be blamed and punished for their wrongdoing.

4. Frustration Reactivity. It is catastrophic when things are not as a person would like.

5. Emotional Irresponsibility. Unhappiness is due to external forces beyond a person's control.

6. Anxious Overconcern. Possible negative consequences should be worried over constantly.

7. Problem Avoidance. It is easier to avoid problems than to face them.

8. Dependency. Individuals must constantly have others to depend on and care for them.

9. Helplessness. A person's past history influences the present and cannot be changed.

10. Perfectionism. Every problem has a perfect solution that must be found.

Reprinted from C.L. Hoglund and B.B. Collison, "Loneliness and Irrational Beliefs Among College Students" in *Journal of College Student Development*, 30, 53–57 (p. 54), January 1989. Copyright © 1989 American Counseling Association. Reprinted with permission. No further reproduction authorized without permission of American Counseling Association.

mood. In other words, lonely individuals tend to withdraw from others, and nonlonely individuals tend to seek others out (Roscoe & Skomski, 1989).

Loneliness is associated with having irrational beliefs, such as those presented in Table 13.6. A few sex differences exist in having irrational beliefs: Men are more likely to have blame proneness and perfectionism beliefs, while women are more likely to endorse anxious overconcern and dependency beliefs. Three of the ten irrational beliefs in Table 13.6 are predictive of loneliness: dependency, anxious overconcern, and frustration reactivity (Hoglund & Collison, 1989).

Loneliness exists in all cultures. A comparison of Japanese and American young adults found that the Japanese were lonelier in romantic/sexual, family, friendship, and community relationship areas (Pearl, Klopf, & Ishi, 1990).

Emotional and Mental Disorders

During the young adulthood years, some individuals experience serious mental disorders. Schizophrenia, phobic disorders, and panic attacks, for example, are most likely to be diagnosed during these years. In the adult population, anxiety disorders are the most common, but more individuals seek help for depression (Strickland, 1988). Among young adults attending college, depression is the most common problem. Student depression often lasts longer than 3 months and sometimes involves suicidal thoughts. Depressed college students are less persistent, less assertive, and less in control of their lives (Vredenburg, O'Brien, & Krames, 1988).

Depression and loneliness are common experiences among college students. Irrational beliefs such as "Nobody ever likes me" or "I'll always be a worthless person" increases negative emotions.

All common forms of deviance—fighting, theft, drug use, drinking, sexual promiscuity, mental illness—peak in the young adulthood years. Violent crimes and disturbance of public order are highest from ages 18 to 24 and steadily decline after age 30. Acting-out and violent deviance show the same age pattern for both males and females, but females have much lower rates of these deviant behaviors (Gove, 1985).

Women are more likely to report problems with stress, anxiety, and depression, and they are more likely to seek help for emotional problems (Strickland, 1988). These sex differences are also found in other cultures (e.g., Ben-Zur & Zeidner, 1988). Table 13.7 shows which mental disorders are more common for each sex.

Men deal more with the acquired risks of smoking, alcohol, sleeping too little, and job hazards, while women deal more with inactivity, nonemployment, stress, unhappiness, and poverty. Women feel less mastery and lower self-esteem. Women have more days of experiencing physical symptoms and emotional upsets and list more total health problems, but men have more chronic health problems and impairments (Verbrugge, 1989). Women may be viewed as turning their emotional problems inward, against themselves; men are more likely to turn their emotional problems outward and to act out.

The adult outcome of mental illnesses that developed during childhood varies by the initial problem. Both autism and conduct disorders have very poor adult outcomes. On the other hand, two thirds of those who were classified as mildly retarded in childhood do not need special services in adulthood. Additionally, adjustment disorders in childhood rarely continue to adulthood (Clarke & Clarke, 1988).

Table 13.7
Gender Differences in Mental Disorder Diagnoses

More Common Among Women	More Common Among Men
Depression	Alcohol hallucinosis
Cyclothymic disorder	Substance use disorders
Dysthymic disorder	Transsexualism
Agoraphobia	Paraphilias (fetishes)
Simple phobias	Factitious disorder
Panic disorder	Impulse control disorder
Somatization disorder	Paranoid personality disorder
Psychogenic pain disorder	Antisocial personality disorder
Multiple personality	Compulsive personality disorder
Inhibited sexual desire	
Histrionic personality disorder	
Borderline personality disorder	
Dependent personality disorder	

From B.R. Strickland, "Sex-Related Differences in Health and Illness" in *Psychology of Women Quarterly,* 12, 381–390, (table 1, p. 394), 1988. Copyright © 1988 Cambridge University Press, New York, NY.

guided review

1. True or false: Physical aging does not begin until at least the middle adult years.
2. Cultural sexual scripts include the _____ (differing expectations for male-female sexuality).
3. Physical health benefits and greater longevity result from following seven basic health habits: eat _____; avoid _____; maintain normal _____; don't _____; drink _____ moderately, if at all; _____ regularly 7 to 8 hr a night; and _____ moderately and regularly.
4. Research indicates that decreasing the amount of _____ in your diet and increasing the amount of _____ reduce the risk of developing cancer and other diseases.
5. Individuals with _____ personalities characteristically are depressed, anxious, and to some degree, angry and hostile, while individuals with _____ personalities exhibit optimism, energy, self-confidence, and self-discipline.
6. Mental disorders most typically diagnosed during the young adult years include _____, _____, and _____.

answers

1. False [LO-1]. **2.** double standard [LO-2]. **3.** breakfast; snacks; weight; smoke; alcohol; sleep; exercise [LO-5]. **4.** fat; fiber [LO-5,6]. **5.** disease-prone; physically fit [LO-7]. **6.** schizophrenia; phobic disorders; panic attacks [LO-9].

Cognitive Development of Young Adults

Intelligence in Adulthood

Longitudinal Studies of Intelligence

What happens to intelligence during the adult years? Early cross-sectional studies indicated that intelligence peaked by the early 20s and then gradually declined throughout the adult years. Fortunately, much of this decline was actually due to educational differences of the various cohorts in the study, rather than to actual declines in ability. Longitudinal studies of intelligence provide more useful information in understanding the true course of intelligence in adulthood.

In 1919, 363 Iowa State University freshmen took the Army Alpha Test. In 1950, 127 were retested; in 1961, more data were collected from 96 of the subjects. Comparisons of 1919 and 1950 data showed that verbal scores increased significantly, relations scores increased somewhat, and numerical scores decreased slightly. By 1961, on numerical scores showed a significant decrease (Cunningham & Owens, 1983).

A second longitudinal study followed the intellectual development of twins from 1946 until 1973. The results showed that cognitive functioning on an untimed test remained steady until at least the age of 75 (Jarvik & Bank, 1983).

The 1956 to 1977 results of a Seattle longitudinal study are shown in Figure 13.2. Using the Thurstone Primary Mental Abilities test, researchers found that IQ remains basically stable throughout young adulthood; in fact, only small changes occur until the substantial declines of late adulthood (Schaie, 1983).

Changes in Types of Intellectual Abilities

Changes in intelligence during adulthood differ for fluid and crystallized abilities. **Fluid abilities** involve aspects that are related to maturation and biological condition, such as speed, flexibility, adaptation to new situations, and abstract reasoning. Fluid intelligence declines in adulthood. **Crystallized abilities** are aspects related to experiences, learning, and culture. Examples of crystallized intelligence include vocabulary, logical reasoning, and mechanical knowledge. Crystallized intelligence tends to remain constant or to improve with age (Cattell, 1971).

---

successful study tip

Fluid and Crystallized Abilities

Fluid abilities involve speed and flexibility of processing and decline with age. Crystallized abilities involve set knowledge and procedures that remain stable or increase with age. To help you differentiate between the two, remember the phrase: Fluids when frozen crystallize.

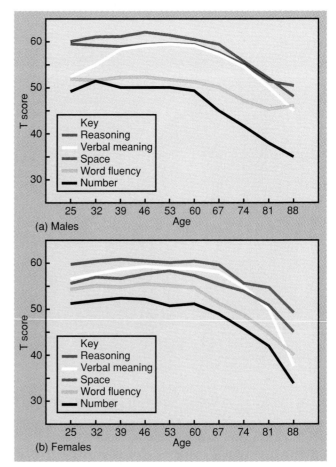

Figure 13.2

Longitudinal estimates of age changes in intelligence for (a) males and (b) females in the Seattle longitudinal study.

Source: Data from K. W. Schaie, (ed.) *Longitudinal Studies of Adult Psychological Development,* fig. 4.6, p. 105, 1983. Guilford, New York.

Another way to conceptualize intelligence is to distinguish between the mechanics and pragmatics of intelligence (Baltes, Dittmann-Kohli, & Dixon, 1984). The basic content-free components of intelligence, or mechanics, become less efficient with age, but the pragmatic aspects of intelligence, which are related to specific knowledge systems, remain stable or improve with age.

This is also true for memory. Age differences in memory are small when test stimuli are pragmatically or meaningfully organized (e.g., Hess & Slaughter, 1990; Waddell & Rogoff, 1987). Figure 13.3 shows how memory items can be placed to change the degree of organization. Figure 13.3a helps adults of all ages to remember material. How do you organize material you are learning to help you remember it?

Adult Stages of Thinking

Formal and Postformal Operational Thought

In earlier chapters, we discussed Piaget's four stages of cognitive thought—sensorimotor, preoperational, concrete operations, and formal operations. In formal operations, individuals learn how to use logical arguments, analyze

(a) Organized

(b) Unorganized

Figure 13.3

Examples of (a) organized and (b) unorganized scenes used in memory studies.

Table 13.8
Schaie's Stages of Adult Cognitive Development

I. "What Should I Know?"	II. "How Should I Use What I Know?"		
Childhood and Adolescence	*Young Adulthood*	*Middle Adulthood*	*Later Adulthood*
Acquisition (Get Knowledge)	Achieving (Use Knowledge)	Responsible (Concern for Others) Executive (Concern for Social Systems)	Reintegrative (Wisdom)

From K. W. Schaie, "Toward A Stage Theory of Adult Development" in *International Journal of Aging and Human Development,* 8, 129–138, 1977/78. Copyright © Baywood Publishing Company, Inc., Amityville, NY.

mathematical and scientific reasoning, and solve abstract problems. Formal operational thought is useful in solving problems with a limited number of variables that can be analyzed and combined into a correct answer, such as in algebraic equations.

However, many of life's decisions occur in overlapping settings and deal with unlimited numbers of ambiguous variables. Formal operations are too strict and rigid to effectively deal with everyday concerns involving family, work, friends, and society. Another adult type of thinking, called postformal operational thought, handles these situations. Postformal operational thought develops with extended education and life experiences, rather than by maturation.

Compared to formal thought, postformal thought is less abstract and less absolute. Gisela Labouvie-Vief (1985) suggested that the adaptive logic of postformal thought adds the elements of subjective feelings and personal experiences to logical thinking, allowing thought to be flexible for dealing with life's inconsistencies.

Another major feature of postformal operational thought is dialectic thought, which involves considering both sides of an issue and forming a synthesis out of the opposing positions (Basseches, 1984; Leadbeater, 1986). For example, the dialectic thought process is involved when an individual is exposed to a different culture. The different way of life initially challenges the individual's cultural values, followed by new insights in appreciating the individuals own culture. Similarly, this process may develop from grappling with work challenges, health problems, or family crises.

Schaie's Model of Adult Thought

Warner Schaie (1977, 1978) developed a more complex stage approach to adult thinking (see Table 13.8). According to this model, childhood and adolescence involve the basic question of "What should I know?" while adulthood deals with "How should I use what I know?" Schaie's model is compatible with both Piaget's stages and Erikson's psychosocial stages.

Schaie proposed three stages during adulthood. The first stage, the **achieving stage,** involves goal-directed learning. Young adults apply the knowledge that was acquired earlier in life to all arenas—career, relationships, and leisure activities. Of course, acquisition of knowledge continues during this stage; in fact, many young adults invest much of their energies in higher education. Going to college improves critical thinking abilities (Pascarella, 1989).

The achieving stage forms the basis for Schaie's middle adulthood cognitive stage, which has two components: the **responsible stage** and the **executive stage.** Now, cognitive development focuses on concern for others. Later in life, the cognitive goal is **reintegrative** with generalized purpose and wisdom.

Schaie's Stages of Adult Cognitive Development

Use the phrase "A ARE R" to remember Schaie's stages of *Acquisition* in childhood, *Achieving* in young adulthood, *Responsible* and *Executive* in middle adulthood, and *Reintegrative* in later adulthood.

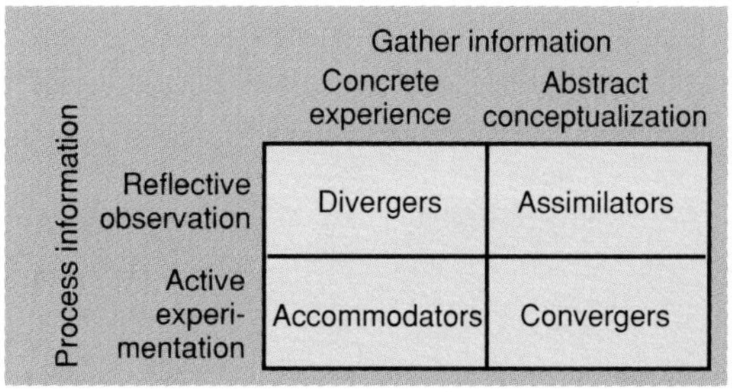

Figure 13.4
Kolb's four learning styles.
Source: From D. A. Kolb, *Experiential Learning: Experience as the Source of Learning and Development,* 1984, Prentice Hall, Englewood Cliffs, NJ.

Thinking Styles

What do you consider important mental activities, and what is your style of thinking? Elementary schoolchildren view mental activities largely in terms of memory. As adults, the four main categories are memory, comprehension, attention, and inference. Not until adulthood do individuals truly recognize features that distinguish comprehension and attention (Fabricus, Schwanenflugel, Kyllonen, Barclay, & Denton, 1989). Individuals use these basic mental activities in different ways and develop different skills.

One of the most useful frameworks for looking at adult thinking styles is Robert Sternberg's (1988b) **model of mental self-government.** Sternberg proposed that people learn to function most comfortably when they operate like the legislative, executive, and judicial branches of government—or as planners, implementers, and evaluators, respectively.

Planners think in terms of formulating, planning, creating, and defining problems. Individuals who are primarily planners like to create their own rules, do things their own way, solve problems that are not prestructured, and be creative and constructive. Planners often prefer careers as writers, scientists, artists, sculptors, policymakers, architects, and investment bankers.

Implementers involve themselves in carrying out plans. They are efficient at encoding, combining, and comparing information. In contrast to planners, implementers like to follow rules, figure out which existing methods to use, and deal with prestructured problems and defined activities. Implementers find compatible careers as lawyers, police officers, builders, surgeons, soldiers, and lower-level managers.

Evaluators judge, monitor, and provide feedback. These individuals are skilled in evaluating rules, judging systems, analyzing problems, and critiquing and giving opinions. Fitting careers can be as judges, critics, program evaluators, admission officers, and consultants.

Do your career plans reflect your primary thinking style? Does your thinking style influence which aspects of college come easiest for you? You probably can identify which thinking style is most typical for you, although you likely do not use this style exclusively. Balance in thinking styles helps you to avoid becoming stuck on problems. A deficiency in a thinking style can produce career problems when a promotion requires proficiency in another style. For example, lower management may require implementer skills, while moving higher in management may require thinking largely as a planner or an evaluator (Sternberg, 1988b).

Learning Styles

Kolb's (1984) learning styles, summarized in Figure 13.4, provide another way to look at differences in cognitive abilities. According to this model, individuals develop preferences for gathering and processing information. Individuals who gather information through concrete experience favor affective learning skills; those who prefer abstract conceptualization use symbolic learning skills. Individuals who process information through reflective observation use perceptual learning skills; those who prefer active experimentation focus on behavioral learning skills. These preferences are combined into four learning styles: accommodators, divergers, assimilators, and convergers. As with Sternberg's model, these learning styles influence career choices. For example, utilizing Holland's model discussed in Chapter 12, divergers are predominantly social and artistic types, while convergers are strongest in investigative (Atkinson, Murrell, & Winters, 1990).

Adult Values

An important way in which people use their thought processes is in developing values. The young adult years are most important in establishing and stabilizing values. Values have been shifting among young adults since the mid-1960s. As shown in Figure 13.5, the percentages of college freshmen who strongly endorse the importance of "being very well off financially" and the importance of "developing a meaningful philosophy of life" have shifted significantly. Accompanying these changes is a drop in political and social activism among this age group (Astin, Green, & Korn, 1987; Conger, 1988). To what do you attribute these changes? Which values do you hold as most important?

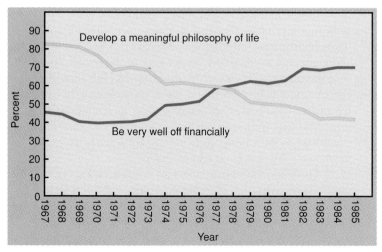

Figure 13.5

Changing American values: Freshman life goals, 1967–1985.
Source: Data reprinted from A. W. Astin, K. C. Green, and W. S. Korn, *The American Freshman: Twenty Year Trends*, p. 23, 1987. University of California at Los Angeles, Higher Education Research Institute.

guided review

7. True or false: Most research studies indicate that cognitive abilities decline significantly across the adult years.
8. _____ abilities decline with age, while _____ abilities remain the same or increase with age.
9. Compared to the stage of formal operations, postformal thinking is _____ (more, less) abstract and _____ (more, less) absolute, and features _____ thinking, in which both sides of an issue are considered.
10. Schaie proposed that children _____ knowledge, while young adults _____ knowledge.
11. According to Sternberg, _____ define problems, _____ carry out plans, and _____ provide feedback.

answers

7. False [LO-10]. 8. Fluid; crystallized [LO-10]. 9. less; less; dialectical [LO-11]. 10. acquire; use [LO-12]. 11. planners; implementers; evaluators [LO-12].

Psychosocial Development of Young Adults

Intimacy

Erikson's Psychosocial Stage

According to Erik Erikson (1963, 1978), young adults are in the sixth psychosocial stage, called **intimacy versus isolation.** In intimacy, one is able to relate hopes, goals, and regrets to another and to accept the other's expression of the same. Sexual intimacy may be an important aspect of an intimate relationship, but intimacy also involves a willingness to regulate work and leisure cycles with another, to share a mutual trust, and to abide by commitments.

The opposite of intimacy (or solidarity) is distantiation (isolation), or the readiness to distance self from others when threat is perceived. Much of adulthood involves a vacillation between intimacy and distantiation. This vacillation may be strongest in young adulthood because of increased vulnerability in sharing areas of self in which identity is still not stable. A significant move toward distantiation results in isolation.

Stages of Intimacy

Recently, psychologists have extended Erikson's ideas about intimacy and isolation to include developmental stages of intimacy (e.g., Bar-Yam Hassan & Bar-Yam, 1987; Paul, 1989; Paul & White, 1990). In one version, individuals move through three levels of intimacy (Paul & White, 1990). At the **self-focused level,** individuals are only concerned with how the relationship affects them. In other words, commitment is defined in terms of convenience and dependency. Couples at this level focus on concrete, external communication topics, and sexuality is based on meeting personal needs, rather than on mutual satisfaction. Adolescent relationships and some young adult relationships are primarily at this level.

In the second, **role-focused level,** individuals make acknowledging and respecting the other person a part of the intimate relationship. Caring is most typically expressed through activities and some sharing of feelings, rather than in total and articulated commitment.

By the third, **individuated-connected level,** individuals have acquired an emotional, intuitive perspective of the other person. Their understanding of both their own and the other person's needs and motivations often allows them to anticipate the needs and wishes of the other person. During this stage, individuals are committed, are willing to discuss concerns and to resolve conflicts, and engage in a more complete, tender sexuality.

Another extension of Erikson's concept of intimacy includes the developmental tasks of interpersonal connectedness (Bar-Yam Hassan, 1989; Bar-Yam Hassan & Bar-Yam, 1987) as summarized in Table 13.9. The five stages presented in the table, like the three-level model just discussed, begin with self-interests, move to sharing through conformity to roles, and blossom with the ability to be both a distinct individual and a committed partner in a relationship.

Gender Differences in Intimacy

Both males and females emphasize the importance of sharing, trust, physical closeness, and openness in intimate relationships, but males place more importance on sexual interaction, and women place more emphasis on openness (Paul & White, 1990).

Table 13.9
Stages of Interpersonal Development in Young Adulthood

1. Social Relatedness Versus Self-Insistence (Need for Approval)
   Relationships are essentially self-serving and concrete, and others are viewed as necessary for taking care of individual's needs.
   Social Relatedness = Cooperation for self-benefit—to obtain concrete goals or psychological rewards (i.e., approval and liking).
   Self-Insistence = Manipulative exploitation and disregard for others.

2. Affiliation Versus Exclusion (Need for Affiliation)
   Relationships are dominated by an anxious, conformity-oriented need for social approval and acceptance.
   Affiliation = Relationships characterized by a high investment in similarity, conformity, identity fusion, and the use of consensual validation.
   Exclusion = Social rejection—experienced as devastating to the self and contributes to persistent social anxiety and low self-esteem.

3. Belonging Versus Alienation (Need for Belongingness)
   Relationships are more differentiated and complex, reflecting a more clearly individuated sense of self in connection with others.
   Belonging = Relationships that reflect an active choice to belong to reference groups, roles, and institutions that support the sense of self.
   Alienation = Emerging sense that self does not fit in—self is experienced as unacceptable; there is interpersonal distancing, estrangement, and anomie.

4. Intimacy Versus Isolation (Need for Intimacy)
   Relationships reflect a need for deeper personal sharing, intimate connection, and mutuality in coordinating dependency and autonomy.
   Intimacy = Deeper involvement in communication, mutual concern, respect, support, and responsibility.
   Isolation = Lack of deeper sharing and mutuality which leads to a sense of personal isolation, loneliness and meaninglessness.

5. Interdependence Versus Interpersonal Constriction (Need for Reciprocity)
   Relationships reflect a need for reciprocity and an appreciation of dynamic and complex interrelatedness. There is awareness of the need to balance multiplicity.
   Interdependence = Active social participation based on a full awareness of both distinct, unique individuality and interpersonal connectedness.
   Interpersonal Constriction = Lack of reciprocity, decline in connectedness, social estrangement, and interpersonal impoverishment.

Source: Aureet Bar-Yam Hassan, "Stages in Interpersonal Development in Young Adulthood" in a paper presented at the 97th Annual Convention of the American Psychological Association in New Orleans, August 14, 1989, page 8. Charles River Counseling Center, Newton Center, MA.

The difference in typical communication patterns for men and women has a significant impact on intimacy. Among young adults, more women than men have capacity for advanced levels of intimacy. Moreover, in female-male communications, the male is likely to experience more than his *typical* amount of intimacy, but the female may be dissatisfied with the level of intimacy because more is *typically* expressed in female-female communication.

In current society, intimacy is influenced by two growing movements. The first is a movement toward more individualism, and this stronger emphasis on self-reliance and autonomy is especially challenging to the female concept of intimacy. However, Erikson (1978) felt that this change might help women to achieve real intimacy. In earlier times, women were socialized to have incomplete identities until they were married; today's emphasis on knowing and being oneself means that both husband and wife have the opportunity to achieve real intimacy.

The second movement involves pressure on men to be more expressive—that is, more empathic, self-expressive, and intimate (Paul & White, 1990). As with the added pressure on women to have more complete identities, this movement holds the opportunity for increased genuine intimacy.

While the development of intimacy is a major focus of young adults, identity issues may still be part of the picture. In particular, gender and ethnic identity issues may be involved in the establishment of intimacy.

Gender Identity

Gender as Differences
Psychological studies of gender have emphasized the differences between males and females. Journal articles emphasize a statistically significant 2 percent difference between men and women, while a 98 percent similarity goes fairly unnoticed. Moreover, the small differences between the genders are often due to cultural and historical, rather than biological, causes. Therefore, societal changes can demolish even these small differences (Hare-Mustin & Marecek, 1988).

Gender as Stereotypes
What characteristics do you associate with being a male? A female? Typically, the male construct is more restricted than that of the female. This rigidity reflects the more constricted socialization of boys compared to girls. In describing characteristics of the opposite gender, females stereotype males more than males stereotype females. In fact, the "ideal female" image presented by males is quite androgynous (Hort, Fagot, & Leinbach, 1990).

The expectation that males act in traditionally masculine terms may account for the findings that low masculinity men have less secure gender identities and more depression, anxiety, and social maladjustment (O'Heron & Orlofsky, 1990). Therapists respond differently to nontraditional male clients and are more likely to diagnose mood disorders and to focus on marital and domestic arrangements for therapeutic intervention (Robertson & Fitzgerald, 1990). However, when male socialization is even more constrained, the result is a macho pattern.

Macho Personalities
Some men undergo a hypermasculine socialization and live their lives as **macho men,** following a life script consisting of (1) callous sexual attitudes, (2) violence as manly, and (3) danger as exciting (Mosher & Tomkins, 1988).

The dynamics behind this personality type are, first, that these men have learned to stop emotionality—"real men" do not attend to the distress of others and do not express their own distress. They learn to turn their sadness and fear into anger and into acting against others. Second, these men learn to inhibit the expression of fear by continually facing fearful situations and by habituating to fear and disgust. Instead of experiencing fear, macho men learn to exhibit bravery in these situations. Third, macho men learn to have manly pride in acting aggressively and in daring and humiliating others. Fourth, they have disgust and contempt for others who display weakness, emotions, and "inferior femininity." Fifth, a hostile-dominant interpersonal style helps macho men to displace a sense of inferiority. Sixth, macho men learn to use surprise to activate fears in others and to increase their own level of excitement. They learn to like risk taking and callous toughness. Seventh, macho men prefer excitement to relaxed enjoyment, which is viewed as weak, inferior, and feminine (Mosher & Tomkins, 1988).

Males who are in the macho world have rites of passage in adolescence and young adulthood. These physical rites can involve fighting, risking danger, and having callous sex. It is important to "fight one's way" into the macho world. The macho script peaks in young adulthood, when physical condition is at its best. In this period, the macho male acts out a counteractive script, seizing opportunities, challenging, and threatening by using daring and violence.

Toward the end of young adulthood, a defensive script emerges because negative effects of the macho lifestyle increase as physical ability declines. Now, macho men try to preserve esteem while being challenged by younger macho men. In some cases, the manly "hard drinking" of youth becomes one of the few tolerated excuses for retiring from this lifestyle. Another outcome is the pseudo-reparative script, in which macho men embrace heroic death. A recovering reparative script is possible, but long-held beliefs in "born to lose," "death before dishonor," and "female inferiority" make it difficult for macho men to embrace a full life with acceptance of their feminine aspects and permission to love others (Mosher & Tomkins, 1988).

Same-Sex and Opposite-Sex Relationships

In childhood, same-sex play is more compatible than mixed-sex play, and children often segregate themselves in same-sex groups. As adults, many social interactions are still sex-segregated. In these sex-segregated groups, males and females build different styles of interacting, and these styles have enduring impact on opposite-sex communications.

Males develop a **restrictive interaction style,** in which self-disclosure is minimized and well-defined roles and dominance hierarchies exist. Females develop an **enabling interaction style** that facilitates communication, acknowledges others comments, and seeks agreement. When a man and a woman interact, therefore, the woman is likely to receive less reciprocal agreement and shared self-disclosure than she receives from other females. On the other hand,

the man receives more acceptance, encouragement, and less competition than he receives from other males. Therefore, most male-female interaction is more rewarding for males than for females (Maccoby, 1990).

Some of the implications of these gender interaction differences are (DeAngelis, 1989; Maccoby, 1990):

- Women are more influenced by opinions of group members than are men.
- Men who feel they are not under surveillance are more willing to yield to a partner's opinion than if they feel they are under surveillance.
- Some women in mixed groups continue their typical female style—smiling, waiting to speak, and talking less; others adapt by becoming more like men—interrupting, raising voices, and being assertive.
- In cross-sex debates, men's self-esteem increases but women's decreases.
- Women may be dissatisfied with the amount of self-disclosure from their husbands, and they may feel like they and their husbands do not talk enough with each other.
- Many married men prefer a more feminine communication style, but in times of marital conflict, they may revert to the masculine style, resulting in increased marital conflict levels.

Ethnic Identity

Ethnic identity is an individual's identification and psychological relationship with their ethnic group. It includes knowledge, values, and emotional significance about an ethnic group. For ethnic minority members, this identity involves more than personal involvement in their ethnic culture—they must also deal with the dominant group's attitudes toward their ethnic group (Phinney, 1990).

Stages of Ethnic Identity

Jean Phinney (1990) proposed a three-stage developmental model of ethnic identity that parallels Marcia's stages of identity formation. The first stage is an unexamined ethnic identity. This initial stage may indicate a diffuse status in which individuals have not considered aspects of their ethnicity, or it may indicate a foreclosure status in which individuals have accepted the ethnic identity of their parents without thinking through their own issues. In the second stage, which is similar to Marcia's moratorium status, individuals explore their ethnic identity. This stage is a period of immense immersion in ethnic culture and may begin with one significant event, such as hearing a speech of a noted ethnic member or enrolling in an ethnic studies course. Exploration may include interpersonal communication, reading, or participating in cultural events. Sometimes, the dominant culture is rejected. The third stage is having a committed ethnic identity, comparable to Marcia's achieved status. In this stage, individuals have a clear, confident sense of their own ethnicity. One positive effect is that ethnic minorities in this stage have higher self-esteem.

African-Americans who celebrate Kwanza have developed their ethnic identity. Some who also identify with the majority group are bicultural.

Table 13.10
Ethnic Identity According to Degree of Identification With Both Personal Ethnic Group and the Majority Culture

Identification With Majority Group	Identification With Ethnic Group	
	Strong	Weak
Strong	Bicultural	Assimilated
Weak	Ethnically Identified	Marginal

From J. S. Phinney, "Ethnic Identity in Adolescents and Adults: Review of Research" in *Psychological Bulletin,* 108, 499–514, Table 1, p. 502, 1990. Copyright 1990 by the American Psychological Association. Reprinted by permission.

Types of Ethnic Identification

Individuals differ in how they identify with the dominant culture, as well as their own ethnic culture. As summarized in Table 13.10, individuals who are strong in both cultures can be labeled bicultural, or integrated. Individuals who are weak in both dominant culture and ethnic culture identity are labeled marginal. Others identify strongly with only one culture. Those who exclusively identify with the dominant culture are assimilated, and those who exclusively identify with their own ethnic culture are ethnically identified, or separated. This last group is the most likely to emphasize ethnic distinctiveness.

The United States is a multicultural society. About 30 percent of 15- to 25-year-olds are minority members. Aspects of adult ethnic identity need to be studied to help individuals to develop identities that build healthy self-concepts. For example, different labels provide ethnic group members with varying connotations. The labels Mexican American, Hispanic, Latino, or Chicano all have different meanings. Self-perceptions can change according to whether an individual is labeled African American,

Black American, Negro, or Colored (Phinney, 1990). Psychologists also need to explore the effects of social and political policies on ethnic identity. For example, current affirmative action policies may have helped African-American women to achieve, while increasing difficulties for African-American men (Bell, 1989).

guided review

12. Erikson' sixth stage is _____ versus _____.
13. Intimacy develops through stages, beginning with _____-interest, moving to sharing through _____ conformity, and eventually reaching a stage of _____ with _____.
14. Regarding gender differences in intimacy, males emphasize _____ interaction, while females emphasize _____.
15. Males develop a _____ interaction style in which self-disclosure is minimized, while females develop an _____ interaction style that facilitates communication.
16. Individuals who identify strongly with both their minority ethnic group and the dominant cultural group are called _____.

answers

12. intimacy; isolation [LO-13]. **13.** self; role; individuality; commitment [LO-13]. **14.** sexual; openness [LO-14]. **15.** restrictive; enabling [LO-14]. **16.** bicultural [LO-15].

Young Adult Relationships

Single Adults

The Growing Acceptance of a Single Lifestyle

Over the last three decades, the number of single adults living separately from relatives has doubled. About three fourths of the men and half of the women between the ages of 20 and 25 are single adults. Today, well over 20 million adults are never-married singles. However, being single is different from choosing to remain single. Most young adults are likely to be single while obtaining an education. Many adults return to the single lifestyle during adulthood as the result of divorce or a spouse's death.

Contributing to the growth of this lifestyle is the greater number of educational and career opportunities for women, with accompanying greater acceptance of women pursuing career opportunities over family opportunities. Another factor is greater tolerance for sexual relationships outside of marriage, and a number of single adults choose cohabitation instead of marriage when making a commitment to another person. The number of cohabiting adults has grown by more than 500 percent since 1960. In fact, nearly a third of American single women in their 20s are in a cohabitation lifestyle (Davis, 1985; Tanfer, 1987).

Compared to married couples, single adults are more likely to develop an extensive network of friends. Single persons divide their leisure time between activities with friends and solitary activities (Cargan, 1981; Haggstrom, Kanouse, & Morrison, 1986).

Homosexual Lifestyle

Some single adults have homosexual lifestyles. Although states do not allow homosexuals to legally marry, some homosexuals consider themselves to be in committed marital relationships. Homosexuals live as varied lifestyles as heterosexuals. While a minority lifestyle, homosexuality is not an abnormal lifestyle. Since 1974, the American Psychiatric Association has not listed homosexuality among its categories of mental illness. In fact, no major psychological differences can be established between heterosexuals and homosexuals.

Although some research on heterosexual couples can also be applied to homosexual relationships, much of the information cannot be applied in an identical way. For example, research on heterosexual couples often features the effects of gender differences on the quality of the relationship; an understanding of homosexual couples requires looking at the effects of gender similarity. Other differences are that more homosexual couples are dual-career couples and that homosexuals are affected differently by legal issues (Eldridge & Gilbert, 1990).

Moving Toward Marriage: Mate Selection

How do individuals choose marriage partners? The potential pool of possible mates is reduced by several general factors. First of all, persons are likely to marry individuals who meet the propinquity, or physical nearness, requirement. After all, if you never "run into" that perfect person who lives a thousand miles away, that person cannot become your mate. Other filters are social class, ethnic background, and religion. While individuals might not marry persons with the same socioeconomic and ethnic backgrounds, they usually make decisions that lead to homogamy (selecting mates with similar backgrounds and characteristics).

Another initial filter in the mate selection process is physical attractiveness. In one study, subjects rated the degree of facial resemblance among pairs of photographs that represented either actual couples (some engaged couples and some married couples) or randomly paired, same-age, opposite-sex individuals. The actual couples were rated higher in facial resemblance (Hinsz, 1989). Several possible explanations exist for these findings, but Hinsz suggested:

People probably do not consciously select mates so that they resemble themselves, but through repeated exposure to their own face and faces of others genetically similar to themselves, they develop an attraction to the combination of features that is characteristic of their own face. Thus, in a mate selection process, people may be more attracted to others who have faces that resemble their own.
(p. 228)

Mate selection involves a number of individual factors—personality traits, behavioral interests, values, role compatibility, self-disclosure styles, empathy, and compatible sexuality, for example (Adams, 1980). Overall, similarity is important, but compatible, complementary characteristics also play a role in determining marital satisfaction (Vinacke, Shannon, Palazzo, Balsavage, & Cooney, 1987).

In recent times, greater numbers of individuals have married persons of dissimilar ethnic and religious backgrounds. As a whole, society has become more tolerant of dissimilar couples who choose to make a lifetime commitment. Another recent trend is women choosing to marry younger men. This trend is most noted for men ages 24 to 29, for women over 30, and for both men and women who are remarrying. Although men are still more likely to marry younger women, a growing minority will likely follow the opposite trend (Wheeler & Gunter, 1987).

The timing of mate selection is also important in the long-term outcome of marriages. Individuals who choose a mate at a young age and get married as adolescents experience more marital disruption than individuals who get married as adults (Teti, Lamb, & Elster, 1987).

Engagement

For many single adults, the transition to marriage is preceded by a period of formal **engagement** in which individuals announce their exclusive commitment to each other. During this time period, couples can reexamine their compatibility in interests and values and discuss both short-term and long-term goals. Engaged individuals determine whether or not their expectations of and for each other are realistic and workable; if they are not, the couple may break the engagement and not require legal procedures to separate.

Often, couples use the engagement period to get better acquainted with future in-laws and the customs of each family of origin. This time period also is often used to make decisions about the wedding and honeymoon and to do the necessary legal procedures for getting married (Broderick, 1984; Coleman, 1984).

Marriage

Reasons for Getting Married and Marital Expectations

Why do people get married? Many reasons center on aspects of intimacy—wanting to make a commitment, needing companionship and a sharing relationship, and desiring an enduring relationship with one person. Marriage is viewed as a way to fulfill the need for love and happiness.

Marriage may occur because "it's about the right time to get married" or to provide economic or emotional security. Some individuals get married to escape loneliness or an unhappy family environment. For many individuals, marriage is viewed as the way to legitimize sexual relationships and as the proper setting in which to raise children (Ammons & Stinnett, 1980; Berkley, 1981; Conger, 1981; Stinnett, Walters, & Kaye, 1984).

Persons with relatively short courtships before making a marital commitment tend to provide intrapersonal-normative reasons, such as the time was right for marriage and the relationship seemed to be desirable. Persons with long courtships give mostly circumstantial reasons, such as finishing their education or becoming established in a career (Surra, Arizzi, & Asmussen, 1988).

Young adults who experienced a parental divorce while growing up do not differ from other young adults in their expectations and ideals about marriage and family life. However, experiencing a parental divorce may provide more permission to leave an unsatisfactory marriage (Carson & Pauly, 1990).

One aspect that helps couples to meet their marital expectations is that committed individuals tend to see their partners as they want them to be. In other words, the more an individual is in love, the higher the marital satisfaction; the more commitment to the relationship, the more the individual minimizes problems in the mate. Research findings support the adage that "love is blind" (Kingsbury & Minda, 1988).

In the first year of marriage, men tend to believe that they are receiving fewer benefits from the marriage than are their wives. In other words, husbands report that their wives are overbenefiting from the marriage and that they are underbenefiting. Nevertheless, newlywed husbands and wives do not differ in their perceptions of overall marital happiness, competence, or control (Crohan & Veroff, 1989).

Types of Marriages

One classification system of marital relationship styles was developed by studying over 200 upper-middle-class marriages (Cuber & Harroff, 1965). All of the subjects in this research project were married at least 10 years and had never seriously considered divorce. After hours of informal interviews with the subjects, the researchers develop a typology of five major kinds of marital relations. These five patterns underscore the perception that American marriages show great variation. The researchers found that 80 percent of marriages fit into the first three types of marriages described here:

1. **Conflict-habituated marriages.** These marriages are characterized by conflict and tension. Although incompatibility is pervasive, couples attempt to hide the degree of discord from the children, relatives, and friends. These couples seem to use conflict as a way of expressing their attachment to each other.
2. **Devitalized marriages.** These marriages begin with passion and deep love, but over time, these features diminish and are replaced by apathy and routine. During the course of the marriage, the number of shared activities declines. Despite the loss of positive

energy, the couple continues the relationship because of established comforts and habits.
3. **Passive-congenial marriages.** From the beginning, these are low-keyed marriages of convenience and comfort. The marriages conform to societal expectations, have high order, and are a way to solve everyday concerns. Passion and expression of love are never strong features in these marriages.
4. **Vital marriages.** These marriages involve high commitment, mutual satisfaction, and strong psychological involvement between partners. These couples enjoy doing things together and prefer shared activities to individual ones.
5. **Total marriages.** These marriages involve total enmeshing of all aspects of the relationship. The couples take the time to resolve differences in the relationship, want to share all important aspects of life, and view themselves as being essentially one.

Marital Power Structures

The power and decision making attributed to husbands and wives vary from couple to couple. Many marriages are patriarchal marriages in that males are considered the head of the family. Sometimes, wives have the authority in such areas as child care and domestic arrangements, but overall, husbands dominate. This pattern is still common but occurs less frequently than in previous generations.

Matriarchal marriages are female dominated. Some cultures, such as the traditional Hawaiian culture, are largely matriarchal, but this type of marriage is less common than patriarchal. In the United States, matriarchal power structures are more common among the lower classes because of higher numbers of absent husbands. With the number of single-parent households growing in all socioeconomic levels, there are now more matriarchal families than before.

Another growing marital power structure is the egalitarian marriage, in which couples share authority, chores, and responsibilities. Rather than the husband or the wife being the undisputed head of household, decision making is mutually shared. This pattern is more common in middle-class families than at other socioeconomic levels (Haas, 1985; Sennett, 1980).

Since 1960, a growing number of college women expect to have egalitarian marriages (Weeks & Botkin, 1987). Indeed, women appear to have moved more toward wanting egalitarian marriages than have men. Carol Holahan (1984) compared 30-year-olds in 1940 who were part of the Terman Study of the Gifted with 30-year-old married Stanford University graduates since 1979. Marital attitudes about male dominance in marriage dramatically changed for women in those 40 years, with women moving away from husband dominance to egalitarianism. Over this same time period, men continued to endorse husband dominance in marriages. For example, women in 1979 felt that wives should be fully aware of family finances; men in 1979 did not think that wives needed to be informed about family finances. By 1979, however, both men and women thought that women should be financially independent and that men should play an active role in child-rearing.

Sons and daughters view the parental power patterns differently. Sons tend to see a patriarchal pattern and attribute power to fathers and support to mothers. However, daughters perceive an egalitarian pattern in which power and support roles are shared (McDermott et al., 1987).

Domestic Violence

In some marital situations, power tactics evolve into violent tactics. Domestic violence has existed for all of human history, but only in the last few decades have some societies tried to understand, stop, and resolve the problem. Because husbands are usually the perpetrators and wives the victims of abuse, the problem is sometimes referred to as **battered wives syndrome** (Walker, 1979). However, domestic violence also includes incidents in which the woman is the perpetrator and the man is the victim. Domestic violence also may occur in homosexual couples. Heterosexual male victims and homosexual victims receive less support and assistance than do heterosexual female victims, and help is insufficient for this group as well (Minnesota Coalition for Battered Women, 1991).

Domestic violence is a common phenomenon. About half of all marriages have at least one incidence of violence. Probably one in five marriages have ongoing violence, defined as five or more violent episodes a year (Straus, Gelles, & Steinmetz, 1980). In these ongoing situations, the batterer constricts the victim's social world, forcing the spouse to be completely dependent. Arguments focus on the spouse's failures in domestic duties, sexual jealousies, and financial disagreements (Sonkin, Martin, & Walker, 1985).

What behaviors are part of the domestic violence situation? Besides the actual physical abuse, batterers make explicit threats of violence (e.g., "If you don't stop right now, I'm going to beat you"), make implicit threats of violence (e.g., "If you keep opening your big mouth, there's no telling what I will do"), take extreme control over the spouse's behavior and whereabouts, exhibit pathological jealousy, say mentally degrading things about the spouse, and force the couple to live an isolated existence (Sonkin et al., 1985).

When battered women attempt to leave the violent home, their risk for being hurt or killed increases. Often, they receive little or no help, or at least insufficient help, from police, prosecutors, and religious figures. Until victims can be made safe, many will continue to risk their lives and well-being in dangerous homes. Moreover, sufficient and well-funded treatment programs for the batterers are needed to reduce this problem.

Parenting

Choosing Parenthood

Young adulthood is the most typical time for individuals to decide whether or not to become parents. Increasingly, young adults are deciding to remain childless or to have

For many expectant mothers, a baby shower is a predictable ritual of celebration.

only one or two children. During the 1980s, for example, about 70 percent of American 20- to 24-year-old women stated that they wanted two or fewer children; in 1971, the majority of women wanted more than two children (Neal, Groat, & Wicks, 1989).

Young adults give several advantages for having children, including needing children to have a real family life, as a source of love and affection, and to prevent loneliness and give purpose to life. Primary disadvantages include children causing drastic changes in lifestyle, especially changes in finances and in employment. Other disadvantages include contributing to the world population problem, dealing with childhood and teenage problems from toilet training to teenage sex and drug use, and negative effects on health and stamina (Neal et al., 1989).

Whether or not individuals perceive many advantages or disadvantages in having children primarily determines their attitude about becoming parents. Figure 13.6 summarizes the four principal positions. In a study of 600 couples, 30 percent of individuals were pro-children, and 30 percent were anti-children. Another 20 percent were indifferent, and 20 percent were ambivalent. Nonclose couples were more likely to hold anti-child attitudes; indifference and ambivalence were not related to marital closeness (Neal et al., 1989). Couple compatibility on attitudes toward children makes decision making about whether to become parents easier. Figure 13.6 is useful for charting changes in attitudes over time.

Once adults have made a commitment to becoming parents, they face the task of developing a parental identity. The "Exploring the Parent/Child Relationship" feature is about the process of acquiring a parental identity.

How does an adult acquire a sense of being a parent? What aspects go into the psychological birth of a parent? The process involves affective and cognitive changes resulting from a reexploration of individuals' relationship with their own parents, sociocultural images of parents, and actual parenting experiences (Partridge, 1988).

Personal History Aspects

Brand-new parents' sense of being parents is influenced by their interactions with their parents—images of being the child of their parents. On conscious and unconscious levels, parents relive aspects of their own development while interacting with and observing their own child. Unresolved conflicts from childhood may intrude and create obstacles in building a healthy parental identity (Benedek, 1970). Unresolved childhood traumas are called "ghosts in the nursery" because of their potential for negative impact on current parental identities (Fraiberg, Adelson, & Shapiro, 1980). Reworking these emotional traumas can alleviate parenting difficulties.

Contemporary Influences

Societal factors influence the development of a parental identity. Although individuals absorb cultural images of parenting roles throughout life (e.g., viewing television mothers from June Cleaver to Marge Simpson, reading articles in popular magazines on how to deal with parenting issues), this process is heightened when actual parenthood is anticipated. Pregnant women pay more attention to information about how other mothers behave, think, and appear and begin to select those images that seem appropriate. Mothers center on five major images: the fun mother, the involved mother, the traditional mother, the protective mother, and the knowledgeable mother (Ruble et al., 1990).

Although information is actively sought out and incorporated into parenting images before the birth of a child, after the birth, self-definitions of parenthood shift to actual experiences with child care (Deutsch, Ruble, Felming, Brooks-Gunn, & Stangor, 1988; Reilly, Entwisle, & Doering, 1987; Ruble et al., 1990).

Personal Parenting Experiences

Of course, personal parental awareness is significantly based on actual parenting experiences. Initially, a mother's primary parenting sense may develop from feeding and caring for her infant; over time, she incorporates the baby's satisfaction into her own identity as the mother (Benedek, 1970).

Parents differ in their ability to balance their own needs and the needs of their children. Parents who are fairly sophisticated in these balancing skills are unlikely to abuse their children (Newberger, 1980).

Personal parental identity depends partly on personal personality style, partly on societal messages, and partly on the child (Belsky, 1984). Strengths in any of these three areas aid parents in dealing with difficulties in the other area(s). People who feel good about themselves and have a strong sense of self are likely to be more effective parents. Children's characteristics, such as sex, appearance, birth order, handicaps, temperament, and health status, can all influence parenting quality and, therefore, parental identity.

Figure 13.6
Value of children typology.

Establishing Parenting Style

Many parenting topics—for example, parenting styles and discipline styles—were covered in earlier chapters. Although the focus was on how the styles affected children, parents choose parenting styles that fit their personal needs and their parental beliefs. For example, parents who use punitive discipline methods tend to view children as disobedient, aggressive, and difficult to control (Kandel, 1990).

Two parents may agree or differ on parenting practices. Degree of parental agreement, or value-concordance, affects children's psychological functioning. Between the ages of 3 and 7, boys with concordant parents rate higher in intelligence, moral judgment, and personality. However, the assertive and independent behavior of girls from these homes is more likely to be viewed as noncompliant and as causing problems. By the end of adolescence, the effects of high parental agreement on females is viewed more positively: Adolescent girls with concordant parents are seen as more assertive, competent, self-confident, independent, responsible, helpful, and socially skilled (Vaughn, Block, & Block, 1988).

Mothers and Fathers and Child-Rearing

Mothering and fathering roles seem to be undergoing a transformation in definition and function. After all, more mothers are combining parenting and work, and more fathers are taking part in child-rearing activities. Joseph Pleck (1987) talked about the three historical phases of fatherhood. Until the mid-20th century, fathers tended to be viewed as distant breadwinners. In the 1960s, the view of fathers as gender role models emerged. Now, the image is that of the involved father.

An involved father is referred to as an **androgynous father,** described as:

an active participant in the details of day-to-day childcare . . . [has a] more expressive and intimate way with his children, and he plays a larger part in the socialization process that his male forebears had long since abandoned to their wives. (Rotundo, 1985, p. 17)

Children with androgynous fathers have fewer stereotypes about paternal and maternal roles (Carlson, 1984).

However, cultural beliefs about fatherhood have actually changed more than men's conduct as fathers (LaRossa, 1988). Rotundo (1985) wrote, "There are more *women* who *advocate* 'Androgynous Fatherhood' than there are *men* who *practice* it" (p. 20). For example, when children get sick, mothers are still the parents that stay home (Bailey, 1989).

In comparing the conduct of fatherhood and motherhood, researchers look at three aspects: engagement, accessibility, and responsibility (Lamb, 1987). Engagement is one-to-one interaction with a child—for example, helping with homework, playing ball together, or feeding. Accessibility is less intense interaction, with the adult being available by doing an activity near the child—for example, the parent is in the kitchen cooking or is watching television near the child. Responsibility is being accountable for the child's welfare and care—for example, scheduling doctor appointments and washing the child's clothes (LaRossa, 1988).

Between 1975 and 1981, fathers' engagement increased 26 percent. In other words, paternal engagement finally increased to one third of maternal engagement. Fathers in 1981 engaged in chid care 2.88 hr a week, compared to 8.54 a week for mothers. Thus, in 1981, fathers were investing 5 min more a day in active child care than they were in 1975 (Lamb, 1987).

Moreover, when researchers asked fathers why they wanted to be with their children, the most typical answer was, "A father has to put in some time with his kids." This has been described as the **technically present father,** and this type of father often experiences guilt about his ambivalence toward active parenting (LaRossa, 1988).

A study that compared 90 nonindustrial societies found (1) a great deal of variation in father-child relationships and (2) that male participation in child-rearing enhances the public status of women (Coltrane, 1988). In societies that feature high levels of father-child proximity, women are likely to be active participants in community decision making. Societies with frequent father-child contact also are likely to exhibit significant female public authority and status. One way to interpret these findings is that gender division of labor in child care serves to maintain and reinforce sex discrimination in public affairs, which cycles back into reinforcing the idea that child care is women's work.

Table 13.11

Difference Between New Zealand Men and Women Regarding Emotional and Therapeutic Support, Sharing of Personal Problems, and Canceling an Engagement

	Men	Women
Derive emotional support from:		
Same-sex friends	18%	58%
Opposite-sex friends	48	10
Share personal problems:		
More with same-sex friends	36	72
More with opposite-sex friends	32	9
With both same- and opposite-sex friends	26	18
Derive therapeutic value from:		
Same-sex friendships	21	37
Opposite-sex friendships	44	18
Would cancel an engagement with a same-sex friend to go with an opposite-sex friend	55	36

From R. Sukett, et al., "Gender Differences in Friendship Patterns" in *Sex Roles,* 19, 57-66, Table II page 63, 1988. Copyright © Plenum Publishing Corporation, New York, NY.

Friends

Gender Differences in Friendships

A number of studies have found that men and women form different friendship patterns. These differences are based on women's and men's disparate communication patterns discussed earlier in the chapter. The impact of these gender communication styles is tremendous, influencing intimate relationships, marital satisfaction, parenting styles, and friendships.

The gender differences in friendship are found in several cultures, and Table 13.11 summarizes differences between New Zealand men and women in their same-sex and opposite-sex friendships. As found in American research (e.g., Bell, 1981; Caldwell & Peplau, 1982; Davis & Todd, 1982; Jones, Bloys, & Wood, 1990; Sapadin, 1988), women are more intimate and emotional in same-sex friendships and place a higher value on these friendships than do men. Male friendships emphasize shared activities, and female friendships emphasize talking, emotional sharing, and dealing with personal problems (Aukett, Ritchie, & Mill, 1988).

Studies show that men derive more emotional and therapeutic support from cross-sex relationships than from same-sex relationships, and the opposite tends to be true for women (Aukett, Ritchie, & Mill, 1988; Bell, 1981). These findings are compatible with the more general findings of differences in female and male communication. For many men, friendships with women are a new experience in emotional sharing and intimate self-disclosure, while women make adjustments to novices in their style of communication (Tschann, 1988). Indeed, some men are unable to adjust to a cross-sex platonic friendship and report no nonsexual friendships with women (Levinson,

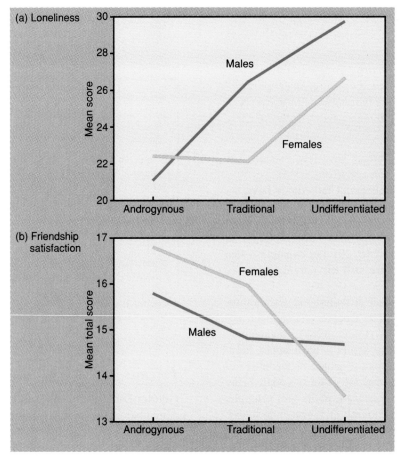

Figure 13.7

(a) loneliness and (b) friendship satisfaction scores by sex role and sex.

Source: Data from D. C. Jones, et al., "Sex Roles and Friendship Patterns" in *Sex Roles,* 23, 133–145, fig. 1, page 143, 1990.

1978). After marriage, women continue to make intimate self-disclosures to their female friends; however, men, who were already low in self-disclosures to other men, make fewer intimate self-disclosures to male friends after marriage (Tschann, 1988).

Emphasizing gender differences in friendship patterns can lead to the erroneous conclusion that male friendships and female friendships are completely different. In fact, they are more similar than different. Both genders find trust, respect, acceptance, and enjoyment in their friendships (Davis & Todd, 1982; Helgeson, Shaver, & Dyer, 1987).

Friendships by Androgynous and Traditional Individuals

More than gender, gender-role characteristics are a factor in the expression of friendships. For both males and females, androgyny contributes to positive friendship experiences, including more trust in friends, more positive views of

friends' attributes, and higher levels of friendship satisfaction. As shown in Figure 13.7, undifferentiated individuals (those who are neither androgynous nor traditional) have lower friendship satisfaction than traditional individuals. Undifferentiated adults have fewer friends and are less adept at recognizing their friends' needs, have less trust in their friends, and feel more isolated in their relationships (Jones et al., 1990).

The friendship patterns of androgynous males and androgynous females are different. Androgynous males have better same-sex friendships (both in quantity and in quality) than do other males. However, androgynous females have enhanced cross-sex friendships compared to other females. In fact, androgynous females express a strong sense of trust in male friends and tend to devalue female friends and rank them as less trustworthy than male friends (Jones et al., 1990).

17. True or false: Contributing factors to a growing acceptance of the single lifestyle include a greater number of career opportunities for women and greater tolerance for sexual relationships outside of marriage. _____
18. Eighty percent of marriages are _____, _____, or _____.
19. Which of the following is a source of parental identity?
    A. Personal parenting experiences
    B. Sociocultural images of parents
    C. Relationship with own parents
    D. All of the above
20. True or false: Cross-culturally, male participation in child-rearing is positively correlated with enhanced status for women. _____
21. In same-sex friendships, males tend to engage in shared _____, while women engage in _____ sharing.

answers

17. True [LO-16]. 18. conflict-habituated; devitalized; passive-congenial [LO-18]. 19. D [LO-19]. 20. True [LO-20]. 21. activities; emotional [LO-21].

Exploring Human Development

1. Using Sternberg's model of mental self-government, compose an essay question and a term-paper topic that would be preferred by each of Sternberg's three thinking styles: planners, implementers, and evaluators.
2. Adopt better nutritional and exercise habits for a 2-week trial period. Write about your attempts in a journal: What did you try? How did you feel about these changes? What were the results? Will you keep any of the changes past the 2 weeks?
3. Interview three couples who became parents for the first time in different decades. What were the similarities and differences in their acquisition of a parental identity?
4. Design a treatment model for dealing with one of the following societal problems: domestic violence, sexual abuse, or sexual addiction.

Discussing Human Development

1. Discuss the gender differences in communication, intimate relationships, parenting, and friendships. What advantages and disadvantages do men and women each bring into these arenas? Do you think that these same gender patterns will exist in the future?
2. In earlier chapters, you studied different parenting styles (authoritarian, permissive, authoritative). How do you think adults establish their parenting style when they are acquiring a parental identity?
3. Why is narcissism growing in society? What impact does this have on work, family, and friendship patterns?

Reading More About Human Development

Carnes, P. (1983). *Out of the shadows: Understanding sexual addiction.* Minneapolis: CompCare.

Gannon, J.P. (1989). *Soul survivors: A new beginning for adults abused as children.* New York: Prentice-Hall.

Lamb, M.E. (Ed.). (1987). *The father's role: Cross-cultural perspectives.* Hillsdale, NJ: Lawrence Erlbaum.

Osborne, P. (1989). *Parenting for the '90s.* Intercourse, PA: Good Books.

Pearsall, P. (1990). *The power of the family.* New York: Doubleday.

Woititz, J.G. (1989). *Healing your sexual self.* Deerfield Beach, FL: Health Communications.

Summary

I. Physical condition of young adults
   A. Adults typically reach their peak physical strength and health during early adulthood.
      1. Muscular strength continues to increase during the 20s, and the body proportions of males and females continue to change.
      2. Weight gain typically continues throughout the early and middle adulthood years, leading to body dissatisfaction for many individuals.
      3. Age-related changes in the elasticity of skin may first be noticed by the late 20s, but young adults are more likely to focus on changes in body shape and weight as external signs of aging.
      4. The organ reserve of young adults causes age-related internal changes, such as slower homeostatic adjustments, to go largely unnoticed.
   B. The sexual motivation of young adults aids individuals in meeting their needs for intimacy, belongingness, power, submission, playfulness, and passion.
      1. Adult sexual values, attitudes, and behaviors are governed by sexual scripts learned from early childhood onward.
      2. Cultural sexual scripts include a double standard in which men are expected to be more sexually active than women and in which women receive greater disapproval for their sexual activity.
      3. Personality dimensions of instrumentality and expressiveness are predictive of adult sexual scripts and behaviors.
      4. Men and women with high instrumentality tend to be more sexually active, but the pattern is more complex for women when the level of expressiveness is also a factor.
      5. The sexual behavior of young adults is influenced also by family background, with females from divorced families, stepfamilies, or high-conflict families being more sexually active.
      6. Young adults who did not receive help for sexual abuse as a child may have difficulty forming intimate relationships and may exhibit posttraumatic stress disorder.
      7. Some adults display a compulsive sexuality in the form of sexual addiction.

C. Maintaining a healthy lifestyle has positive benefits throughout adulthood.
   1. Individuals who follow seven basic health habits not only live longer but have healthier lives.
   2. Many Americans forego breakfast, snack between meals, are dieting, do not get enough sleep each night, abuse alcohol, smoke, and do not exercise regularly.
   3. Multicultural nutrition studies show a correlation between high-fiber, low-fat diets and low rates of cancer.
   4. Participating in regular exercise has immediate effects of increasing energy level and decreasing tension and a long-term effect of increasing longevity.
   5. Research suggests the presence of disease-prone personalities, characterized by depression, anxiety, and hostility, and hardy or physically fit personalities, characterized by optimism, self-confidence, and self-discipline.
   6. Adults under age 30 express lower levels of psychological well-being than older adults.
   7. The relationships among personality characteristics, stress, and health are complex, with emotionality adding another factor.
   8. Different types of loneliness, especially situational loneliness, affect the physical and mental well-being of young adults.
   9. The diagnoses of mental disorders typically differ between men and women.

II. Cognitive development of young adults
   A. Although earlier cross-sectional studies indicated that intellectual abilities declined after the early 20s, longitudinal studies consistently find that intellectual abilities generally remain stable or continue to increase across the adult years.
      1. Increases in crystallized abilities across adulthood are somewhat offset by decreases in fluid abilities.
      2. Age differences in memory abilities are a function of the test situation, with only small differences observed when test stimuli are pragmatically (meaningfully) arranged.
   B. Theorists studying adult cognitive development suggest that Piaget's stage of formal operations is followed by the development of postformal thought, resulting from continued education and life experiences.
      1. With increased experience, adults move from the idealistic, strict logic, and correct-solution focus of the formal stage to less abstract and less absolute thinking, creating flexibility for dealing with the inconsistencies of adult life.
      2. Dialectic thought is a major feature of postformal thinking, allowing adults to synthesize opposing viewpoints.
      3. Schaie's stage model of cognitive development in adulthood proposes that the knowledge acquired in childhood and adolescence is put to use in different ways at different times in adulthood.
      4. According to Schaie, young adults use their knowledge to achieve; middle-aged adults focus on concern for others and the larger social system; and older adults use their knowledge to establish a sense of purpose and wisdom.

C. Sternberg's model of mental self-government proposes three thinking styles.
   1. Planners, like the legislative branch of government, like to define the problems and make the rules.
   2. Implementers, like the executive branch, like to carry out plans.
   3. Evaluators, like the judicial branch, like to evaluate and provide feedback.
   4. Sternberg's cognitive styles are related to career choices.
D. Kolb's approach to adult cognitive abilities distinguishes four learning styles, based on individual preferences for gathering and processing information.
   1. Kolb's four learning styles are accommodators, divergers, assimilators, and convergers.
   2. Like Sternberg's cognitive styles, Kolb's learning styles are related to career choices.
E. The values established and stabilized during the young adult years have been shifting since the mid-1960s.

III. Psychosocial development of young adults
   A. According to Erikson, young adults experience the sixth psychosocial stage of intimacy versus isolation.
      1. Achieving intimacy includes establishing sexual intimacy but also involves developing mutual trust, honoring commitments, and being willing to accommodate the needs and interests of others.
      2. Isolation, or distantiation, is the readiness to distance oneself from others when a threat is perceived.
      3. Intimacy may move from a self-focused level through a role-focused level to an individuated-connected level of mature intimacy.
      4. Bar-Yam Hassan's five-stage model proposes a similar sequence for the development of intimacy, as individuals move from a position of self-interest to a mature, committed, intimate relationship.
      5. Men's and women's views of intimate relationships are similar, but men put more emphasis on sexual activity, while women stress openness.
      6. Young adult men and women differ in the degree of intimacy expressed in their communication patterns, with women expressing a greater degree of intimacy in both female-female and female-male communications.
   B. An emphasis on distinct gender identities for males and females often obscures the high degree of similarity between men and women.
      1. Men and women hold more rigid gender stereotypes for males than for females.
      2. Macho men exhibit personalities that reflect callous sexual attitudes and identification of manliness with violence and dangerous excitement.
      3. The hypermasculine socialization of macho men develops scripts for adulthood that are problematic and difficult to change.
      4. The sex-segregated groupings of childhood and adolescence extend into adulthood and result in gender differences in styles of interacting.
      5. Typically, males develop a restrictive interaction style that limits self-disclosure and establishes well-defined roles.

6. Females develop an enabling interaction style that enhances self-disclosure and seeks agreement among different points of view.
7. The gender differences in interaction styles usually result in male-female interactions that are more rewarding for males than for females.

C. Ethnic identity is an individual's identification and psychological relationship with his or her ethnic group.
   1. Identity issues for ethnic minorities also include the dominant ethnic group's attitudes and behaviors toward the minority group.
   2. Phinney proposed a three-stage model of ethnic identity development in which individuals move from a position of unexamined ethnic identity to a final stage of committed ethnic identity.
   3. Individuals in an ethnic minority may develop identities than reflect both minority and majority cultures, either one or the other, or neither.
   4. About 30 percent of Americans ages 15 to 25 are ethnic minority members.

IV. Young adult relationships
A. The number of single adults living separately from relatives has doubled in the last three decades.
   1. As a group, single adults are comprised of those who have chosen to remain single, those who are planning to marry, and those who are divorced or widowed.
   2. Factors contributing to the increase in the single lifestyle include a delay in marrying while individuals pursue educational and career goals, greater educational and career opportunities for women, greater tolerance of sexual relationships outside of marriage, and a large increase in cohabitation.
   3. Single adults who live homosexual lifestyles are as diverse as heterosexual single adults.
   4. Homosexual couples may not legally marry, but many maintain long-term, committed relationships.
   5. Many single adults plan to marry, and their selection of marriage partners is affected by such factors as propinquity (physical nearness), social class, ethnic background, and religion.
   6. Physical attractiveness is also a factor in mate selection, as are perceived similarity or complementarity of characteristics.
   7. Mate selection often includes a formal period of engagement in which a couple announce their exclusive commitment to each other and make plans for their marriage.

B. People marry for many reasons, but most focus on establishing intimacy; timing, economic and emotional security, and legal sanctioning of sexual activity may also be involved.
   1. The marriage expectations of young adults from divorced families do not differ from the expectations of young adults from intact families.
   2. Research supports the idea that "love is blind" in that, the more committed the relationship, the more each partner minimizes the faults of the other.

3. Marriages have been classified as conflict-habituated, devitalized, passive-congenial, vital, and total, underscoring the idea that American marriages are diverse.
4. Marital power and decision making vary greatly, from patriarchal (male-dominated) to matriarchal (female-dominated) to egalitarian (the couple share authority and responsibility).
5. Since 1960, women have moved more toward wanting egalitarian marriages than men have.
6. The use of marital power sometimes results in domestic violence and may produce battered wives syndrome, in which the husband is the perpetrator and the wife is the victim.

C. Young adults also typically make lifestyle decisions about becoming parents.
   1. Since the 1970s, young adults have been choosing to have fewer children (two, one, or none).
   2. The relative balance of the perceived advantages and disadvantages of having children and the couples' compatibility of views are important factors in the decision to become parents.
   3. Parental identity develops from past family experiences, contemporary influences during the pregnancy, and actual experiences with the baby after birth.
   4. Parents adopt parenting styles that fit their personal needs and their parental beliefs.
   5. Parental agreement regarding parenting practices positively affects the psychological functioning of the children.
   6. The role of the father has changed during the 20th century, from that of distant breadwinner to that of the involved (androgynous) father.
   7. Cultural beliefs about fatherhood have changed more than men's behavior as fathers; for example, fathers' actual time spent in active child care has increased but remains well below the time spent by mothers.
   8. In nonindustrial societies where fathers are highly involved in child-rearing, the public status of women is enhanced.

D. Men and women form different friendship patterns as a result of their differing communication patterns.
   1. Women are more intimate and emotional in same-sex friendships and place more value on the friendships than men do.
   2. Male friendships emphasize shared activities, while female friendships emphasize talking, emotional sharing, and dealing with personal problems.
   3. Men derive more emotional and therapeutic support from cross-sex relationships than from same-sex relationships, with the opposite true for women.
   4. Despite the differences, men and women are more alike in their friendships than they are different.
   5. Androgynous gender characteristics are positive factors for both male and female friendships, resulting in more trust, more friends, and higher levels of friendship satisfaction.

1. The organ reserve refers to one's
   a. potential to deal with certain bodily injuries because the body has two of certain organs instead of just one.
   b. total physical capacity that is not normally used.
   c. self-consciousness in engaging in physical activities when others are present.
   d. ability to recover from illness by action of the immune system.

2. Which of the following is part of the "double standard" sexual script?
   a. Males are more sexually active than females.
   b. Females support the double standard more than males.
   c. Sexually active females receive more disapproval than sexually active males.
   d. All of the above are correct.

3. Which of the following groups has the lowest sexual experience?
   a. women high in instrumentality and low in expressiveness
   b. men high in instrumentality
   c. women high in both instrumentality and expressiveness
   d. women high in expressiveness and low in instrumentality

4. Which of the following statements is correct?
   a. Extramarital sex is common for husbands but infrequent for wives.
   b. Females from intact families have significantly fewer premarital sexual behaviors than other females.
   c. American women are less likely to approve of extramarital sex than to engage in its practice.
   d. Individuals who experienced sexual abuse during childhood seldom have this experience affect their adult sexual relationships.

5. Which of the following is *not* one of the seven basic health habits proposed by the pioneer health psychology study of adults in Alameda County, California?
   a. Eat healthy small snacks frequently.
   b. Do not smoke.
   c. Exercise moderately and regularly.
   d. Sleep regularly 7 to 8 hr a night.

6. Which of the following is *not* an accurate comparison of the typical Chinese diet with the typical American diet?
   a. Chinese men consume more calories than American men.
   b. Americans consume more fats than do the Chinese.
   c. The Chinese consume more meats and vegetables.
   d. The Chinese consume more dietary fiber than the Americans.

7. Which of the following is associated with a disease-prone personality?
   a. perfectionism
   b. anger
   c. optimism
   d. competition

8. Which of the following irrational beliefs is predictive of loneliness?
   a. Individuals must have love and approval from everyone.
   b. Individuals must be blamed and punished for their wrongdoing.
   c. Every problem has a perfect solution that must be found.
   d. Individuals must constantly have others to depend on and care for them.

9. The emotional problem for which the most adults seek help is
   a. anxiety.
   b. anger.
   c. depression.
   d. boredom.

10. In the Iowa State longitudinal study of intelligence, which area showed a significant decrease in the adult years?
    a. numerical scores
    b. verbal scores
    c. relations scores
    d. all of the above

11. Which of the following is more typical of postformal operational thought than of formal operational thought?
    a. logical arguments
    b. mathematical and scientific reasoning
    c. abstract problem solving
    d. dialectic thought

12. Which of the following careers would be a good choice for someone who fits Sternberg's evaluator thinking style?
    a. judge
    b. police officer
    c. scientist
    d. artist

13. In Bar-Yam Hassan's stages of interpersonal development of young adulthood, which is the most advanced stage?
    a. need for approval
    b. need for reciprocity
    c. need for intimacy
    d. need for affiliation

14. The most intimate communication tends to occur in _____ relations.
    a. male-male
    b. female-male
    c. female-female
    d. No significant differences exist.

15. The assimilated ethnic orientation results from _____ identification with one's ethnic group and _____ identification with one's majority group.
    a. strong-strong
    b. strong-weak
    c. weak-strong
    d. weak-weak

16. Researchers studying homosexual couples rather than heterosexual couples must consider all of the following factors *except*
    a. the effects of gender similarity, which are more important than gender differences.
    b. that homosexuality is an abnormal lifestyle.

c. that homosexuals are more likely to be dual-career couples.

d. that homosexuals are affected differently by legal issues.

17. Which of the following is an accurate statement about marital expectations?

a. In the first year of marriage, men believe that their wives are receiving more marriage benefits than they are.

b. In the mate selection process, people are attracted to others whose faces resemble their own.

c. Young adults who experienced a parental divorce do not differ from others in their marital expectations and ideals.

d. All of the above are correct.

18. Which of the following marital types is the least common pattern?

a. total marriages

b. conflict-habituated marriages

c. devitalized marriages

d. passive-congenial marriages

19. What are "ghosts in the nursery?"

a. parents' unresolved childhood traumas

b. parents' memories of a baby lost to miscarriage, stillbirth, or infant death

c. parents' scripts from society or family about how to rear their children

d. parents' doubts about their ability to rear children

20. Which of the following typifies male friendships rather than female friendships?

a. talking

b. emotional sharing

c. dealing with personal problems

d. shared activities

Answers

1. B [LO-1].	8. D [LO-8].	15. C [LO-15].
2. D [LO-2].	9. C [LO-9].	16. B [LO-16].
3. C [LO-3].	10. A [LO-10].	17. D [LO-17].
4. B [LO-4].	11. D [LO-11].	18. A [LO-18].
5. A [LO-5].	12. A [LO-12].	19. A [LO-19].
6. C [LO-6].	13. B [LO-13].	20. D [LO-21].
7. B [LO-7].	14. C [LO-14].	

chapter 14

Physical and Cognitive Development in Middle Adulthood

Learning Objectives

1. Describe the normal age-related changes in the sensory systems of middle-aged adults.
2. Explain the conditions of presbyopia and presbycusis.
3. Describe the normal age-related changes in physical appearance of middle-aged adults.
4. Explain the relationship between changes in collagen and the changes in physical appearance in middle age.
5. Identify the middle adulthood changes in physical functioning of the muscular, cardiac, and respiratory systems.
6. Discuss the double standard of aging.
7. Distinguish between the terms *menopause* and *climacteric*.
8. Identify the major physical changes of the climacteric, and describe the symptoms that accompany these changes.
9. Discuss how attitudes regarding menopause vary across cultures and have changed over the years.
10. Describe the sexual response cycle in men and women and the changes in the cycle that are the result of aging.
11. Identify causes of impotence, and explain the biological-psychological interaction view of impotence.
12. Discuss the risks associated with midlife childbearing, and compare the advantages and disadvantages from both the parents' and child's perspectives.
13. Distinguish between the concepts of absolute, relative, and population-attributable health risks.
14. Explain the cross-cultural relationships between socioeconomic status and obesity.
15. Evaluate the research findings on Type A personality as a predictor of heart attacks.
16. Describe the relationship between stressful life events and health status.
17. Identify common health problems of middle-aged adults.
18. Illustrate the relationship between lifestyle choices and disease incidence with information about cancer.
19. Describe the symptoms of Type-II, adult-onset diabetes and the health complications associated with this disease.
20. Identify the characteristics of postformal thinking.
21. Explain how memory functions in the middle adulthood years.
22. Distinguish among the characteristics of mature thinkers, experts, and individuals with wisdom.

> In the middle of the journey of our life
> I came to myself within a dark wood
> Where the straight way was lost
> (Dante, *Inferno* I:1–3)

As Dante suggested, in midlife, there is no blueprint for how to conduct life, and middle-aged people choose diverse paths: Some have remained single, some have been married for years, some marry during middle adulthood, and others get divorced or have been divorced for years. Some middle-agers are finishing their years of active parenting, while others are choosing to become parents for the first time. Some become grandparents before they are 40, while others will have to wait three more decades. Careers may remain steady or take new directions. Some middle-aged adults attend college, while others retire. Moreover, the middle adulthood years are one of personality changes and reevaluation of life goals. Although most middle-aged individuals have good physical health and cognitive functioning, a minority are affected by serious health problems and cognitive disorders.

Exploring Your Own Development

When will you enter middle age? Or have you already passed that point in adulthood? No definite chronological age marker exists for middle adulthood. In today's youth-centered culture, many would put the start of middle age off until age 59. More practical persons will admit that the 40s are part of middle adulthood. In actuality, 35 would be a more appropriate age to choose for the start of middle adulthood.

If you have not yet reached your middle years, what script do you anticipate following for middle adulthood? How have your choices as a young adult set the stage for your middle adulthood years? If you have already entered middle adulthood, are the middle adulthood years meeting your expectations? What changes have you made in your script for these years? What further changes do you anticipate? How will the choices you make in these middle years set the stage for your later years? Compare your ideas about middle adulthood with the information presented in this chapter.

Physical and Sensory Development in Middle Adulthood

Although physical and sensory development peaks during the young adult years, decline during middle adulthood is usually gradual, and individuals can compensate for the changes. Rate and type of changes are influenced by heredity, health habits, environmental factors, and diseases.

Most middle-aged individuals do not notice any loss in physical or sensory functioning at first. When the decline is finally noticed, individuals may then begin to label themselves as middle-aged. If the middle-aged label is viewed in terms of deterioration, then the dread about being middle-aged is not surprising. Perhaps the time has come to change the middle-age stereotypes. Most middle-aged adults (as well as most older adults) have high-quality and satisfying lives.

Changes in Sensory Functioning

Visual Changes

While most of the senses function at high levels well into middle age, vision decline may become noticeable earlier. Because the lens of the eye gradually loses its elasticity, **presbyopia,** or farsightedness as the result of aging (near objects are seen with difficulty), begins to develop around age 40. By age 50, most people need reading glasses or bifocals. In addition, age-related changes in the cornea result in more astigmatism problems. Especially after age 50, individuals exhibit poorer dark adaptation and less depth perception. Gradually, individuals have more problems adjusting to the darkness of theaters, dimly lit restaurants, and driving at night (Katchadourian, 1987; Schuster & Ashburn, 1986; Whitbourne, 1985).

Hearing Changes

Hearing ability peaks at age 20 and then gradually diminishes. For many individuals, hearing loss is not significant until late adulthood. However, some middle-aged individuals have difficulty understanding speech amid background noise, as typified by crowded restaurants and family gatherings.

Presbycusis is hearing loss specifically related to aging that characteristically is greatest in upper sound frequencies. People of all ages can also experience **noise-induced hearing loss** from repeated exposure to loud noise or extended exposure to moderate noise. Industrialized cultures such as the United States are noisy, and studies have shown that hearing loss is more common in the United States than in African tribes (Katchadourian, 1987; Timiras, 1972b).

---

successful study tip

Presbyopia and Presbycusis

Decipher these words to remember their meanings. *Presby* (prez-be) is a prefix that refers to old age or the elderly. Thus, both of these terms refer to a sensory loss resulting from aging. *Opia* (o-pe-a) refers to vision, while *cusis* (kyoo-sis) refers to hearing.

    Presbyopia = Farsightedness from less elasticity in the lens due to aging.

    Presbycusis = Loss of hearing (primarily high pitches) from aging.

Table 14.1
Examples of Harmful Noise Levels and Guidelines for
Determining if Noises are Harmful

Everyday sounds that can cause damage:

Firearms	140 dBs
Air Raid Sirens	140 dBs
Jackhammer	130 dBs
Jet Plane Taking Off	120 dBs
Rock music	110 dBs
Snowmobile	100 dBs
Chain Saw	100 dBs

You may be experiencing harmful noise levels if:

1. You must raise your voice to be heard.

2. You cannot hear someone a few feet away.

3. Speech around you sounds muffled or dull after you leave a noisy area.

4. You have pain or ringing in your ears (tinnitus) after exposure to noise.

Source: Information from "Noise: Too Much Causes Hearing Loss" in *Good Health,* pp. 6–7, Spring 1990, University of Osteopathic Medicine and Health Sciences, Des Moines, IA.

In middle age, physical aging is apparent, yet most middle age persons are attractive, active, and healthy.

Most Americans are exposed to potentially damaging noises. For example, 59 million are exposed to urban traffic noise, and 11 million Americans are exposed to potentially harmful noise levels (85 or more dB) on their jobs. At least a fourth of agricultural, mining, manufacturing, and construction workers are around hazardous noise levels. Rural adolescents exposed to noisy farm machinery for 40 hr a week may have hearing more typical of 50-year-olds ("Noise," 1990). Stereo headphones, lawn mowers, motorboats, motorcycles, guns, and power tools can all cause auditory harm. Even some children's toys (e.g., cap guns, walkie-talkies, toys with sirens) can be used in ways that can damage hearing. Also, individuals participating in noisy recreational sports should take better precautions. Specific examples of potentially harmful sounds and some general guidelines for determining if sounds are hazardous are provided in Table 14.1.

The Other Senses
The other senses show less decline during middle age. Although the number of taste buds are fewer, taste shows only little decline during the 50s. Touch and pain sensitivities decline slightly from age 45 on. Smell abilities are the most stable, although losses may begin during middle adulthood.

Changes in Physical Appearance

Graying of Hair and Baldness
During middle adulthood, signs of aging appear in individual's external appearance (Doress, Siegal, & Midlife and Older Women Book Project, 1987; Katchadourian, 1987; Schuster & Ashburn, 1986). During adulthood, the production of hair pigment decreases, and during middle age, graying of hair becomes marked. Because the timing and pattern of graying is influenced by genetic factors, individual variation is great. Traditionally, gray hair is considered unbecoming on women and distinguished on men, but these social messages are subject to change. Today, some women believe that their graying hair looks good, and some men dye their hair to hide the gray.

Baldness is another possible middle adulthood physical change. Since baldness is controlled by both genetic factors and male hormones, more males than females experience balding. By age 45, 45 percent of men have significant baldness. Men tend to have more negative views of baldness than of gray hair.

Wrinkles and Other Skin Changes
Both men and women develop wrinkles during the middle adulthood years. These wrinkles are caused by structural changes in the connective tissue that supports the skin. Connective tissue is composed of collagen fibers, elastin fibers, and a gel called ground substance. Collagen is a large protein structure consisting of three intertwining chains that are quite flexible and stable. However, with aging, cross-bonding occurs among the three chains, and they become less resilient. Elastin also changes over the years, making connective tissue stiffer and less flexible. As a result, the skin collapses and forms wrinkles that are commonly called laugh lines, crow's feet, and frown lines. Individuals' typical emotional expressions influence the pattern of wrinkles.

With age, water content in the body decreases, which influences the dryness of the skin. In addition, the epidermis, or outer layer of skin, is covered by a protective coating of dead cells that by middle adulthood is shed less frequently. As a result, the skin has a coarser appearance.

These changes also lead to "bags" under the eyes as underlying muscle and fibrous tissues weaken. Unlike earlier years, rapid loss of weight after age 40 is accompanied by slow receding of excessive skin, causing some middle-age weight-reducers to temporarily appear older, even though they may feel and act younger.

Height and Weight

Height growth ends in the late teens or early adulthood, and by the middle adulthood years, individuals are beginning to "shrink." Height decreases slightly for three reasons: First, bone mass begins to decrease, and at a faster pace for women than for men. Second, degeneration of the discs in the spinal column narrows the size of the discs and increases the curvature of the spine. Third, with aging, the angle of the hip-femur joint gradually moves from a 135-degree angle to a 105-degree angle. This angle change, which is more pronounced in women, results in a slight height decrease.

Weight changes in middle adulthood are variable, but the most typical pattern is to become progressively heavier into the 50s and then to gradually lose weight. Patterns are influenced by heredity and by lifestyle. Those with sedentary lifestyles typically gain the most and appear the flabbiest. Some interesting ongoing research looks at how weight and body shape changes affect health. For example, research findings suggest that weight gain in the midsection (giving the individual an apple shape) is more predictive of heart attacks and diabetes than is weight gain in the hips and thighs (pear shape).

Changes in Physical Functioning

Muscular Functioning

Along with changes in external physical appearance, organs are changing during middle age. Individuals have little if any awareness of these changes until an organ is significantly altered or disturbed (Katchadourian, 1987; Schuster & Ashburn, 1986).

Muscle strength and mass during middle age depend on muscle use. Physically active early middle-aged persons and persons who increase their exercise may improve in this area. Sedentary middle-aged persons, however, exhibit a slow decline in muscle mass, structure, and strength.

Eventually, muscle loss is caused by actual physical aging involving changes in collagen fibers. As these fibers thicken and become less elastic, facial, breast, and abdominal muscles sag and droop. Aging of the hamstring muscles decreases back and hip flexibility and increases the risk of lower back pain. During a person's 50s, back strength is about 90 percent of its maximum level but declines more rapidly in later years.

Cardiovascular and Respiratory Functioning

Most middle-aged persons have normal fist-sized hearts, but the left sides of some individuals' hearts enlarge due to arterial hardening. Another change during middle age is that the upper heart chambers become stiffer as they increase in collagen.

Middle-aged smokers experience more respiratory problems than do non-smoking peers.

During a person's 40s, the coronary arteries start to narrow, even in healthy individuals. Changes also occur in the peripheral vascular system, which leads to increased blood pressure. Nearly half of individuals close to the end of middle age have **hypertension,** or chronic elevated blood pressure. Hypertension is associated with strokes, heart attacks, and other diseases.

Middle-aged smokers experience poorer functioning of respiratory tissues. For nonsmokers without repeated respiratory illnesses (e.g., pneumonia, asthma, bronchitis), respiratory tissues maintain full capacity for a significant period of middle age. However, the natural aging process of lung tissues becoming thicker, less elastic, and stiffer means that, by the late 50s, breathing capacity is reduced.

Other Bodily Changes

Throughout middle adulthood, the gastrointestinal system experiences some changes—notably, decreases in gastric juice secretion, free acid content, and pepsin. Pancreatic digestive enzymes also gradually decrease during these years. Some middle-aged adults drop specific foods from their diets because these physiological changes result in digestive "disagreement."

Through early middle age, the kidneys are at full capacity. With aging, however, the number of functioning nephrons gradually decreases. Adequate daily fluid consumption can help to prolong proper kidney functioning.

Sex hormones—especially female sex hormones—change significantly during middle age. These changes are discussed later in the chapter, in the section about the climacteric and menopause.

Loss of Reserve Capacity

An important bodily change during middle age is the loss of reserve capacity. Reserve capacity is the ability of the body's systems to put forth extra effort in times of stress. A variety of changes contribute to the loss, including lowered ability to pump blood, weakened diaphragm, diminished kidney functioning, and changes in the gastrointestinal tract. Loss of reserve capacity contributes to health problems in middle and later adulthood.

Attitudes Toward Physical Aspects of Aging

The Double Standard of Aging

Traditionally, *her* wrinkles and graying hair have meant that she is over the hill, while *his* wrinkles and graying temples have meant distinguished maturity. According to the **double standard of aging,** women undergo more negative aging experiences than do men. They are more likely to experience a decrease in appeal to others and to judge themselves more negatively. However, the effects are not all positive for males either. Some men miss out on job promotions because of their age and because of expectations that younger males are more competitive and more productive. In relationships, aging may have more negative effects for homosexual males than for heterosexual males (Berger, 1982).

The effects of the double standard of aging are evident in long-term relationships. A telephone survey and 3-year follow-up of over 1,500 married persons who were at least 55 years old looked at these effects. The researchers asked questions about weight gain, declines in physical appearance, and sexual problems of subjects and their spouses. Husbands who believed that their wives had become less physically attractive reported less satisfaction with marital sexual relationships, less interest in their wives sexually, and more unfaithfulness to their wives. A similar pattern was not found for wives whose husbands had become less attractive (Margolin & White, 1987).

Are Attitudes Changing?

American culture seems to be confused about its attitudes toward aging. On the one hand, about three quarters of a million Americans have cosmetic surgery each year, with many using collagen injections, fat transfer, chemical peeling, and dermabrasion to get rid of wrinkles (Berkman, 1987). Indeed, some studies report that middle-aged women fight aging by trying to regain a youthful beauty (Jacobs, 1979). On the other hand, more middle-aged and older adults are appearing in magazine and television ads. More adults realize that the middle adulthood years are satisfying and healthy. Some studies find that middle-aged women like their appearance, with some subjects preferring their middle-aged looks to how they looked when they were younger (Berkun, 1983; Pellegrino, 1981).

While some middle-aged persons loathe their changed appearance, others are able to sense that middle age can

In recent years, more middle-aged women are mentioned in the media. Jane Fonda is an example of women's growing influence on social issues.

bring a freedom from the youth culture (a culture that emphasizes youthful appearance, energy, and activities)—a freedom to act without self-consciousness about appearance. Reactions of others and the availability of employment and social opportunities will help to determine whether more middle-aged women will become satisfied with their mature appearance. Middle-aged women who are satisfied with their body image also report higher self-esteem and higher mastery of life events (Vann Rackley, Warren, & Bird, 1988).

Motor Abilities

Unless they live sedentary lives, adults experience only a small decrement in strength and coordination during the middle adulthood years. However, average reaction time slows about 20 percent in the years from 20 to 60 (Birren, Woods, & Williams, 1980). Driving skills are negatively affected by the decline in reaction time and by lessened ability to tolerate glare, but the driving records of middle-aged persons are superior to younger drivers, due to experience and more conservative driving styles (McFarland, Tune, & Welford, 1964).

Sleep Patterns

Middle-aged individuals get only a little less total sleep and REM (rapid eye movement) sleep than do younger adults. In middle adulthood, however, many individuals wake up often during the night and take longer to fall asleep. Therefore, to feel rested, a higher percentage of middle-aged adults add short naps to their daily regimen (Katchadourian, 1987).

Midlife Changes in Reproductive and Sexual Capacity

The Climacteric and Menopause

What is Menopause and the Climacteric?

Menopause is the term used for when menses have ceased. A woman is considered to have reached menopause if she has not had a menstrual period for 1 year. When a woman reaches menopause, she no longer is capable of reproduction.

Menopause typically occurs around age 50 but can take place as early as the late 30s and as late as the mid-50s. Heredity and lifestyle factors play a role in when menopause occurs. For example, smokers average an earlier menopause age. Women whose mothers smoked have a menopause that is 2 years earlier than women whose mothers did not smoke (Everson, Sandler, & Wilcox, 1986). **Premature menopause** (before age 35) can be due to hysterectomy, surgical removal of ovaries, autoimmune response, or abnormal chromosomes (Beard & Curtis, 1988).

The **climacteric** is the 2- to 5-year period of physiological changes that bring on menopause. Often, the years preceding menopause involve shorter regular menstrual cycles. At age 35, menstrual cycles average 28 days; by the mid 40s, menstrual cycles average only 23 days. Toward the end of the 40s, the menstrual cycle becomes more erratic (Whitbourne, 1985).

These changes are related to a drop in estrogen production. Estrogen production decreases as females' ovaries become depleted of ova. Although females are born with thousands of oocytes (immature ova), half are already lost by puberty. By the age of menopause, the rest are gone due to atresia, the atrophy of ovarian follicles. When ova can no longer be released from the ovaries, the ovaries stop producing estrogens and progestins, which results in menopause. Estrogen production does not cease altogether since other areas of the body continue to produce it.

Another hormonal change that occurs during the climacteric is an increase in the pituitary gland's production of gonadotropic hormones (follicle-stimulating hormone [FSH] and luteinizing hormone [LH]). The gonadotropic hormones stimulate the ovaries to release ova, so production of these hormones may increase at this time in an attempt to continue ovulation (Kimmel, 1990).

Symptoms of Menopause

In addition to the cessation of menses, the most common physical symptoms associated with menopause are **hot flashes,** or hot flushes. Hot flashes are brief feelings of warmth and flushing, accompanied by perspiration. During hot flashes, both skin temperature and heart rate measurably increase (Germaine & Freedman, 1984). Hot flashes have been linked to the production of the gonadotropic hormone LH (Harman & Talbert, 1985). Studies have reported that as many as 70 percent of menopausal women (Polit & LaRocco, 1980) or as few as 28 percent (Goodman, Grove, & Gilbert, 1978) experience hot flashes.

Long-term physical symptoms associated with the climacteric include thinning of the vaginal walls, reduced vaginal lubrication, decreased breast sizes, and accelerated loss of bone mass. Many physicians believe that these symptoms can be lessened by **estrogen replacement therapy (ERT),** which involves taking a low dosage of estrogen and progestin so that hormone levels are similar to levels before menopause but not high enough to cause menstrual periods. Estrogen given without progestin increases the risk of breast and cervical cancers (Kimmel, 1990). Table 14.2 lists possible benefits and risks of estrogen replacement therapy.

Table 14.2
Possible Benefits and Risks of Using Estrogen
for Treating the Menopausal Syndrome

Possible benefits:
    Decrease in the frequency and severity of hot flashes
    Prevention or relief of atrophic vaginitis
    Prevention or relief of atrophy of the vulva
    Prevention of thinning of the skin
    Prevention of osteoporosis
    Decrease in mortality

Possible risks:
    Nausea, fluid retention, and facial acne
    Postmenopausal bleeding
    Increased severity of cystic breast disease
    Accelerated growth of uterine fibroid tumors
    Increased risk of gallstones
    Increased risk of uterine and breast cancer (?)
    Deep vein thrombophlebitis and thromboembolism
    Increased blood pressure (rare)
    Decreased sugar tolerance (rare)

Table 2 (p. 71) from *Love and Sex After 40* by Robert N. Butler, M. D. and Myrna I. Lewis. Copyright © 1986 by Robert N. Butler, M. D. and Myrna I. Lewis. Reprinted by permission of HarperCollins Publishers, Inc.

A number of psychological symptoms, including apathy, apprehension, depression, fatigue, forgetfulness, headaches, and irritability, are associated with menopause (Beard & Curtis, 1988). However, most menopausal women do not report problems with these symptoms. Interestingly, menopausal women rate their own physical and psychological symptoms as less frequent and less severe than do physicians. Moreover, physicians are more likely to regard menopausal symptoms as pathological than are the women who experience the symptoms (Cowan, Warren, & Young, 1985b).

Menopause was once believed to involve depression, anxiety, and mental instability (Millette & Hawkins, 1983; Skalka, 1984). At one time, psychiatrists used the diagnosis of **involutional melancholia** for major psychotic depression brought on by menopause. However, recent studies find no association between menopausal status and "menopausal negativism," or depression (Lennon, 1987).

Attitudes Toward Menopause

A few cross-cultural studies on menopause suggest that experiencing menopausal symptoms is heavily influenced by cultural attitudes and expectations. Western European and American women are the most likely to have menopausal symptoms and negative attitudes (Unger, 1979). Nancy Datan looked at the attitudes of North African, European, Arab, Persian, and Turkish middle-aged women living in Israel and found no regret about the loss of fertility (Datan, Antonovsky, & Mooz, 1981).

Although attitudes toward menopause have been becoming more positive in recent years, even surveys done in the 1960s found that only half of middle-aged women found menopause to be disagreeable, and only 4 percent regarded menopause as the worst thing about middle age. Older middle-aged women held more positive attitudes

Table 14.3
Attitudes About Menopause Among
100 White Mothers, Ages 45 to 55

	Percent
1. The best thing about menopause	
Not having to worry about getting pregnant	30%
Not having to bother with menstruation	44
Better relationship with husband	11
Greater enjoyment of sex life	3
None of these	12
2. The worst thing about menopause	
Now knowing what to expect	26%
The discomfort and pain	19
Sign of getting older	17
Loss of enjoyment in sexual relations	4
Not being able to have more children	4
None of these	30
3. How menopause affects a woman's appearance	
Negative changes	50%
No effect	43
Positive changes	1
No response	6
4. How menopause affects a woman's physical and emotional health	
Negative changes	32%
No effect	58
Positive change or improvement	10
5. How menopause affects a woman's sexual relations	
Sexual relations become more important	18%
No effect	65
Sexual relations become less important	17

From B. L. Neugarten, "A New Look at Menopause" in *Psychology Today,* 1, 42–45, 67–69, 71. (15), December 1967. Reprinted with permission from Psychology Today Magazine Copyright © 1967 Sussex Publishers Inc.

about menopause than did younger middle-aged women (Neugarten, 1967). As shown in Table 14.3, many women in the 1960s already viewed menopause in positive ways, despite the medical and popular opinions of that era.

Is There a Male Climacteric?

If a male climacteric exists, it is different from the female experience. During the female climacteric, reproductive ability is lost. For males, a decline in the number of sperm and decreased sperm motility reduce fertility, but fertility is not lost. Psychologists who support the concept of a male climacteric believe that its symptoms include decreased fertility, decreased orgasms, increased impotence, and other varying symptoms, including depression and fatigue; they also believe that the male climacteric occurs about 10 years later than for females (Weg, 1987). On the other hand, only a few studies find even a gradual decline in male testosterone levels in late midlife. Even in old age, some men still have high levels of this hormone. Other researchers argue that what some have labeled as the male climacteric is probably more related to health factors than to normal aging (Butler & Lewis, 1986; Harman & Talbert, 1985).

Sexuality in Middle Age

The Sexual Response Cycle and Aging

The sexual response cycle consists of four phases: excitement, plateau, orgasm, and resolution. The excitement phase occurs more quickly in males than females and is characterized by penile erection and vaginal lubrication. The plateau phase is characterized by blood congestion and sexual tension in the entire pelvic area. The male orgasmic phase involves two stages—one of slight contractions and one of actual ejaculation. The female orgasmic phase is one longer stage. A notable sex difference is the ability of many women to have repeated orgasms. The resolution phase involves decongestion of the blood vessels and occurs more slowly in females. Males, but not females, have a refractory period, during which another orgasm cannot be achieved (Kimmel, 1990).

Barring some physical conditions, the sexual response is viable for the entire life span. However, some aspects of this cycle are modified, especially from age 50 on. Overall, the intensity of the characteristics of the sexual response cycle gradually decrease (Katchadourian, 1987).

With age, males need more time to achieve an erection. Furthermore, erections tend to be softer and the direction of the erect penis is less upward. Although erections are not maintained as long as in youth, males are less likely to experience premature ejaculation during middle adulthood. Middle-aged males' orgasmic reactions are less intense, with fewer contractions and less vigorous ejaculation. Moreover, refractory periods become longer as men age (Katchadourian, 1987; Kimmel, 1990).

The changes in the sexual response cycle are less dramatic in women. Basically, orgasmic contractions are fewer and less intense, and resolution occurs more rapidly. In addition, after menopause, the thinning of vaginal walls and lessened vaginal lubrication can result in painful sexual intercourse. Estrogen replacement therapy or lubricants can alleviate these problems (Katchadourian, 1987).

Impotence

Impotence, the male's inability to achieve an erection, can occur occasionally at any age for a variety of reasons—fatigue, depression, tension, drug usage and medication side effects, illness, and stress. In middle age, problems with impotence increase in frequency, due to illness or other causes, but not due to physical aging itself. In fact, the sexual activity of some males increases as they get older (Butler & Lewis, 1986).

Psychological causes have traditionally been estimated to be responsible for 90 to 95 percent of middle-aged male impotence. However, recent biomedical research has suggested that half of all impotence has a biological component. Impotence is best viewed as a biological-psychological interaction (Butler & Lewis, 1986). Table 14.4 lists the medical conditions that most commonly contribute to impotence. Psychotherapy and various medical treatments are successful in dealing with most cases of impotence.

William Johnson and Virginia Masters did pioneer work on the sexual response cycle. As a result, sex therapy is very helpful for many couples.

Table 14.4
Major Causes of Physically Based Impotence

Physical problem	Approximate Number of Cases
Diabetes mellitus	2,000,000+
Vascular insufficiency (arteriosclerosis, hypertension, antihypertensive medications)	1,500,000
Radical surgery (prostatectomies, colostomies, cystectomies)	650,000
Trauma (spinal cord injuries, pelvic fractures)	400,000
Hypogonadism and other endocrine disorders	300,000
Multiple sclerosis	180,000
Side effects from medications	Unknown

From *LOVE AND SEX AFTER 40* by Robert N. Butler, M.D. and Myrna I. Lewis. Copyright © 1986 by Robert N. Butler, M.D. and Myrna I. Lewis. Reprinted by permission of HarperCollins, Publishers, Inc.

Importance of Sexuality in Middle Age

Many of the sexual concerns of middle age, such as differences in sexual interest between partners, problems with fidelity, and sexual rebuffs, are the same as in earlier adult years. Additional concerns that influence middle-age sexuality include changes in family responsibilities as adult children leave home, additional work responsibilities, illness in a partner, and physical aging. Some individuals at midlife become bored and apathetic to long-term roles and want a change within the relationship or a different relationship. Some couples fall out of love, while other relationships improve. Ability to communicate with one's sexual partner and to work on differences can help to make adjustments possible (Butler & Lewis, 1986).

As in younger years, middle-aged individuals attribute diverse meanings to sexuality, the most typical of which are listed in Table 14.5. As you can see, many of the same meanings would be given by adolescents and young adults.

Sex remains important for most middle-aged persons. Less than a tenth of middle-aged or older males and less than a third of middle-aged or older females express lack of

Of the 3.5 million babies born in the United States each year during the 1980s, around 1 million were born to mothers who were at least 30 years old. For the new parents, many advantages may exist for later-life parenting, but little research has been conducted on how the offspring feel about having older-than-average parents. Monica Morris (1988) did a comprehensive survey on the viewpoints of adult "last-chance" children. Two cautionary statements are offered in interpreting her conclusions: First, only 22 subjects were in Morris's sample. Second, these subjects were raised by older parents during an era in which fewer adults were choosing to delay having children. Today's "last-chance children" may feel differently about their experience just because their parents are not the only ones with gray hair and faded youthful beauty.

The subjects in Morris's study perceived three major advantages to being the children of older parents: First, older parents are often more settled financially and emotionally than younger parents. Second, some subjects believed that older parents were wiser, especially in child-rearing practices, and more patient than younger parents. They perceived that their parents were able to provide good parenting due to hav-ing more experiences and being more mellow. Third, these subjects felt that they benefited from their parents' stable marriages.

However, these last-chance children also perceived six disadvantages to being the children of older parents: First, many of the subjects remembered their parents as being less energetic than younger parents and therefore not as physically active with their children. Several regretted that they had never been able to participate in sports with their parents or that they were not encouraged to participate in many activities. On the other hand, many older parents compensated with lots of time involvement, quiet activities, or even outstanding attendance at sports events.

Second, parents of last-chance children were less likely to live to see their children reach adulthood. Fathers especially were sometimes lost before the end of adolescence. Third, their parents were having problems of old age when the offspring were only adolescents or young adults. Thus when the offspring were making important career and lifestyle decisions, some were also busy caring for parents with serious health problems.

Fourth, many of the subjects felt that older parents "forget what it is like" to be young and dealing with issues like emerging sexuality. Instead of a genera-tion gap, these subjects experienced a double-generation gap. Fifth, despite this double-generation gap, many of the last-chance children found it difficult to accomplish normal adolescent rebellion because it would have been, to some degree, like rebelling against their mellowed-out, settled grandparents.

Finally, almost all of the subjects remembered that their older parents' physical appearance had at times embarrassed them because their parents looked different than most parents. Some remember being upset when others mistook a parent for a grandparent. Some avoided introducing their parents to their friends.

Again, predicting which of these advantages and disadvantages will be perceived when today's last-chance children grow up is difficult. Perhaps the increasing number of older parents and the decreased emphasis on a youth culture will diminish some of the embarrassment and sense of being different. Older parents who regularly exercise and practice good health habits may reduce some of the disadvantages associated with diminished energy and physical activity. However, last-chance children will always experience at a younger age the aging of parents and parents' deaths.

interest in sexuality, although higher percentages report a decline in sexual activity (Kimmel, 1990).

Middle-aged persons are more sexually active than estimated by younger individuals. For example, a study of 646 college students found that over half thought that their parents had sex less than once a month and a fourth believed that their parents were no longer sexually active (Pocs, Godow, Tolone, & Walsh, 1977). However, the majority of men and women 46 to 50 years old report at least weekly sexual intercourse (Pfeiffer, Verwoerdt, & Davis, 1974).

Midlife Childbearing

A trend that began in the early 1970s in the United States is women delaying childbearing until their 30s and 40s. As many middle-aged women are seeing their adult children off to independent lives, other middle-aged women are just starting to have infants. Between 1972 and 1982, first-birth rates for women in their early 30s more than doubled, and for women in their late 30s, the rates increased by more than 80 percent (Mansfield, 1988).

One concern is that delayed childbearing is biologically ill-advised. After all, women over 35 are considered

Table 14.5
Meanings Attributed to Sexuality in Middle Age

- The opportunity for intimacy through the expression of passion, affection, admiration, loyalty, and other emotions
- An affirmation of one's body and its functioning
- A strong sense of self
- A means of self-assertion
- Protection from anxiety
- The pleasure of being touched or caressed
- A sense of romance
- An affirmation of life
- A continued search for growth and experience

From LOVE AND SEX AFTER 40 by Robert N. Butler, M. D. and Myrna I. Lewis. Copyright © 1986 by Robert N. Butler, M. D. and Myrna I. Lewis. Reprinted by permission of HarperCollins, Publishers, Inc.

to be of "advanced maternal age," and their first-time pregnancies are usually labeled as "high risk" on the basis of age alone. In actuality, research findings do not support the notion that maternal age predicts high-risk pregnancies. Maternal age is not associated with toxemia, placental complications, or prolonged labor. It is associated with a higher incidence of cesarean deliveries (Mansfield, 1988). Earlier studies that suggested that maternal age led to higher infant and maternal mortality and to low birthweight were conducted with samples from inner-city clinics, and the complications were actually attributable to poor prenatal care and poor nutrition, rather than to maternal age (Mansfield, 1988).

The continuing misconceptions about the risk of maternal age in pregnancy can lead to higher levels of anxiety and stress in pregnant middle-aged women. It also leads physicians to use more medications during labor and to anticipate the need for cesarean deliveries. One risk that does increase with maternal age is the birth of a baby with Down syndrome (Mansfield, 1988).

Middle-aged men and women who are considering starting a family may have to deal with greater risk of Down syndrome, but the risks of maternal age and pregnancy have been exaggerated. Prospective parents should pay more attention to how parenting demands will affect their lives. Many individuals who beat their "biological clocks" to parenthood believe that they are better parents due to patience, financial stability, and experience. The "Exploring the Parent/Child Relationship" feature looks at delayed parenting from the viewpoint of the children.

guided review

6. The _____ is the 2- to 5-year period of physiological changes that bring on _____ (literally, the cessation of the menses).
7. Which of the following is a common symptom of menopause?
   A. depression
   B. hot flashes
   C. increased vaginal lubrication
   D. all of the above
8. True or false: Men experience a climacteric that is very similar to that of women.
9. In middle adulthood, problems with _____ (the inability to achieve an erection) increase in frequency due to illness and other causes but not due to aging itself.
10. Couples contemplating having a child in their middle years should consider all but which one of the following factors?
    A. decreased energy levels
    B. increased risk of Down syndrome
    C. the high risk of first-time pregnancy in middle age
    D. the impact of being older adults while their children are still relatively young

answers

6. climacteric; menopause [LO-7]. 7. B [LO-8]. 8. False [LO-8]. 9. impotence [LO-11]. 10. C [LO-12].

Health Concerns and Disorders of Middle Adulthood

Health Status and Lifestyle Factors

How Healthy are Middle-Aged Adults?

The majority of middle-aged adults feel healthy and are healthy. Of American adults ages 45 to 64, 82 percent report that their health is good to excellent. Only 7 percent of this age group must curtail important activities due to health (U.S. Department of Health and Human Services, 1985, 1986). During middle adulthood, individuals become increasingly concerned about their health and about how to live their life to maintain their health.

Risk Factors and Lifestyle

Table 14.6 distinguishes the terms *absolute health risks, relative health risks,* and *population-attributable health risks.* These health risks are discussed in news coverage about diet, exercise, seat belts, regular physical checkups, and alcohol use. Some people adjust their behaviors to lower their health risks. For example, more people now use helmets when they ride bicycles, and many people have reduced fat in their diets while increasing fiber. Are your behaviors influenced by what you hear about health risks?

successful study tip

Absolute and Relative Health Risks

To remember the difference between absolute and relative health risks, ask yourself the following questions:

Absolute risk: How likely is it that I will die from this health risk?

Relative risk: How likely is it that I will die from this health risk, compared to someone not exposed to the risk?

Interest in health risks and behavior modification is most likely when an individual's absolute risk and relative risk are both high. For example, researchers found that 50 percent of heart attack survivors quit smoking within a year of their heart attack. For these smokers, the risk of smoking is quite salient. Smokers whose physicians urge them to quit have a 10 percent quitting rate, which is still double that of the general population of smokers (Jeffrey, 1989).

Perhaps due to physical aging and increased awareness of personal mortality, middle-aged adults seem to pay more attention to lifestyle factors related to health risks than do younger adults. Although over a third of middle-aged adults smoke cigarettes, this is the period of life in which many smokers decide to quit the habit and do. Many other middle-aged adults increase their exercise and make healthier decisions about their diets. About a third of individuals in middle adulthood are obese, and the "Exploring Cultural Diversity" feature explores cultural differences in obesity.

Table 14.6
Health Risks

Health researchers often mention the risk of such behaviors as smoking. To determine your personal risk, you must know whether the health risk is given as an absolute, a relative, or a population-attributable risk.

An **absolute health risk** is the risk that an individual will acquire some problem or disease over a defined time period. For a 40-year-old American male, the absolute risk of dying of heart disease this year is 44 in 100,000.

A **relative health risk** is the ratio of the chance of disease in individuals exposed to a risk factor, compared to others who are not exposed to the risk factor. A 40-year-old American male who is a heavy cigarette smoker, compared to a comparable nonsmoker, has a relative risk of 10 to 1 for developing lung cancer. High relative risks suggest (1) causation and (2) a way to modify risk by reducing or removing the risk factor (e.g., quitting smoking).

A **population-attributable health risk** is the number of excess cases of disease that can be attributed to a particular risk factor. For example, 101,000 fewer people would die from lung cancer this year if no one smoked.

From R. W. Jeffrey, "Risk Behaviors and Health: Contrasting Individual and Population Perspectives" in *American Psychologist,* 44, 1194–1202, 1989. Copyright 1989 by the American Psychological Association. Adapted by permission.

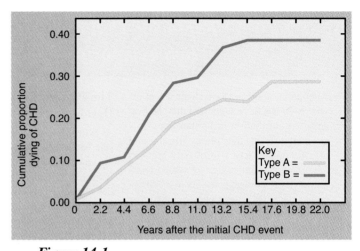

Figure 14.1

Cumulative case fatality rates among 231 patients with coronary heart disease (CHD) who survived for longer than 24 hr after a heart attack, according to Type A and Type B behavior pattern.

Source: Data from D. R. Ragland and R. J. Brand, "Type A Behavior and Mortality From Coronary Heart Disease" in *The New England Journal of Medicine,* fig. 1, p. 68, January 14, 1988.

A newer trend in helping people to adopt lifestyles that lead to better health is for entire communities, colleges, or companies to develop health programs. For example, Pawtucket, Rhode Island, a community of 180,000, actively worked on long-term change in health habits. Over a 10-year period, community members decreased cholesterol levels by 11 percent and smoking by 36 percent, and there were 22 percent fewer deaths from heart diseases (Roberts, 1990).

Stress and Health

A Brief History of the Type A Variable

Personal coping styles influence how stress affects health. Beginning in the 1950s, research literature about a **Type A personality** began to appear. This personality is characterized as being hard-driving, competitive, ambitious, and aggressive. Type A people cannot stand waiting in a grocery line and quickly grow impatient if made to wait at a railroad crossing. Moreover, these individuals are incapable of relaxing on a vacation, are constantly comparing their own performance to that of others or to perfectionistic standards, and even walk at a faster pace than other individuals. Type As convey a sense of time urgency. Most importantly, early research studies suggested that Type A individuals are at higher risk for coronary disease (Dimsdale, 1988; Friedman & Rosenman, 1974).

For example, the Western Collaborative Group Study followed 3,154 healthy men for 8.5 years. During this time, persons with Type A behavior had about twice the chance of acquiring coronary artery disease than others in the study (Rosenman et al., 1975). Three additional studies found that patients with Type A behavior had more extensive coronary artery disease at the time of cardiac catheteriza-

tion than other patients (Blumenthal, Williams, Kong, Schanberg, & Thompson, 1978; Frank, Heller, Kornfield, Sporn, & Weiss, 1978; Zyzanski, Jenkins, Ryan, Flessas, & Everist, 1976). By 1981, Type A behavior was recognized by an independent review board as a coronary artery disease risk factor (Dimsdale, 1988).

However, most of the studies done in the 1980s failed to show a direct relationship between Type A behavior and coronary risk (e.g., Booth-Kewley & Friedman, 1987; Cohen & Reed, 1985; Haynes, Feinleib, & Kannel, 1980; Shekelle, Gale, & Norusis, 1985). Although many Americans continue to believe that the Type A pattern leads to heart attacks, researchers are now redefining the concept. Some researchers suggest that the *hostility* component of Type A personality is the crucial aspect of subsequent coronary problems (MacDougall, Dembroski, Dimsdale, & Hackett, 1985), while others propose that *depression* is the important predictor of coronary problems (Booth-Kewley & Friedman, 1987). A relationship does seem to exist between personality and heart disease, but Type A personality is too simplistic or too broad to describe this relationship (Dimsdale, 1988).

Another interesting study compared the survival rate of Type A and Type B patients who had had a heart attack (Ragland & Brand, 1988). **Type B personality** consists of the relative absence of Type A characteristics. In other words, Type B persons are relaxed, noncompetitive, and nonaggressive. The researchers found that, in the first 24 hr following a heart attack, Type A and Type B patients died in about equal numbers. However, on a long-term basis, Type A persons outsurvived Type B persons—the fatality rate of Type A patients was only 58 percent that of Type B patients. These differences are summarized in Figure 14.1. These findings were the opposite of what had been anticipated. Perhaps Type A behaviors help

Exploring Cultural Diversity: The Relationship Between Socioeconomic Status and Obesity

Although a number of excellent recent research studies have suggested that the biogenetic contribution to human obesity is quite significant, the role of societal and psychological factors in obesity remains important. A recent review of studies looking at the relationship between socioeconomic status (SES) and obesity found that developed societies (i.e., modern, industrialized societies) and developing societies (i.e., more traditional, agricultural societies) exhibit different patterns (Sobal & Stunkard, 1989).

The Pattern in Developed Countries

A very consistent and striking pattern in the United States and in other developed societies was found for women: an inverse relationship between SES and obesity. In other words, more lower SES women are obese, and the higher the SES, the more prevalent thinness is. In 30 studies in the United States, 28 studies (93 percent) found this inverse association for women. Eighteen of 24 studies (75 percent) done in other developed societies (e.g., Britain, Germany, Czechoslovakia, Sweden, Canada) found this same inverse relationship.

The pattern is more mixed for males. In the United States, 44 percent of 27 studies found an inverse relationship, and 44 percent found a direct relationship between SES and obesity. In the studies reporting an inverse relationship, the relationship was weaker than it was for women. Of the 22 studies done on males in other developed societies, 56 percent found an inverse relationship.

In other words, in developed societies, adult females are much more likely to be significantly overweight if they are in lower socioeconomic levels. The pattern for adult males is more variable.

The Pattern in Developing Countries

As with developed societies, the relationship between SES and obesity in developing countries is stronger for women than it is for men. However, the relationship is in the *opposite* direction. Studies done in Africa, Asia, Central America, Mexico, South America, Australia, and the Pacific Islands all found that, the higher the SES, the more prevalent the obesity among women. These studies also found a direct relationship for men. In fact, 91 percent of the studies confirmed a direct relationship for SES and obesity for women, and 86 percent confirmed a direct relationnship for men.

In other words, for both males and females in developing countries, obesity is more common among the upper SES levels than the lower levels. Also, unlike developed countries, males and females in developing countries exhibit similar patterns.

Possible Explanations

In developed countries, great value is placed on dietary restraint and exercise. Over the last three decades, the ideal body shape for women has been becoming thinner (Garner & Garfinkel, 1980), with the result that most adolescent and adult women are on diets (Rosen & Gross, 1987). Even the majority of average-weight female adolescents report that they are fat and need to strictly control their food intake (Wardle & Beales, 1986). Women of higher SES diet more often than other women.

Most jobs, including lower-paying jobs, no longer involve great physical activity. Women in higher SES levels may have more leisure time in which to engage in exercise, and indeed, may experience more societal pressure to exercise. This physical activity helps to control weight levels. By contrast, working women in lower SES levels not only receive less weight-control benefits from exercise on the job, they also experience less societal pressure to exercise to control weight when they are not working.

Being successful at dietary restraint and exercise seems to pay off since upward mobility is easier for thin women than for overweight women. In fact, some American women seriously believe the motto "You can't be too rich or too thin," and structure their lives around its message. Unfortunately, for some women, this obsession leads to eating disorders (discussed in Chapter 10). For other women, obesity limits their options, shatters their self-esteem, and negatively affects their entire lives. Societal attitudes make obesity a personal failure or sin, rather than a health problem.

In developing countries, lack of sufficient food for the poor may affect the low prevalence of obesity in lower SES levels. In some countries, only the higher SES individuals have enough food to become overweight. After all, 47 percent of developing countries have food shortages at least once a year (Brown & Konner, 1987). Under these circumstances, individuals with a tendency to store fat may be envied and admired. In developing countries, females who are plump reflect the ideal of feminine beauty. For both males and females in developing countries, obesity represents social prestige and sexual attractiveness.

---

coronary patients to cope and work on recovery, but further research is needed to support that hypothesis.

In 1981, Type A behavior was believed to be a risk factor in coronary disease. By the end of the same decade, that belief had been severely shaken. Continued research in this area is needed to determine which characteristics put individuals at greater risk and which aid adaptive coping. The Type A personality research clearly shows the need for multiple studies on all topics, even those that seem to have

conclusive evidence. It also points out the need for individuals to stay informed about the most recent medical, psychological, and nutritional research to be able to make the most accurate lifestyle decisions.

Life Events and Stress

Stressful life events can have long-term effects on physical health (Kimmel, 1990, Willis, Thomas, Garry, & Goodwin, 1987). Recent stressful events have a greater impact on physical health than do distant stressful events. Also,

Table 14.7
Examples From the Life Events Questionnaire (Center for the Study of Neuroses, University of California, San Francisco)

The following are some stressors that you may have experienced. For each one that you have experienced, circle the appropriate number for how long ago the event happened. The numbers in parentheses, from left to right, represent the following: (within 1 month, from 1 to 6 months, from 6 to 12 months, from 1 to 2 years, over 2 years). You may circle more than one time period for events that occurred over a long period of time, or you might have experienced some events more than once, and you should check these events as many times as appropriate. Add your total.

Death of a child or spouse/mate	(90/81/67/50/32)
Death of a parent or sibling	(79/70/51/34/22)
Loss of a close friend/relationship to death	(70/53/36/22/12)
Legal troubles resulting in being held in jail	(82/65/51/37/27)
Financial difficulties	(60/43/26/13/7)
Being fired or laid off	(68/46/27/16/8)
A miscarriage or abortion	(71/53/31/18/11)
Divorce or breakup with a lover	(76/63/45/29/16)
Court appearance for a serious violation	(70/41/23/13/5)
An unwanted pregnancy	(72/57/42/25/15)
Serious hospitalization of family member	(69/46/26/14/8)
Unemployment over 1 month	(57/42/20/10/6)
Illness/injury (bedridden over a week)	(65/48/25/12/5)
An extramarital affair	(62/50/37/25/17)
The loss of a personally valuable object	(47/26/13/8/5)
Involvement in a lawsuit (not divorce)	(61/41/23/13/7)
Failing an important examination	(62/37/19/9/5)
Breaking an engagement	(65/47/27/14/7)
Arguments with spouse/mate	(59/40/26/17/11)
Taking on a large loan	(42/29/20/14/10)
Being drafted into the military	(62/51/39/30/17)
Troubles with boss or other workers	(50/23/9/4/3)
Separation from a close friend	(49/36/24/16/10)
Taking an important examination	(45/12/5/2/2)
Separation from spouse because of job demands	(65/51/38/26/15)
A big change in work or in school	(49/30/16/9/5)
A move to another town, state, country	(46/32/20/10/5)
Getting married or returning to spouse	(60/45/34/23/18)
Minor violations of the law	(31/15/7/3/2)
Moved home within the same town	(25/13/7/3/2)
Birth or adoption of a child	(52/39/26/18/15)
Being confused for over 3 days	(62/34/15/10/-)
Being angry for over 3 days	(52/25/10/5/-)
Being nervous for over 3 days	(48/23/10/5/-)
Being sad for over 3 days	(46/24/12/6/-)
Spouse-unfaithful	(68/55/40/27/19)
Attacked, raped, or involved in violent acts	(72/57/42/25/18)

Reprinted from Mardi J. Horowitz, et al., "Life Event Questionnaires For Measuring Presumptive Stress" in *Psychosomatic Medicine* 39: 413–431, 1977, © American Psychosomatic Society. Reprinted by permission of William and Wilkins, Baltimore, MD. Also appeared in Mardi J. Horowitz, *Stress Response Syndromes,* 2nd edition, 1986, Hillsdale: Aronson.

stresses that are perceived as negative have more impact than stresses that are perceived as positive. An example of a common stressful event during middle adulthood is offspring moving out of the home. Some parents view this as a negative event because they focus on the emptiness in the house and the loss of the parenting role. Other parents view this as a positive event because the couple can rejuvenate their marriage, give up much of the burden of parenting, and start on long-awaited projects. The transition is experienced quite differently among parents. One interesting finding is that middle-aged persons often have both greater negative and greater positive stress than other age groups (Chiriboga & Cutler, 1980).

The Life Events Questionnaire in Table 14.7 is an example of a scale that takes into account both the recency of stressors and the great impact of negative life events (Horowitz & Wilner, 1980). Like other scales, it can only provide a typical rating of stress for each event. Thus, some types of events may affect individuals more or less than this scale indicates. Also, the scale does not measure the effect of daily, routine stressors, called **hassles.** Women tend to be more affected by family hassles throughout adulthood. Young adults are hassled the most about family issues, while older adults are hassled the most about health issues and family stress (Chiriboga & Cutler, 1980).

Health Problems

Common, Troubling Problems

One in four middle-aged Americans has hypertension, or chronically elevated blood pressure. Hypertension is associated with risk of strokes, heart attacks, and other diseases. Most hypertensive individuals have no symptoms (Kimmel, 1990).

Blood pressure is the force of blood against the walls of the arteries and veins. The systolic, or upper, number in a blood pressure reading is the blood pressure in the arteries when the heart is pumping blood. The diastolic, or lower, number in a blood pressure reading is the blood pressure in the arteries when the heart is filling with blood for the next beat. The American Heart Association defines hypertension as a reading of 140/90 or higher (Doress et al., 1987).

Mild hypertension can often be controlled by good nutrition and weight management, exercise, and stress reduction. Some hypertension needs to be treated with medications (Doress et al., 1987).

Back problems may occur at any age but are more common from midlife on. Back pain can come from muscle or ligament strain, muscle spasm, disc problems, excessive curvature of the spine, sacroiliac joint strain, and arthritis. An injured back may take several weeks to heal. Exercises that strengthen back muscles, abdominal muscles, and the quadriceps (front thigh muscles) are important in injury prevention. Stretching and warm-up exercises before a workout also are important (Doress et al., 1987).

Hysterectomies, the surgical removal of the uterus, are common operations for middle-aged women. In 1985, 670,000 hysterectomies were performed in the United

States. Some experts believe that 33 to 72 percent of these hysterectomies were unnecessary; therefore, women should consider obtaining more than one medical opinion before having this surgery. Several necessary reasons for having a hysterectomy include: (1) invasive cancer of the uterus, ovaries, cervix, or fallopian tubes; (2) hemorrhaging combined with anemia that does not respond to other medical treatments; (3) fibroid tumors *if* bowel or urinary function is obstructed; (4) advanced pelvic inflammatory disease; (5) severe uterine prolapse; and (6) severe endometriosis (Doress et al., 1987).

Acute and Chronic Diseases

Acute diseases are temporary diseases caused by infection or virus, and they become less frequent as people age. Chronic diseases are long-term illnesses that often cannot be fully cured, and these diseases increase in incidence as individuals age. The most common middle-age diseases are asthma, bronchitis, diabetes, mental disorders, arthritis, rheumatism, and impairments of circulatory and digestive systems.

The incidence of cancer goes up in the second half of life. Cancer is featured in the section that follows because it illustrates the important relationship between lifestyle and disease incidence. Diabetes is the other chronic illness focused on in this chapter. Type-I (insulin-dependent) diabetes, which is also known as diabetes mellitus or sugar diabetes, affects 1 in 20 adults, while Type-II diabetes is diagnosed mainly after the age of 40 (Butler & Lewis, 1986).

Cancer

What are your odds of surviving cancer? What factors contribute to your cancer risk? Is cancer preventable? In the 1990s, the statistics are much more encouraging than in previous decades. For example, in the 1930s, a cancer patient had only a 20 percent chance of surviving for 5 years; in 1990, the 5-year survival rate was 50 percent. In addition, some researchers believe that 80 percent of cancers might be preventable. Despite these encouraging and improving statistics, cancer is the number one cause of death in the middle adult years (Petrus & Vetrosky, 1990).

In cancer, or tumorigenesis, the first step is a change in cellular chromosomal structure, which might be caused by ionizing radiation, chemicals, or oncogenic viruses (e.g., hepatitis B virus or Epstein-Barr virus). Lifestyle factors, including those discussed earlier, greatly influence the development of these abnormal cells. Unavoidable risk factors include heredity, previous malignant disease, chronic disease, and aging (Petrus & Vetrosky, 1990).

Use of tobacco is the number one controllable risk factor for cancer. Probably a third of all cancers are related to tobacco use. Cancer risk increases with the number of cigarettes smoked, and the risk goes down when smoking stops. In fact, 10 to 15 years after quitting, a former smoker's risk is the same as someone who never smoked (Petrus & Vetrosky, 1990).

Some researchers believe that diet plays a role in about a third of all cancers. For example, excessive fat in the diet is associated with increased risk of breast, pancre-

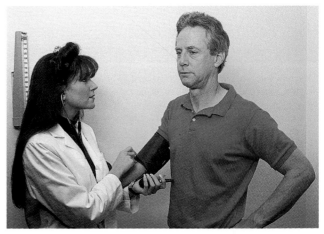

Preventative health check-ups, proper diet and moderate exercise should be important aspects of the middle adulthood lifestyle.

atic, prostate, ovarian, and colon cancers. Obesity is also related to a number of different cancers (Petrus & Vetrosky, 1990). Women of normal weight but with a bulging tummy ("apple shape") have six times greater risk for breast cancer than women with flat stomachs. Apple-shaped women have lower levels of a protein called sex hormone binding globulin; this results in higher levels of free estrogen, which has been implicated as a risk factor for breast cancer. When "apple-shaped" women lose weight in the abdominal region, the level of the protein increases (Van Pelt, 1990a). Other risk factors for breast cancer are provided in Table 14.8.

Other dietary aspects associated with increased cancer risk are high cholesterol levels and low-fiber diets. In a cross-cultural study, smoked, salt-cured, pickled, and nitrate-containing meats were implicated in gastric cancers because of the high incidence of these cancers in Japan and Hawaii, where these meats are a major part of the diet. On the other hand, high-fiber diets; vitamins A, C, and E; and cruciferous vegetables (e.g., broccoli, cabbage, and cauliflower) may help protect against some types of cancers (Petrus & Vetrosky, 1990).

Excessive alcohol use is associated with about 7 percent of cancers and 3 percent of cancer deaths. Alcohol seems to have a stronger effect with smokers than nonsmokers in increasing cancer risks (Petrus & Vetrosky, 1990).

About 10 percent of cancers are probably related to environmental risks, including industrial agents (e.g., asbestos, arsenic, rubber, chromium compounds, nickel, dyes, and polyvinyl chloride), solar radiation, radon gas, and medical radiologic procedures. Solar radiation is related to basal cell and squamous cell skin carcinomas and to melanoma; therefore, using tanning booths or being outdoors without sunscreen can increase the risk of skin cancers. Radon gas, a problem in many homes, is related to lung cancer (Petrus & Vetrosky, 1990).

Reproductive, sexual, and hormonal influences comprise about 3 percent of preventable causes of cancer. For example, cervical cancer is more common in women who had early sexual experiences, multiple sexual partners, and

Table 14.8
Risk Factors for Breast Cancer

One in ten American women develops breast cancer. Some traits are associated with higher- or lower-than-average risks.

Higher Risk	Lower Risk
Older than 50	Younger than age 50
Cancer in other breast	No family history of breast cancer
Family history of breast cancer	Both ovaries removed early in life
No pregnancies	Full-term pregnancy before age 30
Firstborn child after age 30	Menstruation onset after age 12
Menstruation onset before age 12	Early menopause
Menopause after age 50	Slenderness
Obesity	Low-fat diet
High-fat diet	

Source: From E. F. Scanlon and P. Strak, *The American Cancer Society Cancer Book,* edited by A. I. Holleb, 1986. American Cancer Society.

Table 14.9
Ethnic Differences in Cancer Incidence

The incidence of cancer varies among ethnic groups. The following gives research results for cancers in which each group is higher than average:

African Americans: Myeloma, oral cavity cancers, esophagus cancer, colon cancer, pancreas cancer, cancer of the larynx, lung cancer, cervical cancer, prostate cancer

European Americans: Melanoma, Hodgkin's disease, leukemia, lip cancer, breast cancer, ovarian cancer, testicular cancer, bladder cancer, brain cancer, colon and rectum cancer

Chinese Americans: Nasopharynx cancers, liver cancers

Hispanic Americans: Cervical cancer, stomach cancer, biliary tract cancers

Japanese Americans: Stomach cancer, colon and rectum cancer, thyroid cancer

Native Americans: Stomach cancer, biliary tract cancer, cervical cancer, kidney cancer

From J. J. Petrus and D. T. Vetrosky, "Cancer : Risk Factors, Prevention, and Screening" in *Physician Assistant,* 21–38, April 1990. Copyright © 1990 Excerpta Medica, Inc., CORE Publishing Division, Belle Mead, NJ.

partners who had had several sexual partners. Clear cell adenocarcinoma of the vagina in adolescent girls is linked with mothers who took diethylstilbestrol (DES) during pregnancy. High-dose estrogen therapy may be associated with an increased risk of breast cancer. The use of oral contraceptives may increase the risk of cervical and liver cancers but at the same time is associated with lower rates of endometrial and ovarian cancer. Androgen (anabolic steroid) may contribute to liver cancer (Petrus & Vetrosky, 1990).

Sedentary lifestyles are associated with increased risk of colon and reproductive tract cancers. Basically, however, the relationship between physical activity and cancer is an enigma. Research trying to shed light on the relationship often involves animals. Biologist Robert Beyer trained rats to run 7 to 9 mi daily on treadmills. Compared to more sedentary rats, the endurance-trained rats had much lower incidence of cancers (Van Pelt, 1990b).

One of the nonadjustable factors of cancer risk is heredity. Ovarian and breast cancer tend to run in families. Several cancers form a classic Mendelian inheritance pattern, including X-linked recessive cancers, such as Hodgkin's disease and leukemia, and dominant patterns, such as retinoblastoma and familial colon cancer (Petrus & Vetrosky, 1990).

Racial background affects the incidence of cancers. Table 14.9 lists the cancers that occur at higher rates for various subgroups of Americans. Sex differences also occur for cancer risks. Women are at increased risk for breast, thyroid, and gallbladder cancers. Males have higher incidence of cancers in the oral cavity, esophagus, larynx, lung, bladder, kidney, and liver (Petrus & Vetrosky, 1990).

Cancer serves as an excellent example for pointing out the importance of good health habits. Although some cancer risk factors cannot be eliminated, the overall incidence of cancer can be reduced through dietary, smoking, and medical choices. The other important factor is early diagnosis and obtaining the most appropriate treatment. For example, breast cancer can be detected in Stages I, II, or III. Stage I breast cancer means that the underarm lymph nodes are cancer-free. At least 80 percent of these patients will be alive 5 years after the initial diagnosis. When cancer has invaded the underarm nodes, Stage II cancer exists, and the 5-year survival rate drops to 60 percent. Stage III cancer, in which cancer has invaded other organs, has the lowest long-term survival rate (Rennie, 1987).

Diabetes
About 12 million Americans are diabetic, with most diabetics being in the middle-aged and older adult population. Diabetes is more common among African Americans; in all age groups, the prevalence is 33 percent higher for African Americans than European Americans (Lieberman, 1988). Diabetes is also more common among females than males (Clark, 1989).

There are three major types of diabetes. **Gestational diabetes** affects approximately 5 percent of all pregnancies and results in a marked increase in fetal death and pregnancy complications. **Type-I diabetes,** or insulin-dependent diabetes, involves total loss of insulin production in the pancreas. Before insulin treatment became available in the 1920s, Type-I diabetics died within 1 year of diagnosis. Today, treatment can delay the development of complications in this severe form of diabetes that often attacks early in the lifespan (Atkinson & Maclaren, 1990). The most common form of diabetes is **Type-II diabetes,** or adult-onset diabetes, which can usually be controlled without insulin treatment. At least 5 million Americans with Type-II diabetes do not even know that they are diabetic, since this form develops gradually over several years (Clark, 1989).

Research suggests that people with insulin-dependent (Type-I) diabetes have specific genetic markers—beta cells that are gradually killed by the autoimmune system. By identifying specific antibodies to counteract this affect, future doctors may be able to detect insulin-dependent diabetes before the body has destroyed its own insulin-making cells and to prevent the development of Type-I diabetes (Atkinson & Maclaren, 1990; Clark, 1989).

Current research suggest that the symptoms of Type-II diabetes are produced by different mechanisms than for Type-I diabetes. Type-II diabetics continue to produce some insulin, but the body does not utilize this insulin efficiently. Moreover, the diabetic may have no symptoms of this common disorder until 80 percent of insulin-producing cells are destroyed (Atkinson & Maclaren, 1990). High levels of amylin have been found in the pancreas of diabetics, and some researchers suspect that this hormone inhibits insulin production (Clark, 1989).

The classic symptoms of adult-onset diabetes are: (1) polyuria, or frequent urination; (2) polyphagia, or fatigue; (3) polydipsia, or thirstiness; and (4) unexplained weight loss. The most powerful risk factor for Type-II diabetes is obesity—90 percent of those with diabetes have been overweight (Butler & Lewis, 1986; Clark, 1989). Other predictive factors are a family history of diabetes, being over age 35, and giving birth to infants with a birth-weight over 9 lb (Clark, 1989).

Diabetes is associated with a wide range of serious complications. Male diabetics have five times the population rate of chronic impotence (Butler & Lewis, 1986). Type-II diabetes is associated with an increased incidence of hypertension, strokes, and atherosclerotic heart disease. Twice as many diabetics as nondiabetics have a heart condition. Diabetes is highly associated with peripheral vascular disease. More than half of diabetics develop end-stage renal disease. About 15 percent of diabetics have experienced ulcers on their ankles or feet, and diabetes is the leading nontraumatic cause of foot amputation. In 1982, more than 34,500 deaths were attributed to diabetes, and diabetes was a contributing cause in another 95,000 deaths (Clark, 1989).

Diabetes greatly affects the visual system. **Diabetic retinopathy** is the leading cause of new blindness in the United States for adults; it affects 40 percent of Type-II diabetics to some degree after 10 years. Approximately 5,800 diabetics become blind annually. Over the last several years, many individuals have been helped with photocoagulation, a process that uses lasers to seal off leaking retinal blood vessels. This procedure slows visual deterioration (Clark, 1989).

Diabetics carefully monitor their blood glucose level. Treatment may involve medication, but for many diabetics, exercise and diet are the most important treatment components. Many patients need to reduce weight to decrease insulin resistance. A typical diabetic diet is 50 to 60 percent carbohydrates (especially high-fiber foods), 30 percent fat, and 12 to 20 percent protein. Meal distribution typically includes both daytime and bedtime snacks (Engel, 1989).

Middle-Age Deaths

Most people survive the middle adulthood years and enter later adulthood. However, beginning at about age 35, the death rate doubles in each of the next two decades. In middle adulthood, cancer and heart disease overtake accidents and violence as the most common cause of death.

Since 1950, the death rate in midlife has dropped by more than a quarter, mostly because of a decline in the mortality rate from heart disease. Middle-age deaths occur more frequently among males than females, and among African Americans than European Americans.

Cognitive Development in Middle Adulthood

Intelligence in Middle Age

Crystallized and Fluid Intelligence

Some of the changes in middle-age intelligence were discussed in Chapter 13. Recall that crystallized intelligence, or learned knowledge and skills, tends to increase throughout the middle adulthood years (Horn & Donaldson, 1980). On the other hand, fluid intelligence, or innate ability to perceive relationships and to form concepts, typically begins to decline before the start of middle adulthood (Botwinick, 1977).

During middle adulthood, no one pattern of intellectual change emerges. Some middle-aged adults experience increases in their intelligence, some remain stable, and others exhibit intellectual decline. Experiences and health play larger roles than does chronological age.

Speed of Response

A common research finding is that speed of processing slows during middle adulthood. **Reaction time,** the interval between the onset of a stimulus and a person's response to it, increases with age—both in simple key-pressing tasks and in instances where subjects must make more complex choices (Newman, 1982). The slower response time cannot be attributed to differences in motivation between young adults and middle-aged adults. Three biological explanations have been proposed for the effects of aging on speed of response: (1) reduction in speed at which neural impulses travel; (2) neurons increasing their random firing, which makes it difficult to act on desired stimuli versus neural noise; and (3) atherosclerosis reducing neural speed (Botwinick, 1984). Of course, slower responding may be partially due to changes in behavioral style as people age; perhaps by middle age, persons have become more cautious (Welford, 1977).

Although older adults have slower speed of response than younger adults, the reaction time of physically fit middle-aged adults is less affected than that of sedentary middle-aged adults (Salthouse, 1984). Travel experiences, being around intellectually stimulating persons, and challenging careers are factors that influence level of intellectual functioning over the lifespan (Honzik, 1984).

Postformal Thinking

As during the young adulthood years, some middle-aged adults engage in formal operational thinking, which involves using abstract thinking in problem solving. A minority of middle-aged adults engage in postformal operational thinking, or problem-finding thinking (Arlin, 1975, 1984). This type of creative thought involves the ability to define problems in better ways and to discover and formulate new problems. Postformal thinking is responsible for the creation of successful consumer products, such as "White-Out" and "Post-Its." Many feel that this productive creativity is at its peak during the middle-adulthood years (Cole, 1979; Dennis, 1966; Lehman, 1962; Simonton, 1977). Much midlife thinking, however, is more practical in nature than postformal.

Memory in Middle Age

How does memory change during the middle adulthood years? Time needed to activate information from memory increases over 60 percent between age 20 and age 50 (Salthouse, 1982). The most evident decline is in newly learned material (Poon, 1985). Figure 14.2 shows the memory decline in different kinds of memory tasks.

Some aspects of memory change very little through the middle adulthood years. Recognition ability remains stable (Schonfield & Robertson, 1966). Auditory memory declines during early adulthood but remains fairly stable from age 40 on. Visual memory remains fairly constant until about age 60. Changes in short-term memory ability across adulthood are very small (Riege & Inman, 1981;

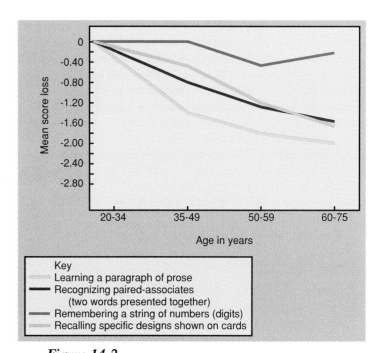

Figure 14.2

Decline on memory tests of different types by age group.

Source: Data from J. G. Gilbert and R. F. Levee, "Patterns of Declining Memory" in *Journal of Gerontology,* 26, 70–75, p. 73, 1971.

Wingfield & Byrnes, 1981). Any reductions in memory abilities seem attributable to an increase in older adults' time to process information (Anders & Fozard, 1973; Salthouse & Kail, 1983).

Memory decline might partly be explained by the amount of memory task practice for young adults versus middle-aged adults. Many young adults are engaged in formal education, while many middle-aged adults have not engaged in formal education for years. In fact, young-adult college students and midlife-adult college students have similar memory scores and use similar memory strategies. Midlife-adult students are more similar to young-adult students than young-adult students are to young-adult nonstudents (Zivian & Darjes, 1983).

Other evidence suggesting that middle-aged adult memory decline is more attributable to experience and strategy than to biological aging comes from studies showing that middle-aged adults' memory abilities improve following instruction in visual imagery and memory organizational techniques (Hultsch, 1975; Mason & Smith, 1977).

Mature Thinkers

How does cognition change between young adulthood and middle adulthood? Middle-aged adults exhibit more pragmatic intelligence and the increased ability to function well in various situations. The characteristics of mature thinkers include: (1) complex thinking, in which inconsistencies can exist side by side; (2) practical thinking, in which idealistic or implausible "ifs" and "whens" are not emphasized; and (3) subjective thinking, with increased reliance on intuition rather than formal, logical rules (Labouvie-Vief, 1986).

Whether young adults or middle-aged adults do better on tasks is partly determined by the type of task. In tasks that require logical thinking, young adults tend to do better. One such task involves showing subjects 42 pictures and having them ask questions until they can figure which is the chosen picture. Young adults do better at asking questions that eliminate several pictures per question. On the other hand, adults in their 40s and 50s tend to be superior in answering questions based on real-life situations and requiring subjectivity and self-reliance. Examples include: "What would you do if you spotted a funnel cloud?" and "What's the best way to survive if you are stranded in a blizzard?" (Denney & Palmer, 1981).

Some, but not all, middle-aged adults may be experts or may be considered wise. What is meant by each of these labels?

Expertise

Experts are individuals who, compared to others, have invested much time and effort into learning an area of knowledge well. Unlike nonexperts, experts rely less on the usage of formal rules and procedures and instead trust their accumulated experience, intuitive reaction to situations, and unique organization of information. Experts make intuitive leaps in their thinking, which allows them to be more rapid and efficient than nonexperts (Rybash, Hoyer, & Roodin, 1986). Exceptional physicians and outstanding auto mechanics often exhibit this type of accurate, intuitive, diagnostic capability.

Compared to others, much of the expert's performance is automated and seems to occur on a nonconscious level. Whether or not you are an expert driver, you can understand **automaticity** by comparing your driving skills as a student driver with your current driving skills. Remember how you used to deliberately think about every response, from turning on the ignition to accelerating or braking? As your driving experience mounted, you became better at just reacting to situations and sensing overall traffic flow and potential driving hazards. Similarly, if you are an amateur typist, you often check your finger position when typing, often hesitate, and need to proofread your paper for errors. The experienced typist types effortlessly, yet senses immediately when a wrong key has been chosen. The shifting of skills from a deliberate processing of information to an automatic processing involves different neural pathways in the brain (Salthouse, 1985).

Experts can process new information in their specialty area faster than others. You may notice that you learn ideas more rapidly and well in your major than you do in your other college subjects. As you build a pool of knowledge in this area, it becomes easier to add more information to the knowledge area. You can quickly determine which ideas are important and which are trivial details. Graduate students learn very intricate and detailed knowledge in their area of expertise, yet learning this difficult material may actually take less time and effort than learning the material of

an introductory course in a nonmajor area. In adulthood, knowledge and skill tend to increase in quite specific areas (Rybash et al., 1986).

Experts have more and better strategies for accomplishing tasks. They are more flexible and willing to experiment with strategies and ideas. Expert musicians and artists give outstanding creative performances by going outside of organized rules—they go with the unexpected as only experts can. Expert physicians can deviate from textbook information to deal with unique medical problems, and top chefs create culinary masterpieces by making subtle adjustments in ingredients and technique, rather than by following recipes. Expert counselors do not work solely out of one theoretical perspective but creatively choose from many sources.

In adulthood, people become more expert in knowledge areas and skills that they choose to develop. However, abilities that are not practiced may decline in these years.

Wisdom

What is **wisdom?** One way to define wisdom is to view it as an ability to use good judgment in important but uncertain matters of life (Dittmann-Kohli & Baltes, 1990). Wisdom enables an individual to grasp basic concerns of human nature and to deal with social, self-knowledge, and interpersonal issues (Clayton, 1982). In other words, wisdom is excellence in pragmatic intelligence and knowledge.

Educated professionals conceptualize wisdom as multidimensional. Wise adults can integrate affective, cognitive, and reflective qualities. Reflective qualities include introspection, intuition, empathy, gentleness, peacefulness, and understanding (Clayton & Birren, 1980).

Characteristics of wisdom include: (1) good judgment and good advice in areas of expertise; (2) ability to recognize important dimensions, alternatives, and comprehensive solutions for problems and crisis situations in major life events; (3) use of a contextual perspective in defining and solving problems; (4) acknowledgement of ambiguity and complexity of problems and the interdependency of issues; and (5) use of relativistic and reflective thinking in dealing with individual differences and in accepting different solutions to real-life problems (Dittmann-Kohli & Baltes, 1990).

Some believe that Eastern and Western cultures define wisdom differently. Both orientations emphasize understanding the meaning of life, but Eastern wisdom emphasizes direct experiential knowledge of life's meaning, and Western wisdom emphasizes the role of intellect and reason (Clayton & Birren, 1980).

Another division of wisdom is into practical and philosophical wisdom. **Practical wisdom** concerns personally relevant situations, such as dealing with the death of a child or going through a midlife crisis. **Philosophical wisdom** concerns the meaning of life and the relationship of the self with the world, such as the self's separateness from others, limited access to knowledge, and mortality (Dittmann-Kohli & Baltes, 1990).

Education can be part of any age group. The college experience is enriched by the diversity of ages in the classroom.

Traditionally, wisdom has been seen as a quality that is achieved with age. Carl Jung, for example, felt that wisdom could not be developed until middle age. Jung defined youth as the time period from puberty to about age 40. According to Jung (1933), in this time period, individuals first have self-doubts, but by the end of this period, they either grow more rigid and intolerant or become the wise guardians of cultural heritage, universal mysteries, and life's purpose.

Actually, wisdom is a fairly rare quality and seems to be equally dispersed across the adulthood years, rather than just among older adults. Interestingly, older adults are the most likely to perceive that wisdom and age are not related. Instead of age, older respondents believe that empathy and understanding are significant parts of wisdom (Clayton & Birren, 1980).

Continuing Education

Several decades ago, high school students made what they thought was a once-in-a-lifetime decision—"Do I go to college after high school graduation or not?" Now, adults of all ages may decide to get more formal education. More than one in every eight adults participate in some adult education course(s) each year.

Middle-aged adults decide to go to college for a variety of reasons. The number one reason is career-related—either more training for their current job or training to facilitate a career change. Others attend school to expand their knowledge and to make their lives more interesting. Some attend college because they no longer want to deny an earlier dream of a college education.

Middle-aged college students are somewhat more anxious and less self-confident than younger college students. They often experience higher levels of fear of failure. Moreover, many older college students have to balance class attendance and studying with external practical problems, such as maintaining both employment and good grades, making arrangements for child care, and balancing being a spouse and a student. Of course, many younger college students have these same difficulties.

Middle-aged college students bring several assets to the classroom. As a group, they are more motivated than younger students, are more eager to learn, have made a conscious commitment to the necessary personal sacrifices, and have more life experiences to contribute to classes (Haponski & McCabe, 1982). They also spend more time studying and asking questions of instructors.

Attending college courses may require middle-aged adults to exercise abstract-thinking and problem-solving skills, and therefore, may help to maintain these skills. Memory abilities also may be strengthened as individuals learn course material. These abilities may be aided through formal instruction in memory strategies and studying skills.

guided review

16. _____, the interval between the onset of a stimulus and a person's response to it, increases with age.
17. Ability to quickly retrieve information from memory _____ (declines, increases) during middle adulthood.
18. The characteristics of mature thinkers include
    A. complex thinking.
    B. practical thinking.
    C. subjective thinking.
    D. all of the above.
19. Wisdom may be _____ or _____ and is _____ (equally, unequally) dispersed across young, middle-aged, and older adults.

answers

16. Reaction time [LO-20]. 17. declines [LO-21].
18. D [LO-22]. 19. practical; philosophical; equally [LO-22].

Exploring Human Development

1. Take the inventory in Table 14.7, and discuss your reactions to this inventory with class members. Daily for a 2-week period, listen to a relaxation or meditation tape, and record your reactions to this experience.
2. Design a college-wide (or class-wide) health program for helping students to develop good exercise, nutrition, and health management habits. Include healthy menus for the school cafeteria, exercise class plans for the school gymnasium, and appropriate health measures (e.g., weight, cholesterol levels) to monitor progress. Find out what healthy options already exist on your campus.
3. Design an informational brochure or poster on some chronic health problem, such as cancer, diabetes, muscular sclerosis, or arthritis.
4. Design a 1-hr memory skill improvement workshop for middle-aged college students.

1. What are common misconceptions about middle adulthood physical development?
2. What is the United States a youth culture? Do you think this preference will change?
3. What are the advantages and disadvantages of midlife childbearing? Compare and contrast the adult experiences of a women who gives birth to two children before she is 20 with one who gives birth to two children after age 35. What are similarities and differences in the experiences of the children?
4. What percentage of middle-aged persons would you describe as being expert? As being wise? Defend your answers.
5. What are the advantages and disadvantages of going to college right after high school versus attending college in middle adulthood?

Reading More About Human Development

Beard, M., & Curtis, L. (1988). *Menopause and the years ahead.* Tucson: Fisher Books.

Butler, R.N., & Lewis, M.I. (1986). *Love and sex after 40: A guide for men and women for their mid and later years.* New York: Harper & Row.

Doress, P.B., Siegal, D.L., and the Midlife and Older Women Book Project. (1987). *Ourselves, growing older.* New York: Touchstone.

Katchadourian, H. (1987). *Fifty: Midlife in perspective.* New York: W.H. Freeman.

Morris, M. (1988). *Last-chance children: growing up with older parents.* New York: Columbia University Press.

Whitbourne, S.K. (1985). *The aging body.* New York: Springer-Verlag.

Summary

I. Physical and sensory development in middle adulthood
   A. Most senses continue to function at a high level during middle adulthood, with vision exhibiting the greatest changes.
      1. Presbyopia (farsightedness as the result of the aging of the lens) often begins to develop around age 40.
      2. After age 50, dark adaptation and depth perception are affected, with the changes often most noticeable when driving at night.
      3. Presbycusis (hearing loss specifically related to aging) is usually not highly noticeable until late adulthood; however, many young and middle-aged adults experience significant noise-induced hearing loss from exposure to loud noises.
      4. Other senses (e.g., taste, touch, pain) decline only slightly during the middle adulthood years.
   B. Middle-aged adults notice signs of aging in their external appearance.
      1. Gray hair from decreased hair pigment production and baldness are two highly noticeable age-related changes in external appearance.
      2. Structural changes in the connective tissue layers of the skin cause wrinkles; the patterns, such as smile and frown lines, are influenced by the individual's typical facial expressions.
      3. The texture of the skin becomes drier and coarser.
      4. Middle-aged adults may experience some shrinkage in height as the result of decreases in bone mass, degeneration of the spinal discs, and changes in skeletal posture.
      5. Weight changes are variable in middle adulthood, but a typical pattern is to gain weight into the 50s and then to gradually lose weight into later adulthood.
   C. The organ systems of middle-aged adults undergo age-related changes.
      1. Muscle strength and muscle mass are more a function of muscle use than aging during middle adulthood; however, eventually, aging changes in collagen result in sagging and decreased flexibility.
      2. Age-related changes in the cardiovascular system lead to increased blood pressure, with nearly half of older middle-aged adults experiencing hypertension and increased risks of strokes, heart attacks and other diseases.
      3. Aging reduces lung capacity by the late 50s, but smoking and chronic respiratory illnesses further reduce the respiratory capacity of many individuals.
      4. Decreases in the secretion of some digestive juices result in digestive upsets for some middle-aged adults that may be controlled by changes in the food eaten.
      5. An important age-related change is the loss of reserve capacity of organs, limiting the body's ability to respond with extra effort during times of stress.
   D. Because of the double standard of aging, women experience more negative reactions to aging than do men.
      1. The effects of the double standard of aging are evident in long-term relationships in that husbands report less marital satisfaction when their wives' appearances age but wives do not report less marital satisfaction when their husbands become less attractive.
      2. Americans' attitudes toward aging are quite varied—from emphasis on regaining a youthful appearance through cosmetic surgery to the greater use of middle-aged and older adults in ads.
   E. A major change in motor abilities in middle adulthood is a 20 percent decrease in reaction time; however, most middle-aged adults adopt more conservative driving styles as one way of compensating.
   F. While the total amount of sleep and dreaming time changes little from the young adult years, many middle-aged adults take longer to fall asleep and wake up more frequently at night.

II. Midlife changes in reproductive and sexual capacity
  A. The climacteric is the 2- to 5-year period of physiological changes that bring on menopause (the cessation of menstruation and ovulation).
    1. Menopause typically occurs around age 50 but varies widely among women, as do the symptoms that accompany the physiological changes.
    2. Hot flashes are the most common symptom associated with the climacteric and may be caused by the woman's body adjusting to changing hormonal levels.
    3. Long-term symptoms associated with the climacteric include thinning of the vaginal wall, reduced vaginal lubrication, decreased breast size, and accelerated loss of bone mass.
    4. Many of these symptoms can be controlled with estrogen replacement therapy, which involves taking low dosages of estrogen and progestin.
    5. Women experiencing the climacteric and postmenopausal women report few problems with the psychological symptoms purportedly associated with menopause.
    6. Cross-cultural studies suggest that the experience of menopausal symptoms is highly influenced by cultural attitudes and expectations.
    7. Since the 1960s, many women—especially older ones—have held positive attitudes regarding menopause.
    8. Men do not experience a climacteric like that of women, and the symptoms of decreased fertility, decreased orgasms, and increased impotence may be due as much to health problems as to the effects of aging.
  B. The sexual response cycle, consisting of excitement, plateau, orgasm, and resolution, remains viable throughout middle and later adulthood but gradually decreases in intensity.
    1. Men experience greater changes in the sexual response cycle with age than do women; middle-aged men need more time to achieve an erection, have less intense orgasms, and experience longer refractory periods.
    2. Impotence (the inability to achieve an erection) can occur for many reasons, with psychological causes estimated to be responsible for over 90 percent of the cases of impotence in middle-aged men.
    3. Sexual activity remains important for most middle-aged men and women, with middle-aged adults expressing the opportunity for intimacy as an important reason for sexual activity.
  C. Beginning in the 1970s, many women began delaying childbearing until their 30s or 40s.
    1. Many misconceptions prevail regarding the risks of later childbearing; however, most are not supported by research evidence.
    2. Increased infertility and a greater risk of Down syndrome are two potential problems associated with later childbearing.
    3. Children of older parents experience several advantages and disadvantages from the age of their parents.

III. Health concerns and disorders of middle adulthood
  A. A large majority of middle-aged Americans report that their health is good to excellent.
    1. An absolute health risk is the risk of acquiring a specific health problem over a defined time period.
    2. A relative health risk defines the risk of individuals exposed to a risk factor, compared to those who are not exposed.
    3. The population-attributable risk is the number of cases of a health problem attributable to a particular risk factor.
    4. Individuals are most likely to change their risky behaviors when absolute and relative health risks are both high.
    5. Middle-aged adults, more than younger adults, pay attention to such lifestyle factors related to health risks as smoking, poor nutrition, lack of exercise, and obesity.
    6. Socioeconomic status is highly related to obesity in women in both developed and developing countries; however, the correlation is the opposite in the two types of countries, with less obesity observed among higher socioeconomic status women in developed countries and more obesity observed among higher socioeconomic status women in developing countries.
  B. Personal coping styles influence how stress affects health.
    1. The Type A coping style has been characterized by competitiveness, aggressiveness, time urgency, and greater risk for coronary heart disease, while the Type B style is easygoing and at much lower risk for coronary heart disease.
    2. More recent research has questioned the overly simplistic relationship between Type A behavior and coronary heart disease, focusing instead on the presence of hostility and depression within the Type A style.
    3. The effects of stressful life events on health vary with such factors as how recently the event occurred and whether the individual perceived the event to be negative or positive.
    4. Hassles (daily routine stressors) affect men and women, and younger and middle-aged adults, differently.
  C. Common middle-age health concerns include hypertension, back problems, and health problems resulting in hysterectomies.
    1. With age, acute, temporary illnesses decrease, while chronic, long-term illnesses increase.
    2. The incidence of cancer increases in middle-age, but continuing medical advances in treatment mean that more individuals survive this class of chronic illness.
    3. Middle-aged adults can control some risks for many types of cancer by not smoking, by watching their nutrition, by not becoming obese, by not abusing alcohol, by exercising, by moderating or eliminating environmental risks, and by regular self-administered and medical physical exams to detect the early symptoms of cancer.

4. Diabetes is also a common chronic health problem in adulthood, occurring more frequently among women and African Americans.

5. The most common form of diabetes in adulthood is Type II—adult onset diabetes that is usually controllable without insulin treatment.

6. The primary symptoms of Type-II diabetes are polyuria (frequent urination), polyphagia (fatigue), polydipsia (thirstiness), and unexplained weight loss.

7. A person with Type-II diabetes is at greater risk for hypertension, strokes, heart disease, kidney and circulatory problems, and visual problems leading to blindness.

8. After age 35, the death rate doubles every 10 years, but since 1950, the death rate in middle adulthood has declined, primarily as the result of better treatments for heart disease.

IV. Cognitive development in middle adulthood

A. During middle adulthood, crystallized intellectual abilities continue to increase, while reaction time, and consequently, fluid intellectual abilities, continue to decline.

    1. The postformal thinking of middle-aged adults leads to problem finding and productive creativity.

    2. Much midlife thinking is more practical than postformal.

B. The ability to quickly retrieve information from memory declines significantly from age 20 to age 50.

    1. The greatest declines in memory retrieval occur for newly learned material.

    2. The ability to recognize information remains relatively stable in middle adulthood.

C. Many middle-aged adults exhibit mature thinking, characterized by complex thinking, practical thinking, and subjective thinking.

    1. By middle age, some individuals have become experts, having learned an area of knowledge well.

    2. The thinking of experts is typically intuitive, relying on accumulated knowledge and experience, and displays automaticity, in which actions are performed and information processed with seemingly little conscious effort.

    3. Experts also employ more and better strategies for accomplishing tasks than do nonexperts.

    4. By middle age, some individuals have gained wisdom—that is, excellence in pragmatic knowledge and intelligence.

    5. Wisdom is multidimensional and involves using good judgment, recognizing important features of problems, using a contextual perspective, tolerating ambiguity, and using relativistic and reflective thinking.

    6. Practical wisdom is used in personally relevant situations, while philosophical wisdom is concerned with the meaning of life.

    7. Wisdom is a fairly rare commodity but can be found among adults of all ages.

D. Continuing education across the adult years is an increasingly frequent occurrence.

    1. Middle-aged adults attend college for career-related and personal fulfillment reasons.

    2. Although middle-aged college students may be more anxious and less confident of their abilities than younger students, their assets include high levels of motivation and commitment and more life experiences to relate to coursework.

Chapter Review Test

1. Americans are more likely than members of African tribes to experience hearing losses due to
  a. presbyopia.
  b. noise-induced hearing loss.
  c. presbycusis.
  d. all of the above.

2. Wrinkles and an increase in skin dryness are due to
  a. cross-bonding of the protein chains of collagen.
  b. decreased water content in the body.
  c. changes in the skin's elastin.
  d. all of the above.

3. Which of the following physical changes is more common for women than for men?
  a. decreasing bone mass
  b. change in angle of the hip-femur joint
  c. both A and B
  d. neither A nor B

4. Which of the following is likely to be true by the end of middle age?
  a. Half of middle-aged adults will have hypertension.
  b. Back strength drops to about 75 percent of its maximum level.
  c. Most experience an increase in gastric juice secretion.
  d. All of the above are correct.

5. Which of the following accurately reflects attitudes toward physical aspects of aging?
  a. Husbands who believe that their wives have become less physically attractive report less satisfaction with marital sex and more unfaithfulness.
  b. Wives who believe that their husbands have become less physically attractive report less satisfaction with marital sex and more unfaithfulness.
  c. Both husbands and wives who believe that their spouses have become less physically attractive report less satisfaction with marital sex and more unfaithfulness.
  d. Beliefs that their spouses have become less physically attractive affect neither husbands' nor wives' unfaithfulness or satisfaction with marital sex.

6. Menopause is to _____ as climacteric is to _____.
  a. females; males
  b. event; period of time
  c. normal; abnormal
  d. physical; psychological

7. During the climacteric, production of estrogen
  a. increases.
  b. remains constant.
  c. drops.
  d. ends.

8. A survey of middle-aged women taken in the 1960s found that they believed that the best thing about menopause was
   a. not having to worry about getting pregnant.
   b. not having to bother with menstruation.
   c. greater enjoyment of their sex life.
   d. a better relationship with their husband.

9. A sex difference in the sexual response cycle is that
   a. males are more likely to experience multiple orgasms.
   b. females experience a two-stage orgasmic phase.
   c. females experience a shorter resolution phase.
   d. males have a refractory period during the resolution phase.

10. Which of the following causes the most physically based impotence?
    a. multiple sclerosis
    b. diabetes mellitus
    c. arteriosclerosis, hypertension, and antihypertensive medications
    d. hypogonadism and other endocrine disorders

11. Which of the following is a risk for midlife childbearing?
    a. Down syndrome
    b. prolonged labor
    c. toxemia and placental complications
    d. all of the above

12. Which type of health risk answers the question: "How likely is it that I will die from this health risk compared to someone not exposed to this risk?"
    a. population-attributable risk
    b. absolute risk
    c. relative risk
    d. all of the above

13. Which statement is most accurate about the relationship between socioeconomic status and obesity?
    a. In developed countries, adult females are much more likely to be obese if they are in lower socioeconomic levels.
    b. In developing countries, adult females are more likely to be obese if they are in higher socioeconomic levels.
    c. In developing countries, adult males are more likely to be obese if they are in higher socioeconomic levels.
    d. All of the above are correct.

14. Although the Type A personality is no longer believed to lead to heart attacks, some researchers believe that its _____ component may be linked to subsequent coronary problems.
    a. hostility
    b. competition
    c. impatience
    d. ambition

15. Which of the following life events is ranked as the most stressful on the Life Events Questionnaire?
    a. victim of rape or other violent act
    b. divorce or breakup with a lover
    c. death of a child or spouse
    d. legal troubles resulting in being held in jail

16. Females have a higher rate of _____ cancer.
    a. liver
    b. lung
    c. esophagus
    d. gallbladder

17. Which of the following is a classic symptom of adult-onset (Type-II) diabetes?
    a. fatigue
    b. thirstiness and frequent urination
    c. unexplained weight loss
    d. all of the above

18. Postformal operational thinking is also called _____ thinking.
    a. practical
    b. problem-finding
    c. abstract
    d. problem-solving

19. Memory changes in middle age are most evident in
    a. increases in time required to process information.
    b. recognition ability.
    c. visual memory.
    d. short-term memory ability.

20. Compared to others, experts are those who
    a. rely strongly on formal rules and procedures.
    b. are less vulnerable to problems created by lapsing into automaticity.
    c. trust their accumulated experience and make intuitive leaps.
    d. tend to work from one preferred theoretical perspective.

Answers

1. B [LO-1,2].	8. B [LO-9].	15. C [LO-16].
2. D [LO-3,4].	9. D [LO-10].	16. D [LO-18].
3. C [LO-3,4].	10. B [LO-11].	17. D [LO-19].
4. A [LO-5].	11. A [LO-12].	18. B [LO-20].
5. A [LO-6].	12. C [LO-13].	19. A [LO-21].
6. B [LO-7].	13. D [LO-14].	20. C [LO-22].
7. C [LO-8].	14. A [LO-15].	

chapter 15

Personality and Social Development in Middle Adulthood

Key Terms

Habituation
Hyperhabituation
Midlife crisis
Generativity versus stagnation or self-absorption
Caring
Transcendence
Animus
Anima
Empty-nest phenomenon
Extended households
Emotional pursuer
Emotional distancer
Parental divorce effect
Joint custody
Serial marriage
Power
Exploitative power
Manipulative power
Competitive power
Nutrient power
Integrative power
Power stress
Reentry career
Early retirement
Burnout
Dysfunctional workplaces

Learning Objectives

1. Identify patterns of personality trait stability and change through the middle adulthood years.
2. Define habituation, hyperhabituation, and midlife crisis.
3. Explain the significance of the midlife crisis from several theoretical perspectives.
4. Discuss various stage theories of personality development in middle adulthood, with particular emphasis on the theories of Erikson, Peck, and Levinson.
5. Describe Jung's views on the change from youth to midlife and the potential personal growth during middle adulthood.
6. Compare and contrast gender differences in personality development in middle adulthood.
7. Assess the effects of historical events, such as the Great Depression and World War II, on attitudes toward parenting, career patterns, and marriage.
8. Explain the effects of the empty-nest phenomenon on marital satisfaction.
9. Describe cultural differences in the prevalence of extended households.
10. Identify different patterns of and factors associated with marital satisfaction.
11. Discuss marital problems, including domestic violence.
12. Explain the impact of divorce on children of different ages.
13. Identify possible causal factors for the upward trend in the divorce rate.
14. Describe the predivorce and recovery phases of divorce.
15. Contrast the characteristics of remarriages with those of first marriages.
16. Identify characteristics associated with middle-aged unmarried individuals.
17. Distinguish among five kinds of power and the steps of power development.
18. Describe career patterns of second careers, reentry careers, and early retirement.
19. Discuss the career problems of burnout and dysfunctional workplaces.
20. Compare and contrast the sharing of household tasks between men and women.
21. Describe gender differences in the use of leisure time.
22. Identify patterns of change in political views, religious beliefs, and church attendance from young adulthood through middle adulthood to older adulthood.

This chapter focuses on typical patterns of middle adulthood personality development; a variety of events that may affect family life during middle adulthood, including divorce, remarriage, and offspring leaving home; and aspects of work, leisure, and political and religious involvement during middle adulthood.

Exploring Your Own Development

As individuals, we are no longer certain about the best time to get married, attend college, be career-oriented, or retire. When will you be (or were you) in the prime of your life? At what age will you (or did you) accomplish the most? Although individualized timing of events is usually welcomed in contemporary life, indefinite guidelines can add to personal anxiety, hesitation, and depression. We sometimes still judge ourselves and others by mythical timetables of how life ought to be led.

As discussed in Chapter 13, recent generations have become less certain about (or more flexible in) how to live their adulthood years. Some of the young adulthood experiences discussed in Chapter 13, such as getting married or having children, might occur during the middle adulthood years instead. Likewise, divorce and remarriage, discussed in this chapter, may occur in young adulthood, late adulthood, or not at all. As shown in Table 15.1, since the middle of the 20th century, adults exhibit less consensus on the most appropriate age range for adult experiences. Compare your own experiences and those of your family and friends with the survey results in Table 15.1. With how many of the age ranges do you agree?

Personality Development in Middle Adulthood

Continuity Versus Transformation

Does personality change much during the adult years? Psychologists have taken both positions. Stage theorists believe that fairly orderly change occurs during adulthood. However, some personality theorists take the position that, although personality can change in the adult years, it typically does not (e.g., McCrae & Costa, 1984; Shanan, 1985). Regardless of social and historical changes, most individuals exhibit stable personality patterns.

Trait Stability

A longitudinal study in which adults from their 20s to their 70s were given personality inventories found strong personality stability (Costa & McCrae, 1980). Young adults who were high in such characteristics as assertiveness and gregariousness typically remained high in these characteristics in middle adulthood.

Norma Haan (1981) found more personality stability in women than men from adolescence through middle age. Stable characteristics included self-confidence, emotional

Many middle-aged couples take the time to appreciate the little pleasures in life.

control, and levels of self-disclosure. Even slowly changing characteristics, such as nurturance, sexuality, and hostility, exhibited some continuity.

Ravenna Helson and Geraldine Moane's longitudinal study (1987) of women as college seniors (1958 and 1960), at age 27, and at age 43 revealed that stability is prevalent during these years but that some changes do occur by middle adulthood. According to this study, during their 20s, women increase in self-control and tolerance and decrease in regression, dependency, impulse expression, and masculinity. By their early 40s, women increase in dominance, independence, and concentration and decrease in responsibility, flexibility, denial, and femininity. As shown in Table 15.2, women in the early middle adulthood years believed that several of their feelings and attitudes had changed.

Hyperhabituation

Kastenbaum (1984) defined aging in terms of **habituation,** the decreasing attention to repetitive stimuli in life. In other words, according to Kastenbaum, middle and later adulthood are marked by a growing tendency to overadapt to daily routines and expectations and a lessening tendency to be flexible and adaptable to change in the world.

The decrease in attention to repetitive stimuli probably is not a handicap of most middle-aged adults. Indeed, some middle-aged adults feel increased appreciation for small, daily events as fewer parenting responsibilities and increased career stability permit time to linger over a cup of coffee, converse with their spouses, or enjoy a gorgeous sunset. Moreover, automated responses to routine work

Table 15.1
Middle-Aged, Middle-Class Consensus on Best Age for Life Events

	Appropriate Age Range	Percentages Agreeing			
		Late 50s		Late 70s	
		Males	Females	Males	Females
Best Age for a Man to Marry	20 to 25	80%	90%	42%	42%
Best Age for a Woman to Marry	19 to 24	85	90	44	36
Best Age to End School and Go to Work	20 to 22	86	82	64	57
When Men Should Be Settling Into a Career	24 to 26	74	64	24	26
When Women Have Most Responsibility	25 to 40	93	91	59	53
When Women Accomplish the Most	30 to 45	94	92	57	48
When Men Have Most Responsibility	35 to 50	79	75	49	50
When Men Accomplish the Most	40 to 50	82	71	46	41
Men's Prime of Life	35 to 50	86	80	59	66
When Men Hold Their Top Jobs	45 to 50	71	58	38	31
When Adults Should Become Grandparents	45 to 50	84	79	64	57
When Adults Should Be Ready to Retire	60 to 65	83	86	66	41

From A. Rosenfeld and E. Stark, "The Prime of Life" in *Psychology Today,* 63–72, May, 1987. Reprinted with permission from Psychology Today Magazine Copyright © 1987 Sussex Publishers, Inc. From B. L. Neugarten, et al., "Age Norms, Age Constraints, and Adult Socialization" in *American Journal of Sociology,* 70, 1965. Reprinted with permission of The University of Chicago Press.

Table 15.2
Statements Rated Higher in Describing Feelings About Life by Women in Early Middle Adulthood Years Than in Young Adulthood

Independence, Confidence, and Competence

Having a Good Sense of Being My Own Person
Feeling More Confident
Having a Wider Perspective
Focusing on Reality; Meeting the Needs of the Day and Not Being Too Emotional About Them
Having Influence in My Community or Area of Interest
Feeling My Life Is Moving Well
Felling Secure and Committed
Feeling Interest in Things Beyond My Own Family
Feeling Powerful

Relationships, Interest in Roots, and Introspection

Appreciating and Being Aware of Older People
Making an Effort to Ensure That Young People Get Their Chance to Develop
Being More Involved With Parents and Siblings
Feeling a New Level of Intimacy
Feeling Women Are More Important to Me Than They Used to Be
Having an Interest in My Family Tree or Ancestral Culture
Having an Intense Interest in Inner Life
Having Religious and Philosophical Interests
Discovering New Parts of Myself

From R. Helson and G. Moane, "Personality Change in Women from College to Midlife" in *Journal of Personality and Social Psychology,* 53, 176–186, Table 3 p. 181, 1987. Copright 1987 by the American Psychological Association. Reprinted by permission.

tasks are required for becoming an expert at a task: Such automaticity allows for faster processing and intuitive leaps (see Chapter 14).

However, some middle-agers seem to exist in a numbing rut. In **hyperhabituation,** adults cling to extreme continuity—fearing all change, resisting the future, and insisting on experiencing life in a consistent way (Datan, Rodeheaver, & Hughes, 1987). Although many teenagers may view their parents' dislike of heavy metal music and clothing fads as hyperhabituation, this extreme aversion to adaptation is rare.

Midlife Crisis

The opposite of midlife as habituation is midlife as crisis-driven. Elliot Jacques (1965) coined the term **midlife crisis** in his study of the effects of aging and change on the artistic styles of 310 artists. Jacques believed that midlife crisis resulted from people dealing with issues of their own mortality.

Of the theorists discussed in this chapter, Carl Jung and Daniel Levinson most strongly write about midlife crisis. George Valliant suggested that midlife crises are rare. Research findings are varied but suggest that midlife crises are not the typical experience of middle-aged persons. Most middle-aged men view themselves as more "together" than they were as young adults (Farrell & Rosenberg, 1981). Norma Haan (1981) found no clear evidence of a midlife crisis among men and women in two longitudinal studies that followed subjects from their adolescence into their 40s.

Script Theory

When script theory was discussed in Chapter 6 on early childhood, the emphasis was on young children asking for stories about how holidays are celebrated and what first days of school are like so that they can structure their behavior to fit an appropriate script. As middle-aged adults, individuals have well-developed, well-rehearsed scripts that have been influenced by their particular environment, culture, and historical period (Tomkins, 1986).

Not only do middle-aged adults have the rules and skills to control later scenes with their scripts by supplementing and replacing scripts, they can also use these skills to rewrite the past. As Carlson (1981) stated:

> *Constructions of the past may be radically changed in the light of later experience; anticipations of the future may color the present and revise the past; old experiences may return to alter the present. (p. 503)*

One implication of these abilities is that individuals may not be able to accurately describe their own experiences and changes over their lifetime. For example, the changes in feelings expressed by middle-aged women in Table 15.2 are based on subjective appraisals. Are they accurate? In this instance, the changes are consistent with score changes on the California Psychological Inventory, taken at ages 21, 27, and 43 (Helson & Moane, 1987). However, in some studies, there are sizable differences between subjective or biographical data and empirical data. Which is more flawed—the life-story memories of individuals or psychologists' statistical representations of adults (Datan et al., 1987)?

Stage Theorists—The Role of Transitions

Growth and Contraction

Charlotte Buhler. Some stage theorists view the first half of life as a period of growth and the second half as a period of contraction. Charlotte Buhler (1968) based her ideas on the studies of 400 biographies and autobiographies collected in Vienna in the 1930s. In studying the course of lives, she compared the parallels of the biological cycle with phases in living. The five biological phases consisted of:

1. Progressive growth (up to the age of 15)
2. Continued growth and ability to reproduce sexually (ages 15 to 25)
3. Stability of growth (ages 25 to 45)
4. Loss of sexual reproductive ability (ages 45 to 65)
5. Regressive growth and biological decline (from age 65 on)

The five phases of living that Buhler matched with the five biological phases were:

1. Being a child at home and not yet having self-determination of goals
2. Being in preparatory expansion and experimentation; a time of self-determination of goals

3. Experiencing culmination and having definitive and specific self-determination of goals
4. Undertaking self-assessment of how well one has strived and achieved one's goals
5. Experiencing either fulfillment of goals or failure; although some original goals and previous activities continue, there can be a reemergence of short-term goals that focus on satisfying immediate needs

As you can see, the first three phases of Buhler's model are fueled by growth or stability of growth, and the last two phases are triggered by the end of growth and the experience of physical losses. In her model, the turning point of middle adulthood is self-assessment, a task that typically occurs in the mid-40s.

Generativity

Erik Erikson. During the middle adulthood years, individuals are in the seventh of Erik Erikson's eight psychosocial stages, that of **generativity versus stagnation or self-absorption.** Characteristics of this stage are given in Table 15.3. Individuals spend more time in this psychosocial stage than in any other stage. Successful stage completion results in the positive quality of **caring,** the widening concern for "what has been generated by love, necessity, or accident" (Erikson, 1976).

Robert Peck. Robert Peck (1968) elaborated on the last two stages of Erikson's model. Since these two psychosocial stages cover about 50 years, Peck suggested that they needed to be split into more specific crises. Of the seven tasks given in Table 15.3, the first four are primarily dealt with during middle age, and the last three are more applicable to old age. According to Peck, during these years, less emphasis is placed on physical powers and sexuality, and more emphasis is placed on wisdom and socializing; middle-aged adults also need to strive for emotional and mental flexibility, rather than rigidity.

George Valliant. George Valliant (1977) viewed midlife as a search for a sense of generativity. He believed that radical and dramatic changes are rare and that most shifts are triggered by the natural transitions occurring in work and family. In midlife, many adults shift away from career achievement emphasis and toward inner exploration. Within the family, middle-aged parents often have adolescent children, which results in thinking about the world in which their offspring and grandchildren will live. Because of differences in timing of events in adult lives, midlife may begin from age 30 to about 50. Valliant found that these years are often more satisfying and happy than early adulthood years.

Defining Pathways and Tasks

Daniel Levinson. Several psychologists have proposed typical pathways and tasks during the adulthood years. Daniel Levinson's stages were discussed in Chapter 12, and Figure 15.1 reviews Levinson's stages. The three major tasks during middle adulthood are: (1) reviewing

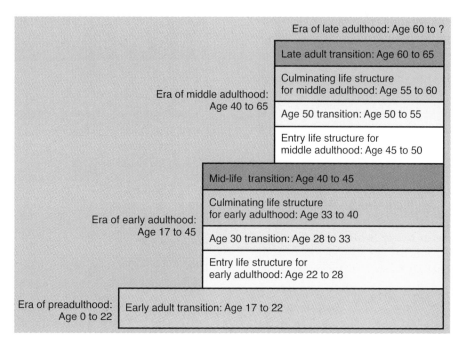

Figure 15.1
Levison's "seasons" of development.
Source: Data from D. J. Levinson, et al., *The Season's of a Man's Life,* 1978. Alfred A. Knopf, Inc.

Table 15.3
Erikson's Generativity Versus Stagnation Psychosocial Stage and Peck's Developmental Tasks

Erikson's Seventh Psychosocial Stage

Generativity

- Concern for Establishing and Guiding the Next Generation
- Concern for Humankind
- Concern for Creativity and Productivity
- Benefiting the Community and the World
- Self-Discovery and Self-Expression

Versus Stagnation and Self-Absorption

- Self-Concern and Self-Indulgence
- Killing Time on the Job
- Obsessive Need for Pseudointimacy Rather Than Real Intimacy
- Personal Impoverishment or Psychological Invalidism

Peck's Elaboration of Erikson's Stage: Seven Tasks of Middle and Late Adulthood (First four are primarily during middle adulthood; last three are primarily in late adulthood)

1. Valuing Wisdom Versus Valuing Physical Powers
2. Socializing Versus Sexuality
3. Emotional Flexibility Versus Emotional Impoverishment
4. Mental Flexibility Versus Mental Rigidity
5. Ego Differentiation Versus Work-Role Preoccupation
6. Body Transcendence Versus Body Preoccupation
7. Ego Transcendence Versus Ego Preoccupation

Sources: Data from E. H. Erikson, *Childhood and Society,* 1950, W. W. Norton and Company, New York, NY; R. C. Peck, "Psychological Developments in the Second Half of Life" in *Middle Age and Aging,* 1968, edited by B. L. Neugarten, University of Chicago Press, Chicago, IL.

and reappraising young adulthood, (2) modifying unsatisfying aspects of life, and (3) resolving issues introduced by entrance into the second half of life (Levinson, 1978).

Levinson's model is characterized by alternation of 6- to 8-year periods of stability and 4- to 5-year periods of transition. Transition periods can be triggered by external events, but Levinson emphasized the role of internal factors. He also suggested that about four out of five people experience tumultuous struggles within the self and with the external world, thereby implying that midlife crises are common (Levinson, 1978).

Levinson's original work was based on the data of one cohort of middle-aged men, but cross-cultural support has been found for the alternating periods of stability and transition, along with substantiation of the age 30 transition and the age 40 to 45 midlife transition (Levinson, 1986). In addition, some support has been established among female samples (Roberts & Newton, 1987).

Roger Gould. Roger Gould (1978) focused on the cognitive challenges of the midlife transition. According to Gould, during this period, several ideas that may have served as guidelines in the first half of life are challenged and modified to be more realistic. Gould wrote, "Childhood delivers most people into adulthood with a view of adults that few could ever live up to" (Rosenfeld & Stark, 1987), and during midlife, these impossible images are addressed. For example, middle-aged adults can no longer believe that "there is no evil or death in the world." The following statements are often dealt with and modified in these years:

1. "The illusion of safety can last forever."
2. "Death can't happen to me or my loved ones."

3. "It is impossible to live without a protector."
4. "There is no life beyond this family."
5. "I am an innocent."

Michael Farrell and Stanley Rosenberg. Michael Farrell and Stanley Rosenberg (1981) proposed four paths for men through middle adulthood (see Table 15.4). They also suggested that men often have trouble negotiating these years because society forces men to conform to a narrow standard of success and masculinity; during midlife, men may feel like failures because they assess themselves as having failed to meet society's standard or because they realize how they set aside their own desires in order to reach society's standard.

Nancy Schlossberg. Nancy Schlossberg is another psychologist who does not believe in a single timetable for adult development. Focusing on female development, she wrote:

> *Give me a roomful of 40-year-old women and you have told me nothing. Give me a case story about what each has experienced and then I can tell if one is going to have a crisis and another a tranquil period. What matters is what transitions she has experienced. . . . It is what has happened or not happened to her, not how old she is, that counts. (Rosenfeld & Stark, 1987, p. 69)*

Schlossberg (1978) made five general propositions about adult development:

1. Behavior in adulthood is determined by social, rather than by biological, clocks.
2. Behavior is at times a function of life stage, at others of age.
3. Gender differences are greater than either age or stage differences.
4. Adults continually experience transitions requiring adaptations and reassessments of the self.
5. The recurrent themes of adulthood are identity, intimacy, and generativity.

Carl Jung's Views of Middle Adulthood

Carl Jung (1875–1961) was a Swiss psychodynamic theorist whose archetypal theory was greatly influenced by Sigmund Freud's psychoanalytic theory, world religions, and cultural mythology. Jung acknowledged the possibility of middle-age rigidity, but he advocated middle adulthood as a time of growth, balance, and increased self-understanding. In fact, Jung is among the first therapists who viewed the second half of life as more important than the first half.

The Ending of Youth

Freud believed that adult personality was basically formed during the first 6 years of life. Jungian theory is quite different. For example, Jung believed that children may be problems to parents and educators but that, normally, children do not have problems of their own—only adults have self-doubt.

Table 15.4
Farrell and Rosenberg's Paths of Development in Middle Age

Path 1: The Transcendent-Generative
- Does Not Experience a Midlife Crisis
- Has Found Adequate Solutions to Major Life Problems
- Finds That Midlife Can Be a Time of Fulfillment and Accomplishment

Path 2: The Pseudo-Developed Man
- Uses Facade of Success to Cover Feelings of Desperation, Loss, and Confusion
- Maintains Facade Through Adherence to Rigid Ways of Thinking and Behaving
- Feels Bored or Has Sense of Having Been Passed by

Path 3: The Midlife Crisis Type
- Has a Sense of Being Confused, Overwhelmed, and Alienated by the Demands of Midlife
- Has the Feeling That the Whole World Is Disintegrating
- Cannot Meet Demands and Solve Problems
- May Continue on Path of Depressive Decline

Path 4: The Punitive-Disenchanted Type
- Shows Signs of Midlife Crisis
- Has Been in a State of Unhappiness and Alienation for Much of Life
- Displays Psychosomatic Symptoms, Distrust, Hostility Toward Others, Depression, and Inability to Improve Life

Source: From Farrell, M. P., & Rosenberg, S. D. 1981. *Men at Midlife*. Auburn House, an imprint of Greenwood Publishing Group, Inc., Westport, CT.

Jung (1933) labeled the period from after puberty to middle adulthood (age 35 to 40) as youth. According to Jung, youth is a time period in which to give up childish dreams and ideas, deal with sexuality, confront feelings of inferiority, and widen life's horizon. Individuals who are unable to leave childhood for youth experience neurotic disturbance.

As people near the age of 40, the period of youth comes to an end. The end of youth does not come with a definitive sign. Jung (1933) observed:

> *It is rather a matter of indirect signs of a change which seems to take its rise in the unconscious. Often, it is something like a slow change in a person's character; in another case, certain traits may come to light which had disappeared since childhood; or again, one's previous inclinations and interests begin to weaken and others take their place.*

Years of Becoming Whole or Rigid

The loss of youth can be traumatic, especially in modern societies that idealize youth over experience and wisdom. For some, the end of youth may be accompanied by acedia, a kind of depressed self-paralysis in which zest for life is gone and the individual is flooded by hurtful memories and remembrances of shortcomings. Individuals may be overwhelmed by sadness and anger. Bianchi (1987) described this experience as the "dark night of the soul" and as being in a "cloud of unknowing."

Two unhealthy patterns may develop from this harsh initiation into middle adulthood. Some individuals try to cling to youth, a choice that Jung thought produced neurotic disturbance. This pattern can be marked by hyperactivity—becoming more competitive, being more frenetic at work, getting involved in more strenuous sports, and increasing number of sexual conquests (Bianchi, 1987).

Other individuals reject the opportunity to break through into growth and fulfillment and choose to become hardened and to rigidly hold onto cherished convictions and principles. In other words, this mode involves the hyperhabituation discussed earlier in the chapter. This midlife reaction is one of hypoactivity—curtailing interests, acting old, complaining about life, and becoming more intolerant and fanatical (Bianchi, 1987).

However, acedia can be a temporary state that transforms individuals into deeper healing (Bianchi, 1987). Carl Jung's personal end to youth occurred in 1913, when he and Freud suddenly ended their relationship. For 3 years, Jung was unable to read a scientific book and instead withdrew into himself and explored his fantasies and dreams. At the end of this "dark period," he was able to formulate his original archetypal theory (Jung, 1961).

The middle adulthood years can be ones in which the most significant personal growth is underway. Jung believed that, during this time period, individuals can grow by changing toward their opposite qualities to achieve personal self-actualization. In other words, intellectuals may become more active and worldly, while those in the business world may become more contemplative in order to balance their psyches. For most adults, growth involves utilization of emotions, symbols, and intuitions, and less reliance on intellectualization and rational reasoning (Squyres, 1987).

Crucial to this period is the turning of attention inward to find meaning and wholeness in life. A second and higher form of self-actualization is **transcendence,** or spiritual self-actualization, involving the striving for unity, wholeness, and integration of the personality and the universe.

Gender Roles in Middle Adulthood

Men and women behave more alike than differently, but gender differences are found—in small habits to large life-shaping behaviors. Can you correctly identify which of the following are more true of men and which are more true of women?

1. Flip channels during a television program
2. Earn a bachelor's or master's degree
3. End a friendship after discovering the friend is a homosexual

Although women continue to do the majority of house cleaning chores, in middle age males may engage in more tasks outside their traditional gender role.

4. Buy greeting cards
5. Be in a traffic accident
6. Take dictation
7. Receive a pension
8. Vote in presidential elections
9. Buy junk food
10. Take vitamins
11. Think it is easier to be a man than a woman

Were the answers easy? All of the even statements are more typical of women, and all of the odd statements are more typical of men—except that number 11 is true of both men and women.

How do gender differences change with age? Some gender-specific behavior, such as differences in the division of responsibility for household tasks (discussed later in this chapter), seems to last a lifetime. However, most research suggests that gender differentiation lessens throughout adulthood. Both men and women tend to become more androgynous with age, with men becoming more expressive and women becoming more assertive and aggressive (Brubaker, 1985).

According to Jung (1933), androgyny occurs because of the midlife trend toward balance or completeness of the psyche. Although persons are born either male or female, the archetype of the other gender in the collective unconscious allows some understanding of the opposite sex. Women have the male symbol **animus** in their unconscious awareness, while men have the female symbol **anima.** Jung believed that, during youth, men and women are basically building their conscious gender identity, but that in middle adulthood, they tap into the unconscious animus or anima and become more androgynous.

A series of studies by Feldman and her associates produced findings consistent with Jung's model (e.g., Abra Feldman, Devin-Sheehan, & Allen, 1981; Feldman & Aschenbrenner, 1983). The studies showed that both young adult males and females increase in gender-typing in the young adult years. Through the middle years, both men and women increase their self-ratings on traits typically judged as more appropriate for the opposite sex. Women especially tend to shift their sense of identity from family to sense of self around the end of their 30s. Women who do revise their goals tend to feel better about their lives than women who do not make this shift (Droege, 1982).

Regardless of whether cultural influences or life stage is largely responsible for the lessening of gender differences during the second half of life, it is important to remember that, throughout the entire life cycle, men and women are more alike than different.

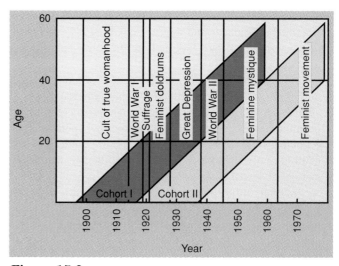

Figure 15.2
Historical experiences of two cohorts of midlife women.

Family Life in Middle Adulthood

Effects of Historical Events on Family Formation

How family life is experienced during middle adulthood partially depends on the Zeitgeist, the historical experiences of a particular time period. As shown in Figure 15.2, females born in the early 1900s were exposed to different experiences than females born in the 1930s. The older group experienced a short suffrage movement, followed by feminist doldrums and the Great Depression, before they were 40. The women in the younger group, however, were children during the Great Depression and young adults during World War II and the feminine mystique period, a time in which traditional gender roles were prevalent. These events influenced attitudes about marriage, the importance of parenting, and career patterns.

The older women's young adulthoods were influenced by getting the right to vote and by family struggles to survive the Great Depression. The younger women might have held traditionally masculine jobs during World War II but then settled into the American dream of marriage, home, and 2.2 children. The feminist movement was beginning as they headed into middle adulthood.

Psychologists tend to study effects in terms of chronological age (e.g., comparing 25-year-olds with 45-year-olds on attitudes toward marital satisfaction) or family units (e.g., effects of preschool versus school-age children on marital satisfaction), and few studies deal with the effects of historical movements on lives. Yet, as shown in Figure 15.3, historical events do influence life patterns. Figure 15.3 shows the modal patterns of family formation for three different time periods. Each bar represents the age range during which 80 percent of those women who ever experienced the transition made it. The postwar pattern addresses the young adulthood experiences of the younger cohort in Figure 15.2. Note how this time period had the most consistent timing of events: A majority of women left their parents' home, got married, became sexually active, and became parents within a relatively short number of years in early young adulthood.

Contrast that pattern with the contemporary pattern. Notice how the bars do not begin and end in the same narrow space. Marriage and parenthood are especially drawn out, indicating that women are now getting married and becoming parents at a variety of ages.

The 19th-century pattern showed the most diversity, and this early pattern is closer to that of the 1980s than the pattern of the 1950s. What do you view as the similarities and differences in the three patterns? What events do you think created these patterns? How do diverse family formation patterns make psychological research harder?

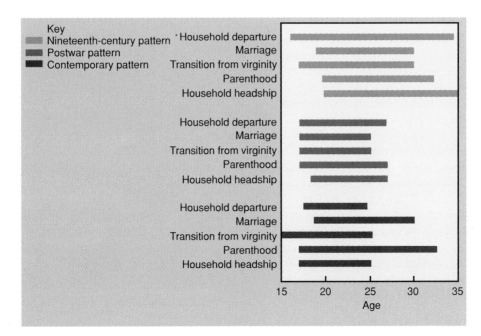

Figure 15.3

Shifts in modal patterns of family formation for women in the United States. (a) Nineteenth-century pattern. (b) Postwar pattern (1950s). (c) Contemporary pattern.

Source: Data from F. F. Furstenberg, Jr. and G. B. Spanier, *Recycling the Family: Remarriage After Divorce*, fig 3.1, page 50, 1987. Sage Publications, Newbury Park, CA.

Relationships with Children and Parents

Parenting Teenagers and Adult Children

As noted in Chapter 14, some middle-aged adults decide to have "last-chance" babies and to begin years of active parenting at a later age. However, more middle-aged adults are dealing with either teenage children or adult children.

Parents often find the years of dealing with adolescent children to be stressful for their marriage (Steinberg & Silverberg, 1987). They struggle with learning how to be more flexible with their children and how to "let go" of control over them. Learning to view their children as emerging adults with their own lives to live is a long and difficult task for parents.

Some parents of adolescents find themselves jealous and resentful of their children's opportunities. Others must deal with their disappointment and frustration regarding their expectations and how their children actually turned out. Some parents of teenagers become more passive in parenting guidance than desired by their children. Another typical problem is parents expressing their viewpoints to adolescent offspring and not trying to understand their teenagers' viewpoints (Hunter, 1985b).

Parents' relationships with adult children, on the other hand, are often easier and more satisfying, especially if parents encourage their children's independence, are nonintrusive consultants on issues, and serve as role models for intimacy and career. In this time period, parents typically are giving more to their adult children than vice versa (Aldous, 1987; Troll, 1986).

The Empty-Nest Phenomenon

Middle-aged parents often must deal with the **empty-nest phenomenon,** which is when the children move out of the household. While the empty-nest phenomenon was once thought to be a transition that led to increased emotional depression for adults, research findings indicate that the most typical emotional experience is relief. When children leave the home, many marriages attain a higher level of happiness. The increase in marital satisfaction can be attributed to: (1) the increase in privacy that encourages more spontaneity and increased intimacy; (2) fewer financial obligations and more money to spend on entertainment, leisure, and travel; and (3) more time to share communication and experiences with each other (Gilford, 1984).

Not all 18- to 21-year-olds leave their parents' household, however. In actuality, over a third of adult offspring ages 18 through 29 are living in one or both parents' home. The reasons for adult children living at home are numerous: The offspring may be single parents, may have low-paying jobs, may still be in school, or may be emotionally immature. In many cases, parents enjoy having adult children at home more than having adolescent children at home because adult children often have more respect for parental values, help out more with household tasks, and are more likely to contribute to household finances. On the other hand, some parent/adult children households are marked by serious conflict and disagreements over independence/dependence issues.

New Roles with Parents

Middle-aged adults modify their relationships with their parents. In a minority of American homes, the parents of middle-aged adults are in their offsprings' homes. In these **extended households,** multiple generations live together. Although the impression is that, historically, extended households were common, they were never the rule. In England from 1574 to 1821, extended households accounted for only 6 percent of families (Kimmel, 1990).

In the United States, Native Americans and African Americans are more likely than European Americans to reside in extended households. The majority of both older Pueblo Indians and older Sioux Indians are members of extended families (Murdock & Schwartz, 1978; Rogers & Gallion, 1978). American families headed by elderly women are more likely to include relatives younger than age 18 in African-American households (48 percent) than in European-American households (10 percent) (Staples, 1976).

Although most middle-aged adults do not have their parents living with them, most do have regular contact with their parents. Ethnic differences exist for frequency of parental contact. For example, 79 percent of Italian Americans and 65 percent of Polish Americans, but only 39 percent of middle-aged American adults of English or Scandinavian heritage, visit their parents weekly (Greeley, 1971). These differences are partially influenced by what group is viewed as the major source of support. Adults of Italian, Mexican, Polish, and Jewish heritage tend to see the family as their major support network. Scandinavians, on the other hand, rely more on social organizations, and individuals of African and Irish heritage rely most on friends (Woehrer, 1978).

During middle adulthood, adults usually learn to view their parents objectively—neither idealizing them nor overblaming them. Sometime during this time period, they are also likely to realize that their parents are old and growing in vulnerability (Kimmel, 1990). However, they are also likely to feel the closest to their parents during this time period. In one study of women ages 35 to 55, relationships with parents were described as emotionally close, rewarding, and lacking conflict (Baruch & Barnett, 1983). Chapter 17 presents more on relationships with elderly parents.

Marriages

At the beginning of the 20th century, marriages lasted around 35 years. Now, marriages not ending in divorce last an average of nearly 45 years. What are the typical patterns of long-term marital satisfaction? What factors are associated with marital satisfaction and marital problems?

Patterns of Marital Satisfaction

Measuring satisfaction with married life is difficult. For example, the question "Would you marry the same person again?" might provide an indication of marital satisfaction. Yet, contradictory results were obtained by national magazines asking this question: A *Woman's Day* 1986 survey reported that only 50 percent of women would marry the

Hispanics are more likely to live in extended families than are Anglo-Americans.

same man, while a *Ladies Home Journal* 1988 survey reported that 88 percent of women would make the same commitment (Associated Press, 1988; Faludi, 1987). Differences in contemporary studies challenge psychologists and readers to explain diverse findings.

When are couples most satisfied with their marriage? Researchers have found more than one pattern (Ade-Ridder & Brubaker, 1983). A few studies suggest that satisfaction peaks early in marriages and then declines (e.g., Blood & Wolfe, 1960; Peterson & Payne, 1975; Pineo, 1961). Several other studies suggest the opposite—that satisfaction and happiness with the marriage grow over time. This result is typically attributed to growing similarity between the spouses (e.g., Kohn, 1987; Scram, 1979).

The most typical pattern of marital satisfaction, especially in recent research, is curvilinear (e.g., Ade-Ridder & Brubaker, 1983; Anderson, Russell, & Schumm, 1983; Gilford, 1989; Gruber-Baldini & Schare, 1986; Miller, 1976; Rollins & Feldman, 1970). As illustrated in Figure 15.4, a common pattern is high initial satisfaction, a significant decrease in satisfaction during active parenting years, and an increase in satisfaction as grown children leave the household. A variation of this pattern is a second lowering of satisfaction after the age of 70 (Gilford, 1984; Miller, 1976).

Parenting responsibilities are not the only influence on this curvilinear pattern: Communication patterns of married couples also can be traced over the life cycle. Positive aspects, such as discussing issues, cooperating with each other, and sharing laughter, tend to follow the U-shaped curve; negative aspects, such as being sarcastic, expressing anger, and disagreeing on issues, tend to decline from the young adulthood years on (Gilford, 1984).

One other trend needs to be mentioned: Until recent surveys, married individuals reported being much happier than individuals who were never married, divorced, or widowed. However, from 1972 to 1986, the number of

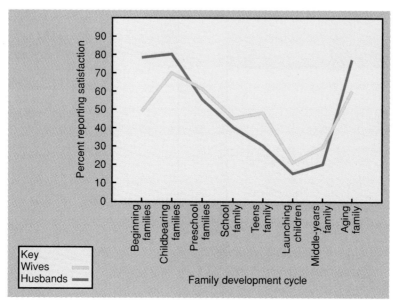

Figure 15.4

Marital-parental satisfaction over the family development cycle.

Source: Data from B. C. Rollins and H. Feldman in "Marital Satisfaction Over the Family Life Cycle" in *Journal of Marriage and the Family*, pp. 20–28, February 1970. National Council on Family Relations, Minneapolis, MN.

married individuals who defined themselves as "very happy" declined, especially among married women. During that period, the never-marrieds reported an increase in happiness (Glenn, 1987; Glenn & Weaver, 1988).

Factors of Marital Satisfaction

Marital satisfaction involves finding meaning in marriage. A recent study of married Roman Catholic couples living in New England found three major meanings of marriage (Guerin, Fay, Burden, & Kautto, 1987): First, marriage can be viewed as having social meaning in that the couple conducts family business and carries out community obligation. Second, the marriage can have sacred meaning and be viewed as a commitment with God and as having a religious-moral dimension. Third, marriage can emphasize individual meaning in that the demands of marriage are subordinate to individual well-being and happiness. In this study, 65 percent of the subjects ranked individual meaning as first; only 10 percent ranked social meaning as the "most important."

What specific factors influence marital satisfaction? Carl Rogers (1972) suggested that long-term intimate relationship focus on the four basic elements listed in Table 15.5. Successful marriages involve a commitment and willingness to work hard on the marriage. Happily married individuals are willing to openly communicate and to express their emotions; they also listen to and empathize with the comments and feelings of their partners. Happily married couples shape their own roles as spouses, rather than accept cultural stereotypes or family and friends' expectations. Finally, although the relationship is important, satisfactorily married persons maintain separate, individual identities.

Table 15.5
Carl Rogers's Four Basic Elements of Long-Term Marriages

1. Dedication of Commitment
2. Communication—The Expression of Feelings
3. Nonacceptance of Roles
4. Becoming a Separate Self

From C. R. Rogers, *Becoming Partners: Marriage and Its Alternatives*, 1972. Copyright © 1972 Doubleday, a division of Bantam, Doubleday, Dell Publishing Group, Inc., New York, NY. Reprinted by permission.

A study of 292 rural Alabama families found that the expressiveness of husbands was the sole significant predictor of both husbands' and wives' marital adjustment (Lamke, 1989). Consistent with several urban studies, marriages in which husbands were sensitive to their wives' needs and expressed their warmth and compassion were the most satisfactory. In American culture, most women are socialized to be expressive in relationships, so female expressiveness does not serve as a predictor, although the expressiveness of wives is also needed for marital satisfaction.

High sexuality does not predict marital satisfaction, although husband-wife similarity in sexual needs and expression is helpful (Fincham & O'Leary, 1983; Lauer & Lauer, 1985). Other specific qualities are more important: Self-confidence, perception of fairness and equity, trust, shared activities and time, friendship, belief in marital commitment, strong religious beliefs, love, and goal agreement aid marital satisfaction (Fincham & O'Leary, 1983; Kohn, 1987; Lauer & Lauer, 1985; Stinett, Sanders, DeFrain, & Parkhurst, 1982; Wilson & Filsinger, 1986).

Table 15.6
Factors Contributing to Marital Dissatisfaction and Sample Items Used in Their Measurement

1. Global Distress. "My marriage has been disappointing in several ways."

2. Affective Communication. "I'm not sure my spouse has ever really loved me."

3. Lack of Problem-Solving Communication. "My spouse and I seem to be able to go for days sometimes without settling our differences."

4. Lack of Time Together. "My spouse and I don't have much in common to talk about."

5. Disagreement About Finances. "My spouse buys too many things without consulting me first."

6. Sexual Dissatisfaction. "My spouse sometimes shows too little enthusiasm for sex."

7. Role Orientation. "A wife should not have to give up her job when it interferes with her husband's career."

8. Family History of Distress. "I was very anxious as a young person to get away from my family."

9. Dissatisfaction With Children. "My children rarely seem to care how I feel about things."

10. Conflict Over Child-Rearing. "My spouse doesn't assume a fair share of taking care of the children."

From D. Snyder, "Multidimensional Assessment of Marital Dissatisfaction" in *Journal of Marriage and the Family*, 41, p. 816, 1979. Copyrighted 1979 by the National Council on Family Relations, 3989 Central Ave. NW, Suite 550, Minneapolis, MN 55421. Reprinted by permission.

Table 15.7
Stereotypes of Typical Power Uses Within Marriage

Female Types of Power
- Helplessness
- Nagging
- Sexuality
- False information
- Indirect information
- Appeal to friendship of other common identity

Male Types of Power
- Expert
- Direct information
- Legitimate (inherent in gender role)
- Coercion
- Reward

From Paula Johnson, "Women and Power" in *Journal of Social Issues*, 32, No. 3, 99–110, 1976. Reprinted by permission of The Society for the Psychological Study of Social Issues.

Marital Problems

Table 15.6 lists some of the factors that contribute to marital dissatisfaction. Several are the opposite of characteristics defining marital satisfaction.

The major personality characteristic predicting low marital satisfaction, marital instability, and divorce is neuroticism (Kelly & Conley, 1987; Kohn, 1987). Neuroticism is associated with emotional instability, marital arguments, emotional overreactions, and sexual problems. Poor impulse control among men is another predictor of marital problems in that it is associated with infidelity, alcohol abuse, and other irresponsible social behavior.

Differences in gender-role preferences also contribute to marital problems. In a study of 331 Air Force couples, the lowest levels of marital adjustment were found among couples in which the husbands had traditional gender roles and wives were nontraditional (G. L. Bowen, 1987). Since many adults become more androgynous with age, mutual adjustment to gender-role changes and other personality changes can help to alleviate marital problems (Zube, 1982).

In traditional marriages, couples may rely on stereotypical uses of power, listed in Table 15.7. Within this model, husbands tend to dominate the marriage, while wives make more concessions and rely on subtle, indirect influences. Because they use more direct power, men are usually more reluctant than women to give up the traditional marriage pattern. Yet, this pattern can create emotional binds that contribute to marital dissatisfaction.

Marriage is not an effortless long-term relationship. In fact, marriage can be described as a constant struggle that can either be enriching or deadly (Guerin et al., 1987). One of the biggest problems occurs when couples get emotionally constrained and locked into old scripts, rather than developing emotional freedom and better relationships.

Marital emotional traps involve either extreme or emotional reaction. One dysfunctional response is to become an **emotional pursuer** who repeatedly brings up painful issues without working toward resolving them. The emotional pursuer, in effect, keeps "pouring salt over open wounds." The other dysfunctional response is to become an **emotional distancer** who prematurely closes a painful issue and compartmentalizes marital hurts and disappointments. Couples who use these patterns can learn better communication patterns (Guerin et al., 1987).

Marital problems can also go unresolved by the use of triangles. Triangles involve using a third person or group to increase marital stability without reducing dysfunctional aspects of the marriage. Common triangle patterns include blaming one of the children for the problems, blaming one or more in-laws, viewing marital problems in terms of a wicked-stepparent or the absent parent, blaming everything on an extramarital affair, or using church or social organizations to stabilize a marital dyad (Guerin et al., 1987).

Domestic Violence

Some marriages are afflicted with domestic violence, or physical abuse. More than one in four couples admit to violent acts in marriage, and some experts estimate that the actual rates are closer to one in two. Shoving and slapping are the most common forms of physical abuse (Flynn, 1987).

The exclusivity, intensity, and commitment of marital relationships not only can lead to intimate happiness—these qualities can also foster violent acts. Risk factors include inequality between husband and wife, high levels of

Shelters for battered women and their children provide safety, support, and insight into the dynamics of abusive relationships.

stress, and males with high need for power (Flynn, 1987; Mason & Blankenship, 1987).

The two most common reactions to abuse are anger and confusion. Some abused persons view the violence in terms of love; a smaller number view the violence as signifying hate. Some tolerance comes from childhood exposure to domestic violence, either as an observer of violence or as a child victim of abuse (Flynn, 1987). Some domestic violence situations involve a high degree of mind control, such as imposing dominance, isolation, fear arousal, guilt induction, enforced loyalty, promotion of powerlessness, pathological jealousy, and secrecy due to shame and bewilderment (Boulette & Andersen, 1985).

Domestic violence is not limited to any socioeconomic group or belief system. However, some religious backgrounds may give messages to the abused person that make it more difficult to end the violence. Messages that emphasize faith, forgiveness, and submission without changes on the part of the batterer may actually increase the amount and severity of the violence. Religious victims may especially have difficulty distinguishing between the temporary expression of remorse and the behavioral commitment involved in repentance (Whipple, 1987).

Divorces

Decisions about divorce are made by adults. Often, however, children are also affected. Effects of divorce on children and parents are discussed in the "Exploring the Parent/Child Relationship" feature.

Divorce Trends

In 1860, only 5 percent of marriages ended in divorce; today, that figure is 50 percent. Throughout the 20th century, the incidence of divorce has risen. The rate of increase slowed during the Great Depression of the 1930s but then sharply increased immediately after World War II and again from the 1960s through the 1980s (Ahrons & Rodgers, 1987; Rice & Rice, 1986).

Factors that contributed to the divorce trend include the Industrial Revolution, which changed the emphasis from survival based on the family unit to that of individual effort. Moreover, industrialization increased urbanization, which further changed the role of the family and increased opportunities outside of the family (Ahrons & Rodgers, 1987; Breault & Kposowa, 1987). Gradually, marriage came to be seen as less crucial, and divorce began to have less social stigma. Older women were the first group to become more approving of divorce, but now younger adults hold the most favorable views (Thornton, 1985).

Also in the last century, the views of organized churches regarding divorce became less important to most individuals. In addition, organized churches often became more flexible in their attitudes toward divorcing couples. The Roman Catholic church's views on divorce influenced parishioners less from 1962 to 1980. Interestingly, during this same time period, the influence of fundamentalist Protestant churches increased (Thornton, 1985).

Another important factor is that divorces became easier to obtain legally. Into the 19th century, a woman's only option for ending a marriage was to desert her husband and children. Then the husband could put notice of the desertion in a newspaper and officially end the marriage. Well into the 20th century, most state laws allowed divorces only for limited reasons that required assignment of blame to either the wife or husband. Today, no-fault divorce is available in every state (Rice & Rice, 1986).

The Divorce Process

Although the stigma of divorce has lessened and fewer legal obstacles to divorce exist, getting a divorce is not an easy decision, and living through the process is quite stressful. Both members of the couple experience about the same amount of stress, but the one who initiates the divorce experiences the stress earlier (Buehler, 1987).

The predivorce phase may be described as "the beginning of the end" (Golan, 1981). During this phase, the couple falls out of love and the partners' attachment to each other erodes. This painful period involves increased anxiety, unhappiness, and distress. Ambivalence is exhibited in erratic sleep patterns, confusion, reconciliation attempts, hostility, and sporadic periods of intimacy.

The predivorce phase involves areas listed in Table 15.8. Although many couples considering these aspects do move on to divorce, fewer than half of couples with high scores on this scale get a divorce within 3 years. Some couples may work out their difficulties, since this phase is a common time for entering counseling (Edwards, Johnson, & Booth, 1987; Storm, Sheean, & Sprenkle, 1983).

Younger couples are more likely to get a divorce. Living in an urban area, unemployment, not attending church, and being childless are other factors that increase the odds of becoming divorced (Rice & Rice, 1986; Thornton, 1985). Interestingly, couples with sons are less likely to get divorces than are couples with daughters (Morgan, Lye, & Condran, 1988).

For those couples who do divorce, the divorce process and immediate period of adjustment are difficult. This phase is often more difficult for men than for women. Men are relatively unaware of marital problems prior to the

Exploring the Parent/Child Relationship: Divorce and the Kids

Effects of Parental Divorce on Children

Although divorce occurs between a husband and a wife, it also affects offspring, even though the children may be told that they are not, and never will be, abandoned by their parents. Each year, over a million American children experience the divorce or separation of their parents; by high school graduation, more than a third of all children will have lived with a divorced parent (Block, Block, & Gjerde, 1986; Santrock, 1987). Effects on children depend on their age at the time of the divorce. Major effects are summarized in the table.

Developmental Changes in Children's Reactions to Divorce

Age	Reaction
2½ to 6	Children have difficulty expressing their feelings. They have poor understanding of divorce and separation concepts. Children tend to blame themselves, even if parents carefully tell them that they are not responsible.
7 to 8	Children often feel rejected. They can more easily verbalize their sadness than their anger. Children tend to blame one parent, rather than to view divorce as a mutual arrangement between the parents. They may fear being abandoned.
9 to 10	Children can express anger toward their parents but often feel a combination of loyalty and anger, or simultaneous loving and hating of a parent. Children often hide their sadness and present a strong facade. They often feel lonely and unloved.
Adolescence	Teenagers often have strong feelings of anger, shame, sadness, and embarrassment. They can exhibit the ability to analyze their parents' marriage and the needs and feelings of each parent.

Source: Data from J. B. Kelly and J. S. Wallerstein, "The Effects of Parental Divorce: Experiences of the Child in Early Latency" in *American Journal of Orthopsychiatry,* 46, 20–32, 1976. From J. S. Wallerstein and J. B. Kelly, "The Effects of Parental Divorce: The Adolescent Experience" in *The Child in His Family: Children at Psychiatric Risk,* Vol. 3, edited by J. Anthony and C. Koupernik, John Wiley & Sons, New York, NY. From J. S. Wallerstein and J. B. Kelly, "The Effects of Parental Divorce: Experiences of the Preschool Child" in *Journal of the American Academy of Child Psychiatry,* 14, 600–616, 1975.

Boys seem to experience more negative effects prior to the actual divorce. Predivorce boys are characterized by poor impulse control, aggression, and excessive energy. Predivorce girls are less affected. This sex difference continues after the divorce. Boys experience stronger negative effects for a longer period of time after their parents' divorce (Block et al., 1986).

Effects of Parental Divorce on Children's Adult Relationships

Girls who grow up in one-parent families due to divorce are more likely to marry and bear children early, to give birth before marriage, and to experience divorces of their own (McLanahan & Bumpass, 1988). One reason for this pattern is that these girls develop an increased interest in and dependency on males; girls whose fathers have died are more likely to have an inhibited relationship with males. Adolescent girls who experience parental divorce are often described as aggressively social, while daughters of widows are more likely to be wallflowers (Hetherington, 1972). A second explanation is that single-parent families provide less supervision, less discipline, and encourage more peer pressure

(Hogan & Kitagawa, 1985; Steinberg, 1987b).

In the United States, especially among white females, there is a significant **parental divorce effect** in that children of divorced parents are more likely to get a divorce than are children of intact marriages (Glenn & Kramer, 1987). According to Judith Wallerstein, children of divorce seem to be quite apprehensive about enduring heterosexual relationships and marriage. As adolescents, they express fear that they might repeat their parents' failure; indeed, a high proportion of them say that they do not plan to ever get married (Wallerstein, 1983). However, they get married at the same rate as others *and* also tend to get married at a younger-than-average age. Perhaps the contradictory aversion and attraction to marriage results in a lower marital commitment (Glenn & Kramer, 1987).

Effects on Parents of Divorcing Adults

Less research has been conducted on how the parents of the divorcing couple are affected by the divorce. It is known that, in the year following the divorce, the amount of interaction between divorced adults and their parents increases. Parental support is associated with ability of the divorcing persons to cope (Lesser & Comet, 1987). In many cases, supportive and understanding grandparents can help children to deal with the divorce of their parents. At times, parents of those going through divorce provide financial as well as emotional support.

Sources: Kelly, J. B., & Wallerstein, J. S. (1976). The Effects of Parental Divorce: Experiences of the Child in Early Latency. *American Journal of Orthopsychiatry,* 46, 20–32. Wallerstein, J. S., & Kelly, J. B. (1974). The Effects of Parental Divorce: The Adolescent Experience. In J. Anthony & C. Koupernik (Eds.), *The Child in his Family: Children at Psychiatric Risk* (Vol. 3). New York: Wiley. Wallerstein, J. S., & Kelly, J. B. (1975). The Effects of Parental Divorce: Experiences of the Preschool Child. *Journal of the American Academy of Child Psychiatry,* 14, 600–616.

divorce, whereas most women find the predivorce phase particularly difficult and experience some relief once the divorce occurs (Chiriboga, 1982).

Some recently divorced persons make extensive attempts to change their self-image. Some become involved in casual sexual relationships to compensate for the loss of marital intimacy. Divorced persons develop new coping strategies for a wide range of changing practical and personal issues (Golan, 1981). According to Bohannan (1971), persons going through a divorce deal with six divorce arenas: emotions, law, economics, coparenting, community, and psychology.

Table 15.8
Indicators of Marital Instability—Assessing
Divorce Proneness

Sometimes, married people think they would enjoy living apart from their spouse. Do you often feel this way?

Even people who get along quite well with their spouse sometimes wonder whether their marriage is working out. Have you thought your marriage might be in trouble within the last 3 years?

As far as you know, has your spouse ever thought your marriage was in trouble?

Have you talked with family members, friends, clergy, counselors, or social workers about problems in your marriage within the last 3 years?

As far as you know, has your spouse talked with relatives, friends, or a counselor about problems either of you were having with your marriage?

Has the thought of getting a divorce or separation crossed your mind in the last 3 years?

As far as you know, has the thought of divorce or separation crossed your spouse's mind in the last 3 years?

Have you or your spouse seriously suggested the idea of divorce in the last 3 years?

Have you talked about dividing up property?

Have you talked about consulting an attorney?

Have you or your spouse consulted an attorney about a divorce or separation?

Because of problems people are having with their marriage, they sometimes leave home either for a short time or as a trial separation. Has this happened in your marriage within the last 3 years?

Have you talked with your spouse about filing for divorce or separation?

Have you or your spouse filed for a divorce or separation petition?

Count the number of Yes answers.

Score	Chance of Divorce in the Next 3 Years
0 to 2	22%
3 to 4	26%
5 to 6	31%
7 to 9	38%
10 to 14	43%

From J. N. Edwards, et al., "Coming Apart: A Prognostic Instrument of Marital Breakup" in *Family Relations*, 36, 168–170, from Table 1, p. 169, 1987. Copyrighted 1987 by the National Council on Family Relations, 3989 Central Ave. NE, Suite 550, Minneapolis, MN 55421. Reprinted by permission.

Divorcing men and women rely on family members during this phase of divorce. Family members rally more around divorcing men than women. Divorced women are more likely to rely on kinfolk if they have children and low incomes; divorced men rely more on kinfolk if they have children and high incomes. Divorced men are more likely to have nonkin help in household tasks (Gerstel, 1988).

In addition to emotional issues, divorcing couples make many practical, economic decisions. About 90 percent of divorcing couples agree upon decisions involving alimony, rehabilitative maintenance, child support, child custody, and division of assets (including the house, retire-ment benefits, and businesses and professional practices) outside of the courtroom (Roha, 1987b).

Maternal custody is more common than paternal custody. Another option is **joint custody,** in which both parents share responsibility for decisions concerning the children. When parents are able to work together and conflict is minimal, joint custody is usually preferable to sole custody (Derdeyn & Scott, 1984; Emery, Hetherington, & Dilalla, 1984). Flexibility in custody decisions is desirable to aid adaptation to children's changing needs. For example, small children may benefit most from frequent, short visits with each parent; older children may need longer but less frequent visits (Wallerstein & Kelly, 1980).

The pattern of maternal custody is consistent with cultural beliefs in women as "kinkeepers." Married couples are usually closer to the wife's mother than to the husband's mother; closer relationships are more likely to develop with daughters-in-law than with sons-in-law. Even in intact families, offspring view their relationships with their mothers as closer and more important (Johnson, Klee, & Schmidt, 1988). Maternal custody may lead to additional distance between offspring and fathers.

Recovery from Divorce

Some divorced persons are negatively affected for at least a decade (Wallerstein, 1986), and being divorced is associated with higher suicide rates (Stack, 1990). However, most divorced persons are rebuilding their lives by the second year following divorce (Golan, 1981). Recovering from divorce is more difficult for individuals in middle and late adulthood (Chiriboga, 1982), and for individuals who did not use the predivorce phase well (Melichar & Chiriboga, 1988).

According to Spira (1981), following the divorce, individuals work through several emotional experiences, including: (1) self-criticism due to beliefs that adequate, lovable persons have spouses who keep fulfilling their needs; (2) depression due to loss of a significant relationship and emotional emptiness; (3) anger and hostility toward the ex-spouse; (4) guilt for initiating the divorce or for being inadequate to maintain the marriage; (5) emotional deprivation or a sense of being cheated in the marriage; (6) euphoria and overexpectations of the fun and freedom of being single; and (7) omnipotence and grandiose fantasies about available and potential lovers. Moreover, divorced individuals must redefine their sense of identity and intimacy (Rice & Rice, 1986).

Remarriages

In the American culture, the majority of divorced persons remarry. However, some cultures show different patterns of divorce and remarriage. The Japanese pattern is the topic of the "Exploring Cultural Diversity" feature.

Incidence of Remarriage

Studies by Bumpass et al. (1990), Cherlin and McCarthy (1985), Furstenberg (1981), and Furstenberg and Spanier (1987) revealed the following about remarriage:

- Half of all marriages involve at least one remarrying individual.

Exploring Cultural Diversity: Marriage, Divorce, and Remarriage in Japan

The Japanese pattern of marriage, divorce, and remarriage differs from the pattern in the United States (Cornell, 1989). For example, Japanese adults marry later than do American adults. Eighty percent of Americans who marry do so between the ages of 18 and 30 (see Figure 15.3). Most Japanese marry in their mid-20s; in other words, their marriage age is more concentrated. Within marriages, husbands and wives have more segregated roles in Japan than is typical in the United States.

American and Japanese divorce rates differ. In America, divorce rates increased during the 20th century, particularly after World War II and from the 1960s on. However, divorce rates in Japan stayed consistently low after World War II. In the 1950s, the number of divorces per 1,000 population was 0.85 in Japan and 2.4 in the United States. The 1970s rate was 1.0 in Japan and 4.6 in the United States (Cornell, 1989).

Perhaps a higher percentage of Japanese married couples are satisfied with their marriages. On the other hand, the divorce rate might be much lower than in the United States because divorce has more social stigma in Japan, especially for women who are referred to as *Kizu mono,* or damaged goods. Helen Hardacre (1984) wrote:

> While marriage is considered necessary for all [Japanese] women, divorce is regarded as a great failure, a lifelong shame. Divorced women and their children are under a heavy stigma in contemporary Japanese society. Furthermore, divorced women with young children typically face dire economic problems, particularly if the former husband is unwilling to support them. Once a woman has left the labor force, it is extremely difficult to reenter it except on a part-time or take-home basis, in which case the pay, unless the woman has rare professional skills, will be extremely low. Thus, there is a great reluctance to divorce, even when there are strong grounds for doing so. (pp. 119–120)

In the United States, the majority of divorced persons want to remarry, and most do. Americans view divorce as a temporary status that is likely to lead to remarriage (Bumpass, Sweet, & Martin, 1990). In Japan, most divorced men want to remarry, but 56 percent of divorced women do *not* want to remarry. Among divorced Japanese women ages 20 to 29, 46.4 percent do not want to remarry, while only 18.6 percent of their male counterparts do not want to remarry; among divorced Japanese in their 50s, 82.2 percent of the women and 45.8 percent of the men do not want to remarry (Cornell, 1989).

Indeed, the gender discrepancy in remarriage rates is higher in Japan than in the United States and other industrialized nations. Japanese men are 1.28 percent more likely to remarry than are women; American men are 1.05 percent more likely to remarry than are women. Japanese women up to the age of 40 are 15 percent more likely to remain divorced than are European-American women; the cultural discrepancy grows after this age (Cornell, 1989).

According to Laurel Cornell (1989), several factors account for the cultural differences in divorce and remarriage rates: First, the Japanese view marriage as practical rather than romantic, and this viewpoint may help to keep the divorce rate low. Moreover, the social stigma associated with divorce in Japan may keep some marriages together that would dissolve in other cultures. Japanese women who do get divorced are likely to have been in the most disappointing marriages and therefore may remain aversive to the institution of marriage. Finally, Japanese women are more likely than American women to blame themselves and to be blamed by society for the failure of the marriage; these attitudes limit both desire for and opportunity to remarry.

- Four of five divorced persons remarry.
- The median number of years from marriage to divorce is about 7 years, and the median number of years from divorce to remarriage is about 3 years.
- One in four children will have more than two parents by age 18.
- Nearly 10 million children live with a biological parent and a stepparent.
- More European-American women remarry than do African-American women.
- Eighty percent of women divorced before the age of 25 remarry within 5 years.
- One in every five households involves at least one remarried person.

Remarriage was almost as common in the 19th century as it is now, but a century ago, widowhood was the antecedent of remarriage rather than divorce. Remarriages involved replacement, rather than rearrangement (Furstenberg, 1981; Furstenberg & Spanier, 1987).

Characteristics of Remarriages

Men are more likely to get remarried than are women. This gender difference is attributed to three factors: (1) More women are available, due to higher rates of male mortality; (2) men tend to marry younger women; and (3) divorced men tend to marry never-married women (Furstenberg & Spanier, 1987). The age of women at the time of their divorce affects their chance of remarriage; remarriage for

Table 15.9
Reported Comparisons of Former and Current Marriages

A. Self-Reports of Communications With Current and Former Spouses

How Often Did the Following Occur in Your Marriages?	Never	Less Than Monthly	Once or Twice Monthly	Once or Twice Weekly	Daily	More Than Daily
Have a stimulating exchange of ideas?						
Former marriage	36%	29%	16%	16%	3%	0%
Current marriage	2	2	10	54	25	8
Laugh together?						
Former marriage	13	8	24	32	18	5
Current marriage	2	0	2	3	52	42
Calmly discuss something?						
Former marriage	21	16	16	26	16	5
Current marriage	2	0	2	13	47	37

B. Frequency of Confiding to Spouses

	Never	Rarely	Occasionally	More Often Than Not	Most of the Time	All of the Time
Former marriage	19%	21%	11%	13%	19%	16%
Current marriage	0	2	0	2	47	50

C. Who is the "Boss" in the Relationship?

	Man	Both	Woman
Males			
Former marriage	31%	46%	23%
Current marriage	19	73	8
Females			
Former marriage	28	47	25
Current marriage	19	75	6

Source: Data from F. F. Furstenberg, Jr. and G. B. Spanier, *Recycling the Family: Remarriage After Divorce,* Tables 3.1 p. 68, 3.2 p. 69, and 3.4 p. 72, 1987, Sage Publications, Newbury Park, CA.

women who divorce after age 40 is much lower than for their male counterparts (Bumpass et al., 1990).

The courtship period for remarriages is shorter than with first marriages. In one study, first marriages averaged courtships of 17 months, and second marriages involved courtships of only 9 months (O'Flaherty & Eels, 1988).

Remarriages themselves are different. They tend to be less romantic and more practical. Those who remarry view marriage in less idealized ways and are more aware of potential hazards. They may have to deal with emotional spillover from the early marriage, such as continued comparisons between the present and the previous relationships or disagreements over issues involving children from the former marriage. Boys tend to adapt more easily to stepparents than do girls (Hobart, 1988).

On the other hand, remarriages are more likely than first marriages to involve egalitarian and overlapped roles, and second-chance marital partners rate themselves as more supportive, tolerant, effective, and open in communication (Furstenberg & Spanier, 1987). As shown in Table 15.9, remarriages are rated much higher than first marriages. Of course, these ratings were done after the first marriage had ended in divorce; if the ratings had been taken during the first marriage, they might have been higher.

Are remarriages satisfactory? In general, men are more satisfied in remarriages than are women (Vemer, Coleman, Ganong, & Cooper, 1989). Although Table 15.9 suggests that remarriages are much improved, remarriages have a higher divorce rate than first marriages (O'Flaherty

As with heterosexual couples, homosexuals in long-term relationships seem to be better adjusted than those who have had several sexual partners.

& Eels, 1988). This high divorce rate may indicate that experiencing one divorce makes that decision easier to make again.

Serial Marriages

One emerging lifestyle is the **serial marriage,** a remarriage pattern in which an individual has been married at least three times. Often, each successive marriage is shorter in length, and with multiple divorces, there is less guilt, anxiety, and depression following the divorce. Persons engaging in the serial marriage pattern tend to be higher in social nonconformity, extroversion, adventurousness, risk taking, and alcohol/drug use, although this typical portrait may change as serial marriage becomes a more common lifestyle (Brody, Neubaum, & Forehand, 1988). Unlike persons in a second marriage, individuals in serial marriages are likely to believe that mistakes from earlier marriages are repeated in remarriage.

Research needs to be conducted on the effects of multiple divorces on children. This lifestyle would likely have the following effects: (1) recurrent exposure to interparental conflict, (2) additional attachment disruptions, and (3) multiple periods of diminished parenting capacity (Brody et al., 1988).

The Unmarried

Unmarried middle-aged adults have not been the focus of as many research studies as married and divorced middle-aged adults. However, studies suggest that unmarried heterosexuals represent "just another way of life." Compared to married individuals, they tend to be more independent, relatively isolated, but rather satisfied with solitary activities (Gubrium, 1976). About 1 in 20 persons is still single at age 50 (Katchadourian, 1987). The number of lifelong, never-married individuals has been declining across the last two decades (Brubaker, 1985).

Some never-married individuals are in cohabitation relationships. In many respects, these relationships are similar to marriages. Cohabitation is increasing among younger adults but decreasing among middle-aged and older adults (Brubaker, 1985).

Finally, long-term homosexual relationships are not uncommon. During middle adulthood, homosexuals in long-term relationships seem to be better adjusted than those who have a number of sexual partners (Katchadourian, 1987).

guided review

6. The most typical emotional reaction of parents experiencing the empty nest is _____.
7. Marital satisfaction follows a typical curvilinear function; that is:
   A. satisfaction is greater before and after the most active parenting years.
   B. satisfaction is greatest during the most active parenting years.
   C. satisfaction increases constantly throughout the marriage.
   D. none of the above.
8. Shoving and slapping are the two most common forms of the major marital problem of _____.
9. In the United States, a significant _____ effect exists in that children of divorced parents are more likely to get a divorce than are children of intact marriages.
10. Which of the following is true of remarriage?
   A. Remarriage occurred almost as frequently in the 19th century as today.
   B. The courtship period is shorter for remarriages.
   C. Remarriages tend to be less romantic and more practical.
   D. All of the above are true.

answers

6. relief [LO-8]. **7.** A [LO-10]. **8.** domestic violence [LO-11]. **9.** parental divorce [LO-12]. **10.** D [LO-15].

Work and Leisure in Middle Adulthood

Need for Power

One feature of middle adulthood that appears in both work and leisure is the exercise of power. **Power** is the ability to cause or prevent change. Power involves the need to have impact upon or control over others (May, 1972; McClelland, 1975). Typically, power is highest around midlife in both career and society (Verloff, Reuman, & Feld, 1984).

Types of Power

What is your image of power? Is power positive or negative? Does it help or hinder others? Are you ambivalent about wanting power? Some individuals equate power with being violent, destructive, and abusive, but power can be used to improve, nurture, and advance. Some idealize innocence over power, but innocence often involves ignorance about real problems. The opposites of power include weakness, helplessness, and impotence—all undesirable characteristics (May, 1972).

Rollo May (1972) proposed the existence of five kinds of power:

1. **Exploitative power** (used on another), the most destructive form, is when an aggressor allows a victim no options. Playground bullies, tyrants, and battering spouses use this type of power.

2. **Manipulative power** (used over another) is another negative power. This power is between individuals of unequal resources, and the more influential person takes advantage. For example, manipulative power can occur between parent and child, teacher and student, boss and employee, and therapist and client.

3. **Competitive power** (used against another) can be either negative or positive. In its negative use, one person gets to advance because another person declines. In its positive use, competitive power is stimulating and constructive. Competitive power is common in business exchanges, athletic games, and sibling rivalry.

4. **Nutrient power** (used for another) is when one person is concerned with another's welfare and uses power to advance or comfort another. Nutrient power typifies parent-child relationships, intimate friendships, and social movements.

5. **Integrative power** (used with another) is the highest, most constructive form of power. Here, power is performed with the other person instead of merely for the other person. Situations that involve nutrient power could also involve integrative power.

Which kinds of power do you typically use? What kinds of power have you experienced with family members? In school systems? In workplaces? How do political and spiritual leaders that you admire address power?

Developmental Steps of Power

David McClelland (1975) proposed a four-step developmental model of power. Each step is learned in order, and all learned steps are available to be used. The first step involves power through dependency and others' support. In this step, a person gains power from being near sources of strength, such as friends, family, organizations, and employees. Individuals in this stage may like serving an important person, bragging about family accomplishments, identifying with winning teams, and choosing friends who are popular and influential.

The second step emphasizes autonomy, self-reliance, and internal control. In this step, individuals want to increase control over body and mind and involve themselves in such activities as bodybuilding, yoga, meditation, and psychology. Or, they may collect possessions that are viewed as extensions of themselves.

The third step is power through competition, assertion, and influence. As with May's competitive power, McClelland views this third step as potentially positive or negative.

The fourth step emphasizes selfless service to an ideal, such as commitment, togetherness, or transcendence. Step 4 individuals satisfy power by subordinating personal goals to a higher authority, possibly in religion, politics, social service, science, or business. This step reflects characteristics of May's nutrient and integrative power types.

Characteristics of Power

Need for and expression of power appear to be strongest around midlife (Verloff et al., 1984). Surprisingly, the nature and level of power seem to be about the same for men and women. The expression of power in careers, for example, is similar for both sexes in the areas of teaching, counseling, journalism, and business (Winter, 1988).

Even in more detailed traits and expressions of power, sex differences rarely exist: Both high-power men and women carry more credit cards, read status magazines, make similar decor and clothing style choices, and act more visibly and impressively in social settings. The few traits associated only with high-need-for-power males are drinking and drug use, physical and verbal aggression, gambling, exploitive sex, and reading sex-oriented magazines (Winter, 1988).

Inhibiting a personal need for power produces **power stress,** a chronic sympathetic activation resulting in high epinephrine levels, high blood pressure, and impaired immune systems. Power stress is associated with high rates of respiratory infections, as well as frequent and severe illnesses (Fodor, 1985; McClelland, 1982). Rather than inhibiting power, efforts should be made to express healthier kinds of power.

Career Stability Versus Career Change

Career Patterns

Some people believe that the optimal career path is having a single lifetime career. However, having more than one career during the working years is more typical: About one in four adults is currently making a career transition (Datan et al., 1987). The reasons for entering a second career (or more) are many. Some career changes are forced by obsolete jobs, unemployment, or an unsatisfying workplace. Sometimes, career patterns change because of a new opportunity. Other career changes are solely due to changes in an employee's motivations. Workers in second careers usually are more productive and higher in achievement motivation than those remaining in a single lifetime career (Schultz & Schultz, 1986).

A career pattern that is more common among women is the **reentry career.** Some adults step out of the work force for a few years, often because of parenting tasks. This choice is so prevalent among women that the popular press has referred to it as "the mommy track." Adults choosing this path often do not advance as far within the workplace.

Burnout involves emotional exhaustion and the overwhelming feeling that one can not accomplish one's work. Nurses experience a high burnout rate.

Table 15.10
Words That Describe Dysfunctional Work Organizations

Confusion	Powerlessness
Poor Communication and Distortions	Secrets and Denial
Dishonesty and Ethical Deterioration	Gossip, Misquotes, and Lies
Spiritually Bankrupt	Judgmentalism
Seduction	Manipulation
Frozen Feelings and Paralysis	Sexism, Racism, and Ageism
Chaos	Crisis Orientation
Quick Fixes and Packaging	Perfectionism
Isolation	Control
Avoiding Responsibility	Conflict Avoidance
Vindictiveness	Forgetfulness
Addictions	

Source: Key Words from J. A. Simons in *Describing Dysfunctional Work Organizations,* at the "Surviving Dysfunctional Workplaces" Workshop in Des Moines, IA, November 1990.

Another career path is **early retirement,** or stepping out of the work force before the mid-60s (and not entering a second career). Since World War II, the number of men ages 55 to 64 who are in the labor force has declined from 89.6 to 80.5 percent (Katchadourian, 1987).

Job Satisfaction

Typically, midlife is the career period in which adults experience the most career satisfaction. Professionals especially experience the peak rewards of the training, experience, contacts, and energy that they have plowed into their work for years. On the other hand, only half of workers seem to be satisfied with their jobs. Although more than 90 percent of university professors would rechoose their same career, only 20 percent of blue-collar workers would make the same choice (Katchadourian, 1987).

Career Problems

Occupational Stress and Burnout

Many middle-aged workers express feelings of stagnation and of being pushed aside by younger workers. Some employees experience temporary feelings of uselessness or of being used. Changes in their work environment or job attitudes can reduce occupational stress levels. So can reevaluating the importance of their work in the total picture of their lives and placing more importance on family or community issues (Katchadourian, 1987).

Some workers, especially those in helping professions, experience a prolonged and unhealthy phenomenon called **burnout.** Burnout involves emotional exhaustion and the overwhelming feeling of not being able to accom-

plish a job. Burned-out workers experience a sense of helplessness and lack of control over their work.

Typically, burnout comes on gradually, with growing symptoms of headaches, fatigue, insomnia, respiratory and digestive health problems, conflict with others, and possible substance abuse. Persons with burnout are often depressed, withdraw from interpersonal relationships, and pull back from work responsibilities (Maslach & Jackson, 1985). Changing stressful aspects of the job, getting a significant break from work, or changing careers are possible ways of alleviating burnout.

Dysfunctional Workplaces

Burnout and other career problems may be attributable to functional problems associated with the workplace itself. Sometimes, occupational stress is related to a few aspects of a job, such as low pay, lack of promotion, a supervisor, repetitive work, or size of work load. These aspects may or may not be tolerable for other workers. In other employment situations, most aspects of the workplace are not functioning well.

In **dysfunctional workplaces,** structural problems or personnel problems create unhealthy work environments. Dysfunctional workplaces are characterized by poor communication patterns, frequent personnel changes and changes in command, exploitation of workers, and deceptive or unethical practices. Increasingly, workers who are dissatisfied with their jobs blame the attitudes and practices of management (Schaef & Fassel, 1988; Simons, 1990). Table 15.10 provides a list of characteristics considered pervasive in dysfunctional workplaces.

Unemployment

A number of individuals become unemployed during middle adulthood. The most difficult aspects of unemployment are loss of income and decreased feelings of self-worth. Persons who have some financial resources and do not blame themselves for being unemployed do better at coping with job loss (Voydanoff, 1983). Persons who have experienced disloyalty from employers, such as being fired to be able to hire "cheaper," younger help, are especially disillusioned (Katchadourian, 1987).

Job loss often has a more severe impact on older workers. Although middle-aged and older adults are better educated, better trained, and more experienced than younger adults, they average being unemployed twice as long as younger unemployed adults. In addition, middle-aged adults expect to be "settled" into careers; unemployment in these years becomes an especially upsetting loss (Mallinckrodt & Fretz, 1988).

Prolonged joblessness produces a distinctive reaction pattern. The initial reaction is disbelief, frustration, and anger, followed by temporary relief, growing relaxation, improved hope, and increased family involvement. However, if joblessness continues, individuals become overwhelmed by self-doubt, hopelessness, and cynicism (Katchadourian, 1987).

Middle-aged unemployed persons who have social support cope better (Voydanoff, 1983). Individuals not perceiving social support during their unemployment period experience higher levels of stress symptoms, more physical health complaints, more depression, lower self-esteem, and a more external locus of control (Mallinckrodt & Fretz, 1988).

Household Work

Attitudes About Employment of Women Outside of the Home

The belief that "a woman's place is in the home" has undergone radical changes. Many women now have paid employment outside of the home, a fact that influences self-satisfaction, family members, and society as a whole. Employment of women is changing society's structure, including day-care needs and latchkey children. How does employment affect women themselves, and how does it influence household labor?

In the 1920s, one in five middle-aged women had paid employment; now the ratio is one in two (Bell, 1983). Employed middle-aged women report a higher sense of well-being than do full-time homemakers (Adelmann, Antonucci, Crohan, & Coleman, 1989). However, many full-time homemakers find the lifestyle rewarding and satisfying. Satisfied homemakers most like the homemaking tasks, autonomy, leisure time, and security-stability aspects. Among dissatisfied homemakers, dislike is directed toward homemaking tasks, lack of autonomy, too much free time, and lack of economic security (Shehan, Burg, & Rexroat, 1986). Notice that the same aspects contribute to satisfaction and dissatisfaction.

Although many women seem to be more satisfied with paid employment, husbands are more ambivalent about their wives' employment. Husbands with employed wives report lower job satisfaction and feeling less adequate as family breadwinners (Staines, Pottick, & Fudge, 1986). The majority of husbands (58 percent) consider it important to earn more than their wives (Hiller & Philliber, 1986). In addition to preserving the stereotype, men may want to be the larger earner to have more power in the relationship. In married couples, cohabiting couples, and gay couples (but not lesbian couples), the partner earning more money has more power in the relationship (Blumstein & Schwartz, 1983).

Women also hold onto images of traditional labor division, even as they become employed in record numbers. Forty-three percent of wives consider it important to be better at childcare than their husbands; 38 percent of them consider it important to be the better housekeeper (Hiller & Philliber, 1986).

Sharing Household Tasks

Table 15.11 shows husbands' and wives' perceptions about the division of household labor. In this study, 58 percent of husbands indicated that housework should be shared, yet fewer than a third help in any tasks except for food shopping and washing dishes. Husbands are more likely to participate in childcare tasks and in less regular household tasks, such as repairs and yard work (Hiller & Philliber, 1986).

Table 15.11 shows that spousal perceptions about how much husbands participate in household duties differ significantly. Spouses think that they carry more responsibility for household duties than their partners think they do. Spouses accurately perceive their partner's expectations about half the time (Hiller & Philliber, 1986).

Numerous studies reveal that employed wives continue to do much more household work than their employed husbands (e.g., Grant, 1988; Rexroat & Shehan, 1987). Women with full-time employment average 28.5 hr of housework per week, while their husbands do 5.2 hr (Rexroat & Shehan, 1987).

Household Tasks Across the Lifespan

More household work is required during active parenting years, and women spend the most hours on household labor during these years. A young female adult without children does about 18 hr a week of household chores. Her counterpart with young children does about 29 hr. Among young male adults, those without children do about 5 hr of household labor and those with young children do about 6 hr (Rexroat & Shehan, 1987).

The impact of this pattern is depicted in Figure 15.5. Throughout the adult lifespan, women who are employed full-time have longer hours of work than do their husbands; the difference is particularly dramatic during the active parenting years (Rexroat & Shehan, 1987). Do you think that this pattern will change in the future?

Leisure Values

Traditionally, the life cycle has been divided into thirds, with the first third largely devoted to learning and apprenticeship, the second third devoted to work and productivity,

Table 15.11
Husbands' and Wives' Perceptions of Division of Household Labor

	Wives' Perception			Husbands' Perception			Percentage of Agreement
	Wife Does	Both Do	Husband Does	Wife Does	Both Do	Husband Does	
Regular household tasks							
Food shopping	70%	20%	10%	67%	23%	10%	86%
Meal preparation	85	10	5	82	13	5	81
Housecleaning	80	17	3	73	23	4	78
Washing dishes	66	29	5	57	36	7	87
Washing clothes	84	10	6	81	14	5	76
Ironing	90	7	3	90	7	3	90
Managing money	42	31	27	39	38	32	65
Less regular tasks							
Household repairs	7%	13%	80%	2%	7%	91%	82%
Yard work	11	29	60	6	24	70	71
Supervision of help	72	24	4	51	34	15	56
Entertaining preparation	52	46	2	44	53	3	61
Major purchases	14	82	4	9	85	6	79
Planning recreation	16	80	4	11	83	7	72
Planning vacations	8	85	7	8	82	10	79
Childcare tasks							
Arranging activities	61%	36%	3%	58%	40%	2%	63%
Take kids to doctor	74	23	3	62	34	4	73
Stay home with sick kids	62	36	2	48	48	4	52
Get kids ready for bed	60	34	6	48	47	5	71
Get kids ready for school	82	11	7	80	16	4	81
Help kids with homework	45	41	14	35	54	11	65

From D. V. Hiller and W. W. Philliber, (Table 3, p. 186), "The Division of Labor in Contemporary Marriage: Expectations, Perceptions, and Performance". Copyright © 1986 by the Society for the Study of Social Problems. Reprinted from *Social Problems,* Vol. 33, 191–201 by permission.

and the final third devoted to retirement and leisure. However, the optimal way to live life might be to "interweave" these thirds (Datan et al., 1987). This interweaving is apparent in the growing number of adolescents who have part-time jobs, of adults who return to educational environments, and of trends involving both early retirement and working in later adulthood.

Table 15.12 indicates the pattern of leisure activities for middle-aged men and women. As you can see, definite gender differences exist, with women engaging in more social, family, and cultural activities and men engaging in more travel, physical, and community activities.

Table 15.12
Most Common Leisure Activities for Men and Women, Ages 40 to 54, From Most Frequently Reported Downward

Women	Men
1. Social activities†	1. Home-based activities
2. Home-based activities*	2. Social activities
3. Family leisure†	3. Family leisure
4. Cultural leisure†	4. Travel*
5. Travel	5. Exercise and sport†
6. Community organizations	6. Cultural leisure
7. Exercise and sport	7. Community organizations*
8. Outdoor recreation	8. Outdoor recreation†

*Reported at somewhat higher rates by this sex
†Reported at much higher rates by this sex
From J. R. Kelly, et al., in "Later Life Leisure: How They Play in Peoria" in *The Gerontologist,* 26, 531–537, 1986. Copyright © 1986 The Gerontological Society of America.

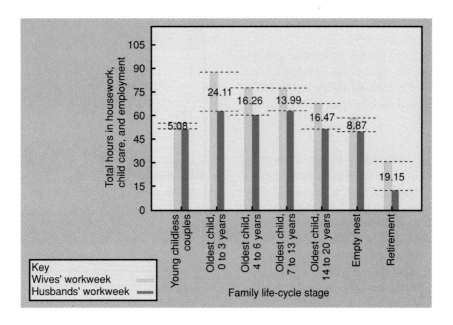

Figure 15.5
Mean total hours in workweek for husbands and wives who are employed full-time, by life-cycle stage.
Source: Data from C. Rexroat and C. Shehan, "The Family Life Cycle and Spouses' Time in Housework" in *Journal of Marriage and the Family*, 49, 737–750, fig. 1 page 746, 1987.

guided review

11. Which one of the following is not one of Rollo May's five kinds of power?
    A. exploitative
    B. machiavellian
    C. competitive
    D. nutrient
12. Career problems at midlife include _____ (feeling overwhelmed by one's job), _____ (unhealthy work environments), and unemployment.
13. Wives with full-time employment average over _____ hr of housework per week, compared to their husbands' average of about _____ hr per week.
14. Middle-aged women and men differ in the ways they are most likely to spend their leisure time, with men engaging in _____ and _____ and _____ recreation at much higher rates than women.

answers

11. B [LO-17]. **12.** burnout; dysfunctional workplaces [LO-19]. **13.** 28; 5 [LO-20]. **14.** exercise; sports; outdoor [LO-21].

World Arenas of Middle-Aged Adults

According to Erik Erikson, the psychosocial task of middle adulthood is generativity versus stagnation or self-absorption. For some, generativity leads to increased activity in the world arenas of politics and religion.

Politics

With middle-aged adults at the peak of their power, politics is often a popular activity. Carl Rogers encouraged political participation with the goals of using positive power forms. He believed that integrative power in politics was very satisfying:

> *I am most satisfied politically when every person is helped to become aware of his or her own power and strength; when each person participates fully and responsibly in every decision which affects him or her. . . . (May, Rogers, & Maslow, 1986, p. 6)*

Americans have a stereotype that older adults are politically conservative. The shift away from liberalism and toward conservatism actually is most typical of early middle adulthood. From young adulthood to middle adulthood, the number of persons labeling themselves as conservatives shifts from one fourth to over one third, a fraction that continues through old age (Russell, 1989).

A larger drop exists in the number of young adults versus middle adults who label themselves as liberals. Moreover, the decline in self-labeled liberals continues through old age. In all age groups, the most common political label is moderate (Russell, 1989).

Religion

Religious Beliefs

Generativity concerns and a growing awareness of personal mortality can lead to a greater interest in religious concerns in the middle adulthood years. Indeed, strong convictions grow from under 35 percent among young adults to 47 percent through middle adulthood. In older adulthood, the percentage who express strong religious beliefs grows to 66 percent (Russell, 1989).

Monthly or more frequent church attendance grows from just over half to more than two thirds in mid-middle adulthood and to about three fourths by the end of middle adulthood. About two thirds of middle-aged adults believe in an afterlife (Russell, 1989).

Spiritual Growth

Scott Peck (1978) suggested that religion has been too narrowly defined in terms of organized religions. According to Peck, all persons have beliefs about human nature and the world; therefore, everyone has a religion. Even if kept from consciousness, persons have and operate from such basic beliefs. For many, the image of God was formed in early childhood and then forgotten. Other areas of knowledge were acknowledged, nurtured, and developed, but many individuals have only a simplistic, childlike view of a "judging God," "loving God," and so on. Views of God are influenced by organized religions but also by the behavior of parents. Peck (1978) wrote:

> Our first (and, sadly, often our only) notion of God's nature is a simple extrapolation of our parents' natures, a simple blending of the characters of our mothers and fathers. . . . If we have loving, forgiving parents, we are likely to believe in a loving and forgiving God. And in our adult view, the world is likely to seem as nurturing a place as our childhood was. If our parents were harsh and punitive, we are likely to mature with a concept of a harsh and punitive monster-god. And if they failed to care for us, we will likely envision the universe as similarly uncaring. (pp. 190–191)

Midlife can be a time in which spiritual growth is sought. Bianchi (1987) thought that resentment toward God is often part of a midlife crisis: "After having lived well, why is God letting my life or physical being fall apart?" Disillusionment with career, possessions, and relationships may also turn individuals within or toward God. Bianchi wrote, "By midlife, the chastened self is ready for the religious journey" (p. 40). As suggested by Jungian theory, self-limitations and psychological pain allow spiritual growth, or self-synthesis. Awareness of personal faults may make forgiveness of others easier in midlife. This ability may enrich relationships and help middle-aged adults to move toward generativity. Ideally, the second half of adulthood allows heightened appreciation of the complexity of humanity.

In contrast, Erich Fromm (1976) suggested that people can hide their need to become by focusing on having things. Modern, materialistic society can mislead people into thinking that having more possessions leads to higher self-esteem, satisfaction, and happiness. People can become obsessed with work in order to buy things, rather than to find meaning in life and relationships.

Exploring Human Development

1. In small groups, list the similarities and differences among the three patterns given in Figure 15.3. Propose reasons for these patterns. Try to predict what the corresponding bars for men would be in these three time patterns. Draw a pattern for what your group thinks the chart would look like 20 years from now.
2. Develop a workshop on either occupational stress and burnout or dysfunctional workplaces.
3. Develop a list of topics that you would include in a book either on building better relationships between adult children and their parents or advice for first-time middle-aged parents.
4. Interview three middle-aged married couples on what aspects of their married lives are most satisfying.
5. Compare the impact of divorce on children by interviewing classmates whose parents are divorced. Group their responses by their age when their parents divorced (0 to 5, 6 to 10, etc.) and look for differences by ages in their recollections and reactions to their parents' divorces.

Discussing Human Development

1. Do you think that many middle-aged adults have midlife crises? Are midlife crises ever desirable? Can adolescents or young adults experience the equivalent of a midlife crisis?
2. How do you think middle adulthood is different and the same for persons in their 50s who have no children, have young children, have teenage children, or have adult children?
3. How are baby boomers experiencing middle age? Do you think their midlife experiences are similar or dissimilar to those of earlier generations? Why?
4. What are the most important factors in enjoying a job? How would you advise a person who is experiencing job stress or job discrimination?
5. How do you think general values, religious orientation, and political orientation change in the second half of life?

Reading More About Human Development

Atwood, W. (1982). *Making it through middle age: Notes while in transit.* New York: Atheneum.

Bianchi, E. C. (1987). *Aging as a spiritual journal.* New York: Crossroad.

Brubaker, T. H. (1985). *Later-life families.* Beverly Hills, CA: Sage.

Farrell, M. P., & Rosenberg, S. D. (1981). *Men at midlife.* Dover, MA: Auburn House.

Katchadourian, H. (1987). *Fifty: Midlife in perspective.* New York: W. H. Freeman.

Morris, M. (1988). *Last-chance children: Growing up with older parents.* New York: Columbia University Press.

Summary

I. Personality Development in Middle Adulthood
   A. Personality during the adult years is viewed by some theorists as continuous and mostly unchanged, while others maintain that some changes are predictable.
      1. Research on personality trait stability supports the idea that traits are relatively stable across the adult years, especially in women.
      2. One longitudinal study shows that, by middle adulthood, women have increased in concentration, dominance, independence, and some other traits.
      3. Kastenbaum believed that middle-aged adults habituate to their daily routines, which causes them to become less flexible and adaptable.
      4. In some rare situations, individuals hyperhabituate and come to fear change and greatly overemphasize continuity and consistency in their lives.
      5. Somewhat the opposite of habituation is the concept of the midlife crisis, in which individuals confront their aging and mortality, but theorists are divided in their support of this concept.
      6. Middle-aged adults have well-developed and well-rehearsed scripts with which to guide their lives and anticipate their futures, but their memories of past experiences may have changed as they have aged.
   B. Numerous theorists have proposed that personality development in adulthood is a sequence of predictable changes.
      1. Buhler's theory is based on the idea that the first half of life is a growth period, while the second half is a period of contraction, and that individuals set specific goals for adulthood and then periodically reassess them.
      2. Erikson believed that middle adulthood is characterized by his seventh psychosocial stage of generativity versus stagnation or self-absorption, in which successful resolution results in caring for others.
      3. Within Erikson's last two stages, Peck defined seven tasks that represent adaptive personality changes during middle and later adulthood.
      4. Valliant viewed midlife personality development as a shift away from concentration on career achievement toward inner exploration and generativity.
      5. Levinson's stage theory proposes that middle-aged adults experience alternating periods of transition and stability and that most middle-aged adults experience a midlife crisis.
      6. Gould's theory focuses on how middle-aged adults face the challenge of changing a number of significant cognitive beliefs that they hold about the world and their place in it.
      7. Farrell and Rosenberg, in proposing four separate pathways for the midlife psychosocial development of men, suggested that many men feel like failures because they judge themselves against society's narrow standards of male success and masculinity.
      8. Schlossberg emphasized: the role in adulthood of social, rather than biological, clocks; gender differences in psychosocial development; and the recurrent themes of identity, intimacy, and generativity.
   C. Jung's archetypal theory proposes that middle age is a time of growth and increased understanding or rigidity, depending on how an individual ends the youthful period of his or her life.
      1. Individuals who react negatively to the ending of their youth may either neurotically cling to being youthful or become rigid and unchanging.
      2. Individuals who react positively to the ending of youth may experience growth of personal self-actualization and transcendence (spiritual self-actualization), resulting in a sense of meaning and wholeness in life.
   D. Both men and women tend to become more androgynous as they age, with men becoming more expressive and women becoming more assertive and aggressive.
      1. Jung believed that the move to greater androgyny was the result of the midlife trend to seek balance in life.
      2. Even with the move toward greater androgyny in middle adulthood, the similarities between men and women are always far greater than the differences at any age of development.

II. Family Life in Middle Adulthood
   A. Family life experiences are influenced greatly by historical events; the differences across generations can be quite varied, making interpretation of developmental research more difficult.
   B. The middle adulthood family years can be a stressful time, since most parents are dealing with teenagers as well as aging parents.
      1. Although the stereotypical view of the empty nest is negative, the emotional response of most parents is relief, and many parents report greater marital satisfaction after the children leave home.
      2. One third of adult children between the ages of 18 and 29 still live with one or both parents, often for economic reasons.
      3. Middle-aged parents are also often middle-aged children of older parents, and middle adulthood is a time for modifying their relationships with their parents.

4. Extended households, where multiple generations of relatives live together, have never been common, but in the United States, native Americans and African Americans are more likely than others to live in extended households.

5. Most middle-aged adults have regular contact with their parents, report feeling closest to their parents during middle adulthood, and come to view their parents more objectively.

C. In 1900, marriages lasted about 35 years, and today, marriages not ending in divorce last about 45 years.

1. Past research has supported varied patterns of marital satisfaction, but contemporary research supports a pattern in which marital satisfaction is higher both before having children and after the children leave home.

2. When the meaning or satisfaction that couples find in their marriages is characterized as having social meaning (marriage as a joint obligation), sacred meaning (marriage as a religious commitment), or individual meaning (marriage as a way to achieve individual well-being), couples rate individual meaning as most important.

3. Rogers suggested that, in marriages and other long-term intimate relationships, commitment, communication, the nonacceptance of stereotyped roles, and the maintaining of separate identities were important factors in producing satisfaction with the relationship.

4. According to some studies, the more open and expressive the husband is in communicating, the higher the level of marital satisfaction.

5. Several factors contribute to marital dissatisfaction, including inability to communicate effectively, disagreements over finances and child-rearing, emotional instability, and sexual problems.

6. Marital satisfaction is often low in couples where the husband has a traditional gender role and the wife has a nontraditional role.

7. Stereotypical uses of power in marriages may be problematic for achieving higher levels of marital satisfaction.

8. The dysfunctional scripts of the emotional pursuer and the emotional distancer limit the ability of couples to achieve marital satisfaction.

9. Violence between spouses is a problem in many marriages and is not related to socioeconomic or religious background.

D. Currently, about half of all marriages end in a divorce.

1. The effects of divorce on children depend on the age of the children at the time of the divorce, with young children having difficulty in expressing their feelings and teenagers having strong feelings, such as anger and sadness.

2. The adult lives of children whose parents divorce may also be affected, with girls who grow up in single-parent families as the result of divorce more likely to marry and bear children at earlier ages.

3. In the United States, a significant parental divorce effect exists in which adult children of divorced parents are more likely to divorce than are adult children from intact marriages.

4. Many factors contribute to the high rate of divorce, including changing economic circumstances, easing of laws and social sanctions against divorce, and changes in religious influences.

5. Divorce is a stressful experience for both spouses, with couples moving from a predivorce phase, during which the decision to divorce is made, through obtaining the divorce, to adjusting to the divorce and entering a recovery phase.

6. Emotional support for divorcing couples often comes from relatives, with men receiving more support than women.

7. Divorcing couples are faced with many practical and economic decisions, including custody decisions if they have children.

8. The negative effects of divorce may last for 10 years, with middle-aged and older adults experiencing more adjustment problems.

E. In the United States, the majority of divorced persons remarry, but the patterns of divorce and remarriage are different in Japan.

1. In the United States, four out of five divorced persons remarry, half within 3 years of their divorce and with men more likely to remarry than women.

2. Remarriages tend to be less romantic and more practical, involve more egalitarian and overlapped roles, and are more satisfying for men than for women.

3. That remarriages have a higher divorce rate than first marriages may contribute to an emerging lifestyle of serial marriages, in which individuals have been married three or more times.

F. The diverse group of unmarried middle-aged adults has received little research scrutiny and represents about 5 percent of the population of 50-year-olds.

III. Work and Leisure in Middle Adulthood

A. Middle-aged adults exercise power to cause or prevent change in both their work and their leisure activities and are at a time in life when they wield their greatest power.

1. May identified five types of power: exploitative, manipulative, competitive, nutrient, and integrative.

2. McClelland proposed a four-step model of power development, moving from childhood dependency in step 1 to selfless service to an ideal or a higher authority in step 4.

3. The need for and expression of power appears to be greatest during the middle adulthood years, and few gender differences are found.

4. Inhibiting a personal need for power causes power stress, a condition associated with high rates of respiratory illnesses, as well as other frequent and severe illnesses.

B. Several career paths emerge in middle adulthood, including remaining in a single career and entering a second career.

    1. Workers in second careers are often higher in achievement motivation and more productive than individuals who remain in one career.

    2. Women often follow a career path of establishing a reentry career after having left a career at an earlier time because of marriage or parenting responsibilities.

    3. Some middle-aged adults alter their career tracks by adopting early retirement before their mid-60s.

C. Occupational stress and burnout are two problems encountered by middle-aged workers.

    1. Occupational stress may be heightened by changing work demands, a sense of being pushed aside by younger workers, and the middle-aged workers' own sense of stagnation.

    2. Burnout often occurs in such helping careers as social work and teaching and involves feelings of helplessness, lack of control, emotional exhaustion, and physical distress.

    3. Occupational stress and burnout can result from dysfunctional workplaces, in which structural or personnel problems create unhealthy work environments.

    4. Some middle-aged adults must cope with unemployment and the accompanying loss of income and decreased feelings of self-worth.

    5. Prolonged unemployment produces a typical reaction pattern of disbelief, frustration, and anger, followed by temporary relief, increased hope, and increased family involvement; continued joblessness yields overwhelming self-doubt, hopelessness, and cynicism.

D. The large increase in women with paid employment outside the home has had an impact in many areas.

    1. Employment generally enhances the sense of well-being of middle-aged women.

    2. Despite increasing reliance on two incomes, a majority of husbands still believe that earning more money than their wives is important.

    3. A majority of husbands believe that housework should be shared, but fewer than a third share any of the work except for food shopping and washing dishes.

    4. Wives with full-time employment average 28.5 hr of housework per week, while their husbands average 5.2 hr.

    5. Parenting significantly lengthens the amount of time spent in housework for wives but not for husbands.

E. The pattern of leisure activities varies between middle-aged women and men, with women engaging in more social, family, and cultural activities and men engaging in more travel, physical, and community activities.

IV. World Arenas of Middle-Aged Adults

    A. Many middle-aged adults exercise power through participation in political activities.

        1. A shift toward more conservative political views typically occurs in early middle adulthood.

        2. Although the conservative shift continues into later adulthood, the most common political label is moderate.

    B. The generativity issues of middle adulthood may lead to greater interest in religious and spiritual concerns.

        1. Church attendance increases substantially across the middle adulthood years.

        2. Middle-aged adults may examine their belief systems and experience spiritual growth as they strive to resolve generativity issues and find meaning in life and relationships.

Chapter Review Test

1. Ravenna Helson and Geraldine Moane's longitudinal study found that all but which of the following characteristics *increased* from when women were college seniors until when they were in their early 40s?

    a. concentration
    b. dominance
    c. flexibility
    d. independence

2. The minority of middle-aged adults who experience hyperhabituation dislike

    a. consistency.
    b. the past.
    c. inattention.
    d. change.

3. Which of the following psychologists is *least likely* to view midlife crises as common?

    a. Carl Jung
    b. Daniel Levinson
    c. George Valliant
    d. Elliot Jacques

4. Which of the following tasks proposed by Robert Peck is an elaboration of Erik Erikson's seventh stage of generativity versus stagnation or self-absorption?

    a. valuing wisdom versus valuing physical powers
    b. ego differentiation versus work-role preoccupation
    c. body transcendence versus body preoccupation
    d. ego transcendence versus ego preoccupation

5. Which pattern of middle-aged development does Carl Jung view as healthy and as one of personal growth?

    a. A pattern marked by hyperactivity in which the individual becomes more competitive, more work productive, and more physical.
    b. A pattern marked by building underdeveloped characteristics, increasing use of intuition, and turning inward.
    c. A pattern marked by some lessening of activity but also by increased conviction of cherished principles.
    d. Jung believed that all three of the above patterns are healthy and growth-oriented for middle-aged adults.

6. Which of the following is true of gender roles in middle adulthood?
   a. Both men and women tend to become more androgynous with age.
   b. Men tend to become more expressive with age.
   c. Jung believed that women have animus in their unconscious awareness.
   d. All of the above are correct.

7. Typically, the empty-nest phenomenon is associated with
   a. emotional relief.
   b. emotional depression.
   c. less marital satisfaction.
   d. both emotional depression and less marital satisfaction.

8. Which of the following ethnic groups tends to visit their parents the least during the middle adulthood years?
   a. Italian
   b. Mexican
   c. Polish
   d. Scandinavian

9. Which of the following is *not* one of Carl Rogers's four basic elements of long-term marriages?
   a. dedication of commitment
   b. communication—the expression of feelings
   c. acceptance of roles
   d. becoming a separate self

10. What is the major personality characteristic predicting low marital satisfaction?
    a. traditional gender roles
    b. neuroticism
    c. emotional freedom
    d. wanting to change marital scripts

11. Which of the following is a correct statement about the effects of divorce on children?
    a. Boys experience more negative effects prior to the actual divorce of their parents.
    b. Girls experience stronger negative effects for a longer period of time after their parents' divorce.
    c. Children of divorced parents are less likely to get a divorce than are children of intact marriages.
    d. All of the above are correct.

12. Which of the following is a significant factor in the increase in divorces in the 20th century?
    a. It became easier to obtain legal divorces.
    b. The Industrial Revolution and urbanization changed the role of the family.
    c. The view of organized churches became less prominent, as well as more flexible.
    d. All of the above are correct.

13. Which of the following statements is correct about predivorce and recovery from divorce?
    a. Persons who divorce during middle adulthood have an easier recovery than do young adults.
    b. Women find the predivorce phase more difficult than do men and often experience some relief once the divorce has occurred.
    c. Couples with sons are more likely to get divorces than are couples with daughters.
    d. Being divorced is associated with lower-than-average suicide rates.

14. Which statement correctly compares marriage, divorce, and remarriage in Japan and America?
    a. Unlike their American counterparts, most divorced Japanese women do not want to remarry.
    b. The Japanese tend to marry at earlier ages than do Americans.
    c. Japanese men are more likely to remarry than Japanese women; in America, the opposite trend is true.
    d. Japanese women are more likely to remarry than Japanese men; in America, the opposite trend is true.

15. Integrative power can be characterized as being used
    a. with another.
    b. against another.
    c. for another.
    d. over another.

16. Which career pattern statement is correct?
    a. Midlife is typically the period of lowest job satisfaction.
    b. Workers who enter a second career usually have lower productivity and motivation than those who remain in one career.
    c. About one in four adults is currently making a career transition.
    d. In the last few decades, the number of men choosing early retirement has actually declined.

17. Which of the following is associated with a dysfunctional workplace?
    a. poor communication patterns
    b. frequent personnel changes
    c. exploitation of workers
    d. all of the above

18. Of the following tasks, which is the task that most husbands get involved in (or do with their wives)?
    a. managing money
    b. household repairs
    c. food shopping
    d. housecleaning

19. Which leisure activity is more common for middle-aged women than for middle-aged men?
    a. travel activities
    b. cultural activities
    c. physical activities
    d. all of the above

20. The most common political label in middle adulthood is
    a. liberal.
    b. conservative.
    c. moderate.
    d. disinterested.

Answers

1. C [LO-1].	**8.** D [LO-9].	**15.** A [LO-16].
2. D [LO-2].	**9.** C [LO-10].	**16.** C [LO-17].
3. C [LO-3].	**10.** B [LO-11].	**17.** D [LO-18].
4. A [LO-4].	**11.** A [LO-12].	**18.** B [LO-19].
5. B [LO-5].	**12.** D [LO-13].	**19.** B [LO-20].
6. D [LO-6].	**13.** B [LO-14].	**20.** C [LO-21].
7. A [LO-8].	**14.** A [LO-15].	

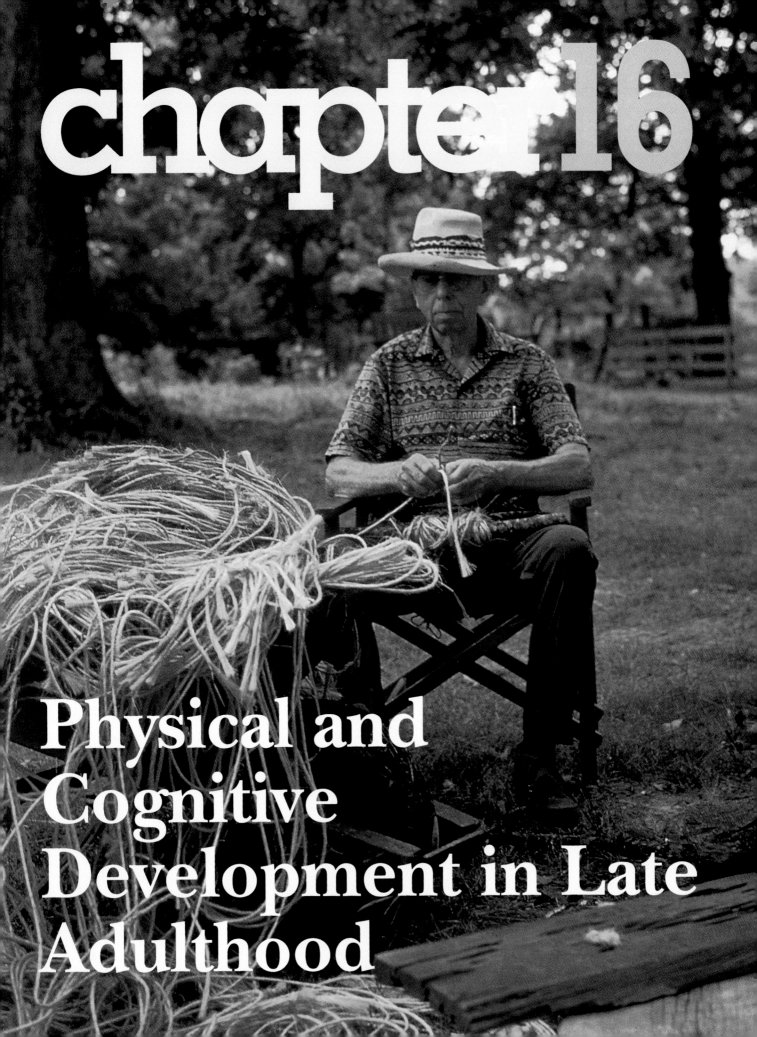

chapter 16

Physical and Cognitive Development in Late Adulthood

Key Terms

Young-old
Old-old
Lifespan
Life expectancy
Primary aging
Secondary aging
"Wear-and-tear" theory
Genetic programming
Hayflick limit
Immunological theories
Clocks of aging
Osteoporosis
Apnea
Myopic
Astigmatism
Cataracts
Glaucoma
Macular degeneration
Errors of omission
Errors of commission
Remote memories
Priming
Classical pattern of
    intellectual aging
Birren hypothesis
Terminal drop
Self-actualizing
    creativeness
"Ulyssean adult"
Special talent creativity
Dementia
Benign forgetfulness
General confusion
Inability to care for self
Alzheimer's disease (AD)
Multi-infarct dementia
    (MID)
Parkinson's disease
Polypharmacy

Learning Objectives

1. Identify the young-old and the old-old in later adulthood.
2. Define the terms *lifespan* and *life expectancy.*
3. Discuss factors associated with living beyond the normal life expectancy.
4. Contrast primary aging with secondary aging.
5. Explain the aging theories of wear-and-tear, genetic programming, immunological, genetic mutation, and ancestral factor.
6. Explain the Hayflick limit.
7. Describe the internal and external physical changes that occur with aging.
8. Identify normal changes in sleeping patterns in older adulthood.
9. Discuss sexuality among older adults, including their attitudes about sexuality, the frequency and kinds of sexual activity among older adults, and the problems encountered.
10. List common health problems among the elderly.
11. Describe the condition of osteoporosis.
12. Discuss the relationship between risk factors and accidents among the elderly.
13. Describe the general age-related changes in vision in later adulthood.
14. Identify the causes and the visual defects produced by cataracts, glaucoma, and macular degeneration.
15. Discuss how practical learning experiences affect the cognitive functioning of older adults.
16. Compare and contrast the problem-solving performance of older adults with younger adults, including the strategies they use and their rates of errors of omission and commission.
17. Describe the changes in short-term and long-term memory in later adulthood.
18. Contrast the abilities of older adults to recall remote and recent memories.
19. Distinguish between the results of cross-sectional and longitudinal studies of intellectual functioning in adulthood.
20. Describe the classical pattern of intellectual aging.
21. Summarize patterns of changes in IQ scores across adulthood.
22. Define self-actualizing creativeness and special talent creativity, and describe the relationship between creativeness and age.
23. Define dementia, and give examples of different types of dementia.
24. Describe the symptoms of Alzheimer's disease, and discuss theoretical explanations of the disorder.
25. Describe the polypharmacy disorders that may occur in older adults.

419

This chapter and the next focuses on older adults. Unlike society's limited images of the aged sitting in rocking chairs, being doting grandparents, or wasting away in nursing homes, older adults are as diverse as younger adults.

Exploring Your Own Development

What would you be willing to do to slow the process of aging and to live longer? Research from animal studies provides some clues about how to prolong life (Begley, Hager, & Murr, 1990). For instance, would you be willing to live in a much colder environment? Flies kept at 18 degrees Celsius live twice as long as those living at 30 degrees. Roy Walford (1983) was successful in developing long-living fish simply by lowering their body temperature. Similarly, most hibernating animals have longer lifespans, and animals with rapid metabolisms die the earliest.

Would you be willing to delay childbearing until late in life? Michael Rose developed long-living superflies by not letting fruitflies reproduce for 70 days (Begley, Hager, & Murr, 1990). Within 10 generations, the offspring had 40 percent longer lives than their ancestors. Late reproduction allows only longevity genes to be passed on.

Would you be willing to exist on a starvation diet? Thousands of mice and rats that were fed 40 percent fewer calories than they would have eaten by appetite alone lived more than twice as long as a control group of rats.

Not enough reliable information exists to know whether these radical, harsh, lifestyle changes would result in greater longevity. For example, in McCay's 1935 pioneer study of the effects of severe diet on life expectancy, many rats lived extraordinarily long lives, but half of the rats died very early, and the long-living rats had retarded physical growth (Watkin, 1983).

However, evidence does indicate that moderate lifestyle changes not only improve the quality of life but also increase longevity. Are you willing to stop smoking, using drugs, and consuming excessive alcohol? Are you willing to engage in regular, moderate exercise, to eat more nutritiously, and to develop better sleep habits? These positive changes would improve your chances of a long life.

Of course, some people with healthy lifestyles die young, and some overweight, sedentary smokers live to be a hundred. However, since 1977, many elderly have been willing to make moderate lifestyle changes and have increased their likelihood of living longer (Manuel, 1988). For the most part, elderly Americans and many younger adults are beginning to take good lifestyle choices more seriously.

The Time Period of Old Age

What is Old Age, and Who are the Older Adults?

Defining the age period of late adulthood is difficult, since it has no definite starting marker. Many persons think of old age as beginning at age 65 because it is the traditional retirement age (but many people retire in their 50s, and others work through their 70s). Using such roles as grandparenting to define old age is also unsatisfactory—some persons are grandparents in their 30s but in no other way resemble older adults.

In spite of the problems with using chronological age to define late adulthood, it is convenient to define late adulthood as beginning during a person's 60s. Because late adulthood has expanded in length during the 20th century, thinking in terms of the **young-old** (60s to about age 85) and the **old-old** (about age 85 on) is helpful. The majority of young-old are healthy, vital, active individuals, and although some of the old-old have good physical and intellectual capabilities, more members of this population are frail, infirm, and declining in abilities (Neugarten & Neugarten, 1986).

Lifespan and Life Expectancy

Lifespan and *life expectancy* are not identical terms. **Lifespan** refers to the biological limit to life. Each species has a characteristic lifespan—from the mayfly's single day to the tortoise's estimated 170 years. The maximum human lifespan is believed to be around 115 years—and has been for centuries. Although **life expectancy,** the average lifetime in a culture, has increased significantly in the 20th century, lifespan has not (Cohen, 1988). Factors associated with decreased life expectancy are listed in Table 16.1. As with all species except horses and Syrian hamsters, females tend to live longer than males. This sex difference reflects a difference in life expectancy, and because it is nearly species universal, it may even reflect a difference in lifespan (Cohen, 1988).

Claims of Being Extraordinarily Old

From time to time, the popular press has reported on isolated villages (e.g., the Abkhazia of the Soviet Union, the Hunzakut of Pakistan) in which large numbers of people live to be well over 100—even as old as 150. However, scientific research has never been able to verify the claims that individuals can defy the human lifespan limit.

For example, researchers thoroughly checked out the claims made by individuals in Vilcabamba, Ecuador (Mazess & Forman, 1979). They interviewed most of the population and gathered proofs of ages from birth and baptismal records from 1860 to 1940 and all 20th-century death and marriage records. In this way, they could verify current age by knowing an individual's age on an old official document. The researchers concluded that most people

Table 16.1
Factors That Decrease Life Expectancy, Expressed in Days Lost From Average Life Expectancy

The following health habits, lifestyle choices, diseases, and other factors reduce life expectancy. The reduction is indicated in the number of days lost from the 75-year average life expectancy for Americans today. For example, on the *average,* an unmarried male experiences a 9.5-year loss from the average life expectancy.

Risk Factor	Days Lost
Being an unmarried male	3,500
Being male and smoking cigarettes	2,250
Heart disease	2,100
Being an unmarried female	1,600
Being 30 percent overweight	1,300
Being a coal miner	1,100
Cancer	980
Being 20 percent overweight	900
Being female and smoking cigarettes	800
Being poor	700
Stroke	520
Having a dangerous job	300
Increasing daily calorie intake by 100	210
Driving a motor vehicle	207
Alcohol	130
Walking down the street	37
Drinking coffee	6
Drinking diet sodas	2

From I. S. Lee and B. L. Cohen, "A Catalog of Risks", 1979. Reproduced from the journal *Health Physics* with permission from The Health Physics Society.

revealed their correct age up to age 70 but exaggerated their ages thereafter. Persons who claimed to be 80 were usually in their late 70s; persons claiming to be between 100 and 130 were likely to be in their 80s and 90s. Why? In this Ecuadorian culture, older adults exaggerate their ages because the oldest individuals receive the most respect and prestige. Compare this to the tendency for Americans to shave a few years off their age because youth is so highly valued.

Although the isolated communities that claim to have individuals of extraordinary age do not have exceptional lifespans, they do have exceptional life expectancies—a large percentage of their population is elderly. Regions where many individuals live long lives have several characteristics in common (Pitskhelauri, 1982): (1) inhabitants eat moderate diets, featuring vegetables and herbs and small amounts of meat and fat; (2) they continue working throughout life; (3) integration into intergenerational families and community activities occurs;

and (4) exercise and relaxation are a part of the daily routine. These characteristics may serve as recommendations for improving life expectancies.

Life Expectancy and Population Changes

As life expectancy improves, the makeup of the population changes, and the result in the United States has been "the graying of America" (it is actually "the graying of the world"). Population used to form a demographic pyramid because there were more children than young adults, and young adults outnumbered older adults. Now, with an increasing older population, society is moving toward a demographic rectangle (Fries & Crapo, 1981; Pifer & Bronte, 1986). The shape is not yet fully rectangular, since mortality rate after age 30 doubles every 8 years (Upton, 1977).

As more individuals live nearer to the lifespan, the proportion of older adults grows. In 1985, one in eight individuals in the United States was over age 65. In the year 2030, one in five individuals will be over age 65. The older adult population will have a growing impact in all aspects of life—politics, economics and consumerism, health, and other areas.

guided review

1. The _____ are likely to be healthy, vital, and active; the _____ are likely to be frail, infirm, and declining in abilities.
2. _____ is the average time that people live; the _____ is the biological limit for life.
3. True or false: In some isolated communities, many people live well beyond the normal lifespan of 115 years.
4. Living beyond the normal life expectancy is associated with
   A. moderate diets with limited intake of meats and fat.
   B. continuing to work throughout life.
   C. including exercise and relaxation as a part of the daily routine.
   D. all of the above.

answers

1. young-old; old-old [LO-1]. 2. Life expectancy; lifespan [LO-2]. 3. False [LO-3]. 4. D [LO-3].

Theories of Physical Aging

Without exception, the human body ages over time. Aging has two components: (1) **primary aging,** due to intrinsic biogenetic processes of aging; and (2) **secondary aging,** due to external factors, such as abuse or disuse of the body, that lead to various diseases and disabilities and that often are controllable (Cohen, 1988). Understanding aspects of secondary aging has dramatically increased life expectancy. The improvement in dealing with secondary aging led Nathan Shock to say, "As we learn more and more about diseases and come to be able to control them, there won't be much left to old age except aging" (Cohn, 1987, p. 102).

Some researchers believe that an understanding of primary aging may someday expand the lifespan. Many theories of primary aging have been proposed.

Wear-and-Tear Theory

One of the oldest and most general theories about primary aging is the **"wear-and-tear" theory.** The theory was influenced by Newton's second law of thermodynamics, which stated that energy becomes increasingly unavailable to do work or to maintain order (entropy). Accordingly, the body tends to run down or to move toward disorganization due to energy loss—in other words, it wears out due to living (Bowles, 1981; Cohen, 1988; Hayflick, 1987).

If you buy a blender with a 2-year guarantee, how long do you expect it to last? Manufacturers do not want to replace blenders for free, so they hope to make a blender that will last at least 2 years under heavy use. With moderate use and good care, your blender should last longer than 2 years, but there is a "blender lifespan" that you will not exceed. If you drop your blender or use it for unsuitable tasks, such as grinding nails, it might break before its 2-year life expectancy. Occasionally, the manufacturer makes a dud, which breaks 6 weeks after purchase. Does your body work like the blender? Well, it is designed to make it through reproduction and child-rearing, with some built-in reserve for life's variations. And careless behavior can shorten a human life as well as the life expectancy of a blender. However, the analogy of the body to machines falls short. Unlike machines, the human body, through regular work and exercise can maintain better shape and experience less exhaustion.

Genetic Programming Theories

Genetic programming or cell death theories propose that primary aging is controlled by the life and death of body cells. Each cell's life has a genetically built-in limit. The aging cell undergoes about 150 changes, including becoming larger, changing in chromosomal number, declining in cellular enzymes, and altering of lysosomes, which destroy old or nonfunctional proteins (Cohn, 1987).

According to the **Hayflick limit,** cells divide only about 50 times before divisions cease (Hayflick, 1977). Hayflick found that (1) embryonic tissue divides about 50 times and then dies; (2) cells from young adults divide about 30 times; (3) embryonic cells that divide 30 times, are frozen, and then thawed, divide only 20 more times; (4) later divisions take longer; (5) cells produced later are structurally different and have lower metabolic rates; and (6) cells from conditions with accelerated aging (e.g., progeria, Down syndrome) have fewer than 50 divisions (Tice & Setlow, 1985). Not all cells fit the Hayflick limit—cancer cells seem to exhibit immortality (Cohn, 1987).

Immunological Theories

Immunological theories purport that older individuals experience alterations in their immune system that make the body more vulnerable to infection and general breakdown. The nondividing cardiac muscle cells and neurons become

The "wear and tear" theory fails to account for why regular strenuous exercise extends the length of life.

increasingly vulnerable to adverse immune system responses; cardiac disorders and Alzheimer's disease among the elderly support the idea that the heart and brain are the most vulnerable to the aging process (Cohen, 1988).

An example of the immunological approach involves the thymus gland. The thymus forms T cells, an important part of the immune system. T cells reject foreign cell tissue, including cancer cells. Yet, the thymus begins to degenerate shortly after sexual maturity, resulting in an increased risk of cancer in middle and late adulthood (Cohen, 1988).

Clocks of Aging Theories

Clocks of aging theories focus on how hormones affect aging. Noting that the endocrine system is central in other markers of the lifespan—puberty and menopause, for example—Denckla (1974) proposed the concept of "death hormones." The thymus, pituitary gland, and hypothalamus have been targeted as having central roles. In one variation, the pituitary gland secretes a "killer hormone" after puberty. Over time, accumulation of the "killer hormone" progressively blocks the action of the thyroid hormone, which is vital to metabolism. The end result is death (Cohen, 1988; Maranto, 1984).

Genetic Mutation Theories

Genetic mutation theories, or error catastrophe theories, focus on how external factors alter intrinsic cell factors, with the accumulation of impairment in different cell types causing aging (Cohen, 1988; Cohn, 1987). In these theories, aging is due to a breakdown of the body's DNA damage repair mechanism. The cell enzymes of an average 70-year-old are estimated to have made about 128 billion repairs (Maranto, 1984). Eventually, the repairs

Water aerobics done in warm water reduces the pain and stiffness in many adults with arthritis.

become less efficient and less thorough. A variety of theories, including the cross-linkage theory, the free-radical theory, and the lipofuscin theory, have proposed what external factors increase aging and how.

Cross-Linkage Theory
The cross-linkage theory or collagen theory of aging proposes that heavy caloric intake contributes to the aging process by increasing the buildup of harmful by-products that interfere with normal cell function. Collagen, which makes up about a third of the body's protein, contributes to abnormal biochemical cross-linkage between cells (e.g., collagen and elastin), resulting in more rigidity and less elasticity (Cohen, 1988).

Free-Radical Theory
Free radicals are produced when the body's metabolic processes cause electrons to separate from their atoms; these short-lived compounds can change into other compounds. Abnormal free-radical reactions, increased by radiation and air pollution, may be a source of cell damage and early aging. Some researchers believe that free radicals contribute to illness, while doubting researchers believe that free-radicals' cell products are harmless (Cohen, 1988; Cohn, 1987; Harman, 1984).

Antioxidants, such as Vitamin E and carotene, may help to keep radical reactions in check, although research does not support the concept that large amounts of Vitamin E prevent aging (Maranto, 1984). Some doctors believe that giving pure oxygen to patients can increase the number of free radicals (Marx, 1987).

Lipofuscin Theory
Lipofuscin is a pigmented substance that increases within the cells with aging. In the old-old, a third of total heart muscle volume is lipofuscin. Some researchers speculate that lipofuscin interferes with the cell's basic components and influences aging. Others believe that lipofuscin is simply cellular waste (Cohen, 1988).

Ancestral Factor
Over the last three decades, researchers have made great strides in understanding the aging process, and the future should produce more ideas on how to delay primary aging. From your personal experiences with others, you are aware of individual differences in aging. While some of these differences are due to lifestyle choices, such as sun tanning, alcohol consumption, and smoking, others are attributable to inherited differences. Significant relationships have been found between parental longevity and offspring longevity (Palmore, 1983), and monozygotic twins are more similar than dizygotic twins in their aging process characteristics (Jarvik & Falek, 1962).

Secondary Aging: Use, Abuse, and Disuse
As discussed in previous chapters, lifestyle choices can hasten or slow the aging process. Consider the impact of the following lifestyle choices on life expectancy:

A longitudinal study of 17,000 Harvard alumni confirmed the importance of moderate exercise for longevity (Paffenbarger, Hyde, Wing, & Hsieh, 1986). Men who exercised moderately and regularly (e.g., 5 hr of walking or 4 hr of jogging a week) had mortality rates one fourth to one half lower than men with sedentary habits. Moderate exercise was even helpful in counteracting some effects of bad risks. Exercising men with hypertension had half the mortality rate of their less active counterparts. Exercising smokers reduced their mortality rate by 30 percent, compared to sedentary smokers.

Unfortunately, many older adults have negative attitudes toward exercise, and 60 to 70 percent are physically unfit (Burrus-Bammel & Bammel, 1985)—just like many American youngsters and younger adults. Research suggests, however, that even moderate exercise (e.g., sustained aerobic activity, including walking) three or four times a week provides nearly as many benefits as more vigorous exercise (Siegel & Milvy, 1990; Slattery, Jacobs, & Nichaman, 1989).

Improved eating habits are also important. American diets include too much fat and not all the necessary nutrients. Beginning long before their elderly years, humans need enough calcium in their diets to build good bone mass and to delay the effects of osteoporosis in old age. Cardiovascular risks can be reduced by eating foods that help to lower the cholesterol level. As mentioned earlier, world regions with many older persons generally have moderate diets that feature fresh vegetables and herbs instead of meat and fat (Pitskhelauri, 1982).

Some researchers have estimated that one third to one half of health problems among the elderly are related to nutrition, dehydration, and obesity. Of individuals over age 50, 84 percent of males and 71 percent of females are overweight (Saxon & Etten, 1978).

The development of good eating habits before later adulthood, plus good sleep habits, an optimistic outlook, the employment of coping mechanisms for stress, the use of seat belts, the practice of safe sex, involvement in enjoyable leisure activities and hobbies, and availability of companionship can all add to longevity. Of course, you can also increase your longevity by exaggerating your age!

Physical Manifestation of Aging

What are the actual bodily changes in aging? Aging affects all internal organs and radically alters physical appearance by the older adult years. Discussed here are just a few of the central and highly noticeable aspects of physical aging.

External Aging

Skin

Changes in skin characteristics begin before the later years—young adults may notice wrinkles and dryer skin. By later adulthood, however, individuals have dryer (less fluid is retained), thinner, and less elastic skin. Wrinkling is prominent, and blood vessels and fat pockets are quite visible. "Age spots," consisting of areas of dark pigmentation, are present for 25 percent by age 60, 70 percent by age 80, and about 100 percent by age 100. Skin cells of young adults last 100 days, but skin cells of the elderly live under 50 days. Also, nerve cells and sweat glands are fewer in the later years (Kart, 1981; Kermis, 1984).

The following skin test illustrates the effects of aging on skin: Place your wrist and palm flat on a table and stretch the fingers far apart. Using your other hand, take a pinch of skin on the back of the hand between the thumb and forefinger. Pull this skin as far up as you can without discomfort and hold for 5 sec. When you release the skin, count the number of seconds for the skin to become smooth again. From adolescence through age 45, the skin usually returns to normal within 2 to 3 sec. By age 65, about 20 sec are needed, and by age 80, 5 min may be required (Walford, 1983).

Hair

Through the later years, the hair becomes thinner (about 65 percent of males become bald) and loses pigmentation, first turning gray and then white. Hair loss occurs on the arms and legs, and in men's beards. Older men typically grow coarse hair in their eyebrows, ears, and nostrils, and older women usually get more facial hair on their upper lip and chin (Pesman, 1984).

Height, Posture, and Body Shape

The elderly typically lose an inch of their height as the spinal disks shrink and as muscles that hold the vertebrae lose flexibility. Some of the elderly have additional postural changes due to **osteoporosis,** a disorder involving gradual loss of bone mass.

With age, most individuals experience a redistribution of fat. Typically, older individuals lose fat in their arms, legs, and upper face and gain fat in the torso and lower face.

Mouth

About half of the elderly have lost all of their teeth, and many use dentures (Kermis, 1984). With better dental care and nutritional knowledge, the elderly of the future may be more likely to have their own teeth. Tooth degeneration is influenced by dental hygiene habits, wear-and-tear from eating and brushing, and the lessened salivation of the older years.

Internal Aging

The Brain

The brain reaches its maximum weight of about 1,400 g (over 3 lb) around age 20. Less than 10 percent of this weight is lost across the lifespan (90 to 100 g). In this loss, the cerebral cortex is affected more than is the brain stem, and the majority of loss is attributed to cell shrinkage rather than to cell loss. The belief that adult humans lose 100,000 neurons a day is *not* supported. Except with neurodegenerative diseases (e.g., Alzheimer's disease), the number of neurons in most peripheral and central pathways is not reduced during aging. Human brains vary in number of neurons and in neural distribution in various brain functions. Some believe that this diversity among individuals may influence the outcome of aging (Cohen, 1988; Finch, 1989).

Synapses, the spaces between neurons, are a likely site of age changes that result in the slowing of brain functions. Aging decreases the numbers of receptors and the time of neurotransmitter turnover, especially with catecholamines (Finch, 1989). Brain-wave patterns are slower. Yet, using positron emission tomography (PET), researchers have found that brain metabolic activity in *healthy* older adults closely resembles that found in younger persons (deLeon, Ferris, & George, 1985).

The Cardiovascular System

After age 55, the heart's rhythm is slower and more irregular. In aging, the aorta loses elasticity, and the arteries become more rigid and shrink, making it difficult for blood to circulate. Therefore, the heart has to work harder, and blood pressure increases. Deposits of fat accumulate around the heart, and cardiac muscle strength weakens (Kart, 1981).

The elderly have less reserve capacity, compared to younger adults. Reserve capacity is the extra capacity of body systems that are used when the body is stressed. Reserve capacity allows organs to put forth from 4 to 10 times the typical effort (Fries & Crapo, 1981). Older persons' lowered reserve capacity means that they become more exhausted from physical activities, such as mowing the lawn or shoveling snow, and that they are less likely to survive illnesses, such as pneumonia. The heart's lowered reserve capacity is illustrated by the changes in the maximum heartbeats per minute during exercise. The average 30-year-old's maximum is 200; at age 50, the maximum is 171; at age 60, the maximum is 159; and at age 70, the maximum is 150. Of course, being healthy and physically fit can modify these maximum heartbeats (Winter & Groch, 1984). Aging aspects of the other body systems are provided in Table 16.2.

Other Physical Changes

Sleeping Patterns in Older Adulthood

As individuals age, their sleeping patterns change. Among older adults, total night sleep decreases, and night sleep is often characterized by frequent wakings, an average of over 20 times a night (Hayachi & Endo, 1982). In a study of individuals over age 70, many of the subjects were awake up to 20 percent of the night. Often, the elderly take small naps or rests throughout the day to compensate for the decrease in night sleep. The sleep itself is changed, too, with less REM sleep (the sleep associated with dreaming) and much less deep, delta sleep. The elderly take longer to fall asleep and awaken more easily than younger adults (Whitbourne, 1985; Woodruff, 1985).

About a third of the elderly complain about sleep problems, with insomnia (chronic inability to get to sleep or to stay asleep) being the most common complaint. Although some individuals who complain of insomnia are simply not realizing the decreased need for sleep, more common contributors to insomnia are pain, anxiety, fear, depression, grief, lack of exercise, and bodily aches. Elderly persons who have insomnia might try relaxation techniques (e.g., reading, listening to soft music, engaging in easy exercises) or adding daytime naps, rather than taking medications to sleep at night. About 5 million elderly in the United States receive prescriptions for sedatives—in other words, they are 12 percent of the population but receive nearly 40 percent of the sedative prescriptions (Moran, Thompson, & Nies, 1988).

Apnea, or periods without breathing during sleep, is another characteristic of sleep for some older adults. Individuals with apnea may stop breathing for 2 sec to 2 min several hundred times a night. They are usually unaware of having apnea, but they are aware that sleep has been restless and that they have daytime fatigue. In obstructive apnea, muscles controlling the airway relax enough to block the airway. This type of apnea is associated with obesity, sleeping on the back, and having a narrow airway. In central sleep apnea, the brain fails to signal the lungs and

As individuals age, naps become more frequent as night sleeping is shortened and involves more frequent waking.

Table 16.2
Some Physiological Changes Associated With the Body's Aging

- The maximum breathing capacity decreases, and the lungs become less flexible as collagen changes lung tissue and blood vessel walls. An increase in the number of red blood cells compensates for these changes and helps to maintain appropriate oxygen levels in the blood.

- The ciliary mechanism of the lungs is reduced, due to drying of the epithelial lining of the lungs.

- Less digestive juice is produced, and peristaltic action (contractions that push the digestive system's contents downward) is reduced.

- The elderly absorb fewer nutrients into their system.

- Constipation is more common among the elderly.

- There is a decline in muscle mass; the decline is greater for sedentary than active older adults.

- Bone density decreases. The incidence of bone breakage increases.

- Mineral salt deposits in the bones increase, synovial fluid (lubricant in the joints) is reduced, and stiffness and pains in the joints of the lower spine, hips, and knees are more common.

- The bladder becomes less elastic with age, and the bladder of an older person has half the capacity of a young adult.

- Many older males have frequent urination, caused by an enlarged prostate gland. About 75 percent of older males have enlarged prostate glands.

- Small blood vessels near the skin surface can become so fragile that elderly persons bruise easily.

- Kidney functions are slowed due to internal changes (e.g., increase in nonfunctional nephrons) and decreased blood circulation.

Source: Data from R. B. Weg, (1983). "Changing Physiology in Aging: Normal and Pathological" in *Aging, Scientific Perspectives and Social Issues*, 1983, edited by D. S. Woodruff & J. E. Birren, Brooks/Cole, Monterey, CA. From M. D. Kermis, *The Psychology of Aging: Theory, Research, and Practice*, 1984, Allyn & Bacon, Boston. From C. S. Schuster and S. S. Ashburn, the *Process of Human Development*, 2d edition, 1986, Little, Brown, Boston.

Table 16.3
Age-Related Changes in Sexual Physiology

Males:	Erection that occurs more slowly and is not as full
	Minimal or even absent: testicular elevation, engorgement of the testes, and preejaculatory fluid
	More ejaculatory control
	Reduced ejaculation force and less seminal fluid
	Briefer orgasm
	Almost immediate return of penis to a flaccid state
	Lengthened refractory period (time period in which another erection cannot physically be achieved)
Females:	Delayed vaginal lubrication
	Thin and atropic vaginal walls
	Slower vaginal expansion
	No loss in clitoral stimulation
	Shorter orgasmic phase
	Shorter resolution phase

From W. H. Masters and V. E. Johnson, *Human Sexual Inadequacy,* 1970. Copyright © 1970 Masters and Johnson Institute.

Table 16.4
Sixty- to Eighty-Year-Old Swedish Subjects' Rating of the Importance of Sexuality

Responses to: How important is sexuality to you?

	Males	Females
Very Important	8%	1%
Fairly Important	46	15
Not Very Important at All	32	34
Not at All	12	44

Reprinted from the *Journal of Sex Research,* a publication of The Society for the Scientific Study of Sex; P.O. Box 208; Mount Vernon, IA 52314, USA.

diaphragm to breathe during sleep. This type of apnea becomes more common with aging (Dement, Miles, & Bliswise, 1982).

Another symptom that increases with age is nocturnal myoclonus, characterized by leg spasms, jerks, and kicking up to a hundred times a night. Nocturnal myoclonus can be reduced by keeping regular bed and wake times, losing weight, and exercising (Dement et al., 1982).

Elderly Sexuality

Until the 1960s, little research was done on any aspect of sexuality among older adults. Research conducted in the last few decades has revealed that stereotypes of the elderly as asexual beings are quite wrong. Most older adults stay physically capable of sexual response and maintain sexual interest; many are sexually active.

Changes in sexual physiology related to age are summarized in Table 16.3. These changes can be accommodated and need not deter older adults from sexual activity. In fact, males who had premature ejaculation problems in younger years often find that the longer latency period prior to orgasm results in a normal male sexual response pattern in their later years (Davidson, 1985).

No evidence indicates that female orgasmic capacity declines with age (Comfort, 1980). Males often have erectile or ejaculatory dysfunctions (Cohen, 1988). About 10 million American men (many of them not elderly) have problems with impotence, the inability to achieve an erection. In addition to psychological factors, such as stress and performance anxiety, impotence can be caused by various medical conditions, including diabetes, hardening of the arteries, alcoholism, multiple sclerosis, kidney disease, liver

disease, major pelvic operations for cancer removal, and inadequate hormone levels. Impotence can be a side effect of medications, including some nasal sprays and hypertensive medications. Eighty percent of impotence cases are treatable, temporary conditions; other cases can be treated with penile prostheses or surgically implanted pumps (Mercy Medical Hospital Center, 1987).

Many Americans still hold negative attitudes about sexuality in older people. Although intercourse is more typical than masturbation among the elderly with an available partner, younger adults find older adults having coitus as less believable than older adults masturbating (Lunde, 1981). Among the elderly themselves, the majority remain interested in sexuality. As shown in Table 16.4, a majority of Swedish men and some women over 60 rate sexuality as fairly or very important. Two thirds of men and one fourth of women over 60 experience sexual desire (Kivela, Pahkala, & Honkakoski, 1986). Are older adults in Scandinavian countries more or less sexually active than those in the United States? The answer to this question is found in the "Exploring Cultural Diversity" feature.

One study looked at stability in preferred sexual activity from young adulthood to old age and found that 47 percent stayed consistent. More women than men expressed changes in preferred sexual activity. Preference changes were related to physical changes in both sexes and to opportunity factors among women (Turner & Adams, 1988). In fact, several research studies suggested that a major determinant of female sexuality in late adulthood is availability of a suitable partner (e.g., Bergstrom-Walan & Nielsen, 1990; Comfort, 1980; Ludeman, 1981). For women, husband's age is a significant factor in frequency of coitus; because women often marry older males, women cease sexual activity an average of 8 years younger than males. Additionally, elderly women have limited available sexual partners—four unmarried women over 65 exist for each unmarried man over 65. In the United States, if each single, older man married an older woman, there would still be 7 million single, older women (Ludeman, 1981).

A number of recent studies confirmed that a sizable portion of the elderly in both the United States and in Scandinavian countries are sexually active:

- A 1968 American study reported that half of individuals ages 60 to 70 were having sexual intercourse. In fact, nearly 20 percent of those older than 78 were sexually active. A higher proportion of males than females reported being sexually active (Pfeiffer, Verwoerdt, & Wang, 1968).
- A 1986 Danish study found that 22 percent of 70-year-old females still were engaging in coitus (Lunde et al., 1986).

- A 1986 Finnish study reported that 50 percent of males and 20 percent of females over 60 were having sexual intercourse (Kivela et al., 1986).
- A 1988 Swedish study found that, among all elderly, half of married men and a third of married women were still sexually active; at age 75, 30 percent of males and 15 percent of females were having coitus (Skoog, 1988).
- A 1990 Swedish study found that, of elderly couples, over half of the men and a third of the women had intercourse every month. This same study reported that 55 percent of

elderly males and 42 percent of elderly females masturbated at least a few times a year (Bergstrom-Walan & Nielsen, 1990).

These data indicate that the elderly in the Scandinavian countries of Denmark, Finland, and Sweden engage in relatively similar rates of sexual activity to those of elderly adults in the United States. Are you surprised by the overall rates of sexual activity reported by these groups of older adults?

Health Concerns

Chronic and Acute Diseases

The majority of older adults consider their physical health to be good or excellent. Yet, the majority of those over age 65 have at least one chronic condition—for example, arthritis, hypertension, heart disease, cataracts, and hearing impairments. Chronic diseases are long-term and usually progressive and irreversible. The most common chronic disorder in the elderly is heart disease: 40 percent of the elderly die of heart disease. In fact, if both heart disease and kidney ailments could be eliminated, life expectancy would jump more than 11 years. If cancers could also be eliminated, life expectancy would go up another 3 years (Fries & Crapo, 1981).

One chronic condition affecting 24 million Americans, especially postmenopausal women, is osteoporosis. In this disease, bone mass gradually diminishes because the body cannot rejuvenate bone as quickly as it is being absorbed back into the bloodstream. By age 60, 20 to 25 percent of females and 5 percent of males show signs of osteoporosis. Over time, this disorder is associated with fractures from falls. Of persons with osteoporosis who get a hip fracture, approximately 17 percent die from complications. Individuals with osteoporosis often develop a stooping posture.

In one study, the bone mass of premenopausal daughters of women with and without signs of osteoporosis was examined. Daughters whose mothers had osteoporosis had lower bone mineral content than did daughters whose mothers were free of osteoporosis. This research suggests that below-average bone mass in adulthood could be a cause of osteoporosis, rather than only an excessive rate of bone loss (Seeman et al., 1989).

Researchers are trying to develop medicines that re-strengthen bones (fluoride does not, while etidronate is promising), but for now, preventive measures are best. Beginning in childhood, diets should contain enough calcium, and postmenopausal women may benefit from estrogen replacement therapy.

Acute diseases occur suddenly and last a short time. Persons over age 65 seem to have fewer colds, flu infections, and acute digestive problems than younger persons. However, the lower reserve capacity means that acute illnesses last longer and can have more serious consequences among the elderly.

Accidents

Children have more accidents than the elderly, but the elderly have more serious disabilities and deaths from accidents. A fall for a youngster is likely to mean a scraped knee or possibly a few stitches. A fall for an older adult can mean broken bones because of osteoporosis, and falls are mentioned as a contributing factor in 40 percent of nursing-home admissions (Tinetti, Speechley, & Ginter, 1988).

Researchers conducted a 1-year prospective investigation using 336 subjects who were at least 75 years old. At the beginning of the study, all subjects were evaluated on mental status, reflexes, balance, gait, medications, and other factors. One year later, the subjects were contacted and asked about any falls during the year. Thirty-two percent of the subjects fell at least once; 108 of the subjects fell a total of 272 times. The researchers found six principal risk factors for falls, which are listed in order of importance in Table 16.5. Only 8 percent of elderly persons with no risk factors fell, but as shown in Figure 16.1, 78 percent of those with four or more risk factors fell (Tinetti et al., 1988).

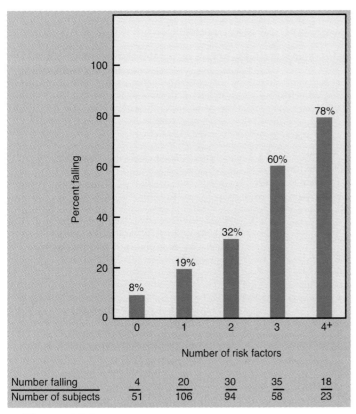

Number falling	4	20	30	35	18
Number of subjects	51	106	94	58	23

Figure 16.1

Occurrence of falls according to the number of risk factors. The risk factors are listed in Table 16.5. As elderly subjects had more of these risk factors, they were more likely to fall.

Source: Data from M. E. Tinetti, et al., "Risk Factors For Falls Among Elderly Persons Living in the Community" in *New England Journal of Medicine,* 319, 1701–1707, fig. 1 page 1705, December 29, 1988.

Table 16.5
Risk Factors for Falls for the Elderly (Age 75 and Up)

Risk Factor	Adjusted Odds Ratio
1. Use of sedatives	28.3
2. Cognitive impairment	5.0
3. Lower-extremity disability	3.8
4. Palmomental reflex	3.0
5. Foot problems	1.8
6. Balance-and-gait abnormalities	
6 to 7	1.9
3 to 5	1.4
0 to 2	1.0

Adapted from information appearing in the *New England Journal of Medicine,* by M. E. Tinetti, et al., "Risk Factors For Falls Among Elderly Persons Living in the Community," 319, 1701–1707, Table 3, December 29, 1988.

Like young drivers, elderly drivers have more than their share of accidents, especially fatal accidents. However, young and old drivers have different kinds of accidents. Individuals under age 25 have accidents because of excessive speed, fatigue, driving on the wrong side of the road, and impairment from alcohol or drugs. Old drivers are likely to have accidents from ignoring traffic signals, failing to yield right of way, improper lane changes, and improper turning. Most older drivers recognize their diminished visual capacities and lowered reaction times and compensate by adjusting driving habits. They drive more slowly, take less busy roads, and avoid most nighttime driving (Sterns, Barrett, & Alexander, 1985).

Visual Sensation and Perception in the Elderly

Due to physiological changes associated with primary aging, various disease disorders, and constant use over the years, the elderly's sensations and perceptions are different than in younger years. Older adults must adapt their environment and adjust their activities to fit their declining sensory abilities. This section discusses how the elderly's visual sensations and perceptions change.

General Age-Related Changes

By the time you reach age 60, your eyes have been exposed to more light energy than would be unleashed by a nuclear war (Sekuler & Blake, 1987). No wonder that our visual abilities change over our lifetime! Around age 40, individuals begin to experience loss of sharpness in close-up vision due to presbyopia, the lens' lessening ability to change shape. **Myopic** (near-sighted) individuals may initially notice some improvement in vision and for the first time in years read without glasses (Ainlay, 1988; Cohen,

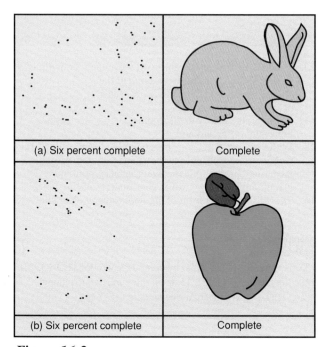

Figure 16.2

Illustrations of the 6 percent complete and complete versions of the (a) rabbit and (b) apple stimuli used in perceptual closure experiments.

1988). **Astigmatism,** which results in more than one point of focus and blurred vision, is an increasing problem as aging corneas begin to flatten. With aging, the iris becomes more rigid, and the resulting reduced pupil size in dim light hampers night vision. In low-light situations, only 10 to 33 percent as much light may hit the retina of an elderly person, compared to a younger person (Sekuler & Blake, 1987).

Other physical changes affect internal and external features of the eye. The retina has decreased blood circulation, which leads to increased risk of detached retinas and other optical disorders. Aging also leads to "floaters" in the vitreous fluid inside the eyeball. "Floaters" cause dots, lines, or cobweb patterns in the vision. The sclera, or "white" of the eye, becomes less elastic and yellowed as a result of fatty deposits. Externally, the eyelids wrinkle, and the muscle tone weakens to the degree that eyelashes may interfere with corneas. With aging, tear secretion lessens and may result in discomfort and severe inflammation (Ainlay, 1988).

Beginning about the mid-50s, individuals begin to lose some ability to discriminate among colors. Green and blue fade the most and red the least, and solid colors provide fewer problems than patterns, stripes, or checks. The following exercise can help younger adults to understand changes in color discrimination that occur with aging:

> *For younger persons to get some idea of what colors look like to an elderly person, they need only put on a pair of yellow or yellowish-brown sunglasses and*

wear them for a time indoors. They will find it difficult—if not impossible—to distinguish between pastel blues, lavenders, yellows, and pinks; and darker shades of brown and blue and even grey will be hard to tell apart. (Dickman, 1983, p. 25)

Visual changes affect visual perceptual abilities in many areas. For example, ability on perceptual closure tasks declines with age. Perceptual closure is the ability to identify objects from incomplete pictures. In one study, young adults and older adults were compared on a variety of closure tasks involving stimuli such as the two examples in Figure 16.2 (Salthouse & Prill, 1988). The older adults performed significantly lower than the younger adults on all measures and experimental variations.

About 80 percent of the elderly use glasses, and only 10 percent do not need glasses. Of persons at least 100 years old, 9 percent still do not need glasses, 62 percent see well with glasses, and only 29 percent have visual deficits that glasses cannot correct (Segerberg, 1982).

Severe Visual Impairments

All elderly persons experience the changes in eye structure and visual abilities just discussed. Some older adults also experience severe visual impairments, even to the point of becoming legally blind (defined as 20/200 vision, or only being able to see at 20 ft what a person with 20/20 vision could see at 200 ft; about 80 percent of legally blind persons can see *something*). Three common severe impairments among the old are cataracts, glaucoma, and macular degeneration. Each of these conditions leaves the sufferer with a different type of limited vision (Ainlay, 1988; Dickman, 1983).

The majority of the elderly have some symptoms of cataracts, with about a fourth of individuals in their 70s actually having cataracts. With **cataracts,** the eye's lens becomes cloudy and yellowish, and the remaining vision is troubled by an inability to see details and seeing glare around lights. Cataract treatment may involve surgery, which has become routine and highly successful, and drug therapy. Microsurgery techniques allow the removal of the clouded lens and the insertion of an artificial lens with an incision so small that only one stitch may be required to close the opening.

Glaucoma is caused by the thickening of the eye's drainage system, resulting in increased pressure within the eye. Glaucoma destroys peripheral vision and leaves "tunnel vision." Regular eye checkups can pick up potential glaucoma problems, and eye drops can prevent the increased pressure that leads to irreversible changes in the optic nerve and retinal vessels. Glaucoma is an inherited pattern in some families and is also associated with diabetes.

The symptoms of **macular degeneration** include the bending of straight lines and multiple images of letters and numbers. This condition is the most common form of blindness among persons over age 60, with about 30 percent of the elderly sustaining a gradual loss of central vision. Such

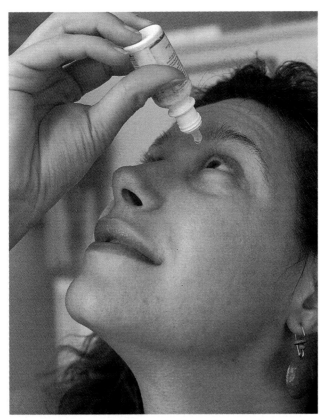

Preventative eyedrops can be used to keep glaucoma from causing permanent damage to the optic nerve and retinal vessels.

disorders as diabetes and hypertension increase the risk for macular degeneration, as does lifelong exposure to bright lights, such as welders experience. Macular degeneration results in the loss of central vision, making reading or close work difficult. Treatment can involve laser therapy and optical aids and lenses.

successful study tip

Severe Visual Impairments

To help you remember the various visual impairments, make doodles that can help you distinguish among them:

Cataract—Draw an eyeball, and on the front where the lens is, write the word *cataract*. If you have colors, tint the lens yellow.

Glaucoma—Draw an eyeball and inside it write the word *pressure*. Next to it draw a tunnel and write the word *glaucoma* inside the tunnel. Together, these images will help you to remember both the cause and effect of glaucoma.

Macular degeneration—Write the name of this impairment as it would be viewed by someone with this condition— with bending lines and multiple images.

guided review

13. The elderly's decreased ability to see at night or in dimly lit situations may result from aging of the _____ or from several severe visual impairments, such as _____, _____, or _____ of the retina.
14. With age, the ability to discriminate _____ decreases, especially for greens and _____.
15. With cataracts, the _____ becomes cloudy and yellowish; with glaucoma, changes in the drainage system result in increased _____ within the eye; cataracts result in the inability to see _____, while glaucoma results in _____.
16. The most common form of blindness among older adults is _____.

answers

13. iris; cataracts; glaucoma; macular degeneration [LO-13, 14]. 14. colors; blues [LO-13]. 15. lens; pressure; details; tunnel vision [LO-14]. 16. macular degeneration [LO-14].

Cognitive Aspects of Aging

What do you think happens to your ability to learn, memorize, and create as you become older? As you age, will your intelligence rise, fall, or stay the same? Do you believe that older people are slow, forgetful, and dull, or practical and wise? This section examines typical cognitive aspects of aging.

Learning

Classical Conditioning

Classical conditioning eyelid response studies with older subjects help in understanding the effects of aging on learning. In these studies, a light is flashed just prior to a puff of air hitting the eye; this puff of air results in an automatic blink. Conditioning occurs when the blink occurs to the light before the puff of air hits the eye. In one study, younger (averaging 20 years of age) and older (averaging 67 years of age) subjects were conditioned for 60 trials. At this point, younger subjects gave conditioned responses 50 percent of the time, but older subjects gave conditioned responses only 30 percent of the time (Kimble & Pennypacker, 1963). Overall, eyelid response studies have found sizable age differences (Woodruff-pak, 1989).

Two areas of the brain—the hippocampus and the cerebellum—have been explored to understand age-related differences in memory. The memory itself is not stored in the hippocampus, but the hippocampus influences the memory storage process. Rabbit studies indicate that an abnormal hippocampus has a negative effect on conditioning but that a missing hippocampus does not alter learning. Interestingly, the hippocampus is an area of the brain affected early and consistently in the pathological aging of Alzheimer's disease. Research findings further indicate that the memory trace for all classically conditioned somatic motor responses occurs in the cerebellum; in aging, the cerebellum loses up to 25 percent of its output cells. Future research on these cells may lead to better understanding of age-related changes in classical conditioning and memory (Woodruff-pak, 1989).

Practical Learning

You may have heard that "you can't teach old dogs new tricks," but if it is true, how are the many exceptions explained? For example, widowed traditional women learn to figure household finances (Cohen, 1988). Furthermore, more than 340,000 persons 65 years of age or older are enrolled in college, and education is increasingly thought of as a lifelong activity (Peterson, 1985). Older adults not only continue to learn—research has even shown that older adults can improve both their speed and accuracy at video games (Clark, Lanphear, & Riddick, 1987)—so watch out for all those "Nintendo Nanas."

In one study, elderly subjects and college students were told to respond to target letters by pressing a corresponding key for each letter (Madden, 1985). Both older subjects and college subjects did better when cues preceded the letter's appearance. Elderly subjects were superior to college students when the interval between the cue and target letter was brief. However, older subjects took longer to press the key. In other words, elderly participants could learn to do this unfamiliar task and could do it accurately, but they could not do it as quickly as younger individuals.

Compared to younger adults, older adults tend to emphasize experience over logical reasoning, and tradition over innovation. Many adults are cautious about trying something new when their typical life strategies have worked so far (Botwinick, 1967). For the elderly, practical solutions are often preferred over logical solutions. Is this true because life has demanded more practical than logical solutions, or because many of today's elderly have had little formal education, which is associated with better logical reasoning strategies?

Another explanation may be that science has undervalued the positive aspects of thinking practically. The virtues of practical thinking are underscored in the following example (Denney, 1982): One research problem had subjects determine whether same-sized barns on the same-sized pasture would leave equal amounts of grazing land if barns were placed adjacent to each other or spread apart. The logical answer is, of course, "yes." However, one knowledgeable older subject did not give this answer because "no two fields ever grow grass the same way."

Problem Solving

In logical, problem-solving studies, elderly subjects usually do worse than younger subjects. In one study, subjects were asked to determine which 2 of 12 food dishes were poisoned. Subjects were given descriptions of three-course meals, with four alternative dishes per course. Subjects could make up versions of three-course meals, and then the experimenter would tell them whether the meal had been "fatal"—that is, whether one or two foods in the meal were poisonous. More young and middle-aged adults than older

adults solved the puzzle correctly. Older adults who were successful required more tries than the others because they used less efficient and more redundant questioning (Hartley, 1981). This age difference could be due to aging or to educational background. When the puzzle was given to well-educated older adults with high fluid intelligence, the older adults did well (Reese & Rodeheaver, 1985).

In a study with similar results, elderly subjects were shown a group of pictures and allowed to ask questions until they could pick out the picture chosen by the experimenter. Older subjects asked less efficient questions, and therefore used more questions, than either young-adult or middle-aged subjects (Denney & Denney, 1982).

Another experimenter had younger adults and elderly subjects group objects into categories. In one task, younger subjects usually ended up with "utensils" and "appliances" categories; elderly subjects were more likely to make functional choices, such as putting a frying pan and stove together because they are used together (Cicirelli, 1976). The strategy of the younger subjects is considered representative of superior logical thinking.

Improving Learning Strategies

Whether inefficient learning strategies are due to aging factors, lack of formal education, or decrement due to disuse of skills (Willis, 1985), many psychologists are interested in whether older adults can be taught to improve their problem-solving skills. Research indicates that training elderly persons in problem-solving skills can be quite successful. In the picture study mentioned in the previous section (Denney & Denney, 1982), trained elderly subjects learned to choose the appropriate picture using fewer questions than before.

Older subjects in research often have lower scores because of a tendency to make **errors of omission**—answering only when they can be accurate, rather than taking guesses. Younger subjects tend to make **errors of commission**—taking guesses even when they are likely to be giving the wrong answer (Botwinick, 1967). The disadvantage of the elderly person's "failure to guess" on many problem-solving tasks is obvious if you think about what would happen to your grades if you only answered multiple-choice questions for which you were certain you knew the correct choice. In real life, however, the elderly may have learned that errors of commission can be too risky and costly. The elderly can be instructed to "make guesses" in tasks. Other suggestions for improving the learning in older adults are given in Table 16.6.

Memory

What happens to memory ability as a person ages? Older adults talk about increased forgetfulness, confusing details, misplacing objects, and mixing up people's names (Sunderland, Watts, Baddeley, & Harris, 1986). A minority of older adults have severe memory deficits due to dementia (discussed later in the chapter). Memory capabilities of healthy adults, however, stay remarkably good. Recognition abilities remain steady, and the elderly can recall well, but

Primary source: Newton, N., & Modahl, C. (1978, March). Pregnancy: The closest human relationship. *Human Nature*, pp. 40–49.

slower than when younger. Encoding new material, though, does take longer (Craik, 1977). Therefore, many of the aging changes probably occur in short-term memory (STM) processing.

Short-Term Memory
Older adults do not do as well as younger adults at remembering details of a passage just read or heard. Although they are worse at reporting something verbatim, they do as well in summarizing essential meaning of material (Hultsch, Hertzog, & Dixon, 1984; Rice & Meyer, 1986).

The decline in short-term memory abilities is also illustrated in a study in which older and younger adult subjects were asked to identify ambiguous pronoun references (Light & Capps, 1986). When the pronoun came soon after the names, old and young subjects performed equally, as they would in these two examples:

Martha worked in the kitchen, while Mary read her textbook. She was preparing sandwiches.
Martha worked in the kitchen, while Mary read her textbook. She was studying for her class examination.

However, when more material was placed between the nouns and the pronouns, younger subjects performed better than older subjects. Younger subjects would be more accurate with this example:

Martha worked in the kitchen, while Mary read her textbook. Both were quite happy in their activities. She was preparing sandwiches.

Results of this study can be explained in more than one way. One explanation is that the STM cannot process as much in older adults as in younger adults. Supporting this explanation are forward-span tasks that find that young adults average a seven-digit memory span, but that by the late 50s, the average is down to six (Wingfield & Byrnes, 1981). A second explanation is that older adults have more

difficulty paying attention to several things at once. In other words, they become more distracted by the sentence in the middle of the task (Welford, 1985).

Serial learning paradigms involve learning a list of words or syllables in verbatim order under strict experimental control. In one experimental variation, 16 unrelated words were presented 4 sec apart. After the last word in the series was presented, subjects did simple arithmetic for 30 sec. Then they were shown the entire list of 16 words and asked to put the words in the order of appearance on the original list. Younger adults did better than both middle-aged adults and elderly adults, but middle-aged adults did not perform much better than elderly adults (Kausler, Salthouse, Saults, 1988).

Paired-associate learning paradigms involve learning pairs of words or syllables (e.g., water-block; college-hammer) and then recalling the second word in the pair when only the first is provided (e.g., water-***; college-***). Longitudinal memory experiments using both paired-associate and serial learning paradigms indicate that performance declines with aging (Arenberg & Robertson-Tchabo, 1977), and the major problem once again is in encoding the material.

Long-Term Memory
Aging seems to affect long-term memory (LTM) less than it does STM. As mentioned earlier, recognition abilities remain steady, but retrieval of material is slower. In comparisons of adults in their 30s and in their 70s, ability to accurately name objects declines less than 10 percent (Albert, Heller, & Milberg, 1988; Nicholas, Obler, Albert, & Goodglass, 1985). For healthy older adults, memory abilities remain quite good if they are given time to recall. Outside of major cognitive disorders, called dementia, the best predictor of poor memory abilities among the elderly is depression (O'Hara, Hinrichs, Kohout, Wallace, & Lemke, 1986).

A research study that illustrated the memory abilities of older adults compared how much Spanish was remembered by younger adults who had had a Spanish class within the last 3 years and older adults who had studied Spanish 50 years ago. Not surprisingly, the younger adults performed better than the older adults; however, the elderly remembered 80 percent of what the young adults remembered, even though it had been 47 years longer since they studied Spanish! Moreover, the elderly who had received grades of A 50 years ago remembered more than young adults who received Cs just 12 months before (Bahrick, 1984).

Remote Versus Recent Memory
One commonly held misconception about late adulthood is that older people remember childhood memories (**remote memories**) with more clarity than they remember recent memories. When older adults were asked to respond to single-word cues (e.g., Easter, school, picnic) with "the first life event that occurs to you," persons in their 70s did not differ from younger college students in their pattern of

Although younger people tend to see older adults as always discussing the "good old days," both younger and older adults talk about recent events most of the time.

reminiscences. Both groups gave recent memories two-thirds of the time (Holding, Noonan, Pfau, Holding, 1986). If remote memories were more prominent and more easily retrievable for the elderly, more of their responses in this study would have been from their own childhood.

Assessing the older adult's ability with remote memories is difficult (Salthouse, 1982). First, researchers have trouble determining the accuracy of early memories. If Bob, a middle-aged man, vividly remembers having his childhood television viewing severely curtailed because of poor eyesight, but neither his parents nor his sister has any memory of his "TV deprivation," is the memory accurate? Perhaps yes, perhaps no. Bob is likely to remember his own childhood better than others would. On the other hand, he might be inferring that he could not watch much television because it hurt his eyes to watch much, and as a child, he may have blamed his eye doctor. Verifying the remote memories of the elderly is even harder because persons who could verify the memories are likely to be deceased.

Second, while the elderly may indeed provide many remote memories, the entire memory bank of childhood probably is not available. Only highly important and memorable childhood memories may be accessible, and yesterday may be hard to remember because it was fairly routine.

Third, how remote are remote memories? Individuals do not have to recall a childhood memory from 60 years ago if it is a well-rehearsed story that gets told at every family reunion. That 60-year-old memory may actually only be 6 weeks old!

Metamemory

Metamemory, self-awareness of memory strategies and whether particular information is held in memory, plays an important role in the everyday world of remembering outside of research studies. Older people can benefit from the memory strategy of **priming,** the use of related material to help recall desired material. The value of priming as a memory aid is shown in a case study in which the researcher prepared questions about trips, celebrations, friends, and family concerns from letters written in youth

by two siblings who were now 80 and 75 years old. When asked the questions individually, one sibling answered 4 of 20 questions, and the other 3 of 20 questions, correctly. The researcher then reunited the siblings and asked both of them the 20 questions, plus 10 new questions. Benefiting from each other's reminiscing, the siblings could now answer 19 of the 20 original questions and 9 of the 10 new questions (Hulicka, 1982).

Because older adults are more aware of forgetfulness than younger adults, they have a tendency to use more mnemonic devices and written notes to remember tasks. Therefore, when older and younger subjects were asked to call a telephone-answering service every day for 2 weeks at a specific time, the majority of younger subjects relied on their memory to remind them to call, but the majority of older subjects marked a calendar or used a written note to remind themselves. As a result, only 20 percent of the younger subjects but 90 percent of the older subjects remembered to make each call in the 2-week period (Perlmutter, 1986).

Yet, the elderly employ fewer sophisticated memory strategies, such as clustering and visualization. As with learning skills, however, the elderly can be given instruction in memory strategies, and their new (or reacquired) metamemory knowledge improves their abilities on memory tasks (Craik, 1977).

Intelligence

Beliefs about the course of intelligence have radically changed over the last few decades. When Janet graduated from high school in the late 1960s, she decided to go to college immediately, while she "still was smart enough to pass." In her first psychology class, she learned that her intelligence would peak during the time she was enrolled in college and that around age 20, her intelligence would begin a gradual decline for the rest of her life. Janet was relieved that she had enrolled in college right after high school. In the 1990s, as a middle-aged college professor, Janet presents a different picture of adult intelligence in her lectures. She tells her students that much of intelligence remains stable through most of adulthood, that some aspects increase, and that a few aspects show a gradual decline. Much of the current material is reassuring to older, returning students enrolled in Janet's course. Why has the information on intelligence presented in psychology courses changed over the years?

Cross-Sectional Versus Longitudinal Studies

One of the main reasons why information on intelligence has changed over the years is that Janet's professor had to draw his conclusions from available cross-sectional studies on adult intelligence. Cross-sectional studies depict the relationship of age to intelligence as a progressive decline, as shown in Figure 16.3. David Wechsler (1944) interpreted the graph in this manner:

> *Every human intellectual capacity, after attaining a maximum, begins an immediate decline. The decline is very slow but after a while increases perceptibly.*

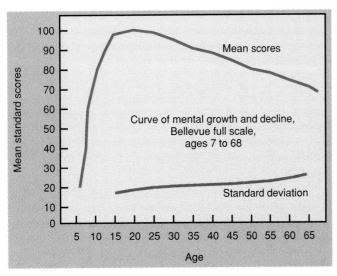

Figure 16.3

Cross-sectional data on the relationship between age and intelligence. As with other cross-sectional data, Wechsler (1944) found a progressive decline in intelligence from early young adulthood on.

Source: Data from D. Wechsler, *The Measurement of Adult Intelligence*, 3d edition, 1944. The Williams & Wilkins Company, Baltimore, MD.

The age at which the maximum is attained varies from ability to ability but seldom occurs beyond 30 and in most cases somewhere in the early 20s. (p. 55)

However, Wechsler's research and other cross-sectional studies of intelligence do not principally illustrate the effects of aging on intelligence. Rather, these studies reflect different life experiences for the younger and older subjects in the studies. For example, older subjects averaged fewer years of formal education, which is associated with lower intelligence scores.

To avoid cohort differences, longitudinal studies follow the same individuals across time. The first study to raise serious doubts about the assumed decline in intelligence during adulthood used 96 males who were freshmen at Iowa State University in 1919. From age 20 to 50, the subjects showed increases in total IQ, especially in verbal ability, and a slight decline in numerical ability. From age 50 to 60, IQ scores changed little (Owens, 1966). Other longitudinal studies also have indicated that intelligence typically peaks in early midlife, plateaus until the late 50s or early 60s, and then shows some decline (Birren, Butler, Greenhouse, Sokoloff, & Yarrow, 1974; Manton, Siegler, & Woodbury, 1986; Schaie, Schaie, & Hertzog, 1983). One 12-year longitudinal study of elderly men even suggested that declines before the 70s may be due more to illness than to aging. The study found that, from the 70s to 80s, vocabulary and ability to arrange pictures improved, but speed of response, quality of sentence completion, and draw-a-person results declined (Birren et al., 1974).

One of the most ambitious studies of cognitive change in adulthood is the cross-sequential Seattle longitudinal study (Schaie, 1983, 1989; Schaie & Hertzog, 1983).

The study began in 1956 with 500 volunteers (10 groups of 25 females and 25 males each, with the first group beginning with 20-year-olds and with each succeeding group five years older). Every 7 years, the original subjects were retested, and new subjects were added to the study. By 1984, 2,000 subjects had been tested, and eighty-eight subjects had had their intelligence measured five times during the course of the research. Along with other longitudinal studies, the Seattle longitudinal study has been helpful in composing a classical pattern of intellectual aging.

The Classical Pattern of Intellectual Aging

According to the **classical pattern of intellectual aging** (Cunningham, 1989; Salthouse, 1982; Schaie, 1989): Vocabulary either remains stable or increases, often up to the age of 70. Information shows no age-related pattern. Comprehension exhibits great individual difference in decline, but for many, declines after age 50 or 60. Arithmetic is relatively stable to age 50 and then declines somewhat. Digit-span tests indicate poorer performance in old age. Spatial abilities (e.g., ability to rotate objects mentally in two-dimensional space, block design) show the most negative age changes and may begin to decline in early adulthood. From childhood on, males do better at spatial abilities tasks than do females. This gender difference is still exhibited in old age, and the size of the gender difference remains fairly constant. However, in a 14-year longitudinal study of changes in mental rotation ability, females improved more than males when given training on the spatial abilities task (Willis & Schaie, 1988).

Earlier chapters discussed crystallized intelligence and fluid intelligence. The results of longitudinal studies of intelligence confirm that elderly adults experience more decline in fluid than crystallized intelligence. In fact, except for speed of response, significant IQ decrements before the age of 60 are likely to be attributable to either disease or lack of effort (Hofland, Willis, & Baltes, 1981; Schaie & Hertzog, 1983).

The most consistent finding is that, as people age, their rate of response slows. The slowing of reaction time was noted by intelligence assessment pioneer Irving Lorge in 1936. He gave subjects three intelligence tests that varied in their time factors. Lorge found the most age difference in the highly timed test and the smallest age difference when time was the least factor (Cunningham, 1989).

In 1948, James Birren proposed the **Birren hypothesis,** which stated that older persons are slower on a wide variety of tasks and that changes in reaction time help to explain behavioral changes seen in the elderly (Cunningham, 1989). In other words, changes in such factors as reaction times and learning, perceptual, and memory abilities cause older adults to act more cautiously, drive automobiles more slowly, and make behavioral adjustments in all areas of their lives.

If the elderly are given no time limits, their performance often is as good as younger adults. For example, subjects from 66 to 83 years of age did as well as younger persons on a mental rotation ability task, as long as they took enough time (Sharps & Gollin, 1987). Moreover, other recent experiments have questioned whether all older individuals experience slower speed of response. One study found that healthy older adults can react about as fast as younger adults who are out of condition (Salthouse, 1985). Another reaction time study used highly active female subjects in their late 60s. "Highly active" was defined as having at least 30 min of vigorous exercise three times a week for the last 10 years. This group of older adults performed *equally* as well as highly active college students.

Over 12 years, Kleemeier (1961) tested the intelligence scores of elderly men four times. He noticed that four men who died soon after the fourth testing had exhibited a significant drop in intelligence, and Kleemeier speculated that there might be a **terminal drop** in intelligence prior to dying. Several research studies since his speculation have found not only a terminal drop in intelligence scores preceding death, but also decreases in perceptual abilities and abilities on psychomotor tasks, as well as personality changes (Lieberman, 1983).

Variations in Aging and Intelligence

While the classic pattern of intellectual aging may be typical, it is not universal. Staying healthy and physically active can counteract at least some of the effects of aging on reaction times and perhaps other aspects of intelligence functioning (Powell, 1974). In addition, well-practiced tasks may not show the typical decline, or may even improve. For example, the work of proofreaders over 60 years of age was shown to be superior to that of younger proofreaders (Clay, 1956). Likewise, many scholars and artists produce their most important work at advanced ages. Training in the elderly years is also effective in forestalling or reversing decrements in skills (Birkhill & Schaie, 1975; Schaie & Willis, 1986).

Overall, patterns of aging and intelligence vary: Some persons have fairly stable IQs, some exhibit an early decline and then recover to previous levels, some exhibit a regular decline, and others show a slow decline. Some aspects of intelligence may increase through most of the life-span, while other aspects decline. Many variations in individuals' lives—such as educational level, number of tests taken, test-taking style, exposure to information through television, health, and personality characteristics—affect a particular pattern (Schaie, 1983). The possible patterns of changes in cognitive functioning are (Willis, 1985): (1) irreversible decrement, (2) decrement with compensation, (3) decrement due to disuse, (4) continued increment, and (5) stability.

Creativity

Self-Actualizing Creativeness

"Self-actualizing creativeness," a term used by Abraham Maslow (1959), describes the "personal intelligence" that older persons can pass down to younger individuals. It is the creative wisdom that comes from experiencing a long life. McLeish (1981) called an individual rich in this creativity a "Ulyssean adult" because of the person's questing spirit and exhibition of courage and resourcefulness.

Special Talent Creativity

Special talent creativity is exhibited by artists, writers, musicians, scientists, and inventors who excel in original ways in specified fields (McLeish, 1981). Also called "emergentive originality," this creativity involves the capacity to create original or essentially new ideas. Older persons can exhibit exceptional talent, as shown by Pablo Picasso, Thomas Edison, Sigmund Freud, Goethe, Benjamin Franklin, Chaucer, Sophocles, Grandma Moses, Eubie Blake, and Albert Einstein (Cohen, 1988). Are these individuals exceptions to the rule or typical? Emergentive originality seems to flourish from the late 50s on through late adulthood (Taylor, 1974).

Indeed, scholarly scientific creativity persists into old adulthood. In a study of scholars ages 20 to 80, creative productivity was more prominent in the scholars' 60s than in their 40s, and during their 70s was equal to the creative productivity of their 40s (Dennis, 1966).

Dementia: Cognitive Disorders of Old Age

Dementia is the pathological loss of intellectual functioning. General symptoms include severe memory loss, rambling conversation, language lapses, disorientation for place and time, and personality changes. Although dementia can occur at any age, it is much more prevalent in old age. Table 16.7 uses studies done in the United States, Japan, Australia, New Zealand, Britain, and Sweden to estimate the prevalence of dementia in the world.

Although people fear Alzheimer's disease most, dementia from all causes goes through the same three stages (Roth, Wischik, Evans, & Mountjoy, 1985). The first stage is **benign forgetfulness,** characterized by forgetting names and places and by misplacing items. This stage is commonly experienced in old age, and many elderly persons acknowledge the increase in forgetfulness and cope by writing reminder notes and using appointment books. Some individuals do not progress to the more serious second stage.

The second stage is one of **general confusion** caused by noticeable short-term memory deficits, lack of concentration, and wandering, repetitive conversations. Second-stage individuals often misplace items, frequently mix up words, and become moody, withdrawn, and out of touch. In contrast to first-stage individuals, who openly acknowledge memory deficits, second-stage individuals usually deny their problems.

The third stage involves the **inability to care for self** because tremendous memory loss creates dangerous, life-threatening situations. Many individuals in this terminal stage exhibit anger or paranoid behaviors. Near the end of this last stage, the individual cannot communicate and fails to recognize relatives.

Alzheimer's Disease

Alzheimer's disease (AD), present in about two-thirds of all dementia, is a brain disorder involving degeneration of neurons that results in tangles and plaques. However, neurons only degenerate in some regions of the brain, particularly the frontal cortex and subcortical areas; plaques are most dense in the hippocampus. The cerebellum, on the other hand, is not affected (Finch, 1989; Woodruff-pak, 1989).

AD is a disease of gradual, but steady decline. If it first appears in late adulthood, the disease may progress over 10 years or longer; however, early appearance in middle age produces a faster progression of typically only 3 to 5 years until death. During the decline, spouses and adult children of the AD victim usually play a growing role in patient care. Caring for a parent with AD is the focus in the "Exploring the Parent/Child Relationship" feature.

Symptoms of Alzheimer's

Alzheimer's disease does not simply involve more severe memory impairment than in normal aging. AD persons experience memory impairment in areas that remain essen-

Table 16.7
Estimated Prevalence of Dementia Among the Elderly

Age Groups	Prevalence
65 to 69	2%
70 to 74	3
75 to 79	6
80 to 84	12
85 to 89	22
90 +	41

From G. A. N. Preston, "Dementia in Elderly Adults: Prevalence and Institutionalization" in *Journal of Gerontology,* 41, 281–287, 1986. Copyright © 1986 The Gerontological Society of America.

tially unchanged in normal aging. Semantic memory (memory for words, concepts, meanings, and knowledge) is severely disrupted in AD patients but not in normal older adults. One of the first symptoms of AD is word-finding difficulty; until fairly late into the disease, content is affected, but syntax is not (Nebes, 1989).

Verbal fluency steadily declines during AD, as shown by studies that asked subjects to name items found in various supermarket categories. Normal older subjects average three to four items from such categories as fruits or meats. AD patients, however, usually can name only one item per category, and sometimes just repeat the category's name itself (e.g., "vegetables") as their example (Martin & Fedio, 1983; Ober, Dronkers, Koss, Delis, & Friedland, 1986). Likewise, over the course of AD, patients have an increasing problem with object naming. In spite of these problems, AD patients retain much of their ability to actually sort items by categories or to answer "yes" or "no" to a question about whether an item belongs in a category (Nebes, 1989).

One noncognitive characteristic of many cases of AD is depression. Compared to nondepressed AD patients, depressed AD patients are more cognitively impaired and more disabled (Rovner, Broadhead, Spencer, Carson, & Folstein, 1989).

Possible Causes of Alzheimer's

Five types of theories have been proposed to explain AD: (1) vascular theories, (2) slow virus theories, (3) chemical and toxin theories, (4) autoimmune theories and (5) genetic theories. Vascular theories represent some of the earliest ideas about the causes of AD. In fact, the first seriously considered theory was that cerebral arteriosclerosis ("hardening of the arteries") caused AD, but this cause has been ruled out. Research in this arena now focuses on features of the blood-brain barrier, the walls of the brain's blood vessels. For example, the blood-brain barrier of Alzheimer's patients accumulates amyloid, a protein-rich substance. Amyloid has been proposed as both a cause and an effect of Alzheimer's. Whichever it is, researchers hope that knowledge about amyloid will lead to an accurate diagnostic skin

Exploring the Parent/Child Relationship: Caring for a Parent With Alzheimer's Disease

A diagnosis of Alzheimer's disease (AD) means that family members, especially the spouse and adult children, must begin to deal immediately with what will happen in the future. Legal, financial, medical, and nurturing decisions must be made, and family members need to know what changes to expect during the remaining years of the patient's life.

One of the first shocks is a financial one. The majority of Americans falsely assume that Medicare will cover most of the medical costs, including nursing-home care. In actuality, Medicare only covers about 2 percent of nursing-home costs, and Medicaid helps to pay only when the family's own resources have been exhausted. The average cost for one AD patient in a nursing home is over $20,000 a year (Overman & Stoudemire, 1988).

Therefore, the spouse and adult offspring can benefit from legal advice on financial and legal issues. Concerns that lawyers should address include:

1. What can be done to financially protect the able spouse from losing the couple's life savings because of the AD spouse's health?
2. Can some of the estate be protected for heirs?
3. Which family member(s) should be given legal authority for making decisions about the patient's finances? About the patient's health-care decisions?
4. Should a will be updated while the AD patient is cognitively able to understand the will?
5. Should a living will be drawn up so that physicians will know the patient's desires about medical life supports?

Families that understand AD can better handle living with an AD patient; families that do not understand the disease sometimes view its symptoms as the patient's uncooperative or lazy behavior. Many families do manage to adjust to this situation (Suitor & Pillemer, 1988).

The table provides adult children (and nursing-home workers) eight useful guidelines for working with AD patients. Other suggestions for working with AD patients include (Zygola, 1987):

- In the early stages of AD, use notes to help the patient to remember things.
- Present multisensory experiences (e.g., seeing and hearing something) when possible.
- Because of memory impairment, AD patients often continually repeat the same questions. Attention problems include having difficulty getting started on a task, doing one of the task's details over and over, and perseveration, the inability to stop a behavior. Remember that these characteristics are part of AD, rather than behaviors designed to annoy.
- Try to get the AD patient to perform "automatic," well-practiced behaviors, since these behaviors take longer to forget. This also means that skills such as piano playing are present in the beginning and that household tasks, such as drying dishes, are behavior options for quite awhile.
- Utilize the AD patient's senses—by using magazine pictures, photo albums, music, rhythm (which is retained for a long time), easy exercises, and body movement. Patients often like to dance, go on walks, and make simple crafts

(e.g., bookmarks, cloth flowers, holiday decorations).
- Many AD patients can participate in bingo games, repetitive tasks such as envelope stuffing, sing-alongs, and so forth.

The Eight Major Rules for Working With Alzheimer's Patients

1. Avoid confrontation.
2. Use residual skills.
3. Avoid ambiguities.
4. Eliminate distractions.
5. Give step-by-step directions.
6. Give concrete visual cues.
7. Eliminate options.
8. Reduce chance of failure.

Source: Data from J. M. Zgola, *Doing things,* p. 74, 1987. Johns Hopkins University, Baltimore, MD.

Adult children need to take care of their own needs while meeting the needs of a mother or father with AD. Other family members may take over care for periods of time, or community groups or churches may have a "Day Away" program for caretakers. A growing trend seems to be elderly day-care centers, a concept that allows family members to be employed or to raise children in the daytime, yet have their AD parent home in the evenings.

Sometimes, counseling helps in dealing with the anger, anxiety, depression, and stress of dealing with an AD parent. If institutional living is an anticipated possibility for the AD patient, family members should look at whatever facilities are available before the actual need for the institution develops. Not all nursing homes are equipped to handle AD patients.

---

test for AD. Until the 1990s, autopsy examination of the brain was the only way to verify the diagnosis of Alzheimer's (Cohen, 1988).

Although no slow virus has been identified for Alzheimer's, researchers explore this area because one rare type of dementia, kuru, is caused by a slow virus. Kuru exists only in isolated New Guinea tribal groups that practice ritualistic cannibalism. Because of this practice, the slow virus was transmitted to new victims, who died 4 to 20 years after contact (Cohen, 1988).

A variety of chemical and toxin theories are being explored. The cholinergic connection theory explores the role of deficit levels of neural transmitter substance—acetylcholine (ACh). Areas of the brain that influence the production of ACh are affected in AD. In one research study, young subjects who were given drugs that interfere with ACh levels developed transient memory and behavioral impairments that mimicked AD. Research is also being conducted on the excessive aluminum found in the brains of AD patients. Evidence suggests, however, that the accumulation of aluminum in the brain is an effect, rather than a cause, of Alzheimer's (Cohen, 1988).

Autoimmune theories argue that late-life changes in brain neurons may fool the individual's immune system into thinking that foreign bodies are present. Researchers have found that the amount of plaques in the AD patient's brain highly correlates with the degree of dementia. Plaques consist of debris from degenerating neurons, scavenger cells that react to the degeneration, and amyloid that gets deposited under conditions of altered immunity (Cohen, 1988).

Finally, genetic theories are being explored because the general risk of getting AD is under 1 percent, but a close relative with the disease increases the risk four times. Other genetic research compares characteristics of Down syndrome with AD. Plaques and tangles are found in all Down syndrome individuals over age 35, and about a third also have the clinical picture of dementia. Because chromosome 21 plays a role in Down syndrome, researchers are exploring a chromosome 21 marker (in a different location) for a familial pattern (about 10 percent of all cases) of AD (Barnes, 1987; Cohen, 1988; DeAngelis, 1988).

One unique theory is that A68, a protein found in the brains of AD patients but not in the brains of normal elderly, is involved in "programmed killing" of brain cells. A68 appears in human fetuses around the 32nd week and disappears again around the age of 2 years; during the first 2 years of life, the brain has too many brain cells, and A68 may help the excess neurons to die. The reappearance of A68 may be an error in gene regulation (Weiss, 1987).

As researchers learn more about the causes of AD, they come closer to creating better diagnostic tests and treatment that will delay the course of the disease. As the puzzle is solved, the disease may become preventable or curable. If not, the incidence of AD will grow as the "baby boomers" enter old age.

Multi-Infarct Dementia

Multi-infarct dementia (MID) makes up about 20 percent of all dementia. Infarcts are ministrokes caused by temporary blood vessel obstructions that prevent oxygen from getting to the brain. As a result, some brain tissue is damaged. An infarct causes an increase in dementia and altered behaviors, but over time, other areas of the brain may compensate for the lost brain tissue, and the patient may improve until the next infarct. After several infarcts, however, the brain can no longer compensate for all the losses and does not recover. With Alzheimer's disease, the patient steadily declines; initially, MID patients display ups-and-downs in symptoms. Eventually, however, Alzheimer's and MID are indistinguishable.

Parkinson's Disease

Parkinson's disease affects 600,000 Americans, most of them older adults (only 8 percent are diagnosed before age 40). The disease features both dementia and muscular tremors. Dementia is not an initial symptom and occurs only when the brain can no longer compensate for neuron loss. The neuron loss in Parkinson's disease occurs in an area of the brain that produces dopamine, a neurotransmitter that helps people to move easily and smoothly (Ferry, 1987; Lewin, 1987; Roth et al., 1985). Although this disease has no cure, patients can be helped temporarily with medications called l-dopa and deprenyl.

Other organic causes of dementia are Huntington's disease, Pick's disease, AIDS, brain tumors, late-life schizophrenia, and head injury. Two nonorganic causes of dementia can be medications and alcohol.

Polypharmacy Disorders

Some dementia is caused by **polypharmacy,** excessive medication due to the number of prescription and over-the-counter drugs an individual uses. Some cases may be iaotrogenic (physician-induced), in that prescription doses have not been altered sufficiently to deal with physical changes of aging. In other words, Aunt Luanne may act looney because her brain is going through "a whole chemistry set's worth of reactions." In nursing homes, patients may be on a half dozen or more prescriptions at one time. The interactions of all these medications may alter patient behavior, but because the very old are "expected" to have cognitive disorders, the dementia is not blamed on the medication. With intervention, many of these dementias are reversible (Tideiksaar, 1990).

Alcohol Abuse and Dementia

Alcohol affects older adults more than younger adults. When blood alcohol levels are identical, older adults experience more physiological effects than do younger adults. Yet, many older Americans regularly consume alcohol. About a third of older Americans are likely to down five or more drinks in a sitting (Manuel, 1988), and a larger number of elderly Americans are likely to engage in steady, measured drinking (LaRue, Dessonville, & Jarvik, 1985). Just under two-thirds of older Americans are active drinkers of alcoholic beverages (Akers, LaGreca, Cochran, & Sellers, 1989).

The number of alcoholics over the lifespan varies by gender. For males, the incidence of alcoholism is higher among younger adults than among older adults. For females, the reverse is true. Elderly women have more drinking problems than young women. Also, older widows have more drinking problems than older married women (Nathan, 1983). Like younger individuals, elderly persons

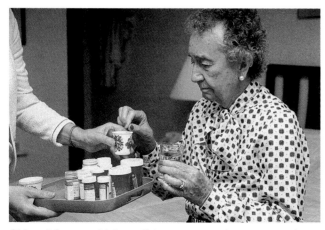

Older adults on multiple medicines may experience memory loss and other physical problems because of the interactions of the various drugs or because too large of doses are being used.

are likely to use alcohol as their family and friends use alcohol; older adults who drink too much are likely to have their excessive norm validated by friends and relatives (Akers et al., 1989).

Alcohol abuse in later adulthood contributes to many physical disorders, one of which is a cognitive disorder that resembles dementia. Whether brought on by alcohol abuse, Alzheimer's disease, multiple infarcts, Parkinson's disease or polypharmacy, dementia is a tragic experience for the elderly person and the person's family and friends and devastates the family's emotional and financial resources. As a societal problem, it requires better solutions for care; as a medical and scientific problem, it requires better understanding and treatment. Remember, however, that the majority of older adults have strong cognitive abilities. They remain able to learn, to think, to express themselves, and to remember.

guided review

22. _____ is the pathological loss of intellectual functioning.
23. True or false: The three stages of all dementias, in order, are: general confusion, benign forgetfulness, and inability to care for self.
24. _____ disease is a progressive neural degeneration disorder that typically proceeds more quickly the _____ (earlier, later) it develops in adulthood.
25. True or false: Alzheimer's disease is caused by hardening of the arteries.
26. Dementia caused by _____ disorders results from overmedication or from the interaction of drugs prescribed for and used by older adults.

answers

22. Dementia [LO-23]. 23. false [LO-23]. 24. Alzheimer's; earlier [LO-24]. 25. False [LO-24]. 26. polypharmacy [LO-25].

Exploring Human Development

1. Interview an elderly neighbor, friend, or relative about what being old is like. Ask them how it approximates their expectations about old age. What aspects are better than anticipated? Worse than anticipated?
2. Peruse several different magazines (e.g., *Modern Maturity, Good Housekeeping, Time, Ebony, National Geographic*) for (a) advertisements using older adults (Are there many ads using older adults? What images are portrayed? What kinds of products are they selling?), (b) types of articles directed toward the elderly, and (c) an analysis of how these images and articles compare to images and articles about other age groups.
3. Try the skin pinch test described in this chapter on yourself and other adults of varying ages. How long did it take for your skin to become smooth again? How do your data compare with the data presented in the chapter?
4. Experience the color vision of the elderly by wearing yellowish or yellowish brown sunglasses, as suggested in the chapter. After 2 hr of wearing the glasses, write a paragraph about your visual experience.
5. Look through the last few months of medical and psychological journals (e.g., *New England Journal of Medicine, Gerontology, Psychology and Aging, Developmental Psychology*), and locate an article on one of the dementias. Tell classmates about the new information you locate.
6. Design the building and the program for a nursing home that will house several Alzheimer's patients.

Discussing Human Development

1. What aspects of a culture do you think influence its members to either "shave a few years off" to be younger or to "pad" their age to appear older?
2. How do you think scientists will influence physical aging in the future? Do you think that the human lifespan will be increased?
3. What can colleges do to encourage older adults to take courses? What kinds of programs do you think the elderly would like to see on college campuses? What services could colleges provide to help older adults to be successful students?
4. How would life be different if the human lifespan was half of what it is? If it was twice as long? If it was endless?

Reading More About Human Development

Cohen, G. D. (1988). *The brain in human aging.* New York: Springer.
Gaitz, C. M., & Samorajski, T. (Eds.). (1985). *Aging 2000: Our health care destiny.* New York: Springer-Verlag.
Jackson, J. S. (Ed.). (1988). *The Black American elderly: Research on physical and psychosocial health.* New York: Springer.
Lumsden, D. B. (Ed.). (1985). *The older adult as learner.* Washington, DC: Hemisphere.
Pifer, A., & Bronte, L. (Eds.). (1986). *Our aging society: Paradox and promise.* New York: Norton.
Whitbourne, S. K. (1985). *The aging body: Physiological changes and psychological consequences.* New York: Springer-Verlag.

Summary

I. The time period of old age
   A. No clear boundary exists for the end of middle age and the beginning of later adulthood.
      1. A majority of the young-old (60s to about age 85) are relatively healthy, vital, and active.
      2. The old-old (those older than 85) are more likely to be frail, infirm, and declining in abilities.
   B. The term *lifespan* refers to the biological limit to life within a species, while *life expectancy* refers to the average lifetime of a species.
      1. The human lifespan is about 115 years, while the human life expectancy is about 75 years.
      2. Health habits, lifestyle choices, diseases, and other factors affect life expectancy, with females of almost all species having longer life expectancies than males.
      3. Investigations of claims of extraordinary age have revealed no evidence to support the claim to longer lifespans but have shown that some communities have higher-than-average life expectancies.
      4. Regions with exceptional life expectancies share several commonalities, including moderate diets high in fiber and low in fat, active involvement in work throughout adulthood, intergenerational family and community activities, and routine exercise and relaxation.
      5. As life expectancy has increased worldwide, the greater proportion of older adults in the population has resulted in the demographic pyramid shifting to a more rectangular shape.

II. Theories of physical aging
   A. Aging has two components: primary aging (internal, biogenetic factors) and secondary aging (external, environmental factors).
      1. Improvement in dealing with secondary aging has resulted in increased life expectancy.
      2. An understanding of primary aging may eventually lead to increasing the lifespan.
   B. The "wear-and-tear" theory of primary aging proposes that the body wears out due to living.
   C. Genetic programming theories of primary aging propose that each cell's life is genetically limited.
      1. According to the Hayflick limit, cells are programmed to divide only about 50 times before they die.
      2. Cancer cells, unlike normal body cells, appear to be able to divide an unlimited number of times.
   D. Immunological theories attribute primary aging to changes in the body's immune system that make the body more vulnerable.
   E. Clocks of aging theories highlight the role of the endocrine gland system and the hormones it produces—specifically, the accumulation of "death" hormones that cause aging and eventual death.
   F. Genetic mutation theories suggest that aging occurs because the body is increasingly less able to repair the damage to the genetic material DNA from external factors.
      1. The cross-linkage or collagen theory of aging proposes that, over time, collagen contributes to abnormal biochemical cross-linkages between cells that disrupt normal cell functioning and result in aging.
      2. The free-radical theory suggests that free-radical reactions increased by environmental factors are the cause of abnormal cell functioning and aging.
      3. Some researchers believe that increases with age of the pigmented substance lipofuscin disrupt the normal functions of body cells.
   G. Ancestry is a definite factor in aging. A significant relationship exists between parental longevity and offspring longevity.
   H. Many facets of secondary aging are controllable by such lifestyle choices as exercising regularly, improving eating habits, not smoking, wearing seat belts, and developing skills for managing harmful stress.

III. Physical manifestation of aging
   A. The effects of aging in older adults are readily apparent in their external appearances.
      1. The skin becomes noticeably dryer, thinner, and less elastic.
      2. Hair becomes thinner and loses pigmentation.
      3. Height, posture, and body shape change as older adults typically experience shrinkage of spinal disks, loss of muscle and bone mass, and redistribution of fat within the body.
      4. With better dental care, future generations of the elderly may not notice the changes in the appearance of the mouth due to loss of teeth.
   B. Changes in internal organs with age are not directly visible but are just as great as those affecting external appearance.
      1. Except in cases of neurodegenerative diseases, the number of neurons in the nervous system does not decrease with aging, but some shrinkage in cell size does occur.
      2. The cardiovascular system has less organ reserve capacity, and other changes associated with aging cause the heart to work harder and blood pressure to increase.
      3. Additional internal changes include decreased breathing capacity, reduced digestive functions, reduced bladder capacity, and slowed kidney functions.
   C. Other physical changes associated with aging include altered sleep patterns and changes in sexual functioning.
      1. Total night sleep decreases in the elderly and is characterized by frequent wakings, with a third of older adults experiencing insomnia and other sleep problems.
      2. Older adults also experience increased apnea, or cessation of breathing while sleeping, which prevents them from experiencing restful sleep.
      3. Most older adults stay physically capable of sexual response and maintain sexual interest; many are sexually active.

4. Many older adult males may experience impotence related to other physical conditions and medications.

5. Despite the sexual capabilities of older adults, many Americans hold negative attitudes about sexual activity in older adults.

6. Research indicates that older adults in America and Scandinavia are sexually active, with availability of a suitable partner a major determinant of how active they are.

D. The majority of older adults consider their physical health to be good or excellent, but a majority also have at least one chronic health condition.

1. The most common chronic disorder is heart disease.

2. Osteoporosis, the loss of bone mass, affects many postmenopausal women, appears to involve hereditary factors, and can be best treated with preventive measures, such as maintaining adequate calcium levels from childhood on, engaging in regular exercise to strengthen bones, and receiving estrogen replacement therapy.

3. Older adults have fewer accidents than children but are more likely to die or experience disabilities as a result of their accidents.

4. The more risk factors that elderly persons have for falls, the greater the likelihood that they will accidently fall.

IV. Visual sensation and perception in the elderly

A. Presbyopia and astigmatism are two common visual changes associated with aging.

1. Other common visual changes include poorer night vision, the appearance of "floaters" in the visual field, and reduced tearing.

2. The ability to discriminate colors decreases during the later years, with greens and blues fading the most and reds the least.

3. Visual changes associated with aging decrease visual perceptual abilities.

B. Three severe visual impairments experienced by many older adults are cataracts, glaucoma, and macular degeneration.

1. With cataracts, the clouding of the lens reduces the ability to see details and increases the effects of glare, while with glaucoma, increased pressure within the eye produces tunnel vision.

2. Macular degeneration is the most common form of blindness for persons over age 60 and results first in the gradual loss of central vision.

V. Cognitive aspects of aging

A. Age-related changes in the hippocampus and cerebellum of the brain may produce detectable learning and memory deficits for older adults but do not prevent most older persons from learning many practical things in their later years.

1. Younger and older persons do not differ in their ability to learn new things, but older adults exhibit slower performance of learned responses.

2. In logical, problem-solving studies, in which elderly subjects usually do worse than younger subjects, the difference may be due more to educational background than to aging.

3. Elderly adults appear to be quite capable of learning new problem-solving strategies, but the strategies they normally use cause them to make more errors of omission, while younger subjects make more errors of commission.

B. Memory capabilities of older adults remain remarkably good, despite the emphasis on forgetfulness as a sign of aging.

1. While recognition memory remains relatively stable, changes in short-term memory are most noticeable, with the key factor being declines in the ability to encode new material.

2. Aging affects long-term memory less than short-term memory, but retrieval of material from long-term memory is slower.

3. The misconception that older adults remember remote childhood memories more easily than more recent memories is not supported by research.

4. The remote memories of older adults are harder to investigate, partly because verifying the accuracy of the memories is difficult.

5. When older adults use priming and other memory aids, they may be more successful at recall of a past experience or in remembering to do a task than younger adults who rely on memory alone.

C. Cross-sectional studies of intelligence in the later years present a picture of gradually declining functions, while longitudinal studies often find intellectual gains.

1. The Seattle longitudinal study has helped to define a classical pattern of intellectual aging in which vocabulary remains stable or increases, spatial abilities may begin to decline in early adulthood, and other abilities may decline or remain stable.

2. Except for declines in fluid abilities related to slower reaction times, significant declines in IQ scores before age 60 are more likely due to disease or lack of effort.

3. The Birren hypothesis proposes that changes in reaction time can explain a variety of behavioral changes seen in older adults.

4. Activity levels may moderate the effects of slowing reaction time in that one study found that highly active older female subjects can perform equally as well as highly active college students.

5. Research supports the observation that elderly persons may experience a terminal drop in intelligence and perceptual functioning that is indicative of approaching death.

6. The classical pattern of intellectual aging is not universal, and much diversity exists in the patterns of intellectual functioning of older adults.

D. Creativity in older adulthood may take the form of self-actualizing creativeness, in which the "Ulyssean adult" possesses wisdom gathered from experiencing a long life, or may be exhibited as the special talent creativity of older artists, scientists, and musicians.

VI. Dementia: Cognitive disorders of old age

A. Dementia is the pathological loss of intellectual functioning, and its incidence increases during older adulthood.

1. Dementia progresses first through a stage of benign forgetfulness and then through a stage of general confusion.

2. The third and final stage is inability to care for self, with many individuals exhibiting anger and paranoid behaviors, as well as tremendous memory loss.

B. Alzheimer's disease (AD), present in about two-thirds of all dementia, is a degenerative brain disorder.

   1. In AD, neurons in specific regions of the brain degenerate, forming tangles and plaques of dysfunctional cells.

   2. AD is a disease of gradual but steady decline; families require many financial and supportive resources to successfully meet the needs of a stricken family member.

   3. AD patients experience severe disruption of semantic memory, and verbal fluency also declines.

   4. Many AD patients also experience depression.

   5. Vascular, slow virus, chemical and toxin, autoimmune, and genetic theories have been proposed to explain AD.

   6. No one theory has successfully explained AD, but continuing research holds the promise of better diagnostic tests and treatments to delay or stop the advance of the disease.

C. Multi-infarct dementia (MID) represents about 20 percent of all dementia.

   1. Infarcts are ministrokes caused by temporary blood vessel obstructions in the brain.

   2. Initial infarcts are compensated for by other brain areas, but multiple infarcts eventually cause losses for which compensation is inadequate, and memory loss and other symptoms then become more severe.

D. Parkinson's disease features both dementia and muscle tremors, specifically from the loss of neurons in the area of the brain that produces the neurotransmitter dopamine.

E. Polypharmacy (excessive medication) can cause some cases of dementia that may be reversible when the level of medication is reduced or eliminated.

F. Alcohol abuse among older adults can cause a physical disorder that resembles dementia.

   1. Alcohol affects older adults more easily than younger adults, and nearly two-thirds of older Americans regularly consume alcohol.

   2. Among males, alcoholism is higher among younger adults, but the opposite is true for females, with older widows experiencing more drinking problems than older married women.

1. Which of the following represents the trend of the 20th century?
   a. Lifespan has increased significantly, but life expectancy has remained the same.
   b. Life expectancy has increased significantly, but lifespan has remained the same.
   c. Both lifespan and life expectancy have increased significantly.
   d. Both lifespan and life expectancy have remained the same.

2. Life expectancy can increase when individuals deal with aspects of _____; increased lifespan is possible only when _____ is understood and altered.
   a. primary aging; primary aging
   b. secondary aging; secondary aging
   c. primary aging; secondary aging
   d. secondary aging; primary aging

3. Which theories of physical aging emphasize how external factors alter intrinsic cell factors?
   a. genetic mutation theories
   b. wear-and-tear theories
   c. genetic programming
   d. clocks of aging

4. Which of the following phrases would be essential to explain the Hayflick limit?
   a. finite number of cell divisions
   b. wearing out due to living
   c. alterations to the immune system
   d. buildup of harmful by-products

5. Which of the following is *not* an accurate statement about the physical manifestations of aging?
   a. Skin cells of the elderly live less than half as long as those of young adulthood.
   b. The majority of males become bald.
   c. Adult humans lose about 100,000 brain cells each day.
   d. Salivation and digestive juice production decreases.

6. Compared to younger adults, the sleep of the elderly is characterized by
   a. more dreaming.
   b. more frequent awakenings.
   c. less time to fall asleep.
   d. all of the above.

7. All of the following are age-related changes in male sexual physiology *except*
   a. briefer orgasm.
   b. slower erection.
   c. lessened ejaculatory control.
   d. longer refractory period.

8. Available evidence suggests that, currently, the best way to reduce problems with osteoporosis is to
   a. end estrogen replacement therapy.
   b. use fluoride to restrengthen bones.
   c. have a calcium-rich diet throughout adulthood.
   d. all of the above.

9. In a 1-year study of persons at least 75 years old, the number one risk factor associated with falls was
   a. foot problems.
   b. cognitive impairment.
   c. balance-and-gait abnormalities.
   d. use of sedatives.

10. _____ involves increased pressure within the eye, is an inherited pattern, and is also associated with diabetes; regular eye drops can be used to keep peripheral vision from being destroyed.
    a. Glaucoma
    b. Macular degeneration
    c. Cataracts
    d. Diabetic retinopathy

11. The elderly do not do as well as younger adults in a practical learning situation when it comes to
    a. learning an unfamiliar task.
    b. speed of response.
    c. accuracy.
    d. relying on experience.

12. Compared to younger subjects, elderly subjects are more prone to
    a. errors of commission.
    b. errors of omission.
    c. both errors of commission and omission.
    d. neither errors of commission or omission.

13. _____ is the memory system most affected by aging.
    a. Long-term memory
    b. Sensory shortage system
    c. Short-term memory
    d. Remote-memory system

14. Remote memories are
    a. those we remember from life stories told of others.
    b. those that have little emotional consequence to an individual.
    c. those that have been repressed due to traumatic experiences.
    d. memories of childhood.

15. Cross-sectional studies of intelligence led researchers to believe that intelligence peaked
    a. in the early 20s.
    b. around the 35th birthday.
    c. in the 50s.
    d. in the 60s.

16. Which of the following tasks would typically have the most decline over the adult years?
    a. digit-span tests
    b. vocabulary tests
    c. arithmetic tasks
    d. spatial abilities tasks

17. A Ulyssean adult is to _____, as special talent creativity is to _____.
    a. crystallized intelligence; fluid intelligence
    b. creative wisdom; personal intelligence
    c. self-actualizing creativeness; emergentive originality
    d. verbal intelligence; artistic intelligence

18. Individuals in the _____ stage of dementia often openly acknowledge memory deficits.
    a. second
    b. general confusion
    c. third
    d. benign forgetfulness

19. Which of the following areas of memory would be the last to be affected by Alzheimer's disease?
    a. syntax
    b. word finding
    c. verbal fluency
    d. meanings and knowledge

20. Polypharmacy disorders have to do with
    a. errors made in medications by pharmacists.
    b. excessive prescription and over-the-counter drug use.
    c. mixing alcohol and sedatives.
    d. suicide attempts because of overconsumption of many medications.

Answers

1. B [LO-2].	8. C [LO-10, 11].	15. A [LO-19].
2. D [LO-4].	9. D [LO-12].	16. D [LO-20, 21].
3. A [LO-5].	10. A [LO-14].	17. C [LO-22].
4. A [LO-6].	11. B [LO-15].	18. D [LO-23].
5. C [LO-7].	12. B [LO-16].	19. A [LO-24].
6. B [LO-8].	13. C [LO-17].	20. B [LO-25].
7. C [LO-9].	14. D [LO-18].	

chapter 17

Psychosocial Development in Late Adulthood

Learning Objectives

1. Identify historical and current examples of positive and negative stereotypes of the elderly.
2. Explain the double standard of aging.
3. Describe how children, adolescents, and young adults view the elderly.
4. Give cultural examples of modernization theory.
5. Describe older adults' views of other older adults.
6. Discuss research findings regarding positive and negative emotions in older adults.
7. Compare evidence for and against the idea of personality stability in later adulthood.
8. Identify Neugarten's four personality types and their related subtypes.
9. Discuss Erikson's eighth crisis of ego integrity versus despair and the resulting virtue of wisdom.
10. Explain Peck's three developmental tasks of older adulthood.
11. Compare and contrast the activity and disengagement styles of successful aging.
12. Identify factors that should be considered in preparing for retirement.
13. Describe Atchley's seven phases of retirement.
14. Discuss the work and leisure activities of men and women in retirement.
15. Identify Duvall's developmental tasks for aging couples.
16. Discuss factors associated with marital satisfaction for wives and husbands.
17. Describe the transitions brought about by death of spouse, divorce, and remarriage in later adulthood.
18. Identify characteristics associated with the never-married elderly.
19. Discuss the quality of relationships between older parents and their adult children and the factors that affect the relationships.
20. Describe different grandparenting styles.
21. Give examples of the experiences of childless individuals as older adults.
22. Describe the developmental tasks of siblings during old age.
23. Contrast the independent living arrangements of older adults with dependent living arrangements.

Now that life expectancy has risen to the 70s and greater numbers are living into their 80s, 90s, and even 100s, old age has more potential years than any other life stage. Childhood only lasts 11 years, adolescence is but 8 years, young adulthood is about 20 years, and middle age is about 25 years, but old age can be upward of 40 years for those who live long enough to be centenarians.

Because of worldwide increases in life expectancies, a larger percentage of the population soon will be composed of individuals 65 and older. As the number of older people and the number of years spent in late adulthood have grown, psychologists have begun to focus more on developmental aspects of old age. In this chapter, we examine how older adults are viewed by others, how they view themselves, their personality and emotional development, and typical lifestyle activities, relationships, and living arrangements.

Exploring Your Own Development

How do you feel about becoming older? Are you looking forward to retirement? To being 70? What are your current views of older adults? Think about your present attitudes toward the elderly and about being old yourself, and then complete the following sentences:

I will be old when I _____.
When I am old, I will never _____.
When I am old, I will _____.
The thing I will hate most about being old is _____.
The thing I most look forward to about being old is _____.
Old people always _____.
Old people never _____.
When I am old, nobody will _____.
When I am old, other people will _____.

Do you know someone who is older than 60? 70? 80? 90? 100? How would these people complete the previous sentences? Ask them, and then compare your responses with those of your classmates and with the information that follows.

Images and Stereotypes of Older Adults

Society's Views of Older Adults

In many ways, the older adult population is the most diverse segment of the population, with less consistency in physical and cognitive aspects, educational background, work experience and decisions, and relationships. Yet, in many ways, society has more rigid stereotypes of the elderly than of any other age group. Two dominant images persist—one negative image of declining abilities and opportunities and one positive image of growing wisdom

and fortitude, although more individuals emphasize negative over positive stereotypes.

Historical Stereotypes
Many believe that negative images of old people are a 20th-century phenomenon and that, before this century, old people had more power and prestige. This belief is founded on the assumptions that old people were fewer in number before modern medical advances, that old people often owned valuable agricultural land, and that old people had stable job skills that they could pass directly on to younger generations (Fischer, 1978; vonKondratowitz, 1984). However, the dichotomous good-bad image of the elderly already existed by the Middle Ages (Goodich, 1990).

One common 13th-century image of the old was that the physical decline of old age was a symptom of moral decline. Pope Innocent III wrote:

> If anyone reaches old age, his heart is impaired, his head is disturbed, his breath is labored, his mouth smells, his face is wrinkled, his posture is bent, his eyes grow dim, his joints totter, his nose runs, his hair falls out, his fingers tremble, his deeds are undone, his teeth stink, his ears are dirty. Old men are easily provoked, but forgive reluctantly; quick to belief, they slowly withdraw their faith; tenacious and greedy, sad and querulous, they are quick to speak, slow to hear, but not slow to anger; they praise the old, spurn the new, disparage the present, praise the past; they sigh and are troubled, stiff and infirm. (cited in Goodich, 1990, p. 123)

The other 13th-century image emphasized the wisdom of the old. As a result of the reintroduction of Aristotle's writings, the translation of Arabic medical writings, and the growing Christian belief in working toward spiritual perfection, elderly persons were also viewed as growing in wisdom as they prepared for eternity.

From the 17th through 19th centuries, the elderly in America apparently experienced increasingly negative stigmas (Fischer, 1978). Early churches reserved the seats of highest honor for the oldest members, but by the end of the 18th century, the richest members used these seats because churches began to auction pews to the highest bidders. Aging was somewhat fashionable in the 18th century—men wore powdered wigs and long coats and practiced "age-heaping," the overstating of their age. However, in the 19th century, youth-oriented men used their natural hair, wore tight-fitting waistcoats, and tended to understate their age. Eighteenth-century family portrait paintings featured the elder male higher than the rest of the family, but one century later, the elder male was typically painted on the same level as other members. In the 19th century, the number of children named after grandparents also declined.

Since psychological research on the elderly is a 20th-century phenomenon, social scientists cannot easily explore stereotypes of the aged in earlier centuries. Since they do not have early research findings to examine, they try to

Table 17.1
Sample Song Lyrics About Older Adults

"Silver Threads Among the Gold" (1873) by Eden E. Rexford

Darling, I am growing old
Silver threads among the gold
Shine upon my brow today
Life is fading fast away.
When your hair is silver white
And your cheeks no longer bright.

"Stick to Your Mother, Mary" (1913) by Thomas Allen

Stick to your mother, Mary
Don't leave your old home now
She's old and gray and she wants you to stay
So don't take a year of her life away.
Those wedding bells can wait, dear
Don't make her old heart sigh
You'll never miss her till the last time you kiss her
And she says goodbye.

"Get Away Old Man, Get Away" (1927) by Frank Crumit

Don't ever marry an old man
I'll tell you the reason why
His lips are all tobacco juice
His chin is never dry.
For an old man he is old
For an old man he is grey
But a young man's heart is full of love
Get away old man, get away.

"I Wish I Was Eighteen Again" (1978) by Sonny Throckmorton

Oh, I wish I was eighteen again,
And going where I've never been.
But old folks and old oaks
Standing tall just pretend;
I wish I was eighteen again.

From E. S. Cohen and A. L. Kruschwitz, "Old Age in America Represented in Nineteenth and Twentieth Century Popular Sheet Music" in *The Gerontologist,* 30, 345–354, 1990. Copyright © 1990 The Gerontological Society of America.

The "Golden Girls" television show broke television barriers by showing older women as competent, independent, active, caring, creative, and sensuous. Typically television ignores older characters or portrays them as stubborn, eccentric, and foolish.

analyze materials that were created in these previous eras—for example, the content of popular magazine articles, elderly characters in children's literature, the images in early sermons, family portrait paintings, and even the content of popular sheet music.

One study of popular sheet music analyzed about 300 songs published from the 1830s through the 1950s (Cohen & Kruschwitz, 1990). The researchers found that popular songs featured common themes and more negative than positive images regarding the elderly across the entire time period. As shown by the examples in Table 17.1, songs have dealt with physical aspects of aging, family responsibilities, elderly sexuality, and preferences for youth.

Historically as well as currently, a double standard of aging has existed: Women face more negative consequences than males for growing old. In the 19th century, women were viewed as being old by menopause. In 1837, Burdach wrote that women at menopause lose generative power and some of their gender. In 1840, Pierer wrote that age 35 was the "last perfect time in the life of a female" (Sontag, 1972; vonKondratowitz, 1984).

Current Stereotypes

Ageism is a societal pattern of widely held devaluative attitudes and stereotypes about the aging process and old people. Many elderly persons are segregated from other population segments, are the subject of hostile humor, and face discriminatory practices (Gatz & Pearson, 1988; Nahemow, 1986). Ageism is most strongly directed toward single, female, and poor elderly (Kimmel, 1988).

Some ageist traits commonly applied to the elderly are being ill, tired, asexual, isolated, depressed, slow, and not intellectually alert (Runback & Carr, 1984). Old people are perceived as primarily involved in nonsocial behaviors and passive activities and as having more negative than positive attributes (Kimmel, 1988; Rodin & Langer, 1980). People, including psychologists, tend to lump all old people into one category, although some old people are merely in their 60s and others are over 90 (Schaie, 1988).

On television shows, the elderly are largely "invisible" and make up only about 2 percent of dramatic television characters, except for a somewhat higher percentage on daytime soap operas (Passuth & Cook, 1985). A 1980 survey of older adult television characters found that the majority of them were portrayed as stubborn, eccentric, and foolish (Gerbner, Gross, Signorielli, & Morgan, 1980). Many times, old people in advertisements are portrayed as having childlike personalities and moods (Arluke & Levin, 1984).

Jokes about old people, especially old women, are often disparaging. Consistent with the superiority theory of humor, people enjoy exposing the weakness or deformity of others—it humiliates and punishes others, while leaving the self triumphant. Of course, old people may make fun of old people in jokes that can reaffirm their integrity, despite the imperfections of aging. However, when jokes are in intense conflict areas, they backfire and make people more anxious (Nahemow, 1986). Two limericks about old age are given in Table 17.2. Analyze why some adults think that they are humorous.

In a survey of 700 children's literature books, researchers found that the aged were stereotyped as unimportant, unimaginative, unintelligible, dependent, and boring. For example, old kings are typically described as good but foolish (Ansello, 1977).

Others' Stereotypes of the Elderly

Views of Children, Adolescents, and Young Adults

When preschoolers are asked, "Would you like to be old?" they respond negatively. In one study, young children used such terms as "tired," "ugly," "helpless," and "ready to die" in describing older adults, and in a second study, older people were depicted as "all wrinkled and short," "have gray hair," "chew funny," "don't go out much," and "have heart attacks and die" (Dellman-Jenkins, Lambert, Fruit, & Dinero, 1986). Other studies found that children basically see old people as positive but as physically incapable of many things (e.g., Mitchell, Wilson, Revicki, & Parker, 1985). Preschoolers exhibit less ageist prejudice than school-age children (Isaacs & Bearison, 1986), and attempts to alter preschoolers' negative views toward old people have been successful (Dellman-Jenkins et al., 1986).

A study of 157 inner-city, lower-middle-class preadolescents found that males and females held about the same attitudes toward the elderly. Surprisingly, attitudes were not affected by amount of contact with elderly persons. The study also found that European-American preadolescents had more positive attitudes toward the elderly than either African-American or Mexican-American preadolescents (Harris & Fiedler, 1988). The "Exploring Cultural Diversity" feature takes a more extensive look at cultural differences in attitudes toward older adults.

Some of the earliest studies of attitudes toward older people used the Tuckman-Lorge Old People Scale, consisting of 137 stereotypes and common misconceptions of old people. The initial study found that old age was viewed as a time of economic insecurity, loneliness, resistance to change, failing mental and physical powers, and poor health. Subsequent studies using the same technique with preadolescents, high school students, and college students confirmed that young adults hold similar unfavorable images of the aged (e.g., Goebel, 1984; Harris & Fiedler, 1988; Lane, 1964).

Views of Nurses and Politicians

Goebel (1984) looked at the attitudes of 72 European-American female student nurses toward children, adolescents, young adults, middle-aged adults, and older adults. The nursing students held the most negative attitudes toward older adults and the most favorable attitudes toward young and middle-aged adults. Older adults were viewed as

Table 17.2
Limericks on Old Age

My bifocals are the best you can find
My teeth fit and don't bind
My ear plug's O.K.
And so's my toupee
But I sure do miss my mind.

Three things age does to you
First you forget who's who
That's not so bad
What makes me sad
I can't recall the next two.

Laughs and Limericks on Aging in Large Print by Reggie the Retiree, 1982, pp. 16 & 19. Reggie the Retiree Company, 6946 Myerlee Country Club Blvd., Fort Myers, FL 33919.

most insecure and as having the most negative habits and mental problems (see Figure 17.1).

That nurses often hold negative views of the elderly is disheartening, since some older persons have extended hospitalizations or stay in medically supervised settings and depend on the care of nurses. Also, if student nurses hold negative views of the old and in their jobs work with the most frail of old persons, will their views become even more negative over the years?

One researcher analyzed the content of published congressional speeches and statements made during a 1981 national debate on aging programs after President Reagan proposed changes in the Social Security Program (Lubomudrov, 1987). As shown in Table 17.3, legislators hold stereotypes of the elderly that resemble those held by the population as a whole. And, like the overall population, members of Congress consistently estimate the seriousness of each problem for older persons to be greater than that assumed by the elderly themselves. Although the majority of stereotypes in the speeches were negative in nature (82.5 percent), in a political sense, these negative stereotypes become "compassionate stereotypes" because they helped to create laws that provided benefits for the elderly. How do you think other professions, in addition to nurses and politicians, are influenced by their stereotypes of the elderly?

Older Adults' Views of Older Adults

Table 17.4 presents what four well-known individuals have written about their experiences of old age. These quotes reflect some fairly typical attitudes of the elderly about themselves: They are surprised at being old; they must deal with cognitive and physical problems; they look for meaning in their lives; and they believe in the value of wisdom and the experience of a long life. Indeed, an elderly person's view of the elderly includes the same stereotypes held by other persons, but held to a less extreme; in addition, the elderly individual often views himself or herself as an exception to the elderly stereotype. Overall, older African Americans have more positive attitudes about their own aging and exhibit more respect for other older adults (Chatters, 1988).

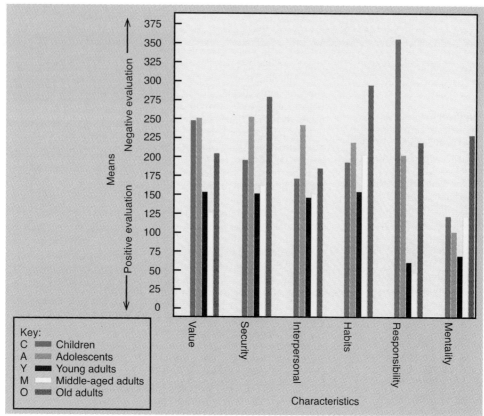

Figure 17.1

Mean ratings of five age groups on six characteristics by student nurses.

Source: Data from B. L. Goebel, "Age Stereotypes Held by Student Nurses" in *The Journal of Psychology*, 116, 249–254, fig. 1 page 252, 1984.

Table 17.3
Frequency of Expression of Negative and Positive Stereotypes Regarding the Elderly in Congressional Statements and Speeches

Types of Negative Stereotypes (n = 913)	Percent
1. Elderly are inadequate employees (e.g., inefficient, accident-prone).	23.0%
2. Elderly are primarily in poor health.	21.2
3. Most older persons are poor.	18.6
4. Elderly are socially isolated.	13.6
5. Older persons are largely conservative.	6.9
6. Elderly are mentally slower than younger people.	5.1
7. Other	11.6

Types of Positive Stereotypes (n = 193)	Percent
1. Old age is a period of being relatively well-off (i.e., old age as the "Golden Years").	31.1%
2. Older persons are mostly wise.	22.8
3. Most older persons are kind and generous.	16.6
4. Older persons are friendly all or most of the time.	12.4
5. Other	17.1

From S. Lubomudrov, "Congressional Perceptions of the Elderly: The Use of Stereotypes in the Legislative Process" in *The Gerontologist*, 27, 77–81 (Table 2, p. 79), 1987. Copyright © 1987 The Gerontological Society of America.

Table 17.4
Four Elders on the Experience of Old Age

"When we are grown up, we hardly think about our age anymore. We feel that the notion does not apply to us; for it is one which assumes that we look back towards the past and draw a line under the total, whereas in fact we are reaching out towards the future, gliding on imperceptibly from day to day, from year to year. Old age is particularly difficult to assume because we have always regarded it as something alien, a foreign species: 'Can I have become a different being while I still remain myself?' " [Simone de Beauvoir]

"To put it simply, I no longer have the arrogant confidence that I can master the new ideas and developments in the field. I'm also aware that old men outlive their abilities without realizing it, and can easily make fools of themselves, or at least not do their past reputations any good. . . . However, I'm not quite senile, not yet. I can still keep up appearances, and there are points on which I can still outtalk younger colleagues. But—between you and me, privately—the picture is one of a slow, inevitable loss of cognitive capacity. For one of my theoretical persuasion, it's fascinating to watch." [Donald O. Hebb]

"The most positive therapy is to perpetuate the life force, and whether the patient is a mechanic or U.S. Senator, he or she has a motivation which must prevail over the illness." [Senator Jacob K. Javits]

"I want you to know that I also will not make age an issue in this campaign. I am not going to exploit for political purposes my opponent's youth and inexperience." [Ronald Reagan to 56-year-old Walter Mondale]

Source: Data from S. DeBeauvoir, *The Coming of Age*, p. 420, Warner Books, NY. From D. O. Hebb, "On Watching Myself Get Old" in *Psychology Today*, p. 23, November 1978. Quotes from Javits and Regan in R. N. Butler, "Productive Aging" in *The Course of Later Life: Research and Reflections*, edited by V. L. Bengston & K. W. Schaie, p. 55, 1989, Springer, NY.

The following aspects of cultures are associated with higher levels of respect and better treatment of the elderly:

1. **Modernization theory** states that preindustrial societies accord more status to the aged than do industrial societies, and most studies find that less industrialized societies accord higher status to the elderly (Cowgill, 1974, 1986; Gilleard & Gurkan, 1987; Lehr, 1983). These societies may give the elderly higher status because fewer people live to old age. More likely, these societies have high status for the elderly because the elderly control something of value in the society, such as spiritual rites, land ownership, money, or valued skills and information to teach the younger generations. For example, the Kikuyu society of 1890 practiced riika, a system of age grading. Each stage of the life cycle had clearly defined transitions, marked by ritual, role learning, and meaning. For the Kikuyu male, marriage was the transition to junior elder status. He became a senior elder when his eldest son was initiated. The roles of the senior elder were to keep peace and to make judgments. All cultures experience aging, but not all experience elderhood as did the Kikuyu (Whiting, 1981). Industrialization often removes the valuable aspects of old age, and as a result, status of the elderly falls (Rosenmary, 1985). In addition, industrialization often results in young adults moving to cities and leaving behind the elderly to fend for themselves.

2. The status of the elderly is higher in societies in which conformity is highly valued than in societies that emphasize self-reliance. If conformity is valued, children learn to obey and respect parents and grandparents; if self-reliance is valued, independence from older generations leads to lower status for the aged. Therefore, most agricultural societies exhibit high levels of status for older adults, and lower status is apparent in hunting-and-gathering societies and in industrialized societies (Ishii-Kuntz & Lee, 1987).

3. Societies with ancestor worship show higher status for the elderly than do other societies. In these cultures, older individuals are closer to ancestor status, and therefore, younger individuals are motivated to please them. The Japanese tradition of honoring the elderly may be based in Japanese roots of ancestor worship (Ishii-Kuntz & Lee, 1987).

4. In some societies, younger persons are legally required to provide care for older persons. For example, Hungary requires families to take care of older family members. Neglecting the health of older individuals unable to care for themselves is against the law (Nusberg, 1983).

5. Societies that emphasize extended families exhibit higher status for the elderly. For example, older Australians are much more likely than older Americans to live with family members (Kendig & Rowland, 1983), the Igbo of Nigeria hold strong beliefs about caring for aged parents (Ohuche & Littrell, 1989), and the majority of elderly in Latin American countries live in extended family households (de Vos, 1990). Within the American culture, African Americans are more likely than European Americans to reside in extended family households, and as a group, they have more positive attitudes toward their own aging (Chatters, 1988; Taylor, 1988). Social changes may disrupt traditional extended family patterns. When rural areas of Zaire, Africa, underwent economic upheaval, many young adults chose autonomy and mobility, and the elderly could no longer count on family cohesiveness provided by extended family dwellings (Masamba ma Mpolo, 1984).

Cultures differ in who is likely to care for elderly parents. In the United States, females assume a greater burden of caregiving for aging parents (Finley, 1989). Female Igbo of Nigeria also take more responsibility for elderly care than do male Igbo (Ohuche & Littrell, 1989). In India, the majority of elderly live with a married son (Goldstein, Schuler, & Ross, 1983), and the elderly of Japan are most likely to live with the eldest son (Havighurst, 1978; Maeda, 1978; Tobin, 1987).

Societal changes can also affect this gender preference. Although the majority of Chinese adults believe that their aged parents should live with their sons, they do not express a preference for themselves eventually living with a son or daughter. The one-child policy of China is thought to be the major reason for this change in beliefs (Yu, Yu, & Mansfield, 1990).

Another cultural difference is whether the elderly are encouraged to be independent or dependent. The majority of older Americans value independence and do not wish to live with their adult children (Hamon & Blieszner, 1990). They like the Swedish system of a social-service network of meals-on-wheels, housekeeping aids, free medical care, and economic assistance because these services maximize the possibility of independence and quality living for as long as possible (Tobin, 1987). However, Hindu cultures such as India's idealize the dependence aspect of aging (Goldstein et al., 1983). Japan has traditionally expected dependence of older adults on their children. When elderly Japanese move in with their eldest sons, the aged persons are expected to be dependent on their offspring. The Japanese saying "When old, obey your children" illustrates this practice of dependence on adult children (Havighurst, 1978; Maeda, 1978; Tobin, 1987).

Finally, beware of pseudo-idealization of old age in other cultures. Some cultures (e.g., Hong Kong, Nepal, Taiwan) that profess belief in high reverence for the elderly do not appear to practice their respect (Fry, 1985).

Americans often idealize old age in Japan yet would be unwilling to play the dependent role of the Japanese aged. In addition, modern Japan is dealing with a decline in extended families, the reluctance of young adults to care for their aging parents, the "graying" of Japan's population, and elderly poverty created by rigid mandatory retirement systems (Tobin, 1987). Review the five characteristics that are typical of societies that highly respect the elderly and notice how these aspects have changed in Japan and in the United States in the 20th century.

Across cultures, older adults express three major concerns about old age (Butler, 1989): First, they have fears about being a burden to others and about not being able to deal with the costs of old age. Fears in this area may be expressed in terms of the antecedents of being institutionalized: declining mobility, memory, and urinary control. One specific symbol of not becoming a burden is maintaining a driver's license. The license wards off the stigma of an old-age identity (Eisenhandler, 1990). A second concern is possible intergenerational conflicts. Although the old and the young are not "natural enemies," misinformation, ideology, and competing interests can fuel conflicts. For example, political debates on Social Security policy can generate young-old conflict. A third concern involves the stagnation of societies. This concern is for both future generations and for creation of meaningful roles for the elderly. Seniors in Peace Corps and in community volunteer programs help to deal with this concern (Butler, 1989).

Emotional and Personality Development in Late Adulthood

Emotions in Old Age

Positive Emotions

Research findings indicate little relationship between age and happiness (Kozma & Stones, 1983). Such factors as good health, relationships, life activities, and earlier attitudes are better predictors of happiness than is age (Cutler, 1979). Overall, elderly persons have high levels of life satisfaction and happiness (Harris et al., 1975), although European Americans self-report higher levels than African Americans (Chatters, 1988).

A good indicator of the positive emotional experience of older adults is the finding that, for every person who feels life is worse than expected over the age of 65, three

say that it is better than expected (Horn & Meer, 1987; Kaufman, 1987). Positive experiences among older adults appear to be the norm across cultures. In a 13-nation international survey on values and well-being over the lifespan, persons over 50 had the highest levels of contentment, satisfaction, and stability (Butt & Beiser, 1987).

Depression in the Elderly

Despite the high levels of contentment and happiness among older adults, depression is also more prevalent in the elderly than in other age groups (Billig, 1987). In fact, depression is the most common emotional problem of the elderly, with 6 percent having a major depression and 15 percent sufficiently depressed that counseling would be helpful (LaRue, Dessonville, & Jarvik, 1985).

Symptoms of depression in the elderly are identical to depression symptoms in younger adults: sadness, slowness, sleep disturbance, dramatic appetite change, tiredness, feelings of worthlessness and hopelessness, inability to concentrate, weight changes, loss of interest in activities, distorted speech, lowered sexual drive, and worrying (Billig, 1987; Klerman, 1983). However, depression in older adults more frequently is first manifested as a physical problem (e.g., headaches, low back pain, chest symptoms, or bowel disturbances) (Billig, 1987).

Sometimes, depression in the elderly is due to the cumulative effect of intense losses in their life. Elderly persons experience numerous losses, including a decline in bodily functions and stamina, deaths of friends and relatives, lowered status, impaired senses, poor health, a diminishing social network, the loss of career, and the "reliving" of losses via reminiscence. Physical disabilities may be the most difficult loss with which to deal (Billig, 1987; Jarvik, 1983). The role of losses in interpersonal relationships was supported by a study of elderly subjects in independent living situations. Individuals with more depression symptoms reported receiving less emotionally satisfying and consistent support from relatives (Grant, Patterson, & Yager, 1988).

Physical illnesses can also cause depression. Half of those who have a stroke are depressed within 2 years. Alzheimer's disease, Parkinson's disease, chronic lung disorders, kidney disorders, thyroid abnormalities, and nutritional abnormalities are all associated with increased rates of depression (Billig, 1987). Depression rates for older men with several chronic illnesses and recent surgery are very high (LaRue et al., 1985). Depression can also be a side effect of medications (Klerman, 1983).

Helping older adults to deal with depression involves the same tasks as helping younger depressed persons. Supportive family and friends can talk with the depressed person, encourage a good diet, ensure that medications are taken correctly, and help to increase the person's activities and socialization. The elderly person also should undergo a physical examination to rule out potential physical causes (Billig, 1987).

Personality Characteristics in Older Adulthood

Personality Stability

Do you expect your personality to change or to be stable during your adult years? Do you think that your personality in old age will undergo radical changes? Many researchers suggest that most older people do not experience dramatic personality transformations (e.g., Neugarten & Neugarten, 1986).

Finn (1986) explored the issue of personality stability throughout adulthood, using two age groups of male subjects who took the Minnesota Multiphasic Personality Inventory (MMPI) in both 1947 and 1977 as part of a longitudinal medical study. He compared the test-retest results on 17 characteristics of a group that had been 17 to 25 years old and a group that had been 43 to 53 years old at the time of the initial testing (see Table 17.5).

Ten characteristics in Finn's study changed more from young to middle adulthood than from middle to older adulthood, suggesting that personality traits change less in the older adult years. The one exception was the characteristic of denying physical complaints, and this exception may be explained by the increase in actual physical illness in older adults compared to younger adults.

Finn found that more than half of the traits had high stability for older adults, while only two characteristics were very stable for younger subjects. Interestingly, delinquency and religious fundamentalism showed high stability for both age groups. The high stability suggests little change in behaviors and beliefs about both delinquency and religious fundamentalism throughout adulthood.

The characteristics of depression and somatization (e.g., fatigue, aches, and pains) showed low stability for both age groups. That is, levels of depression and somatization in 1977 could not be predicted by scale scores in 1947. These characteristics are probably influenced more by current life events than by internal personality traits.

While results of Finn's study suggest that, throughout the adult years, personality becomes more stable, the results may indicate that people's beliefs about themselves become more consistent, while their actual behaviors continue to change throughout their lives (Finn, 1986).

Gender Differences in Older Adults

Table 17.6 shows personality characteristics that older men and women perceive as common traits in the elderly. Compared to similar studies with younger subjects, older adults view themselves as less stereotypically feminine and masculine. Older males perceive themselves as sympathetic and compassionate, two traits often associated with females. Likewise, older females perceive themselves as dominant, adventurous, and assertive, traditionally masculine traits. The two lists have some characteristics in common, and both appear quite androgynous; yet, several traits that appear in each list are unique to that gender (Windle & Sinnott, 1985).

Table 17.5

Stability of Personality Characteristics Over 30 Years as Measured by 17 MMPI Factor Scales

Group 1: Middle to Old Age

Low Stability:
  Denial of physical complaints*
  Depression
  Somatization

Moderate Stability:
  Optimism versus pessimism
  Neurotic anxiety
  Social extroversion
  Paranoia
  Phobias

High Stability:
  Restraint
  Psychoticism
  Cynicism
  Traditional femininity
  Delinquency
  Traditional masculinity
  Family attachment
  Intellectual interests
  Religious fundamentalism

Group 2: Young to Middle Adult

Low Stability:
  Paranoia*
  Depression*
  Somatization

Moderate Stability:
  Optimism versus pessimism
  Restraint*
  Neurotic anxiety
  Psychoticism*
  Cynicism*
  Denial of physical complaints
  Social extroversion
  Traditional femininity*
  Traditional masculinity
  Phobias*
  Family attachment*
  Intellectual interests*

High Stability:
  Delinquency
  Religious fundamentalism*

*Indicates that the age group changed significantly more than did the other age group. From S. E. Finn, "Stability of Personality Self-Ratings Over 30 Years: Evidence For an Age/Cohort Interaction" in *Journal of Personality and Social Psychology,* 50, 816, 1986. Copyright 1986 by the American Psychological Association. Reprinted by permission.

Neugarten's Personality Types

Bernice Neugarten's Kansas City Studies of Adult Life involved following several hundred persons ages 50 to 80 for a 6-year period (Neugarten, Havighurst, & Tobin, 1968). The results of this longitudinal study suggested four personality types (and seven subtypes) in old age.

Table 17.6
Personal Characteristics of Elderly Males and Females
Based on Responses to the Bem Sex-Role Inventory

Characteristics of Elderly Men	
*Feminine: Sympathetic, Shy, Understanding	Leadership
Sensitive: Compassionate, Warm	*Bitter
*Resourceful	*Dominant
*Achievement-Oriented	Kind

Characteristics of Elderly Women	
*Resourceful	Adventurous
*Feminine	Self-Reliant and Nurturant
*Achievement-Oriented	Involved With Others
*Dominant	Assertive and Loyal
*Bitter	

*Characteristics perceived by both men and women.
From M. Windle and J. D. Sinnot, "A Psychometric Study of the Bem Sex Role Inventory With an Older Adult Sample" in *Journal of Gerontology*, 40, 336–343, 1985. Copyright © 1985 The Gerontological Society of America.

The **integrated personality** is mature, flexible, and open to new stimuli, and has high life satisfaction and complex and intact cognitive functioning. Three subtypes are: (1) **reorganizers**—highly active persons who have substituted new activities for no longer appropriate activities; (2) **focused persons**—moderately active persons who concentrate on selective, satisfying roles; and (3) **disengaged persons**—low-activity persons with self-contained yet content lives.

The **armored-defended personality** is striving, ambitious, and achievement-oriented. Individuals with this personality type have a strong need to control impulses and to defend themselves against anxiety. Two subtypes are: (1) **holding-on persons,** who try to live a middle-age lifestyle as long as possible; and (2) **constricted persons,** who limit energy expenditure and social interaction in an effort to slow aging.

The **passive-dependent personality** depends on others to meet personal needs. Two subtypes are: (1) **succorance-seeking persons,** who have good life satisfaction as long as they have someone to lean on; and (2) **apathetic persons,** who are passive and low in achievement.

The final personality type is the **unintegrated personality,** a pattern of disorganized, dysfunctional living.

Change in Psychological Orientation

Carl Jung proposed that a fundamental psychological reorientation occurs from middle age through old age in that individuals shift from dealing with external issues and focus more on internal feelings and interpersonal relationships.

Older men may do more nuturant, active grandparenting than they did as parents. This change is due partly to a lessening of gender roles in older adulthood and partly to having more time after retirement from a career.

successful study tip

Remembering Neugarten's Personality Types

Map out Neugarten's four personality types and seven subtypes to increase the meaningfulness of this material:

Integrated (mature)	Armored-Defended (striving)
Reorganizers	Holding-on
Focused	Constricted
Disengaged	
Passive-Dependent (dependent on others)	Unintegrated (disorganized, dysfunctional)
Succorance-seeking	
Apathetic	

This interiority is a reflective and philosophical assessment of accomplishments and failures and is associated with becoming more introspective, more cautious, slower, and more practical (Campbell, 1972; Siegler, 1980). At the same time, levels of openness and extroversion remain rather stable (Costa et al., 1986).

Carol Ryff (1982) found that both men and women report a change from instrumental values (e.g., ambition, courage, capability) to terminal values (e.g., sense of accomplishment, freedom) as they get older—that is, there is a move from "doing" to "being." It seems that men initiate this shift somewhat earlier than do women.

An internal orientation forces the individual to focus on how his or her life has been lived. Robert Butler (1963) suggested that older adults participate in a **life review** in which they recall and recount aspects of their lives—both the highs and lows, the past and the present. Ideally, older individuals can relate their life stories to the next generation and perceive the passing on of generational links.

When college-age individuals interviewed elderly relatives regarding their views on personal well-being and effective living, the following major themes were apparent (Long, Anderson, & Williams, 1990):

1. The primary contributors to a sense of well-being throughout life are family, religion, and good health.
2. Older adulthood is more satisfying than either young adulthood or middle adulthood.
3. The greatest accomplishment in life is successful rearing of children; successful marriages, careers, and religious choices were mentioned by some persons.
4. If older adults could change something about their earlier life, they would get more education or use their education better.
5. Older adults' most important advice to younger people was to live by high religious or moral principles.
6. As they get older, adults worry less about money and pay more attention to satisfying personal needs and to viewing life as intrinsically precious.

You might want to interview elderly relatives or friends to see if their responses are similar to the life reflections given in this study.

Developmental Tasks in Old Age

Erikson's Ego Integrity Versus Despair

According to Erik Erikson (1964, 1985), older adults experience the eighth and final psychosocial crisis, **ego integrity versus despair.** Ego integrity is achieved through a life review in which individuals accept and take responsibility for mistakes, faults, failures, and disappointments, while also acknowledging their positive impact in the world. Contentment with significant others in their life and a view that life is acceptable the way it was played out develops. However, individuals who cannot accept the characteristics and flavor of what life has been experience a sense of despair and hopelessness. Ego integrity leads to acceptance of mortality, but despair leads to fear of death.

Successful resolution of this last psychosocial crisis leads to the virtue of wisdom, a characteristic that for centuries has been associated with old age. However, there are two basic problems with this idea. One problem is that some research indicates that wisdom is no more common in older adulthood than in other adulthood stages (e.g., Smith & Baltes, 1990). The second, and more fundamental, problem is how to define wisdom. Wisdom is a common concept, yet its definition is elusive. If wisdom is defined as the recognition of and response to human limitation (Taranto, 1989), then wisdom is indeed a likely outcome of a successful last psychosocial stage.

Peck's Challenges of Late Adulthood

Robert Peck (1968) believed that three tasks need to be resolved during Erikson's eighth psychosocial stage and that successfully dealing with these three challenges helps people to become less concerned with concrete work and physical condition, and more focused on self-understanding and the meaning of life. According to Peck, the three challenges are:

1. **Ego differentiation versus work-role preoccupation.** This task involves dealing with one's work identity and being able to define oneself in broader terms than one's career. If not self-initiated, events such as retirement or last child leaving home force individuals to address this issue. For many older persons, this switch involves a shift from determining self-meaning on the basis of action to using an affective, or feeling, identity (Mutran, 1987).
2. **Body transcendence versus body preoccupation.** Preoccupation with one's body often decreases in young adulthood, but if not, physical decline and chronic illnesses force this issue in old age. Having a satisfactory life depends on having good, meaningful relationships in spite of physical discomfort.
3. **Ego transcendence versus ego preoccupation.** This most important task involves dealing with one's own mortality and the fear of death. Ego can be transcended by seeing enduring personal achievements, whether through career, offspring, or cultural contributions, and by contributing to the happiness or well-being of others.

Thus, according to both Erikson and Peck, personality changes that occur in later adulthood are more a change in focus than a major shift. Personality factors remain relatively stable in older adults, and older adults remain relatively content with themselves.

guided review

5. True or false: Depression is the most common emotional problem of the elderly.
6. Compared to similar studies with younger subjects, older adults view themselves in _____ (more, less) stereotypically feminine and masculine ways.
7. Older adults with _____ personalities are striving, ambitious, and achievement-oriented.
8. Erikson's eighth and final stage is _____ versus _____, and successful resolution of this crisis leads to the virtue of _____.

answers

5. True [LO-6]. 6. less [LO-7]. 7. armored-defended [LO-8]. 8. ego integrity; despair; wisdom [LO-9].

Lifestyle Activities of Older Adults

Styles of Successful Aging

What is the "appropriate" way to age? Should you drop out of activities and spend most of your days in a rocking chair or in front of the television set? Should you continue your career and other activities as long as possible? Or, should you remain active but in different roles than you had in earlier adult years? All of these patterns have been suggested as successful ways to age—and indeed, any of these models can lead to a satisfactory life *if* the older person can make the choice, rather than having the style dictated from external sources.

Disengagement Theory

One of the earliest proposed theories of psychosocial aging was the **disengagement theory** of Elaine Cumming and William Henry (1961). According to this theory, aging is a progressive process of withdrawal from work and other institutions. It is a double withdrawal in that, as older persons withdraw from society, society withdraws from the elderly.

Disengagement is viewed as beginning in late middle age, a time period in which people often narrow their social sphere, find that their worker and parental roles are becoming less central, and lose some friends through death. During disengagement, persons become more passive and fail to acquire new roles. Over time, they give up more roles.

Although these changes can be viewed as a loss of important ties, induced isolation, and a move to passivity and social inactivity, disengagement theory was proposed as a successful aging pattern because it permits escape from excessive stress, allows better coping with decreases in physical health and cognitive skills, and leads to tranquility and increased introspection.

Disengagement theory may explain the aging pattern of some elderly, but research findings do not generally support the notion that most elderly disengage. Rather, participation and associations continue. Of course, some roles do drop out—parenting, for example, becomes less central. However, disengagement in one area is likely to mean involvement in one or more new activities (Adams, 1987; Babchuk, Peters, Hoyt, & Kaiser, 1979; Cutler, 1979; Kahana, Kahana, & McLenigan, 1980; Longino & Kart, 1982).

Activity Theory

Quite different from disengagement theory, Robert Havighurst's **activity theory** proposes that most successfully aging people do not disengage but maintain the activities and attitudes of middle age (Havighurst, 1961; Havighurst, Neugarten, & Tobin, 1968). Quite simply, the more roles, the more life satisfaction in the later years.

Of course, some specific activities cannot be maintained due to changed circumstances (e.g., parenting diminishes when children leave home; retirement affects work activity) or changed abilities (e.g., sports activities may be dropped as physical capabilities decline). However, successful aging within this model includes substitution of ac-

tivities. Most older adults maintain a fairly stable level of activity—if some activities must be dropped, others are added (Longino & Kart, 1982).

A survey of more than a thousand older adults about their activities and satisfaction with life found that highest life satisfaction levels involved friends and family in informal activities. Solitary activities (e.g., television watching, reading, some hobbies) did not seem to affect life satisfaction levels, but formal, structured group activities had a negative effect on life satisfaction among older adults (Longino & Kart, 1982).

successful study tip

Disengagement and Activity Theories of Psychosocial Aging

Use the following figures to form a strong visual image of the contrasts between the disengagement and activity theories of psychosocial aging:

Disengagement (decreasing activities and involvement)

Activity (continued activities and involvement)

Role Exit Theory

Zena Smith Blau (1981) proposed **role exit theory,** which deals with the effect on older adults of a loss in a major life role. Occupational and marital statuses are core identities or anchoring points for adult identity. Throughout adulthood, transitions in these arenas (e.g., unemployment, divorce) can be shattering, undermining experiences. Yet, with time, many adults view these "role exits" as transitional points that led to other experiences.

For some older adults, however, the "role exits" of retirement and widowhood are overwhelming experiences from which they do not fully recover. Destruction of one or both of these anchoring points in old age can severely undermine feelings of social usefulness. However, if society provides options of social worth for older adults (e.g., volunteerism, church status, grandparenting roles, remarriage), then the loss of a core identity does not have to remain devastating.

Retirement

Attitudes Toward Retirement

Do you want to "work until you drop," or do you hope to opt for early retirement? What types of preparations are you making now for your eventual retirement? What kinds of activities do you hope to be involved in when you retire?

Do you expect life to be better or worse after retirement? The attitudes that you have toward retirement influence how you prepare for it and how easily you will adjust to your retirement years.

Adjusting to retirement is important since the average adult spends about one-fifth of life in retirement (Schick, 1986). About a third of workers look forward to retirement, about a third have some misgivings, and about a third are fatalistic or avoid thinking about retirement. Positive attitudes about retirement are related to wanting to end an unsatisfactory work experience and to believing that personal income will remain sufficient (Belbin, 1983). Groups such as African Americans, other minorities, and women, who have had disadvantaged work experiences (e.g., lower-status jobs, sporadic work patterns, low earnings), have a more difficult time saving for a secure retirement (Gibson, R.C., 1988).

Some individuals decide not to retire—about 1 in 6 older men and 1 in 10 older women remain a part of the labor force. Another 20 percent of retirees work part-time. More older white males than black males continue employment, but more older black females than white females keep working (Donovan, 1984; George, 1988). Over 80 percent of the working elderly are satisfied with their work experience (Glenn & Weaver, 1985).

Although today most elderly retire, retirement is basically a 20th-century phenomenon. In 1900, two of three elderly men worked, and in 1950, one in two were working. Part of the increase in retirement came from mandatory retirement policies that stipulated that employees must retire at a specific chronological age, usually 65. (Mandatory retirement age actually varied by occupation. In the 1960s, most airlines required flight attendants to "retire" in their 30s.)

Most mandatory retirement policies are now outlawed, yet older adults continue to choose retirement, often opting to retire at earlier ages. About a third of men and half of women choose to retire between the ages of 55 and 65, often due to job dissatisfaction or health concerns. More women may choose early retirement because their husbands are older and they want to retire when their spouses retire (Palmer et al., 1982).

Prior attitudes, expectations, and preparation (including maintaining health and adequate income) are the most important predictors of successful adjustment to retirement (Horn & Meer, 1987; Parnes & Less, 1985). Involuntary retirement, especially retirement for health reasons, is the most important predictor of unsuccessful retirement adjustment. Excessive free time and feelings of aimlessness also lead to negative retirement views (Monsesian, 1987). Most retirees are satisfied with retirement—only 12 percent of retired individuals would like to be working.

Retirement Preparation

By middle age, adults should be well into making preparations for retirement: Financial experts suggest setting aside 10 percent of salary specifically for retirement. If you hope to retire with an annual income of at least $20,000, you

Like former president and first lady, Jimmy and Rosalynn Carter's work for Habitat for Humanity, many older adults enrich our society through volunteer work.

will need to have nearly 80 percent of that income from sources other than Social Security (Reid, 1988). Middle-aged adults need to gradually cut living costs to suit retirement income, get major bills out of the way, review adequacy of insurance policies, and make investment decisions regarding retirement income (Brammer, Nolen, & Pratt, 1982; Ferraro, 1990).

Retirement preparations involve more than financial planning. Individuals also need a plan for maintaining good health (e.g., realistic exercise plan, good nutrition, regular checkups), for developing appropriate leisure activities and anticipating how additional free time will be spent, and for considering future living arrangement options (Bramer et al., 1982; Ferraro, 1990).

Ability to plan for retirement is influenced by economic climate and political policies. Between 1974 and 1981, for example, the retirement preparation index decreased: Savings decreased, home ownership remained stable, but will preparation increased. Since that time period, an increase in retirement preparation programs, Individual Retirement Accounts (IRAs), and rising saving rates suggest that more people are now making retirement preparations (Ferraro, 1990).

Gradual Retirement Policies in Europe

In the United States, retirement is typically a sudden event. After years of employment, an individual has a last day of work, a brief retirement party, and then full retirement. Many European corporations have phased retirement policies. Over a period of months or even years, workers gradually reduce their working time in stages, often without wage or benefit reductions (Swank, 1982).

Sweden has nationally legislated retirement policies that affect all companies. Persons 60 to 64 years of age may reduce their work hours and receive partial compensation for lost earnings from the national pension fund. These partial pensioners have more than doubled since the program was initiated in 1976, and they work an average of 26.7 hr a week. What is your view of such phased-in retirement plans?

Phases of Retirement

Robert Atchley (1971, 1976) proposed seven phases to retirement. Although people do not necessarily experience every phase, each stage poses specific adjustment tasks:

1. The remote preretirement phase begins when individuals enter the work force. Although young workers recognize that retirement will occur, it is still far in the future. Therefore, the beginning worker is more focused on current earnings and work conditions than pension plans. However, young workers who invest in long-term savings enhance their eventual retirement adjustment.

2. The near preretirement phase occurs as workers determine a specific retirement plan or even a specific retirement date. Besides planning for retirement realities, workers increasingly fantasize about how time will be spent during retirement. Another task is emotionally withdrawing from their career or company.

3. The honeymoon phase, which immediately follows retirement, is a time of joy, excitement, and living out preretirement dreams. Many new retirees increase their favorite leisure activities, such as golf, fishing, gardening, and travel. Others become more involved grandparents. The first 6 months of retirement seem to be the most positive, but for some retirees, the honeymoon phase extends for years (Ekerdt, Bosse, & Levkoff, 1985).

4. The disenchantment phase begins when the newness of retirement wears off, and retirees settle into a daily routine. If retirement fantasies have been unrealistic, if excessive time leads to boredom or depression, or if health or financial problems occur, retirees may become disenchanted. Typically, satisfaction with retirement life and levels of activity are lowest at the end of the first year of retirement (Ekerdt et al., 1985).

5. The reorientation phase involves looking for new opportunities in social, leisure, community, or even work activities. During this phase, retirees search for realistic choices that will result in satisfaction with living. Often, by the end of the second year of retirement, retirees are increasing their activity levels and feeling more satisfaction with life's options (Ekerdt et al., 1985).

6. Once the reorientation has resulted in some satisfactory options, retirees enter the stability phase. Although individuals may still make some changes, they are living a retirement that suits them. They are experiencing a comfortable and satisfying lifestyle and have become a "master retiree." Some retirees, of course, move directly from the honeymoon phase to the stability phase.

7. The final phase, called the terminal phase, is marked by three options: (1) a return to the worker role, (2) a loss of independence and a move into a sick and disabled role, or (3) death.

Adjusting to Retirees

The retiree is not the only one who has to adjust to retirement: Family members, especially the spouse, must make adjustments, too. Spouses who have been in the traditional role of homemaker may face the most dramatic changes (Hill & Dorfman, 1982; Keating & Cole, 1980). For example, homemaker wives must adjust to husbands' increased time around the house, and only 28 percent of retired husbands begin to help more with housework. Moreover, some wives become fed up with retired husbands who want to "reteach" them how to vacuum or dry dishes when the wives have managed these tasks efficiently for years. Common complaints are that husbands do not have enough to do and that there is too much togetherness. However, many spouses enjoy the role of helping the newly retired spouse to find new interests and keeping them busy. Many spouses like the increase in joint activities, especially travel. Adjustment is higher if husbands and wives allow each other some privacy. Retirement tends to highlight both the positive and negative qualities within marriages (Brubaker, 1985).

Activities of Older Adults

Work and Leisure Activities

How do older adults spend their time? Compared to younger adult, retirees do more exercise, reading, hobbies, visiting, home maintenance, and volunteer work (Parnes & Less, 1985). Table 17.7 lists the activities in which older males and females of three ethnic groups engage. Statistically significant differences were found for five of the activities: church activities, volunteering, working, doing child care, and farming (Harris, Begay, & Page, 1989). Additional studies have found that older African Americans are more likely than older European Americans to participate in senior citizen centers and to be active in church, but older European Americans are more likely to engage in educational and informational organizations (George, 1988).

Table 17.7 also reveals significant gender differences. The six activities that older women do more than older men are: reading, thinking, housework, church activities, cooking, and crafts. Child-care activities, typically seen as

Table 17.7
Percentage of Older Males and Females Within Each Ethnic Group Engaging in Each Activity

Overall		Native Americans		European Americans		Hispanic Americans	
		Males	Females	Males	Females	Males	Females
79%	Reading	50%	81%	61%	88%	92%	86%
78	Friends	75	89	61	79	75	71
77	TV watching	75	78	72	77	92	71
74	Traveling	75	64	72	80	75	43
68	Thinking	25	89	39	80	58	43
67	Housework	25	83	39	74	58	86
65	Church activities	63	86	33	59	75	57
62	Cooking	38	81	33	71	42	71
60	Exercising	63	70	56	59	67	43
54	Making crafts	38	72	22	68	8	57
53	Gardening	88	53	22	62	58	29
50	Volunteering	63	70	22	41	42	43
42	Sitting	38	61	17	32	50	29
30	Working	75	42	22	18	17	14
29	Doing child care	50	50	6	18	33	29
13	Hunting	38	14	17	6	17	0
12	Farming	50	20	6	0	8	0

From Mary B. Harris, et al., "Activities, Family Relationships and Feelings About Aging in a Multicultural Elderly Sample" in *International Journal of Aging and Human Development*, 29, 103–117, Table 1, p. 108, 1989. Copyright © 1989 Baywood Publishing Company, Inc., Amityville, NY.

"women's work," do not have a gender difference in old age. Many older men have more time to take pleasure in caring for children after retirement, and some women avoid child-care activities because they have "already done enough of that." Many older adults change activities to improve their health. An interview of nearly all senior citizens residing in Willsboro, New York, found that 83 percent had attempted one or more lifestyle changes in the past year, with nearly half maintaining the change for at least 6 months. Table 17.8 shows the percentage of elders who attempted change.

Some older adults make huge changes because they change cultures late in life. A study of older Vietnamese refugee adults found that language acquisition was harder for them than for younger refugees. Many did not have enough command of English to shop for food, to apply for aid, or to contact emergency services. Generally, older Vietnamese men did better than older Vietnamese females in the ability to use English. This sex difference may be due to Vietnamese women's socialization to accept lower status and less involvement outside of the family realm (Tran, 1990). Being an older refugee is a challenging and sometimes overwhelming situation.

Table 17.8
Types of Lifestyle Change Attempts Reported by Elders

Change Type	Percentage of Elders Reporting Attempted Change
Stop smoking	18%
Engage in regular exercise	35
Increase muscle flexibility	19
Control weight	35
Balance diet	38
Manage alcohol use	6
Control medications	11
Reduce stress	22
Add excitement	12
Improve social lives	19
Increase community service	26

From J. Allen, "New Lives For Old: Lifestyle Change Initiatives Among Older Adults" in *Health Values*, 10, 8–18, Table 2 page 12, November/December 1986. Copyright © 1986 PNG Publications, P.O. Box 4593, Morgantown, WV 26504–4593.

Compared to younger persons, older adults are more likely to attend church, read the Bible, and pray.

Community Service

About a third of older adults become involved in some form of community service. Volunteering at a museum, visiting nursing-home residents, and participating in foster grandparents programs are some of the ways in which older adults add meaningful life experiences and feel like they are contributing to future generations (Rosel, 1986).

Older adults also are more active than others in political voting. They are more likely to be registered and to vote. In fact, elders vote at twice the rate of the youngest voting group of 18- to 20-year-olds (Rosel, 1986). Older males are more likely to vote than older females, and elder European Americans are more likely to vote than elder African Americans; however, the gender difference and the race difference in voting are each less than 5 percent (George, 1988).

Table 17.9 Spiritual Values and Religious Activities of Younger and Older Adults		
Spiritual Values		
	Percentages Replying "Yes"	
	Under 65	**Over 65**
1. Is religious faith the most important influence in your life?	56%	82%
2. Do you get personal comfort and support from religion?	69	87
3. Do you try to put religious beliefs into practice?	69	89
Church Attendance		
Age Group	**Weekly Church Attendance**	
65 and over	48%	
50 to 64	45	
30 to 49	40	
18 to 29	31	

Source: Data from The Gallup Report, June-July 1982.

Religious and Spiritual Values

Persons over age 65 value religion more than younger individuals. Studies show an increase in religious faith, prayer, Bible reading, listening to religious programs, and spirituality among the elderly (Achenberg, 1985; George, 1988; Schick, 1986; Ward, 1984). Table 17.9 compares older adults with other adults on religion.

Relationships in Older Adulthood

After the child-rearing years and once "launching of adult children" has begun, the nuclear family unit is in a contracting, rather than expanding, phase (Brubaker, 1985). This does not mean that family becomes less important and more distant. In fact, across all races (see Table 17.10), most older adults report feeling closer to their families than in previous years (Harris et al., 1989; Taylor, 1988).

Marriage

Over the years, the number of older adults who have been single, married, divorced, or widowed has varied. Figure 17.2 shows the marital status of three cohorts as they entered old age. Comparisons of the first and third cohorts show several changes: Divorces increased fourfold, but the

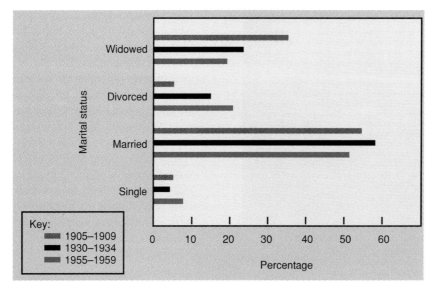

Figure 17.2
Marital status distribution at ages 65 to 69 by cohort.
Source: Data from P. Uhlenberg, et al., "Divorce For Women After Midlife" in *Journal of Gerontology: Social Sciences, 45,* S3–11, fig. 2 page S7, 1990.

Table 17.10
Changes in Family Relationships for People Over Age 60

	More	No Change	Less
Time Spent With Family	47%	10%	43%
Closeness to Family	73	12	15
Dependence on Family	32	9	59
Amount of Arguing With Family	10	14	76
Enjoyment of Family	83	10	7

From M. B. Harris, et al., "Activities, Family Relationships and Feelings About Aging in a Multicultural Elderly Sample" in *International Journal of Aging and Human Development,* 29, 103–117, Table 2, p. 109, 1989. Copyright © 1989 Baywood Publishing Company, Inc., Amityville, NY.

number widowed was halved. Being married is the most common status for all three cohorts (Uhlenberg, Cooney, Boyd, 1990).

Most married older persons married before entering old age. In fact, only 1 percent of brides and 2 percent of bridegrooms are 65 years or older. Very long-term marriages are more common than brand-new married older couples. About 3 percent of all marriages involve couples who will celebrate golden wedding (50 years) anniversaries. In fact, one in five first marriages lasts this long. These long-term couples tend to be very satisfied with their relationships, describing them as "give-and-take" relationships with much sharing of activities (Brubaker, 1985).

Developmental Tasks for Older Couples
Evelyn Duvall (1977) suggested that aging couples (from retirement to death of a spouse) have eight developmental tasks:
1. Making satisfying living arrangements as aging progresses

2. Adjusting to retirement income
3. Establishing comfortable routines
4. Safeguarding physical and mental health
5. Maintaining love, sex, and marital relations
6. Remaining in touch with other family members
7. Keeping active and involved
8. Finding meaning in life

Marital Satisfaction
Most studies have found that marital satisfaction is never higher than in old age. Older couples share more activities, communicate more, and emphasize expressive, honest relationships (Anderson, Russell, & Schumm, 1983; Brubaker, 1985; Gilford & Bengston, 1979; Keating & Cole, 1980; Stinnett, Carter, & Montgomery, 1972; Swensen & Tranaug, 1985). The majority of couples find that marital satisfaction increases when child-rearing activities are completed (Brubaker, 1985).

Over the years of marriage, husbands and wives become more similar to each other, and the happiest of old couples are the most alike (Goleman, 1987). During old age, couples use less distinctive gender roles, and women gain in power within the marital relationship (Ward, 1984). In other words, older married men become more expressive, and older married women become more aggressive (Brubaker, 1985).

According to older couples, the two most rewarding aspects of marriage are companionship and ability to express true feelings, and the two most important characteristics are respect and sharing common interests. The two most troublesome aspects of the marital relationship are having different values and lacking mutual interests (Stinnett et al., 1972).

Retirement and the aging process can increase interdependence within the marital relationship. For example, poor health in one spouse makes that spouse dependent on

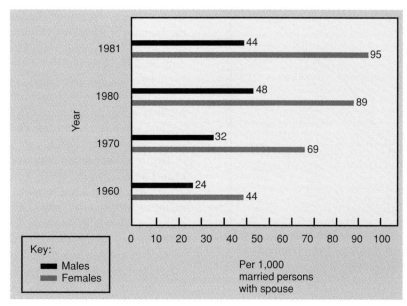

Figure 17.3

Divorced persons Ages 65 years and over per 1,000 married persons with spouse present.

Source: Data from "Marital Status and Living Arrangements: March 1981" in *Current Population Reports,* Series P. 20, No. 372, p. 3, 1982. Bureau of Census.

the other for care. Typically, an older husband's dependence on his wife increases at a faster pace than her dependence on him (Antonucci & Akiyama, 1987; Kelley, 1981). Because husbands tend to be older than wives, more wives are placed in the caretaker role (Atchley & Miller, 1983). Changes in interdependence often change levels of marital satisfaction.

Marriage Transitions

Divorce

About 1 percent of divorces involve at least one person 65 years of age or older (Brubaker, 1985). The process and aftermath of divorce is stressful at any age, but divorce for the elderly poses additional problems, especially for older women. Many experience financial problems and have trouble finding employment; some had only married couples for social contact and find themselves fairly isolated after the divorce. Some conclude that it is too late to start over and become resigned to a limited existence.

Figure 17.3 shows that the number of divorced elderly has grown since 1960. Of course, only a minority of the divorced elderly are newly divorced. Others are considered career divorced because they were divorced in their early or middle adulthood years and never remarried. More women than men fit this category. A third group experienced serial divorces, or going through more than one divorce (Brubaker, 1985).

Widowhood

The majority of marriages involve wives younger than their husbands. Even with equal-aged couples, women can expect to outlive their mates by 7.5 years. Therefore, the majority of widowed individuals are women. Three out of

four women will be a widow. In the United States, there are about 10 million widows, but fewer than 2 million widowers (Barrow, 1986). Incidentally, women who are married to younger men tend to live longer than expected, while women married to older men tend to die sooner than expected (Klinger-Vartabedian & Wispe, 1989). Widows and widowers experience an increase in mortality rate, suicide rate, and loneliness, and a decrease in health (Barrow, 1986).

Research findings suggest that the elderly who are in need of the most socioemotional and tangible support are older widowed women. Although many are quite self-sufficient, some need help to deal with loneliness, finances, or decision making. Widows' attitudes about receiving support greatly influence the amount of overall help they get from others. Number of children, children's income, and perceived willingness of children to help affect what proportion of the help comes from adult offspring (O'Bryant & Morgan, 1990). Sibling support is important to many widows; in fact, interaction with married sisters is second only to health in predicting positive emotions among widows (O'Bryant, 1988).

Remarriage

More elderly males than females remarry. After divorce, older men remarry at a rate of 31 per 1,000, and women at 9 per 1,000. After a spouse's death, 20 of 1,000 widowers remarry, and 2 of 1,000 widows. Of the small number of widowed elderly who choose to remarry, the widower waits an average of 1.5 years, and the widow waits an average of 3.8 years. Widowed African Americans wait longer before remarriage (Brubaker, 1985).

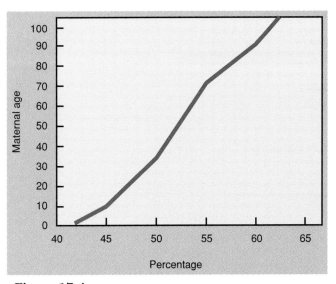

Figure 17.4
Cumulative percentage of maternal age at which the youngest child turns 21.

Source: Data from A. Rossi, "Aging and Parenthood in the Middle Years" in *Life-Span Development and Behavior*, 3, Fig 6 page 167, 1980. Academic Press, New York.

Never-Married Elderly

One in 20 elderly men and 1 in 18 elderly women (i.e., about 5 percent) are never-married individuals, and most never-married elderly remain single. The remarriage rates among those divorced or widowed during old age are low, but both rates are higher than the marriage rate of lifelong single elderly (Brubaker, 1985). Reasons for never marrying include career decisions, homosexual orientation, gender or other demographic imbalances, and family responsibilities that precluded marriage (Rubenstein, 1987).

Of the more than 1 million never-married elderly, a small number are lifelong isolates, but most have close friends, varied lifestyles, and social lives. Women who live in urban areas are the most likely to have frequent contacts with friends and to engage in the most activities; rural men have the fewest diverse social relationships and activities (Keith & Nauta, 1988). Rather than being lonely and desolate, most never-married elderly are autonomous and self-reliant (Keith, 1983). Surprisingly, fewer never-married elderly live alone than divorced or widowed elderly (Rubenstein, 1987).

Adult Children

Relationships Between Older Parents and Adult Children

Eighty percent of the elderly have living children, with 10 percent of the elderly having a child who is also in the late adulthood years (Aizenberg & Treas, 1985; Cicirelli, 1983). Figure 17.4 shows the cumulative percentage of maternal age at which the youngest child turns 21. In their early 50s, the majority of mothers still have a child under the age of 21, but by age 60, fewer than 10 percent of mothers do

(Rossi, 1980). Therefore, the years preceding old age are the busiest for launching children (when children begin independent living), and most elderly have relationships with only adult children.

One task for older adults is to adapt their relationship with their children to a more peerlike adult relationship. Mothers are more successful in this than fathers, probably because some fathers have been in a traditional, authoritarian, head-of-the-household role and find it difficult to not dictate rules and restrictions for their adult children (Fischer, 1986).

The cultural norm for older parents and adult children seems to be distant intimacy, a pattern of both attachment and separation with two-way help during crises (Fischer, 1986; Stevens-Long, 1984). Attachment is visible in many forms, including long-distant communications, periodic visits, and residential proximity (Cicirelli, 1983). Over three-fourths of the elderly see an adult child at least weekly, and more than four-fifths live within an hour of an adult child (Hagestad, 1987; Miller, 1981).

Both elderly parents and adult children see their relationship as (1) a source of emotional support, (2) one in which important matters can be discussed, and (3) a source of available resources. Less important, but agreed upon, is the advantage of either living nearby or communicating regularly (Hamon & Blieszner, 1990). Living nearby seems to be more predictive of a close relationship in rural families than in urban families (Mercier, Paulson, & Morris, 1988). Elderly parents are less likely than adult children to think that adult children should give them assistance, provide a home, or adjust their work schedule to meet a parent's needs (Brody & Lang, 1982; Hagested, 1987; Hamon & Blieszner, 1990).

Another important role of intergenerational ties is that persons are allowed to both "preview" and "review" other phases of life (Hagestad, 1987; Miller, D. A. 1981). Adult children get to review childhood through their own children and to preview late adulthood through their parents. Elderly parents can only "review" through the other generations. However, they can review more than one generation—their own children, their children's children, and sometimes even their grandchildren's children. The "Exploring the Parent/Child Relationship" features focuses on grandparenting.

Adult Children's Attitudes Toward and Support of Elderly Parents

The adult children/elderly parents time period in the parent-child relationship is often one of renewed closeness (Fischer, 1986). Most adult children feel close to both elderly parents: 87 percent feel close to fathers and 91 percent feel close to mothers. Interestingly, adult children feel less close to a widowed parent than to two living parents (Cicirelli, 1983). Perhaps, the surviving parent places more stressful demands on the adult offspring. When adult children are supporting their elderly parents, problems can develop (see Table 17.11). Two common problems are an overcontrolling,

Table 17.11
Six Problems That Can Make Families
Unable to Support Aging Parents in Need

Caretaker-Based Problems

1. Caretaker fatigue

2. Competing demands (e.g., parent versus spouse versus children)

Old-Pattern Problems

3. Depression and anger (i.e., unable to deal with parental decline, so use denial)

4. Wrong survivor (i.e., expectations that the other parent would die first)

5. Sibling rivalry (e.g., one does most of the work of caretaking, but the other sibling gets most of the credit)

6. Unemancipated offspring who regret dependence and lost time

Work from M. G. Schmidt, "Failing Parents, Aging Children" was originally published in *Journal of Gerontological Social Work*, 2, 1980. © 1980 Haworth Press Inc., 10 Alice Street, Binghamton, NY 13904.

intrusive elderly parent and an elderly parent who is embarrassed over dependency issues (Brubaker & Brubaker, 1981). These problems are usually surmountable but are difficult to handle for adult children whose parents were rejecting, unloving, and uncaring when the children were growing up (Miller, D. A., 1981). Some adult children abuse or neglect their elder parents, although this is not typical (Steinmetz, 1988).

Female adult children typically provide more help and companionship to their elderly parents than male adult children. Regardless of time available, attitudes about obligations, or amount of available external resources, female adult children do the most in providing for their elderly parents. On money issues and decision making, the gender difference disappears (Finley, 1989).

Elderly Parents' Support of Adult Children

Many adult children provide financial support, direct care, and housing for their parents; however, elderly parents are more likely to provide resources for their adult children. Although adult children help parents to deal with such transitions as health conditions and widowhood, elderly parents are just as involved in helping adult children to deal with transitions of marriage, parenthood, and divorce (Johnson, 1981).

Although most adult children are eager to leave their parents' home before marriage (Goldscheider & Goldscheider, 1989), a surprising number of adult children continue to live in their parents' homes. In a study of 146 adult children (average age of 32) residing in the homes of their elderly parents, 63 percent had always resided with their parents (Suitor & Pillemer, 1987). Seventy-five percent had never married, 17 percent were formerly married, and 8 percent were currently married. More daughters (55 percent) than sons lived with their parents. The researchers

found that sharing a residence with adult children had no effect on marital conflict. This finding is somewhat surprising in that studies have shown that marital satisfaction improves when offspring are "launched" from the home. Apparently, regardless of whether launching actually occurs, the parents' marital relationship improves once primary child-rearing is finished.

Childless Elderly

In earlier adult years, childless adults are often warned that, if they stay childless, they will regret the decision when they grow old. Some individuals view their children as "old-age insurance" (Johnson & Catalono, 1981; Keith, 1983). Are these proscriptions reflective of reality? While some studies suggest that elderly parents have more friends and higher life satisfaction (e.g., Rempel, 1985), the majority of research suggests that the childless elderly do not experience more loneliness, lower life satisfaction, less acceptance of death, or lower levels of family support (Glenn & McLanahan, 1981; Johnson & Catalono, 1981; Keith, 1983).

In fact, childless elderly in good health have more contact with friends and neighbors than do other elderly. Indeed, the high level of nonkin contact leads to low isolation, which psychologists suggest can offset the absence of interaction with adult children. Only the childless in poor health, who no longer have high contact with friends, experience high levels of isolation. Even then, the childless who maintain close ties with family members have as much support as the elderly with offspring (Keith, 1983).

The patterns for childless marrieds and childless unmarrieds are somewhat different. Childless marrieds are often socially isolated in that the only relative support is from spouses. Only 20 percent of this group see another relative weekly. On the other hand, over 80 percent of childless unmarrieds have at least weekly contact with one or more relatives. Siblings are the most important source of support. The childless unmarrieds also have wider social networks than their childless married counterparts. The childless unmarrieds are more active in friendships, neighborhoods, and churches (Johnson & Catalono, 1981).

Having children does not guarantee help for the elderly, and not having children certainly does not take away support. The childless elderly follow the **principle of substitution**—that is, when adult children are not available, another family member provides assistance. For childless married persons, care comes from the spouse; for childless unmarried persons, help comes from siblings, nieces and nephews (Johnson & Catalono, 1981).

Siblings

Sibling Patterns

For most, sibling relationships are their longest-lasting relationships in life. About 80 percent of the elderly have at least one living sibling, and about one in five see a sibling at least weekly and one in three see a sibling monthly. At

Grandparents have never been more important in the lives of their grandchildren. For children, these relationships are second in emotional power and influence only to parent-child relationships (Kornhaber & Woodward, 1981). People now live longer, so more children have living grandparents, and most of these grandparents are around for years of interaction. Although some men and women become grandparents in their 30s, the most common age for becoming a grandparent is 49 to 51 for females and 51 to 53 for males (Troll, 1983). Since most people live into their 70s or longer, many children form relationships with grandparents that last into their adult years. In fact, many children get to know at least one great-grandparent or even great-great-grandparent.

Other important changes over previous generations are the health, wealth, and time available to grandparents. A high percentage of grandparents are in good health and can provide their grandchildren with positive stereotypes of the elderly. More grandparents have financial security and are retired (or work only part-time). The combination of good health, financial resources, and free time make grandparents the perfect companions for small children. They have the time and ability to do activities with the youngsters when often their parents are busy working and managing family affairs. Grandparents seem to be most important in assisting single-parent units and teenage mothers. Mobility of families may create geographical distances that limit grandparent-grandchild contact; however, modern transportation systems provide affluent grandparents with continued contact opportunities (Bengston & Robertson, 1985; Kornhaber & Troll, 1986; Kornhaber & Woodard, 1981; Rodeheaver & Thomas, 1986; Tinsley & Parke, 1984; Troll, 1980).

In many divorced families, one set of grandparents has better contact than the other. This may be one reason why some studies find that grandchildren are more likely to be closer to maternal than paternal grandparents (Matthews & Sprey, 1985). The high societal divorce rate has also resulted in a growing number of stepgrandparents. A recent study found that the majority of stepgrandchildren maintain contact with stepgrandparents beyond their high school years and that about half rate relationships with stepgrandparents as important (Trygstad & Sanders, 1989).

Most older adults enjoy their grandparenting role. In conversations, grandparents refer spontaneously to their grandchildren about 27 percent of the time. Grandchildren also often refer spontaneously to their grandparents (Troll, 1983). Ninety-seven percent of grandparents and 85 percent of young adult grandchildren view the grandparent-grandchild relationship as important (Hartshone & Manaster, 1982). Some researchers have suggested that grandparenting has a "Goldilocks effect"—that too much grandparenting is as bad as too little (Hess & Waring, 1978). They found that grandparents are most satisfied with the role when they have some regular (but not overwhelming) contact with their grandchildren.

More grandmothers than grandfathers express satisfaction with the role of grandparenting (Bergston, 1985; Thomas, 1986, 1989). The most active and involved grandparents are found in African-American, Asian-American, Italian-American, and Hispanic-American ethnic groups (Bengston, 1985; Taylor, 1988).

The grandparenting role offers satisfaction in five major aspects: (1) it provides meaning for life; (2) it allows grandparents to be advisors and mentors; (3) it instills a sense of personal immortality through descendants; (4) it allows the reliving of earlier experiences and memories; and (5) it grants grandparents the enjoyment of indulging their grandchildren (Kivnick, 1982). Grandfathers are more likely than grandmothers to emphasize the aspects of family extension and indulgence (Thomas, 1989). Grandparents who emphasize the advising role do not report as much satisfaction with the grandparenting role as others (Thomas, 1986).

Grandparents play the role of upholders of social order—they are in the position to transmit and preserve values and customs through interacting with their grandchildren (Bengston, 1987). Many young children enjoy "gramps" and "nana" telling tales about the "good old days," as well as stories about "what Mommy/Daddy was like as a child."

Grandparents get to smooth out the differences between generations within families (lineage effect) and generations as a whole (cohort effect), while sharing the events and attitudes of their own time period compared to their grandchildren's time period (period effect).

But as grandparents teach grandchildren about traditions and stabilities, grandchildren teach their grandparents about change and renewal (Bengston, 1987). Adjusting to rapid societal changes is difficult for many older adults, and grandchildren often provide just the right approach to introducing their grandparents to new technology (e.g., personal computers), political movements, and fads and fashions. The grandparent-grandchild dyad is often a nurturing and accepting teaching unit.

Of course, not all grandparents operate in the same way. Age is one factor in grandparenting style. In fact, the older the grandparent, the less central the role is seen (Cherlin & Furstenberg, 1986). Younger grandparents have many styles for the role; old grandparents tend to be more formal and distant (Neugarten & Weinstein, 1964). Grandparents from their 50s through their 70s tend to enjoy the role more than grandparents who are either younger than 50 or older than 80. Most grandparents are most satisfied when their grandchildren are young (Troll, 1983). Advanced age is a major reason why great-grandparents are less involved than grandparents; great-grandparents prefer younger children and short visits (Wentowski, 1985).

Grandparenting styles have been described in many ways. The following system divides grandparenting styles into five major types (Neugarten & Weinstein, 1964):

1. *Formal.* While these grandparents are interested in their grandchildren, they take over few of the caretaking aspects.
2. *Fun-seeker.* These grandparents have mutually self-indulgent relationships with their grandchildren. The relationships feature informality and play.

continued

3. *Surrogate parent.* These grandparents (more often the grandmothers) are involved in major caretaking responsibilities with their grandchildren.
4. *Reservoir of family wisdom.* Grandparents (especially grandfathers) are viewed as individuals who can provide skills and resources. In this type, grandparents are somewhat authoritarian and powerful.
5. *Distant figure.* These grandparents have little contact with their grandchildren. Most contacts occur on birthdays and other holidays.

Which style best represents your grandparents? What roles did they play in your life? Which style of grandparent do you want to be/become?

---

least two-thirds of the elderly with siblings feel close to their siblings, and only a fifth feel hostile or indifferent toward siblings (Atchley, 1980; Barrow, 1986; Cicirelli, 1980; Stark, 1988).

Typically, siblings are a crucial part of each other's childhood and adolescence; then drift apart as each is involved with careers, marriage, and parenting; and then grow increasingly closer in the later adult years. Critical events, such as parental sickness or death, often bring older siblings closer together—or drive rivaling siblings further apart (Stark, 1988).

Developmental Tasks with Siblings During Old Age

Sibling developmental tasks occur throughout the lifespan, and in old age, sibling tasks include (Cicirelli, 1980; Goetting, 1986; Stark, 1988):

1. Siblings often provide companionship and emotional support. This role is more important for childless elderly and for widowed elderly. Although the sibling relationship is valued, elderly sibling interaction does not seem to affect an older adult's morale (Lee & Ihinger-Tallman, 1980).
2. Siblings may provide direct aid and services. In some cases, siblings fill some of the roles of a deceased spouse. Other siblings provide financial help as needed.
3. Many former sibling jealousies and rivalries are transformed into respect, loyalty, and empathy in older adulthood.
4. As friends and relatives die, the number of contact/support services declines, and siblings may help to fill gaps in nurturance and comfort.
5. Siblings often find that reviewing the past together is a rewarding activity. Siblings provide the most central link to each other's past.

Among the elderly, sister-sister relationships are typically the closest, with sister-brother relationships being intermediate in closeness and brother-brother relationships being least close. One reason is that sisters tend to provide more sibling help than do brothers; sisters are more likely to be in the kin-keeping role (Kivett, 1985; Stark, 1988).

Friends and Acquaintances

During late adulthood, the number of friendships often decreases, but the importance of friends increases. Most elderly have at least one close friend, and as in earlier years, older females tend to have more friends than older males. Friends play several roles: They can be buffers against stress, co-participants in leisure activities, and confidants. For older women, the most crucial role of friendships seems to be understanding and support; for older men, friends are most viewed as persons with whom to participate in activities (Antonucci, 1985; Antonucci & Akiyama, 1987; Ebersole & Hess, 1981).

The key to long-term friendships tends to be reciprocity. Over the years, both partners in a friendship have at times been indebted to the other (Roberto & Scott, 1986). The most satisfying relationships are those in which give-and-take is fairly equal, and equal reciprocity is more related to satisfaction with friends than it is to relationships with adult children (Rook, 1987).

guided review

13. True or false: As is the case with many aspects of old age, marital satisfaction in later adulthood declines.
14. The term _____ describes that pattern of both separation and attachment that characterizes the cultural norm for the relationship between older adults and their adult children.
15. Grandparenting styles include the _____ style, in which grandparents are interested but provide little childcare, and the _____ style, in which grandparents engage in mutually self-indulgent activities with their grandchildren.
16. True or false: People who choose to remain childless regret it in old age.

answers

13. False [LO-16]. 14. distant intimacy [LO-19]. 15. formal; fun-seeker [LO-20]. 16. False [LO-21].

Living Arrangements

Independent Living

Living with Spouse or Alone

Seventy-five percent of American elders own the dwelling in which they live. Of this group, 80 percent have paid off their mortgages. Therefore, the home represents a major economic asset that no longer requires a monthly payment. More important is the emotional significance of staying in one's own home, with its history of attachments and reminiscences (Danigelis & Fengler, 1990).

However, the physiological changes that accompany aging, the loss of a spouse, and lowered income after retirement may make it difficult to maintain a home. The house may deteriorate as the owner finds it difficult to make and to afford repairs. Eventually, maintaining an independent home may be impossible.

Another concern is that elderly individuals living alone or with an elderly spouse may develop a significant fear of crime. Table 17.12 shows the responses of 1,185 persons residing in Albany-Schenectady-Troy, New York. Overall, 84 percent felt fairly safe in their own neighborhoods, but a significant minority were fearful. The elderly who lived in urban areas were the most likely to perceive danger, and they often eliminated activities because of their fears. Besides urban residence, variables associated with higher-than-average fear of crime are: female, African American, lower socioeconomic status, living alone, and former crime victim (Ward, LaGory, & Sherman, 1986).

Home sharing and retirement communities provide means to independent living while also allaying concerns about deteriorating health, limited incomes, and fears of crime.

Home Sharing

Home sharing is a living arrangement in which two or more unrelated individuals share a single-family dwelling owned by one of them. Although home sharing may seem like a brand-new idea, at the start of the 20th century, 15 percent of the population lived with nonrelatives; this figure dropped substantially after World War II, as economic conditions became more favorable and there was a boom in home building. Currently, with longer life expectancies and persons unable to buy their own homes, home sharing is again increasing (Danigelis & Fengler, 1990; Givens & Starr, 1989).

Both home owners and home sharers tend to be satisfied with home-sharing arrangements, especially if they give prior consideration to lifestyle compatibility and desired amounts of social interaction. Some arrangements involve rent only, while others emphasize caregiving to the elderly home owner (Danigelis & Fengler, 1990; Givens & Starr, 1989).

Retirement Communities

Retirement communities, living arrangements in which older adults live near other elderly persons, come in a vari-

Retirement communities provide the elderly with many opportunities for social interactions.

Table 17.12
Perceived Safety by Degree of Urbanism

	City	Suburb	Rural
Safe all of the time	45%	62%	67%
Safe most of the time	32	25	26
Safe during the day, not at night	11	9	5
Unsafe most or all of the time	12	4	3

From R. A. Ward, et al., "Fear of Crime Among the Elderly as Person/Environment Interaction" in *The Sociological Quarterly*, 27, Table 1, p. 333, 1986. Copyright © 1986 JAI Press, Greenwich, CT. Carbondale, IL.

ety of forms. Some are entire retirement villages in which dwellings are single-family houses or apartments, and both shopping centers and recreational facilities are on-site. Another form is a single, high-rise building in which the elderly live in apartments and share lounges and a recreation room. A third kind is a life-care home in which residents live in individual apartments or cottages, have meals provided, and have accessibility to medical care and housekeeping assistance. Life-care homes provide such common areas as activity rooms, lounges, and dining rooms.

Retirement communities provide many benefits: (1) they allow longer maintenance of independent living and gradual increase in assistance as abilities decline; (2) living with other older adults provides opportunities for social interaction, a need that can be great after the death of a spouse or close friends; (3) most older adults enjoy living around their peers more than living in the home of an adult child and grandchildren; (4) when medical-care facilities are provided, fears about nursing homes are reduced; (5) fears about being a crime victim are decreased. However, retirement communities are not a desirable option for everyone. Some elderly want to stay in their original neighborhood or prefer to live with individuals from a wide age range.

Table 17.13
Questions That Adult Children Should Answer When Considering Forming a Multigenerational Household

1. How do you feel about helping your older parents?
2. Do you believe that you owe your parents your home and care just because they raised you?
3. How do you feel about old age? Do you see your parents as old?
4. What needs do your parents have, and how can you meet these needs?
5. What is your relationship with your parents?
6. Do you get along well with your parents? Are you close to them?
7. How does your family deal with illness?
8. How does your family deal with financial problems?
9. When your family deals with problems, do family members come together? Feel resentment? Deny?
10. If parents move in, will everyone have enough privacy?
11. If parents move in, will you have to do any remodeling, such as wheelchair ramps, railings?
12. If parents move in, is there enough room in your house?
13. Will there be enough money when all the resources are pooled?
14. Does your community have a transportation program for the elderly?
15. Is there a senior center near your home?
16. Is there an adult day-care center?
17. Is there a respite program at a local nursing home?
18. Are home-delivered meals available?
19. Are home health care, telephone reassurances, and housekeeping assistance services available in your community?
20. Are there support groups for caretakers in your community?

From T. H. Brubaker, *Later Life Families,* page 60, 1985. Copyright © 1985 Reprinted by permission of Sage Publications, Inc.

Dependent Living

Living with Relatives

Some older adults cannot maintain independent living and move in with relatives, most often their adult children. As noted earlier, older adults usually do not want to live with their adult offspring, but in some instances, a multigenerational household may be a desirable option. Some families, such as those raised in the Amish tradition, may cherish the opportunity to care for aged parents. In other families, the elderly parents may be mobile and healthy enough to assist in rearing the grandchildren. In some situations, it is the best option of several inadequate options. The formation of a multigenerational household should be based on realities and not just emotions and obligations. Individuals thinking about having an older parent move into their home should consider the questions posed in Table 17.13. In addition, they should seek the opinion of their older parents—some elders would prefer a life-care retirement community or a nursing home (Brubaker, 1985; Hennon, Brubaker, & Baumann, 1983).

Adult Day-Care Centers

Adult day-care centers, which provide elderly persons with supervised care and activities during the day, are a growing trend in the United States. Although these centers first appeared only in the early 1970s, by 1990 over two thousand existed. Most centers are open from early morning to late afternoon, and a few have overnight and weekend services. Some provide transportation.

Well-run centers have a variety of craft projects, exercise games, tasks (such as baking and yardwork), fenced-in walk areas, and visits from pets, children, and entertainers. They provide meals with decent nutrition and programs that challenge clients to utilize their fullest abilities.

Adult day-care centers help to keep elderly persons out of nursing centers, slow down physical and cognitive deterioration, and provide relief for families that are trying to care for elderly parents (Beck, 1990).

Nursing Homes

One of the biggest fears expressed by aging persons is that they will spend time in a nursing home—about 40 percent expect to be in a nursing home at some point. In actuality, only 5 percent of the elderly are residing in a hospital or nursing home (Brubaker, 1985). The typical nursing-home resident is a widowed female experiencing multiple physical problems. Most residents need help with everyday activities: 78 percent need assistance to get dressed, 40 percent need help in eating, 63 percent have elimination problems, and 91 percent need assistance in bathing (National Center for Health Statistics, 1987).

One problem is that some nursing homes serve as warehouses in which residents spend the majority of time doing nothing. In some nursing homes, residents have little interpersonal contact with each other, and this isolation increases depression (Gottesman & Bourestom, 1974).

A second problem is that many nursing homes employ physical and chemical restraints to keep the residents manageable. In some cases, the number of medications used causes cognitive decline. Nursing-home managers say that physical and chemical restraints keep patients safer and are a necessity in homes with staff shortages. Others claim that acting-out behaviors should not be controlled with restraints, since problematic behaviors are attempts by residents to reestablish a sense of control and dignity (Friedman & Ryan, 1986).

Nursing homes that have stimulating environments, multiple activities, and patient-to-patient contact, that encourage family visitations and interaction, and that let residents take control and responsibility produce healthier, less depressed patients (Gottesman & Bourestom, 1974; Langer & Rodin, 1976).

Even under ideal living conditions, older adults face with greater immediacy than at any other time in their lives the final stage of development—death, the topic of the final chapter in this text.

17. At any given time in America, _____ percent of elderly Americans live in their own homes, while _____ percent live in nursing-care facilities.

18. _____, a living arrangement in which two or more nonrelated individuals live together, is one solution for helping older adults to continue living semi-independently in their own homes.

19. Retirement communities provide many benefits. Which of the following is *not* a benefit?
    A. lengthening of independent living
    B. a gradual phase of assistance as needed
    C. intergenerational living arrangements
    D. opportunities to interact with peers

20. A problem that may occur at some nursing homes is
    A. an overreliance on drugs to control residents.
    B. low amounts of interpersonal contact.
    C. inadequate staff.
    D. all of the above.

answers

17. 75; 5 [LO-23]. **18.** Home sharing [LO-23]. **19.** C [LO-23]. **20.** D [LO-23].

Exploring Human Development

1. Analyze the stereotypes that are being portrayed in magazine advertisements that feature older adults. Compare a variety of magazines (e.g., *Ladies' Home Journal, Modern Maturity, Newsweek*). You might wish to get some magazines from other decades and compare old images with new images.

2. Interview six elderly persons about the advantages and disadvantages of old age. What aspects are most enjoyable and most troublesome? What activities are most meaningful? How is old age different from what they anticipated?

3. Locate five couples who have been married 50 years or more. Ask them to identify the most satisfying aspects of their marriages. Are their responses similar? How similar are the husband's and wife's responses for each couple? Are there gender differences in the responses?

4. Interview individuals who have worked in nursing-home settings. Do they think that the stereotypes about nursing homes reflect reality? What did they like and dislike about their job?

5. Write a job description for the role of grandparent. What personality characteristics are desirable? What tasks will the person have to perform?

Discussing Human Development

1. Videotape segments from popular television programs and commercials that include older adults. View the tape with your classmates, and critique the ways in which older adults are portrayed.

2. List the ways in which American society reinforces both feelings of integrity in older adults and feelings of despair. Discuss ways to eliminate the despairing messages about old age.

3. When long-term marriages end in divorce, how should pensions and Social Security be divided? Does it make any difference whether both spouses worked or one stayed at home? How long must a marriage last for the nonemployed spouse to have a right to retirement benefits?

4. Discuss the advantages and disadvantages of moving to "sunny states" (or other geographical relocation) during the retirement years versus staying in your hometown. Would you consider a move to a retirement community? How have older relatives decided on this issue?

5. What kinds of legislation and enforcement are needed to improve the quality of nursing homes? How can nursing homes deal with mental illness among the elderly (e.g., Alzheimer's, severe depression)? What responsibility does government versus family have for paying for nursing homes? Are nursing homes dumping grounds for impaired elderly, or are they communities? How would you design an ideal nursing home, and what activities would you have at the nursing home?

Reading More About Human Development

Bengston, V. L., & Robertson, J. F. (Eds.). (1985). *Grandparenthood.* Beverly Hills, CA: Sage.

Bengston, V. L., & Schaie, K. W. (Eds.). (1989). *The course of later life: Research and reflections.* New York: Springer.

Bould, S., Sanborn, B., & Reif, L. (1989). *Eighty-five plus: The oldest old.* Belmont, CA: Wadsworth.

Brubaker, T. H. (1985). *Later-life families.* Beverly Hills, CA: Sage.

Fisher, L. R. (1986). *Linked lives: Adult daughters and their mothers.* New York: Harper & Row.

Jackson, J. S. (Ed.). (1988). *The Black American elderly: Research on physical and psychosocial health.* New York: Springer.

Summary

I. Images and stereotypes of older adults
   A. The older adult population is the most diverse, yet most rigidly stereotyped, age group.
      1. A negative stereotype of old people that emphasizes declining abilities and opportunities competes with a positive stereotype of growing wisdom and fortitude.
      2. Historically, the good-bad image of the elderly had emerged by the Middle Ages.
      3. An investigation of popular songs from the 1830s to the 1950s revealed more negative than positive images of aging and older adults.
      4. The double standard of aging has existed for many years.
      5. Ageism is a societal pattern of prejudice against aging and toward older adults.
      6. From television shows to advertising to jokes about older adults, ageism is prevalent in contemporary society.
   B. Ageism varies across cultures and age groups.
      1. Children and adolescents often hold ageist attitudes, but their attitudes can be changed through education.
      2. Modernization theory states that preindustrial societies accord higher status to the aged than do industrialized societies.

3. The status of older adults is higher in societies with ancestor worship, with extended families, and in which conformity is highly valued.

4. Two groups who often work with and for the elderly—nurses and politicians—also often hold negative, ageist views of the elderly.

C. Interestingly, older adults often have the same stereotypes of the elderly as other segments of the population.

1. Cross-culturally, older adults express concerns about becoming a burden to others, about financial insecurity, and about intergenerational conflicts.

2. Older adults also express more global concerns involving the stagnation of societies.

II. Emotional and personality development in late adulthood

A. Older adults experience a variety of positive and negative emotions, but generally have high levels of life satisfaction and happiness.

1. European Americans report higher levels of life satisfaction than do African Americans.

2. Three times as many elderly Americans say that old age is better than they expected, compared to those who say it is worse, and the positive reaction also is found in many other countries.

3. Depression is the most common emotional problem of the elderly and is more prevalent in the elderly than in other age groups.

4. Depression may be caused by physical illnesses or may be due to older adults experiencing the cumulative effects of many losses.

5. Older adults can be helped to deal with depression in the same ways that younger depressed persons are.

B. While research results indicate that personality characteristics remain relatively stable across the adult years, the findings could indicate that only people's beliefs about themselves become more consistent, while their actual behaviors continue to change.

1. Neugarten observed four personality types in old age, including the integrated personality with the subtypes of the reorganizers, the focused, and the disengaged.

2. The armor-defended personality has two subtypes: the holding-on type and the constricted type.

3. The passive-dependent personality includes types that are succorance-seeking and that are apathetic.

4. Individuals with an unintegrated personality type display a pattern of disorganized and dysfunctional living.

5. A shift toward interiority (focusing on internal feelings and interpersonal relationships) in old age is accompanied by a shift from instrumental values to terminal values and, often, by a life review.

C. Several developmental tasks related to psychosocial development in later adulthood have been suggested.

1. Erikson's eighth and final psychosocial stage is ego integrity versus despair, in which ego integrity is achieved by self-acceptance.

2. Ego integrity leads to acceptance of mortality, but despair leads to fear of death.

3. According to Erikson, individuals who successfully resolve this last crisis acquire the virtue of wisdom.

4. Peck identified three tasks to be resolved during Erikson's eighth stage: ego differentiation versus work-role preoccupation, body transcendence versus body preoccupation, and ego transcendence versus ego preoccupation.

III. Lifestyle activities of older adults

A. Several patterns of successful aging have been identified.

1. According to disengagement theory, successful aging involves a progressive withdrawal from work and other social involvements.

2. Activity theory predicts that the most successful aging involves maintaining the activities and attitudes of middle age.

3. Role exit theory explains how the losses of major life roles affect people as they grow older.

B. Preretirees' attitudes about retirement influence how they prepare for and adjust to retirement.

1. The average adult spends a fifth of his or her life in retirement, but 1 in 6 men and 1 in 10 women do not retire, and 20 percent of retirees work part-time.

2. Mandatory retirement policies greatly increased the number of retirees, but even now, when such policies are illegal, most older adults choose to retire.

3. Involuntary retirement, particularly for health reasons, is the most important predictor of unsuccessful retirement adjustment.

4. Preparation for retirement involves financial planning, plans for maintaining good health, the development of leisure activities, and consideration of future living arrangements.

5. Many European businesses use phased retirement, rather than the sudden, abrupt shift to total retirement typical in the United States.

6. Atchley proposed seven phases that people may experience as they approach and live through their retirement years.

7. Spouses and other family members also have to adjust to the retirement of another family member.

C. Retired older adults typically spend their leisure in the pursuit of many varied activities, with activities varying among ethnic groups and by gender.

1. Many older adults begin activities to improve their health.

2. Older adults increase their involvement in religious and spiritual activities.

3. About a third of older adults become involved in community service.

4. Older adults vote in elections at a higher rate than other age groups.

IV. Relationships in older adulthood

A. Most older adults are married or have been married and report feeling closer to their families than in previous years.

1. Duvall identified eight developmental tasks for aging couples, including making satisfying living arrangements, adjusting to retirement income, and finding meaning in life.

2. Typically, marital satisfaction is never higher than in old age.

3. Older couples report that the most rewarding aspects of marriage are companionship and the expression of true feelings, while value differences and lack of mutual interests are the most troublesome.

B. A small number of older couples divorce, but many more experience a transition to being single again as the result of the death of a spouse.
   1. The number of divorced elderly has grown since 1960, with many having become divorced in their early and middle adulthood years.
   2. The majority of widowed individuals are women since wives are usually younger than their husbands and women have a longer life expectancy than men.
   3. Widowhood is associated with increased mortality, suicide rates, and loneliness, as well as declining health.
   4. Divorced or widowed elderly men are much more likely to remarry than divorced or widowed elderly women.

C. About 5 percent of older adults have never married and are a diverse group, with most being self-reliant and autonomous.

D. Most older adults have living adult children.
   1. By age 60, most mothers no longer have a child under age 21.
   2. Distant intimacy describes the pattern of both attachment and separation that is characteristic of the relationships between many older parents and their adult children.
   3. Intergenerational ties allow individuals to both preview and review other phases of life.
   4. Grandparenting is an important, but varied, role for older adults that provides many satisfactions as well as the opportunity to learn from grandchildren while teaching them about family and cultural traditions.
   5. Female adult children typically provide more help and companionship to their elderly parents than male adult children.
   6. While adult children may help to provide for their elderly parents' care, older parents are more likely to provide resources for their adult children.

E. Stereotypes of the childless elderly are generally false.
   1. The childless elderly are no more lonely, dissatisfied with life, or isolated than other elderly.
   2. Having children does not guarantee help for the elderly, and not having children does not eliminate support for the elderly.

F. For most people, sibling relationships are the longest-lasting relationships in their lives.
   1. In later adulthood, siblings often provide companionship and emotional support.
   2. Among the elderly, sister-sister relationships are typically the closest, and brother-brother relationships the least close.

G. As the number of friendships decreases in later adulthood, the importance of friends increases.
   1. Elderly women find understanding and support in friendships, while elderly men value friends for the opportunity to participate in activities.
   2. Reciprocity is the key to long-term friendships.

V. Living arrangements
   A. Most older Americans live in houses that they own.
      1. Independent living in one's own home may become more difficult on reduced retirement income and limited pension benefits and with declining health.
      2. Older adults living alone or with a spouse may develop a significant fear of crime.
      3. Home sharing, in which two or more unrelated individuals share a single-family dwelling, is an effective alternative for continued independent living for many older adults.
      4. Retirement communities are another alternative for independent living that provide many benefits, often including the opportunity to move to more dependent conditions as the need arises.
   B. Dependent living in later adulthood may take the form of living with relatives or residing in nursing-care facilities.
      1. The choice to form multigenerational households should be based on realities and not just on emotions and feelings of obligation.
      2. Adult day-care centers can provide positive experiences for dependent older adults, while providing relief for families caring for their dependent elders.
      3. While many elderly both fear and expect to live for a time in a nursing home, only 5 percent of the elderly reside in a hospital or nursing home.
      4. Nursing homes are often stereotyped as impersonal with overreliance on physical and chemical restraints to manage residents, but high-quality nursing homes do not commit those abuses.

Chapter Review Test

1. Which of the following is true about the stereotypes of older adults?
   a. Negative images of old people are a 20th-century phenomenon.
   b. From the 17th through 19th centuries, the stereotypes of older adults increasingly became more positive.
   c. Society has more rigid stereotypes of the elderly than of other age groups.
   d. All of the above are correct.

2. Which of the following is true about children's attitudes toward the elderly?
   a. Preschoolers exhibit less ageist prejudice than school-age children.
   b. Children's attitudes toward the elderly are affected by their amount of contact with elderly persons.
   c. Among preadolescents, no ethnic differences are found in attitudes toward the elderly.
   d. All of the above are correct.

3. All of the following societal aspects are associated with higher levels of respect and better treatment of the elderly *except*
   a. preindustrial.
   b. value self-reliance.
   c. ancestor worship.
   d. value conformity.

4. Which of the following is a major concern that older adults express about old age?
   a. becoming a burden to others
   b. possible intergenerational conflicts
   c. concern for meaningfulness and for future generations
   d. all of the above

5. Which of the following statements about emotions in old age is accurate?
   a. The majority of older adults say that old age is worse than they had expected.
   b. Elderly persons have lower rates of happiness than other adults.
   c. Elderly European Americans report lower levels of happiness than elderly African Americans.
   d. Depression is more prevalent in the elderly than in other age groups.

6. Which of the following traits exhibits the most stability throughout adulthood?
   a. religious fundamentalism
   b. depression
   c. optimism versus pessimism
   d. social extroversion

7. Which of the following is *not* a subtype of Neugarten's integrated personality?
   a. disengaged persons
   b. focused persons
   c. holding-on persons
   d. reorganizers

8. Which of the following is associated with a positive resolution of Erikson's eighth psychosocial crisis?
   a. self-acceptance
   b. wisdom
   c. acceptance of mortality
   d. all of the above

9. Which of the following is *not* one of the late adulthood developmental tasks proposed by Peck?
   a. ego differentiation versus work-role preoccupation
   b. body transcendence versus body preoccupation
   c. spiritual concerns versus worldly concerns
   d. ego transcendence versus ego preoccupation

10. Which of the following has a negative effect on the life satisfaction levels of older adults?
    a. solitary activities
    b. formal, structured group activities
    c. informal activities
    d. activities with family or friends

11. According to Atchley, the _____ after retiring tends to have the lowest satisfaction level and is often a time of boredom or depression.
    a. end of the first year
    b. time immediately
    c. end of the second year
    d. fifth year

12. In which of the following activities do older adults engage in most?
    a. reading
    b. church activities
    c. volunteering
    d. traveling

13. Older married couples tend to
    a. communicate less than when younger.
    b. be more satisfied now that child-rearing is complete.
    c. rely more heavily on gender roles than do younger couples.
    d. grow less similar in values and activities.

14. _____ out of four women will be a widow.
    a. Less than one
    b. One
    c. Two
    d. Three

15. Which of the following is a true statement about the never-married elderly?
    a. Most describe themselves as lonely and desolate.
    b. Women who live in urban areas have fewer contacts than other never-married elderly.
    c. Fewer never-married elderly live alone than divorced or widowed elderly.
    d. None of the above is correct.

16. Which of the following statements is true regarding older parents and their adult children?
    a. Less than half of elderly parents see an adult child at least weekly.
    b. Living nearby is more predictive of a close relationship for rural families than for urban families.
    c. Fathers are more successful than mothers at transforming the parent/child relationship into a more peerlike adult relationship.
    d. Elderly parents are more likely than adult children to think that the offspring should provide assistance for the parents.

17. Which grandparenting style involves interest but little caretaking?
    a. formal
    b. distant figure
    c. fun-seeker
    d. all of the above

18. Which of the following is more true of the childless elderly than of elderly parents?
    a. lower satisfaction with life
    b. more loneliness
    c. more contact with friends
    d. less acceptance of death

19. The typical relationship between elderly siblings can best be described as
    a. indifferent.
    b. close.
    c. hostile.
    d. dependent.

20. What percentage of the elderly are residing in a hospital or nursing home?
    a. 40 percent
    b. 22 percent
    c. 13 percent
    d. 5 percent

Answers

1. C [LO-1].	8. D [LO-9].	15. C [LO-18].
2. A [LO-3].	9. C [LO-10].	16. B [LO-19].
3. B [LO-4].	10. B [LO-11].	17. A [LO-20].
4. D [LO-5].	11. A [LO-13].	18. C [LO-21].
5. D [LO-6].	12. A [LO-14].	19. B [LO-22].
6. A [LO-7].	13. B [LO-16].	20. D [LO-23].
7. C [LO-8].	14. D [LO-17].	

chapter 18

Death, Dying, and Bereavement

Key Terms

Death system
Irreversibility of death
Nonfunctionality of death
Universality of death
Survivor's guilt
Acknowledgment stage
Grieving stage
Reconciliation stage
Detachment stage
Memorialization
Postbereavement mourning
Reunion
Reverence
Retribution
Chronic living-dying
  interval
Denial
Anger
Bargaining
Depression
Acceptance
Brain death
Cognitive death
Living wills
Near-death experiences
  (NDEs)
Reincarnation
Hospice
Euthanasia
Grief
Bereavement
Mourning
Anniversary reaction

Learning Objectives

1. Explain the concept of cultural death systems.
2. Identify the four major historical time periods of attitudes about death.
3. Describe how attitudes and concepts about death develop during childhood and adolescence.
4. Identify the chronic living-dying interval and its relationship to terminal illness.
5. Discuss factors associated with survivor's guilt.
6. Describe types of sudden death due to heart attack, accidents, homicides, and suicides in adolescents and adults.
7. Give examples of Kübler-Ross's five stages of dying, and explain the processes involved in each stage.
8. Describe Pattison's three-stage model of adjusting to the idea of dying.
9. Distinguish among traditional definitions of death, brain death, and cognitive death.
10. Describe the normal physiological changes that occur during the dying process.
11. Explain various interpretations of the near-death experience.
12. Identify major belief systems' views of the nature of existence after death.
13. Discuss reasons for why death education is needed.
14. Describe the goals and typical services of the hospice movement.
15. Discuss the issues of euthanasia, cryonics, and organ transplants and implants.
16. Distinguish between passive and active euthanasia.
17. Differentiate among the concepts of bereavement, grief, and mourning.
18. Describe historical changes in American mourning rituals.
19. Identify the typical components and decisions involved in contemporary American funerals and other mourning rituals.
20. Explain the different types of grieving experienced during the grieving process.
21. Discuss complications that may occur in resolving grief.
22. Give examples of helpful ways to assist others in their grief process.
23. Discuss the relationship between grief and losses other than death that people experience throughout their lifetime.

"Nothing is certain except death and taxes," according to an old adage. Certainly, dying is the final stage in lifespan development. While we have come to expect that people will die after living into older adulthood, we also are aware that individuals die in all stages of the lifespan. Sometimes, this final developmental stage is sudden and unexpected, as when death results from an accident or a heart attack, and sometimes, this stage is longer and death is expected, as when a person develops an incurable, terminal illness. Whether death is sudden or lingering, expected or unexpected, an understanding of death, dying, and grief is critical to the study of human development.

Exploring Your Own Development

Who died in your first experience with death? If you were born after 1960, you probably had your first encounter with death while watching a television program. The first death experience for many older adults may have occurred at the movies. But, you may be protesting, "Everyone knows that the people don't really die in the movies or on TV!" So, who died in your first personal encounter with real death? If you are like many children, the first real death you observed was that of an animal, perhaps a dead bird in the backyard or an animal killed on the highway. How death was explained to you as a child and how you observed death, mourning, and funeral rituals in movies and on television shows all affected your current ideas and feelings about dying, death, and the cultural rituals surrounding death.

Before beginning this final chapter, survey your attitudes about death and funerals. Have you thought much about death? Have close friends and relatives died? Have you attended a funeral? How many? Have you made plans for your own death? Do you have a will? Have you made plans for your funeral? Do you own a cemetery plot? Have you considered donating your body to science? Do you wonder about what happens after you die? Even if you would prefer to not think about these things, death is the final chapter in lifespan development.

Death and Society

Historical Views

Death Systems
The term **death system** refers to the manner in which a society comprehends death and dying. Death system is a broad concept that includes the culture's ideas about health and sickness, dependence and independence, life and death, the dying process, and bereavement. In addition, the death system includes the many persons and institutions involved in dying and death—patients, family members, physicians, nurses, clergy, funeral directors, police, lawyers, cemetery directors and personnel, hospitals, hospices, morgues, funeral homes, and churches (Morgan, 1988). Your attitudes about death can be gathered by considering your beliefs and feelings about each aspect of the death system. Moreover, your attitudes and values are influenced by how the people just listed feel about death and by how the involved institutions help to structure the death experience. For example, medical doctors have higher death anxiety than does the general population (Feifel, Hannon, Jones, & Edwards, 1972). Does this high death anxiety of physicians affect how they tell families about patients' conditions or what procedures they try to prolong life?

What is the death system of the United States? Is the United States a country that denies the reality of death and fails to accept the mortality of human lives? Or is this country overfascinated with death, as indicated by the death images abundantly displayed in the media? In modern times, Americans seem to have both a flight from dealing with death and a perverse attentiveness to distorted death scenes. Some children grow up without experiencing the death of a family member or close friend but witnessing more than 10,000 deaths on television by the time they graduate from high school. Are attitudes regarding death limited by inexperience with actual deaths and distorted by deaths of fictional characters (Morgan, 1988)?

Four Historical Views
How do modern attitudes about death differ from those of previous generations? One proposed model suggests four major historical periods of attitudes about death (Aries, 1981; Morgan, 1988). The first time period, labeled Tamed Death, occurred during the early Middle Ages. During this historical period, all people were constantly exposed to death—after all, life expectancy was only 33 years (Stillion, 1985). The only unacceptable death was the sudden death. Ideally, the dying person announced his or her physical condition and summoned friends and family members to be at the deathbed. Unlike today, dying was a public act. The death scene included the dying person recalling both achievements and regrets, asking for forgiveness from God and from loved ones, and leaving behind worldly possessions. The Tamed Death period represents the era in which people were most secure in the knowledge that death was a transition from earthly life to a better afterlife.

The second historical period, Death of Self, was from the 12th to 15th centuries. As people became less certain that death was a passageway to eternity rather than a doorway to eternal nothingness, death lost some of its peacefulness and gained a self-conscious uneasiness. Plagues killed off a third of the world's population, resulting in the development of a sense of "uncontrolled mortality" and a fascination with macabre images and physical decomposition. Death images moved from souls entering heaven to bodies decaying. Dying also became less of a public event, and instead, more attention was paid to elaborate funerals and tombs—all that might remain of a person. Although fewer believed wholeheartedly in a blissful afterlife, many hoped for such an option. Therefore, the ideal was a deathbed confession (i.e., an 11th-hour conversion) in case of an afterlife.

Gradually, death and love became more and more linked together, so that by the 19th century, a third historical period emerged, called Death of the Other. The ideal death became one of "beauty," with much grief expressed by surviving family and loved ones. During this century, few wills were made because it was believed that loved ones would want to voluntarily carry out the dying person's wishes. By now, public deathbeds were a scene of the past, as death became the last act of an intimate relationship.

The fourth and current historical period of death is called Denial of Death. As one sociologist put it:

> We pushed the idea of death and decay as far from our consciousness as possible. The dying no longer announced the coming of death. That role was given to the medical profession. We are now informed, and even then resist the final verdict as much as possible. The moment of death is also isolated, taken out of view and away from friends and relatives, with the dying person deposited in the hospital or nursing home. Even there, the medical professionals who witness death are socially insulated, as they confront it only in their medical roles and not as more vulnerable private selves. Because of its disruptive terror, modern death threatens social order and has to be isolated as much as possible. Hence, its denial and elimination from conversation, family life, and even eyesight. If we do not acknowledge the possibility of our own death, we seem to do so indirectly by worrying over the death of others. In effect, the fear of our own death has been projected on the possible loss of loved ones, whose death we can consciously acknowledge, worry about, and publicly grieve. It is as if the constant knowledge of our own temporal nature is too much to handle, and so we have transplanted the fear of our own death to the possible death of the other. We can acknowledge the limited quality of our own existence only by seeing it in others, where it is kept at a safe distance. (Bergesen, 1984, p. 437)

In actuality, modern society is not unified in how its members deal with death. While denial of death is a common response, the hospice movement, living wills, and donor organ banks show that some people deal with the concept of death. People may no longer have to deal with many deaths in childbirth and childhood, but they still deal with diseases of longevity and with dying with dignity in old age. Death may not come to Americans personally on a daily basis, but death is present in the media (e.g., coverage of wars, urban violence, terrorism), in ethical issues (e.g., euthanasia, abortion), in deaths from disease (e.g., AIDS, cancer), and in fear of megadeath, mass death resulting from nuclear warfare (Kahn, 1960; Kamerman, 1988). Assess your own attitudes about death by using the short inventory in Table 18.1.

The Mayan Culture's View of Death

Just as attitudes about death have changed over time, different cultures deal with dying and bereavement in diverse ways. Some cultures make elaborate preparations for death, while others have simple preparations. Some hide death, while others accept death as an ordinary part of life. Cultures

---

Table 18.1
A Personal Death and Dying Inventory

Assess your views and beliefs about death by answering the following questions. Discuss your answers with family members, friends, and other students in your class.

1. I expect to live to age (circle your answer):
   25 30 35 40 45 50 55 60 65 70 75 80 85 90 95 100

2. I want to live to age (circle your answer):
   25 30 35 40 45 50 55 60 65 70 75 80 85 90 95 100

3. Who died in your first personal involvement with death?
   a. Grandparent or great-grandparent
   b. Parent
   c. Brother or sister
   d. Other family member
   e. Friend or acquaintance
   f. Stranger
   g. Public figure
   h. Animal

4. What aspect of your own death is the most distasteful to you?
   a. I could no longer have any experiences.
   b. I am afraid of what might happen to my body after death.
   c. I am uncertain as to what might happen to me if there is a life after death.
   d. I could no longer provide for my dependents.
   e. It would cause grief to my relatives and friends.
   f. All of my plans and projects would come to an end.
   g. The process of dying might be painful.

5. What does death mean to you?
   a. The end, the final process of life
   b. The beginning of a life after death; a transition, a new beginning
   c. A joining of the spirit with a universal cosmic consciousness
   d. A kind of endless sleep; rest and peace
   e. Termination of this life but with survival of the spirit
   f. Don't know

6. If you had a choice, what kind of death would you prefer?
   a. Tragic, violent death
   b. Sudden, but not violent death
   c. Quiet, dignified death
   d. Death in line of duty
   e. Death after a great achievement
   f. Suicide
   g. Homicide victim

7. For whom or what might you be willing to sacrifice your life?
   a. For a loved one
   b. For an idea or a moral principle
   c. In combat or a grave emergency where a life could be saved
   d. Not for any reason

8. To what extent do you believe in a life after death?
   a. Strongly believe in it
   b. Tend to believe in it
   c. Uncertain
   d. Tend to doubt it
   e. Convinced it does not exist

9. Regardless of your belief about life after death, what is your wish about it?
   a. I strongly wish there were a life after death.
   b. I am indifferent as to whether there is a life after death.
   c. I definitely prefer that there not be a life after death.

Sources: Questions 1 & 2 from R. J. Kastenbaum, *Death, Society, and Human Experience*, 1981, 2d edition, C. V. Mosby Co., St. Louis, MO. Questions 3–9 from E. S. Shneidman. Reprinted with permission of *Psychology Today Magazine*. Copyright © 1970 Sussex Publishers, Inc.

Many school-age children fear dying in a nuclear war.

Some areas of the Mayan empire did not bury noblemen. Instead, they cremated the bodies and put the ashes in hollow statues of pottery or wood. In one region, the corpses of noblemen were boiled until the flesh separated from the bones. The front of the skull was then used to make a death face.

Whatever the specific local customs, funeral rituals were designed to help the spirit of the departed leave earth and enter the afterlife. The soul was believed to leave the body through the tongue and to linger near the body for 8 days following illness and for 20 days following a violent death. During this transitional period, family and friends performed specific mourning rituals to end emotional ties with the deceased.

The Maya Indians believed that paradise—an afterlife setting with abundant food, drink, and pleasant shaded shelter—was most accessible to those who committed suicide, were killed in battle or sacrifice, died in childbirth, or were priests. Others might go to the lower region of Mitnal, where they were hungry, cold, tired, and sad. The Mayans accepted death and used specific tasks to help both the dying and the bereaved (Steele, 1977).

Developing Attitudes Toward Death

As mentioned earlier, one modern attitude toward death involves denial and avoidance. People can be partially successful in death denial because they have few direct experiences with death, as the following 20th-century changes in the demography of death exemplify (Rain, 1988; Stillion, 1985):

- In 1900, more than 16 of 100 babies died before 1 year of age. In 1983, only 1 in 100 babies died the first year.
- In 1900, a higher proportion of the population died before their first birthday than died before their 75th birthday in 1970.
- In 1900, 1 in 4 children experienced the death of at least one parent by age 15. In 1976, only 1 in 20 children had a parent die by age 15.
- In 1900, the average life expectancy was only 47 years; by 1940, it was 63 years; and by 1980, it was 74 years.

Regardless of direct personal experiences with death, all individuals progress through similar stages in developing attitudes about death. Children who have a personal experience with death develop an earlier accurate understanding of death. Both Zeitgeist and Ortgeist factors affect understanding of death, and European children during World War II were more mature in their death attitudes than are children in Des Moines, Iowa, in the 1990s (Stambrook & Parker, 1987).

Preschoolers' Attitudes About Death

As soon as children have developed the concept of object permanence, they are capable of showing emotional reaction to the death of loved ones, but they do not understand that death is permanent and irreversible until they are in Piaget's stage of concrete operations. Furthermore, a complete understanding of death as irreversible, universal, and part of the natural order of things may not occur until the formal operations stage (Wass, 1984).

develop ideas about an afterlife, but this afterlife has many faces. This section discusses the ancient Mayan culture's views of death, while the "Exploring Cultural Diversity" feature focuses on the death system of the Amish culture.

The ancient Mayans believed that evil winds brought the diseases that led to death. When winds entered the body, sorcerers used magical rituals, symbolism, bleeding, and medicinal herbs to force the wind-caused disease from affected bodies. Sorcerers would rub patients' legs and observe the resultant muscle twitching to know if patients would survive. When sorcerers forecast death instead of recovery, patients would accept the prediction, ask the date of death, lie down on a hammock, and refuse food and drink until death occurred.

Dreams were believed to contain symbols that could foretell death. When someone dreamed about floating on air, intense pain, a pulled tooth, or a broken water jug, it meant that a close family member would die. Dreaming about red tomatoes foretold a baby's death.

After death, the body was washed and wrapped in a shroud. Either a jade bead or a bit of corn was placed in the corpse's mouth to provide the soul with food for the journey to the afterlife. In much of the Mayan empire, the dead person's dog was sacrificed so that the dog's soul could guide the person's soul to paradise. Other household and career possessions were also buried with the body. While a nobleman was buried at a pyramid, a common person was buried beneath the mud floor of the home. After several people were buried under one house, the family would change homes and use the old home as a family shrine.

Exploring Cultural Diversity: The Amish Death System

The Amish have been dealing with death in the same manner for centuries, and their lifestyle incorporates an acceptance of death as a natural part of life. The Amish strongly believe in the teachings of the New Testament, and they view death as the connection between the temporary human state and divine eternity.

Unlike the rest of American society, almost all Amish people die in family homes, with family members around them to care for them. Family members seem to cherish the opportunity to take care of the elderly and the terminally ill. Caring for the sick and old provides the Amish the opportunity to work out grief before the death occurs and aids the transition in family patterns. Amish children are more familiar with dying and death than are other children in the United States.

Death itself is made less frightening through unshakable belief in immortality and through support of family and friends. Although the dead person's soul is joyfully released, the Amish do recognize the loss and sadness in the survivors. Other Amish families who have had a similar death often travel long distances to be a new support system for the grieving family. The immediate family is relieved of most of the decisions about the funeral; the family decides who to invite to the funeral and then appoints a family to make and carry out funeral arrangements.

The embalmed body is back in the family home within a day, and the body is dressed in white garments as prescribed in Revelation 3:5:

> For a man, this consists of white trousers, a white shirt, and a white vest. For a woman, the usual clothing is a white cape and apron that were worn by her at both her baptism and her marriage. At baptism, a black dress is worn with the white cape and apron; at marriage, a purple or blue dress is worn with the white cape and apron. It is only at her death that an Amish woman wears a white dress with the cape and apron that she put away for the occasion of her death. This is an example of the lifelong preparation for death, as sanctioned by Amish society. The wearing of white clothes signifies the high ceremonial emphasis on the death event as the final rite of passage into a new and better life. (Bryer, 1979, p. 257)

Funerals are held in the barn in warm months and in the home at other times. The service is always the same—about 1 1/2 hr long and conducted in German. The mourners view the body in a plain, wooden coffin when they first arrive, when the service is over, and one last time at the cemetery. Silence is observed while the body is placed in the grave and covered with earth. Then scriptures are read, and prayers are said. Following the ceremony at the cemetery, family and neighbors return to the family's home, where the families in charge have prepared a meal.

The bereaved family receives much support in the following year. Others visit regularly and help with such tasks as child-rearing and quilting. Although mourning is substantial, the Amish believe that life goes on and that families that lose a member need to make up the loss. One example of this is the Amish rate of remarriage after death of a spouse, which is higher than any other culture (Bryer, 1979).

During the preschool years, children's conceptualization of death is incomplete due to cognitive limitations. Typically, 3- to 5-year-olds believe that death is similar to sleep or a temporary departure, and they believe that death is reversible if the correct procedures are followed, such as praying, using magic, or observing specific rituals (Speece & Brent, 1984; Stambrook & Parker, 1987).

Preschoolers view death as life under different circumstances. For example, they might believe that the dead person's senses continue but that the dead person can no longer move. Some children may develop concepts of this altered life as being lonely and scary because the individual is trapped in a coffin (Stambrook & Parker, 1987). Young children believe that some functions, such as heartbeat and breathing, stop at death, while other functions, especially cognitive and emotional aspects, continue on (Kane, 1979).

A belief held by preschoolers and older children is that death occurs only in old age. This belief is fortified in modern culture because fewer children and young adults are dying now. This misconception also keeps young children from more realistically considering the possibility of their own immediate death (Stambrook & Parker, 1987).

Children who have a personal experience with death develop an earlier accurate understanding of death. Here children visit their grandfather's grave.

Perhaps it is surprising that young children have as much understanding of death as they do. After all, preschoolers are still confused in understanding differences between animate and inanimate objects. In one study, 5- and 6-year-olds were asked the following questions about 12 objects (boy, tree, car, flower, wind, snake, moon, plant, bird, sun, fish, and grass): "Is _____ alive or not alive? Why do you say that _____ is (not) alive?" and "Can a _____ die or not die? Why do you say that the _____ can (not) die?" Young children were accurate in answering questions about animals but made numerous errors about inanimate objects and plants (Berzonsky, 1987). Children may need to understand the basic classification of living and nonliving before they learn the fundamental, unchanging aspects of death. Death-attribution accuracy is made more difficult by diverse meanings of the word *dead*: "The dog is dead," "Whew, I feel dead," "The battery is dead," "He's a deadbeat," and "What a dead night at this place."

School Children's Attitudes About Death

By age 7, most children have acquired three important components of a mature concept of death: death is irreversible, death involves becoming nonfunctional, and death is universal. **Irreversibility of death** is knowing that the death of a living being means that the physical body cannot come alive again; death is permanent and final. Irreversibility belief can be measured by asking "Can a dead person come back to life?" or "How can you make dead things come back to life?" **Nonfunctionality of death** means that the child understands that a dead person cannot see, move, grow, eat, know, hear, feel, dream, talk, or think. **Universality of death** means that children understand that everybody, including themselves, will die. In testing this aspect, researchers ask children, "Does everybody die?" "Will you die?" and "Can you think of someone who might not die?" (Speece & Brent, 1984; Stambrook & Parker, 1987).

Although most 7-year-olds do understand the irreversibility, nonfunctionality, and universality of death, they may still believe that only the old die or that illness and death is a punishment for bad behavior. Children in this age group often personify death and believe that death requires an external agent, such as a bad driver or a murderer. Older children understand that death is an internal biological process that adheres to natural laws (Stambrook & Parker, 1987).

Between the ages of 9 and 12, many children have greater interest in the rituals and ceremonies surrounding death. They want to know what happens in hospitals, during funerals, and at gravesites; they are beginning to deal with religious beliefs about death, such as distinguishing between body and soul (Stambrook & Parker, 1987). Most experts believe that children's questions require concrete, understandable answers. While the majority of children ultimately benefit from participating in funeral rituals, participation should not be forced. Parents may prefer to keep young children from viewing the body and from seeing the coffin being lowered into the grave (Salk, 1983).

Adolescents' and Adults' Attitudes About Death

Teenagers are usually quite mature in their understanding of death. They know that death is final and irreversible and that it can occur at any age. This accuracy seems to increase their level of death anxiety, compared to 9- to 12-year-olds. On the other hand, teenagers are subject to their personal fable, the magical thinking that their specialness provides protection from harm and death.

Adults hold a variety of attitudes about death and dying. Typically, however, in the young adult years, individuals ponder the personal inevitability of death. During middle adulthood, people often shift their focus from "time since birth" to "time left to live." Middle-aged individuals are the most likely to experience the death of parents and an increase in deaths among peers; these experiences usually influence attitudes and behaviors concerning death. In old age, people lose more friends and possibly a spouse to death. Many older adults do life reviews and prepare for death; overall, older adults have lower levels of death anxiety than younger adults.

Early childhood attitudes may affect adolescent and adult attitudes about death. For example, suicidal behavior in adolescent and adult years may be rooted in suicidal tendencies of early childhood. Suicidal children have higher repulsion for life and greater attraction to death beliefs than do other children (Orbach, Feshbach, Carlson, Glaubman, & Gross, 1983; Orbach, Feshbach, Carlson, & Ellenberg, 1984).

Attitudes and Length of Life

Adult death attitudes affect carefulness in a variety of behaviors. In one study, cautious, conservative pedestrians had the following average responses to questions about death: They believed that their lives were in danger about 2.1 percent of the time, 8 percent had attempted or thought of suicide, they expected to live until they were 81 years old, and they wanted to live until they were age 92. On the other hand, risk-taking pedestrians believed that their lives were in danger about 16.1 percent of the time, 32 percent had attempted or thought of suicide, they expected to live only until they were 67 years old, and they wanted to live only until they were age 69 (Kastenbaum & Briscoe, 1975). Apparently, people who do not expect or want to live long lives engage in more behaviors that increase their chances of shortening their lives.

People can decrease the length of their lives by engaging in risk-taking behavior and unhealthy lifestyle choices, but less is known about the ability to personally sustain life. Can people postpone the date of their death? David Phillips compared birthdates and death dates of 1,251 famous Americans and found that public figures were more than twice as likely to die in the month following their birthday than in the month preceding their birthday. Furthermore, Phillips found that famous Americans with publicly celebrated birthdays during their lifetimes were the most likely to die after their birthdays (Koenig, 1972).

Support groups like the Empty Arms help parents deal with the death of a child.

Age of Death

Death in Infancy

Of the 40,000 deaths among infants in the United States each year, over half are attributed to four causes: congenital anomalies (problems present at birth), sudden infant death syndrome (SIDS, also called "crib death"), respiratory distress syndrome, and disorders relating to short gestation and low birthweight (National Center for Health Statistics, 1987).

Sudden infant death syndrome is responsible for several thousand deaths each year. With SIDS, apparently healthy infants, usually between 2 and 4 months of age, die suddenly in their sleep. Although SIDS occurs in all cultures and at all socioeconomic levels, suspected risk factors include: male babies, between 1 and 6 months of age, low birthweight, low Apgar score at birth, jaundice and respiratory problems at birth, prolonged apnea, increased REM (rapid eye movement) sleep, bottle-fed, young mother, mother who smokes, and shortened pregnancy (Navelet, Payan, Guilhaume, & Benoit, 1984). Researchers are exploring a wide range of possible causes of SIDS: lesions in the brain stem, sleep apnea (temporary halts in breathing during sleep), head colds, viruses, overheating, and insufficient levels of physical stimulation from being rocked, jiggled, and bounced (Lipsitt, Sturner, & Burke, 1979; Navelet et al., 1984; Schulte, Albani, Schnizer, Bentele, & Klingspron, 1982; Shannon & Kelly, 1982; Stanton, 1984; Steinschneider, 1975; Thoman, Korner, & Beason-Williams, 1977).

Families who have an infant die from SIDS feel guilty and can become a target of societal criticism. Some people believe that the parents must have been negligent in parenting, and some parents internalize these criticisms. Siblings experience an increase in nightmares and school adjustment problems. Most families need at least 18 months to recover from the grief (DeFrain, Taylor, & Ernst, 1982).

Among the 20 leading industrialized nations, the United States, Belgium, East Germany, and West Germany have the highest infant mortality rates. In the United States, black infants have a significantly higher rate of death than

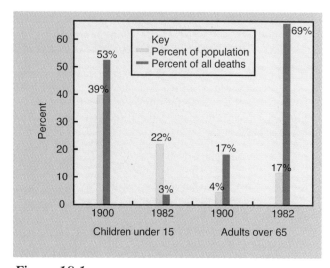

Figure 18.1

Changes in population and age of death from 1900 to 1982.
Source: From J. B. Kamerman, *Death in the Midst of Life: Social & Cultural Influences on Death, Grief & Mourning.* Prentice-Hall, Englewood Cliffs, NJ.

do white infants. "A black infant born within 5 miles of the White House is more likely to die in the first year of life than an infant born in Third World countries like Trinidad" ("Born in the U.S.A.," 1987). The U.S. infant mortality rate would decrease with better access to medical care and better nutrition among the poor.

Death in Childhood and Adolescence

As illustrated in Figure 18.1, in the 20th century, childhood death has moved from being fairly common to being atypical. Still, about 54,000 individuals between the ages of 1 and 24 die each year (Knapp, 1987). One result of the lower infancy and childhood death rate is that many parents who survive the death of a child experience survivor's guilt, the topic of the "Exploring the Parent/Child Relationship" feature.

Childhood death is considered especially tragic because it represents lost hopes and future experiences. Because the deaths seem unfair, grief tends to be longer-lasting and to involve more despair and anger. Believing that the dead child will be remembered and talking about the death seem to be helpful in resolving grief issues. Death of offspring is often associated with a shift away from interest in careers and money and toward new commitments to values (Knapp, 1987).

One of the major consequences of the high rate of survival through the childhood years is the impact on parent-child relationships. In 1900, over 60 percent of all families experienced the death of a child; by 1976, that figure had dropped to 4 percent. Therefore, at the turn of the century, most parents probably guarded against strong emotional bonds with their children. Today, parents are much more likely to have intimate parent-child relationships (Uhlenberg, 1980).

Death in Adulthood

Changes in death demographics also affect family relationships of adults. In modern times, most individuals are able to reach adulthood without becoming orphans; in fact, most

In expressing his grief and guilt following the death of his adolescent son after a long illness, a father showed the **survivor's guilt** experienced by many parents who have had children die:

> Missing him now, I am haunted by my own shortcomings, how often I failed him. I think every parent must have a sense of failure, even of sin, merely in remaining alive after the death of a child. One feels that it is not right to live when one's child has died, that one should somehow have found the way to give one's life to save his life. Failing there, one's failures during his too brief life seem all the harder to bear and forgive. (Gunther, 1949)

Survivor's guilt is experienced in greater intensity as the death of children becomes an extraordinary rather than typical event. Until the 20th century, most parents lost children to death. For example, in colonial days, Puritan parents lost an average of a fourth to a third of their children. Since children's deaths were as expected as the deaths of the old, parents did not feel like failures when their children died (Kamerman, 1988).

Today, parents with dying children are a minority group. The relative rarity of childhood deaths can make believing that death will occur difficult, and therefore, parents who have a terminally ill child may experience a lengthy **acknowledgment stage,** in which they must come to realize the inevitability of their child's death. Next, parents typically experience **grieving** and **reconciliation stages** while their child is still alive. During these anticipatory grief stages, parents partially come to terms with their impending loss, help their child to deal with dying, and learn to appreciate the remaining time they have with their child.

The **detachment stage** often begins before the child's death. Parents accept the impending death, become less emotionally distraught, and focus on how death can be a release from suffering. Unfortunately, friends and hospital staff may misinterpret these changes as callousness and uncaring and may make comments that later add to parents' survivor's guilt. Yet, parents who detach somewhat before their child's death have an easier adjustment after the death than do parents who begin detachment afterward. After the child dies, parents go through two additional stages: **memorialization** (formation of a permanent positive image of the child) and **postbereavement mourning,** the intensity and duration of which is less if parents experienced anticipatory grief (Futterman & Hoffman, 1983).

Parents of children who die suddenly (e.g., from accidents) have longer grieving periods because they had no opportunity for anticipatory grief. In addition, when children die from accidents, parents are more likely to think that they should have been able to save their children. Illness has an aura of being beyond personal control, but with accidents, parents may have haunting thoughts, such as, "If only I hadn't let my child play outside . . . ," "If only I hadn't bought my child a bicycle . . . ," "If only I hadn't let my child go on that canoeing trip . . .". Hindsight may make accidents seem avoidable, and therefore, parents may overblame themselves (Knapp, 1987). In a study of the long-term effects of losing a child in a car accident, a large number of parents (from 30 to 85 percent, depending on the questions) indicated that they still could not accept the death, could not find meaning in the death, and continued to think about what they could have done to prevent the accident (Lehman, Wortman, & Williams, 1987). In a similar pattern, about a third of women who have a miscarriage suffer significantly from survivor's guilt (Cole, 1987).

Survivor's guilt involves intense feelings of guilt and vulnerability, and the syndrome typically involves an acute phase that lasts from 2 weeks to 3 months and a chronic phase that lasts longer than a year. In the acute phase, parents feel depressed and desolate and want to escape life. In the chronic phase, parents typically develop a somewhat nonchalant attitude toward death, with the majority of parent-survivors having an absence of fear of death (Knapp, 1987).

In resolving survivor's guilt and grief, many parents turn to religion to find meaning and justification for their loss (Knapp, 1987). Parents often choose one of three pathways to resolve grief: reunion, reverence, and retribution (Cook & Wimberley, 1983). In **reunion,** the major focus is on an eventual reunion with the dead child. In **reverence,** parents choose to use their child's death as an inspiration to do well and live well. This excerpt from *Death Be Not Proud* suggests that a person can learn to appreciate life more as a result of dealing with a child's death:

> Today, when I see parents impatient or tired or bored with their children, I wish I could say to them, "But they are alive, think of the wonder of that! They may be a care and a burden, but think, they are alive! You can touch them—what a miracle!" (Gunther, 1949)

In the third pathway **retribution,** parents conclude that the child died because of parental sins. This group has the most survivor's guilt. The retribution theme is prevalent in this brief selection from Maeve Brennan's *The Eldest Child:*

> Perhaps she had let herself get too proud. She had seen at once that the child was unique. She had been thankful, but perhaps not thankful enough. (Brennan, 1968)

Grief support groups and professional counseling may help to ease survivor's guilt.

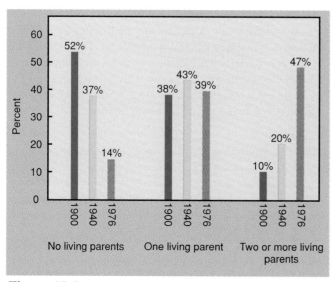

Figure 18.2

Percentage of middle-aged couples with living parents.

Source: From P. Uhlenberg, Death and Family in *Journal of Family History*, 315–322, Fall 1980.

Americans will have living parents even in their middle adulthood years, as illustrated in Figure 18.2. Along with having parents throughout much of adulthood, adults today are more likely to have living grandparents and less likely to be widowed in the young and middle adulthood years. Individuals who marry in their early 20s and do not divorce are likely to have marriages that last 45 years before one of the spouses dies (Uhlenberg, 1980). Obviously, any changes in death rates affect the way individuals live out their lives.

Among younger adults, a proportionally high number of deaths are caused by accidents and suicides. From time to time, death rates among young male adults is increased by wars. Death from disease does occur in young adulthood but is viewed by most people as a more likely possibility in the middle and later adulthood years. Awareness that life expectancy is shortened increases whenever there is an incurable disease epidemic. The AIDS epidemic, for example, will result in a large increase in deaths among young and middle-aged adults.

Deaths in middle age are more likely to be due to heart disease and cancer than to accidents. While lifestyle, attitudes, and health habits can significantly affect length and quality of life, genetic background also influences adult mortality. If you want to live a long life, choose your ancestors carefully. Researchers looked at 960 families to evaluate the relative effects of premature (before the age of 50) deaths of both biological and adoptive parents (Sorensen, Nielson, Andersen, & Teasdale, 1988). The study found that premature deaths in adults, especially those due to infections and vascular causes, have a strong genetic influence. Environmental influences were somewhat more noticeable in deaths from cancers.

In Table 18.1, you probably marked some elderly year for when you expected to die and for when you hoped to die. Elderly people were asked how long they believed they would live. Half of those from ages 64 to 75 thought that they would live at least 10 more years. Nearly 30 percent of those from ages 76 to 84 believed that they would live at least 10 more years. Only 10 percent of those from ages 85 to 96 expected to be alive in 10 years (Marshall, 1975). The decreasing expectations of longevity as chronological years increase make some sense, but these subjects based their estimates on more than just chronological age—they also considered the age of their parents at death. Persons who are older than the death ages of their parents do not expect to live as long as those individuals who are younger than the age of death of at least one parent.

Although most people want long lives, many people want to live long lives only if the quality of life is good. Among older adults, overall fear of death seems to decrease, but fear of senility, long-lingering deaths, nursing homes, and physical incapacitation increases (Dumont & Foss, 1972; Kamerman, 1988). At the same time, some younger adults resent the time, effort, and expenses involved in extending the lives of the elderly. Some individuals have proposed that physicians not perform life-extending procedures on persons over a specified age, such as 80 (Callahan, 1987; Lawren, 1988).

Terminal Illnesses

Table 18.2 lists the 10 leading causes of death in the United States. Deaths from these 10 causes account for just over 83 percent of all deaths. Two of these 10 causes have been decreasing for several years: atherosclerosis has been declining since 1950, and chronic liver disease and cirrhosis have been declining since 1979. Mortality levels for all 10 causes of death are higher for males than for females, with the largest sex difference occurring for accidental deaths (National Center for Health Statistics, 1987).

Although all persons know that they will die, the diagnosis of a terminal illness abruptly changes a person's life. Pattison (1977) called the time period between knowledge of impending death and actual death the **chronic living-dying interval.** Many people use this time period to rearrange their priorities and activities and to share the remaining time with family and friends. When dying patients share memories and emotions with loved ones, this anticipatory grief period helps family and friends to deal better with bereavement.

Sudden Deaths

Heart Attacks

The leading cause of death in the United States and other industrialized nations is sudden cardiac death. One in five Americans—about 330,000 a year—die of instant heart failure. Most people are familiar with the other kind of heart attack—myocardial infarction (MI), the result of

Table 18.2
Top Ten Leading Causes of Death in United States in 1985

Rank	Cause of Death	Percentage of Total Deaths
1	Heart Diseases	37.0%
2	Cancers (Malignant Neoplasms)	22.1%
3	Cerebrovascular Diseases	7.3%
4	Accidents	4.5%
5	Chronic Obstructive Pulmonary Diseases	3.6%
6	Pneumonia and Influenza	3.2%
7	Diabetes Mellitus	1.8%
8	Suicide	1.4%
9	Chronic Liver Disease and Cirrhosis	1.3%
10	Atherosclerosis	1.1%

Source: Data from the National Center for Health Statistics, 1987. Advance Report of Final Mortality Statistics, 1985. Monthly Vital Statistics Report, Washington, D.C., U.S. Department of Health and Human Services.

months or years of battling coronary atherosclerosis. Persons with MI have breathlessness and angina, and eventually, death results when heart muscle dies from lack of oxygenated blood (Monagan, 1986).

Sudden-death heart attacks begin with a storm of electrical impulses that abruptly disrupt the pumping of the heart. About 75 percent of sudden-death victims have no previous MIs, and nearly half have no smoking, high cholesterol, hypertension, and obesity histories. Research is being conducted on why and when these electrical misfirings occur and how they can be prevented. One research area involves an improperly functioning chemical in the frontal lobe of the brain (Monagan, 1986).

Along with biochemical research, psychological research is exploring what life events increase the probability of a sudden-death heart attack. Widowers are 40 percent more likely to have a sudden heart attack than are married men of the same age. The rate of sudden heart attacks dramatically increases during the first year of retirement (Monagan, 1986).

People are also more likely to die suddenly during fear, rage, grief, joy, or humiliation. In a study of 275 cases of sudden death, 135 deaths were due to a disruption of a close relationship, with 50 of these deaths occurring during the first 2 weeks after a significant loss (e.g., death of a spouse) and with 20 deaths occurring when someone important was in danger. In 103 cases, the person who died was in personal danger, and in 21 cases, death was associated with failure, defeat, or loss of self-esteem. Sixteen individuals died while achieving recognition of an important goal or during a joyous reunion (Engel, 1977).

Accidents and Homicides

In the United States, accidents are the fourth leading cause of deaths, while homicides are the twelfth. These deaths are disproportionate among younger persons and among men. Homicides occur 3.3 times more frequently among men than among women; accidents are 2.8 times more common for men (National Center for Health Statistics, 1987).

Suicides

Suicides are the eighth most frequent cause of deaths in America, and males are 3.8 times more likely to die from suicide than are females (National Center for Health Statistics, 1987). Suicides are growing dramatically among adolescents: Currently, more than 5,000 15- to 24-year-olds commit suicide annually (Sanders et al., 1988).

Among teenagers ages 15 to 19, suicides are the third leading cause of death (Gispert, Wheeler, Marsh, & Davis, 1985). Among adolescents, the suicide rate tripled from the mid-1950s to the mid-1980s (Kamerman, 1988). For every death, 50 to 200 suicide attempts are made (Sanders et al., 1988). In other words, 1 of every 10 teenagers has made at least one suicide attempt. Compared to older individuals, teenagers are more likely to commit cluster suicides, multiple suicides in one geographical location within a short time period (Sanders et al., 1988). Teenagers are more likely to use revenge as a motive for suicide and to imitate suicidal behaviors from television and movies.

guided review

1. A _____ is a culture's attitudes and rituals about dying, death, and bereavement.
2. The _____ period is considered to be generally representative of the attitudes toward death in the United States today.
3. As children's cognitive development advances, they eventually achieve a mature concept of death that incorporates the understanding that death is _____, that death involves becoming _____, and that death is _____.
4. Lower mortality rates, especially among infants and children, have resulted in increases in _____ _____ among parents who do have children die.
5. True or false: Among the 10 leading causes of death in adulthood, males have higher rates of mortality than females in 6 of the 10 categories.

answers

1. death system [LO-1]. 2. Denial of Death [LO-2].
3. irreversible; nonfunctional; universal [LO-3].
4. survivor's guilt [LO-5]. 5. False [LO-6].

The Process of Dying

Theoretical Perspectives of Dying

Elisabeth Kübler-Ross: Stages of Dying

Elisabeth Kübler-Ross began interviewing hundreds of dying patients when little research was being done on dying. She found that all of the patients knew that they were going to die soon, yet 40 percent of them had not been officially told by either doctors or family members that their illness was terminal. (Today, most terminally ill patients are informed about their medical condition.) She found that persons who were terminally ill wanted to talk about the experience. From her interviews, Kübler-Ross (1969) concluded that dying persons, if they live long enough, progress through five stages.

The first stage is **denial,** a stage of shock and disbelief that the illness is that serious. This stage can last from a few seconds to a few months; Kübler-Ross found that fewer than 1 percent of her subjects remained in the denial stage until they died.

Anger is the second stage. When patients can no longer deny that they will soon die, they become difficult, demanding, complaining, and critical of everything. Patients may express anger at God, and they pose the unanswerable question, "Why me?" Family and medical staff should remind themselves that patients are not directly angry at them but that the health and energy of others remind patients of their own diminishing lives. Patients need to openly express anger and to wrestle with "Why me?"

During the third stage, called **bargaining,** patients promise something in exchange for extension of life or lessening of pain. Promises may be made to God or to members of the medical staff. Patients may bargain for one more time out of the hospital, for going to a daughter's wedding, or for seeing the next grandchild. Typically, patients bargain for a particular event; if they get their wish, they then try to strike another bargain.

The fourth stage is **depression.** Depression is a normal response of dying because patients must deal with the impending loss of life and everything and everyone they love. The grief needs to be expressed because patients are dealing with the separation from others.

Kübler-Ross's last stage is **acceptance.** During the beginning of this stage, most patients want to see their relatives and friends to say goodbye. Then, many choose one primary person as a companion to provide comfort. This stage is not resignation; they would rather go on living, but they are ready for death and therefore finish their mission.

> ### successful study tip
> #### Kübler-Ross's Stages
> Use the acronym DABDA to help you remember Kübler-Ross's five stages: Denial, Anger, Bargaining, Depression, and Acceptance.

Elisabeth Kübler-Ross did much work on how persons deal with the process of dying.

Kübler-Ross's ideas are accepted by professionals working with the terminally ill, but some researchers have been unable to replicate these stages (Butler & Lewis, 1982). Some have expressed concern that busy medical personnel might force dying persons through the five stages to simplify their jobs and at the same time feel good that dying persons in the acceptance stage have made spiritual progress (Rosenbaum, 1982).

Kübler-Ross herself and others (Kalish, 1981; Shneidman, 1978) did not see these stages as always present. Just as there are many ways in which to live, there are many ways in which to die. Shneidman (1978) suggested that, rather than following a linear process through five stages, dying individuals alternate between hope and despair, between denial and acceptance. According to Shneidman, the various emotions do not occur in neat, tidy packages.

The following excerpt, written by Jacob Javits (1984) when he was terminally ill from amyotrophic lateral sclerosis (ALS), a gradually disabling muscle disease, illustrates how acceptance of dying status is intertwined with aspects of earlier stages, including denial:

> *Now a few observations on my own life as a "sick man," which may be helpful to others carrying comparable serious disabilities. I do lecture, I do read, and I do write. I dedicate my life to the issues that have dominated it for many decades now, and to my profession as a lawyer. I believe that I can still be useful in many ways.*
>
> *In short, life does not stop with terminal illness. Only the patient stops if he does not have the intellectual and moral wherewithal to go forward with life until death overtakes him. That happens to*

everybody. We can be inspired by our disabilities and carry on what is truly life, or we can be dismayed and downed by them.

The greatest therapy is to forget about terminal illness. Everybody is terminal. That is the great message that can perpetuate the useful life of the patient and be of solace and comfort to the patient's family and friends. What is really worthwhile in life is the excitement and the expectation of living, and the giving and receiving, which is, after all, life's essence. (p. 31)

E. Mansell Pattison's Three Phases of Dying

E. Mansell Pattison (1977) did not create dying stages that revolved around emotional experiences. Instead, he proposed a three-phase model in which dying persons experience a wide range of individual responses. The three phases are the acute phase, the chronic living-dying interval, and the terminal phase.

According to Pattison, the acute phase commences when patients realize that death is imminent. Anxiety is typically the predominant emotion, but other emotions, such as fear, anger, and resentment, are also present.

The second phase, the chronic living-dying interval, was discussed earlier in the chapter and is characterized by less anxiety but by diverse emotional experiences, such as fear of the unknown, sorrow, loneliness, suffering and pain, loss of self-control, and loss of identity. Some people in this phase find ways to make their remaining time very fulfilling.

The last phase is the terminal phase, the actual process of dying. While many emotional states may continue to exist, Pattison felt that the most typical reaction in this phase was withdrawal. Of course, theoretical positions can only deal with persons who are terminally ill, rather than those who die suddenly.

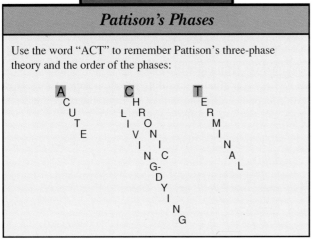

successful study tip

Pattison's Phases

Use the word "ACT" to remember Pattison's three-phase theory and the order of the phases:

A
C
U
T
E

C
H
L
R
I
O
V
N
I
C
N
G-
D
Y
I
N
G

T
E
R
M
I
N
A
L

Definitions of Death

Traditionally, death was defined as occurring when the heart stopped beating, the lungs ceased breathing, the pupils were fixed and dilated, and tendon reflexes were absent. As medical treatment advanced, increased use of life-support systems and organ transplants made this traditional definition inadequate. Modern definitions of death focus on **brain death** (Kamerman, 1988). Doctors at the Harvard Medical School proposed the following criteria for brain death (Jeffko, 1980): (1) totally unreceptive and unresponsive, (2) no movements for 1 hr, (3) no breathing for 3 min when the respirator is removed, (4) no reflexes, (5) no brain stem activity, and (6) a flat electroencephalogram (EEG).

Some professionals believe that these criteria are too strict and that they prolong the vegetative existence of some individuals. The death of the cerebral cortex (**cognitive death),** rather than the whole brain, has been proposed as an alternative determinant of death. The attending physician usually determines which criteria are used. Some terminally ill individuals enact a **living will,** which informs family members and medical professionals about their preferences for sustaining life or allowing death.

Physiological Changes at Death

Most individuals have not directly experienced the death of another person. What happens in the body as death draws near? Dying persons gradually lose sensations in their limbs and the ability to move their legs and then their arms. As peripheral circulation diminishes, the dying person may frequently be very sweaty and feel cool at the body surface. Sight and hearing are failing, so patients often turn their heads toward light and need visitors to speak loudly. The touch sensation also decreases, but most patients feel comforted by touch from others. Shortly before death, patients seem to be in less pain and at peace. The majority of dying patients are conscious until the moment of death (Gray, 1984).

After death, the remaining bodily processes diminish and then stop. Hair continues to grow for several hours, and the liver continues for awhile to convert glycogen to glucose. Most noticeably, rigor mortis, the contraction of muscles, begins about 2 hr after death and continues for 30 hr.

Near-Death Experiences

About 35 to 40 percent of people who almost die but recover have **near-death experiences (NDEs);** this includes about 8 million Americans (Ring, 1984). A book by Moody (1976) called *Life After Life* popularized NDEs. However, NDEs may have nothing to do with dying, since only some people who are close to clinical death have NDEs, since some people experience out-of-body experiences (OBE) without nearly dying, and since descriptions of NDEs match many individuals' experiences on hallucinogens (Kastenbaum, 1981; Siegel, 1980). Others believe that NDEs may help in understanding what goes on after death (Ring 1980, 1984; Ring & Franklin, 1981).

Ring (1980) suggested five progressive stages to a prototypical NDE, but only 10 percent experience all five stages: (1) a sense of peace and well-being, (2) body separation (OBE), (3) entering the darkness, (4) seeing the light, and (5) entering the light. Many individuals who made it to steps 3 and 4 found that they were allowed (or told) to return to human life. This decision period often included a life review, awareness of a "presence," encounters with deceased loved ones, and the actual decision to return. Some NDErs believe that, in addition to a life review, they experienced previews of the future—personal flash-forwards, memories of future life events, and prophetic visions of a more general nature (Ring, 1984). A general description of a near-death experience follows:

> *The realm that the NDEr enters at the time of the experience is one of timelessness, infinite space, and total freedom. One feels enormously expanded in all ways and filled with divine love and knowledge. Usually, with all one's heart, one desires to remain in this state forever.* (Ring, 1984, p. 90)

In general, people who have NDEs have reduced fears about death (Kamerman, 1988). Suicide attempters who had NDEs experienced peace and well-being and lowered suicide desires (Greyson, 1981; Ring & Franklin, 1981). Most people who experience an NDE believe that the experience changes their values, increasing their appreciation for life and their concern for others. They become less concerned with materialistic goals and with impressing others. Many NDErs believe that the event served as a catalyst for spiritual awakening (Ring, 1984).

After Death

A majority of Americans (70 percent) believe that existence does not end with death, but the existence of life after death cannot be tested scientifically. Early psychologists, such as Gustav Fechner and William James, tried to investigate life after death, ghosts, and communication with the dead, but the work of these early psychologists looks quaint and questionable by today's scientific standards. One of the most curious studies was done by MacDougall. He weighed bodies at the time of death and used the immediate weight loss to calculate how much a human soul weighed—his answer was 1 oz (Siegel, 1980).

One belief is that death is the absolute end of existence and that, after death, the body disintegrates and is reabsorbed into the environment and that consciousness also ends (Toynbee, 1976). However, most people do not believe that death represents annihilation.

One detailed analysis of what occurs after death is found in the *Tibetan Book of the Dead,* written in the 14th century and translated into English in 1927. The Tibetan Buddhists' descriptions of the first moments of dying are very similar to contemporary descriptions of near-death experiences: initial confusion, sounds, a tunnel, light, a presence, and a life review. For the next 49 days, the soul is said to experience bardos, distinct periods of heavens and hells. Each bardo can trap or liberate the soul, depending on the dying person's fear and attraction for the content of the bardos. According to the *Tibetan Book of the Dead,* to progress through the bardos, the dead person must view these scenes without confusion and terror. The soul is said to be aided in moving through the bardos if survivors do not grieve too much (Goleman, 1977).

Globally, most people believe in **reincarnation,** the idea that everyone lives a series of human lives within different bodies. Believers use dream content, interest in other time periods, and resemblances to ancestors as support for their beliefs (Siegel, 1980).

In the United States, the most common belief is that each person experiences one human life, followed by eternal afterlife in heaven or hell. All religions promise immortality (in some religions, immortality comes only after many earthly lives). Christians receive grace, Hindus achieve Atman, and Buddhists reach Dharma.

Psychology has basically ignored what occurs after death. Carl Jung's concept of the collective unconscious is one of the few that can be used in beliefs about afterlife. On the other hand, Sigmund Freud viewed belief in immortality as a denial of death (Siegel, 1980).

Dying with Dignity

Death Education

Because individuals have become fairly isolated from personal experiences with death, and because modern society is just emerging from an era of death denial, formal instruction about death is needed. In recent years, many medical schools, colleges, high schools, and even some elementary schools have added courses on death and dying.

More journals are publishing articles on death and bereavement, and even popular magazines are giving death topics more coverage (Woodward, Gosnell, Reese, Coppola, & Liebert, 1978).

More therapists are now counseling the dying and their survivors (Carey, 1976; Insel, 1976; Sinick, 1976). Dying persons need counseling in both tangible (e.g., providing for survivors, medical decisions) and intangible (e.g., the meaning of life) areas. Survivors can be assisted in dealing with their grief, guilt, and anger.

As individuals become more knowledgeable about death, they take an increasing interest in making the decisions about how they die and where they die. As professionals become more efficient in lengthening life by medical procedures, ethical issues increase.

The Hospice Movement

Most people used to die in their own homes, but homes are no longer the most common place in which to die. By the 1980s, over 60 percent of deaths in the United States occurred in hospitals, and another 14 percent occurred in other institutions, such as nursing homes (Bendiet, 1988). Nursing homes increased in numbers after World War II. Today, the average nursing home resident is an 80-year-old widow or spinster with three or four chronic ailments who spends 2.6 years in the nursing home, with residence ending in death 30 percent of the time (Bendiet, 1988).

Dying persons in hospitals and nursing homes typically lack control over daily decisions and the course of dying. Care for dying patients is worked around the needs of other patients. Patients must constantly adjust to different styles of workers on different shifts, deal with overhearing discussions about themselves and other patients, and become institutionalized. In some hospital settings, patients who have died near the end of one work shift have been ignored so that the next shift's personnel must deal with the corpse (Kamerman, 1988).

Recently, the **hospice** movement has provided another option in care for the terminally ill. *Hospice* is a medieval term for a rest stop for travelers, but by the end of the 19th century, the term was applied to places where nuns cared for dying persons (Woodward et al., 1978). A hospice is a specialized health-care program that serves terminally ill patients during their final days and focuses on in-home care, relief from pain, and preparation for dying. The first hospice in the United States was established in 1971 in Connecticut (Leming & Dickinson, 1985).

Hospice personnel help patients to find quality in their remaining lifetime with as little discomfort as possible. For example, medication is provided before pain begins, rather than when patients cannot tolerate more pain. In England, hospice residents are given "Brompton cocktails," a mixture of heroin, cocaine, alcohol, syrup, and chloroform water so that pain can be avoided. In the United States, morphine and thorazine are often substituted for the illegal heroin and cocaine, but this combination often leaves dying patients feeling tired and sluggish. Some programs have resolved this dilemma by using morphine alone (Woodward et al., 1978).

Many insurance plans provide benefits for hospice care. Since 1983, Medicare has provided for hospice care as long as the following criteria are met: (1) patients have life expectancies under 6 months; (2) patients no longer benefit from curative intervention; (3) patients receive 80 percent of care at home; and (4) relatives or friends assume responsibility for custodial care and legal decisions (Bulkin & Lukashok, 1988).

Hospice care can be adapted to all ages, but most hospice patients are over 60 (Leming & Dickinson, 1985). Currently, 90 percent of all hospice patients have cancer. Patients who have AIDS could also benefit greatly from hospice services, but two of the necessary criteria are hard to meet. Doctors find it quite difficult to estimate when AIDS patients have less than a 6-month life expectancy, and hospice residents are not allowed to be given experimental drugs (Bulkin & Lukashok, 1988).

Family members of terminally ill persons also may benefit from hospice care. Hospice personnel provide support and information while patients are still alive, and hospice programs later help survivors in their grief processing (Leming & Dickinson, 1985).

Although the hospice movement provides many services and humane care, for dying individuals to avail themselves of these services, they must make the decision to stop life-sustaining efforts and to wait for death. Because of the linkage between stopping curative interventions and receiving insurance coverage for hospice services, some individuals may be counseled to stop medical interventions while the individuals are still focused on living. Likewise, the shift to a focus on dying may cause some individuals to consider assisted suicides and other forms of euthanasia.

Euthanasia and Other Issues

Euthanasia

The literal translation of **euthanasia** is "the good death," and euthanasia refers to the means for producing a gentle and easy death (Leming & Dickinson, 1985). Many people have used euthanasia to end the suffering of cats and dogs with unbearable pain from an incurable disease, but most people hesitate to advocate an injection to end the suffering of a loved one.

On the other hand, medical advances over the last 50 years have made it very difficult to die from "natural causes":

> *For almost any life-threatening condition, modern medical technology can now delay the moment of death. Death will often not occur until and unless the decision has been made to withhold or withdraw life-sustaining treatment. In other words,* when *and* how *a patient dies is increasingly the outcome of a deliberate human decision. (Kuhse, 1987, p. 145)*

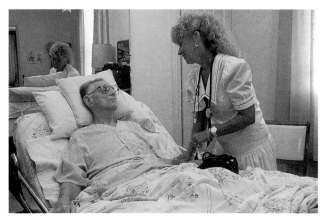

Medical advances have improved the quality of the "living-dying interval," but also created new ethical issues such as when to stop life-support systems.

People with pneumonia are often saved with antibiotics, and people who have cardiac arrest are subjected to "Code Blue" treatment of electrical jump-started hearts (Capron, 1987). Life-support systems can keep people in permanent vegetative states for years. This sophisticated medical ability necessitates questions about which measures should be taken to keep persons alive and who should make the decisions about the use of life-support systems.

On what basis should decisions regarding continuation or discontinuation of life-support systems be made? According to the quality-of-life position, persons should be kept alive *if* the quality of life meets or exceeds minimal human standards. Some people view minimal human standards as being near animal nature; others support more rigorous standards, such as intellectual criteria and ability to communicate. According to the sanctity-of-life position, *all* life, regardless of quality, is worth preserving. This position is associated with the Judeo-Christian tradition; the early Greek writers Plato and Pythagoras also held this position (Pinch, 1986). The sanctity-of-life position calls for more conservative decisions about euthanasia.

Who makes life-support decisions? Sometimes, the decisions can be made by the patients themselves. Living wills written by people when they are healthy inform medical personnel of their personal decisions regarding life support in the event that, in the future, they are no longer capable of communicating their decisions. One possible problem is that healthy individuals may not be able to accurately predict what their wishes will be under critical medical circumstances. Sometimes, patients who are suffering and wish to die may have a chance to recover and achieve good quality of life. Should doctors follow patients' wishes or not? One burn patient who pleaded with his doctor to help him die but was kept alive later stated:

> *In terms of how happy I am now, I have a very good quality of life. . . . I have had some very, very good experiences and happy experiences that I, of course, would not have had if I had died. My contention is that I should have been the one to make that choice at that time. (Pinch, 1986, p. 3)*

Medical personnel may make the decisions about euthanasia. Medical staff have to balance legal concerns, medical concerns, patient interests, and personal values regarding the quality and sanctity of life. Because of these conflicts, many right-to-die issues are becoming judicial decisions. In one court decision, permission was given to stop artificially feeding a patient in a vegetative state. Currently, 10,000 comatose Americans who are unable to swallow are kept alive through feeding tubes (Ostling, 1987b). Who do you believe should make the decisions about continuing artificial feeding of comatose patients? How about conscious patients who are unable to swallow—should they be allowed to determine that they no longer want to be kept alive by means of artificial feeding?

Passive euthanasia consists of *omitting* a medical procedure (such as artificial feeding), with the eventual result being death. Active euthanasia consists of *doing* a medical procedure to bring about an earlier death. In other words, in passive euthanasia, the patient is *allowed* to die, and in active euthanasia, the patient is *helped* to die. More individuals approve of passive euthanasia than voluntary active euthanasia—perhaps, because it is viewed as nonaggressive and painless. Few realize that passive euthanasia can cause lingering suffering. When kidneys fail and dialysis is not performed, patients remain conscious for several days or weeks while experiencing nausea, gastrointestinal hemorrhage, vomiting of blood, neuromuscular twitching, and convulsions. Untreated respiratory death is experienced as air hunger, in which panicky gasping may go on for hours (Kuhse, 1987).

Voluntary active euthanasia (or "mercy killing") may be performed by the patient, a loved one, or a medical professional. A physician could, for example, use injections of drugs to cause death. In 1939, Sigmund Freud, who was suffering from cancer, asked his physician to help him end his life with morphine injections (Gay, 1988). Although voluntary active euthanasia is currently illegal in all countries but the Netherlands, some see it as an appropriate solution to ending life (Pinch, 1986). Others argue that greater acceptance of voluntary active euthanasia makes choosing to continue life-support systems and curative interventions more difficult.

Cryonics

Between 1900 and 1920, scientific advancements allowed many to believe that, soon, people would only die from old age. They believed that scientists would learn how to cure old age and make physical immortality a possibility. During those years, people bought lots of yogurt and buttermilk because those substances were believed to fight the body toxins associated with old age (Leming & Dickinson, 1985).

Similarly, some people believe that the diseases from which they are dying will be curable in the future. Therefore, they join cryonics societies, and when they die, their bodies are frozen to the temperature of solid carbon dioxide. These individuals believe that they will someday be thawed, brought back to life, and cured, although the success of cryonics is doubtful (Aiken, 1985).

Organ Transplants and Heart Implants

One way to prolong life is through organ transplants. Many persons have had extended, quality lives because of receiving a new kidney or heart. Yet, this medical arena has several ethical issues:

- Since needy recipients outnumber donors, who decides who receives donor organs? On what basis are these decisions made? Greatest need? Most likely to have a successful transplant? Likelihood of future contributions to society? Chronological age? Ability to financially pay?
- Who can be used as an organ donor? Can anencephalic babies (born with no brain except for the brain stem) be used? Can head-injured patients in a permanent vegetative state be declared dead and their organs donated? Could a healthy person sell a kidney or eye to the highest bidder?
- Should patients or family members make appeals in the media to try to acquire one of the limited number of available organs?

Less successful and more controversial than organ transplants are artificial heart implants (Bernstein, 1985). The first recipient of a permanent artificial heart was Barney Clark, who survived for 112 days. During that time, he repeatedly asked to be allowed to die. The second recipient was William Schroeder, who suffered at least two strokes, had great memory loss (sometimes, he could not recognize family members), and was depressed during his 6-month survival. His wife stated, "If he had anticipated the hardship, he might not have done it. . . . Bill thought he'd either die or be better" (Bernstein, 1985, p. 87). Ethical concerns include the quality of life, the use of human beings in experimental surgery, and the huge expenditure of money ($250,000 per heart implant patient per year) to try to save one life. What is your opinion about such procedures?

---

guided review

11. _____ provides many services to assist dying individuals and their families.
12. The practices of euthanasia and _____ transplants raise many _____ issues that are not easily resolved.
13. In _____ euthanasia, the patient is allowed to die, while in _____ euthanasia, the patient is helped to die.

answers

11. Hospice care [LO-14]. 12. organ; ethical [LO-15].
13. passive; active [LO-16].

Bereavement, Mourning, and Grief

This section focuses on the experiences of the survivors of those who have died. What do loved ones experience, and what do they do to recover from their losses? The terms *grief, bereavement,* and *mourning* are distinctly different terms, even if the differences are often lost in everyday usage. **Grief** is the sadness, sorrow, and distress experienced because of **bereavement**. Bereavement is the status of having a significant person in your life die. Bereavement causes the emotions of grief. **Mourning** is the term for the culturally prescribed ways of expressing grief—the process by which grief is gradually controlled (Jackson, 1974).

Table 18.3 describes some cross-cultural and historical mourning rites. Some of these ideas may seem quite foreign and perhaps repulsive to you, but if you were a member of the Kapauku Papuans, you would find your mourning rituals ordinary and comforting, and American funeral customs might seem alien and barbaric instead.

Funerals and Other Death Rituals

Before learning about modern-day funerals, read the material that follows about typical American mourning customs in 1700 and 1850. Learning about these historical customs will help you to see how rituals have evolved over the last 300 years. As you read, pay attention to your reactions to the various customs and beliefs. Are some of the older customs appealing to you? Do other customs seem odd or inappropriate? Why?

The American Way of Mourning: 1700

America in 1700 was in the midst of the Puritan tradition. Puritans believed that people deserved death and damnation because of original sin and because of their own sins. People could not do anything or believe anything that would guarantee salvation—salvation was only for persons chosen by God. Nevertheless, dying persons were aided in "lifting toward heaven" by spending their remaining time praying, reading the Bible, and accepting God's will.

Most deaths occurred in the homes, and homes and cemeteries were the two most common sites of funerals. Corpses were considered shells of souls, so bodies were simply washed, wrapped in shrouds, and placed in coffins. When possible, midwives prepared the corpses.

Townfolk would learn about death by the tolling of the town's church bells. Persons who would be part of the funeral rites (e.g., ministers and pallbearers) were invited to the funeral with a gift of gloves. Rich individuals would send extravagant symbols of mourning, such as memorial rings or scarves. Funerals focused on comforting and instructing the living. Often, funeral sermons were given at the next church meeting (Leming & Dickinson, 1985).

Table 18.3
Cross-Cultural and Historical Funeral Rites

- The Parsee of India place the corpse on a high scaffold called a dakhmas. The bones are picked over by vultures.

- The ancient Romans cremated the body except for one severed finger that was buried. This custom was called os resectum.

- The ancient Egyptians embalmed cadavers over a 30-day period. The Egyptians believed that souls went on a 3,000-year journey and then returned to use their bodies.

- Widows among the Swazi in Africa express their mourning by shaving their heads.

- The Kapauku Papuans of West New Guinea express grief by weeping, eating ashes, cutting off fingers, and smearing their bodies with mud, ashes, or clay.

- Among Cheyenne Indians, female relatives of the dead person cut off their long hair and gash their foreheads. Male relatives merely let down their hair.

- The Kapauku Papuans of West New Guinea bind the corpse by the limbs to a pole and carry it in procession to the burial location.

- The Tausug in the Philippines prepare the corpse with ritualized bathings. After cleaning all body orifices, they plug the openings with cotton.

- In the French West Indies, bodies are washed with rum, rum is placed inside the corpse, and orifices are sealed with small pieces of lime.

- The Konyak Nagar in India separate the head from the rest of the corpse 6 days after the funeral. The cleaned skull is placed in an urn.

- For the Somai of Malaya, graves are only 2 to 3 ft deep. The cadaver is buried in an east-west direction, with the head to the west (to coincide with the setting sun).

- The Kapauku Papuans of West New Guinea bury their most honored tribe members in special huts on high stilts. The corpse is placed in a squatting position, and a pointed pole is driven through the rectum, abdomen, chest cavity, and neck. The cadaver is placed so that its face can be seen at the window. After several years, the skull is cleaned and stuck on a pole near surviving relatives' residences.

- The Yanomamo Indians in Venezuela and Brazil burn the corpse on a pyre of logs. Later, the bones are retrieved and crushed into a black powder. This powder is added to boiled plantain soup and eaten during a feast.

Source: Data from Leming & Dickinson, 1985; and Aikens, 1985.

The American Way of Mourning: 1850

Religious ideas had modified significantly by 1850. Now, Christians believed that they could influence their eternal salvation by wanting it and praying for it. Death became less scary because (1) more people believed they would be saved, and (2) death was assumed to have some special purpose that God had temporarily concealed from His people. In 1850, people emphasized self-control and control over nature.

People were also influenced by romanticism and sentimentalism; therefore, mourning rituals and funerals were no longer simple. Funerals were a mixture of excessive emotion, beautified and made-up corpses, funeral music, fancy caskets, and elaborate mourning costumes. People were invited to funerals with hand-delivered printed cards. The homes of mourners were radically changed. Front doors had black door badges placed on them, windows were draped, and black crepe was placed over pictures on the walls. Funerals had the same general format as many funerals today—condolences to the family, viewing the body, the funeral, the funeral procession to the cemetery, and graveyard comments.

However, the bereaved in the 1850s had more elaborate mourning rituals than is typical today. Widows typically did 1 year of deep mourning, during which they wore dull black. In the second year, the mourning costumes were lightened by using colored accessories. Consolation literature (e.g., obituary poems and memoirs) and embroidered mourning portraits were also customs of the 19th century.

The 1850s signaled the start of several trends, including the availability of painkillers for dying persons, the beginning of the life insurance business, and the establishment of the funeral service director as a separate career (Leming & Dickinson, 1985).

Dying persons and survivors of the latter 20th century have different preferences about which aspects to include as mourning rituals, so the rituals of death are as individualized as the rituals of life. Think about what you would like your funeral, obituary, and memorial to be, using the questions in Table 18.4 to guide you.

Autopsies

Autopsies, the examination of bodies after death, are performed in about 20 percent of deaths. Complete autopsies involve examination of organs of three major body cavities: abdomen, chest, and head (Leming & Dickinson, 1985). Autopsies are done for several reasons, such as checking on the accuracy of diagnosis and medical history. For example, Alzheimer's disease can only be diagnosed without error in an autopsy. A second medical reason is that information is gained about the appropriateness of medical and surgical procedures. Third, autopsies are done for research information. Persons in experimental drug research studies may be required to allow autopsies in the event of their death. A fourth reason for autopsies is to clarify the cause of death. Autopsies provide information in cases of suspicious deaths. Finally, autopsies can be done to provide organ and tissue donations for others (Roberts, 1978).

Autopsies may be required by law when the death is a coroner's case. Otherwise, they are at the discretion of relatives. Relatives may request an autopsy to obtain definite information about the cause of death, or they may view an autopsy as an "assault" on the corpse and forbid it. Autopsies do create some difficulties for funeral directors: They result in time delays, render the corpses harder to embalm, and make the task of preparing the body for public viewing more difficult (Leming & Dickinson, 1985).

Embalming

Embalming, the replacement of body fluids with preserving chemicals, did not become widespread in the United States until the germ theory of disease. Although the ancient

Here are some suggestions for items to prepare ahead of time about your own funeral. Having an up-to-date and detailed list of information both makes planning easier for survivors who make funeral plans and reassures them that they are following your wishes.

1. Who do you want to be notified about your death as soon as possible? List name, relationship, address, telephone number. If any person should be informed in person rather than by telephone, mention this.
2. List your clergy, physician, lawyer, and funeral director preferences.
3. Provide information about you for official certification and for information in an obituary. For example: Name, usual residence, birth date and birthplace, usual occupation and employer, spouse, parents, Social Security number, service serial number and dates of service, children.
4. List your designation for executor and where your will can be found.
5. Name of bank and safety deposit box number. List of valuable papers not in this box and where they can be found.
6. The funeral ceremonies:
   a. Who do you want in charge of decisions?
   b. Preferred clergy
   c. Preferred funeral director
   d. Preferred location of ceremony (church, residence, funeral home)
   e. Cremation (disposition of cremated remains) or burial (where, lot number)
   f. Comments on costs/quality of caskets, vaults, funeral services
   g. Comments on details, such as clothing, hairdresser, pallbearers, flowers
   h. Comments on details of the funeral service, such as preferred scripture, music
   i. Preferences such as open or closed casket, flowers or donation to a charity (which one?)
7. Comments on donation of tissue or organs for medical research.

Funeral rites help bereaved individuals come to terms with the death of a loved one.

Egyptians embalmed bodies because they expected the soul to return in 3,000 years, modern embalming is done for ordinary reasons of health and disease control. Nationally, about four of every five corpses are embalmed and bathed. Most undertakers use cosmetics to restore a more natural coloring because 75 percent of all funerals have a viewing of the body (Leming & Dickinson, 1985).

Notification of Others About the Death

People no longer use hand-printed cards, the deliverance of gloves, or tolling bells to tell others about deaths. Today, the three most typical ways of informing others of a death are in person, by telephone, and in the newspaper. Obituaries maintain the sex-role biases that the individuals dealt with during their lifetimes. Death notices of males are about 20 percent longer and 10 times more likely to include a photo than death notices of females. The obituaries of females are more likely to mention spousal relationships; this sex difference is most evident when the spouse is already dead: Female obituaries list deceased husbands more often than male obituaries list deceased wives (Halbur & Vandagriff, 1987).

Funerals

The funeral director or undertaker profession evolved from roles played by cabinetmakers (who originally made the caskets) and livery owners (who owned the hearse and carriages for mourners). As Americans moved funerals out of their own homes, the largest house in town often became the town's funeral home. Today, half of all funerals are conducted in churches, and most of the rest are conducted in one of 22,000 funeral homes nationwide (Leming & Dickens, 1985).

Starting in the 1890s, states began to regulate embalmers and funeral directors. States require from 9 months to 2 years of training and a period of apprenticeship. Besides specific skills and knowledge of health practices, undertakers need skills in working with people. Funeral directors specialize in dealing with people in crisis, and they take on the roles of crisis intervener, caregiver, and liaison (Leming & Dickinson, 1985).

Details of funerals—from music to flowers to scripture choices—vary, but most funerals have several common factors. After death, bodies are taken to funeral homes, where they are bathed, embalmed, dressed, and put into a casket. Ceremonies often include viewing of the body, condolences to the family, one or more services, and a procession to the graveyard.

What purposes do funeral rites serve? Cross-culturally, funerals have numerous functions: to maintain ancestral spirits, to send the soul to another world, to commemorate the person, to allow expression of grief, to solidify family ties, to reinforce social status, to ensure rebirth, and to appease the deceased's spirit so that it will not haunt the living or bring misfortune (Leming & Dickinson, 1985). Most Americans believe that the major purpose of funerals is to help the bereaved persons. Funerals introduce reality to the irreversibility of death, provide a way to express grief, meet a need for social support, help in the search for meaning in death, and assist bereaved individuals in realizing that death is final (Irion, 1956).

Final Disposition of the Corpse

Interment is the most common means of corpse disposition. About 85 percent of corpses in the United States are buried, mostly in cemeteries. When people buy plots in cemeteries, they do not purchase the land itself but the "right to interment." In addition to the casket, a burial vault or outer receptacle is used. Cemeteries, not the survivors, control how graves can be marked. Disposition of about 5 percent of corpses occurs by entombment, in which caskets are sealed in specially designed buildings called mausoleums (Leming & Dickinson, 1985).

In the United States, approximately 10 percent of bodies are cremated, while in Japan, that figure is 90 percent (Leming & Dickinson, 1985). Cremation can be done by extreme heat or by direct flame and takes about 2 hr. Until recently, crematories were only located within cemeteries, but now, some funeral homes also have them.

Another way to dispose of the corpse is through body bequest programs to medical schools. Of the nearly 2 million U.S. deaths annually, only 7,000 bodies are disposed of through these programs (Leming & Dickinson, 1985).

Methods of corpse disposition in other cultures include open-air disposal, water burial, and mortuary cannibalism. The Parsee of India use open-air disposal, which in their culture consists of placing the dead on scaffolds so that vultures can pick the flesh from the bones. This disposition method is consistent with the Parsee's Zoroastrian beliefs that other methods offend the elements of earth, fire, water, and air. Water burial is used with some deaths at sea. Other cultures may float corpses in boats. A final method is mortuary cannibalism. In endocannibalism, the deceased is eaten by others: Either the body is cremated and the powdered ash is consumed by family members or warriors, or family members eat a bit of the flesh from the bones. Although endocannibalism is not part of American culture, transubstantiation, or symbolic cannibalism, is. One example of transubstantiation is the Christian ritual of Holy Communion, in which the bread and wine are symbolically turned into Christ's body and blood (Aiken, 1985).

Wills

About 25 percent of adults (70 percent of the elderly) have wills, but a number of people die intestate—that is, no valid will is located. When people leave no will, material possessions are distributed according to state law. Nuncupative wills (oral wills) are considered valid if spoken in a situation of imminent death. Holographic wills, which are wills in the testator's own handwriting, are valid if correctly drawn and witnessed.

Lawyers usually draw up wills. The document should include: name, address, age, date, statement of testamentary capacity (the will is made voluntarily by a capable person of "sound mind and body"), specific dispositions, heirs, executor, and signatures of two witnesses (Aiken, 1985).

Table 18.5
Styles of Mourning

1. Denial of Mourning. For some individuals, strong religious beliefs may eliminate the need to grieve.
2. Absence of Mourning. Persons without emotional ties to the deceased do not need to grieve.
3. Mourning Before Death. When there is knowledge ahead of time that a person is dying, persons may have anticipatory grief.
4. Hiding Grief. Some individuals experience grief but do not express it outwardly. These individuals believe that it is important to "carry on" despite bereavement.
5. Time-Limited Mourning. A typical model, these individuals experience intense grief and then move back into normal activities.
6. Unlimited Mourning: "Never Get Over It." For these individuals, grief is never resolved. Although they move back into normal activities, grief is still evident at least part of the time.
7. Unlimited Mourning: Mummification. These individuals deal with long-term grieving by trying to keep things the same as before the death. For example, they may keep the deceased person's room exactly as the person had kept it.
8. Unlimited Mourning: Despair. Not only do these individuals not resolve their grief, they become despondent and depressed over the bereavement. They may also experience anxiety and guilt. These individuals could most benefit from grief therapy.

Sources: From G. Gorer, *Death, Grief, and Mourning,* 1965, Doubleday, New York, NY. From J. Kamerman, *Death in the Midst of Life,* 1988, Prentice Hall, Englewood Cliffs, NJ.

The Experience of Grief

The Grieving Process

Grief, the emotions associated with bereavement, involves stages similar to those proposed by Kübler-Ross (1969) for dying. Kavanaugh (1972) suggested that a typical pattern is shock and denial, disorganization, volatile emotions, guilt, loss and loneliness, relief, and reestablishment. People have different styles of mourning (see Table 18.5).

How long do the bereaved usually grieve? One researcher proposed that the bereavement process takes an average of 90 to 190 days (Lindemann, 1944). Another researcher proposed that individuals typically grieve from 18 to 24 months because bereaved persons need to experience each holiday and special event at least once without the dead person (Davidson, 1975). Both researchers believed that people never completely resolve their feelings of grief—they just learn to live with the loss.

Grieving often has an **anniversary reaction,** called anniversary grief. Each year around the time a loved one died, survivors may experience a vague depression as grief reactions reappear. Survivors often cope better if they set aside death anniversaries to acknowledge loss and to remember the dead person.

Complications in Resolving Grief

Grieving is harder to resolve with some kinds of deaths than with others. The following factors make the grieving process more difficult (Breckenridge, Gallagher, Thompson, & Peterson, 1986; Leming & Dickinson, 1985; Parkes & Weiss, 1983): (1) suicides and deaths due to self-neglect; (2) untimely deaths (e.g., young people or newlyweds); (3) homicide and accident victims; (4) unconfirmed deaths with no body found; (5) sudden, unexpected deaths; (6) drawn-out, lingering deaths; (7) persons on whom survivors were dependent; (8) people toward whom ambivalence was felt; and (9) deaths that cannot be publicly acknowledged (e.g., abortions and spontaneous abortions).

Grief and Abortion

Approximately 400 abortions occur for every 1,000 live births. Since most women do not discuss their abortion experiences openly, they typically grieve in private, thereby prolonging grieving. Called "abortion hangover" or "postabortion blues," grieving may be partly explained by the hormonal changes following an abortion but is mostly attributable to dealing with the loss of imagining what might have been under different circumstances (Stillion, 1985). A temporary but severe grief also follows spontaneous abortions and stillborns. About 15 percent of those who lose a baby have severe anxiety reactions (Stillion, 1985). Losses are harder to take when medical staff and family try to hurry the grieving parents through the bereavement process.

Grief and the Death of a Parent

Deaths of parents hit individuals especially hard, since it is an end to the longest relationship a person can have. The death of the last parent symbolizes the offspring's transition into the oldest generation, a position that can have awesome responsibilities and also may be a reminder of mortality. The death of a parent is associated with depression, and if it occurs during childhood, can serve as a predisposition to depressive illness. Even among adults, parental death is associated with mental illness, an increase in admissions to mental hospitals, and an increase in suicide attempts (Stillion, 1985).

Grief and the Death of a Spouse

One in 20 Americans is a widow or widower. Widows are much more common than widowers, since men are more likely to marry younger women, and women have a longer life expectancy. In the United States, there are about 10 million widows, and three of four currently married women will someday be a widow (Stillion, 1985).

Widowers are more likely than widows to be affected physically after losing a spouse (Helsing & Szklo, 1981). However, widows seem to suffer more psychologically. Women experience higher levels of psychological problems because: (1) many married women build their identities around their husbands' identities; (2) fewer widows remarry; (3) some women do not know how to handle finances and make other decisions; and (4) some widows begin to worry about their physical safety (Stillion, 1985).

Table 18.6
How to Help the Bereaved

- Try to avoid platitudes and rationalizations, such as "It was God's will," "God is testing you," "There's a reason for everything. Don't question God's will."
- Do say something like "We will all miss her," "I'll be here to talk if you wish."
- Do not say, "I know how you feel," unless you have lost someone in a similar situation.
- Do talk about the positive qualities of the deceased. Share memories of the person's life.
- Offer some concrete help, such as extra rooms in your house for out-of-town relatives to use or housesitting during the funeral to avoid problems with burglaries.
- Help out around the house.
- Respect the family's wishes about flowers and donations. Some families would prefer a tree planted in memory of the deceased than cut flowers.
- Visit the funeral home and express condolences to the bereaved individuals.
- Send a sympathy card and put a personal note in the card. Bereaved individuals may read the cards several times while they are grieving.
- Be a person who will listen when the survivors need to talk.

Source: adapted from D. Braun, "They No Longer Walk Alone" in *Farm Journal*, 46–50, March 1984. Reprinted courtesy of Farm Journal Publishers, Inc.; and data from W. E. Wallace, "What to Say to the Bereaved" in *Lutheran*, March 20, 1985.

Most widows and widowers adapt to the loss of their spouse. Prolonged grief is associated with unexpected spousal death, the death of a young spouse, the death of a spouse in a conflicted marriage (freedom from an unhappy marriage is mixed with anxiety and guilt), and the death of a spouse who made all the decisions (Breckenridge et al., 1986; Parkes & Weiss, 1983).

Helping the Bereaved

Cultures with definite mourning rites have prescribed ways in which friends can aid bereaved survivors. (see the "Exploring Cultural Diversity" feature earlier in the chapter). Compared to the Amish, most Americans do not know how to help those who are experiencing grief. According to one study, 80 percent of what individuals say to mourners is not useful (Wallace, 1985). Sometimes, comments offer only superficial reassurance ("God calls the best home to Him") or callously compare the dead person to survivors ("Well, I'm sorry about the death of your dear child, but at least you have other children to comfort you"). Table 18.6 offers suggestions for constructively helping the bereaved. Individuals with prolonged grief, depression, and anxiety should be encouraged to see counselors to help them resolve their grief.

Grieving Death and Other Losses

Grief over someone's death is difficult, in part, because of the death's permanence. Much as individuals wish it, nothing will bring back the life of the other person. On the other hand, many grieving situations in life do not involve the

The Vietnam Memorial in Washington, D.C. helps individuals and the United States heal from the losses of the Vietnam War.

deaths of other people. Some, but not all, of these losses, however, may involve the same sense of permanence as deaths of persons. You may have experience grieving over some of these losses:

Loss of childhood
Loss of dreams and aspirations
Loss of a significant friendship or intimate relationship
Loss of marriage
Loss of innocence
Loss of career
Loss of hope
Loss of spirituality
Loss of integrity
Loss of purpose
Loss of income
Loss of achievements
Loss of direction

These and other losses may be as real and as painful to you as losses due to death. However, with these types of losses, you may have the ability to begin renewal: Adults can regain a touch of childhood, new dreams and aspirations can be developed, new friends and intimates can be made, the jaded thought can be made fresh with innocence, careers can blossom in a new direction. But when renewal is not achieved, grief over losses can last for years.

The Renewal of Life Through Death

Believe that life is worth living, and your belief will help to create the fact. (William James)

There is a test to find whether your mission on earth is finished: If you're alive, it isn't. (Richard Bach)

Deaths of other individuals often lead us to evaluation of our lives, our relationships, and our priorities. They may serve as a reminder of our own mortality and help us in our resolve to use the rest of our lifetime more wisely. If we know that we are dying, we are likely to assess how we have led our lives and hopefully have a sense of accomplishment and integrity.

What lies beyond death remains a mystery. Death may represent the end, a transition into a different existence or afterlife, or a return to another life on earth. If the latter should be true, what lies ahead is a return to Chapter 1.

Exploring Human Development

1. Write a plan for the funeral you would like your survivors to have for you. What influenced your choices?
2. Take a field trip to a local cemetery. Compare older gravesites with newer ones. In the older sections of the cemetery, did you notice more grave markers for children? What other differences based on the date of death did you notice?
3. Talk to individuals who deal with the dying on frequent occasions (e.g., ministers, medical personnel, funeral-home workers, hospice workers). What are their attitudes about death? How do they deal with dying persons and their families? What are the effects of frequent exposure to death?
4. Design a survey interview to use with individuals under the age of 18. Interview children of different ages to see how attitudes and beliefs about death change from the preschool years to adulthood.
5. Find examples of death and dying in children's literature (e.g., "Rock-a-Bye-Baby," "Now I Lay Me Down to Sleep," "Humpty Dumpty," "Cock Robin," "Old Mother Hubbard," "Solomon Grundy," "Jack and the Beanstalk"). Discuss why so many death images occur in children's literature.

1. What criteria would you use to call a death a suicide? For example, when would you label automobile accidents and drug overdoses as suicides? Why is it necessary to identify suicidal deaths?

2. Would you rather die a sudden death or from a terminal illness? What are the advantages and disadvantages of these types of death? Which is better for the survivors?

3. If you had a terminal illness and had only 6 months to 2 years to live, would you live differently than you do now? What changes would you make? Why do you not live that way now?

4. Should there be death education in the public schools? Give reasons for your position.

5. Discuss near-death experiences. How many in your class believe that they are real experiences? How do other students explain this phenomenon?

Reading More About Human Development

Gordon, S. (1985). *When living hurts*. New York: Union of American Hebrew Congregations.

Kamerman, J. B. (1988). *Death in the midst of life: Social & cultural influences on death, grief, & mourning*. Englewood Cliffs, NJ: Prentice-Hall.

Kübler-Ross, E. (1969). *On death and dying*. New York: Macmillan.

Leming, M. R., & Dickinson, G. E. (1985). *Understanding dying, death, and bereavement*. New York: Holt, Rinehart & Winston.

Mitford, J. (1963). *The American way of death*. New York: Simon & Schuster.

Moffat, M. J. (Ed.) (1982). *In the midst of winter: Selections from the literature of mourning*. New York: Vintage.

Moody, R. A. (1976). *Life after life*. New York: Bantam.

Stillion, J. M. (1985). *Death and the sexes*. Washington, DC: Hemisphere.

Summary

I. Death and society
   A. The term *death system* refers to a society's beliefs and attitudes about dying and death.
      1. Many characterize the death system of the United States as denial of death.
      2. During the Middle Ages, the Tamed Death system was prominent in that many people believed that death was a transition from earthly life to a better afterlife.
      3. A second historical death system, occurring from the 12th to the 15th centuries and known as the Death of Self, viewed dying and death more negatively.
      4. Death and love were linked in a third death system, called Death of the Other, in the 19th century.
      5. A fourth and current death system is called Denial of Death.
   B. The Mayan and Amish death systems exhibit the cultural diversity that exists with regard to attitudes and practices associated with dying and death.

   C. All individuals progress through similar stages in developing attitudes about death.
      1. The development of object permanency makes young children capable of reacting to death, but they do not understand the irreversible, permanent nature of death until Piaget's concrete operations stage.
      2. Many preschoolers and older children believe that death only occurs in old age.
      3. By age 7, most children recognize that death is irreversible, involves becoming nonfunctional, and is universal (everyone will die eventually).
      4. Older children become interested in the rituals and ceremonies surrounding death.
      5. Teenagers' greater understanding of death is accompanied by higher levels of anxiety about dying and death.
      6. Attitudes about death change across the adult years, with older adults experiencing less anxiety about death than younger adults.
      7. Attitudes about death can result in behaving in ways that either increase or decrease chances of dying.
   D. Likely causes of death and attitudes regarding the death vary with the age at which death occurs.
      1. The leading causes of death in infancy are congenital anomalies, sudden infant death syndrome, respiratory distress syndrome, and complications of prematurity and low birthweight.
      2. Among the 20 leading industrialized nations, the United States has one of the highest infant mortality rates.
      3. Many parents experience survivor's guilt when their children die before they do.
      4. Parents and other relatives of terminally ill children may pass through several stages in dealing with the child's impending and eventual death: acknowledgment, grieving and reconciliation, detachment, memorialization, and postbereavement mourning.
      5. Parents who experience survivor's guilt may follow one of three pathways in resolving their grief: reunion, reverence, and retribution.
      6. Changes in death rates among adults today translate into fewer children being raised as orphans and more children having living grandparents.
      7. Many deaths in early adulthood are due to accidents and suicide; in middle adulthood, heart disease and cancer are the leading causes of death.
   E. According to Pattison (1977), the diagnosis of a terminal illness begins a time period called the chronic living-dying interval, in which dying individuals may make plans for and resolve issues surrounding their impending deaths.
   F. The leading cause of death in the United States and other industrialized countries is sudden heart attacks.
      1. Widowers are much more likely than married men of the same age to die from sudden heart attacks.
      2. The rate of sudden heart attacks increases dramatically during the first year of retirement.

3. Other sudden deaths include accidents and homicides, both of which occur more often in younger adults and men.
4. Suicides are a frequent cause of death in the United States.
5. Among teenagers, suicides are the third most frequent cause of death.
6. Cluster suicides are also more typical among teenagers.

II. The process of dying
A. Kübler-Ross and Pattison formulated theories regarding the process of dying.
1. From her interviews with dying patients, Kübler-Ross concluded that dying persons may progress through five stages: denial, anger, bargaining, depression, and acceptance.
2. Pattison's model identifies three phases through which dying persons may progress: the acute phase, the chronic living-dying interval, and the terminal phase.
B. Traditional definitions of death focused on heart stoppage, cessation of breathing, dilation of pupils, and absence of reflexes, while recent definitions focus on different aspects of brain death as the most important criteria.
C. Many physiological changes are experienced at the time of death.
1. Dying persons gradually lose sensations and movement in the limbs, and sight and hearing begin to fail.
2. The majority of dying patients are conscious until the moment of death.
3. After death, other physiological changes, such as the continued growth of hair, continue for several hours.
D. Near-death experiences (NDEs) are reported by about 35 to 40 percent of people who almost die.
1. NDEs are controversial, with some people maintaining that they have nothing to do with dying and others believing that they may help in understanding what goes on after death.
2. Typical NDEs proceed through five stages, from a sense of peace to entering the light.
3. Those who have experienced NDEs have reduced fears of death, and their lives are altered in other significant ways.
E. A majority of Americans believe in an existence after death.
1. The existence of life after death cannot be tested scientifically.
2. Another belief is that death is the absolute end of existence.
3. Worldwide, the most common belief about existence after death is reincarnation.
4. All religions promise immortality as a part of existence after death.
5. Psychology has basically ignored the issue of what occurs after death.

III. Dying with dignity
A. One way to counteract the denial of death in the American culture is through death education.
B. The hospice movement is an alternative for caring for terminally ill individuals that focuses on in-home care, relief from pain, and preparation for dying.
1. Hospice workers provide humane care and support for family members, as well as for the dying person.
2. The requirement to stop life-sustaining efforts before receiving hospice care raises several ethical issues.
C. Ending a fellow human's suffering through euthanasia is an extremely complex legal/medical/ethical issue, as are other medical procedures, such as organ transplants.
1. Passive euthanasia consists of omitting a medical procedure, with the eventual result being death.
2. Active euthanasia consists of performing a medical procedure to cause an earlier death.
3. Who is eligible to receive transplants is a major issue, as is who can be used as donors.
4. The lack of available donors means that some people will die before a suitable donor is found.
5. The need for donors may mean that some individuals kept alive on life-support systems may be requested to die in order to provide donor organs.

IV. Bereavement, mourning, and grief
A. Bereavement is the status of having a loved one die; grief is the set of emotions experienced as the result of bereavement; and mourning is the set of culturally prescribed ways of expressing grief.
B. Funerals and other mourning rituals have evolved throughout history.
1. In colonial America, most deaths occurred in the home, and homes and cemeteries were the sites for funerals.
2. By the 1850s, mourning rituals and funerals had become quite elaborate.
3. Contemporary funeral practices may first involve an autopsy to determine the cause of death.
4. The body is prepared for viewing and burial by embalming and cosmetic restoration of facial features.
5. The role of the funeral director has evolved to the point where most funerals are managed by professional firms.
6. Funerals serve numerous functions, including helping the bereaved individuals to honor the dead person and to deal with their grief.
7. The final disposition of the corpse is most often by burial in a cemetery, but cremation and body bequests to medical schools are also used.
8. An important adjunct of mourning is the enacting of the deceased's will, which specifies disposition of a person's material possessions after his or her death.
C. Grief involves stages similar to those proposed by Kübler-Ross for dying.
1. A typical pattern is shock and denial, disorganization, volatile emotions, guilt, loss and loneliness, relief, and reestablishment.

2. Grieving may last from a few months to up to 2 years or more, with many individuals experiencing anniversary reactions of renewed grieving as the anniversary of the loved one's death approaches.

3. Grieving over sudden death and suicides may be harder to resolve.

4. Abortions, miscarriages, and stillbirths also bring about grieving.

5. Death of a parent or spouse often results in problematic grieving and related emotional disturbances.

D. Grieving individuals are helped by definite cultural mourning rituals and by supportive friends who openly talk about the dead person and who make themselves available to listen and to assist the grieving person.

E. Grieving can occur for losses other than death.

   1. The loss of a marriage or employment can be as painful and disturbing as a loss due to death.

   2. The grieving of any loss can lead to reevaluation and renewal in the lives of those experiencing the loss.

F. Deaths of others often lead us to increase our resolve to use the rest of our lifetime wisely.

Chapter Review Test

1. The current death system is called
   a. Denial of Death.
   b. Death of the Other.
   c. Death of Self.
   d. Tamed Death.

2. Which of the following is an essential component of a mature concept of death?
   a. irreversibility
   b. nonfunctionality
   c. universality
   d. all of the above

3. In a comparison of current and turn-of-the-century statistics,
   a. children under age 15 have gone from accounting for over half of U.S. deaths to a very small percentage.
   b. individuals over age 65 are now a smaller portion of the total population but a larger percentage of the deaths.
   c. about half of all families used to experience a death of a child, and now the figure is about half of that.
   d. all of the above are correct.

4. According to Pattison, the chronic living-dying interval is
   a. the communication and relationship between a survivor and a dying person.
   b. the rest of your life.
   c. the time between knowledge of impending death and actual death.
   d. another name for a near-death experience.

5. Which age group is most likely to have cluster suicides?
   a. the elderly
   b. teenagers
   c. young- to middle-aged adults
   d. There is no trend by age.

6. Helena seems to be losing her battle to AIDS, but she is trying to hold on until her son graduates from high school. She often prays to God that "If you just let me see him complete the school year, I'll be ready to go, and I won't be a bother to the medical staff or to my family." Helena is in the _____ stage, according to the Kübler-Ross stages of dying model.
   a. acceptance
   b. anger
   c. bargaining
   d. denial

7. Using Pattison's three-phase model of dying, the acute phase is to _____ as the terminal phase is to _____.
   a. sorrow; suffering
   b. anxiety; withdrawal
   c. nonemotional; emotional
   d. fear; depression

8. Which of the following statements about the physiological changes during dying is *incorrect?*
   a. There is a gradual loss of sensations in the limbs, and although touch sensation decreases, touch is usually comforting.
   b. Rigor mortis, the contraction of muscles, begins about 2 hr after death and continues for about 30 hr.
   c. After death, hair continues to grow for several hours.
   d. The majority of dying patients are not conscious at the moment of death.

9. Compared to others, persons who have experienced near-death experiences (NDEs)
   a. are identical except for the NDE experience.
   b. are more likely to support suicide, risky behaviors, and termination of medical treatments because death is now viewed as a positive and welcomed experience.
   c. have reduced fears about death.
   d. are less likely to be concerned with human, materialistic, and spiritual issues.

10. Psychologists rarely study "life after death" because
   a. few psychologists believe in any form of existence after death.
   b. most people no longer view "life after death" as anything but a misconception.
   c. it cannot be tested scientifically.
   d. psychologists honor a separation between religion and science.

11. Currently, the most common place for a person to die is in
    a. a hospital.
    b. a nursing home.
    c. a hospice setting.
    d. their own home.
12. A "Brompton cocktail" is associated with
    a. hospice residents.
    b. cryonics.
    c. embalming.
    d. active euthanasia.
13. Which of the following is more common for animals than for people?
    a. organ transplants
    b. passive euthanasia
    c. cryonics
    d. active euthanasia
14. _____ is the culturally prescribed ways of expressing _____, the emotion caused by _____, which is the status of having a significant person in your life die.
    a. Bereavement; mourning; grief
    b. Grief; mourning; bereavement
    c. Mourning; bereavement; grief
    d. Mourning; grief; bereavement
15. Which of the following aspects of modern dying and bereavement was a new trend in the 1850s?
    a. life insurance business
    b. painkillers for dying persons
    c. the funeral service director career
    d. all of the above
16. Which of the following is more typical in obituaries of women than of men?
    a. a photo
    b. mention of a spouse
    c. longer
    d. all of the above
17. In the type of mourning called mummification, the survivor
    a. experiences grief but does not express it outwardly.
    b. does not grieve because there was no emotional tie with the deceased.
    c. tries to keep things the same as before the death.
    d. becomes despondent, depressed, and anxious for a very long time.

18. "Postabortion blues" are mostly attributable to
    a. imagining what might have been under different circumstances.
    b. hormonal changes.
    c. change in attitude toward the abortion act.
    d. lack of input into the abortion decision by significant others.
19. Which of the following comments might be most helpful when talking to bereaved survivors?
    a. "I know how you feel."
    b. "God calls the best home to Him."
    c. "We will all miss her."
    d. "I'm sorry about the death of your child, but at least you have other children to comfort you."
20. Losses other than death (e.g., loss of career, aspirations, purpose, income) are different from losses from death in that
    a. they are not as painful as someone's death.
    b. they may not be permanent.
    c. they are not as real as someone's death.
    d. they do not lead to possible renewal or self-evaluation, while the death of a loved one almost always does.

Answers

1. A [LO-1, 2].	8. D [LO-10].	15. D [LO-18].
2. D [LO-3].	9. C [LO-11].	16. B [LO-19].
3. A [LO-3].	10. C [LO-12].	17. C [LO-20].
4. C [LO-4].	11. A [LO-14].	18. A [LO-21].
5. B [LO-6].	12. A [LO-14].	19. C [LO-22].
6. C [LO-7].	13. D [LO-15,16].	20. B [LO-23].
7. B [LO-8].	14. D [LO-17].	

Appendix A

Developmental Researchers and their Theories

This appendix contains brief biographical sketches and summaries of the basic concepts of important developmental researchers and theorists. No attempt has been made to create a comprehensive listing of all developmental theorists; rather, those selected are representative of each of the five major psychological perspectives presented in chapter 1. Special attention is given to such theorists as Piaget, Freud, and Erikson, whose ideas appear throughout the book.

The following is a brief outline of Appendix A:

I. The Biological Perspective
   a. Darwin
   b. Bowlby
II. The Behavioral-Learning Perspective
   a. Pavlov and Watson
   b. Skinner
   c. Bandura
III. The Cognitive Perspective
   a. Piaget
   b. Kohlberg
IV. The Psychodynamic Perspective
   a. Freud
   b. Erikson
   c. Adler
V. The Humanistic-Existential Perspective
   a. Maslow
   b. Rogers

The Biological Perspective

Charles Darwin (1809–1882): Evolution and Child Study

Charles Darwin was born into a prominent family of English doctors. However, he became a naturalist scientist. His book *The Origin of Species,* published in 1859, was a major force in changing scientific views of human development and in focusing attention on the study of children.

Darwin first studied medicine, then theology, and then by chance was recommended to be a naturalist on the *H.M.S. Beagle* as it sailed around the world. Observations that Darwin made on that voyage formed the basis for his ideas about evolution and natural selection.

Darwin's ideas about the origin of living beings were controversial and remain so for some people today because he proposed the concept of evolution—that living organisms evolved from a common ancestor, rather than appearing completely formed as according to theological interpretations. Because he was a religious person who had studied theology, these ideas were troubling to Darwin. In fact, he delayed publishing his observations and his theory based on those observations for 20 years.

A second major concept in Darwin's theory was the idea of natural selection. Darwin discarded the notion that characteristics acquired during one's lifetime were passed on to one's offspring in favor of the idea that those individuals who inherited characteristics that favored survival were more likely to reproduce and pass on those survival characteristics. Thus, natural selection led to the survival of the fittest in each species. Darwin's theory proposed that whole species would become extinct if they did not possess traits that favored survival in the environment. Darwin also believed that, among humans, natural selection occurred for reasoning abilities and social behaviors that favored survival.

Darwin's theory of evolution and natural selection influenced many scientists. These Darwinians, as they were called, believed that they found further evidence of evolution in the observation that development of individuals within a species (ontogeny) recapitulates the evolution of the species across generations (phylogeny).

While mistaken in this belief, the Darwinians succeeded in focusing interest on the scientific study of child development. Darwin also contributed to this movement by keeping a detailed diary of his own son's development.

Darwin worked on his theory for over 40 years and was widely recognized for his scientific achievements. At his death, he was buried beside Sir Isaac Newton at Westminster Abbey. Today, his ideas, augmented with data from genetics, are generally accepted but remain controversial for some.

John Bowlby (1907–1990): Biological Attachment Theory

Bowlby's biological attachment theory is an extension of Darwin's ideas to explain the bond that develops between a human infant and its primary caregiver, usually its mother. Like Darwin, Bowlby was born in England, but 100 years later. He taught school, studied medicine, received training in Freudian psychoanalysis, and in 1936, became involved in child guidance work. His work with children led Bowlby to become concerned about the disturbances experienced by children living in orphanages. He observed that children raised in institutions often displayed an inability to form lasting, intimate relationships with others. Bowlby attributed this difficulty to the lack of opportunity for development of a mother/infant bond.

Bowlby believed that an attachment bond between mother and infant had survival value similar to that found in other species but that, in humans, the attachment process occurred over a much longer time period. He proposed four phases of attachment from birth to the end of childhood (see Table A1.1).

For human infants, who remain relatively defenseless throughout much of childhood, attachment and attachment behaviors serve to maintain the closeness of an adult protector and aid in survival. Thus, Bowlby's views are an example of natural selection of social behaviors for survival. Bowlby proposed that the attachment system was one of four adaptive systems. (The other three are fear-wariness, affiliation, and exploration.) He believed that deprivation through institutionalization as a baby or disruption of the attachment system through early prolonged separation from caregivers resulted in children at risk for emotional problems.

Bowlby's theory places crying, smiling, and other attachment behaviors within an evolutionary context. And, contrary to folk wisdom, Bowlby's theory predicts that parents who respond promptly and consistently to their baby's cries will not spoil the child but will have instead a child who is securely attached.

The Behavioral-Learning Perspective

Ivan Pavlov (1849–1936): Classical Conditioning

Pavlov was born in Ryazan, Russia, and planned on becoming a priest like his father. In his early 20s, however, he became interested in a scientific career, focusing on physiological research. His studies of the digestive system earned him a Nobel Prize in 1904 and also were the basis for his pioneering scientific research on basic learning mechanisms, now called classical conditioning.

Table A1.1
Bowlby's Four Phases of Attachment

Phase	Phase Name	Typical Attachment Behaviors
Phase 1 (birth to 3 months)	Indiscriminate Responsiveness to Humans	Babies display such attachment behaviors as crying and smiling indiscriminately. That is, babies in this phase react to most people in similar ways.
Phase 2 (3 to 6 months)	Focusing on Familiar People	At 3 months of age, babies become selective and begin to limit their smiles to familiar people, while staring at strangers. Babies are most responsive to two or three people, with one person becoming the principal attachment figure.
Phase 3 (6 months to 3 years)	Intense Attachment and Active Proximity Seeking	Attachment to one person becomes increasingly intense and exclusive. Child shows separation anxiety and stranger fear, and uses the attachment figure as a secure home base from which to explore.
Phase 4 (3 to 12 years)	Partnership Behavior	Child increasingly is able to tolerate not always being close to the attachment figure, becomes less dependent on the caregiver, and develops more of a partnership with the caregiver.

While studying salivation in dogs, Pavlov observed that, over time, the dogs began to salivate before food was put in their mouths. Investigations into this phenomenon led to Pavlov's formulation of some of the basic components of modern learning theory. Pavlov's key concepts and terms are listed in Table A1.2. While Pavlov's idea of associations as the basis of learning was not unique, he was the first person to test the idea with scientific laboratory investigations.

John B. Watson (1878–1958): Behaviorism

Watson was born in South Carolina and, after a somewhat lackluster academic record, earned his doctorate in psychology from the University of Chicago. He obtained a position at Johns Hopkins University, where he proceeded to make a name for himself in several ways.

First, in 1913, Watson published a paper titled "Psychology as the Behaviorist Views It," in which he presented a strong case against the use of introspectionism in psychological research and argued that the only proper subject matter for scientific psychology was overt behavior. This

Table A1.2
Classical Conditioning Terms and Concepts

Term	Definition
Unconditioned stimulus (US)	Any stimulus that produces an immediate unlearned response
Unconditioned response (UR)	An immediate, unlearned reaction to an unconditioned stimulus
Conditioned stimulus (CS)	A neutral stimulus that, after pairing with an unconditioned stimulus, produces a learned, conditioned response
Conditioned response (CR)	A learned reaction to a previously neutral conditioned stimulus
Classical conditioning	The learning that results when a signal (CS) reliably predicts the occurrence of a second stimulus (US)
Stimulus generalization	The tendency for a CR to be elicited by stimuli similar to the CS
Stimulus discrimination	The situation when a response reinforced in the presence of a specific CS is not reinforced in the presence of other stimuli
Higher order conditioning	The conditioning that occurs when an established CS serves as the US in a new conditioning task
Extinction	The condition that occurs when the CS is presented without the US, or when a response is not reinforced
Spontaneous recovery	The recurrence, after a lapse of time, of a previously extinguished classically conditioned response

paper pegged Watson as an extreme environmentalist, a position from which he did not retreat, as evidenced by his famous quote:

> Give me a dozen healthy infants, well-formed, and my own specified world to bring them up in and I'll guarantee to take any one at random and train him to become any type of specialist I might select—doctor, lawyer, artist, merchant, chief, and yes, even beggar-man and thief. (Watson, 1924, p. 104)

Shortly thereafter, Watson read Pavlov's research on conditioning and began to actively use classical conditioning to study childhood problems. This led to his famous study on the conditioning of emotions in children with "Little Albert." Watson and his associate Rosalie Raynor successfully conditioned fear in an orphan boy name Albert, but Albert was adopted before Watson and Raynor were able to extinguish the fear. Later, Watson devised an approach, now called systematic desensitization, for extinguishing classically conditioned fears.

Watson's tenure at Johns Hopkins and his academic career abruptly ended with his sensationalized divorce in 1929. He later married Rosalie Raynor and pursued a business career, but he continued to publish his ideas about child development in the popular press.

B. F. Skinner (1904–1990): Operant Conditioning

B. F. Skinner, born in a small town in Pennsylvania, became one of the premier American psychologists. As a child, he displayed a number of talents, including writing stories and poetry. He majored in English literature in college but turned to psychology two years after graduating, when he discovered to his dismay that he had nothing to say. Skinner spent the bulk of his academic career at Harvard University, where he remained until his death a committed behaviorist.

While in graduate school, Skinner became interested in operant conditioning. Unlike Pavlovian classical conditioning, in which stimuli elicit behavior, in operant conditioning, organisms emit certain behaviors that are followed by specific consequences. Skinner investigated the factors that influenced operant learning, focusing primarily on various types of reinforcers and schedules of reinforcement. Key terms and concepts related to operant conditioning are presented in Table A1.3.

Skinner not only greatly expanded the sphere of learning theory but also challenged several basic tenets of traditional developmental psychology. As a strict behaviorist, Skinner emphasized the external environment and the consequences of overt behavior as the determiners of development. He dismissed the role of stages and maturational factors in behavior development. While the developmental role of the environment and external consequences cannot be denied, contemporary research continues to find that internal organismic factors and maturation also affect development.

Albert Bandura (1925–): Social Learning Theory

Albert Bandura was born in a small town in the province of Alberta, Canada. He earned his undergraduate degree in British Columbia and his doctorate in psychology from the University of Iowa. He was hired by Stanford University in 1953 and has remained there ever since.

The strict behaviorism of Skinner maintained that individuals had to actively respond in order to learn. Bandura argued that individuals learn many things simply by observing others. Thus, observational learning is a cornerstone of Bandura's theory.

Bandura proposed four components of observational learning: (1) The learner must attend to a model; (2) the learner must be able to cognitively retain what he or she has observed; (3) the learner must possess the motor skills necessary to reproduce the observed behavior; and

Table A1.3
Operant Conditioning Terms and Concepts

Term	Definition
Operant conditioning	The process of learning to operate on the environment to obtain certain consequences
Positive reinforcer	A stimulus whose occurrence increases the probability of the recurrence of a response that precedes it
Negative reinforcer	A stimulus whose removal increases the probability of the recurrence of a response that precedes it
Positive punisher	A stimulus whose occurrence decreases the probability of the recurrence of a response that precedes it
Negative punisher	A stimulus whose removal decreases the probability of the recurrence of the response that precedes it
Schedules of reinforcement	Various ways of reinforcing behavior based on fixed (predictable) or variable (unpredictable) presentation of reinforcers and on the number of responses made (ratio) or amount of time between reinforcers (interval). Four basic schedules are: fixed ratio, variable ratio, fixed interval, and variable interval.
Shaping	The reinforcing of successive approximations until a desired response is learned
Behavior modification	The application of operant conditioning techniques to the treatment of behavior problems
Programmed instruction	A method of instruction allowing for independent, self-paced learning in which the units of instruction are based on small, incremental steps, requiring active responding, and presenting the opportunity for immediate feedback and reinforcers

(4) while the learner may acquire the response without reinforcement, the reinforcement contingencies are necessary for the performance of the observed behavior. Thus, according to Bandura, learning involves a reciprocal determinism among behavior, environment, and cognitive factors.

According to Bandura, in reciprocal determinism, behavior, environment, and cognition interact and influence each other. A behavior might change the environment, which then changes a cognition. Or a change in cognition might change the environment, thereby modifying behavior in that altered environment. Therefore, according to Bandura, children can actively shape the environment that influences their behavior and personality.

Although in some ways Bandura's social learning theory is a bridge between Skinner's strict behaviorism and the organismic approach of the cognitive developmental-

ists, Bandura clearly emphasizes environmental factors over internal factors. Social learning theory has proven to be especially useful in studying the development of aggression, prosocial behaviors, and gender roles through investigations of the influence of modeling on behavior.

The Cognitive Perspective

Jean Piaget (1896–1980): Theory of Cognitive Development

Jean Piaget was born in Switzerland and had a remarkably long, productive, and influential career researching children's thinking. Trained as a biologist, he published his first research on mollusks when he was 16. Later, while studying in France as a young adult, he helped to give intelligence tests to children and became intrigued by the kinds of errors children made on test items. Piaget took a detour in his career as a biologist and studied the ways in which children acquire knowledge about the world and mentally represent that knowledge. Fortunately for the field of cognitive development, Piaget's career detour lasted for the remaining 60-plus years of his life.

Due in part to his training as a marine biologist, Piaget based his theories about cognitive development on careful observations of children. Piaget studied how children come to reason and know about physical reality, but he did not use traditional laboratory experiments. Rather, he relied on simple demonstrations and on adept use of clinical interviews to assess children's cognitive abilities.

The clinical method is the hallmark of Piaget's approach to studying children. Typically, Piaget would work with one child at a time. He would pose a simple task for the child, asking questions as the child worked with the task and listening intently to the child's answers. Later, Piaget would examine the answers for what they indicated about the child's reasoning.

After collecting volumes of observations, Piaget studied his notes and searched for commonalities that would allow him to generalize about children's thought processes. Piaget's efforts were enormous, and his insights were brilliant. Almost single-handedly, he created cognitive development as a field of psychology.

Piaget's ideas about cognitive development became quite popular in Europe in the 1930s, but behaviorism was so strong in the United States that many U.S. psychologists did not know much about Piaget's ideas until the 1960s. Since then, his ideas have not only influenced American psychologists but American parents and educators as well.

From his observations of children, Piaget developed a four-stage theory of cognitive development. The four stages are outlined in Table A1.4, while some of his basic terms and concepts are presented in Table A1.5.

Because Piaget's observations were based on loosely structured interviews, and because his clinical approach lacked the precise control measures of more traditional laboratory studies, other researchers have criticized his method

Table A1.4
Piaget's Four Stages of Cognitive Development

Stage	Approximate Age Range	Representative Skills
Sensorimotor	Birth to 24 months	Coordination of simple behaviors and perceptions Simple means-ends separation Object permanence
Preoperational	2 to 7 years	Early representational ability Use of language, symbols, and pretend play Elementary concepts of cause, number, spatial relationships
Concrete operational	7 to 12 years	Sensitive to viewpoints of others Conventional notions of time, cause, number, and spatial relationships Ability to apply logical thinking to real events
Formal operational	Age 12 on	Ability to use hypothetical-deductive logic Introspective thought Ability to use abstract concepts and metaphors

Table A1.5
Piagetian Terms and Concepts

Term	Definition
Adaptation	The process of cognitively adjusting to the environment
Schema	A mental structure that denotes what is essential about category membership
Assimilation	The process by which a new experience is incorporated into an already existing schema
Accommodation	The process by which a schema is modified to fit a new experience or an entirely new schema is created for the experience
Equilibration	The internal drive that assures, through assimilation and accommodation, that schemas are sufficient to make sense of experience
Object permanence	The capacity of an infant to recognize that people and objects continue to exist even when the infant is not in sensory contact with them
Egocentrism	The inability to view the world from a reference point other than oneself
Centration	The inability to focus on more than one aspect of a problem at a time
Irreversibility	The inability to mentally reverse operations
Conservation	The principle that such properties as number, volume, and mass remain the same despite apparent changes in appearance

and his results. For example, critics contend that children who are given Piaget's conservation tasks may fail to understand the questions asked or may misinterpret the tasks and the questions.

Despite these valid criticisms, the main body of Piaget's ideas remain supported by research findings. In recent years, other cognitive researchers have proposed an additional stage of cognitive development—postformal operations—that appears to be more characteristic of the thinking of middle-aged and older adults.

Lawrence Kohlberg (1927–1987): Theory of Moral Reasoning

Lawrence Kohlberg developed a stage theory of moral reasoning in which developmental changes in moral reasoning were linked to cognitive development. Kohlberg's ideas were developed not only from his research, which was directly influenced by Piaget's theory, but also by his own life experiences and his reflections on them.

Kohlberg spent his childhood in Bronxville, New York, and attended high school at the prestigious Andover Academy in Massachusetts. After graduation at the end of World War II, he enlisted in the Israeli cause and helped to transport European refugees to Israel, defying British blockades. In 1948, he entered the University of Chicago,

where his exceptionally high entrance scores allowed him to complete a bachelor's degree in one year. In graduate school at the University of Chicago, Kohlberg encountered Piaget's theory and became interested in the moral reasoning of children and adolescents. His doctoral dissertation in 1958 was the initial form of his own stage theory of moral reasoning. Kohlberg continued to research and develop his theory throughout his academic career, which ended with his death in 1987. Throughout much of his career, Kohlberg suffered from a tropical disease and depression. At age 59, he made the moral decision to end his life by drowning.

Kohlberg's theory was a detailed extension of Piaget's ideas about children's moral development. The theory evolved as Kohlberg and his students conducted research on the development of moral reasoning and as Kohlberg sought to answer criticisms of his ideas.

Kohlberg's six stages of moral development are listed in Table A1.6. Despite such changes as reducing Stage 6 to a potential stage, since no one in his research studies reasoned at this stage, Kohlberg remained faithful to basic Piagetian ideas. For example, he maintained that each stage represented a qualitatively different universal pattern of reasoning and that the stages unfolded in an invariant sequence that represented an integrated hierarchy of cognitive structures.

Table A1.6
Kohlberg's Six Stages of Moral Development

Level I: Preconventional Morality

    Stage 1: Obedience and Punishment Orientation
    Stage 2: Instrumental Purpose and Exchange

Level II: Conventional Morality

    Stage 3: Interpersonal Orientation and Conformity
    Stage 4: Social Accord and System Maintenance

Level III: Postconventional Morality

    Stage 5: Social Contract, Utility, Individual Rights
    Stage 6: Universal Ethical Principles

Kohlberg continually advocated the application of his ideas for helping people to reach higher levels of moral reasoning. Some of his critics, however, argued that having large numbers of individuals placing their own personal codes of morality above society's needs and laws was not beneficial to society.

Additional questions have been raised regarding the cultural and gender biases of Kohlberg's theory. Of these two, the gender issue has been most thoroughly pursued by one of Kohlberg's colleagues at Harvard, Carol Gilligan. Kohlberg's research was conducted exclusively with males, which Gilligan maintains reflects masculine preference for justice reasoning based on rights and rules. Females, Gilligan asserts, are socialized to prefer caring reasoning based on compassion and responsibility for others. Despite criticisms, Kohlberg's theory remains a detailed framework capable of generating many future investigations into moral development.

The Psychodynamic Perspective

Sigmund Freud (1856–1939): Psychoanalytic Theory

Sigmund Freud was the firstborn son of his then 20-year-old mother and 40-year-old father. His father's financial difficulties forced the family to move to Moravia (in the former Czechoslovakia) and to eventually settle in Vienna, where Freud remained for much of his life. Freud was very bright and did very well in school. His interests were varied, and he had difficulty choosing a field of study to pursue. Eventually, he chose medicine because he liked doing research.

Freud spent his early and middle career years attempting to make important discoveries that would assure his position and make a name for himself. By his mid-40s, he had begun to consolidate his ideas from earlier investigations into his grand theory of psychoanalysis. These ideas included the techniques of free association and dream analysis to uncover repressed thoughts and feelings and the notion that childhood sexuality was a major developmental force.

Freud continued to expand and revise his theory of psychoanalysis throughout the remainder of his life. He never completely overcame financial difficulties and had to contend with painful cancer of the jaw during the last 16 years of his life. His ideas were widely discussed in Europe and the United States, but were repressed by the Nazis of Germany. In 1938, he was forced to leave Vienna and move to London, where he died the next year.

Freud's ideas were controversial when he proposed them and remain somewhat so today. Many people have heard about Freud and have heard what other people have to say about him, but few people have actually read and studied his writings. While aspects of his theory can be validly criticized, his theory was a major force in changing views of child development.

Libido and Thanatoes

If you have heard anything about Freud, it probably was that he was "obsessed with sex." This impression comes from two sources: (1) the Zeitgeist of Freud and (2) current misunderstanding of libido, the sex drive. The Zeitgeist of Freud was the Victorian era, a time of significant sexual repression and strict sexual morality. Therefore, many of Freud's patients were dealing with sexual problems. Working with his patients led Freud to believe strongly in infantile sexuality—that is, that young children have biological sexual feelings. In particular, he believed that preschoolers fall in love with their parents.

The second source of misunderstanding comes from Freud's concept of libido or sex drive. Freud used the term *libido* very broadly. In fact, Freud's libido might better be translated as sensuality drive. Freud believed that all of one's psychic energy is expressed through the libido, a pleasure-seeking drive.

Influenced by World War I and the ominous Nazi atmosphere of pre-World War II, Freud proposed a second drive called thanatoes, or death-seeking drive. He used thanatoes to explain humankind's aggression, violence, destructiveness, and activities, such as war and suicide. Freud believed that thanatoes was also involved in risk-taking behaviors, such as smoking cigarettes, driving cars too fast, and riding roller coasters. Although thanatoes was never fully integrated into psychoanalytic theory, it provides a useful way to explain children's symbolic aggression in play.

Id, Ego, and Superego

According to Freud, at birth, all of one's libido is expressed in the id, the first of three major personality structures. The id is governed by the pleasure principle, which means that the id seeks immediate gratification. Parents of newborns can probably view their baby as merely a "bundle of id," displaying a calm, satisfied countenance when all needs are gratified, but a screaming, agitated one when milk, cuddling, or dryness demands are not immediately met.

Table A1.7
Freud's Psychosexual Stages of Personality Development

Stage	Age	Source of Pleasure	Possible Personality Traits If Fixations Occur
Oral	0–1 year	Sucking, biting, chewing	Dependent, gullible, generous, argumentative, sarcastic
Anal	1–3 years	Elimination and retention of feces	Excessively shy, clean, shameful, impulsive, stingy, stubborn, hostile, aggressive
Phallic	3–6 years	Gential stimulation	Homosexuality, flirtatious behavior, excessive guilt
Latency	6–12 years	Need for pleasure is repressed	A period of learning; no definite effect on personality development
Genital	Adolescence	Sexual and affectual relationships with the opposite sex	Inability to form lasting, meaningful adult relationships

Id is all the newborn baby may need, but other aspects of personality must develop because no parents are willing to meet every need of their offspring for life. Therefore, within a few months, the second personality structure—the ego—begins to develop. The ego, the most important aspect of personality, is guided by the reality principle; that is, the ego seeks to fulfill needs realistically. Like the id, the ego wants gratification, but unlike the id, the ego is *able to delay* gratification.

In toddlerhood, the third and final personality structure begins to develop. The superego is the moral arm of the personality; as such, its goal is to be good and moral rather than to experience gratification. As a result, the superego is often in conflict with the id, and the ego serves as the mediator between the two. The superego is made up of the conscience, which can punish the self with guilt for wrongdoing, and the ego ideal, which can reward the self with pride for doing well.

Psychosexual Stages of Personality Development

Freud thought that personality development occurred in five psychosexual stages (see Table A1.7), which he named for the region of the body in which libido is most expressed.

Over the years, Freud's ideas have been soundly attacked from all quarters, with even many of his early adherents distancing themselves from his work. Yet, his writings rank among the best of the great books for the depth of his analyses and the forcefulness of his insights. Despite the sociohistorical limits of his ideas and the difficulties of testing his theoretical positions with rigorous scientific experiments, Freud remains one of the most influential psychologists of all time.

Erik Erikson (1902–): Psychosocial Development

Erik H. Erikson, whose parents was Danish, was born in Frankfurt, Germany, because his parents separated shortly before he was born, and his mother went to Germany to be with friends. When he was 3, his mother married a local physician (Erikson's middle initial actually stands for his stepfather's surname, Homburger). Partly because he was not a particularly good student (he liked art) and partly because he disliked formal schooling, Erikson did not go to college. Instead, he traveled around Europe as a young adult, supporting himself through his artwork and trying to discover his role in life.

At age 25, he began working at Anna Freud's school for children in Vienna. While there, he studied psychoanalysis with Anna Freud and others. With the rise of Nazism, Erikson moved with his family to the United States, where he continued his work as a child analyst and pursued his interests in native American Indian tribes. Eventually, he was hired to teach at Harvard University, a remarkable achievement, considering he had never earned a formal college degree.

Erikson has written broadly about his views on development. In his book *Childhood and Society,* he presented an eight-stage theory of personality that (1) shifted from Freudian emphasis on sexuality to social factors in development, (2) enlarged on each of Freud's stages, and (3) added three stages for adulthood. As Erikson has grown older, he has further expanded on his ideas about the stages in adulthood.

As shown in Table A1.8, Erikson proposed eight psychosocial stages across the life cycle. According to Erikson, the goals of one's life cycle are to "round oneself out" and to form links with both previous and future generations. Individuals then come to view themselves as a link in the chain of generations.

Each of Erikson's stages represents a growing arena of social interaction. In stage I, mother is the most important social link; by stage VIII, individuals feel a connection with humankind. The social interactions of each stage, along with growing biological and cognitive abilities, form the setting for acting out the crisis at each stage.

Erikson thought that crises were turning points in one's life—crucial moments with both increased vulnerability and heightened potential. Therefore, Erikson posed each stage in terms of a potential growth and a potential shortcoming, as in the first stage's basic trust versus basic mistrust. Of course, dealing with the crisis is not an all-or-none proposition—no one can be totally trusting or totally mistrusting. Rather, the goal in each crisis is to resolve the ratio of development in favor of the desired aspect. Such healthy resolution provides individuals with an outstanding characteristic from each stage—hope, will, purpose, competence, fidelity, love, care, and wisdom. Unhealthy resolutions can produce opposite characteristics.

Table A1.8
Stages of Psychosocial Development

Stage	Age	Psychosocial Crises	Basic Social Modalities
I	Infancy (0–1 year)	Trust Versus Mistrust	To receive To give in return
II	Early child (1–3 years)	Autonomy Versus Shame and Doubt	To hold on To let go
III	Play age (3–5 years)	Initiative Versus Guilt	To make = go after To make life = playing
IV	School age (6–11 years)	Industry Versus Inferiority	To make things (completing) To make things together
V	Adolescence	Identity Versus Identity Diffusion	To be oneself To share being oneself
VI	Young adulthood	Intimacy Versus Isolation	To lose and find oneself in others
VII	Middle Adulthood	Generativity Versus Self-Absorption	To make be To take care of
VIII	Late adulthood	Integrity Versus Despair	To be through having been and having made to be To face not being

	Radius of Significant Persons	Desired Outcome	Equivalent Freudian Stage
I	Maternal person	Hope	Oral
II	Parental persons	Will	Anal
III	Basic family	Purpose	Phallic
IV	Neighborhood, school	Competence	Latency
V	Peer group and outgroups Models of leadership	Fidelity	Genital
VI	Friends and spouse Patterns in friendship, sex, competition, cooperation	Love	Genital
VII	Family interactions and job acquaintances Divided labor and shared households	Care	Genital
VIII	"Humankind," "My kind"	Wisdom	Genital

Erikson's theory fits strongly in the traditional stage theories of Freud and Piaget. He views the psychosocial stages as qualitatively different from each other, universal across cultures, and invariant in their sequence. In a significant departure from Freudian emphasis on abnormal development, Erikson stresses the potential for healthy development in his stages. However, like Freudian theory, Erikson's ideas have been criticized for their theoretical vagueness. Nonetheless, like Freud, Erikson has provided a theoretical framework around which many aspects of development can be organized.

Alfred Adler (1870–1937): Individual Psychology

Alfred Adler was raised in Vienna, Austria. The second of six children of a successful merchant, his difficult, unhappy childhood included rickets, pneumonia, accidents, and the death of a sibling. For most of his school years, Adler was only an average student, but he later excelled and became a medical student at the University of Vienna, where he trained as an eye specialist. He had a general practice and later specialized in neurology and psychiatry.

Adler's ideas were always different from Freud's, and Adler was neither Freud's student nor ever psychoanalyzed. Yet Adler and Freud benefitted from an exchange of ideas that influenced the separate development of both their theories. In 1902, Adler was invited to join Freud's weekly discussion group on psychoanalysis. When this group became the Vienna Psychoanalytic Society, Adler became the first president. However, by 1911, Adler and Freud differed so significantly in their approaches to psychoanalysis that the two ended their association. Nearly one third of the Vienna Psychoanalytic Society members left with Adler. In the 1930s, to escape the Nazis, Adler moved to New York City, where he had a private practice and taught medical psychology.

Adler called his theory individual psychology to indicate the uniqueness of the individual and the individual's responses to any situation. Adler believed that social factors are more important than the sex drive in shaping personality. He thought that people are motivated primarily by social interests and that basic life problems—work, friendship, and loving relationships—are social.

Adler believed that all people are striving for superiority (Adler used the term *superiority* as other psychologists use the term *self-actualization*). According to Adler, the drive for superiority is a response to a universally experienced sense of inferiority, which develops out of relationships with others. As babies and young children, individuals are dependent on parents and others, and this dependency makes them feel inferior. Children also compare themselves to their siblings, playmates, and schoolmates and sometimes conclude that others are nicer, more competent, and more talented. As a response to these unpleasant feelings of inferiority, individuals strive to improve. Inferiority feelings, therefore, are largely responsible for personal growth.

Adler also believed that each individual developed a lifestyle, or characteristic theme or life plan, in interacting with people and the environment. In his writings, Adler compared the individuality of people's lifestyles with the differences in pine trees:

> *If we look at a pine tree growing in a valley, we will notice that it grows differently from one on top of a mountain. It is the same kind of a tree, a pine, but*

Table A1.9
Adlerian Concepts

Term	Definition
Birth Order	An individual's age ranking among siblings
Family atmosphere	The emotional relationships among family members
Family constellation	The representative positions within a family in terms of the presence or absence of parents and the birth order and gender among siblings
Sibling rivalry	The competition among siblings for the affections and approval of their parents
Compensation	The mechanism by which people attempt to overcome imagined or real inferiorities or weaknesses
Overcompensation	The denial rather than the acceptance of a real situation and the exaggerated effort to cover up a weakness
Inferiority complex	An overcompensation pattern in which the individual feels highly inadequate
Superiority complex	An overcompensation pattern in which the individual exaggerates self-importance to cover up an inferiority complex

there are two distinct styles of life. Its style on top of the mountain is different from its style when growing in the valley. The style of life of a tree is the individuality of a tree expressing itself and molding itself in an environment. We recognize a style when we see it against a background of an environment different from what we expect, for then we realize that every tree has a life pattern and is not merely a mechanical reaction to the environment.

It is much the same way with human beings. We see the style of life under certain conditions of environment, and it is our task to analyze its exact relation to the existing circumstances, inasmuch as mind changes, with alteration of the environment. As long as a person is in a favorable situation, we cannot see his style of life clearly. In new situations, however, where he is confronted with difficulties, the style of life appears clearly and distinctly. (Adler, 1929, p. 98)

According to Adler, each person develops a self-consistency and goal-directedness based on his or her lifestyle. In simplified terms, individuals can base their lives on themes of victims, martyrs, controllers, drivers, babies, or go-getters. Adler believed that lifestyles are influenced by family factors, such as family atmosphere and birth order. These and other important Adlerian concepts are presented in Table A1.9.

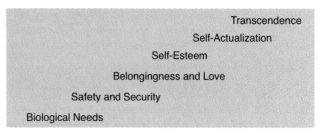

Figure A1.1
Maslow's Hierarchy of Needs

Humanistic-Existential Perspective

Abraham Maslow (1908–1970): Metamotivational Theory

Abraham Maslow was born in Brooklyn, New York, to uneducated Russian Jewish immigrants. His was the only Jewish family in the neighborhood, and Maslow was shunned and taunted. He described himself as a "shy and neurotic" child, and he retreated to books, libraries, and academic achievement. Maslow enrolled in law school after high school graduation, but he disliked law classes and dropped out after 2 weeks. He subsequently enrolled in a liberal arts college program and graduated from the University of Wisconsin.

Maslow first was behavioristic in perspective and then was influenced by Freudian and Gestalt psychology. Parenting and World War II led him to believe in both the complexity of human nature and the need for a positive psychology whose goal was peace and harmony. Out of his optimistic beliefs, humanism, the "third force" of psychology, was created. (The first two forces are psychoanalysis and behaviorism.)

Maslow's popular hierarchy of needs was first published in 1941 (see Figure A1.1), and his prominence as a personality theorist began in 1954 with the publication of *Motivation and Personality.*

Maslow's metamotivational theory of personality underscored the universal tendency for growth. Maslow believed that normal children choose to move toward positive growth because growth choices are satisfying, feel good, and bring pleasure. In contrast, their parents and other adults often try to get children to pick safety choices over growth choices. Children's growth choices enhance attractions but overlook inherent dangers. Adults' safety choices focus on danger at the expense of growth's attractiveness. Children usually learn to pick safety choices over growth choices in order to receive adult approval. At times during their lives, adults may need to relearn taking growth risks over safety in order to make changes in their personalities and life circumstances. People who overrely on safety may feel as if they are living their lives according to the rules of others. Only by taking risks can their personalities develop toward their potential.

Carl Rogers (1902–1988): Self Theory

Carl Rogers was born the fourth of six children in a middle-class family in suburban Chicago. He considered careers in agriculture, history, and religion, but while attending seminary classes, he enrolled in psychology courses at Columbia University, receiving his doctoral degree in counseling psychology in 1931.

Rogers worked for the Society for the Prevention of Cruelty to Children in New York, taught, and wrote. He believed that all people possess an actualizing tendency, a tendency to grow in positive ways once circumstances are supportive. He developed a theory—called self theory—that is based on this and other humanistic principles.

Rogers emphasized the self, or integrated person. Each person has an image of an ideal self, which represents the person one would like to be. Congruence occurs when similarity exists between the real and ideal self, between experience, awareness, and expression of what one is and what one wants to be. Incongruence exists when the real and ideal selves are quite dissimilar and when self-awareness and self-expression are inconsistent.

Rogers believed that all people would like to decrease incongruence and strive to be more like their ideal selves and that individuals achieve this goal if the environment supports their task. According to Rogers, the goal of life is to become a fully functioning person by moving toward the image of the ideal self.

While the image of the ideal self is certainly influenced by social/environmental factors, Rogers emphasized the internal mechanism of the self-actualizing tendency as the primary force for personality development. Rogers believed that, to move toward becoming fully functioning persons, individuals must stop fulfilling someone else's goals for their life and learn how to please themselves, trust themselves, and make their own decisions.

Appendix B

Creating a Developmental Autobiography

At the core of developmental psychology is the analysis of human lives, both individually and collectively. One way to make the contents of this text personally meaningful is to conduct a developmental analysis of your own life—that is, create a developmental autobiography.

Psychobiography—"the systematic use of psychological (especially personality) theory to transform a life into a coherent and illuminating story" (McAdams, 1988)—has a rich history, beginning with Freud's analytical biography of Leonardo da Vinci (Freud, 1910). Writing in *Explorations in Personality,* Henry Murray (1938) emphasized the importance of biographical accounts of human development:

> *The organism consists of an infinitely complex series of temporarily related activities extending from birth to death. Because of the meaningful connection of sequences, the life cycle of a single individual should be taken as a unit, the long unit of psychology. It is feasible to study the organism during one episode of its existence, but it should be recognized that this is but an arbitrarily selected part of the whole. The history of the organism is the organism. The proposition calls for biographical studies. (p. 39)*

Erik Erikson, following Freud's lead, skillfully used psychobiographies of Martin Luther and Gandhi to enhance his explanations of personality development (Erikson, 1958, 1969). More recently, other developmental psychologists have recognized biography as a valuable tool for gathering information about human lives (Bruner, 1986; Cohler, 1982; Mandler, 1984).

While your personal life narrative may seem insignificant to you when compared with the life of Gandhi, a developmental autobiography can aid you in understanding your own development in several ways (Elms, 1988; Runyon, 1982). In the process of writing your life story, you may discover new aspects about life, relate the circumstances of your life to psychological theories and cultural contexts, develop new insights about your past development, and synthesize a more coherent sense of yourself and the meaning of your life.

Other benefits that may occur in writing your autobiography or the biography of another family member have been noted by William Zimmerman (1981). Biographies:

1. Provide a way by which a family can be drawn more meaningfully together
2. Preserve the special and unique circumstances of your life
3. Help you to recognize and preserve family values and traditions
4. Help you to work on personal problems
5. Provide a source of personal satisfaction and accomplishment

Ways of Constructing Autobiographies

There is no one best way for creating your autobiography. The several approaches presented here can be used separately or combined in any number of creative ways. Whichever approach you choose, you will probably want to consider dividing your project into two phases. In Phase I, do background work. Attempt to discover as much information about your past development as possible. Do not overlook the seemingly insignificant or trivial happenings in your life. In Phase II, use your background research to construct an autobiography. Be as comprehensive or as focused as you choose. For some people, the comprehensive approach may turn into a mini-book that may become a treasured family heirloom. For others, a more focused approach may allow them to concentrate on one aspect or time period of their development.

A Factual Chronology

One approach is to assemble the chronological facts of your life. You might begin with the circumstances of your birth but could also include information about your conception and prenatal development. From birth onward, record important facts from each stage of your physical, cognitive, and psychosocial development. A partial listing might include answers to the following questions:

What were the conditions of your mother's pregnancy?

What were your vital statistics at birth?

Were you an "easy" or "difficult" baby?

Were you breast- or bottle-fed?

When were you weaned, toilet-trained, etc.?

When did you sit up, crawl, walk, talk, etc.?

What childhood illnesses did you have, and when did you have them?

Who were your first playmates?

When did you have growth spurts?

What were your most favorite and least favorite subjects in schools?

How would you rate your progress in school? Was school easy or difficult?

Who were your friends in the fifth grade?

What are your best and worst memories of school?

When did puberty begin for you? Your voice change? Your body shape change? Menstruation begin?

When did the changes that accompany the onset of adolescence stabilize?

Are you still growing, and is your body still changing shape?

Have you found making friends easy? Have you considered yourself a shy person?

When did you begin dating? What were the circumstances of your first serious romance?

Who were your idols or models?

How many times have you moved?

What was your first job? What jobs have you held since then?

How many times have you changed your career plans?

Have you married? Divorced?

Do you have children?

Where are you now in your development?

Obviously, this list can be limited or expanded as your own situation dictates. This factual chronology may also serve as the background research for the autobiography that you eventually create.

An Important Document File

This approach is similar to the factual chronology, but instead of recording the facts of your life, you collect your actual life records. If writing about your life appears difficult, this approach may appeal to you. Whether you collect your documents in a file or a display album, you may be amazed at what can be learned about your development by studying the contents.

As in the factual chronology, begin at your beginning. Do you have a copy of your birth certificate? Include birth announcements and newspaper clippings, if you can find them. Did your parents keep a baby book? Put in copies of pertinent medical records. Do you have a record of your childhood immunizations?

For each stage of your life, search diligently for documents that record your physical, cognitive, and psychosocial development. Search broadly. Use photos, school records and papers, programs for educational and religious activities in which you participated, newspaper clippings, and personal letters. You may want to include small mementos or photos of mementos and past experiences.

An Oral Interview

If the first two approaches to recording your life history do not appeal to you, perhaps you would prefer to make an oral record of your life. William Zimmerman (1981) wrote an easy-to-use guide entitled *How to Tape Instant Oral Biographies*. The basis for this approach is a structured interview. Working from a set of prepared questions about which the interviewee has had time to think, the interviewer tape-records the interview. Zimmerman's paperback guide provides simple step-by-step directions for the entire project.

While Zimmerman's book is directed toward interviewing other family members, you can easily be the subject of your own interview. If interviewing yourself seems awkward, ask another person to interview you. Zimmerman provides a standard set of questions, but feel free to add, delete, and modify the set to fit your individual circumstances.

With this approach, you likely will create a more personal account of your life, one that not only includes the facts of your life but also personal and family anecdotes, special memories, and stories about events in your earlier development. In addition, this approach can easily become a family project in which the life stories of grandparents, parents, and children are recorded. With the increasing availability of video camcorders, you might want to consider creating a video as well as an audio record of your life.

Life Narratives

In considering the oral interview approach, you may have thought of several family or personal stories that you would tell if interviewed. In the life narrative approach, you write down the stories that you have heard about your early development or that you recall from your own experiences. In essence, you create a collection of short stories about your life.

The emphasis in life narratives is not on the accuracy of the accounts but in telling the stories as you recall them. Some of your stories may be only a paragraph or two long, while other experiences may require one or more pages. You may decide to tell stories from across your lifespan, or perhaps, focus on the stories from just one period of your life.

To help you think of stories to tell, consider the following suggestions:

Do you recall any stories about your parents naming you at birth? Can you tell about how you acquired a nickname? Can you write about your feelings regarding changing your name when marrying?

Do you remember any stories that your parents tell about your very early development? Are you the subject in your mother's stories about her pregnancy or birthing experiences? Have your parents or other relatives regaled you (or more likely your friends) with stories about embarrassing moments in your early childhood?

Recall your first vivid memory. Write a brief story about a pleasant memory from each stage of your development. Do the same for unpleasant memories. Tell the stories about your escapades as a child, teenager, and young adult.

Which stories about your school experiences are most vivid in your memory? Can you remember being in day care or preschool or the first day of kindergarten? Tell about your activities in school. Write about your friendships, pals, and chums. Tell the stories you recall about your first days in junior high, high school, and college.

Tell the stories of your crushes and romances across the years. What do you remember about your first date? If appropriate, write stories about your experiences with courtship, cohabitation, marriage, estrangements, divorce, and the ending of relationships.

Write about your experiences with pregnancy, childbirth, adoption, raising children, blended families, in-laws, grandparents, babysitters, and child care.

Tell the stories that accompany the mementos that you keep in your room, office, or home. Write about the cars you have owned, favorite articles of clothing, pets, or other things that have been important to you.

Recall your favorite stories from the different jobs you have held. Tell about how you have made career choices. Tell about your experiences in seeking jobs, getting promoted or obtaining raises, and leaving or losing jobs.

Write stories that illustrate how you have been influenced by different people and events. Tell about your idols and mentors. Do you recall stories about the influence of musicians, writers, teachers, political figures, or relatives? What stories can you tell about the impact on your life of major events, such as wars, economic conditions, and international crises? What stories can you tell about personal events, such as religious or spiritual experiences, the deaths of family members and friends, illnesses, and peak experiences?

The life narratives approach is your opportunity to be a storyteller. As the foregoing list illustrates, everyone has many stories to tell. Do not be overwhelmed by trying to tell every story evoked by thinking about the list. Instead, focus on your best, favorite, and most meaningful stories to create a collection that provides insight about you and your development.

Making Your Autobiography into a Psychobiography

After you have completed one or a combination of the previous approaches to creating your autobiography, consider analyzing its content from a developmental perspective. Creating a psychobiography will provide you with opportunities to apply the knowledge you have gained in reading this text and from studying developmental psychology. This knowledge should be the basis for greater insights about your past, present, and future development. Test the effectiveness of developmental theories in accounting for the circumstances and outcomes of your development. When a theoretical perspective fails to adequately explain your experiences, you may discover new concepts that need to be added to the theory. In short, creating a psychobiography allows you to go beyond writing your life story to applying your skills as a developmental psychologist.

One way to begin your developmental analysis is to apply one or more of the psychological perspectives to your life. Look for examples of the biological, behavioral, psychodynamic, cognitive, and humanistic/existential perspectives in what you have written about your life. From the biological perspective, what has been the impact of inherited characteristics on your development? From the behavioral perspective, how have you been influenced by your parents' use of specific rewards and punishments? Similar analyses can be made for each of the perspectives. Analyze the material you have collected about yourself for examples that illustrate the different perspectives.

From the general perspectives, move to specific theories. For example, Erikson's psychosocial stages provide a convenient framework for analyzing your development at different ages. You may be able to apply contrasting theories, such as those of Kohlberg and Gilligan in the area of moral development, to draw a clearer picture of the factors that influenced your development.

However you choose to approach the task of writing a psychobiography, begin with the idea that the project will be an enjoyable experience. Have fun exploring your development. Do not fret about making "correct" analyses; instead, view the project as an opportunity for further growth and development. Pause often in your work to reflect, as Henry Murray did over 50 years ago, on the uniqueness of being you:

In the organism, the passage of time is marked by rhythms of assimilation, differentiation, and integration. The environment changes. Success and failure produce their effects. There is learning and there is maturation. Thus, new and previously precluded combinations come into being, and with the perishing of each moment, the organism is left a different creature, never to repeat itself exactly. No moment nor epoch is typical of the whole. Life is an irreversible sequence of nonidentical events. (Murray, 1938, p. 43)

References

Bruner, J. (1986). *Actual minds, possible worlds.* Cambridge, MA: Harvard University Press.

Cohler, B. J. (1982). Personal narrative and life course. In P. Baltes & O. G. Brim, Jr. (Eds.), *Life span development and behavior* (Vol. 4, pp. 205–241). New York: Academic Press.

Elms, A. C. (1988). *The psychologist as biographer.* Paper presented at the American Psychological Association annual meeting, Atlanta, GA, August 14.

Erikson, E. H. (1958). *Young man Luther: A study in psychoanalysis and history.* New York: Norton.

Erikson, E. H. (1969). *Gandhi's truth: On the origins of militant nonviolence.* New York: Norton.

Freud, S. (1910). Leonardo da Vinci and a memory of his childhood. In J. Strachey (Ed. & Trans.), *The standard edition of the complete psychological works of Sigmund Freud* (1957, Vol. 11, pp. 59–137). London: Hogarth Press.

McAdams, D. P. (1988). Biography, narrative, and lives: An introduction. *Journal of Personality, 56* (1), 1–18.

Mandler, J. M. (1984). *Stories, scripts, and scenes: Aspects of schema theory.* Hillsdale, NJ: Erlbaum.

Murray, H. A. (1938). *Explorations in personality.* New York: Oxford University Press.

Runyon, W. M. (1982). *Life histories and psychobiography.* New York: Oxford University Press.

Zimmerman, W. (1981). *How to tape instant oral biographies.* New York: Guarionex Press.

Glossary

A

abortion The expulsion of the fetus as the result of a medical procedure to end the pregnancy by voluntary choice.

acceptance Kübler-Ross's fifth and final stage experienced by terminally ill individuals, in which the inevitability of death is accepted.

accepted children Children accepted by their peers.

accommodation The process by which an existing schema is modified or an entirely new schema is created in order to adapt to a new experience.

achieving stage Schaie's first stage of adult cognitive development, in which young adults apply the knowledge they acquired earlier in life to their careers, relationships, and leisure activities.

acknowledgment stage A stage in which survivors of terminally ill individuals must come to realize the inevitability of their loved one's death.

activity theory A theory of aging that proposes that successful aging results, not from disengaging, but from maintaining the activities and attitudes of middle age.

adaptation In Piaget's cognitive development theory, the process of adjusting to the environment.

adolescent egocentrism A concept proposed by Elkind in which adolescents display an inability to think beyond their own perspectives. Characterized by an inability to differentiate between what is unique to the individual adolescent and universal to all adolescents or people.

adoptive parents Individuals who become parents through the legal process of assuming the parental rights of and responsibilities for someone else's child.

age-graded Events that occur for all individuals at about the same age.

ageism A societal pattern of widely held devaluative attitudes and stereotypes about the aging process and old people.

altruistic behaviors Prosocial behaviors intentionally done for the benefit of others.

Alzheimer's disease A brain disorder of older adults, involving degeneration of neurons, that eventually results in death of the individual after a period of several years of gradual, but steady decline.

ambivalent attached-resistant infants Ainsworth's term describing attachment between infants and their mothers that is characterized by the infants' inability to leave their mothers to play or to be separated from their mothers without distress. When reunited with their mothers, these infants cry, pout, and push their mothers away.

amniocentesis A test performed around the 16th week of pregnancy in which amniotic fluid is withdrawn through a needle inserted in the mother's abdomen and is analyzed for indications of genetic disorders and lung development.

amniotic sac The fluid-filled sac surrounding the embryo and fetus that acts as a shock absorber to cushion and protect the developing baby.

anal stage Freud's second stage of psychosexual development, during which the anal region of the body and urination and bowel movements become the primary sources of pleasure. Occurs from ages 1 to 3.

androgynous Term used to describe the ability of males and females to express the positive qualities of both genders.

androgynous fathers Fathers who are involved in their children's lives as active participants in the details of day-to-day childcare and who are more expressive and intimate with their children than traditional fathers.

androgynous parents Parents who do not rigidly adhere to traditional mother and father roles.

anger Kübler-Ross's second stage experienced by terminally ill individuals, in which their eventual death is no longer denied, and anger and outrage are expressed regarding their terminal condition.

anima Jung's archetypal symbol for the female gender.

animism The belief that inanimate objects have a consciousness and are alive.

animus Jung's archetypal symbol for the male gender.

anniversary reaction The experiencing again of grief each year around the time of a loved one's death.

anxiously attached-avoidant infants Ainsworth's term describing attachment between infants and their mothers that is characterized by the infants' ability to leave their mothers to play, to be separated from their mothers, but when reunited, to only casually greet them or avoid them.

apathetic persons A subtype of Neugarten's older adult passive-dependent personality type. Typical of persons who are passive and low in achievement.

Apgar scale A quick medical assessment of newborns that measures heart rate, respiration, muscle tone, reflex irritability (nervous system functioning), and color.

apnea Brief periods during sleep in which breathing stops.

appropriate-for-gestational-age (AGA) Term used to describe preterm babies whose birthweight is appropriate for their gestational age at birth.

archetypal theory Carl Jung's personality theory that was influenced by Freud's psychoanalytic theory, world religions, and cultural mythology and that focused on adult personality development.

armor-defended personality One of Neugarten's older adult personality types. Typical of striving, ambitious, achievement-oriented persons with a strong need to control impulses and to defend themselves against anxiety.

artificialism The belief that human beings cause natural phenomena to occur.

artistic Holland's personality type and work environment that is characterized by people who use creative skills, imagination, and expressiveness and who are viewed as nonconforming and sensitive.

assimilation The process by which a new experience is incorporated into an already existing schema.

astigmatism A condition produced by irregularities in the shape of the cornea that result in more than one point of focus and in blurred vision.

attachment A relatively enduring emotional tie to a specific person, as in the emotional tie that develops between an infant and its caregiver.

authenticity Being true to and acting consistently with one's beliefs.

authoritarian Baumrind's parenting style describing traditional, autocratic, demanding, unresponsive to children's views, power-oriented parents.

authoritative Baumrind's parenting style describing democratic, demanding, power-oriented, responsive to children's views, reasoning parents.

automaticity A characteristic of experts in that their performance, compared to others, appears automated and seems to occur on a nonconscious level.

autonomous motivation Veroff's first stage of achievement motivation, in which children orient themselves to internal, self-generated norms.

autonomy versus shame and doubt Erikson's second psychosocial stage of personality development, during which toddlers acquire the strength of self-control (willpower).

B

babbling The production by infants of consonant/vowel sound combinations. An early stage in language acquisition.

baby-talk register Adults' alterations in tone and inflection when speaking to babies.

bargaining Kübler-Ross's third stage experienced by terminally ill individuals, in which the person promises something in exchange for extension of life or lessening of pain.

basic trust versus basic mistrust Erikson's first psychosocial stage of personality development, in which consistent, good, nurturant care and a sense of safety help to develop the psychosocial strength of hope in infants.

battered wives syndrome A term for domestic violence in which the husband is the perpetrator and the wife is the victim of the abuse.

behavioral-learning perspective The psychological perspective that emphasizes environmental factors in explaining development.

belief in a just world The adult belief that, sooner or later, justice will prevail (good people will be rewarded and bad people will be punished).

benign forgetfulness The first stage of dementia. Characterized by forgetting names and places and by misplacing items.

bereavement The status of having a significant person in your life die.

biological attachment theory Bowlby's theory that infants have a biologically based predisposition for social interchange, which in the first few months of life becomes focused on one specific adult.

biological perspective The psychological perspective that emphasizes the relationships of biological systems to behavior and mental processes.

Birren hypothesis The idea that increases in reaction time as adults age can help to explain the behavioral changes seen in older adults.

birth order Adler's belief that one's position in the family constellation, as well as the number of siblings, their gender and ages, and spacing, influence one's personality development.

blended families The family unit that results when individuals with children from a previous family marry.

body transcendence versus body preoccupation According to Peck, a psychological task of older adults involving being able to move beyond one's physical condition.

bonding A strong, emotional attachment formed between parents and newborns in the first minutes after birth.

brain death Death defined by no brain stem activity and a flat electroencephalogram, accompanied by total unresponsiveness, no breathing for 3 min, and no reflexes.

brain lateralization The separation and integration of functional systems within the cerebral hemispheres of the brain.

Brazelton neonatal behavioral assessment scale (BNAS) A test that rates 3- to 9-day-old infants on 26 categories that measure aspects of physiological, motor, state of consciousness, and social interaction behavior.

bulimia (bulimarexia) An eating disorder (also called binge-purge syndrome and dietary chaos syndrome) in which individuals binge-eat and then use fasting, self-induced vomiting, and other techniques to purge themselves.

burnout A work-related problem resulting from prolonged job stress. Individuals experience emotional exhaustion, an overwhelming feeling of not being able to accomplish a job, and a sense of helplessness and lack of control over their work, as well as physical symptoms of headaches, fatigue, insomnia, respiratory and digestive problems, conflict with others, and possible substance abuse.

C

career The pursuit of a specific vocation for a number of years.

career adaptability Super's concept of adult readiness for career decision making.

career maturity Super's concept about the extent to which a person has completed stage-appropriate career developmental tasks.

caring 1. A cluster of a love relationship. Consists of nurturance, support, and advocation. 2. The positive quality achieved with successful resolution of Erikson's seventh psychosocial crisis.

castration anxiety According to Freud, the anxiety of preschool boys that, if they compete with their fathers for their mother's affection, their fathers will castrate them.

cataracts A visual impairment caused by the clouding and yellowing of the lens with age, resulting in inability to see details and seeing glare around lights.

centering Young children's inability to pay attention to more than one factor or dimension at a time.

cephalocaudal principle The developmental principle describing how development occurs first and strongest in the head region and proceeds down the body trunk (literally, head to tail or, more appropriately, head to toe development).

cesarean section (c-section) A surgical procedure to remove the baby from the uterus by making an incision in the lower abdomen.

child care The overall term for educational and day-care services for children younger than kindergarten age.

child-centered parents Parents who are responsive to their children but less demanding than authoritative parents.

chromosomes The genetic maps found in the nucleus of every cell, consisting of arrangements of genes or genetic blueprints. The nuclei of human cells contain 23 pairs of chromosomes (except the gametes or sex cells).

chronic living-dying interval According to Pattison, the time period between knowledge of impending death and actual death.

classical conditioning Learning to respond to signals (stimuli) that have previously been associated with other stimuli that produce automatic or involuntary responses.

classical pattern of intellectual aging A description of how intellect changes with age. Derived from the results of several longitudinal studies of intellectual functioning in adulthood, in which some abilities start to decline in early adulthood (spatial abilities), while others remain stable or increase throughout adulthood (vocabulary).

classification The ability to place similar objects into groups, such as separating objects into groups by shape or by color.

climacteric The 2- to 5-year period of physiological changes that bring on menopause.

clocks of aging Theories of aging that focus on how hormones affect aging.

cluttering A type of dysrhythmia in which rapid, nervous speech is marked by omission of syllables.

cognitive death An alternative definition of death based on the cessation of activity in the cerebral cortex, rather than in the whole brain.

cognitive modifiability The ability to change mental structures and contents through mediated learning experiences.

cognitive perspective The psychological perspective that emphasizes the individual's active role in selecting and processing information about the world to create a meaningful internal representation of the world.

cognitive style Stable preferences for mentally organizing and manipulating perceptions and information.

commitment According to Perry, the idea that continued college experience leads to support of specific positions based on available evidence, adoption of specific values and ideas, and awareness of responsibility for the positions and values one adopts.

communal relationships Relationships based on mutual responsibility for each other's welfare.

competitive power According to May, a type of power that, when used against another person, can be either negative (one gains while the other loses) or positive (both persons gain).

complementarity of needs A factor in interpersonal attraction in which people are attracted to individuals of opposite characteristics when those characteristics fit their needs.

conflict-habituated marriages Marriages that are characterized by conflict and tension and in which couples use conflict as a way of expressing their attachment to each other.

conservation The ability to recognize that quantities remain the same (are conserved) even when appearances change. Includes conservation of number, mass, and volume.

constricted persons A subtype of Neugarten's older adult armored-defended personality type. Typical of persons who limit energy expenditure and social interaction in an effort to slow aging.

contextual model The developmental model based on the idea that living systems act upon their environments and are reactive to them and that each individual develops in a unique set of bio-socio-historical circumstances.

conventional Holland's personality type and work environment that is characterized by people who are practical, conscientious, and conforming and who prefer work that features systematic organization and manipulation of data.

conventional morality Kohlberg's second level of moral reasoning (ages 10 to 13), in which children seek approval by upholding society's standards.

coping The effortful or purposeful responses of individuals to stress in order to manage external and internal demands.

critical periods Developmental time periods of greatest sensitivity to environmental influences.

cross-sectional studies Research studies designed to look at how people of various ages differ on one or more factors, while providing the convenience of measuring all age groups in one time period.

crowning The event of the baby's head emerging from the vagina during the delivery stage of childbirth.

crystallized abilities Cognitive abilities related to experiences, learning, and culture, including general information and knowledge, vocabulary, logical reasoning, and mechanical knowledge.

D

day care Physical-nurturing child care without an educational emphasis.

death system The manner in which a society comprehends death and dying.

deductive reasoning Reasoning from general ideas to reach specific conclusions.

delayed language development The condition in which children by age 2 do not use words to communicate.

dementia The pathological loss of intellectual functioning.

denial Kübler-Ross's first stage experienced by terminally ill individuals in which individuals are in a state of shock and disbelief.

depression Kübler-Ross's fourth stage experienced by terminally ill individuals, in which persons become depressed as they try to cope with their impending loss of life.

depth perception The ability to judge the distance of objects from the observer.

detachment stage A stage in which survivors of terminally ill individuals accept the impending death and focus on how death can be a release from suffering.

developmental quotient (DQ) A score on the Gesell Preschool Test that indicates the rate of development compared to others of the same age.

devitalized marriages Marriages that began with passion and deep love, which, over time, were replaced with apathy and routine.

diabetic retinopathy A leading cause of blindness in the United States for adults. Produced by diabetic conditions that cause retinal blood vessels to leak, resulting in loss of vision.

dialectical thinking A characteristic of adult postformal operational cognitive development. Characterized by the ability to recognize and resolve self-contradictory experiences and paradoxes of adulthood.

difficult babies Babies whose temperaments result in irregular eating and sleeping schedules, strong negative reactions to change and novelty, and generally long periods of intense negative emotions.

dilation The enlargement of the cervical opening during the labor stage of childbirth.

disease-prone personality A personality type characterized by depression, anxiety, and to some degree, anger and hostility. Associated with increased risk for coronary heart disease, asthma, peptic ulcers, rheumatoid arthritis, and headaches.

disengaged persons A subtype of Neugarten's older adult integrated personality type. Typical of low-activity persons with self-contained yet content lives.

disengagement theory A psychosocial theory of aging in which aging is viewed as a progressive process of withdrawal from work and other institutions.

DNA (deoxyribonucleic acid) The complex protein molecule of which genes are composed and that forms the basis of the genetic code and heredity.

dominant inheritance The appearance in the individual's phenotype of a physical trait when either one or both of the alleles in the individual's genotype carry the trait.

double standard of aging The idea that women undergo more negative aging experiences than men do.

dualism The world view that is represented by the belief that all questions have either absolutely right or absolutely wrong answers and that the two different kinds of answers are knowable.

dysfunctional workplaces Workplaces in which structural problems or personnel problems create unhealthy work environments.

E

early retirement Leaving the work force before the mid-60s and not entering another career.

easy babies Babies whose temperaments result in regular eating and sleeping schedules, ready adaptation to change and new situations, and generally positive emotional reactions.

effacement The thinning of the cervix during the labor stage of childbirth.

egocentrism The inability to view or experience the world from another's point of view and the belief that other people experience the world in the same way that you do.

ego differentiation versus work-role preoccupation According to Peck, a psychological task for older adults involving being able to define oneself in broader terms than one's career.

ego identity versus role confusion Erikson's fifth psychosocial stage, in which adolescents who achieve ego identity develop an integrated, internal sense of self that can operate compatibly with external roles, and in which role confusion is characterized by feelings of aimlessness and purposelessness.

ego integrity versus despair Erikson's eighth stage of psychosocial personality development, in which successful resolution of the crisis results in a sense of acceptance of and contentment with one's life and the achievement of the virtue of wisdom.

ego transcendence versus ego preoccupation According to Peck, a psychological task of older adults involving dealing with one's own mortality and finding meaning in one's life.

electra complex Freud's explanation of gender-role identification in girls, in which preschool girls first fall in love with their mothers and then their fathers, eventually block their feelings for their fathers, and adopt the female gender role of their mothers.

embryonic stage The second stage of prenatal development, from 2 to 8 weeks of gestation, during which all of the major body systems and individual organs develop. This is the stage of greatest vulnerability to birth defects.

emotional distancer A marital partner who engages in the dysfunctional response of prematurely closing a painful issue and compartmentalizing marital hurts and disappointments.

emotional pursuer A marital partner who engages in the dysfunctional response of repeatedly bringing up painful issues without working toward resolving them.

empty-nest phenomenon The transition period and time after the children move out of the family household.

enabling interaction style An interaction style that develops among females that facilitates communication, acknowledges others, comments, and seeks agreement.

enactive mode Cognitive representation of the world in terms of motor actions.

engagement A period preceding marriage in which individuals announce their exclusive commitment to each other.

enterprising Holland's personality type and work environment that is characterized by people who tend to be extraverted, dominant, self-confident, and ambitious and who thrive in work environments that utilize manipulation and persuasion.

episiotomy A surgical incision designed to enlarge the birth canal and to minimize vaginal tearing. Usually performed during the second stage of labor.

episodic memory Memories consisting of sequences of events set within the context of time.

equilibration Piaget's term for the drive to maintain a balance between existing cognitive schemas and current experience.

equity theory A theory of interpersonal attraction that holds that the ratio of each person's inputs relative to his or her outcomes should be equal.

erotophilia Positive attitudes toward and pleasure in sexuality. Accompanied by receptivity to sexual information and behavior.

erotophobia Negative attitudes toward, avoidance of, or distaste for sexuality. Accompanied by significant anxiety and guilt about sexual behavior.

errors of commission Errors resulting from wrongly answering questions on a test.

errors of omission Errors resulting from not answering (omitting an answer) questions on a test.

estrogen replacement therapy A therapy used to lessen the symptoms of menopause by administering low dosages of estrogen and progestin.

ethnic identity Individuals' identification and psychological relationship with their ethnic group.

euthanasia Literally, "the good death." The means for producing a gentle and easy death by choice.

evaluators In Sternberg's model of mental self-government, individuals who judge, monitor, and provide feedback.

exchange theory A theory of interpersonal attraction that holds that relationships are usually maintained only as long as the costs are less than the benefits.

executive stage A component of Schaie's middle adulthood cognitive stage in which concern is shown for others.

experts Individuals who, compared to others, have invested much time and effort into learning an area of knowledge well.

exploitative power According to May, the most destructive form of power, in which an aggressor allows a victim no options.

exploratory systems The programmed action and sensory systems that allow infants to discover what the world is like.

expressive language The ability to produce speech.

expressiveness A personality dimension defined by such terms as *warm, tender, affectionate,* *sympathetic, care-taking,* and *compassionate* and that is predictive within each sex of differences in sexual scripts and behaviors.

extended family A nuclear family in which the children have left home and have begun nuclear families of their own. Extended families may extend across several generations.

extended households Households in which two or more generations live together.

F

familial retardation Intellectual retardation for which no known biological cause can be identified.

family life cycle The stages experienced in a family, from establishment of the family, through childbearing and child-rearing, to retirement with children launched as adults on their own.

family of origin An individual's family when raised by his or her biological parents.

family of procreation The family unit formed when individuals marry and have children.

family triangles Conditions that exist when parents confuse marital conflicts with parenting by developing a serious conflict with one or more of their children.

fantasy stage Ginzberg's first stage of career decision making (up to about age 11), in which children are unrealistic about careers and their own abilities and interests.

fertilization The act of conception, when a sperm penetrates an ovum and a zygote is formed.

fetal alcohol syndrome (FAS) The pattern of birth defects and problems of retarded growth, mental development, and motor development associated with maternal alcohol abuse during prenatal development.

fetal monitor A sensing device either placed around the woman's abdomen to measure fetal heart rate and contractions during labor or attached to the fetus's scalp to measure oxygen levels in the fetal bloodstream.

fetal stage The third and longest stage of prenatal development, from 8 weeks to birth, during which there is much physical growth and behavioral development.

fidelity The strength of loyalty and competence developed with successful resolution of Erikson's fifth psychosocial stage of personality development.

fluid abilities: General, innately determined aspects of thinking that relate to speed of processing, flexibility of thinking, adaptation to novel situations, and abstract reasoning.

focused persons A subtype of Neugarten's older adult integrated personality type. Typical of moderately active persons who concentrate on selective, satisfying roles.

formal operations Piaget's fourth and final stage of cognitive development. Occurs in early adolescence and is characterized by hypothetico-deductive reasoning, convergent problem solving, and the ability to do abstract thinking.

friendship A cluster of a love relationship. Consists of acceptance, trust, respect, enjoyment, confidence, understanding, spontaneity, and assistance.

G

gain-loss theory A theory of interpersonal attraction that holds that people are more attracted to each other in relationships in which gains in liking occur and less attracted in relationships in which losses in liking occur than they are in relationships in which there are no changes in liking or disliking.

gametes The sex cells (either eggs or sperm) that contain only half as much genetic information as other cells.

gender constancy Awareness that one's sex will always remain the same.

gender differences Psychological and behavioral differences between females and males that may or may not be of biological origin.

gender roles Culturally defined behaviors, attitudes, skills, and interests that a society considers appropriate for females and males.

gender schema A mental structure used to organize information about gender and to organize behaviors related to gender.

gender schema theory Bem's theory that incorporates elements of the cognitive-developmental (the creation of gender schemas) and social-learning (societal expectations shape gender roles) views of gender-role development.

gender stereotypes Exaggerated generalizations about female or male behavior.

gender-typing The acquisition of appropriate gender roles.

general confusion The second stage of dementia, in which older adults exhibit noticeable short-term memory deficits, lack of concentration, and wandering, repetitive conversations.

generativity versus stagnation or self-absorption Erikson's seventh psychosocial stage of personality development, occurring during middle adulthood. Successful resolution results in concern for establishing and guiding the next generation and for the development of the strength of caring.

genes The basic building blocks of life, consisting of base pairs of basic proteins strung together in strands of deoxyribonucleic acid (DNA).

genetic programming A set of theories about primary aging that propose that aging occurs because each cell's life has a genetically built-in limit.

genetics The study of heredity, the inborn influences on development from genes inherited from parents.

genital stage Freud's fifth and final psychosexual stage, in which adolescents change from a narcissistic sexual drive to a mature, interpersonal sexual drive.

genotype An individual's actual genetic makeup, consisting of the specific allele configurations inherited by the individual.

gentle birth hypothesis Leboyer's thesis that minimizing the harshness of being born produces happier babies and, later, happier adults.

germinal stage The first 2 weeks of prenatal development, from conception to implantation. Highlighted by repeated cell division and cellular differentiation.

gestational diabetes Diabetes resulting from pregnancy that may cause pregnancy complications and fetal death.

gestational neurohormonal theory The proposal that gender orientation in humans is the result of prenatal actions of hormones between the second and fifth months of gestation.

glaucoma An eye disorder caused by the thickening of the eye's drainage system, resulting in increased pressure within the eye and reduced vision.

grief The sadness, sorrow, and distress experienced because of bereavement.

grieving stage A stage of anticipatory grief in which individuals who have terminally ill loved ones mourn their impending loss and partially come to terms with it.

H

habituation 1. The diminished response to a sensory stimulus as the result of repeated exposure to the stimulus. 2. Kastenbaum's definition of aging in terms of decreasing attention to repetitive stimuli in life.

hardiness A factor in the physically fit personality type. Involves the qualities of commitment, challenge, and control that are associated with positive health effects.

hassles Daily, routine stressors, as compared to such major life event stressors as marriage, job loss, and the death of a loved one.

Hayflick limit The idea from genetic programming theories of aging that human cells divide only about 50 times before divisions cease.

Head Start A federally funded compensatory preschool program that began in 1965 for socioeconomically disadvantaged children.

helpless children Children who have high levels of discouragement, low levels of effort, and deteriorating performance over time.

heredity The inborn influences on development from genes inherited from parents.

holding-on persons A subtype of Neugarten's armored-defended personality type, in which older adults try to live a middle-age lifestyle as long as possible.

hospice A specialized health-care program that serves terminally ill patients and focuses on in-home care, relief from pain, and preparation for dying.

hot flashes Brief feelings of warmth and flushing, accompanied by perspiration. Experienced by many women during the climacteric and linked to changes in the production of the gonadotropic hormone LH.

humanistic-existential perspective The psychological perspective that emphasizes individuals' active striving to fulfill their potentials for growth and to find meaning in their existence.

"the hurried child" Elkind's term to denote a modern style of raising children in which parents push their children educationally, schedule their free time with organized activities, and have them take care of themselves as "latchkey" children.

hyperhabituation A condition in which adults cling to extreme continuity in their lives, fearing all change, resisting the future, and insisting on experiencing life in a consistent way.

hypertension Chronic elevated blood pressure associated with strokes, heart attacks, and other diseases.

I

iconic mode Cognitive representation of the world in terms of mental images.

identity The sense of knowing oneself.

identity achievement Marcia's identity state in which individuals have experienced identity crises and have committed to definite identities.

identity crises Crucial, inescapable turning points of development during which individuals confront aspects of themselves. Successful resolution of identity crises leads to the ego strength of fidelity.

identity diffusion Marcia's identity state in which individuals have not experienced identity crises and have not committed to definite identities.

identity foreclosure Marcia's identity state in which individuals have made premature identity decisions without experiencing identity crises.

identity moratorium Marcia's identity state in which individuals are experiencing identity crises but have not committed to definite identities.

identity panic According to Erikson, the result of historical crises that increase the difficulties of adolescents trying to assimilate their identities with society-at-large.

imaginary audience The feelings of self-consciousness and the exaggerated sense of how often an individual is at the center of others' thoughts that adolescents develop as the result of their newly emerging cognitive abilities.

imitation The ability to model behaviors observed in others. Requires coordinated motor activity and a mental representation of what one wants to imitate.

immanent justice The childhood belief that every misdeed will be followed by a misfortune that serves as a punishment from God.

immunological theories Theories that attribute physical aging to changes in the immune system that make the body more vulnerable to infection and general breakdown.

implantation The process by which cells in the blastocyst penetrate and attach to the lining of the uterine wall and begin to receive nourishment from the mother's body.

implementers Individuals in Sternberg's model of mental self-government who involve themselves in carrying out plans.

impotence A males's inability to achieve an erection.

inability to care for self The third stage of dementia, in which older adults can no longer care for themselves because tremendous memory loss creates dangerous, life-threatening situations.

individuated-connected level The third level of developing intimacy, in which individuals acquire an emotional, intuitive perspective of the other person, are committed, and are willing to discuss concerns and to resolve conflicts.

induction Hoffman's discipline style in which parents direct attention to their children's reasoning, pride, concern for others, and desire to be mature to control their behavior.

inductive reasoning Reasoning from specifics to reach general conclusions.

industry versus inferiority Erikson's fourth psychosocial stage of personality development (ages 5 to 12), in which individuals either have experiences that develop a sense of accomplishment and the virtue of competence or they feel inferior in their performance of tasks.

infanticide The killing of unwanted babies. A common practice before the 19th century.

infantile amnesia The nearly complete lack of memory of one's life before age 3.

initiative versus guilt Erikson's third psychosocial stage of personality development, during which preschoolers learn to take initiative and to be goal-oriented and also acquire the strength of purpose.

innate theory of language development The theory that the development of language is built into the human system and that the order of language acquisition is at least partially determined by brain maturation.

instrumentality A personality dimension defined by such terms as *independent, assertive, forceful, risk-taking, dominant,* and *aggressive* and that is predictive within each sex of differences in sexual scripts and behaviors.

integrated motivation Veroff's third stage of achievement motivation (ages 10 to 12), in which children use both autonomous and social comparison motivation.

integrated personality Neugarten's personality type characterized by persons who are mature, flexible, and open to new stimuli, and who have high life satisfaction and intact cognitive functioning.

integrative power According to May, a type of power used with another person, in which persons work together to use their shared power constructively.

intelligence quotient (IQ) A formula for converting scores on tests of mental ability to a single number to represent a person's intelligence. The formula, IQ = (MA/CA) × 100, involves dividing the score on the test by the person's age and multiplying by 100.

interdependent friendships Committed friendships (ages 12 and up), in which individuals respect their friends' needs for both dependency and autonomy.

intimacy versus isolation Erikson's sixth psychosocial stage of personality development, in which successful resolution of the crisis results in being able to relate hopes, goals, and regrets to another person and to develop the virtue of love.

investigative Holland's personality type and work environment that is characterized by people who are analytical, introspective, and intellectual and who are most satisfied with scientific and mathematical work environments.

involutional melancholia A former psychiatric diagnostic category for major psychotic depression brought on by menopause.

irreversibility The inability of young children to begin at the end of a mental operation and work back to the start.

irreversibility of death One component of a mature concept of death, in which a person knows that, once dead, the physical body cannot come alive again.

J

job A specific employment position within an occupational area.

joint custody The situation in which both divorced parents share legal responsibility for their children.

L

larche The budding of the breasts. One of the first physical changes of pubescence in girls.

large-for-gestational-age (LGA) Term used to describe a condition often associated with diabetic mothers in which preterm or full-term babies' birthweights are exceptionally large for their gestational age at birth.

"last-chance" children The children of parents who delayed childbearing until middle adulthood.

latency stage Freud's fourth psychosexual stage of personality development (ages 6 to 12), in which sexual and aggressive conflicts are minimized.

learning theory of language development The theory that language is a product of social interaction in which adults systematically reinforce babies for language acquisition. This theory emphasizes the environmental factors that shape the particular language an infant learns.

life expectancy The average age to which people live in a given culture.

life review An activity in which persons recall aspects of their lives—the highs and lows, the past and the present.

life structure The basic patterns or designs of people's lives that shape and are shaped by people's interactions with the world.

lifespan The maximum age to which members of given species live. The biological limit to life.

lifespan developmental psychology The study of changes in people's lives from conception to death.

living wills A legal document for informing family members and medical professionals about an individual's preferences for sustaining life or allowing death during times of treatment for terminal illnesses or other critical medical conditions.

longitudinal studies Research studies designed to follow the same subjects over an extended period of time to note developmental changes in variables.

love relationships A category of interpersonal relationships consisting of three clusters: friendship, passion, and caring.

love-withdrawal Hoffman's discipline style in which parents use their children's fear of losing parental emotional support, approval, and affection to control their behavior.

low-birthweight babies Newborns who weigh less than 5 1/2 lb.

M

macho men Men who have undergone a hypermasculine socialization and follow a life script consisting of callous sexual attitudes and the attitudes that violence is manly and danger is exciting.

macular degeneration An eye disorder producing the most common form of blindness among persons over age 60, in which the central area of the retina responsible for seeing detail deteriorates, causing loss of central vision.

manipulative power According to May, a type of power used over another person, in which a person with greater resources takes advantage of someone with less influence.

mastery-oriented children Children who display sustained levels of high motivation, exhibit good concentration, and persist in problem-solving attempts.

maturation Qualitative developmental change that occurs as the unfolding of one's unique genetic plan.

mechanistic model The developmental model based on the idea that living systems are reactive to their environments and more like machines whose actions can be comprehended by an analysis of their functional parts and the environmental factors that influence them.

memorialization The stage of grief after a terminally ill loved one has died in which grieving individuals form a permanent positive image of the dead person.

menarche The first menstrual period. One of the last physical changes accompanying sexual maturity in girls.

menopause The term used for when menses have ceased, ending a woman's reproductive capability. Defined as not having a menstrual period for 1 year.

mental age The average cognitive capabilities of an individual relative to others of the same age.

metalinguistic awareness Intuitive awareness of how language works. Emerges around age 5.

metamemory Self-awareness of memory strategies and of whether particular information is held in memory.

midlife crisis A popular term for the emotional turmoil that may be experienced by some middle-aged persons.

model of mental self-government Sternberg's proposal that people learn to function most comfortably when they operate like the legislative, executive, and judicial branches of government.

modeling (imitation) Learning by copying another person's behavior.

modernization theory The idea that preindustrial societies accord more status to the aged than do industrial societies.

Montessori school A preschool program that emphasizes motor, sensory, and language development, while fostering patience, self-control, cooperation, and responsibility.

morality of caring The idea that moral judgments should be based on concern for others. Gilligan proposed that this type of reasoning is more characteristic of women, who focus on interpersonal connectedness to and responsibility for others, than of men.

morality of constraint Piaget's first stage of moral reasoning, in which children exhibit a rigid morality. In this stage, something is either right or it is wrong, everyone agrees on what is right and wrong, rules are unchangeable, adult authority is to be respected and obeyed, and those who do wrong are expected to be severely punished.

morality of cooperation Piaget's second stage of moral reasoning in which children exhibit a more flexible morality. In this stage, intentions as well as other points of view are considered, and rules can be changed.

morality of justice The idea, similar to the morality of rights, that moral judgments should be based on the rights of individuals above those of groups, a morality typified by Kohlberg's highest level and criticized by Gilligan as male gender-biased.

morality of rights The idea that moral judgments should be based on a system of laws and principles, an idea that Gilligan believes characterizes males' moral reasoning more than females'.

motor skills Controlled and coordinated movements of various parts of the body.

mourning The culturally prescribed ways of expressing grief. The process by which grief is gradually controlled.

multi-infarct dementia (MID) Dementia resulting from a series of ministrokes caused by temporary blood vessel obstructions that prevent oxygen from getting to the brain.

mutual friendships Friendships (ages 9 to 15) defined in terms of being intimate, shared, and mutually desirable. In these friendships, loyalty is important, and the friendships continue for longer periods of time.

myopic Visual near-sightedness.

N

nature The philosophical position that emphasizes innate hereditary factors as the prime determinants of development.

near-death experiences (NDEs) The experiences of people who have almost died but recover.

need for achievement (nAch) The motivation for accomplishing difficult tasks, competing to do more than others, and working toward a standard of excellence.

negative identity Role repudiation exhibited as adoption of an identity that is opposite of expectations.

neglected children Children ignored by their peers.

neonates A label for newborn babies during the first month after birth ("neo-" for *new* and "nate" for *born*).

neonatology A medical specialty involving care for and study of newborn infants.

night terrors Experiences of strong panic during a non-REM stage of sleep.

nightmares Disturbing dreams that occur during the REM stage of sleep. Are most common among preschoolers.

nocturnal emissions Ejaculations during sleep. One of the changes occurring in pubescence as boys reach sexual maturity.

noise-induced hearing loss Hearing loss from repeated exposure to loud noise or extended exposure to moderate noise.

nonfunctionality of death One component of a mature concept of death, in which it is understood that a dead person cannot see, feel, think, talk, or have any other functions.

nonnormative life events Events that are experienced by people at times other than when they are expected to occur for most people.

normative age-graded life event An event that is predictable for most people of the same age group.

nuclear family The prototypical family, consisting of a father, a mother, and their children.

nurture The philosophical position that emphasizes the effects of environmental experience and learning as the prime determinants of development.

nutrient power According to May, a type of power used for another person, in which one person is concerned with another's welfare and uses power to help the other person.

O

object permanence The recognition that people and objects continue to exist even when one is not in sensory contact with those people and objects.

occupation The principal work activity in which a person is employed.

Oedipus complex Freud's explanation of gender-role identification in boys, in which preschool boys form sexual attachments to their mothers, are conflicted about these attachments, and resolve the conflict through gender-role identification with their fathers.

old-old A term referring to adults age 85 and older.

operant conditioning Learning to increase responses that are followed by pleasant consequences (reinforcers) and to decrease responses that are followed by unpleasant consequences (punishers).

operational thinking The mental manipulation of symbols and the use of logical thought processes.

oral stage Freud's first psychosexual stage of personality development, during which the mouth is the most pleasure-producing body area. Occurs during the first year of life.

organ reserve The part of total physical capacity not normally used but called upon during times of greater physical exertion.

organic retardation Genetically or biologically caused intellectual retardation.

organismic model The developmental model based on the underlying themes of biological structure and the self-directed activity of living systems.

Ortgeist A German word translated as the "spirit of the place." Used developmentally to refer to the contexts of locations and cultures.

ossification The process whereby cartilage is hardened into bone by deposits of calcium and phosphorous. Used as a measure of physical maturation.

osteoporosis A disorder most frequently observed in postmenopausal women and involving gradual loss of bone mass, increased susceptibility to broken bones, and decreased height.

ovulation The release of a mature ovum from its follicle in the ovary.

P

parental divorce effect The greater likelihood that children of divorced parents will themselves be more likely to divorce than children of intact marriages.

parentification When children and adolescents are assigned roles and responsibilities normally reserved for parents.

parkinson's disease A disease affecting primarily older adults, whose symptoms include both dementia and muscle tremors resulting from neuron loss in an area of the brain that produces the neurotransmitter dopamine.

parturition A medical term for childbirth, which is divided into three stages.

passion A cluster of a love-relationship. Involves fascination, sexual desire, and exclusiveness.

passive-congenial marriages Marriages characterized by convenience, comfort, and conformity to societal expectations but lacking strong passion and expression of love.

passive-dependent personality One of Neugarten's personality types, in which older persons depend on others to meet their personal needs.

penis envy According to Freud, preschool girls' longing for the return of their penises (which they believe their mothers took away) and their envy of their fathers' penises.

perceptual constancy The ability to perceptually adapt to changing and distorted information from sense receptors by perceiving some aspects of objects as constant and unchanging.

permissive Baumrind's parenting style describing nurturing, child-centered, undemanding, responsive to children's views, affirming, nonpower-oriented parents.

personal fable The feelings of being special, unique, and eternal that adolescents develop because of their new cognitive abilities. Contributes to a sense of personal strength and comfort but can lead to an inappropriate sense of indestructibility.

phallic stage Freud's third psychosexual stage of personality development, in which the primary source of pleasure is the genital region and during which preschoolers achieve gender-role identification.

phenotype An individual's outward appearance, or actual physical makeup, based on his or her genotype.

philosophical wisdom Wisdom concerned with the meaning of life and the relationship of the self with the world.

physically fit personality A personality type characterized by optimism, energy, self-confidence, and self-discipline. Associated with good health and decreased risk for coronary heart disease, asthma, peptic ulcers, rheumatoid arthritis, and headaches.

pioneer careers Career choices for females that are still male-dominated.

placenta The transfer organ that allows for the exchange of nutrients and oxygen from the mother's system and waste products and carbon dioxide from the developing baby.

planners Individuals in Sternberg's model of mental self-government who think in terms of formulating, planning, creating, and defining problems.

polygenic inheritance An inheritance pattern in which information for the trait is carried on the alleles of more than two chromosomes.

polypharmacy A condition of excessive medication due to the number of prescription and over-the-counter drugs an individual uses. Can cause dementia.

postbereavement mourning A stage of grief after a terminally ill loved one has died, the intensity and duration of which is less if the grieving individuals have experienced anticipatory grief.

postconventional morality Kohlberg's third level of moral reasoning (reached by some teens and adults), in which moral judgments are based on the development of a set of autonomous moral principles.

postformal operations An additional stage of cognitive development beyond Piaget's fourth stage, occurring in adulthood and characterized by the acceptance and integration of contradiction (dialectism), divergent problem solving, and the realization that knowledge is relative and not absolute.

postpartum depression Depression experienced by mothers following childbirth that varies from milder and more frequent postnatal maternity blues to more severe and less frequent puerperal psychosis.

power The ability to cause or prevent change and involving the need to have impact upon or control over others.

power-assertion Hoffman's discipline style in which parents use their greater physical and verbal power to control their children's behavior.

power stress A condition produced by the inhibition of a person's need for power, resulting in chronic activation of the sympathetic nervous system and impaired immune reactions.

practical wisdom Wisdom exhibited in personally relevant situations, such as dealing with the death of a loved one.

preconventional morality Kohlberg's first level of moral reasoning (before age 9 or 10), in which children make moral judgments based on self-interests to avoid punishment or to receive rewards.

premature menopause Onset of menopause before age 35.

premature (preterm) babies Babies born before the 38th week of gestation.

preoperational stage Piaget's second stage of cognitive development (ages 2 to 7). Characterized by transductive reasoning and by such limitations on thinking as egocentrism, centering, and irreversibility.

presbycusis Hearing loss as the result of primary aging.

presbyopia Visual farsightedness as the result of primary aging.

preschool Educationally oriented child care.

primary aging Aging due to intrinsic biogenetic processes.

priming A memory strategy in which related information is used to help recall the desired material.

principle of substitution The pattern of care observed among childless older persons, in which other family members (spouses, siblings, nieces, and nephews) help care for the older adults.

productive love According to Fromm, the most complete and basic love. Involves care, responsibility, knowledge, and respect for another person.

professions Occupational choices that require extensive specialization and academic preparation.

propinquity In interpersonal attraction, the physical proximity of a person. A necessary requirement for forming an initial relationship with someone.

prosocial behaviors Behaviors that benefit other people and that include sharing, rescuing, comforting, cooperating, complimenting, and helping.

proximodistal principle The developmental principle describing the direction of development from the center of the body outward (literally, near to far development).

psychodynamic perspective The psychological perspective that emphasizes that development is the result of the unconscious interaction of dynamic inner forces.

psychosexual stages Freud's five stages of personality development (oral, anal, phallic, latent, and genital) that he named for the region of the body in which libido (the pleasure-seeking drive) is most expressed.

psychosocial stages Erikson's eight stages of personality development across the lifespan that emphasize conflicts arising from social interactions.

pubarche Pubic hair growth, a secondary sex characteristic that is often the second physical change to appear in pubescence in boys and girls.

pubertal timing The individual rate of maturation in achieving puberty. The timing affects adolescents' interpersonal statuses and life experiences.

puberty The end of pubescence, when individuals are capable of producing mature sex cells (eggs and sperm).

pubescence The time period of approximately 2 years during which sexual maturation occurs and secondary sex characteristics appear.

Q

quickening The mother's awareness of spontaneous fetal movements, such as kicking.

R

radical departers A variation of identity foreclosure in which individuals depart from their families' values and goals by joining cults or ideological communes.

reaction time The interval between the onset of a stimulus and a person's response to the stimulus. Increases with age.

realism The attribution of real physical properties to mental phenomena.

realistic Holland's personality type and work environment that is characterized by people who are concrete, practical problem-solvers and who like work environments that are mechanical, technical, manual, or agricultural.

realistic stage Ginzberg's third career decision-making stage, during which, at the end of adolescence, most individuals explore careers, select a career field, and decide on a specific job.

receptive language The ability to comprehend speech.

recessive inheritance The appearance in the individual's phenotype of a physical trait only when both of the alleles in the individual's genotype carry the trait.

reconciliation stage A stage of anticipatory grief in which individuals with loved ones who are terminally ill partially come to terms with their impending loss.

reentry career A career pattern more common among women, in which some adults step out of the work force for a few years and then reenter a career.

reflexes Automatic behaviors in response to external stimulation.

rejected children Children actively disliked by their peers.

rejecting/neglecting Baumrind's parenting style describing laissez-faire, abusive, unresponsive to children's views, undemanding, nonpower-oriented, nonaffirming, noninvolved parents.

reincarnation The idea that everyone lives a series of lives within different bodies.

reinforcement-affect model A theory of interpersonal attraction that holds that people like individuals more when the individuals are associated with events that arouse positive feelings.

reintegrative stage Schaie's older adulthood cognitive stage, in which the cognitive goal is generalized purpose and wisdom.

relativism The world view that is represented by the belief that all viewpoints are equally valid because any answer can be right or wrong, depending on the situation.

REM sleep-Rapid-eye-movement sleep. A stage of sleep during which the eyes move rapidly under the closed lids, indicative of dreaming. The dreaming stage of sleep.

remote memories Older adults' memories of childhood and other distant events.

reorganizers A subtype of Neugarten's integrated personality type in which older persons remain highly active, substituting new activities for no longer appropriate ones.

repression-sensitization A personality style existing on a continuum, from repressors (individuals who tend to neglect or avoid information in threatening situations) on one extreme to sensitizers (individuals who focus their attention on situational cues that indicate possible danger) on the other.

resilient children Children who are able to survive tough situations and have high self-esteem, supportive families, and positive role models.

responsible stage A component of Schaie's middle adulthood cognitive stage in which concern is shown for others.

restrictive interaction style An interaction style that develops among males, in which self-disclosure is minimized and well-defined roles and dominance hierarchies exist.

retribution A pathway for resolving grief for individuals experiencing survivor's guilt in which grieving persons conclude that the loved one died because of the grieving individual's sins.

reunion A pathway for resolving grief for individuals experiencing survivor's guilt in which the major focus is on an eventual reunion with the dead person.

reverence A pathway for resolving grief for individuals experiencing survivor's guilt, in which grieving individuals choose to use the loved one's death as an inspiration to do well and to live well.

rites of passage In some societies, rituals that mark the transition from childhood to adulthood.

role exit theory Blau's theory that deals with the effect on older adults of loss of such major life roles as occupational and marital statuses.

role-focused level The second stage of developing intimacy, in which individuals acknowledge and respect the other person as part of an intimate relationship.

role repudiation According to Erikson, the result of failing to resolve an identity crisis. Roles and values are seen as alien to the self.

S

schema Mental structures that denote what is essential about category membership.

scripts Verbal and cognitive descriptions of appropriate sequences of events in specific situations. Largely unconscious, culturally determined cognitive plans that individuals use to organize and guide their behavior.

secondary aging Aging due to such external factors as lifestyle and abuse or disuse of the body.

securely attached infants Ainsworth's term describing attachment between infants and their mothers that is characterized by the infants' ability to leave their mothers to play, to be separated from their mothers, and to react positively when reunited.

self The system of concepts individuals develop to define themselves and to indicate their awareness of their separation from other people and the environment.

self-actualizing creativeness A term used by Maslow to describe the "personal intelligence" that older persons can pass down to younger individuals.

self-concept theory Super's five-stage theory of career development.

self-directed regulatory behaviors The coping behaviors of infants exhibiting some self-control over their own crying and negative emotions.

self-focused level The first stage of developing intimacy, in which individuals are only concerned with how a relationship affects them.

self-recognition The ability to recognize one's image, which emerges gradually during the first 2 years of life.

self theory Roger's humanistic personality theory, which proposes that all people possess an actualizing tendency that directs them to grow in positive ways.

sensorimotor stage Piaget's first stage of cognitive development, from birth to 24 months, during which infants become able to coordinate simple behaviors and perceptions and achieve object permanence.

separation anxiety The tendency of infants to cry and to protest being separated from their usual caretaker.

sequential designs The combinations of cross-sectional and longitudinal research designs in which individuals of different age groups are observed repeatedly over an extended period of time.

serial marriage A remarriage pattern in which an individual has been married at least three times.

seriation The ability to order items according to size or some other characteristic.

sex differences Physical differences between females and males.

sex-limited inheritance An inheritance pattern in which both males and females inherit the characteristic, but usually only one gender displays the trait because it is triggered by specific levels of hormones.

sex-linked inheritance The appearance in the individual's phenotype of a physical trait when the relevant trait information is carried on a sex chromosome (usually the X chromosome).

sexual addiction Compulsive sexuality involving preoccupation with sexual thoughts and stimulation, ritualization of sexual behavior, and despair and feeling of powerlessness over the sexual compulsiveness.

sexual orientation The continuum representing an individual's sexual attraction to members of the opposite gender, the same gender, or both genders.

sexual scripts Largely unconscious, culturally determined cognitive plans that individuals use to organize and guide their sexual behavior.

sexually transmitted diseases (STDs) Genital infections and other diseases usually contracted by sexual contact with an already infected person.

shyness The condition in which behavioral inhibition (the inability to initiate action) is the response to unfamiliar situations, new persons, and mild mental stress.

sibling rivalry According to Adler, the competition between siblings for the affection and approval of their parents.

sincerity The quality of honesty to self and others.

"sissy boy syndrome" A condition in which young boys wish to become members of the opposite sex and exhibit a liking for feminine objects and activities. Predictive of later homosexual or bisexual orientation.

slow-to-warm-up babies Babies whose temperaments result in some irregularity in eating and sleeping, initial negative reactions to change and novelty but with an eventual shift to positive reactions, and generally negative emotions initially, followed by positive emotions.

small-for-gestational-age (SGA) Term used to describe preterm or full-term babies whose birthweights are low for babies born at that gestational age.

social Holland's personality type and work environment that is characterized by people who value interpersonal relationships and work in social, educational, and therapeutic areas.

social clocks The times in a person's life when certain life events are expected to occur.

social comparison motivation Veroff's second stage of achievement motivation (age 6), in which children direct themselves according to social norms.

social smiles Smiles that represent the intentional responses of infants to attention from parents and others.

special talent creativity The creativity exhibited by artists, writers, musicians, scientists, inventors, and others who display the capacity to create original ideas in specific areas of endeavor.

spontaneous abortion The natural expulsion of the fetus and ending of a pregnancy by the 25th week of pregnancy. Also called a miscarriage.

stage of concrete operations Piaget's third stage of cognitive development, in which school-age children become capable of operational thinking and can mentally represent objects and events symbolically.

stuttering A type of dysrhythmia in which speech rhythm and fluency are disturbed by periodic blocking, repetition, or prolongation of sounds and words.

succorance-seeking persons A subtype of Neugarten's passive-dependent personality type, in which older adults have good life satisfaction as long as they have someone on which to lean.

superego According to Freud, the moral arm of the personality. Represents society's rules and values, especially as taught and modeled by parents.

survivor's guilt Guilt experienced by those who survive a loved one, especially parents of children who die. Involves intense feelings of guilt and vulnerability.

symbolic mode Cognitive representation of the world in terms of symbols, especially language.

T

technically present father Traditional fathers who are involved in their children's lives out of a sense of obligation, who experience guilt over their ambivalence toward parenting, and who spend significantly less time in day-to-day childcare than either mothers or androgynous fathers.

temperament A set of inborn personality traits that appear early in life and consist of individual differences in arousal, primary emotions, activity level, and persistence.

tentative stage Ginzberg's career decision-making stage in which adolescents begin more serious and realistic exploration, definition, and clarification of possible career options.

teratogen Any agent that can produce harmful effects in the fetus. Teratogens primarily pass from the mother across the placental barrier to the fetus. From *tera,* the Greek work for "monster."

terminal drop In older adults, a condition in which death is preceded by a significant drop in intelligence scores, as well as by personality changes and decreases in perceptual and psychomotor abilities.

theory of separation-individuation Mahler's three-stage theory describing the emergence of the psychological self during infancy and toddlerhood.

total marriages Marriages that are characterized by total enmeshing of all aspects of the relationship and in which the couple view themselves as being essentially one.

transcendence Jung's term for spiritual self-actualization, involving the striving for unity, wholeness, and integration of the personality and the universe.

transductive reasoning Reasoning from particular to particular.

transformations The transitions or changes from one event to another.

Type A Personality A personality type characterized as being hard-driving, competitive, ambitious, and aggressive, with hostility a crucial factor in Type A's association with higher risk for coronary disease and heart attacks.

Type B Personality A personality type consisting of the relative absence of Type A characteristics—that is, Type B individuals are relaxed, noncompetitive, and nonaggressive.

type-I diabetes Insulin-dependent diabetes resulting from total loss of insulin production in the pancreas.

type-II diabetes Adult-onset diabetes resulting from the body's inefficient use of insulin. Often controllable without insulin treatment.

U

ultrasound A technique using acoustic pulses sent into the pregnant woman's body from a probe placed on the abdomen. The reflected pulses are then computer analyzed to map the fetus's body structure.

"Ulyssean adult" McLeish's term for an individual rich in self-actualizing creativeness. Based on the person's questing spirit and exhibition of courage and resourcefulness.

unintegrated personality One of Neugarten's personality types, in which older adults exhibit a pattern of disorganized, dysfunctional living.

universality of death One component of a mature concept of death, in which the person understands that everybody, including themselves, will die.

V

visual accommodation The ability to visually focus on near and far objects by changing the shape of the lens in the eye.

visual acuity The ability to detect the separate parts of an object. This ability is limited in newborns but greatly improves in 6 to 12 months.

vital marriages Marriages characterized by high commitment, mutual satisfaction, and strong psychological involvement between partners and in which couples enjoy doing things together rather than apart.

vocation The specific occupational choice for which training and employment is sought.

W

"wear-and-tear" theory One of the oldest and most general theories of primary aging that proposes that the body ages due to the wear and tear of living.

wisdom The ability to use good judgment in important but uncertain matters of life. Excellence in pragmatic intelligence and knowledge.

Y

young-old A term referring to older adults in their 60s to about age 85.

youth Keniston's developmental stage describing an extended transitional period for entering adulthood in which the tasks of adolescence have been completed but the responsibilities and commitments of adulthood have not been fully assumed.

Z

Zeitgeist A German word translated as the "spirit of the age" or the "sign of the times." Used developmentally to refer to the contexts experienced by different cohorts (groups of individuals of the same age or generation).

References

A

Abelson, R. (1981). Psychological status of the script concept. *American Psychologist, 36,* 715–729.

Abramovitch, R., Corter, C., Pepler, D. J., & Stanhope, L. (1986). Sibling and peer interaction: A final follow-up and a comparison. *Child Development, 57,* 217–229.

Abrams, M. (1959). *The teenage consumer.* London, England: Press Exchange.

Abroms, K., & Bennett, J. (1981). Changing etiological perspectives in Down's syndrome: Implications for early intervention. *Journal of the Division for Early Childhood, 2,* 109–112.

Achenberg, W. A. (1985). Religion in the lives of the elderly. In G. Lesnoff-Caravalglia (Ed.), *Values, ethics and aging.* New York: Human Sciences Press.

Adams, B. N. (1980). *The family: A sociological interpretation* (3rd ed.). Boston: Houghton Mifflin.

Adams, D. M., & Fuchs, M. (1986, November). The video media and cultural misunderstanding. *USA Today,* pp. 79–81.

Adams, G. R., Abraham, K. G., & Markstrom, C. A. (1987). The relations among identity development, self-consciousness, and self-focusing during middle and late adolescence. *Developmental Psychology, 23,* 292–297.

Adams, R. G. (1987). Patterns of network change: A longitudinal study of friendship of elderly women. *Journal of Gerontology, 27,* 222–227.

Adams, R. J. (1987). An evaluation of color preference in early infancy. *Infant Behavior and Development, 10,* 143–150.

Adamson, L. B., Bakeman, R., Smith, C. B., & Walters, A. S. (1987). Adults' interpretations of infants' acts. *Developmental Psychology, 23,* 383–387.

Adelmann, P. K., Antonucci, T. C., Crohan, S. E., & Coleman, L. M. (1989). Empty nest, cohort, and employment in the well-being of midlife women. *Sex Roles, 20,* 173–189.

Adelmann, P. K., & Zajonc, R. B. (1989). Facial efference and the experience of emotion. *Annual Review of Psychology, 40,* 249–280.

Ade-Ridder, L., & Brubaker, T. H. (1983). The quality of long-term marriages. In T. H. Brubaker (Ed.), *Family relationships in later life.* Beverly Hills, CA: Sage.

Adler, A. (1929). *The science of living.* New York: Greenberg.

Adler, A. (1931). *What life should mean to you.* Boston: Little, Brown.

Adler, A. (1946). *Understanding human nature.* New York: Greenberg.

Adler, J. (1987, March 16). Cause for concern—and optimism. *Newsweek,* p. 66.

Adubato, S. A. (1984). Father involvement, sex typing, and the toy play of children. *Dissertation Abstracts International, 46,* 1353B (University Microfilm No. DA85-083).

Ahrons, C. R., & Rodgers, R. H. (1987). *Divorced families: A multidisciplinary developmental view.* New York: W. W. Norton.

Aiken, L. R. (1985). *Dying, death, and bereavement.* Boston: Allyn & Bacon.

Ainlay, S. C. (1988). Aging and new vision loss: Disruptions of the here and now. *Journal of Social Issues, 44,* 79–94.

Ainsworth, M. D. S., Blehar, M., Waters, E., & Wall, S. (1978). *Patterns of attachment.* Hillsdale, NJ: Erlbaum.

Ainsworth, M. D. S., & Wittig, B. A. (1969). Attachment and exploratory behavior of one-year-olds in a strange situation. In B. M. Foss (Ed.), *Determinants of infant behavior.* London: Metheun.

Aizenberg, R., & Treas, J. (1985). The family in later life. In J. E. Birren & K. W. Schaie (Eds.), *Handbook of the psychology of aging* (2nd ed., pp. 169–190). New York: Van Nostrand Reinhold.

Akers, R. L., La Greca, A. J., Cochran, J., & Sellers, C. (1989). Social learning theory and alcohol behavior among the elderly. *Sociological Quarterly, 30,* 625–638.

Alan Guttmacher Institute. (1985). *Issues in brief* (Vol. 5). Washington, DC: Alan Guttmacher Institute.

Albert, M. S., Heller, H. S., & Milberg, W. (1988). Changes in naming ability with age. *Psychology and Aging, 3,* 173–178.

Aldous, J. J. (1987). Family life of the elderly and near-elderly. *Journal of Marriage and the Family, 49,* 227–234.

Aldwin, C. M., Levenson, M. R., Spiro III, A., & Bosse, R. (1989). Does emotionality predict stress? Findings from the normative aging study. *Journal of Personality and Social Psychology, 56,* 618–624.

Allen, J. (1986, November/December). New lives for old: Lifestyle change initiatives among older adults. *Health Values,* pp. 8–18.

Allore, R., O'Hanlon, D., Price, R., Neilson, K., Willard, H. F., Cox, D. R., Marks, A., & Dunn, R. J. (1988). Gene encoding the B subunit of S100 protein is on chromosome 21: Implications for Down syndrome. *Science, 239,* 1311–1313.

Allred, K. D., & Smith, T. W. (1989). The hardy personality: Cognitive and physiological responses to evaluative threat. *Journal of Personality and Social Psychology, 56,* 257–266.

Almy, M. (1949). *Children's experiences prior to first grade and success in beginning reading* (Contributions to Education, No. 954). New York: Bureau of Publications, Teachers College, Columbia.

Als, N., Tronick, E., Lester, B. M., & Brazelton, T. B. (1979). Specific neonatal measures: The Brazelton neonatal behavior assessment scale. In J. D. Osofsky (Ed.), *Handbook of infant development.* New York: John Wiley.

Alter, R. C. (1984). Abortion outcome as a function of sex-role identification. *Psychology of Women Quarterly, 8,* 211–233.

Amato, P. R. (1988). Parental divorce and attitudes toward marriage and family life. *Journal of Marriage and the Family, 50,* 453–461.

American Psychiatric Association. (1980). *Diagnostic and statistical manual of mental disorders* (3rd ed.). Washington, DC: American Psychiatric Association.

Ames, L. B., Gillespie, C., Haines, J., & Ilg, F. (1980). *The Gesell Institute's child from one to six: Evaluating the behavior of the preschool child.* London: Hamish Hamilton.

Ames, L. B., Metraux, R. W., Roedell, J. L., & Walker, R. N. (1974). *Child Rorschach responses: Developmental trends from two to ten years.* New York: Brunner/Mazel.

Ammons, P., & Stinnett, N. (1980). The vital marriage: A closer look. *Family Relations, 29,* 37–42.

Anand, K. J. S., & Hickey, P. R. (1987). Pain and its effects in the human neonate and fetus. *New England Journal of Medicine, 317,* 1321–1329.

Anders, T., Caraskadon, M., & Dement, W. C. (1980). Sleep and sleepiness in children and adolescents. *Adolescent Medicine, 27,* 29–44.

Anders, T. R., & Fozard, J. L. (1973). Effects of age upon retrieval from primary and secondary memory. *Developmental Psychology, 9,* 411–416.

Anderson, G. C., Burroughs, A. K., & Measel, C. P. (1983). Nonnutritive sucking opportunities. In T. Field & A. Sostek (Eds.), *Infants born at risk.* New York: Grune & Stratton.

Anderson, S. A., Russell, C. S., & Schumm, W. R. (1983). Perceived marital quality and family life-cycle categories: A further analysis. *Journal of Marriage and the Family, 45,* 127–139.

Andrews, L. B. (1984, December). Yours, mine and theirs. *Psychology Today,* pp. 20–29.

Angier, N. (1984, September). Medical clues from babies' cries. *Discover,* pp. 49–51.

Angier, N. (1987, March). Light cast on a darkling gene. *Discover,* pp. 85–96.

Ansello, E. F. (1977). Age and ageism in children's first literature. *Educational Gerontology, 2,* 255–274.

Antell, S. E., & Keating, D. P. (1983). Perception of numerical invariance in neonates. *Child Development, 54,* 695–701.

Anthony, K. H. (1985). The shopping mall: A teenage hangout. *Adolescence, 20,* 307–312.

Antonucci, T. C. (1985). Personal characteristics, social support, and social behavior. In R. H. Binstock & E. Shanas (Eds.), *Handbook of aging and the social sciences.* New York: Van Nostrand.

Antonucci, T. C., & Akiyama, H. (1987). An examination of sex differences in social support among older men and women. *Sex Roles, 17,* 737–749.

Aoki, C., & Siekevitz, P. (1988, December). Plasticity in brain development. *Scientific American,* pp. 56–64.

Apgar, V. A. (1953). A proposal for a new method of evaluation of a newborn infant. *Anesthesia and Analegia . . . Current Research, 32,* 260–267.

Apgar, V., & Beck, J. (1973). *Is my baby all right?* New York: Trident.

Apgar, V., & Beck, J. (1974). *Is my baby all right?* New York: Pocket Books.

Apgar, V., Holaday, D. A., James, L. S., Weisbrot, I. M., & Berrien, C. (1958). Evaluation of the newborn infant—Second report. *Journal of the American Medical Association, 168,* 1985–1988.

Archer, C. J. (1984). Children's attitudes toward sex-role division in adult occupational roles. *Sex Roles, 10,* 1–9.

Arenberg, D., & Robertson-Tchabo, E. (1977). Learning and aging. In J. E. Birren & K. W. Schaie (Eds.), *Handbook of the psychology of aging.* New York: Van Nostrand Reinhold.

Aries, P. (1962). *Centuries of childhood: A social history of family life* (R. Baldick, Trans.). New York: Knopf.

Aries, P. (1973). *Centuries of childhood.* Hammondsword, England: Penguin.

Aries, P. (1981). *The hour of our death.* New York: Knopf.

Arlin, P. K. (1975). Cognitive development in adulthood: A fifth stage? *Developmental Psychology, 11,* 602–606.

Arlin, P. K. (1984). Adolescent and adult thought: A structural interpretation. In M. L. Commons, F. A. Richards, & C. Armon (Eds.), *Beyond formal operations: Late adolescent and adult cognitive development* (pp. 258–271). New York: Praeger.

Arluke, A., & Levin, J. (1984, August/September). Another stereotype: Old age as a second childhood. *Aging,* pp. 7–11.

Aronson, E., & Linder, D. (1965). Gain and loss of esteem as determinants of interpersonal attractiveness. *Journal of Experimental Social Psychology, 1,* 156–171.

Ashburn, S. S. (1986). Biophysical development of the infant. In C. S. Schuster & S. S. Ashburn, *The process of human development: A holistic life-span approach* (2nd ed.). Boston: Little, Brown.

Asher, J. (1987, April). Born to be shy? *Psychology Today,* pp. 56–64.

Ashmead, D. H., Clifton, R. K., & Perris, E. E. (1987). Precision of auditory localization in human infants. *Developmental Psychology, 23,* 641–647.

Ashmead, D. H., & Perlmutter, M. (1980). Infant memory in everyday life. In M. Perlmutter (Ed.), *New directions in child development.* San Francisco: Jossey-Bass.

Ashton, E. (1983). Measures of play behavior: The influence of sex-role stereotyped children's books. *Sex Roles, 9* (1), 43–47.

Aslin, R. N., & Smith, L. B. (1988). Perceptual development. *Annual Review of Psychology, 39,* 435–473.

Associated Press. (1988, May 10). 88% of women say they would marry the same man again. *Des Moines Register,* A:2.

Astin, A. W. (1977). *Four critical years.* San Francisco: Jossey-Bass.

Astin, A. W., Green, K. C., & Korn, W. S. (1987). *The American freshman: Twenty-year trends.* Los Angeles: University of California at Los Angeles, Higher Education Research Institute.

Atchley, R. C. (1971). Retirement and work orientation. *The Gerontologist, 2,* 29–32.

Atchley, R. C. (1975). The life course, age grading, and age-linked demands for decision making. In N. Datan & L. Ginsberg (Eds.), *Life-span developmental psychology: Normative life crises.* New York: Academic Press.

Atchley, R. C. (1976). *The sociology of retirement.* New York: Halstead Press.

Atchley, R. C. (1980). *The social forces in later life* (3rd ed.). Belmont, CA: Wadsworth.

Atchley, R. C., & Miller, S. J. (1983). Types of elderly couples. In T. H. Brubaker (Ed.), *Family relationships in later life.* Beverly Hills, CA: Sage.

Atkin, C., Hocking, J., & Block, M. (1984, Spring). Teenage drinking: Does advertising make a difference? *Journal of Communication,* pp. 157–167.

Atkinson, G., Jr., Murrell, P. H., & Winters, M. R. (1990). Career personality types and learning styles. *Psychological Reports, 66,* 160–162.

Atkinson, J., & Braddick, O. (1988). Infant precursors of later visual disorders: Correlation or causality? In A. Yonas (Ed.), *Perceptual development in infancy. The Minnesota Symposia on child psychology* (Vol. 20). Hillsdale, NJ: Lawrence Erlbaum.

Atkinson, J. W. (1974). The mainspring of achievement-oriented activity. In J. W. Atkinson & J. O. Raynor (Eds.), *Motivation and achievement.* Washington, DC: Winston.

Atkinson, M. A., & Maclaren, N. K. (1990, July). What causes diabetes? *Scientific American,* pp. 62–71.

Aukett, R., Ritchie, J., & Mill, K. (1988). Gender differences in friendship patterns. *Sex Roles, 19,* 57–66.

Awalt, S., Snowden, L. R., & Schott, T. L. (1987). Personal and marital adjustment in the transition to parenthood. Cited in Snowden, L. R., Schott, T. L., Awalt, S. J., & Gillis-Knox, J. (1988). Marital satisfaction in pregnancy: Stability and change. *Journal of Marriage and the Family, 50,* 325–333.

Azrin, N., & Foxx, R. M. (1981). *Toilet training in less than a day* (2nd ed.). New York: Pocket Books.

B

Babchuk, N., Peters, G. R., Hoyt, D. R., & Kaiser, M. A. (1979). The voluntary associations of the aged. *Journal of Gerontology, 34,* 579–587.

Bachman, J. G. (1987). An eye on the future. *Psychology Today, 23,* 292–297.

Bachman, J. G., Johnston, L. D., O'Malley, P. M., & Humphrey, R. H. (1988). Explaining the recent decline in marijuana use: Differentiating the effects of perceived risks, disapproval, and general lifestyle factors. *Journal of Health and Social Behavior, 29,* 92–112.

Backman, C. W., & Secord, P. F. (1959). The effect of perceived liking on interpersonal attraction. *Human Relations, 12,* 379–384.

Bahrick, H. P. (1984). Semantic memory content in permastore: Fifty years of memory for Spanish learned in school. *Journal of Experimental Psychology: General, 113,* 1–35.

Bailey, W. T. (1989, May). *"Who stays home when you're sick?" Fathers' involvement in health care.* Paper presented at the meeting of the Midwestern Psychological Association, Chicago.

Baker, S. (1987, October). Mothering hormone. *Omni,* p. 39.

Baker, S. A., Thalberg, S. P., & Morrison, D. M. (1988). Parents' behavioral norms as predictors of adolescent sexual activity and contraceptive use. *Adolescence, 23,* 265–282.

Baldwin, J. D., & Baldwin, J. I. (1988). Factors affecting AIDS-related sexual risk-taking behavior among college students. *Journal of Sex Research, 2,* 181–196.

Baldwin, J. M. (1895). *Mental development in the child and the race: Methods and processes.* New York: Macmillan.

Baldwin, J. M. (1906–1915). *Thought and things: A study of the development and meaning of thought, or genetic logic* (4 vols.). New York: Macmillan (Vols. 1–3); Putnam (Vol. 4).

Bales, J. (1986, November). Explaining sexuality? Consider the Sambia. *APA Monitor,* p. 18.

Ball, J. A. (1987). *Reactions to motherhood.* New York: Cambridge University Press.

Baltes, P. B. (1979a). Life-span developmental psychology: Some converging observations on history and theory. In P. B. Baltes & O. G. Brim (Eds.), *Life-span development and behavior* (Vol. 2). New York: Academic Press.

Baltes, P. B. (1979b, Summer). On the potential and limits of child development: Life-span developmental perspectives. *Newsletter of the Society for Research in Child Development,* pp. 1–4.

Baltes, P. B. (1983). Life-span developmental psychology: Observations on history and theory revisited. In R. M. Lerner (Ed.), *Developmental psychology: Historical and philosophical perspectives.* Hillsdale, NJ: Erlbaum.

Baltes, P. B., Featherman, D. L., & Lerner, R. M. (Eds.). (1986). *Life-span development and behavior* (Vol. 7). Hillsdale, NJ: Erlbaum.

Baltes, P. B., & Reese, H. W. (1984). The life-span perspective in developmental psychology. In M. H. Bornstein & M. E. Lamb (Eds.), *Developmental psychology: An advanced textbook.* Hillsdale, NJ: Erlbaum.

Baltes, P. B., Reese, H. W., & Lipsitt, L. P. (1980). Life-span developmental psychology. *Annual Review of Psychology, 31,* 65–110.

Baltes, P. B., & Schaie, K. W. (Eds.). (1973). *Life-span developmental psychology: Personality and socialization.* New York: Academic Press.

Baltes, P. B., & Schaie, K. W. (1974). The myth of the twilight years. *Psychology Today, 7,* 35–40.

Band, E. B., & Weisz, J. R. (1988). How to feel better when it feels bad: Children's perspectives on coping with everyday stress. *Developmental Psychology, 24,* 247–253.

Bandura, A. (1965). Influence of models' reinforcement contingencies on the acquisition of imitative responses. *Journal of Personality & Social Psychology, 1,* 589–595.

Bandura, A. (1973). *Aggression: A social learning analysis.* Englewood Cliffs, NJ: Prentice-Hall.

Bandura, A. (1977). *Social learning theory.* Englewood Cliffs, NJ: Prentice-Hall.

Bandura, A. (1978). The self system in reciprocal determinism. *American Psychologist, 33,* 344–358.

Bandura, A., Ross, D., & Ross, S. A. (1963). A comparative test of the status envy, social power and secondary reinforcement theories of identificatory learning. *Journal of Abnormal and Social Psychology, 67,* 527–534.

Banks, M. S., & Salapatek. (1983). Infant visual perception. In P. H. Mussen (Ed.), *Handbook of child psychology* (4th ed.). M. H. Harth & J. J. Campos (Vol. Eds.), *Infancy and developmental psychology.* New York: Wiley.

Barker, R. G., & Wright, H. F. (1955). *Midwest and its children.* New York: Harper & Row.

Barnes, D. M. (1987, February). Defect in Alzheimer's is on chromosome 21. *Science,* pp. 846–847.

Barnes, K. E. (1971). Preschool play norms: A replication. *Developmental Psychology, 5,* 99–103.

Barnett, L. A., & Fiscella, J. (1985, Spring). A child by any other name—A comparison of the playfulness of gifted and nongifted children. *Gifted Child Quarterly,* pp. 61–66.

Barol, B. (1987, November 30). The grueling baby chase. *Newsweek,* pp. 78–83.

Barr, H. M., Streissguth, A. P., Martin, D. C., & Herman, C. S. (1984). Infant size at 8 months of age: Relationship to maternal use of alcohol, nicotine, and caffeine during pregnancy. *Pediatrics, 74,* 336–341.

Barr, R. G., & Elias, M. F. (1988, April). Nursing interval and maternal responsivity: Effect on early infant crying. *Pediatrics,* pp. 529–536.

Barrow, G. M. (1986). *Aging, the individual, and society* (3rd ed.). St. Paul: West.

Bar-Tal, D., Raviv, A., & Goldberg, M. (1982). Helping behavior among preschool children: An observational study. *Child Development, 53,* 396–402.

Baruch, G., & Barnett, R. (1983). Adult daughters' relationships with their mothers. *Journal of Marriage and the Family, 45,* 601–606.

Baruch, G., Barnett, R., & Rivers, C. (1983). *Lifeprints: New patterns of love and work for today's woman.* New York: McGraw-Hill.

Bar-Yam Hassan, A. (1989, August 14). *Stages in interpersonal development in young adulthood.* Paper presented at American Psychological Association Convention, New Orleans.

Bar-Yam Hassan, A., & Bar-Yam, M. (1987). Interpersonal development across the life span: Communication and its interaction with agency in psychosocial development. *Contributions to Human Development, 18,* 102–128.

Basseches, M. (1984). *Dialectical thinking and adult development.* Norwood, NJ: Ablex.

Baumrind, D. (1968). Authoritarian versus authoritative parental control. *Adolescence, 3,* 255–272.

Baumrind, D. (1971). Current patterns of parental authority. *Developmental Psychology Monographs, 4,* (1, Pt. 2).

Baumrind, D. (1982). Are androgynous individuals more effective persons and parents? *Child Development, 53,* 44–75.

Beard, M., & Curtis, L. (1988). *Menopause and the years ahead.* Tucson: Fisher Books.

Beautrais, A. L., Fergusson, D. M., & Shannon, F. T. (1982). Life events and childhood morbidity: A prospective study. *Pediatrics, 70,* 935–940.

Becher, R. M. (1985, September/October). Parent involvement and reading achievement: A review of research and implications for practice. *Childhood Education,* pp. 44–50.

Beck, M. (1990, July 2). A home away from home. *Newsweek,* pp. 56–58.

Becque, M. D., Katch, V. L., Rocchini, A. P., Marks, C. R., & Moorehead, C. (1988). Coronary risk incidence of obese adolescents: Reduction by exercise plus diet intervention. *Pediatrics, 81,* 605–612.

Begley, S., Hager, M., & Murr, A. (1990, March 5). The search for the fountain of youth. *Newsweek,* pp. 44–48.

Behrman, R. E. (1987). Premature births among black women. *New England Journal of Medicine, 317,* 763–765.

Belbin, R. M. (1983). The implications of gerontology for new work roles in later life. In J. E. Birren (Ed.), *Aging: A challenge to science and society* (Vol. 3, pp. 214–225). New York: Oxford University Press.

Belenky, M., Clinchy, B., Goldberger, N., & Tarule, J. (1986). *Women's ways of knowing.* New York: Basic Books.

Bell, A. P., Weinberg, M. S., & Hammersmith, S. K. (1981). *Sexual preferences: Its development in men and women.* Bloomington, IN: Indiana University Press.

Bell, D. (1989). The effects of affirmative action on male-female relationships among African Americans. *Sex Roles, 21,* 13–24.

Bell, D., & Bell, L. (1983). Parental validation and support in the development of adolescent daughters. In H. Grotevant & C. Cooper (Eds.), *Adolescent development in the family: New directions in children's development.* San Francisco: Jossey-Bass.

Bell, R. R. (1981). Friendships of women and men. *Psychology of Women Quarterly, 5,* 402–417.

Bell, R. R. (1983). *Marriage and family interaction.* Homewood, IL: Dorsey.

Bell, S. M., & Ainsworth, M. D. S. (1972). Infant crying and maternal responsiveness. *Child Development, 43,* 1171–1190.

Belloc, N. B., & Breslow, L. (1972). Relationship of physical health status and health practices. *Preventive Medicine, 1,* 409–421.

Belmont, N. (1976). Levana: Or how to raise up children. In F. Forster & O. Ranum (Trans. & Eds.), *Family and society.* Baltimore: Johns Hopkins University.

Belsky, J. (1984). The determinants of parenting: A process model. *Child Development, 55,* 83–96.

Belsky, J., Gilstrap, B., & Rovine, M. (1984). The Pennsylvania infant and family development project I: Stability and change in mother-infant and father-infant interaction in a family setting at one, three, and nine months. *Child Development, 55,* 692–705.

Belsky, J., Lang, M. E., & Rovine, M. (1985). Stability and change in marriage across the transition to parenthood: A second study. *Journal of Marriage and the Family, 47,* 855–865.

Belsky, J., & Rovine, M. J. (1988). Nonmaternal care in the first year of life and the security of infant-parent attachment. *Child Development, 59,* 157–167.

Bem, S. L. (1983). Gender schema theory and implications for child development: Raising gender-aschematic children in a gender-schematic society. *Signs: Journal of Women in Culture and Society, 8,* 598–616.

Bem, S. L. (1985). Androgyny and gender schema theory: A conceptual and empirical integration. In T. B. Sonderegger (Ed.), *Nebraska symposium on motivation, 1984: Psychology and gender.* Lincoln, NE: University of Nebraska Press.

Benacerraf, B. R., Gelman, R., & Frigoletto, F. D. (1987). Sonographic identification of second-trimester fetuses with Down syndrome. *New England Journal of Medicine, 317,* 1371–1376.

Benbow, C. P. (1986, April). *Home environments and toy preferences of extremely precocious students.* Paper presented at the meeting of the American Educational Research Association, San Francisco, CA.

Benderly, B. L. (1987, December). Kids and smoking: Informed consent? *Psychology Today,* p. 24.

Bendiet, J. (1988). Institutional dying: A convergence of cultural values, technology, and social organization. In H. Wass, F. M. Berardo, & R. A. Weimeyer (Eds.), *Dying: Facing the facts* (2nd ed.). Washington, DC: Hemisphere.

Benedek, T. (1970). The family as a psychologic field. In E. J. Anthony & T. Benedek (Eds.), *Parenthood: Its psychology and psychopathology.* Boston: Little, Brown.

Bengtson, V. L. (1985). Diversity and symbolism in grandparents' role. In V. L. Bengtson & J. F. Robertson (Eds.), *Grandparenthood.* Beverly Hills, CA: Sage.

Bengtson, V. L. (1987). Parenting, grandparenting, and intergenerational continuity. In J. B. Lancaster, J. Altmann, A. S. Rossi, & L. R. Sherrod (Eds.), *Parenting across the lifespan: Biosocial dimensions.* New York: Aldine de Gruyter.

Bengtson, V. L., & Robertson, J. F. (Eds.). (1985). *Grandparenthood.* Beverly Hills, CA: Sage.

Benson, R. C. (1983). *Handbook of obstetrics and gynecology* (8th ed.). Los Altos, CA: Lange Medical Publications.

Ben-Zur, H., & Zeldner, M. (1988). Sex differences in anxiety, curiosity, and anger: A cross-cultural study. *Sex Roles, 19,* 335–347.

Berberian, K. E., & Snyder, S. S. (1982). The relationship of temperament and stranger reaction for younger and older infants. *Merrill-Palmer Quarterly, 28,* 79–94.

Berg, J. H., & McQuinn, R. D. (1986). Attraction and exchange in continuing and noncontinuing dating relationships. *Journal of Personality and Social Psychology, 50,* 942–952.

Berger, R. M. (1982). *Gay and gray: The older homosexual male.* Urbana: University of Illinois Press.

Bergesen, A. (1984). Review essay: Centuries of death and dying. *American Journal of Sociology, 90,* 435–439.

Bergstrom-Walan, M., & Nielsen, H. H. (1990). Sexual expression among 60- to 80-year-old men and women: A sample from Stockholm, Sweden. *Journal of Sex Research, 27,* 289–295.

Berkman, S. (1987, January). New ways to get rid of wrinkles. *Good Housekeeping,* p. 151.

Berkman, S. (1987, August). Child asthma alert. *Good Housekeeping,* p. 187.

Berko, J. (1958). The child's learning of English morphology. *Word, 14,* 150–177.

Berkowitz, L. (1965). The concept of aggressive drive: Some additional considerations. In L. Berkowitz (Ed.), *Advances in experimental social psychology* (Vol. 2). Orlando, FL: Academic Press.

Berkowitz, L. (1974). Some determinants of impulsive aggression: Role of mediated association with reinforcement for aggression. *Psychological Review, 81,* 165–176.

Berkowitz, L. (1984). Some effects of thought on anti- and prosocial influences of media events: A cognitive-neoassociation analysis. *Psychological Bulletin, 95,* 410–427.

Berkun, C. (1983). Changing bodies, changing selves. In E. W. Markson (Ed.), *Older women: Issues and prospects.* Lexington, MA: Lexington Books.

Berndt, T. (1979). Developmental changes in conformity to peers and parents. *Developmental Psychology, 15,* 608–616.

Berndt, T. J., Hawkins, J. A., & Hoyle, S. G. (1986). Changes in friendship during a school year: Effects on children's and adolescent's impressions of friendship and sharing with friends. *Child Development, 57,* 1284–1297.

Bernstein, B. (1985, July). A moratorium on heart implants? *Discover,* p. 87.

Berscheid, E. S., & Walster, E. (1978). *Interpersonal attraction* (2nd ed.). Reading, MA: Addison-Wesley.

Berthenthal, B. E. (1987). Emerging discontinuities in the Piagetian legacy. *Contemporary Psychology, 32,* 9–11.

Berthenthal, B. I., & Fischer, K. W. (1978). Development of self-recognition in the infant. *Developmental Psychology, 14,* 44–50.

Berti, A. E., & Bombi, A. S. (1981). The development of the concept of money and its value: A longitudinal study. *Child Development, 52,* 1179–1182.

Berzonsky, M. D. (1987). A preliminary investigation of children's conceptions of life and death. *Merrill-Palmer Quarterly, 33,* 505–513.

Bettelheim, B. (1962). *Symbolic words.* New York: Collier.

Bettelheim, B. (1983). *Freud and man's soul.* New York: Alfred A. Knopf.

Bettelheim, B. (1985, November). Punishment versus discipline. *Atlantic Monthly,* pp. 51–59.

Bettelheim, B. (1987, March). The importance of play. *Atlantic Monthly,* pp. 35–46.

Bianchi, E. C. (1987). *Aging as a spiritual journey.* New York: Crossroads.

Bibby, R. W., & Posterski, D. C. (1985). *The emerging generation: An inside look at Canada's teenagers.* Toronto, Canada: Irwin.

Bichard, S. L., Alden, L., & Walker, L. J. (1988). Friendship understanding in socially accepted, rejected, and neglected children. *Merrill-Palmer Quarterly, 34,* 33–46.

Bigelow, B. J. (1977). Children's friendship expectations: A cognitive developmental study. *Child Development, 48,* 246–253.

Billig, N. (1987). *To be old and sad: Understanding depression in the elderly.* Lexington, MA: Lexington Books.

Bindra, S. (1985). Motivation, the brain, and psychological theory. In S. Koch & D. E. Leary (Eds.), *A century of psychology as science.* New York: McGraw-Hill.

Binkin, N. J., Yip, R., Fleshood, L., & Trowbridge, F. L. (1988). Birth weight and childhood growth. *Pediatrics, 82,* 828–833.

Birkhill, W. R., & Schaie, K. W. (1975). The effect of differential reinforcement of cautiousness in intellectual performance among the elderly. *Journal of Gerontology, 30,* 578–583.

Birnholz, J. C., & Benacerraf, B. R. (1983). The development of human fetal hearing. *Science, 22,* 516–518.

Birren, J. E., Butler, R. N., Greenhouse, S. W., Sokoloff, L., & Yarrow, M. R. (Eds.). (1974). *Human aging I: A biological and behavioral study* (DHEW Publication No. (ADM) 74–122). Rockville, MD: National Institute of Mental Health.

Birren, J. E., Woods, A. M., & Williams, M. V. (1980). Behavioral slowing with age: Causes, organization, and consequences. In L. W. Poon (Ed.), *Aging in the 1980s.* Washington, DC: American Psychological Association.

Blakemore, J. E. O., LaRue, A. A., & Olejnik, A. B. (1979). Sex-appropriate toy preference and the ability to conceptualize toys as sex-role related. *Developmental Psychology, 15,* 339–340.

Blau, Z. S. (1981). *Aging in a changing society* (2nd ed.). New York: Franklin Watts.

Blinn, L. M. (1987). Phototherapeutic intervention to improve self-concept and prevent repeat pregnancies among adolescents. *Family Relations, 36,* 252–257.

Block, J. (1981). Some enduring and consequential structures in personality. In A. I. Rubin, J. Aronoff, R. M. Barclay, & R. A. Zucker (Eds.), *Further explorations in personality* (pp. 27–43). New York: Wiley.

Block, J., Block, J. H., & Keyes, S. (1988). Longitudinally foretelling drug usage in adolescence: Early childhood personality and environmental precursors. *Child Development, 59,* 336–355.

Block, J. H. (1979). *Personality development in males and females: The influence of different socialization.* Master Lectures Series of the American Psychological Association, New York.

Block, J. H., Block, J., & Gjerde, P. F. (1986). The personality of children prior to divorce: A prospective study. *Child Development, 57,* 827–840.

Blomberg, J. F. (1981). Sex-typed channeling behavior in the preschool peer group: A study of toy choice in same-sex and cross-sex play dyads. *Dissertation Abstracts International, 42,* 3066A (University Microfilms No. 82-00, 028).

Blood, R. O., & Wolfe, D. M. (1960). *Husbands and wives, the dynamics of married living.* New York: Free Press.

Bloom, B. S. (1984). *Developing talent in young people.* New York: Ballantine.

Bloom, D. (1981). *What's happening to the age at first birth in the United States?* Paper presented at the annual meeting of the Population Association of America, Washington, DC.

Blos, P. (1962). *On adolescence.* New York: Free Press.

Blos, P. (1967). The second individuation process of adolescence. *Psychoanalytic Study of the Child, 22,* 162–185.

Blumberg, S. H., & Izard, C. E. (1985). Affective and cognitive characteristics of depression in 10- and 11-year-old children. *Journal of Personality and Social Psychology, 49,* 194–202.

Blumenthal, J. A., Williams, R. G. J., Kong, Y., Schanberg, S. M., & Thompson, L. W. (1978). Type A behavior pattern and coronary angiographic findings. *Journal of the American Medical Association, 240,* 761–763.

Blumstein, P., & Schwartz, P. (1983). *American couples: Money, work, sex.* New York: William Morrow.

Blyth, D. A., Bulcroft, R., & Simmons, R. G. (1981, August). *The impact of puberty on adolescents: A longitudinal study.* Paper presented at the annual meeting of the American Psychological Association, Los Angeles.

Boden, M. (1979). *Piaget.* Glasgow, Scotland: Fontana.

Bogatz, G., & Ball, S. (1971). *The second year of "Sesame Street," A continuing evaluation.* Princeton, NJ: Educational Testing Service.

Boggiano, A. K., Main, D. S., & Katz, P. A. (1988). Children's preference for challenge: The role of perceived competence and control. *Journal of Personality and Social Psychology, 54,* 134–141.

Bohannan, P. (1971). *Divorce and after.* New York: Anchor Books.

Borke, A. (1975). Piaget's mountains revisited: Changes in the egocentric landscape. *Developmental Psychology, 11,* 240–243.

Borman, K. M., & Kurdek, L. A. (1987). Grade and gender differences in and the stability and correlates of the structural complexity of children's playground games. *International Journal of Behavioral Development, 10,* 241–251.

Born in the U. S. A. (1987, February 16). *Time,* p. 31.

Borstelmann, L. J. (1983). Children before psychology: Ideas about children from antiquity to the late 1800s. In W. Kessen (Ed.), *Handbook of child psychology: Vol. 1. History, theory and methods.* New York: Wiley.

Boskind-White, M., & White, W. C. (1987). *Bulimarexia: The binge/purge cycle* (2nd ed.). New York: W. W. Norton.

Botkin, J. R. (1988). Anencephalic infants as organ donors. *Pediatrics, 82,* 250–256.

Botwinick, J. (1967). *Cognitive processes in maturity and old age.* New York: Springer.

Botwinick, J. (1977). Intellectual abilities. In J. Birren & K. W. Schaie (Eds.), *Handbook of the psychology of aging.* New York: Van Nostrand Reinhold.

Botwinick, J. (1984). *Aging and behavior: A comprehensive integration of research findings* (3rd ed.). New York: Springer.

Boulette, T. R., & Andersen, S. M. (1985). "Mind control" and the battering of women. *Community Mental Health Journal, 21,* 109–118.

Bovet, M., Parrat-Dayan, S., & Kamii, C. 1986. Early conservation: What does it mean? *Journal of Psychology, 120,* 21–35.

Bowen, E. (1987, May 25). Looking to its roots. *Time,* pp. 26–29.

Bowen, G. L. (1987). Changing gender-role preferences and marital adjustment: Implications for clinical practice. *Family Therapy, 14,* 17–33.

Bower, T. G. R. (1982). *Development in infancy* (2nd ed.). San Francisco: W. H. Freeman.

Bower, T. G. R., Broughton, J. M., & Moore, M. K. (1970). Infant responses to approaching objects: An indicator of response to distal variables. *Perception and Psychophysics, 9,* 193–196.

Bowlby, J. (1951). *Maternal care and mental health.* Geneva, Switzerland: World Health Organization.

Bowlby, J. (1958). The nature of the child's tie to his mother. *International Journal of Psychoanalysis, 39,* 350–373.

Bowlby, J. (1969). *Attachment and loss: Vol. 1. Attachment.* New York: Basic Books.

Bowlby, J. (1973). *Attachment and loss: Vol. 2. Separation.* New York: Basic Books.

Bowlby, J. (1981). *Attachment and loss: Vol. 3. Loss.* New York: Basic Books.

Bowles, L. T. (1981). Wear and tear: Common biological changes of aging. *Geriatrics, 32,* 77–86.

Boyes, M. C., & Walker, L. J. (1988). Implications of cultural diversity for the universality claims of Kohlberg's theory of moral reasoning. *Human Development, 31,* 44–59.

Boyle, H., & Offord, D. R. (1986). Smoking, drinking, and use of illicit drugs among adolescents in Ontario: Prevalence, patterns of use and sociodemographic correlates. *Canadian Medical Association Journal, 135,* 1113–1121.

Bozett, F. W. (Ed.). (1987). *Gay and lesbian parents.* New York: Praeger.

Brackbill, Y. (1970). Continuous stimulation and arousal levels in infants: Additive effects. *Proceedings of the 78th Annual Convention, American Psychological Association, 5,* 271–276.

Brackbill, Y. (1982). Lasting effects of obstetrical medication on children. In J. Belsky (Ed.), *In the beginning.* New York: Columbia University Press.

Brammer, L. M., Nolen, P. A., & Pratt, M. (1982). *Joys and challenges of middle age.* Chicago: Nelson-Hall.

Bray, G. A. (1986). Effects of obesity on health and happiness. In K. D. Brownell & J. P. Foreyt (Eds.), *Handbook of eating disorders.* New York: Basic Books.

Brazelton, T. B., Yogman, M., Als, H., & Tronick, E. (1979). The infant as a focus for family reciprocity. In M. Lewis & L. A. Rosenblum (Eds.), *The child and his family.* New York: Plenum.

Brazzell, J. F., & Acock, A. C. (1988). Influence of attitudes, significant others, and aspirations on how adolescents intend to resolve a premarital pregnancy. *Journal of Marriage and the Family, 50,* 413–425.

Breault, K. D., & Kposowa, J. (1987). Explaining divorce in the United States: A study of 3,111 counties, 1980. *Journal of Marriage and the Family, 49,* 549–558.

Breckenridge, J. N., Gallagher, D., Thompson, L. W., & Peterson, J. (1986). Characteristic depressive symptoms of bereaved elders. *Journal of Gerontology, 41,* 163–168.

Breitmayer, B. J., & Riccuiti, H. N. (1983). *Impact of neonatal temperament on care-giver behavior.* Paper presented at the biennial meeting of the Society for Research in Child Development.

Bremner, J. H. G. (1980). The infant's understanding of space. In M. V. Cox (Ed.), *Are young children egocentric?* London: Concord.

Brennan, M. (1968). The eldest child. *The New Yorker, 44,* 30–33.

Bretherton, I., & Beeghly, M. (1982). Talking about internal states: The acquisition of an explicit theory of mind. *Developmental Psychology, 18,* 906–921.

Bridges, K. M. B. (1932). Emotional development in early infancy. *Child Development, 3,* 324–341.

Bridges, K. M. B. (1933). A study of social development in early infancy. *Child Development, 4,* 36–49.

Brislin, R. W., & Lewis, S. A. (1968). Dating and physical attractiveness. *Psychological Reports, 22,* 976.

Broderick, C. (1984). *Marriage and the family* (2nd ed). Englewood Cliffs, NJ: Prentice-Hall.

Brody, E. M., & Lang, A. (1982, Winter). They can't do it all: Aging daughters with aged mothers. *Generations*, pp. 18–20.

Brody, G. H., Neubaum, E., & Forehand, R. (1988). Serial marriage: A heuristic analysis of an emerging family form. *Psychological Bulletin, 103*, 211–222.

Brody, G. H., & Shaffer, D. R. (1982). Contributions of parents and peers to children's moral socialization. *Developmental Review, 2*, 31–75.

Brody, J. E. (1990, May 8). Huge study of diet indicts fat and meat. *New York Times*, Section C.

Brodzinsky, P. M., Singer, L. M., & Braff, A. M. (1984). Children's understanding of adoption. *Child Development, 55*, 869–878.

Bronfenbrenner, U. (1960). Freudian theories of identification and their derivatives. *Child Development, 31*, 15–40.

Bronfenbrenner, U. (1979). *The ecology of human development: Experiments by nature and design.* Cambridge, MA: Harvard University Press.

Bronson, G. W. (1969). Fear of visual novelty: Developmental patterns in males and females. *Developmental Psychology, 2*, 33–40.

Bronson, G. W. (1972). Infants' reactions to unfamiliar persons and novel objects. *Monographs of the Society for Research in Child Development, 37*, no. 3.

Brooks, G. A., & Fahey, T. D. (1984). *Exercise physiology: Human bioenergetics and its application.* New York: Wiley.

Brooks-Gunn, J., & Lewis, M. (1984). The development of early visual self-recognition. *Developmental Review, 4*, 215–239.

Broughton, J. (1980). The divided self in adolescence. *Human Development, 24*, 13–32.

Broughton, J. (1981). The divided self in adolescence. *Human Development, 24*, 13–32.

Broughton, J. M., & Freeman-Moir, D. J. (1982). *The cognitive-developmental psychology of James Mark Baldwin.* Norwood, NJ: Ablex.

Brown, A. L., Branford, J. D., Ferrara, R. A., & Campione, J. C. (1983). Learning, remembering, and understanding. In P. H. Mussen (Ed.), *Handbook of child psychology* (4th ed.). *Vol. 3. Cognitive development.* J. H. Flavell & E. M. Markman (Eds.). New York: Wiley.

Brown, B. B., Clasen, D. R., & Eicher, S. A. (1986). Perceptions of peer pressure, peer conformity dispositions, and self-reported behavior among adolescents. *Developmental Psychology, 22*, 521–530.

Brown, B. B., & Lohr, M. J. (1987). Peer-group affiliation and adolescent self-esteem: An integration of ego-identity and symbolic-interaction theories. *Journal of Personality and Social Psychology, 52*, 47–55.

Brown, G., & Desforges, C. (1979). *Piaget's theory: A psychological critique.* London, England: Routledge & Kegan Paul.

Brown, J. D. (1975). Adolescent initiation rites: Recent interpretations. In R. E. Grinder (Ed.), *Studies in adolescence: A book of readings in adolescent development* (3rd ed.). New York: Macmillan.

Brown, P., & Eliot, R. (1965). Control of aggression in a nursery school class. *Journal of Experimental Child Psychology, 2*, 103–107.

Brown, P. J., & Konner, M. (1987). An anthropological perspective on obesity. *Annals of the New York Academy of Sciences, 499*, 29–46.

Brown, T. (1988). Ships in the night: Piaget and American cognitive science. *Human Development, 31*, 60–64.

Brubaker, T. H. (1985). *Later life families.* Beverly Hills, CA: Sage.

Brubaker, T. H., & Brubaker, E. (1981, May). Adult child and elderly parent household: Issues in stress for theory and practice. *Alternative Lifestyles*, pp. 242–256.

Bruner, J. S. (1966). *Toward a theory of instruction.* Cambridge, MA: Belknap Press.

Bruner, J. S., Olver, R. R., & Greenfield, P. M. (1966). *Studies in cognitive growth.* New York: Wiley.

Bryant, P. E., Jones, P., Claxton, V., & Perkins, J. (1972). Recognition of shapes across modalities by infants. *Nature, 240*, 303–304.

Bryer, K. B. (1979). The Amish way of death: A study of family support systems. *American Psychologist, 34*, 251–261.

Buehler, C. (1987, January). Initiator status and the divorce transition. *Family Relations*, pp. 82–86.

Buhler, C. (1968). The developmental structure of goal setting in group and individual studies. In C. Buhler & F. Massarik (Eds.), *The course of human life* (pp. 27–54). New York: Springer.

Bulkin, W., & Lukashok, H. (1988). Rx for dying: The case for hospice. *New England Journal of Medicine, 318*, 376–378.

Bullock, M. (1985). Animism in childhood thinking: A new look at an old question. *Developmental Psychology, 21*, 217–226.

Bumpass, L., Sweet, J., & Martin, T. C. (1990). Changing patterns of remarriage. *Journal of Marriage and the Family, 52*, 747–756.

Bumpers, D. (1984). Securing the blessings of liberty for posterity: Preventive health care for children. *American Psychologist, 39*, 896–900.

Burgdorff, K. (1980). *Recognition and reporting of child maltreatment: Findings from the national incidence and severity of child abuse and neglect.* Washington, DC: National Center on Child Abuse and Neglect.

Burroughs, M. (1972). *The stimulation of verbal behavior in culturally disadvantaged three-year-olds.* Unpublished doctoral dissertation, Michigan State University, East Lansing, MI.

Burrus-Bammel, L. L., & Bammel, G. (1985). Leisure and recreation. In J. E. Birren & K. W. Schaie (Eds.), *Handbook of the psychology of aging* (2nd ed.). New York: Van Nostrand Reinhold.

Buss, A. H., & Plomin, R. (1984). *Temperament: Early developing personality traits.* Hillsdale, NJ: Erlbaum.

Buss, D. M. (1988). Love acts: The evolutionary biology of love. In R. J. Sternberg & M. L. Barnes (Eds.), *The anatomy of love.* New Haven, CT: Yale University Press.

Butler, R. N. (1963). The life review: An interpretation of reminiscence in the aged. *Psychiatry, 26*, 65–76.

Butler, R. N. (1989). Productive aging. In V. L. Bengtson & K. W. Schaie (Eds.), *The course of later life: Research & reflections.* New York: Springer.

Butler, R. N., & Lewis, M. I. (1977). *Aging and mental health: Positive psychosocial approaches.* St. Louis, MO: C. V. Mosby.

Butler, R. N., & Lewis, M. I. (1982). *Aging and mental health* (2nd ed.). St. Louis, MO: C. V. Mosby.

Butler, R. N., & Lewis, M. I. (1986). *Love and sex after 40: A guide of men and women for their mid and later years.* New York: Harper & Row.

Butt, D. S., & Beiser, N. (1987). Successful aging: A theme for international psychology. *Psychology and Aging, 2*, 87–94.

Butterfield, H. (1957). *The origins of modern science, 1300–1800.* New York: Macmillan.

Butterworth, G. (1978). Thoughts and things: Piaget's theory. In A. Burton and J. Radford (Eds.), *Perspectives on thinking.* London, England: Methuen.

Butterworth, G., & Hicks, L. (1977). Visual proprioception and postural stability in infancy: A developmental study. *Perception, 6*, 255–262.

Byrne, D. (1964). Repression-sensitization as a dimension of personality. In B. A. Maher (Ed.), *Progress in experimental personality research* (Vol. 1). New York: Academic Press.

Byrne, D., & Clore, G. L. (1970). A reinforcement model of evaluation responses. *Personality: An International Journal*, 103–128.

Byrne, J., Mulvihill, J. J., Myers, M. H., & Connelly, R. R. (1987). Effects of treatment on fertility in long-term survivors of childhood or adolescent cancer. *New England Journal of Medicine, 317*, 1315–1321.

Byrne, J. M., & Horowitz, F. D. (1981). Rocking as a soothing intervention: The influence of direction and type of movement. *Infant Behavior and Development, 4*, 207–218.

C

Cairns, R. B., Cairns, B. D., Neckerman, H. J., Gest, S. D., & Gariepy, J. (1988). Social networks and aggressive behavior: Peer support or peer rejection? *Developmental Psychology, 24*, 815–823.

Caldwell, M. A., & Peplau, L. A. (1982). Sex differences in same-sex friendship. *Sex Roles, 8*, 721–732.

Calkins, D. (1988, August). The hidden handicap. *American Baby*, pp. 7–8.

Callahan, D. (1987). *Setting limits: Medical goals in an aging society.* New York: Simon & Schuster.

Campbell, A. (1981). *The sense of well-being in America.* New York: McGraw-Hill.

Campbell, D. T. (1965). Ethnocentric and other altruistic motives. In D. Levine (Ed.), *Nebraska symposium on motivation* (Vol. 13.). Lincoln, NE: University of Nebraska Press.

Campbell, J. (Ed.). (1972). *The portable Jung.* New York: Viking Press.

Campbell, J. F. (1988). The primary personality factors of younger adolescent Hawaiians. *Genetic, Social, and General Psychology Monographs, 114,* 141–171.

Campbell, J. F. (1991). The primary personality factors of Hawaiian, middle adolescents. *Psychological Reports, 68,* 3–26.

Campbell, T. C., Junshi, C., Brun, T., Parpia, B., Yinsheng, Q., Chunming, C., & Geissler, C. (1990). *China: From diseases of poverty to diseases of affluence. Policy implications of the epidemiological transition.* Ithaca, NY: Division of Nutritional Sciences, Cornell University.

Campbell, T. C., & Junyao, L. (Eds.). (1990). *Diet, lifestyle, and mortality in China: A study of the characteristics of 65 Chinese counties.* Ithaca, NY: Cornell University Press.

Campos, J. J., Barrett, K. C., Lamb, M. E., Goldsmith, H. H., & Stenberg, C. (1983). Socioemotional development. In P. H. Mussen (Ed.), *Handbook of child psychology* (4th ed., Vol. 2). New York: Wiley.

Campos, J. J., Langer, A., & Krowitz, A. (1970). Cardiac responses on the visual cliff in prelocomotor human infants. *Science, 170,* 196–197.

Cannella, G. S. (1986, March/April). Praise and concrete rewards: Concerns for childhood education. *Childhood Education,* pp. 297–301.

Capron, A. M. (1986). Legal and ethical problems in decisions for death. *Law, Medicine & Health Care, 14,* 141–144.

Carey, W. B. (1970). A simplified method for measuring infant temperament. *Journal of Pediatrics, 77,* 188–194.

Cargan, L. (1981). Singles: An examination of two stereotypes. *Family Relations, 30,* 377–385.

Carlson, B. E. (1984). The father's contribution to child care: Effects on children's perceptions of parental roles. *American Journal of Orthopsychiatry, 54,* 123–136.

Carlson, R. (1981). Studies in script theory: 1. Adult analogs of a childhood nuclear scene. *Journal of Personality and Social Psychology, 40,* 501–510.

Carnes, P. (1983). *Out of the shadows: Understanding sexual addiction.* Minneapolis, MN: CompCare Publishers.

Caron, J. J., Caron, R. F., Caldwell, R. C., & Weiss, S. J. (1973). Infant perception of the structural properties of the face. *Developmental Psychology, 9,* 385–399.

Carroll, L. (1988). Concern with AIDS and the sexual behavior of college students. *Journal of Marriage and the Family, 50,* 405–411.

Carson, D. K., & Pauly, K. M. (1990). Perceptions of marriage and family life of young adults with and without histories of parental divorce. *Psychological Reports, 66,* 33–34.

Carter-Saltzman, L. (1980). Biological and sociocultural effects on handedness: Comparison between biological and adoptive families. *Science, 209,* 1263–1265.

Case, R. (1984). The process of stage transition: A neo-Piagetian view. In R. J. Sternberg (Ed.), *Mechanisms of cognitive development.* New York: W. H. Freeman.

Cash, T. F., & Brown, T. A. (1989). Gender and body images: Stereotypes and realities. *Sex Roles, 21,* 361–373.

Caspi, A., Elder, G., & Bem, D. J. (1987). Moving against the world: Life-course patterns of explosive children. *Developmental Psychology, 22,* 303–308.

Caspi, A., Elder, G., & Bem, D. J. (1988). Moving away from the world: Life-course patterns of shy children. *Developmental Psychology, 24,* 824–831.

Castro, F. G., Maddahian, E., Newomb, M. D., & Bentler, P. M. (1987). A multivariate model of the determinants of cigarette smoking among adolescents. *Journal of Health and Social Behavior, 28,* 273–289.

Cattell, R. B. (1971). *Abilities: Their structure, growth, and action.* Boston: Houghton Mifflin.

Cattell, R. B., Wagner, A., & Cattell, M. D. (1970). Adolescent personality structure in Q-data, checked in the High School Personality Questionnaire. *British Journal of Psychology, 61,* 39–54.

Cella, D. F., DeWolfe, A. S., & Fitzgibbon, M. (1987). Ego identity status, identification, and decision-making style in late adolescence. *Adolescence, 22,* 849–861.

Cernoch, J. M., & Porter, R. H. (1985). Recognition of axillary odors by infants. *Child Development, 56,* 1593–1598.

Chafel, J. A. (1988). Social comparisons by children: An analysis of research on sex differences. *Sex Roles, 18,* 461–485.

Chance, P. (1987, April). Master of mastery. *Psychology Today,* pp. 43–46.

Charlesworth, W. R. (1986). Darwin and developmental psychology: 100 years later. *Human Development, 29,* 1–35.

Chatters, L. (1988). Subjective well-being among older black adults: Past trends and current perspectives. In J. S. Jackson (Ed.), *The Black American elderly: Research on physical and psychosocial health.* New York: Springer.

Cherlin, A., & Furstenberg, F. F., Jr. (1986). *The new American grandparent: A place in the family.* New York: Basic Books.

Cherlin, A., & McCarthy, J. (1985). Remarried couple households: Data from the June 1980 Current population survey. *Journal of Marriage and the Family, 47,* 23–30.

Chess, S. & Thomas, A. (1984). *Origins and evolution of behavior disorders: Infancy to early adult life.* New York: Brunner/Mazel.

Chess, S., & Thomas, A. (1987). *Know your child.* New York: Basic Books.

Chiam, H. (1987). Change in self-concept during adolescence. *Adolescence, 22,* 69–76.

Chilman, C. (1986). Some psychosocial aspects of adolescent sexual and contraceptive behaviors in a changing American society. In J. B. Lancaster & B. A. Hamburg (Eds.), *School-age pregnancy and parenthood: Biosocial dimensions.* New York: Aldine De Gruyter.

Chiriboga, D. A. (1982). Adaptation to marital separation in later and earlier life. *Journal of Gerontology, 37,* 109–114.

Chiriboga, D. A., & Cutler, L. (1980). Stress and adaptation: Lifespan perspectives. In L. W. Poon (Ed.), *Aging in the 1980s* (pp. 347–363). Washington, DC: American Psychological Association.

Chollar, S. (1987, December). Latchkey kids: Who are they? *Psychology Today,* p. 12.

Chomsky, C. (1969). *The acquisition of syntax in children from five to ten.* Cambridge, MA: MIT Press.

Chomsky, N. (1972). *Language and mind.* New York: Harcourt.

Chomsky, N. (1978). *Syntactic structures.* The Hague, The Netherlands: Mouton.

Christie, J. F., & Johnsen, E. P. (1987). Reconceptualizing constructive play: A review of the empirical literature. *Merrill-Palmer Quarterly, 33,* 439–452.

Christopher, F. S. (1988). An initial investigation into a continuum of premarital sexual pressure. *Journal of Sex Research, 25,* 255–266.

Chugani, H. T., & Phelps, M. E. (1986). Maturational changes in cerebral function in infants determined by [18]FDG Positron Emission Tomography. *Science, 231,* 840–843.

Cicirelli, V. G. (1976). Categorization behaviors in aging subjects. *Journal of Gerontology, 31,* 676–680.

Cicirelli, V. G. (1980). Sibling relationships in adulthood. In L. W. Poon (Ed.), *Aging in the 1980s* (pp. 455–463). Washington, DC: American Psychological Association.

Cicirelli, V. G. (1983). Adult children and their elderly parents. In T. H. Brubaker (Ed.), *Family relationships in later life.* Beverly Hills, CA: Sage.

Clark, C. M., Jr. (1989, April). Diabetes: Past, present, and future. *Hospital Medicine,* pp. 13–16.

Clark, J. E., Lanphear, A. K., & Riddick, C. C. (1987). The effects of videogame playing on the response selection processing of elderly adults. *Journal of Gerontology, 42,* 82–85.

Clark, M. S., & Reis, H. T. (1988). Interpersonal processes in close relationships. *Annual Review of Psychology, 39,* 609–672.

Clark, R., & Delia, J. (1976). The development of functional persuasive skills in childhood and early adolescence. *Child Development, 47*, 1008–1014.

Clarke, A. M., & Clarke, A. D. B. (1988). The adult outcome of early behavioral abnormalities. *International Journal of Behavioral Development, 11*, 3–19.

Clarke-Stewart, K. A. (1979). Evaluating parental effects on child development. In L. Shulman (Ed.), *Review of research in education* (Vol. 6). Itasca, IL: F. E. Peacock.

Clarke-Stewart, K. A. (1988). Parents' effects on children's development: A decade of progress? *Journal of Applied Developmental Psychology, 9*, 41–84.

Clausen, J. A. (1987). Health and the life course: Some personal observations. *Journal of Health and Social Behavior, 28*, 337–344.

Clay, H. M. (1956). A study of performance in relation to age at two printing works. *Journal of Gerontology, 11*, 417–424.

Clayton, V. (1982). Wisdom and intelligence: The nature and function of knowledge in the later years. *International Journal of Aging and Human Development, 15*, 315–321.

Clayton, V., & Birren, J. E. (1980). The development of wisdom across the lifespan: A reexamination of an ancient topic. In P. B. Baltes & O. G. Brim, Jr. (Eds.), *Lifespan development and behavior* (Vol. 3, pp. 103–135). New York: Academic Press.

Clifford, E. (1971). Body satisfaction in adolescence. *Perceptual and Motor Skills, 33*, 119–125.

Clifton, R., Morrongiello, B., Kulig, J., & Dowd, J. (1981). Developmental changes in auditory localization in infancy. In R. Aslin, J. Alberts, & M. R. Petersen (Eds.), *The development of perception: Psychobiological perspectives: Vol. 1. Audition, somatic perception, and the chemical senses.* New York: Academic Press.

Cohen, E. S., & Kruschwitz, A. L. (1990). Old age in America represented in nineteenth and twentieth century popular sheet music. *The Gerontologist, 30*, 345–354.

Cohen, G. D. (1988). *The brain in human aging.* New York: Springer.

Cohen, J. B., & Reed, D. (1985). The type A behavior pattern and coronary heart disease among Japanese men in Hawaii. *Journal of Behavioral Medicine, 8*, 343–352.

Cohen, L. A. (1987, November). Diet and cancer. *Scientific American, 257*, 42–48.

Cohen, L. B., DeLoache, J. S., & Strauss, M. S. (1979). Infant visual perception. In J. D. Osofsky (Ed.), *Handbook of infant development.* New York: John Wiley.

Cohn, J. P. (1987). The molecular biology of aging. *Bioscience, 37*, 99–102.

Cohn, V. (1975, November). New method of delivering babies cuts down "torture of the innocent." *Capital Times.*

Coie, J. D., & Dodge, K. A. (1983). Continuities and changes in children's social status: A five-year longitudinal study. *Merrill-Palmer Quarterly, 19*, 261–282.

Coie, J. D., Dodge, K. A., & Coppotelli, H. (1982). Dimensions and types of social status: A cross-age perspective. *Developmental Psychology, 18*, 557–570.

Cole, C., & Rodman, H. (1987). When school-age children care for themselves: Issues for family life educators and parents. *Family Relations, 36*, 92–96.

Cole, D. (1987, July). It might have been: Mourning the unborn. *Psychology Today,* pp. 64–65.

Cole, S. (1979). Age and scientific performance. *American Journal of Sociology, 84*, 958–977.

Cole, S. (1980, July). Send our children to work? *Psychology Today,* pp. 44–66.

Cole, S. (1981). *Working kids on working.* New York: Lothrop, Lee & Shephard.

Coleman, J. C. (1980). Friendship and the peer group in adolescence. In J. Adelson (Ed.), *Handbook of adolescent psychology.* New York: Wiley.

Coleman, J. C. (1984). *Intimate relationships, marriage, and the family.* Indianapolis, IN: Bobbs-Merrill.

Collins, J. K. (1974). Adolescent dating intimacy: Norms and peer expectations. *Journal of Youth and Adolescence, 3*, 317–328.

Collins, J. K., & LaGanza, S. (1982). Self-recognition of the face: A study of adolescent narcissism. *Journal of Youth and Adolescence, 11*, 317–328.

Collins, L. M., Sussman, S., Rauch, J. M., Dent, C. W., Johnson, C. A., Hansen, W. B., & Flay, B. R. (1987). Psychosocial predictors of young adolescent cigarette smoking: A sixteen-month, three-wave longitudinal study. *Journal of Applied Social Psychology, 17*, 564–573.

Collins, R. C., & Deloria, D. (1983). Head Start research: A new chapter. *Children Today, 12*, 15–19.

Coltrane, S. (1988, March). Father-child relationships and the status of women: A cross-cultural study. *American Journal of Sociology, 5*, 1060–1095.

Comer, J. P. (1988). Educating poor minority children. *Scientific American, 259*, 42–48.

Comfort, A. (1980). Sexuality in later life. In J. E. Birren & R. B. Sloane (Eds.), *Handbook of mental health and aging.* Englewood Cliffs, NJ: Prentice-Hall.

Committee on Environmental Hazards. (1986). Involuntary smoking—A hazard to children. *Pediatrics, 77*, 755–757.

Compas, B. E. (1987). Coping with stress during childhood and adolescence. *Psychological Bulletin, 101*, 393–403.

Condon, W. S., & Sander, L. W. (1974). Neonate movement is synchronized with adult speech: Interactional participation and language acquisition. *Science, 183*, 99–101.

Condry, J. C., & Ross, D. F. (1985). Sex and aggression: The influence of gender label on the perception of aggression in children. *Child Development, 56*, 225–233.

Conger, J. J. (1981). Freedom and commitment: Families, youth, and social change. *American Psychologist, 36*, 1470–1484.

Conger, J. J. (1988, April). Hostages to fortune: Youth, values, and the public interest. *American Psychologist, 43*, 291–300.

Conger, J. J., & Peterson, A. C. (1984). *Adolescence and youth.* New York: Harper & Row.

Constanzo, P. (1970). Conformity development as a function of self-blame. *Journal of Personality and Social Psychology, 14*, 366–374.

Constanzo, P. R., & Shaw, M. E. (1966). Conformity as a function of age level. *Child Development, 37*, 967–975.

Consumer Product Safety Commission Product Summary Report. (1988). Cited in: Parent alert: Danger on wheels. *Good Housekeeping,* May 1988, p. 227.

Cook, J. A., & Wimberley, D. W. (1983). If I should die before I wake: Religious commitment and adjustment to the death of a child. *Journal for the Scientific Study of Religion, 22*, 222–238.

Coombs, R. H., & Landsverk, J. (1988). Parenting styles and substance use during childhood and adolescence. *Journal of Marriage and the Family, 50*, 473–482.

Cooper, C., Grotevant, H., & Condon, J. (1983). Individuality and connectedness in the family as a context for adolescent identity formation and role-taking skill. In H. Grotevant & C. Cooper (Eds.), *Adolescent development in the family: New directions in child development.* San Francisco: Jossey-Bass.

Cooper, S. (1987). The fetal alcohol syndrome. *Journal of Child Psychology and Psychiatry, 28*, 223–227.

Cornell, L. L. (1989). Gender differences in remarriage after divorce in Japan and the United States. *Journal of Marriage and the Family, 51*, 457–463.

Costa, P. T., & McCrae, R. R. (1980). Still stable after all these years: Personality as a key to some issues in adulthood and old age. In P. B. Baltes & O. G. Brim, Jr. (Eds.), *Life-span development and behavior* (Vol. 3). New York: Academic Press.

Costa, P. T., McCrae, R. R., Zondeman, A. B., Barbano, H. E., Lebowitz, B., & Larson, D. M. (1986). Cross-sectional studies of personality in a national sample: Stability in neuroticism, extroversion, and openness. *Psychology and Aging, 1*, 144–150.

Covell, K., & Abramovitch, R. (1987). Understanding emotion in the family: Children's and parents' attributions of happiness, sadness, and anger. *Child Development, 58*, 985–991.

Cowan, C. P., Cowan, P. A., Heming, G., Garrett, E., Coysh, W. S., Curtis-Boles, H., & Boles, A. J. (1985). Transition to parenthood: His, hers, and theirs. *Journal of Family Issues, 6*, 461–481.

Cowan, G., Warren, L. W., & Young, J. L. (1985). Medical perceptions of menopausal symptoms. *Psychology of Women Quarterly, 9*, 3–14.

Cowan, P. A. (1978). *Piaget, with feeling: Cognitive, social and emotional dimensions.* New York: Holt, Rinehart and Winston.

Cowan, R. (1987). When do children trust counting as a basis for relative number judgments? *Journal of Experimental Child Psychology, 43,* 328–345.

Cowen, E. L., Pederson, A., Babigan, H., Izzo, L. D., & Trost, M. A. (1973). Long-term follow-up of early detected vulnerable children. *Journal of Consulting and Clinical Psychology, 41,* 438–446.

Cowgill, D. O. (1974). Aging and modernization: A revision of the theory. In J. F. Gubrium (Ed.), *Late life.* Springfield, IL: Charles C. Thomas.

Cowgill, D. O. (1986). *Aging around the world.* Belmont, CA: Wadsworth.

Craik, F. I. M. (1977). Age differences in human memory. In J. E. Birren & K. W. Schaie (Eds.), *Handbook of the psychology of aging* (pp. 384–421). New York: Van Nostrand Reinhold.

Cramer, P. (1987). The development of defense mechanisms. *Journal of Personality, 55,* 597–630.

Crano, W. D. (1986). Research methodology: The interaction of substance with investigative form. In V. P. Makosky (Ed.), *The G. Stanley Hall lecture series* (Vol. 6). Washington, DC: American Psychological Association.

Cratty, B. J. (1970). *Perceptual and motor development in infants and children.* New York: Macmillan.

Crockenberg, S. (1987). Predictors and correlates of anger toward and punitive control of toddlers by adolescent mothers. *Child Development, 58,* 964–975.

Crockett, L., Losoff, M., & Petersen, A. C. (1984). Perceptions of the peer group and friendship in early adolescence. *Journal of Early Adolescence, 4,* 155–181.

Crockett, L. J., & Petersen, A. C. (1987). Pubertal status and psychosocial development: Findings from early adolescence study. In R. M. Lerner & T. T. Foch (Eds.), *Biological-psychological interactions in early adolescence: A life-span perspective.* Hillsdale, NJ: Erlbaum.

Crohan, S. E., & Veroff, J. (1989, May). Dimensions of marital well-being among white and black newlyweds. *Journal of Marriage and Family, 51,* 373–383.

Crooks, C. (1988, June). Healing the unborn. *Parents,* pp. 138–143.

Cryan, J. R. (1985, January/February). Research position statement. *Childhood Education,* pp. 219–220.

Crystal, D. (1986). *Listen to your child: A parent's guide to children's language.* Harmondsworth, England: Penguin.

Cuber, J. F., & Harroff, P. B. (1965). *The significant Americans.* New York: Appleton-Century-Crofts.

Cumming, E., & Henry, W. (1961). *Growing old.* New York: Basic Books.

Cunningham, W. R. (1989). Intellectual abilities, speed of response, and aging. In V. L. Bengston & K. W. Schaie (Eds.), *The course of later life: Research and reflections.* New York: Springer.

Cunningham, W. R., & Owens, W. A. (1983). The Iowa State study of the adult development of intellectual abilities. In K. W. Schaie (Ed.), *Longitudinal studies of adult psychological development.* New York: Guilford.

Cutler, N. E. (1979). Age variations in the dimensionality of life satisfaction. *Journal of Gerontology, 34,* 573–578.

D

Dale, P. S. (1976). *Language development* (2nd ed.). New York: Holt, Rinehart & Winston.

Damon, W., & Hart, D. (1982). The development of self-understanding from infancy through adolescence. *Child Development, 53,* 841–864.

Daniels, D., Plomin, R., & Greenhalgh, J. (1984). Correlates of difficult temperament in infancy. *Child Development, 55,* 1184–1194.

Danigelis, N. L., & Fengler, A. P. (1990). Homesharing: How social exchange helps elders live at home. *The Gerontologist, 30,* 162–170.

Darwin, C. (1877). A biographical sketch of an infant. *Mind, 2,* 285–294.

Darwin, C. (1955). *The expression of the emotions in man and animals.* New York: Philosophical Library. (Original work published 1872.)

Darwin, C. R. (1859). *The origin of species.* London: Murray.

Datan, N., Antonovsky, A., & Maoz, B. (1981). *A time to reap: The middle age of women in five Israeli subcultures.* Baltimore, MD: Johns Hopkins University Press.

Datan, N., Rodeheaver, D., & Hughes, F. (1987). Adult development and aging. *Annual Review of Psychology, 38,* 153–180.

David, H. P., Dytryck, Z., Matejcek, Z., & Schuller, V. (1988). *Born unwanted: Developmental effects of denied abortion.* New York: Springer.

Davidson, G. W. (1975). *Living with dying.* Minneapolis, MN: Augsburg.

Davidson, J. M. (1985). Sexuality and aging. In R. Andres, E. L. Bierman, & W. R. Hazzards (Eds.), *Principles of geriatric medicine.* New York: McGraw-Hill.

Davis, J. M., Wheeler, R. W., & Willy, E. (1987). Cognitive correlates of obesity in a nonclinical population. *Psychological Reports, 60,* 1151–1156.

Davis, K. (1985). The future of marriage. In K. Davis (Ed.), *Contemporary marriage: Comparative perspectives on a changing institution.* New York: Russell Sage.

Davis, K. E. (1985). Near and dear: Friendship and love compared. *Psychology Today, 19,* 22–30.

Davis, K. E., & Todd, M. (1982). Friendship and love relationships. In K. E. Davis and T. O. Mitchell (Eds.), *Advances in descriptive psychology* (Vol. 2). Greenwich, CT: JAI Press.

Day, R. D., & Hooks, D. (1987). Miscarriage: A special type of family crisis. *Family Relations, 36,* 305–310.

DeAngelis, T. (1986, November). Twins: Mirror image more than skin deep. *APA Monitor,* p. 21.

DeAngelis, T. (1988, February). Microtubules called Alzheimer's clue. *APA Monitor,* p. 8.

DeAngelis, T. (1989, November). Men's interaction style can be tough on women. *APA Monitor,* p. 12.

DeCasper, A. J., & Fifer, W. P. (1980). Of human bonding: Newborns prefer their mothers' voices. *Science, 208,* 1174–1176.

Deci, E. L., & Ryan, R. M. (1985). *Intrinsic motivation and self determination in human behavior.* New York: Plenum Press.

Decker, M. D., Dewey, M. J., Hutcheson, R. H., & Shafner, W. (1984). The use and efficacy of child restraint devices. *Journal of the American Medical Association, 252,* 2571–2575.

DeFrain, J., Taylor, J., & Ernst, L. (1982). *Coping with sudden infant death.* Lexington, MA: D. C. Heath.

Dellmann-Jenkins, M., Lambert, D., Fruit, D., & Dinero, T. (1986, January/February). Old and young together: Effect of an educational program on preschoolers' attitudes toward older people. *Childhood Education,* pp. 206–212.

DeLoache, J. S., Cassidy, D. J., & Carpenter, C. J. (1987). The three bears are all boys: Mothers' gender labeling of neutral picture book characters. *Sex Roles, 17,* 163–178.

DeLoache, J. S., & DeMendoza, O. A. P. (1987). Joint picturebook interactions of mothers and 1-year-old children. *British Journal of Developmental Psychology, 5,* 111–123.

DeLoache, J. S., Sugarman, S., & Brown, A. L. (1985). The development of error correction strategies in young children's manipulative play. *Child Development, 56,* 928–939.

DeLucia, L. A. (1963). The toy preference test: A measure of sex-role identification. *Child Development, 34,* 107–117.

deMause, L. (1974). The evolution of childhood. In L. deMause (Ed.), *The history of childhood.* New York: Harper & Row.

Dement, W. C., Miles, L. E., & Bliswise, D. L. (1982). Physiological markers of aging: Human sleep pattern changes. In M. E. Reff & E. L. Schneider (Eds.), *Biological markers of aging.* Bethesda, MD: National Institute of Health (Publication No. 82-2221).

Demo, D. H., & Acock, A. C. (1988). The impact of divorce on children. *Journal of Marriage and the Family, 50,* 619–648.

Denckla, W. D. (1974). Role of the pituitary and thyroid glands in the decline of minimal 02 consumption with age. *Journal of Clinical Investigation, 53,* 572–581.

Denney, N. (1982). Aging and cognitive changes. In B. Wolman (Ed.), *Handbook of developmental psychology.* Englewood Cliffs, NJ: Prentice-Hall.

Denney, N. W., & Denney, D. R. (1982). The relationship between classification and questioning strategies among adults. *Journal of Gerontology, 37,* 190–196.

Denney, N. W., & Palmer, A. M. (1981). Adult age differences on traditional and practical problem-solving measures. *Journal of Gerontology, 36,* 323–328.

Dennis, W. (1966). Creative productivity of persons engaged in scholarship, the sciences, and the arts. *Journal of Gerontology, 21,* 1–8.

Dennis, W., & Dennis, M. G. (1940). The effects of cradling practice upon the onset of walking in Hopi children. *Journal of Genetic Psychology, 56,* 77–86.

Dennison, B. A., Straus, J. H., Melits, E. D., & Charney, E. (1988). Childhood physical fitness tests: Predictor of adult physical activity levels? *Pediatrics, 82,* 324–329.

Derdeyn, A., & Scott, E. (1984). Joint custody: A critical analysis and appraisal. *American Journal of Orthopsychiatry, 54,* 199–209.

deRosenroll, D. A. (1987). Early adolescent egocentrism: A review of six articles. *Adolescence, 22,* 791–802.

Deutsch, F. M., Ruble, D. N., Felming, A., Brooks-Gunn, J., & Stangor, C. (1988). Information-seeking and maternal self-definition during the transition to motherhood. *Journal of Personality and Social Psychology, 55,* 420–431.

de Vaus, D. A. (1983). The elative importance of parents and peers for adolescent religious orientation: An Australian study. *Adolescence, 4,* 147–158.

deVilliers, P. A., & deVilliers, J. G. (1979). *Early language.* Cambridge, MA: Harvard University Press.

de Vos, S. (1989). Leaving the parental home: Patterns in six Latin American countries. *Journal of Marriage and the Family, 51,* 615–626.

de Vos, S. (1990). Extended family living among older people in six Latin American countries. *Journal of Gerontology, 45,* S87–S94.

Dewsberry, D. A. (1984). *Comparative psychology in the twentieth century.* Stroudsburg, PA: Hutchinson Ross.

Diamont, L. (1987). Introduction. In L. Diamont (Ed.), *Male and female homosexuality.* Washington, DC: Hemisphere.

Dickman, I. R. (1983). *Making life more livable.* New York: American Foundation for the Blind.

DiLeo, J. C., Moely, B. E., & Sulzer, J. L. (1979). Frequency and modifiability of children's preferences for sex-typed toys, games, and occupations. *Child Study Journal, 9,* 141–159.

Dimsdale, J. E. (1988, January 14). A perspective on type A behavior and coronary disease. *New England Journal of Medicine,* pp. 110–112.

Dinsmore, K. E. (1988, April). Baby's first books. *Childhood Education,* pp. 215–219.

Dion, K. K., Berscheid, E., & Walster, E. (1972). What is beautiful is good. *Journal of Personality and Social Psychology, 24,* 285–290.

Directs, A., & Holmes, H. B. (1986, November). Miracle drug, miracle baby. *New Scientist, 6,* 53–55.

Dittmann-Kohli, F., & Baltes, P. B. (1986). Toward a neofunctionalist conception of adult intellectual development: Wisdom as a prototypical case of intellectual growth. In C. Alexander & E. Langer (Eds.), *Beyond formal operations: Alternative endpoints to human development.* New York: Oxford University Press.

Dodd, D. H., & White, R. M. (1980). *Cognition: Mental structures and processes.* Boston, MA: Allyn & Bacon.

Dodge, K. A. (1986). A social information processing model of social competence in children. In M. Perlmutter (Ed.), *Minnesota symposia on child psychology* (Vol. 18, pp. 77–125). Hillsdale, NJ: Erlbaum.

Dollard, J., Doob, L. W., Miller, N. E., Mowrer, O. H., & Sears, R. R. (1939). *Frustration and aggression.* New Haven, CT: Yale University Press.

Dollard, J., & Miller, N. E. (1950). *Personality and psychotherapy.* New York: McGraw-Hill.

Donaldson, M. (1978). *Children's minds.* Glasgow, Scotland: Collins.

Donovan, R. (1984, February/March). Planning for an aging workforce. *Aging,* pp. 4–7.

Doress, Paula Brown, Siegal, Diana Laskin, and the Midlife and Older Women Book Project. (1987). *Ourselves, growing older.* New York: Touchstone Books.

Dornbusch, S. M., Ritter, P. L., Leiderman, P. H., Roberts, D. F., & Fraleigh, M. J. (1987). The relation of parenting style to adolescent school performance. *Child Development, 58,* 1244–1257.

Douvan, E., & Adelson, J. (1966). *The adolescent experience.* New York: Wiley.

Dowie, M. (1985, January). Manhattan project for the unborn. *Mother Jones,* p. 20.

Drabman, R. S., Cordus, C. D., Hammer, D., Jarvie, G. J., & Horton, W. (1979). Developmental trends in eating rates of normal and overweight children. *Child Development, 50,* 211–216.

Dreikurs, R. (1972). *The challenge of child training.* New York: Hawthorne.

Dreikurs, R., & Soltz, V. (1964). *Children: The challenge.* New York: Hawthorne.

Droege, R. (1982). A psychological study of the formation of the middle adult life structure in woman. *Dissertation Abstracts International, 43,* 1635B (University Microfilms No. 82-23517).

Drotar, D. (1987). Implications of recent advances in neonatal and infant behavioral assessment. *Developmental and Behavioral Pediatrics, 8,* 51–53.

Dubow, E. F., Huesmann, L. R., & Eron, L. D. (1987). Child correlates of adult ego development. *Child Development, 58,* 859–869.

Dumont, R. G., & Foss, D. C. (1972). *The American view of death: Acceptance or denial?* Cambridge, MA: Schenkman.

Dunn, J. (1975). Patterns of early interaction: Continuities and consequences. In H. R. Schaffer (Ed.), *Studies in mother-infant interaction.* London: Academic Press.

Dunn, J., Kendrick, C., & MacNamee, R. (1981). The reaction of first-born children to the birth of a sibling: Mother's reports. *Journal of Child Psychology and Psychiatry, 22,* 1–18.

Dunphy, D. C. (1963). The social structure of urban adolescent peer groups. *Sociometry, 26,* 230–246.

Dunst, C. J., & Lingerfelt, B. (1985). Maternal ratings of temperament and operant learning in 2- to 3-month-old infants. *Child Development, 56,* 555–563.

Durkheim, E. (1961). *Moral education: A study in the theory and application of the sociology of moral education* (E. K. Wilson & H. Schnurer, Trans.). New York: Free Press. (Original work published 1925)

Durkin, D. (1966). *Children who read early.* New York: Teachers College Press.

Duvall, E. M. (1977). *Marriage and family development* (5th ed.). Philadelphia, PA: Lippincott.

Duvall, E. M., & Hill, R. L. (1948). *Report of the committee on the dynamics of family interaction.* Working paper prepared for the National Conference on the Family, Washington, DC.

E

Eagleston, J. R., Kirmil-Gray, K., Thoresen, C. E., Wiedenfeld, S. A., Bracke, P., Heft, L., & Arnow, B. (1986). Physical health correlates of Type A behavior in children and adolescents. *Journal of Behavioral Medicine, 4,* 341–362.

Earle, J. R., & Perricone, P. J. (1986). Premarital sexuality: A ten-year study of attitudes and behavior on a small university campus. *Journal of Sex Research, 22,* 304–310.

Eberhard, M. T. W. (1975). The evolution of social behavior by kin selection. *Quarterly Review of Biology, 50,* 1–33.

Ebersole, P., & Hess, P. (1981). *Toward healthy aging: Human needs and nursing response.* St. Louis, MO: Mosby.

Eckerman, C. O., & Whatley, J. L. (1977). Toys and social interaction between peers. *Child Development, 48,* 1648–1656.

Eden, A. N. (1988, June). Toilet-training tips. *American Baby,* pp. 55, 62.

Edwards, C. P. (1982). Moral development in comparative cultural perspective. In D. A. Wagner & H. W. Stevenson (Eds.), *Cultural perspectives in child development.* San Francisco, CA: W. H. Freeman.

Edwards, D., & Middleton, D. (1988). Conversational remembering and family relationships: How children learn to remember. *Journal of Social and Personal Relationships, 5,* 3–25.

Edwards, J. N., Johnson, D. R., & Booth, A. (1987, April). Coming apart: A prognostic instrument of marital breakup. *Family Relations, 36,* 168–170.

Egeland, B., & Farber, E. A. (1984). Infant-mother attachment: Factors related to its development and changes over time. *Child Development, 55,* 753–771.

Eichorn, D. H. (1979). Physical development. In J. D. Osofsky (Ed.), *Handbook of infant development*. New York: John Wiley & Sons.

Eimas, P. D. (1975). Speech perception in infancy. In L. B. Cohen & P. Salapatek (Eds.), *Infant perception* (Vol. 2). New York: Academic Press.

Eimas, P. D. (1985). The perception of speech in early infancy. *Scientific American, 252,* 46–52.

Eisenberg, L. (1965, July/August). A developmental approach to adolescence. *Children Today,* pp. 131–135.

Eisenberg, N., Lennon, R., & Roth, K. (1983). Prosocial development: A longitudinal study. *Developmental Psychology, 19,* 846–855.

Eisenhandler, S. A. (1990). The asphalt identikit: Old age and the driver's license. *International Journal of Aging and Human Development, 30,* 1–14.

Ekerdt, D. J., Bosse, R., & Levkoff, S. (1985). An empirical test for phases of retirement. *Journal of Gerontology, 40,* 95–101.

Ekerdt, D. J., Bosse, R., & LoCastro, J. D. (1983). Claims that retirement improves health. *Journal of Gerontology, 38,* 231–236.

Ekman, P., & Oster, H. (1979). Facial expressions of emotions. *Annual Review of Psychology, 30,* 527–554.

Elder, G. (1963). Parental power legitimation and its effect on the adolescent. *Sociometry, 26,* 50–65.

Eldredge, L., & Salamy, A. (1988). Neurobehavioral and neurophysiological assessment of healthy and "at-risk" full-term infants. *Child Development, 59,* 186–192.

Eldridge, N. S., & Gilbert, L. A. (1990). Correlates of relationship satisfaction in lesbian couples. *Psychology of Women Quarterly, 4,* 43–62.

Eliade, M. (1958). *Birth & rebirth: The religious meaning of initiation in human culture.* New York: Harper & Brothers.

Elias, S., & Annas, G. J. (1987). Routine prenatal genetic screening. *New England Journal of Medicine, 317,* 1407–1408.

Elkind, D. (1975). Perceptual development in children. *American Scientist, 63,* 33–41.

Elkind, D. (1978). *The child's reality: Three developmental themes.* Hillsdale, NJ: Erlbaum.

Elkind, D. (1981). *The hurried child: Growing up too fast too soon.* Reading, MA: Addison-Wesley.

Elkind, D. (1987, May). The child yesterday, today, and tomorrow. *Young Children,* pp. 6–11.

Elkind, D. (1988, July). Bound for college. *Parents,* p. 175.

Elkind, D., & Bowen, R. (1979). Imaginary audience behavior in children and adolescents. *Developmental Psychology, 15,* 38–44.

Ellis, L., & Ames, M. A. (1987). Neurohormonal functioning and sexual orientation: A theory of homosexuality-heterosexuality. *Psychological Bulletin, 101,* 233–258.

Ellis, S., Rogoff, B., & Cromer, C. C. (1981). Age segregation in children's social interactions. *Developmental Psychology, 17,* 399–407.

Ellis-Schwabe, M., & Thornburg, H. D. (1986). Conflict areas between parents and their adolescents. *Journal of Psychology, 120,* 59–68.

Elster, A. B., & Lamb, M. E. (1986). Adolescent fathers: The understudied side of adolescent pregnancy. In J. B. Lancaster & B. A. Hamburg (Eds.), *School-age pregnancy and parenthood: Biosocial dimensions.* New York: Aldine De Gruyter.

Emery, R. E., Hetherington, E. M., & Dilalla, L. F. (1984). Divorce, children and social policy. In H. W. Stevenson & A. E. Siegel (Eds.), *Child development research and social policy.* Chicago, IL: University of Chicago Press.

Emmerich, W. (1966). Continuity and stability in early social development: II. Teacher's ratings. *Child Development, 37,* 17–27.

Emmerich, W., Goldman, K. S., Kirsh, B., & Sharabany, R. (1976). *Development of gender constancy in economically disadvantaged children.* Report of the Educational Testing Service, Princeton, New Jersey.

Engel, G. (1977, November). Emotional stress and sudden death. *Psychology Today,* pp. 114–115, 153.

Engel, S. S. (1989, April). Prescribing a proper diabetic diet. *Hospital Medicine,* pp. 20–26.

Engler, B. (1985). *Personality theories: An introduction* (2nd ed.). Boston: Houghton Mifflin.

Entwisle, D. R., & Alexander, K. L. (1987). Long-term effects of cesarean delivery on parents' beliefs and children's schooling. *Developmental Psychology, 23,* 676–682.

Entwisle, D. R., & Alexander, K. L. (1988). Achievement in the first two years of school: Patterns and processes. *Monographs of the Society in Child Development, 53,* 1–157.

Erens, P. (1985, October). Bodily harm: Help for women trapped in the binge-purge cycle. *Ms/Campus Times,* pp. 62–66, 82.

Ericsson, R. J., & Glass, R. H. (1982). *Getting pregnant in the 1980s: New advances in infertility treatment and sex preselection.* Berkeley, CA: University of California Press.

Erikson, E. H. (1959). Identity and the life cycle. *Psychological Issues,* monograph *1,* 1–171. New York: International Universities Press.

Erikson, E. H. (1963). *Childhood and society* (2nd ed.). New York: Norton.

Erikson, E. H. (1964). *Insight and responsibility.* New York: Norton.

Erikson, E. H. (1968). *Identity: Youth and crisis.* New York: Norton.

Erikson, E. H. (1972). Eight ages of man. In C. S. Lavatelli & F. Stendler (Eds.), *Readings in child behavior and child development.* San Diego, CA: Harcourt Brace Jovanovich.

Erikson, E. H. (1976). Reflections on Dr. Borg's life cycle. *Daedalus, 105,* 1–28.

Erikson, E. H. (1978). *Adulthood.* New York: W. W. Norton.

Erikson, E. H. (1980). *Identity and the life cycle.* New York: Norton.

Erikson, E. H. (1981). *Youth, change, and challenge.* New York: Basic Books.

Erikson, E. H. (1982). *The life cycle completed: A review.* New York: Norton.

Erikson, E. H. (1985). *The life cycle completed.* New York: Norton.

Erikson, E. H., & Erikson, J. (1987). The power of the newborn. In S. P. Schlein (Ed.), *A way of looking at things: Selected papers from 1930 to 1980. Erik Erikson.* New York: W. W. Norton. (Originally published in 1953.)

Eron, L. (1982). Parent-child interaction, television, violence, and aggression of children. *American Psychologist, 37,* 197–211.

Evans, R. I. (1981). *Dialogue with Jean Piaget* (Eleanor Dickworth, Trans.). New York: Praeger.

Eveleth, P. B. (1986). Timing of menarche: Secular trend and population differences. In J. B. Lancaster & B. A. Hamburg (Eds.), *School-age pregnancy and parenthood: Biosocial dimensions.* New York: Aldine de Gruyter.

Everson, R. B., Sandler, D. P., & Wilcox, A. J. (1986, September 27). Effect of passive exposure to smoking on age at natural menopause. *British Medical Journal, 293,* 792.

F

Fabricus, W. V., Schwanenflugel, P. J., Kyllonen, P. C., Barclay, C. R., & Denton, S. M. (1989). Developing theories of the mind: Children's and adults' concepts of mental activities. *Child Development, 60,* 1278–1290.

Fagan, J. F., III, & Singer, L. T. (1979). The role of simple feature differences in infants' recognition of faces. *Infant Behavior and Development, 2,* 39–45.

Fagot, B. I., Hagan, R., Leinbach, M. D., & Kronsberg, S. (1985). Differential reactions to assertive and communicative acts of toddler boys and girls. *Child Development, 56,* 1499–1505.

Fallon, A. E., Rozin, P., & Pliner, P. (1984). The child's conception of food: The development of food rejections with special reference to disgust and contamination sensitivity. *Child Development, 55,* 566–575.

Faludi, S. (1987, July/August). The marriage trap. *Ms.,* pp. 62–66, 191.

Fantz, R. L. (1961). The origin of form perception. *Scientific American, 204,* 66–72.

Fantz, R. L. (1965). Visual perception from birth as shown by pattern selectivity. *Annals of the New York Academy of Science, 118,* 793–814.

Fantz, R. L. (1970). Visual perception and experience in infancy: Issues and approaches. In B. Lindsly & F. Young (Eds.). *Early experience and visual information processing in perceptual and reading disorders.* Washington, DC: National Academy of Sciences.

Farber, S. (1981, January). Telltale behavior of twins. *Psychology Today*, pp. 58–64.

Farrell, M. P., & Rosenberg, S. D. (1981). *Men at midlife*. Boston, MA: Auburn.

Fehr, B. (1987). Prototype analysis of the concepts of love and commitment. Cited in Clark, M. S., & Reis, H. T. (1988). Interpersonal processes in close relationships. *Annual Review of Psychology, 39*, 609–672.

Feifel, H., Hannon, S., Jones, R., & Edwards, L. (1972). Physicians consider death. In R. Kastenbaum & R. Aisenberg (Eds.), *The psychology of death*. New York: Springer.

Feiring, C., & Lewis, M. (1987). The child's social network: Sex differences from three to six years. *Sex Roles, 17*, 621–636.

Feldman, J. F., Brody, N., & Miller, S. A. (1980). Sex differences in non-elicited neonatal behaviors. *Merrill-Palmer Quarterly, 26*, 63–73.

Feldman, R. S., Devin-Sheehan, L., & Allen, V. L. (1976). Children tutoring children: A critical review of research. In V. L. Allen (Ed.), *Children as teachers: Theory and research on tutoring*. New York: Academic Press.

Feldman, S. S., & Aschenbrenner, B. (1983). Impact of parenthood on various aspects of masculinity and femininity. *Developmental Psychology, 19*, 278–289.

Feldman, S. S., Biringen, Z. C., & Nash, S. C. (1981). Fluctuations of sex-related self-attributions as a function of stage of the family life cycle. *Developmental Psychology, 17*, 24–35.

Ferraro, K. F. (1990). Cohort analysis of retirement preparation: 1974–1981. *Journal of Gerontology: Social Sciences, 45*, S21–S44.

Fetuses weigh less if father smokes. (1986). *New Scientist, 28*, 19.

Feuerstein, R. (1980). *Instrumental enrichment: An intervention program for cognitive modifiability*. Baltimore, MD: University Park Press.

Field, J. (1976). Relation of young infants' reaching behavior to stimulus distance and solidity. *Developmental Psychology, 12*, 444–448.

Field, T. M. (1981). Infant arousal, attention, and affect during early interaction. In L. P. Lipsitt (Ed.), *Advances in infancy* (Vol. 1, pp. 57–100). Norwood, NJ: Ablex.

Field, T. M., Woodson, R., Greenberg, R., & Cohen, D. (1982). Discrimination and imitation of facial expressions by neonates. *Science, 218*, 179–181.

Finch, C. E. (1989). The brain, genes and aging. In V. L. Bengtson & K. W. Schaie (Eds.), *The course of later life: Research and reflections*. New York: Springer.

Fincham, F., & O'Leary, K. D. (1983). Causal inferences for spouse behavior in maritally distressed and nondistressed couples. *Journal of Clinical and Social Psychology, 1*, 42–57.

Fine, M. J. (1980). *Intervention with hyperactive children: A case study approach*. New York: Spectrum.

Fine, S. (1987). Children in divorce, custody and access situations: An update. *Journal of Child Psychology and Psychiatry, 28*, 361–364.

Fingarette, H. (1988). *Heavy drinking: The myth of alcoholism as a disease*. Berkeley, CA: University of California Press.

Finley, N. J. (1989, February). Theories of family labor as applied to gender differences in caregiving for elderly parents. *Journal of Marriage and the Family, 51*, 79–86.

Finn, S. E. (1986). Stability of personality self-ratings over 30 years: Evidence for an age/cohort interaction. *Journal of Personality and Social Psychology, 50*, 816.

Fischer, D. H. (1978). *Growing old in America*. (2nd ed.). New York: Oxford University Press.

Fischer, K. W., & Silvern, L. (1985). Stages and individual differences in cognitive development. *Annual Review of Psychology, 36*, 613–648.

Fischer, L. R. (1986). *Linked lives: Adult daughters and their mothers*. New York: Harper & Row.

Fischman, J. (1987, December). Getting tough. *Psychology Today*, pp. 26–28.

Fisher, L. A., & Bauman, K. E. (1988). Influence and selection in the friend-adolescent relationship: Findings from studies of adolescent smoking and drinking. *Journal of Applied Social Psychology, 18*, 289–314.

Fisher, W. A., Byrne, D., White, L. A., & Kelley, K. (1988). Erotophobia-erotophilia as a dimension of personality. *Journal of Sex Research, 25*, 123–151.

Fisher, W. A., & Gray, J. (1988). Erotophobia-erotophilia and sexual behavior during pregnancy and postpartum. *Journal of Sex Research, 25*, 379–396.

Fitzgerald, H. E., & Brackbill, Y. (1976). Classical conditioning in infancy: Development and constraints. *Psychological Bulletin, 83*, 353–376.

Flavell, J. (1977). *Cognitive development*. Englewood Cliffs, NJ: Prentice-Hall.

Flavell, J. H. (1985). *Cognitive development* (2nd ed.). Englewood Cliffs, NJ: Prentice-Hall.

Flavell, J. H. (1986). The development of children's knowledge about the appearance-reality distinction. *American Psychologist, 41*, 418–426.

Flavell, J. H., Flavell, E. R., Green, F. L., & Wilcox, S. A. (1981). The development of three spatial perspective-taking rules. *Child Development, 52*, 356–358.

Flavell, J. H., Shipstead, S. G., & Croft, K. (1978). Young children's knowledge about visual perception. *Child Development, 49*, 1208–1211.

Fleming, A. S., Ruble, D. N., Flett, G. L., & Shaul, D. L. (1988). Postpartum adjustment in first-time mothers: Relations between mood, maternal attitudes and mother-infant interactions. *Developmental Psychology, 24*, 71–81.

Fletcher, A. B. (1987). Pain in the neonate. *New England Journal of Medicine, 317*, 1347–1348.

Floderus-Myrhed, B., Pedersen, N., & Rasmuson, I. (1980). Assessment of heritability or personality, based on a short form of the Eysenck Personality Inventory. *Behavior Genetics, 10*, 153–162.

Flynn, C. P. (1987). Relationship violence: A model for family professionals. *Family Relations, 36*, 295–299.

Fodor, E. (1985). The power motive, group conflict and physiological arousal. *Journal of Personality and Social Psychology, 49*, 1408–1415.

Fomon, S. J., Filer, L. J., Anderson, T. A., & Ziegler, E. E. (1979). Recommendations for feeding normal infants. *Pediatrics, 63*, 52.

Fost, N. (1988, October/November). Organs from anencephalic infants: An idea whose time has not yet come. *Hastings Center Report*, pp. 5–10.

Fost, N. C., Bartholome, W. G., & Bell, W. R. (1988). Fetal therapy: Ethical considerations. *Pediatrics, 81*, 898–899.

Foulkes, D. (1982). *Children's dreams: Longitudinal studies*. New York: Wiley.

Fraiberg, S., Adelson, E., & Shapiro, V. (1980). Ghosts in the nursery: A psychoanalytic approach to the problems of impaired infant-mother relationships. *Journal of the American Academy of Child Psychiatry, 14*, 387–421.

Frank, D. A., Zuckerman, B. S., & Amaro, H. (1988). Cocaine use during pregnancy: Prevalence and correlates. *Pediatrics, 82*, 888–895.

Frank, K. A., Heller, S. S., Kornfeld, D. S., Sporn, A. A., & Weiss, M. B. (1978). Type A behavior pattern and coronary angiographic findings. *Journal of the American Medical Association, 240*, 761–763.

Franzoi, S. L., & Herzog, M. E. (1987). Judging physical attractiveness: What body aspects do we use? *Personality and Social Psychology Bulletin, 13*, 19–33.

Fraser, L. (1986, December). Oh boy, let's have a baby! *Mother Jones*, pp. 16–17.

Freedman, D. G. (1971). Behavioral assessment in infancy. In G. A. B. Stoelinga & J. J. Van Der Werff Ten Bosch (Eds.), *Normal and abnormal development of brain and behavior*. Leiden, The Netherlands: Leiden University Press.

Freeman, E. B. (1985, November/December). When children face divorce: Issues and implications of research. *Childhood Education*, pp. 130–134.

Freud, A. (1958). Adolescence. *Psychoanalytic Study of the Child, 16*, 225–278.

Freud, A. (1965). *Normality and pathology in childhood*. New York: International Universities Press.

Freud, A., & Dann, S. (1951). An experiment in group upbringing. *Psychoanalytic Study of the Child, 6*, 127–168.

Freud, S. (1905). Three essays on the theory of sexuality. In J. Strachey (Ed. & Trans.), *The standard edition of the complete psychological works of Sigmund Freud* (Vol. 7). London: Hogarth Press.

Freud, S. (1940). *An outline of psychoanalysis*. New York: Norton.

Freud, S. (1953). *Introductory lectures on psycho-analysis* (J. Riviere, Trans.). London, England: Allen & Unwin. (Original work published 1923.)

Freud, S. (1959a). The defense neuro-psychoses. In E. Jones (Ed.), *Collected papers* (Vol. 1, J. Riviere, Trans.). New York: Basic Books. (Originally published in 1894.)

Freud, S. (1959b). Repression. In E. Jones (Ed.), *Collected papers* (Vol. 4, J. Riviere, Trans.). New York: Basic Books. (Originally published in 1915.)

Freud, S. (1961). Some psychical consequences of the anatomical distinction between the sexes. In J. Strachey (Ed.), *The standard edition of the complete psychological works of Sigmund Freud* (Vol. 19). London: Hogarth Press. (Original work published 1925.)

Freudenheim, J. L., Graham, S., Marshall, J. R., Haughey, B. P., & Wilkinson, G. (1990). A case-control study of diet and rectal cancer in western New York. *American Journal of Epidemiology, 131,* 612–624.

Fried, P. A., & Oxorn, H. (1980). *Smoking for two: Cigarettes and pregnancy.* New York: Free Press.

Friedman, H. S., & Booth-Kewley, S. (1987). The "disease-prone personality": A meta-analytic view of the construct. *American Psychologist, 42,* 539–555.

Friedman, M., & Rosenman, R. H. (1974). *Type A behavior and your heart.* New York: Alfred A. Knopf.

Friedman, S., & Ryan, L. S. (1986). A systems perspective on problematic behaviors in the nursing home. *Family Therapy, 13,* 265–273.

Friedrich, O. (1983, August 15). What do babies know? *Time,* pp. 52–59.

Fries, J. A., & Crapo, L. M. (1981). *Vitality and aging: Implications of the rectangular curve.* San Francisco, CA: Freeman.

Frisch, R. E. (1988). Fatness and fertility. *Scientific American, 258,* 88–95.

Fromm, E. (1947). *Man for himself.* New York: Rinehart.

Fromm, E. (1956). *The art of loving.* New York: Harper & Row.

Fromm, E. (1976). *To have or to be?* New York: Harper & Row.

Fry, C. L. (1985). Culture, behavior, and aging in the comparative perspective. In J. E. Birren and K. W. Schaie (Eds.), *Handbook of the psychology of aging* (2nd ed.). New York: Van Nostrand Reinhold.

Fuqua, R. W., Bartsch, T. W., & Phye, G. D. (1975). An investigation of the relationship between cognitive tempo and creativity in preschool-age children. *Child Development, 466,* 779–782.

Furman, W., & Bierman, K. L. (1983). Developmental changes in young children's conceptions of friendship. *Child Development, 54,* 549–556.

Furstenberg, F. (1976). *Unplanned parenthood: The social consequences of teenage childbearing.* New York: Free Press.

Furstenberg, F. F., Jr. (1981). Remarriage and intergenerational relations. In R. W. Fogel, E. Hatfield, S. B. Kiesler, & E. Shanas (Eds.), *Aging: Stability and change in the family.* New York: Academic Press.

Furstenberg, F. F., Jr., Herceg-Baron, R., Shea, J., & Webb, D. (1986). Family communication and contraceptive use among sexually active adolescents. In J. B. Lancaster & B. A. Hamburg (Eds.), *School-age pregnancy and parenthood: Biosocial dimensions.* New York: Aldine de Gruyter.

Furstenberg, F. F., Jr., & Spanier, G. B. (1987). *Recycling the family: Remarriage after divorce.* Newbury Park, CA: Sage.

Futterman, E. H., & Hoffman, E. (1983). Mourning the fatally ill child. In J. E. Schowalter & P. R. Patterson (Eds.), *The child and death.* New York: Columbia University Press.

G

Gagnon, J. H., & Simon, W. (1987). The sexual scripting of oral genital contacts. *Archives of Sexual Behavior, 16,* 1–25.

Galambos, N. L., & Garbarino, J. (1983, July/August). Identifying the missing links in the study of latchkey children. *Children Today,* pp. 2–4ff.

Gallup, G. G., Jr. (1970). Chimpanzees: Self-recognition. *Science, 167,* 86–87.

Garbino, J. (1986). Troubled youth, troubled families: The dynamics of adolescent maltreatment. In D. Cicchetti & V. Carlson (Eds.), *Research and theoretical advances on the topic of child maltreatment.* Hawthorne, NY: Aldine de Gruyter.

Garbino, J., & Gilliam, G. (1980). *Understanding abusive families.* Lexington, MA: Lexington Books.

Garcia-Barrio, C. (1988, September). High-tech help for high-risk mothers. *American Baby,* pp. 9–10.

Gardner, H. (1983). *Frames of mind: The theory of multiple intelligences.* New York: Basic Books.

Gardner, J. L. (Ed.). (1982). *Eat better, live better.* Pleasantville, NY: Reader's Digest Association.

Garner, D. M., & Garfinkel, P. E. (1980). Cultural expectations of thinness in women. *Psychological Reports, 47,* 483–491.

Garnica, O. K. (1977). Some prosodic and paralinguistic features of speech to young children. In C. E. Snow & C. A. Ferguson (Eds.), *Talking to children.* Cambridge, England: Cambridge University Press.

Gatz, M., & Pearson, C. G. (1988, March). Ageism revised and the provision of psychological services. *American Psychologist,* pp. 184–188.

Gay, P. (1988). *Freud: A life for our times.* New York: Norton.

Geber, M. (1962). Longitudinal study and psychomotor development among Baganda children. *Proceedings of the Fourteenth International Congress of Applied Psychology, 3,* 50–60.

Geber, M., & Dean, R. F. A. (1957). The state of development of newborn African children. *Lancet, 1,* 1216–1219.

Geismar-Ryan, L. (1986, October). Infant social activity: The discovery of peer play. *Childhood Education,* pp. 24–29.

Gelman, D. (1986, December 15). The mouths of babes. *Newsweek,* pp. 84–86.

Gelman, S. A. (1988). Children's expectations concerning natural kind categories. *Human Development, 31,* 28–34.

Genishi, C. (1988, November). Children's language: Learning words from experience. *Young Children,* pp. 16–23.

Georgaklis, C. C. (1987). Relationship between parental views and romantic happiness in college women. *Psychological Reports, 61,* 75–78.

George, D. T., Ladenheim, J. A., & Nutt, D. J. (1987). Effect of pregnancy on panic attacks. *American Journal of Psychiatry, 144,* 1078–1079.

George, L. K. (1988). Social participation in later life: Black-white differences. In J. S. Jackson (Ed.), *The Black American elderly: Research on physical and psychosocial health.* New York: Springer.

Gerbner, G., Gross, L., Signorielli, N., & Morgan, M. (1980). Aging with television: Images in television drama and conceptions of social reality. *Journal of Communication, 30,* 37–47.

Germaine, L. M., & Freedman, R. R. (1984). Behavioral treatment of menopausal hot flashes: Evaluation by objective methods. *Journal of Consulting and Clinical Psychology, 52,* 1072–1079.

Gerstel, N. (1988). Divorce and kin ties: The importance of gender. *Journal of Marriage and the Family, 50,* 209–219.

Gibbons, S., Wylie, M. L., Echterling, L., & French, J. (1986). Patterns of use among rural and small-town adolescents. *Adolescence, 21,* 887–900.

Gibbs, J. C., Arnold, K. D., & Burkhart, J. E. (1984). Sex differences in the expression of moral judgment. *Child Development, 55,* 1040–1043.

Gibbs, J. C., & Schnell, S. V. (1985). Moral development "versus" socialization. *American Psychologist, 40,* 1071–1080.

Gibson, E. J. (1988). Exploratory behavior in the development of perceiving, acting, and the acquiring of knowledge. *Annual Review of Psychology, 39,* 1–41.

Gibson, E. J., & Levin, H. (1975). *The psychology of reading.* Cambridge, MA: MIT Press.

Gibson, E. J., & Walk, R. D. (1960). The "visual cliff." *Scientific American, 202,* 64–71.

Gibson, J. J. (1966). *The senses considered as perceptual systems.* Boston, MA: Houghton Mifflin.

Gibson, J. J. (1979). *The ecological approach to visual perception.* Boston, MA: Houghton Mifflin.

Gibson, R. C. (1988). The work, retirement, and disability of older black Americans. In J. S. Jackson (Ed.), *The Black American elderly: Research on physical and psychosocial health.* New York: Springer.

Giddings, M., & Halverson, C. F. (1981). Young children's use of toys in home environments. *Family Relations, 30,* 69–74.

Gilford, R. (1984). Contrasts in marital satisfaction throughout old age: An exchange theory analysis. *Journal of Gerontology, 39,* 325–333.

Gilford, R., & Bengtson, V. L. (1979). Measuring marital satisfaction in three generations: Positive and negative dimensions. *Journal of Marriage and the Family, 41,* 387–398.

Gilford, R., & Black, D. (1972). The grandchild-grandparent dyad: Ritual or relationships. In L. E. Troll & V. L. Bengston (Eds.), 1982. Intergenerational relations throughout the life span. In B. B. Wolman (Ed.), *Handbook of developmental psychology.* Englewood Cliffs, NJ: Prentice-Hall.

Gilleard, C. J., & Gurkan, A. A. (1987). Socioeconomic development and the status of elderly men in Turkey: A test of modernization theory. *Journal of Gerontology, 42,* 353–357.

Gilligan, C. (1982). *In a different voice: Psychological theory and women's development.* Cambridge, MA: Harvard University Press.

Gilligan, C. (1984, August). *Remapping the moral domain in personality research and assessment.* Invited address given at the American Psychological Association Convention in Toronto, Canada. Cited in Muuss, R. E. (1988). Carol Gilligan's theory of sex differences in the development of moral reasoning during adolescence. *Adolescence, 23,* 229–243.

Gilligan, C., & Attanucci, J. (1988). Two moral orientations: Gender differences and similarities. *Merrill-Palmer Quarterly, 34,* 223–237.

Gillis, J. R. (1974). *Youth and history: Tradition and change in European age relations 1770-present.* New York: Academic Press.

Gilmartin, B. G. (1979, February). The case against spanking. *Human Behavior,* pp. 18–23.

Ginott, H. G. (1969). *Between parent and child.* New York: Avon.

Ginsburg, H. J., & Miller, S. M. (1982). Sex differences in children's risk-taking behavior. *Child Development, 53,* 426–428.

Ginzberg, E. (1984). Career development. In D. Brown & L. Brooks (Eds.), *Career choice and development: Applying contemporary theories to practice.* San Francisco, CA: Jossey-Bass.

Gispert, M., Wheeler, K., Marsh, L., & Davis, M. S. (1985). Suicidal adolescents: Factors in evaluation. *Adolescence, 20,* 753–762.

Givens, R., & Starr, M. (1989, March 20). Sharing a house of one's own. *Newsweek,* p. 74.

Glasberg, R., & Aboud, F. (1982). Keeping one's distance from sadness: Children's self-reports of emotional experience. *Developmental Psychology, 18,* 287–293.

Glenn, N. D. (1987, October). Marriage on the rocks. *Psychology Today,* pp. 20–21.

Glenn, N. D., & Kramer, K. B. (1987). The marriages and divorces of the children of divorce. *Journal of Marriage and the Family, 49,* 811–825.

Glenn, N. D., & McLanahan, S. (1981). The effects of offspring on the psychological well-being of older adults. *Journal of Marriage and the Family, 43,* 409–421.

Glenn, N. D., & Weaver, C. N. (1985). Age, cohort, and reported job satisfaction in the United States. In Z. S. Blau (Ed.), *Current perspectives on aging and the life cycle* (Vol. 1, pp. 89–111). Greenwich, CT: Jai.

Glenn, N. D., & Weaver, C. N. (1988, May). The changing relationship of marital status to reported happiness. *Journal of Marriage and the Family, 50,* 317–324.

Glick, P. C. (1989). The family life cycle and social change. *Family Relations, 38,* 123–129.

Gnepp, J., & Hess, D. L. R. (1986). Children's understanding of verbal and facial display rules. *Developmental Psychology, 22,* 103–108.

Goebel, B. L. (1984). Age stereotypes held by student nurses. *Journal of Psychology, 116,* 249–254.

Goethals, G. W., & Klos, D. S. (1970). *Experiencing youth: First-person accounts.* Boston, MA: Little, Brown.

Goetting, A. (1986). The developmental tasks of siblingship over the life cycle. *Journal of Marriage and the Family, 48,* 703–714.

Golan, N. (1981). *Passing through transitions.* New York: Free Press.

Gold, J. A., Ryckman, R. M. & Mosley, N. R. (1984). Romantic mood induction and attraction to a dissimilar other: Is love blind? *Personality and Social Psychology Bulletin, 10* (3), 358–368.

Goldberg, B., Rosenthal, P. P., Robertson, L. S., & Nicholas, J. A. (1988). Injuries in youth football. *Pediatrics, 81,* 255–261.

Goldberg, S. (1979). Premature birth: Consequences for the parent-infant relationship. *American Scientist, 67,* 214–220.

Golden, N. L., Sokol, R. J., Kuhnert, B. R., & Bottoms, S. (1982). Maternal alcohol use and infant development. *Pediatrics, 70,* 931–934.

Goldfarb, C. S. (1988). The folklore of pregnancy. *Psychological Reports, 62,* 891–900.

Goldfarb, W. (1947). Variations in adolescent adjustment of institutionally reared children. *American Journal of Orthopsychiatry, 17,* 449–459.

Goldscheider, F. K., & Da Vanzo, J. (1985). Living arrangements and the transition to adulthood. *Demography, 22,* 545–563.

Goldscheider, F. K., & Goldscheider, C. (1989, February). Family structure and conflict: Nest-leaving expectations of young adults and their parents. *Journal of Marriage and Family, 51,* 87–97.

Goldsmith, H. H. (1983). Genetic influences on personality from infancy to adulthood. *Child Development, 54,* 331–335.

Goldsmith, H. H., Buss, A. H., Plomin, R., Rothbart, M. K., Thomas, A., Chess, S., Hinde, R. A., & McCall, R. B. (1987). Roundtable: What is temperament? Four approaches. *Child Development, 58,* 505–529.

Goldsmith, M. F. (1985). Possible herpes virus role in abortion studies. *Journal of the American Medical Association, 251,* 3067–3070.

Goldstein, M. C., Schuler, S., & Ross, J. L. (1983). Social and economic forces affecting intergenerational relations in extended families in a Third-World country: A cautionary tale from South Asia. *Journal of Gerontology, 38,* 715–724.

Goleman, D. (1977, April). Back from the brink. *Psychology Today,* pp. 56–59.

Goleman, D. (1987, September 11). Long-married couples do look alike, study finds. *New York Times,* pp. 13, 17.

Goodell, & Gurin, J. (1984, January/February). Where should babies be born? *American Health,* pp. 66–75.

Goodich, M. (1990). The virtues and vices of old people in the late middle ages. *International Journal of Aging and Human Development, 30,* 119–127.

Goodman, M. J., Grove, J. S., & Gilbert, F., Jr. (1978). Age at menopause in relation to reproductive history in Japanese, Caucasian, Chinese, and Hawaiian women living in Hawaii. *Journal of Gerontology, 33,* 688–694.

Gordon, T. (1980). *Parent effectiveness training* (2nd ed.). New York: Peter H. Wyden.

Gorski, P. A., Lewkowicz, D. J., & Huntington, L. (1987). Advances in neonatal and infant behavioral assessment: Toward a comprehensive evaluation of early patterns of development. *Developmental and Behavioral Pediatrics, 8,* 39–50.

Goswami, U. (1988). Children's use of analogy in learning to spell. *British Journal of Developmental Psychology, 6,* 21–33.

Gottesman, L., & Bourestom, N. (1974). Why nursing homes do what they do. *The Gerontologist, 14,* 501–506.

Gottfried, A. W., & Bathurst, K. (1983). Hand preference across time is related to intelligence in young girls, not boys. *Science, 221,* 1074–1075.

Gottlieb, G. (1983). The psychobiological approach to developmental issues. In P. H. Mussen (Ed.), *Handbook of child psychology* (4th ed.), M. M. Haith & J. J. Campos (Vol. Eds.), *Infancy and developmental psychobiology.* New York: Wiley.

Gould, R. L. (1978). *Transformations: Growth and change in adult life.* New York: Simon & Schuster.

Gould, R. L. (1980). Transformations during early and middle adult years. In N. J. Smelser & E. H. Erikson (Eds.), *Themes of work and love in adulthood.* Cambridge, MA: Harvard University Press.

Gove, W. R. (1985). The effect of age and gender on deviant behavior: A biopsychological perspective. In A. S. Rossi (Ed.), *Gender and the life course*. New York: Aldine.

Grady, D. (1985, August). Preemies: A $2 billion dilemma. *Discover*, pp. 53–65.

Grady, D. (1987, June). The ticking of a time bomb in the genes. *Discover*, pp. 26–39.

Granrud, C. E. (1987). Size constancy in newborn human infants. *Supplement Investigative Ophthalmology and Visual Science, 28*, 5.

Granrud, C. E., Yonas, A., & Pettersen, L. (1984). A comparison of monocular and binocular depth perception in 5- and 7-month-old infants. *Journal of Experimental Child Psychology, 38*, 19–32.

Grant, E. (1988, January). The housework gap. *Psychology Today*, p. 10.

Grant, I., Patterson, T. L., & Yager, J. (1988, October). Social supports in relation to physical health and symptoms of depression in the elderly. *American Journal of Psychiatry, 145*, 1254–1257.

Grant, W. V. (1984). Trends in college enrollments: 1972–1982. In *Statistical highlights of the National Center for Educational Statistics* (Publication no. NCES 84–403). Washington, DC: U. S. Department of Education.

Gray, V. R. (1984). The psychological response of the dying patient. In P. S. Chaney (Ed.), *Dealing with death and dying* (2nd ed.). Springhouse, PA: International Communications/Nursing Skillbooks.

Greeley, A. M. (1971). *Why can't they be like us*. New York: Dutton.

Green, R. (1987). *The "Sissy boy syndrome" and the development of homosexuality*. New Haven, CT: Yale University Press.

Greenberg, J. (1985). Birth trauma linked to adolescent suicide. *Science News, 127*, 183.

Greenberger, E., & Steinberg, L. (1986). *When teenagers work: The psychological and social costs of adolescent employment*. New York: Basic Books.

Greenfield, P. (1966). On culture and conservation. In J. S. Bruner, R. R. Olver, & P. M. Greenfield, (Eds.), *Studies in cognitive growth*. New York: Wiley.

Greenfield, P. M. (1984). *Mind and media: The effects of television, video games, and computers*. Cambridge, MA: Harvard University Press.

Greyson, B. (1981). Near-death experiences and attempted suicide. *Suicide and Life-Threatening Behavior, 11*, 10–16.

Grieser, D. L., & Kuhl, P. K. (1988). Maternal speech to infants in a tonal language: Support for universal prosodic features in motherese. *Developmental Psychology, 24*, 14–20.

Grossman, F. K., Pollack, W. S., & Golding, E. (1988). Fathers and children: Predicting the quality and quantity of fathering. *Developmental Psychology, 24*, 82–91.

Grotevant, H. D., & Cooper, C. R. (1986). Individuation in family relationships. *Human Development, 29*, 82–100.

Gruber-Baldini, A., & Schaie, K. W. (1986, November 21). *Longitudinal sequential studies of marital assortivity*. Paper presented at the annual meeting of the Gerontological Society of America, Chicago.

Gruber, E., & Chambers, C. V. (1987). Cognitive development and adolescent contraception: Integrating theory and practice. *Adolescence, 22*, 661–670.

Gubrium, J. F. (1976). Being single in old age. In J. F. Gubrium (Ed.), *Time, roles and self in old age* (pp. 179–195). New York: Human Sciences Press.

Guerin, P. J., Jr., Fay, L. F., Burden, S. L., & Kautto, J. G. (1987). *The evaluation and treatment of marital conflict: A four-stage approach*. New York: Basic Books.

Gunther, J. (1949). *Death be not proud*. New York: Harper & Row.

H

Haaf, R. (1974). Complexity and facial resemblance as determinants of response to facelike stimuli by 5- and 10-week-old infants. *Journal of Experimental Child Psychology, 18*, 480–487.

Haan, N. (1981). Common dimensions of personality development: Early adolescence to middle life. In D. H. Eichorn, J. A. Clausen, N. Haan, M. P. Honzik, & P. H. Mussen (Eds.), *Present and past in middle life* (pp. 117–151). New York: Academic Press.

Haas, L. (1985). Role-sharing couples. In L. Cargan (Ed.), *Marriage and family: Coping with change*. Belmont, CA: Wadsworth.

Hagestad, G. O. (1987). Parent-child relations in later life: Trends and gaps in past life. In J. B. Lancaster, J. Altman, A. S. Rossi, & L. R. Sherrod (Eds.), *Parenting across the lifespan*. New York: Aldine de Gruyter.

Haggstrom, G. W., Kanouse, D. E., & Morrison, P. A. (1986). Accounting for educational shortfalls of mothers. *Journal of Marriage and the Family, 48*, 175–186.

Haith, M. M., Bergman, T., & Moore, M. J. (1977). Eye contact and face scanning in early infancy. *Science, 198*, 853–854.

Hajnal, J. (1982). Two kinds of preindustrial household formation systems. *Population and Development Review, 8*, 449–494.

Halbur, B., & Vandagriff, M. (1987). Societal responses after death: A study of sex differences in newspaper death notices for Birmingham, Alabama, 1900–1985. *Sex Roles, 17*, 421–436.

Hale, R. W. (1984). Diagnosis of pregnancy and associated conditions. In R. C. Benson (Ed.), *Current obstetric and gynecological diagnosis and treatment* (5th ed.). Los Altos, CA: Lange.

Halford, S., & Boyle, F. M. (1985). Do young children understand conservation of number? *Child Development, 56*, 165–176.

Hall, G. S. (1883). The contents of children's minds. *Princeton Review, 11*, 249–272.

Hall, G. S. (1904). *Adolescence: Its psychology and its relations to physiology, anthropology, sociology, sex, crime, religion, and education* (Vol. 1). New York: Appleton.

Hall, J. A. (1987). Parent-adolescent conflict: An empirical review. *Adolescence, 22*, 767–789.

Halpern, S. (1989, January/February). Infertility: Playing the odds. *Ms*, pp. 147–151.

Hamburg, B. A. (1986). Subsets of adolescent mothers: Developmental, biomedical and psychosocial issues. In J. B. Lancaster & B. A. Hamburg (Eds.), *School-age pregnancy and parenthood: Biosocial dimensions*. New York: Aldine de Gruyter.

Hamon, R. R., & Blieszner, R. (1990). Filial responsibility expectations among adult child-older parent pairs. *Journal of Gerontology: Psychological Sciences, 45*, P110–P112.

Hancock, J. A. (1894). A preliminary study of motor ability. *Pedagogical Seminary, 3*, 9–29.

Hansen, S. L. (1977). Dating choices of high school students. *The Family Coordinator, 26*, 133–138.

Hanson, J. W., Streissguth, A. P., & Smith, D. W. (1978). The effects of moderate alcohol consumption during pregnancy on fetal growth and morphogenesis. *Journal of Pediatrics, 92*, 457–460.

Hanson, S. L., Myers, D. E., & Ginsburg, A. L. (1987). The role of responsibility and knowledge in reducing teenage out-of-wedlock childbearing. *Journal of Marriage and the Family, 49*, 241–256.

Haponski, W. C., & McCabe, C. E. (1982). *Back to school: The college guide for adults*. Princeton, NJ: Peterson's Guides.

Hardacre, H. (1984). *Lay buddhism in contemporary Japan: Reiyukai Kyodan*. Princeton, NJ: Princeton University Press.

Hardyck, C., & Petrinovich, L. F. (1977). Left-handedness. *Psychological Bulletin, 84*, 385–404.

Hare-Mustin, R. T., & Marecek, J. (1988). The meaning of difference: Gender theory, postmodernism, and psychology. *American Psychologist, 43*, 455–464.

Harman, D. (1984). Free radicals and the origination, evolution, and present status of the free radical theory of aging. In D. Armstrong, R. S. Sohol, R. G. Cutler, & T. P. Slater (Eds.), *Free radicals in molecular biology, aging, and disease*. New York: Raven Press.

Harman, S. M., & Talbert, G. B. (1985). Reproductive aging. In C. E. Finch & E. L. Schneider (Eds.), *Handbook of the biology of aging* (2nd ed.). New York: Van Nostrand Reinhold.

Harre, R. (1980, January). What's in a nickname? *Psychology Today*, pp. 78–84.

Harris, J., & Fiedler, C. M. (1988, Summer). Preadolescent attitudes toward the elderly: An analysis of race, gender, and contact variables. *Adolescence, 23*, 335–340.

Harris, L. (1987). *Inside America*. New York: Vintage.

Harris, L., & Associates. (1975). *The myth and reality of aging in America.* Washington, DC: National Council on Aging.

Harris, M. B., Begay, C., & Page, P. (1989). Activities, family relationships and feelings about aging in a multicultural elderly sample. *International Aging and Human Development, 29,* 103–117.

Harris, P. L. (1983). Infant cognition. In P. H. Mussen (Ed.), *Handbook of child psychology* (4th ed.), M. H. Harth & J. J. Campos (Vol. Eds.), *Infancy and developmental psychobiology.* New York: Wiley.

Harris, P. L., Donnelly, K., Guz, G. R., & Pitt-Watson, R. (1986). Children's understanding of the distinction between real and apparent emotion. *Child Development, 57,* 895–909.

Harris, P. L., Olthof, T., & Terwogt, M. (1981). Children's knowledge of emotions. *Journal of Child Psychology and Psychiatry, 22,* 247–261.

Harris, P. L., Olthof, T., Terwogt, M. M., & Hardman, C. E. (1987). Children's knowledge of the situations that provoke emotion. *International Journal of Behavioral Development, 10,* 319–343.

Hart, D. (1988a). The development of personal identity in adolescence: A philosophical dilemma approach. *Merrill-Palmer Quarterly, 34,* 105–114.

Hart, D. (1988b). A longitudinal study of adolescents' socialization and identification as predictors of adult moral judgment development. *Merrill-Palmer Quarterly, 34,* 245–260.

Hart, L. (1987). *The winning family: Increasing self-esteem in your children and yourself.* New York: Dodd, Mead.

Hartley, A. A. (1981). Adult age differences in deductive reasoning processes. *Journal of Gerontology, 36,* 700–706.

Hartmann, E. (1981). The strangest sleep disorder. *Psychology Today, 15,* 14–18.

Hartmann, E., Baekeland, F., & Zwilling, G. (1972). Psychological differences between long and short sleepers. *Archives of General Psychiatry, 26,* 463–468.

Hartshorne, T. S., & Manaster, G. J. (1982). The relationship with grandparents: Contact, importance, role conception. *International Journal of Aging and Human Development, 15,* 233–245.

Hartup, W. W. (1983). Peer relations. In P. H. Mussen (Ed.), *Handbook of child psychology* (4th ed.), E. M. Hetherington (Ed.), *Socialization, personality, and social development* (Vol. 4). New York: Wiley.

Hartup, W. W., & Moore, S. G. (1963). Avoidance of inappropriate sex-typing by young children. *Journal of Counseling Psychology, 6,* 467–473.

Hartup, W. W., & Sancilio, M. (1986). Children's friendships. In E. Schopler & G. Mesibov (Eds.), *Social behavior in autism.* New York: Plenum.

Haskins, R. (1985). Public school aggression among children with varying day-care experience. *Child Development, 56,* 689–703.

Hass, A. (1979). *Teenage sexuality: A survey of teenage sexual behavior.* New York: Macmillan.

Hatfield, E., Traupmann, J., Sprecher, S., Utne, M., & Hay, J. (1985). Equity and intimate relations: Recent research. In W. Ickes (Ed.), *Compatible and incompatible relationships.* New York: Springer-Verlag.

Havighurst, R. J. (1948). *Developmental tasks and education.* New York: David McKay.

Havighurst, R. J. (1956). Research on developmental task concept. *School Review, 64,* 215–223.

Havighurst, R. J. (1961). Successful aging. *The Gerontologist, 1,* 8–13.

Havighurst, R. J. (1972). *Developmental tasks and education* (3rd ed.). New York: D. McCay.

Havighurst, R. J. (1978). Aging in western societies. In D. Hobman (Ed.), *The social challenge of aging.* New York: St. Martin's Press.

Havighurst, R. J., Neugarten, B. L., & Tobin, S. S. (1968). Disengagement and patterns of aging. In B. L. Neugarten (Ed.), *Middle age and aging.* Chicago, IL: University of Chicago Press.

Hayachi, Y., & Endo, S. (1982). All-night sleep polygraphic recordings of healthy aged persons: REM and slow wave sleep. *Sleep, 5,* 277–283.

Hayes, D. S., Chemelski, B. E., & Palmer, M. (1982). Nursery rhymes and prose passages: Preschoolers' liking and short-term retention of story events. *Developmental Psychology, 18*(1), 49–56.

Hayes, D. S., & Ross, C. E. (1987). Concern with appearance, health beliefs, and eating habits. *Journal of Health and Social Behavior, 28,* 120–130.

Hayflick, L. (1977). The cellular basis for biological aging. In C. E. Finch & L. Hayflick (Eds.), *Handbook of the biology of aging.* New York: Van Nostrand Reinhold.

Hayflick, L. (1987). Biological theories of aging. In G. L. Maddox (Ed.), *The encyclopedia of aging.* New York: Springer.

Haynes, H., White, B. L., & Held, R. (1965). Visual accommodation in human infants. *Science, 148,* 528–530.

Haynes, S. G., Feinleib, M., & Kannel, W. B. (1980). The relationship of psychosocial factors to coronary heart disease in the Framingham Study. III. Eight-year incidence of coronary heart disease. *American Journal of Epidemiology, 111,* 37–58.

Hazan, C., & Shaver, P. (1987). Romantic love conceptualized as an attachment process. *Journal of Personality and Social Psychology, 52,* 511–524.

Hebdige, D. (1984). Framing the youth "problem": The construction of troublesome adolescence. In V. Garms-Homolova, E. M. Hoerning, & D. Schaeffer (Eds.), *Intergenerational relationships.* Lewiston, NY: C. J. Hogrefe.

Heckhausen, J. (1987). How do mothers know infants' chronological age or infants' performance as determinants of adaptation in maternal instruction? *Journal of Experimental Child Psychology, 43,* 212–226.

Heibert, E. H. (1978). Preschool children's understanding of written language. *Child Development, 49,* 1231–1234.

Helgeson, V., Shaver, P., & Dyer, M. (1987). Prototypes of intimacy and distance in same-sex and opposite-sex relationships. *Journal of Social and Personal Relationships, 4,* 195–233.

Helmholtz, H. (1962). *Treatise on physiological optics* (Vol. 3) (J. P. Southall, Ed. and Trans.). New York: Dover Press. (First German edition, 1866)

Helsing, K. J., & Szklo, M. (1981). Mortality after bereavement. *American Journal of Epidemiology, 114,* 41–52.

Helson, R., & Moane, G. (1987). Personality change in women from college to midlife. *Journal of Personality and Social Psychology, 53,* 176–186.

Hendrick, C., & Hendrick, S. (1986). A theory and method love. *Journal of Personality and Social Psychology, 50,* 392–402.

Hendrick, C., Hendrick, S., Foote, F. H., & Slapion-Foote, M. J. (1985). Do men and women love differently? *Journal of Social and Personal Psychology, 48,* 1630–1642.

Hendrick, S., & Hendrick, C. (1987). Multidimensionality of sexual attitudes. *Journal of Sex Research, 23,* 502–526.

Hennon, C. B., Brubaker, T. H., & Baumann, S. A. (1983). Your aging parent: Deciding whether to live together. In *Cooperative Extension Service Bulletin.* Madison, WI: University of Wisconsin Extension.

Henri, V., & Henri, C. (1898). Earliest recollections. *Popular Science Monthly, 53,* 108–115.

Henton, C. L. (1961). The effect of socio-economic and emotional factors on the onset of menarche among Negro and White girls. *Journal of Genetic Psychology, 98,* 255–264.

Hess, T. M., & Slaughter, S. J. (1990). Schematic knowledge influences on memory for scene information in young and older adults. *Developmental Psychology, 26,* 855–865.

Hetherington, E. M. (1972). Effects of father absence on personality development in adolescent daughters. *Developmental Review, 7,* 313–326.

Hetherington, E. M., Cox, M., & Cox, R. (1979). Play and social interaction in children following divorce. *Journal of Social Issues, 35,* 26–49.

Hetherington, E. M., Cox, M., & Cox, R. (1985). Long-term effects of divorce and remarriage on the adjustment of children. *Journal of the American Academy of Child Psychiatry, 24,* 518–530.

Hiatt, S. W., Campos, J. J., & Emde, R. N. (1979). Facial patterning and infant emotional expression: Happiness, surprise, and fear. *Child Development, 50,* 1020–1035.

Hill, E. A., & Dorfman, L. T. (1982). Reaction of housewives to the retirement of their husbands. *Family Relations, 31*, 195–200.

Hill, J. P., Holmbeck, G. N., Marlow, L., Green, T. M., & Lynch, M. E. (1985). Menarcheal status and parent-child relations in families of 7th-grade girls. *Journal of Youth and Adolescence, 14*, 301–316.

Hill, R. L. (1986). Life cycle stages for types of single-parent families: Of family development theory. *Family Relations, 35*, 19–29.

Hiller, D. V., & Philliber, W. W. (1986). The division of labor in contemporary marriage: Expectations, perceptions, and performance. *Social Problems, 33*, 191–201.

Hinsz, V. B. (1989). Facial resemblance in engaged and married couples. *Journal of Social and Personal Relationships, 6*, 223–229.

Hobart, C. W. (1988). Perception of parent-child relationships in first married and remarried families. *Family Relations, 37*, 175–182.

Hofferth, S. L., & Phillips, D. A. (1987). Child care in the United States, 1970 to 1995. *Journal of Marriage and the Family, 49*, 559–571.

Hoffman, L. (1979). Maternal employment. *American Psychologist, 34*, 859–865.

Hoffman, L. W., & Manis, J. (1979). The value of children in the United States: A new approach to the study of fertility. *Journal of Marriage and the Family, 41*, 583–596.

Hoffman, M. L. (1983). Affective and cognitive processes in moral internalization. In E. T. Higgins, D. N. Ruble, & W. W. Hartup (Eds.), *Social cognition and social development: A sociocultural perspective.* Cambridge, England: Cambridge University Press.

Hoffman, M. L. (1984). Moral development. In M. H. Bornstein & M. E. Lamb (Eds.), *Developmental psychology: An advanced textbook* (3rd ed.). Hillsdale, NJ: Erlbaum.

Hoffman, M. L., & Saltzstein, H. D. (1967). Parent discipline and the child's moral development. *Journal of Personality and Social Psychology, 5*, 45–57.

Hofland, B. F., Willis, S. L., & Baltes, P. B. (1981). Fluid intelligence performance in the elderly: Intraindividual variability and conditions of assessment. *Journal of Educational Psychology, 73*, 573–587.

Hogan, D. P. (1987). Demographic trends in human fertility, and parenting across the life span. In J. B. Lancaster, J. Alman, A. S. Rossi, & L. R. Sherrod (Eds.), *Parenting across the life span: Biosocial dimensions.* New York: Aldine de Gruyter.

Hogan, J. (1989). Personality correlates of physical fitness. *Journal of Personality and Social Psychology, 56*, 284–288.

Hoglund, C. L., & Collison, B. B. (1989, January). Loneliness and irrational beliefs among college students. *Journal of College Student Development, 30*, 53–57.

Holahan, C. K. (1984). Marital attitudes over 40 years: A longitudinal and cohort analysis. *Journal of Gerontology, 39*, 49–57.

Holden, C. (1987, September). Genes and behavior: A twin legacy. *Psychology Today,* pp. 18–19.

Holding, D. H., Noonan, T. K., Pfau, H. D., & Holding, C. S. (1986). Data attribution, age, and the distribution of lifetime memories. *Journal of Gerontology, 41*, 481–486.

Holland, E. I. M. (1987, June). Granny midwives. *Ms.,* pp. 48–51, 73–74.

Holland, J. (1985). *Making vocational choices* (2nd ed.). Englewood Cliffs, NJ: Prentice-Hall.

Holmes, D. L., Reich, J. N., & Pasternak, J. F. (1984). *The development of infants born at risk.* Hillsdale, NJ: Lawrence Erlbaum.

Holmes, L. (1987, June). The insurance crisis. *Ms.,* p. 74.

Holroyd, K. A., & Coyne, J. (1987, June). Personality and health in the 1980s: Psychosomatic medicine revisited? *Journal of Personality, 55*, 359–375.

Holzgreve, W., Beller, F. K., & Buchholz, B. (1987). Kidney transplantation from anencephalic donors. *New England Journal of Medicine, 316*, 1069–1070.

Honzik, M. P. (1984). Life-span development. *Annual Review of Psychology, 35*, 309–331.

Honzik, M. P., McFarlane, J. W., & Allen, L. (1948). The stability of mental test performance between two and eighteen years. *Journal of Experimental Education, 17*, 309–324.

Horn, J. C., & Meer, J. (1987). The vintage years. *Psychology Today, 21*, 76, 77, 80–84, 88–90.

Horn, J. L., & Donaldson, G. (1980). Cognitive development in adulthood. In J. Kagan & O. G. Brim, Jr. (Eds.), *Constancy and change in development.* Cambridge, MA: Harvard University Press.

Horney, K. (1967). *Feminine psychology.* New York: Norton.

Horowitz, M. J., & Wilner, N. (1980). Signs and symptoms of posttraumatic stress disorder. *Archives of General Psychiatry, 37*, 85–92.

Hort, B. E., Fagot, B. I., & Leinbach, M. D. (1990). Are people's notions of maleness more stereotypically framed than their notions of femaleness? *Sex Roles, 23*, 197–212.

Horwitz, A. V., & White, H. R. (1987). Gender-role orientations and styles of pathology among adolescents. *Journal of Health and Social Behavior, 28*, 158–170.

Howes, C. (1988). Relations between early child care and schooling. *Developmental Psychology, 24*, 53–57.

Huesmann, L. R., Eron, L. D., Lefkwitz, M. M., & Walder, L. O. (1984). Stability of aggression over time and generations. *Developmental Psychology, 20*, 1120–1134.

Hughey, M. J., McElin, T. W., & Young, T. (1978). Maternal and fetal outcome of Lamaze-prepared patients. *Obstetrics and Gynecology, 51*, 643–647.

Huitt, W. G., & Ashton, P. T. (1982). Parents' perception of infant development: A psychometric study. *Merrill-Palmer Quarterly, 28*, 95–109.

Hulicka, I. M. (1982). Memory functioning in late adulthood. In F. I. M. Craik & S. Trehub (Eds.), *Aging and cognitive processes.* New York: Plenum.

Hull, J. G., Van Treuren, R. R., & Virnelli, S. (1987). Hardiness and health: A critique and alternative approach. *Journal of Personality and Social Psychology, 53*, 518–530.

Hultsch, D. F. (1975). Adult age differences in retrieval: Trace-dependent and cue-dependent forgetting. *Developmental Psychology, 11*, 197–201.

Hultsch, D. F., Hertzog, C., & Dixon, R. (1984). Temporal memory for performed activities: Intentionality and adult age differences. *Developmental Psychology, 20*, 1193–1210.

Hunter, F. T. (1985a). Adolescents' perception of discussions with parents and friends. *Developmental Psychology, 20*, 1092–1100.

Hunter, F. T. (1985b). Adolescents' perception of discussions with parents and friends. *Developmental Psychology, 21*, 443–450.

Hunziker, U. A., & Barr, R. G. (1986). Increased carrying reduces infant crying: A randomized controlled trial. *Pediatrics, 77*, 641–648.

Hurley, D. (1986, August). A sound mind in an unsound body. *Psychology Today,* pp. 34–43.

Hurlock, E. B., & Schwartz, R. (1932). Biographical records of memory in preschool children. *Child Development, 3*, 230–239.

Huston, A. C. (1983). Sex-typing. In P. E. Mussen (Ed.), *Handbook of child psychology* (4th ed., Vol. 4). New York: Wiley.

Huston, A. C., Carpenter, C. J., & Atwater, J. B. (1986). Gender, adult structuring of activities, and social behavior in middle childhood. *Child Development, 57*, 1200–1209.

Hutchinson, M. G. (1982). Transforming body image: Your body, friend or foe? *Women & Therapy, 1*, 59–67.

Hyde, J. S. (1984). Children's understanding of sexist language. *Developmental Psychology, 20*, 697–706.

I

Identity crisis. (1988, March). *Discover,* p. 22.

Inhelder, B., & Piaget, J. (1958). *The growth of logical thinking from childhood to adolescence.* New York: Basic Books.

Inoff-Germain, G., Arnold, G. S., Nottelmann, E. D., Susman, D. J., Cutler, G. B., Jr., & Chrousos, G. P. (1988). Relations between hormone levels and observational measures of aggressive behavior of young adolescents in family interaction. *Developmental Psychology, 24*, 129–139.

Insel, S. A. (1976). On counseling the bereaved. *Personnel and Guidance Journal, 55*, 127–129.

Intons-Peterson, M. J. (1988). *Gender concepts of Swedish and American youth.* Hillsdale, NJ: Lawrence Erlbaum.

Intons-Peterson, M. J., & Reddel, M. (1984). What do people ask about a neonate? *Developmental Psychology, 20*, 358–359.

Irion, P. E. (1956). *The funeral: An experience of value.* Milwaukee, WI: National Funeral Directors Association.

Isaacs, L. W., & Bearison, D. J. (1986). The development of children's prejudice against the aged. *International Journal of Aging and Human Development, 23,* 175–194.

Isenberg, J., & Quisenberry, N. L. (1988, February). Play: A necessity for all children. *Childhood Education,* pp. 138–145.

Ishii-Kuntz, M., & Lee, G. R. (1987, May). Status of the elderly: An extension of the theory. *Journal of Marriage and the Family, 49,* 413–420.

Isotoma, Z. M. (1975). The development of voluntary memory in children of pre-school age. *Soviet Psychology, 13,* 5–64.

Izard, C. E. (1978). On the ontogenesis of emotions and emotion-cognition relationships in infancy. In M. Lewis & L. Rosenblum (Eds.), *The development of affect.* New York: Plenum.

Izard, C. E., Huebner, R. R., Resser, D., McGinness, G. C., & Dougherty, L. M. (1980). The young infant's ability to produce discrete emotional expressions. *Developmental Psychology, 16,* 132–140.

J

Jacklin, C. N., & Maccoby, E. E. (1978). Social behavior at 33 months in the same-sex and mixed-sex dyads. *Child Development, 49,* 557–569.

Jacklin, C. N., Maccoby, E. E., & Doering, C. H. (1983). Neonatal sex-steroid hormones and timidity in 6- 18-month-old boys and girls. *Developmental Psychobiology, 16,* 163–168.

Jackson, E. (1974). The mourning process. In E. A. Grollman (Ed.), *Concerning death: A practical guide for the living.* Boston, MA: Beacon Press.

Jacobs, G., & Kerrins, J. (1987). *The AIDS file.* Woods Hole, MA: Cromlec Books.

Jacobs, R. H. (1979). *Life after youth: Female, 40—what next?* Boston, MA: Beacon Press.

Jacobson, S. W., & Kagan, J. (1979). Interpreting "initiative" responses in early infancy. *Science, 205,* 215–217.

Jacques, E. (1965). Death and the mid-life crisis. *International Journal of Psychoanalysis, 46,* 502–514.

Jarvik, L. F. (1983). The impact of immediate life situation on depression. In L. D. Breslau & M. R. Haug (Eds.), *Depression and aging.* New York: Springer.

Jarvik, L. F., & Bank, L. (1983). Aging twins: Longitudinal psychometric data. In K. W. Schaie (Ed.), *Major psychological assessment instruments.* Boston, MA: Allyn & Bacon.

Javits, J. B. (1984, August). When should doctors let a patient die? *Discover,* pp. 30–31.

Jeffko, W. G. (1980). Redefining death. In E. S. Schneidman (Ed.), *Death: Current perspectives* (2nd ed.). Palo Alto, CA: Mayfield.

Jeffrey, R. W. (1989). Risk behaviors and health: Contrasting individual and population perspectives. *American Psychologist, 44,* 1194–1202.

Jensen, L. C., & Kingston, M. (1986). *Parenting.* New York: Holt, Rinehart and Winston.

Jimenez, S. L. M. (1988, June). Cleft lip and palate. *American Baby,* pp. 66, 80–81.

Johnson, C. L., & Catalano, D. J. (1981, December). Childless elderly and their family supports. *The Gerontologist, 21,* 610–618.

Johnson, C. L., Klee, L., & Schmidt, C. (1988). Conceptions of parentage and kinship among children of divorce. *American Anthropologist, 90,* 136–144.

Johnson, E. S. (1981). Older mothers' perceptions of their child's divorce. *The Gerontologist, 21,* 395–401.

Johnson, M. P., & Leslie, L. (1982). Couple involvement and network structure. A test of the dyadic withdrawal hypothesis. *Social Psychology Quarterly, 4,* 34–43.

Johnson, N. (1967). *How to talk back to your television set.* Boston, MA: Little, Brown.

Johnson, P., & Salisbury, D. W. (1975). Breathing and sucking during feeding in the newborn. In *Parent-infant interaction* (Vol. 33). Amsterdam, The Netherlands: CIBA Foundation Symposium.

Johnson, W. F., Emde, R. N., & Pannabecker, B. J. (1982). Maternal perception of infant emotion from birth through 18 months. *Infant Behavior and Development, 5,* 313–322.

Johnston, L. D., O'Malley, P. M., & Bachman, J. G. (1987). *National trends in drug use and related factors among American high school students and young adults, 1975–1986.* Rockville, MD: National Institute on Drug Abuse.

Jones, D. C., Bloys, N., & Wood, M. (1990). Sex roles and friendship patterns. *Sex Roles, 23,* 133–145.

Jones, M. A., & Hendrickson, N. J. (1970). Recognition by preschool children. *Journal of Home Economics, 62,* 263–267.

Josselson, R. (1982). Personality structure and identity status in women as viewed through early memories. *Journal of Youth and Adolescence, 11,* 293–299.

Juhasz, A. M., & Sonnenshein-Schneider, M. (1987). Adolescent sexuality: Values, morality and decision making. *Adolescence, 22,* 579–590.

Jung, C. G. (1961). *Memories, dreams and reflections.* New York: Random House.

Jung, C. G. (1971). The stages of life (R. F. C. Hull, Trans.). In J. Campbell (Ed.), *The portable Jung* (pp. 3–22). New York: Viking. (Original work published 1933.)

Jurich, A. P., Polson, C. J., Jurich, J. A., & Bates, R. A. (1985). Family factors in the lives of drug users and abusers. *Adolescence, 20,* 143–155.

K

Kagan, J. (1982a). The emergence of self. *Journal of Child Psychology and Psychiatry, 23,* 363–381.

Kagan, J. (1982b, July). The fearful child's hidden talents. *Psychology Today,* pp. 50–59.

Kagan, J. (1984). *The nature of the child.* New York: Basic Books.

Kahana, B., Kahana, E., & McLenigan, P. (1980). Cited in B. Kahana, Social behavior and aging. In B. B. Wolman (Ed.). (1982). *Handbook of developmental psychology.* Englewood Cliffs, NJ: Prentice-Hall.

Kahn, H. (1960). *On thermonuclear war.* Princeton, NJ: Princeton University Press.

Kail, R. (1984). *The development of memory in children.* New York: W. H. Freeman.

Kaitz, M., Meschulach-Sarfaty, O., & Auerbach, J. (1988). A reexamination of newborns' ability to imitate facial expressions. *Developmental Psychology, 24,* 3–7.

Kalat, J. W. (1981). *Biological psychology.* Belmont, CA: Wadsworth.

Kalish, R. A. (1981). *Death, grief, and caring relationships.* Monterey, CA: Brooks/Cole.

Kalter, N. (1987). Long-term effects of divorce on children: A developmental vulnerability model. *American Journal of Orthopsychiatry, 57,* 587–600.

Kalter, N., Riemes, B., Brickman, A., & Chen, J. W. (1985). Implications of parental divorce for female development. *Journal of the American Academy of Child Psychiatry, 24,* 538–544.

Kamerman, J. B. (1988). *Death in the midst of life: Social & cultural influences on death, grief & mourning.* Englewood Cliffs, NJ: Prentice-Hall.

Kamii, C., & deVries, R. (1980). *Group games in early education.* Washington, DC: National Association for Education of Young Children.

Kandel, D., & Lesser, G. (1972). *Youth in two worlds: U. S. and Denmark.* San Francisco, CA: Jossey-Bass.

Kandel, D. B. (1990, February). Parenting styles, drug use, and children's adjustment in families of young adults. *Journal of Marriage and the Family, 52,* 183–196.

Kane, B. (1979). Children's concepts of death. *Journal of Genetic Psychology, 134,* 141–153.

Kanin, E. J., & Parcell, S. R. (1977). Sexual aggression: A second look at the offended female. *Archives of Sexual Behavior, 6,* 67–76.

Kantrowitz, B. (1987, October 12). Teenagers and abortion. *Newsweek,* p. 81.

Kantrowitz, B., Wingert, P., & Hager, M. (1988, May 16). Preemies. *Newsweek,* pp. 62–67.

Kaplan, H., & Dove, H. (1987). Infant development among the Ache of East Paraguay. *Developmental Psychology, 23,* 190–198.

Karpoe, K. P., & Olney, R. L. (1983). The effect of boys' and girls' toys on sex-typed play in preadolescents. *Sex Roles, 9,* 507–514.

Kart, C. S. (1981). *The realities of aging.* Boston, MA: Allyn & Bacon.

Kastenbaum, R. (1981). *Death, society and human experience* (2nd ed.). St. Louis, MO: C. V. Mosby.

Kastenbaum, R. J. (1984). When aging begins: A lifespan developmental approach. *Research Aging, 6,* 105–117.

Kastenbaum, R., & Briscoe, L. (1975). The street corner: A laboratory for the study of life-threatening behavior. *Omega, 6,* 33–44.

Katchadourian, H. (1987). *Fifty: Midlife in perspective.* New York: W. H. Freeman.

Kaufman, A. S., & Kaufman, N. L. (1983). *Kaufman assessment battery for children interpretive manual.* Circle Pines, MN: American Guidance Service.

Kaufman, S. R. (1987). *The ageless self: Sources of meaning in late life.* Madison, WI: University of Wisconsin Press.

Kausler, D. H., Salthouse, T. A., & Saults, J. S. (1988, Summer). Temporal memory over the adult lifespan. *American Journal of Psychology, 101,* 207–215.

Kavanaugh, R. E. (1972). *Facing death.* Baltimore, MD: Penguin.

Keating, N. C., & Cole, P. (1980). What do I do with him 24 hours a day? Changes in the housewife role after retirement. *The Gerontologist, 20,* 84–89.

Keener, M. A., Zeanah, C. H., & Anders, T. F. (1988). Infant temperament, sleep organization, and nighttime parental interventions. *Pediatrics, 81,* 762–771.

Keil, F. (1979). *Semantic and conceptual development.* Cambridge, MA: Harvard University Press.

Keith, P. M. (1983). A comparison of the resources of parents and childless men and women in very old age. *Family Relations, 32,* 403–409.

Keith, P. M., & Nauta, A. (1988, January). Old and single in the city and in the country: Activities of the unmarried. *Family Relations, 37,* 79–83.

Kelley, H. H. (1981). Marriage relationships and aging. In R. W. Fogel, E. Hatfield, S. B. Kiesler, & E. Shanas (Eds.), *Aging: Stability and change in the family.* New York: Academic Press.

Kellman, P. J., Spelke, E. S., & Short, K. R. (1986). Infant perception of object unity from translatory motion in depth and vertical translation. *Child Development, 57,* 72–86.

Kelly, E. L., & Conley, J. J. (1987). Personality and compatibility: A prospective analysis of marital stability and marital satisfaction. *Journal of Personality and Social Psychology, 52,* 27–40.

Kendig, H. L., & Rowland, D. T. (1983). Family support of the Australian aged: A comparison with the United States. *The Gerontologist, 23,* 643–649.

Keniston, K. (1975). Youth as a stage of life. In R. Havighurst & P. H. Dreyer (Eds.), *Youth* (74th Yearbook of National Society for the Study of Education). Chicago, IL: University of Chicago Press.

Kerchoff, A. C., & Davis, K. E. (1962). Value consensus and need complementarity in mate selection. *American Sociological Review, 27,* 295–303.

Kermis, M. D. (1984). *The psychology of aging: Theory, research and practice.* Boston: Allyn & Bacon.

Kienhorst, C. W. M., Wolters, W. H. G., Diekstra, R. F. W., & Otte, E. (1987). A study of the frequency of suicidal behavior in children aged 5 to 14. *Child Psychology and Psychiatry, 28,* 153–165.

Kiff, R. S., & Lepard, C. (1966). Visual response of premature infants. *Archives of Ophthalmology, 75,* 631–633.

Kimble, G. A., & Pennypacker, H. S. (1963). Eyelid conditioning in young and aged subjects. *Journal of Genetic Psychology, 103,* 283–289.

Kimmel, D. C. (1988, March). Ageism, psychology, and public policy. *American Psychologist, 43,* 175–178.

Kimmel, D. C. (1990). *Adulthood and aging.* New York: John Wiley & Sons.

Kimmel, M. M., & Segel, E. (1983). *For reading out loud!* New York: Delacorte.

Kinard, E. M., & Reinherz, H. (1984). Behavioral and emotional functioning in children of adolescent mothers. *American Journal of Orthopsychiatry, 54,* 578–591.

Kingsbury, N. M., & Minda, R. B. (1988). An analysis of three expected intimate relationship states: Commitment, maintenance and termination. *Journal of Social and Personal Relationships, 5,* 405–422.

Kinnaird, K., & Gerrard, M. (1986). Premarital sexual behavior and attitudes toward marriage and divorce among young women as a function of their mothers' marital status. *Journal of Marriage and the Family, 48,* 757–765.

Kirby, M. D. (1987). Medical technology and new frontiers of family law. *Law, Medicine & Health Care, 14,* 113–119.

Kitchener, K., & King, P. (1981). Reflective judgment: Concepts of justification and their relationship to age and education. *Journal of Applied Developmental Psychology, 2,* 89–116.

Kitchener, P. (1985). *Vaulting ambition: Sociobiology and the quest for human nature.* Cambridge, MA: MIT Press.

Kivela, S. L., Pahkala, K., & Honkakoski, A. (1986). Sexual desire, intercourse, and related factors among elderly Fins. *Nord Sexol, 4,* 18–27.

Kivett, V. R. (1985). Consanguinity and kin level: Their relative importance to the helping network of older adults. *Journal of Gerontology, 40,* 228–234.

Klass, C. S. (1987, March). Childrearing interactions within developmental home- or center-based early education. *Young Children,* pp. 9–13, 67–70.

Klaus, M., & Kennell, J. (1976). *Maternal-infant bonding.* St. Louis, MO: C. V. Mosby.

Kleemeier, R. W. (1961). Intellectual change in the senium or death and the I.Q. Cited in J. Botwinick. (1984). *Aging and behavior* (3rd ed.). New York: Springer.

Klein, R. P. (1985). Caregiving arrangements by employed women with children under 1 year of age. *Developmental Psychology, 21,* 403–406.

Kleinman, J. C., & Kessel, S. S. (1987). Racial differences in low birthweight. *New England Journal of Medicine, 317,* 749–753.

Klerman, G. L. (1983). Problems in the definition and diagnosis of depression in the elderly. In L. D. Breslau & M. R. Haug (Eds.), *Depression and aging.* New York: Springer.

Klinger-Vartabedian, L., & Wispe, L. (1989, February). Age differences in marriage and female longevity. *Journal of Marriage and the Family, 51,* 195–202.

Knapp, R. J. (1987, July). When a child dies. *Psychology Today,* pp. 60–67.

Knittle, J. (1972). Obesity in childhood: A problem in adipose tissue cellular development. *Journal of Pediatrics, 81,* 1948.

Koenig, P. (1972, November). Death doth defer. *Psychology Today,* pp. 83–87.

Kohlberg, L. (1958). *The development of modes of moral thinking and choice in the years ten to sixteen.* Unpublished doctoral dissertation, University of Chicago, Chicago. Cited in Gibbs, J. C., & Schnell, S. V. (1985). Moral development "versus" socialization. *American Psychologist, 40,* 1071–1080.

Kohlberg, L. (1966). A cognitive-developmental analysis of children's sex-role concepts and attitudes. In E. E. Maccoby (Ed.), *The development of sex differences.* Stanford, CA: Stanford University Press.

Kohlberg, L. (1969). Stage and sequence: The cognitive-developmental approach to socialization. In D. Goslind (Ed.), *Handbook of socialization theory and research.* Chicago, IL: Rand McNally.

Kohlberg, L. (1981). *The philosophy of moral development: Moral stages and the ideal of justice* (Vol. 1). San Francisco, CA: Harper & Row.

Kohlberg, L. (1984). *The philosophy of moral development: Essays on moral development* (Vol. 2). San Francisco, CA: Harper & Row.

Kohlberg, L. (1986). *The stages of ethical development from childhood through old age.* San Francisco, CA: Harper & Row.

Kohlberg, L., Levine, C., & Hewer, A. (1983). Moral stages: A current formulation and response to critics. *Contributions to Human Development, 10,* 1–174.

Kohlberg, L., & Ullman, D. Z. (1974). Stages in the development of psychosexual concepts and attitudes. In R. C. Friedman, R. M. Richart, & R. L. VandeWille (Eds.), *Sex differences in behavior.* New York: Wiley.

Kohn, A. (1987, December). Making the most of marriage. *Psychology Today,* pp. 6–8.

Kohut, H. (1977). *The restoration of the self.* New York: International Universities Press.

Kolata, G. B. (1986). Obese children. *Science, 232,* 20–21.

Kolata, G. B. (1987). Early signs of school age IQ. *Science, 236,* 774–775.

Kolb, D. A. (1984). *Experiential learning: Experience as the source of learning and development.* Englewood Cliffs, NJ: Prentice-Hall.

Koops, B. L., & Battaglia, F. C. (1987). The newborn infant. In C. H. Kempe, H. K. Silver, D. O'Brien, & V. A. Fulginiti (Eds.), *Current pediatric diagnosis & treatment 1987.* Norwalk, CT: Appleton & Lange.

Korner, A. F. (1973). Sex differences in newborns with special reference to differences in the organization of oral behavior. *Journal of Child Psychology and Psychiatry, 14,* 17–29.

Korner, A. F., Zeanah, C. H., Linden, J., Berkowitz, R. I., Kraemer, H. C., & Agras, W. S. (1985). The relation between neonatal and later activity and temperament. *Child Development, 56,* 38–42.

Kornhaber, A., & Woodard, K. L. (1981). *Grandparents/grandchildren: The vital connection.* Garden City, NJ: Anchor.

Koslow, R. E. (1988). Age-related reasons for expressed interest in exercise and weight control. *Journal of Applied Social Psychology, 18,* 349–354.

Koslowski, B. (1980). Quantitative and qualitative changes in the development of seriation. *Merrill-Palmer Quarterly, 26,* 391–405.

Koss, M. P., & Oros, C. J. (1982). Sexual experiences survey: A research instrument investigating sexual aggression and victimization. *Journal of Consulting and Clinical Psychology, 50,* 455–457.

Kowalski, B. (1988). *Cholesterol and children.* New York: Harper & Row.

Kozlov, A. (1988). Women of the year: The old girl network. *Discover, 9,* 30–31.

Kramer, D. A. (1983). Post-formal operations? A need for further conceptualization. *Human Development, 26,* 91–105.

Krenzke, T. L. (1981). The relationship between cognitive levels of play and child-selected play activities in younger and older preschool children. *Dissertation Abstracts International, 42,* 1472A (University Microfilms No. 81–20, 504).

Kreutzer, M., Leonard, C., & Flavell, J. (1975). An interview study of children's knowledge about memory. *Monographs of the Society for Research in Child Development, 40,* (1, Serial No. 159).

Krohne, H. W., & Rogner, J. (1982). Repression-sensitization as a central construct in coping research. In H. W. Krohne & L. Laux (Eds.), *Achievement, stress, and anxiety.* Washington, DC: Hemisphere.

Krosnick, J. A., & Judd, C. M. (1982). Transition in social influence at adolescence. *Developmental Psychology, 18,* 359–368.

Krueger, H. K., & Bornstein, P. H. (1987). Depression, sex-roles, and family variables: Comparison of bulimics, binge-eaters, and normals. *Psychological Reports, 60,* 1196.

Kruger, S., & Maetzold, L. D. (1983). Practices of tradition for pregnancy. *Maternal-Child Nursing Journal, 12,* 135–139.

Kübler-Ross, E. (1969). *On death and dying.* New York: Macmillan.

Kuhl, P. K., & Meltzoff, A. N. (1988). Speech as an intermodal object of perception. In A. Yonas (Ed.), *Perceptual development in infancy. The Minnesota Symposia on Child Psychology* (Vol. 20). Hillsdale, NJ: Lawrence Erlbaum.

Kuhl, P. K., & Miller, J. D. (1982). Discrimination of auditory target dimensions in the presence or absence of variations in a second dimension by infants. *Perception and Psychophysics, 31,* 279–292.

Kuhn, D., Nash, S. C., & Brucken, L. (1978). Sex-role concepts of two- and three-year-olds. *Child Development, 49,* 445–451.

Kuhse, H. (1986). The case for active voluntary euthanasia. *Law, Medicine & Health Care, 14,* 445–451.

L

Labouvie-Vief, G. (1985). Intelligence and cognition. In J. E. Birren & K. W. Schaie (Eds.), *Handbook of the psychology of aging* (2nd ed.). New York: Van Nostrand Reinhold.

Labouvie-Vief, G. (1986). Modes of knowledge and the organization of development. In M. L. Commons, L. Kohlberg, F. Richards, & J. Sinnott (Eds.), *Beyond formal operations 3: Models and methods in the study of adult and adolescent thought.* New York: Praeger.

Lagercrantz, H., & Slotkin, T. A. (1986, April). The "stress" of being born. *Scientific American,* pp. 100–107.

Lamanna, M. A., & Reidmann, A. (1988). *Marriages and families: Making choices and facing change* (3rd ed.). Belmont, CA: Wadsworth.

Lamaze, F. (1970). *Painless childbirth: Psychoprophylactic method.* Chicago, IL: Regnery.

Lamb, M. E. (1981). The development of father-infant relationships. In M. E. Lamb (Ed.), *The role of the father in child development.* New York: Wiley.

Lamb, M. E. (1987). Introduction: The emergent American father. In M. E. Lamb (Ed.), *The father's role: Cross-cultural perspectives* (pp. 3–25). Hillsdale, NJ: Erlbaum.

Lamb, M., & Hwang, C. P. (1982). Maternal attachment and mother neonate bonding: A critical review. In M. E. Lamb & A. L. Brown (Eds.), *Advances in developmental psychology* (Vol. 2). Hillsdale, NJ: Erlbaum.

Lamb, M. E., Pleck, J. H., Charnov, E. L., & Levine, J. A. (1987). A biosocial perspective on paternal behavior and involvement. In J. B. Lancaster, J. Altmann, A. S. Rossi, & L. R. Sherrod (Eds.), *Parenting across the lifespan: Biosocial dimensions.* New York: Aldine de Gruyter.

Lamke, L. K. (1989). Marital adjustment among rural couples: The role of expressiveness. *Sex Roles, 21,* 579–590.

Lancioni, G. E. (1980). Infant operant conditioning and its implications for early intervention. *Psychological Bulletin, 88,* 516–534.

Land, H. (1987, March/April). Children having children. *Society,* pp. 36–40.

Landers, S. (1988, January). Study finds "latchkey kid" alarm to be exaggerated. *APA Monitor,* p. 28.

Landwirth, J. (1988). Should anencephalic infants be used as organ donors? *Pediatrics, 82,* 257–259.

Lane, B. (1964). Attitudes of youth toward the aged. *Journal of Marriage and the Family, 26,* 229–231.

Langer, E. J., & Rodin, J. (1976). The effects of choice and enhanced personal responsibility for the aged: A field experiment in an institutional setting. *Journal of Personality and Social Psychology, 34,* 191–198.

Langlois, J. H., Roggman, L. A., Casey, R. J., Ritter, J. M., Rieser-Danner, L. A., & Jenkins, V. Y. (1987). Infant preferences for attractive faces: Rudiments of a stereotype? *Developmental Psychology, 23,* 363–369.

Langsdorf, P., Izard, C. E., Rayias, M., & Hembree, E. A. (1983). Interest expression, visual fixation, and heart rate changes in 2- and 8-month old infants. *Developmental Psychology, 19,* 375–386.

Lansbaum, J., & Willis, R. (1971). Conformity in early and late adolescence. *Developmental Psychology, 4,* 334–337.

Lansky, V. (1985, February). Your child's friends & foes: In praise of friendship. *Parents,* pp. 68–76.

LaRossa, R. (1988, October). Fatherhood and social change. *Family Relations, 37,* 451–457.

LaRossa, R., & LaRossa, M. M. (1981). *Transition to parenthood: How infants change families.* Beverly Hills, CA: Sage.

Larson, R. (1989). Is feeling "in control" related to happiness in daily life? *Psychological Reports, 64,* 775–784.

Larson, R., & Csikszentmihalyi, M. (1978). Experiential correlates of time alone in adolescence. *Journal of Personality, 46,* 677–693.

LaRue, A., Dessonville, C., & Jarvik, L. F. (1985). Aging and mental disorders. In J. E. Birren & K. W. Schaie (Eds.), *Handbook of the psychology of aging* (2nd ed., pp. 664–703). New York: Van Nostrand Reinhold.

Lau, R. R., & Klepper, S. (1988). The development of illness orientations in children aged 6 through 12. *Journal of Health and Social Behavior, 29,* 149–168.

Lauer, J., & Lauer, R. (1985). Marriages made to last. *Psychology Today, 19,* 22–26.

Lauer, R. H., & Lauer, J. C. (1987). Development: Men versus women. *Psychological Reports, 61,* 706.

Lauer, R. H., & Lauer, J. C. (1988). *Watersheds: Mastering life's unpredictable crises.* New York: Little, Brown.

Lawren, B. (1988, May). We're sorry, your time is up. *Omni,* p. 31.

Lazar, I., Darlington, R., Murrar, J., Roysce, J., & Snipper, A. (1982). Lasting effects of early education. *Monographs of the Society for Research in Child Development, 47,* (1–2, Serial No. 194).

Lazarus, R. S., & Folkman, S. (1984). *Stress, appraisal and coping.* New York: Springer.

Leach, P. (1982). *Your baby & child: From birth to age five.* New York: Knopf.

Leadbeater, B. (1986). The resolution of relativism in adult thinking: Subjective, objective, or conceptual. *Human Development, 29,* 291–300.

Leary, M. R., & Snell, W. E., Jr. (1988). The relationship of instrumentality and expressiveness to sexual behavior in males and females. *Sex Roles, 18,* 509–521.

Leboyer, F. (1975). *Birth without violence.* New York: Random House.

Lee, D. N., & Aronson, E. (1974). Visual proprioceptive control of standing in human infants. *Perception & Psychophysics, 15,* 529–532.

Lee, G. R., & Ihinger-Tallman, M. (1980, September). Sibling interaction and morale: The effects of family relations on older people. *Research on Aging,* pp. 367–391.

Lee, I. S., & Cohen, B. L. (1979). A catalog of risks. *Health Physics, 36*, 707–722.

Lee, J. A. (1973). *The colors of love: An exploration of the ways of loving.* Englewood Cliffs, NJ: Prentice-Hall.

Lee, J. A. (1977). A typology of styles of loving. *Personality and Social Psychology Bulletin, 3*, 173–182.

Leekam, S. R. (1988). *Children's understanding of intentional falsehood.* Unpublished doctoral dissertation, Sussex University, Brighton, England. Cited in Mant, C. M., & Perner, J. (1988). The child's understanding of commitment. *Developmental Psychology, 24*, 343–351.

Lehman, D. R., Wortman, C. B., & Williams, A. F. (1987). Long-term effects of losing a spouse or child in a motor vehicle-crash. *Journal of Personality and Social Psychology, 52*, 218–231.

Lehman, H. C. (1962). The creative production rates of present versus past generations of scientists. *Journal of Gerontology, 17*, 409–417.

Lehr, U. (1983). Stereotypes of aging and age norms. In J. E. Birren (Ed.), *Aging: A challenge to science and society* (Vol. 3, pp. 101–112). New York: Oxford University Press.

Leming, M. R., & Dickinson, G. E. (1985). *Understanding dying, death, and bereavement.* New York: Holt, Rinehart and Winston.

Lemonick, M. D. (1988, January 4). It's a boy, and here's why. *Time*, p. 60.

Lempers, J. D., Flavell, E. R., & Flavell, J. H. (1977). The development in very young children of tacit knowledge concerning visual perceptions. *Genetic Psychology Monographs, 95*, 3–53.

Lenneberg, E. H. (1967). *Biological foundations of language.* New York: Wiley.

Lennon, M. C. (1987). Is menopause depressing? An investigation of three perspectives. *Sex Roles, 17*, 1–16.

Leo, J. (1986, November 24). Sex and schools. *Time*, pp. 54–63.

Leon, M. (1987). Somatic aspects of parent-offspring interactions. In J. B. Lancaster, J. Altmann, A. S. Rossi, & L. R. Sherrod (Eds.), *Parenting across the lifespan: Biosocial dimensions.* New York: Aldine de Gruyter.

Lepper, M. R., Greene, D., & Nisbett, R. E. (1973). Undermining children's intrinsic interest with extrinsic rewards. *Journal of Personality and Social Psychology, 18*, 129–137.

Lerner, J. V. (1984). The import of temperament for psychosocial functioning: Tests of a goodness-of-fit model. *Merrill-Palmer Quarterly, 30*, 177–188.

Lerner, R. M. (1983). The history of philosophy and the philosophy of history in developmental psychology: A view of the issues. In R. M. Lerner (Ed.), *Developmental psychology: Historical and philosophical perspectives.* Hillsdale, NJ: Erlbaum.

Lerner, R. M. (1985). Individual and context in developmental psychology: Conceptual and theoretical issues. In J. R. Nesselroade & A. Von Eye (Eds.), *Individual development and social change: Explanatory analysis.* New York: Academic Press.

Lesser, E. K., & Comet, J. J. (1987). Help and hindrance: Parents of divorcing children. *Journal of Marital and Family Therapy, 13(2)*, 197–202.

Lester, B. M., & Boukydis, C. F. Z. (1985). *Infant crying: Theoretical and research perspectives.* New York: Plenum.

Levine, S. V. (1984, August). Radical departures. *Psychology Today*, pp. 20–27.

Levinson, D. J. (1978). *The seasons of a man's life.* New York: Knopf.

Levinson, D. J. (1986). A conception of adult development. *American Psychologist, 41(1)*, 3–13.

Levinson, D. J., Darrow, C. M., Klein, E. B., Levinson, M. H., & McKee, B. (1976). Periods in the adult development of men: Ages 18–45. *The Counseling Psychologist, 6*, 21–25.

Levinson, R., Powell, B., & Steelman, L. C. (1986). Social location, significant others and body image among adolescents. *Social Psychology Quarterly, 49*, 330–337.

Levitan, S. A. (1984, September/October). The changing workplace. *Society*, pp. 41–48.

Levitt, M. J., Weber, R. A., Clark, M. C., & McDonnell, P. (1985). Reciprocity of exchange in toddler sharing behavior. *Developmental Psychology, 21*, 122–123.

Levoy, G. (1987). Birth controllers. *Omni, 30*, 100.

Levy-Shiff, R., & Israelashvili, R. (1988). Antecedents of fathering: Some further exploration. *Developmental Psychology, 24*, 434–440.

Lewin, R. (1987). More clues to the cause of Parkinson's disease. *Science, 237*, 978.

Lewis, A. B., & Mayer, R. E. (1987). Students' miscomprehension of relational statements in arithmetic word problems. *Journal of Educational Psychology, 79*, 363–371.

Lewis, M., & Brooks-Gunn, J. (1979). *Social cognition and the acquisition of self.* New York: Plenum Press.

Lewis, T. L., & Maurer, D. (1977, March). *Newborns' central vision: Whole or hole?* Paper presented at the meeting of the Society for Research in Child Development, New Orleans.

Lewkowicz, D., & Turkewitz, G. (1981). Intersensory interaction in newborns: Modification of visual preferences following exposure to sound. *Child Development, 52*, 827–832.

Lieberman, E., Ryan, K. J., Monson, R. R., & Schoenbaum, S. C. (1987). Risk factors accounting for racial differences in the rate of premature birth. *New England Journal of Medicine, 317*, 743–748.

Lieberman, L. S. (1988). Diabetes and obesity in elderly black Americans. In J. S. Jackson (Ed.), *The Black American elderly: Research on physical and psychosocial health.* New York: Springer.

Lieberman, M. A. (1983). Studies of terminal decline: Implications for a developmental theory of personality. In J. E. Birren (Ed.), *Aging: A challenge to science and society* (Vol. 3). New York: Oxford University Press.

Liebert, R. M., Sprafken, J. N., & Davidson, E. S. (1982). *The early window: Effects of television on children and youth* (2nd ed.). New York: Pergamon Press.

Light, L. L., & Capps, J. L. (1986). Comprehension of pronouns in young and older adults. *Developmental Psychology, 22*, 580–585.

Lin, S., & Lepper, M. R. (1987). Correlates of children's usage of videogames and computers. *Journal of Applied Social Psychology, 17*, 72–93.

Lindemann, E. (1944). Symptomatology and management of acute grief. *American Journal of Psychiatry, 101*, 141–148.

Linkletter, A. (1961). *Kids still say the darndest things!* New York: Pocket Books.

Linn, R. (1987). When an AIDS child enters the classroom: Moral-psychological research questions. *Psychological Reports, 61*, 191–197.

Lipman-Blumen, J., Handley-Isakin, A., & Leavitt, H. J. (1983). Achieving styles in men and women: A model, an instrument, and some findings. In J. T. Spence (Ed.), *Achievement and achievement motives: Psychological and sociological approaches.* San Francisco, CA: W. H. Freeman.

Lipsitt, L. (1977). Taste in human neonates: Its effects on sucking and the heart rate. In J. M. Weiffenbach (Ed.), *Taste and development: The genesis of sweet preference.* Washington, DC: U. S. Government Printing Office.

Lipsitt, L., Engen, T., & Kaye, H. (1963). Developmental changes in the olfactory threshold of the neonate. *Child Development, 34*, 37–46.

Lipsitt, L. P., Sturner, W. Q., & Burke, B. (1979). Perinatal indicators and subsequent crib death. *Infant Behavior and Development, 2*, 325–328.

Loehlin, J. S., & Nichols, R. C. (1976). *Heredity, environment, and personality.* Austin, TX: University of Texas Press.

Long, J. D., Anderson, J., & Williams, R. L. (1990). Life reflections by older kinsmen about critical life issues. *Educational Gerontology, 16*, 61–71.

Long, T. J., & Long, L. (1982). *Latchkey children.* Washington, DC: Catholic University of America (ERIC Document Reproduction Service No. ED 211 229).

Longino, C. F., & Kart, C. S. (1982). Explicating activity theory: A formal replication. *Journal of Gerontology, 37*, 713–721.

Lorenz, K. (1957). Comparative study of behavior. In C. H. Schiller (Ed.), *Instinctive behavior.* New York: International Press.

Lorenz, K. (1966). *On aggression.* London, England: Methuen.

Lounsbury, M. L., & Bales, J. E. (1982). The cries of infants of differing levels of perceived temperamental difficultness: Acoustic properties and effect on listeners. *Child Development, 53,* 677–686.

Lovell, K., & Shayer, M. (1978). The impact of the work of Piaget on science curriculum development. In J. M. Gallagher & J. A. Easley, Jr. (Eds.), *Knowledge and development. Vol. 2. Piaget and education.* New York: Plenum Press.

Lubomudrov, S. (1987). Congressional perceptions of the elderly: The use of stereotypes in the legislative process. *The Gerontologist, 27,* 77–81.

Ludeman, K. (1981). The sexuality of the older person: Review of the literature. *The Gerontologist, 21,* 203–208.

Lunde, N. I., Fog, E., Larsen, G. K., Maden, J., Garde, K., & Kelstrup, J. (1986). 70-aarige kvinders seksuelle adfard, oplevelse, viden og holdning. *Ugeskr Lager, 148,* 2863–2866.

Lyons-Ruth, K. (1977). Bimodal perception in infancy: Response to auditory visual incongruity. *Child Development, 48,* 820–827.

M

Maccoby, E. E. (1980). *Social development.* San Diego, CA: Harcourt Brace Jovanovich.

Maccoby, E. E. (1990, April). Gender and relationships: A developmental account. *American Psychologist, 45,* 513–520.

Maccoby, E. E., & Jacklin, C. N. (1980). Sex differences in aggression: A rejoinder and reprise. *Child Development, 51,* 964–980.

Maccoby, E. E., & Martin, J. A. (1983). Socialization in the context of the family: Parent-child interaction. In P. H. Mussen (Ed.), *Handbook of child psychology: Vol. 4. Socialization, personality and social development.* New York: Wiley.

MacFarlane, A. (1978). What a baby knows. *Human Nature, 1,* 74–81.

MacFarlane, J. W. (1964). Perspectives on personality consistency and change from the guidance study. *Vita Humana, 7,* 115–126.

Macklin, E. (1987). Nontraditional family forms. In M. S. Sussman & S. K. Steinmetz (Eds.), *Handbook of marriage and the family.* New York: Plenum Press.

Macklin, E. D. (1988). AIDS: Implications for families. *Family Relations, 37,* 141–149.

Maclean, M., Bryant, P., & Bradley, L. (1987). Rhymes, nursery rhymes, and reading in early childhood. *Merrill-Palmer Quarterly, 33*(3), 255–281.

Madden, D. J. (1985). Adult age differences in memory-driven selective attention. *Developmental Psychology, 21,* 654–665.

Madison, L. S., Madison, J. K., & Adubato, S. A. (1986). Infant behavior and development in relation to fetal movement and habituation. *Child Development, 57,* 1475–1482.

Maeda, D. (1978). Aging in eastern society. In D. Hobman (Ed.), *The social challenge of aging.* New York: St. Martin's Press.

Magenis, R. E., Overton, K. M., Chamberlin, J., Brady, T., & Lorrein, E. (1977). Parental origin of the extra chromosome in Down's syndrome. *Human Genetics, 37,* 7–16.

Magnusson, D., Stattin, H., & Allen, V. L. (1986). Differential maturation among girls and its relations to social adjustment: A longitudinal perspective. In P. B. Baltes, D. L. Featherman, & R. M. Lerner (Eds.), *Life-span development and behavior* (Vol. 7). Hillsdale, NJ: Lawrence Erlbaum.

Mahler, M. S. (1968). *On human symbiosis and the vicissitudes of individuation.* New York: International Universities Press.

Main, W. E., & Weston, D. R. (1981). The quality of the toddler's relationship to mother and to father: Related to conflict and the readiness to establish new relationships. *Child Development, 52,* 932–940.

Malatesta, C. Z., & Izard, C. E. (1984). *Emotion in adult development.* Beverly Hills, CA: Sage.

Malina, R. M. (1979). Secular changes in size and maturity: Causes and effects. In A. F. Roche (Ed.), *Monographs of the Society for Research in Child Development, 44,* Nos. 3–4.

Mallinckrodt, B., & Fretz, B. R. (1988). Social support and the impact of job loss on older professionals. *Journal of Counseling Psychology, 35,* 281–286.

Maloney, B. D. (1988). The legacy of AIDS: Challenge for the next century. *Journal of Marital and Family Therapy, 14,* 143–150.

Mandler, J. M. (1983). Representation. In P. H. Mussen (Ed.), *Handbook of child psychology* (4th ed., Vol. 3. pp. 420–495). New York: Wiley.

Mandler, J. M., & Robinson, C. A. (1977). Developmental changes in picture recognition. *Journal of Experimental Child Psychology, 3,* 386–396.

Mansfield, P. K. (1988). Midlife childbearing: Strategies for informed decision making. *Psychology of Women Quarterly, 12,* 445–460.

Mant, C. M., & Perner, J. (1988). The child's understanding of commitment. *Developmental Psychology, 24,* 343–351.

Manton, K. G., Siegler, I. C., & Woodbury, M. A. (1986). Patterns of intellectual development in later life. *Journal of Gerontology, 41,* 486–499.

Manuel, R. C. (1988). The demography of older Blacks in the United States. In J. S. Jackson (Ed.), *The Black American elderly: Research on physical and psychosocial health.* New York: Springer.

Maranto, G. (1984). Choosing your baby's sex. *Discover, 5,* 24–27.

Marcia, J. E. (1966). Development and validation of ego-identity status. *Journal of Personality and Social Psychology, 3,* 551–558.

Marcia, J. E. (1980). Identity in adolescence. In J. Adelson (Ed.), *Handbook of adolescent psychology.* New York: Wiley.

Margolin, L., & White, L. (1987). The continuing role of physical attractiveness in marriage. *Journal of Marriage and the Family, 49,* 21–27.

Markman, E. M. (1977). Realizing that you don't understand: A preliminary investigation. *Child Development, 48,* 986–992.

Marks, I. (1987). The development of normal fear: A review. *Journal of Child Psychology and Psychiatry, 28,* 667–697.

Marquand, R. (1987, October 16). Nailing down the numbers on U. S. students and schools. *Christian Science Monitor,* p. 18.

Marshall, V. W. (1975). Age and awareness of finitude in developmental gerontology. *Omega, 6,* 113–129.

Martin, A., & Baenen, N. R. (1987). School-age mothers' attitudes toward parenthood and father involvement. *Family Therapy, 14,* 97–103.

Martin, A., & Fedio, P. (1983). Word production and comprehension in Alzheimer's disease: The breakdown of semantic knowledge. *Brain and Language, 25,* 323–341.

Martin, N., & Jardine, R. (1986). Eysenck's contributions to behavior and controversy. In S. Modgil & C. Modgil (Eds.), *Hans Eysenck: Consensus and controversy* (pp. 13–47). Philadelphia, PA: Falmer.

Marx, J. L. (1987). Oxygen-free radicals linked to many diseases. *Science, 235,* 529–531.

Marzollo, J. (1988, May). Talking to kids about AIDS. *Parents,* pp. 118–122, 196–206.

Masamba ma Mpolo. (1984). *Older persons and their families live in a changing village society: A perspective from Zaire.* Washington, DC: International Federation on Aging.

Masangkay, Z. S., McCluskey, K. A., McIntyro, C. W., Simi-Knight, J., Vaughan, B. E., & Flavell, J. H. (1974). The early development of inferences about the visual percepts of others. *Child Development, 45,* 357–366.

Maslach, C., & Jackson, S. E. (1985). Burnout in health professions: A social psychological analysis. In G. Snagers & J. Suls (Eds.), *Social psychology of health and illness.* Hillsdale, NJ: Lawrence Erlbaum.

Maslow, A. (1959). Creativity in self-actualizing people. In H. H. Anderson (Ed.), *Creativity and its cultivation.* New York: Harper & Row.

Maslow, A. (1968). *Toward a psychology of being.* Princeton, NJ: Van Nostrand.

Maslow, A. (1970). *Motivation and personality* (rev. ed.). New York: Harper & Row.

Mason, A., & Blankenship, V. (1987). Power and affiliation motivation, stress, and abuse in intimate relationships. *Journal of Personality and Social Psychology, 52,* 203–210.

Mason, S. E., & Smith, A. D. (1977). Imagery in the aged. *Experimental Aging Research, 3,* 17–32.

Matas, L., Arend, R. A., & Sroufe, L. A. (1978). Continuity in the adaptation in the second year: The relationships between quality of attachment and later competence. *Child Development, 49,* 547–556.

Matheny, A. (1986). Stability and change of infant temperament: Contributions from the infant, mother, and family environment. In G. Kohnstamm (Ed.), *Temperament discussed* (pp. 49–55). Berwyn, PA: Swets North America.

Mattessich, P., & Hill. R. L. (1987). Life cycle and family development. In M. S. Sussman & S. K. Steinmetz (Eds.), *Handbook of marriage and the family*. New York: Plenum Press.

Matthews, S. H., & Sprey, J. (1985). Adolescents' relationships with grandparents: An empirical contribution to conceptual clarification. *Journal of Gerontology, 40,* 621–626.

Maudry, M., & Nekula, M. (1939). Social relations between children of the same age during the first two years of life. *Journal of Abnormal and Social Psychology, 27,* 243–269.

Maurer, D. M., & Salapatek, P. (1976). Developmental changes in the scanning of faces by young infants. *Child Development, 47,* 523–527.

May, R. (1972). *Power and innocence: A search for the sources of violence.* New York: Norton.

May, R., Rogers, C., & Maslow, A. (1986). *Politics and innocence: A humanistic debate.* Dallas, TX: Saybrook.

Mayer, J. E. (1988). The personality characteristics of adolescents who use and misuse alcohol. *Adolescence, 23,* 383–404.

Maykovich, M. K. (1976). Attitudes versus behavior in extramarital sexual relations. *Journal of Marriage and the Family, 38,* 693–699.

Mazess, R. B., & Forman, S. H. (1979). Longevity and age exaggeration in Vilcabamba, Ecuador. *Journal of Gerontology, 34,* 94–98.

McAnarney, E. R., & Greydanus, D. E. (1987). Adolescence. In C. H. Kempe, H. K. Silver, D. O'Brien, & V. A. Fulginiti (Eds.), *Current pediatric diagnosis & treatment 1987.* Norwalk, CT: Appleton & Lange.

McAuliffe, K. (1985, October). Making of a mind. *Omni,* pp. 62–67, 74.

McBride, S., & Belsky, J. (1988). Characteristics, determinants, and consequences of maternal separation anxiety. *Developmental Psychology, 24,* 407–414.

McCabe, M. P. (1984). Toward a theory of adolescent dating. *Adolescence, 19,* 159–170.

McCall, R. B., Applebaum, M. I., & Hogarty, P. S. (1973). Developmental changes in mental performance. *Monographs of the Society for Research in Child Development, 38,* (Serial No. 150).

McCarthy, K. (1990, November). If one spouse is sick, both are affected. *APA Monitor,* p. 7.

McCartney, K., Scarr, S., Phillips, D., & Grajek, S. (1985). Day care as intervention: Comparisons of varying quality programs. *Journal of Applied Developmental Psychology, 6,* 247–260.

McClelland, D. C. (1975). *Power: The inner experience.* New York: Irvington.

McClelland, D. C. (1982). The need for power, sympathetic activation, and illness. *Motivation and Emotion, 6,* 31–39.

McClelland, D. C. (1984). *Achievement motivation.* New York: Free Press.

McClelland, D. C., Atkinson, J. W., Clark, R. A., & Lowell, E. L. (1953). *The achievement motive.* New York: Appleton-Century-Crofts.

McClelland, D. C., Constantian, C. A., Regalado, D., & Stone, C. (1978). Making it to maturity. *Psychology Today, 12,* 42–53, 114.

McCormick, S. (1977). Should you read aloud to your children? *Language Arts, 54*(2), 139–143, 163.

McCrae, R. R., & Costa, P. T. (1984). *Emerging lives, enduring dispositions: Personality in adulthood.* Boston, MA: Little, Brown.

McDavid, J. W., & Harari, H. (1966). Stereotyping of names and popularity in grade children. *Child Development, 37,* 453–459.

McDermott, J. F., Jr., Waldron, J. A., Char, W. F., Ching, J., Izutsu, S., Mann, E., Ponce, D. E., & Fukunaga, C. (1987, August). New female perceptions of parental power. *American Journal of Psychiatry, 144,* 1086–1087.

McFarland, R. A., Tune, G. B., & Welford, A. (1964). On the driving of automobiles by older people. *Journal of Gerontology, 19,* 190–197.

McGee, L. M. (1983). May I take your order? *First Teacher, 4,* 5, 13.

McGee, L. M. (1986, December). Young children's environmental print reading. *Childhood Education,* pp. 118–125.

McGhee, P. E. (1974). Cognitive mastery and children's humor. *Psychological Bulletin, 81,* 721–730.

McGraw, M. B. (1940). Neural maturation as exemplified in achievement of bladder control. *Journal of Pediatrics, 16,* 580–589.

McKim, M. K. (1987, January). Transition to what? New parents' problems in the first year. *Family Relations,* pp. 22–25.

McLanahan, S., & Bumpass, L. (1988). Intergenerational consequences of family disruption. *American Journal of Sociology, 94*(1), 130–152.

McLeish, J. A. B. (1981). The continuum of creativity. In P. W. Johnston (Ed.), *Perspective on aging: Exploding the myth.* Cambridge, MA: Ballinger.

McNurlen, C. (1986, November). Giving birth: New options for expectant parents. *Better Homes and Gardens,* pp. 97–99.

Mead, M. (1928). *Coming of age in Samoa.* New York: Morrow.

Mead, M. (1935). *Sex and temperament in three primitive societies.* New York: Morrow.

Mechanic, D., & Hansell, S. (1987). Adolescent competence, psychological well-being, and self-assessed physical health. *Journal of Health and Social Behavior, 28,* 364–374.

Mehler, J., Bertoncini, J., Barriere, M., & Jassik-Gerschenfeld, D. (1978). Infant recognition of mother's voice. *Perception, 7,* 491–497.

Meikle, S., Peitchinis, J. A., & Pearce, K. (1985). *Teenage sexuality.* San Diego, CA: College Hill Press.

Meilman, P. W. (1979). Cross-sectional age changes in ego identity status during adolescence. *Developmental Psychology, 15,* 230–231.

Melhuish, E. C. (1982). Visual attention to mother's and stranger's faces and facial contrast in 1-month-old infants. *Developmental Psychology, 18,* 229–231.

Melichar, J. F., & Chiriboga, D. A. (1988). Significance of time in adjustment to marital separation. *American Journal of Orthopsychiatry, 58,* 221–227.

Melson, G. F., & Fogel, A. (1988, January). Learning to care. *Psychology Today,* pp. 39–45.

Meltzoff, A. N. (1985). Immediate and deferred imitation in 14- and 24-month-old infants. *Child Development, 56,* 62–72.

Meltzoff, A. N., & Moore, M. K. (1977). Imitation of facial and manual gestures by human neonates. *Science, 198,* 800–802.

Melzack, R. (1984). The myth of painless childbirth. *Pain, 19,* 321–337.

Menning, B. E. (1988). *Infertility: A guide for the childless couple* (2nd ed.). New York: Prentice-Hall.

Mensch, B. S., & Kandel, D. B. (1988). Do job conditions influence the use of drugs? *Journal of Health and Social Behavior, 29,* 169–184.

Mercer, J. R., & Lewis, J. F. (1978). *System of multicultural pluralistic assessment.* New York: Psychological Corporation.

Mercier, J. M., Paulson, L., & Morris, E. W. (1988). Rural and urban elderly: Differences in the quality of the parent-child relationship. *Family Relations, 37,* 68–72.

Mercy Hospital Medical Center, Des Moines. Impotence. (1987, July). *Journal,* pp. 2–3.

Mereson, A. (1988). Monkeying around with the relatives. *Discover, 9,* 26–27.

Merimee, T. J., Zapf, J., Hewlett, B., & Cavalli-Sforza, L. L. (1987). Insulin-like growth factors in pygmies. *New England Journal of Medicine, 316,* 906–911.

Miall, C. E. (1986). The stigma of involuntary childlessness. *Social Problems, 33,* 268–282.

Mika, P., Bergner, R. M., & Baum, M. C. (1987). The development of a scale for the assessment of parentification. *Family Therapy, 14,* 229–235.

Milan, R. J., Jr., & Kilmann, P. R. (1987). Interpersonal factors in premarital contraception. *Journal of Sex Research, 23,* 289–321.

Miller, B. C. (1976). A multivariate development model of marital satisfaction. *Journal of Marriage and Family, 8,* 643–657.

Miller, D. A. (1981, September). The "sandwich" generation: Adult children of the aging. *Social Work,* pp. 419–423.

Miller, G. A. (1956). The magical number seven, plus or minus two: Some limits on our capacity to process information. *Psychological Review, 63,* 81–97.

Miller, J. A. (1985, February 2). Window on the womb. *Science News, 127,* 75–77.

Miller, J. A. (1987). Building a better mouse. *Bioscience, 37,* 103–106.

Miller, J. D. (1981). Epidemiology of drug use among adolescents. In D. J. Lettier & J. P. Ludford (Eds.), *Drug abuse and the American adolescent.* Rockville, MD: National Institute on Drug Abuse.

Miller, L. B., & Bizzell, R. P. (1983). Long-term effects of four preschool programs: Sixth, seventh, and eighth grades. *Child Development, 54,* 727–741.

Miller, S. A. (1988). Parents' beliefs about children's cognitive development. *Child Development, 59,* 259–285.

Miller, S. A., Harris, Y., & Blumberg, R. (1988). Children's judgments of peers' abilities. *Merrill-Palmer Quarterly, 34,* 421–435.

Miller, S. M., & Green, M. L. (1984). Coping with stress and frustration: Origins, nature, and development. In M. Lewis & C. Saarni (Eds.), *The socialization of emotions.* New York: Plenum Press.

Miller, V., Onotera, R. T., & Deinard, A. S. (1984). Denver Developmental Screening Test: Cultural variations in southeast Asian children. *Journal of Pediatrics, 104,* 481–482.

Millette, B., & Hawkins, J. (1983). *The passage through menopause: Women's lives in transitions.* Reston, VA: Reston Publishing.

Mills, J., & Clark, M. S. (1982). Exchange and communal relationships. In L. Wheeler (Ed.), *Review of personality and social psychology* (Vol. 3, pp. 121–144). Beverly Hills, CA: Sage.

Milunsky, A. (1988). Harvesting organs for transplantation from dying anencephalic infants. *Pediatrics, 82,* 274–276.

Minnesota Coalition for Battered Women. (1991). *Confronting lesbian battering.* St. Paul, MN: Coalition for Battered Women.

Minuchin, P. P., & Shapiro, E. K. (1985). The school as a context for social development. In P. H. Mussen (Ed.), *Handbook of child psychology* (Vol. 4). New York: Wiley.

Mischel, W. (1966). A social learning view of sex differences. In E. E. Maccoby (Ed.), *The development of sex differences.* Stanford, CA: Stanford University Press.

Mischel, W. (1984). Convergences and challenges in the search for consistency. *American Psychologist, 39,* 351–364.

Mitchell, J. (1972). Some psychological dimensions of adolescent sexuality. *Adolescence, 7,* 447–458.

Mitchell, J., Wilson, K., Revicki, D., & Parker, L. (1985). Children's perceptions of aging: A multidimensional approach to differences by age, sex, and race. *The Gerontologist, 25,* 182–187.

Miyake, K., Chen, S. J., & Campos, J. J. (1985). Infant temperament, mother's mode of interaction, and attachment in Japan: An interim report. In I. Bretherton & E. Waters (Eds.), *Growing points of attachment theory*

and research. Monographs of the Society for Research in Child Development, 50 (Serial No. 209, Nos. 1–2), 276–297.

Monagan, D. (1986, January). Sudden death. *Discover,* pp. 64–71.

Money, J., & Ehrehardt, E. (1972). *Man & woman, boy & girl.* Baltimore, MD: Johns Hopkins University.

Monmaney, T. (1988, May 16). Preventing early births. *Newsweek,* p. 70.

Moody, R. A. (1976). *Life after life.* New York: Bantam.

Moore, C., Williams, J., & Gorczynska, A. (1987). View specificity, array specificity, and egocentrism. *Canadian Journal of Psychology, 41,* 74–79.

Moore, K. (1979). *The developing human: Clinically oriented embryology.* Philadelphia, PA: W. B. Saunders.

Morales, R. W., Shute, V. J., & Pellegrino, J. W. (1985). Developmental differences in understanding and solving simple word problems. *Cognition and Instruction, 2,* 41–57.

Moran, M. G., Thompson, T. L., & Nies, A. S. (1988, November). Sleep disorders in the elderly. *American Journal of Psychiatry, 145,* 1369–1378.

Morgan, J. D. (1988). Living our dying: Social and cultural considerations. In H. Wass, F. Berardo, & R. Neimeyer (Eds.), *Dying: Facing the facts.* Washington, DC: Hemisphere.

Morgan, S. P., Lye, D. N., & Condran, G. A. (1988). Sons, daughters, and the risk of marital disruption. *American Journal of Sociology, 94,* 110–129.

Morris, M. (1988). *Last-chance children: Growing up with older parents.* New York: Columbia University Press.

Morrongiello, B. A., & Rocca, P. T. (1987). Infants' localization of sounds in the horizontal plane: Effects of auditory and visual cues. *Child Development, 58,* 918–927.

Mosher, D. L., & Tomkins, S. S. (1988, February). Scripting the macho man: Hypermasculine socialization and enculturation. *Journal of Sex Research,* pp. 60–84.

Mullins, H. P. (1987, March). The rocky courtship of teens and birth control. *Ms.,* p. 25.

Murdock, S. H., & Schwartz, D. F. (1978). Family structure and the use of agency services: An examination of patterns among elderly Native Americans. *The Gerontologist, 18,* 475–481.

Murphy, J. (1987, March 16). Tracing Fragile X syndrome. *Time,* p. 78.

Murray, A. D., Dolby, R. M., Nation, R. L., & Thomas, D. B. (1981). Effects of epidural anesthesia on newborns and their mothers. *Child Development, 52,* 71–82.

Murray, J. B., & Gallahue, L. (1987). Postpartum depression. *Genetic, Social, and General Psychology Monographs, 113,* 193–212.

Murstein, B. E., Chalpin, M. J., Heard, K. V., & Vyse, S. A. (1989, Spring). Sexual behavior, drugs, and relationship patterns on a college campus over thirteen years. *Adolescence, 24,* 125–139.

Mutran, E. (1987). Family, social ties and self-meaning in old age: The development of an affective identity. *Journal of Social and Personal Relationships, 4,* 463–480.

Muuss, R. E. (1986). Adolescent eating disorder: Bulimia. *Adolescence, 21,* 257–267.

Muuss, R. E. (1988). Carol Gilligan's theory of sex differences in the development of moral reasoning during adolescence. *Adolescence, 23,* 229–243.

Myers, B. J. (1982). Early intervention using Brazelton training with middle-class mothers and fathers of newborns. *Child Development, 53,* 462–471.

Myers, B. J. (1984). Mother-infant bonding: The status of this critical period hypothesis. *Developmental Review, 4,* 240–274.

Myers, N. A., Clifton, R. K., & Clarkson, M. G. (1987). When they were very young: Almost-threes remember two years ago. *Infant Behavior and Development, 10,* 123–132.

N

Naeye, R. L. (1981). Influence of maternal cigarette smoking during pregnancy on fetal and childhood growth. *Obstetrics & Gynecology, 57,* 18–21.

Nahemow, L. (1986). Humor as a data base for the study of aging. In L. Nahemow, K. A. McClusky-Fawcett, & P. E. McGhee (Eds.), *Humor and aging.* Orlando, FL: Academic Press.

Nathan, P. E. (1983). Failures in prevention: Why we can't prevent the devastating effect of alcoholism and drug abuse. *American Psychologist, 38,* 459–467.

National Center for Health Statistics. (1987, August 28). *Monthly vital statistics report.* Washington, DC: U. S. Department of Health and Human Services.

National Institute on Drug Abuse. (1984). *Are you a drug quiz whiz?* DHHS Publication No. (ADM) 84–1084. Washington, DC: U. S. Department of Health and Human Services.

National Institute on Drug Abuse. (1986, April). Cocaine use in America. *Prevention Networks.* DHHS Publication No. (ADM) 86–1433. Washington, DC: U. S. Department of Health and Human Services.

Navelet, Y., Payan, C., Guilhaume, A., & Benoit, O. (1984). Nocturnal sleep organization in infants "at risk" for sudden infant death syndrome. *Pediatric Research, 18,* 654–657.

Neal, A. G., Groat, H. T., & Wicks, J. W. (1989, May). Attitudes about having children: A study of 600 couples in the early years of marriage. *Journal of Marriage and the Family, 51,* 313–328.

Nebes, R. D. (1989). Semantic memory in Alzheimer's disease. *Psychological Bulletin, 106,* 377–394.

Nelson, C. A. (1987). The recognition of facial expressions in the first two years of life: Mechanisms of development. *Child Development, 58,* 889–909.

Nelson, K. (1978). How children represent knowledge of their world in and out of language: Preliminary report. In R. S. Siegler (Ed.), *Children's thinking: What develops.* Hillsdale, NJ: Lawrence Erlbaum.

Nelson, K., & Ross, G. (1980). The generalities and specifics of long-term memory in infants and young children. In M. Perlmutter (Ed.), *Children's memory: New directions for child development.* San Francisco, CA: Jossey-Bass.

Nelson, M. (1985, December). Listening in the womb. *Omni,* p. 24.

Nelson, N. M., Enkin, M. W., Saroj, S., Bennett, K. J., Milner, M., & Sackett, S. L. (1980). A randomized clinical trial of the Leboyer approach to childbirth. *New England Journal of Medicine, 302,* 655–660.

Nerlove, S. B., & Snipper, A. S. (1981). Cognitive consequences of cultural opportunity. In R. H. Munroe, R. L. Munroe, & B. B. Whiting (Eds.), *Handbook of cross-cultural human development.* New York: Garlan Publishing.

Nesdale, A. R., & McLaughlin, K. (1987). Effects of sex stereotypes on young children's memories, predictions and liking. *British Journal of Developmental Psychology, 5,* 231–241.

Neugarten, B. L. (1964). *Personality in middle and late life.* New York: Atherton Press.

Neugarten, B. L. (1967, December). A new look at menopause. *Psychology Today, 1,* 42–45, 67–69, 71.

Neugarten, B. L. (1969). Continuities and discontinuities of psychological issues in adult life. *Human Development, 12,* 121–130.

Neugarten, B. L. (1980a). Acting one's age: New rules for old. *Psychology Today, 15,* 66–80.

Neugarten, B. L. (1980b, February). Must everything be a mid-life crisis? *Prime Time* pp. 263–264.

Neugarten, B. L., Havighurst, R. J., & Tobin, S. S. (1968). Personality and patterns of aging. In B. L. Neugarten (Ed.), *Middle age and aging.* Chicago: University of Chicago Press.

Neugarten, B. L., Moore, J. W., & Lowe, J. C. (1965). Age norms, age constraints, and adult socialization. *American Journal of Sociology, 70,* 712.

Neugarten, B. L., & Neugarten, D. A. (1986). Changing meanings of age in the aging society. In A. Pifer & L. Bronte (Eds.), *Our aging society: Paradox and promise.* New York: Norton.

Neugarten, B. L., & Neugarten, D. A. (1987, May). The changing meanings of age. *Psychology Today,* pp. 29–33.

Neugarten, B. L., & Weinstein, K. (1964). The changing American grandparent. *Journal of Marriage and the Family, 26,* 199–204.

Newacheck, P. W., & Halfon, N. (1988). Preventive care use by school-aged children: Differences by socioeconomic status. *Pediatrics, 82,* 462–468.

Newberger, C. (1980). The cognitive structure of parenthood: Designing a descriptive measure. *New Directions for Child Development, 7,* 45–67.

Newcomer, S., & Udry, J. R. (1987). Parental marital status effects on adolescent sexual behavior. *Journal of Marriage and the Family, 49,* 235–240.

Newman, B. M. (1982). Mid-life development. In B. Wolman (Ed.), *Handbook of developmental psychology.* Englewood Cliffs, NJ: Prentice-Hall.

Newman, J. (1987). Psychological effects on college students of raising the drinking age. *Adolescence, 22,* 503–510.

Newton, N., & Modahl, C. (1978, March). Pregnancy: The closest human relationship. *Human Nature,* pp. 40–49.

Nezu, A. M., Nezu, C. M., & Blissett, S. E. (1988). Sense of humor as a moderator of the relation between stressful events and psychological distress: A prospective analysis. *Journal of Personality and Social Psychology, 54,* 520–525.

Nicholas, M., Obler, L. K., Albert, M., & Goodglass, H. (1985). Lexical retrieval in healthy aging. *Cortex, 21,* 595–606.

Nicol, A. R., Willcox, C., & Hibbert, K. (1985). What sort of children are suspended from school and what can we do for them? In A. R. Nicol (Ed.), *Longitudinal studies in child psychology and psychiatry,* Chichester, New York: John Wiley & Sons.

Nielsen, A. C. (1985). *Nielsen television index: National audience demographic report* (30th ed.). Northbrook, IL: A. C. Nielsen.

Ninio, A. (1988). The effects of cultural background, sex, and parenthood on beliefs about the timetable of cognitive development in infancy. *Merrill-Palmer Quarterly, 34,* 369–388.

Noise: Too much causes hearing loss (pp. 6–7). (1990, Spring). Des Moines, IA: University of Osteopathic Medicine and Health Sciences.

Nolan, K. (1988, October/November). Anencephalic infants: A source of controversy. *Hastings Center Report,* p. 5.

Norwood, C. (1985, January). Terata. *Mother Jones,* pp. 15–21.

Nottelman, E. D., Susman, E. J., Blue, J. H., Inoff-Germain, G., Dorn, L. D., Loriaux, D. L., Cutler, G. B., & Chrousos, G. P. (1985). Gonadal and adrenal hormone correlates of adjustment in early adolescence. In R. M. Lerner & T. T. Foch (Eds.), *Biological-psychosocial interactions in early adolescence: A lifespan perspective.* Hillsdale, NJ: Erlbaum.

Nusberg, C. (1983). Filial responsibility still required in Hungary. *Aging International, 9,* 7–9.

O

Ober, B. A., Dronkers, N. F., Koss, E., Delis, D. C., & Friedland, R. P. (1986). Retrieval from semantic memory in Alzheimer-type dementia. *Journal of Clinical and Experimental Neuropsychology, 8,* 75–92.

O'Brien, M., & Nagle, K. J. (1987). Parents' speech to toddlers: The effect of play context. *Journal of Children Language, 14,* 269–279.

O'Bryant, S. L. (1988, February). Sibling support and older widows' well-being. *Journal of Marriage and the Family, 50,* 173–183.

O'Bryant, S. L., & Morgan, L. A. (1990). Recent widows' kin support and orientations to self-sufficiency. *The Gerontologist, 30,* 391–398.

O'Connell, J. C., & Farran, D. C. (1982). Effects of day-care experience on the use of intentional communicative behaviors in a sample of socioeconomically depressed infants. *Developmental Psychology, 18,* 22–29.

O'Connor, M. J., Cohen, S., & Parmelee, A. H. (1984). Infant auditory discrimination in preterm and full-term infants as a predictor of 5-year intelligence. *Developmental Psychology, 20,* 159–165.

Offer, D., & Offer, J. (1975). *From teenage to young manhood.* New York: Basic Books.

Offer, D., Ostrov, E., & Howard, K. I. (1981). *The adolescent: A psychological self-portrait.* New York: Basic Books.

Offer, D., & Sabshin, M. (1984). Adolescence: Empirical perspectives. In D. Offer & M. Sabshin (Eds.), *Normality and the life cycle.* New York: Basic Books.

O'Flaherty, K. M., & Eells, L. W. (1988). Courtship behavior of the remarried. *Journal of Marriage and the Family, 50,* 499–506.

O'Hara, M. W., Hinrichs, J. W., Kohout, F. J., Wallace, R. B., & Lemke, J. H. (1986). Memory complaint and memory performance in the depressed elderly. *Psychology and Aging, 1,* 208–214.

O'Heron, D., & Orlofsky, J. L. (1990). Stereotypic and nonstereotypic sex role trait and behavior orientations, gender identity, and psychological adjustment. *Journal of Personality and Social Psychology, 58,* 134–143.

Ohuche, N. M., & Littrell, J. M. (1989). Igbo students' attitudes toward supporting aged parents. *International Journal of Aging and Human Development, 29,* 259–267.

Olney, J. (1980). Biography, autobiography, and the life course. In K. W. Back (Ed.), *Life course: Integrative theories and exemplary populations* (AAAS Selected Symposium 41). Boulder, CO: Westview Press for the American Association for the Advancement of Science.

Olsho, L. W., Schoon, C., Sakai, R., Turpin, R., & Sperduto, V. (1982). Preliminary data on frequency discrimination in infancy. *Journal of the Acoustical Society of America, 71,* 509–511.

Olson, G. M., & Sherman, T. (1983a). Attention, learning, and memory in infants. In P. H. Mussen (Ed.), *Handbook of child psychology* (4th ed., Vol. 2). New York: Wiley.

Olson, G. M., & Sherman, T. (1983b). A conceptual framework for the study of infant mental processes. In L. P. Lipsitt (Ed.), *Advances in infancy research* (Vol. 3). Norwood, NJ: Ablex.

Olweus, D. (1982). Development of stable aggressive reaction patterns in males. In R. Blanchard & C. Blanchard (Eds.), *Advances in the study of aggression* (Vol. 1). New York: Academic Press.

Onuf, N. G. (1987). Rules in moral development. *Human Development, 30,* 257–267.

Oppenheim, D., Sagi, A., & Lamb, M. E. (1988). Infant-adult attachments on the Kibbutz and their relation to socioemotional development 4 years later. *Developmental Psychology, 24,* 427–433.

Orbach, I., Feshbach, S., Carlson, G., & Ellenberg, L. (1984). Attitudes toward life and death in suicidal, normal, and chronically ill children: An extended replication. *Journal of Consulting & Clinical Psychology, 52,* 1020–1027.

Orbach, I., Feshbach, S., Carlson, G., Glaubman, H., & Gross, Y. (1983). Attraction and repulsion by life and death in suicidal and normal children. *Journal of Consulting & Clinical Psychology, 51,* 661–670.

Osipow, S. H. (1987). Counseling psychology: Theory, research, and practice in career counseling. *Annual review of psychology, 38,* 257–278.

Osofsky, J. D. (Ed.) (1987). *Handbook of infant development* (2nd ed.). New York: Wiley.

Ostling, R. (1987b, February 23). Is it wrong to cut off feeding? *Time,* p. 71.

Ostling, R. N. (1987a, March 23). Technology and the womb. *Time,* pp. 58–59.

Overman, W., Jr., & Stoudemire, A. (1988, December). Guidelines for legal and financial counseling of Alzheimer's disease patients and their families. *American Journal of Psychiatry, 145,* 1495–1500.

Owens, W. A. (1966). Age and mental abilities: A second adult follow-up. *Journal of Educational Psychology, 57,* 311–325.

P

Paffenbarger, R. S., Hyde, R. T., Wing, A. L., & Hsieh, C. C. (1986). Physical activity, all-cause mortality, and longevity of college alumni. *New England Journal of Medicine, 314,* 605–613.

Paige, K. E., & Paige, J. M. (1973). The politics of birth practices: A strategic analysis. *American Sociological Review, 38,* 663–676.

Palkovitz, R. (1985). Fathers' birth attendance, early contact, and extended contact with their newborns: A critical review. *Child Development, 56,* 392–406.

Palla, B., & Litt, I. F. (1988). Medical complications of eating disorders in adolescents. *Pediatrics, 81,* 613–623.

Palmer, E. L., & McDowell, C. N. (1979). Program/commercial separators in children's television programming. *Journal of Communication, 29,* 197–201.

Palmore, E. B. (1983). Social class, sex differences, and longevity. In J. E. Birren (Ed.), *Aging: A challenge to science and society* (Vol. 3, pp. 41–48). New York: Oxford University Press.

Papousek, H. (1967). Experimental studies of appetitional behavior in human newborns and infants. In H. W. Stevenson, E. H. Hess, & H. L. Rheingolds (Eds.), *Early behavior.* New York: Wiley.

Papousek, H., & Papousek, M. (1987). Intuitive parenting: A didactic counterpart to the infant's precocity in integrative capacities. In J. D. Osofsky (Ed.), *Handbook of infant development* (2nd ed.). New York: Wiley.

Parke, R. D., & Tinsley, B. R. (1981). The father's role in infancy: Determinants of involvement in caregiving and play. In M. E. Lamb (Ed.), *The role of the father in child development* (2nd ed.). New York: Wiley.

Parker, C. (1985). *Alcohol: Simple facts about combinations with other drugs.* Phoenix, AZ: Do It Now Publications.

Parkes, C. M., & Weiss, R. S. (1983). *Recovery from bereavement.* New York: Basic Books.

Parmellee, A. H., Jr. (1986). Children's illnesses: Their beneficial effects on behavioral development. *Child Development, 57,* 1–10.

Parnes, H. S., & Less, L. (1985). Variation in selection forms of leisure activity among elderly males. In Z. S. Blau (Ed.), *Current perspectives on aging and the life cycle: Work retirement and social policy.* Greenwich, CT: JAI Press.

Parten, M. (1932). Social play among preschool children. *Journal of Abnormal and Social Psychology, 27,* 243–269.

Partridge, S. E. (1988). The parental self-concept: A theoretical exploration and practical application. *American Journal of Orthopsychiatry, 58,* 281–287.

Pascarella, E. T. (1989, January). The development of critical thinking: Does college make a difference? *Journal of College Student Development, 30,* 19–26.

Pascoe, J. M., Chessare, J., Baugh, E., Urich, L., & Ialongo, N. (1987). Help with prenatal household tasks and newborn birthweight: Is there an association? *Developmental and Behavioral Pediatrics, 87,* 207–212.

Pascual-Leone, J. (1980). Constructive problems for constructive theories: The current relevance of Piaget's work and a critique of information-processing simulation psychology. In R. H. Kluwe & Y. H. Spada (Eds.), *Developmental models of thinking.* New York: Academic Press.

Pasley, K., & Gecas, V. (1984). Stresses and satisfactions of the parental role. *Personnel and Guidance Journal, 62,* 400–404.

Passuth, P. M., & Cook, F. L. (1985). Effects of television viewing on knowledge and attitudes about older adults: A critical reexamination. *The Gerontologist, 25,* 69–77.

Patrusky, B. (1980, July/August). Diagnosing newborns. *Science,* pp. 26–29.

Patterson, G. R. (1980). Mothers: The unacknowledged victims. *Monographs of the Society for Research in Child Development, 45* (5, Serial No. 186).

Pattison, E. M. (1977). *The experience of dying.* Englewood Cliffs, NJ: Prentice-Hall.

Paul, E. L. (1989, August 14). *Individual differences in young adult intimacy development.* Presented at American Psychological Association Conference in New Orleans, LA.

Paul, E. L., & White, K. M. (1990, Summer). The development of intimate relationships in late adolescence. *Adolescence, 225,* 375–400.

Payne, B. D., & Manning, B. H. (1984). Sex of preferred pupil in relation to student teachers' projected and self-reported personality characteristics. *College Student Personnel Journal, 18,* 345–351.

Pearl, T., Klopf, D. W., & Ishi, S. (1990). Loneliness among Japanese and American college students. *Psychological Reports, 67,* 49–50.

Peck, M. S. (1978). *The road less traveled.* New York: Touchstone.

Peck, R. C. (1968). Psychological developments in the second half of life. In B. L. Neugarten (Ed.), *Middle age and aging.* Chicago, IL: University of Chicago Press.

Pedersen, N. L., Plomin, R., McClearn, G. E., & Friberg, L. (1988). Neuroticism, extraversion, and related traits in adult twins reared apart and reared together. *Journal of Personality and Social Psychology, 55,* 950–957.

Pellegrini, A. D. (1988). Elementary-school children's rough-and-tumble play and social competence. *Developmental Psychology, 24,* 802–806.

Pellegrino, V. Y. (1981). *The other side of 30.* Rauson, NJ: Wade.

Perlmutter, M. (1986). A life-span view of memory. In P. B. Baltes, D. L. Featherman, & R. M. Lerner (Eds.), *Life-span development and behavior.* (Vol. 7). Hillsdale, NJ: Lawrence Erlbaum.

Perlmutter, M., & Hall, E. (1985). *Adult development and aging.* New York: John Wiley & Sons.

Perry, D. G., Kusel, S. J., & Perry, L. C. (1988). Victims of peer aggression. *Developmental Psychology, 24,* 807–814.

Perry, D. G., Perry, L. C., & Rasmussen, P. (1986). Cognitive social learning mediators of aggression. *Child Development, 57,* 700–711.

Perry, W. (1968a). *Forms of intellectual and ethical development in the college years.* New York: Holt, Rinehart & Winston.

Perry, W. (1968b). *Patterns of development in thought and values of students in a liberal arts college: A validation of a scheme.* Washington, DC: U. S. Department of Health, Education, and Welfare, Office of Education, Bureau of Research. (Final report)

Perry, W. (1981). Cognitive and ethical growth. In A. Chickering (Ed.), *The modern American college.* San Francisco, CA: Jossey-Bass.

Peters, R. D., & Bernfeld, G. A. (1983). Reflection-impulsivity and social reasoning. *Developmental Psychology, 19,* 78–81.

Petersen, A. C. (1988). Adolescent development. *Annual Review of Psychology, 39,* 583–607.

Petersen, A. C., & Crockett, L. J. (1985). Pubertal timing and grade effects on adjustment. *Journal of Youth & Adolescents, 14,* 191–206.

Peterson, D. A. (1985). A history of education for older learners. In D. B. Lumsden (Ed.), *The older adult as learner.* Washington, DC: Hemisphere.

Peterson, J. A., & Payne, B. (1975). *Love in the later years.* New York: Association Press.

Petrus, J. J., & Vetrosky, D. T. (1990, April). Cancer: Risk factors, prevention, and screening. *Physician Assistant,* pp. 21–38.

Pezdek, K. (1987). Memory for pictures: A life-span study of the role of visual detail. *Child Development, 58,* 807–815.

Pfeiffer, E., Verwoerdt, A., & Davis, G. C. (1974). Sexual behavior in middle life. In E. Palmore (Ed.), *Normal aging II: Reports from the Duke longitudinal studies, 1970–1973* (pp. 243–251). Durham, NC: Duke University Press.

Phillips, D. (1984). The illusion of incompetence among academically competent children. *Child Development, 55,* 2000–2016.

Phillips, D. A. (1987). Socialization of perceived academic competence among highly competent children. *Child Development, 58,* 1308–1320.

Phillips, D., McCartney, K., & Scarr, S. (1987). Child-care quality and children's social development. *Developmental Psychology, 23,* 537–543.

Phillips, J. L. (1975). *The origins of intellect: Piaget's theory* (2nd ed.). San Francisco, CA: W. H. Freeman.

Phillips, J. R. (1973). Syntax and vocabulary of mothers' speech to young children: Age and sex comparisons. *Child Development, 44,* 182–185.

Phillips, S. D. (1982). Career exploration in adulthood. *Journal of Vocational Behavior, 20,* 129–140.

Phillips, S. D., & Johnson, S. L. (1985). Attitudes toward work roles for women. *Journal of College Student Personnel, 26,* 334–338.

Phinney, J. S. (1990). Ethnic identity in adolescents and adults: Review of research. *Psychological Bulletin, 108,* 499–514.

Piaget, J. (1929). *The child's conception of the world.* New York: Harcourt Brace.

Piaget, J. (1932). *The moral judgement of the child.* New York: Harcourt Brace.

Piaget, J. (1951). *Play, dreams, and imitation in childhood.* New York: Norton.

Piaget, J. (1952a). *The child's conception of numbers.* London, England: Routledge & Kegan Paul.

Piaget, J. (1952b). *The origin of intelligence in children* (M. Cook, Trans.). New York: International Universities Press. (Original work published 1936)

Piaget, J. (1954). *The construction of reality in the child.* New York: Basic Books. (Original work published 1937)

Piaget, J. (1962). The stages of intellectual development of the child. *Bulletin of the Menninger Clinic, 26,* 120–128.

Piaget, J. (1970). A conversation with Jean Piaget. *Psychology Today, 3,* 25–32.

Pifer, A., & Bronte, L. (1986). Introduction: Squaring the pyramid. In A. Pifer & L. Bronte (Eds.), *Our aging society: Paradox and promise.* New York: Norton.

Pillard, R. C., & Weinrich, J. D. (1987). The periodic table model of the gender transpositions: Part I. A theory based on masculinization and defeminization of the brain. *Journal of Sex Research, 23,* 425–454.

Pinch, W. J. (1986). Quality of life as a philosophical position. *Health Values, 10,* 3–7.

Pinderhughes, E., & Zigler, E. (1985). Cognitive and motivational determinants of children's humor responses. *Journal of Research in Personality, 19,* 185–196.

Pineo, P. E. (1961). Disenchantment in the later years of marriage. *Marriage and Family Living, 23,* 3–11.

Pines, M. (1978, September). Invisible playmates. *Psychology Today,* pp. 38–42.

Pines, M. (1982, February). Baby, you're incredible. *Psychology Today,* pp. 48–53.

Pitskhelauri, G. Z. (1982). *The long-living of Soviet Georgia.* New York: Human Sciences Press.

Planned Parenthood. (1985). *Frontiers in fertility.* Chicago: Planned Parenthood Federation of America.

Planned Parenthood of Mid-Iowa. (1987). *Sexually transmitted diseases.* Des Moines, IA: Planned Parenthood.

Pleck, J. (1975). Masculinity-femininity: Current and alternative paradigms. *Sex Roles, 1,* 161–178.

Pleck, J. H. (1987). American fathering in historical perspective. In M. S. Kimmel (Ed.), *Changing men: New directions in research on men and masculinity* (pp. 83–97). Beverly Hills, CA: Sage.

Plotkin, S. A., Evans, H. E., & Fost, N. C. (1988). Perinatal human immunodeficiency virus infection. *Pediatrics, 82,* 941–944.

Pocs, O., Godow, A., Tolone, W. L., & Walsh, R. H. (1977, June). Is there sex after 40? *Psychology Today, 11,* 54–56, 87.

Pogrebin, L. C. (1980). *Growing up free.* New York: McGraw-Hill.

Pogrebin, L. C. (1988, March). What wonders kids are. *Ms.,* p. 94.

Polit, D. F., & LaRocco, S. A. (1980). Social and psychological correlates of menopause symptoms. *Psychosomatic Medicine, 42,* 335–345.

Polit-O'Hara, D., & Kahn, J. R. (1985). Communication and contraceptive practices in adolescent couples. *Adolescence, 20,* 33–43.

Pollock, L. (1983). *Forgotten children: Parent-child relations from 1500 to 1900.* Cambridge, England: Cambridge University Press.

Pongratz, L. H. (1967). *Problemgeschichte der Psychologie.* Bern, Switzerland: Francke.

Poon, L. W. (1985). Differences in human memory with aging: Nature, causes, and clinical implications. In J. E. Birren & K. W. Schaie (Eds.), *Handbook of the psychology of aging* (2nd ed., pp. 427–462). New York: Van Nostrand Reinhold.

Pope, H. G., & Hudson, J. I. (1984). *New hope for binge eaters: Advances in the understanding and treatment of bulimia.* New York: Harper & Row.

Powell, R. R. (1974). Psychological effects of exercise therapy upon institutionalized geriatric mental patients. *Journal of Gerontology, 29,* 157–161.

Powers, P. S., Schulman, R. G., Gleghorn, A. A., & Prange, M. E. (1987). Perceptual and cognitive abnormalities in bulimia. *American Journal of Psychiatry, 144,* 1456–1460.

Powers, S., Hauser, S., Schwartz, J., Noam, G., & Jacobson, A. (1983). Adolescent ego development and family interaction. In H. Gotivant & C. Cooper (Eds.), *Adolescent development in the family.* San Francisco, CA: Jossey-Bass.

Prather, P. A., & Bacon, J. (1986). Developmental differences in part/whole identification. *Child Development, 57,* 549–558.

President's Council on Physical Fitness and Sports. (1985). *Fitness fundamentals: Guidelines for personal exercise programs.* Washington, DC: Department of Health & Human Services.

Presser, H. B. (1988). Shift work and child care among young dual-earner American parents. *Human Development, 50,* 133–148.

Presser, H. B., & Baldwin, W. (1980). Child care as a constraint on employment: Prevalence, correlates, and bearing on the work and fertility nexus. *American Journal of Sociology, 85,* 1202–1213.

Pressley, M., Cariglia-Bull, T., & Deane, S. (1987). Short-term memory, verbal competence, and age as predictors of imagery instructional effectiveness. *Journal of Experimental Child Psychology, 43,* 194–211.

Preventing early death: The western way to die. (1985, August 31). *The Economist,* pp. 75–78.

Price, G. G. (1984). Mnemonic support and curriculum selection in teaching by mothers. *Child Development, 55,* 659–668.

Price, R. A., Cadoret, R. J., Stunkard, A. J., & Troughton, E. (1987). Genetic contributions to human fatness: An adoption study. *American Journal of Psychiatry, 144,* 1003–1008.

Ptashne, M. (1989, January). How gene activators work. *Scientific American,* pp. 40–47.

Q

Quilitch, H. R., & Risely, T. R. (1973). The effects of play materials on social play. *Journal of Applied Behavior Analysis, 6,* 573–578.

Quilligan, L., & Kretchmer, N. (1980). *Fetal and maternal medicine.* New York: Wiley.

R

Radman, M., & Wagner, R. (1988, August). The high fidelity of DNA duplication. *Scientific American,* pp. 40–46.

Ragland, D. R., & Brand, R. J. (1988, January 14). Type A behavior and mortality from coronary heart disease. *New England Journal of Medicine, 318,* 65–69.

Rain, E. L. (1988). Trends in the demography of death. In H. Wass, F. Berardi, & R. Neimeryer (Eds.), *Dying: Facing the facts.* Washington, DC: Hemisphere.

Ramsey, C. N., Abell, T. C., & Baker, L. C. (1986). The relationship between family functioning, life events, family structure, and the outcome of pregnancy. *Journal of Family Practice, 22,* 521–527.

Rapaport, K., & Burkhart, B. R. (1984). Personality and attitudinal characteristics of sexually coercive college males. *Journal of Abnormal Psychology, 93,* 216–221.

Raper, J., & Aldridge, J. (1988, February). What every teacher should know about . . . AIDS. *Childhood Education,* pp. 146–149.

Raymond, C. (1989, January). A miracle goes sour. *Discover,* p. 72.

Rebecca, M., Hefner, R., & Oleshansky, B. (1976). A model of sex-role transcendence. *Journal of Social Issues, 32,* 197–206.

Reese, H. W., & Rodeheaver, D. (1985). Problem solving and complex decision making. In J. E. Birren & K. W. Schaie (Eds.), *Handbook of the psychology of aging* (2nd ed.). New York: Van Nostrand Reinhold.

Reggie the Retiree. (1982). *Laughs and limericks on aging in large print.* Wells, ME: Reggie the Retiree.

Reid, J. L. (1988, April). How to reach your goals. *Money,* p. 76.

Reif, G. (1985). *Fitness for youth.* Unpublished report. Ann Arbor, MI: Department of Physical Education, University of Michigan. Cited in Zigler, E. F., & Finn-Stevenson, M. (1987). *Children: Development and social issues.* Lexington, MA: D. C. Heath.

Reilly, T. W., Entwisle, D. R., & Doering, S. G. (1987). Socialization into parenthood: A longitudinal study of the development of self-evaluations. *Journal of Marriage and the Family, 49,* 295–308.

Reis, J. S., & Herz, E. J. (1987). Correlates of adolescent parenting. *Adolescence, 22*(87), 599–609.

Remley, A. (1988, October). From obedience to independence. *Psychology Today, 22,* 56–59.

Rempel, J. (1985). Childless elderly: What are they missing? *Journal of Marriage and the Family, 47*(2), 343–348.

Rennie, S. (1987, November). Breast cancer: When chemotherapy works. *Ms.,* pp. 70–74.

Rexroat, C., & Shehan, C. (1987). The family life cycle and spouses' time in housework. *Journal of Marriage and the Family, 49,* 737–750.

Rice, G. E., & Meyer, B. J. F. (1986). Prose recall: Effects of aging, verbal ability, and reading behavior. *Journal of Gerontology, 41,* 469–480.

Rice, J. K., & Rice, D. G. (1986). *Living through divorce.* New York: Guilford Press.

Richards, J. E., & Rader, N. (1981). Crawling-onset age predicts visual cliff avoidance in infants. *Journal of Experimental Psychology: Human Perception and Performance, 7,* 382–387.

Richards, M., & Light, P. (Eds.). (1986). *Children of social worlds: Development in a social context.* Cambridge, MA: Harvard University Press.

Richardson, R. A., Galambos, N. L., Schulenberg, J. E., & Petersen, A. C. (1984). Young adolescents' perceptions of the family environment. *Journal of Early Adolescence, 4,* 131–154.

Richman, C. L., Niden, S., & Pittman, L. (1976). Effects of meaningfulness on child free-recall learning. *Developmental Psychology, 12,* 460–465.

Rickert, V. I., & Johnson, C. M. (1988). Reducing nocturnal awakening and crying episodes in infants and young children: A comparison between scheduled awakenings and systematic ignoring. *Pediatrics, 81,* 203–212.

Ridenour, M. V. (1982). Infant walkers: Development tool or inherent danger. *Perceptual & Motor Skills, 55,* 1201–1202.

Riege, W. H., & Inman, V. W. (1981). Age differences in nonverbal memory tasks. *Journal of Gerontology, 36,* 51–58.

Riegel, K. F. (1973). Dialectic operations: The final period of cognitive development. *Human Development, 16,* 346–370.

Riegel, K. F. (1976). The dialects of human development. *American Psychologist, 31,* 689–700.

Riegel, K. F. (1979). *Foundations of dialectical psychology.* New York: Academic Press.

Rieser, J., Yonas, A., & Wilkner, K. (1976). Radial localization of odors by human newborns. *Child Development, 47,* 856–859.

Ring, K. (1980). *Life at death: A scientific investigation of the near-death experience.* New York: Coward, McCann & Geoghegan.

Ring, K. (1984). *Heading toward Omega.* New York: William Morrow.

Ring, K., & Franklin, S. (1981). Do suicide survivors report near-death experiences? *Omega, 12,* 191–207.

Risman, B. J., Hill, C., Rubin, Z., & Peplau, L. A. (1981). Living together in college: Implications for courtship. *Journal of Marriage and the Family, 43,* 77–83.

Rist, R. C. (1970). Student social class and teacher expectations: The self-fulfilling prophecy in ghetto education. *Harvard Education Review, 40,* 411–451.

Rivara, F. P., & Mueller, B. A. (1987). The epidemiology and causes of childhood injuries. *Journal of Social Issues, 43,* 13–31.

Roberto, K. A., & Scott, J. P. (1986). Equity considerations in the friendships of older adults. *Journal of Gerontology, 41,* 241–247.

Roberts, C. W., Green, R., Williams, K., & Goodman, M. (1987). Boyhood gender identity development: A statistical contrast of two family groups. *Developmental Psychology, 23,* 544–557.

Roberts, L. (1992). Two chromosomes down, 22 to go. *Science, 258,* 28, 30.

Roberts, M. (1988, February). Schoolyard menace. *Psychology Today,* pp. 53–56.

Roberts, M. (1990, June 18). Little towns that could. *U. S. News & World Report,* pp. 74–75.

Roberts, M. C., Fanurik, D., & Layfield, D. A. (1987). Behavioral approaches to prevention of childhood injuries. *Journal of Social Issues, 43,* 105–118.

Roberts, M. C., & Turner, D. S. (1984). Preventing death and injury in childhood: A synthesis of child safety seat efforts. *Health Education Quarterly, 11,* 25–36.

Roberts, M. C., & Turner, D. S. (1986). Rewarding parents for their children's use of safety seats. *Journal of Pediatric Psychology, 11,* 25–36.

Roberts, P., & Newton, P. M. (1987). Levinsonian studies of women's adult development. *Psychology and Aging, 2,* 154–163.

Roberts, W. C. (1978). The autopsy: Its decline and a suggestion for its revival. *New England Journal of Medicine, 299,* 332–338.

Robertson, J., & Fitzgerald, L. F. (1990). The (mis) treatment of men: Effects of client gender role and life-style on diagnosis and attribution of pathology. *Journal of Counseling Psychology, 37,* 3–9.

Robinson, B. E., Rowland, B. H., & Coleman, M. (1986). Taking action for latchkey children and their families. *Family Relations, 35,* 473–478.

Robinson, I. E., & Jedlicka, D. (1982). Change in sexual behavior of college students from 1965 to 1980: A research note. *Journal of Marriage and the Family, 44,* 237–240.

Rochat, P. (1983). Oral touch in young infants: Response to variations of nipple characteristics in the first months of life. *International Journal of Behavioral Development, 6,* 123–133.

Roche, A. F. (1981). The adipocyte-number hypothesis. *Child Development, 52,* 31–43.

Roche, A. F. (Ed.). (1979). Secular trends in human growth, maturation, and development. *Monographs of the Society for Research in Child Development, 44,* (3–4, serial no. 179).

Roche, J. P. (1986). Premarital sex: Attitudes and behavior by dating stage. *Adolescence, 21,* 107–121.

Rodeheaver, D., & Thomas, J. L. (1986). Family and community networks in Appalachia. In N. Datan, A. L. Greene, & H. W. Reese (Eds.), *Life-span developmental psychology: Intergenerational relations.* Hillsdale, NJ: Erlbaum.

Rodin, J., & Hall, E. (1987). A sense of control. In E. Hall (Ed.), *Growing and changing.* New York: Random House.

Rodin, J., & Langer, E. (1980). Aging labels: The decline of control and the fall of self-esteem. *Journal of Social Issues, 36,* 12–29.

Roff, M. F., Sells, S. B., & Golden, M. M. (1972). *Social adjustment and personality development in children.* Minneapolis, MN: University of Minnesota Press.

Roffwarg, H. P., Muzio, J. N., & Dement, W. C. (1966). Ontogenetic development of the human sleep-dream cycle. *Science, 152,* 604–619.

Rogers, C. J., & Gallion, T. (1978). Characteristics of elderly Pueblo Indians in New Mexico. *The Gerontologist, 18,* 479–481.

Rogers, C. R. (1951). *Client-centered therapy: Its current practice, implications and the theory.* Boston, MA: Houghton Mifflin.

Rogers, C. R. (1961). *On becoming a person: A therapist's view of psychotherapy.* Boston, MA: Houghton Mifflin.

Rogers, C. R. (1972). *Becoming partners: Marriage and its alternatives.* New York: Dell (Delacorte Press).

Rogoff, B. (1981). Schooling and the development of cognitive skills. In H. C. Triandis & A. Heron (Eds.), *Handbook of cross-cultural psychology: Developmental psychology* (Vol. 4). Boston, MA: Allyn & Bacon.

Roha, R. R. (1987a, November). The bundle a baby costs. *Changing Times,* pp. 85–93.

Roha, R. R. (1987b, May). The dollar side of divorce. *Changing Times,* pp. 94–100.

Rollins, B. C., & Feldman, H. (1970, February). Marital satisfaction over the family life cycle. *Journal of Marriage and the Family,* pp. 20–28.

Rook, K. S. (1987). Reciprocity of social exchange and social satisfaction among older women. *Journal of Personality and Social Psychology, 52,* 145–154.

Roscoe, B., Diana, M. S., & Brooks, R. H., II. (1987). Early, middle, and late adolescents' views on dating and factors influencing partner selection. *Adolescence, 22,* 59–68.

Roscoe, B., Kennedy, D., & Pope, T. (1987). Adolescents' views of intimacy: Distinguishing intimate from nonintimate relationships. *Adolescence, 22,* 511–516.

Roscoe, B., Krug, K., & Schmidt, J. (1985). Written forms of self-expression utilized by adolescents. *Adolescence, 20,* 841–844.

Roscoe, B., & Kruger, T. L. (1990). AIDS: Late adolescents' knowledge and its influence on sexual behavior. *Adolescence, 25,* 39–48.

Roscoe, B., & Skomski, G. G. (1989, Winter). Loneliness among late adolescents. *Adolescence, 24,* 947–955.

Rose, K. J. (1988). *The body in time.* New York: Wiley.

Rose, R. J. (1979). Genetic variance in nonverbal intelligence: Data from the kinship of identical twins. *Science, 205,* 1153–1155.

Rose, R. J., Koskenvuo, M., Kaprio, J., Sarna, S., & Langinvainio, H. (1988). Shared genes, shared experiences, and similarity of personality. *Journal of Personality and Social Psychology, 54,* 161–171.

Rose, S. A. (1983a). Differential rates of visual information processing in full-term and preterm infants. *Child Development, 4,* 1189–1198.

Rose, S. A. (1983b). Behavioral and psychophysiological sequelae of preterm birth. In T. Field & A. Soslek (Eds.), *Infants born at risk.* New York: Grune & Stratton.

Rose, S. A., & Blank, M. (1974). The potency of context in children's cognition. *Child Development, 45,* 499–502.

Rose, S. A., & Wallace, I. F. (1985). Visual recognition memory: A predictor of later cognitive functioning in preterms. *Child Development, 56,* 843–852.

Rosel, N. (1986). Growing old together: Neighborhood, communality among the elderly. In T. R. Cole & S. A. Gadow (Eds.), *What does it mean to grow old?* Durham, NC: Duke University Press.

Rosen, C. M. (1987, September). The eerie world of reunited twins. *Discover,* pp. 36–46.

Rosen, J. C., & Gross, J. (1987). Prevalence of weight reducing and weight gaining in adolescent girls and boys. *Health Psychology, 6,* 131–147.

Rosenbaum, R. (1982, July). Turn on, tune in, drop dead. *Harper's,* pp. 32–42.

Rosenfeld, A. H. (1987, November). Coping with a partner's depression. *Psychology Today,* p. 24.

Rosenfeld, A., & Stark, E. (1987, May). The prime of life. *Psychology Today,* pp. 63–72.

Rosenman, R. H., Brand, R. J., Jenkins, C. D., Friedman, M., Straus, R., & Wurm, M. (1975). Coronary heart disease in the Western Collaborative Group Study: Final follow-up experience of 8 ½ years. *Journal of the American Medical Association, 233,* 872–877.

Rosenmary, L. (1985). Changing values and positions of aging in western culture. In J. E. Birren & K. W. Schaie (Eds.), *Handbook of the psychology of aging* (2nd ed.). New York: Van Nostrand Reinhold.

Rosenthal, A. (1988, May). How fantasy helps kids grow. *Parents,* pp. 90–94.

Rosenthal, M. K. (1982). Vocal dialogues in the neonatal period. *Developmental Psychology, 18,* 17–21.

Rosett, H. L., Weiner, L., Lee, A., Zuckerman, B., Dooling, E., & Oppenheimer, E. (1983). Patterns of alcohol consumption and fetal development. *Obstetrics and Gynecology, 61,* 539–546.

Rossi, A. S. (1980). Aging and parenthood in the middle years. In P. B. Baltes & O. G. Brim, Jr. (Eds.), *Life-span development and behavior* (Vol. 3). New York: Academic Press.

Rossi, A. S. (1987). Parenthood in transition: From lineage to child to self-orientation. In J. B. Lancaster, J. Altmann, A. S. Rossi, & L. R. Sherrod (Eds.), *Parenting across the lifespan: Biosocial dimensions.* New York: Aldine de Gruyter.

Rossi, M. J. M. (1988, September). An early start on art. *American Baby,* pp. 30, 34, 36.

Roth, M., Wischik, C. M., Evans, N., & Mountjoy, C. (1985). Convergence and cohesion of recent neurobiological findings in relation to Alzheimer's disease and their bearing on its etiological basis. In M. Bergener, M. Ermini, & H. B. Stahelin (Eds.), *Thresholds in aging.* London, England: Academic Press.

Rothbaum, F. (1988). Maternal acceptance and child functioning. *Merrill-Palmer Quarterly, 34,* 163–184.

Rothenberg, R., Woelfel, M., Stoneburner, R., Milberg, J., Parker, R., & Truman, B. (1987). Survival with the acquired immunodeficiency syndrome. *New England Journal of Medicine, 317,* 1297–1302.

Rothman, B. K. (1987). *The tentative pregnancy: Prenatal diagnosis and the future of motherhood.* New York: Penguin.

Rothman, B. K., Grant, S., & Strahorn, J. (1988, March 12). *Tentative pregnancy workshop.* Iowa Methodist School of Nursing, Des Moines, IA.

Rotundo, E. A. (1985). American fatherhood: A historical perspective. *American Behavioral Scientist, 29,* 7–25.

Rovee-Collier, C. (1987). Learning and memory in children. In J. D. Osofsky (Ed.), *Handbook of infant development* (2nd ed.). New York: Wiley.

Rovee-Collier, C. K. (1992, April). *Relating cognition and learning to information acquisition.* Paper presented at the International Conference on Infant Studies, Miami Beach, FL.

Rovee-Collier, C. K., Sullivan, M. W., Enright, M. L., Lucas, D., & Fagen, J. W. (1980). Reactivation of infant memory. *Science, 208,* 1159–1161.

Rovner, B. W., Broadhead, J., Spencer, M., Carson, K., & Folstein, M. F. (1989). Depression and Alzheimer's disease. *American Journal of Psychiatry, 146,* 350–353.

Rowe, D. C., Clapp, M., & Wallis, J. (1987). Physical attractiveness and the personality resemblance of identical twins. *Behavior Genetics, 17,* 191–201.

Rubenstein, C. (1984, September). The Michael Jackson syndrome. *Discover,* pp. 69–70.

Rubenstein, R. L. (1987). Never-married elderly as a social type: Re-evaluating some images. *The Gerontologist, 27,* 108–113.

Rubin, J., Provenzano, F., & Luria, Z. (1974). The eye of the beholder: Parents' views of sex and newborns. *American Journal of Orthopsychiatry, 43,* 720–731.

Rubin, K. H. (1977). The social and cognitive value of preschool toys and activities. *Canadian Journal of Behavioral Science, 9,* 382–385.

Rubin, K. H., Fein, G. G., & Vandenberg, B. (1983). Play. In P. H. Mussen (Ed.), *Handbook of child psychology* (4th ed., Vol. 4). New York: Wiley.

Rubin, Z. (1980). *Children's friendships.* Cambridge, MA: Harvard University Press.

Rubin, Z., & Sloman, J. (1984). How parents influence their children's friendships. In M. Lewis (Ed.), *Beyond the dyad.* New York: Plenum Press.

Ruble, D. N., & Brooks-Gunn, J. (1982). The experience of menarche. *Child Development, 53,* 1557–1577.

Ruble, D. N., Brooks-Gunn, J., Fleming, A. S., Fitzmaurice, G., Stangor, C., & Deutsch, F. (1990). Transition to motherhood and the self: Measurement, stability, and change. *Journal of Personality and Social Psychology, 58,* 450–463.

Runback, R. B., & Carr, T. S. (1984). Schema-guided information search in stereotyping of the elderly. *Journal of Applied Social Psychology, 14,* 57–68.

Runyon, W. M. (1982). *Life histories and psychobiography.* New York: Oxford University Press.

Russell, C. H. (1989). *Good news about aging.* New York: John Wiley.

Rutter, M. (1979). *Changing youth in a changing society.* London, England: Nuffield Provincial Hospitals Trust.

Rutter, M., Maugham, B., Mortimer, P., & Ouston, J. (1979). *Fifteen thousand hours.* London, England: Open Books.

Ryan, R. M. (1982). Control and information in the intrapersonal sphere: An extension of cognitive evaluation theory. *Journal of Personality and Social Psychology, 43,* 450–461.

Rybash, J. M., Hoyer, W. J., & Roodin, P. A. (1986). *Adult cognition and aging: Developmental changes in processing, knowing, and thinking.* New York: Pergamon.

Ryff, C. D. (1982). Self-perceived personality change in adulthood and aging. *Journal of Personality and Social Psychology, 42,* 108–115.

S

Sabatelli, R. M., & Cecil-Pigo, E. F. (1985). Relational interdependence and commitment in marriage. *Journal of Marriage and the Family, 47,* 931–937.

Sachs, A. (1988, December 5). Abortion on the ropes. *Time,* pp. 58–59.

Sachs, B. P., McCarthy, B. J., Rubin, G., Burton, A., Terry, J., & Tyler, C. W. (1983). Cesarean section. *Journal of the American Medical Association, 250,* 2157–2159.

Salapatek, P. (1975). Pattern perception in early infancy. In L. B. Cohen & P. Salapatek (Eds.), *Infant perception: From sensation to cognition* (Vol. 1). New York: Academic Press.

Salk, L. (1983). *What every child would like his parents to know* (pp. 306, 959–965, & 1022–1028). New York: Fireside Books.

Salthouse, T. A. (1982). *Adult cognition: An experimental psychology of human aging.* New York: Springer-Verlag.

Salthouse, T. A. (1984). Effects of age and skill in typing. *Journal of Experimental Psychology: General, 113,* 345–371.

Salthouse, T. A. (1985). Speed of behavior and its implications for cognition. In J. E. Birren & K. W. Schaie (Eds.), *Handbook of the psychology of aging* (2nd ed., pp. 400–427). New York: Van Nostrand Reinhold.

Salthouse, T. A., & Prill, K. A. (1988, Summer). Effects of aging on perceptual closure. *American Journal of Psychology, 101,* 217–238.

Salvatore, D. (1987, February). Teen rage. *Ladies' Home Journal,* pp. 95–97, 154–156.

Sameroff, A. J. (1982). Development and the dialectic: The need for a systems approach. In W. A. Collins (Ed.), *The concept of development. Minnesota symposia on child psychology* (Vol. 15). Hillsdale, NJ: Lawrence Erlbaum.

Sameroff, A. J. (1983). Developmental systems: Contexts and evolution. In P. H. Mussen (Ed.), *Handbook of child psychology: Vol. 1. History, theory, and methods.* New York: Wiley.

Sameroff, A. J., & Cavanagh, P. J. (1979). Learning in infancy: A developmental perspective. In J. D. Osofsky (Ed.), *Handbook of infant development.* New York: John Wiley & Sons.

Samet, N., & Kelly, E. W., Jr. (1987). The relationship of steady dating to self-esteem and sex-role identity among adolescents. *Adolescence, 22,* 231–245.

Sandberg, D. E., Ehrhardt, A. A., Mellins, C. A., Ince, S. E., & Meyer-Bahlburg, H. F. L. (1987). The influence of individual and family characteristics upon career aspirations of girls during childhood and adolescence. *Sex Roles, 16,* 649–668.

Sanders, J. M., Beach, R. K., Brookman, R. R., Brown, R. R., Creene, J. W., & McAnarney, E. (1988). Suicide and suicide attempts in adolescents and young adults. *Pediatrics, 81,* 322–324.

Santrock, J. W. (1987). The effects of divorce on adolescents: Needed research perspectives. *Family Therapy, 14*(2), 147–159.

Sapadin, L. A. (1988). Friendship and gender: Perspectives of professional men and women. *Journal of Social and Personal Relationships, 5,* 387–403.

Saslaw, R. (1981, Fall). A new student for the eighties: The mature woman. *Educational Horizons,* pp. 41–46.

Savage, W. (1986). *A savage enquiry: Who controls childbirth.* London, England: Virago.

Saxby, L., & Bryden, M. P. (1985). Left visual-field advantage for processing visual information. *Developmental Psychology, 21,* 253–261.

Saxon, S. V., & Etten, M. J. (1978). *Physical change and aging.* New York: Tiresias.

Scafidi, F. A., Field, T. M., Schanberg, S. M., Bauer, C. R., Vega-Lahr, N., Garcia, R., Poirier, J., Nystrom, G., & Kuhn, C. M. (1986). Effects of tactile/kinesthetic stimulation on the clinical course of sleep/wake behavior of preterm neonates. *Infant Behavior and Development, 9,* 91–105.

Scarpitti, F. R., & Datesman, S. K. (1980). *Drugs and the youth culture.* Beverly Hills, CA: Sage.

Scarr, S. (1984). *Mother care/other care.* New York: Basic Books.

Scarr, S., & McCartney, K. (1983). How people make their own environments: A theory of genotype-environment effects. *Child Development, 54,* 424–435.

Schaef, A. W., & Fassel, D. (1988). *The addictive organization.* San Francisco, CA: Harper & Row.

Schaeffer, C. (1987). "Will the baby be okay?" *Changing Times, 41,* 97–103.

Schaffer, H. R., & Emerson, P. E. (1964). The development of social attachments in infancy. *Monographs of the Society for Research in Child Development, 29,* 3, Serial No. 94.

Schaffer, J., & Kral, R. (1988). Adoptive families. In C. S. Chilman, E. W. Nunnally, & F. M. Cox (Eds.), *Variant family forms* (Vol. 5). Newbury Park, CA: Sage.

Schaie, K. W. (1977/1978). Toward a stage theory of adult development. *International Journal of Aging and Human Development, 8,* 129–138.

Schaie, K. W. (1983). The Seattle longitudinal study: A twenty-one-year investigation of psychometric intelligence. In K. W. Schaie (Ed.), *Longitudinal studies of adult personality development.* New York: Guilford.

Schaie, K. W. (1988, March). Ageism in psychological research. *American Psychologist, 43,* 179–183.

Schaie, K. W. (1989). Individual differences in rate of cognitive change in adulthood. In V. L. Bengtson & K. W. Schaie (Eds.), *The course of later life: Research and reflections.* New York: Springer.

Schaie, K. W., & Hertzog, C. (1983). Fourteen-year cohort-sequential analyses of adult intellectual development. *Developmental Psychology, 19,* 531–544.

Schaie, K. W., Labouvie, G. V., & Buech, B. V. (1973). Generational and cohort-specific differences in adult cognitive functioning: A fourteen-year study of independent samples. *Developmental Psychology, 9,* 151–166.

Schaie, K. W., & Willis, S. L. (1986). *Adult development and aging* (2nd ed.). Boston, MA: Little, Brown.

Schick, F. L. (Ed.). (1986). *Statistical handbook on aging Americans.* Phoenix, AZ: Oryx Press.

Schlossberg, N. K. (1978). Five propositions about adult development. *Journal of College Student Personnel, 19,* 418–423.

Schnaiberg, A., & Goldenberg, S. (1989). From empty nest to crowded nest: The dynamics of incompletely launched young adults. *Social Problems, 36,* 251–269.

Schoenborn, C. A., & Cohen, B. H. (1986, June 30). Trends in smoking, alcohol consumption, and other health practices among U.S. adults, 1977 and 1983. *Advance Data from Vital and Health Statistics.* No. 118. DHHS Pub. No. 86–1250.

Schonfield, D., & Robertson, B. A. (1966). Memory storage and aging. *Canadian Journal of Psychology, 20,* 228–236.

Schulte, F. J., Albani, M., Schnizer, H., Bentele, K., & Klingspron, R. (1982). Neuronal control of neonatal respiration—sleep apnea and the sudden infant death syndrome. *Neuropediatrics, 13,* 3–14.

Schultz, D. P., & Schultz, S. E. (1986). *Psychology and industry today* (4th ed.). New York: Macmillan.

Schumacher, G., & Cattell, R. B. (1974). Factor analysis of the German HSPQ: Investigations of the cross-cultural constancy of primary personality factors. *Zeitschrift fur Experimentelle und Angewandte Psychologie, 21,* 621–636. Cited in J. F. Campbell. (1991). The primary personality factors of Hawaiian, middle adolescents. *Psychological Reports, 68,* 3–26.

Schumaker, J. F., Small, L., & Ward, D. S. (1985). Eating behavior among Thais and Americans. *Journal of Psychology, 119,* 469–474.

Schuster, C. S., & Ashburn, S. S. (1986). *The process of human development: A holistic life-span approach* (2nd ed.). Boston, MA: Little, Brown.

Schutte, N. S., Malouff, J. M., Post-Gorden, J. C., & Rodasta, A. L. (1988). Effects of playing videogames on children's aggressive and other behaviors. *Journal of Applied Social Psychology, 18,* 454–460.

Schwartz, D. B., & Darabi, K. F. (1986). Motivations for adolescents' first visit to a family planning clinic. *Adolescence, 21,* 535–545.

Schwartz, J. (1988, May). Risky business. *Omni,* p. 36.

Schwartz, J. C. (1972). Effects of peer familiarity on the behavior of preschoolers in a novel situation. *Journal of Personality and Social Psychology, 24,* 276–284.

Schwartz, R. C. (1987). Working with "internal and external" families in the treatment of bulimia. *Family Relations, 36,* 242–245.

Schwartzberg, N. S. (1988a). Born too soon. *Parents, 63,* 114–118.

Schwartzberg, N. S. (1988b). The popularity factor. *Parents, 63,* 144–148.

Scram, R. W. (1979). Marital satisfaction over the family life cycle: A critique and proposal. *Journal of Marriage and the Family, 411,* 7–12.

Scribner, S., & Cole, M. (1973). Cognitive consequences of formal and informal education. *Science, 182,* 553–559.

Seeman, E., Hopper, J. L., Bach, L. A., Cooper, M. E., Parkinson, E., McKay, J., & Jerums, G. (1989, March 2). Reduced bone mass in daughters of women with osteoporosis. *New England Journal of Medicine, 320,* 554–558.

Segerberg, O. (1982). *Living to be 100: 1,200 who did and how they did it.* New York: Scribners.

Seidner, L. B., Stipek, D. J., & Fesbach, N. D. (1988). A developmental analysis of elementary school-aged children's concepts of pride and embarrassment. *Child Development, 59,* 367–377.

Sekaran, U. (1986). *Dual-career families.* San Francisco, CA: Jossey-Bass.

Selman, R. (1980). *The growth of interpersonal understanding.* New York: Academic Press.

Selman, R. L., & Selman, A. P. (1979, October). Children's ideas about friendship: A new theory. *Psychology Today,* pp. 71–80.

Seltzer, J. A., & Bianchi, S. M. (1988). Children's contact with absent parents. *Journal of Marriage and the Family, 50,* 663–677.

Sennett, R. (1980). *Authority.* New York: Knopf.

Serbin, L. A., & Sprafkin, C. (1986). The salience of gender and the process of sex typing in three- to seven-year-old children. *Child Development, 57,* 1188–1199.

Shaffer, D. R. (1988). *Social and personality development* (2nd ed.). Pacific Grove, CA: Brooks/Cole.

Shanan, J. (1985). Personality types and culture in later adulthood (monograph). In *Contributions to human development* (Vol. 12). Basel, Switzerland: Kargen.

Shannon, D. C., & Kelly, D. H. (1982). SIDS and Near-SIDS. *New England Journal of Medicine, 306,* 1022–1028.

Shapiro, J. L. (1987, January). The expectant father. *Psychology Today,* pp. 36–42.

Sharps, M. J., & Gollin, E. S. (1987). Speed and accuracy of mental image rotation in young and elderly adults. *Journal of Gerontology, 42,* 342–344.

Shaver, P., & Hazan, C. (1987). Being lonely, falling in love: Perspectives from attachment theory. *Journal of Social and Behavioral Personality, 2,* 105–124.

Shaver, P., Hazan, C., & Bradshaw, D. (1988). Love as attachment: The integration of three behavioral systems. In R. J. Sternberg & M. L. Barnes (Eds.), *The anatomy of love.* New Haven, CT: Yale University Press.

Shaver, P., Schwartz, J., Kirson, D., & O'Connor, C. (1987). Emotion knowledge: Further exploration of a prototype approach. *Journal of Personality and Social Psychology, 52,* 1061–1086.

Shehan, C. L., Burg, M. A., & Rexroat, C. A. (1986). Depression and the social dimensions of the full-time housewife role. *Sociological Quarterly, 27,* 403–421.

Sheingold, K., & Tenney, Y. J. (1982). Memory for a salient childhood event. In U. Neisser (Ed.), *Memory observed.* San Francisco, CA: W. H. Freeman.

Shekelle, R. B., Gale, M., & Norusis, M. (1985). Type A score (Jenkins Activity Survey) and risk of recurrent coronary heart disease in the Aspirin Myocardial Infarction Study. *American Journal of Cardiology, 56,* 221–225.

Shepard, M. J., Hellenbrand, K. G., & Bracken, M. B. (1986). Proportional weight gain and complications of pregnancy, labor, and delivery in healthy women of normal prepregnant stature. *American Journal of Obstetrics and Gynecology, 155,* 947–954.

Sher, G. I., & Marriage, V. A. (1988). *From infertility to in vitro fertilization.* New York: McGraw-Hill.

Shereff, R. (1989, November). Small doses: A ton of prevention. *Ms.,* p. 22.

Sherman, L. W. (1984). Development of children's perceptions of internal locus of control: A cross-sectional and longitudinal analysis. *Journal of Personality, 52,* 338–354.

Shneidman, E. (1978). Death work and the stages of dying. In R. Fulton (Ed.), *Death and dying.* Reading, MA: Addison-Wesley.

Shneidman, E. (1985). *The definition of suicide.* New York: Wiley.

Shneidman, E. (1987, March). At the point of no return. *Psychology Today,* pp. 54–58.

Siegel, A. J., & Milvy, P. (1990, May). Physical activity levels and altered mortality from coronary heart disease with an emphasis on marathon running: A critical review. *Cardiovascular Reviews & Reports,* pp. 96–99.

Siegel, L. S. (1978). The relationship of language and thought in the preoperational child: A reconsideration of non-verbal alternatives to Piagetian tasks. In S. Siegel & C. Brainerd (Eds.), *Alternatives to Piaget.* New York: Academic Press.

Siegel, R. K. (1980). The psychology of life after death. *American Psychologist, 35,* 911–931.

Siegler, I. C. (1980). The psychology of adult development and aging. In E. W. Busse & D. G. Blazer (Eds.), *Handbook of geriatric psychiatry.* New York: Van Nostrand Reinhold.

Siegler, R. S. (1981). Developmental sequences within and between concepts. *Monographs of the Society for Research in Child Development, 46,* no. 189.

Siegler, R. S. (1986). *Children's thinking.* Englewood Cliffs, NJ: Prentice-Hall.

Siegler, R. S., & Richards, D. D. (1982). The development of intelligence. In R. J. Sternberg (Ed.), *Handbook of human intelligence.* Cambridge, England: Cambridge University Press.

Sigall, H., Page, R., & Brown, A. C. (1971). Effect of expenditure as a function of evaluation and evaluator attractiveness. *Representative Research in Social Psychology, 2,* 19–25.

Silber, T. J. (1987). Adolescent marijuana use: Screening and ethics. *Adolescence, 22,* 1–6.

Silberstein, L. R., Striegel-Moore, R. H., Timko, C., & Rodin, J. (1988). Behavioral and psychological implications of body dissatisfaction: Do men and women differ? *Sex Roles, 19,* 219–230.

Silver, H. K. (1987). Growth & development. In C. H. Kempe, H. K. Silver, D. O'Brien, & V. A. Fulginiti (Eds.), *Current pediatric diagnosis & treatment 1987.* Norwalk, CT: Appleton & Lange.

Silverstein, B., & Perdue, L. (1988). The relationship between role concerns, preferences for slimness, and symptoms of eating problems among college women. *Sex Roles, 18,* 101–106.

Simmons, R. G., & Blyth, D. A. (1987). *Moving into adolescence: The impact of pubertal change and school context.* New York: Aldine de Gruyter.

Simmons, R. G., Rosenberg, F., & Rosenberg, M. (1973). Disturbance in the self-image at adolescence. *American Sociological Review, 38,* 553–568.

Simons, J. A. (1990, November). *Surviving the dysfunctional workplace.* Presentation at Des Moines Area Community College, Des Moines, IA.

Simons, J. A., Irwin, D. B., & Drinnin, B. A. (1987). *Psychology: The search for understanding.* St. Paul: West.

Simonton, D. K. (1977). Creativity, age and stress. *Journal of Personality and Social Psychology, 35,* 791–804.

Simpson, E. (1987). The development of political reasoning. *Human Development, 30,* 268–281.

Singer, D. G. (1982). The research connection. *Television and Children, 5,* 25–35.

Singer, D. G., & Singer, J. L. (1980). Television viewing and aggressive behavior in preschool children: A field study. *Forensic Psychology & Psychiatry, 347,* 289–303.

Singer, J. L., Singer, D. G., & Rapaczynski, W. S. (1984). Family patterns and television viewing as predictors of children's beliefs and aggression. *Journal of Communication, 34,* 73–89.

Sinick, D. (1976, November). Counseling the dying and their survivors. *Personnel and Guidance Journal,* pp. 122–123.

Siwolop, S., & Mohs, M. (1985, February). The war on Down syndrome. *Discover,* pp. 67–73.

Skalka, P. (1984). *The American Medical Association guide to health and well-being after fifty.* New York: Random House.

Skinner, B. F. (1953). *Science and human behavior.* New York: Macmillan.

Skinner, B. F. (1957). *Verbal behavior.* New York: Appleton-Century-Crofts.

Skinner, B. F., & Vaughan, M. E. (1983). *Enjoy old age.* New York: Warner Books.

Skipper, J. K., & Nass, G. (1966). Dating behavior: A framework for analysis and illustration. *Journal of Marriage and the Family, 28,* 412–420.

Skoog, I. (1988). Sexualitet hos aldre. In *Medicinsk sexologi.* Stockholm, Sweden: Svenska Lakaresallskapet & Spri.

Skrimshire, A. (1987). Children's moral reasoning in the context of personal relationships. *Human Development, 30,* 99–104.

Slattery, M. L., Jacobs, D. R., & Nichaman, M. Z. (1989). Leisure time physical activity and coronary heart disease death. The U. S. Railroad Study. *Circulation, 79,* 304.

Smart money, money survey. (1989, November). *Ms.,* pp. 53–57.

Smetana, J. G. (1986). Preschool children's conceptions of sex-role transgressions. *Child Development, 57,* 862–871.

Smilansky, S. (1968). *The effects of sociodramatic play on disadvantaged preschool children.* New York: Wiley.

Smilgis, M. (1987, February 16). The big chill: Fear of AIDS. *Time,* pp. 50–59.

Smith, C., & Lloyd, B. (1978). Maternal behavior and perceived sex of infant: Revisited. *Child Development, 49,* 1263–1265.

Smith, E. A., & Udry, J. R. (1985, October). Coital and non-coital sexual behavior of white and black adolescents. *American Journal of Public Health,* pp. 1200–1218.

Smith, F. (1977). Making sense of reading—and of reading instruction. *Harvard Educational Review, 47,* 386–395.

Smith, J., & Baltes, P. B. (1990). Wisdom-related knowledge: Age/cohort differences in response to life-planning problems. *Developmental Psychology, 26,* 494–505.

Smotherman, W. P., & Robinson, S. R. (1987). Prenatal influences on development: Behavior is not a trivial aspect of fetal life. *Developmental and Behavioral Pediatrics, 8,* 171–176.

Snarey, J. R. (1985). Cross-cultural universality of social-moral development: A critical review of Kohlbergian research. *Psychological Bulletin, 97,* 202–232.

Snarey, J. R. (1987, June). A question of morality. *Psychology Today,* pp. 6–8.

Snow, M. E., Jacklin, C. N., & Maccoby, E. E. (1983). Sex-of-child differences in father-child interaction at one year of age. *Child Development, 54,* 227–232.

Snowden, L. R., Schott, T. L., Awalt, S. J., & Gillis-Knox, J. (1988). Marital satisfaction in pregnancy: Stability and change. *Journal of Marriage and the Family, 50,* 325–333.

Sobal, J. (1987). Health concerns of young adolescents. *Adolescence, 22,* 739–750.

Sobal, J., Klein, H., Graham, D., & Black, J. (1988). Health concerns of high school students and teachers' beliefs about student health concerns. *Pediatrics, 81,* 218–223.

Sobal, J., & Stunkard, A. J. (1989). Socioeconomic status and obesity: A review of literature. *Psychological Bulletin, 105,* 260–275.

Sollie, D. L., & Miller, B. C. (1980). The transition to parenthood as a critical time for building family strengths. In N. Stinnett, B. Chesser, J. DeFain, & P. Kraul (Eds.), *Family strengths: Positive models of family life.* Lincoln, NE: University of Nebraska Press.

Somerville, S. C., Wellman, H. M., & Cultice, J. C. (1983). Young children's deliberate reminding. *Journal of Genetic Psychology, 143,* 87–96.

Sommer, B. B. (1978). *Puberty and adolescence.* New York: Oxford University Press.

Sonkin, D. J., Martin, D., & Walker, L. E. A. (1985). *The male batterer: A treatment approach.* New York: Springer.

Sontag, S. (1972, September 2). The double standard of aging. *Saturday Review,* pp. 29–38.

Sorce, J. F., Emde, R. N., Campos, J. J., & Klinnert, M. D. (1985). Maternal emotional signaling: Its effects on the visual cliff behavior of 1-year-olds. *Developmental Psychology, 21,* 195–200.

Sorel, N. (1984). *Ever since Eve: Personal reflections on childbirth.* New York: Oxford University Press.

Sorensen, T. I. A., Nielsen, G. G., Andersen, P. K., & Teasdale, T. W. (1988). Genetic and environmental influences on premature death in adult adoptees. *New England Journal of Medicine, 318,* 727–732.

Sorenson, R. C. (1973). *Adolescent sexuality in contemporary America: Personal values and sexual behavior, ages thirteen to nineteen.* New York: World.

Sosa, R., Kennell, J., Klaus, M., Robertson, S., & Urrutia, J. (1980). The effect of a supportive companion on perinatal problems, length of labor, and mother-infant interaction. *New England Journal of Medicine, 303,* 597–600.

Speece, M. W., & Brent, S. B. (1984). Children's understanding of death: A review of three components of a death concept. *Child Development, 55,* 1671–1686.

Spees, E. R. (1987). College students' sexual attitudes and behaviors, 1974–1985: A review of the literature. *Journal of College Student Personnel, 28,* 135–140.

Spence, J. T., & Helmreich, R. L. (1983). Achievement-related motives and behaviors. In J. T. Spence (Ed.), *Achievement and achievement motives: Psychological and sociological approaches.* San Francisco, CA: Freeman.

Spencer, S. (1979, May). Childhood's end. *Harper's,* pp. 16–19.

Spira, L. (1981). The experience of divorce for the psychotherapy patient: A developmental perspective. *Clinical Social Work Journal, 9,* 258–270.

Spock, B. J. (1985, October). Kids and superkids. *Omni,* pp. 28, 159.

Sprecher, S., McKinney, K., & Orbuch, T. L. (1987). Has the double standard disappeared? An experimental test. *Social Psychology Quarterly, 50,* 24–31.

Squyres, E. M. (1987). Approaches to the self: An examination of the work of Bowen and Jung. *Family Therapy, 14,* 165–178.

Sroufe, L. A. (1974). Wariness of strangers and the study of infant development. *Child Development, 48,* 731–748.

Sroufe, L. A. (1978, October). Attachment and the roots of competence. *Human Nature,* pp. 50–57.

Sroufe, L. A. (1979). Socioemotional development. In J. Osofsky (Ed.), *Handbook of infant development.* New York: Wiley.

Stack, S. (1990). New micro-level data on the impact of divorce on suicide, 1959–1980: A test of two theories. *Journal of Marriage and the Family, 52,* 119–127.

Staines, G. L., Pottick, K. J., & Fudge, D. A. (1986). Wives' employment and husbands' attitudes toward work and life. *Journal of Applied Psychology, 71,* 118–128.

Stake, J., & Lauer, M. L. (1987). The consequences of being overweight: A controlled study of gender differences. *Sex Roles, 17,* 31–47.

Stambrook, M., & Parker, K. (1987). The development of the concept of death in childhood: A review of the literature. *Merrill-Palmer Quarterly, 33,* 133–157.

Stanton, A. N. (1984, November 24). Overheating and cot death. *The Lancet,* pp. 1199–1201.

Staples, R. (1976). The Black American family. In C. H. Mindel & R. W. Habenstein (Eds.), *Ethnic families in America* (2nd ed., pp. 217–244). New York: Elsevier.

Stark, E. (1986, October). Young, innocent and pregnant. *Psychology Today,* pp. 28–35.

Stark, E. (1988, April). Beyond rivalry. *Psychology Today,* pp. 61–63.

Stark, R. E. (1986). Prespeech segmental feature development. In P. Fletcher & M. Garman (Eds.), *Language acquisition* (2nd ed.). New York: Cambridge University Press.

Starkey, P., & Cooper, R. G., Jr. (1980). Perception of numbers by human infants. *Science, 210,* 1033–1035.

Stechler, G., & Halton, A. (1982). Prenatal influences on human development. In B. B. Wolman (Ed.), *Handbook of developmental psychology.* Englewood Cliffs, NJ: Prentice-Hall.

Steele, R. (1977, December). Dying, death, and bereavement among the Maya Indians of Mesoamerica: A study in anthropological psychology. *American Psychologist,* pp. 1066–1068.

Stein, A. H., & Friedrich, L. K. (1972). Television content and young children's behavior. In J. P. Murray, E. A. Rubinstein, & G. A. Comstock (Eds.), *Television and social behavior: Vol. II. Television and social learning* (pp. 202–317). Washington, DC: U. S. Government Printing Office.

Stein, R. F. (1987). Comparison of self-concept of nonobese and obese university junior female nursing students. *Adolescence, 22,* 77–90.

Stein, Z., Susser, M., Saenger, G., & Marolla, F. (1975). *Famine and human development: The Dutch hunger winter of 1944–1945.* New York: Oxford University Press.

Steinbacher, R., & Gilroy, F. D. (1986). Preference for sex of child among primiparous women. *Journal of Psychology, 119,* 541–547.

Steinberg, C. S. (1980). *TV facts.* New York: Facts on File.

Steinberg, L. (1981). Transformations in family relations at puberty. *Developmental Psychology, 17,* 883–850.

Steinberg, L. (1987a, September). Bound to bicker. *Psychology Today,* pp. 36–39.

Steinberg, L. (1987b). Single parents, stepparents, and the susceptibility of adolescents to antisocial peer pressure. *Child Development, 58,* 269–275.

Steinberg, L. (1988). Reciprocal relation between parent-child distance and pubertal maturation. *Developmental Psychology, 24,* 122–128.

Steinberg, L. D., & Silverberg, S. B. (1986). The vicissitudes of autonomy in early adolescence. *Child Development, 57,* 841–851.

Steinberg, L. D., & Silverberg, S. B. (1987). Influences on marital satisfaction during the middle stages of the family life cycle. *Journal of Marriage and the Family, 49,* 751–760.

Steiner, J. E. (1979). Facial expressions in response to taste and smell stimulation. In H. W. Resse & L. P. Lipsitt (Eds.), *Advances in child development and behavior* (Vol. 13). New York: Academic Press.

Steinmetz, S. K. (1988). *Duty bound: Elder abuse and family care.* Newbury Park, CA: Sage.

Steinschneider, A. (1975). Implications of the sudden infant death syndrome for the study of sleep in infancy. *Minnesota Symposia on Child Psychology, 9,* 106–134.

Stephan, C. W., & Langlois, J. H. (1984). Baby beautiful: Adult attributions of infant competence as a function of infant attractiveness. *Child Development, 55,* 576–585.

Steri, H., & Pecheux, M. (1986). Tactual habituation and discrimination of form in infancy: A comparison with vision. *Child Development, 57,* 100–104.

Stern, C., & Stern, W. (1931). *Monographien ueber die seelische Entwicklung des Kindes: 2 Band. Erinnerung, Aussage und Luege in der ersten Kindheit* (4th ed.). [Monographs on the psychological development of the child: Vol. 2. Remembering, informing and lying in early childhood.] Leipzig, Germany: Barth. (Original work published 1909. Cited in Mant, C. M., & Perner, J. [1988]. The child's understanding of commitment. *Developmental Psychology, 24,* 343–351.)

Stern, D. J. (1985). *The interpersonal world of the infant.* New York: Basic Books.

Sternberg, R. J. (1984). Toward a triarchic theory of human intelligence. *Behavioral & Brain Sciences, 7,* 269–315.

Sternberg, R. J. (1985). *Beyond IQ: A triarchic theory of human intelligence.* Cambridge, England: Cambridge University Press.

Sternberg, R. J. (1988a). *Intelligence applied.* San Diego, CA: Harcourt Brace.

Sternberg, R. J. (1988b). Mental self-government: A theory of intellectual styles and their development. *Human Development, 31,* 197–224.

Sterns, H. L., Barrett, G. V., & Alexander, R. A. (1985). Accidents and the aging individual. In J. E. Birren & K. W. Schaie (Eds.), *Handbook of the psychology of aging* (2nd ed., pp. 703–725). New York: Van Nostrand Reinhold.

Stevens-Long, J. (1984). *Adult life* (2nd ed.). Palo Alto, CA: Mayfield.

Stillion, J. (1985). *Death and the sexes.* Washington, DC: Hemisphere.

Stinnett, N., Carter, L. M., & Montgomery, J. E. (1972, November). Older persons' perceptions of their marriages. *Journal of Marriage and the Family,* pp. 665–670.

Stinnett, N., Sanders, G., DeFrain, J., & Parkhurst, A. A. (1982). A nationwide study of families who perceive themselves as strong. *Family Perspective, 16,* 15–22.

Stinnett, N., Walters, J., & Kaye, E. (1984). *Relationships on marriage and the family* (2nd ed.). New York: Macmillan.

Storfer, M. D. (1990). *Intelligence and giftedness: The contributions of heredity and early environment.* San Francisco, CA: Jossey-Bass.

Storm, C. L., Sheean, R., & Sprenkle, D. H. (1983). The structure of separated women's communication with their nonprofessional and professional social networks. *Journal of Marital and Family Therapy, 9,* 423–429.

Strahan, R. (1978). Personal communication.

Strange, C. C., & King, P. M. (1981). Intellectual development and its relationship to maturation during the college years. *Journal of Applied Developmental Psychology, 2,* 281–295.

Straus, M. A., Gelles, R. J., & Steinmetz, S. K. (1980). *Behind closed doors: Violence in the American family.* New York: Anchor-Doubleday.

Streissguth, A. P., Barr, H. M., & Martin, D. C. (1983). Maternal alcohol use and neonatal habituation assessed with the Brazelton Scale. *Child Development, 54,* 1109–1118.

Streissguth, A. P., Martin, D. C., Sandman, B. M., Kirchner, G. L., & Darby, D. S. (1984). Intra-uterine alcohol and nicotine exposure: Attention and reaction time in four-year-old children. *Developmental Psychology, 20,* 533–541.

Strickland, B. R. (1988). Sex-related differences in health and illness. *Psychology of Women Quarterly, 12,* 381–399.

Strickland, D. M., Saeed, S. A., Casey, M. L., & Mitchell, M. D. (1983). Stimulation of prostaglandin biosynthesis by urine of the human fetus may serve as a trigger for parturition. *Science, 220,* 521–522.

Striegel-Moore, R. H., Silberstein, L. R., & Rodin, J. (1986). Toward an understanding of risk factors for bulimia. *American Psychologist, 41,* 246–263.

Suitor, J. J., & Pillemer, K. (1987, November). The presence of adult children: A source of stress for elderly couples' marriages? *Journal of Marriage and the Family, 49,* 717–725.

Suitor, J. J., & Pillemer, K. (1988, November). Explaining intergenerational conflict when adult children and elderly parents live together. *Journal of Marriage and the Family, 50,* 1037–1047.

Sunderland, A., Watts, K., Baddeley, A. D., & Harris, J. E. (1986). Subjective memory assessment and test performance in elderly adults. *Journal of Gerontology, 41,* 376–384.

Super, D. E. (1980). A life-span, life-space approach to career development. *Journal of Vocational Behavior, 16,* 282–298.

Surra, C. A., Arizzi, P., & Asmussen, L. A. (1988). The association between reasons for commitment and the development and outcome of marital relationships. *Journal of Social and Personal Relationships, 5,* 47–63.

Sutton-Smith, B. (1986). *Toys as culture.* New York: Gardner Press.

Swank, C. (1982). Phased retirement: The European corporate experience. *Aging International, 9,* 10–15.

Swensen, C. H., & Tranaug, G. (1985). Commitment and the long-term marriage relationship. *Journal of Marriage and the Family, 47,* 939–945.

Swick, K. J., & Graves, S. B. (1986, October). Locus of control and interpersonal support as related to parenting. *Childhood Education,* pp. 41–49.

T

Tamashiro, R. T. (1979). Children's humor: A developmental view. *Elementary School Journal, 80,* 69–75.

Tan, L. E. (1985). Laterality and motor skills in four-year-olds. *Child Development, 56,* 119–124.

Tanfer, K. (1987). Patterns of premarital cohabitation among never-married women in the United States. *Journal of Marriage and the Family, 49,* 483–497.

Tanner, J. (1970). Physical growth. In P. H. Mussen (Ed.), *Carmichael's manual of child psychology* (3rd ed.). New York: Wiley.

Tanner, J. M., & Davies, P. S. W. (1985). Clinical longitudinal standards for height and height velocity for North American children. *Journal of Pediatrics, 107,* 317–329.

Tanner, V. L., & Holliman, W. B. (1988). Effectiveness of assertiveness training in modifying aggressive behaviors of young children. *Psychological Reports, 62,* 39–46.

Tanzer, D., & Block, J. L. (1976). *Why natural childbirth?* New York: Schocken Books.

Taranto, M. A. (1989). Facets of wisdom: A theoretical synthesis. *International Journal of Aging and Human Development, 29,* 1–21.

Taylor, I. A. (1974). Patterns of creativity and aging. In E. Pfeiffer (Ed.), *Successful aging.* Durham, NC: Duke University, Center for the Study of Aging and Human Development.

Taylor, R. J. (1988). Parents, children, siblings, in-laws, and non kin as sources of emergency assistance to black Americans. *Family Relations, 37,* 298–304.

Taylor, N. B., & Pryor, R. G. L. (1985). Exploring processes of compromise in career decision making. *Journal of Vocational Behavior, 27,* 171–190.

Taylor, S. E., & Brown, J. D. (1988). Illusion and well-being: A social psychological perspective on mental health. *Psychological Bulletin, 10,* 193–210.

Teachman, J. D., Polonko, K. A., & Scanzoni, J. (1987). In M. S. Sussman & S. K. Steinmetz (Eds.), *Handbook of marriage and the family.* New York: Plenum Press.

Teeven, R. C., & McGhee, P. E. (1972). Childhood development of fear of failure motivation. *Journal of Personality and Social Psychology, 21,* 345–348.

Tellegen, A., Lykken, D. T., Bouchard, T. J., Jr., Wilcox, K. J., Segel, N. L., & Rich, S. (1988). Personality similarity in twins reared apart and together. *Journal of Personality and Social Psychology, 54,* 1031–1039.

Tellerman, K., & Medio, F. (1988). Pediatricians' opinions of mothers. *Pediatrics, 81,* 186–189.

Teti, D. M., Lamb, M. E., & Elster, A. B. (1987, August). Long-range socioeconomic and marital consequences of adolescent marriage in three cohorts of adult males. *Journal of Marriage and the Family, 49,* 499–506.

Thayer, R. E. (1987). Energy, tiredness, and tension effects of a sugar snack versus moderate exercise. *Journal of Personality and Social Psychology, 52,* 119–125.

Theirot, R., & Bruce, B. (1988, June). Teenage pregnancy: A family life curriculum. *Childhood Education,* pp. 276–279.

Thibaut, J. W., & Kelly, H. H. (1959). *The social psychology of groups.* New York: Wiley.

Thoman, E. B., Korner, A. F., & Beason-Williams, L. (1977). Modification of responsiveness to maternal vocalization in the neonate. *Child Development, 4,* 563–569.

Thomas, A., & Chess, S. (1977). *Temperament and development.* New York: Brunner/Mazel.

Thomas, A., Chess, S., & Birch, H. G. (1968). *Temperament and behavior disorders in children.* New York: New York University Press.

Thomas, A., Chess, S., & Korn, S. (1982). The reality of difficult temperament. *Merrill-Palmer Quarterly, 28,* 1–20.

Thomas, B. (1984). Early toy preferences of four-year-old readers and nonreaders. *Child Development, 55,* 424–430.

Thomas, E. (1986, May 19). Growing pains at 40. *Time,* pp. 22–41.

Thomas, J. L. (1989). Gender and perceptions of grandparenthood. *International Journal of Aging and Human Development, 29,* 269–282.

Thompson, A. P. (1983, February). Extramarital sex: A review of the research literature. *Journal of Sex Research, 19,* 1–22.

Thompson, R. A., & Lamb, M. E. (1986). Infant-mother attachment: New directions for theory and research. In P. B. Baltes, D. L. Featherman, & R. M. Lerner (Eds.), *Life-span development and behavior* (Vol. 7). Hillsdale, NJ: Lawrence Erlbaum.

Thornberry, O. T., Wilson, R. W., & Golden, P. M. (1986, September 19). Health promotion data for the 1990 objectives: Estimates from the National Health Interview Survey of Health Promotion and Disease Prevention: United States, 1985. *Advance Data from Vital and Health Statistics.* No. 126. DHHS Pub. No. 86–1250.

Thorndike, R. L., Hagen, E. P., & Sattler, J. M. (1985). *Stanford-Binet* (4th ed.). Chicago, IL: Riverside Publishing.

Thornton, A. (1985). Changing attitudes toward separation and divorce: Causes and consequences. *American Journal of Sociology, 90,* 856–872.

Tice, D. M., Buder, J., & Baumeister, R. F. (1985). Development of self-consciousness: At what age does audience pressure disrupt performance? *Adolescence, 20,* 301–305.

Tice, R. R., & Setlow, R. B. (1985). DNA repair and replication in aging organisms and cells. In C. E. Finch & E. L. Schneider (Eds.), *Handbook of the biology of aging* (2nd ed.). New York: Van Nostrand.

Tideiksaar, R. (1990, February). Principles of drug therapy in the elderly. *Physician Assistant,* pp. 29–46.

Tiggemann, M., & Rothblum, E. D. (1988). Gender differences in social consequences of perceived overweight in the United States and Australia. *Sex Roles, 18,* 75–86.

Timiras, P. S. (1972). *Developmental physiology and aging.* New York: Macmillan.

Tinbergen, N. (1969). *The study of instinct.* New York: Oxford University Press. (Original work published 1951)

Tinetti, M. E., Speechley, M., & Ginter, S. F. (1988, December 29). Risk factors for falls among elderly persons living in the community. *New England Journal of Medicine, 319,* 1701–1707.

Tinsley, B. R., & Parke, R. D. (1984). Grandparents as support and socialization agents. In M. Lewis (Ed.), *Beyond the dyad.* New York: Plenum.

Tobin, J. J. (1987). The American idealization of old age in Japan. *The Gerontologist, 27,* 53–58.

Tomkins, S. S. (1979). Script theory: Differential magnification of affects. In H. E. Howe, Jr. & R. A. Dienstbier (Eds.), *Nebraska symposium on motivation: 1978* (Vol. 26, pp. 201–236). Lincoln, NE: University of Nebraska Press.

Tomkins, S. S. (1986). Script theory. In J. Aronoff, R. A. Zucker, & A. I. Rabin (Eds.), *Structuring personality.* Orlando, FL: Academic.

Tomkins, S. S. (1987). Script theory. In J. Aronoff, A. I. Rabin, & R. A. Zucker (Eds.), *The emergence of personality.* New York: Springer.

Tomkins, S. S. (1988). Script theory. In J. Aronoff (Ed.), *The structuring of personality.* New York: Academic Press.

Tompkins, G. E. (1984). Use product packaging to teach skills. *Early Years, 15,* 36–37.

Tovey, D. R., Johnson, L. G., & Szporer, M. (1988, June). Beginning reading: A natural language learning process. *Childhood Education,* pp. 288–292.

Toynbee, A. (1976). Man's concern with life after death. In A. Toynbee & A. Koestler (Eds.), *Life after death.* New York: McGraw-Hill.

Tracy, D. M. (1987). Toys, spatial ability, and science and mathematics achievement: Are they related? *Sex Roles, 17,* 115–138.

Tran, T. V. (1990). Language acculturation among refugee adults. *The Gerontologist, 30,* 94–99.

Trilling, L. (1968). *From sincerity to authenticity.* Cambridge, MA: Harvard University Press.

Trilling, L. (1972). *Sincerity and authenticity.* Cambridge, MA: Harvard University Press.

Troll, L. E. (1980). Grandparenting. In L. W. Poon (Ed.), *Aging in the 80's: Psychological issues.* Washington, DC: American Psychological Association.

Troll, L. E. (1983). Grandparents: The family watchdogs. In T. H. Brubaker (Ed.), *Family relationships in later life.* Beverly Hills, CA: Sage.

Troll, L. E. (1986). Parents and children in later life. *Generations, 10,* 23–25.

Tronick, E. Z. (1989). Emotions and emotional communication in infants. *American Psychologist, 44,* 112–119.

Trotter, R. J. (1983). Baby face. *Psychology Today, 20* (8), 56–62.

Trotter, R. J. (1987a, January). The play's the thing. *Psychology Today,* pp. 27–34.

Trotter, R. J. (1987b, May). You've come a long way, baby. *Psychology Today,* pp. 35–47.

Trygstad, D. W., & Sanders, G. F. (1989). The significance of stepgrandparents. *International Journal of Aging and Human Development, 29,* 119–134.

Tschann, J. M. (1988). Self-disclosure in adult friendship: Gender and marital status differences. *Journal of Social and Personal Relationships, 5,* 65–81.

Turkington, C. (1984, December). Psychologists help spot danger in crib. *APA Monitor,* p. 38.

Turner, B. F., & Adams, C. G. (1988). Reported change in preferred sexual activity over the adult years. *Journal of Sex Research, 25,* 289–303.

U

Udry, J. R., & Eckland, B. K. (1984). Benefits of being attractive: Differential payoffs for men and women. *Psychological Reports, 4,* 47–56.

Uhlenberg, P. (1980, Fall). Death and the family. *Journal of Family History,* pp. 313–322.

Uhlenberg, P., Cooney, T., & Boyd, R. (1990). Divorce for women after midlife. *Journal of Gerontology: Social Sciences, 45,* S3–S11.

Ullman, C. (1987). From sincerity to authenticity: Adolescents' views of the "true self." *Journal of Personality, 55,* 583–595.

Umberson, D., & Hughes, M. (1987). The impact of physical attractiveness on achievement and psychological well-being. *Social Psychology Quarterly, 50,* 227–236.

Unger, R. K. (1979). *Female and male: Psychological perspectives.* New York: Harper & Row.

Upton, A. C. (1977). Pathology. In L. E. Finch & L. Hayflick (Eds.), *Handbook of the biology of aging.* New York: Van Nostrand Reinhold.

Urwin, C. A. (1988). AIDS in children: A family concern. *Family Relations, 37,* 154–159.

U. S. Bureau of the Census. (1989). *Changes in American family life* (Current Population Reports, Series P-20, No. 401). Washington, DC: U.S. Government Printing Office.

U. S. Department of Health and Human Services (USDHHS). (1985). *Health, United States, 1985* (DHHS Publication No. PHS 86–1232). Washington, DC: U.S. Government Printing Office.

U. S. Department of Health and Human Services (USDHHS). (1986). *Health, United States, 1986 and Prevention Profile* (DHHS Publication No. PHS 87–1232). Washington, DC: U. S. Government Printing Office.

V

Valliant, G. E. (1977). *Adaptation to life.* Boston, MA: Little, Brown.

Vance, B. K., & Green, V. (1984). Lesbian identities: An examination of sexual behavior and sex-role attribution as related to age of initial same-sex sexual encounter. *Psychology of Women Quarterly, 8,* 293–307.

Vandell, D. L., Owen, M. T., Wilson, K. S., & Henderson, V. K. (1988). Social development in infant twins: Peer and mother-child relationships. *Child Development, 59,* 168–177.

van Pancake, R. (1985, April). *Continuity between mother-infant attachment and ongoing dyadic peer relationships in preschool.* Paper presented at the biennial meeting of the Society for Research in Child Development, Toronto, Canada.

Van Pelt, D. (1990a, March 5). Midbody fat tied to breast cancer. *Insight,* p. 55.

Van Pelt, D. (1990b, April 23). Athletic rats resist carcinogens. *Insight,* p. 45.

Vann Rackley, J., Warren, S. A., & Bird, G. W. (1988). Determinants of body image in women at midlife. *Psychological Reports, 62,* 9–10.

Vaughan, V. C., McKay, J. R., & Behrman, R. E. (1984). *Nelson textbook of pediatrics* (12th ed.). Philadelphia, PA: W. B. Saunders.

Vaughn, B. E., Block, J. H., & Block, J. (1988). Parental agreement on child rearing during early childhood and the psychological characteristics of adolescents. *Child Development, 59,* 1020–1033.

Vemer, E., Coleman, M., Ganong, L. H., & Cooper, H. (1989). Marital satisfaction in remarriage: A meta-analysis. *Journal of Marriage and the Family, 51,* 713–725.

Venesky, R. L. (1975). Prereading skills: Theoretical foundations and practical applications. In T. A. Brigham, R. Hawkins, J. W. Scott, & T. F. McLaughlin (Eds.), *Behavior analysis in education: Self-control and reading.* Dubuque, IA: Kendall/Hunt.

Verbrugge, L. M. (1989). The twain meet: Empirical explanations of sex differences in health and mortality. *Journal of Health and Social Behavior, 30,* 282–304.

Verloff, J., Reuman, D., & Feld, S. (1984). Motives in American men and women across the adult life span. *Developmental Psychology, 20,* 1142–1158.

Vinacke, W. E., Shannon, K., Palazzo, V., Balsavage, L., & Cooney, P. (1987). Similarity and complementarity in intimate couples. *Genetic, Social, and General Psychology Monographs, 114,* 51–76.

Vinal, D., Wellman, C., Tyser, K., Stites, I., Leaf, J., Larson, A., & Graves, J. (1986). A determination of the health-protective behaviors of female adolescents: A pilot study. *Adolescence, 21,* 87–105.

Vines, G. (1990, December). China's long march to longevity. *New Scientist,* pp. 37–45.

von Hofsten, C., & Lindhagen, K. (1979). Observations on the development of reaching for moving objects. *Journal of Experimental Child Psychology, 28,* 158–173.

vonKondratowitz, H. (1984). Long-term changes in attitudes toward "old age." In V. Garms-Homolova, E. M. Hoerning, & D. Schaeffer (Eds.), *Intergenerational relationships.* Lewiston, NY: C. J. Hogrefe.

Voydanoff, P. (1983). Unemployment: Family strategies for adaptation. In C. R. Figley & H. L. McCubbin (Eds.), *Stress and the family: Vol. II. Coping with catastrophe.* New York: Brunner/Mazel.

Vredenburg, K., O'Brien, E., & Krames, L. (1988). Depression in college students: Personality and experiential factors. *Journal of Counseling Psychology, 35,* 419–425.

Vurpillot, E. (1968). The development of scanning strategies and their relation to visual differentiation. *Journal of Experimental Child Psychology, 6,* 632–650.

Vurpillot, E. (1976). *The visual world of the child* (W. E. C. Gillham, Trans.). New York: International Universities Press.

W

Waddell, K. J., & Rogoff, B. (1987). Contextual organization and intentionality in adults' spatial memory. *Developmental Psychology, 23,* 514–520.

Wagner, J. A. (1987). Formal operations and ego identity in adolescence. *Adolescence, 22,* 23–35.

Waldman, S. (1988, April 18). Kids in harm's way. *Newsweek,* pp. 47–48.

Walford, R. L. (1983). *Maximum life span.* New York: Norton.

Walker, L. E. (1979). *The battered woman.* New York: Harper & Row.

Walker, L. J. (1984). Sex differences in the development of moral reasoning: A critical review. *Child Development, 55,* 677–691.

Walker-Andrews, A. S., & Lennon, E. M. (1985). Auditory-visual perception of changing distance by human infants. *Child Development, 56,* 544–548.

Wallace, W. E. (1985, March 20). What to say to the bereaved. *The Lutheran,* pp. 12–14.

Wallerstein, J. S. (1983). Children of divorce: The psychological tasks of the child. *American Journal of Orthopsychiatry, 53,* 230–243.

Wallerstein, J. S. (1986). Women after divorce: Preliminary report from a ten-year follow-up. *American Journal of Orthopsychiatry, 56,* 64–77.

Wallerstein, J. S. (1987). Children of divorce: Report of a ten-year follow-up of early latency-age children. *American Journal of Orthopsychiatry, 57,* 199–211.

Wallerstein, J. S., & Kelly, J. B. (1980). *Surviving the breakup: How children and parents cope with divorce.* New York: Basic Books.

Walster, E., Aronson, V., Abrahams, D., & Rottman, L. (1966). Importance of physical attractiveness in dating behavior. *Journal of Personality and Social Psychology, 5,* 508–516.

Walster, E., & Walster, G. W. (1978). *Love.* Reading, MA: Addison-Wesley.

Walters, G. C., & Grusec, J. E. (1977). *Punishment.* San Francisco, CA: Freeman.

Walters, J. W., & Ashwal, S. (1988, October/November). Organ prolongation in anencephalic infants: Ethical & medical issues. *Hastings Center Report,* pp. 19–27.

Ward, R. A. (1984). *The aging experience: An introduction to social gerontology* (2nd ed.). New York: Harper & Row.

Ward, R. A., LaGory, M., & Sherman, S. R. (1986). Fear of crime among the elderly as person/environment interaction. *Sociological Quarterly, 27,* 327–341.

Ward, S., Reale, G., & Levinson, D. (1972). Child's perceptions, explanations, and judgments of television advertising: A further exploration. In E. A. Rubenstein, G. A. Comstock, & J. P. Murray (Eds.), *Television and social behavior. Vol. IV. Television in day-to-day life: Patterns of use* (pp. 468–490). Washington, DC: U.S. Government Printing Office.

Ward, S., & Wackman, D. (1972). Television advertising and intrafamily influence: Children's purchase influence attempts and parental yielding. In E. A. Rubenstein, G. A. Comstock, & J. P. Murray (Eds.), *Television and social behavior. Vol. IV. Television in day-to-day life: Patterns of use* (pp. 516–525). Washington, DC: U.S. Government Printing Office.

Wardle, J., & Beales, S. (1986). Restraint, body image and food attitudes in children from 12 to 18 years. *Appetite, 7,* 209–217.

Washington, J., Minde, K., & Goldberg, S. (1986). Temperament in preterm infants: Style and stability. *Journal of the American Academy of Child Psychiatry, 25,* 493–502.

Wass, H. (1984). Concepts of death: A developmental perspective. In H. Wass & C. A. Coris (Eds.), *Childhood and death.* Washington, DC: Hemisphere.

Wassarman, P. M. (1988, December). Fertilization in mammals. *Scientific American,* pp. 78–84.

Waterman, A. S. (1984). *The psychology of individualism.* New York: Praeger.

Watkin, D. M. (1983). *Handbook of nutrition, health, and aging.* Park Ridge, NJ: Noyes.

Watkins, B. A., Huston-Stein, A., & Wright, J. C. (1980). Effects of planned television programming. In E. L. Palmer & A. Dorr (Eds.), *Children and the faces of television: Teaching, violence, selling.* New York: Academic Press.

Watson, E. H. (1978). *Growth and development of children.* Chicago, IL: Year Book Medical Publishers.

Watson, J. B. (1919). *Psychology from the standpoint of a behaviorist.* Philadelphia, PA: Lippincott.

Watson, R., Coppola, V., Wang, P., Moreau, R., Copeland, J. B., Cardwell, D., McDonald, D. H., Sandza, R., Robinson, T. L., Burgower, R., & Bailey, E. (1984, September 10). What price day care? *Newsweek,* pp. 14–21.

Watson-Gegeo, K. A., & Gegeo, D. W. (1989). The role of sibling interaction in child socialization. In P. Goldring Zukow (Ed.), *Sibling interaction across cultures: Theoretical and methodological issues.* New York: Springer-Verlag.

Wechsler, D. (1944). *The measurement of adult intelligence* (3rd ed.). Baltimore, MD: Williams & Wilkins.

Weeks, M. O., & Botkin, D. R. (1987). A longitudinal study of the marriage role expectations of college women: 1961–1984. *Sex Roles, 17,* 49–58.

Weg, R. B. (1987). Menopause: Biomedical aspects. In G. L. Maddox (Ed.), *The encyclopedia of aging* (pp. 433–437). New York: Springer.

Weggemann, T., Brown, J. K., Fulford, G. E., & Minns, R. A. (1987). A study of normal baby movements. *Child: Care, Health and Development, 13,* 41–58.

Weiffenback, J., & Thach, B. (1975). *Taste receptors in the tongue of the newborn human: Behavioral evidence.* Paper presented at the biennial meeting of the Society for Research in Child Development, Denver, CO.

Wein, B. (1988, May). Tiny dancers. *Omni,* p. 122.

Weinberg, K. (1989). *The relation between facial expressions of emotion and behavior in 6 month old infants.* Unpublished master's thesis, University of Massachusetts, Amherst. Cited in Tronick, E. Z. (1989). Emotions and emotional communication in infants. *American Psychologist, 44,* 112–119.

Weiner, B., Graham, S., Stern, P., & Lawson, M. E. (1982). Using affective cues to infer causal thoughts. *Developmental Psychology, 18,* 278–286.

Weinrach, S. G. (1984). Determinants of vocational choice: Holland theory. In D. Brown & L. Brooks (Eds.), *Career choice and development: Applying contemporary theories to practice.* San Francisco, CA: Jossey-Bass.

Weinraub, M., Brooks, J., & Lewis, M. (1977). The social network: A reconsideration of the concept of attachment. *Human Development, 20,* 31–47.

Weisner, T. S. (1987). Socialization for parenthood in sibling caretaking societies. In J. B. Lancaster, J. Altmann, A. S. Rossi, & L. R. Sherrod (Eds.), *Parenting across the lifespan: Biosocial dimensions.* New York: Aldine de Gruyter.

Weiss, R. (1987, November 28). Alzheimer's: A cancer-like mechanism? *Science News, 132,* 348.

Weissberg, J. A., & Paris, S. G. (1986). Young children's remembering in different contexts: A reinterpretation of Istomina's. *Child Development, 57,* 1123–1129.

Weissbluth, M. (1985). *Crybabies. Coping with colic: What to do when your baby won't stop crying.* New York: Berkley.

Weitkamp, L. R., & Schachter, B. Z. (1985). Transferrin and HLA: Spontaneous abortion, neural tube defects, and natural selection. *New England Journal of Medicine, 313,* 925–932.

Welford, A. T. (1977). Motor performance. In J. E. Birren & K. W. Schaie (Eds.), *Handbook of the psychology of aging.* New York: Van Nostrand.

Welford, A. T. (1985). Changes of performance with age: An overview. In N. Charness (Ed.), *Aging and human performance.* New York: Wiley.

Wellman, H. M., & Estes, D. (1986). Early understanding of mental entities: A reexamination of childhood realism. *Childhood Development, 57,* 910–923.

Wellman, H. M., Somerville, S. C., Revelle, G. L., Haake, R. J., & Sophian, C. (1984). The development of comprehensive search skills. *Child Development, 55,* 472–481.

Wentowski, G. J. (1985). Older women's perceptions of great-grandmotherhood: A research note. *The Gerontologist, 25,* 593–596.

Werker, J. F., & Tees, R. C. (1984). Cross-language speech perception. *Infant Behavior and Development, 7,* 49–63.

Werner, H. (1948). *Comparative psychology of mental development.* New York: International Universities Press.

Werner, J. S., & Perlmutter, M. (1979). Development of visual memory in infants. In H. W. Reese & L. P. Lipsitt (Eds.), *Advances in child development and behavior* (Vol. 14). New York: Academic Press.

Wertlieb, D., Weigel, C., & Feldstein, M. (1987). Measuring children's coping. *American Journal of Orthopsychiatry, 57,* 548–560.

Werts, C. E. (1968). Paternal influence on career choice. *Journal of Counseling Psychology, 15,* 48–52.

Wheeler, R. H., & Gunter, B. G. (1987). Change in spouse age difference at marriage: A challenge to traditional family and sex roles? *Sociological Quarterly, 28,* 411–421.

Whipple, V. (1987). Counseling battered women from fundamentalist churches. *Journal of Marital and Family Therapy, 13,* 251–258.

Whitbourne, S. K. (1985). *The aging body: Physiological changes and psychological consequences.* New York: Springer-Verlag.

White, B. L. (1985). *The first three years* (rev. ed.). Englewood Cliffs, NJ: Prentice-Hall.

White, B. L., Kaban, B., & Attanucci, J. (1979). *The origins of human competence.* Lexington, MA: Heath.

White, L. K. (1988). Gender differences in awareness of aging among married adults ages 20 to 60. *Sociological Quarterly, 29,* 487–502.

White, S. H. (1983). The idea of development in developmental psychology. In R. M. Lerner (Ed.), *Developmental psychology: Historical and philosophical perspectives.* Hillsdale, NJ: Lawrence Erlbaum.

Whitehead, A., & Mathews, A. (1986). Factors related to successful outcome in the treatment of sexually unresponsive women. *Psychological Medicine, 16,* 373–378.

Whiting, B. B., & Whiting, J. W. M. (1975). *Children of six cultures: A psycho-cultural analysis.* Cambridge, MA: Harvard University Press.

Whiting, J. W. M. (1981). Aging and becoming an elder: A cross-cultural comparison. In R. W. Fogel, E. Hatfield, S. B. Kiesler, & E. Shanas (Eds.), *Aging: Stability and change in the family.* New York: Academic Press.

Whiting, J. W. M., Burbank, V. K., & Ratner, M. S. (1986). The duration of maidenhood across cultures. In J. B. Lancaster & B. A. Hamburg (Eds.), *School-age pregnancy and parenthood: Biosocial dimensions.* New York: Aldine de Gruyter.

Whitt, J. K., & Prentice, N. M. (1977). Cognitive processes in the development of children's enjoyment and comprehension of joking riddles. *Developmental Psychology, 13,* 129–136.

Wideman, M. V., & Singer, J. E. (1984). The role of psychological mechanisms in preparation for childbirth. *American Psychologist, 39,* 1357–1371.

Widerstrom, A. H., & Dudley-Marling, C. (1986, May/June). Living with a handicapped child: Myth and reality. *Childhood Education,* pp. 359–367.

Widmayer, S., & Field, T. (1980). Effects of Brazelton demonstrations on early interactions of preterm infants and their teen-age mothers. *Infant Behavior and Development, 3,* 79–89.

Willats, P. (1985). *Development and rapid adjustment to means-ends behavior in infants aged six to eight months.* Presented at meeting of the International Society for the Study of Behavioral Development, Tours, France. Cited in Gibson, E. J. (1988). Exploratory behavior in the development of perceiving, acting, and the acquiring of knowledge. *Annual Review of Psychology, 39,* 1–41.

Williams, R. J. (1956). *Biochemical individuality.* Los Angeles, CA: Career Control Society.

Williamson, D. A., Kelley, M. L., Davis, C. J., Ruggiero, L., & Blovin, D. C. (1985). Psychopathology of eating disorders: A controlled comparison of bulimic, obese and normal subjects. *Journal of Consulting and Clinical Psychology, 3,* 161–166.

Willis, L., Thomas, P., Garry, P. J., & Goodwin, J. S. (1987). A prospective study of response to stressful life events in initially healthy elders. *Journal of Gerontology, 42,* 627–630.

Willis, S. L. (1985). Towards an educational psychology of the older adult learner: Intellectual and cognitive bases. In J. E. Birren & K. W. Schaie (Eds.), *Handbook of the psychology of aging* (2nd ed.). New York: Van Nostrand Reinhold.

Willis, S. L., & Schaie, K. W. (1988). Gender differences in spatial ability in old age: Longitudinal and intervention findings. *Sex Roles, 18,* 189–203.

Wilson, E. O. (1975). *Sociobiology: The new synthesis.* Cambridge, MA: Harvard University Press.

Wilson, E. O. (1978). *Sociobiology.* Cambridge, MA: Harvard University Press.

Wilson, M. R., & Filsinger, E. E. (1986). Religiosity and marital adjustment: Multidimensional interrelationships. *Journal of Marriage and the Family, 48,* 147–151.

Wimmer, H. (1979). Processing of script deviations by young children. *Discourse Processes, 2,* 301–310.

Windle, M., & Sinnott, J. D. (1985). A psychometric study of the Bem Sex-Role Inventory with an older adult sample. *Journal of Gerontology, 40,* 336–343.

Winer, G. A., Hemphill, J., & Craig, R. K. (1988). The effect of misleading questions in promoting nonconservation responses in children and adults. *Developmental Psychology, 24,* 197–202.

Wingfield, A., & Byrnes, D. L. (1981). *The psychology of human memory.* New York: Academic Press.

Winter, D. G. (1988). The power motive in women—and men. *Journal of Personality and Social Psychology, 54,* 510–519.

Winter, R., & Groch, J. (1984, May). Biomarkers: Beating body burnout. *American Health,* pp. 70–80.

Winterbottom, M. (1958). The relation of need for achievement to learning experiences in independence and mastery. In J. Atkinson (Ed.), *Motives in fantasy, action, and society.* Princeton, NJ: Van Nostrand.

Witkin, H. A., & Goodenough, D. R. (1981). *Cognitive styles: Essence and origins.* New York: International Universities Press.

Wittemore, R. D., & Beverly, E. (1989). Trust in the Mandinka way: The cultural context of sibling care. In P. Goldring Zukow (Ed.), *Sibling interaction across cultures: Theoretical and methodological issues.* New York: Springer-Verlag.

Woehrer, C. E. (1978). Cultural pluralism in American families: The influence of social aspects of aging. *Family Coordinator, 27,* 329–339.

Woititz, J. G. (1989). *Healing your sexual self.* Deerfield Beach, FL: Health Communications.

Wolfe, D. A. (1987). *Child abuse: Implications for child development and psychopathology.* Newbury Park, CA: Sage.

Wolfenstein, M. (1954). *Children's humor: A psychological analysis.* Glencoe, IL: Free Press.

Wolff, P. H. (1963). Observations on the early development of smiling. In B. M. Foss (Ed.), *Determinants of infant behavior* (Vol. 2). London, England: Methuen.

Wolff, P. H. (1969). The natural history of crying and other vocalizations in early infancy. In B. Foss (Ed.), *Determinants of infant behavior* (Vol. 4). New York: Wiley.

Wood, W., Rhodes, N., & Whelan, M. (1989). Sex differences in positive well-being: A consideration of emotional style and marital status. *Psychological Bulletin, 106,* 249–264.

Woodruff, D. C. (1985). Arousal, sleep, and aging. In J. E. Birren & K. W. Schaie (Eds.), *Handbook of the psychology of aging.* (2nd ed., pp. 261–296). New York: Van Nostrand Reinhold.

Woodruff-pak, D. C. (1989). Neurobiological models of learning, memory, and aging. In V. L. Bengston & K. W. Schaie (Eds.), *The course of later life: Research and reflections.* New York: Springer.

Woodward, K. L., Gosnell, M., Reese, M., Coppola, V., & Liebert, P. (1978, May 1). Living with dying. *Newsweek,* pp. 52–63.

Worobey, J., & Belsky, J. (1982). Employing the Brazelton Scale to influence mothering: An experimental comparison of three strategies. *Developmental Psychology, 18,* 736–743.

Worth, D. M. (1988). Age/grade and social-class differences in descriptions and inquiries about games. *Psychological Reports, 62,* 247–255.

Yager, J., Kurtzman, F., Landsverk, J., & Wiesmeier, E. (1988). Behaviors and attitudes related to eating disorders in homosexual male college students. *American Journal of Psychiatry, 14,* 495–497.

Yager, J., Landsverk, J., & Edelstein, C. K. (1987). A 20-month follow-up study of 628 women with eating disorders. I: Course and severity. *American Journal of Psychiatry, 144,* 1172–1177.

Yalisove, D. (1978). The effect of riddle structure on children's comprehension of riddles. *Developmental Psychology, 14,* 173–180.

Yarrow, M. R., & Waxler, C. Z. (1976). Dimensions and correlates of prosocial behavior in young children. *Child Development, 47,* 118–125.

Ylisto, I. (1967). *An empirical investigation of early reading responses of young children.* Unpublished doctoral dissertation, University of Michigan, Ann Arbor.

Yogman, M. W., & Zeisel, S. H. (1983). Diet and sleep patterns in newborn infants. *New England Journal of Medicine, 309,* 1147–1149.

Yonas, A. (1981). Infants' responses to optical information for collision. In R. N. Aslin, J. R. Alberts, & M. R. Peterson (Eds.), *Development of perception: Psychobiological perspectives. Vol. 2: The visual system.* New York: Academic.

Yost, E. B., & Corbishley, M. A. (1987). *Career counseling: A psychological approach.* San Francisco, CA: Jossey-Bass.

C. M., Young, (Ed.), (1977). Ages, reasons and sex differences for children leaving home. In *Australian Family Formation Project Monograph 6: The Family Life Cycle.* Canberra, Australia: Australian National University.

Young-Loveridge, J. M. (1987). Learning mathematics. *British Journal of Developmental Psychology, 5,* 155–167.

Youniss, J. (1980). *Parents and peers in social development: A Sullivan-Piaget perspective.* Chicago, IL: University of Chicago.

Yu, L. C., Yu, Y., & Mansfield, P. K. (1990, March). Gender and changes in support of parents in China: Implications for the one-child policy. *Gender & Society, 4,* 83–89.

Z

Zabin, L. S., Kantner, J. F., & Zelnick, M. (1979). The risk of adolescent pregnancy in the first months of intercourse. *Family Planning Perspectives, 11,* 215–222.

Zacharias, L., & Wurtman, R. J. (1969). Age at menarche. *New England Journal of Medicine, 260,* 868–875.

Zakin, D. F., Blyth, D. S., & Simmons, R. G. (1984). Physical attractiveness as a mediator of the impact of early pubertal changes for girls. *Journal of Youth & Adolescents, 13,* 439–450.

Zelazo, P. R., Zelazo, N. A., & Kolb, S. (1972). "Walking" in the newborn. *Science, 176,* 314–315.

Zelnick, M., & Kantner, J. (1977). Sexual and contraceptive experience of young unmarried women in the United States, 1976 and 1971. *Family Planning Perspectives, 9,* 55–71.

Zeskind, P. S., & Marshall, T. R. (1988). The relation between variations in pitch and maternal perceptions of infant crying. *Child Development, 59,* 193–196.

Zigler, E., Rubin, N., & Kaufman, J. (1988). Do abused children become abusive parents? *Parents, 63,* 100–106.

Zivian, M. T., & Darjes, R. W. (1983). Free recall by in-school and out-of-school adults: Performance and metamemory. *Developmental Psychology, 19,* 513–520.

Zube, M. (1982). Changing behavior and outlook of aging men and women: Implications for marriage in the middle and later years. *Family Relations, 31,* 147–156.

Zuckerman, P., Ziegler, M., & Stevenson, H. W. (1978). Children's viewing of television and recognition memory of commercials. *Child Development, 49,* 96–104.

Zygola, J. M. (1987). *Doing things.* Baltimore, MD: Johns Hopkins University.

Zytowski, D., & Hay, R. (1985). Do birds of a feather flock together? A test of the similarities within and the differences between five occupations. *Journal of Vocational Behavior, 24,* 242–248.

Zytowski, D. G. (1976). Predictive validity of the Kuder Occupational Interest Survey: A 12- to 19-year follow-up. *Journal of Counseling Psychology, 23,* 221–233.

Zyzanski, S. J., Jenkins, C. D., Ryan, T. J., Flessas, A., & Everist, M. (1976). Psychological correlates of coronary angiographic findings. *Archives of Internal Medicine, 136,* 1234–1237.

Credits

Line Art

Chapter 1

Figure 1.1 From R. C. Atchely, "The Life Course, Age Grading, and Aged Linked Demands for Decision Making" in *Lifespan Developmental Psychology: Normative Life Crisis,* edited by N. Datan and L. Ginsberg. Copyright © 1975 Academic Press, Inc., San Diego, Ca.

Chapter 2

Figure 2.4 Modified from Moore, K. L. and Persuad T. V. N.: *The Developing Human: Clinically Oriented Embryology,* 5th edition. W.B. Saunders, 1993.

Chapter 3

Figure 3.1 From Kent M. Van De Graaff, *Concepts of Human Anatomy and Physiology,* 3d edition, Copyright © 1989 Wm. C. Brown Communications, Inc., Dubuque, Iowa. All Rights Reserved. Reprinted by permission.
Figure 3.3 Source: Data from Ronald Melzack, "The Myth of Painless Childbirth" in *Pain,* 19:321–337, 1984.
Figure 3.4 Source: Adapted from an illustration by Alex Senenoick in "The Origin of Form Perception" by Robert L. Fantz, *Scientific American,* 204, pp. 66–72. Copyright © Scientific American, New York, NY.
Figure 3.5 From M. Kaitz, et al., "A Reexamination of Newborns' Ability to Imitate Facial Expressions" in *Developmental Psychology,* 24, 3–7, fig. 1, 1988. Copyright © 1988 by the American Psychological Association. Reprinted by permission.

Chapter 4

Figure 4.2 From Lester M. Sdorow, *Psychology,* 2d edition, Copyright © 1993 Wm. C. Brown Communications, Inc., Dubuque, Iowa. All Rights Reserved. Reprinted by permission.
Figure 4.5 From P. Langsdorf, et al., "Interest Expression, Visual Fixation, and Heart Rate Changes in 2–8 Month Old Infants" in *Developmental Psychology,* 19, 375–386, 1983. Copyright © 1983 American Psychological Association. Reprinted by permission.

Chapter 5

Figure 5.1 From J. Kagan, "Emergent Themes in Human Development" in *American Scientist,* 64, p. 190, 1976. Copyright © 1976 Scientific Research Society. Reprinted by permission of American Scientist, journal of Sigma Xi, The Scientific Research Society.

Chapter 6

Figure 6.1 Source: Adapted from Prather & Bacon article in *Child Development,* Vol. 57, p. 552, 1986. Copyright © 1986 The Society for Research in Child Development, Inc.

Chapter 7

Figure 7.2 From *Social and Personality Development,* Second Edition by David R. Shaffer. Copyright © 1988, 1979 by Wadsworth, Inc. Reprinted by permission of Brooks/Cole Publishing Company, Pacific Grove, California, 93950.
Figure 7.3 From L. A. Serbin and C. Sprafkin, "The Salience of Gender and the Process of Sex Typing in Three-to-Seven-Year-Old Children" in *Scientific American,* 57, p. 1195, 1986. Copyright © 1986 The Society for Research in Child Development, Inc.

Chapter 8

Figure 8.3 From R. J. Comer, "Educating Poor Minority Children" in *Scientific American,* 259, p. 45, 1988. Copyright © 1988 Scientific American, New York, NY.
Figure 8.4 From R. J. Comer, "Educating Poor Minority Children" in *Scientific American,* 259, p. 47, 1988. Copyright © 1988 Scientific American, New York, NY.

Chapter 9

Figure 9.1 From A. H. Maslow, *Toward a Psychology of Being,* 2d edition, p. 47, 1968. Copyright © 1968 Van Nostrand Reinhold, New York, NY.
Figure 9.4A Adapted from D. Wertlieb, et al., "Measuring Children's Coping" in *American Journal of Orthopsychiatry,* 57, 548–560, 1987. Reprinted by permission, from the American Journal of Orthopsychiatry. Copyright © 1987 by the American Orthopsychiatric Association, Inc.
Figure 9.6 Figure 1 from L. W. Sherman, "Development of Children's Perceptions of Internal Locus of Control" in *Journal of Personality,* 52:4, pp. 338–354. Copyright Duke University Press, 1984. Reprinted with permission of the publisher.
Figure 9.7 From A. Caspi, G. H. Elder, Jr., and D. J. Bem, "Moving Away From the World: Life-Course Patterns of Shy Children" in *Developmental Psychology,* 24, 824–831, 1988. Copyright © 1988 American Psychological Association. Reprinted by permission.
Figure 9.8 From E. Ellis, B. Rogoff, and C. C. Cromer, "Age Segregation in Children's Social Interactions" in *Developmental Psychology,* 17, 399–407, 1981. Copyright © 1981 American Psychological Association. Reprinted by permission.

Chapter 13

Figure 13.6 From A. G. Neal, et al., "Attitudes about Having Children: A Study of 600 Couples in the Early Years of Marriage" in *Journal of Marriage and the Family,* 51, 313–328, Fig. 1 page 321, 1989. Copyrighted 1989 by the National Council on Family Relations, 3989 Central Ave. NE, Suite 550, Minneapolis, MN 55421. Reprinted by permission.

Chapter 16

Figure 16.2 From T. A. Salthouse and K. A. Prill in "Effects of Aging on Perceptual Closure" in *American Journal of Psychology,* 101, 217–238, figure 1, Summer 1988. Copyright © 1988 University of Illinois Press, Champaign, IL. Reprinted by permission.

Photographs

Chapter 1

Opener: © Bill Bachman/PhotoEdit; **p. 6:** © Robert L. Simons; **p. 10:** © Mary Evans/Sigmund Freud Copyrights; **p. 13:** © Suki Hill; **p. 19:** Sharon Beals for "Insight Magazine"; **p. 24:** © Laura Dwight/Peter Arnold, Inc.

Chapter 2

Opener: © David M. Phillips/Photo Researchers, Inc.; **p. 32:** © Michael Newman/PhotoEdit; **2.2:** © Rawlins/Custom Medical Stock Photo; **p. 36:** © Hank Morgan/Photo Researchers, Inc.; **p. 41:** © Petit Format/Nestle/Science Source/Photo Researchers, Inc.; **p. 44:** © Chas Cancellare/Picture Group; **p. 45:** © Vanessa Vick/Photo Researchers, Inc.; **p. 47:** © Amy C. Etra/PhotoEdit; **p. 49:** © Lennart Nilsson/Bonnier Alba; **p. 52:** AP/Wide World Photos

Chapter 3

Opener: © Tom McCarthy/PhotoEdit; **p. 62:** © Charles Gupton/Stock Boston; **p. 66:** © SUI/Photo Researchers, Inc.; **p. 64:** © David Leah/Science Photo Library/Photo Researchers, Inc.; **p. 67:** © Brownie Harris/The Stock Market; **p. 69:** © Hank Morgan/Science Source/Photo Researchers, Inc.; **p. 71:** © Petit Format/J. Da Cunha/ Photo Researchers, Inc.; **p. 75:** © Myrleen Ferguson/ PhotoEdit; **p. 79:** © Robert Brenner/PhotoEdit

Chapter 4

Opener: © Robert L. Simons; **p. 86:** © Robert L. Simons; **p. 88:** © Suzanne Szasz/Photo Researchers, Inc.; **p. 89:** © Laura Dwight/Peter Arnold, Inc.; **p. 92:** © Harold Hoffman/Photo Researchers, Inc.; **p. 93:** © Laura Dwight/Peter Arnold, Inc.; **p. 94:** © Michael Newman/PhotoEdit; **4.3:** © Erico Ferrolli; **p. 99:** © Robert L. Simons; **p. 101 left:** © Laura Dwight/Peter Arnold, Inc.; **p. 101 right:** © Robert L. Simons; **p. 103:** © James Prince/Photo Researchers, Inc.; **4.6:** Courtesy of Carolyn Rovee-Collier; **p. 108:** © Steve Niedorf/The Image Bank, Texas

Chapter 5

Opener: © James H. Karales/Peter Arnold, Inc.; **p. 116:** © Laura Dwight/Peter Arnold, Inc.; **p. 118:** © Chris Hackett/Image Bank Texas; **p. 120:** © Robert Brenner/PhotoEdit; **p. 123:** © Spencer Grant/Photo Researchers, Inc.; **p. 125:** Bettmann; **p. 126:** © Ray Ellis/Photo Researchers, Inc.; **p. 133:** © James Prince/Photo Researchers, Inc.

Chapter 6

Opener: © Laura Dwight/Peter Arnold, Inc.; **p. 143 top left:** © Mary Kay Denny/PhotoEdit; **p. 143 top right, middle left:** © Robert Brenner/PhotoEdit; **p. 143 middle right, bottom left:** © Tony Freeman/PhotoEdit; **p. 143 bottom right:** © David Young-Wolff/PhotoEdit; **p. 145:** © Robert L. Simons; **p. 146:** © Matt Meadows/Peter Arnold, Inc.; **p. 148:** © Lawrence Migdale/Photo Researchers, Inc.; **p. 149:** © Mary Kate

Denny/PhotoEdit; **p. 151:** © Earl Roberge/Photo Researchers, Inc.; **p. 156:** © Hattie Young/Science Photo Library/Photo Researchers, Inc.; **p. 154:** © Myrleen Ferguson/PhotoEdit; **p. 158:** © Robert L. Simons; **p. 160:** AP/Wide World Photos; **p. 162:** © Paul Conklin/PhotoEdit

Chapter 7

Opener: © Myrleen Ferguson/PhotoEdit; **p. 173:** © Suzanne Szasz/Photo Researchers, Inc.; **p. 176, p. 177, p. 179:** © Robert L. Simons; **p. 180:** © Ken Gaghan/Jeroboam; **p. 183 top left:** © Laima Druskis/Photo Researchers, Inc.; **p. 183 bottom left:** © Richard Hutchings/Photo Researchers, Inc.; **p. 183 top right:** © Michael P. Gadomski/Photo Researchers, Inc.; **p. 183 bottom right:** © Myrleen Ferguson/PhotoEdit; **p. 187:** © Tony Freeman/PhotoEdit; **p. 192:** © Miro Vintoniv/Stock Boston

Chapter 8

Opener: © Spencer Grant/Photo Researchers, Inc.; **p. 201:** © Mary Kate Denny/PhotoEdit; **p. 202:** © Richard Hutchings/Photo Researchers, Inc.; **p. 204:** © Elizabeth Crews/The Image Works; **p. 208:** © Doug Menuez/Stock Boston; **p. 211:** © Yves DeBraine/Black Star; **p. 213:** © Keith Carter; **p. 217:** © Richard Hutchings/Photo Researchers, Inc.

Chapter 9

Opener: © Richard Hutchings/Photo Researchers, Inc.; **p. 231:** © Mary Kate Denny/PhotoEdit; **p. 233:** © Richard Hutchings/Photo Researchers, Inc.; **p. 239:** © Mark Richards/PhotoEdit; **p. 241:** © John-Clare du Bois/Photo Researchers, Inc.; **p. 248:** © Jeff Isaac Greenberg/Photo Researchers, Inc.

Chapter 10

Opener: © Spencer Grant/Photo Researchers, Inc.; **p. 259:** © David Young-Wolff/PhotoEdit; **p. 261:** © David R. Frazier/Photo Researchers, Inc.; **p. 265:** © Tony Freeman/PhotoEdit; **p. 268:** © Robert Brenner/PhotoEdit; **p. 272:** © Michael Newman/PhotoEdit; **p. 275:** © Tom Prettyman/PhotoEdit; **p. 279:** © Myrleen Ferguson/PhotoEdit

Chapter 11

Opener: © Will and Deni McIntyre/Photo Researchers, Inc.; **p. 289:** © James Marshall; **p. 291:** © Conrad Collette/Shooting Star; **p. 294:** © Michael Newman/PhotoEdit; **p. 299, p. 301:** © Jeff Isaac Greenberg/PhotoEdit; **p. 303:** © Alan Dorow/Actuality, Inc.

Chapter 12

Opener: © Michael Newman/PhotoEdit; **p. 314:** © Leslye Borden/PhotoEdit; **p. 317:** © Joseph Nettis/Photo Researchers, Inc.; **p. 321:** © Robert Brenner/PhotoEdit; **p. 322, p. 326:** © Will and Deni McIntyre/Photo Researchers, Inc.

Chapter 13

Opener: © Robert L. Simons; **p. 338:** © Myrleen Ferguson/PhotoEdit; **p. 341:** © Mark Richards/PhotoEdit; **p. 345:** © Cleo Photography/PhotoEdit; **p. 352:** © David Young-Wolff/PhotoEdit; **p. 355:** © Michael Newman/PhotoEdit

Chapter 14

Opener: © Tom McCarthy/PhotoEdit; **p. 367:** © Tony Freeman/PhotoEdit; **p. 368:** © Martin/Custom Medical Stock Photo; **p. 369, p. 372:** AP/Wide World Photos; **p. 378:** © ATC Productions/Custom Medical Stock Photo; **p. 383:** © Elena Rooraid/PhotoEdit

Chapter 15

Opener: © Robert L. Simons; **p. 390:** © Myrleen Ferguson/PhotoEdit; **p. 395:** © Robert Brenner/PhotoEdit; **p. 398:** © Bob Daemmrich/Stock Boston; **p. 401:** © Michael Newman/PhotoEdit; **p. 406:** © Deborah Davis/PhotoEdit; **p. 408:** © Custom Medical Stock Photo

Chapter 16

Opener: © Robert L. Simons; **p. 422:** © Jerry Wachter/Photo Researchers, Inc.; **p. 423:** © Polly Brown/Actuality, Inc.; **p. 425:** © Tony Freeman/PhotoEdit; **p. 430:** © Martin/Custom Medical Stock Photo; **p. 433:** © Kenneth Murray/Photo Researchers, Inc.; **p. 439:** © Martin/Custom Medical Stock Photo

Chapter 17

Opener: © Michael Austin/Photo Researchers, Inc.; **p. 447:** AP/Wide World Photos; **p. 453:** © Robert L. Simons; **p. 456:** © Margaret Miller/Photo Researchers, Inc.; **p. 459, p. 466:** © Blair Seitz/Photo Researchers, Inc.

Chapter 18

Opener: © Charles Harbutt/Actuality, Inc.; **p. 476:** © Los Alamos National Laboratory/Science Photo Library/ Photo Researchers, Inc.; **p. 477:** © Dennis MacDonald/PhotoEdit; **p. 479:** © Larry Mulvehill/Photo Researchers, Inc.; **p. 483:** UPI/Bettmann; **p. 487:** © Blair Seitz/Photo Researchers, Inc.; **p. 490:** © Michael Newman/PhotoEdit; **p. 493:** © Paul Conklin/PhotoEdit

Index

Androgyny, 183–184
androgynous father, 357
androgynous parents, 237
development of, 184
and friendships, 358
in midlife, 395
Anecephalic infants, use in medical research, 19
Anger, stage of dying, 483
Animism, and preschoolers' thinking, 150
Animus and anima, 395
Anniversary reaction, grief, 491
Anorexia nervosa, 265–266
Anxiously attached-avoidant infants, 129, 130
Apathetic persons, 453
Apgar Scale, 70–71
Apnea, 425–426
Appropriate-for-gestational age infants, 68
Aries, Philippe, 6
Arithmetic, and aging, 434
Armored-defended personality, 453
Articulation disorders, 156
Artificial insemination, 36
Artificialism, and preschoolers' thinking, 150
Assimilation, Piagetian, 101
Astigmatism, 429
Attachment, 128–131
ambivalent attached-resistant infants, 129, 130
anxiously attached-avoidant infants, 129, 130
biological attachment theory, 128–129
Bowlby's attachment theory, 500
definition of, 128
individual differences in, 129
and later love relationships, 324
and parent-child relationships, 129–130
and peer relationships, 130
and personality, 130–131
securely attached infants, 129, 130
and separation-individuation theory, 129
stages in development of, 129, 500
Authenticity, 293
Authoritarian parenting, 185, 237, 297–298
Authoritative parenting, 21, 185, 237, 298
Autism, 52
Autobiographies
chronology, 510
document file, 510
life narratives, 510–511
oral interview, 510
psychobiographies, 511
Automaticity, 382
Autonomous motivation, 216
Autonomy
autonomy versus shame and doubt, 125–126
and identity development, 292
Autopsies, 489

B

Babbling, 106
Baby-talk register, 107
Baby Temperament Scales, 121
Back problems, 377
Baldness, 367
Baldwin, James Mark, 8
Bandura, Albert, 176, 501, 501–502
Bargaining, stage of dying, 483
Battered wife syndrome, 355

Behavioral-learning theory
behaviorism, 500–501
classical conditioning, 100, 500
history of, 9–10
of language development, 106
as mechanistic model, 11, 12
modeling, 101
operant conditioning, 101, 501
theories in, 9–10
Behaviorism, Watson's formulation of, 500–501
Behavior modification, for toilet training, 93
Belief in just world, 211
Bereavement, definition of, 488
Bias, in experimental research, 20
Binet, Alfred, 7
Binet, Armande, 7
Binge-eating, 266
Biological theory
of aggression, 178
of attachment, 128–129, 500
Bowlby's contribution, 500
Darwin's contribution, 499
of emotions, 117
history of, 9–10
as organismic model, 11–12
sexual orientation, 274
theories of, 9
Birren hypothesis, 434–435
Birth centers, 67
Birth order, 175–176
effects of, 175
Blank slate, 9
Blastocyst, 38
Blended family, 318
Body image, 256–257
research findings related to adolescents, 257
Bonding, parents-newborn, 66
Bone
ossification of, 200
osteoporosis, 427
Books, and infants, 134
Bowlby, John, 500
Brain
activity in infants, 88
and aging, 424
development in infancy, 88–89
lateralization, 88–89
myelination, 88
Brain death, 484
Brazelton Neonatal Assessment Scale, 71
Brazelton training, 71
Breast cancer, 379
Bronfenbrenner, Urie, 12
Buhler, Charlotte, 11
Bulimia, 266
Burnout, 408

C

Caesarean delivery, 64–65
Canalization, 25
Cancer, 378–379
ethnic differences in, 379
risk factors, 378–379
survival factors, 378
Cardiovascular disease, risk factors in children, 201
Cardiovascular system
in middle age, 368
and old age, 424–425

Care, middle/late childhood, 202
Career development, 304–305, 324–327
career adaptability, 304
career changes, 407–408
career maturity, 304–305
and college attendance, 326–327
decision-making, stages in, 304
gender differences, 305, 325–326
job satisfaction, 408
male attitudes about female employment, 409
personality types and work environment, 325
self-concept theory, 304–305
Career, meaning of, 324
Career problems, 408–409
burnout, 408
dysfunctional workplaces, 408
unemployment, 408–409
Caring, 322
Carus, Friedrich August, 7, 12
Case studies, 14
Castration anxiety, 173
Cataracts, 429
Centering, and preschoolers' thinking, 151
Cephalocaudal principle, 24, 72, 90
Child abuse, 187–188
characteristics of abusive parents, 187–188
historical view, 187
Childbirth, 60–68
Caesarean delivery, 64–65
cross cultural view, 67
fetal monitoring, 65
first stage, 60
home deliveries, 67
hospital settings, 66
initiation of, 62
Lamaze strategy, 65
Leboyer method, 65–66
low birthweight babies, 68–70
medication, use in, 64
midwives, 67–68
pain of, 62
postpartum depression, 63
second stage, 60–61
stress hormones, 62–63
third stage of, 61
Child care, 162–164
advantages/disadvantages of, 162, 164
cross cultural view, 163–164
types of, 162
Child-centered parents, 237
Childhood. See Middle/late childhood;
Preschoolers
Children
historical views of, 6–7
as research subjects, 19
Chlamydia, 270
Chorionic villus sampling, 53
Chromosomes, 48
defects transmitted by, 52
and gender determination, 48
Cigarette smoking
in adolescence, 268
effects of, 201, 378
and fetal development, 44
quitting, 374
Circular model, 4
Classical conditioning, 9, 500
learning by, 100
Pavlov's contribution, 500

Fertility rates, 35
Fertilization, 32, 34–35
  developmental events following, 38–47
  and gender determination, 34–35
  process of, 34
Fetal alcohol syndrome, 44
Fetal monitoring, 65
Fetus
  fetal stage, 40
  treatment of, 38
Fidelity, 290
Field dependence, 205
Field independence, 205
Fine motor skills
  infancy, 91
  middle/late childhood, 200
  preschoolers, 142
Fluid intelligence, 215, 346, 380
Focused persons, 453
Fol, Hermann, 32
Follicle-stimulating hormone, 33, 258
Formal operations stage, 259–260
Fragile X syndrome, 52
Free-radical theory, aging, 423
Freud, Anna, 10, 14, 289
Freud, Sigmund, 10, 172–173, 228, 504
Freudian theory
  of aggression, 178
  anal stage, 124
  castration anxiety, 173
  defense mechanisms, 174
  ego, 505
  Electra complex, 173
  formulation of, 504–505
  gender identification, 181
  genital stage, 288–289
  id, 504–505
  latency stage, 228
  libido in, 504
  Oedipus complex, 172–173
  oral stage, 124
  penis envy, 173
  phallic stage, 172
  sexual orientation, 273
  superego, 174, 505
Friendships, 192, 245–247
  and accepted/rejected/neglected children, 247–248
  in adolescence, 298
  and androgyny, 358
  cliques and crowds, 299
  gender differences, 298, 357–358
  interdependent friendships, 246
  mutual friendships, 246
  older adults, 465
  stages of, 245–247
  trouble making friends, 248
Frustration-aggression hypothesis, 178
Functional play, 189–190
Funerals, 488–491
  functions of, 490

G

Gain-loss theory, of interpersonal attraction, 302
Galton, Francis, 20
Games
  games-with-rules play, 191
  of infant, 133, 134
  middle/late childhood, 244

parent/child game playing, 245
  stages in learning of, 244
  video games, 244
Gardnerella, 271
Gastrointestinal system, in middle age, 368
Gender
  expectations of parents, 45–46, 78
  genetic mechanisms in, 48
  timing of intercourse and, 34–35
Gender constancy, meaning of, 180
Gender differences
  activities of older adults, 457–458
  in adult development, 314–315
  in attitudes toward dating, 300
  career development, 305, 325–326
  communication, 351
  friendships, 298, 357–358
  grandparenting, 464
  identity development, 292
  intimacy, 349–350
  meaning of, 180
  mental disturbances, 345
  moral development, 213–214
  older adults, perception of self, 452
  physical growth, 200
  sexual attitudes, 276
Gender identification, 180–184
  cognitive developmental theory, 182
  Freudian theory, 181
  gender-schema theory, 182
  meaning of, 180
  social learning theory, 181–182
Gender identity
  gender as differences, 350
  gender as stereotypes, 350
  macho personalities, 350–351
  and same-sex relationships, 351
Gender roles
  acquisition of, 180–181
  androgyny, 183–184
  cross cultural view, 184
  definition of, 180
  and marital problems, 400
  middle adulthood, 395–396
  and sexual orientation, 274
  traditional roles, 182–183
Gender schema theory, gender identification, 182
Gender stereotypes, meaning of, 180
Gender typing
  meaning of, 180
  and toys, 161
Generativity versus stagnation, 313, 392
Genes, 48
Genetic counseling, 52–53
Genetic disorders, 51–52
  achondroplasia, 51
  cystic fibrosis, 52
  Down syndrome, 52
  Fragile X syndrome, 52
  hemophilia, 52
  Huntington's disease, 51–52
  prenatal testing for, 53
  sickle cell anemia, 52
  Tay-Sachs disease, 52
Genetic mutation theory, aging, 422–423
Genetic programming theory, aging, 422
Genetics
  meaning of, 48
  See also Heredity
Genital stage, 288–289

Genotype, 49
Germinal stage, 38–39
Gesell, Arnold, 9
Gesell Preschool Test, 157–158
Gestational diabetes, 379
Gestational neurohormonal theory, sexual orientation, 274
Gilligan, Carol, 213–214
Gilligan's moral development theory, 213–214
  morality of caring in, 214
  morality of justice in, 214
  morality of rights in, 213
  stages of, 213
Glaucoma, 429
Gonadotropin-releasing hormone, 258
Gonorrhea, 270
Gordon, Thomas, 229
Gould's theory, adult development, 314
Grandparenting, 464–465
  gender differences, 464
  styles of, 464–465
Greece, ancient
  study of human development, 4
  view of children, 6
Grief, 491–493
  and abortion, 492
  anniversary reaction, 491
  and death of parent, 492
  and death of spouse, 492
  definition of, 488
  factors complicating process, 492
  helping bereaved, 492
Gross motor skills
  infancy, 91
  middle/late childhood, 200
  preschoolers, 142

H

Habituation, 73, 390–391
  hyperhabituation, 391
Hair
  graying/baldness in middle age, 367
  and old age, 424
Hall, G. Stanley, 7–8, 9, 288
Handedness
  development of, 142
  preschoolers, 142
Hardiness, components of, 341
Hassles, 377
Head Start, 162
Health
  acute illness, 378
  health risks, types of, 274, 375
  and lifestyle, 374–375
  and personality, 341, 343
  problems in middle age, 377–378
  and stress, 375–376
  in young adulthood, 338–343
  See also Illness
Hearing
  impairments in infants, 98
  infant abilities, 76, 98
  loss in middle adulthood, 366–367
Heart attack, 481–482
  sudden death in, 482
Height
  and aging, 424
  in middle age, 368
Helplessness, coping style, 234
Hemophilia, 52